Project Management in Practice

Project Management in Practice

3e

Pearson

Larson

Gray

McGraw Hill

National Library of Australia Cataloguing-in-Publication Data

Authors: Neil Pearson, Erik W Larson, Clifford F Gray
Title: *Project Management in Practice*
Edition: 3
ISBN: 9781760427085 (paperback)

A catalogue record for this book is available from the National Library of Australia

Published in Australia by
McGraw-Hill Education (Australia) Pty Ltd
Level 33, 680 George St, Sydney, NSW 2000
Publisher: Sarah Cook
Production editor: Elmandi Du Toit
Digital specialist: Bethany Ng
Research coordinator: Daniel Harkins
Permissions editor: Debbie Gallagher, Legend Images
Copyeditor: Rosemary Moore
Proofreader: Paul Hines
Indexer: Straive, India
Cover design: Christa Moffitt, Christabelladesigns
Cover image: Mystery Kit/Shutterstock.com
Internal design: Simon Rattray, Squirt Creative
Typeset by Straive, India
Printed in Australia by Pegasus Media & Logistics Pty Ltd

Brief contents

PART 1 Setting the scene · 1

  1 Contemporary project management · 2

PART 2 Project establishment and performance · 27

  2 Popular frameworks and methodologies · 28
  3 The Scrum (Agile) approach · 71
  4 Strategy, project selection and the Business Case · 122
  5 Organisational change management and cultures · 169

PART 3 Performing project initiation · 203

  6 Project integration management · 204
  7 Governance and projects · 236

PART 4 Performing project planning · 259

  8 Defining the scope of a project · 260
  9 Estimating · 297
  10 Project resource management · 323
  11 Project schedule management · 343
  12 Project cost management · 384
  13 Project quality management · 408
  14 Project stakeholder management · 445
  15 Project information and communications management · 469
  16 Project risk management · 504
  17 Project procurement management · 539

PART 5 Performing project execution · 573

  18 Project execution · 574
  19 Project leaders and project teams · 593
  20 Complex project management · 649

PART 6 Performing project closure · 669

  21 Project closure · 670

Contents

Preface   xi
About the authors   xiv
Text at a glance   xv

PART 1
Setting the scene

CHAPTER 1

Contemporary project management   2

1.1   Introduction   3
1.2   What is a project and what is project
      management?   8
1.3   Standards, frameworks and methodologies:
      An introduction   11
1.4   The importance of project management   16
1.5   Contemporary project management:
      A holistic approach   22

      Summary   24
      Review questions   25
      Exercises   25
      References   26

PART 2
Project establishment and performance

CHAPTER 2

Popular frameworks and methodologies   28

2.1   Introduction   29
2.2   Life cycle types and their selection   33
2.3   An overview of PRINCE2   39
2.4   An overview of ISO 21500:2021
      "Project, programme and portfolio
      management—context and concepts"   43
2.5   An introduction to the Agile
      (Scrum) approach   46
2.6   An overview of the APM framework   50
2.7   An introduction to Lean Six Sigma and the
      DMAIC process   51
2.8   An overview of the Praxis framework   54
2.9   An overview of the P3.express system   57
2.10 An introduction to the *Project Management
      Body of Knowledge* (PMBOK)   59

      Summary   67
      Review questions   68
      Exercises   69
      References   69

CHAPTER 3

The Scrum (Agile) approach   71

3.1   Introduction   72
3.2   Overview of Scrum   76
3.3   Scrum roles   78
3.4   Scrum events (ceremonies)   87
3.5   Scrum artefacts   96
3.6   Scrum and procurement   112
3.7   Agile under PRINCE2 and PMBOK   113
3.8   Large-Scale Scrum (LeSS)   116
3.9   DevOps   118

      Summary   119
      Review questions   119
      Exercises   119
      References   120

CHAPTER 4

Strategy, project selection and the
Business Case   122

4.1   Introduction   123
4.2   Why project leaders need to understand
      strategy   123
4.3   An overview of the strategic management
      process   124
4.4   The need for an effective portfolio,
      program and project management
      system   132
4.5   An introduction to portfolio management   136
4.6   Applying a selection model   149
4.7   Managing the portfolio management
      system   153
4.8   Project portfolio management   157
4.9   Benefits management integration
      with project management   160

      Summary   164
      Review questions   165
      Exercises   165
      References   167

CHAPTER 5
Organisational change management
and cultures   169

5.1	Introduction to Part 1	170
5.2	OCM and the predictive life cycle	175
5.3	OCM approaches and tools	177
5.4	OCM summary	190
5.5	Introduction to Part 2	190
5.6	Organisational culture	190
5.7	Implications of organisational cultures when leading projects	195
5.8	Working across international cultures	198

Summary   198
Review questions   198
Exercises   200
References   200

PART 3
Performing project initiation

CHAPTER 6
Project integration management   204

6.1	Introduction	205
6.2	Project chartering and the project leader	208
6.3	Project design and the integrated Project Management Plan	212
6.4	Executing the work and delivering	216
6.5	Managing project control	218
6.6	Managing variations (change requests)	219
6.7	Managing project finalisation	220
6.8	Managing project knowledge	221
6.9	Integrative thinking	223

Summary   233
Review questions   234
Exercises   235
References   235

CHAPTER 7
Governance and projects   236

7.1	Introduction to governance in the project context	237
7.2	Identify governance	242
7.3	Develop governance plans	244
7.4	Monitor governance	251
7.5	Review governance	252
7.6	The project (program) management office	253

Summary   256
Review questions   257
Exercises   257
References   258

PART 4
Performing project planning

CHAPTER 8
Defining the scope of a project   260

8.1	Introduction	261
8.2	Planning scope management	262
8.3	Defining the project scope	265
8.4	Capturing requirements	275
8.5	Creating the work breakdown structure (WBS)	279
8.6	Integrating the WBS with the organisation	286
8.7	Estimating the WBS	287
8.8	Variation request management	289

Summary   293
Review questions   294
Exercises   294
References   296

CHAPTER 9
Estimating   297

9.1	Introduction	298
9.2	Factors influencing the quality of estimates	300
9.3	What is being estimated?	303
9.4	Estimating guidelines for resources, duration (time) and costs	305
9.5	Top-down versus bottom-up estimating	307
9.6	Methods for estimating project resources, durations (time) and costs	310
9.7	Additional estimating considerations	317

Summary   319
Review questions   320
Exercises   321
References   322

CHAPTER 10
Project resource management   323

10.1	Introduction	324
10.2	Planning resource management	326
10.3	Resource identification and assignment	330
10.4	Acquiring resources	338
10.5	Monitoring and controlling resources	340
10.6	Resource closure	341

Summary   341
Review questions   342
Exercises   342
References   342

CHAPTER 11

Project schedule management 343

11.1	Introduction	344
11.2	Planning schedule development	346
11.3	Developing the project schedule	347
11.4	From work package/task to network	348
11.5	From network to project schedule	357
11.6	Advanced scheduling techniques	363
11.7	Advanced schedule efficiency techniques	367
11.8	The resource scheduling challenge	371
11.9	Assigning and monitoring project work	379
11.10	Multi-project resource optimisation	380

Summary	381
Review questions	381
Exercises	382
References	383

CHAPTER 12

Project cost management 384

12.1	Introduction and important considerations for cost management	385
12.2	Cost management planning	390
12.3	Identification, estimation and categorisation of costs	391
12.4	Time-phased project budgets	394
12.5	Project cost control and monitoring	401
12.6	Contingency planning	402
12.7	Cost closure	405

Summary	406
Review questions	406
Exercises	406
References	407

CHAPTER 13

Project quality management 408

13.1	Introduction	409
13.2	Quality and project management	410
13.3	Continuous improvement	413
13.4	Planning for quality	417
13.5	Quality of the project management	423
13.6	Carrying out quality control	429
13.7	Reporting quality performance	437
13.8	Root-cause analysis	438

Summary	442
Review questions	443
Exercises	443
References	444

CHAPTER 14

Project stakeholder management 445

14.1	Introduction	446
14.2	Stakeholder co-creation	447
14.3	Planning stakeholder management	450
14.4	Identifying stakeholders	451
14.5	Analysing stakeholders	457
14.6	Engage and monitor stakeholders	463
14.7	Closing stakeholder relationships	466

Summary	467
Review questions	467
Exercises	467
References	467

CHAPTER 15

Project information and communications management 469

15.1	Introduction	470
15.2	Background to communications in projects	471
15.3	Communication models	475
15.4	Further communication considerations	479
15.5	The Communications Management Plan	485
15.6	Planning, developing and tracking communications	488
15.7	Project reporting	494
15.8	Project management information systems (PMIS)	496

Summary	501
Review questions	501
Exercises	502
References	502

CHAPTER 16

Project risk management 504

16.1	Introduction	505
16.2	Risk management overview	507
16.3	The Risk Management Plan	509
16.4	Step 1: Establishing the risk context	511
16.5	Step 2: Risk identification	511
16.6	Step 3: Risk analysis	516
16.7	Further complexity in risk analysis	518
16.8	Step 4: Risk evaluation	521
16.9	Step 5: Risk treatment	522
16.10	Step 6: Contingency planning	527
16.11	Opportunity risk explored	529
16.12	Common approaches to handling risk	530
16.13	Budgets, contingency and risk	532

16.14 Risk monitoring and review   533
16.15 Communication and consultation   535
16.16 Close risk management   536
16.17 Risk management tools   536

Summary   536
Review questions   537
Exercises   538
References   538

CHAPTER 17

Project procurement management   539

17.1 Introduction   540
17.2 Procurement and projects   541
17.3 Identifying procurement requirements   542
17.4 Procurement Management Plan   546
17.5 Decision: Purchase order   547
17.6 Decision: Tender, including
      supplier selection   548
17.7 Decision: Contracts and contract types   551
17.8 Outsourcing project work   561
17.9 Partnering practices   564
17.10 Procurement closure activities   569

Summary   571
Review questions   571
Exercises   572
References   572

PART 5
Performing project execution

CHAPTER 18

Project execution   574

18.1 Introduction   575
18.2 Moving from Planning to Execution   576
18.3 A day in the life   581

Summary   590
Review questions   591
Exercises   592
References   592

CHAPTER 19

Project leaders and project teams   593

19.1 Introduction   594
19.2 Understanding the role of a contemporary
      project leader   596
19.3 Managing versus leading a project   601

19.4 Building and leveraging your networks   602
19.5 Ethics and the project leader   608
19.6 Building trust: The key to exercising
      influence   610
19.7 The project leader as a leader   613
19.8 Project teams   614
19.9 Building project teams   617
19.10 Managing project teams   630
19.11 Disbanding project teams   642
19.12 Servant leadership   642

Summary   645
Review questions   646
Exercises   646
References   647

CHAPTER 20

Complex project management   649

20.1 Introduction   650
20.2 Thinking practices to assist the
      project leader   653
20.3 Evaluating project complexity   656
20.4 A generic complexity framework   657
20.5 Framework part A: Pre-project complexity
      assessment   658
20.6 Framework part B: Detailed complexity
      assessment   662
20.7 Framework part C: Monitor project
      complexity   664
20.8 Framework part D. Review and capture
      knowledge   665
20.9 Framework part E: Assess handover and
      operational complexity   666

Summary   667
Review questions   667
Exercises   668
References   668

PART 6
Performing project closure

CHAPTER 21

Project closure   670

21.1 Introduction   671
21.2 Types of project closure   673
21.3 Closure activities   674
21.4 Performance evaluation   680
21.5 Lessons learned   687

21.6 The Business Case, benefits and
       scope realisation   693
21.7 Project celebration   695
       Summary   695
       Review questions   696
       Exercises   696
       References   697
Glossary   698
Index   711

Preface

SINCE YOU ARE READING THIS TEXT, you have made a decision that learning more about project management will have a positive impact for you. You are absolutely right! Project management has become an organisation-wide core competency; nearly every manager, regardless of discipline, is involved in projects. This text is designed to provide project managers and prospective project managers with the knowledge and skills that are transferable across industries and countries.

Our motivation for writing this text was to provide students and practitioners alike with a holistic, integrative, practice-driven view of project management. The linkages for integration include the process of selecting projects that best support the strategy of a particular organisation and that in turn can be supported by the technical and managerial processes made available to bring projects to completion. The goals for prospective project managers are to understand the role of a project in their organisation and to master the project management tools, techniques and interpersonal skills necessary to orchestrate projects from conception to completion.

The role of projects in organisations is receiving increasing attention, visibility, and accountability. Projects are the major tool for implementing and achieving the strategic goals of the organisation. In the face of intense, worldwide competition, many organisations have reorganised around a philosophy of innovation, renewal and organisational learning to survive. This philosophy suggests a structure that is flexible and project driven. Project management has developed to the point where it is a professional discipline having its own body of knowledge and skills. Today it is nearly impossible to imagine anyone at any level in the organisation who would not benefit from some degree of expertise in the process of managing projects. The text covers traditional life cycle project management but also has a detailed chapter on Agile (Scrum) project management to complement any project managers knowledge, as it is likely we will be applying different approaches to different types of "project" work.

Audience

This text is written for a wide audience. Although it is aligned to the Australian VET sector training package for the Certificate IV and Diploma of Project Management and the *Project Management Body of Knowledge* (making links to both the sixth and seventh editions), it covers concepts and skills that are used by managers to propose, plan, secure resources, budget and lead project teams to successful completion. The text should prove useful to students and prospective project managers in helping them understand why organisations have developed a formal project management process to gain a competitive advantage. Readers will find the concepts and techniques discussed in enough detail to be immediately useful in any project situation. Practising project managers will find the text to be a valuable guide and reference when dealing with typical problems that arise in the course of a project.

Managers will also find the text useful in understanding the role of projects in the missions of their organisations. Facilitators of VET may use this text as a replacement to course notes, as the text is aligned to and covers all subject material at the Certificate IV and Diploma levels. Members of the Project Management Institute will find the text is well structured to meet the needs of those wishing to prepare for PMP (Project Management Professional) or CAPM (Certified Associate in Project Management) certification exams. Those wishing to understand the concepts of Agile (Scrum) will also gain a wealth of knowledge from the extended change on Agile (Scrum) Project Management.

The text has in-depth coverage of the most critical topics found in PMI's *Project Management Body of Knowledge* (PMBOK®). People at all levels in the organisation assigned to work on projects will find the text useful not only in providing them with a rationale for the use of project management tools and techniques but also because of the insights they will gain on how to enhance their contributions to project success.

Our emphasis is not only on how the management process works but, more importantly, on why it works. The concepts, principles and techniques are universally applicable. That is, the text does not specialise by industry type or sector. Instead, the text is written for the individual who will be required to manage a variety of projects in a variety of different organisational settings. In the case of some small projects, steps need to be tailored to meet the size, complexity, risk, etc. of the project, but the conceptual framework applies to all organisations in which projects are important to survival. The approach can be used in pure project organisations such as construction, research and engineering consultancy. At the same time, this approach will benefit organisations that carry out many small projects while the daily effort of delivering products or services continues.

Content

In this third Australian edition of the book, we have responded to valuable feedback received from both students and teachers. As a result of this feedback, the following changes have been made:

- Extended coverage of all ten areas of the *Project Management Body of Knowledge* sixth edition (2017), with a new chapter covering the aspects of project integration management (Chapter 6).
- Acknowledgement of the *Project Management Body of Knowledge* seventh edition (2021) with its move away from a detail knowledge resource to guidance and principles around the application of project management to life cycle and more Agile practices.
- Further recognition and explanation of other project management methodologies, such as Scrum (Agile), PRINCE2, ISO 21500:2012, APM, Praxis, P3.express and Lean Six Sigma.
- An extended chapter covering Agile (Scrum) in greater detail (Chapter 3).
- Localisation of the text to the Australian marketplace, including mapping to the VET competency framework for the Certificate IV and Diploma of Project Management.
- Development of a number of additional online resources to provide students and facilitators (teachers) with a rich set of content, including a full suite of project management templates covering the 10 areas of knowledge and beyond.
- Complete update of content to bring it in line with current project management thinking.
- Coverage of key project management documents (artefacts) typical of most projects managed under a life cycle approach.
- Greater consideration of the integrative nature of project management.
- New chapter on project complexity, a benefit to us all to identify and therefore better prepare for project complexity. This new chapter also covers the new VET competency on Managing Complex Projects.
- New dedicated chapter on organisational change management (OCM) to represent a developing set of skills project managers are increasingly drawing on in the implementation of projects.
- New chapter on project governance, with material from other chapters of the book consolidated and expanded into a dedicated chapter on project governance, with the author's (Pearson's) Governance Planning Canvas tool to assist in the planning of project governance.
- New chapter on project execution to bring to life some day-in-the-life scenarios of what can happen to projects during the Execution stage.

Overall, the text addresses the major questions and issues the authors have encountered over their 80 combined years of teaching project management and consulting with practising project managers in domestic and overseas environments.

The following questions represent the issues and problems practising project managers find consuming most of their effort:

- What is the strategic role of projects in contemporary organisations?
- How are projects prioritised?
- What organisational and managerial styles will improve chances of project success?

- How do project managers orchestrate the complex network of relationships involving vendors, subcontractors, project team members, senior management, functional managers, and customers that affect project success?
- What factors contribute to the development of a high-performance project team?
- What project management system can be set up to gain some measure of control?
- How do managers prepare for a new international project in a foreign culture?
- How is the impact of organisational change management activities increasingly being integrated into the design of projects?

Project managers must deal with all these concerns to be effective. All the issues and problems listed represent links to an integrative project management view. The chapter content has been placed within an overall framework that integrates these topics in a holistic manner, and cases and snapshots are included from the experiences of practising managers. The future for project managers is promising.

About the authors

Dr. Neil Pearson

NEIL PEARSON (PhD) is a freelance corporate educator and management consultant. Neil teaches at various universities, corporate businesses and professional training institutes, and is highly versed in a number of subjects, including traditional portfolio, program and project management, strategy design, Lean Six Sigma and Agile/Scrum and business analysis.

Neil holds a PhD in a business and ICT-related discipline, having studied project management in both his bachelor and masters degrees. He also has an Advanced Diploma of Project Management, obtained through the Australian vocational education system and has facilitated many hundreds of training sessions at vocational level (Certificate IV, Diploma and Advanced Diploma) in Australia. Throughout his long and distinguished career in program and project management, Neil has inspired and led many professional teams, working across three continents: the United Kingdom, North America, South America, Europe and Australia. His experience includes a variety of organisations including large corporates, small-to-medium enterprises, educational establishments and government-related entities.

If you require non-accredited project management courses, either PMI-based or Agile, please contact us for a bespoke delivery. Neil is also building a library of high-quality supplemental trainers delivery material. For expressions of interest please contact Neil at: info@drneilpearson.com.

Additional materials can be found at the following eCommerce store: https://projectdoctor.gumroad.com/

Originating author: Erik W. Larson

ERIK W. LARSON is Professor of Project Management at the College of Business, Oregon State University. He teaches executive, graduate, and undergraduate courses on project management, organisational behaviour and leadership. His research and consulting activities focus on project management. He has published numerous articles on matrix management, product development and project partnering. He has been honoured with teaching awards from both the Oregon State University MBA program and the University of Oregon Executive MBA program. He has been a member of the Portland, Oregon, chapter of the Project Management Institute since 1984. He is a certified project management professional (PMP) and Scrum Master.

Originating author: Clifford F. Gray

CLIFFORD F. GRAY is Professor Emeritus of Management at the College of Business, Oregon State University. His research and consulting interests have been divided between operations management and project management. He has published numerous articles and has conducted research in the International Project Management Association.

Cliff has been a member of the Project Management Institute since 1976 and was President of Project Management International, Inc. 1977–2005. He received his BA in economics and management from Millikin University, MBA from Indiana University, and doctorate in operations management from the College of Business, University of Oregon. He is a certified Scrum Master.

Text at a glance

THIS TEXT IS DESIGNED to provide a holistic integrative view of project management for students and practitioners. We want students to get the most from this book, and we realise that students have different learning styles and study needs. We therefore present a number of study features to appeal to a wide range of students which are designed to test their knowledge of theory and practical skills. The text also includes a variety of real-life case studies and examples to help explain the key topics in each chapter.

Learning elements

1A   Develop an understanding of the background to project management.

1B   Understand how projects differ from routine operational work.

1C   Understand the difference between a standard, a framework and a methodology.

◀ Learning elements These elements map out the important topics and learning goals to help guide students through the chapter. They are mapped against the relevant heading level.

1.1 | Introduction   LE 1A

Welcome to the third edition of *Project Management in Practice*, which finally sees a shift in the industry in project management thinking, led by the Project Management Institute (PMI) in its seventh edition of *A Guide to the Project Management Body of Knowledge (PMBOK® Guide)* (PMI 2021a), which includes *The Standard for Project Management* (PMI 2021b).

▶ In Theory This feature explains a tool or a technique widely used in the field of project management. Some provide a fascinating background to the rationale behind the management and teamwork strategies described in this book, and give an insight into the way these strategies are developed and verified.

IN THEORY   The INVEST acronym

A popular technique that is often used as an aid to writing better story cards is the INVEST acronym. It stands for:

- Independent of all other story cards
- Negotiable, the results of engaging with business stakeholders to collect the user story (or conversation)
- Valuable to the business
- Estimable to a reasonable accuracy (preferably story points)
- Small enough to fit within a sprint
- Testable (in principle, even if there isn't a test for it yet).

This is much like applying the SMART acronym (specific, measurable, achievable, realistic and timely) to project objectives.

 Tool—Project Vision Statement

◀ Template When you see this icon, it indicates that a template is available. There are over sixty templates to help you save time in the workplace. Please contact your trainer or RTOs for copies of these.

▶ Snapshot from Practice
A series of short case studies demonstrating real-life project management problems and creative solutions. The snapshots provide a fascinating insight into projects from Australia as well as internationally and give practical examples of how the key topics discussed in the text play out in a real-world context.

SNAPSHOT *from* PRACTICE   Key project management bodies

The Project Management Institute (PMI) (www.pmi.org) was founded in 1969 as an international society for project leaders. Today, the PMI has chapters in more than 300 countries, with a total membership in excess of 700 000. PMI professionals work in almost every major industry, including aerospace, automotive, business management, construction, engineering, financial services, information technology, pharmaceuticals, health care and telecommunications.

The PMI offers an industry-recognised certification for project leaders: the Project Management Professional (PMP). This is available only to someone who has sufficient documented project experience, agrees to follow the PMI Code of Professional Conduct and demonstrates mastery of the field of project management by passing a comprehensive examination. The number of people earning PMP status has grown dramatically in recent years. In 1996 there were fewer than 3000 certified project management professionals. By the end of 2021, there were more than one million PMPs across the globe.

Passing the PMP (or an equivalent industry-recognised exam/certification) is becoming a mandatory standard for project leaders. Some companies require that all their project leaders are PMP certified. Numerous job postings indicate that applications will only be accepted from project leaders holding an industry-recognised project management certification (and/or qualification). Being PMP certified therefore potentially offers candidates a positive leveraging point in today's marketplace from a globally recognised body.

Summary

Powerful economic forces are contributing to the rapid expansion of project management approaches to business problems and opportunities. A project is defined as a non-routine, one-time effort that is limited by time and resources and by performance specifications designed to meet customer needs.

Effective project management begins with selecting and prioritising projects that support the organisation's mission and strategy and deliver value to the customer. Successful implementation requires both technical (hard skills) and competent leadership and engagement (soft skills). Project leaders must plan and budget projects as well as orchestrate and lead the contributions of others with often diverse backgrounds.

In summarising this chapter, it is helpful to reflect on and learn from some of the typical reasons projects fail, and conversely to learn why others are successful. Reflecting on this chapter, the reader will be able to identify and embellish on the positive lessons and negative lessons in relation to why we carry out project management—refer to Table 1.10 for some of the author's (Pearson's) reflections.

◀ **Chapter summary** Each chapter contains a summary of the key points and topics.

▶ **Review questions** These end-of-chapter questions are designed to help you revise and test your understanding of the key topics.

Review questions

1. What are the main characteristics that help differentiate projects from other functions carried out in the daily operations of an organisation?
2. What are the important factors in contemporary project management which are requiring a project leader to understand factors beyond just the project?
3. Why is the implementation of projects important to strategic planning and the project leader?
4. "The yin and yang of project management are two sides of the same coin." Explain.
5. What is meant by an integrative (holistic) approach to project management? Why is this approach important in today's environment?
6. What are the key reasons for challenged projects according to the Standish Group?
7. What are the main stages in the PMI's *Project Management Body of Knowledge* (PMBOK) life cycle? What is the purpose of each stage?

Exercises

1. Use the internet to identify all the infrastructure projects currently taking place in your local area. How many are you able to find? What is the value of the projects and how long are they planned to take?
2. Individually identify what you consider to be the greatest achievements accomplished by humankind in the last decade. Now share your list with other students in the class and come up with an expanded list. Review these accomplishments in terms of the definition of a project. What does your review suggest about the importance of project management?
3. Individually identify a recent project you have either worked on or been impacted by. Can you identify evidence of both the yin and yang of project management?

◀ **Exercises** These exercises can be used in group discussions as practical activities to embed knowledge and improve skills.

▶ **Key terms** Within each chapter key terms are highlighted the first time they appear. Key terms are defined in the Glossary at the end of the book.

Included within this text is wider thinking on good governance, ethics, principles, cultures, organisational change management, integrative business systems thinking, the voice of the customer and project design.

This is a good time to be reading an up-to-date text about project management as many business leaders and experts have proclaimed that project management is a strategic imperative. Project management provides employees with a powerful set of tools that can improve their ability to design, plan, implement and manage activities to accomplish specific organisational or customer objectives. But project management is more than just a set of tools and techniques; it is a results-oriented management style that places a premium on building collaborative relationships among a diverse

PART 1

Setting the scene

CHAPTER 1

Contemporary project management

Learning elements

1A Develop an understanding of the background to project management.

1B Understand how projects differ from routine operational work.

1C Understand the difference between a standard, a framework and a methodology.

1D Understand, at a broad level, the concept of a project life cycle.

1E Appreciate the current trends impacting the management of projects.

In this chapter

1.1 Introduction

1.2 What is a project? What is project management?

1.3 Standards, frameworks and methodologies: An introduction

1.4 The importance of project management

1.5 Contemporary project management: A holistic approach

Summary

1.1 : Introduction

LE 1A

Welcome to the third edition of *Project Management in Practice,* which finally sees a shift in the industry in project management thinking, led by the Project Management Institute (PMI) in its seventh edition of *A Guide to the Project Management Body of Knowledge (PMBOK® Guide)* (PMI 2021a), which includes *The Standard for Project Management* (PMI 2021b).

The approach in each edition of this text has been to (1) promote the soft side of project management, upholding good ethics, a self-mandated set of principles and a mindset that a well-led and empowered project team will more likely deliver success for all, including the project leader; and to (2) emphasise that most project management tools, techniques and models are as applicable to predictive (traditional) approaches as they are to adaptive (Agile) approaches, and in fact techniques between these approaches frequently blend.

This edition, through the update and addition of material, integrates a more rounded exploration of the multifaceted project leader (Figure 1.1), who embraces contemporary thinking and the skills needed to operate in a 21st century project environment.

This edition has not reduced the discussion of the technical side of project management (after all, this is expected as baseline knowledge at interviews) but articulates and incorporates other, less tangible, *soft* skills that make a successful project leader. Project leaders are often leading a team of people on a journey—a journey that results in a customer (whether internal or external to the organisation) receiving something of **value**. Increasingly, customer and project are working hand in hand, with neither subservient to the other—almost akin to the Scrum team being equal to the product owner in an Agile project environment. This joint involvement starts from the project outset in the selection of the most suitable project management approach to guide project delivery.

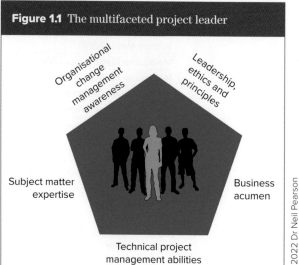

Figure 1.1 The multifaceted project leader

Organisational change management awareness

Leadership, ethics and principles

Subject matter expertise

Business acumen

Technical project management abilities

In Chapter 2 "Popular frameworks and methodologies", this decision is examined as part of the good governance of projects, whereby selecting the most suitable approach to the management of the project will undoubtedly enhance its success.

Included within this text is wider thinking on good governance, ethics, principles, cultures, organisational change management, integrative business **systems thinking**, the voice of the customer and project design.

This is a good time to be reading an up-to-date text about project management as many business leaders and experts have proclaimed that project management is a strategic imperative. Project management provides employees with a powerful set of tools that can improve their ability to design, plan, implement and manage activities to accomplish specific organisational or customer objectives. But project management is more than just a set of tools and techniques; it is a results-oriented management style that places a premium on building collaborative relationships among a diverse cast of characters. Exciting opportunities await people who are well-skilled and passionate about the management of projects.

The *project approach* has long been the preferred style of doing business in the construction and mining industries, in government, as well as in big consulting firms. Projects are found in all avenues of work in today's global marketplace. Project teams carry out everything: from port expansions, to hospital restructuring, to upgrading information systems, to changing the way an organisation operates internally. Project teams are creating next-generation fuel-efficient vehicles, developing sustainable sources of energy, exploring the farthest reaches of outer space and delving beneath our seas to explore offshore resource possibilities. The impact of project management is arguably most profound in the software industry, where the new folk heroes are those professionals whose Herculean efforts lead to a constant flow of new hardware innovations and software products that penetrate all aspects of our business and personal lives.

It is nearly impossible to read a newspaper or business periodical and not find something about projects! Project management is a discipline that can be applied to all industries, whether in the private sector, the public sector (government) or not-for-profit organisations. It can be applied to endeavours as varied as providing emergency aid (e.g. during Cyclone Yasi, in Queensland), to devising and implementing strategies for reducing crime and illicit drug abuse within a city, to changing the way serious crime is investigated; to large global investment initiatives such as China's Belt and Road Initiative (BRI), where an estimated USD1 trillion equivalent is being spent across the globe in what President Xi Jinping describes as a 21st century silk road. Australia is investing substantial spending within its borders (Table 1.1), with an ever-increasing value of projects to meet the demands of a growing population.

Table 1.1 Large infrastructure projects, Australia 2022

Project name	Value AUD billion
WestConnex (NSW)	16
Sydney Metro (NSW)	12
Melbourne Metro Tunnel (Victoria)	11
Melbourne to Brisbane Inland Rail (national)	9.3
Bruce Highway Upgrade Program (Queensland)	8.5
West Gate Tunnel (Victoria)	6.8
Cross River Rail (Queensland)	5.4
Western Sydney Airport (NSW)	5.3
Melbourne Airport Rail Link (Victoria)	5
Western Sydney Infrastructure Plan (NSW)	2.9
M80 Ring Road Upgrade (Victoria)	2.25
METRONET (WA)	1.84

Source: Adapted from iseekplant 2017, "A complete list of Australian infrastructure projects", https://blog.iseekplant.com.au/australian-infrastructure-guide

To meet the demands of such projects, the project management discipline is fast entering a new era of even more integrated and complex projects.

A strong indicator of the demand for project management can be seen in the continued expansion of the PMI, a professional organisation for project leaders. PMI membership has grown from 93 000 in 2002 to more than 700 000 in 2022 (PMI 2022). See "Snapshot from Practice: Key project management bodies" for information regarding professional certification in project management.

The discipline of project management is not without its problems. The Standish Group has tracked the management of information and communication technology (ICT) projects since 1994. This firm's periodic landmark reports summarise some of the factors behind the continued need for improved project management and the importance of continually learning from past projects, so future projects have smoother pathways.

Looking across the Standish Group's chaos reports for 2011–20 (Table 1.2), there was marginal year-on-year resolution of information technology projects (resolution being on time and on cost with a satisfactory result). The survey goes on to unpack various dimensions of projects—it is evident that the project management discipline has stalled in improving the resolution of projects.

Table 1.2 Information technology project success (%)

	2011	2012	2013	2014	2015	2020
Successful	29	27	31	28	29	31
Challenged	49	56	50	55	52	50
Failed	22	17	19	17	19	19

Source: Adapted from Krasner H 2021, *The Cost of Poor Software Quality in the US,* CISQ, https://www.it-cisq.org/pdf/CPSQ-2020-report.pdf, accessed December 2021

Underlying these figures has been a change in the project management approach: a big shift from *Waterfall* or traditional (predictive) project management, towards an adaptive *Agile* approach.

Table 1.3 indicates this shift. Note the success rates of the Agile approach over Waterfall in the context of software development.

Table 1.3 Waterfall versus Agile approaches (%)

	2012		2015		2020	
	Waterfall	Agile	Waterfall	Agile	Waterfall	Agile
Successful	14	42	12	39	13	42
Challenged	57	49	56	52	59	47
Failed	29	9	32	9	28	11

Source: Adapted from Vitality Chicago, "Why Agile is better than Waterfall (based on Standing Group Chaos Report 2020", https://www.it-cisq.org/pdf/CPSQ-2020-report.pdf, accessed December 2021

Closer to the Australian market are reports from Blake Dawson indicating current trends in scoping issues in the Australian construction and infrastructure industry. Survey responses and interviews revealed these five key findings:

1. a high prevalence of deficient scoping in Australian construction and infrastructure projects (52%)
2. scoping inadequacies are being discovered far too late, and the consequences of poor scoping are significant (64%)
3. cost overruns (61%)
4. delayed completion (57%)
5. disputes (30%) (Dawson 2008, p. 12).

More recently, the Australian Institute of Project Management (AIPM), in its "Project Delivery Performance in Australia" survey and report (AIPM and KPMG 2020) observed that:

- 48% of respondents felt their organisation managed projects and programs effectively or very effectively
- 25% of projects were delivered successfully, at least most of the time
- 52% of projects were delivered with stakeholder satisfaction
- 51% of projects were likely to meet original goal and business intent
- 42% of projects were likely to be delivered on time
- 40% of projects were likely to be delivered on budget
- 61% of sponsors had actively engaged sponsors
- 32% of organisations with formal change (variation) management activities considered them to be very or extremely effective.

The Standish Group Chaos Manifesto (2014) confirmed that time has not improved many issues encountered in managing projects (Table 1.4).

Table 1.4 Project challenge factors

1995	2014	2020
1. Incomplete requirements	1. Lack of user input	1. Lack of user input
2. Lack of user involvement	2. Incomplete requirements and specifications	2. Incomplete requirements and specifications
3. Lack of resources	3. Changing requirements and specifications	3. Changing requirements and specifications
4. Unrealistic expectations	4. Lack of executive support	4. Lack of executive support
5. Lack of executive support	5. Technology incompetence	5. Technical incompetence

Note: A challenged project would have met only two out of the three constraints of scope, time and cost.
Sources: Adapted from The Standish Group, www.standishgroup.com (data from various Standish Group sources sighted and referenced); Open Door 2021, "The Standish Group reports 83.9% of IT projects fail – How to save yours", https://www.opendoorerp.com/the-standish-group-report-83-9-of-it-projects-partially-or-completely-fail/

On the flip side, the Standish Group has reported (through its chaos reports) some project success factors (Table 1.5).

Table 1.5 Project success factors

1994	2012	2016	2020
1. User involvement	1. Executive support	1. Executive sponsorship	1. User involvement
2. Executive management support	2. User involvement	2. Emotional maturity	2. Executive management support
3. Clear statement of requirements	3. Clear business objectives	3. User involvement	3. Clear statement of requirements
4. Proper planning	4. Emotional maturity	4. Optimisation	4. Proper planning
5. Realistic expectations	5. Optimising scope	5. Skilled resources	5. Realistic expectations

Sources: Adapted from The Standish Group, www.standishgroup.com (data from various Standish Group sources sighted and referenced); Open Door 2021, "The Standish Group reports 83.9% of IT projects fail – How to save yours", https://www.opendoorerp.com/the-standish-group-report-83-9-of-it-projects-partially-or-completely-fail/

Professional project leaders will regularly review these types of reports and subscribe to industry journals and publications to learn lessons from the project profession's wider context (and from more focused industry reports, where these are available).

As the Dawson, AIPM/KPMG and Standish Group surveys all suggest, project performance (on time, on cost, to scope, to customer happiness), continues to offer challenges to the project management profession.

Many people who excel at managing projects never actually hold the title of project leader. This includes accountants, lawyers, administrators, scientists, contractors, public officials, teachers and community advocates, whose success depends on being able to lead and manage project work. For them, project management is not a title but an integral job requirement. It is hard to think of a profession or a career path that could not benefit from applying project management techniques, from predictive (traditional life cycle) through to adaptive (Agile) techniques.

The skillset required in project management is transferable across many sectors, industries, businesses and professions. Project management fundamentals are universal: the same project management methodology used to develop a new product can be adapted to create new services, organise events, refurbish ageing operations (and so forth). In a world where it is estimated that each person is likely to experience three to four career changes over the course of their professional working life, being able to manage projects is a skill worth developing, whether for your professional career or personal life (such as building a new home, organising events for charities or planning a round-the-world exploration!)

The significance of project management is also evident in the classroom: 20 years ago, major universities offered one or two classes or courses in project management (primarily for engineers). Today, most universities offer several project management courses that are geared towards not only engineers, but also business students majoring in marketing, human resources, information systems and finance, as well as students from other disciplines, such as oceanography, health sciences, earth sciences and the liberal arts. Students often find that their knowledge of project management provides them with a distinct advantage when it comes time to seek employment. More and more employers are looking for graduates with project management skills. RMIT University describes how qualifications in project management may help to future-proof students' careers (Johnson 2016).

More information on project management qualifications and certifications is provided in Table 1.6.

Refer also to "Snapshot from Practice: Project management in action" later in this chapter.

Table 1.6 Project management qualifications and certifications (Australia and international)

Role	Qualifications	Certifications						
		Project Management Institute (PMI)	Australian Institute of Project Management (AIPM)	International Project Management Association (IPMA)	Best Management Practice	Scrum/Agile (many variants of Agile/Scrum)	Praxis	Lean Six Sigma
Project officer Project coordinator	Certificate IV*	Certified Associate in Project Management (CAPM)	Certified Practising Project Practitioner (CPPP)	Certified Project Management Associate (IPMA Level D)	PRINCE2 Foundation	Scrum Fundamentals Certified (through SCRUMstudy)	Praxis Foundation	Yellow Belt
Project leader Senior project leader	Diploma* Undergraduate degree	Project Management Professional (PMP)	Certified Practising Project Manager (CPPM) Certified Practising Senior Project Manager (CPSPM)	Certified Project Manager (IPMA Level C) Certified Practising Senior Project Manager (IPMA Level B)	PRINCE2 Practitioner	Scrum Master Certified (SMC) Scrum Developer Certified (SDC) Scrum Product Owner Certified (SPOC) (through SCRUMstudy) PMI–Agile Certified Practitioner (PMI–ACP) PRINCE2 Agile Scrum Master Scrum Product Owner	Praxis Practitioner	Green Belt Black Belt
Program manager Portfolio manager	Advanced diploma* Undergraduate degree Postgraduate degree	Program Management Professional (PgMP) Portfolio Management Professional (PfMP)	Certified Practising Project Director (CPPD) Certified Practising Portfolio Executive (CPPE)	Certified Project Director (IPMA Level A)	Managing Successful Programs (MSP Practitioner) Advanced MSP	Scaled Scrum Master Certified (SSMC) Scaled Scrum Product Owner Certified (SSPOC) (through SCRUMstudy)		Black Belt Master Black Belt
Maturity assessment		Organizational Project Management Maturity Model (OPM3®)	Project Managed Organisation (award-based)		Portfolio, Program, and Project Management Maturity Model (P3M3®)		Praxis 360° Capability Assessment	

* Australian Vocational Education and Training (VET) or equivalent

© 2022 Dr Neil Pearson

Key project management bodies

The Project Management Institute (PMI) (www.pmi.org) was founded in 1969 as an international society for project leaders. Today, the PMI has chapters in more than 300 countries, with a total membership in excess of 700 000. PMI professionals work in almost every major industry, including aerospace, automotive, business management, construction, engineering, financial services, information technology, pharmaceuticals, health care and telecommunications.

The PMI offers an industry-recognised certification for project leaders: the Project Management Professional (PMP). This is available only to someone who has sufficient documented project experience, agrees to follow the PMI Code of Professional Conduct and demonstrates mastery of the field of project management by passing a comprehensive examination. The number of people earning PMP status has grown dramatically in recent years. In 1996 there were fewer than 3000 certified project management professionals. By the end of 2021, there were more than one million PMPs across the globe.

Passing the PMP (or an equivalent industry-recognised exam/certification) is becoming a mandatory standard for project leaders. Some companies require that all their project leaders are PMP certified. Numerous job postings indicate that applications will only be accepted from project leaders holding an industry-recognised project management certification (and/or qualification). Being PMP certified therefore potentially offers candidates a positive leveraging point in today's marketplace from a globally recognised body.

The PMI also offers other certifications, such as Certified Associate in Project Management (CAPM). CAPM is designed for project team members and entry-level project leaders, as well as qualified undergraduate and graduate students who want a credential that identifies their comprehension and competency in the PMBOK. CAPM does not require the level of extensive project management experience that is associated with the PMP.

In Australia, the primary professional body for project leaders is the Australian Institute of Project Management (AIPM) (www.aipm.com.au). Like the PMI, it has practice-based certification based on three levels of competency: the Certified Practising Project Administrator (CPPA), which is comparable to the PMI's Certified Associate in Project Management (CAPM); the Certified Practising Project Manager (CPPM) and Certified Practising Senior Project Manager (CPSPM), which is comparable to the PMI's PMP; and the Certified Practising Project Director (CPPD) and Certified Practising Portfolio Executive (CPPE), which is comparable to the PMI's Program Management Professional (PgMP) certification.

If further international certification is required, project leaders can seek certification through the International Project Management Association (IPMA) (www.ipma.world). IPMA has a network of member associations across 50+ countries.

1.2 What is a project and what is project management?

What do the following headlines have in common?

- "Free wi-fi to be made available in public parks and in bus, train and tram stations"
- "1000-acre wind farm to replace a coal-fired power station"
- "The world's largest lithium battery to be built in 100 days"
- "City receives stimulus funds to expand its light rail system after winning the bid to hold the next Commonwealth Games"
- "Shopping mall to be constructed—replacing 40-year-old city eye-sore buildings"

Figure 1.2 Peak Gold Mine in Cobar, NSW, Australia

The answer is that all these events represent projects.

The general definition of a *project* would include terms like *temporary* and *unique*, with the aim of producing a product, service or result (PMI 2021b). Figure 1.2 is a photo of part of the immense Peak Gold Mine project in NSW, Australia.

As for most organisations' efforts, the major goal of a project is to satisfy a customer's need. Yet beyond this fundamental similarity, the characteristics of a project differ from other endeavours of the organisation. The six major characteristics of a project are:

1. an established objective
2. a defined life span, with a defined beginning and end (i.e. it is temporary)
3. usually, the involvement of several departments and/or stakeholders
4. typically, doing something that has never been done before (unique)
5. specific time, cost, scope and performance requirements
6. delivery of something that is of value.

The first characteristic pertains to how projects have a defined objective. For example, this may be to construct a 12-storey apartment complex by 1 January or to release version 2.0 of a software package by a specific date. This singular purpose is often not present in daily *business as usual* where workers perform repetitive operations each day.

The second characteristic comes into play because, as there is a specified objective, the project will have a defined endpoint (this differs in nature from the ongoing duties and responsibilities of operational work). In many cases, individuals will move from one project to the next (as opposed to staying in one job). For example, after helping to install a security system, a telecommunications engineer may be assigned to commission a telephone switch.

Third, unlike much organisational work that is often segmented according to functional departments, projects typically require the combined efforts of a variety of specialists from across multiple departments of a business (cross-functional). Instead of working in separate offices under separate managers, project participants (whether they be engineers, financial analysts, marketing professionals or quality control specialists) will work closely together under the guidance of a project leader to complete the work as one project with one shared vision and goal.

The fourth characteristic of a project is that it is non-routine and has some unique elements. This is not an issue but a matter of degree. A project may accomplish something that has never been done before, such as building a new type of hybrid (electric/petrol) vehicle or returning rocket fuel tanks to earth for reuse on another mission. Both examples would typically require solving previously unsolved problems and potentially applying breakthrough technology. On the other hand, even small projects involving established sets of routines and procedures will require some degree of customisation that makes them unique. For example, the refit of one floor of an office would likely be different from the refit of another floor; there may be different requirements from the fit-out (office space versus meeting rooms versus training rooms), different stakeholders, different budget, and so on.

The fifth characteristic—specific time, cost, scope and performance requirements—bind projects. Projects are evaluated according to the accomplishment of scope, cost and time. These *triple constraints* impose a higher degree of accountability than is typically found in many operational situations. They also highlight one of the primary functions of project management, which is balancing the trade-offs between time, cost and performance (scope), while ultimately satisfying the customer (quality).

The sixth characteristic—delivery of something that is of value—implies that at the start of the project we as project leaders grasp and understand the concept of value from the customer's perspective, and what we ultimately design, build and deliver is something of value to the customer.

1.2.1 What a project is not

Projects should not be confused with everyday business-as-usual work (operational activity). A project is not routine, repetitive work! Ordinary daily work typically requires doing the same or similar work over and over, while a project is done only once, and a new product service or result will exist when the project is completed. Table 1.7 compares routine work and projects. Recognising this difference is important because all too often resources can be used up on daily operations that may not contribute to longer range organisational strategies that require innovative new products.

Table 1.7 Comparison of routine (operational) work with project work

Routine (operational) work	Projects
■ Entering expense claims into an accounting system	■ Constructing a house
■ Responding to a customer service enquiry	■ Relocating a department to a new office building
■ Attaching price tags to sales inventory before they are placed on the shop floor	■ Extending a railway line by 5 km to reach a new suburb
■ Assembling the components of a smartphone	■ Designing new digital TV leveraging developments in OLED technology
■ Analysing management reports to make operational decisions	■ Installing smart tags to allow scan-free checkout and payment at a large supermarket
■ Carrying out team members' performance reviews	■ Building a new state-of-the-art hospital in a large city
■ Supervising a hospital ward	■ Building a large battery resource to protect the energy supply of a region
	■ Developing, trialling and certifying a vaccine in response to a global pandemic

1.2.2 What is project management?

If a project is a unique, temporary (time-bound) piece of work with defined objectives, what is project management? Project management is the selection and application of an appropriate project management approach (discussed in Chapter 2 "Popular frameworks and methodologies"), in order for a project team to successfully deliver the project to the customer's requirements.

This book considers the following:

- predictive life cycle based on the traditional Initiate, Plan, Execute, Close, and Monitor and Control life cycle (the bulk of this text)
- adaptive (iterative) life cycle, or the Agile/Scrum approach to the management of projects (refer to Chapter 3 "Agile (Scrum) project management")
- hybrid approach, where predictive and perhaps adaptive are combined in designing the project's approach (refer to Chapter 2 "Popular frameworks and methodologies").
- Continuous improvement (sometimes referred to as *business improvement*), and the Lean Six Sigma technique of Define, Measure, Analyse, Improve and Control (DMAIC) as introduced in Chapter 13 "Project quality management".

Selecting the most appropriate approach to manage the project is discussed in Chapter 2 "Popular frameworks and methodologies", Figure 2.5, as selecting the project management approach is a key consideration before any work takes place on the project and will ultimately influence the success of the project. Project management today is not seen as a cookie cutter approach and requires careful consideration and *tailoring* to consider the environment within which the project is going to deliver results of value to a customer (internal or external to the organisation).

1.2.3 Program versus project

In practice, the terms *project* and *program* can cause confusion as they are often used synonymously. A **program** is a group of related projects designed to accomplish a common goal over an extended period to realise a greater set of benefits (and more value) than a single project could achieve alone. Each project within a program has a project leader. The major differences lie in scale and time span.

A program is generally defined as a collection of projects brought together to deliver a greater benefit (and value) than projects could have delivered individually (i.e. the sum is greater than the parts). Management of a program and its component projects should:

- be consistent with the organisation's strategy
- enable the program's delivery
- ensure that parts (e.g. schedule, resources, scope) are managed to ensure the program has the best outcome

- consider risk holistically
- consider assumptions, constraints and conflict across the whole program
- control upstream and downstream dependencies
- occur under the control of standard governance and program management office
- be overseen and guided by a suitable program manager.

1.2.4 Program versus portfolio

Just as there is a clear difference between a project and a program, the same is true for portfolios. **Portfolios** provide an overarching umbrella for an organisation to manage all investment activity, which may be managed as a mix of programs and/or major projects and operational activity. A portfolio is a true mix of investment activity designed to ensure business-as-usual (BAU) work and investment opportunities are blended, to not only keep the organisation running but also to innovate and stay competitive.

Program management is the process of managing a group of ongoing, interdependent, related projects in a coordinated way to achieve strategic objectives and defined business benefits. For example, a pharmaceutical organisation could have a program for working towards curing cancer. The cancer research program includes and coordinates all cancer research projects that continue over an extended time horizon. Coordinating all cancer research projects under the attention of a cancer research team provides benefits not available from managing the projects individually. This team also oversees the selection and prioritising of projects that are included in their cancer research portfolio. Although each project retains its own goals and scope, the project leader and team are also motivated by the higher program goal. Program goals are closely aligned to the organisation's strategic goals. This link is important, as the results of achieving a program will move the organisation further towards achieving its strategic goals and objectives.

1.3 | Standards, frameworks and methodologies: An introduction

The terms *standards*, *frameworks* and *methodologies* appear frequently throughout this text and in other resources such as the *PMBOK® Guide* (PMI 2021a). Noting the difference between these terms helps to determine the implied level of flexibility or rigidity of the approach being discussed.

1.3.1 Standard

The Cambridge Dictionary definition of a standard is "a pattern or model that is generally accepted: This program is an industry standard for computers" (Cambridge Dictionary n.d.). ISO's definition is a "document, established by a consensus of subject matter experts and approved by a recognized body that provides guidance on the design, use or performance of materials, products, processes, services, systems, or persons" (ISO n.d.).

(Source: https://www.iso.org/sites/ConsumersStandards/1_standards.html# Reproduced by McGraw Hill LLC with the permission of Standards Australia Limited under licence CLE0822MGH. Copyright in ISO vests in ISO. Users must not copy or reuse this work without the permission of Standards Australia or the copyright owner).

- The PMI publishes the *PMBOK® Guide* (along with other practice standards) to guide a project leader in the management of projects. PMBOK is a recognised standard with the American National Standards Institute (ANSI/PMI 99-001-2017 6th edition, and ANSI/PMI 99-001-2021 7th edition).
- The AIPM, IPMA and VET sectors all use a competency baseline: a standard against which to accredit the skill level of various project management roles.
- ISO 21500:2021 "Project, programme and portfolio management—Context and concepts" applies to most organisations, irrespective of their industry or size at the portfolio, program or project levels.

1.3.2 **Framework**

The Cambridge Dictionary definition of a framework is "a system of rules, ideas, or beliefs that is used to plan or decide something: a legal framework for resolving disputes" (Cambridge Dictionary n.d.).

- Scrum is a framework: The Scrum Guide states that, "Scrum is a framework for developing, delivering, and sustaining complex products" (Schwaber & Sutherland 2017).
- The PMI promotes the *PMBOK® Guide* as a framework for managing a project (it is also an American National Standards Institute standard).
- ISO 31000:2018 "Risk management" offers a framework for managing organisational risks (it is also a standard).
- ISO 21500:2021 "Project, programme and portfolio management—Context and concepts" contains a high-level framework for the management of projects (it is also a standard).

  A framework allows a degree of flexibility (i.e. permitting some poetic licence over how it is applied, akin to tailoring in project management terminology).

1.3.3 **Methodology**

The Cambridge Dictionary definition of methodology is "a system of ways of doing, teaching, or studying something: The methodology and findings of the research team have been criticized" (Cambridge Dictionary n.d.).

- PRINCE2 is a methodology (albeit tailoring is considered!).
- XP, or eXtreme Programming, is considered a methodology.
- Agile PM (formerly known as *dynamic systems development methodology* or DSDM) would be considered a methodology, as it has a defined (prescriptive) method of approaching the management of a project in an *agile* manner.

  A methodology is different from a framework, as a methodology means there must be a certain (more defined) way of carrying out something.

The above definitions are provided to assist the reader in determining the degree of rigidity in the approaches that are further described in later chapters.

1.3.4 **Project life cycle**

Another way of illustrating the unique nature of project work is the **project life cycle** (often referred to as the *traditional* or *predictive* project life cycle). Some project leaders find it useful to use the project life cycle as the cornerstone for managing projects. The life cycle recognises that projects have a limited life span and that there are predictable changes in the level of effort and focus over the life of the project. For example, a new software development project may consist of five stages: definition, design, code, integration/test and maintenance. A generic predictive life cycle, based on PMBOK, is depicted in Figure 1.3.

The generic predictive project life cycle typically passes through four stages: Initiation, Planning, Execution and Closure, with Monitor and Control traversing the life cycle. The starting point begins the moment the project is given the go-ahead. Typically, project effort starts slowly, builds to a peak and then declines as the project's deliverables are delivered to the customer.

1. *Initiation stage:* This stage ensures agreement between the project sponsor (the accountable business stakeholder) and the project leader of the key dimensions of the project based on discussions with key project stakeholders. It is typically captured in the Project Charter document.

2. *Planning stage:* The level of effort increases and the project scope document is defined based on the parameters captured in the Project Charter, along with the work breakdown structure (project design). These (upon interim approval) are then detailed to determine what the project will entail, when it will be scheduled, who it will benefit, what quality level should be maintained, what the budget will be, what risks there might be, how the project will be communicated, what

Figure 1.3 Generic predictive project life cycle

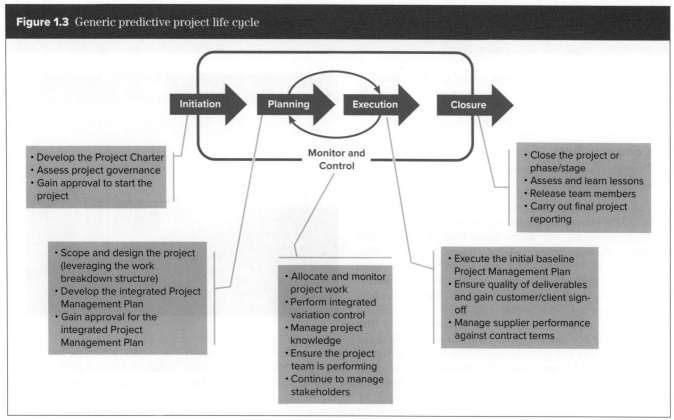

is to be procured, and how resources will be assigned and managed (to name but a few project leader activities). These detailed documents make up the integrated Project Management Plan (integrated PMP). This plan is then approved and becomes the **baseline** plan from which the project is subsequently executed.

3. *Execution stage:* The baseline integrated PMP is executed. This is where a major portion of the project work takes place—both physical and mental. The product, service or result is produced (e.g. a bridge, report, software program). Time, cost and specification measures are used for control—to check whether the project is on schedule, within budget and meeting customer specifications.

4. *Closure stage:* Closing includes three key activities: delivering the project's final product, service or result to the customer, redeploying project resources and conducting a post-implementation review.

Monitor and Control: Although not a stage in its own right, there is an overarching expectation that the project will be astutely monitored and controlled throughout its life cycle. One key process commonly applied during monitoring and controlling a project is the variation (change) management process. This process is defined during the project Planning stage and applied to control the scope (and other dimensions) of the project once baselines have been approved. Changes can include changes to the scope of the project, addition of costs not previously identified, or even slippage of work activities. Scope, cost and time are commonly referred to as the *triple constraints* and are discussed in Chapter 8 "Defining the scope of a project".

In practice, the project life cycle is used by some project groups to depict the timing of major tasks over the life of the project. For example, the design team might plan a major commitment of resources in the Initiating stage, while the quality team would expect their major effort to increase during the Execution stage of the project life cycle. Because most organisations have a portfolio of projects taking place concurrently, each at a different stage of each project's life cycle, careful planning and management at the organisation and program/project levels are imperative.

This predictive (traditional) project life cycle will form the basis of the framework that will be used throughout this text. Chapter 2 "Popular frameworks and methodologies" provides further detail on the

SNAPSHOT *from* PRACTICE | Project management in action

Businesses thrive and survive based on their ability to manage projects that produce products and services that meet market needs. Below is a small sample of projects that are important to their company's future.

Figure 1.4 Hornsdale Power Reserve

© NEON

Company: Tesla

Project: Hornsdale Power Reserve (online battery), South Australia

This is a 100-MW power reserve stored in the largest (as of 2020) lithium battery in the world. Located in South Australia, at the Hornsdale Wind Farm, the Hornsdale Power Reserve (online battery) (Figure 1.4) can (within fractions of a second) "kick into action" to cover peaks in electricity demand or provide safety in supply should traditionally fuelled power plant(s) fail. The project was constructed by Tesla within 100 days (after receiving regulatory approval), completing in December 2017. The project was of interest around the world not only because it pertained to the world's largest lithium battery, but also because Tesla's CEO claimed the battery would be handed over free if the project was not delivered to its deadline. As of April 2020, the Hornsdale Battery Extension project has added 50 MW/64.5 MWh of capacity at the site, bringing the total to 150 MW/193.5 MWh. This has doubled the capacity of the battery storage. The battery storage is reported to have cost Neon (the current operators of the Hornsdale battery and adjacent wind farm) AUD66 million but has brought benefits to consumers valued at AUD116 million per year. (More information at: https://electrek.co/2020/04/17/tesla-completes-massive-expansion-big-battery/)

Company: Korean Midland Power Co.

Project: World's largest tidal turbine farm, South Korea

Korean Midland Power Co. signed an agreement with Lunar Energy, Britain's leading tidal power company, to build a colossal 300-turbine field in the Wando Hoenggan waterway off the South Korean coast. The KRW$800 million-plus project provided 300 MW of renewable energy, enough to power 200 000 homes. The project entailed installing a series of 18-metre-high tidal turbines in deep ocean water. A 1-MW pilot plant was installed first to evaluate the environmental impact before the full-blown turbine was allowed. The ecological impact was much less than that of conventional tidal barges, which destroy bird habitats and hinder the passage of migratory fish such as salmon and eels. The project completed successfully in 2011.

Company: Apple Inc.

Project: Apple watch

Apple is reported to be developing the next generation of its smartwatch that will integrate advanced health functions (e.g. body temperature and blood sugar levels). Whether the marketplace is ready for another industry attempt at integrating watch technology with big data and analytics to watch over the health of individuals remains to be seen. The persistent, and often invasive, use of technology in every aspect of daily life may be at a turning point—but which way will it go?

Company: Crossrail

Project: Elizabeth line construction, London, England

A new railway being delivered by Crossrail Ltd runs for over 100 km through central London from Shenfield and Abbey Wood in the east to Reading and Heathrow in the west, with a total of 41 stations (10 of which are major stations). Costing GBP18.9 billion on an original budget of GBP14.8 billion, the Elizabeth line connects London's main employment centres and supports new journeys through central London out to Essex, Buckinghamshire and Berkshire. The Elizabeth line services commenced on 24 May 2022 as part of a phased opening plan completing in 2023. Crossrail can be categorised as a large, complex project. (More information at: www.crossrail.co.uk)

Company: Brisbane Airport Corporation

Project: Brisbane Airport new runway, Queensland, Australia

At AUD1.1 billion, the 3300-metre second runway took around eight years to build. It was started in 2012 and completed in 2020. It has been built on 360 hectares of swampland that is parallel to the existing main runway. Built to cater for the expected increase in flights—from 227 000 in 2015 to over 360 000 in 2025—the runway's capacity will rival that of the Hong Kong and Singapore airports. By 2035, the runway project is anticipated to have created around 7800 local jobs, delivering a local economic benefit of circa AUD5 billion annually. (More information at: www.bne.com.au)

Figure 1.5 Apple headquarters

Company: Apple Inc.

Project: Apple Park, California, United States

Apple Park (Figure 1.5) acts as the campus headquarters for 12 000 employees. It is a unique space-ship-like building, and its construction, design and operation are environmentally considerate. The massive 66-hectare site had proposed costs that came in at USD500 million. By 2011, these were raised to USD3 billion and, as of 2017, the estimated cost of completion had risen to circa USD5 billion. This goes to show that even with best project estimates, costs can (and almost always will) overrun! A lot of the costs have been attributed to the development of eco-friendly features, such as landscaping (7000 trees), rooftop solar panels and water recycling. (More information at: www.macworld.co.uk)

Company: SingHealth

Project: National Cancer Centre, New Building, Singapore

As people live longer and many lifestyles and environments remain unhealthy, cancer incidence increases. SingHealth is involved in the state-of-the-art construction of a new dedicated building and resources to meet forecast demand for such facilities. The now completed facility is a patient-centric design, with access and connections to existing site resources. It houses advanced therapy centres (based on proton therapy), and research and innovation hubs. The project demonstrates a commitment to the needs of the patient (the customer) in all aspects of design through to operations.

PMBOK-based project management life cycle, with each subsequent chapter targeting a specific area of knowledge within the project management life cycle. The reader must remember that although the central part of this text takes a knowledge area approach, this is the key: it is knowledge that will assist you as a contributor in an Agile team, as it would a project leader for a traditional life cycle approach.

1.3.5 The project leader

In some ways, project leaders perform similar functions to generic managers, because they plan, schedule, motivate and monitor work. However, what makes them dissimilar is the fact that they manage temporary, non-repetitive activities to complete a fixed duration project. Unlike functional managers who take over existing operations, project leaders create a project team where none previously existed. They must decide *what* and *how* things should be done, instead of simply managing set processes. They must meet the challenges of each stage of the project life cycle, and even oversee the dissolution of efforts when the project is completed.

Project leaders must work with a diverse group of characters to complete projects. They are typically the direct link to the customer and must manage the tension between customer expectations and what is feasible, reasonable and agreed within the project. Project leaders provide direction, coordination and integration to the project team, which is often made up of part-time participants who are loyal to their functional departments. They must often work with a cadre of outsiders—vendors, suppliers, subcontractors—who may not necessarily share the same project allegiance.

Project leaders are ultimately responsible for performance (frequently with too little authority). They must ensure that appropriate trade-offs are made between the time, cost and performance requirements of the project. At the same time, unlike their functional counterparts, project leaders generally possess only rudimentary technical knowledge to make such decisions. Instead, they must orchestrate the completion of the project by having the right people, at the right time, to address the right issues, make the right decisions and carry out the project's activities.

While project management is not for the timid, working on projects can be an extremely rewarding experience. Life on projects is rarely repetitive; each day is different from the last. Since most projects are directed at solving some tangible problem or pursuing some useful opportunity, project leaders usually find their work personally meaningful and satisfying. They enjoy the act of creating something new and innovative. Project leaders and project team members can feel immense pride in their accomplishment, whether it is a new bridge, a new product or a needed service. Project leaders are often stars in their organisation and can be remunerated well.

Good project leaders are always in demand. Every industry is looking for effective people who can get (the right) things done, on time, on cost and to the customer's satisfaction. Undoubtedly, project management is both a challenging and exciting profession!

Chapter 19 "Project leaders and project teams" reviews the skills that a typical, competent, project leader will possess. From leadership skills to change management abilities—an adept project leader is truly a multifaceted individual (Figure 1.1). This is recognised in this text by changing the term *project manager* to *project leader* to represent the approach we should now be taking (leading goes beyond managing).

1.4 The importance of project management

Project management is no longer a sidelined management technique. It is rapidly becoming a standard way of doing business. An increasing percentage of a typical organisation's effort is being devoted to projects; others are completely *projectised*, where all work is accomplished via projects and there is minimal organisational and administrative people and processes. The future promises an increase in both the importance and role of projects in contributing to the strategic direction of organisations. Several reasons are briefly discussed below.

1.4.1 Value and the customer experience

This concept of projects, programs and portfolio is not new; however, *why* we are doing this is changing from a strategic alignment perspective to a business systems perspective, where the focus is on value-delivery to the customer. A business system is composed of the people, organisation, processes, information that flows and technology that enables (Yeates, Cadle & Paul 2014). These business systems are all geared towards delivery of value to a customer. To achieve delivery of these end-to-end value streams, many different functions (departments) in the organisation may be crossed. Refer to Figure 1.6. The top tier represents the value chain to the customer (value identification), which is delivered through a combination of processes, people, technology that enables and information that flows; this is carried out within an organisation (i.e. the business system) (value creation and delivery). Where value to the customer has been identified, this is frequently delivered by end-to-end cross-functional business processes. These end-to-end value-adding processes that operate within a business system are frequently delivered and improved through programs and projects.

1.4.2 Compression of the product or service life cycle

One of the most significant driving forces behind the demand for project management is the shortening of the product life cycle. For example, today in high-tech industries, the product life cycle averages one to three years. Only 30 years ago, life cycles of 10 to 15 years were not uncommon. Time to market for new products/services with short life cycles has become increasingly important. A common rule of thumb in the world of high-tech product development is that a six-month project delay can result in a 33 per cent loss in product revenue share, or competitors gaining a market advantage. Speed, therefore, becomes a

Figure 1.6 Value identification, and value creation and delivery

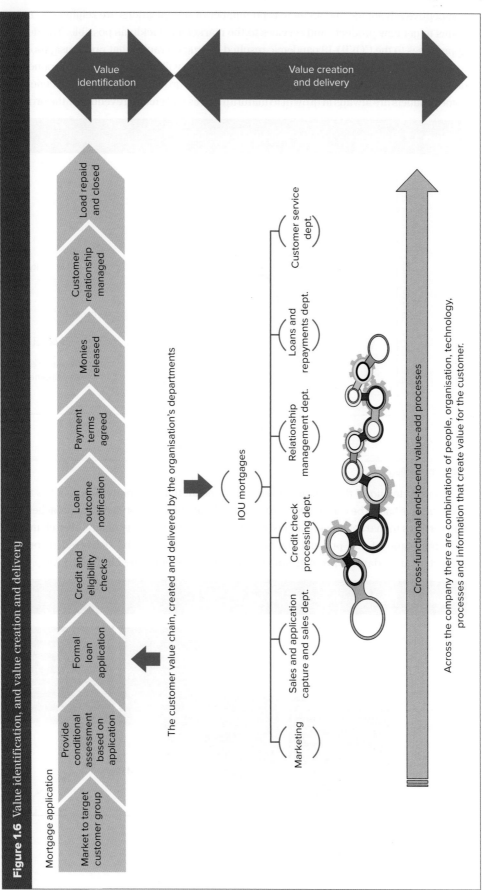

Mortgage application

Market to target customer group → Provide conditional assessment based on application → Formal loan application → Credit and eligibility checks → Loan outcome notification → Payment terms agreed → Monies released → Customer relationship managed → Load repaid and closed

Value identification

Value creation and delivery

The customer value chain, created and delivered by the organisation's departments

IOU mortgages

Marketing — Sales and application capture and sales dept. — Credit check processing dept. — Relationship management dept. — Loans and repayments dept. — Customer service dept.

Cross-functional end-to-end value-add processes

Across the company there are combinations of people, organisation, technology, processes and information that create value for the customer.

competitive advantage and an increasing number of organisations are relying on cross-functional project teams to get new products and services to the market as quickly as possible. The development of various approaches to the COVID-19 pandemic resulted in drug therapies that previously took many years to bring to market. Figure 1.7 illustrates that most organisations will have a pipeline of products in various stages of development: research and development, introduction, growth, maturity and decline; organisations ensure some products are always in growth to maturity as this will ensure revenue for the organisation is sustained.

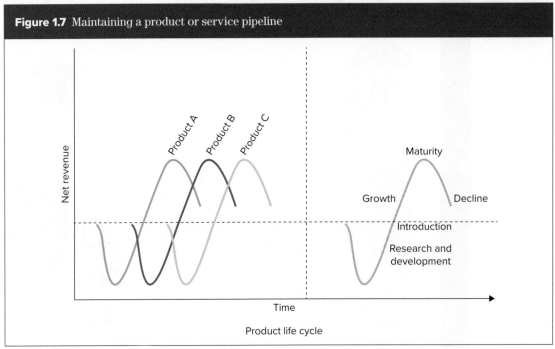

Figure 1.7 Maintaining a product or service pipeline

© 2022 Dr Neil Pearson

The shortening of the product life cycle has meant that alternative approaches to the management of projects have had to be considered. Scrum and Agile are often the preferred approaches for bringing products and services to market quicker and with better alignment with customers' ever-changing requirements.

Each stage of the product (or service) life cycle could be delivered through combinations of predictive and adaptive projects; an example of this is portrayed in Figure 1.8.

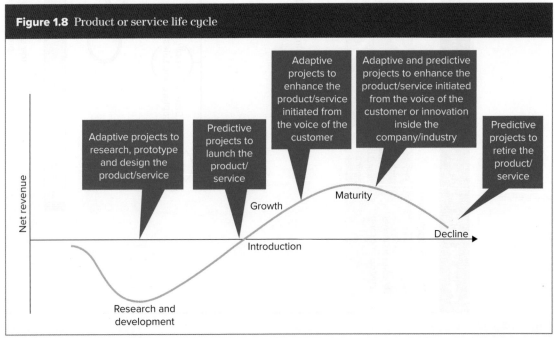

Figure 1.8 Product or service life cycle

© 2022 Dr Neil Pearson

1.4.3 Complexity

The growth of new knowledge has increased the complexity of projects, as projects typically encompass the latest advances in technology, materials and thinking. For example, building a road 30 years ago was a relatively simple process. Today, each area has increased in complexity, including material selection, specifications, codes, legislation, aesthetics, equipment and required specialists. Similarly, in today's digital age, it is becoming hard to find products that do not leverage the internet in some aspect of their function. Product complexity has increased the need to integrate divergent technologies. Project management has emerged as an important discipline for achieving the task of managing such complexity; even if this requires moving away from the predictive life cycle approaches of project management to Agile/Scrum approaches to solve the problem successfully. To recognise this, the Australian VET framework has introduced a new unit of competency to specifically address complexity in projects; this is further discussed in Chapter 20 "Complex project management".

1.4.4 Business systems and systems thinking

When undertaking any project, it is important that the project leader considers the system within which their project is taking place. For an internal project that is establishing a new ICT system, the business system in which the project is being implemented would need to be considered: for example, upstream processes, downstream processes and how these interact with the system. What other stakeholders or users identified that could be impacted by the project? What aspects of the organisation could be impacted by carrying out the project (decision-making protocols, leadership hierarchy, organisational culture)? What information needs to flow into and out of the business system to the wider system of events taking place? The same technique can be applied to physical external projects. What physical systems interact with the project: are there environmental aspects that now need to be considered? From a people perspective, are there further stakeholders (citizens in the community) who are now important to the project? What external interfaces interact with the organisation: are there lobby groups, unions and government departments that should be considered? From a technology perspective, are there opportunities to further explore?

Thinking in systems expands the project leader's ability to discover connections between the project and the wider system that exists. These could, for example, be captured as risks (either threat risks or opportunity risks), as additional packages of work to be included in the project, as new stakeholders that need to be managed in the project, or as additional communications to be formalised with the project's communication register. Table 1.8 lists some challenging vocabulary to apply to change from linear thinking to a systems thinking.

Table 1.8 Systems thinking-inspired vocabulary

Traditional thinking	Systems thinking
Elements assessed in isolation	Relationships
Disconnected elements	Interconnectedness and patterns
Linear and sequential	Circular
The parts	The whole
Analysis	Synthesis
Ring fenced, constrained	Big picture, open
Problem fixing	Root-cause identification
Control and master	Sustainable and sympathetic
Orderly	Chaotic
Seek simplicity	Understand complexity
Immediate response	Deeper considerations

© 2022 Dr Neil Pearson

Practising thinking and working in systems will assist the project leader in many ways: from a better integrated project design considerate of the system within which the project is to deliver, to ultimately greater success in the deliverables (outputs and outcomes) from the project being accepted by the business system and its actors. This concept of a *business system* is an underpinning principle in the way project leaders think, work and react. The system thinking technique is also a prerequisite for the manner in which complex projects are assessed (see Chapter 20 "Complex project management").

1.4.5   Triple bottom line (planet, people and profit)

The threat of climate change has brought sustainable business practices to the forefront. Businesses can no longer simply focus on maximising profit to the detriment of the environment (and indirectly therefore, society). Efforts to reduce the carbon footprint and use renewable resources are realised through effective project management. The impact of this movement towards **sustainability** can be seen in changes in the objectives and techniques used to complete projects (see "Snapshot from Practice: Gold Coast sustainable teaching hospital"). Tomorrow's projects will be heavily influenced not only in leading sustainability-focused projects, but also as a key consideration in any project we deliver. Project sustainability plans are an up-and-coming trend we should consider with all projects.

Sustainability covers:

- designing, planning and executing a sustainable project with sound environmental principles embedded in the design, so that in execution everything possible is being done to protect the environment
- operationally handing over and running the product or service for the life of the product or service to ensure a sustainable endeavour. Is the product producing net-zero emissions in operations? Is it adding new pollutants to the environment? We only have to go back to our customers and understand value: most would rather pay a few cents more for a product or service if they know sustainability goals are being truly addressed.

1.4.6   Corporate rightsizing

The last decade has seen a dramatic restructuring of organisational life. Downsizing (or rightsizing) and focusing on core competencies have become necessary for the survival of many organisations. The structure of middle management is thankfully a mere skeleton of the past. In today's flatter and leaner organisations, where change is a constant, project management is replacing middle management as a way of ensuring goals are achieved. Corporate rightsizing has also changed the way organisations approach projects. Companies outsource significant segments of project work, and project leaders must manage not only their own people, but also resources in different organisations under differing contractual conditions, with different cultural nuances.

Organisations seek to achieve more with the same, using technology and automation to assist in the fulfilment of roles.

1.4.7   Increased customer focus

Increased competition and the age of social media has placed a premium on customer satisfaction. Customers no longer simply settle for generic products and services. They want bespoke products and services that cater to their specific needs. This mandate requires a much closer working relationship between the customer and the organisation.

Increased customer focus has also prompted the development of bespoke products and services to segments, sub-segments and individuals (personas). Understanding the voice of the customer (VOC), the customer value proposition sold to the customer, how we deliver value to the customer through the value chain and being mindful of customer feedback are all critical elements to comprehend as project leaders. We now need to understand how value is realised and turned into the end-product, service or result that the customer (internal or external to the organisation) receives. This is not a new concept, as in the Lean Six Sigma world we drive the process from understanding the customer, we as project leaders need to discover and be given access to the customer so this value can be captured, understood, defined and form the focus of the project's deliverables and goals.

1.4.8 Organisational change management

Managing projects (large or small) can bring new challenges to an organisation, its departments, teams and individuals. Managing organisational change is an accepted norm in organisations today. However, too much change in one specific area of an organisation can have negative effects. An example of this might be the impact on day-to-day operations, the loss of key personnel and not being able to balance the introduction of new projects with operational activities. Managing a group of projects as a program enables the organisation to take a holistic view of organisational change impact across and within areas of the organisation, facilitating an easier, thorough preparation of staff and activities for the required changes to occur. It also allows for the smoother embedding of change post-project within the operational business. This text introduces a new chapter to review organisational change in the context of project management (Chapter 5 "Organisational change management and cultures"); the subject is also integrated into the latest edition of the *PMBOK® Guide* (PMI 2021a).

1.4.9 Small projects represent big problems

The velocity of change required to remain competitive, or to simply keep up, has created an organisational climate in which hundreds of projects may be implemented concurrently. This climate has created a multi-project environment with a plethora of new problems. Sharing and prioritising resources across a portfolio or program of projects is a major challenge for senior management. Many organisations have no idea of the problems involved, with inefficient management of multiple small projects. Small projects typically carry the same or more risk as large projects. Small projects are perceived as having little impact on the bottom line because they do not demand large numbers of scarce resources and/or amounts of money. Because so many small projects are going on concurrently and because the perception of the inefficiency impact is small, measuring inefficiency is usually non-existent. Unfortunately, many small projects soon add up to large sums of money. Many customers and millions of dollars are lost each year on small projects in product and service organisations. The failure of small projects can represent hidden costs to an organisation, yet often these costs are not measured.

SNAPSHOT *from* PRACTICE ┊ **Gold Coast sustainable teaching hospital**

Construction of one of Australia's largest ever public health infrastructure projects, a teaching hospital on the Gold Goast, was completed in 2012 at a cost of AUD1.76 billion.

The hospital site includes state-of-the-art healthcare facilities, 750 hospital beds (170 000 square metres of floorspace), onsite research facilities, relaxation areas for patients' family and friends, retail areas, car parking for over 2000 cars, easy access to the public light rail system and a private hospital co-located on the site.

Providing a mix of teaching, research and health care, the hospital has become an example of how to build with the public in mind. The project had numerous environmental considerations to meet, and a profit model formed on the grounds of activity-based funding, as opposed to a traditional block funding of services. Examples of the environmental and sustainability elements included in the construction are water harvesting, energy-efficient lighting, recycling and waste reduction, an energy-efficient façade, the use of recycled materials and a reduction in the use of polyvinyl chloride (and polyurethane-based glues).

This fit of planet, people and profit provides a benchmark for future teaching hospital construction and no doubt will be replicated in other Australian states.

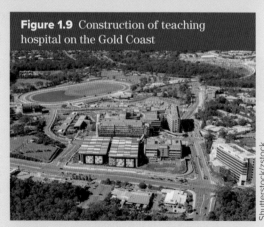

Figure 1.9 Construction of teaching hospital on the Gold Coast

The building of this teaching hospital on the Gold Coast is a large project that might lead to other, similar projects.

Shutterstock/zstock

Source: Adapted from Lend Lease n.d., "Stage 1 Entry Gold Coast University Hospital, Australian Construction Achievement Award", https://acaa.net.au/wp-content/uploads/2020/02/Gold-Coast-University-Hospital-%E2%80%93-Queensland.pdf

Organisations with many ongoing, concurrent small projects face the most difficult project management problems. A key question becomes how to create an organisational environment that supports multi-project management. A process is needed to prioritise and develop a portfolio or program of small projects that supports the mission of the organisation.

A variety of forces interact in today's world that contribute to the increased demand for good project management across all industries and sectors. Project management is ideally suited for a business environment that requires accountability, flexibility, innovation, speed and continuous improvement.

1.5 | Contemporary project management: A holistic approach

Competing in a global market that is influenced by rapid change, innovation and time-to-market challenges means organisations are increasingly becoming involved in managing projects. Being able to coordinate and manage projects in such a changing environment is therefore essential. To meet this challenge, organisations are increasingly centralising their project management processes and practices. For example, Dell, IBM and ANZ Bank will often have thousands of projects being delivered concurrently across different countries. But how do these organisations oversee the management of so many projects? How were these projects selected? How do they ensure performance measurement and accountability? How can project management continually be improved?

Centralisation entails the integration of all project processes and practices to improve project management. Integration is designed to improve project management in the whole organisation over the long haul. The rationale for the integration of project management to the wider organisation is to provide senior management with:

■ an overview of all project management activities

■ a big picture of how organisational resources are being used

■ an assessment of the risk their portfolio or program of projects represents

■ a metric for measuring the improvement of managing projects, relative to others in the industry

■ linkages to senior management with sponsorship, accountability and performance

■ performance management of projects, and linkages to executive pay and remuneration

■ a clear definition of the benefits from projects, and the tracking and delivery of these benefits across and beyond the life of a project, in support of the delivery of a program and portfolio into an organisation.

Full insight of all components of the organisation is crucial for aligning internal business resources with the requirements of the changing environment. Integration enables management to have greater flexibility and better control of all project management activities.

Operationally, what does project management integration mean? It necessitates combining all the major dimensions of project management under one umbrella. Each dimension is connected in one seamless, integrated domain (Figure 1.10). Integration means applying knowledge, skills, tools and techniques to a collection of projects to move the organisation towards its strategic goals. This integration is central to project-driven organisations, across all industries.

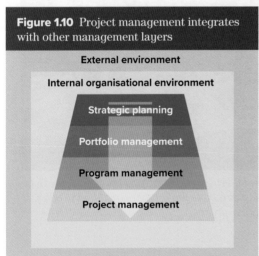

Figure 1.10 Project management integrates with other management layers

External environment

Internal organisational environment

Strategic planning

Portfolio management

Program management

Project management

1.5.1 Alignment of projects with organisational strategy

Today, projects are the *modus operandi* for delivering strategy. Yet in some organisations, the selection and management of projects often fail to support the strategic plan of the organisation and add unconfirmed value to the customer. Strategic plans are written by one group of managers, projects may be selected by a different group and projects may be implemented by yet another. Independent decisions made by different groups of managers create a set of conditions that can lead to conflict, confusion and (frequently) a dissatisfied customer. Under such conditions, the resources of the organisation are wasted on non-value-adding activities and related projects.

Since projects are often the preferred modus operandi, the strategic alignment of projects is of major importance to conserving and effectively using an organisation's resources. Selection criteria are needed to ensure each project is prioritised and contributes to the organisation's strategic goals. Anything less wastes scarce organisational resources—people, capital, materials and equipment—and may lead to unethical business practices. Ensuring alignment requires a selection process that is systematic, open, consistent and balanced. All the projects selected become part of a portfolio that balances the total risk for the organisation. Management of the portfolio ensures that only the most valuable projects are approved and managed across the entire organisation. Strategic alignment and value systems are the focus of Chapter 4 "Strategy, project selection and the Business Case".

1.5.2 Management of projects through portfolio management

Portfolio management provides the capability to zoom out to a wide-angle view or "zoom in" to a specific element of a specific project activity or process. Full insight into all components of the organisation is crucial for aligning internal business resources with the requirements of the changing environment. Project portfolios are frequently managed by a portfolio or program office that serves as a bridge between senior management and project leaders and their teams. The major functions of portfolio management are to:

- oversee project selection and prioritisation
- monitor aggregate resource levels and skills
- encourage best practices
- balance projects in the portfolio to represent a risk level appropriate to the organisation
- improve communication among all stakeholders
- create a total organisational perspective that goes beyond silo thinking
- monitor the delivery of benefits across the portfolio into the organisation
- educate and train project leaders
- instigate communities of practices where project leaders can share lessons learned
- undertake continuous improvement of best practice methodology, processes and templates
- report on progress and provide updates on cost, time and scope dimensions to executive management
- manage cross-dependencies between programs and projects
- establish governance and approval *gates* so the business needs are continually validated to ensure project activity delivers the requirements for an ever-changing business
- manage risk across the portfolio, program and projects.

Portfolio management manages the integration of elements of organisational strategy with projects (along with their interdependencies). At the project level, the management of the portfolio is directed towards creation and use of best practices.

1.5.3 **The yin and yang of project management**

Project management is often described as a *yin and yang* situation, where the technical project management hard skills are complemented and interconnected with the soft skills. These are opposite forces that, when combined, deliver better project success. The author (Pearson), in his early project management career, was given this advice by his mentor: "You don't manage projects from sitting behind your desk". This implied the yin (technical project management) was not being supplemented with enough of the yang (managing stakeholders and relationships).

Table 1.9 indicates some of these yin and yang qualities of managing a project.

Table 1.9 Yin and yang of project management

Yin	Yang
Project kick-off	Gaining commitment and buy-in
Scoping activities	Understanding customer value
Stakeholder management strategies and formal communications	Engaging and building relationships in a face-to-face situation
Planning activities dealing with facts	Using subject matter experts, knowledge and relationships to gain a border understanding
Metrics and measurement	Understanding and realism
Following due process	Working with customers to deliver value
Managing the triple constraints	Intimately understanding the customer's requirements and their value proposition
Ignoring organisational change management impacts to departments and people	Empathetically understanding the impact the project has on the organisation and its people

© 2022 Dr Neil Pearson

Figure 1.1 emphasises this distinction, with two-fifths of the skills coming from a technical project management and subject matter expertise perspective (the yin) and the other three-fifths from the yang perspective: business acumen (understanding the customer and what the organisation value-adds); leadership, ethics and principles; and organisational change management awareness.

Summary

Powerful economic forces are contributing to the rapid expansion of project management approaches to business problems and opportunities. A project is defined as a non-routine, one-time effort that is limited by time and resources and by performance specifications designed to meet customer needs.

Effective project management begins with selecting and prioritising projects that support the organisation's mission and strategy and deliver value to the customer. Successful implementation requires both technical (hard skills) and competent leadership and engagement (soft skills). Project leaders must plan and budget projects as well as orchestrate and lead the contributions of others with often diverse backgrounds.

In summarising this chapter, it is helpful to reflect on and learn from some of the typical reasons projects fail, and conversely to learn why others are successful. Reflecting on this chapter, the reader will be able to identify and embellish on the positive lessons and negative lessons in relation to why we carry out project management—refer to Table 1.10 for some of the author's (Pearson's) reflections.

Table 1.10 Positive and negative lessons in relation to managing projects

Positive lessons	Negative lessons
■ The project has a defined project Steering Committee, an agreed committee charter and appropriate levels of accountability. ■ There is a sound Business Case that informs and guides the ongoing business need for the project. ■ There is a well-articulated story of the strategic alignment of the project, supported by an active, positive sponsor who is respected across all levels of the business. ■ Project leader and project team skills are matched to the complexity and challenges of the project. ■ An approved methodology is used that is actively applied to the project and is communicated to the project team and stakeholders beyond the immediate project. ■ There is tightly defined and communicated governance, including team roles and responsibilities, and transparency of the governance across the project environment. ■ A gateway review process actively assists the project in a positive manner, as opposed to a blame culture. ■ There is a planned and prepared stakeholder and communication strategy. ■ Organisational change management is considered early in the project and incorporated into the design of the project.	■ The project is not aligned to organisational strategy. ■ The value to be delivered to the customer is vague. ■ There is a lack of top management/sponsor support. ■ Political discord exists within the organisation to the detriment of the project. ■ There is poor/inadequate estimating of time, resources and costs. ■ The project works backwards from a given *drop-dead* date and takes on an unachievable profile from the outset. ■ Too many expectations are placed on inexperienced project management personnel. ■ There is a fragmented team and team values. ■ There are poorly/vaguely defined requirements (scope). ■ There is a lack of user (customer) involvement. ■ The testing and piloting stages are reduced/skipped to meet a slipping schedule. ■ Unrealistic requirements/expectations are set from the outset. ■ There is scope creep and a lack of formal variation control process. ■ There is poor/lack of communication. ■ Project early warning indicators (e.g. cost and time variances) are ignored. ■ There are poor governance and control mechanisms.

© 2022 Dr Neil Pearson

If lessons learned are implemented into daily practice by the project leader, negative lessons should be avoidable in future.

Review questions

1. What are the main characteristics that help differentiate projects from other functions carried out in the daily operations of an organisation?
2. What are the important factors in contemporary project management which are requiring a project leader to understand factors beyond just the project?
3. Why is the implementation of projects important to strategic planning and the project leader?
4. "The yin and yang of project management are two sides of the same coin." Explain.
5. What is meant by an integrative (holistic) approach to project management? Why is this approach important in today's environment?
6. What are the key reasons for challenged projects according to the Standish Group?
7. What are the main stages in the PMI's *Project Management Body of Knowledge* (PMBOK) life cycle? What is the purpose of each stage?
8. What are PMI and PRINCE2?
9. What are the differences between a framework, a methodology and a standard?
10. What are the stages of a product life cycle?

Exercises

1. Use the internet to identify all the infrastructure projects currently taking place in your local area. How many are you able to find? What is the value of the projects and how long are they planned to take?
2. Individually identify what you consider to be the greatest achievements accomplished by humankind in the last decade. Now share your list with other students in the class and come up with an expanded list. Review these accomplishments in terms of the definition of a project. What does your review suggest about the importance of project management?
3. Individually identify a recent project you have either worked on or been impacted by. Can you identify evidence of both the yin and yang of project management?

4. Review the PMI site (www.pmi.org).
   - Review general information about the PMI, as well as membership information.
   - See if there is a PMI chapter in your state/territory. If not, where is the closest one? Would you consider attending to build you knowledge and expand your network?
   - Use the search function on the PMI home page to find information on PMBOK. What are the major knowledge areas of PMBOK?
   - Explore other links provided by the PMI. What do these links tell you about the nature and future of project management?
5. Review the AIPM site (www.aipm.com.au).
   - Read the general information about the AIPM, as well as its membership information.
   - Take note of the benefits of being a member of the AIPM.
6. Review the Apple predictions at: https://www.macworld.co.uk/news/new-apple-products-3510027/
   - Choose one of the product streams and draft a hypothetical product life cycle diagram depicting the current stage of the product (i.e. development, growth, maturity or decline).
   - Indicate product releases you would like to see, using your own innovative ideas.

References

AIPM and KPMG 2020, *Project Delivery Performance in Australia,* https://assets.kpmg/content/dam/kpmg/au/pdf/2020/aipm-australian-project-delivery-performance-survey-2020.pdf, accessed January 2022.

Blake Dawson, *Scope for Improvement 2008, A Report on Scoping Practices in Australian Construction and Infrastructure Projects,* https://mosaicprojects.com.au/PDF-Gen/BDW_Scope_FI_2008.pdf, accessed May 2022.

Cambridge Dictionary n.d., "Meaning of 'standard' in the English dictionary", "Meaning of 'framework' in the English dictionary", "Meaning of 'methodology' in the English dictionary", https://dictionary.cambridge.org/dictionary/english, accessed February 2018.

iseekplant 2017, "A complete list of Australian infrastructure projects", https://blog.iseekplant.com.au/australian-infrastructure-guide, accessed December 2021.

ISO n.d., "Consumers and Standards: Partnership for a Better World. 1.1 What are standards and how do they help?", https://www.iso.org/sites/ConsumersStandards/1_standards.html#, accessed February 2018.

ISO 2021, ISO 21500:2021 "Project, programme and portfolio management—Context and concepts", https://www.iso.org/standard/75704.html, accessed March 2022.

Johnson C 2016, "How project management can future-proof your career", RMIT University, 6 October, https://www.rmit.edu.au/news/all-news/2016/october/why-is-project-management-the-business-degree-of-the-21st-century, accessed February 2018.

Open Door 2021, "The Standish Group reports 83.9% of IT projects fail – how to save yours", https://www.opendoorerp.com/the-standish-group-report-83-9-of-it-projects-partially-or-completely-fail/, accessed March 2022.

Project Management Institute (PMI) 2021a, *A Guide to the Project Management Body of Knowledge (PMBOK® Guide),* 7th edition, Newton Square, PA.

Project Management Institute (PMI) 2021b, *The Standard for Project Management (ANSI/PMI 99-001-2021),* 7th edition, Newton Square, PA.

Project Management Institute (PMI) 2022, "Membership", https://www.pmi.org, accessed March 2022.

Schwaber K & Sutherland J 2017, *The Scrum Guide: The Definitive Guide to Scrum, The Rules of the Game,* https://scrumguides.org/docs/scrumguide/v2020/2020-Scrum-Guide-US.pdf#zoom=100, accessed December 2021.

Yeates D, Cadle J & Paul D 2014, *Business Analysis,* 3rd edition, BCS Learning & Development, The Chartered Institute for IT.

PART 2

Project establishment and performance

CHAPTER 2
Popular frameworks and methodologies

Learning elements

2A Understand the different life cycles, frameworks and approaches to the management of projects.

2B Be able to select one life cycle, framework or approach over another.

2C Achieve a high-level understanding of PRINCE2.

2D Achieve a high-level understanding of ISO 21500:2021.

2E Achieve a high-level understanding of Agile and Scrum.

2F Achieve a high-level understanding of the APM framework.

2G Achieve a high-level understanding of Lean Six Sigma.

2H Achieve a high-level understanding of the Praxis framework.

2I Achieve a high-level understanding of the P3.express system.

2J Further develop knowledge of the *Project Management Body of Knowledge* (PMBOK).

In this chapter

2.1 Introduction

2.2 Life cycle types and their selection

2.3 An overview of PRINCE2

2.4 An overview of ISO 21500:2021 "Project, programme and portfolio management—context and concepts"

2.5 An introduction to the Agile (Scrum) approach

2.6 An overview of the APM framework

2.7 An introduction to Lean Six Sigma and the DMAIC process

2.8 An overview of the Praxis framework

2.9 An overview of the P3.express system

2.10 An introduction to the *Project Management Body of Knowledge* (PMBOK)

Summary

2.1 | Introduction

Advances in project management as a discipline have improved substantially over the last 40 years and today's project leader has a plethora of relatively mature frameworks and methodologies to select from. All are well documented, supported by training programs, backed by professional communities, and generally have a ready pool of skilled project leaders available. Although the focus of this text is the Project Management Institute's (PMI) *life cycle* approach (as this is globally one of the most common approaches to managing projects), the reader needs to be aware that other widely used major frameworks and methodologies also exist in the global marketplace, which are often used within specific industry sectors (such as **Agile** in software engineering projects, and PRINCE2 in large government departments.

Regardless of the approach selected, the knowledge captured in this text will almost certainly assist the project leader, Scrum master or business analyst in applying best practice to the situation they find themselves in.

Although we often refer to *generic* project management approaches, the developers of the approaches discussed in this chapter have determined whether their approach is a methodology (i.e. a set of prescriptive principles, tools and practices) or a framework (i.e. a looser and more flexible structure that allows room for the inclusion of other practices, tools and techniques).

A good project management resource on the subject is located at: https://www.projectmanagement. com/articles/278600/Why-Youre-Confusing-Frameworks-with-Methodologies.

In relation to the approaches discussed in this chapter, the developers classify them as:

- PRINCE2—methodology
- ISO 21500:2021 "Guidance on Project Management"—standard (and framework)
- Scrum (Scrum Guide)—framework
- Association for Project Management Body of Knowledge (APM BOK)—framework
- Lean Six Sigma and DMAIC—framework
- Praxis—framework
- PMI's *A Guide to the Project Management Body of Knowledge*—good practice framework (also a standard—ANSI/PMI 99-001-2021).

The approaches introduced in this chapter are:

- ***PRINCE2***: Projects IN Controlled Environments was developed by the UK Office of Government Commerce (now known as the *Cabinet Office*) and is used extensively by the UK Government (Gov.UK 2021). It is now recognised and applied globally and has gradually been adopted by governments and large information and communication technology (ICT) providers. The PRINCE2 methodology offers non-proprietary best-practice guidance on project management. AXELOS (www.axelos.com) controls accreditation and standards for the PRINCE2 method, which it publishes through best-practice guidance. Like the PMI's PMBOK, PRINCE2 is part of a large suite of methodologies incorporating portfolio, program, risk, value (benefits) and ITIL (service management).

- **ISO 21500:2021**: This standard called "Project, programme and portfolio management—context and concepts" provides a high-level description of concepts and processes that are considered to form good practice in project management. This guidance also considers a wider context by including elements such as the organisation's strategy, governance, company operations and benefits. Elements of ISO 21500:2021 appear to be modelled on elements of the PMI's PMBOK, and therefore at its core takes a similar life cycle approach (Initiation, Planning, Execution, Closure, and Monitor and Control). This is in a context of operating in a strategically aligned organisation, where each investment (project) has a valid Business Case and delivers benefits back to the business as a result of undertaking the project work.

  A series of standards are modelled around the ISO 21500:2021 standard, including (ISO 2021):

  - ISO 21502 "Project, programme and portfolio management—Guidance on project management"
  - ISO 21503 "Project, programme and portfolio management—Guidance on programme management"
  - ISO 21504 "Project, programme and portfolio management—Guidance on portfolio management"
  - ISO 21505 "Project, programme and portfolio management—Guidance on governance"
  - ISO/TR 21506 "Project, programme and portfolio management—Vocabulary"
  - ISO 21508 "Earned value management in project and programme management"
  - ISO 21511 "Work breakdown structures for project and programme management".

- **Scrum:** The term *Scrum* was introduced by Takeuchi and Nonaka (1986) when they observed that projects that use small, cross-functional teams historically tend to produce the best results. Scrum was one of the earliest implementations of "the new new product development game" that emerged out of this work (Takeuchi & Nonaka 1986). Jeff Sutherland set about formalising and realising this new way of working by applying it to software product development. Using the study by Takeuchi and Nonaka as a platform, Jeff Sutherland subsequently published *Scrum: The Art of Doing Twice the Work in Half the Time* (Sutherland 1993). Ken Schwaber (software developer, product manager and industry consultant) is also associated with the development of Scrum. He presented Scrum as a formal development process at an Object-Oriented Programming, Systems, Languages and Applications conference in 1995. In 2001, the Agile Manifesto (a formal declaration of four key values and 12 principles towards an iterative and people-centric approach to software development) was born. This started the ever-expanding world of Agile and since then, many variants of Scrum have since emerged.

  - Kanban—based on the much earlier Toyota Production System, which came into existence post-World War II (commonly known as Lean thinking in today's business language)
  - XP or eXtreme Programming—created by Kent Beck as a part of the Chrysler Comprehensive Compensation System (C3) in approximately 1996. Focused on micro-increments (smaller groups of requirements) and a test-first approach where tests are determined up-front for each micro-increment
  - Scrum of Scrums—a way of carving up large (development) teams into sub-teams and cascading the reporting and management of *stories* both upwards and downwards among the teams via ambassadors
  - Large-Scale Scrum (LeSS) framework—a framework to guide in the scaling of multiple concurrent scrums. Also LeSS Huge, where area product owners report to a product owner for

large product developments where a single product owner cannot cope with the demands of multiple concurrent sprints

- AgilePM (formerly known as dynamic system development model (DSDM) framework)—a formalisation of the rapid application development methodology. AgilePM was created in 1994 to address problems associated with a traditional approach to development. A founding member of the Agile Alliance, AgilePM supports the Agile Manifesto and principles and has been expanded to provide governance around the context of Agile

- Scaled Agile Framework (SAFe)—often described as a knowledge base of proven, integrated patterns for Lean–Agile implementations and truly brings together aspects of both Lean and Agile approaches. It incorporates aspects of DevOps and the Continuous Delivery Pipeline

- SCRUMstudy is another popular approach to Agile project management.

This text (in Chapter 3 "Agile (Scrum) project management") will take the SCRUMstudy approach, since it incorporates the original Scrum thinking, but extends the Scrum approach to include necessary project management activities and is somewhat scalable. The SCRUMstudy Scrum Body of Knowledge (SBOK) is also free to access (https://www.scrumstudy.com).

- **■** ***Lean Six Sigma*** *and the* ***DMAIC*** *process*: Lean Six Sigma combines the benefits of Lean thinking (which originated out of the Toyota Production System in Japan in the 1940s) and the statistical techniques of Six Sigma (originating from Motorola in the United States in the 1980s), into a single approach for the management of continuous improvement projects. In recent times, this approach to the management of continuous improvement projects has become popular, with the DMAIC approach being applied to the routine management of continuous improvement project work.

DMAIC (Define, Measure, Analyse, Improve, Control) is applied to the improvement of existing processes. For the development of new processes, the DMADV (define, measure, analyse, design, verify) approach is used. Lean Six Sigma has become extremely popular in recent years as the approach for continuous improvement projects of all sizes and complexities. It is interesting to note that some of the values, principles and techniques adopted in Scrum are to be found in Lean Six Sigma (no doubt furthering the popularity of the approach, as organisations look to become more agile in their day-to-day operations).

- **■** *Praxis:* This is a free framework for the management of projects, programs and portfolios. It includes a body of knowledge, methodology, competency framework and capability maturity model. The framework is supported by a knowledge base of resources and an encyclopaedia. (Praxis n.d., accessed May 2022).

> *The challenge now facing the profession is to find consistency and consensus across the many guides so that they may be used together in an integrated framework.*
>
> *Praxis is designed to provide that integration. It takes the principles of existing, proven guides and adapts them so that they have a common terminology, structure and approach. It also supports these with a library of information drawn from published experts and the practical experience of the P3M community (PFL 2015).*

The framework consists of four interconnected sections:

1. body of knowledge, definition of the portfolio, programme and project building blocks
2. method, the processes and descriptions based on a life cycle approach
3. capability maturity modelling, guidance in support of delivery of an organisations portfolios, programmes and projects
4. competency framework, supporting the maturity, method and knowledge sections.

Although not currently a mainstream approach to the management of projects, Praxis has recently gained support from APMG International, which now offers a certification option. Additionally, the Praxis framework has recognised Agile and includes guidance on how to integrate Agile with the Praxis framework (hybrid approach). The Praxis framework was adopted by the Australian Institute of Project Management as its base for a body of knowledge in 2019 (AIPM 2019).

- *APM life cycle and approach*: The Association for Project Management (APM) is the UK's arm of the International Project Management Association (IPMA). It is:

  > *a federation of around 70-member association across the globe which provides qualification standards for individuals working in project, programme and portfolio management. IPMA qualifications are internationally recognised and designed for project professionals at all levels in their careers. APM are the certification body in the UK for the IPMA and offer the full suite of qualifications* (APM 2021).

  Founded in 1965, the IPMA exists as arguably the world's first project management association. Its national associations collaborate to advance the profession's achievements in project and business success; evidence of their strategic vision is offered in the way the association changed its name from INTERNET to IPMA in the early 1970s.

  The APM is associated with the IPMA, but it also offers a (popular) project management framework in its own right, as documented in the APM's Body of Knowledge (APM 2019). It is essentially a predictive life cycle approach that is inclusive of the wider environment in which projects operate.

- *The PMBOK® Guide sixth edition (PMI 2017a), upon which this text is based:* It provides a generic life cycle approach that can be applied to projects of all sizes and complexities and in all industries (including the public sector).

  In 2021 the PMI launched the seventh edition of the *PMBOK® Guide*, this time making more radical changes to the structure and reduction in depth of content. The two volumes within the guide are:

  - *The Standard for Project Management*, which discusses what the PMI terms the "system for value delivery" and introduces and defines a principle approach to the management of projects, of which there are 12 principles: stewardship, team, stakeholders, value, systems thinking, leadership, tailoring, quality, complexity, risk, adaptability and resiliency, and change.
  - *A Guide to the Project Management Body of Knowledge*, which moves away from the previous 10 knowledge areas to *performance domains*. The eight performance domains are stakeholders, team, development approach and lifecycle, planning, project work, delivery, measurement, and uncertainty. The domains are accompanied by a discussion on tailoring and lists of models, methods and artefacts.

  Some concepts introduced in the seventh edition of the *PMBOK® Guide* have always been present in the Australian adaptation of this text (e.g. value generation, change management, coverage of different project management approaches and systems thinking). The *PMBOK® Guide* is now a more focused publication with less detail (dropping from 756 to 274 pages), placing more emphasis on texts such as this to extrapolate, illustrate and discuss the models, methods and artefacts. To assist the reader in seeing how content in the seventh edition of the *PMBOK® Guide* maps to chapters within this text, a mapping table is included as Table 2.8(a) and 2.8(b) later in this chapter. Unless expressly stated, this text pins its discussion to the sixth edition, while also covering a large amount of the *PMBOK® Guide* seventh edition.

  The *PMBOK® Guide* provides a valuable body of knowledge around project management in general as it provides an understanding of some of the key tools and techniques that are used and applied within other frameworks and methodologies, such as PRINCE2, Praxis, ISO 21500:2021 and to some extent Scrum/Agile—for example, we still apply quality techniques and assess risk, although they are packaged differently! The PMI has become a globally accepted body of knowledge that is practised around the world. There are many PMI chapters dotted across the globe who support, promote and further develop the profession of project management—it is beyond doubt the largest and most widespread of all the approaches that are described in this text, and forms the basis of knowledge within the current Australian Certificate IV and Diploma in project management, from professional development courses right up to universities' offerings around the world.

As will be discussed in this chapter, there is no single framework or methodology that suits all organisations, working cultures and industries. In practice, an overarching methodology is usually chosen and internalised within the organisation, providing the basis for project management governance, best-practice guidance, templates and education programs. Selecting the best framework or methodology for your organisation is not only key for embedding best-practice project management, but also for providing a common understanding and vocabulary with other project leaders in your organisation and with suppliers and peers within your industry. In today's project environments there is also less focus on having a single project management approach; rather, there is access to multiple approaches, with the decision about a defined approach based on the project content, customer delivery requirements and other project environmental factors.

This chapter provides an overview of each of the popular approaches described (PRINCE2, ISO 21500:2021, Scrum/Agile project management, Lean Six Sigma, APM, Praxis and PMBOK) in the management of projects within organisations.

2.2 Life cycle types and their selection

Before launching into an overview of each of the previously mentioned frameworks, this section seeks to position the discussions and decisions a project leader will typically consider many times during their project management career, in terms of which project management approach should be applied to a particular project.

The project leader has to consider the type of work being undertaken, as this will fundamentally influence the approach taken in the management of a project. We could, for example, leverage a decision-making taxonomy known as the *Cynefin framework* to assist us (Cynefin Co 2022). This is explored in Chapter 20 "Complex project management".

- For projects where there is a low degree of technical uncertainty and low degree of requirements uncertainty, we would be tempted to use more linear predictive approaches to the management of projects (i.e. simple approaches).

- For projects where there is a medium degree of technical uncertainty and medium degree of requirements uncertainty, we would be tempted to use more **adaptive** approaches (i.e. complicated or even complex approaches).

- Where there is a high degree of technical uncertainty and high degree of requirements uncertainty, we would be tempted to question the ability to solve these with more adaptive approaches as they are inherently risky.

This can potentially facilitate choosing the type of project management framework that may feasibly be applied. Table 2.1 considers *requirements uncertainty* and *technical degree of uncertainty*; with the zones of *simple, complicated, complex* and *chaos* indicated for the type of work being considered in the project. These zones help to influence the choice of project management life cycle approach.

Table 2.1 Uncertainty informs approach

	Technical degree of uncertainty		Requirements uncertainty		
	High ⟵⟶ Low		High ⟵⟶ Low		
Chaos	●		●		Fundamentally risky, reassess before addressing
Complex		●		●	Most suited to adaptive approaches
Complicated	●			●	
Simple		●		●	Most suited to predictive approaches

© 2022 Dr Neil Pearson

Figure 2.1 A simple predictive project life cycle

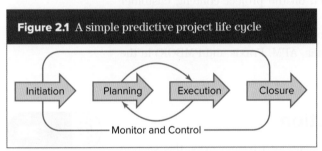

Initiation → Planning → Execution → Closure

— Monitor and Control —

© 2022 Dr Neil Pearson

A project life cycle describes the stages a project goes through from beginning to end, regardless of the project management approach. Some generic project life cycles include predictive, incremental, adaptive (iterative) and hybrid. General definitions of these follow.

■ *Predictive:* A predictive arrangement relies on the up-front initiation, planning and capturing of requirements before any execution activity. Variations (changes) to the project are tolerated (but carefully managed) via a variation (change) management process. The predictive approach is the main focus of this book. Figure 2.1 provides a simple visual of this life cycle, which is discussed in further detail over the subsequent chapters.

A project is initiated with agreement between the project leader and project sponsor (captured in the Project Charter), then further scoped and planned, the result being the integrated Project Management Plan (integrated PMP); after approval the integrated PMP is baselined and then executed, until completion of the defined deliverables, at which point the project will be closed out.

Due to the nature of many projects, the predictive approach is very popular and is often customised to meet industry specific requirements. Table 2.2 provides some examples of predictive life cycles the author (Pearson) has explored in doing and teaching project management.

■ *Incremental:* In approaching a project incrementally, we would have a confirmed idea about what we are to deliver (e.g. a five-storey block of apartments). However, the project is delivered in increments against the confirmed idea. We would build the foundations based on the original floor plan of the building, then erect the building's structure, subsequently fit out and finally landscape. The project has effectively delivered the initial idea, but via a number of increments. Each increment could pass through each stage of Initiation, Planning, Execution and Closure before the next increment is started (i.e. sequentially). More often, increments are run in some degree of parallelism. For example, the fit-out would be started on the completed first floor, as the construction of the second floor continues. Large increments of work are handed over (delivered) incrementally over the duration of the project. The subsequent increment is also influenced (lessons and feedback) and inclusive of changes from the previous increment (Figure 2.2).

Table 2.2 Tailored predictive approaches from different industries

Start ➝ End

Initiation / Feasibility / Start-up	Planning / Design / Plan	Execution / Build / Development	Monitor and Control / Test / Test	Closure / Deploy / Deploy	Close / Close			PMBOK, sixth edition / PMBOK, seventh edition (indicative) / PMBOK, seventh edition (indicative)
Requirements definition	Design development	Manufacturing	Test and checkout	Delivery	Operations			Aerospace industry
Discovery	Scoping	Build Business Case	Development	Testing and validation	Launch			New product development
Material solution analysis	Technology development	Engineering and manufacturing development	Production and deployment	Operations and support				Acquisition-based life cycle
Conceptual planning	Feasibility study	Design and engineering	Procurement and construction	Start-up and occupancy	Operation and maintenance	Disposal of facility		Construction
Pre-planning	Design	Procurement	Construction	Start-up				Construction
Concept	Development	Design	Construction	Commissioning	Operations			Construction
Design	Pre-construction	Procurement	Construction	Commissioning	Occupancy	Closeout		Construction
Feasibility analysis	Requirements analysis	System design	Development and testing	Implementation	Operation and maintenance			Software development
Initiation	System concept development	Planning	Requirements analysis	Design	Integration and test	Implementation	Operation and maintenance	Software development
Assess markets	Create strategy	Plan product releases	Design and develop products	Launch products	Rollout products			General product development
Conceptualisation	Literature review	Detailed research	Data collection	Analysis of findings	Write-up	Review		Research life cycle
Define opportunity	Develop research proposal	Submit and negotiate research direction	Establish project	Data collection and analysis	Write-up and hypothesis testing	Publication		Research life cycle
Plan book	Write book	Edit book	Design book	Print book	Promote book			Publishing
Conception and initiation	Definition and planning	Execution and launch	Performance and control	Project close				Generic
Concept	Definition	Development	Handover and closure	Benefits realisation	Operations			Generic
Define marketing objectives	Analyse opportunities	Research and select target markets	Design marketing strategies	Plan marketing "programs"	Implement marketing efforts	Optimise and control marking efforts		Marketing
Geology assessment	Preliminary economic assessment	Preliminary feasibility study	Feasibility study	Bankable feasibility study	Initiation	Execution		Mining
Exploration	Economic appraisal	Engineering design	Execution	Operations	Mine reclamation	Operations		Mining
Acquire	Develop	Operate	Divest					Real estate
Design brief	Procurement	Design	Construction					Real estate
Pre-project	Concept	Scope	Planning	Delivery	Performance manage	Post-project		Extended generic

Note: Columns in table do not indicate project phase alignment

Figure 2.2 A simple incremental approach

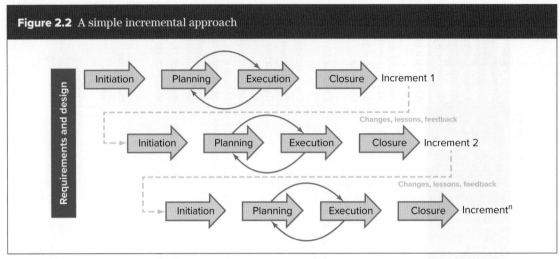

© 2022 Dr Neil Pearson

- *Adaptive (also referred to as* iterative*):* This approach is often referred to as *Agile* or *Scrum*. In Agile, a businessperson (the product owner) agrees a set amount of work to be completed by the Scrum team (development team) within a defined time, referred to as a *sprint* or *timebox*. At the end of the sprint, a potentially shippable product that can be handed over to the business (or implemented) is produced. Each sprint iteratively adds (usually) small amounts of functionality to the item under development, therefore iteratively increasing its functionality (Figure 2.3).

Figure 2.3 A simple iterative (Scrum-based) approach

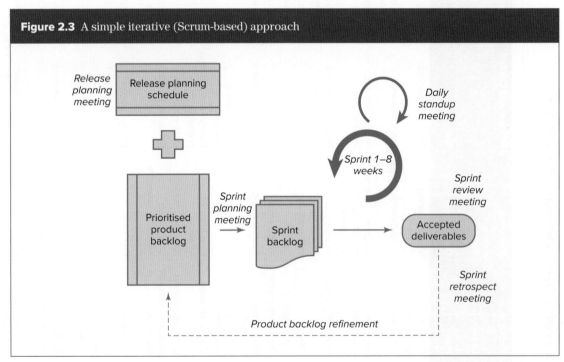

© 2022 Dr Neil Pearson

- *Hybrid:* This is where a degree of predictive approach (e.g. during Initiation and Planning) is applied to ascertain a set or suite of requirements (up-front planning), but will later change to a different approach, such as iterative (e.g. during Execution). These are becoming more often applied as the transition to Agile/Scrum is taken by organisations, causing a cultural shift to take place. Media often report this approach as either TAGILE (traditional and Agile) or WAGILE (Waterfall and Agile). A TAGILE example is provided in Figure 2.4 where a project is initiated and planned in its entirety (the requirements were in this case relatively static), but due to the customer demanding frequent customer deliveries, and a pay-as-you-build agreement with the client for remuneration, the execution of the project adopted an adaptive (iterative) approach. The project, once all iterations (sprints) had been completed, was subsequently closed out in a predictive manner.

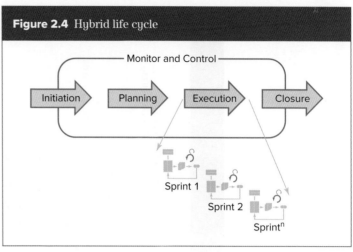

Figure 2.4 Hybrid life cycle

© 2022 Dr Neil Pearson

Table 2.3 indicates which life cycle approach is more commonly applied against the factors of frequency of delivery, technical degree of uncertainty and requirements uncertainty.

Table 2.3 Approach selection factors

	Frequency of delivery		Technical degree of uncertainty		Requirements uncertainty	
	High ⟷ Low		High ⟷ Low		High ⟷ Low	
Predictive		● (Low)		● (Low)		● (Low)
Incremental	● (High)			● (Low)		● (Low)
Adaptive (Iterative)	● (High)		● (High)		● (High)	
Hybrid	● (High)		● (Low)		● (Low)	

© 2022 Dr Neil Pearson

2.2.1   Survey tools to support approach selection

Choosing which approach to use (or even hybrids of different approaches to use) can be a somewhat difficult task. It may be that the choice of approach is driven more by internal standards than by what is the most fitting choice. To assist the project leader in making informed recommendations, there are several assessment tools available. For example, the PMI's Agile Practice Guide (Appendix X3) has an Agile suitability filter tool. The presence and use of these tools is also common in other Agile approaches such as AgilePM. The PMI's approach differs as it considers not just Agile and predictive approaches, but also hybrid approaches in its recommendations when handling responses to a survey (PMI 2017b, pp. 125–38).

To summarise, Figure 2.5 captures the decision that the project leader will be making at the pre-project or Initiation stages, with suggestions as to what commercial approach the decision might result in. Ideally, a decision tree similar to this would be embedded as governance at the project management office (PMO) level. In today's contemporary world of project management the phrase *one size fits all* does not apply.

Figure 2.5 Project management approach selection

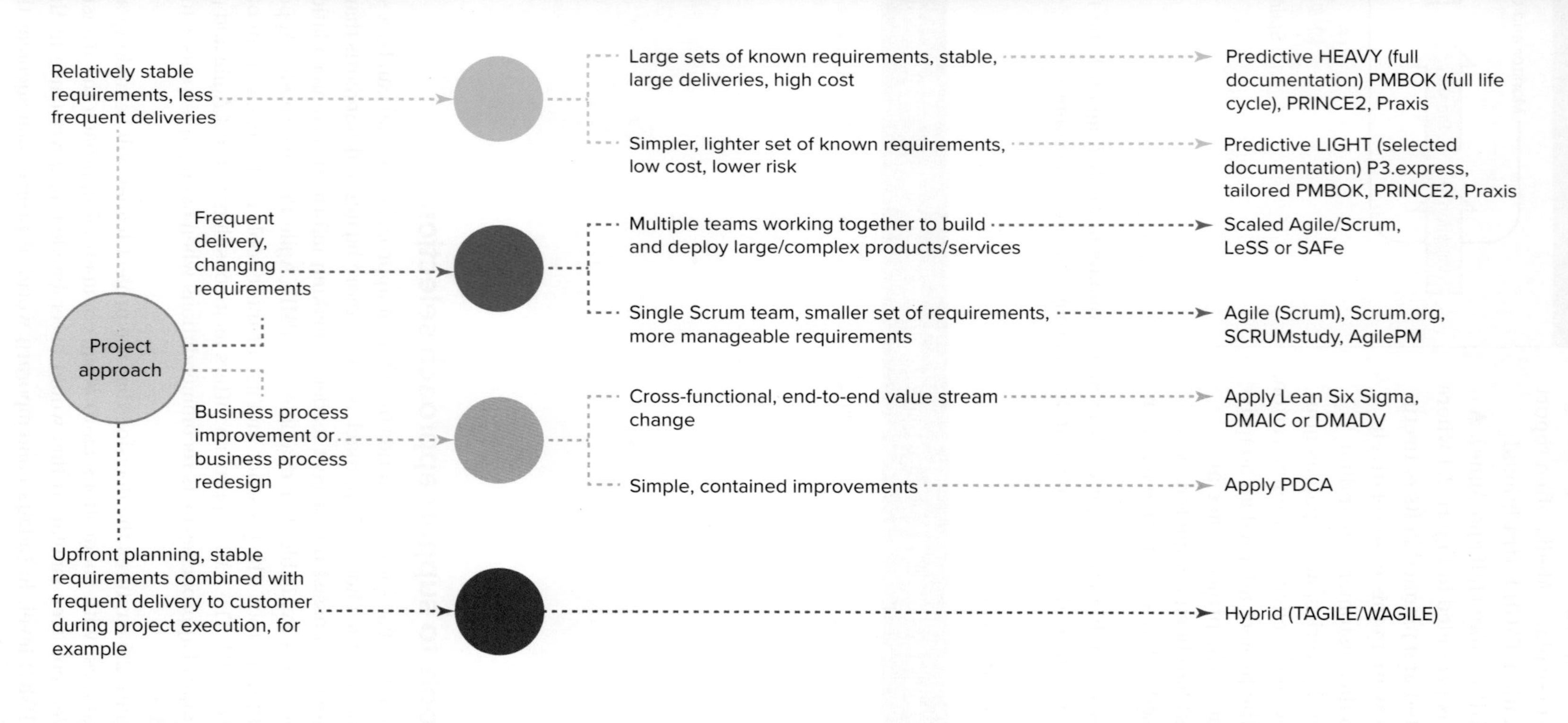

Project approach

- Relatively stable requirements, less frequent deliveries → Large sets of known requirements, stable, large deliveries, high cost → Predictive HEAVY (full documentation) PMBOK (full life cycle), PRINCE2, Praxis
- Frequent delivery, changing requirements → Simpler, lighter set of known requirements, low cost, lower risk → Predictive LIGHT (selected documentation) P3.express, tailored PMBOK, PRINCE2, Praxis
  - Multiple teams working together to build and deploy large/complex products/services → Scaled Agile/Scrum, LeSS or SAFe
  - Single Scrum team, smaller set of requirements, more manageable requirements → Agile (Scrum), Scrum.org, SCRUMstudy, AgilePM
- Business process improvement or business process redesign → Cross-functional, end-to-end value stream change → Apply Lean Six Sigma, DMAIC or DMADV
  - Simple, contained improvements → Apply PDCA
- Upfront planning, stable requirements combined with frequent delivery to customer during project execution, for example → Hybrid (TAGILE/WAGILE)

The following sections take a more detailed look at a selection of the project management commercial approaches from predictive to adaptive (iterative).

2.3 | An overview of PRINCE2

PRINCE2 (PRojects IN Controlled Environments) features a full life cycle outside what was seen as traditional project management, and includes richer start-up and governance structures than some other methodologies. Continual alignment checks are an integral part of the PRINCE2 methodology and require the project leader to ask the questions: Are the outputs and outcomes—to be delivered by the project—still required by the business? and What benefits are to be delivered, and how are these managed (owned) beyond project delivery?

PRINCE2 has four components to its structure: principles, themes, processes and tailoring.

2.3.1 Principles

There are seven principles in PRINCE2 and all must be applied in order for the project to be PRINCE2. The principles represent guiding obligations and good practice. They also help to determine whether the project is genuinely being project managed as a PRINCE2 project. The principles are summarised in Table 2.4.

Table 2.4 Seven principles in PRINCE2

Principles	Description
Continued business justification	There is a valid business justification (business case) to start the project and the project remains required throughout its duration.
Learn from experience	Learn from previous lessons at the start-up of a project and during each stage of the project, and record lessons at the end of the project.
Defined roles and responsibilities	PRINCE2 has defined roles and responsibilities to ensure responsibilities of key roles within the project and the business are clearly understood.
Manage by stages	Defined stages are built into the process in PRINCE2 and, aside from the start-up and closing stages, there are repeatable stages within the project delivery.
Manage by exception	Projects in PRINCE2 define tolerances for scope, time, cost, quality and additional risk and benefits. These are tightly controlled in a PRINCE2 project, and if tolerances are exceeded, escalations must take place to the appropriate person in the defined role.
Focus on products	Products are a key focus of PRINCE2 projects. There are two key categories of products: project management products, and products relating to the outcomes and outputs of the project itself.
Tailor to suit project environment	PRINCE2 is a comprehensive process and is suitable for both simple and complex projects. It can be tailored to suit the environment. Tailoring does not mean omitting any parts of the methodology, but instead (for example) adjusting the methodology to the structure and governance of the organisation.

2.3.2 Themes

PRINCE2 encompasses seven themes. These themes describe aspects of project management that must continually be attended to throughout the life of the project. The themes are summarised in Table 2.5.

Table 2.5 Seven themes in PRINCE2

Themes	Description
Business Case	The Business Case is critical in PRINCE2. It is created at the start of the project and progresses with the project to ensure its continued justification. At key decision points, the Business Case is verified to ensure continued business justification.
Organisation	The organisation theme addresses the roles and responsibilities of a PRINCE2 project from the business, user and supplier perspectives, in addition to the PRINCE2 defined roles.
Quality	Quality, in relation to the products produced from the project, is key in PRINCE2. Quality is defined within products and appraised to ensure products are produced within defined tolerances.
Plans	Plans define where and to whom products are delivered. PRINCE2 has three main types of plans: project plan, stage plan(s) and team plan(s) (optional).
Risk	Risk is present in all projects. PRINCE2 integrates risk management into all aspects of the project management methodology. Both negative risk (threats) and positive risks (opportunities) are considered in a proactive approach to the identification, evaluation and management of risk.
Change	Change (or variation) management is attended to within PRINCE2 by putting in place processes, roles and actions that can be invoked as a response to issues raised around quality, or other issues within the project.
Progress	This theme validates the ongoing viability of plans, performance-monitoring plans, and the escalation process in the event of the project not proceeding to plan.

2.3.3 **Processes**

There are seven processes and these provide detail around the steps to be taken throughout the life of a PRINCE2 project. The processes are summarised in Table 2.6.

Table 2.6 Seven processes in PRINCE2

Processes	Description
Starting up (SU) a project	The SU process focuses on the question: "Do we have a viable and worthwhile project?" The project executive and the project leader is appointed within the SU process: the outline Business Case is prepared, previous lessons are captured, the project brief is prepared and the initiation stage is planned.
Initiating a project (IP)	The IP process defines the foundational information and prepares the key plans for the risk management strategy, the quality management strategy, the configuration management strategy and the communications management strategy. The Business Case is further refined and the Project Plan is assembled. Additionally, project controls are established (according to PRINCE2 guidelines).
Directing a project (DP)	DP is a critical project-control process. Overseen by the project board, DP establishes the controls between the project leader and the project board. The project board is accountable for making key decisions (continued business justification), while day-to-day management of the project is delegated to the project leader.
Managing a stage boundary (SB)	In SB, the interfaces between the project board and the project leader come into play. The project board must ensure that the current stage of the project has been successful and that the Stage Plan for the next stage is approved while ensuring the Project Plan and business justification remain valid, in light of the current risk profile.
Controlling a stage (CS)	The focus of CS is to control the delivery of the stage's products, ensuring work remains within tolerance, and raising exception reports where tolerances are breached. Assigning *work to be done* to the managing product delivery (MP) process, reporting on that work, and managing issues are all components of this process.
Managing product delivery (MP)	The MP process is the domain of the team managers (the CS process agrees and sets the work to be done). It is in MP, under the direction of a team manager, that the work actually occurs to agreed specifications and within defined tolerances. The MP process delivers one or more of the project's products.
Closing a project (CP)	CP is the formal process entered into to close the project and can be planned or invoked for premature closure. CP is entered into when the objectives, as defined in the project initiation document, have been achieved (including any approved changes). User acceptance is verified, the business is prepared to take on running and maintenance activities post-project closure, baseline and actual performance is reviewed, benefits are declared or handed over to the business, and open risks and issues are handed to the business, with any follow-on plans.

An overarching process map for PRINCE2 is depicted in Figure 2.6, which indicates the key interactions between the seven PRINCE2 processes.

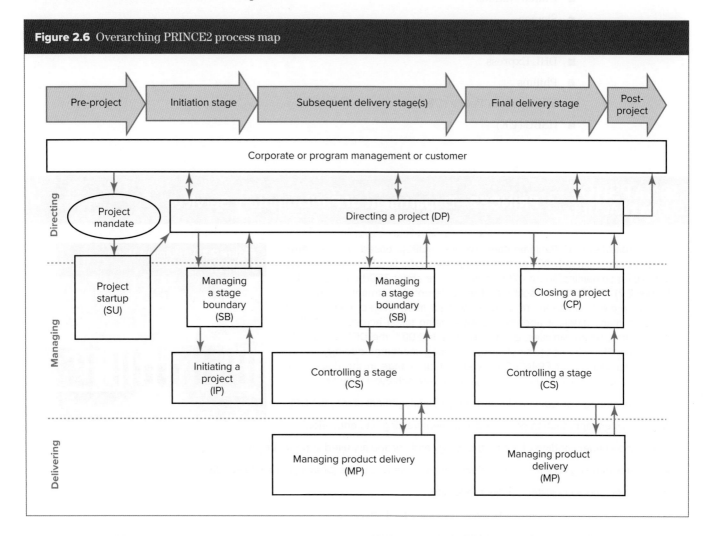

Figure 2.6 Overarching PRINCE2 process map

2.3.4 Tailoring

PRINCE2 is a comprehensive process in its own right; however, it can be tailored to suit an organisational environment, to manage large or small, simple or complex projects. Tailoring does not mean omitting any parts of the methodology.

2.3.5 PRINCE2 around the world

PRINCE2 has a particularly strong following in Europe. The Queensland Government (in Australia) has adopted this methodology as its mandated methodology for ICT projects over certain cost/ risk thresholds. Examples of other organisations and governments entities that have implemented PRINCE2 (as reported in trade press and media sites) include:

- TRANSPOWER: New Zealand's high-voltage transmission company
- University of Western Australia
- Australian Department of Parliamentary Services (see "Snapshot from practice—Department of Parliamentary Services")
- NRMA (Australian insurance company)

■ SUN Microsystems (now part of Oracle Corporation)

■ United Nations

■ Siemens

■ Vodafone

■ DHL Express

■ Phillips

■ Metropolitan Police (UK)

■ HSBC (UK).

SNAPSHOT *from* PRACTICE   PRINCE2—Department of Parliamentary Services

The Department of Parliamentary Services (DPS), based in Canberra, employs approximately 800 staff as an agency supporting Parliament House (a building containing about 4700 rooms, where about 3500 people work—Figure 2.7). The DPS was split into three different departments each using its own project management system. With so many project management systems, many different approaches were being taken across the DPS to governance, responsibilities, quality and risk. In 2007, the DPS decided to implement PRINCE2 as the single project management methodology.

Figure 2.7 Parliament House, Canberra

© Phillip Minnis/Alamy Stock Photo

The introduction of PRINCE2 caused a stark change in the delivery of projects and several benefits to the business were achieved including:

■ a more strategic perspective towards project management across the DPS

■ a consistent approach to project management training and education

■ common understanding of the methodology and vocabulary used in project management

■ benefits of being able to reuse project management resources (people) across the department

■ improved, more consistent, project reporting

■ application of lessons learned to avoid repeating past mistakes

■ greater effectiveness in the engagement of stakeholders

■ clearer governance and improved decision-making arising out of having PRINCE2 defined roles.

The DPS is receiving direct business benefits in response to having adopted a PRINCE2 approach towards project management, with some of the (indirect) benefits going beyond project delivery.

Source: Best Management Practice Case Study, www.apmg-international.com/offices/au/case-study-aus.aspx/, accessed February 2013

PRINCE2 offers a comprehensive methodology with a defined process and distinct roles (which form an integrated set of governance guidelines) that can be tailored to any environment, whether complex or simple. Note that PRINCE2 is documented in the official PRINCE2 guide available from AXELOS (www.axelos.com).

As the next framework of ISO 21500:2021 is introduced, the reader should begin to draw some parallels, and note some differences, between the approaches being covered.

2.4 An overview of ISO 21500:2021 "Project, programme and portfolio management—context and concepts"

In November 2007, the International Organization for Standardization (ISO) began the development of ISO 21500:2021 "Guidance on project management" as an international approach and standard for the management of projects. To move development of the standard forward, a project committee (ISO/PC 236) was established, involving 20 countries in the development process, plus a further three observing. This standard had a large amount of interest from the outset, and in 2012, the first release was made public. Since 2012 the series of standards relating to project, program and portfolio management have been extended and in 2020 and 2021 a new release was undertaken. The standard takes account of project governance through a high-level set of interactions between projects, programs and portfolios; the reason to initiate these is via a Business Case in response to the organisation's strategy, considerate of the organisational environment and external environment. Figure 2.8 replicates this relationship between these components.

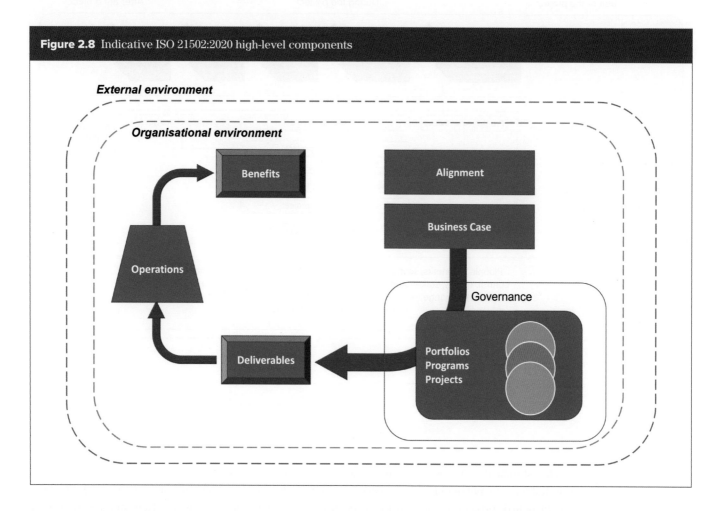

Figure 2.8 Indicative ISO 21502:2020 high-level components

In ISO 21500:2021 there is this initial focus on positioning projects in the wider context of the organisation. Credit is given to the strategic alignment of projects in terms of the alignment of the need for the project, from a top-down direction, not just the continued justification for the project in the form of a Business Case (discussed further in Chapter 4 "Strategy, project selection and the Business

Case"). The value creation chain outlined in the standard discusses the organisation's strategy for identifying opportunities delivered by projects with defined benefits: the diagram implying these benefits could be delivered inside or external to the organisation.

Taking the project component of this standard, this is further extrapolated into a predictive arrangement with implications though that Agile and hybrid approaches could also be applied. This is indicated in Figure 2.9, where a predictive gated life cycle is supported by a number of practices (a blend of PMBOK phase and PRINCE2 stages) is presented. This is underpinned what are referred to as management practices (akin to PMBOK knowledge areas or in the seventh edition of the *PMBOK® Guide* performance domains), which can be delivered via any combinations of approaches (e.g. PMBOK, PRINCE2 (predictive) or Agile (adaptive)).

Figure 2.9 ISO 21502:2020 project context for delivering projects

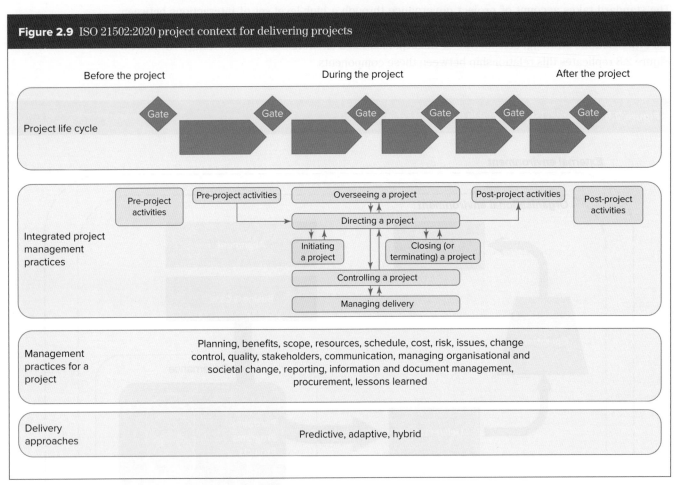

© 2022 Dr Neil Pearson

The standard outlines the requirements for project governance among various groups of stakeholders, in particular, the governance arrangements between the sponsoring organisation, project board, project sponsor, project assurance, project leader, project office and a new role of work package leader. The project management practices (life cycle)—taking a familiar predictive life cycle approach—has been remodelled with project management activities that resemble components of both PRINCE2 and PMBOK. The integrated project management practices (life cycle) is illustrated in Figure 2.10.

Figure 2.10 ISO 21502:2020 project management life cycle

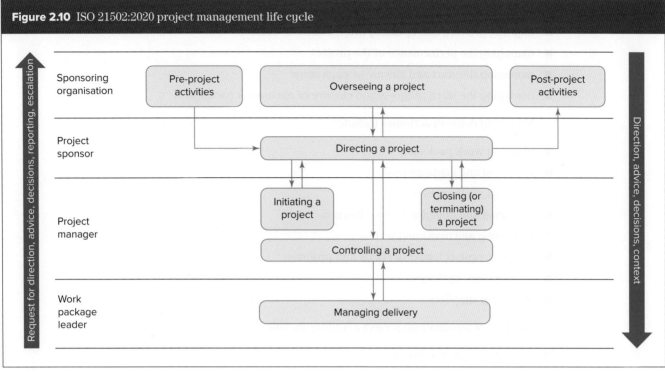

© 2022 Dr Neil Pearson

Pre-project activities include:

- establishing the projects objectives, benefits and rationale
- links to program or portfolio and/or the customers' needs
- identifying the project sponsor and project leader and establishing roles and responsibilities
- defining initial governance arrangements
- identifying indicative funding and the arrangements for funding.

Overseeing project activities include:

- reporting and decison-making
- assurance audits and reviews
- escalations and interventions.

Directing project activities include:

- ongoing justification (of the Business Case) and therefore the project (terminated when no longer justified)
- continued validation of the benefits, outcomes and outputs and their delivery
- resourcing appropriate to the project requirements.

Initiating project activities include:

- mobilising the project team
- specifying governance arrangements
- checking project justification
- initial project planning.

Controlling project activities include:

- ongoing delivery and updating of the Business Case
- managing the performance of the project
- managing the start and closure of each stage
- managing the start, progress and closure of each work package.

Managing delivery activities include:

- planning work packages
- assessing and managing risk
- managing deliverables
- capturing and applying lessons learned
- mobilising and managing teams
- updating project leader of status and progress
- closing work packages
- managing suppliers.

Closing (or terminating) project activities include:

- confirming scope delivery
- completing all work packages
- demobilising the team, resources and facilities
- returning remaining risks and issues to the programs and portfolios
- closure review
- lessons learned
- final stakeholder communications.

The management practices for a project further unpack some of the knowledge and activities that should be considered throughout the project, bearing in mind that some projects have greater focus on some areas whereas another project might have a different focus. These 17 management practices include: planning, benefits, scope, resources, schedule, cost, risk, issues, change control, quality, stakeholders, communications, organisational and societal change, reporting, information and documentation management, procurement, and lessons learned. As mentioned previously, these resemble the PMBOK knowledge areas or (in the seventh edition) performance domains, being a mix of application and knowledge.

The ISO 21500:2021 series of standards provides a useful standard (governance) for establishing a project management function within an organisation. In essence, it captures the *pre-project, initiating and stage aspects* of PRINCE2 and the *knowledge areas or the newer performance domains* of PMBOK. The full list of standards relating to the ISO 21500:2021 series can be located at www.iso.org.

2.5 | An introduction to the Agile (Scrum) approach

Agile project management (based on the original Scrum framework) was predominately used in software engineering, but this approach has now been adopted across many industries for many types of projects. Both PRINCE2 and the PMI have extensions on how to integrate Agile (Scrum) into their respective frameworks or, in the case of the seventh edition of PMBOK (PMI 2021a), use Agile as the sole project management approach. Chapter 3 "Agile (Scrum) project management" provides a detailed description of Agile/Scrum and the SCRUMstudy (www.scrumstudy.com), which is the *flavour* of Agile project management that this text uses as basis for our knowledge on Scrum/Agile.

First, let's take a look at a brief history of Scrum and the original description of Scrum. Scrum has been in circulation, especially in the software development industry, for longer than most people imagine. However, over the last 40+ years the approach has become more harmonised, despite there being dozens of "flavours" of Scrum/Agile. Two seminal moments are worth noting: "The new new product development game" research paper (Takeuchi & Nonaka 1986), which introduced the concept of Scrum based on the English game of rugby; and the coming together of influential players in the software development industry creating the Agile Manifesto (Agile Manifesto 2021a) and later the Agile Principles (Agile Manifesto 2021b). From this point (February 2001), the various flavours of Scrum and Agile take on a much more harmonised approach with variations rather than divergent/competing approaches. Figure 2.11 indicates

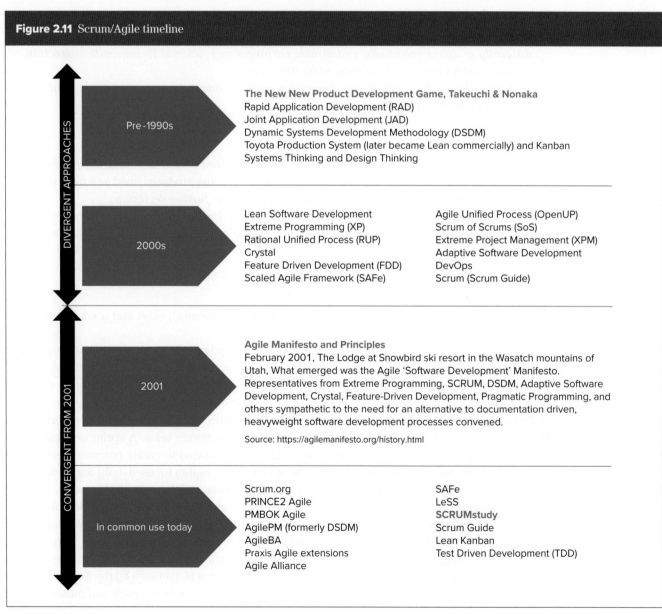

Figure 2.11 Scrum/Agile timeline

DIVERGENT APPROACHES

Pre-1990s

The New New Product Development Game, Takeuchi & Nonaka
Rapid Application Development (RAD)
Joint Application Development (JAD)
Dynamic Systems Development Methodology (DSDM)
Toyota Production System (later became Lean commercially) and Kanban
Systems Thinking and Design Thinking

2000s

Lean Software Development
Extreme Programming (XP)
Rational Unified Process (RUP)
Crystal
Feature Driven Development (FDD)
Scaled Agile Framework (SAFe)

Agile Unified Process (OpenUP)
Scrum of Scrums (SoS)
Extreme Project Management (XPM)
Adaptive Software Development
DevOps
Scrum (Scrum Guide)

CONVERGENT FROM 2001

2001

Agile Manifesto and Principles
February 2001, The Lodge at Snowbird ski resort in the Wasatch mountains of Utah, What emerged was the Agile 'Software Development' Manifesto. Representatives from Extreme Programming, SCRUM, DSDM, Adaptive Software Development, Crystal, Feature-Driven Development, Pragmatic Programming, and others sympathetic to the need for an alternative to documentation driven, heavyweight software development processes convened.

Source: https://agilemanifesto.org/history.html

In common use today

Scrum.org
PRINCE2 Agile
PMBOK Agile
AgilePM (formerly DSDM)
AgileBA
Praxis Agile extensions
Agile Alliance

SAFe
LeSS
SCRUMstudy
Scrum Guide
Lean Kanban
Test Driven Development (TDD)

the divergent approaches taking place before the 2001 meeting, and subsequently the flavours of Scrum/Agile that materialise after this meeting, largely based on a consensus definition of what Agile is.

According to *The Scrum Guide* (Schwaber K & Sutherland J 2020), Scrum is based on the following.

Transparency

The emergent process and work must be visible to those performing the work as well as those receiving the work. With Scrum, important decisions are based on the perceived state of its three formal artifacts. Artifacts that have low transparency can lead to decisions that diminish value and increase risk.

Transparency enables inspection. Inspection without transparency is misleading and wasteful.

Inspection

The Scrum artifacts and the progress toward agreed goals must be inspected frequently and diligently to detect potentially undesirable variances or problems. To help with inspection, Scrum provides cadence in the form of its five events.

Inspection enables adaptation. Inspection without adaptation is considered pointless. Scrum events are designed to provoke change.

Adaptation

If any aspects of a process deviate outside acceptable limits or if the resulting product is unacceptable, the process being applied or the materials being produced must be adjusted. The adjustment must be made as soon as possible to minimize further deviation.

Adaptation becomes more difficult when the people involved are not empowered or self-managing. A Scrum team is expected to adapt the moment it learns anything new through inspection.

Source: https://scrumguides.org/docs/scrumguide/v2020/2020-Scrum-Guide-US.pdf#zoom=100

Scrum is based around a simple process, meetings (ceremonies), roles and a small number of artefacts.

Figure 2.12 outlines the Scrum approach. The Scrum cycle begins with a stakeholder meeting, during which the product vision is created. The product owner then develops a prioritised product backlog that contains a prioritised list of business (customer) requirements written in the form of user stories. Each sprint begins with a sprint planning meeting during which high-priority user stories are considered for inclusion in the sprint; user stories that are accepted into a sprint from the sprint backlog; a sprint goal is established to focus the Scrum team. A sprint generally lasts between one and six weeks and involves the Scrum team working to create potentially shippable deliverables or product increments. During the sprint, short, highly focused daily Scrum meetings are conducted where team members discuss daily progress. At the end of the sprint, a sprint review meeting is held during which the product owner and relevant business stakeholders are provided a demonstration of the deliverables (user stories). The product owner accepts the deliverables only if they meet the predefined acceptance criteria. The cycle ends with a sprint retrospect meeting where the team and product owner discusses ways to improve processes and product as they move forward into the next sprint. This process is overseen by the **Scrum master,** who ensures the manifesto and principles are adhered to and steps in to coach and mentor any of the other roles.

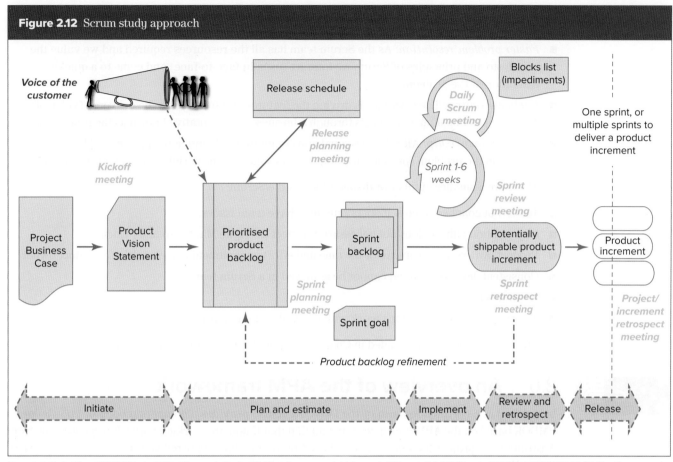

Figure 2.12 Scrum study approach

Source: Adapted from SCRUMStudy 2012, "Scrum study sheet", https://www.scrumstudy.com/pdf/Scrumstudy%20Process%20Chart-2-%2018-10-2012.pdf, accessed December 2021

2.5.1 Benefits/disbenefits to applying the Agile/Scrum approach

The benefits to applying Agile project management are numerous.

- *Adaptability:* Empirical (based on applying and gaining feedback on what is actual being done) and iterative delivery ensures projects are considerate of change.
- *Transparency:* Artefacts such as the product backlog, Scrumboard and sprint burndown chart are visual, open and shared leading to a transparent work environment.
- *Continuous feedback:* Through ceremonies such as the daily stand-up and the sprint review meeting, constant feedback is provided.
- *Continuous improvement:* The deliverables are improved sprint by sprint (through continuous feedback. The product backlog artefact is also refined and reprioritised between sprints
- *Continuous delivery of value:* There is potentially shippable product, service or result at the end of each sprint. If delivered and place into production then delivery is effectively being delivered. It might be the customer has demanded often and frequent delivery—Scrum is an ideal way to meet this demand.
- *Sustainablility:* Only work that is estimated to be do-able is put into a sprint.
- *High value delivered first:* Due to the way the product backlog is prioritised, the highest value feature or functions of the product, service or result are delivered first.

- *Sprints (or timeboxes) are efficient ways to do work:* Scrum is also lean so the amount of work not done is also important to consider.

- *Faster problem resolution:* As the Scrum team has all the resources required and we value the manifesto and principles of Scrum we interact (usually face-to-face) and come to a quicker resolution of the problem.

- *Customer centric:* The customer is driving the features and functions to be delivered (voice of the customer) channelling all requests through a business representative known as the product owner.

- *Collective ownership:* All roles are equal and committed to being in the project and have a shared interest in the problem (product backlog) and its solution (the sprint backlog and sprint goal).

There are a smaller number of disbenefits to Agile/Scrum:

- Teams not coached to be self-sustaining may have team issues.

- Organisation culture does not necessarily respect the Agile Manifesto and Principles.

- Product owners are not aware of the time and effort commitment in their role as a product owner.

- Consistent, level resourcing cannot be achieved in a Scrum team.

- No finite end.

- Too rigid contracts that don't work with the Agile/Scrum approach.

This whole process is expanded in Chapter 3 "Agile (Scrum) project management".

2.6 ┊ **An overview of the APM framework**

Introduced as a certification arm of the IMPA, APM also provides a competing body of knowledge to PMBOK based on the APM life cycle. You may find that if you are working with UK organisations from Australia their project life cycle may be based on regionally supported standards such as the APM, PRINCE2 or even the British Standards Institute BS 6079:2019 "Project management: Principles and guidance for the management of projects". The APM life cycle is illustrated in Figure 2.13.

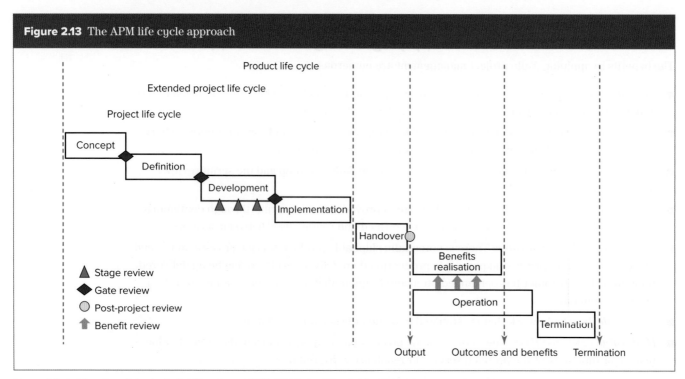

Figure 2.13 The APM life cycle approach

Source: Adapted from Association for Project Management 2019, *APM Body of Knowledge* (APM BOK), seventh edition, APM, 2019

The phases of the APM life cycle are (adapted from APM 2019):

- *Concept phase*: This involves developing the initial idea. High-level requirements captured and assessment of viability, including the outline business case.
- *Definition phase*: Detailed definition (including plans) and a statement of requirements is prepared.
- *Development phase*: The implementation of the plans and checking of project performance through project assurance activities to ensure the intended outputs, outcomes and benefits are achieved.
- *Handover*: The project's outputs (and outcomes) are handed over to the business and are accepted by the sponsor on behalf of the business.
- *Benefits realisation*: Continued tracking of benefits until all the projects benefits have been reported on and realised.

Further phases include:

- *Operation*: Continuing support and maintenance of the outputs in the business.
- *Termination*: Close down (or disposal) at the end of the product's useful life.

These two additional phases are important considerations in some industries, such as the construction of a nuclear power station, as there has to be an approach to decommissioning the plant (i.e. termination of the plant at the end of its useful life) at the start of the larger program of work.

The APM approach considers not only an extended project life cycle that includes the realisation of benefits beyond the traditional project closure but also the concept that work (often occurring after a period of extended time) will need to keep the product or service in operation and ultimately decommission (take down) the product or service at the end of its useful life.

2.7 An introduction to Lean Six Sigma and the DMAIC process

Organisations taking a Lean Six Sigma approach to the development and maintenance of processes (and all the holistic components of operating process in the business) will use the DMADV and DMAIC processes to approach the project.

If the process (and supporting business system) is new (does not currently exist in the organisation) or the current process is deemed to be far off delivering what the customer wants (or has been promised) then the DMADV (also known as Design for Six Sigma—DFSS) approach is applied. DMADV stands for:

- *Define* the project and its goals
- *Measure* the critical-to-quality aspects that are important to the customer, as this is the basis for the later design
- *Analyse* data to inform the best design possible
- *Design* and pilot (including testing) the new product or service process
- *Verify* that the designed process will deliver and meet the customer's critical-to-quality requirements.

Whereas, DMAIC is the most predominant approach used for the improvement of existing processes. As illustrated in Figure 2.14, each stage of the DMAIC process has defined outcomes.

Figure 2.14 The DMAIC process

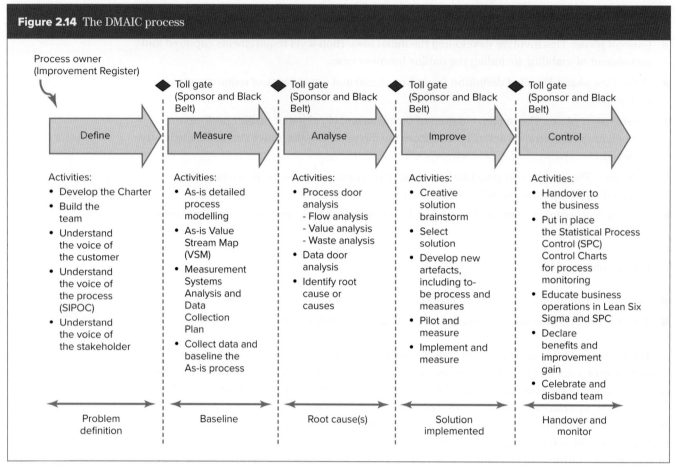

© 2022 Dr Neil Pearson

As per Figure 2.14:

- *Define* is concerned with defining and understanding the problem and results in a charter being produced for the project. The Project Charter is validated at a toll gate by the sponsor representing the business interests and a Lean Six Sigma black belt (a senior practitioner of the Lean Six Sigma approach). Linking back the requirements to what the customer of the process requires is referred to as the *voice of the customer* (VOC).

- *Measure* focuses on understanding the details of the existing process and coming to an agreed way of working. Once this has been ascertained, the *as-is* process can be baselined, against which future improvements made at the Improve stage can be measured.

- *Analyse* is where the process and the data are analysed in detail to ascertain root cause(s). The *process door* looks at waste (in particular the eight wastes of transport, inventory, motion, waiting (delays), over-production, over-processing, defects and skills), flow and value (value-adding activities, non-value-adding activities, and business non-value-adding activities). Various visualisations of data are used from a *data door* perspective. The results indicate improvement opportunities in the process under review, from which a root-cause analysis can be carried out. Two popular root-cause analysis techniques are the *fishbone diagram* and the *5 whys* (refer to Chapter 13 "Project quality management").

- *Improve* means that once the root cause(s) has been confirmed, the process of identifying the best solution(s) to be implemented takes place; these are prioritised with input from the business.

The selected solutions are developed ready for piloting (including the *to-be* process and other artefacts, after which measuring takes place, to ensure the baseline established (at the Measure stage) has been improved upon. The solution will be implemented in the business after piloting and after further improvements have been made, as required. The implemented process is measured again post-implementation, to ensure the improvements being sought are actually achieved.

■ *Control* includes the activities of embedding the solution in business-as-usual operations and leaving necessary measures and charts in place, including the all-important statistical process control (SPC) control charts.

The Lean Six Sigma approach is highly problem oriented and typically generates only a few project-related documents such as the Project Charter, a Pilot Plan, an Implementation Plan and a Control Plan (which is handed over to the business during the Control stage). Governance is contained in the toll gates, which give the go-ahead to move into the next stage of DMAIC. DMAIC projects can be of any reasonable length of time (e.g. from days, months for larger, more complex improvement projects). The environment is very Agile when applying DMAIC, as techniques such as the Kanban board (Scrum board), daily stand-ups and self-managing work, are applied—refer Snapshot from Practice: Lean Six Sigma at an Australian water company.

Some project leaders apply either the **Plan-Do-Study-Act (PDSA)**, also known as the **Plan-Do-Check-Act (PDCA)**, or the DMIAC approach to improve the project's processes or on occasions within the project to find solutions to process and business systems components of a project. DMAIC and PDCA approaches are discussed further in Chapter 13 "Project quality management".

SNAPSHOT *from* PRACTICE : Lean Six Sigma at an Australian water company

Seqwater is a large water service provider in Queensland, Australia. It provides domestic drinking water (plus water for irrigation) across Southeast Queensland. In recent years it has experienced significant organisational change through a series of mergers, throughout which it has still been required to deliver an efficient service to its customers. A case study was carried out to demonstrate how Lean Six Sigma could be applied to the water industry (using internal resources, leveraged by external consultants).

An area that was flagged as requiring a review was externally provided with water quality and environmental monitoring. Seqwater's current monitoring program is separated according to historic business divisions, which are catchment, water treatment, bulk supply system and environmental.

Each program has largely been developed independently to meet specific business needs and regulatory requirements. In addition to independent programs, data are also stored across multiple databases and systems. With the creation of the Queensland Bulk Water Supply Authority (trading as Seqwater) there was an incentive to integrate these programs. By taking a holistic approach to water quality monitoring it is hoped that a better understanding of the schemes could be developed (Howey & Middleton 2015).

The project utilised a DMAIC process to manage the process improvement. Table 2.7 summarises the key activities undertaken at each stage of the DMAIC process by the improvement team.

In the conclusion to the paper, the authors note that:

> *Statistical analysis showed in many cases that the rationale for monitoring was not being demonstrated by the results and value for money was not being achieved. Recommendations for improvement were applied to seqwater's routine monitoring program, removing high cost low risk monitoring and a saving of up to 45% was possible, whilst still maintaining regulatory compliance and effective risk management (Howey & Middleton 2015).*

(Continues)

Table 2.7 DMAIC at Seqwater

Stage	Indicative activities undertaken
Define	Definition of the problem statement: "Through a series of restructures and amalgamations Seqwater's combined water quality monitoring program has grown large. The rational[e] behind the monitoring program needs to be reviewed in order to focus monitoring on achieving stated objectives in risk management and compliance. It is considered with a more focused monitoring program significant savings could be achieved" (Howey & Middleton 2015). Clarification of the project's scope, along with identification of the project's key objectives of identify efficiencies, improve risk management, maintain regulatory compliance and fulfil contractual (other monitoring) commitments. Listening to the voice of the customer, with the customer being represented through regulatory and other requirements reviews, benchmarking to other water providers, and a focus group workshop.
Measure	In order to baseline (measure) the current (as-is) process, the improvement team had to understand the as-is process of routine and non-routine sampling and analysis. "Historic financial information was gathered for all of the components of the program. In addition to this the current documented routine monitoring program was costed, which included 61 test suites and over 220,000 analyses per annum" (Howey & Middleton 2015). Risks across 40 water treatment plants were also collected, in addition to financial data. If this risk data had not been available, the project could have carried out a current analysis of risk (of the as is process) using a technique known as a FMEA (failure mode and effects analysis).
Analyse	"A vital question that [the] project needed to answer was whether the monitoring data collected actually fulfilled the rationale that justified the monitoring in the program (i.e. was it being used and was it valuable)" (Howey & Middleton 2015). The improvement team used a popular Lean Six Sigma data analysis tool (Minitab) to visualise the various criteria of water quality using charts such as boxplots, graphical summaries, interval plots, correlation (scatter graphs) and Pareto charts. Root causes (findings) were taken forward from the Data Analysis stage (carried out in the Analysis stage) to the Improve phase of the project.
Improve	Recommendations (solutions) were made and developed for each finding. These recommendations were subsequently applied to a test site and (following measurement) were considered for deployment to the entire monitoring program.
Control	The control processes, measurements and the tool used (Minitab) were all passed back to Seqwater for further consideration. The project's success was considered: "Based on these changes the routine analysis budget was reduced by 45%. However, even if all the recommendations were to be applied it is not anticipated that a final saving of this magnitude would be achieved, as there will be an increase in non-routine monitoring as the program moves to a more risk-based approach and a considerable cost still exists for sample collection" (Howey & Middleton 2015). This open and transparent declaration, regarding its final impact, provided an example of an important understanding of Lean Six Sigma projects.

Source: © James Howey, Duncan Middleton - Viridis Consultants P/L, Brisbane and Seqwater, Ipswich

This Lean Six Sigma project example demonstrates the focus of such projects: most effort was focused around the project, analysis and later solutions for implementation, rather than a heavy focus on the project management aspects (as in predictive project management approaches). This is one of the reasons that the uptake of Lean Six Sigma practices has grown significantly across the globe.

Source: Howey J & Middleton D 2015, "Lean Six Sigma application to water utilities: getting value for money out of water quality monitoring", https://www.academia.edu/33737919/LEAN_SIX_SIGMA_APPLICATION_TO_WATER_UTILITIES_GETTING_VALUE_FOR_MONEY_OUT_OF_WATER_QUALITY_MONITORING, accessed May 2022

2.8 | An overview of the Praxis framework

The Praxis framework is described as a free framework for the management of projects, programs and portfolios. The Praxis project management approach (which considers programs and portfolios in its wider framework) also includes a capability maturity model and competency framework (much like the PMI approach). Figure 2.15 shows a simplified version of the process model for projects and programs.

Figure 2.15 The Praxis approach

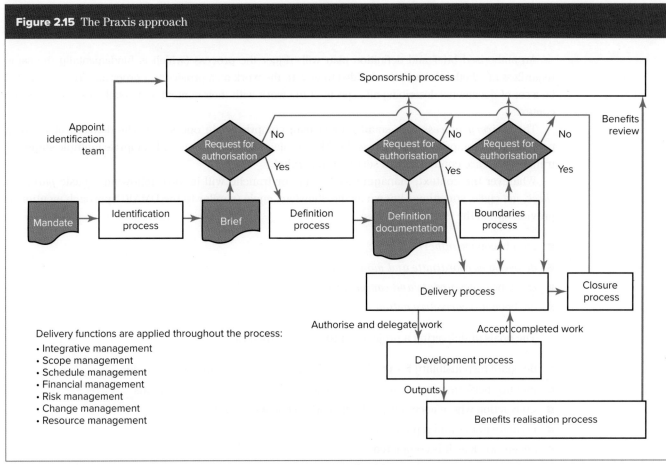

Source: Adapted from Praxis 2019, "Process infographic", https://www.praxisframework.org/en/resource-pages/praxis-process-infographic, accessed December 2021

The process groups are described as follows.

The *identification process* manages the first phase of the project's or program's life cycle. Its goals are to:

- develop an outline of the project or program and assess whether is it likely to be justifiable
- determine what effort and investment is needed to define the work in detail
- gain the sponsor's authorisation for the definition phase.

This process is designed to achieve the goals of the sponsorship function, which are to:

- provide ownership of the Business Case
- act as champion for the objectives of the project or program
- make go/no-go decisions at relevant points in the life cycle
- address matters outside the scope of the manager's authority
- oversee assurance
- provide ad hoc support to the management team.

The *definition process* manages the definition phase of the project or program life cycle. Its goals are to:

- develop a detailed picture of the project or program
- determine whether the work is justified

- describe governance policies that describe how the work will be managed
- gain the sponsor's authorisation for the delivery phase.

An authorised brief and definition plan will trigger the process (which is fundamentally the same regardless of whether it has been decided to govern the work as a project or a program). The output will be a set of documents describing all aspects of the work with their content and detail varying to suit the context.

The *delivery process* of a small project may comprise only one stage. The delivery phase of a program may comprise only one tranche. Most projects and programs will comprise multiple stages or tranches that are conducted in a series or in parallel.

Whatever the context, managing each stage or tranche will involve following a basic *plan, do, check, act* cycle, sometimes known as the Shewhart cycle (similar to the DMAIC approach mentioned previously). In the delivery process:

- *plan* becomes *authorised work*
- *do* becomes *coordinate and monitor progress*
- *check* becomes *update and communicate*
- *act* becomes *corrective action.*

The goals of delivering a project or program are then to:

- delegate responsibility for producing deliverables to the appropriate people
- monitor performance of the work and track this against the delivery plans
- take action where necessary to keep work in line with plans
- escalate issues and replan if necessary
- accept work as it is completed
- maintain communications with all stakeholders.

The *closure process* goals are to:

- close a project or program that has delivered all of its outputs
- close a project or program that is no longer justifiable
- review the management of work and to learn lessons.

Closure is principally concerned with a temporary organisation (the project) handing over responsibility for its objectives and disbanding. Where that occurs in the life cycle will depend on how the project or program was constituted in the first place.

It is usually the case that benefits are not automatically realised simply by producing an output. In most cases, an output is used to change some aspect of an organisation's mode of operation, or environment. Implicit within the word *change* is a quantifiable improvement in one or more performance indicators to which value has been assigned. The goals of the *benefits realisation process* are to:

- establish the current state of what is being changed
- co-ordinate the delivery of outputs with the management of change
- ensure changes are permanent
- establish whether benefits have been achieved.

In its simplest form, realising benefits is about measuring current performance, helping people who make up the organisation through the period of change (the transition) and measuring the improvement in performance (adapted from: https://www.praxisframework.org/en/method/identification-process).

Praxis (much like PRINCE2 and the PMI) supports the integration of Agile in the delivery process of the life cycle. As illustrated in Figure 2.16, the delivery process is broken down further, with the Agile approach effectively replacing the traditional deliverable-based approach.

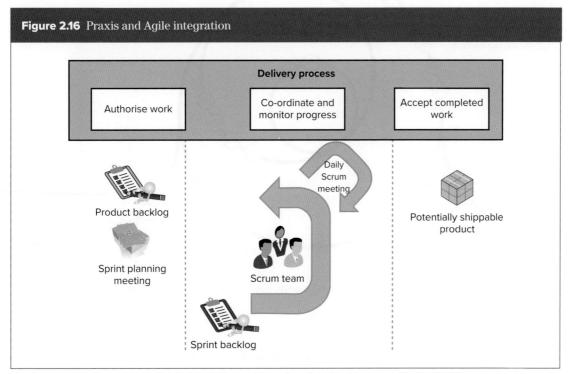

Figure 2.16 Praxis and Agile integration

Source: Adapted from "Using Scrum with Praxis", Praxis, https://www.praxisframework.org/en/resource-pages/using-scrum-with-praxis, accessed February 2018

Certification is available through a variety of providers including APMG International (2022). As noted in Chapter 1 "Contemporary project management", this is the approach adopted by the Australian Institute of Project Management (AIPM) as the underpinning body of knowledge for its members.

2.9 An overview of the P3.express system

Before providing a quick overview of **P3.express,** it must be stated that most of the approaches covered in this chapter can be tailored to suit projects of most sizes and complexity. That said, let's take a quick look into the motivations of P3.express.

If you are a project leader seeking an inherently simplified project management approach, then look no further than P3.express. It has a simple flow with attached activities (denoted by the numbers and letters) (Figure 2.17).

A P3.express project is planned, executed and controlled on a monthly cycle basis. The seven areas of management activities in summary are:

1. *Project Initiation:* Prepare the environment and develop a high-level plan. In Figure 2.17, Activity A08 represents a go/no-go decision, after which in A09 the project is kicked off.
2. *Monthly Initiation:* At the start of each month several activities take place to prepare the project for the month to come. A check is made to ask whether to continue the project (Figure 2.17, Activity B03).
3. *Weekly Management:* Activities run weekly accompanied by measurements and controls such as the planning of responses to deviations (Figure 2.17, C02).

Figure 2.17 P3.express flow

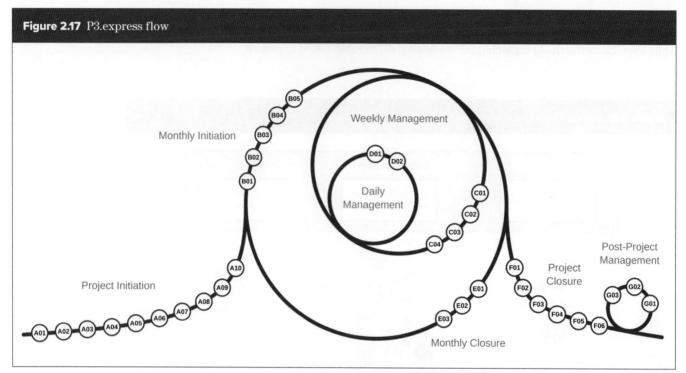

4. *Daily Management:* Activities which are run daily—risk, issue and change request management. At D02 in Figure 2.17, completed deliverables are (potentially) accepted.

5. *Monthly Closure:* Activities run at the end of the month to prepare the project for the next cycle, including where lessons are captured (Figure 2.17, E02).

6. *Project Closure:* When the work is done, activities are carried out to close the project (Figure 2.17, F01), hand over the product and celebrate successes (Figure 2.17, F05).

7. *Post-Project Management:* This is where benefit evaluation takes place (Figure 2.17, G0). Also, new ideas are generated to improve upon the benefits delivered. These could be a new project in the future or continuous improvement opportunities in the business operations (Figure 2.17, G02).

The approach appears relatively simple to follow and has a small number of carefully designed activities; however, it still requires knowledge that comes from other sources. For example, how risk and issues are handled is not stipulated in the P3.express approach, so the project leader would have to turn to other approaches such as PMBOK, or even industry standards such as ISO 31000:2018 "Risk management—Guidelines". P3.express also refers to a set of principles known as **NUPP.** "NUPP is a collection of nearly universal principles of projects: those we'd do well to follow in all projects, regardless of the methodologies and approaches that we use, to maximize our success" (NUPP 2019). It is interesting that P3.express picked up the NUPP guide to introduce the concept of a defined set of principles designed to influence behaviours of project leaders in a positive manner, as defined by the PMI in the seventh edition of *The Standard for Project Management* (PMI 2021b).

The NUPP principles are described as follows.

■ "NUP1: prefer results and the truth to affiliations. We all have a natural tendency to belong to groups, a tendency that often goes beyond its basic form, creates strong affiliations, and causes problems. We lose a lot more than we gain because of affiliations. We can become more professional and effective experts if we don't limit our identity and preferences to certain groups.

- NUP2: preserve and optimize energy and resources. Resources are limited. Resources available to the project are limited, as is the mental energy you have to make good decisions. You should preserve and optimize this resource for yourself and for the project, and help other team members do the same.

- NUP3: always be proactive. There's a natural tendency in us to be reactive. It can help us preserve our energy dealing unimportant matters, or it may give us better results when we are dealing with something in which we're completely incompetent. Those situations are different from our projects, and here we can get better results by being proactive.

- NUP4: remember that a chain is only as strong as its weakest link. There are various domains in projects, and they all need attention; we must have a holistic perspective of the project. Paying attention to a seemingly important domain (e.g., time) is not enough, because all domains interact and they don't work properly unless they all receive adequate attention.

- NUP5: don't do anything without a clear purpose. You shouldn't do anything unless it has a clear purpose. Imagine two parallel worlds where everything is the same except for the thing that you're considering doing: How different would those worlds be? Is the difference worth the effort to do that thing?

- NUP6: use repeatable elements. An ad hoc approach to the project takes too much energy and resources, and always runs the risk of missing some of the necessary elements. The best way of simplifying what has to be done is to use repeatable elements, and preferably to take them in repeatable cycles." (NUPP 2019)

(**Source:** https://nupp.guide, accessed February 2022, CC BY 4.0, https://creativecommons.org/licenses/by/4.0/)

2.10 An introduction to the *Project Management Body of Knowledge* (PMBOK)

To further develop understanding of PMBOK, let's now look at a brief history of PMI's PMBOK. PMBOK was first published as a white paper, "Ethics, Standards, and Accreditation Committee final report" (discussed in Duncan 1996) to document and standardise generally accepted project management information and practices. A PMBOK white paper was published in 1987, with an exposure draft of the PMBOK in 1994. The first edition of *A Guide to the Project Management Body of Knowledge* (*PMBOK® Guide*) was published in 1996 (originally 176 pages) and had a structure reminiscent of many of the later editions with the five process groups (Initiation, Planning, Execution, Control and Closure) complete with the original nine knowledge areas (project integration management, project scope management, project time management, project cost management, project quality management, project human resource management, project communications management, project risk management and project procurement management). The second edition followed in 2000 (216 pages) with only minor updates. The *PMBOK® Guide* received a major overhaul with the release of a third edition in 2004 and this was subsequently built upon in the fourth edition, released in 2008 and reinforcing the nine knowledge areas.

The fifth edition of the *PMBOK® Guide* was released in January 2013 with some Agile considerations and recognition of the tenth knowledge area referred to as *project stakeholder management*. In 2017, the sixth edition of the *PMBOK® Guide* was released and included extensive consideration of the Agile approach and was supplemented with an additional guide the "Agile

Practice Guide", which took Scrum/Agile theory and indicated how this can be leveraged instead of and within the traditional predictive PMBOK life cycle. The sixth edition also split the book into two distinct parts: *The Standard for Project Management* and *A Guide to the Project Management Body of Knowledge*; additionally, *project human resource management* changed to *project resource management* to reflect the identification and management of any resource: human, physical or other.

PMBOK	Seventh edition updates (PMI 2021)

In 2021 the seventh edition of the *PMBOK® Guide* radically reworked the approach and moved away from a heavily biased predictive approach to a more holistic guide applicable to many of the approaches describe in the earlier section of this chapter. As noted in the Chapter 1 "Contemporary project management", this text focuses on the sixth edition (as it aligns well with a staged life cycle approach), but also introduces elements of the seventh edition. A summary of where material from both editions of the *PMBOK® Guide* can be located in this text is in Table 2.8(a) and Table 2.8(b).

Table 2.8(a) *A Guide to the Project Management Body of Knowledge*, sixth edition versus seventh edition, mapped to chapters in this text

A Guide to the Project Management Body of Knowledge			
The ten knowledge areas		The eight performance domains	
PMBOK sixth edition	In this text	PMBOK seventh edition	In this text
Chapter 4 Project Integration Management	Chapter 6 Project integration management Chapter 7 Governance and projects	Chapter 2.1 Stakeholder Performance Domain	Chapter 14 Project stakeholder management
Chapter 5 Project Scope Management	Chapter 8 Defining the scope of a project	Chapter 2.2 Team Performance Domain	Chapter 19 Project leaders and project teams
Chapter 6 Project Schedule Management	Chapter 9 Estimating Chapter 11 Project schedule management	Chapter 2.3 Development Approach and Life Cycle Performance Domain	Chapter 2 Popular frameworks and methodologies Chapter 3 Agile (Scrum) project management
Chapter 7 Project Cost Management	Chapter 9 Estimating Chapter 12 Project cost management	Chapter 2.4 Planning Performance Domain	Chapter 8 Defining the scope of a project Chapter 9 Estimating Chapter 10 Project resource management Chapter 11 Project schedule management Chapter 12 Project cost management Chapter 15 Project information and communications management Chapter 16 Project risk management Chapter 17 Project procurement management
Chapter 8 Project Quality Management	Chapter 13 Project quality management	Chapter 2.5 Project Work Performance Domain	Chapter 18 Project execution
Chapter 9 Project Resource Management	Chapter 9 Estimating Chapter 10 Project resource management Chapter 19 Project leaders and project teams	Chapter 2.6 Delivery Performance Domain	Chapter 13 Project quality management Chapter 16 Project risk management Chapter 18 Project execution
Chapter 10 Project Communications Management	Chapter 15 Project information and communications management	Chapter 2.7 Measurement Performance Domain	Chapter 4 Organisational strategy and project selection Chapter 18 Project execution Chapter 19 Project leaders and project teams Chapter 21 Project closure
Chapter 11 Project Risk Management	Chapter 16 Project risk management	Chapter 2.8 Uncertainty Performance Domain	Chapter 20 Complex project management
Chapter 12 Project Procurement Management	Chapter 17 Project procurement management	Chapter 3 Tailoring	Chapter 2 Popular frameworks and methodologies
Chapter 13 Project Stakeholder Management	Chapter 14 Project stakeholder management	Chapter 4 Models, Methods, and Artifacts	Dispersed throughout this text where used in a project environment

Table 2.8(b) *The Standard for Project Management,* sixth edition versus seventh edition, mapped to chapters in this text

The Standard for Project Management			
The 5 process groups		The 12 project management principles	
PMBOK sixth edition	**In this text**	**PMBOK seventh edition**	**In this text**
Initiation	Chapter 4 Organisational strategy and project selection Chapter 6 Project integration management Chapter 7 Governance and projects Chapter 14 Project stakeholder management	Chapter 3.1 Be a diligent, respectful and caring steward	Chapter 14 Project leaders and project teams
Planning	Chapter 8 Defining the scope of a project Chapter 9 Estimating Chapter 10 Project resource management Chapter 11 Project schedule management Chapter 12 Project cost management Chapter 13 Project quality management Chapter 14 Project stakeholder management Chapter 15 Project information and communications management Chapter 16 Project risk management Chapter 17 Project procurement management	Chapter 3.2 Create a collaborative project team environment	Chapter 14 Project leaders and project teams
Execution	Chapter 6 Project integration management Chapter 18 Project execution	Chapter 3.3 Effectively engage with stakeholders	Chapter 15 Project stakeholder management
Monitor and Control	Chapter 8 Defining the scope of a project Chapter 6 Project integration management Chapter 18 Project execution	Chapter 3.4 Focus on value	Chapter 1 Contemporary project management Chapter 4 Organisational strategy and project selection
Closure	Chapter 6 Project integration management Chapter 21 Project closure	Chapter 3.5 Recognize, evaluate, and respond to system interactions	Chapter 1 Contemporary project management
		Chapter 3.6 Demonstrate leadership behaviours	Chapter 14 Project leaders and project teams
		Chapter 3.7 Tailor based on context	Chapter 2 Popular frameworks and methodologies
		Chapter 3.8 Build quality into processes and deliverables	Chapter 12 Project quality management
		Chapter 3.9 Navigate complexity	Chapter 20 Complex project management
		Chapter 3.10 Optimize risk responses	Chapter 17 Project risk management
		Chapter 3.11 Embrace adaptability and resiliency	Chapter 14 Project leaders and project teams
		Chapter 3.12 Enable change to achieve envisioned future state	Chapter 5 Organisational change management and cultures

© 2022 Dr Neil Pearson

The *PMBOK® Guide* seventh edition is substantially shorter than a number of the previous editions and lists numerous models, methods and artefacts; this text aims to detail and provide examples where space allows.

The shift from PMBOK sixth edition to PMBOK seventh edition:

- moves from focusing on deliverables to creating value

- widens its audience from just project leaders to others involved in a project

- moves from processes (49) and process groups (5) to the 12 project management principles, which influence our behaviours as project leaders; therefore, a move from knowledge areas (10) to performance domains (8).

(Continues)

Organisational change management is also formally recognised in the seventh edition, a request the principal author of this third Australian edition of *Project Management in Practice* has been making for several years. Refer to Chapter 5 "Organisational change management and cultures".

The PMBOK indicative life cycle was introduced in Chapter 1 "Contemporary project management", Figure 1.2; this will now be explored further. Figure 2.18 presents the stages of the life cycle in a more predictive format.

Figure 2.18 Predictive life cycle stages

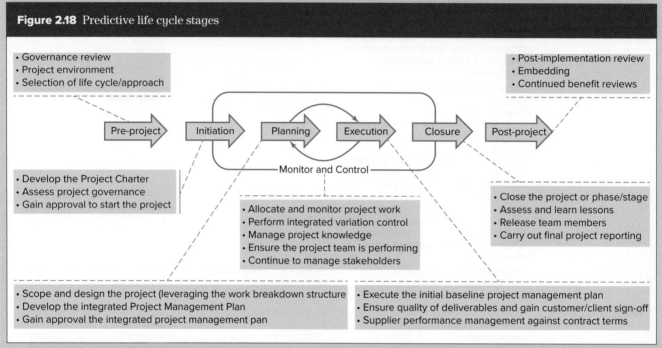

© 2022 Dr Neil Pearson

The process groups indicated in Figure 2.18 are described as:

- *Pre-project:* Assessment of the project environment and establishment of overarching governance. Selection of the most appropriate life cycle/approach in which to undertake the project.

- *Initiation process group:* The processes carried out in relation to the definition of a project (or project stage), generating an approved Project Charter.

- *Planning process group:* The processes carried out in relation to defining the detail required before executing the plan (or stages), further clarifying the Charter as a scope document, and the development of the integrated PMP.

- *Execution process group:* The processes carried out in relation to completion of the planned work according to the approved Project Management Plan.

- *Closure process group:* The processes (or stage) carried out in relation to formally closing the project (or stage).

- *Monitor and Control processes group:* The processes carried out in relation to the review, tracking, reporting and management of change (variations) across the life cycle of the project (or stage).

- *Post-project:* Further learnings and the post-implementation review, accompanied by the continuous delivery of benefits for benefits not realised at project handover. From a business perspective continued execution of the project's Organisational Change Management Plan.

2.10.1 PMBOK and tailoring

Both the sixth and seventh edition of the *PMBOK® Guide* recognise the need for tailoring. Tailoring is taking the good practice of the *PMBOK® Guide* and adjusting it to the factors relevant and important to your project within the project environment that you are operating. The act of tailoring can be compared to cooking a quality steak: tailoring can be both *undercooked*, where too much is removed from the process that results in critical components of project management not being attended to; or *overcooked* where too much process is included, which detracts from the product, service or result being produced. Either way the customer does not receive what they wanted or value.

Project leaders consider a number of factors when tailoring, for example, the size of the project, project complexity, and the strategic and customer value the project adds.

Similarly in the seventh edition of the *PMBOK® Guide,* the PMI discusses that each performance domain can be adapted according to the unique needs of each project (PMI 2021a). Remember that in the seventh edition the 12 principles guide behaviours over the project leader doing the work in the eight performance domains, so any or all of the eight performance domains could be tailored:

- Stakeholder Performance Domain
- Team Performance Domain
- Development Approach and Life Cycle Performance Domain
- Planning Performance Domain
- Project Work Performance Domain
- Delivery Performance Domain
- Measurement Performance Domain
- Uncertainty Performance Domain.

Once the project environment (approach, governance and processes), have been tailored to consider the external environment and internal environment, the project leader would capture this information within relevant management plans, or even an overarching project Governance Management Plan. This plan would then be communicated to all project team members and other interested/impacted stakeholders to ensure consistent application of governance. Furthermore, the tailored project environment would be placed within the continuous improvement protocols established as a part of the quality and continuous improvement management plan for the project. PDSA and DMAIC are the continuous improvement approaches typically applied to the ongoing improvement of the project's processes and systems. PDSA and DMAIC are discussed in Chapter 13 "Project quality management".

2.10.2 **Applying the predictive approach**

It is important to consider how a project leader might leverage the PMBOK life cycle approach in the design (approach) of the project. It is perfectly feasible and normal to phase a project. Phases of a project are natural separations in the work to be performed, often occurring where approvals need to be sought before proceeding onto the next phase of the project. The *PMBOK® Guide* outlines three phased approaches: sequential relationship, overlapping relationship and the rolling wave planning approach.

Sequential relationship, where one phase of a project can only start on completion of a previous phase, is depicted in Figure 2.19. In this figure, Phase 1—Design factory must complete before Phase 2—Acquire and prepare land; and Phase 3—Build and commission factory can only start after Phase 2 has been completed.

Overlapping relationship is when a future phase of the project can start before a previous phase has completed, as shown in Figure 2.20. Towards the two-thirds point of Phase 1—Design factory, Phase 2—Acquire and prepare land is initiated (overlapping with Phase 1), as once the basic factory parameters have been defined the act of finding and shortlisting suitable land can be started in parallel to the detailed factory design. In this example Phase 3—Build and commission factory can only take place sequentially after Phase 2—Acquire and prepare land.

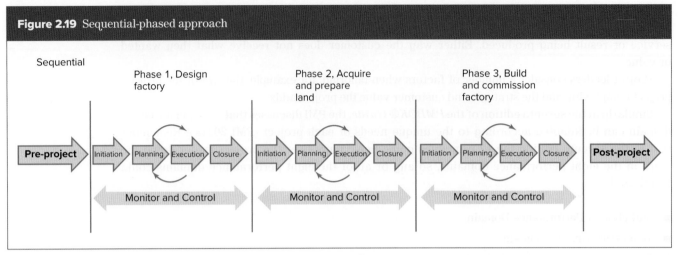

Figure 2.19 Sequential-phased approach

© 2022 Dr Neil Pearson

Note: Each phase is in itself a complete life cycle from Initiation to Closure.

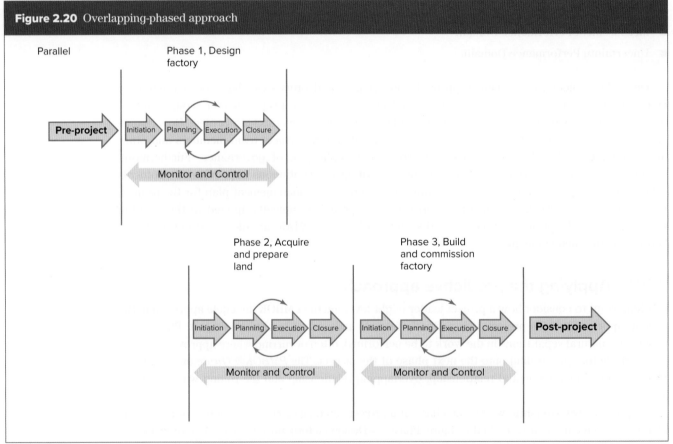

Figure 2.20 Overlapping-phased approach

© 2022 Dr Neil Pearson

Rolling wave planning is where the next phase is planned (and influenced) by the current phase, as the current phase is being delivered, as depicted in Figure 2.21. While Phase 1—Factory design is being delivered, Initiation and Planning processes are taking place in Phase 2—Acquire and prepare land (i.e. this work is getting closer, therefore more detail will be added to the plans). Phase 3—Build and commission will not receive much attention until Phase 2 is nearing Closure. Remember, the principle of rolling wave planning is of progressive elaboration. Therefore, project work can exist in various

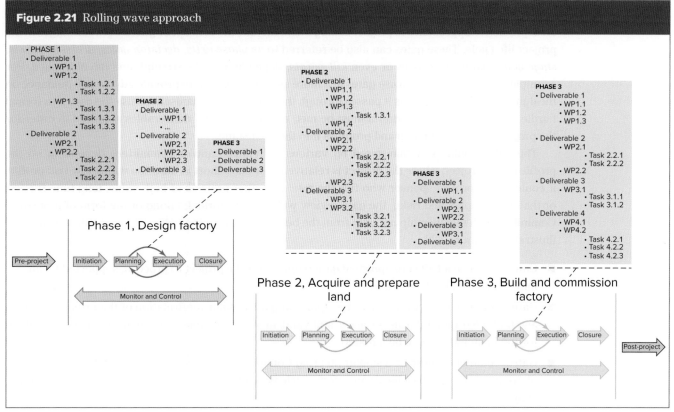

Figure 2.21 Rolling wave approach

© 2022 Dr Neil Pearson

levels of detail, depending on where it is in the overall project life cycle. Work that is about to occur will be planned in detail, while work in future phases will not be planned in detail until closer in proximity.

2.10.3 Integrative project management

The importance of taking an integrative approach to the 10 knowledge areas cannot be stressed enough. The project leader may focus on a particular area of the project; however, a good project leader will play forward the consequences of any decisions made across all the other knowledge areas: referred to in this text as **integrative thinking** (what PMI refers to in the sixth edition as *Integration at the Cognitive Level*, PMI 2017a, p. 67).

For example, you may be a project leader who is early in the Planning stage of the project when the customer requests a change to the end-date of the project to bring it forward by a number of weeks. As project leader, your decision cannot be made purely on time. Adjusting the delivery schedule will necessitate a review of many factors, including resource availability, additional equipment expenses, potential effects on the quality of the outcomes and changes to the risk profile of the project, among a host of other factors.

PMBOK : Seventh edition updates (PMI 2021)

In the seventh edition of the *PMBOK® Guide* there is no performance domain that covers the equivalent of project integration management; it is assumed this will be taking place across the life cycle, integrative thinking is what a project leader should be considering in all activities carried out.

In this text we build integration and associated activities within each stage of the project life cycle into the relevant knowledge chapter. Other aspects of project integration the PMI considers in the sixth edition of the *PMBOK® Guide* are discussed in Chapter 6 "Project integration management".

2.10.4 Gates and the project life cycle

Most predictive approaches to project management include the concept of **gates** between stages in the project life cycle. These gates can also be referred to as *phase exits, decision gates, decision points, stage gates, gateway reviews* or even *kill points*, depending on the strength and intent implied. For example, some organisations use gates in a more assistive context, to provide advice and guidance on the dynamics of the project as it passes through the gate. Other organisations use the gate as a formal hurdle where performance criteria must be met, or approvals and deliverables achieved in order for the project to receive funding and progress into the next stage.

The gates could be administered by various individuals and/or committees depending on the profile of the project; where the project is relatively low cost, short in duration with a low risk profile, it could be the project sponsor who fills the role. For other projects of high value, long time frames, or that are complex and risky, the gate review will be more formal, taking of the form of a Steering Committee with membership not only from the business but also the PMO. A typical gated scenario is illustrated in Figure 2.22.

- Gate 1 could be a PMO pre-approval gate required for the project to proceed, supported by an initial approved Business Case.
- Gate 2 could be a Steering Committee approval gate seeking confirmation of the Project Charter and that the original Business Case is still valid, or where the release of funds would be approved for the Planning stage to be initiated.
- Gate 3 could once more be a similar Steering Committee approval gate, where detailed plans are approved (baselined) and monies released for the project to progress to the Executing stage.
- Gate 4, at the end of the Execution stage, would be the required verification of final deliverable acceptance, before formal project closure is initiated.
- Gate 5 could be a governance, benefit and final post-implementation review assessment. The gated process would be adjusted to suit the governance established at project initiation and would be influenced by the organisation's governance on benefit management, business case validity, performance measurement and any other relevant governance.

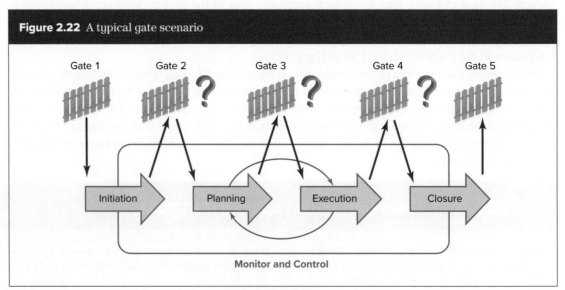

Figure 2.22 A typical gate scenario

© 2022 Dr Neil Pearson

Additionally, the scope (e.g. objectives, deliverables) plus variations would be assessed to ensure delivery occurred against what was originally proposed mindful or any approved variations.

Governance related to gates and the tailored project management approach with governance that does not cleanly fall into a knowledge area management plan, would be captured into an overarching project Governance Management Plan (refer to Chapter 7 "Governance and projects").

The seventh edition of the *PMBOK® Guide* mentions stage gates (or a phase gate review) in its definition of an indicative predictive life cycle (Feasibility, Design, Build, Test, Deploy, Close) to ensure that all outcomes have been achieved before moving on to the next stage.

Summary

There are many project management frameworks and methodologies available to a project leader. This chapter has focused on some of the more popular, commonly used methodologies including PRINCE2, ISO 21500:2021, Agile, Lean Six Sigma, APM, Praxis, P3.express and PMI's PMBOK. There are no hard and fast rules around which frameworks and methodology should be used. However, there are some noticeable patterns that can potentially assist with demonstrating the use of one methodology over another.

- PRINCE2 was, historically, principally used by governments and for large ICT projects or by large corporations. It is characterised by strong governance, defined roles and a continued business justification throughout the project.

- ISO 21500:2021 offers guidance where the adoption of a standards-based approach to project management at a high level is sought. It is ideal for when businesses require only high-level guidance to establish a project management presence supplementing the detail behind the guidance with other approaches, such as PMI or Praxis. ISO 21500:2021 does consider external, internal and project environment and reinforces strategic alignment and benefit delivery.

- Scrum (Agile) is the approach of the moment as organisations seek more agility in the management of projects, building only features that deliver value to the business/customer. This approach is based on a small number of roles (product owner, Scrum master and Scrum team), supports by a small number of ceremonies/events (sprint planning, daily Scrum, sprint review and sprint retrospective) and a small number of prudent artefacts (release roadmap, product backlog, sprint backlog, story cards, burndown/up charts and the finished product). It provides a principles-based approach to the management of projects that have uncertain requirements and/or are complex.

- Lean Six Sigma is gaining a lot of traction for the ongoing continuous improvement of business processes. It is administered through the belt system of roles: a Yellow Belt (for a subject matter expert), a Green Belt (for a project lead) or a Black Belt (for a more senior role e.g. complex project lead). Like Agile/Scrum it inherits some principles from Lean, such as being customer focused, Kanban boards, visual management and value. Lean Six Sigma does not have a large project management footprint.

- APM remains popular as an alternative to the PMI's PMBOK. Although the APM Body of Knowledge (APM 2019) is not as content rich, its overarching process encompasses the key elements of the extended project life cycle and also the wider product life cycle.

- Praxis is an open source framework for the management of portfolios, programs and projects. Gaining mainstream popularity for the management of projects, it is built on community-based empirical evidence from practising project leaders. It provides a solid body of knowledge, templates and other artefacts, and has a community through which support can be found.

- PMI's PMBOK is a generic, de facto, project management framework. It is applied across all industries (private and government) and is supported by a rich knowledge-based approach. It takes a truly global approach towards project management and offers easily accessible training and education programs. PMBOK is often adapted and internalised within organisations and supported by other business processes and governance (such as procurement or human resource processes and policy) to provide a wide, comprehensive methodology.

Deciding which standard, methodology or framework to use is often not a simple process and this decision can be influenced by any number of factors, including:

- the project management maturity of the organisation
- the presence of any partly implemented project management methodologies already in place within the organisation
- methodologies being adopted in the organisation's supply chains
- methodologies predominately used by customers or clients
- the maturity of business processes that support project management, such as Business Case development and approval, business planning and investment prioritisation, and benefits management
- the degree of customisation and internalisation versus the acceptance of a common industry-led approach to project management
- project management skills available in the marketplace
- the agility of the organisation
- the stability of requirements
- the frequency of delivery the customer would like to experience.

Referring back to Figure 2.5, remember there is no longer one size that fits all. You need to be able to select the most appropriate approach according to the customer's needs, amount of change, complexity and other factors. Contemporary organisations that apply project management will have multiple approaches available.

KPMG's 2017 project management survey indicates that the use of Agile has increased by 43% since the last survey was carried out in 2013. KPMG comments, "it is hardly surprising that agile methods are becoming more and more popular as organisations seek to respond faster and more effectively to an increasing pace of change, especially in the way they manage projects that produce improved ways of working or new products" (KPMG 2017).

Chapter 3 "Agile (Scrum) project management" takes an in-depth look at the Scrum (Agile) approach, and subsequent chapters look at each of the knowledge areas in more detail, since they:

- form large sections of PMBOK and other competing bodies of knowledge (PRINCE2, Praxis, APM and ISO 21500:2021)
- underpin the many competency-based certifications that exist globally (such as IPMA, AIPM, APM and many others)
- form the knowledge component of formal qualifications (such as the Australian VET sector Certificate IV, Diploma and Advanced Diploma in Project Management).

Review questions

1. Why is a traditional project management approach less effective when project scope and technology are not well known?
2. What are the four types of approaches to project management? Explain briefly and draft a diagram.
3. What are the advantages of Agile? What are the disadvantages of Agile?
4. How does Praxis integrate Agile into its project management approach?
5. Why does the project leader need to think beyond the project, as captured in a number of the approaches described in the chapter?
6. Why does ISO 21500:2021 appeal to organisations that have limited project management experience?
7. What are the 10 knowledge areas within the PMI Body of Knowledge?
8. What do all the methodologies have in common in relation to knowledge?
9. What factors influence the selection of one approach over another approach?
10. What type of project(s) is the Lean Six Sigma approach best suited for?
11. How does PMBOK sixth edition differ from PMBOK seventh edition?

Exercises

1. Break into small groups and discuss the differences between PMBOK sixth and PMBOK seventh editions. Carry out research (on the internet) to assist your understanding.

2. For a project you are currently working on, use:

   ■ Table 2.1 Uncertainty informs approach

   ■ Table 2.3 Approach selection factors

   ■ Figure 2.5 Project management approach selection

   to assess which approach would be most suited to the management of that project. Does it differ from the approach currently being used? If so, can you see the benefits of using the approach the book directs you towards?

References

Agile Manifesto 2021a, "Manifesto for Agile software development", http://agilemanifesto.org, accessed February 2021.

Agile Manifesto 2021b, "Principles behind the Agile Manifesto", http://agilemanifesto.org/principles.html, accessed February 2021.

APMG International 2022, "Praxis framework", https://apmg-international.com/product/praxis-framework, accessed December 2021.

Association for Project Management (APM) 2019, *APM Body of Knowledge* (APM BOK), 7th edition, APM, 2019.

Association for Project Management (APM) 2021, "IPMA qualifications", https://www.apm.org.uk/qualifications-and-training/ipma/, accessed March 2022.

Australian Institute of Project Management (AIPM) 2019, "AIPM choose Praxis Framework™ as their body of knowledge partner for members", https://www.aipm.com.au/articles/national/aipm-praxis-framework, accessed December 2021.

Cynefin Co. 2022, "The Cynefin framework", https://thecynefin.co/about-us/about-cynefin-framework/, accessed December 2021.

Duncan W 1996, "A guide to the project management body of knowledge", http://nutek-us.com/PMBOK_1996.pdf, accessed May 2022.

Gov.UK 2021, "Best practice management portfolio", https://www.gov.uk/government/publications/best-management-practice-portfolio/about-the-office-of-government-commerce#links

Howey J & Middleton D 2015, "Lean Six Sigma application to water utilities: getting value for money out of water quality monitoring", https://www.academia.edu/33737919/LEAN_SIX_SIGMA_APPLICATION_TO_WATER_UTILITIES_GETTING_VALUE_FOR_MONEY_OUT_OF_WATER_QUALITY_MONITORING, accessed May 2022.

International Project Management Association (IPMA), "About us", IPMA, www.ipma.world/about-us/, accessed December 2021.

ISO 2021, "Improving project management: Two new standards join the ISO series", https://www.iso.org/news/ref2645.html, accessed December 2021.

ISO 21502:2020 "Project, programme and portfolio management — Guidance on project management", https://www.iso.org/standard/74947.html, accessed December 2021.

KPMG 2017, "Driving business performance: Project management survey 2017", https://assets.kpmg.com/content/dam/kpmg/nz/pdf/July/projectmanagementsurvey-kpmg-nz.pdf, accessed December 2021.

NUPP 2019, "NUPP – Nearly universal principles of projects", https://nupp.guide, accessed February 2022.

P3.express n.d., "The minimalist project management system", https://p3.express/manual/v2/, accessed December 2021.

Praxis n.d., "Praxis", https://www.praxisframework.org, accessed May 2022.Praxis Framework Ltd (PFL) 2015, "Praxis introduction", PFL, https://www.praxisframework.org/en/resource-pages/praxis-introduction, accessed February 2018.

Praxis 2019, "Process infographic", https://www.praxisframework.org/en/resource-pages/praxis-process-infographic, accessed December 2021.

Project Management Institute (PMI) 2013, *A Guide to the Project Management Body of Knowledge,* 5th edn, PMI.

Project Management Institute (PMI) 2017a, *A Guide to the Project Management Body of Knowledge,* 6th edition, PMI.

Project Management Institute (PMI) 2017b, *Agile Practice Guide,* PMI.

Project Management Institute (PMI) 2018, Standards & Publications, PMI, https://www.pmi.org/pmbok-guide-standards, accessed May 2022.

Project Management Institute (PMI) 2021a, *A Guide to the Project Management Body of Knowledge (PMBOK® Guide),* 7th edition, Newton Square, PA.

Project Management Institute (PMI) 2021b, *The Standard for Project Management (ANSI/PMI 99-001-2021),* 7th edition, Newton Square, PA.

SCRUMStudy 2012, "Scrum study sheet", https://www.scrumstudy.com/pdf/Scrumstudy%20Process%20Chart-2-%2018-10-2012.pdf, accessed December 2021.

Schwaber K & Sutherland J 2017, *The Scrum Guide™,* https://www.scrumguides.org/docs/scrumguide/v1/scrum-guide-us.pdf, accessed February 2018.

Schwaber K & Sutherland J 2020, *The Scrum Guide™,* https://scrumguides.org/docs/scrumguide/v2020/2020-Scrum-Guide-US.pdf#zoom=100 , accessed May 2022.

Sutherland J 1993, *The Scrum: The Art of Doing Twice the Work in Half the Time,* Random House Business Books

Takeuchi H & Nonaka I 1986, "The new new product development game", *Harvard Business Review,* January–February.

CHAPTER 3
The Scrum (Agile) approach

Learning elements

3A Understand the history of Scrum and Agile and the key thinking behind the Agile/Scrum approach.

3B Gain an understanding of the Agile/Scrum adaptive project management approach.

3C Understand the key roles within the Scrum approach.

3D Understand the key events (ceremonies) of the Scrum approach.

3E Understand the key artefacts of the Scrum approach.

3F Gain an overview of how contracts and procurement may need to be revised when taking the Agile/Scrum approach.

3G Appreciate how Agile/Scrum are packaged within PRINCE2 and PMBOK.

3H Learn how Scrum can be scaled.

3I Relate Scrum practices to the developing DevOps approach.

In this chapter

3.1 Introduction

3.2 Overview of Scrum

3.3 Scrum roles

3.4 Scrum events

3.5 Scrum artefacts

3.6 Scrum and procurement

3.7 Agile under PRINCE2 and PMBOK

3.8 Large-Scale Scrum (LeSS)

3.9 DevOps

Summary

3.1 | Introduction

The term **Scrum** was introduced in a Harvard Business Review paper titled, "The new new product development game" (Takeuchi & Nonaka 1986). In this paper, the authors observed that projects that use small, cross-functional teams historically tend to produce the best results. They relate such high-performance teamwork to rugby scrum (Figure 3.1) formations:

Figure 3.1 A rugby scrum

Shutterstock/Patrimonio Designs Ltd

Companies are increasingly realizing that the old, sequential approach to developing new products simply won't get the job done. Instead, companies in Japan and the United States are using a holistic method— as in rugby, the ball gets passed within the team as it moves as a unit up the field.

This holistic approach has six characteristics: built-in instability, self-organizing project teams, overlapping development phases, "multi-learning," subtle control, and organizational transfer of learning. The six pieces fit together like a jigsaw puzzle, forming a fast, flexible process for new product development (Takeuchi & Nonaka 1986).

Scrum was one of the earliest implementations of the new product development game that emerged out of this work. Jeff Sutherland set about formalising and realising this new way of working by applying it to software product development. Using the study by Takeuchi and Nonaka as a platform, Sutherland published *Scrum: The Art of Doing Twice the Work in Half the Time* (1993). Ken Schwaber—software developer, product manager and industry consultant—is also associated with the development of Scrum. He presented Scrum as a formal development process at an Object-Oriented Programming, Systems, Languages and Applications (OOPSLA) conference in 1995.

In 2001, the Agile Manifesto (a formal declaration of 4 key values and 12 principles towards an iterative and people-centric approach to software development) was born. This started the ever-expanding world of Scrum and Agile and since then, many variations have emerged, including:

- *Kanban:* based on the Toyota Production System (commonly known as *Lean Thinking*), which includes at its core the Kanban Board.
- *AgilePM:* formerly called *Dynamic System Development Model* (DSDM), this is a formalisation of the Rapid Application Development (RAD) methodology, one of the heavier implementations of Agile.
- ***Large-Scale Scrum*** or ***LeSS***: a scalable version of Scrum where multiple teams contribute to a product's development simultaneously.
- *SAFe:* Scaled Agile Framework, a more comprehensive implementation of scaling Agile.
- *SCRUMstudy:* an Agile project management approach embracing Scrum at its core.

The Agile Alliance, formed in 2002 by Ken Schwaber and Jeff Sutherland, was the first formal body to provide a certification: the Certified Scrum Master. In 2010, Schwaber and Sutherland wrote the first version of *The Scrum Guide* to help people worldwide understand Scrum (Schwaber & Sutherland 2020). The guide is a compact guide to the (now globally accepted) Scrum approach.

In recent times, there have been many so-called *flavours* of Scrum/Agile (refer to Chapter 2 "Popular frameworks and methodologies", Figure 2.11). Among these approaches have been supplements to two globally accepted frameworks on predictive project management: PRINCE2 (Bennet 2017) and the Project Management Institute's (PMI's) *Project Management Body of Knowledge* (PMI 2017a).

This text leverages the freely available Scrum Body of Knowledge (SBOK), available from the SCRUMstudy (www.Scrumstudy.com), as SCRUMstudy embraces the concept of Agile project management; at its core is the definitive approach of *The Scrum Guide*.

3.1.1 **So what is Scrum?**

According to Schwaber and Sutherland (2017), Scrum is:

A framework within which people can address complex adaptive problems, while productively and creatively delivering products of the highest possible value.

[It] is:

- *Lightweight*
- *Simple to understand*
- *Difficult to master.*

Scrum is seen as a subset of Agile project management. In fact, the author (Pearson) observes that since 2001, Scrum appears central to all flavours (based in software development as captured in scrumguides.org), with each flavour adding extras to handle aspects of, for example, project management or scalability.

The Agile Manifesto (http://agilemanifesto.org) consists of the manifesto and a set of accompanying principles. The manifesto is burned into the memory of just about every Agile practitioner and as such is repeated here verbatim.

Manifesto for Agile Software Development
We are uncovering better ways of developing
software by doing it and helping others do it.
Through this work we have come to value:

Individuals and interactions over processes and tools
Working software over comprehensive documentation
Customer collaboration over contract negotiation
Responding to change over following a plan

That is, while there is value in the items on
the right, we value the items on the left more.

Kent Beck	James Grenning	Robert C. Martin
Mike Beedle	Jim Highsmith	Steve Mellor
Arie van Bennekum	Andrew Hunt	Ken Schwaber
Alistair Cockburn	Ron Jeffries	Jeff Sutherland
Ward Cunningham	Jon Kern	Dave Thomas
Martin Fowler	Brian Marick	

Source: https://agilemanifesto.org, accessed December 2011

1. We can replace the phrase *software development* with *product*, *service* or *result*; Agile is applicable to any industry, globally.

2. Note the use of the word *value*. The implication is that we value the left more than the right; it does not say we are not doing the right.

3. You will find that a lot of work when implementing Agile is behaviour based, therefore the manifesto and corresponding principles will become key to accomplishing this goal of changing behaviours.

The reader is encouraged to review the narrative of the history behind the formation of the Agile Manifesto on its website.

The items in the manifesto are seen as critical to the successful implementation of Agile, Scrum and all variants. They underpin the essence of all Agile projects. The manifesto is further supported by an expanded set of principles, as outlined in "In Theory: Principles behind the Agile Manifesto".

They are captured here as they are symbolic and a mainstay behind the manifesto, and to changing the behaviours of all those in and around the Agile project. We follow these principles.

Our highest priority is to satisfy the customer through early and continuous delivery of valuable software.

Welcome changing requirements, even late in development. Agile processes harness change for the customer's competitive advantage.

Deliver working software frequently, from a couple of weeks to a couple of months, with a preference to the shorter timescale.

Business people and developers must work together daily throughout the project.

Build projects around motivated individuals. Give them the environment and support they need and trust them to get the job done.

The most efficient and effective method of conveying information to and within a Scrum team is face-to-face conversation.

Working software is the primary measure of progress.

Agile processes promote sustainable development. The sponsors, developers, and users should be able to maintain a constant pace indefinitely.

Continuous attention to technical excellence and good design enhances agility.

Simplicity–the art of maximizing the amount of work not done–is essential.

The best architectures, requirements, and designs emerge from self-organizing teams.

At regular intervals, the team reflects on how to become more effective, then tunes and adjusts its behaviour accordingly.

Kent Beck	James Grenning	Robert C. Martin
Mike Beedle	Jim Highsmith	Steve Mellor
Arie van Bennekum	Andrew Hunt	Ken Schwaber
Alistair Cockburn	Ron Jeffries	Jeff Sutherland
Ward Cunningham	Jon Kern	Dave Thomas
Martin Fowler	Brian Marick	

© 2001, the above authors

This declaration may be freely copied in any form, but only in its entirety through this notice

Source: https://agilemanifesto.org, accessed December 2011

The original *Scrum Guide* was updated in 2013–16; included were values in support of the successful application of Scrum, with the following comment (Schwaber & Sutherland 2017):

> *When the values of commitment, courage, focus, openness, and respect are embodied and lived by the Scrum Team, the Scrum pillars of transparency, inspection, and adaptation come to life and build trust for everyone. The Scrum Team members learn and explore those values as they work with the Scrum roles, events, and artifacts.*
> *Successful use of Scrum depends on people becoming more proficient in living these five values.*

Agile and Scrum have developed over time. They have largely been convergent (while remaining different), stemming from the Agile Manifesto and its principles. Agile and Scrum have grown from deep, strong, empirically-based roots.

Agile/Scrum reaches out across many industries. Some reasons behind its success will be revealed as we look at how Scrum works (based on the SCRUMstudy flavour).

Note: The benefits of adopting Agile are outlined in Chapter 2 "Popular frameworks and methodologies", section 2.5.

When a project is managed under the Agile/Scrum approach, the dynamics of the triple constraints change. Instead of dealing with relatively fixed features (scope) in the predictive world where scope is defined and agreed up-front, in Scrum requirements (user stories) change on a daily basis as the **product owner** maintains the list of user stories on the prioritised product backlog. In Scrum, time and cost are viewed as more fixed than features (scope), as a sprint will have a known cost in terms of staffing, which will deliver the agreed content within a set time period (e.g. a two-week sprint) (timebox). This turning of the triple constraints is illustrated in Figure 3.2(a).

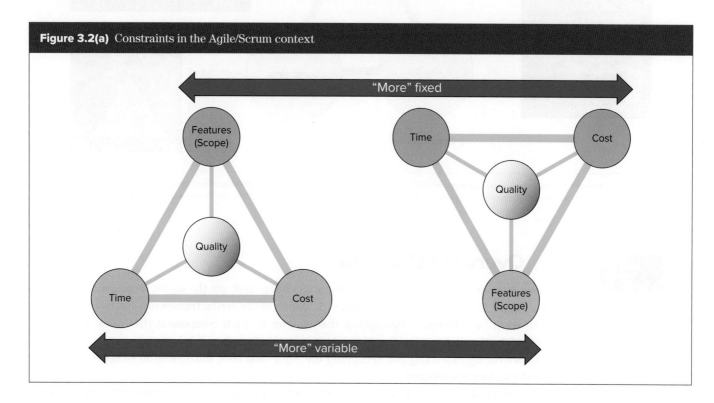

Figure 3.2(a) Constraints in the Agile/Scrum context

Jim Highsmith went on to form what is now known as the *Agile triangle:*

- Value is for the customer a released product or deliverable.
- Quality is continuous delivery of high-quality and adaptive products or services.
- Constraints are the traditional scope, schedule (time) and cost.

This is illustrated in Figure 3.2(b). *Note:* Value constitutes extrinsic quality (i.e. quality to the customer), whereas quality constitutes intrinsic quality to the project team—does it comply with our internal definition of quality (i.e. the *definition of done* or *DoD*)?

Scrum teams consider both, and frequently use the terms:

- *Done* to indicate it meets the acceptance criteria at the user story level by means of testing the story against its acceptance criteria (note that the acceptance criteria are written by the product owner at the same time as writing the user story).
- *Done-Done* to indicate it meets all the criteria of the DoD. The DoD will be established at the kick-off meeting along with the product vision, product roadmap and team charter, as these are all artefacts that cross the Agile project from start to finish.

Figure 3.2(b) Constraints according to Jim Highsmith

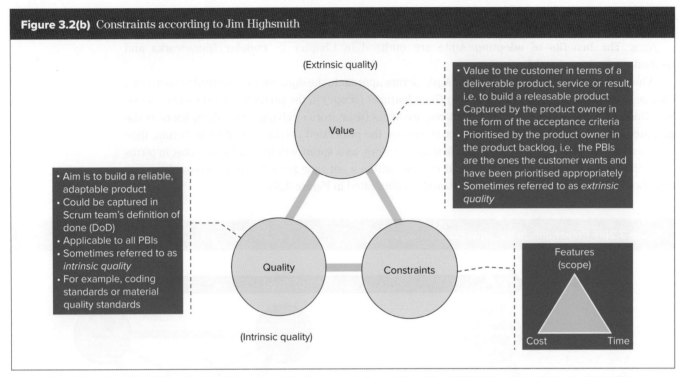

Source: Adapted from Highsmith J 2009, *Agile Project Management: Creating Innovative Product*, 2nd edition, 2009 Addison-Wesley Professional; https://blog.
cutter.com/2009/08/10/beyond-scope-schedule-and-cost-measuring-agile-performance/, accessed December 2021; and https://www.projectmanagement.com/blog/
blogPostingView.cfm?

3.2 │ Overview of Scrum

The Scrum framework is often said to be simple to understand, yet the secret to its use lies in all its
nuances. Figure 3.3 represents an often-seen articulation of the Scrum framework and its components.
This figure will be referred to throughout this chapter as each component (the roles, events and
artefacts) of the Scrum framework are introduced and discussed.

Let's start off by extending and recapping the Agile overview introduced in Chapter 2 "Popular
frameworks and methodologies".

The Scrum cycle begins with a kick-off (product visioning meeting), during which the product
vision statement is crafted. At this meeting the team charter (which describes the behaviours
and principles the team wishes to adhere to) and the DoD (as described in Figure 3.2(b)) are also
established. The product owner then develops a prioritised product backlog that contains a prioritised
list of business (customer) requirements written in the form of user stories (As a <persona> I want to
<do something> so that <I gain a benefit>).

Each **sprint** (a timebox usually between one and eight weeks) begins with a **sprint planning
meeting** during which high-priority user stories are considered for inclusion in the sprint. User stories
are accepted into a sprint from the **sprint backlog** and a sprint goal is established to focus the **Scrum
team**. A sprint generally lasts between one and eight weeks and involves the Scrum team working
to create potentially shippable deliverables or product *increments*. During the sprint, short, highly
focused **daily Scrum meetings** are conducted where team members discuss daily progress and any
impediments to the work being achieved. At the end of the sprint, a **sprint review** meeting is held
during which the product owner and relevant business stakeholders are provided with a demonstration
of the deliverables (user stories). The product owner accepts the deliverables only if they meet the
predefined acceptance criteria (defined at the same time as the user story). The cycle ends with a
sprint retrospective meeting (lessons learned) where the team and product owner discuss ways to
improve processes and product as they move forward into the next sprint. This process is overseen

Figure 3.3 The Scrum framework

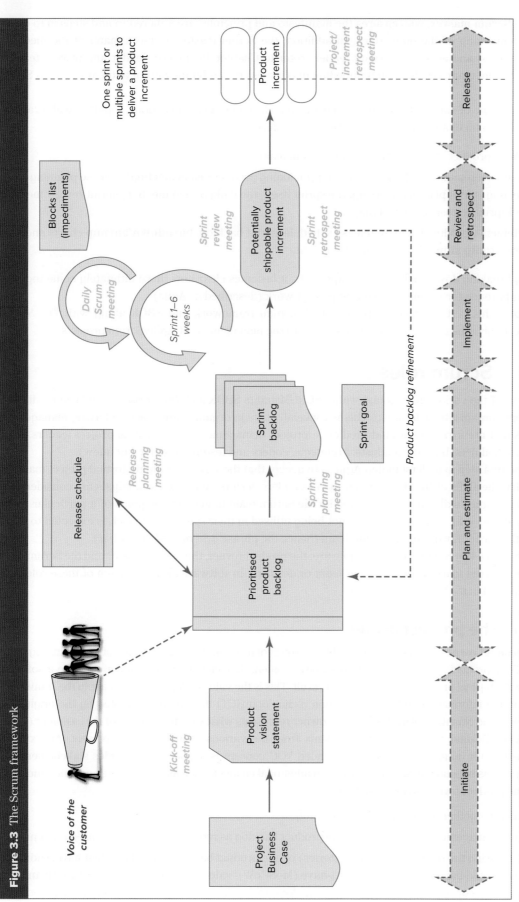

Source: Adapted from SCRUMStudy 2012, "Scrum flow", https://www.Scrumstudy.com/pdf/Scrumstudy%20Process%20Chart-2-%2018-10-2012.pdf, accessed December 2021

by the **Scrum master**, who ensures the manifesto and principles are adhered to and steps in to coach and mentor any of the other roles. In addition, the Scrum master oversees many of the meetings (ceremonies) and acts as a servant leader (refer to Chapter 19 "Project leader and project teams") to the Scrum team, resolving any impediments (issues) raised by the Scrum team at the daily Scrum meeting.

An outline of each of these components is introduced in the next sections, together with practical examples to facilitate understanding. These sections cover the:

■ roles—product owner, Scrum master, Scrum team

■ events (ceremonies)—kick-off meeting (including product vision meeting), release planning meeting, sprint planning meeting, the sprint itself, the daily Scrum meeting, sprint review meeting and sprint retrospective meeting

■ artefacts—product backlog, release schedule, sprint backlog, **burndown/burnup** charts and **potentially shippable product** increment.

By breaking down each of the components, it becomes clear how these ultimately come together as an approach for the management of project work (described as Agile).

Note: This text leverages both the SCRUMstudy framework and SBOK along with *The Scrum Guide*, to give the reader a rounded approach to the management of Agile/Scrum projects.

3.3 | Scrum roles

Aspects of the various roles found within SCRUMstudy's SBOK and *The Scrum Guide* can be difficult for some organisations to grasp. This is especially true in organisations used to having management teams that are arranged around predictive project management roles such as project leaders, team leads, schedulers, business analysts, architects, coders and testers (to name but a few).

The first step in understanding Agile is to accept that there is generally no formal project manager and that the skills of traditional roles such as coders, testers and business analysts are considered as being specialist skills that are required by the Scrum team to achieve the goals of a particular sprint being attended to. A specialist, when not being utilised in their specialist skillset, is expected to carry out other general work in the Scrum team (hence the phrase *generalised specialist*).

The three key roles involved in Agile are: the product owner, the Scrum master and the Scrum team (often referred to as the *development team* or *dev team* in software projects); each of these roles will be explored in the following sections.

3.3.1 The product owner

The **product owner** is a single accountable person (not a committee) and is responsible for driving value out of the product, service or result under development. Remember that a product could be a software product, physical product, service or just a result. This is the value of Agile—we can apply the framework beyond the information and communication technology (ICT) domain, as promoted by the originators Takeuchi and Nonaka (1986). The product owner represents what we call the *voice of the customer* (VOC), receiving, fielding and probing requirements from the various channels they represent. An example is illustrated in Figure 3.4, where an extended VOC concept is applied that includes stakeholders and requirements beyond the customer, including additional channels such as competitors and innovations.

The product owner is responsible for:

1. pulling together the initial product backlog

2. daily management (refinement) of the product backlog as requirements change based on Figure 3.4

3. prioritising the requirements (user stories) on the product backlog, based on must-have, should-have, could-have and want-but-won't-have (MoSCoW), value, dependency, time criticality and risk (reduction or opportunity enhancement), along with other organisational factors as required.

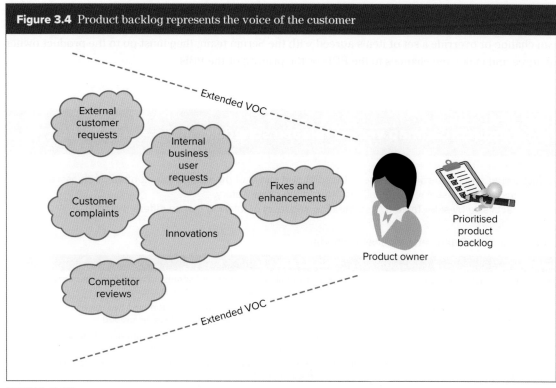

Figure 3.4 Product backlog represents the voice of the customer

© 2022 Dr Neil Pearson

a. When the product backlog has been prioritised using the MoSCoW (or similar) technique, it is referred to as the *prioritised product backlog*.

b. When the product backlog has been prioritised and adjusted to consider what risk the *epic* or user story is addressing, it is referred to as the *risk-adjusted prioritised product backlog*.

4. ensuring a product vision and product roadmap exists

5. ensuring a release schedule is maintained with more detail in releases that are closer (rolling-wave planning principles) (refer to: "In Theory: Product roadmap versus release schedule")

6. ensuring wider organisational goals and missions are also considered in the ordering of product backlog items (or PBIs)

7. optimising the value of the work to be performed by the Scrum team

8. ensuring the product backlog is visible to the business/customer and, in doing so, becoming a collection/negotiation point for requests from the business/customer and ensuring the business/customer is aware of the ordering (prioritisation) of requests as only high-priority PBIs will be fed into the **sprint planning meeting**

9. ensuring the Scrum team understands the items on the product backlog and acting as a conduit for questions about the items on the product backlog during a sprint.

The product owner in today's busy business environments often has a delegate. For example, a senior manager who is a product owner for a global service desk business system may devolve responsibility for fielding requests, writing the PBIs (i.e. user stories), and prioritisation to a business analyst. The business analyst is the responsible person for doing the work; at all times, the product owner remains accountable for these role-specific duties. The business analyst in this role is often referred to as the *proxy product owner*.

If the product owner is unable to delegate any of their duties, they must be willing and able to make regular representations and allocate dedicated time to the management of the product backlog.

The business must respect the role of the product owner and empower the person in this role to make all required decisions (often on a quick turn-around basis). For example, no one in the business can change or override a set of items agreed with the Scrum team; they must go to the product owner to agree and make any changes to the PBIs or the priority of the PBIs.

IN THEORY   Product roadmap versus release schedule

Produced by the product owner and often confused, these two different views of the same product often need assistance from the Scrum master to ensure both visual representations provide the correct story.

We can put the two artefacts side by side (Table 3.1) so the type and level of thinking can be differentiated.

Table 3.1 Product or service roadmap versus release schedule

Product or service roadmap	Release schedule
■ Is a high-level vision for the product or service	■ Ties detail (user stories and sprints) to high-level elements of the features and functions of the roadmap
■ Is long term for the full lifecycle of the product or service (e.g. 12–18 months)	■ Is accurate for the short term (e.g. the next two releases of three sprints each); longer term, less developed
■ Focuses on delivering a strategy	■ Focuses on committing work based on priority (of the user story in the product backlog) into the sprint
■ Is used to communicate the big picture, typically with managers and executives (and customers)	■ Is used to communicate what work is being scheduled to be carried out in the short term

© 2022 Dr Neil Pearson

An example of a product roadmap could resemble Figure 3.5.

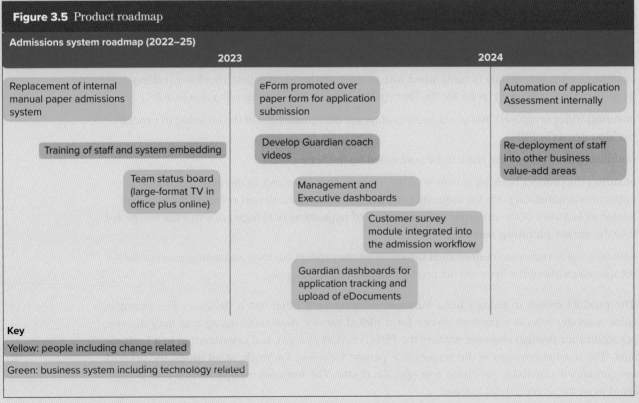

Figure 3.5 Product roadmap

Admissions system roadmap (2022–25)

2023   2024

Replacement of internal manual paper admissions system

Training of staff and system embedding

Team status board (large-format TV in office plus online)

eForm promoted over paper form for application submission

Develop Guardian coach videos

Management and Executive dashboards

Customer survey module integrated into the admission workflow

Guardian dashboards for application tracking and upload of eDocuments

Automation of application Assessment internally

Re-deployment of staff into other business value-add areas

Key

Yellow: people including change related

Green: business system including technology related

© 2022 Dr Neil Pearson

The detail on what/when is planned to be undertaken in terms of sprints and increments (multiple sprints that make up a feature to be delivered) is captured in the release schedule (Figure 3.6).

Figure 3.6 Example: Release schedule

Release 1 Core functionality	Release 2 Customer focus	Release 3 Team/Supervisor focus	Release 4 Manager/Director focus
Sprint 1	**Sprint 1**	**Sprint 1**	**Sprint 1**
As a Governance and Policy Director I want to ensure all users of the system have individual secure logins so I comply with medical standards and policy.	As a Guardian I want to view the status of my application on a mobile device so I can be assured progress is being made without having to continually call for updates.	As a Admission Clerk Supervisor I want to be alerted when there is an escalation of the application so I can ensure that complaints/non-compliances are brought to the Supervisor's attention in the shortest possible time.	As a Admissions Director I want to automate the EM* dashboard report so that I can use my time to carry out more urgent operational work.
As a Guardian I want to be able to lodge my application via a requestable form so I can make an application without having to use technology.	As a Guardian I want to upload medical records to the application so I don't have to send confidential items by expensive recorded/tracked mail.	As a Admission Clerk Supervisor I want to be able to escalate a case to the supervisor so I can, in a timely manner, gain feedback on what should be done in non-routine circumstances.	As a Governance and Policy Director I want to be able to audit who entered what information at what time so I comply with any medical/legislative audits.
As a Guardian I want to be able to lodge applications via my mobile device so I can make an application at any time.			
Sprint 2	**Sprint 2**	**Sprint 2**	**Sprint 2**
As a Admission Clerk Supervisor I want to manually scan and attach medical records to an application so I can ensure the medical staff have all information available to make decisions on acceptance of the patient on medical grounds.	As a Guardian I want to cancel an application so I can inform Golden Years that the application is no longer required.		
Sprint 3	**Sprint 3**	**Sprint 3**	**Sprint 3**

© 2022 Dr Neil Pearson

Note: There are many tools available to assist the product owner in building and managing the information on the product roadmap and the release schedule. One such product, by Atlassian, is Jira Align. For information and sample screen dumps of what this product can offer, refer to https://www.atlassian.com/software/jira/align.

3.3.2 The Scrum master

The **Scrum master** is an independent overseer of the Agile/Scrum framework and its implementation (workflow driven), including the manifesto and principles (behaviour driven). This role is probably the most difficult in practice. It is not a project leader role or a team leader role (as the Scrum team is self-maintaining) and they also decide and agree on what tasks need to be done to accomplish a user story (i.e. they are not given or directed to do tasks by a project leader or team leader). The Scrum master's focus is to build confidence in the use of Agile/Scrum practices, to coach and mentor the other roles and to ensure that, whichever flavour of Agile/Scrum has been selected, it is applied in a fair and consistent manner.

Activities in the Scrum master's role encompass:

- promoting all aspects of the Agile/Scrum approach selected (theory, practices, processes, rules, values and principles)
- actively applying the servant-leadership style of management

- understanding Agile deeply and having the ability to adjust the behaviours of the business employees, customer, the product owner and the Scrum team accordingly
- assisting in the planning of sprints at the sprint planning meeting
- enabling changes to the environment to promote Agile practices (e.g. the co-location of Scrum team members and protecting the Scrum team from unnecessary interruptions such as walk-ups by employees in the business)
- working with other Scrum masters in a scaled Scrum implementation to ensure consistency of practices and achievement of goals.

The Scrum master assists the product owner by:

- ensuring the wider team (Scrum master, product owner and Scrum team) understand the product vision and product roadmap
- advising about the techniques (and tools) needed for the management of the product backlog to ensure a consistent approach is applied and practised
- helping the product owner by ensuring the items on the product backlog are clear and devolved to a consistent level of detail, especially for potential PBIs that are closer on the release schedule and could be taken into the sprint planning meeting
- assisting the product owner in continually reviewing and refining the product backlog; this occurs while the Scrum team works from the sprint backlog so that the product backlog is ready for consideration at the next sprint planning meeting. There could also be last-minute changes to the product backlog as a result of the sprint review meeting (at the end of the sprint) which need to be incorporated
- helping the product owner in the ordering (prioritisation) techniques of the items in the product backlog whether MoSCoW or another prioritisation technique is used (refer to "In Theory: The MoSCoW prioritisation technique"). With the ongoing ordering and reordering of items (and potential constant changes to ordering), the Scrum master is essentially promoting agility—items are not fixed until they are agreed to be the content for a sprint at the sprint planning meeting. Prioritisation is an important concept as it assists the business in determining the high-value items that should be attended to first. For example, if a product owner sees a lot of value (benefits) in implementing workflows in a human resource management system, then these features would be given a higher priority in the product backlog
- assisting the product owner to understand the Scrum events (or at the request of the product owner to even facilitate some Scrum events).

The Scrum master assists the Scrum team by:

- coaching them in self-organisation, conflict negotiation and communication, among other servant-leadership skills
- helping them in the creation of high-value products from the sprint
- removing impediments (such as a lack of a particular skill, a lack of access to a tool) by taking these away from the Scrum team and working on them, leaving the Scrum team to focus on the user stories and tasks they have committed to in the sprint backlog to achieve the sprint goal
- creating a safe environment for those who have committed to the work (e.g. stopping interruptions to the Scrum team by employees in the business or stopping the product owner potentially changing the content of a sprint that is in progress)
- coaching them in respect to the Scrum/Agile approach, practices and principles.

To do this, the Scrum master must be respected for their approach and should possess excellent people, negotiation and communication skills. They are not a project leader, nor are they a team leader as the Scrum team is self-organising—they allocate and report on the work at the daily Scrum meeting (often referred to as the *daily stand-up*).

As the Scrum master is an overseer of the practices of Agile/Scrum, it is not uncommon for an experienced Scrum master to oversee multiple (two to three) Scrum projects simultaneously.

Before moving on to the role of the Scrum team, review "In Theory: Are you committed?" This applies to all roles: the product owner, Scrum team and Scrum master. Are you committed to your Agile/Scrum project, or only interested—in which case is it the right project for you to be on?

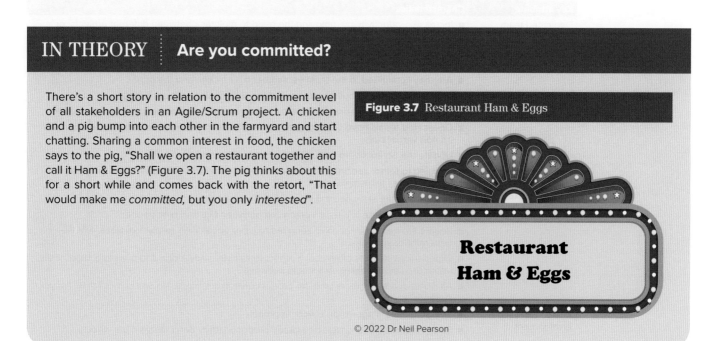

IN THEORY : **Are you committed?**

There's a short story in relation to the commitment level of all stakeholders in an Agile/Scrum project. A chicken and a pig bump into each other in the farmyard and start chatting. Sharing a common interest in food, the chicken says to the pig, "Shall we open a restaurant together and call it Ham & Eggs?" (Figure 3.7). The pig thinks about this for a short while and comes back with the retort, "That would make me *committed,* but you only *interested*".

Figure 3.7 Restaurant Ham & Eggs

Restaurant Ham & Eggs

© 2022 Dr Neil Pearson

3.3.3 **The Scrum team**

The Scrum team is made up of people with the skills required to achieve the contents of the sprint backlog and achieve the sprint goal. Typically, a product backlog, and therefore a sprint backlog, contains similar types of work; therefore, the make-up of the Scrum team will remain relatively static in terms of skillsets.

Characteristics of the Scrum team are:

- The team is self-organising—not even the Scrum master will tell the Scrum team what tasks must be done to turn a sprint backlog item (user story) into a done-done state. The Scrum master will coach and advise only if asked.

- The team has the correct skills to achieve the contents of the sprint backlog; as introduced earlier in this chapter, Scrum team members are seen as generalised specialists.

- There are no sub-teams and no hierarchy. The Scrum team works as one team to achieve the sprint goal jointly and supports each other to achieve this.

The Scrum team is a truly empowered team whose focus is delivering the agreed sprint goal and the PBIs that were agreed to be placed in the sprint backlog. This arrangement can be challenging for traditional environments where developers are used to operating under a team lead or project leader and operating separately from other functional teams, such as testers and business analysts.

The team's size should therefore be such that this arrangement can be achieved. Usually, a team size of 5–9 members can produce excellent results. Any smaller and the achievements may be limited; any larger and self-organisation and communication may become problematic.

Typically, the team is co-located (in the same office space) to facilitate ease of communication, cohesiveness and rapport. If co-location is not possible and the team is virtual, careful consideration will need to be given to enabling technology that can provide some of the benefits of co-location (e.g. shared online spaces, videoconferencing, intelligent whiteboards). Refer to Table 3.2 for a summary of Scrum team characteristics.

Table 3.2 Scrum team characteristics

Key attribute	Characteristics
Dedicated team members	▪ Increase productivity by removing the need to multitask between different projects, or projects and operational work. ▪ Focus on the product vision and, more specifically, the sprint goal: a single agreed goal statement for the sprint. ▪ Are they committed to the team (remember the chicken and the pig)? ▪ Trust each other and build a strong working relationship with each other.
Co-location	▪ Physical co-location is preferred—extra consideration needs to be given to virtual teams. ▪ Co-located teams have superior team dynamics. Teams communicate better and can draw on non-verbal cues. ▪ Update the Scrum board, including Kanban and burndown charts.
Teams combining specialist and generalist expertise	▪ Bringing together specialist expertise and the flexibility of generalists calls for greater flexibility from team members. ▪ Teams have the skills needed to achieve the sprint goal. ▪ The ideal team size is a team comprising between five and nine people. ▪ People are trained in the skills required to carry out all their respective tasks, whether generalist or specialist. ▪ Experienced skillsets often coach others to transfer knowledge and therefore share tasks rather than being reliant on a single individual. ▪ All Scrum team members (and the product owner) are equal. No one can call that "I'm your superior" card!
Known work environment	▪ The Scrum team agrees on a work approach. ▪ Scrum teams build on artefacts already produced (they don't reinvent the wheel). ▪ Teams know they depend on each other to deliver the outcomes of the sprint—no single person can achieve these goals. ▪ Teams share the work and take credit as a team. ▪ No sub-teams within the team, the team operate as one team.

© 2022 Dr Neil Pearson

3.3.3.1 Who makes up the Scrum team?

This is often a difficult concept to grasp in a Scrum environment. The Scrum team will comprise all the resources required to be able to fulfil the DoD for the sprint. Therefore, the skills required could vary from sprint to sprint. For example, one sprint may require a business analyst capability to refine story cards into more granular requirements suitable for later coding and testing, while another sprint may require more technical capability to establish environments and databases. Some sprints may require elements of all capabilities to deliver the sprint goal for that sprint.

However, a Scrum team member typically has multiple skills: they will have a key specialist skill but also be capable of other, more generalists duties. For example, a business analyst (specialist skill) might also have user interface design skills and be capable of carrying out acceptance testing (these are seen as generalist skills). This concept is key to ensuring the Scrum team is not overloaded with skillsets that are only used for a small amount of time, and cannot be fully utilised in the sprint.

There are also other reasons for keeping the Scrum team consistent in a sprint and across multiple sprints.

▪ It enables the team to build as a team and form as a team. The initial team would progress through the forming–storming–norming–performing cycle of Tuckman (1965) (refer to Chapter 19 "Project leaders and project teams"). However, if we use the same team members of high emotional intelligence in subsequent sprints then the team will have been through the forming, storming and norming stages and should be able to start performing as a team from Sprint 1. Obviously, if the team rebuilds each time at the start of every sprint, we are not being very lean and will undoubtably not be able to complete as much work within a sprint.

■ With the same team members for the same sprint duration, we know the costs. It is also possible to work out what work is produced from the Scrum team (referred to as *velocity*); therefore, we will have a ratio of cost to work output that stays the same across multiple sprints—we know what amount of work can be achieved for what cost.

■ Team dynamics, communication preferences, relationships, skillsets and a host of other factors are established during the first few sprints. These do not need challenging or re-establishing at the start of every sprint when the same Scrum team is rolled forward to the next sprint.

SNAPSHOT *from* PRACTICE | Trello and Scrum

In a recent Scrum project, the Scrum team members were geographically dispersed. A software tool (Trello) was used to create a virtual version of the Kanban component of the Scrum board. As user stories and tasks were being actively updated, they were moved across the board, from the *to-do* stack to the *doing* stack and so on. The key tracking screen of Trello was displayed on a large-screen TV in each location, so visual progress could easily be followed 24/7. This was combined with videoconferencing (using the respective TVs), enabling the daily Scrum to take place with geographically dispersed members of the team being able to see the Scrum board and see/hear each other.

Another example of using a simple Kanban Scrum board arrangement was during the update of this text to its third edition. Figure 3.8(a) indicates the stacks of the Kanban board customised to the workflow for publishing: Chapters, TO-DO; Chapters DOING; Chapters, McGraw Hill, 1st review; Chapters, McGraw-Hill / Author Cycle; Final PDF check; and Chapters, DONE-DONE. The Chapters, TO-DO list represents the product owners, product backlog and the cards in this stack are effectively the product backlog items. Figure 3.8(b) indicates some of the detail that can be captured behind each card (user story) such as coloured labels, assignment of team members, checklists, attachments, and a commentary of dialog, questions and answers (Q&A).

For a greater understanding of the features of Trello, refer to https://trello.com. *Note:* Many dozens of Scrum/Agile tools include Kanban boards: assess your project's needs before making a purchasing decision. A discussion on tools follows later in this chapter.

Figure 3.8(a) Example of a Trello board

Figure 3.8(b) Example of a user story card

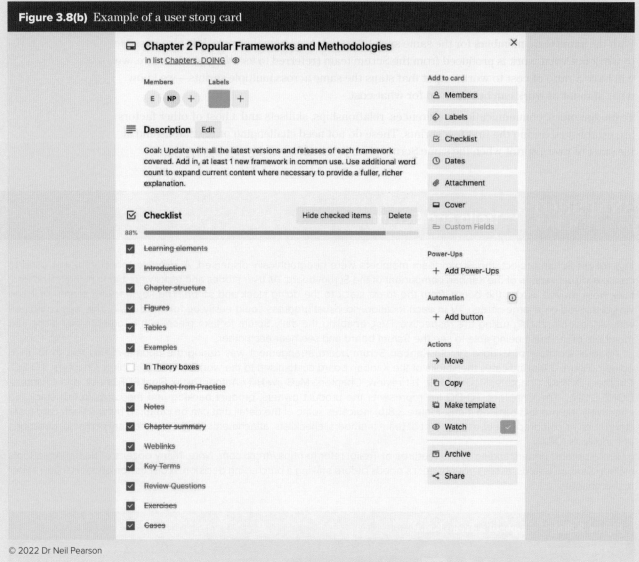

© 2022 Dr Neil Pearson

IN THEORY : The MoSCoW prioritisation technique

MoSCoW is a simple method that assists in prioritising product backlog items. Each item is classified by the product owner (as the empowered decision-maker) as being one of the following.

M is a must-have item—it must be attended to by the Scrum team. The word *must* has further importance because it is the Minimum Usable SubseT of items needed to produce a *done* (or implementable) feature of the end-product. These are features that the product must have if it is to provide any value to the customer, so they are included in the first increments.

S is a should-have item—it is important but is not a must-have item. There could be an interim manual or other workaround in the business until this feature is accommodated in a future sprint or increment of the product, but it will be in the final product.

C is a could-have item—it is a feature that is desirable but does not have to be attended to, in order to support the implementation of the must-have or should-have PBIs (at this time). It may be accommodated if time and money permit.

W is a want-to-have but won't-have item—it is not considered to be a priority at this time and no effort will be made in refining it as a user story. It is usually held for consideration in future projects.

MoSCoW helps us to remember these four classifications. The product owner must understand the value of each item on the product backlog, and be able to classify each item accordingly. Remember that part of the Scrum master's role is to support the product owner in being able to understand and apply such techniques.

3.4 | Scrum events (ceremonies)

These are few in nature but effective in use. They include the kick-off (product visioning meeting), the sprint planning meeting, the daily Scrum, the sprint review and the sprint retrospective.

3.4.1 The kick-off meeting

At the start of the Agile/Scrum project, the Business Case is reviewed by the product owner, Scrum master and Scrum team. From this review several artefacts are jointly created. These include the:

- product vision statement, which describes in a visionary nature what the end state of the product, service or result will resemble. This should not be so tight that it needs revising when the product backlog changes (and it will as we are agile and expect change)
- product roadmap (refer to "In Theory: Product roadmap versus release schedule")
- key stakeholders (refer to Chapter 14 "Project stakeholder management" for a discussion on techniques to identify stakeholders and devise stakeholder management strategies)
- team charter, which could include items such as:
  - the team vision and mission
  - team rituals
  - tools and what purpose the tool is to be used for
  - how conflict will be handled (consensus versus majority)
  - behavioural expectations
  - escalation procedures
- sprint length, the type of work to be undertaken and how stable the requirements are will be discussed at this meeting, combined with factors such as complexity and frequency of delivery required by the customer. All will influence the sprint length. Where there is likely to be a lot of changing requirements, complexity unpacking sprints tend to be shorter in duration (one to three weeks). Where requirements are more stable, and the team is dealing with more known-knowns, the sprint will tend to be longer in duration (three to eight weeks)
- project's success criteria (refer to "In Theory: Success criteria").

IN THEORY : Success criteria

At the project kick-off meeting it is important to discuss with the product owner what is important to the project. Rob Thomsett's *Radical Project Management* includes a tool to assist the Scrum master and Scrum team discuss with the product owner which factors are more or less important than other factors. These factors will no doubt influence the product vision, team charter and how work is prioritised in the product backlog.

Mountain Goat Software (www.mountaingoatsoftware.com/tools/project-success-sliders) has an online tool which can assist in facilitating this discussion. The basis of the tool is that you cannot have everything. Factors must be kept in balance. If one factor is seen as more important than another, another factor must be adjusted down by the same amount to keep the factors in balance. Refer to Figure 3.9.

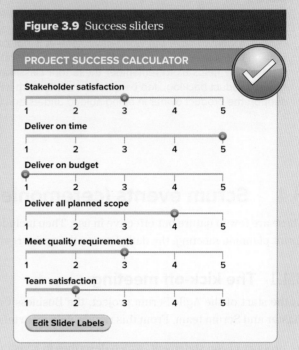

Figure 3.9 Success sliders

Source: Mountain Goat Software n.d., "Project success calculator", https://www.mountaingoatsoftware.com/uploads/blog/sliders3.jpg, accessed December 2021

3.4.2   The release planning meeting and the initial creation of the product backlog

Once the project kick-off meeting has been successfully held, the next event is the creation of the initial product backlog. This usually takes place over several workshops, with the Scrum master facilitating discussions with the product owner and relevant business/customer representative to capture the requirements of the customer (internal or external to the business). These requirements will then be packaged using techniques such as an affinity diagram until a reasonably complete initial product backlog has been created with some structure. Groupings that could provide some formal structure to the product backlog are indicated in Figure 3.10. *Note:* There appears to be no industry standard above the epic level.

Capability is a large component or goal of the customer: for example, "As a customer of age and low technology awareness I want to ensure a paper process is available for to me to make an application and receive notifications on status".

The capability could be elaborated into several *features*—if we deliver all the features, we deliver the capability. For example, there could be two key features of the above capability: Feature 1—To provide a paper-based application and Feature 2—To provide paper-based status on application progress.

Features could then be elaborated into several epics (a collection of user stories). If all the epics within a feature are delivered, the feature is delivered and so on up. For example, Feature 2 could be elaborated into two epics, Epic 1—To provide notification of receipt of application, and Epic 2—To provide notification of status.

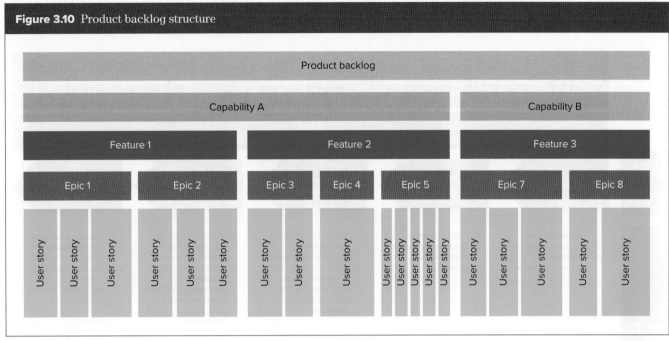

Figure 3.10 Product backlog structure

© 2022 Dr Neil Pearson

Epics are then elaborated into *user stories*, which are singular estimable requirements written in the user story format. In relation to Epic 2, one of the user stories could have been "As an aged care organisation, a declined letter with further support brochure will be sent on application decline so that the customer is provided with other avenues of support".

Remember, there are no tasks on the product backlog. Tasks are identified during the sprint planning meeting by the Scrum team and are transferred with the user story straight to the to-do column of the Kanban board (or Scrum board) discussed later in this chapter.

An interesting example of what Mountain Goat Software refers to as "early version of the Scrum Alliance website" product backlog is available at www.mountaingoatsoftware.com/agile/Scrum/Scrum-tools/product-backlog/example.

Another approach attracting a lot of attention from the marketing and design thinking community is customer journey maps.

> *Customer journey maps show an end-to-end view of the touchpoints where customers engage with an organisation and the perceptions of the customer experience offered during the delivery of the organisation's operational processes. Each touchpoint offers an opportunity for an organisation to excel, and the analysis of a customer journey map helps to identify where the service provided is lacking and process improvements are needed* (Paul et al. 2020).

For a product owner, customer journey mapping provides a more holistic customer-centric view of the business system in which they engage. The customer journey mapping opportunities for improvement will be identified for the existing customer journey or may lead to the creation of a new customer journey. Either way, as a product owner the improvements are potential capabilities, features, epics or user stories that can be included in the development of the product backlog (Figure 3.11).

Figure 3.11 Customer journey map for an aged care home admissions process

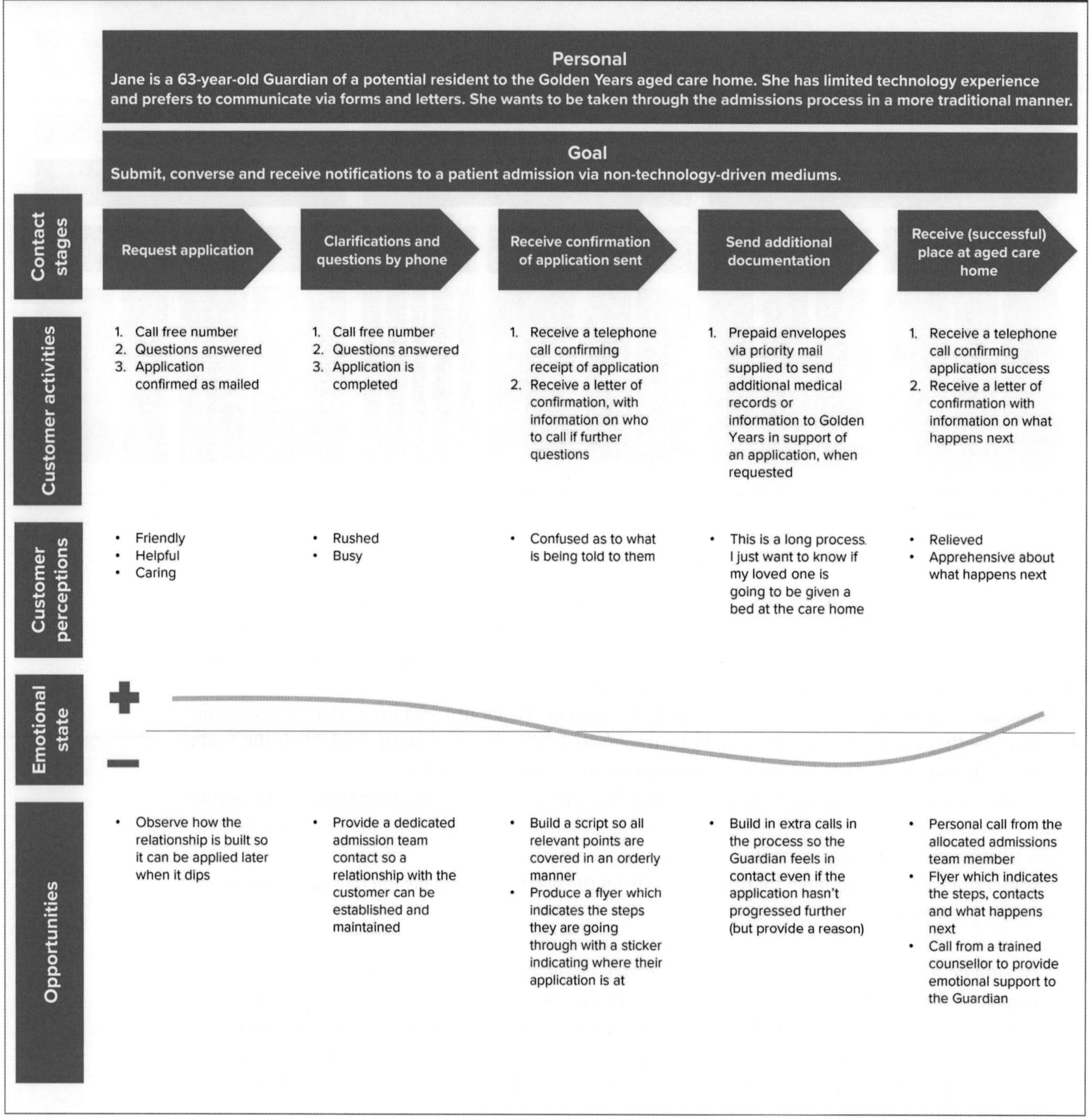

Personal
Jane is a 63-year-old Guardian of a potential resident to the Golden Years aged care home. She has limited technology experience and prefers to communicate via forms and letters. She wants to be taken through the admissions process in a more traditional manner.

Goal
Submit, converse and receive notifications to a patient admission via non-technology-driven mediums.

	Request application	Clarifications and questions by phone	Receive confirmation of application sent	Send additional documentation	Receive (successful) place at aged care home
Customer activities	1. Call free number 2. Questions answered 3. Application confirmed as mailed	1. Call free number 2. Questions answered 3. Application is completed	1. Receive a telephone call confirming receipt of application 2. Receive a letter of confirmation, with information on who to call if further questions	1. Prepaid envelopes via priority mail supplied to send additional medical records or information to Golden Years in support of an application, when requested	1. Receive a telephone call confirming application success 2. Receive a letter of confirmation with information on what happens next
Customer perceptions	• Friendly • Helpful • Caring	• Rushed • Busy	• Confused as to what is being told to them	• This is a long process. I just want to know if my loved one is going to be given a bed at the care home	• Relieved • Apprehensive about what happens next
Emotional state					
Opportunities	• Observe how the relationship is built so it can be applied later when it dips	• Provide a dedicated admission team contact so a relationship with the customer can be established and maintained	• Build a script so all relevant points are covered in an orderly manner • Produce a flyer which indicates the steps they are going through with a sticker indicating where their application is at	• Build in extra calls in the process so the Guardian feels in contact even if the application hasn't progressed further (but provide a reason)	• Personal call from the allocated admissions team member • Flyer which indicates the steps, contacts and what happens next • Call from a trained counsellor to provide emotional support to the Guardian

Once content has been sourced, the next step is to prioritise the PBIs across several different dimensions, but often starting with the MoSCoW technique (refer to "In Theory: MoSCoW prioritisation technique"). In addition to the MoSCoW technique, other factors might come into play when prioritising the product backlog, for example:

- Does the PBI mitigate a significant risk in the business? If so, should it be considered higher priority? In other words, by carrying out the development of a user story we mitigate risk(s) in the business.

- Does the PBI have dependency(ies) with other PBIs? Even if lower priority, the PBIs have to be prioritised as a set as they have dependencies and must be developed together.

■ Does the PBI have time constraints around it? Again, it might be a high-priority PBI item, but if materials are not available (e.g. due to pandemic supply chain issues), its priority is constrained and cannot yet be taken forward into sprint planning.

Once the product backlog is ready, a further workshop with the Scrum team will typically take place to carry out what is often referred to as *T-shirt sizing* (estimation) of PBIs. Refer to Figure 3.12 for an example of the T-Shirt sizing scale. Each PBI is estimated, and an indicative estimate of effort (to later develop) is provided by the Scrum team. This enables the product owner to then take the prioritised, estimated product backlog and create the release schedule (refer to "In Theory: Product roadmap versus release schedule").

Figure 3.12 T-shirt sizing scale

The result is the creation of the initial prioritised product backlog (Table 3.3).

Table 3.3 Simple prioritised product backlog

Product backlog ID	Story (front of card)			Concatenated story sentence	Priority (business value)	T-shirt size estimate
	As a . . .	I want to . . .	So that . . .			
1	website visitor	be able to reset my password	I can still access my account even if I forget my password	\<As a/an\> website visitor \<I want to\> be able to reset my password \<so that\> I can still access my account even if I forget my password	Must	S
2	website visitor	be able to recover my username	I can access my account if I have forgotten my username	\<As a/an\> website visitor \<I want to\> be able to recover my username \<so that\> I can access my account if I have forgotten my username	Must	M
3	authenticated website visitor	see a customised homepage	I am more engaged with the website	\<As a/an\> authenticated website visitor \<I want to\> see a customised homepage \<so that\> I am more engaged with the website	Could	S
4	website visitor	view a home page	I can see the most important content at a glance and quickly understand the site navigation	\<As a/an\> website visitor \<I want to\> view a home page \<so that\> I can see the most important content at a glance and quickly understand the site navigation	Should	M
5	website visitor	be able to log in to the site	I can see tailored content and manage my relationship with the company	\<As a/an\> website visitor \<I want to\> be able to log in to the site \<so that\> I can see tailored content and manage my relationship with the company	Must	M
6	website visitor	be able to register for an account	I can log in and gain all the benefits of being an authenticated user	\<As a/an\> website visitor \<I want to\> be able to register for an account \<so that\> I can login and gain all the benefits of being an authenticated user	Must	M
7	authenticated website visitor	be able to manage my profile details	I can update incorrect or changed details and view current records	\<As a/an\> authenticated website visitor \<I want to\> be able to manage my profile details \<so that\> I can update incorrect or changed details and view current records	Should	S
8	authenticated website visitor	be able to log out of the website	my private information is kept secure when accessing the site on a shared computer	\<As a/an\> authenticated website visitor \<I want to\> be able to log out of the website \<so that\> my private information is kept secure when accessing the site on a shared computer	Must	S

3.4.3 **The sprint**

The **sprint** is a timebox of typically between one and eight weeks. Organisations usually move into a routine of using the same timebox (two-week sprints are the most popular in practice). Estimating the work that can be done in this timebox may be done accurately through the repeated use of the burndown chart, and in the understanding of velocity (discussed later in this chapter). At the end of the sprint, a set of done-done work will be accomplished. This work is what we call *potentially shippable* (e.g. it could be production-ready code). Some individual sprints produce work that can be implemented or put into production; normally it takes several sprints that have delivered a number of features and together they can be released or put into production.

1. Quality is at the forefront of the sprint approach. Quality must not be jeopardised by attempts to put more into a sprint to get more done, only to have to correct more defects later! Sometimes Scrum teams talk about done-done, which effectively affirms the work has been done according to the story card and the story has been tested according to the acceptance criteria, and further to this meets the definition of done (DoD); therefore, it is done-done!

2. The sprint contents generally are not changed—this would endanger the sprint goal; the sprint goal is agreed at the sprint planning meeting and is encapsulated in what is to be achieved in the sprint. It is developed by the Scrum team during the sprint planning meeting.

3. Each day in the sprint, usually in the morning before work commences, the team carries out the daily Scrum meeting or daily stand-up to update all on progress in a transparent manner (the daily stand-up meeting is described later in this section).

Each sprint could be considered a mini project, where the work is planned, designed, developed and potentially implemented. The product owner is the only person who can cancel a sprint before it is over. The cancellation of sprints rarely occurs in practice; sprints are timeboxes of relatively short duration so work is usually allowed to be completed. A sprint may be cancelled if business circumstances have significantly changed, or the product's development has been suspended.

Often a sprint 0 is a *get-ready sprint* that is used by the Scrum master and the Scrum team to establish the environments, software tools, protocols and standards to be used across the entire Scrum project. As such, the sprint may be shorter in duration and may not directly produce any business-related potentially shippable product. The sprint will still adhere to the DoD, will apply the Agile Manifesto and will provide a test of confidence in the Scrum team's ability to work together as an empowered team under the servant-leadership arrangement with the Scrum master.

The final sprint is often an integrative sprint where the potentially shippable products from previous sprints are integrated and shipped or implemented in the business.

3.4.4 **The sprint planning meeting**

Sprint planning (Figure 3.13) takes place at the start of each and every sprint. The work will be estimated using the popular story point technique (refer to "In Theory: Planning Poker") and a sprint goal will be crafted for the entire sprint, which will become the focus for the Scrum team. Sprint planning is put into the hands of the Scrum team. They, with input from the product owner, will decide which PBIs are to form the content for the sprint. The sprint planning meeting covers two aspects:

1. agreeing on what can be achieved in the sprint (i.e. deciding which PBIs are to go into the sprint backlog with input from the product owner)

2. deciding how the chosen sprint backlog items will be done by the Scrum team. This usually results in a user story card being broken down into several tasks, which the Scrum team must accomplish in order to accomplish the story card. These tasks are typically allocated to different members of the Scrum team. Further explanation of the story card is provided in section 3.5.

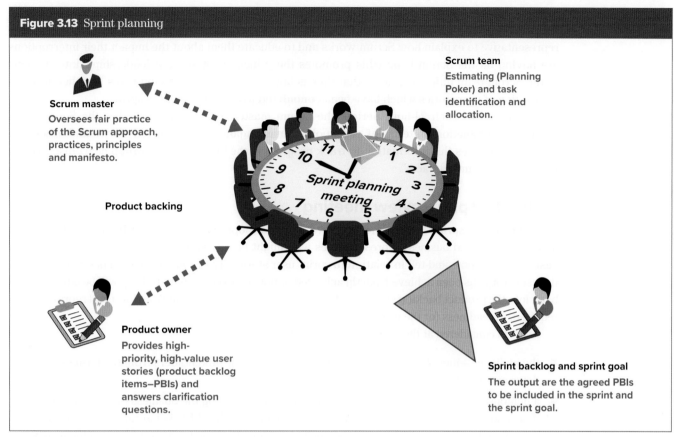

Figure 3.13 Sprint planning

Scrum master
Oversees fair practice of the Scrum approach, practices, principles and manifesto.

Product backing

Product owner
Provides high-priority, high-value user stories (product backlog items—PBIs) and answers clarification questions.

Scrum team
Estimating (Planning Poker) and task identification and allocation.

Sprint planning meeting

Sprint backlog and sprint goal
The output are the agreed PBIs to be included in the sprint and the sprint goal.

The sprint goal will be established at the sprint planning meeting. This is the Scrum team's understanding and agreement of the *what* and *why* it is building in the sprint towards delivery of the increment of potentially shippable product. The sprint goal becomes the focus for the sprint and could be printed out as a banner in the Scrum team's workplace: it is the sprint's North Star, which anyone in the team can glance up to see and refocus their direction.

3.4.5 The daily Scrum meeting

The daily Scrum meeting is a short, 15-minute (timeboxed) ceremony, where the Scrum team synchronises activities and plans the next 24 hours. Referencing the visual Scrum board (and the Kanban board from where the sprint backlog stories are managed), the Scrum team (in a self-organising manner) gathers around the board, and each discusses the following three key topics:

1. what they have achieved in the previous 24 hours towards their allocated stories and associated tasks, moving task cards along the Kanban board as they move from to-do, doing, done and done-done

2. what they are planning to do today (i.e. in the next 24 hours) to help the Scrum team meet the sprint goal

3. what impediments (issues) they envisage are in the way of them achieving the story, tasks or sprint goal and how they plan to overcome these and what assistance they may need from, for example, the Scrum master.

Each member of the Scrum team must speak and will have about two minutes to do so. They must therefore come fully prepared for the daily Scrum meeting (or daily stand-up).

Remember that although the Scrum master makes sure this meeting occurs, they are not a team lead for the meeting—instead, the Scrum team must collectively act as an empowered team as no team lead role exists in Agile/Scrum. The Scrum master may take away information about some of the impediments and action them; for example, if a business representative is approaching the Scrum team directly, it is the Scrum master who will take this impediment away by working with the business representative to explain how Scrum works and to educate them about the impact their interruptions are having on the Scrum team (this promotes the principles of servant leadership). Interruptions to the Scrum team ultimately mean that time is taken away from achieving tasks and therefore the completion of user stories which have been **committed** to at the start of the sprint.

At the end of each 24-hour period, the Scrum master will also request that the Scrum team update the completion (in terms of story points) made against their selected stories and tasks. The Scrum master uses this information to track progress in the burndown or burnup chart discussed in section 3.5 "Scrum artefacts".

3.4.6 The sprint review meeting

At the end of the sprint, the increment is reviewed and (hopefully) is accepted by the product owner and any associated business representatives who might be invited to this meeting. The Scrum team basically do a show-and-tell in relation to sprint user stories. The product owner has several options: the user story has been achieved, partly achieved or not achieved. Note that these will be later updated back into the product backlog so the product owner can refine the product backlog and reprioritise, as required, in readiness for the next sprint planning meeting.

Aspects considered at the sprint review include:

■ the audience—including the product owner and other key stakeholders from the business, as determined by the product owner

■ a demonstration of what has been done, to gain acceptance by the business of what has been done and to answer any questions. This could result in further PBIs being raised by stakeholders attending the review, which would then be represented back on to the product backlog as new stories. This often happens when an increment is released, as the stakeholder may see a way of enhancing this feature to extract further value from it

■ any problems encountered by the Scrum team (when working with the business) and how any such problems were resolved

■ a review by the product owner of any changes to the business environment and inputting these into the *what to do next* discussion

■ a general review of the increment, the sprint, the resources used and the budget for the next increment.

The normal outcome from a sprint review meeting is acceptance of the user stories, as these would have been developed and tested according to the acceptance criteria (written by the product owner) and the team's internal definition of done checks. New features are sometimes identified as a result of the work completed; as mentioned, these are added to the product backlog, which is reprioritised in readiness for the next sprint planning meeting.

3.4.7 The sprint retrospective meeting

A **sprint retrospective** is a shorter meeting that takes place after the sprint review meeting. The sprint retrospective covers the traditional questions of:

■ What went well?
■ What didn't go so well?
■ What could have been done better?

Another popular Agile format to this is the 4 Ls—loved, loathed, longed for and learned. (An example of this technique can be found at www.atlassian.com/team-playbook/plays/4-ls-retrospective-technique#instructions.)

The Scrum master participates in this meeting as a peer member of the Scrum team. It is an opportunity to reflect on the Scrum framework and make changes to it. Items could be raised on any matter, but often includes discussions about:

■ working with the business—people, relationships and politics

■ application of the Scrum framework—where this went well, but also where improvements can be made and who will action the improvement, preferably before the next sprint (recall the Agile principle *Simplicity—the art of maximising the amount of work not done—is essential*)

■ a discussion and allocation of the outstanding impediments that need to be actioned

■ considerations around product quality and how well this is being achieved, potential revision to the DoD and coaching of the product owner in the writing of user stories and acceptance criteria

■ environmental considerations—not only in terms of the physical environment, but also in terms of the tools used (whiteboards or virtual Scrum boards) through to team reward(s) and acknowledgement of achievements.

The sprint retrospective is an opportunity for the whole Scrum team to be able to inspect and adapt (known in some circles as *action learning*).

For the time typically allocated to the various Scrum ceremonies (events), refer to Table 3.4. These can be scaled-up for sprints longer than four weeks in duration.

Table 3.4 Event durations

	Sprint length			
Event	4 weeks	3 weeks	2 weeks	1 week
Sprint planning meeting	8 hours	6 hours	4 hours	2 hours
Daily Scrum	15 minutes	15 minutes	15 minutes	15 minutes
Sprint review meeting	4 hours	3 hours	2 hours	1 hour
Sprint retrospective meeting	4 hours	3 hours	2 hours	1 hour

© 2022 Dr Neil Pearson

IN THEORY   Planning Poker

Planning Poker is an Agile technique used to estimate (and later track) the amount of work effort in story points for each story (or item) on the product backlog. *Points* are an arbitrary unit of measure for expressing an estimate of the overall effort that will be required to fully implement a product backlog item (PBI). Some Scrum teams use half-day increments or hours. However, when this story point principle is adopted and the Scrum team becomes comfortable with *effort to story points,* the process of estimating becomes more accurate. This is because the Scrum team is focused on discussing the relative complexity of each item on the product backlog rather than on time. For example, this could be expressed as PBI A being 13 times more complex than PBI B.

As seen in Figure 3.14, the Scrum team typically uses a set of Planning Poker cards. The standard number sequence is normally based on the Fibonacci sequence, with additional cards used for higher story points. For example, a question

Figure 3.14 Planning Poker in action

Bartosz Budrewicz/Shutterstock.com

(Continues)

In Theory: Planning Poker (*Continued*)

mark (?) for "I don't understand, I need more information", and the infinity symbol (∞) for a number greater than the largest number in the deck of cards being used (i.e. too large to estimate).

Scrum team members typically sit around a table with the product owner and the Scrum master, with the sequence events taking place based around the following steps:

1. The product owner reads and describes the highest-prioritised item (story) on the product backlog list being considered for inclusion into the sprint (as per the release schedule). Remember: The product owner would have assessed the value of each PBI and prioritised this using the MoSCoW technique.

2. The Scrum team then carry out two to three minutes of quiet thinking where individually they identify all the tasks they think the team must do to accomplish the user story.

3. The Scrum team next votes on the story points they individually see the story being worth (given the tasks they have identified). Simultaneously, all the Scrum team members place (face-up) in the centre of the table an individual card from their personal set of cards, so that its value can be seen. Examples of the differing scenarios that could arise from Planning Poker include:

   a. If the presented card values are the same, then the PBI would be added to the sprint backlog and the Scrum team would progress onto the next prioritised item from the product backlog list, but not before discussing the tasks each Scrum team member identified individually to make sure they have not estimated on different sets of tasks. If they have, everyone will outline the tasks in more detail, discuss and then another round of quiet thinking would take place before a further round of Planning Poker.

   b. If the presented card values are vastly different, the tasks would be shared so the team gain exposure to the specialist thinking each team member brings to the table. Another round of quiet thinking would take place before a further round of Planning Poker.

   c. If the Scrum team started playing the question mark card, the product owner needs to add clarification (i.e. it may be that the user story requires breaking down) and then the story is re-estimated, by playing Planning Poker.

   d. If the Scrum team puts down an infinity symbol card, the story would be broken down into more discrete stories with input from the product owner, given that the Scrum team have indicated that the story is too large for them to estimate in its current form.

How do you know when to stop adding user stories from the product backlog to the sprint backlog?

This typically lies in tracking completion rate of user stories from previous sprints (termed *sprint velocity* in Scrum). The Scrum master will be able to advise on how many story points are being achieved across sprints (of the same nature). This will inform the maximum number of story points that can be packed into the current sprint. (Refer to later sections in this chapter on how to calculate sprint velocity.)

(A helpful resource for this process, in the form of a Planning Poker app, can be found at: www.mountaingoatsoftware. com/tools/planning-poker.)

Advanced topic: In this description of Planning Poker, the phrase *story points* was introduced. This is the Agile/Scrum preferred way of estimating relative effort consistently across all stories and all sprints (instead of using, for example, effort-hours). Readers are encouraged to view "What are story points?" by Mike Cohn (www.youtube.com/watch?v=VsSaoIMtkKU).

3.5 | Scrum artefacts

Several Scrum artefacts have been mentioned in this chapter. This section provides further details.

The artefacts considered include the product backlog, the sprint backlog, burndown/burnup charts and the finished work (the potentially shippable product).

Note: The product roadmap and the release schedule were discussed previously (refer to "In Theory: Product roadmap versus release schedule").

3.5.1 The product vision

One of the first artefacts developed at the kick-off meeting is the product vision statement, which brings together all the key roles in the Scrum project to gain understanding and agreement on what the vision is (for the product, service or result). There are several techniques to assist in drafting the product vision statement:

■ The product vision box is where the cereal box principle is used to inspire discussion. The front of the box sets out the value proposition, with the imagery, slogan and key features clearly displayed. The back of the box contains the objects behind the vision, and the sides contain yet further detail. Although seen as a creative workshop, it can really focus a team on the key aspects of what the product, service or result is setting out to deliver. A general internet search of *product vision box* will return examples to provide inspiration.

■ The formula style is another popular way of capturing what the vision of the product is all about (Figure 3.15).

Figure 3.15 Product vision statement

For	<who is buying the product/service>
Who	<statement of need or opportunity>
The <product name>	Is a <product category>
That	<statement of key benefit>
Unlike	<competitors or alternative situation>
Our product	<statement of key differentiation that will address the pain or support the gain>

© 2022 Dr Neil Pearson

■ Using Simon Sinek's Why—How—What approach. Only Simon Sinek himself can provide the animated discussion on this powerful combination. The reader is encouraged to view the TED talk at the following link: www.ted.com/talks/simon_sinek_how_great_leaders_inspire_action?language=en

 Tool—Project Vision Statement

3.5.2 **The product backlog**

The product backlog is a changeable list of the business requirements, also known as PBIs, user stories, features or just plain requirements. The product backlog is ordered according to the value the business sees from the requirement being implemented. It is therefore owned by the business (in particular, the product owner).

The product owner is the accountable, empowered owner of the list: they liaise with the business, user groups in the business and customers, and provide a single entity (i.e. a single person, not a group of people) for the Scrum team to liaise with in relation to the PBIs and the priorities set. The product owner has the final say as to the contents of the product backlog, and therefore must be respected and empowered to represent the business (customer) and have suitable decision-making authority—hence

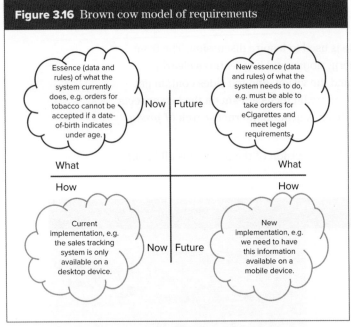

Figure 3.16 Brown cow model of requirements

© 2022 Dr Neil Pearson

Source: Adapted from Atlantic Systems Guild 2009, "How now brown cow", https://www.volere.org/wp-content/uploads/2019/02/howNowBrownCow.pdf

product owners typically are managers or senior managers in an organisation. There are many techniques the product owner could use with the business to extract high-level requirements, for example, the *brown cow* technique. As illustrated in Figure 3.16, the grid aims to differentiate between *what* the business wants to do from *how* it wants to do it, across the time dimensions of *now* and *in the future*.

This technique could also be used at other points in the Scrum proceedings, such as in the sprint event itself, by members of the Scrum team in extrapolating and clarifying requirements. Carrying out workshops with business users of a business system is also popular where (when creating the initial cut of the product backlog) a brainstorm session using sticky notes would start the generation of *requirements*. The product owner as facilitator of this session could then apply the affinity diagram technique, where they get the group to look for likeness between the sticky notes. By grouping (and sub-grouping) the sticky notes, themes should start to emerge and gaps might be identified. These sticky notes would then be transferred to:

- a manually maintained set of story cards (Figure 3.17) pinned to a visual Scrum board, or
- virtual equivalents in a software tool such as a Trello (Figure 3.8(a)), or a more comprehensive tracking tool such as Jira could be used. The more comprehensive tools allow customisation to include information on estimating and prioritisation that can be later reported on for sprint monitoring purposes in the form of burndown and/or burnup charts.

Once prioritised, the must-have requirements, collated into the first sprints to deliver an increment, represent what is often referred to as the:

- minimum usable subset (MUST), or
- minimum viable product (MVP).

A more tech-savvy product owner could employ *use case diagrams* (Figure 3.18).

Figure 3.17 Coloured story cards

Ken Cavanagh/McGraw Hill

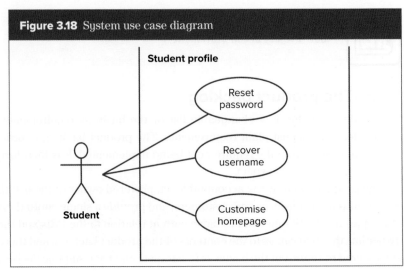

Figure 3.18 System use case diagram

© 2022 Dr Neil Pearson

Whatever combination of facilitation techniques and tools are used, the goal is to draft the initial version of the product backlog. Whichever medium (tool or story card) is used, the accepted format for a user story is:

> **As a < persona > I want < to do something > so that < I can gain a benefit >**

The first part of the user story is the *persona*. Personas are not stakeholders, nor are they actors. A persona is a rich description of a particular group of users (or customers) that are using the product, service or system. Remember, in Agile/Scrum we take a customer-centric perspective. Refer to Figure 3.19. If personas have not yet been defined, then the more generic term *actor* could be used.

Figure 3.19 Personas

Users of a travel booking system

Casual, bargain-hunting travellers

Vanessa, 39 years old,
The Backpacker
"My backpack is always ready for me to pick up so I can jet off and explore the world."

Vanessa is a 39-year-old resident of San Francisco. She is pursuing her passion for travelling after having a highly successful career as an attorney. She likes to have options for air travel and accommodations so that she can pick the best and most affordable ones. She gets frustrated by slow and cluttered websites.

Business professionals

"I like a website that is simple and convenient and lets me plan my itinerary quickly."

Matt, 25 years old,
The Business executive

Matt is a business consultant who travels extensively around the world. He plans his itinerary while he is on the go and does not like spending too much time on travel websites. He needs convenient access to the air travel and accommodation locations he visits frequently.

Source: Adapted from https://www.Scrumstudy.com, accessed December 2021

The second part of the user story is *what* the persona wants to do. Be careful when writing the *what* as often it is too large to be estimated and later must be broken down into more granular (atomic) user stories. Thinking in atomic, singular, compact requirements will get you at the correct level, unless you are deliberately writing the user story at an epic (group of user stories) level, for later breaking down into more granular user stories that are estimable.

The third part of the user story is the *why* or benefit. *Why* and specifically what benefit is the persona going to get from the user story? This must convince the product owner that the story has importance to the overall product vision. Refer to the following user story examples:

> As a *website visitor* I want to *be able to reset my password* so that I *can still access my account even if I forget my password.*
>
> As an *online store user* I want to *securely enter card details* so that I *can store credit card details for future transactions.*

A useful acronym to refer to when writing user stories is INVEST (independent, negotiable, valuable, estimable, small and testable) (refer to "In Theory: The INVEST acronym"). This technique could be used by the Scrum master when coaching the product owner to write quality story cards for the Scrum team, potentially helping to avert questions and issues in estimating the story during the sprint planning meeting.

So, that is the front of card taken care of. On the back of the story card are the *acceptance criteria* (Figure 3.20). Elements of quality in Agile/Scrum are geared around the extrinsic quality of the results (whether it adds value). If a user story (a statement of something that the customer wants) is seen to add value to the customer's experience and it meets the acceptance criteria for testing that user story, we are achieving some confirmation that is has delivered what the customer requires. The user story is about *what* and *why*, and the acceptance criteria ensure we have tested what was developed—and therefore confirms the story.

The Scrum team later use these acceptance criteria to verify the user story has been *done* in the sprint, and at the sprint review meeting to show that the user story meets the acceptance criteria (as defined by the product owner) at the review meeting.

Figure 3.20 Example story card

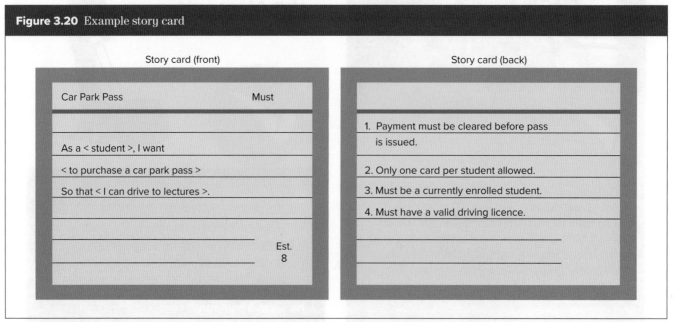

Story card (front)

| Car Park Pass | Must |

As a < student >, I want

< to purchase a car park pass >

So that < I can drive to lectures >.

Est. 8

Story card (back)

1. Payment must be cleared before pass is issued.

2. Only one card per student allowed.

3. Must be a currently enrolled student.

4. Must have a valid driving licence.

As the Scrum project progresses and a number of sprints have been delivered, the items on the product backlog could expand to include story cards beyond pure business/customer requirements. User stories are often grouped into the following categories:

- user story—the source of most of these is the product owner (representing the business / voice of the customer), supplemented by additional stories raised by the Scrum team
- bug (defect)—potentially raised by anyone, at any time, but more frequently raised as a result of applying testing (i.e. acceptance criteria on the back of the story card)
- technical work—work that needs to be accomplished to put down technical foundations, such as creation and configuration of databases, installation of hardware, or software installation and configuration
- knowledge acquisition (research, or sometimes referred to as *spikes*)—activities from training to research. This is accounted for in a sprint as a story card because effort will be exerted in carrying out the activity.

If the Scrum team is using manual story cards and the storyboard wall technique, different-coloured story cards can be used to represent each of these types of items on the storyboard. This renders it easier to be able to identify the product backlog, and ultimately to facilitate what gets carried forward and is worked on by the Scrum team in the sprint backlog (after the sprint planning meeting: refer to Figure 3.14).

The story card (or its equivalent) is based on a concept that Ron Jeffries documented in 2001 as part of his approach to XP (eXtreme Programming). He proposed to distinguish *social* user stories from *documentary* requirement practices such as use cases, and so the story card emerged, and along with it the acronym, the 3C's. In his *card, conversation, confirmation* model, Jeffries defines:

1. a *card* (or often a sticky note) as a physical token giving tangible and durable form to what would otherwise only be an abstraction
2. a *conversation* as taking place at different times and places during a project between the various people concerned with a given feature of a software product: customers, users, developers, testers. This conversation is largely verbal but is usually supplemented by documentation
3. a *confirmation* as occurring once the objectives the conversation revolved around have been reached (Jeffries 2001).

So, where does the confirmation get documented? On the reverse of the story card. Figure 3.20 gives a simple example of a completed story card. Note that confirmation criteria in Scrum are more commonly called *acceptance criteria* and appear on the reverse of the card.

As described, the product backlog might be maintained using physical story cards. However, with anything but the simplest of projects, this can be become an arduous task. Many practitioners therefore use spreadsheets or software tools to assist with defining and managing the items on the product backlog, as illustrated in Figure 3.8(a).

Note: More comprehensive software tools are available and the reader is encouraged to research a tool appropriate to their Agile project requirements.

These story cards are an important concept for capturing the business system requirements, and as such might be referred to as *functional requirements* in a traditional business analyst context.

The stories could be likened to a business analyst capturing the system use case diagram and the individual user cases captured within the system use case diagram. This necessitates a more advanced discussion with your Scrum team members. Be warned, there are often differences in the level of abstraction of user cases. Some system use case diagrams will indicate quite high-level requirements (epics), and will require further detail when pushed into the sprint planning meeting if not extrapolated before—as should occur.

IN THEORY   The INVEST acronym

A popular technique that is often used as an aid to writing better story cards is the INVEST acronym. It stands for:

- **I**ndependent of all other story cards
- **N**egotiable, the results of engaging with business stakeholders to collect the user story (or conversation)
- **V**aluable to the business
- **E**stimable to a reasonable accuracy (preferably story points)
- **S**mall enough to fit within a sprint
- **T**estable (in principle, even if there isn't a test for it yet).

This is much like applying the SMART acronym (specific, measurable, achievable, realistic and timely) to project objectives.

Figure 3.18 shows a partial system use case diagram for three items as indicated in the product backlog list (Figure 3.4). A *student to reset password* would be referred to as a *user case* (or use case) and form an individual story card (at the epic level requiring further breakdown). The same would apply for the *student to recover username*, which would be captured on a second story card, and so on.

Discussion on the elicitation of business requirements would take place with the Scrum team at the outset of the project, so that a consistent approach is taken.

3.5.3 Sprint backlog

The **sprint backlog** is, in essence, a subset of PBIs (from the product backlog) that have been accepted for development by the Scrum team (refer to the above section on sprint planning) into the current sprint. However, note that the sprint backlog will contain additional information as defined by the Scrum team and Scrum master. For example:

- The Scrum master might require that the Scrum team record progress made towards completion of the story at the end of each day. This information would be recorded on the burndown or burnup charts, indicating progress referred to as *monitoring sprint progress* (later in this chapter we discuss the burndown, burnup and velocity in detail). Expanding on Figure 3.10, we layer on the concept of the sprint backlog and tasks (Figure 3.21).

- The Scrum team will break a story down into its requisite tasks, which they need to individually complete for the story to be completed or *done*.

- The Scrum team will allocate the tasks determined at the sprint planning meeting (refer to "In Theory: Planning Poker") to members of the team (remember there is no project manager and no team lead). The team is responsible for planning and managing the work (tasks) that take place within the sprint in order to achieve the sprint goal. See Figure 3.22 for a breakdown of user stories into allocated tasks.

- The Scrum team (from a business analysis perspective) might then have information recorded against each task, in relation to the stakeholder who was consulted, a record of discussion, and so on.

- The Scrum team (from a tester's perspective) might want to record further details about the quality/testing of acceptance criteria.

Tip: This is where, from a practical perspective, applying Scrum (in the business) and the Agile Manifesto collide. The Scrum team must agree on the extent of documentation required; the Agile Manifesto states, "Working software over comprehensive documentation". The Scrum wall is based on the lean visual management system—the Kanban board. A Scrum team will generally take over a whole room and allocate a wall when running Agile/Scrum projects to be the visual Scrum wall. Figure 3.23 provides

Figure 3.21 Sprint backlog

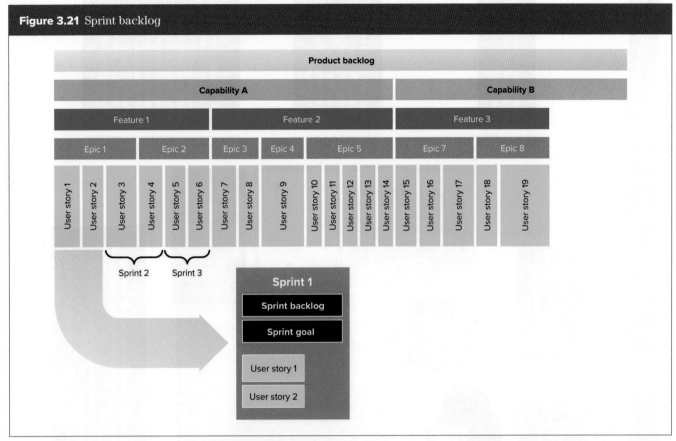

Figure 3.22 User stories and allocated tasks

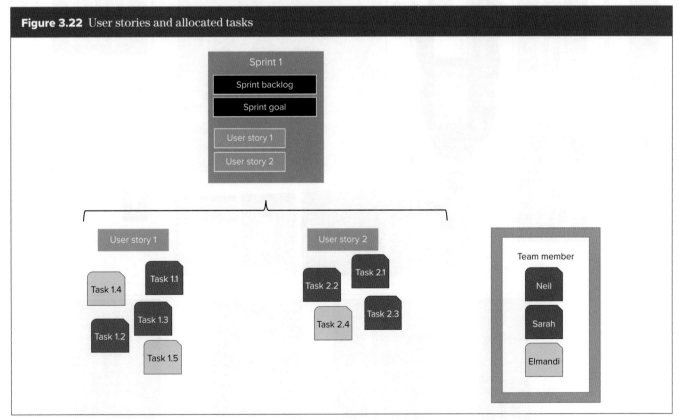

Figure 3.23 Visual Scrum wall

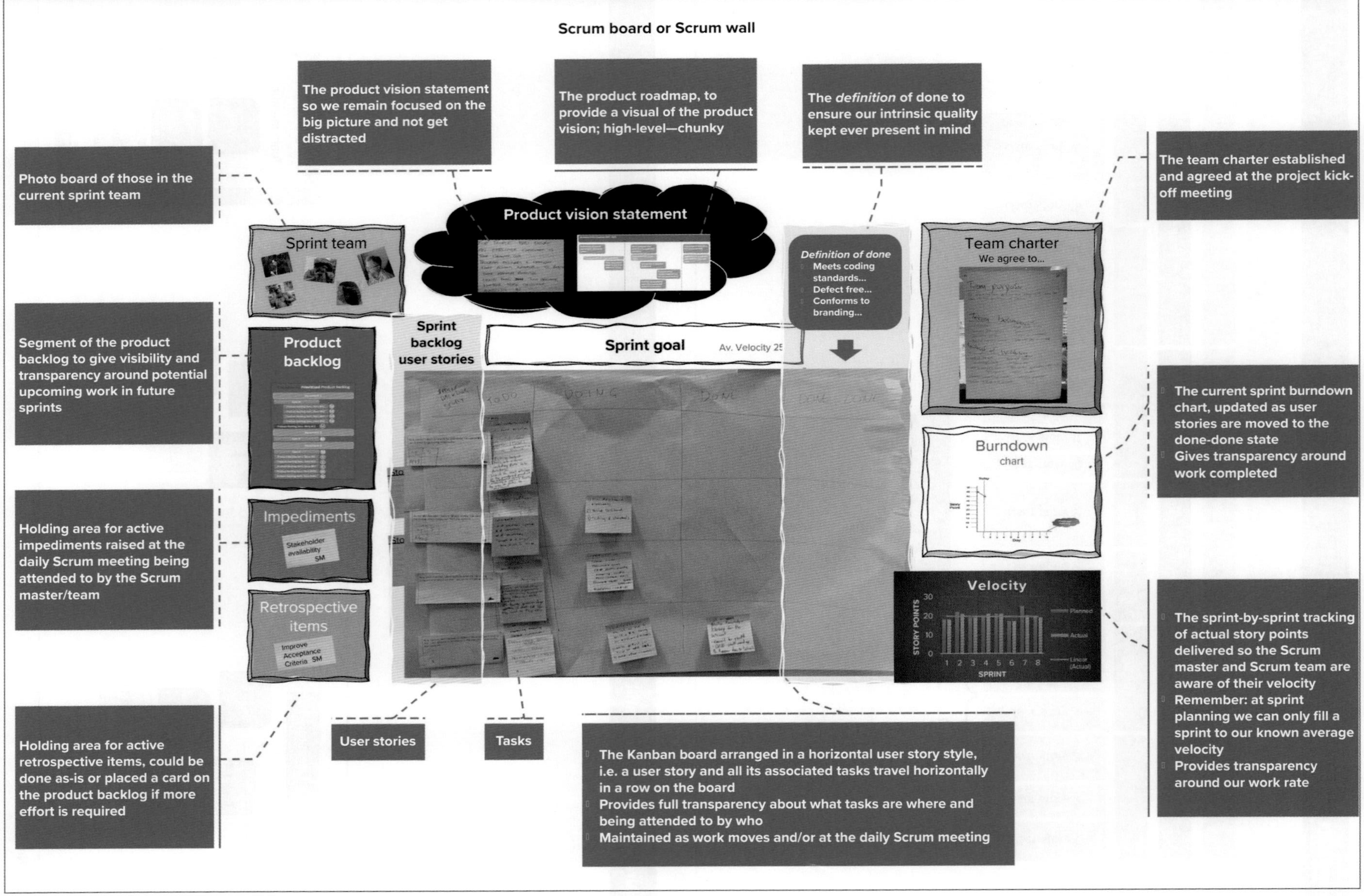

Scrum board or Scrum wall
Photo board of those in the current sprint team
The product vision statement so we remain focused on the big picture and not get distracted
The product roadmap, to provide a visual of the product vision; high-level—chunky
The *definition* of done to ensure our intrinsic quality kept ever present in mind
The team charter established and agreed at the project kick-off meeting
Sprint team
Product vision statement
Definition of done
Meets coding standards...
Defect free...
Conforms to branding...
Team charter
We agree to...
Segment of the product backlog to give visibility and transparency around potential upcoming work in future sprints
Product backlog
Sprint backlog user stories
Sprint goal
Av. Velocity 25
The current sprint burndown chart, updated as user stories are moved to the done-done state
Gives transparency around work completed
Burndown
chart
Holding area for active impediments raised at the daily Scrum meeting being attended to by the Scrum master/team
Impediments
Stakeholder availability SM
Retrospective items
Improve Acceptance Criteria SM
Velocity
STORY POINTS
SPRINT
Planned
Actual
Linear (Actual)
The sprint-by-sprint tracking of actual story points delivered so the Scrum master and Scrum team are aware of their velocity
Remember: at sprint planning we can only fill a sprint to our known average velocity
Provides transparency around our work rate
Holding area for active retrospective items, could be done as-is or placed a card on the product backlog if more effort is required
User stories
Tasks
The Kanban board arranged in a horizontal user story style, i.e. a user story and all its associated tasks travel horizontally in a row on the board
Provides full transparency about what tasks are where and being attended to by who
Maintained as work moves and/or at the daily Scrum meeting

a mock-up of such a Scrum wall using Scrum artefacts from many different projects, to provide the inspiration to research and build a Scrum wall that visually appeals to your team and is rich in transparent information.

The author (Pearson) has used online tools to create such Scrum boards (a popular tool has been a collaborative virtual whiteboard tool https://miro.com or https://excalidraw.com).

At the centre of the Scrum wall is the Scrum board or Kanban board. It has the traditional To-Do, Doing, Done columns supplemented with the Agile Done-Done column. This enables the movement of tasks across these different states to be tracked as the Scrum team completes them. When all tasks for a user story have been done-done then the user story is ready to take to the sprint review meeting. When all user stories are done-done the sprint will be nearing its end and all user stories will be taken to the sprint review meeting for approval (sign-off) by the product owner.

Note: The user stories and associated tasks are arranged in rows, so it can be seen which tasks have been completed for which user stories. This is also represented in Figure 3.24.

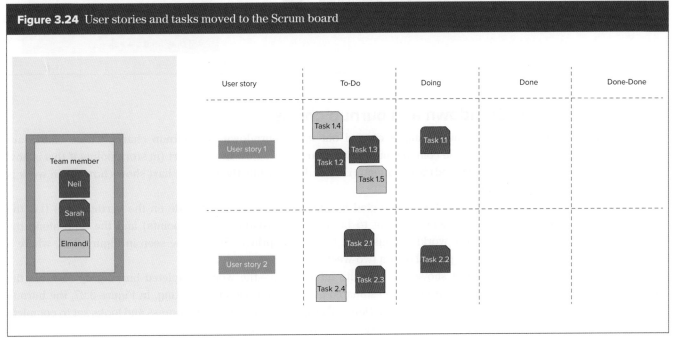

Figure 3.24 User stories and tasks moved to the Scrum board

© 2022 Dr Neil Pearson

3.5.4 Potentially shippable product

The output of every sprint is called a *potentially shippable product*. This is a key concept in the way Scrum operates. A sprint should be planned so it will deliver a potentially shippable product increment. *Potentially shippable* means that the product (whether software or other) could be put into a production environment and released to its customers. This concept would be reinforced by the Scrum master at the sprint planning meeting and in interactions with the product owner when reviewing and maintaining the PBIs on the product backlog.

When an increment (typically several sprints) is put into production, this is mapped out on the release schedule. Whether this can be done at the end of the sprint or requires a special, shorter sprint with different skillsets to move the increment into production will depend on what and how much work needs to be done. Figure 3.25 represents two typical scenarios that are often encountered.

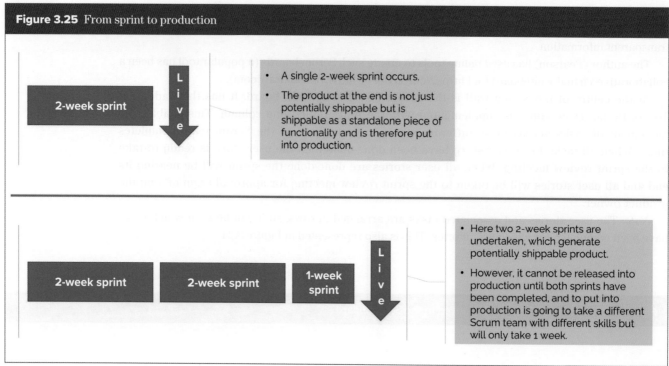

Figure 3.25 From sprint to production

- A single 2-week sprint occurs.
- The product at the end is not just potentially shippable but is shippable as a standalone piece of functionality and is therefore put into production.

- Here two 2-week sprints are undertaken, which generate potentially shippable product.
- However, it cannot be released into production until both sprints have been completed, and to put into production is going to take a different Scrum team with different skills but will only take 1 week.

© 2022 Dr Neil Pearson

3.5.5   Burndown and burnup charts

Sprint progress monitoring is carried out using burndown and burnup charts. These charts are flipsides of the same coin: the burndown chart shows how much effort (in story points if this is how the PBI was estimated) is remaining (i.e. not done), while the burnup chart shows how much work is left to be done.

A burndown chart is constructed by putting the story point scale on the vertical axis (i.e. the scope of the increment or sprint to be achieved, usually in story points) and the time along the horizontal axis (10 working days for a two-week sprint). This can be seen in Figure 3.26, where a burndown chart is plotted over a two-week sprint.

A burnup chart shows the opposite information—the work completed burning up towards the amount of scope (story points) estimated at the sprint planning meeting. In Figure 3.27, the burnup chart shows a two-week sprint on Day 9. The sprint has made good progress and looks set to complete the estimated story points at the end of the sprint on Day 10.

Burndown and/or burnup charts should be plotted for the purpose of monitoring progress. The Scrum master can use these charts to raise questions about progress and impediments to pursuing the objective of achieving the sprint goal within the sprint length. The Scrum team can also use these charts to monitor their own progress, and in some Scrum teams it will be the team members that plot the chart as they complete user stories into the done-done state, the updating of the chart usually taking place at the daily Scrum meeting.

3.5.6   Contemporary Agile status reporting

Combining burndown charts and other project and sprint information in the form of an *information radiator* is becoming a popular artefact in Agile projects. An example is captured in Figure 3.28.

3.5.7   Advanced topic cumulative flow diagram

In some organisations that are wholly committed to the Agile/Scrum approach, more information is required to track progress of many user stories and see into how work (tasks) are progressing. To accomplish these insights behind the burndown, a cumulative flow diagram can be used. The reader is encouraged to review the information at https://zepel.io/agile/reports/cumulative-flow-diagram/.

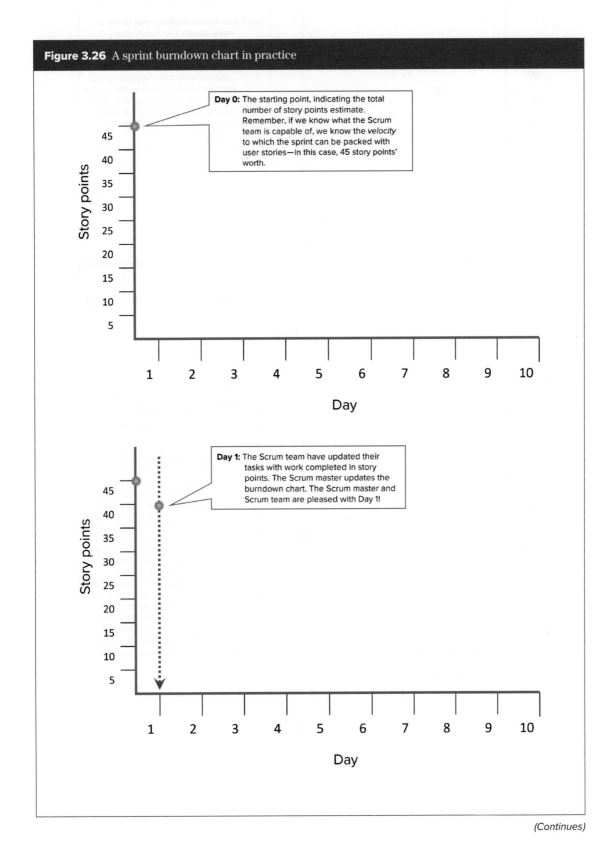

Figure 3.26 A sprint burndown chart in practice

(Continues)

Figure 3.26 A sprint burndown chart in practice (*Continued*)

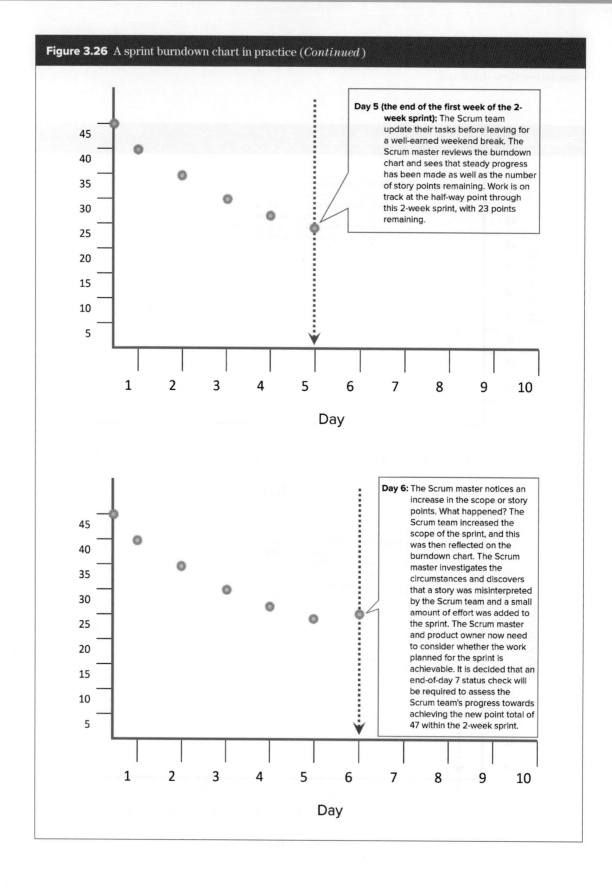

Day 5 (the end of the first week of the 2-week sprint): The Scrum team update their tasks before leaving for a well-earned weekend break. The Scrum master reviews the burndown chart and sees that steady progress has been made as well as the number of story points remaining. Work is on track at the half-way point through this 2-week sprint, with 23 points remaining.

Day 6: The Scrum master notices an increase in the scope or story points. What happened? The Scrum team increased the scope of the sprint, and this was then reflected on the burndown chart. The Scrum master investigates the circumstances and discovers that a story was misinterpreted by the Scrum team and a small amount of effort was added to the sprint. The Scrum master and product owner now need to consider whether the work planned for the sprint is achievable. It is decided that an end-of-day 7 status check will be required to assess the Scrum team's progress towards achieving the new point total of 47 within the 2-week sprint.

Figure 3.26 A sprint burndown chart in practice (*Continued*)

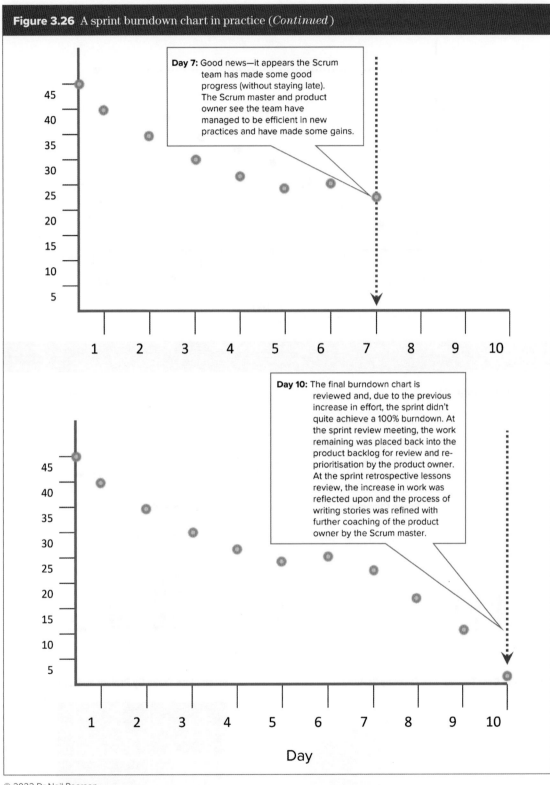

Day 7: Good news—it appears the Scrum team has made some good progress (without staying late). The Scrum master and product owner see the team have managed to be efficient in new practices and have made some gains.

Day 10: The final burndown chart is reviewed and, due to the previous increase in effort, the sprint didn't quite achieve a 100% burndown. At the sprint review meeting, the work remaining was placed back into the product backlog for review and re-prioritisation by the product owner. At the sprint retrospective lessons review, the increase in work was reflected upon and the process of writing stories was refined with further coaching of the product owner by the Scrum master.

Day

3.5.8 Sprint velocity

Another useful metric to track is the sprint velocity. This is simply the number of story points achieved at the end of the sprint. If this metric is tracked over several sprints, it can help to inform (sometimes very accurately, if the sprints are of the same nature) the amount of work that can go into a sprint during sprint planning.

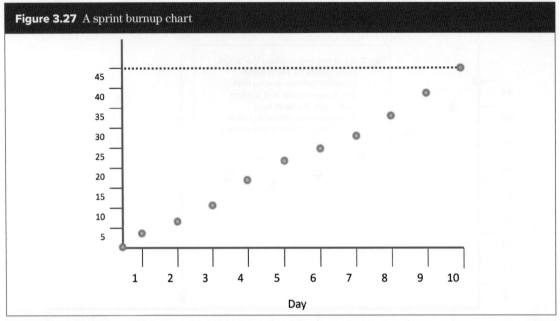

Figure 3.27 A sprint burnup chart

© 2022 Dr Neil Pearson

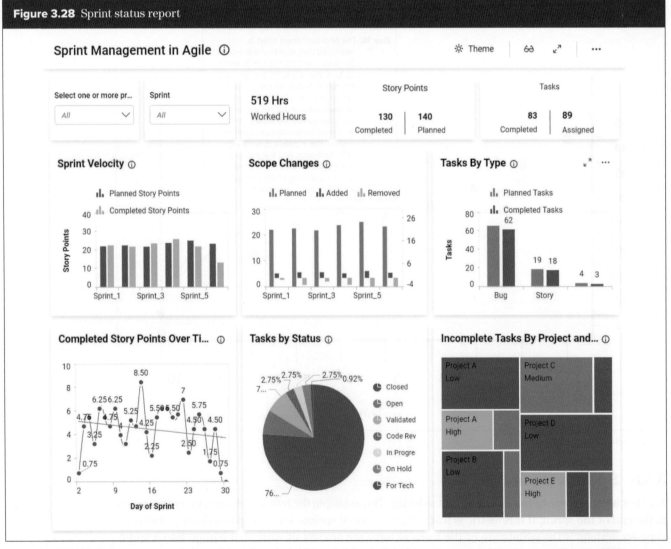

Figure 3.28 Sprint status report

Source: Bold BI 2022, "Sprint management dashboard", https://samples.boldbi.com/solutions/agile/sprint-management-dashboard, accessed February 2022

Figure 3.29 shows the average sprint velocity across a number of sprints. The resulting sprint velocity number would be used to inform the number of story points that can be included in a sprint in future sprint planning meetings.

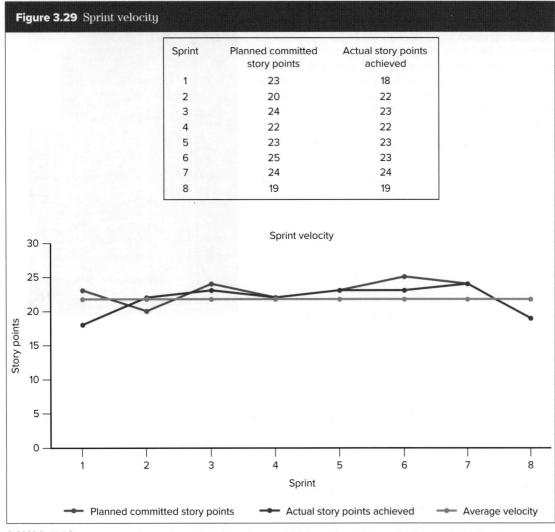

Figure 3.29 Sprint velocity

Sprint	Planned committed story points	Actual story points achieved
1	23	18
2	20	22
3	24	23
4	22	22
5	23	23
6	25	23
7	24	24
8	19	19

© 2022 Dr Neil Pearson

"Snapshot from Practice: Suncorp's adoption of Agile methods" illustrates the use of Agile at Suncorp Bank, Australia. The reader should now be familiar with the terminology used.

SNAPSHOT *from* PRACTICE : Suncorp's adoption of Agile methods

Suncorp is a banking and insurance company that has its headquarters in Brisbane, Australia (Figure 3.30). The company employs more than 16 000 people and has over 7 million customers and an AUD8 billion asset base.

Suncorp started its transition across the company to the Agile approach to project management in 2007, with the arrival of a new Chief Information Officer, Jeff Smith.

With over 4000 people employed in the ICT department alone, Agile became "the way we work around here" where previously a heavyweight *Waterfall*, approach had been used. In support of its Agile implementation, Suncorp invested in an Agile:

■ change program to change-manage the introduction of Agile into and across the business

■ education program to develop the skills required (enabled via The Agile Academy, an external training organisation specialising in the Agile approach)

(Continues)

Snapshot from Practice: Suncorp's adoption of Agile methods (*Continued*)

■ coaching and mentoring programs to build on existing skills and to leverage benefits from experienced practitioners (Couzens 2009).

Figure 3.30 Suncorp headquarters in Brisbane

An example of the Agile approach being applied within Suncorp appears in Case Study: Standardised Enterprise Bargaining Agreements (Presence of IT n.d.). The project was to standardise enterprise bargaining agreements using Agile and set out to merge eight agreements into one single agreement, subsequently translating the single agreement into the PeopleSoft Human Capital Management (v9) system. Some of the recognised benefits of taking an Agile approach to this project included:

1. flexibility—reducing the risk of delays caused by changes in business requirements

2. management of unknowns—components with uncertain requirements can be developed last to allow maximum time for clarification

3. facilitating the incremental testing of changes

4. more efficient use of resources—streams can operate in parallel (Presence of IT n.d.).

The team used key aspects of Agile during implementation, including:

■ incorporating the customer as part of the Agile product team

■ including the business subject matter expert (SME) as part of the team, ensuring that any changing requirements were met in a timely and practical fashion. The SME was able to influence what features were added, changed or removed based on priority and value. The SME gained insight into project complexities and was able to inform business decisions

■ writing requirements as acceptance tests before coding commenced

■ ensuring acceptance criteria were agreed with the SME, and a representative of each team role, at the time of elaboration. This ensured that business, development, testing, processing and communication perspectives were raised and addressed to find the best-fit solution

■ automated testing where possible

■ writing independent testing and verification scripts alongside the code-line development to support traditional testing methods. This was critical in building a repeatable suite that could be used for the iterative nature of the Agile methodology

■ negotiating schedules rather than assigning them

■ iteration planning to give the business a chance to determine the work to be completed in the next iteration and allowed for course correction. The entire team participated in the sessions, and was encouraged to identify risks, dependencies, and bottlenecks. The team then committed to the work identified (Presence of IT n.d.).

The great success of Agile within Suncorp is evident not only from a customer's perspective in the innovative products and services that have been brought to market, but also in the many positive press articles reported in trade and professional magazines across Australia.

Sources: Couzens JA 2009, 'Implementing an enterprise system at Suncorp using Agile development', www.agileacademy.com.au/agile/sites/default/files/ASWEC2009-IndustryPaperJamesCouzens.pdf, accessed December 2012; Presence of IT n.d., 'Suncorp standardized EB agreements using Agile', www.presenceofit.com.au/case-studies/suncorp-standardised-eb-agreements-using-agile, accessed December 2012

3.6 | **Scrum and procurement**

As we know, there is a stark difference between the approach of predictive project management (i.e. the PMI's approach) and that of Scrum/Agile (adaptive) project management. One key difference that has affected the way contracts are developed and applied is the lack of firm up-front requirements. When requirements are only agreed for inclusion in the sprint at the sprint planning meeting and, at this point, the contracting supplier is being issued with the work, how can a contract be formed? Even if the supplier was consulted at the outset when an emerging product backlog was being developed (before any epics, increments or sprints were outlined), the supplier still does not know what will end up in the sprint until the sprint planning meeting has taken place. This uncertainty (risk) is one of the key drivers to changing relationships that organisations have to accommodate when moving to an Agile approach. Listed below are some of the dynamics that need to be considered when building contracts for an adaptive approach towards outsourcing the sprint development activities.

1. Involve the supplier early on as this helps to foster trust. Although there can be no guarantee about the total amount of work that will be contracted out, the supplier can be engaged on the premise that whatever work is carried out, they will be the selected supplier.

2. Sprint goals are useful for driving performance: consider how measures of success can inform reward (pay) (e.g. the number of stories completed to quality acceptance criteria).

3. Risk/reward is shared between the organisation and the supplier in equal proportions. Rewards (savings) are shared back with the project, and risks realised are appropriately shared between the project and supplier according to predetermined criteria.

4. Access by the supplier to various stakeholders in the business can be a sticking point. As this situation can quickly cause delays within a sprint, the conditions of access need to be defined very carefully.

5. Scrum projects are liable to fail faster—feedback to the business is immediate at the sprint review and the next sprint may not go ahead based on the changing business environment. If there is the possibility that a supplier will be providing services for only a short period of time, the standard clauses of contract termination may now need adjusting.

6. Consider evolving new contract types, such as:

   ■ Capped time and materials: This is a modified time and materials (T&M) contract, where a fixed agreed upper cap is placed on the contract. The supplier benefits in being able to recover up-front expense early on in charges, and the organisation benefits by having a cap on costs.

   ■ Cost targeted contracts: A realistic price for the final product is agreed up-front. Work is paid based on this final price. These types of contracts are more often used in the manufacturing and construction industries but could be adapted for use in an Agile (Scrum) project.

   ■ Modified piece work: Not in the realms of turn-of-the-century Victorian industry, but a price associated with story points, or a sprint/increment (of a standard duration).

Generally, because of the unknown duration of a Scrum (Agile) project in total, do not be surprised if a risk/reward arrangement cannot be entered into, and that you as an organisation may be paying inflated prices to cover the risk of the potential short-term nature of the project from sprint to sprint. The outsourcing or contracting out of sprint development work is an evolving area of the Scrum (Agile) approach to project management; the reader is encouraged to search the internet for current practices in this area.

3.7   Agile under PRINCE2 and PMBOK

Although the ultimate would be to adopt Scrum in its purest form—to really drive value from the adaptiveness of the framework—in reality this is often not practical. It is for this reason that we often see the terms *TAgile* and *WAgile* bandied about. TAgile is the combination of traditional project management and Agile used together from a project management perspective. WAgile is often used from a development perspective, blending the waterfall method of software development with Agile techniques. As this text does not cover the development realm, we will focus on the project management phrase: TAgile.

Enhancements have occurred in recent years to both **PRINCE2** and the PMI's *Guide to the Project Management Body of Knowledge* (*PMBOK® Guide*) (PMI 2017a), which cover the use of Agile within their respective approaches. Hence, the term *TAgile* has emerged.

The following sections consider how the PMBOK and PRINCE2 each consider Agile within their respective predictive frameworks, where the majority of up-front planning is carried out.

Generally, for projects with:

1. a low degree of change and an infrequent delivery, we would adopt predictive approaches
2. a low degree of change and frequent delivery, we would adopt incremental approaches
3. a high degree of change and an infrequent delivery, we would adopt iterative approaches
4. a high degree of change and frequent delivery, we would adopt an Agile approach.

Refer to Chapter 2 "Popular frameworks and methodologies" for definitions of predictive, incremental and adaptive approaches.

Table 3.5 indicates which approach is more commonly applied.

Table 3.5 The life cycle continuum

	Frequency of delivery		Technical degree of uncertainty		Requirements uncertainty	
	High ◄————► Low		High ◄————► Low		High ◄————► Low	
Predictive		●		●		●
Incremental	●			●		●	
Adaptive (iterative)	●			●		●	
Hybrid	●			●		●	

© 2022 Dr Neil Pearson

3.7.1 **PMBOK and Agile**

In the *PMBOK® Guide* 2021, the three distinct life cycles introduced in Chapter 2 "Popular frameworks and methodologies" are now confirmed: predictive, incremental and adaptive (or iterative); the latter has been the focus of this chapter. However, as also mentioned in Chapter 2, numerous organisations are actually creating hybrid life cycles based on combinations of these life cycles.

One of the most common hybrid combinations is to carry out predictive Initiation and Planning, followed by iterative Execution. Refer to "Snapshot from Practice: Queensland Tertiary Admissions Centre—a hybrid approach" for an example of such a hybrid combination.

SNAPSHOT *from* PRACTICE : **Queensland Tertiary Admissions Centre—a hybrid approach**

The Queensland Tertiary Admissions Centre (QTAC) operates a centralised tertiary application service for:

1. publicly funded Queensland universities
2. Bond University's medical program
3. TAFE Queensland
4. the Australian Maritime College
5. some courses at publicly funded universities in Northern New South Wales
6. some private tertiary education providers.

Over the past three years, QTAC has invested in the replacement of legacy systems and has also invested in a program of redevelopment and enhancement to meet the demands of a changing business environment. A program was established using a largely traditional approach, initiated by the development of a comprehensive feasibility analysis and Business Case.

The approach involved initially taking a traditional project management approach. Initial requirement elicitation produced a detailed understanding of the *as-is* processes. The activity for redeveloping the legacy systems supporting these processes and updates to the process and other new enhancements to the systems were moved into a more Agile manner of working.

Development teams were formed to take subsets (the sprint backlog) of the prioritised list of *to-be* requirements (the product backlog) to build increments of potentially shippable product. Depending on the subset of stories in the sprint, this determined the mix of resources employed in each Scrum team. The Scrum teams typically comprised multi-skilled workers who were capable of refining requirements, coding, testing and implementing the product.

Modules of shippable product were implemented once understanding and momentum in the business had been gained using an Agile approach. These shippable products ranged in scope from complete modules (replacing elements of legacy systems) and enhancements to processes (and systems) through to modules enabling new functionality to end-users of QTAC's systems—a truly successful implementation of traditional and Agile approaches working together.

3.7.2 **PRINCE2 Agile**

PRINCE2 is a popular, globally expanding, structured project management method. Since its release in 2015, the Agile version of PRINCE2 has gained a significant following. PRINCE2 and Agile are both seen as having strengths as individual approaches to project management. However, contemporary thinking recognises that the two approaches complement each other and can be used to create a holistic approach towards managing projects, in an Agile way.

The strength of PRINCE2 particularly lies in the areas of project direction and project management. However, it is generally now viewed as having little focus on the field of product delivery. Conversely, Agile has a strong focus on product delivery, but relatively little focus on project direction and project management. When used in tandem, and therefore in a more holistic, TAgile way, the strengths of each can be drawn upon at the relative stages of a project. As illustrated in Figure 3.31, PRINCE2's

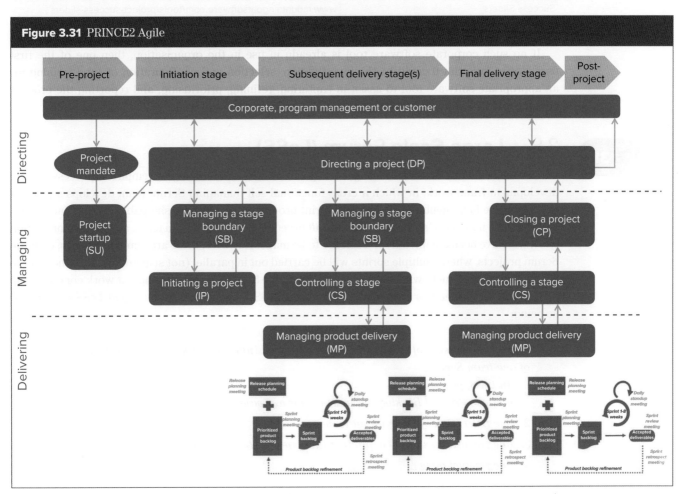

Figure 3.31 PRINCE2 Agile

directing and *managing* aspects are largely retained, with the inclusion of Agile (sprints) for the *delivery* aspects of the project.

3.7.3 Agile/Scrum software tools

As indicated in Figure 3.23, *visual management* is a key concept of Agile (Scrum) that has been adopted from lean management concepts. It is sometimes referred to as a *Kanban board*. However, as discussed earlier in this chapter, when the Scrum team is geographically dispersed or there are many dozens of PBIs to manage, using manual techniques such as physical story cards may not be possible. Therefore, the use of software tools to assist the product owner in maintaining the product backlog, and help the Scrum team in the breakdown of stories on the sprint backlog, may be required.

At the time of writing, there are dozens of software tools in circulation that can facilitate these processes. They are (for the most part) fundamentally different tools to those used by a traditional project manager—you will, of course carry out your own research into such tools.

Table 3.6 highlights some of the Scrum/Agile-based tools that have successfully been used by the authors in past and current Agile/Scrum projects.

Table 3.6 Agile/Scrum tools

Tool	Link
Jira (Atlassian software)	www.atlassian.com/software/jira
Trello (Atlassian software)	www.atlassian.com/software/trello
Pivotaltracker	www.pivotaltracker.com
Scrumwise	www.Scrumwise.com/features.html
AgileScout	https://agilescout.com
Zepel	https://zepel.io/agile/reports/cumulative-flow-diagram/
Success Sliders	www.mountaingoatsoftware.com/tools/project-success-sliders

© 2022 Dr Neil Pearson

If no such corporate software tool is already in use in the organisation, then one of the first user stories in Sprint 0 could be the investigation, selection and configuration of (and training in) an appropriate software tool to assist in capturing, refining, prioritising, and reporting the product backlog and PBIs, release schedule and sprint backlog for example.

3.8 | Large-Scale Scrum (LeSS)

Ken Schwaber and Jeff Sutherland generally discuss Scrum as being an empirical-process-control development framework, in which a cross-functional self-managing Scrum team develops a product in an iterative incremental manner. Each sprint produces a potentially shippable product increment, and usually a number of sprints are carried out in sequence by one Scrum team, at which point enough work will have been completed for a release to be made. However, there are many occasions, on large Scrum projects, where multiple sprints will be carried out in parallel (not sequential), and where there will be multiple product owners involved, with multiple Scrum teams carrying out work concurrently.

To cater for the need for scalability in Scrum, the LeSS framework was developed. LeSS is described as being:

> *a scaled-up version of one-team Scrum, and it maintains many of the practices and ideas of one-team Scrum.*
>
> *In LeSS, you will find:*
> 1. *a single Product Backlog (because it's for a product, not a team),*
> 2. *one Definition of Done for all teams,*
> 3. *one potentially shippable product increment at the end of each sprint,*
> 4. *one product owner,*

5. *many complete, cross-functional teams (with no single-specialist teams)*,

6. *one Sprint* (LeSS.works 2018).

LeSS is truly scalable, being suitable for up to eight teams (of eight people each) while the LeSS Huge framework can operate for up to a few thousand people on one product.

Figure 3.32 provides a visual diagram of an increment (under a single accountable product owner) being developed though three parallel sprints. Additional complexity for the Scrum master comes in the form of interactions across the sprints, which must now be managed. Given the essence of Scrum, it is not necessary for the Scrum master to ensure integration takes place, but to empower the Scrum teams to integrate the components and communicate across the three parallel sprints with different Scrum teams. The Scrum master will of course assist in removing any relevant impediments raised (e.g. at the daily Scrum). The Scrum master will also attend each of the three different sprints' daily Scrums, ensuring these are scheduled at different times, of course.

In Figure 3.33, the Scrum environment is taken to a further level of complexity. There is still one product owner ultimately accountable for the product, but due to the size of the product, multiple

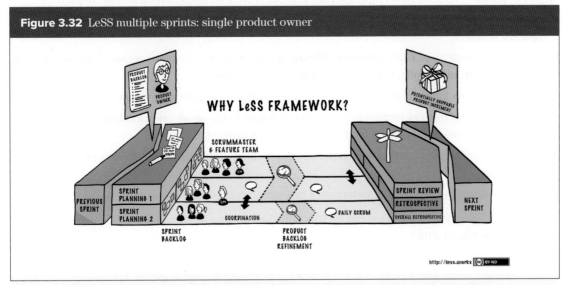

Figure 3.32 LeSS multiple sprints: single product owner

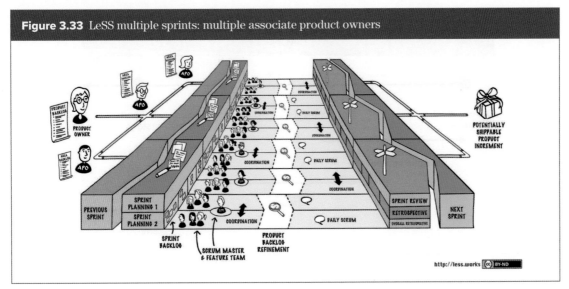

Figure 3.33 LeSS multiple sprints: multiple associate product owners

assistant product owners have been assigned who need to coordinate the master PBIs into the sprints, which are to deliver the required DoD (from each sprint and combined sprints).

The LeSS website provides a rich resource of information for more complex Scrum projects. Note that as with all things Scrum, complexity is managed by breaking tasks down into increments and sprints to deliver prioritised, high-value PBIs into potentially shippable product increments (releases).

3.9 | DevOps

DevOps is a relatively recent approach emerging from two related trends. It aims to unify software development (Dev) and software operation (Ops), which are traditionally two independent functions of an ICT department.

The need for DevOps arose from the increasing success of the Agile approach to software development, which led to Scrum teams releasing software quicker and more frequently. This in turn placed more pressure on the release and support functions. As illustrated in Figure 3.34, the three components are:

1. development—very much an Agile (Scrum/lean) approach as documented in this chapter

2. quality—leveraging process and practices of, for example, the International Software Testing Quality Board

3. operations—here an ICT infrastructure library approach to service management is often pursued, but in a lighter, more agile, manner. This approach is reported to:

   ■ make the development process more efficient, by linking software development to delivery

   ■ create more stable operating environments as issues in the production environment are identified sooner and pushed back into the DevOps process

   ■ improve team collaboration across the development, quality and service teams (serving the business)

   ■ reduce times to market in contemporary fast-paced competitive environments.

Further information on DevOps can be found at the DevOps Institute (www.devopsinstitute.com; Kim, Behr & Spafford 2016).

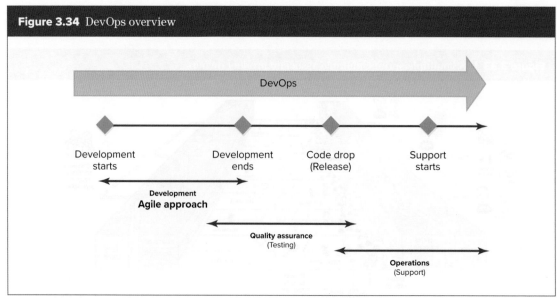

Figure 3.34 DevOps overview

Summary

This chapter has covered:

1. the history of Agile, starting with the origins of the new product development game, which later became the inspiration for Scrum

2. the Scrum framework, which includes the Scrum roles (product owner, Scrum master and Scrum team), events (the sprint, the sprint planning meeting, the daily Scrum, the sprint review and the sprint retrospective) and the artefacts (the product backlog, the sprint backlog, the burndown/burnup charts and the finished work)

3. a brief insight into how both the PMI and PRINCE2 have recognised and adopted Agile concepts into their respective approaches to project management

4. the acknowledgement that visual management (e.g. the Kanban board) is a key concept within the Agile approach. With geographically dispersed or complex projects, there may a requirement to use software Agile tools to assist with the management of an Agile approach

5. an overview of how Scrum can be scaled by applying the LeSS framework

6. how DevOps is taking elements of Scrum and integrating further with quality and operations to transform the traditional development through to production and services functions of an organisation.

Review questions

1. What are the Scrum roles and the key expectations of each?
2. What are the Scrum artefacts, and what is the purpose of each?
3. What are the Scrum events, when do they take place and what is the purpose of each event?
4. How could Scrum be integrated with predictive project management?
5. What does MoSCoW mean and how is it used?
6. What is the purpose of the Kanban or the Scrum board?
7. How long does a daily Scrum meeting take?
8. How long would a sprint review take for a two-week sprint?
9. What's the format for writing the front of story card?
10. What's on the back of the story card?
11. What does INVEST stand for?
12. What is a burndown and burnup chart used for?
13. What is sprint velocity and how is it leveraged in sprint planning?
14. What types of problems are Scrum projects best suited for?
15. What approach provides for the scalability of Scrum?
16. What are the three key elements of a DevOps environment?

Exercises

Sarah, the Human Resources Manager, is approached by the Scrum master, Fred. Fred has heard that the HR department is to undertake further development of the human resource management system, but all development is to take place using a Scrum (Agile) approach. Fred starts to outline what Sarah's duties as a product owner will be, including asking whether Sarah has a product roadmap. Sarah does not, but she does have lots to say in relation to what the business and internal customers (or users) of the system are saying, and the features the vendor is promising in the next release. Fred, being a proactive Scrum master, discusses the issues with Sarah and starts to draft a product roadmap (Figure 3.35) with her input, and suggests she continues developing with input from the business. At this first meeting, Fred has drafted a basic roadmap to capture Sarah's great ideas. On explaining the product backlog, Fred explains that in her work in producing the product roadmap, Sarah will initially feed the high-level stories for the product backlog, from which further detail will be added. Sarah now feels her ideas for the human resource management system are being listened to and makes a commitment to further develop and maintain the product roadmap.

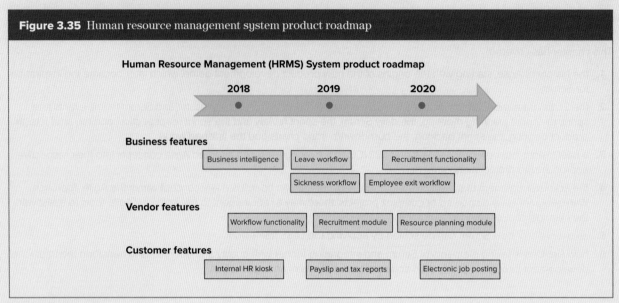

Figure 3.35 Human resource management system product roadmap

© 2022 Dr Neil Pearson

1. Using the above product roadmap with your own understanding of a human resource management system and any additional research, build a partial product backlog for a feature of your choosing.

2. Prioritise your product backlog using the MoSCoW technique.

3. From the prioritised product backlog, design an appropriate sprint backlog for 20 story points of effort including some tasks (as if you were part of a development team).

References

Agile Manifesto 2001a, "Manifesto for Agile software development", http://agilemanifesto.org, accessed February 2018.

Agile Manifesto 2001b, "Principles behind the Agile Manifesto), http://agilemanifesto.org/principles.html, accessed February 2018.

Atlantic Systems Guild 2009, "How now brown cow", https://www.volere.org/wp-content/uploads/2019/02/howNowBrownCow.pdf, accessed May 2022.

Axelos 2017, *Managing Successful Projects with PRINCE2,* 6th edition, Stationary Office, UK.

Bold BI 2022, 'Sprint management dashboard', https://samples.boldbi.com/solutions/agile/sprint-management-dashboard, accessed February 2022.

Couzens JA 2009, "Implementing an enterprise system at Suncorp using Agile development", www.agileacademy.com.au/agile/sites/default/files/ASWEC2009-IndustryPaperJamesCouzens.pdf, accessed December 2012.

Highsmith J 2009, *Agile Project Management: Creating Innovative Product,* 2nd edition, 2009 Addison-Wesley Professional.

Jeffries R 2001, "Essential XP: card, conversation, confirmation", https://xprogramming.com/articles/expcardconversationconfirmation/, accessed February 2018.

Kim D 2012, "The Agile triangle", Project management.com https://www.projectmanagement.com/blog/blogPostingView.cfm?blogPostingID=5325&thisPageURL=/blog-post/5325/The-Agile-Triangle#_=_, accessed March 2022.

Kim G, Behr K, Spafford G 2016, *The Phoenix Project: A Novel about IT, DevOps, and Helping Your Business Win',* IT Revolution Press.

LeSS Works 2018, "LeSS Framework", https://less.works/less/framework/index.html, accessed February 2018.

LeSS Works 2018, "LeSS Huge", https://less.works/less/less-huge/index.html, accessed February 2018.

Mountain Goat Software n.d., "Project success calculator", https://www.mountaingoatsoftware.com/uploads/blog/sliders3.jpg, accessed December 2021.

Paul D, Cadle J, Eva M, Rollason C, Hunsley J 2020, *Business Analysis,* 4th edition, BCS Learning & Development Ltd, Kindle Edition.

Presence of IT n.d., "Suncorp standardized EB agreements using Agile", www.presenceofit.com.au/case-studies/suncorp-standardised-eb-agreements-using-agile, accessed December 2012.

Project Management Institute (PMI) 2017a, *A Guide to the Project Management Body of Knowledge,* 6th edition, PMI.

Project Management Institute (PMI) 2017b, *Agile Practice Guide,* PMI.

Project Management Institute (PMI) 2021a, *A Guide to the Project Management Body of Knowledge (PMBOK® Guide),* 7th edition, Newton Square, PA.

Project Management Institute (PMI) 2021b, *The Standard for Project Management (ANSI/PMI 99-001-2021),* 7th edition, Newton Square, PA.

Schwaber K & Sutherland J 2020, *The Scrum Guide. The Definitive Guide to Scrum: The Rules of the Game,* https://scrumguides.org/docs/scrumguide/v2020/2020-Scrum-Guide-US.pdf#zoom=100, accessed December 2021.

Schwaber K & Sutherland J 2017, The Scrum Guide™, https://www.scrumguides.org/docs/scrumguide/v1/scrum-guide-us.pdf, accessed February 2018.

SCRUMStudy 2012, "Scrum flow", https://www.Scrumstudy.com/pdf/Scrumstudy%20Process%20Chart-2-%2018-10-2012.pdf, accessed December 2021.

Sutherland J, 1993. *Scrum: The Art of Doing Twice the Work in Half the Time,* Random House Business Books.

Takeuchi H & Nonaka I 1986, "The new new product development game", Harvard Business Review, January–February.

Tuckman B 1965, 'Developmental sequence in small groups', *Psychological Bulletin,* vol. 63, no. 6, pp. 384–99.

CHAPTER 4

Strategy, project selection and the Business Case

Learning elements

4A Gain an understanding of strategy, the Business Case and benefits as a project leader.

4B Further develop and understand the importance of the methods that define and align an organisation's project activity.

4C Understand the need for an investment Business Case, and the detailed contents of a Business Case, including the financial models and non-financial criteria.

4D Understand the features of portfolio management systems and the role of portfolio management.

4E Be able to create a benefit dependency map, profile benefits and key into the interactions between the benefits management process and project management process.

In this chapter

4.1 Introduction

4.2 Why project leaders need to understand strategy

4.3 An overview of the strategic management process

4.4 The need for an effective portfolio, program and project management system

4.5 An introduction to portfolio management

4.6 Applying a selection model

4.7 Managing the portfolio management system

4.8 Project portfolio management

4.9 Benefits management integration with project management

Summary

4.1 : Introduction

Strategy is (fundamentally) deciding how an organisation will deliver value to its customers in a competitive environment. Organisations use projects and programs to convert strategy into the new products, services and results needed for success. For example, the major strategy of Intel is one of differentiation. Its projects target innovation and time to market. Currently, Intel is directing its strategy towards specialty chips for products other than computers, such as cars, security, mobile phones, tablet computers and home automation. Another goal is to reduce project cycle times. Intel, Suncorp, General Electric, Samsung and Apple have reduced their product cycle times by 20 to 50 per cent (refer to Chapter 1 "Contemporary project management", Figure 1.8 "Product or service life cycle explained", for a discussion on product/service cycle times; for example, Apple brings to market semi-annually updated mobile phones). Projects and project management play the key role in supporting strategic goals. It is vital for project leaders to think—and act—strategically.

Aligning projects with the strategic goals of the organisation is crucial for project success. Today's economic climate is unprecedented in terms of rapid changes in technology, global competition, social cultures and financial uncertainty. These conditions make the quest for the strategic alignment of project activity even more essential for organisational success. Every major project needs to have a clear link to the organisation's Strategic Plan. The larger and more diverse an organisation, the more difficult it is to create and maintain this strong link. Ample evidence suggests that many organisations have not developed business processes that allow for the alignment of project selection with the strategic planning processes, which will result in poor use of the organisation's resources (e.g. people, financial and equipment). Conversely, organisations that have a coherent link of projects (investments) to strategy tend to have more cooperation across the organisation, perform better, have fewer failures and can react more decisively if an unforeseen shift in their external environment occurs.

How can an organisation ensure this link and alignment? The answer involves the alignment of projects to the Strategic Plan—or, more logically, the top-down approach, where the Strategic Plan gives rise to the need for portfolios, with programs and projects that will deliver the strategy. Integration assumes the existence of a Strategic Plan and a process for prioritising investments to deliver that plan. A crucial factor to ensure the success of integrating the plan with projects lies in the creation of a process that is open and transparent for all participants to review.

This chapter presents an overview of the importance of strategic planning and the links the project leader should be able to clearly describe for the projects under their leadership. Problems that are typically encountered when strategy and projects are not linked are discussed. A generic methodology that ensures integration—by creating strong linkages of project selection and priority to the Strategic Plan—is also discussed. The intended outcomes are a clear organisational focus, best use of scarce organisational resources (people, equipment, resources and capital) and improved coordination and communication across projects and departments.

4.2 : Why project leaders need to understand strategy

Project management has (historically) been preoccupied solely with the planning and execution of projects. Strategy was considered to be under the purview of senior management. However, this is old-school thinking. New-school thinking recognises that project management is a key enabler of strategy. It is the authors' belief that strategy is executed through the delivery of the organisation's portfolios, programs and projects.

There are two main reasons why project leaders need to understand their organisation's mission, vision, values and strategic objectives.

The first reason is so they can make appropriate decisions and adjustments. For example, how a project leader would respond to a suggestion to modify the design of a product to enhance performance will vary depending upon whether their company strives to be a product leader through innovation, or to achieve operational excellence through low-cost solutions. Similarly, how a project leader responds to delays may vary depending upon strategic concerns. A project leader will authorise overtime if their organisation places a premium on getting the product or service to market first, whereas a different project leader may accept the delay if speed is not essential.

JP Descamps (1999) observed that project leaders who do not understand the role their project plays in accomplishing the strategy of their organisation tend to make serious mistakes, such as:

- focusing on problems or solutions that have low priority strategically
- focusing on the immediate customer rather than the whole marketplace and value chain
- over-emphasising technology as an end in, and of, itself, resulting in projects that pursue exotic technology that does not fit the strategy or customer needs
- trying to solve every customer issue with a product or service rather than focusing on the features the customer persona truly values
- engaging in a never-ending search for perfection that no-one except the project team really cares about.

The second reason project leaders need to understand their organisation's strategy is so they can be effective project advocates—that is, they understand why the project has been given to them and the significance it has in contributing to the organisation's strategy. Protection and continued support come from being aligned with corporate objectives. Project leaders also need to be able to explain to team members and other stakeholders why certain project objectives and priorities are critical. This is essential for getting buy-in on contentious trade-off decisions. For these reasons, project leaders will find it valuable to have a keen understanding of strategic management and of project selection processes.

4.3 | An overview of the strategic management process

Strategic management is the process of assessing *what we are* and deciding and implementing *what we intend to be* and *how we are going to get there*. Strategy describes how an organisation intends to compete with the resources available in the existing and perceived future environment. This could be visualised using an extremely high-level *as-is* (current) state and *to-be* (future) state diagram (Figure 4.1).

As Figure 4.1 illustrates, it is the astute choice and subsequent successful implementation of investments that move the business from the **current state** to a **future state**; this state of play will be unpacked in this chapter.

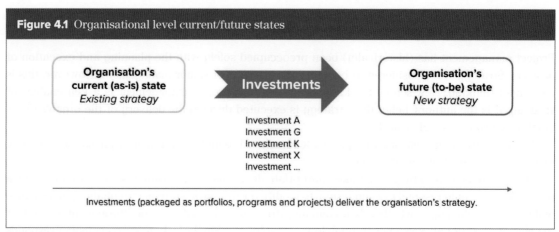

Figure 4.1 Organisational level current/future states

Organisation's current (as-is) state
Existing strategy

Investments

Organisation's future (to-be) state
New strategy

Investment A
Investment G
Investment K
Investment X
Investment ...

Investments (packaged as portfolios, programs and projects) deliver the organisation's strategy.

The three dimensions important to strategic management are:

1. responding to changes in the external environment, including the competition
2. allocating the organisation's scarce resources internally to improve its competitive position
3. intimately understanding the customer and the value being added by the organisation to deliver this value proposition to the customer.

Constant scanning of the external environment for changes is the first requirement for survival in a dynamic, competitive environment. The second requirement is to ensure there are internal responses (programs and projects) that are aimed at enhancing the competitive position of the organisation. The nature of the responses depends on the type of business, environment volatility, competition and the organisational culture.

Strategic management provides the theme and focus of the future direction of the organisation. It supports consistency of action at every level of the organisation. It encourages integration because effort and resources are committed to common goals and strategies. It is a continuous, iterative process, aimed at developing an integrated and coordinated long-term plan of action. Strategic management *positions* the organisation to meet the needs and requirements of its customers for the long term. With the long-term position identified, objectives are set and strategies are developed to achieve these objectives, which are then translated into actions by implementing programs and projects. Strategy can decide the survival of an organisation. Most organisations are successful in formulating strategies for what course(s) they should pursue. However, the problem in many organisations is implementing strategies—that is, making them happen. Moving from strategy formulation to strategy implementation (execution) can be the Achilles' heel of organisations. The components of strategic management are closely linked, and all are directed towards the future success of the organisation.

Strategic management requires strong links among vision, mission, objectives, strategies and tactics (business plans and the projects that deliver them). The vision gives the aspirational long-term desires of the organisation. The mission brings this into focus and makes it more practical. Strategic objectives provide organisational measures and targets within the mission. The objectives require actions to be implemented; this is achieved through the definition of general strategies (e.g. improve customer service), which is delivered through tactics (build a website, implement a free call number, improve engagement processes). These are potentially programs and projects, which, when delivered, ultimately deliver the objectives and therefore move the organisation towards its mission and vision.

Figure 4.2 shows a schematic of a simple strategic management process and major activities undertaken from a program and project perspective.

A typical sequence of activities within the strategic to portfolio management process includes (refer to Figure 4.2):

1. What value are we adding to our customers' experience? Activities include:
   - external analysis of the external environment; popular techniques are the PESTEL (external environment analysis) and Porter's 5 Forces (competitor market analysis)
   - looking at the value chain for the customer (i.e. what identified activities directly add value to the customers' experience)
   - looking internally at the resources (people, plant and machinery) of the organisation. Verifying whether these enable the delivery of value to the customer.

   From a detailed analysis of these three areas a determination of the organisation's future strategic state can be made in the form of a revised Strategic Plan (mission, vison, values and customer value proposition).

2. What is our focus to deliver this value? Activities include:
   - definition of supporting strategic objectives and key performance indicators (KPIs) to measure our journey towards achieving the revised strategy
   - high-level tactics (and strategies) that will deliver the organisation's strategy (vision, mission and customer value proposition).

Figure 4.2 Strategic management process

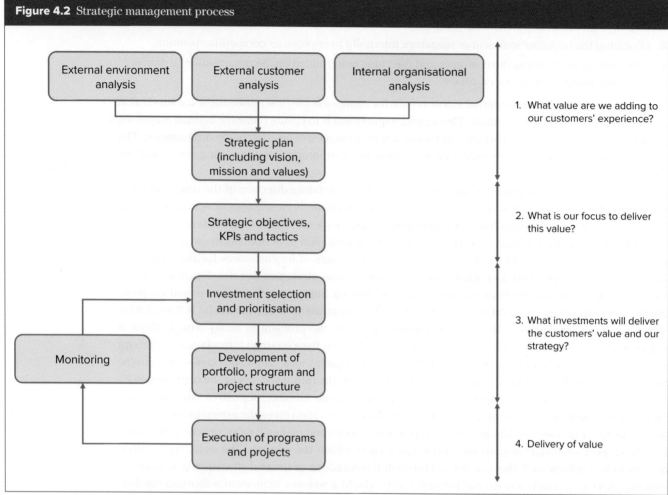

© 2022 Dr Neil Pearson

3. **What investments will deliver value to the customers and realise our strategy?** Activities include:
   - drafting the initial portfolio and of investments and their supporting business cases
   - structuring this investment activity as portfolios, programs and projects so that the tactics can be delivered through a piece of project work. PMI describes this as a part of their system for value delivery (PMI 2021a, p. 8).

4. **Delivery of value.** Activities include:
   - executing the programs and projects
   - monitoring project delivery to ensure the Business Case and value are delivered.

Some of the above terminology is explained further in this chapter. The project leader should be able to use the elements of Figure 4.2 to tell the strategic story of why they are working on their project: this makes a good door-opener with senior stakeholders in the project—even an elevator pitch for the project!

4.3.1 Define and review the organisation's vision, mission and values

The *vision statement* sets the long-term vision of the organisation and how the organisation will be seen within that industry. A mission statement differs from the more aspirational vision statement. The *mission statement* identifies *what we want to become*. Mission statements identify the scope of the organisation in terms of its product or service. A written mission statement provides focus for decision-making when shared by organisational managers and employees. Everyone in the organisation should be clearly aware of its mission and how their role relates to its delivery. The mission statement communicates and identifies the purpose of the organisation to all stakeholders. Mission statements can be used for evaluating organisational performance.

Traditional components of mission statements are major products and services, target customers and markets, and the geographic domain. In addition, statements frequently include the organisation's philosophy, key technologies, public image and contribution to society. Including such factors in mission statements relates directly to business success. Mission statements change relatively infrequently; however, when the nature of the business changes or shifts, a revised mission statement may be required. For example, Steve Jobs (of Apple) envisioned the use of computer technology beyond the personal desktop computer. His mission was to look at computer technology as the vehicle for work and entertainment. As a result, the iPod was developed for selling music. Jobs also masterminded the development of animated movies such as *Toy Story, Finding Nemo* and others through the Pixar organisation. See "Snapshot from Practice: Apple's strategy" to find out more about how Apple's mission shapes new product development projects.

Values are the traits (typically shared beliefs) the company wishes to see in its employees. If the company openly exhibits these values, this fosters positive connections with the customer and sets the standard of cultural interactions the customer can expect to engage in with the organisation (as well as the interactions of the employees internally). Formulating strategy answers the question of what the organisation wants to be, but not how to achieve these strategic objectives. Strategy formulation includes determining and evaluating alternatives that support the organisation's objectives and selecting the best option. The first step is a realistic evaluation of the past and current position of the enterprise. This step typically includes an analysis of who the customers are and their needs are (as the customers see them). This step often includes an assessment of the internal and external environments.

What are the internal strengths and weaknesses of the enterprise, and the external threats and opportunities? A SWOT (internal strengths and weaknesses, external opportunities and threats) analysis is the starting place for exploring these questions. Examples of internal strengths and weaknesses could include core competencies such as technology, product quality, management talent, low debt and dealer networks. Managers can alter (change and influence) internal strengths and weaknesses. Opportunities and threats usually act as external forces for change, such as advancement of technology, industry and competition. To help us understand the implications of SWOT, a TOWS (SWOT backwards) analysis is often carried out. Competitive benchmarking tools are sometimes used to assess current and future directions. Opportunities and threats are the flip sides of each other. That is, a threat can be perceived as an opportunity, or vice versa. Examples of perceived external threats could be a slowing of the economy, a maturing product life cycle, exchange rates or government regulation. Typical opportunities are increasing demand, emerging markets and demographics. Managers and individual organisations have limited opportunities to influence such external environmental factors. However, in recent years, notable exceptions have occurred, such as Apple using the iPhone to create a market to sell online music. The key is to attempt to forecast fundamental industry changes and to stay in a proactive mode rather than a reactive one.

SWOT is a basic strategic planning tool that can provide some perspective for an organisation to consider. Other tools you may have heard of (or used) include: PESTEL, TOWS, Porter's 5 Forces, Porters Value Chains, Blue Ocean Strategy, Kaplan and Norton's Strategy Maps and Balanced Scorecards, and value propositions—to name but a few. The authors encourage you to further research these areas as new approaches are constantly emerging.

Developing an organisation's vision, mission and values is often a complex process. When agreed and promoted throughout the organisation, a focused clarity can be achieved for defining the business's purpose. This can lead to better results through the resulting tighter focus. Clear mission and vision statements decrease the chance of stakeholders taking the wrong direction, customers making incorrect interpretations of them and employees misunderstanding them.

SNAPSHOT *from* PRACTICE   Apple's strategy

When Steve Jobs returned to Apple Computers as its CEO in 1997, he became strikingly successful in developing a turnaround strategy that developed new markets and increased market share. It all began with a strict adherence to the mission statement:

Figure 4.3 Apple devices

Apple is committed to bringing the best personal computing experience to students, educators, creative professionals, and consumers around the world through its innovative hardware, software, and service offerings.

The thrust of this turnaround strategy included mass customisation and targeting market segments. Apple's primary competitive advantage is that it controls both the hardware and software aspects of most of its products. The vision, coupled with this strong strategic advantage, allows Apple to offer innovation in hardware, software and service offerings. Many product strategies were forged from their vision statement. For example, Jobs first segmented Apple's market into *consumer* and *professional*. This segmentation reduced the number of products and sharply targeted products to specific end-users (Figure 4.3). Several specific strategies were developed for the consumer market: for example, iTunes allows users to collate a digital library of music and other media from their personal computer. Users can use iTunes to sync their music files across multiple devices, stored in the cloud and supplemented with purchased music from Apple's music store.

Apple's competitive advantages provide strong support for its product strategies. Some of the more obvious are:

- control over both hardware and software (avoids compatibility problems)
- high quality and innovation
- common architecture (which fits most products and eases development time)
- free software
- ease of use
- a loyal customer base.

For over 10 years, the array of innovative products and services released by Apple Inc. has been spectacular (and there appears to be no end). Each new product and service closely aligns with Apple's mission statement and current strategies. Launching new products in new markets requires executing projects within tight time, cost and scope constraints, and Apple appears to understand this approach, whether delivered via predictive or, more likely, adaptive (iterative) approaches. The key to Apple's success is knowing the full extent of the value chain to the customer and having the financial and other resources to be able to deliver and exceed the customers' expectations.

4.3.2 Set the organisation's strategic objectives

Strategic objectives translate the organisation's mission and vision into specific, concrete, measurable terms. Strategic objectives establish the organisational level measures and targets, subsequently cascaded into the lower levels of the organisation. Objectives pinpoint the direction managers believe the organisation should move towards. Objectives answer in detail where an organisation is headed and when it is going to get there, and with what level of improvement (measured). Typically, objectives for the organisation cover markets, products, innovation, productivity, quality, finance, profitability, employees and consumers. In every case, objectives should be as specific as possible. That is, objectives should include a timeframe and be measurable and be realistic.

Each level below the organisational objectives should support the higher-level objectives in more detail; this is frequently called *cascading* of objectives. For example, if an organisation making leather luggage sets an objective of achieving a 40 per cent increase in sales through a research and development (R&D) strategy, this charge is passed to the marketing, production and other departments (often via KPIs). The R&D department accepts the organisation's strategy as its objective, and its strategy becomes the design and development of (for example) a new pull-type luggage case with hidden retractable wheels and GPS location tracking.

It is useful to apply the SMARTA technique when defining strategic objectives. Objectives written using SMARTA (refer to Table 4.1) give rise to clear statements that progress can be tracked against, for example, to see how the organisation's programs and projects are positively moving the organisation towards its mission. The objective suggested above, *achieving a 40 per cent increase in sales through an R&D strategy*, might be refined to *achieving a 40 per cent increase in sales on a baseline of AUD50 million through an R&D strategy, bringing at least two new products to market, to be achieved within the 2023–24 financial year.*

Table 4.1 SMARTA characteristics of strategic objectives

S	Specific	Be specific in targeting an objective. Don't describe multiple objectives as one objective; separate them out into individual objectives.
M	Measurable	Establish a measurable indicator(s) of progress (preferably with a baseline, so the improvement that has been delivered can be assessed later).
A	Assignable	Make the objective assignable to one group of people for completion.
R	Realistic	State what can realistically be achieved by the investment. This is a business reality check.
T	Time-bound	State when the objective can be achieved. That is, the duration/date it is to be achieved by.
A	Agreed	By all those accountable.

© 2022 Dr Neil Pearson

A critical analysis of the strategies involves asking questions such as:

1. Does the strategy take advantage of our core competencies?
2. Does the strategy exploit our competitive advantage?
3. Does the strategy deliver on the value proposition and does the value proposition deliver what the customer wants?
4. Does the strategy fit within our acceptable corporate risk tolerances?

Once the strategic objectives are clarified, socialisation of these (along with the vision, mission and values) takes place. This cascading of strategy represents an important stage in ensuring a consistent understanding of where the organisation is going, and what each individual's role is in delivering the strategy.

4.3.3 **From strategy to project**

From this analysis, critical issues and a portfolio of strategic alternative investment areas are identified. These alternatives are compared with the current portfolio and available resources. The portfolio of investments identified in support of the strategic objectives is a result of a complex process, potentially involving a line-up of business managers, program managers and other subject matter experts.

A typical process for what is being described here can be found in Figure 4.4. Some organisations will initiate an investment appraisal Business Case (Level 0) in support of these identified investment areas. The Business Case development starts in this step; it continues in the steps described in the next section. A typical investment Business Case so-called *table of contents* will contain elements such as:

- *Strategic alignment criteria* detailing exactly what strategic objectives the investment aligns to and, when delivered, how much it will contribute (e.g. what is the expected impact on the KPIs if the investment is delivered?).
- *Definition of the business problem* being solved, and identification of constraints and assumptions made in developing the Business Case.
- *Benefits identification and analysis* with the inclusion of a **benefit–cost ratio (BCR)** calculation.

Figure 4.4 From strategy to project

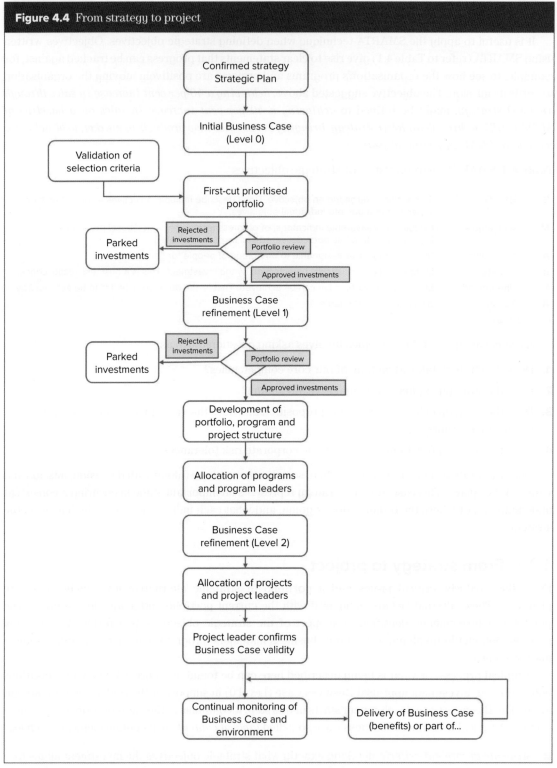

Confirmed strategy
Strategic Plan

Initial Business Case
(Level 0)

Validation of
selection criteria

First-cut prioritised
portfolio

Rejected
investments

Parked
investments

Portfolio review

Approved investments

Business Case
refinement (Level 1)

Rejected
investments

Parked
investments

Portfolio review

Approved investments

Development of
portfolio, program and
project structure

Allocation of programs
and program leaders

Business Case
refinement (Level 2)

Allocation of projects
and project leaders

Project leader confirms
Business Case validity

Continual monitoring of
Business Case and
environment

Delivery of Business Case
(benefits) or part of...

© 2022 Dr Neil Pearson

- *Options analysis* including the do nothing option, the deferred option (e.g. we continue as is for six months and then do something), and usually three other options, highlighting the recommended option (i.e. recommended above the other options presented).
- *Business risk analysis* examining how the investment stacks up against the organisational risk context and the business risks identified.

- *Organisational change management assessment*, maybe using a high-level assessment tool such as Lewin's force field analysis (discussed in Chapter 5 "Organisational change management and cultures").

- *Funding summary* indicating how and from where the investment will be funded and detailing what the estimated cost and return on the investment will be, often accompanied by **payback**, **net present value (NPV)**, **internal rate of return (IRR)** and BCR calculations for each option considered.

Note: The Business Case table of contents is explored in more detail later in this chapter.

Once the Business Case has been prepared for each investment area, a validation check will ensure there is continued alignment between the strategic objectives and the investment areas. After receiving appropriate approvals from the executive level, the investment Business Case is carried forward into the next stage.

Many organisations, as illustrated in Figure 4.4, denote different levels of detail in the Business Case as it progresses further down the investment selection process. For example:

- level 0—strategic high level, indicative with a wide basis for estimates

- level 1—confirmed facts and details sought as time is committed to expand the business case further

- level 2—detailed Business Case—this is what the piece of work (program or project) intends to deliver against.

The New South Wales Treasury and Queensland Treasury both give good examples of Business Case development on their websites.

4.3.4 Implement strategies through portfolios, programs and projects

Implementation answers the question of how strategies will be realised, given available resources, equipment, organisational change tolerance and a host of other factors. The conceptual framework around strategy implementation can often lack the structure and discipline found in strategy formulation. Implementation requires the actioning and completion of pieces of work; the latter frequently means mission-critical projects, meaning that implementation must include attention to five key areas.

1. Completing work will require allocating resources: Resources could include combinations of, for example, funds, people, management talents, technological competencies, raw material availability, plant and equipment. Frequently, the implementation of projects is treated as an addendum rather than an integral part of the strategic management process. However, multiple objectives (operational, strategic and mandatory) place conflicting demands on organisational resources.

2. Implementation requires a formal organisation structure that complements and supports strategy and projects: Authority, responsibility and performance all depend on organisational structure and culture. As the saying goes, "structure follows strategy".

3. Planning and control systems must be in place to be certain that project and program activities are effectively performed, monitored and subsequently achieved.

4. Motivating project contributors will be a major factor for achieving project/program success (e.g. project sponsor selection, consideration of organisational change management and the alignment to the value proposition and strategic statements).

5. An area receiving more attention in recent years is prioritising investments so that when delivered as programs and projects, the project leader knows how they are supporting the delivery of the organisation's strategy.

Although the strategy implementation process is not as clear as strategy formulation, all good managers realise that success is impossible without a solid implementation process.

This section is summarised in Figure 4.5, where the linkages between the organisation's external environment, strategy, portfolios, programs and projects are illustrated. Also shown are some of the tools that can be applied by a strategic analyst in crafting and monitoring strategy through to a project leader looking to confirm a Business Case is still valid before accepting and taking it forward to project chartering. Think of the Business Case as the foundations of a 120-storey block of apartments; without a solid foundation, everything will start to collapse!

Figure 4.5 Strategy alignment to projects, popular techniques

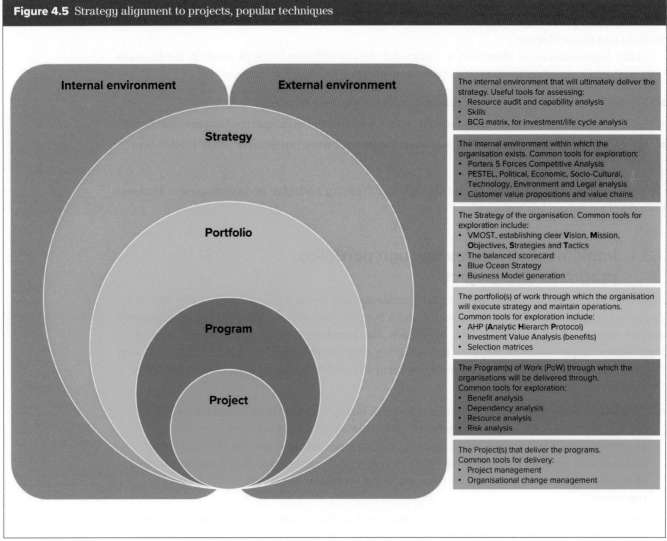

© 2022 Dr Neil Pearson

4.4 | The need for an effective portfolio, program and project management system

As indicated in Figure 4.4, the implementation of projects without a strong portfolio and program management system that is linked to strategy creates problems. Three of the most obvious problems are discussed on the following pages. A portfolio management system can go a long way to reduce, or even eliminate, the impact of these problems.

4.4.1 Problem 1: The implementation gap

In organisations with short product or service life cycles, it is interesting to note that repeated participation in frequent (quarterly) strategic planning and review meetings includes participants from all levels within the organisation. However, in perhaps 80 per cent of the remaining product and service organisations, top management generally formulates strategy and leaves strategy implementation to the functional managers.

The functional managers develop more detailed strategies and objectives within these broad constraints. The fact that objectives and strategies are made independently at different levels by functional groups within the organisation hierarchy causes multiple problems. Some symptoms that an organisation is struggling with *strategy disconnect* and unclear priorities are outlined below.

Conflicts (about conflicting priorities) frequently occur among functional managers and cause a lack of trust. Frequent meetings are called to establish or renegotiate priorities.

People frequently shift from one program/project to another, depending on the organisation's current priority. Employees are confused about which projects are therefore strategically important.

People are working on multiple projects and feel inefficient. There is an inadequate focus on achieving outcomes and outputs within planned timeframes and budgets. The scope of work changes on a frequent basis and no longer delivers the Business Case upon which the work was approved to take place in the first place.

Resources are not adequate to meet the demands of project and operational activities, and conflicts occur in trying to balance these limited resources across the two.

Because clear linkages do not exist, the organisational environment becomes dysfunctional and confused and there is ineffective implementation of organisational strategy, and thus of programs and projects that are to deliver it. The *implementation gap* refers to the lack of understanding and consensus on organisational strategy among top managers, middle-level managers and the employees who are responsible for delivering the work.

A common scenario is that top management picks its top (say, 20) projects for the next planning period, without priorities. Each functional department (marketing, finance, operations, engineering, information technology and human resources) selects projects from the list. Unfortunately, independent department priorities across projects are not homogenous. A project that rates first in the Information and Communications Technology (ICT) department rates tenth in the finance department. Implementation of the projects generates perceived conflicts of interest, and levels of animosity develop over organisational resources. If this kind of situation exists, how is it possible to effectively implement strategy? This type of situation is serious. It is the authors' experience that when consulting across many companies in many industries, there is frequently a misalignment between the strategic direction of a company and the work (investments, portfolios, programs and projects) taking place in the organisation.

Middle managers often consider organisational strategy to be under the purview of others, or not within their own realm of influence. It is the responsibility of senior management therefore to set policies that show a distinct link between organisational strategy and objectives and projects that implement those strategies.

4.4.2 Problem 2: Organisational politics

Politics exist in every organisation and can significantly influence which projects receive funding and high priority (and which do not). This is especially true when the criteria and processes for selecting investments are ill-defined and are not aligned with the organisation's vision, mission and objectives. Investment (project) selection may be based not so much on facts and business drivers, but rather on the persuasiveness and power (the *squeaky wheel syndrome*) of people advocating for a particular investment.

The term *sacred cow* is often used to denote a project that a powerful, high-ranking executive is advocating for. A marketing consultant once explained how he was hired by the marketing director of a large organisation to conduct an independent, external market analysis for a new product the organisation was interested in developing. His extensive research indicated there was insufficient demand to warrant the financing of this new product. The marketing director chose to bury the report and made the consultant promise never to share this information with anyone. The director explained how the new product was the pet idea of the new CEO (who saw it as his legacy to the organisation). The marketing director went on to describe the CEO's irrational obsession with the project. The marketing director believed that he would lose his job if such critical information ever became known. Ethics and transparency did not come into this discussion—in a modern project organisation these situations should never arise.

Project sponsors can play a significant role in the selection and successful implementation of product innovation projects. Project sponsors are typically high-ranking managers who endorse and lend political support for the completion of a specific project. They are instrumental in winning approval for the project and protecting it during the critical development stage. Savvy project leaders recognise the importance of having such sponsors, who can advocate for their case and protect their interests.

The significance of corporate politics can be seen in the often quoted and ill-fated ALTO computer project at Xerox during the mid-1970s. The project was a tremendous technological success; it developed the first workable mouse, the first laser printer, the first user-friendly (GUI) software and the first local area network (LAN). All these developments were five years ahead of their nearest competitor. Over the next five years the opportunity to dominate the nascent personal computer market was squandered because of internal in-fighting at Xerox and the absence of a strong project sponsor. Bill Gates stepped into the market after seeing developments at Xerox, as did Steve Jobs, and, as they say, the rest is history.

Politics can play a role not only in project selection but also in the aspirations behind projects. Individuals can enhance their power within an organisation by managing extraordinary and critical projects. Power and status naturally accrue to successful innovators and risk-takers rather than to steady producers. Many ambitious managers pursue high-profile projects as a means for moving quickly up the corporate ladder. For example, Lee Iacocca's career was built on successfully leading the design and development of the highly successful Ford Mustang. Managers become heroes by leading projects that contribute significantly to an organisation's mission or solve a pressing crisis.

Many would argue that politics and project management should not mix. A more proactive response is that projects and politics invariably mix and that effective project leaders recognise that any significant project has political ramifications. Top management needs to develop a system for identifying and selecting projects that reduce the impact of internal politics and foster the selection of the best projects for achieving the mission and strategy of the organisation.

4.4.3 Problem 3: Resource conflicts and multitasking

Most project organisations exist in a multi-project environment. This environment creates problems of project interdependency and the need to share resources. For example, consider what the potential impact would be on the labour resource pool of a (medium-sized) construction company, should it win a contract it would like to bid on when it is already heavily committed to other projects. Will its existing labour force be adequate to deal with the new project—given the completion date? Will current projects be delayed? Will subcontracting help? Which projects will have priority? Competition among project leaders can be contentious. All project leaders seek to have the best people for their projects. The problems of sharing resources and scheduling resources across projects grows exponentially as the number of projects rises. In multi-project environments, the stakes are even higher and the benefits, or penalties, for good or bad resource scheduling become even more significant than in most single projects. Resource sharing also leads to multitasking. Multitasking involves starting and stopping work on one task to work on another project and then returning to the original task. People working on several tasks concurrently are far less efficient, especially where conceptual or physical shutdown and start-up are significant. Multitasking adds to delays and costs; changing priorities exacerbate the multitasking problems. Likewise, multitasking is more evident in organisations that have too many projects for the resources they command. The number of projects in a portfolio almost always exceeds the available resources (typically by a factor of three to four times). This capacity overload inevitably leads to confusion and the inefficient use of scarce organisational resources. The presence of an implementation gap, power politics and multitasking add to the problem of which projects are allocated resources first. Employee morale and confidence suffer because it is difficult to make sense of an ambiguous system. A multi-program/project organisation environment faces major problems without a priority system that is clearly linked to the Strategic Plan. So, what can be done?

The first and most important change that will go a long way in addressing these and other problems is the development and use of a meaningful *project priority process* for project selection; such a system should answer questions such as:

- How can the implementation gap be narrowed so that understanding and consensus on organisational strategies run through all levels of management? That is, how is strategy cascaded through the organisation?
- How can power politics be minimised?
- Can a process be developed in which investments (programs/projects) are consistently prioritised to support organisational strategies?
- Can the prioritised investments be used to allocate scarce organisational resources (e.g. people and equipment)?
- Can the process accommodate bottom-up initiation of ideas (that later become projects) that support and align with the organisation's strategy?

What is needed is a set of integrative criteria and a process for evaluating and selecting projects that best support the higher-level strategies and objectives that can be resourced. A single-project priority system that ranks projects by their contribution to the Strategic Plan would make life easier. This is easily enough said but difficult to accomplish in practice. Organisations that manage independent programs and projects and allocate resources in an ad hoc manner have shifted focus to selecting the right portfolio of programs and projects (investments) to achieve their strategic objectives. This is an accelerating trend. The advantages of successful portfolio management systems are becoming well-recognised in project-driven organisations. A few of the key benefits (note that this could easily be extended) are that they:

- build discipline into program and project selection and prioritisation
- prioritise program and project proposals across a common set of criteria, rather than based on politics or emotion
- manage dependencies across the set of programs and projects
- facilitate budget tracking across the portfolio of programs and projects
- justify prematurely closing programs and projects that do not or no longer support the organisation's strategy
- improve communication and support agreement on program and project goals
- enable a holistic view of risk and the impact this may have on the organisation to be taken across a portfolio
- enable an *apples with apples* comparison due to a common approach to the financial returns of investments
- enable resources to be optimised across the entire portfolio, thereby ensuring proactive use of often-scarce resources
- build strategically aligned portfolios, increasing success in the execution of strategy
- formalise decision-making into a process that transparently and fairly allows for discussion, debate and confirmation of the investments to be undertaken prior to executing the portfolio through programs and projects.

A portfolio management system is discussed next, with an emphasis on selection criteria (which is where the power of the portfolio system is established—i.e. selecting the correct investments, which are later packaged as programs and projects). We normally refer to the idea for a program or project at this level as an *investment*. Once an investment has been approved, it will be placed into a structure within each portfolio (and an organisation typically has multiple portfolios) and there will typically be several programs and dozens of projects that deliver each portfolio.

4.5 | An introduction to portfolio management

Succinctly put, the aim of portfolio management is to ensure that investments are aligned with strategic goals and are prioritised appropriately. As Foti (2002) points out, portfolio management needs to elicit the rhetorical question: "What is strategic to our organisation?" Portfolio management provides information that allows people to make better business decisions. Since investments typically compete for funding and people usually outnumber available resources, it is important to follow a logical and defined process for selecting which investments (programs and projects) to implement. The design of a portfolio system should include (at minimum) the classification of investment(s), selection criteria depending upon classification, sources of proposals, proposal evaluations and managing the portfolio of programs and projects.

4.5.1 Classification of investments

Many organisations find they have three different kinds of investments in their portfolio: compliance and emergency (must-do) investments, operational investments and strategic investments.

- *Compliance investments* are typically those that are needed to meet regulatory conditions or legal compliance; hence, they are called *must-do* investments. Emergency work, such as rebuilding a warehouse that has been destroyed by floods, would also meet the must-do criteria. Compliance programs/projects usually have penalties if they are not implemented.

- *Operational investments* are those that are needed to support current operations. These investments are designed to improve efficiency of operational systems and processes, reduce product costs and improve performance. Continuous improvement (sometimes referred to as *business improvement*) investments are examples of operational projects.

- *Strategic investments* are those that directly support the organisation's vision, mission, objectives, strategies and tactics. They are frequently directed towards increasing revenue, market share or customer retention/satisfaction. Examples of strategic investments are new products, R&D or changing the way the business operates to better service the customer (refer to Table 4.2).

Table 4.2 Some examples of compliance (must-do), strategic and operational investments

Category	Theme	Investment
Compliance	Workplace health and safety	Implement fully Reporting of Injuries, Diseases and Dangerous Occurrences Regulations 2013 (UK)
	Financial	Implement European Union General Data Protection Regulation
	Financial	Implement updated Company Director Guidance
	Financial	Ensure compliance with the Australian Consumer Law
Strategic	Customer	Review competitor product and customer complaints and create a better aligned service
	Market	Introduce a new service to compete with competitor offerings
	Research and development (R&D)	Research the impact of the Internet of Things on existing products to enable delivery of this functionality
Operational	Process	Improve the recruitment process and shorten the lead-time to employment
	Equipment	Replace ageing elevators with a more energy-efficient solution

Remember: A portfolio is a mix of strategic work and operation work. The strategic work is typically delivered through programs and projects, while operational improvement work could be delivered through the organisation's preferred business improvement approach, such as Lean Six Sigma.

Most organisations that carry out strategic alignment of investments will use a portfolio or investment management solution to assist them in this prioritisation activity. The strategic value of a proposed investment must be determined before it can be placed in the portfolio. Under some circumstances, there are investments that must be selected. Compliance (typically legal, government or legislation) or emergency investments are those that must be implemented, or the organisation will fail or suffer dire penalties or consequences (e.g. where a manufacturing plant must install an electrostatic filter on top of a smokestack within six months or close down, or where loss of life or injury has occurred and practices need to be adjusted as a matter of urgency). European Union (EU) courts are trying to force Microsoft to open its software architecture to allow competing software organisations to be compatible and interact with Microsoft. This decision may become a compliance investment for Microsoft. The EU is also introducing laws that all phone manufacturers must use the same charging port to reduce the amount of e-waste (imagine what challenges this would pose Apple with its **proprietary** lightning port!). Any project placed in the must category ignores other selection criteria. A rule of thumb for placing a proposed project in this category is that most of the organisation's stakeholders would agree that the project must be implemented; there is no perceived choice but to implement the project. All other projects are selected using selection criteria linked to an organisation's strategy.

4.5.2 Selection criteria

Although there are many criteria for selecting projects, selection criteria are typically identified as financial and non-financial. A short description of each is given next, followed by a discussion of their use, in practice. Remember that these financial calculations can be carried out for several situations the project leader may find themselves in, for example to:

- compare options within a Business Case
- compare two or more investments for strategic prioritisation
- make decisions about which terms to accept from a supplier.

4.5.2.1 Financial criteria models

Many managers prefer using financial criteria models to evaluate investments. These models are appropriate when there is a high level of confidence associated with estimates of future cash flows. The four models (with examples) that are demonstrated in this next section are the payback, NPV, IRR and BCR.

The examples are based on the following two simple investments:

- Investment A has an initial investment of $700,000 and projected cash inflows of the same amount of $225,000 for five years.
- Investment B has an initial investment of $400,000 and projected cash inflows of the same amount of $110,000 for five years.

The payback model measures the time it will take to recover the project investment. Shorter paybacks are more desirable. Payback is the simplest and most widely used model. Payback emphasises cash flows: a key factor in business. Some managers use the payback model to eliminate unusually risky projects (those with lengthy payback periods). The two major limitations of payback are that it:

- ignores the time value of money (i.e. money received in the future is worth less in today's money)
- does not consider cash inflows after the payback year.

Figure 4.6 compares the payback for Investment A and Investment B. The payback for Investment A is three years two months and for Investment B is three years eight months. Using the payback method alone, both investments are acceptable, since both return the initial investment in less than four years (if that was the baseline set by the Finance department for this business). However, Investment A is looking like the preferred option at this point as it pays back marginally sooner by six months.

Figure 4.6 Payback

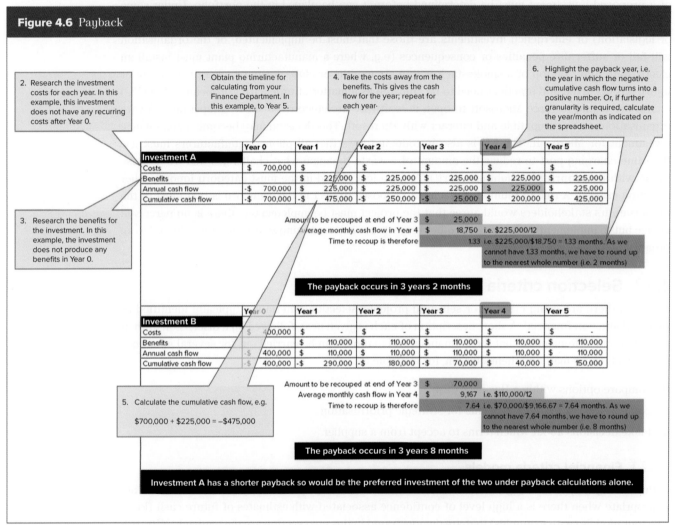

Payback is usually a part of the overall financial decision-making; it informs us that money returned sooner to the organisation suffers less devaluation and can be put to other users quicker (e.g. fund that next investment).

Let's consider the time value of money and how this now affects our decision. Remember, a typical Business Case will call for multiple financial models to be applied so that a more rounded financial decision can be input into the overall recommendation across all sections of the Business Case.

The NPV model (Figure 4.7) uses the Finance Department's desired discount rate (15%) to calculate the present value of all cash inflows annually, and subsequently the net present value. The calculations take into account that money over time devalues, and we must consider that in the selection of investments.

Explanation of Figure 4.7.

1. Obtain the discount rate from your finance department. The discount rate is a complex calculation affected by many factors, including what rate the business can borrow funds (money) at to finance the investments it wishes to make.

Figure 4.7 Net present value (NPV)

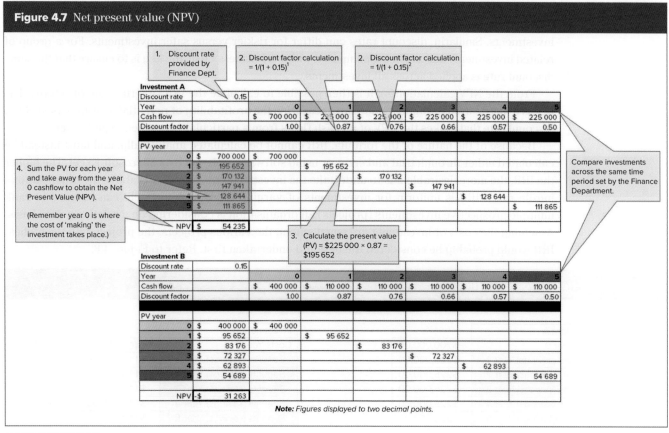

© 2022 Dr Neil Pearson

2. Calculate the discount factor based on this discount rate with the formula 1/(1+ discount rate)^year.

   a. Where discount rate is 15% = 0.15 so 1 plus the discount rate = 1.15

   b. Where year 1 year is 1, where year 2 year is 2 etc.

   c. Where the ^ symbol indicates to the power of.

   So 1/(1 + 0.15) ^2 = 0.76 (i.e., at the end of Year 2 we are discounting the money by 0.76 to equate this to today's value of that money. This is because money devalues over time).

3. Multiply the net cashflow for the year (costs minus benefits—refer to payback table (Figure 4.6) for an example of how this number was arrived at) by the discount factor to get the present value (PV) for the year. Repeat this for each year.

4. Sum all the year 1 through year 5 PVs and subtract from the Year 0 PV. This will give you the NPV of the investment.

5. Repeat the process for each investment.

   The NPV is used to assist in the financial decision. The general rules applied to the resulting NPV are:

   ■ If the NPV is positive, it is eligible for further consideration, given all the other factors in the Business Case.

   ■ If the NPV is 0 (zero), the investment is termed *breakeven* and would probably be rejected on the grounds of the tangible costs and benefits.

   ■ If the NPV is negative, the project is rejected (as it will cost more than it returns).

   ■ If you have multiple investments, all with positive NPVs based on NPV alone (not considering any other Business Case factor), the investment that returns the highest NPV would be selected.

   Compare the NPV results with the payback results. The NPV model is more realistic because it considers the time value of money and all cash flows (payback considered cashflow up to the payback year and not after). When using the NPV model, the discount rate can differ for different types of projects. For example, strategic investments are frequently set higher than operational investments. Similarly, discount rates can differ for riskier versus safer investments. For a group of related investments that are being compared within a Business Case, the key is to ensure that the same discount rate is applied across all investments.

From the NPV calculation(s), it is then possible to calculate the IRR (internal rate of return). The IRR is a metric used in capital budgeting, measuring the profitability of potential investments. IRR is a discount rate that makes the NPV of all cash flows from a particular investment equal to zero.

Because of the nature of the formula, IRR cannot be calculated analytically, and must instead be calculated either through trial and error or using software tools, such as Microsoft Excel. The higher the IRR, the more desirable it is to undertake the investment (so long as it is above the organisation's hurdle rate). IRR is uniform for investments of varying types and, as such, can be used to rank multiple prospective investments (projects) an organisation is considering on a relatively even basis. Assuming the costs of investment are equal among the various projects, the project with the highest IRR would probably be considered the best and undertaken first. Refer to Figure 4.8.

Figure 4.8 Internal rate of return (IRR)

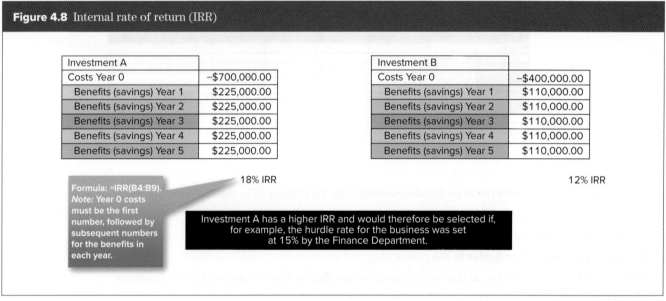

© 2022 Dr Neil Pearson

The benefit–cost ratio (BCR) model provides a simple ratio of the benefits to be delivered by the investment against the cost to deliver those benefits (i.e. the cost of doing the investment). The formula for BCR is:

$$\text{Benefit–cost ratio} = \frac{\text{sum of all present values (PV) for benefits}}{\text{sum of all present values (PV) for costs}}$$

Note: Stipulate whether this is based on present-value figures adjusted for the time value of money, or plain non-adjusted figures.

Using the same investments, Figure 4.9 confirms that the higher BCR of Investment A means that Investment A would be the preferred investment to take forward over Investment B. This is based on BCR alone, when applying the following generally accepted rules:

- BCR > 1: Investment option is profitable (benefits are greater than costs).
- BCR = 1: Investment option is neither profitable nor a loss leader (benefits are equal to costs).
- BCR < 1: Investment option generates losses (benefits are less than costs).

A positive whole number is good; it represents that the money invested returns greater value in benefits delivered to the organisation. A negative number is bad, as costs would outweigh the benefits.

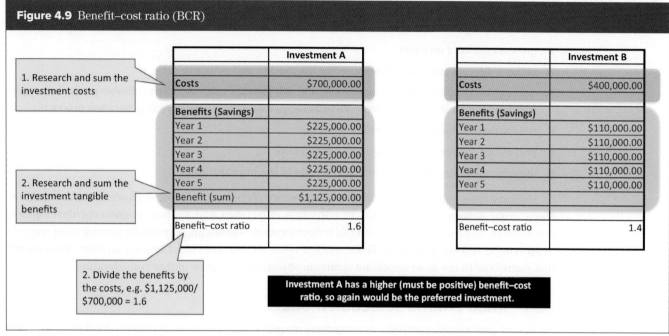

Figure 4.9 Benefit–cost ratio (BCR)

© 2022 Dr Neil Pearson

With BCR and the previously mentioned financial models, only *tangible benefits* for the investment have been considered as we are looking at the financial viability of the investment. Considering *intangible benefits* (benefits to which we cannot attach a direct tangible dollar value), the organisational change impact and risk factors from other parts of the investment business case will allow ultimately a more rounded decision to be taken on the investment which considers other factors beyond the hard $ values.

Unfortunately, pure financial models fail to include many projects where financial return is impossible to measure and/or other factors are vital to the accept or reject decision. One research study by Foti (2002) showed that companies using predominantly financial models to prioritise projects yielded unbalanced portfolios and projects that were not strategically oriented. Other studies make similar claims.

The general decision criteria for each model are summarised in Table 4.3.

Table 4.3 Summary of financial models

Technique	Looking for . . .	Comment
Payback	The sooner, the better	Cash flows after the payback year are ignored. Money returned sooner to the organisation suffers less devaluation and can be put to other users faster.
NPV	A positive number greater than zero The higher the number, the better	Takes into consideration the time value of money. Negative numbers indicate investments should not be backed.
IRR	The higher the percentage, the better	Most organisations specify a threshold (hurdle rate) over which the investment must return.
Benefit–cost ratio (BCR)	Ratio must be greater than one The higher the ratio, the better	BCR values less than one indicate the investments costs outweigh the benefits. Only considers tangible benefits.

© 2022 Dr Neil Pearson

4.5.2.2 Non-financial criteria

Financial return, while important, does not always reflect strategic importance. The 1960s and 1970s saw organisations become overextended by diversifying too much. Now the prevailing thinking is that long-term survival is dependent upon developing and maintaining core competencies. Companies must be disciplined enough to say no to potentially profitable investments that are outside the realm of their core mission. This requires other criteria be considered beyond direct financial return. For example, an organisation may support investments that do not have high profit margins for other strategic reasons, including to:

■ grow a customer segment

■ make it difficult for competitors to enter the market and compete

■ develop an enabler product, if its introduction will increase sales in more profitable products/services now or in the future (e.g. develop core technology that will be used in next-generation products)

■ reduce dependency on unreliable suppliers

■ prevent government intervention and regulation

■ improve the ethical and sustainability profile of the organisation.

Organisations may support investments to restore corporate image or enhance brand recognition. Many organisations are committed to corporate citizenship and support community development investments. Since no single criterion can reflect strategic significance, portfolio management requires multi-criteria screening models. These models often weight individual criteria so those investments that contribute to the most important strategic objectives are given higher consideration.

4.5.3 Multi-criteria selection models

As stated previously, portfolio management requires multi-criteria screening models. Two such models—a checklist and multi-weighted scoring models—are described next.

4.5.3.1 Checklist models

The most frequently used method for selecting projects has been the checklist. This approach uses a list of questions to review potential investments and determine their acceptance or rejection. Several examples of questions typically encountered in practice are listed in Table 4.4.

Table 4.4 Sample selection questions used in practice

Topic	Question
Strategic alignment	What organisational strategy does this investment align with?
Driver	What business problem does the investment solve?
Success metrics	How will we measure success?
Sponsorship	Who is the investment sponsor?
Risk	What is the impact of not making this investment?
Risk	What is the investment risk to our organisation?
Risk	Where does the proposed investment fit in our risk profile?
Benefits, value, return on investment (ROI)	What is the value of the investment to this organisation?
Benefits, value, ROI	When will the investment show results?
Benefits, value, ROI	What is the opportunity cost?
Objectives	What are the investment objectives?
Organisational culture	Is our organisational culture right for this type of investment?
Resources	Will internal resources be available for this investment?
Approach	Will we make (build) or buy?
Schedule	What are dependencies with other investments?
Schedule	Is the timeline realistic?
Training/resources	Will staff training be required?
Finance/portfolio	What is the estimated cost of the investment?
Portfolio	Is this a new initiative or part of an existing initiative?
Portfolio	How does this investment interact with current investments?
Technology	Is the technology mainstream or proven?
Organisational change impact	What is the organisational change impact of the investment?
Organisational change impact	Does the organisational structure require changing?

Checklist models allow great flexibility when selecting from many different types of projects and are easily applied across different divisions and locations.

Although many investments are selected using a variation of the checklist approach, there are serious shortcomings in this approach that the reader should bear in mind. This approach fails to answer the *relative importance* or *value* of a potential investment to the organisation and fails to allow for comparison with other potential investments. Each potential project will have a different set of positive and negative answers. How do you compare them? Ranking and prioritising investments by their importance is difficult, if not impossible. This approach also leaves the door open for potential power plays, political maneuverings and other forms of manipulation. To overcome these serious shortcomings, experts recommend the use of a *multi-weighted scoring* model to select investment.

4.5.3.2 Multi-weighted scoring models

A weighted scoring model typically uses several weighted selection criteria to evaluate investment proposals. Weighted scoring models will generally include qualitative and/or quantitative criteria and each selection criterion is assigned a weight. Scores are assigned to each criterion *for* the project, based on its importance *to* the project being evaluated. The weights and scores are multiplied to get a total weighted score for the project. Using these multiple screening criteria, projects can then be compared using the weighted score. Investments with higher weighted scores are considered better.

Selection criteria need to mirror the critical success factors of an organisation. For example: 3M set a target that 25 per cent of the company's sales would come from products fewer than four years old, versus the old target of 20 per cent. The company's priority system for project selection strongly reflected this new target.

Failure to pick the right factors will render the screening process useless. See Snapshot from Practice: Crisis IT.

Figure 4.10 represents a project-scoring matrix that uses some factors usually found in practice. The selected screening criteria are shown across the top of the matrix (e.g. stay within core competencies, ROI of 18% plus). Management weights each criterion (e.g. a value of zero to a high of three) by its relative importance to the organisation's objectives and Strategic Plan. Project proposals are then submitted to a project priority team or the project portfolio office.

Figure 4.10 Investment (project) weighted criteria selection matrix

Criteria / Weight	Stay within core competencies	Strategic fit	Urgency	25% of sales from new products	Reduce defects to less than 1%	Improve customer loyalty	ROI of 18% plus	Weighted total
	2.0	3.0	2.0	2.5	1.0	1.0	3.0	
Project 1	1	8	2	6	0	6	5	66
Project 2	3	3	2	0	0	5	1	27
Project 3	9	5	2	0	2	2	5	56
Project 4	3	0	10	0	0	6	0	32
Project 5	1	10	5	10	0	8	9	102
Project 6	6	5	0	2	0	2	7	55
⋮								
Project *n*	5	5	7	0	10	10	8	83

Each investment (project) is next evaluated by its relative contribution/value added to the selected criteria. Values of zero to a high of 10 are assigned to each criterion for each project. This value represents the fit to the specific criterion. For example, Project 1 appears to fit well with the strategy of the organisation since it is given a value of eight. Conversely, Project 1 does nothing to support reducing defects (its value is zero). Finally, this model applies the management weights to each criterion by importance—using a value of one to three. For example, ROI and strategic fit have a weight of three, while urgency and core competencies have weights of two. Applying the weight to each criterion, the priority team derives the weighted total points for each project. For example, Project 5 has the highest value of 102 $[(2 \times 1) + (3 \times 10) + (2 \times 5) + (2.5 \times 10) + (1 \times 0) + (1 \times 8) + (3 \times 9) = 102]$ and Project 2 has a low value of 27. If the resources available create a cut-off threshold of 50 points, the priority team would eliminate Projects 2 and 4. (Note: Project 4 appears to have some urgency, but it is not classified as a *must* project. Therefore, it is screened with all other proposals.) Project 5 would receive first priority, Project n second, and so on. In rare cases where resources are severely limited and project proposals are similar in weighted rank, it is prudent to pick the project that places less demand on resources. Weighted multiple criteria models like this are rapidly becoming the preferred choice for prioritising projects.

At this point in the discussion, it is advisable to pause and put things into perspective. While selection models like the one above may yield numerical solutions to investment selection decisions, models should not make the final decisions—the people using the models should. No model, no matter how sophisticated, can capture the total reality it is meant to represent. Models are *tools* for guiding the evaluation process, so the decision-makers consider relevant issues and agree which projects should be supported and not supported. This is a much more subjective process than calculations suggest.

SNAPSHOT *from* PRACTICE : Infrastructure overload

Governments in any country tend to be one of the biggest spenders on large infrastructure projects. However, different countries take different perspectives for the selection of projects. The Australian Government is no different. Not only do government-funded infrastructure projects provide benefits to the citizens of the country, but they also provide jobs and growth opportunities for a region or sector.

Ensuring the correct mix of national and state projects is undertaken over a time period is no simple feat, the media often picking up on the failure side and questioning use of public funds. Many examples have appeared as headlines over the last few years alone.

- NBN rollout—AUD51 billion, issues with new technology overtaking technology being deployed into the ground, inadequate planning on how to get the fibre into existing households from the road, cost overruns and health scares (asbestos in the service ducts and manhole access areas)

- Royal Adelaide Hospital, South Australia—AUD2.3 billion, plagued by delays and cost overruns

- Queensland Health Payroll System—problems included underpaying, overpaying and not paying a large percentage of the 80 000+ staff, ending in costs of AUD1.2 billion on an original AUD6 million contract with IBM

- Victorian Government myki cards—ended up introducing free tram travel in Melbourne's central business district because of the issues in tapping on and off the system.

With so many possible areas into which a limited pot of funds could be invested, governments should be applying a very short-, medium- and long-term strategic process to their selection. But how often does a politician announce project go-ahead as part of political hustling among parties? How often do state priorities overplay the need to think strategically for the long-term good of the country (as opposed to the current political climate)? Enter Infrastructure Australia, the federal statutory body with the mandate to advise governments, industry and the community on the investments and reforms needed to deliver better infrastructure for all Australians. The governing legislation, the *Infrastructure Australia Act 2008* (Cth), defines its role and responsibilities in guiding nationally significant infrastructure investment and reform (Infrastructure Australia 2022a).

As of 2020, Australian national high-priority initiatives included:

■ regional road network safety improvements

■ water supply and resilience for town and city populations

■ strategic planning for water capture, use and management

■ coastal inundation protection strategy for sea-level rise and flooding

■ national waste and recycling management

■ national road maintenance strategy

■ network optimisation program for national urban rail network congestion

■ network optimisation program for national urban road network congestion

■ national strategic planning for future freight initiatives

■ corridor preservation for East Coast High Speed Rail for future rail connectivity between east coast capital cities.

Refer to Figure 4.11.

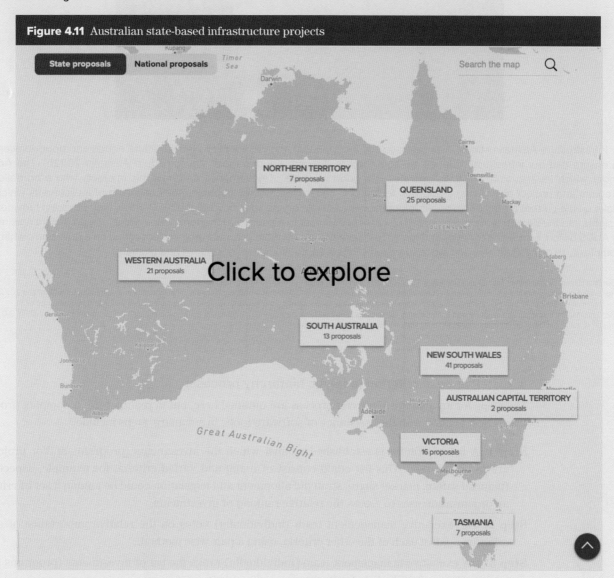

Figure 4.11 Australian state-based infrastructure projects

Figure 4.12 Port of Brisbane dedicated freight rail connection early proposal

Infrastructure Australia states, "Our rigorous and independent analysis identifies infrastructure needs and opportunities, to ensure that our infrastructure funds are spent where they are needed most" (Infrastructure Australia 2022b). The Act under which Infrastructure Australia operates is a good example of governance and how this interacts with a portfolio, program and project environment. So, what techniques underpin how they approach their selection of investments which make up the current portfolio? No public information is available on the specifics, but the AICD article (see Sources) provides insights into the department's operations. It discusses alignment to a country's long-term vision, value of a project increasing to AUD5 billion, competing for skills and resources, learning lessons from previous projects, not acting on a politician's whim, complexity (e.g. meshing new and old road systems together), community expectations and planning.

4.5.3.3 Pair-wise criterion (analytic hierarchy process)

The steps for an analytic hierarchy process are outlined here, but in reality, form a complex process that is best applied with the assistance of software tools. In summary, steps include:

Step 1: A list of criteria is established against which the investments (programs and/or projects) are to be assessed. This list could consist of many and varied criteria, for example, aspects of financial safety, market share, strategic alignment and legislation could be among a set of criteria an organisation uses to assess the relative ranking of investments.

Step 2: The executive management team (individually) votes on the relative importance of each criterion against each of the other criteria, using a pair-wise method.

Step 3: The executive management team (individually) ranks the list of investments (programs and/ or projects) against the list of criteria.

Step 4: The output of these processes is a prioritised list of investments, based on the weighted set of criteria.

This can be a complex process but has been proven to assist organisations of all sizes across varied industries in this complex area of decision-making. Some portfolio management systems include prioritisation tools within their software that are based on the pair-wise criterion method (e.g. Primavera). Other tools, such as Decision Lens (www.decisionlens.com), specialise in providing software and processes that apply this technique across various decision-making contexts in an organisation.

4.5.3.4 Nominal group technique

Another technique commonly encountered in portfolio prioritisation is the nominal group technique (NGT)—viewed as a simple, perceptions-based technique for investment (program/project) selection. NGT is a simple prioritisation technique that helps to take out bias of vocal members of the voting community. NGT is a simple series of steps usually carried out in a brainstorming workshop, as follows:

Step 1: The group is asked for input to creating a list of the items (programs/projects) to be prioritised. The group should be facilitated so only the content of the list is brainstormed, and not the perspectives or opinions of the individuals in the room. The facilitator must also ensure the group understands any item added to the list.

Step 2: The individuals in the group (anonymously) next prioritise the list as: first, second, third, and so on (no duplicate priorities can be used).

Step 3: The facilitator collects the individual lists and totals the scores. As first is the lowest numerically, the project with the lowest total score will be the project that tops the list (and so on, down the totals).

The result is a prioritised, perceptions-based list of programs/projects. When setting the ground rules prior to going into the meeting, it would need to be declared and emphasised that the resulting group vote would be the list that would be taken forward for further development by the portfolio management office. Although lacking in a quantitative basis, NGT can provide a perspectives-based list that is pivoted around experience or the gut feeling of a team of executives (or other managers) about what they perceive to be important investments to pursue. Even if only used as a tool to validate and/or question other methods, NGT is useful.

When applied to an example, the steps would pan out as:

Step 1: The facilitator requests a group of six executive managers to attend a briefing session to prioritise the eight key strategic programs for the year, as determined by the strategic planning process. The list of the eight strategic programs looks like this:

A	Implement a customer relationship management system (including business processes, systems and training).
B	Develop two new products and market test to ensure continuity of products in the marketplace.
C	Grow market share by 15% on a baseline of 33%.
D	Implement social media strategies and technologies across all products and services offered.
E	Update the Enterprise Resource Planning (ERP) system to the latest version to ensure continued software support arrangements can be entered into.
F	Reduce employee headcount by 10% through implementation of efficiency programs.
G	Relocate to a greenfield sustainable technology park to reduce overheads by 10%.
H	Remove one executive management position and five direct management positions to flatten the organisational structure, in line with competitors.

In this step, each investment area (project) is discussed to ensure the achievement of a common understanding. The facilitator steers discussion to ensure that personalities, politics and personal perspectives are kept out of the discussion.

Step 2: After a common understanding of the programs is achieved, each of the individual executive managers is asked to vote (in confidence). For example, the CFO's vote could potentially look like:

CFO voting slip		
A	Implement a customer relationship management system (including business processes, systems and training).	1
B	Develop two new products and market test to ensure continuity of products in the marketplace.	3
C	Grow market share by 15% on a baseline of 33%.	4
D	Implement social media strategies and technologies across all products and services offered.	2
E	Update the ERP system to the latest version to ensure continued software support arrangements can be entered into.	6
F	Reduce employee headcount by 10% through implementation of efficiency programs.	8
G	Relocate to a greenfield sustainable technology park to reduce overheads by 10%.	7
H	Remove one executive management position and five direct management positions to flatten the organisational structure, in line with competitors.	5

Step 3: The facilitator now collects the voting slips from all the participants, tallies the scores, and reveals the totals to the group. The resulting list of priorities could be as shown below:

Investment area (program/project)		Overall group priority
A	Implement a customer relationship management system (including business processes, systems and training).	16
B	Develop two new products and market test to ensure continuity of products in the marketplace.	18
C	Grow market share by 15% on a baseline of 33%.	19
D	Implement social media strategies and technologies across all products and services offered.	20
E	Update the ERP system to the latest version to ensure continued software support arrangements can be entered into.	25
F	Reduce employee headcount by 10% through implementation of efficiency programs.	33
G	Relocate to a greenfield sustainable technology park to reduce overheads by 10%.	39
H	Remove one executive management position and five direct management positions to flatten the organisational structure, in line with competitors.	46

In this example, Investment A—Implement a customer relationship management system (including business processes, systems and training)—was voted by the group as being the most important.

4.6 : Applying a selection model

Investment classification: Experience shows that most organisations use similar criteria across all types of investments, with perhaps one or two criteria specific to the type of investment (e.g. strategic versus operational). Regardless of criteria differences among different types of investments, the most important criterion for selection is the investment's (project's) fit to the organisation's strategy. Therefore, this criterion should be consistent across all types of projects and carry a high priority, relative to other criteria. This uniformity across all priority models used can keep departments from sub-optimising the use of organisational resources. Anyone generating a project proposal should classify their proposal by *type*, so the appropriate criteria can be used to evaluate their proposal.

Selecting a model: In the past, financial criteria were used almost to the exclusion of other criteria. However, in the last two decades we have witnessed a dramatic shift to include multiple criteria in project selection (this supports concepts such as triple bottom line and sustainability reporting discussed elsewhere in this text). Concisely put, profitability alone is simply not an adequate measure of contribution; however, it is still an important criterion, especially for investments that enhance revenue and market share such as breakthrough R&D investments.

Today, senior management is interested in identifying the potential mix of investments that will yield the best use of human and capital resources to maximise return on investment in the long run. Factors such as researching new technology, public image, ethical position, protection of the environment, core competencies and strategic fit might be important criteria for selecting investments. Weighted scoring criteria seem the best alternative to meet this need.

Weighted scoring models bring investments into closer alignment with strategic goals. If the scoring model is published and available to everyone in the organisation, some discipline and credibility are attached to the selection of investments. The number of wasteful investments using resources is reduced. Politics and sacred cow projects are exposed. Investment goals are more easily identified and communicated using the selection criteria as corroboration. Finally, using a weighted scoring approach helps project leaders understand how their investment (program/project) was selected, how their project contributes to organisational goals and how it compares with other investments. Investment selection is one of the most important decisions guiding the future success of an organisation. Criteria for selection are the area where the power of your portfolio starts to manifest itself. New investments are aligned with the strategic goals of the organisation. With a clear method for selecting investments in place, project/program proposals can be solicited.

4.6.1 The Business Case

The Business Case captures all the facts, figures and reasons for the investment. It is the major source of program and project *reason for being* as a result of the strategic and business planning processes. However, there must be an opportunity in the business for the submission of programs/projects from a **bottom-up approach** (Figure 4.13 ②)—for example, programs/projects identified from all levels of the organisation, usually by the people at the coalface of the organisation. Although these projects have been identified from a bottom-up approach in the organisation, they would be subject to the same investment appraisal and prioritisation processes.

In addition to top-down (Figure 4.13 ①) and bottom-up program/project activity, the organisation's innovation processes might also generate potential project briefs for consideration. Again, as with bottom-up identified projects, they would be subject to the same investment appraisal and prioritisation processes. No matter where the investment is sourced from (Figure 4.13), many organisations use the investment Business Case to research and define many aspects of the investment.

It also important to note on Figure 4.13 ③, this link between what we are undertaking as projects in the organisation are in most cases handed over to the operations of the organisation for ongoing embedding, operation and continuous improvement.

Figure 4.13 Investment identification and packaging: top-down, bottom-up or combination

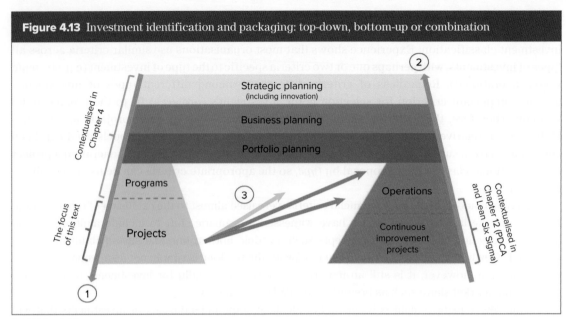

© 2022 Dr Neil Pearson

This list extends the (typical) Business Case table of contents that was introduced earlier in this chapter.

- *Executive summary*: Using the bottom line up front (BLUF) technique, it would include vital elements extracted from each of the sections discussed below—with a particular focus on the overall recommendation and why the investment selected is above and beyond the other investments considered.

- *Glossary of terms*: Ensure any business or technical subject matter terminology is defined in the glossary. Do not assume your reader is at the same knowledge level as the writer/author of the business case.

- *Background*: Describe why the Business Case is being developed.

- *Strategic alignment criteria*: Exactly which strategic objectives does the investment align with? And when delivered, how much will it contribute (i.e. what is the expected impact on the strategic object and supporting KPIs if the investment is delivered)?

- *Business opportunity*: Describe the business opportunity (or problem) that is to be solved by the Business Case.

- *Problem vision statement*: Describe what the world will like if the problem is successfully achieved by the delivery of this Business Case.

- *Impact if not approved*: Describe what will happen in the business if the current situation is left to run as-is and nothing is done. This statement should clearly state the pain to the business in factual (tangible) terms with additional comments made about the softer (intangible) implications.

- *Organisational level benefit assessment*: Describe the overall benefits expected to be delivered from any option later considered. Within each option (later) these may be refined with other option benefits identified in addition to covering the key identified business benefits. Could also be captured in a separate Benefits Plan that accompanies the business case.

- *Organisational level risk assessment*: What enterprise level risks are seeking to be addressed in pursuing this Business Case? Remember a risk being addressed can be a threat risk (negative risk) or an opportunity risk (positive risk). Refer to Chapter 16 "Project risk management".

- *Critical success factors*: Describe what the critical success factors are for the investment. These should be described to maintain focus of the benefits. They should provide clarity, so at the end of the investment, a check-back to the critical success factors and benefits can be made to measure success.

- *Compelling organisational change reason*: In language that is accessible to all employees, what is the compelling change reason?

- *Stakeholder consultation*: Document all consultations with key internal and external stakeholders carried out in building the Business Case. This demonstrates to the review committee that key appropriate stakeholders have been consulted.

- *Governance*: List any company governance and policy around the development of the Business Case and any specific governance and policy in relation to the product, service or result being achieved by delivering the Business Case.

- *Options considered*: Include the do nothing and deferred options, and usually at least three other options. This is a brief description of the options to be analysed in further detail under each option in the next section of the business case.

    a. The do nothing option outlines maintaining the status quo. Usually there is a cost to doing this, such as increased maintenance costs, potential down-time to the business, loss of revenue (customer) or loss of market segment.

    b. The deferred option: What is the cost for deferring actions to a later timeframe?

    c. Other options, as required. Usually, a minimum of three other options would be considered.

- *Options analysis*: duplicated for each option outlined above.

------------- **Start of option** -------------

For each of the options identified (above), carry out a detailed description/analysis of:

- Option description and approach: A description of the option and how it is to be approached.

- Business risks: Examine how the investment stacks up against the organisational risk context (above) and any other business risks identified, whether negative (threat) risks or positive (opportunity) risks.

- Benefits: Examine how well the investment delivers the organisational level benefits expected, how it varies from these if it does not deliver, and what additional benefits it provides. Typically, most benefits will be tangible benefits. On occasions there can be compelling intangible benefits to which a direct dollar amount cannot (or should not) be attributed.

- Disbenefits: Disbenefits are expected undesirable outcomes to a stakeholder, department or customer. Disbenefits can, for example, take the form of a loss of value to a department or person because of the project (termed the *disbeneficiary*).

- Funding analysis: Indicating how, and from where, the investment will be funded. This sub-section also details the estimated cost and return on investment. Often accompanied by payback, NPV, IRR and BCR calculations.

- Opportunity cost: What is being given up in the way of other options, to pursue this option? This would include what the business could do with the money if it invested it in bonds, high-interest account(s) or other such investments.

- Structure/milestone summary: Indicating the approach and major components of work to be carried out.

- Technical viability: Does the option comply with the organisation's enterprise architecture, technology roadmaps or blueprints?

- Organisational change, compelling reasons: In language that is accessible to all employees, what is the compelling change reason?
- Organisational change impact: Identify users/departments where a large organisational change impact is expected. Outline what these are and ensure any associated risks have been captured in the options Business risk section.

------------ **End of option*** ------------

*Repeat whole dashed area for each option being considered: do nothing, deferred, Option A, Option B, Option C, and so on.

- *Overall recommendation*: State clearly, using evidence, why the recommended option is preferred over all the other options considered and presented. A summary of this then becomes the core content for the Executive Summary.
- *Appendices*: With supporting calculations, date and information.

Having this detailed level of information around each investment (program or project level business cases) enables the relevant people involved in the selection and prioritisation process to make well-informed decisions. Later (once approved), it will also provide the necessary background information to the program/project leader for the project's reason for being.

A Business Case template is included with this text, suitable for exploring business cases in support of your Certificate IV, Diploma or Advanced Diploma in project management.

 Business Case

The project leader may find that some organisations require a valid and approved Business Case before a project (or program) can start, and that the Business Case will become a living document that is carried forward with the program/project and is reviewed at each gate. Further to this, the success of the project itself is not only measured against what was declared in the project scope document, but also any additional dimensions declared and approved in the project's Business Case (Figure 4.14).

4.6.2 Ranking proposals and selection of projects

Picking through so many proposals to identify those that add the most value requires a structured process (refer back to Figure 4.4). The flowchart shows a generic screening process, beginning with the creation of a Business Case. Although represented as a flowchart within this text, in practice this is often captured within the strategic and business planning processes of an organisation as a more comprehensive process swimlane diagram with accompanying policy (governance) and detailed work instructions for those carrying out the work.

4.6.3 Responsibility for prioritising

Prioritising can be an uncomfortable exercise for managers. But prioritising projects is a major responsibility for senior management. Prioritising means discipline, accountability, responsibility, constraints, reduced flexibility and loss of power. Top management commitment means more than

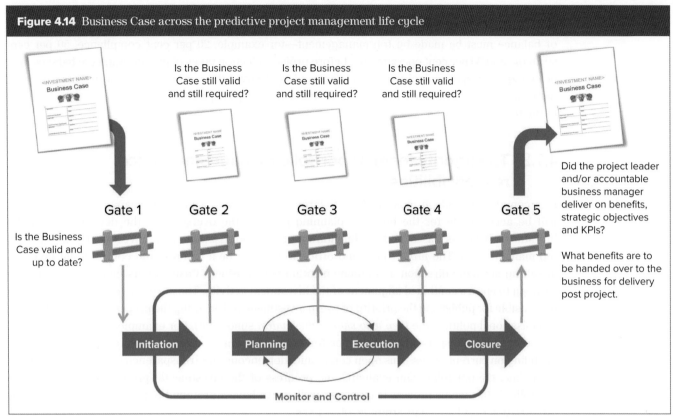

Figure 4.14 Business Case across the predictive project management life cycle

© 2022 Dr Neil Pearson

giving a blessing to the priority system; it means management will have to rank and weigh, in concrete terms, the investments (programs/projects) that best support the organisation's objectives and the strategies they believe to be most critical to the long-term success of the organisation. This public declaration of commitment can be risky if the ranked objectives later prove to be poor choices but setting the course for the organisation is the accountability of top management. The good news is, if management is truly trying to direct the organisation to a strong future position, a good project priority system supports their efforts and develops a culture in which everyone is contributing to the goals of the organisation against a set of mutually agreed selection criteria. The project leader would be seeking a RASCI (**R**esponsible, **A**ccountable, **S**upporting, **C**onsulted, **I**nformed) matrix (refer to Chapter 7 "Governance and projects"), which outlines the accountabilities and responsibilities around the Business Case, as undoubtedly there would be responsibilities allocated to the project leader.

4.7 | Managing the portfolio management system

Managing the portfolio takes the selection system one step higher in that the merits of a particular investment are assessed within the context of existing investments. At the same time, it involves monitoring and adjusting selection and prioritisation criteria to reflect the strategic focus of the organisation. This requires constant management. The priority system can be managed by a small group of key employees in a small organisation. Or, in larger organisations, the priority system may be managed by the portfolio management office or may even be a part of the office of strategy management.

4.7.1 Senior management input

Management of a portfolio system requires two major inputs from senior management. First, senior management must provide guidance in establishing selection criteria that strongly align with the current organisational strategies (e.g. using the pair-wise criterion method). Second, the senior management team must decide annually how to balance the available organisational resources (plant and equipment, people and capital) among the different types of projects. A preliminary decision of balance must be made by top management—for example, 20 per cent compliance, 50 per cent strategic and 30 per cent operational—before project selection takes place, although the balance may be changed when the submitted projects are reviewed. Given these inputs, the priority team can carry out its many responsibilities, which include supporting project sponsors and representing the interests of the total organisation.

4.7.2 The priority team or portfolio management office responsibilities

It is common to find (in most medium-to-large organisations) a portfolio management office that will be accountable for the business planning process, the oversight of the development of the Investment Business Cases, and the facilitation of the prioritisation of the investment activity (with top management). The *project* portfolio office would also be a monitor and control point involved in setting strategic direction and communicating with Business Case owners changes in company strategy to ensure continued alignment of the investment activity. The *portfolio* management office is responsible for publishing the priority of every investment and ensuring the process is open and free of organisational politics (the *they who shouts the loudest* syndrome). For example, most organisations use scorecards to disperse the current portfolio of investments and report back on the status of each, including on current issues. This open communication encourages transparency (for better or worse). Over time, the portfolio team evaluates the progress of the investments (programs/projects) in the portfolio. If this whole process is managed well, it can have a profound impact on the success of an organisation in achieving its strategic objectives.

Constant scanning of the external environment—to determine if organisational focus and/or selection criteria need to be changed—is imperative. Periodic priority reviews and changes need to keep current with the changing environment. Regardless of the criteria used for selection, each investment should be evaluated by the same criteria. If investments are classified by *mandatory* (compliance), *operational* and *strategic*, each investment in its class should be evaluated by the same criteria. Enforcing the priority system is crucial. Keeping the whole system open (transparent) and above board is important to maintaining the integrity of the system and keeping new, young or even seasoned executives from going around the system. For example, communicating which investments are approved, investment ranks, status of in-process investment, and any changes in investment criteria will discourage people from bypassing the system.

4.7.3 Balancing the portfolio for risks and dependencies

A major responsibility of the portfolio management office is to balance projects by type, risk and resource demand. This requires a total-organisation perspective. Hence, a proposed investment that ranks high on most criteria may not be selected because the organisational portfolio already includes too many investments with the same characteristics—for example, risk level, use of key resources, high cost, non-revenue producing and long durations. Balancing the portfolio of investment is as important as investment selection. Organisations need to evaluate each new investment in terms of what value it adds. Short-term needs must be balanced with long-term potential. Resource usage needs to be optimised across all investments, not just the most important investment. Risks associated with investment need to be considered:

■ Do the risks associated with the total portfolio of programs and projects reflect the organisation's risk profile?

■ Are there specific investment risks that can inhibit the execution of a program/project, such as schedule, cost and technical?

In this chapter, we refer only to balancing the organisational risks inherent in the portfolio, such as market risk, ability to execute, time to market and technology advances. Project-specific risks will be covered in detail in Chapter 16 "Project risk management".

Alongside the balancing of risk is the maneuvering of projects, given the set of dependencies that exist among the group of investments at any one time. As programs and projects deliver, as new investments are introduced into the mix, and as delays and issues affect others, the dependencies will be ever-changing and will be another factor in balancing the portfolio. For example, what dependencies exist between the themes (mandatory, strategic and operational) and the programs/projects in Figure 4.15?

Figure 4.15 Portfolio dependencies

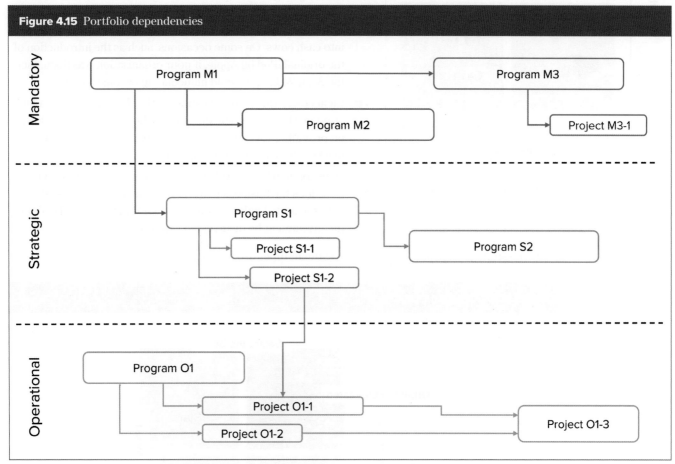

© 2022 Dr Neil Pearson

These styles of dependency schedules, at a strategic level, are common interpretations of how the investment activity will be scheduled—looking at the dependency between elements on the schedule, and as such, any risks associated with delivering the portfolio in the designed manner.

Bruce Henderson proposed BCG's growth share matrix in the 1970s and the principles are still used today (Figure 4.16). Such matrices are usually captured in reports available from products such as Oracle Corporation's Primavera portfolio management tool. A portfolio management office would use many cuts across the data to ensure a balanced and thorough approach is applied to the selection of the investments that ultimately make their way into the final portfolio, programs and projects.

> *A company should have a portfolio of products/services with different growth rates and different market shares. The portfolio composition is a function of the balance between cash flows ... margins and cash generated are a function of market share.* (Reeves, Moose & Venema 2014)

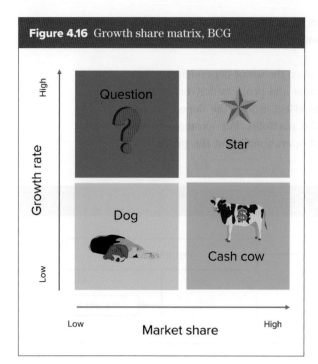

Figure 4.16 Growth share matrix, BCG

Source: Adapted from Reeves M, Moose S & Venema T 2014, "BCG classics revisited: The growth share matrix", BCG, https://www.bcg.com/publications/2014/growth-share-matrix-bcg-classics-revisited.aspx

The BCG matrix is concerned with classifying products and services (investments) into the categories of:

■ Dogs: These are investments that don't have market share and are experiencing low market growth. The question is, what should be done with these investments? Does the business put the dog down and kill off the investment?

■ Stars: These are investments that have high growth and high market share. These are the investments that equate to the maturity stage on the product life cycle. Businesses need to milk these for as long as possible and extend their life as stars. If the marketplace stays stable, these investments typically turn into cash cows. On some occasions, such as the introduction of the original iPod by Apple, if your organisation was Sony, then the Sony Walkman would immediately become a dog.

■ Cash cows: These are investments that have low growth but good market share. The question is, how long they can keep on providing revenue and at what cost to the business if market share potential is capped?

■ Question marks (?): Although seeing good market growth, how does the business convert these investments into stars, with the added value this returns? Or don't they, and should the investment be disinvested (put down)?

Some strategies for handling these investment types are indicated in Figure 4.17.

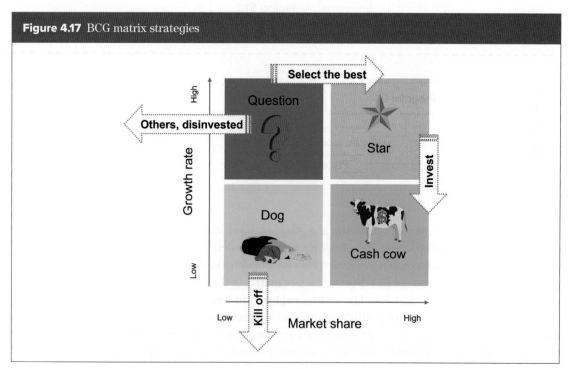

Figure 4.17 BCG matrix strategies

Source: Adapted from Reeves M, Moose S & Venema T 2014, "BCG classics revisited: The growth share matrix", BCG, https://www.bcg.com/publications/2014/growth-share-matrix-bcg-classics-revisited

The result of the portfolio planning, from a project leader's perspective, could be an aligned structure of programs and projects that indicate the position of their particular allocated work, its strategic alignment and contribution to the organisation's strategy, its overall priority and other useful information. The project leader can use this information in multiple ways, for example to:

- position and understand the priority of the project
- build a compelling 60-second story (or elevator pitch) for the project
- gain understanding of the expected benefits (value) to be delivered by the project
- understand upwards reporting requirements
- understand the dependencies between the project and other programs/projects taking place.

Project portfolio management (PPM) can be a complex process in organisations and therefore PPM software is often used to assist strategists and portfolio managers. The next section reviews some of the features of software tools that can assist in such activities.

4.8 : Project portfolio management

Project Management Information Systems (PMISs) are discussed in Chapter 15 "Project information and communications management". **Project Portfolio Management (PPM) systems** have features that are not commonly found in run-of-the-mill PMISs. This short section aims to present some of the key features of PPM software.

4.8.1 Features of Project Portfolio Management (PPM) systems

As with PMISs, there is a lot of focus on cloud solutions in the software industry, and PPM is no different. In the Gartner cloud-based PPM magic quadrant report (Stang & Handler 2012), several trends are identified in the cloud PPM marketspace, including:

- *The PPM sweet spot:* Here, reference is made to the *sweet spot* in communication and reporting. What level of information is captured, at what level in the organisation for effective decisions to be made? Using various grids and other charts to visualise information, refer to Figure 4.18.

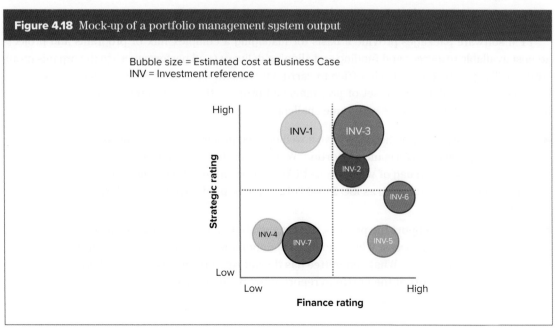

Figure 4.18 Mock-up of a portfolio management system output

- *PPM and Agile development support:* With the rise in the use of Agile methodologies, PPM applications are now supporting elements of the communication, collaboration and reporting nuances associated with Agile development methods.

- *Social networking and collaboration:* Gartner notes that social networking and collaboration in the PPM context seem more like fads than mainstay features of PPM applications.

- *Mobile device support direct into the PPM solution:* PPM providers are using HTML5 to ensure connectivity from popular tablets and smartphones to ensure facilities exist for mobile platforms to allow users to report their time (sheets) and completion of assigned work packages directly into the PPM system, carry out approval of items within a workflow, and carry out executive reporting (dashboards) with drill-down on mobile devices.

These supplement the more traditional business requirements of PPM software, which include the following:

- The ability to strategically align investments to organisational strategy and particularly their contribution towards the delivery of an objective. This has been discussed throughout this chapter as it is the cornerstone of alignment and linking projects to the delivery of strategy.

- PPM tools should not be constrained to portfolio planners as various levels in the organisation should have access to these—portfolio managers to manage the portfolio, executives to see alignment and obtain status on delivery, and managers to see KPIs and their contribution and effect on objectives.

- By ensuring there are various reporting outputs from the package to inform the different roles involved in PPM, the intangible benefit could be to improve speed and accuracy of decision-making in the organisation, as the organisation has a defined source of truth for portfolios and investments.

- PMO can flow down from the information presented in the PPM; this could be captured in a Business Case, for example, from which the Project Charter and scope document would subsequently be developed.

- Having a defined source of truth for portfolio and investment data provides an organisation-wide synergy and truth to the information being presented.

PPM software packages provide a basis for managing a complex mix of programs and projects against available resources and funding and aligning delivery (and performance) to the organisation's strategy. They allow the portfolio office to carry out simulations and be able to rank and prioritise, to provide that ideal, balanced set of programs and projects that the organisation is best placed to deliver. These systems do come with some challenges:

- *Process:* The organisation needs to have a well-defined process for managing investments— from conception to performance reporting. Without this, the content of the PPM system is likely to be a mixed bag of work. Some PPM solutions follow a particular project management approach, such as ISO 21500:2012, Agile or predictive PMI and PRINCE2 approaches.

- *People (roles):* To support the process, the organisation must define the roles of the people participating in the process. Who is going to maintain the mass of information in the PPM system on a daily basis? What committee has the approval of the portfolio? Where is the weekly/monthly status of the portfolio reported to? What access do the project leaders have into the PPM system to maintain project-related information? Remember the adage: *rubbish in, rubbish out!*

■ *Technology (integration):* Integration to existing ICT systems is often critical. For example, is there a requirement for the PPM system to interface with the organisation's finance systems to capture accurate spending and funding? How does the PPM system integrate with any project tracking systems that exist in the organisation? If your organisation leverages Microsoft Project Server, how is milestone and other tracking information integrated with the PPM system, so updates from program and project status are automatically reflected back into the portfolio management solution?

■ *Knowledge:* Is the business ready to harness the information provided by the PPM system, and does it have the right forums, with the right people in place, to harness the collective knowledge of the organisation? Can this knowledge and decision-making capability be harnessed by the PPM system and recorded for future learning?

4.8.2 **Prominent PPM systems**

The authors have experienced many PPM systems in their careers, from inhouse-developed spreadsheets offering complex solutions to mainstream PPM systems, such as those offered by Oracle Corporation's Primavera and Artemis portfolio management software.

The choice of software systems (remember the definition of a *system* here is people, process, technology and knowledge) is complex and a Business Case should be developed to ensure a solution is selected that provides the needs of the business now and in the future.

■ *Alfabet (http://alfabet.softwareag.com):* Software AG's Alfabet IT portfolio management platform.

■ *Aurea Planning Solutions (formerly Artemis) (www.aurea.com/our-acquisitions/artemis/):* Enterprise investment, asset and portfolio management software. Enables real-time reporting and decision-making at the portfolio and investment level, based upon real-time project and resource data.

■ *Planview (www.planview.com):* For planning and monitoring portfolios, from a top-down perspective. Offers a real-time view across the enterprise.

■ *Primavera (www.oracle.com):* Focuses on solutions that support business outcomes that drive C-level strategic metrics and results.

■ *HP Project and Portfolio Management Center (www.hp.com):* Standardises, manages and captures the execution of project and operational activities. It provides critical information in real-time.

SNAPSHOT
from PRACTICE **Ergon Energy**

Program JET (valued at AUD35 million) involved the establishment of a large program of work as part of the business improvement portfolio of work and a strategic investment to replace multiple ICT systems with an integrated enterprise resource planning (ERP) system. The program was jointly sponsored by Ergon Energy, Queensland (the regional energy distributor) and Energex (the city and urban energy distributor). The ERP package was based on the Mincom Ellipse Enterprise Asset Management application suite. This huge program of work, involving more than 200 employees plus contractors over 18 months, was phased into multiple streams of work.

(Continues)

One of the authors was jointly involved in one of the streams of work, to develop a future-state process for investment management and the configuration of a portfolio management system that was to support the process. Artemis 7 was the selected portfolio management solution and had to integrate with aspects of the ERP system and with the program/project management software (based on a combination of Artemis Views (a project management scheduling tool) and Microsoft Project.

By integrating systems and having a defined workflow (process), managing the many hundreds of Investment Business Cases and much management information became a routine process in the organisation. Before this, several ad hoc tools had been used to establish, prioritise and control the AUD millions of competing investment requests (some mandatory, based on regulatory changes, and some strategic, such as asset replacements and some operational improvements). The value of the annual portfolio for the building and maintenance of the assets topped the AUD1 billion mark, so ensuring tight control of the funds and the investment choices was critical to business success and meeting the demands of the customer base, which was spread across a geographic area of 1.7 million km² with 220 000 km of powerlines serving a population of 4.8 million.

Figure 4.19 Power lines

Pixtal/AGE Fotostock

Sources: Mincom 2007, "Ergon Energy goes live with Mincom Ellipse", Business Wire, 30 May, https://www.businesswire.com/news/home/20070530005988/en/Ergon-Energy-Live-Mincom-Ellipse, accessed February 2018; Woodhead B 2007, "Taking care of power business", *The Australian Business Review*, 29 May, www.theaustralian.com.au/business/technology/taking-care-of-power-business/news-story/23272bc58ba896df0ae3f5d48000dc5d, accessed February 2018.

Organisations selecting a PPM system should carefully consider the features and complexity of such software packages and seek professional advice in not only their selection, but also about embedding such systems within their business processes and culture. Selecting and embedding a PPM system is a major project in its own right. Refer to Snapshot from Practice: Ergon Energy.

4.9 | Benefits management integration with project management

In practice, when establishing a project—in, for example, the pre-Initiation stage or as a part of being involved in business planning work drafting early Business Cases—it is important to be aware of any Business Case terminology and the life cycle of a Business Case and how that interacts with the organisation's project management methodology. We have seen one interpretation of this in Chapter 2 "Popular frameworks and methodologies", Figure 2.23. Here, there are implications for the project leader, to ensure currency of the business case as the project progresses. It is within the Business Case that most organisations document benefits and the value of those benefits.

Remember a benefit is a result of achieving the project's deliverables in a holistic manner. If we as project leaders:

- make sure there is alignment between the deliverables, ensuring they will deliver the benefits
- in design, ensure we do not lose sight of these deliverables
- in Execution, ensure that the deliverables are on track to deliver the benefits

We will be positioned for the best possible benefit delivery.

It is the project leader who takes this role on behalf of the leadership team and, more specifically, the project sponsor. The question begs though if a project leader is remunerated sufficiently to take on the delivery of benefits as a senior manager in an organisation would?

Figure 4.20 illustrates a typical benefits management process as it interacts across a traditional project management life cycle.

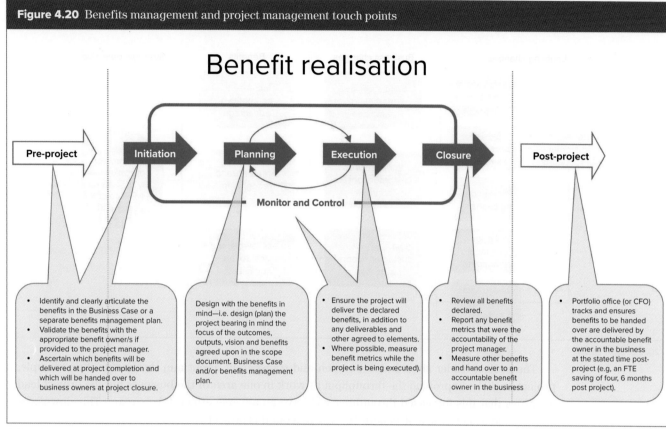

Figure 4.20 Benefits management and project management touch points

© 2022 Dr Neil Pearson

As Kernzer discusses (depicted in Figure 4.20), a project leader can:

- carry out due diligence as a project leader and ensure benefits are correct, owned and have measures at the start of the project
- design with benefits in mind during the Planning stage of the project
- check delivery against benefits and adjust course as necessary, during project Execution and Monitor and Control
- at project Closure, measure and delivery the remaining benefits (or parts of benefits) by handing them back to the business with an accountable owner to be released at a future point in time.

As a project leader it is rare that we see the majority of benefits realised at Closure. Projects are typically enablers for later benefits to be harvested by the business; as Kernzer indicates, the project leader departs the project at Closure, and often is a contractor to the organisation and departs the organisation; it is almost unheard of that the project leader becomes the operational manager and takes on the realisation of the benefits post-project.

4.9.1 The essence of a good Benefits Plan

First, understand the benefits dependency network for the project in relation to the business objective/s of the organisation. Start from the right-hand side of Figure 4.21, identify the *business objective* the project is being aligned to deliver (blue circle). From this, work backwards to the *benefits* the project is being positioned to deliver in support of the *business objective*. Next, work out what must change in the business to deliver the benefits (i.e. the *business changes*; from this the more granular *enabling changes* that will enable the *business change* to take place will drop out).

Figure 4.21 Benefits dependency network

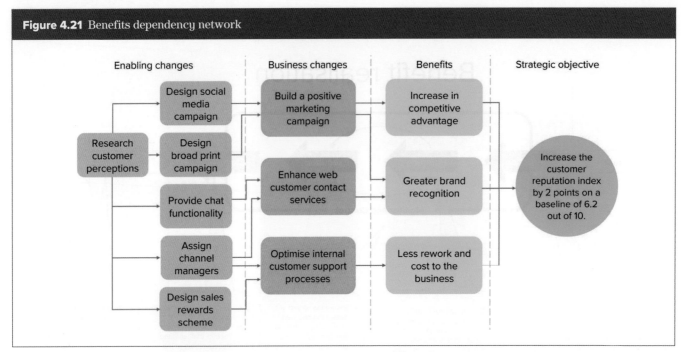

The project leader should also be open and transparent about any disbenefits. For example, a project could be improving the throughput of work in one area of the business but the project leader identifies that this increased throughput will have an adverse effect downstream. This downstream effect could be noted as a disbenefit (in carrying out this project).

Second, create a benefit profile for each benefit. Although the benefits dependency network links our benefits to the business objective/s, from a project leader's perspective these are lacking the detail required to deliver. The project leader, in conjunction with the sponsor, would next create a benefit profile for each of the benefits. The key elements to collect in relation to each benefit include (for example):

- Benefit—greater brand recognition
- Description—to improve the brand recognition of key customer groups
- Measure—net promoter score (refer to www.netpromoter.com/know/)
- Baseline—7.5 out of 10
- Calculation—subtracting the percentage of detractors from the percentage of promoters gives the net promoter score (NPS)
- Target—9 out of 10
- Timeframe—within 12 months
- Category—customer service
- Owner—customer services director
- Success—dependent on delivery of the enabling and business changes
- Risks—new generation-led movement brings product to market.

Documenting benefit profiles for tangible (measurable) benefits is critical but the project leader must also not lose sight of those intangible benefits. Intangible benefits are those benefits to which it can be difficult to attach a direct measurable value.

In Figure 4.21 an intangible benefit could be that employees are more engaged as the products are seen as high-end and trend setting. How would we measure employee engagement with the company?

Remember, benefits can be in support of many organisation facets, for example, product quality, reputation, compliance (laws and legislation), assets, sustainability, financial, risk, data quality, service quality, brand, market share (segment), customer value, performance (process) and culture.

Both the Benefits Plan and the Business Case travel with the project, are updated on approval, are presented at the various gates for verification of benefit and business case delivery, and are used to validate project delivery at the end of the project. The Benefits Plan is typically handed over to an accountable business representative (e.g. corporate benefits manager, reporting to the CFO), and the accountable operational manager now tasked with delivering any post-project benefits (Figure 4.22).

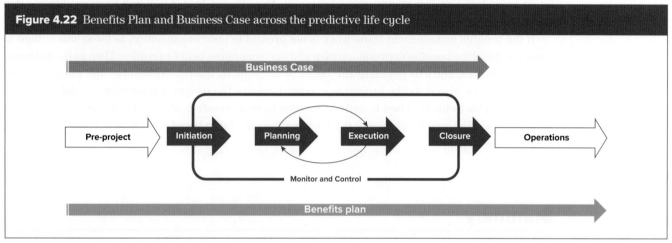

Figure 4.22 Benefits Plan and Business Case across the predictive life cycle

© 2022 Dr Neil Pearson

Third, build the project around delivery of the benefits. If the project is carrying out activities that don't ultimately support realisation of the benefit, then question: Why is this work being carried out in this project? For this, we can use a benefits traceability matrix. This next tool really enables the project leader and team to see what work in this project and other related projects is contributing to the delivery of which benefits (Figure 4.23).

Figure 4.23 Benefits traceability matrix

> Which deliverable or work package directly delivers the whole or a part of the benefit? This ensures we design the project with the benefits in mind!

Benefits traceability

Benefit name	Benefit owner in the business	Benefit measure	Baseline value	Target value	Delivers/contributes to strategic objective/KPI	Deliverable	Work package	Work package	Work package	Work package	Deliverable	Work package	Work package	Work package	Work package
											Project A				
Greater brand recognition	Service director	XYZ brand awareness survey	Segment X rating 3 out of 10 / Segment Y rating 5 out of 10	Segment X rating 7 out of 10 / Segment Y rating 8 out of 10	Improve brand awareness across all customer segments...	*Research customer brand feedback*	WP45	WP23			*Design re-branding marketing package*	WP65-80			

© 2022 Dr Neil Pearson

Note: The mapping to work package level provides an extra level of assurance to the project leader; this relationship between deliverables and work packages would be captured in the project's work breakdown structure, which is generated later in the Planning stage. The project leader would have to come back to this matrix and complete this information at a later stage in planning. It acts as a good cross-reference check to ensure benefits are being designed into the project.

Benefits Profile and Traceability Matrix

In summary, know your organisation's benefits management framework and know how this interacts with the project management approach. As a project leader you will have established this governance at the start of the project.

If the benefits management framework is not present in your organisation as governance, then at minimum build the benefits dependency map and accompanying benefit profiles. Then as the Planning stage progresses, start to populate the benefits traceability matrix—remember the phrase *design with benefits in mind!* As the project is executed, ensure the design components are delivered and the deliverables (with attached benefits) continue to be harvested. At project Closure, measure and review all benefits, and hand over to the business the remaining benefits with an accountable benefit owner in the business.

Summary

1. The key takeaways from this chapter include:
   - As a project leader, insist on a validated, current Business Case upon which to base the Initiation (chartering) of your project.
   - As a project leader, always validate the Business Case at project Initiation. Don't assume this has been done accurately before issuing the Business Case to yourself as project leader. Use some of the tools introduced in this chapter to assist you. Often Business Cases are written at the start of the financial year—if you receive the Business Case 10 months into the financial year, environments and other factors will undoubtedly have changed.
   - As a project leader, ensure you can tell that strategic story of alignment. It could become the basis of your project's elevator pitch.
   - As a project leader, understand how your project has been packaged within the program and portfolio structure, and identify any other project, program and portfolio dependencies.
   - Have a Benefits Plan, and involve the accountable business owners of benefits (post-project) as they are now an interested/impacted stakeholder in the project.
   - As a project leader, understand the external customer, the value that we add as organisations and how we tactically work inside the organisation to deliver this value through programs and projects.

     Refer to the following template for inspiration around activities a project leader should be involved in and carrying out in the lead-up to project Initiation.

Checklist—Pre-project

2. This chapter has introduced the importance of strategically aligning investment activity, and prioritising competing investments to ensure an organisation is considerate of its *external* environment, and customer value chain/customer value proposition:
   - time to market pressures
   - competitive advantage
   - legislative requirements
   - economic conditions
   - technology advancements
   - innovation

- customer value chain
- customer value proposition

  and its *internal* environment:

- skills of its resources
- corporate risk
- finite capital reserves
- tools and equipment.

3. The common techniques that can be applied to the prioritisation of investments include:
   - analytic hierarchy process
   - pair-wise criterion
   - weighted criteria
   - nominal group technique (NGT).

4. The chapter discussed the contents of a Business Case, including financial and non-financial criteria. The financial criteria for consideration discussed include:
   - payback
   - net present value (NPV)
   - internal rate of return (IRR)
   - benefit–cost ratio (BCR)

We also looked at the importance of having a Business Case that starts with the investment and follows this through the life cycle of the program/project and remains valid throughout. In more contemporary project environments this Business Case is supported by a Benefits Plan and a benefits traceability matrix.

Remember, the project leader must be able to clearly identify the strategic link of their projects, the benefits of the project, and the financial cost model associated with their project in order that, at the end of the project, it can be ascertained whether the project has delivered on the promises made within the Business Case and has delivered the expected value (benefits) from the investment made by the organisation.

Review questions

1. Describe the major components of a strategic management process.
2. Explain the role projects play in the delivery of an organisation's strategy.
3. Why should projects be linked to the organisation's Strategic Plan?
4. The portfolio of projects is typically represented by compliance, strategic and operational projects. What impact can this classification have on project selection?
5. Why does the priority system described in this chapter require that it be open and published? Does the process encourage bottom-up initiation of projects? Does it discourage some projects? Why?
6. Why should an organisation not rely only on financial measures to select projects?
7. Reflect on how the pair-wise criterion system could be applied in your organisation. Against which criterion would you carry out prioritisation?
8. What is the BCG matrix and how is it used?

Exercises

1. Using the BCG matrix illustrated in Figure 4.16, review the investments.
   a. Investment A is a new product that has been released into the industry. It seems to be experiencing growth currently.
   b. Investment B has been hanging on, operations have flagged, and we are not making much profit on these products.
   c. Investment C has recently seen a lot of product growth and is producing some good returns. We don't know how long this will be sustained in the current environment so are watching this investment closely.
   d. Investment D has slowed down in terms of growth but is still producing good returns.

e. Investment E is still seeing good returns but seems to be levelling off. We have the marketing director reviewing the marketplace to see what the trajectory is likely to do in the future.

f. Investment F is a product brought to market some months ago, but the marketing director has reported that it is not making any progress in terms of growth or returns.

2. Position where you perceive the Investments A through F sit on the BCG matrix. Further analyse these investments and determine the direction the investment could take—as illustrated in Figure 4.17. Justify your reasoning.

3. In small groups, review the list of investments in Table 4.5, sourced from Infrastructure Australia. Then review section 4.5.1, in particular the categories and themes presented for a list of investments. Using idea storming, come up with a categorisation system for the Australia national and state-based list of infrastructure investments.

Table 4.5 Partial list of Australian infrastructure projects (as of 2021)

Adelaide North–South Corridor upgrade (remaining sections)	Upgrading the remaining sections of the north-south corridor, in Adelaide.
Bindoon Bypass	Constructing a western bypass of Bindoon along the Great Northern Highway, in the Shire of Chittering, north-west of Perth. The bypass would be a two-lane highway, comprising 61.6 km of new highway and 4.4 km of improvements to the existing Great Northern Highway.
Beerburrum to Nambour rail upgrade	Duplication of the existing track between Beerburrum and Nambour, as well as extend passing loops and improve stations, to improve the efficiency of passenger and freight rail services.
Armadale Road bridge	A new bridge and freeway interchange bypassing traffic around Cockburn Central, to provide easier access to the Kwinana Freeway and Armadale Road.
Advanced Train Management System implementation on the interstate rail network	Delivery of a wireless satellite communications-based train control system that will replace line-side signalling to improve rail capacity, transit times and rail safety.
AdeLINK tram network: Adelaide tram network expansion	Expansion of the tram network in Adelaide around the CBD and inner suburbs. The initiative also includes a link to Port Adelaide.
Active transport (walking and cycling) access to Sydney CBD	Upgrade a network of 284 km of dedicated cycling and shared cycling/walking paths, on existing radial and cross-regional corridors within a 10 km radius of the CBD.
A3 and A6 corridor capacity	A range of initiatives aimed at reducing capacity constraints on the A3 and A6 corridors.
Brisbane Metro	A set of infrastructure and non-infrastructure changes to public transport services in inner Brisbane.
Brisbane to Gold Coast transport corridor upgrades	A 10-year, network-wide program for upgrades to transport infrastructure in the corridor, including road, rail, cycling and bus improvements.
Bruce Highway upgrade	A broad package of works to progressively upgrade priority sections of the Bruce Highway to address specific capacity constraints, flood resilience and safety concerns.
Bruce Highway: Deception Bay Road Interchange upgrade	New parallel bridges over the Bruce Highway, near Deception Bay, to increase the capacity of the intersection and improve traffic flow
Bruce Highway: Caboolture-Bribie Island Road to Steve Irwin Way	Widening the Bruce Highway from four to six lanes between Caboolture and Steve Irwin Way.
Bruce Highway: Cairns Southern Access Corridor—Stage 3: Edmonton to Gordonvale	Creating a four-lane highway between Edmonton to Gordonvale and significantly reducing interfaces with properties, the North Coast Railway and arterial roads.
Bunbury Outer Ring Road	Developing a ring road on the outskirts of Bunbury to separate regional traffic accessing the Port of Bunbury and local traffic.
Burnie to Hobart freight corridor improvement	Developing a Burnie to Hobart Freight Corridor Strategy, which will prioritise areas for investment along the corridor, with a focus on improving intermodal freight productivity
Canberra public transport improvements	Developing bus transit corridors between Belconnen and Queanbeyan to central Canberra.
Canning Bridge crossing capacity and interchange	Improving station accessibility and the adjacent road network.

Connection between eastern gas markets and gas suppliers	Developing infrastructure to connect northern and/or western Australian gas reserves to the eastern gas markets.
Corridor preservation for East Coast High Speed Rail	Preserving corridor for a high-speed rail link between Melbourne, Sydney and Brisbane.
Corridor preservation for Melbourne Outer Metropolitan Ring Road/E6	Preserving the corridor for the Outer Metropolitan Ring Road and E6 in Melbourne.
Coastal inundation protection strategy	Developing an infrastructure strategy in advance of the inundation risks materialising. Involving engagement with all levels of government, the strategy will need to consider which areas should be protected for continued use, modified to accommodate floods, or withdrawn from altogether.

Source: © Infrastructure Australia 2022. The information set out in this extract https://www.infrastructureaustralia.gov.au/search-priority-list-map?id=408 was captured January 2022 and reflects a point in time. The Priority List (both the website and the contents within), has been and will continue to be updated, with some of the listings now removed. CC BY 3.0 https://creativecommons.org/licenses/by/3.0/

4. Based on Table 4.6, calculate the net present value (NPV) of each investment. The organisation uses a discount rate of 10%. From purely an NPV perspective, which investment would you select?

Table 4.6 Cash flows for Investments A, B and C

Investment A	Years						NPV	
	0	1	2	3	4	5	− $523,033.08	
Cash flows	− $10,000 000	$2,500,000	$2,500,000	$2,500,000	$2,500,000	$2,500,000		=B4+NPV(10%,C4:G4)
Investment B	Years						NPV	
	0	1	2	3	4	5	$8,157.35	
Cash flows	− $750,000	$200,000	$200,000	$200,000	$200,000	$200,000		=B9+NPV(10%,C9:G9)
Investment C	Years						NPV	
	0	1	2	3	4	5	− $18,138.20	
Cash flows	− $75,000	$15,000	$15,000	$15,000	$15,000	$15,000		=B14+NPV(10%,C14:G14)

© 2022 Dr Neil Pearson

5. Based on the list of infrastructure projects presented Table 4.5, in small groups design a list of selection questions as demonstrated in Table 4.4.

6. Design a generic checklist of items to undertake on receipt of the Business Case (including benefits) as a project leader in the Initiation of a project.

References

Australian Institute of Company Directors 2019, "The 7 biggest infrastructure projects in Australia right now", https://aicd.companydirectors.com.au/membership/company-director-magazine/2019-back-editions/february/infrastructure, accessed April 2022.

Daptiv 2010, *The Essential Buyer's Guide for Project Portfolio Management (PPM)*, www.daptiv.com, accessed February 2018.

Descamps, JP 1999, "Mastering the dance of change: Innovation as a way of life", *Prism*, Second Quarter, pp. 61–7.

Foti R 2002, "Louder than words", *PM Network*, December, pp. 22–9.

Infrastructure Australia, https://www.infrastructureaustralia.gov.au, accessed April 2022.

Infrastructure 2020, "Infrastructure Australia focuses on resilience in $58 billion priority list" https://infrastructuremagazine.com.au/2020/02/26/infrastructure-australia-focuses-on-resilience-in-58-billion-priority-list/, accessed April 2022.

Infrastructure Australia n.d., "Infrastructure priority list", https://www.infrastructureaustralia.gov.au/search-infrastructure-priority-list?nid=&search_api_fulltext_db=, accessed January 2022.

Infrastructure Australia 2022a, "About us", https://www.infrastructureaustralia.gov.au/about-us, accessed April 2022.

Infrastructure Australia 2022b, "What we do", https://www.infrastructureaustralia.gov.au/what-we-do, accessed April 2022.

Kerzner H 2017, "Benefits realization and values management in project management", https://www.axelos.com/resource-hub/blog/benefits-realization-and-value-management-in-project-management, accessed January 2022.

Macrobusiness 2019, "Infrastructure Australia: Failing infrastructure wrecking productivity", https://www.macrobusiness. com.au/2019/06/infrastructure-australia-failing-infrastructure-wrecking-productivity/, accessed April 2022.

Mincom 2007, "Ergon Energy goes live with Mincom Ellipse", *Business Wire*, 30 May, https://www.businesswire.com/ news/home/20070530005988/en/Ergon-Energy-Live-Mincom-Ellipse, accessed February 2018.

Project Management Institute (PMI) 2021a, *A Guide to the Project Management Body of Knowledge* (*PMBOK® Guide*), 7th edition, Newton Square, PA.

Project Management Institute (PMI) 2021b, *The Standard for Project Management* (ANSI/PMI 99-001-2021), 7th edition, Newton Square, PA.

Reeves M, Moose S & Venema T 2014, "BCG classics revisited: The growth share matrix", BCG, https://www.bcg.com/ publications/2014/growth-share-matrix-bcg-classics-revisited.aspx, accessed February 2018.

Stang DB & Handler RA 2012, *Magic Quadrant for Cloud-Based Project, and Portfolio Management Services*, www. mccormickpcs.com/images/Magic_Quadrant_for_Cloud-Based_Project_and_Portfolio_Management_Services.pdf, pp. 1–15, accessed December 2012.

Woodhead B 2007, "Taking care of power business", *The Australian Business Review*, 29 May, www.theaustralian.com. au/ business/technology/taking-care-of-power-business/news-story/23272bc58 ba896df0ae3f5d48000dc5d, accessed February 2018.

CHAPTER 5

Organisational change management and cultures

Learning elements

5A   Understand the importance of organisational change management (OCM) in a project environment.

5B   Be able to identify the types of change, the common change-oriented roles, and the typical change activities across the predictive life cycle.

5C   Have a high-level understanding of the commonly encountered OCM approaches and several OCM-relevant tools.

5D   Realise the importance of an organisation's culture and the effect it can have on the management of a project.

5E   Be able to identify and incorporate cultural considerations across continents, countries and companies.

In this chapter

Part 1   Organisational change management (OCM)

5.1   Introduction to Part 1

5.2   OCM and the predictive life cycle

5.3   OCM approaches and tools

5.4   OCM summary

Part 2   Cultures explored

5.5   Introduction to Part 2

5.6   Organisational culture

5.7   Implications of organisational cultures when leading projects

5.8   Working across international cultures

Summary

Part 1 Organisational change management (OCM)

5.1 Introduction to Part 1

Organisational change management (OCM) is a vast discipline of knowledge in its own right. For a project leader, OCM covers all those aspects of change that delivering the project will impact the organisation, its employees and, ultimately, its customers. These changes to the organisation could include changing the attitudes, leadership style and decision-making model of senior management teams; changing the ways teams are supervised, led and paid; and impact assessments of an individual's role in the organisation.

OCM is preparing groups and individuals for the change associated with the project; in doing so, the project leader may have to overcome much resistance to the proposed change.

Effectively what we are doing is moving a business system (people, processes, organisation, technology, behaviours, culture) from a current (*as-is*) state to a future (*to-be*) state; the gaps between the two states are potentially pieces of work that must be incorporated into the project design led by the project leader, and will be allocated to project team members as work packages or tasks as they occur according to the project schedule. Figure 5.1 indicates this thinking.

Figure 5.1 The gap analysis

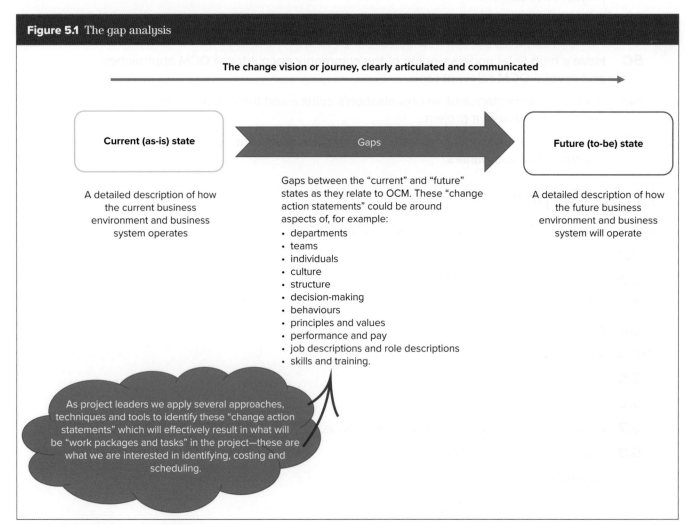

The outputs of applying the approaches, techniques and tools would be project work that is typically captured in the project's organisational change plan, sometimes referred to as the **Organisational Change Management Plan**.

So, why are we interested in this as a project leader? The *Project Management Body of Knowledge,* seventh edition (PMI 2021a), recognised the importance of change to the success of the project by introducing:

- a principle titled *Enable change to achieve the envisioned future state* (PMI 2021a, p. 58)
- several change models, including **ADKAR**, **Kotter's 8-step process**, the **Virginia Satir change model** and the **Bridges transition model** (detailed later in this chapter).

Many influencers have shared their wisdom with us. For example:

- Kurt Lewin: "If you want to truly understand something, try to change it."
- Henry Mintzberg: "Organisations are communities of human beings, not collections of human resources."
- Peter Senge: "People don't resist change. They resist being changed."

As a leader of a project, we are typically not just introducing a change to a business process, a new piece of technology or a new service; we are introducing change to a group of customers (a community) and/or a group of employees (a workforce the company depends on for its existence).

As leaders of projects, with too many lessons captured but not learned, now is the time to truly incorporate OCM into the boundaries of what we enact as project leaders.

Aspects of the wider business system under investigation (refer to Chapter 1 "Contemporary project management") that would be considered during the planning for the change would include the following.

- *Departments:* What impact does the future state have on the department, its purpose, how it is managed, and its fit with other departments and functions within the business?
- *Teams:* How are teams within the department to function in the future state as opposed to how they operate in the current state?
- *Individuals:* What support do individuals require, and how will their job and role change in the future state? Can they fulfil the new purpose in the future? Can they be reskilled and coached or does the project have to consider release and employ (new skills)?
- *Customer:* How will the customer feel about the new product? Is it intuitive, does it require support, does it fulfil a known need or is the project deploying an innovation to fulfil a perceived unknown need?
- *Culture:* Does the culture support the deployment of the project's outputs and outcomes? Does the culture require nudging (refer to the **nudge theory** later in this chapter) or more direct influencing? Do we know what elements of cultures are impacted and require changing (refer to Part 2 of this chapter).
- *Structure:* Does the whole or part of the organisation's structure (as typically represented in the organisational chart) need to be restructured in support of the to-be state? This could include making swathes of middle management redundant or releasing and re-employing people on the ground as a whole new skillset could be required. Remember that structure follows strategy.
- *Decision-making:* Are individuals empowered to make decisions based on defined sets of information? Do they have to always ask supervisors or managers as they feel untrusted? Does the information to make empowered decisions exist, or does the project have to provide this as an output to influence changing behaviours around decision-making?

- *Management versus leadership:* Is the organisation, department or team based around management (micro-management) or transparency and empowerment? Chapter 19 "Project leaders and project teams" discusses these subtle but powerful differences.

- *Principles and values:* Do any principles and values (e.g. in the organisation's values statement) support all aspects of the change taking place? *Note:* Principles, values and culture are typically slow changing and difficult factors to influence and report on in any organisation.

- *Performance and pay:* Do individuals require revised performance agreements to support the future business system and its implementation? Do these require input from managers, supervisors, human resource departments or unions? How does this affect the way the individual is paid? Do new performance measures now have to be achieved where previously none existed?

- *Job descriptions and role descriptions:* Do job descriptions or components of the job need to be revisited, rewritten and assessed? When assessed, do these affect remuneration? Does an individual take on more responsibility (if a RASCI Matrix has been introduced—refer to Chapter 7 "Governance and projects", section 7.3.1), suggesting the job or role should be remunerated at a higher level?

- *Skills and competencies:* What skills and competencies are required to accomplish the revised or new job in the future state? Can these skills and competencies be retrained, or do we have to acquire new people with the new skills? What happens to the old people with the old skills?

- *Knowledge sharing and transfer:* What knowledge is available? Has it been made explicit (e.g. written processes, policy, work instructions) or does it reside in people's heads (tacit knowledge)? If so, how can this be captured and shared?

- *Trust:* Do people feel safe and trusted in their work environments, or do they feel vulnerable and not trusted? No physical evidence may exist—how, as a project leader, are we going to pick up on these vibes and specifically and tactfully address them with the work of the project?

- *Geographic considerations*: Will all cultures and languages receive, react and accept the change outcome in the same manner? What differences must be addressed? Can local resources be leveraged; are further sub-sponsors required within each region or country to add credibility to the change vision?

- *Training and education:* Has a training needs analysis been conducted for all impacted individuals? Do individuals require an individual tailored training plan?

You will have been on the receiving end of organisational changes at some point in your career. How did you feel? Were the factors above considered? Can you identify any other factors? Would you include these in future projects as you take on the role of leading a project?

5.1.1 Types of change

Not all change is equal. Some change is wide and has great impacts, while other change may be contained around a specific business process and the actors involved in that process (the swimlanes in a process swimlane model!).

Generically, change is broken into three types of change. During the pre-project activities, it is critical that the to-be project is correctly assessed as this will influence the amount of change activity that must take place in the project, the roles required, and ultimately the projects budget and schedule.

The three generic types of change (see Figure 5.2) often encountered are:

1. *Transformational change* will completely redesign and reshape an organisation, industry or segment. An organisational transformation can end up transforming a whole industry. Apple did this in 2001 with the original iPod—how quickly did portable cassette players and DVD players disappear off the market? This was much like Tesla did with the electric vehicle industry in 2003—today just about every other major manufacturer is planning to remove petrol (gas) and diesel vehicles from their product portfolios. For example, the Japanese car-maker Honda has committed to completely moving over to research, development and production of electric vehicles by 2040. This long-term transformation is a huge move in technology, skills, raw materials, production and servicing.

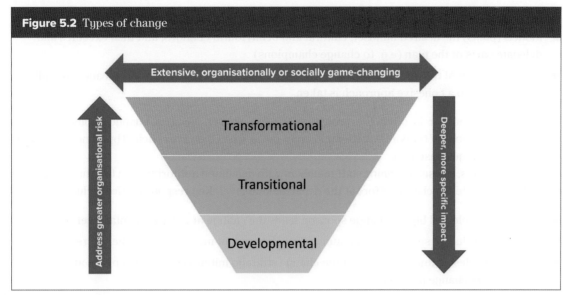

Figure 5.2 Types of change

© 2022 Dr Neil Pearson

2. *Transitional change* is less encompassing but can be equally complex; often, writing a new playbook (transformational) is easier than editing the personas in the existing playbook. Transitional change could include making substantial business changes to remain competitive, leap-frog a competitor or introduce a new cutting-edge technology to market. These typically affect structures, technology and the skills of the people. For example, in a company merger, both companies have business systems for human resources, payroll and finance; however, in the merged company there can only be one instance of each system. This could represent a transitional change to the company that has to replace one of its systems, but a developmental change to the company that stays with the technology but perhaps has to make minor tweaks to its business system.

3. *Development change* is therefore much more contained, and is typically referred to as *business improvement* project work. Components of a business system are changed that could impact, in a less substantial way, the workflow, information, skills of people and how performance is managed. These projects are common and often frequent in organisations in pursuit of perfection. We could use the DMAIC or PDCA process to introduce these changes, discussed in detail in Chapter 13 "Project quality management".

5.1.2 OCM roles

Depending on the type of change, the project leader will be in a better position to identify up-front what additional OCM roles (and later activities) will be required in the project. Due to the nature of projects with a high OCM component, the earlier the change role is brought on board, the sooner change considerations can be accommodated. This is particularly true in transformational and transitional projects where from pre-project and Initiation it is critical to ensure the commitment, sponsorship and leadership is established.

Typical roles found in project environments specific to the OCM components of the project include the following.

Change sponsors: The change sponsor is the champion of the change effort and has authority and influence over the desired outcomes. Key responsibilities include:

- ensures the future state aligns with the organisation's strategic plan
- ensures the future state delivers value to the customer and can articulate this value
- mobilises resources when required to support change management activities
- ensures communication of the future state and what has to be carried out to achieve that desired state
- delegates roles and responsibilities to change leaders

■ assesses and builds readiness and capacity for change

■ models (plans) the desired mindset, cultural and behavioural changes, and then executes and delegate parts of the plan (e.g. to change champions)

■ manages the OCM timeline and identifies milestone events, updates the project leader with all aspects OCM so a cohesive approach is taken.

The change sponsor is often the project sponsor; however, being a change sponsor requires additional dimensions of thinking—better outcomes occur when they are coached by a knowledgeable, experienced change consultant.

Change leaders: These are senior staff members with delegated authority from the change sponsor to lead and execute the change effort at the departmental level. Key responsibilities include:

■ having been selected by the change sponsor, leads the change at a departmental level

■ supports the change sponsor in communicating a consistent message about the future state

■ oversees the design and execution of the change strategy initiatives and each phase and activity of the overall change process

■ clarifies the scope of the change, desired outcomes, heartbeat (timing), conditions for success, constraints and metrics

■ chairs the change leadership team when cross-functional initiatives are considered

■ assesses and builds the organisation's readiness and capacity for change

■ details plans around the desired mindset, cultural and behavioural changes

■ interacts with the project leader and change sponsor on timelines and milestones.

Change champions: These are from across the organisation. They may not be broad subject matter experts, but typically come from the area of the business subject to the change. Key responsibilities include:

■ executes the desired mindset, cultural and behavioural change plans (i.e. the Organisational Change Management Plan)

■ gathers new information about the change effort that may influence how it rolls out and bring this to the attention of the change leader and project leader

■ acts as a feedback loop in a respectful manner, from the on-the-ground individuals and departments to the change leader, change sponsor and project leader.

The selection of this role is critical, as change champions are often the conduit between the plans and the people on the ground being impacted by the change. Change champions must be embedded in the business operations, be respected by all fellow colleagues, be good communicators, be able to influence, and have the trust of those around them.

Change consultants: These are usually independent of the project and the business area under change. Often external consultants are brought into the organisation and the project to address the OCM needs. They often report directly to the project leader and have close ties to the change sponsor. Key responsibilities include:

■ brings a wealth of knowledge and experience to bear on the project, the roles within the project team and the recipients of the project

■ coaches, mentors and advises all the roles in best and good practices

■ contributes and assists all roles in the identification, planning and doing of change management activities

■ reviews and adjusts artefacts beyond the Organisational Change Management Plan (in consultation with the project leader), such as the project stakeholder register, communications register and project schedule.

5.2 : **OCM and the predictive life cycle**

Our discussion on OCM is very much focused around the predictive life cycle, but draws on some key models and theories to base the chapter in good practice research. So, how does OCM fit into the project context? Figure 5.3 indicates some key touch points of OCM with the predictive project management approach. The green overlay represents Project Management Institute (PMI) terminology (PMI 2013).

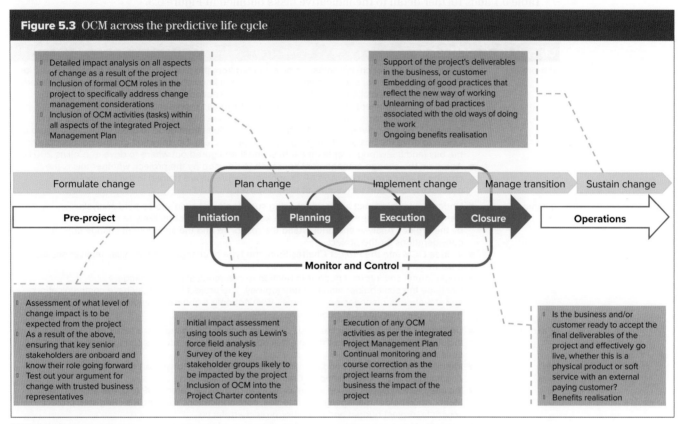

Figure 5.3 OCM across the predictive life cycle

- Detailed impact analysis on all aspects of change as a result of the project
- Inclusion of formal OCM roles in the project to specifically address change management considerations
- Inclusion of OCM activities (tasks) within all aspects of the integrated Project Management Plan

- Support of the project's deliverables in the business, or customer
- Embedding of good practices that reflect the new way of working
- Unlearning of bad practices associated with the old ways of doing the work
- Ongoing benefits realisation

Formulate change — Plan change — Implement change — Manage transition — Sustain change

Pre-project | **Initiation** | **Planning** | **Execution** | **Closure** | **Operations**

Monitor and Control

- Assessment of what level of change impact is to be expected from the project
- As a result of the above, ensuring that key senior stakeholders are onboard and know their role going forward
- Test out your argument for change with trusted business representatives

- Initial impact assessment using tools such as Lewin's force field analysis
- Survey of the key stakeholder groups likely to be impacted by the project
- Inclusion of OCM into the Project Charter contents

- Execution of any OCM activities as per the integrated Project Management Plan
- Continual monitoring and course correction as the project learns from the business the impact of the project

- Is the business and/or customer ready to accept the final deliverables of the project and effectively go live, whether this is a physical product or soft service with an external paying customer?
- Benefits realisation

© 2022 Dr Neil Pearson

With OCM, considerations fall pre-project, during the project and post-project. In pre-project activities a high-level assessment of the overall type of change caused by the project must be considered; this decision will flow into the project at Initiation.

At the pre-project stage, craft a statement of why the change is needed and then leverage a small number of trusted representatives in the business to test out your argument for the change. The greater the degree of organisational change impact, the more activities would have to be built into the scope, project design and eventually detailed planning of the project. Therefore, during project Initiation, the project leader should further understand what the drivers (positive forces) and restrainers (negative forces) to the change are. Here, we could use techniques should as **Lewin's force field analysis** to investigate further. Using this one tool alone would result in the identification of high-level OCM requirements that must be considered as part of the Project Charter. On acceptance of the organisational change impact, the requirements flow into the Planning stage of the project where a detailed **gap analysis** of the project from an organisational change perspective takes place (Figure 5.1). Here, the project leader would look at using a variety of techniques to assess in detail the impact of the project on the organisation, its departments and the employees (and/or customer). Once the plans have been established and approved along the integrated Project Management Plan (integrated PMP), the Project Management Plan and the Organisational Change Management Plan are then executed, in the Execution stage of the project, with course corrections taking place as necessary. As the project nears Closure, the change plans continue to operate. The recipients of the project will continue to require assistance in many forms. This will be transferred out of the project into business operations at project Closure, with the necessary plans and resources handed over to the business for the continued operation of the system and ultimately realisation of final benefits. It is not atypical for a project to have a key subject matter expert from the business involved in all aspects of the project, with the open and transparent expectation that this resource will then move back into the business at project completion and take all the knowledge with them as a *super-user or subject matter expert (SME)*.

Table 5.1 adds further detail to the indicative tasks outlined in Figure 5.3.

Table 5.1 Project-related OCM activities

Life cycle stage	OCM activity
Pre-project	■ Assess what type of change impact is be expected from the piece of work (refer to previous section). ■ Ensure that key senior stakeholders are on board and know their role in the project going forward. ■ Identify any specific change roles (refer to previous section). ■ Test out your argument for change with trusted business representatives. ■ Ensure the project sponsor, project leader and key stakeholders are positive promoters of the change. "The executives who ignited the transformations from good to great did not first figure out where to drive the bus and then get people to take it there. No, they first got the right people on the bus (and the wrong people off the bus) and then figured out where to drive it" (Collins 2001). ■ Agree on the change management approach to be used by the project, whether this is the **change leader's roadmap**, ADKAR or another. Ensure all are trained in the terminology, processes, roles and techniques at their disposal.
Initiation	■ Undertake initial impact assessment using such tools as Lewin's force field analysis. ■ Carry out a change-specific survey of the key stakeholder groups likely to be impacted by the project. Analyse and understand the response and the subsequent change impact considerations for the project. ■ Include OCM into the Project Charter. State the type of change and the initial implications that must be considered. ■ Begin formal and informal nudges in relation to communicating the change. ■ Continue the stakeholder management journey. The project leader may have communications and stakeholder management strategies from not only a general project perspective, but also from a more specific OCM perspective.
Planning	■ Undertake a detailed impact analysis on all aspects of the change as a result of the project. ■ Include formal OCM roles in the project scope to specifically address change management considerations. ■ Identify all work packages and tasks required in the project to support the change as documented in the Organisational Change Management Plan. ■ Include OCM activities (tasks) within all aspects of the integrated PMP (e.g. the Stakeholder Matrix, stakeholder management strategies, communications register, Risk Register, project schedule, project budget and any other project artefacts). ■ Apply OCM tools to assist in identifying all aspects of the change, including the areas of change resistance. What are the key areas of resistance, what actions (activities) are to be done to address the resistance and who is responsible for ensuring the actions are addressed?
Execution	■ Execute any OCM activities as per the Project Management Plan and the Organisational Change Management Plan. Common OCM activities include: 　• additional stakeholder engagements 　• additional communications 　• training development and roll-out 　• negotiating employment-related issues 　• working with unions 　• readiness arrangements and reporting 　• coaching and mentoring (change skills) 　• knowledge transfer arrangements 　• risk assessment. ■ Carry out and act on the all-important business readiness assessment. Is the business and/or customer ready to accept the final deliverables of the project and effectively go live?
Monitor and Control	■ Undertake continual monitoring and course correction as the project learns from the business the impact of the project. ■ Manage and communicate with stakeholders.
Closure	■ Are the business and/or customers ready to accept the final deliverables of the project and effectively go live? ■ Adopt success measurement and benefits realisation. ■ Undertake business readiness assessment and implement any remaining gaps to ensure success at go-live.
Operations	■ Support the project's deliverables (outcomes) in the business or the customer. ■ Embed good practices that reflect the new way of working. ■ Unlearn bad practices associated with the old ways of working. ■ Ongoing benefits realisation.

5.2.1 Business readiness assessment

As outlined in Table 5.1, there are many OCM activities to be considered within a project environment. The authors would like to highlight one of these activities: the business readiness assessment(s). These typically take the form of surveys but could also be a workshop or a series of interviews with key stakeholders. Whichever mode is applied, be sure to check readiness from all levels of the organisation—strategic, tactical and operational (more of this later).

The key question is: Do they truly feel ready in all aspects of their job for the new business system to go live and for them to be successful in their job?

The business readiness assessment (sometimes referred to a *change readiness assessment*) will probe multiple dimensions, for example:

- awareness of the change
- their support level in relation to the change
- their knowledge, skills and competencies in relation any component of the business system, such as technology, equipment or processes
- their capacity to take on the change and make it a success
- the quality and usefulness of any explicit (knowledge) as information; in the form of guidelines, work instructions, procedures and so on
- their role, responsibilities, remuneration and decision-making parameters.

This survey, once administered to all levels of the area impacted by the change, is collated, the results analysed and actions assigned to address any last-minute course corrections or changes.

Several companies specialise in OCM and have pre-written readiness surveys for administering it, including Prosci.

The discussion thus far has been around integrating OCM with project management activities. As indicated in Table 5.1, one of the first activities is to identify, communicate and educate the project team (including OCM roles) around the OCM approach to be taken. The next section considers some of the more popular approaches encountered through consulting, and also through student engagements.

5.3 | OCM approaches and tools

This section summarises various relevant approaches, techniques and tools before expanding each one into further detail. Table 5.2 represents a sample of those available, drawn from the authors' own experiences and feedback from thousands of students through professional training activities.

5.3.1 Prosci and ADKAR

Let's start with Prosci, as this covers ADKAR to some extent. It has an overarching Prosci change triangle model based on the four aspects of:

1. *success*—definition of what this is
2. *leadership and sponsorship*—direction and guidance for the project
3. *project management*—how the change is delivered
4. *change management*—to address the people side of change.

This model is supported by the Prosci three-phase process, as illustrated in Figure 5.4. It is made up of three phases—prepare approach, manage change and sustain outcomes. Note that at the centre is ADKAR (Awareness, Desire, Knowledge, Ability and Reinforcement-to change). ADKAR is the subject of a best-selling personal change book (Hiatt 2006).

Table 5.2 OCM approaches and tools

Name/link	Most suitable for which type of change?	Approach or tool?
Prosci: ADKAR Prosci is an overarching methodology. ADKAR is at the individual level of change. https://www.prosci.com	Transitional/developmental	Approach with tools
Change Management Institute (CMI) *Change Management Body of Knowledge* (CMBOK). This was a collaboration between CMI and APMG; this is also the APMG certification for OCM in support of various approaches such as PRINCE2. https://www.change-management-institute.com	All	Approach with tools
John Kotter's 8-step process for leading change. Kotter is a globally respected author on change leadership. https://www.kotterinc.com/8-step-process-for-leading-change/	Transformational/transitional	Approach
Change leader's roadmap. https://beingfirst.com	Transformational/transitional and developmental	Approach
Lewin's force field analysis.	All	Tool
Lewin's unfreeze, change, refreeze model. Lightweight with intent.	All	Approach
Kübler-Ross. Individual change cure based in psychology and personal grief.	All (when at the individual level)	Tool
Fisher's personal transition curve.	All (when at the individual level)	Tool
McKinsey 7-S. A solid gap analysis tool for investigating between the *as-is* and *to-be* states.	All	Tool
The nudge theory. The psychology of micro nudges.	All	Tool
Virginia Satir change model. Introduced in *Project Management Body of Knowledge* (PMI 2021).	All	Tool
William Bridges's transition model. Introduced in *Project Management Body of Knowledge* (PMI 2021).	All	Tool
Managing Change in Organisations: A Practice Guide (PMI 2013). PMI's overarching approach to change, as overlaid on Figure 5.1.*	All	Approach
Praxis Change Management.* https://www.praxisframework.org/en/knowledge/change-management	All	Approach

* Not covered in this text but included for completeness.

© 2022 Dr Neil Pearson

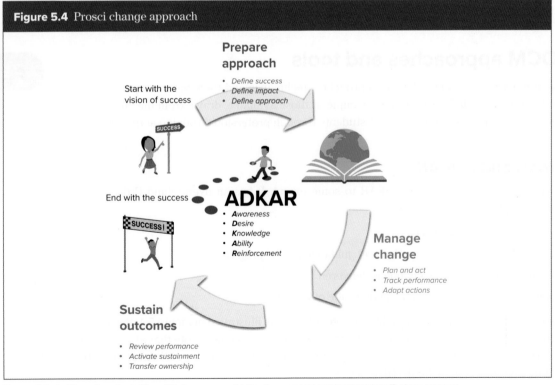

Figure 5.4 Prosci change approach

Source: Adapted from: Prosci n.d., "Prosci 3-phase process", https://www.prosci.com/methodology/3-phase-process

ADKAR is a frequently applied approach to take change down to the individual level in an organisation, department or team. The elements of ADKAR are indicated in Figure 5.5. It promotes the principle that if we all achieve individual (personal) change in support of the vision, then the sum of that coordinated change should go a long way towards achieving success in terms of the vision. The success of implementing an Enterprise Resource Planning (ERP) system, for example, would depend on its end users (across all departments in the organisation) having the awareness, desire, knowledge and ability to use the system. Another example could be the implementation of an improved process for triaging a hospital's accident and emergency admissions, to ensure the hospital can meet its four-hour service level agreement (SLA)—the administration staff, nurses and doctors will all need to have the awareness, desire, knowledge and ability to make this process change a success, suitably reinforced by the business.

Figure 5.5 ADKAR

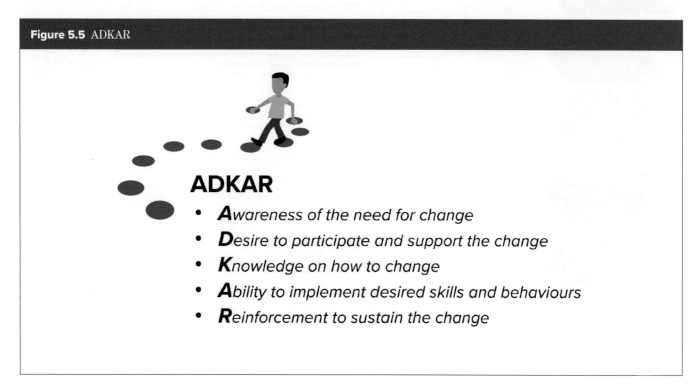

ADKAR

- **A**wareness of the need for change
- **D**esire to participate and support the change
- **K**nowledge on how to change
- **A**bility to implement desired skills and behaviours
- **R**einforcement to sustain the change

Source: Prosci n.d., "The Prosci ADKAR model", https://www.prosci.com/methodology/adkar, accessed January 2022

Refer to the "Snapshot from Practice: ADKAR in action".

SNAPSHOT *from* PRACTICE : **ADKAR in action**

A not-for-profit domestic violence support centre was having to implement a local policy on the use of GPS tracking devices for staff (social workers) out in the field carrying out one-to-one visits. Using the ADKAR approach, the employee's individual response to the introduction of a new policy pertaining to a local government department's implementation of a lone worker GPS tracking device for social workers was captured (Figure 5.6).

Referring to Figure 5.6 (working across a row in the table):

■ The first arrow (in any row) indicates the ADKAR word.

■ The second is a definition from an employer perspective.

■ The third is a question an employee can rhetorically ask themselves.

- The fourth column is an example of an employee's ADKAR to the introduction of a lone worker GPS tracker and alert device.

- The fifth is a score system for the employee to complete, based on their perceptions.

- The circle at the end of each dimension of ADKAR represents the score given.

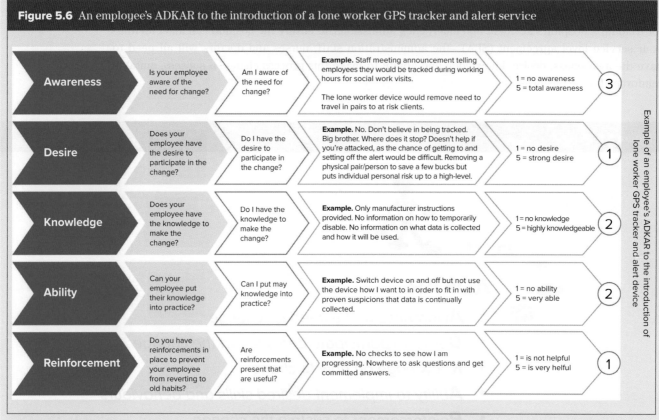

Figure 5.6 An employee's ADKAR to the introduction of a lone worker GPS tracker and alert service

© 2022 Dr Neil Pearson

Source: Adapted from ADKAR®: A Model for Change in Business, Government and Our Community, Prosci Learning Centre Publications, Loveland, Colorado, 2006

The change consultant and change leader would then review the responses: taking the first row that scored 3 (or below), they would start out by trying to understand the root cause (the why) so they can address the concern. For example, in the first row, a score of 3 for Awareness could trigger an exploration of the reasons for and benefits of the change with the individual, both at an organisational level (in terms of budgets and resources) and an individual level (we do care about employee safety). The change consultant and change leader would then move down to the next row scoring 3 or less. In this case, Desire would be investigated with the employee to try and lower their resistant forces and increase their positive forces. All the other sub-3 scores would be addressed. In doing so, the change consultant and change leader works at the coal face with the people directly affected by the change to put in place actions to address the issues. If these types of tools are applied during the project Planning stage (prior to implementation) they have been proven to bring about more successful change that is sustainable in the longer term, as additional much-needed change actions are being built into the work of the project for later execution.

5.3.2 Change Management Body of Knowledge (CMBOK)

The Change Management Institute has recently formalised what was a few years ago a general set of guidelines on change management into a more formal approach to OCM with accreditations offered through APMG. This jointly developed Change Management Body of Knowledge (CBOK) follows patterns we will see in pretty much most of these change management approaches but is geared around 13 knowledge areas. Picking any change management approach that appeals to your business environment will greatly enhance project success!

This CBOK is based around 13 change knowledge areas:

1. *A change management perspective*—the overarching approach behind the change
2. *Defining change*—what the change is, what the new world will look like
3. *Managing benefits*—are the benefits from the change identified and documented?
4. *Stakeholder strategy*—change strategies to engage with stakeholders
5. *Communications and engagement*—additional change communications
6. *Change impact*—what the impact is and measuring progress
7. *Change readiness*—planning and measurement, ensuring a sound change management plan is prepared
8. *Project management*—how the change activities interact with the project (and program if relevant)
9. *Education and learning support*—putting in place the training and support infrastructure for the change to be successful
10. *Facilitation*—the facilitation of change across the change process
11. *Sustaining systems*—ensuring the business has the knowledge and resources to sustain the change
12. *Personal and professional management*—developing the skills, particularly the soft skills
13. *Organisational considerations that will affect the implementation of the change:* structure, leadership, values and so on.

It is based around an indicative process as illustrated in Figure 5.7.

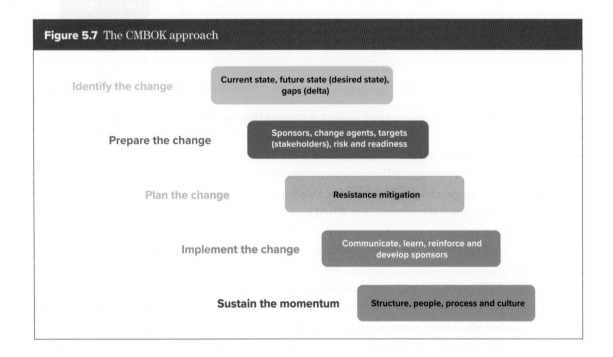

Figure 5.7 The CMBOK approach

Identify the change — Current state, future state (desired state), gaps (delta)

Prepare the change — Sponsors, change agents, targets (stakeholders), risk and readiness

Plan the change — Resistance mitigation

Implement the change — Communicate, learn, reinforce and develop sponsors

Sustain the momentum — Structure, people, process and culture

5.3.3 John Kotter's eight-step process for leading change

The eight-step process was originally developed during the writing of *Leading Change* (Kotter 2012). The eight steps provide guidance around the key activities a change sponsor should be cognizant of and able to delegate to employees working with change in an organisation. It is a generic approach and does not specifically integrate with project management processes. However, the based-on-research approach, guidance and examples provided by Kotter give interesting insights into the OCM discipline. The eight steps are indicated in Figure 5.8.

Figure 5.8 Kotter's eight steps for leading change

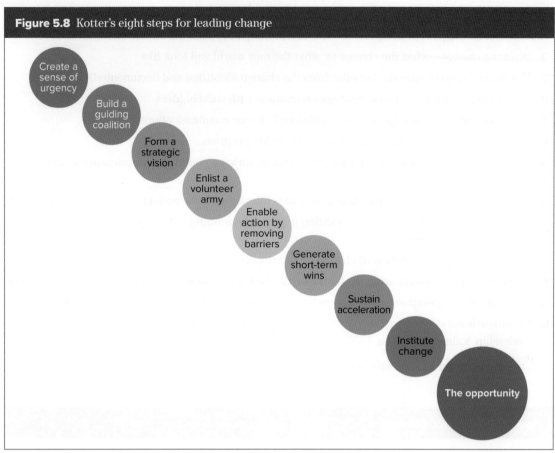

© 2022 Dr Neil Pearson

Source: Adapted from Kotter n.d., "The 8-step process for leading change", https://www.kotterinc.com/8-step-process-for-leading-change/, accessed January 2022

- First, create a sense of urgency. Craft a clear statement that inspires, clearly articulates the WHY and motivates people to go with us on the journey with the required urgency.

- Second, build a guiding coalition. Harness the power of the passionate people from the areas affected and leverage them to influence and guide others.

- Third, form a strategic vision and initiatives. Develop the vision (the WHY) and define the work that is going to support its delivery (the WHAT).

- Fourth, enlist a volunteer army. Create "movement" around the change—successful change is unfortunately like a pandemic virus—catching!

- Fifth, enable action by removing barriers. Provide the means by which roadblocks can be removed, whether people-, process-, organisationally-, technology- (or other) related. We are either on the bus and travelling to a better destination or making a conscious decision to not come along!

- Sixth, generate short-term wins. In future chapters we discuss how introducing deliverables all the way through the project life cycle is so important. Here we are considering the same: what are the quick wins we can design into the project to show positive movement?

- Seventh, sustain acceleration. Push through, keep the vision and move towards it every day—be resilient, we know not everyone is going to like it!

- Eighth, institute change. Make it stick, remove old behaviours and practices, and positively reinforce the new ways of working.

Remember, these approaches can be combined and tailored to create a process that fits with your project and own change management approach. For example, you may choose to regularly take Step 6, seeking opportunities to build this into the project's schedule and communications register.

On the back of this book, Kotter also published the highly likeable and readable book *Our Iceberg is Melting* (https://www.kotterinc.com/book/our-iceberg-is-melting/). It tells the story of various penguins as they discover the iceberg is melting, and unknowingly take on various perspectives (such as change leader penguin, change resistant penguin) and progress through the eight steps of change. This book was used by the author (Pearson) in a business change project where multiple copies were purchased and left around meeting rooms and lunch break rooms. Employees would pick the book up, read and then start to cast character likenesses to the penguins in the book. As a project leader and change leader, the author found that this lightened the mood and opened the door to discussions on various individual employee perspectives on the change about to take place—an unintended consequence of deploying the book. His purpose was just to educate on the eight steps and the move to a new world (or the change vision of the future)!

5.3.4 The change leader's roadmap

This has been around for several years now and has stood the test of time. Often referred to as the *change leader's roadmap methodology* (CLMR), it is positioned at the more transitional and transformational change in an environment (e.g. technology implementations, re-structuring and culture transformations). Within the approach there are elements of Kotter's 8-steps and the Prosci change approach. The CLMR delves more into the three stages (upstream, midstream and downstream); the model indicates the more detailed steps to be taken, suggesting tools/techniques that might assist in collection and analysis of information gained from the various project stakeholders. The result of carrying out the steps is a lot of the content for a typical Organisational Change Management Plan.

Definitions of upstream, midstream and downstream are as follows.

- *Upstream*: Here the focus is on clearly defining what the change is all about—the desired state post the change at a 30 000 m level. This includes the make-up of the initial change team and their change skill level. Also included in this stage is initial high-level readiness and capacity assessments, initial communications and stakeholder assessments and the actual communication of the high-level desired state.

- *Midstream*: Here the focus shifts from the initial design and readiness to the actual detailed design (think of moving from the 30 000 m to 3000 m and 300 m levels). It entails piloting of the desired state, analysing and course correcting before further communicating the details of the design. Finally, this stage also builds the plan for implementation supporting any projects implementation plans from a change management perspective. Further impact analysis at an individual level would also be carried out with actions defined to ensure reactions (behavioural and emotional) are managed (negative) or leveraged (positive).

- *Downstream*: The theme for this stage is the implementation of the change: managing the people side of the change as it is implemented and celebrating the successes of the change, and course correcting the plans and approach in addition to the desired state, if required. This stage also seeks to embed the change in the business as the new way of doing things, supporting people in this activity.

As with ADKAR and Kotter, the reader is encouraged to review the change leader's roadmap book to bolster their OCM knowledge and skills (Ackerman Anderson & Anderson 2010).

5.3.5 Lewin's force field analysis

A tool that the authors find useful, particularly at the Initiation stage of a project (and as part of a readiness check for the implementation of a change), is Kurt Lewin's force field analysis (Figure 5.9). In the analysis, "[a]n issue [future state] is held in balance [equilibrium] by the interaction of two opposing sets of forces—those seeking to promote change (driving forces) and those attempting to maintain the status quo (restraining forces)" (Strategies for Managing Change n.d.). The analysis goes on to state that the driving forces must exceed the restraining forces, thereby moving the equilibrium.

Figure 5.9 Lewin's force field analysis

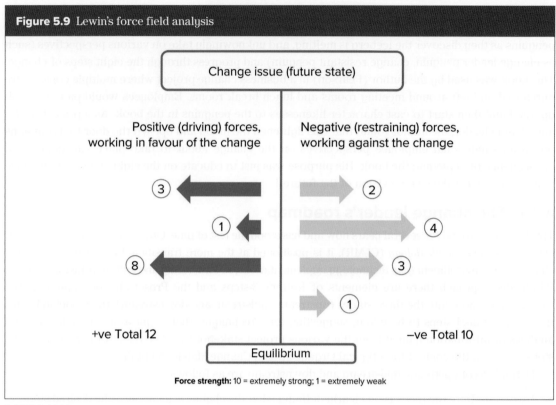

© 2022 Dr Neil Pearson

Source: Graphic adapted from Lewin K 1943, "Defining the 'field at a given time'", *Psychological Review*, vol. 50, no. 3, pp. 292–310 and https://www.valuebasedmanagement.net/methods_lewin_force_field_analysis.html, accessed January 2022

In an OCM context we use the model to visualise the positive and negative forces for the change.

Referring to Figure 5.9, it can be seen how the change leader (CL) and project leader (PL) could leverage this tool in several situations. A typical sequence of events in the Initiation stage could resemble the following.

1. The CL and PL, with the project team, craft a vision statement (e.g. what does the business look like after the change?).

2. The CL and PL hold a workshop with key stakeholders (managers and supervisors of the project's deliverables), and at this workshop they brainstorm all the:
   - positive (driving) forces for the change and rate each force on a scale of 1–10 (10 = extremely strong, 1 = extremely weak)
   - negative (restraining forces) for the change and rate each force on a scale of 1–10 (10 = extremely strong, 1 = extremely weak).

3. The CL and PL can then analyse the results of this brainstorming session and:
   - review the positive forces, which indicate points that can be leveraged in the project. This analysis may result in the requirement for additional communications, the need to build relationships with stakeholders, or even include additional work packages in the project to address new work that has now been identified
   - review the negative forces, which indicate concerns in the project. This analysis may result in the requirement to log risks, issues or address the concern by including additional work packages in the project to address new work that has now been identified
   - by reviewing the overall (total) scores of the positive and negative forces, the PL can see which way the project is weighted and adjust strategies and approaches across the entire project accordingly.

5.3.6 Lewin's unfreeze, change, refreeze model

This is a lightweight way of thinking about what has to occur. This model has three stages: unfreeze, change and refreeze, as indicated in Figure 5.10.

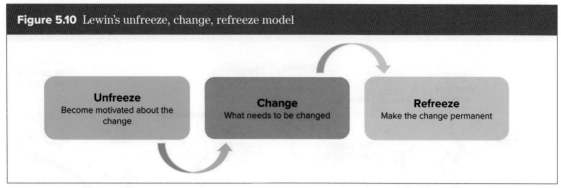

Figure 5.10 Lewin's unfreeze, change, refreeze model

© 2022 Dr Neil Pearson

Unfreeze. *This first stage of change involves preparing the organization to accept that change is necessary, which involves breaking down the existing status quo before you can build up a new way of operating.*

Change. *After the uncertainty created in the unfreeze stage, the change stage is where people begin to resolve their uncertainty and look for new ways to do things. People start to believe and act in ways that support the new direction.*

Refreeze. *When the changes are taking shape and people have embraced the new ways of working, the organization is ready to refreeze. The outward signs of the refreeze are a stable organization chart, consistent job descriptions, and so on* (MindTools n.d.).

5.3.7 Kübler-Ross

Elisabeth Kübler-Ross introduced the world to what is regularly referred to as the *five stages of grief* model in 1969 (within her book *On Death and Dying*). Based in psychiatry, the model proposes that a person who is approaching death or a survivor of an intimate's [partner's] death progresses through the five stages. So, why have we picked up this model in a business context? This is compactly explained as follows.

> *Every organization needs to support the employees in the process of making transitions or changes. These individual transformations can be traumatic and may involve a lot of power loss and prestige issues. The easier it is for the employees to move along on their journey, the easier will it be for the organization to move towards success. Thus, this impacts the success rate and overall profits experienced by the company. The Change Curve in business is thus a powerful model that can help one understand and deal with changes and personal transitions. It helps to fathom how one will react to change and how to provide support during the process of change* (Belyh 2022).

(For a full description of the model and its five stages, refer to the Elizabeth Kübler-Ross Foundation at www.ekrfoundation.org/5-stages-of-grief/5-stages-grief/ and Belyh 2022.)

To a practising project leader, the Kübler-Ross model is a tool that, like Bruce Tuckman's Team Development model (refer to Chapter 19 "Project leaders and project teams"), sits ever present in the back of the mind and is triggered when an individual starts the process of change. Remember, different people impacted by the project will be in different stages of the model at different times; it is an individual model of grief. Like Tuckman, as humans we must progress through all stages.

The Kübler-Ross model led to a more popular variation on the five stages, through the research of John M. Fisher.

5.3.8 Fisher's personal transition curve

John M Fisher was a chartered psychologist who, based on Kübler-Ross's early work in grief, presented how people responded to change; this process is represented in Figure 5.11.

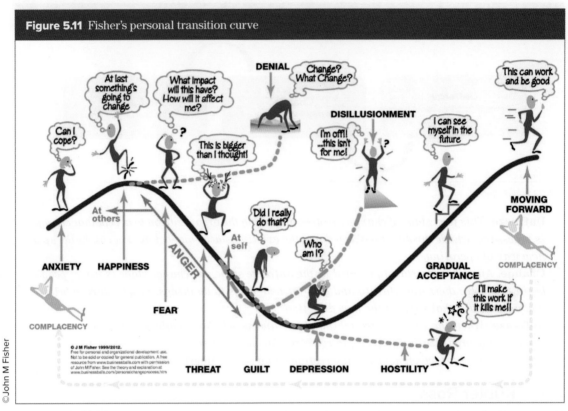

Figure 5.11 Fisher's personal transition curve

Source: Fisher J M 2000, "Creating the future?", in Scheer J W (ed), *The Person in Society: Challenges to a Constructivist Theory*, Geissen, Psychosozial-Verlag

The model is applied in a similar manner to that of Kübler-Ross, tracking each key stakeholder's (those who are most impacted by the project) response to change on the cycle and updating our stakeholder management strategies and communications register to ensure all in the project team are kept current with how these stakeholders should be engaged. It is not a simple or trivial activity for the change leader and project leader to undertake in a change-heavy project.

5.3.9 McKinsey 7-S

If you are specifically looking to, for example, workshop the gaps between the current state and the future state in order to identify change-related activities, then the **McKinsey 7-S** tool provides a wheel to spin around and seek connection between the 7-S's. The 7-S's are the *structure*—the basis for building the organisation will change to reflect new needs for specialisation and coordination resulting from the new strategic direction. Formal and informal business *systems* that supported the old system that must change in the future state. The *style* or culture of the organisation that will be affected by a new strategic direction. The *shared values*, beliefs and norms that developed over time may be revised or even swept away. Shared values are the guiding concepts of the organisation, the fundamental ideas that are its basis. The way *staff* are recruited, developed and rewarded may also change. New strategies may mean relocating people or making them redundant. The *skills* or competencies acquired in the past may be of less use now. The new *strategy* may call for new skills or changes to any of the other 6-S's.

An approach frequently taken to using the McKinsey 7-S as a tool would be as follows. On a large wall pin up on the left-hand-side all the current state artefacts the change leader and project leader have amassed; on the right-hand-side of the wall the change leader and project leader would pin up all the future state artefacts and descriptions. Next, a workshop (for example) could be held with various stakeholders from the business and the project to identify all the gaps between the current state description and the future state description. The gaps can then be taken into the project where change-related activities are identified that need to be attended to by various members of the project team (including the change roles identified earlier in this chapter). This process is illustrated in Figure 5.12.

Figure 5.12 McKinsey 7-S framework

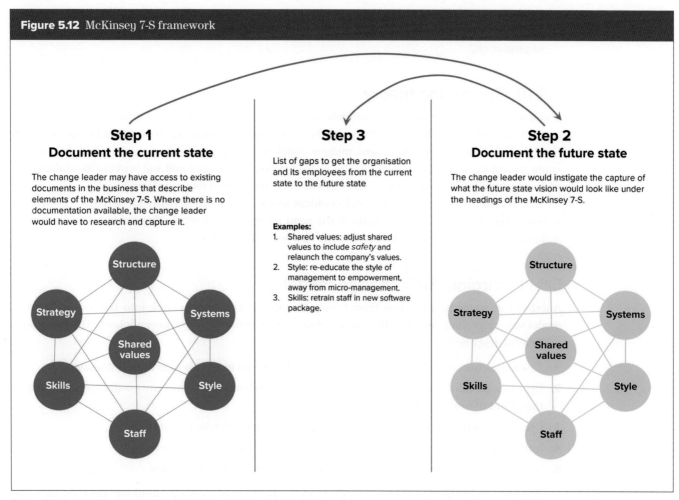

Step 1
Document the current state

The change leader may have access to existing documents in the business that describe elements of the McKinsey 7-S. Where there is no documentation available, the change leader would have to research and capture it.

Step 3

List of gaps to get the organisation and its employees from the current state to the future state

Examples:
1. Shared values: adjust shared values to include *safety* and relaunch the company's values.
2. Style: re-educate the style of management to empowerment, away from micro-management.
3. Skills: retrain staff in new software package.

Step 2
Document the future state

The change leader would instigate the capture of what the future state vision would look like under the headings of the McKinsey 7-S.

Some 7-S questions follow to get your workshop on the move. In relation to the *hard* elements:

■ *Strategy:* What must be challenged strategically and changed for the future to be made a reality. Is the strategy different in the future state? What is the gap? What needs to be done to communicate this?

■ *Structure:* The physical organisational structure and reporting lines—what must be changed for the change to work? Is the current organisation structure deep, with many layers of decision-making, and is the future state structure relatively flat, with empowered autonomy in relation to decision-making? How are changes going to be made to achieve this new structure?

■ *Systems:* The everyday policy, processes and procedures that need to be adopted in the future state—how do these differ from the current ways of working?

In relation to the *soft* elements:

- *Shared values:* Do the core organisational values support the new environment going forward; do they need to be adjusted and re-marketed across the entire organisation?
- *Style:* Of the leadership and supervisor teams—is it *command and control* when it should be about delegation and empowerment?
- *Staff:* What is the profile of the employees and their general abilities?
- *Skills:* Actual competencies (skills) of the employees—do they need upskilling or re-skilling in the future state? How is this going to be done? Do the current staff have the ability to be upskilled or is the new way of working a major shift requiring new skills be acquired into the organisation?

5.3.10 The nudge theory

A nudge is a factor that influences an individual's choice or behaviour and is deliberately deployed to elicit the outcome, which is in the individual's self-interest. (Read more at Plays-in-business.com, "Nudging: the ideas behind it". These nudges could be incorporated into our identified stakeholder management strategies and communications. Nudges are very situational and provide the stakeholder with a positive (often fun) nudge to switch their decision to use a more preferred route.

For example, if we are nudging stakeholders to use a new process design, perhaps this process design allows the job to be done without the need for unpaid overtime. This could be the nudge the stakeholders require in order to switch to the new way of working.

5.3.11 Virginia Satir change model

Another five-stage model comes from family therapy and is coming back into fashion as an OCM model to prompt thinking about the impact of an organisational change on employees. The five stages are briefly described as:

1. Late status quo—employee receives bad news: their role in a process is to be automated.
2. Resistance—the employee resists the change and pushes the *old ways are good ways* mentality—they want to return to the status quo.
3. Chaos—with the status quo absent, the employee perceives a lack of stability.
4. Integration—over time the employee comes to an acceptance of the new state.
5. New status quo—the employee now starts to make the required changes.

Within each of the five stages the effect on the individual's feelings, thinking, performance and physiology is assessed, resulting in actions that a more experienced organisational change consultant could attend to or detail for inclusion in project planning (Figure 5.13).

5.3.12 Bridges transition model

The last model to be included in this overview is William Bridges's transition model. The basis of transition is based on inner psychological routes as the old fades and the new change becomes apparent. Although a vision exists towards which a project will proactively move, as project leaders and change leaders we must not forget to provide support to individuals and build resilience at the organisational level.

Figure 5.14 visualises this model (the reader is encouraged to pursue further reading at https://wmbridges.com).

Figure 5.13 Virginia Satir change model

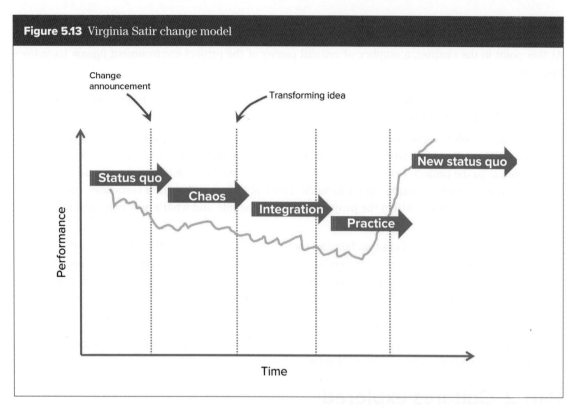

Source: Adapted from "Satir change model", http://www.satirworkshops.com/files/satirchangemodel.pdf, accessed January 2022

Figure 5.14 Bridges transition model

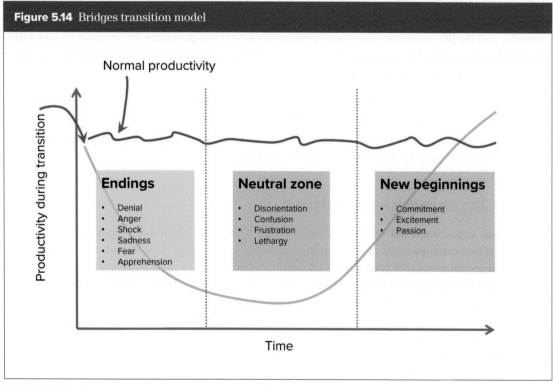

© 2022 Dr Neil Pearson

Source: Adapted from William Bridges Associates n.d., "Bridges transition model", https://wmbridges.com/about/what-is-transition/, accessed May 2022

5.4 OCM summary

At this point in the chapter, a number of critical pieces of the project environment jigsaw have been provided.

- We have defined and know how this can (and should) be integrated with the project management approach, whether predictive or other.

- The project leader will undoubtedly achieve more positive acceptance of the project's outcomes when OCM is taken seriously within the project environment rather than seen as a token addendum to the project. However, by seriously considering OCM, additional activities will be identified in order to carry out OCM work. These activities will require resources, time and materials, and therefore affect the project's budget, schedule and what's now considered to be in scope and out of scope of the project.

- We have presented several approaches and tools. These are far from exhaustive but are indicative of what the authors have used to implement OCM alongside project activities. The advice would be to select an appropriate OCM approach, integrate this approach with your project management life cycle and then draw in other tools as necessary to complete a specific organisational change activity.

The second part of this chapter considers cultures in more detail, these being one element that may require adjusting when carrying out OCM activities.

Part 2 Cultures explored

5.5 Introduction to Part 2

The previous chapter looked at the strategic alignment of investments (portfolios, programs and projects), and the prioritisation of programs and projects within a portfolio. The chapter closed with a resulting list of approved programs and projects to be delivered by the accountable business managers (sponsors). The questions this chapter seeks to answer are:

- What is the organisation's culture and how does this impact the management of the project and the deployment of the product, service or result from the project?

- In relation to the product, service or result being produced from the project, what impact does this have on the organisation, the departments and the employees?

5.6 Organisational culture

So how does **organisational culture** affect the selection of which project organisation to apply? Let's look at two organisations: one is a long-established government department, and the other is a commercial organisation that prides itself on the ability to get products to market quickly.

In the first organisation (a long-established government organisation), people are tasked to both operational day-to-day activities (on tightly defined employment contracts under the auspice of an enterprise bargaining agreement) and, for a percentage of their time, to projects. As the projects cannot be organised (or funded) with dedicated project personnel, the project leaders and the employees resourced to the projects come from across the business and a weak matrix organisational structure takes shape. The managers, who are also the project leaders, closely manage the workload of the employees to ensure that both the operational day-to-day activities are carried out as well as the tasks allocated to the employees in respect to delivering the projects. The arrangement works well as the department has no pressures upon it to bring products to market (although projects do have to be completed to the agreed schedule), so the daily customer-facing activities can be met.

The commercial organisation has great success in using dedicated project teams, is resourced to carry out all aspects of the project, and reports to a full-time project leader who is fully engaged to deliver the project in the most efficient manner possible. The support functions within the business provide services to the project, such as human resource and procurement services. The culture of the organisation is to rotate project resources around the projects and to give the project employees a choice of which projects to participate in. This works well for the organisation, as there are more projects in the pipeline than there are people to carry out the projects. The project employees get to choose the subject nature of the project they wish to be involved in (as opposed to being allocated on a prearranged basis) and the organisation, in most cases, fills the project roles with employees who are interested and passionate about the project.

Gaining efficiencies in the marriage between the organisation's culture and the organisational structure and project's structure is often a learning exercise and one structure (solution) may not fit all projects. Smaller projects could be delivered within a weak matrix structure; however, larger, complex projects often require dedicated project structures.

5.6.1 What is organisational culture?

Organisational culture refers to a system of shared norms, beliefs, values and assumptions that bind people together, thereby creating shared meanings. This system is manifested by customs and habits that exemplify the values and beliefs of the organisation. For example, *egalitarianism* may be expressed in the informal dress worn at a high-tech firm. Conversely, mandated uniforms at a department store reinforce respect for the hierarchy.

Culture reflects the personality of the organisation and, like an individual's personality, can enable us to predict attitudes and behaviours of employees. Culture is also one of the defining aspects of an organisation that sets it apart from other organisations, even in the same industry.

Research suggests that there are 10 primary characteristics that, in aggregate, capture the essence of an organisation's culture:

1. *Member identity:* The degree to which employees identify with the organisation, rather than with their type of job or field of professional expertise.
2. *Team emphasis:* The degree to which work activities are organised around groups rather than individuals.
3. *Management focus:* The degree to which management decisions consider the effect of outcomes on people within the organisation.
4. *Unit integration:* The degree to which units (departments) within the organisation are encouraged to operate in a coordinated or interdependent manner.
5. *Control:* The degree to which rules, policies and direct supervision are used to oversee and control employee behaviour.
6. *Risk tolerance:* The degree to which employees are encouraged to be aggressive, innovative and risk-seeking.
7. *Reward criteria:* The degree to which rewards (such as promotion and salary increases) are allocated, according to employee performance rather than seniority, favouritism or other non-performance factors.
8. *Conflict tolerance:* The degree to which employees are encouraged to air conflicts and criticisms openly.
9. *Means versus end orientation:* The degree to which management focuses on outcomes rather than on techniques and processes used to achieve those results.
10. *Open-systems focus:* The degree to which the organisation monitors and responds to changes in the external environment.

As shown in Figure 5.15, each of these dimensions exists on a continuum. Assessing an organisation according to these 10 dimensions provides a composite picture of the organisation's culture. This picture becomes the basis for feelings of shared understanding that members have about the organisation, how things are done, and the way members are supposed to behave.

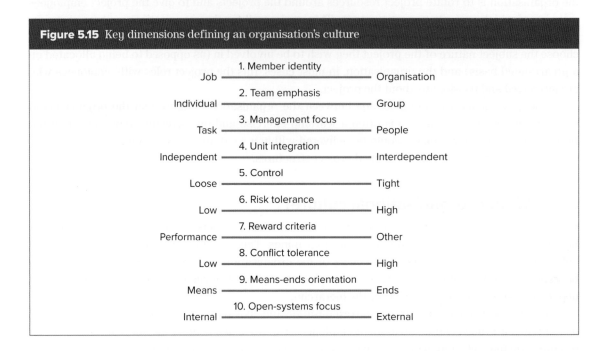

Figure 5.15 Key dimensions defining an organisation's culture

Culture performs several important functions in organisations. An organisation's culture provides a sense of identity for its members. The more clearly an organisation's shared perceptions and values are stated, the more strongly people can identify with their organisation and feel a vital part of it. Identity generates commitment to the organisation and provides reasons for members to devote energy and loyalty to the organisation.

A second important function is that culture helps to legitimise the management system of the organisation. Culture helps to clarify authority relationships. It provides reasons why people are in a position of authority and why their authority should be respected.

Most importantly, organisational culture clarifies and reinforces standards of behaviour. Culture helps to define what is permissible/appropriate and, conversely, what is impermissible/inappropriate behaviour. These standards span a wide range of behaviours: from specifying dress codes and working hours, to how to/when to (and perhaps when not to) challenge the judgement of superiors and how to collaborate with other departments. Ultimately, culture helps create social order within an organisation. Imagine what it would be like if members didn't share similar beliefs, values (but not personal beliefs or values, which may differ) and assumptions—chaos! Equitable *customs*, *norms* and *ideals* that are conveyed by the culture of an organisation can provide stability and predictability of behaviour that is essential for an effective organisation. See Snapshot from Practice: Real-life project teams! for an example of this.

Although this discussion of organisational culture might appear to suggest one culture dominates the entire organisation, this is rarely the case. *Strong* or *thick* are adjectives used to denote a culture in which an organisation's core values and customs are widely shared within the entire organisation. Conversely, a *thin* or *weak* culture is one that is not widely shared or practised within a firm.

Even within a strong organisational culture, there are likely to be subcultures that are often aligned within specific departments or specialty areas. As noted earlier in our discussion on project management structures, it is not uncommon for organisational norms, values and customs to develop within a specific field or profession. People working in a marketing department, for example, may have a different set of norms and values than those working, say, in finance.

SNAPSHOT *from* PRACTICE : Real-life project teams!

Among his many professional experiences of working in project management, one of the authors was involved in various areas of the Business for Oracle Corporation (in the United Kingdom and the United States). This enabled him to experience both leadership and membership of several different project teams. Some of the larger projects (e.g. back-office system consolidations) were run by a small core team of full-time project staff comprising the project leader, communications staff, a change leader and business analysts. However, most other employees utilised by the project were seen as transient and, typically, subject matter experts (SMEs) were drawn in from across the business as and when needed. SMEs ranged from a variety of technical experts to local (in-country) business representatives. The SMEs retained their functional position in the organisation, but also reported to the project leader regarding assigned project activities and tasks. This hybrid structure worked well for the organisation and for the delivery of projects. The culture of the organisation was *empowerment*. Everyone knew what their role was, and they were suitably empowered to carry out their role. The environment was very positive and the SMEs, project leaders and others supported each other in a collective, collaborative manner.

Figure 5.16 Real-life team projects

The author experienced a different situation at an energy utility company in Australia. There was a complex political culture with a predominantly *command and control* ethos. The organisation was (outside of operations) a projectised organisation, with many large and small projects being attended to in a true projectised nature. As an example of a project structure in practice, imagine a project that is designed to deliver changes to core aspects of the business model. Included in the scope of this project was the redesign of the following business processes: strategic planning, business planning, performance management, benefits management and portfolio/program/project management. This, as can be imagined, touched on all senior positions and players in the organisation and was run as a full-time project with a project leader, SMEs, business analysts, a part-time organisational change consultant and a full-time project administrator. The focus of the project was stakeholder management and communications. The project was well supported by other functional departments in terms of human resources, procurement and corporate communications (with these functional departments supporting the day-to-day activities of the business, as well as most large or small projects).

These two examples show the range of differing cultures and project structures that can typically be found across organisations. As a project leader (whether contracted or permanent), you have to quickly be able to adapt to the organisation's culture and to the preferred style of project structure: functional, matrix or projectised.

Countercultures that embody a different set of values, beliefs and customs sometimes emerge within organisations, often in direct contradiction with the culture espoused by top management. Depending on how pervasive these subcultures and countercultures are, they can affect the strength of the culture of the organisation and the extent to which culture influences members' actions and responses.

5.6.2 Identifying organisational cultural characteristics

Deciphering an organisation's culture can be a highly interpretative, subjective process which often requires an assessment of both its current and past history. Someone seeking to learn about organisational culture should not just rely on what people tell them: it's also important to consider the physical environment in which people work, and how people act and respond to different events that occur. Table 5.3 contains a basic analysis of the culture of an organisation. Although by no means exhaustive, this approach can help to yield clues about some of the norms, customs and values of an organisation.

Table 5.3 Organisational culture analysis: National Australia Bank (NAB)

Attribute	Examples of manifestation
Physical characteristics	Head Office: an eight-storey modern building, located at the Docklands in Melbourne, Australia. Smart business attire, banking formalities.
Public documents	Annual reports (including financial statement), sustainability reports, investor reports, risk and capital reports.
Strategy	Focus on the strong Australian franchise and manage international positions for value, maintain balance-sheet strength, reduce complexity and cost, enhance reputation.
Behaviour	Investing in the skills and capabilities of employees, organisational culture, diversity and inclusion, talent management, health and wellbeing, learning and development, performance and reward, industrial relations, flexible working.
Folklore	Stories, anecdotes and history evidenced.

Source: Adapted from NAB 2011, Annual Review 2011, National Australia Bank

Further to Table 5.3, it is helpful to conduct the following culture analysis.

1. *Study the physical characteristics of an organisation:* What does the external architecture look like? What image does it convey? Is it unique? Are the buildings and offices the same quality for all employees? Or are modern buildings and fancier offices reserved for senior executives or managers from a specific department? What are the customs concerning dress? What symbols does the organisation use to signal authority and status within the organisation? These physical characteristics can shed light on who has real power within the organisation, the extent to which the organisation is internally differentiated and how formal the organisation is in its business dealings.

2. *Read about the organisation:* Examine annual reports, mission statements, press releases and internal newsletters. What do they describe? What principles are championed in these documents? Do the reports emphasise the people who work for the organisation and what they do, or the financial performance of the firm? Each emphasis reflects a different culture. The first demonstrates concern for the people who make up the company. The second may suggest a predominant concern for results and the bottom line.

3. *Observe how people interact within the organisation:* What is their pace—is it slow and methodical, or urgent and spontaneous? What rituals exist within the organisation? What values do they express? Meetings can often yield insightful information. Who are the people at the meetings? Who does the talking? To whom do they talk? How candid is the conversation? Do people speak for the organisation or for the individual department? What is the focus of the meetings? How much time is spent on various issues? Issues that are discussed repeatedly and at length are clues about the values of the organisation's culture.

4. *Interpret stories and folklore surrounding the organisation:* Look for similarities among stories told by different people. The subjects highlighted in recurring stories often reflect what is important to an organisation's culture. For example, many of the stories that are repeated at Versatec, a Xerox subsidiary that makes graphic plotters for computers, involve their vibrant cofounder, Renn Zaphiropoulos. According to company folklore, one of the very first things Zaphiropoulos did when the company was formed was to assemble the top management team at his home. They then devoted the weekend to hand-making a beautiful teak conference table around which all future decisions would be made. This table came to symbolise the importance of teamwork and maintaining high standards of performance: two essential qualities of the culture. Try to identify who the heroes and villains are in the folklore of a company. What do these characters suggest about the culture's ideals? Returning to Versatec, when the company was eventually purchased by Xerox, many employees expressed concern that Versatec's informal play hard/work hard culture would be overwhelmed by perceived bureaucracy at Xerox. Zaphiropoulos rallied the employees towards superior levels of performance by arguing that if they exceeded Xerox's expectations, they would potentially be left alone. Autonomy remained a fixture of Versatec's culture, even long after Zaphiropoulos's retirement.

It is also important to pay close attention to the basis of promotions and rewards. What do people see as key to getting ahead within the organisation? What contributes to downfalls? These last two questions can yield important insights into some of the qualities and behaviours the organisation honours, as well as insights into some of the cultural taboos and behavioural land mines that can derail a career. For example, one project leader confided that a former colleague was sent to project management purgatory soon after publicly questioning the validity of a marketing report. From that point on, the project leader was extra careful to privately consult the marketing department whenever they had questions about their data.

With practice, an observer can usually assess how strong the dominant culture of an organisation is and the significance of any subcultures and countercultures. Those who are new to project management can use the 10 cultural dimensions presented in this chapter as a springboard for beginning to discern and identify where the culture of an organisation stands, and, in essence, begin to build a cultural profile for a firm.

5.7 | Implications of organisational cultures when leading projects

Project leaders must be able to operate in several potentially diverse organisational cultures. First, they must interact with the culture of their parent organisation, as well as the subcultures of various departments (e.g. marketing, accounting). Second, they must interact with the project's client or customer organisations. Third, they must interact in varying degrees with a host of other organisations that are connected to the project. These organisations include suppliers and vendors, subcontractors, consulting firms, government and regulatory agencies and, in many cases, community groups. Many of these organisations are likely to have very different cultures. Project leaders must be able to *read and speak* the culture they are working in to develop strategies, plans and responses that are likely to be understood and accepted. Although the focus of this chapter is on the relationship between organisational culture and project management structure, a detailed discussion of leadership, team building and the human dimensions of project management can be found in Chapter 19 "Project leaders and project teams". The linkage between strong relationships, project management structures, organisational culture and successful project management was referred to earlier. To explore this further, let's return to the dimensions that can be used to characterise the culture of an organisation. By using these dimensions, we could, for example, hypothesise that certain aspects of the culture of an organisation would support successful project management, while other aspects would deter or interfere with effective management. Figure 5.17 attempts to identify which cultural characteristics create an environment that is potentially conducive to completing complex projects, involving people from different disciplines.

Note that, in many cases, the ideal culture is not at either extreme. For example, a fertile project culture would likely be one in which management balances its focus on the needs of both the task and the people. An optimal culture would balance concern with output (ends) and processes to achieve those outcomes (means). In other cases, the ideal culture would be on one end of a dimension or the other. For example, because most projects require collaboration across disciplines, it would be desirable that the culture of the organisation emphasises working in teams and identifying with the organisation, not just with the professional domain. Likewise, it is important that the culture supports a certain degree of risk-taking and a tolerance for constructive conflict.

One organisation that appears to fit this ideal profile is 3M, which has received acclaim for creating an entrepreneurial culture within a large corporate framework. The essence of its culture is captured in phrases such as: *Encourage experimental doodling. Hire good people and leave them alone. If you put fences around people, you get sheep. Give people the room they need.* Freedom and autonomy to experiment are reflected in the 15 per cent rule, which encourages technical people to spend up to 15 per cent of their time on projects of their own choosing and initiative. This fertile culture has contributed to 3M branching out into more than 60 000 products and 35 separate business units. Google applies a similar scenario with Google 20, where employees are encouraged to spend 20 per cent of

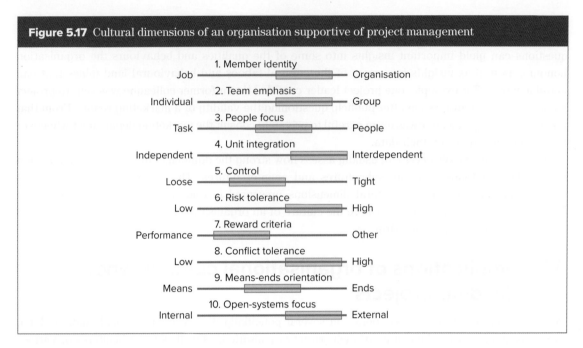

Figure 5.17 Cultural dimensions of an organisation supportive of project management

paid time working on ideas that may (or may not) materialise into a ground-breaking product for the organisation. This is purportedly how ideas for Google News, Gmail and AdSense were born. It has been reported that only about 10 per cent of Googlers are using the 20 per cent time—does this matter? They report that it's the idea that counts: "Typically, employees who have an idea separate from their regular jobs will focus 5 or 10% of their time on it, until it starts to 'demonstrate impact.' At that point, it will take up more of their time and more volunteers will join, until it becomes a real project" (D'Onfro 2015).

A metaphor that aptly describes the relationship between organisational culture and project management is that of a riverboat trip where culture is the river, and the project is the boat. Organising and completing projects within an organisation in which the culture is conducive to project management is akin to paddling downstream (i.e. very little effort is required; balance and steering in the current is all that is required). This is the case for projects that operate in a project-friendly environment, where teamwork and cross-functional cooperation are the norms and there is a deep commitment to excellence. Any healthy conflict is voiced and dealt with quickly and effectively.

Conversely, trying to complete a project in a toxic culture is like paddling upstream: much more time, effort and attention is needed to reach the destination. Such would be the situation in cultures that discourage teamwork and cooperation, that have a low tolerance for conflict, and where getting ahead is based less on performance and more on cultivating favourable relationships with superiors. In such cases, the project leader and their people not only have to overcome the natural obstacles of the project, but also the prevailing negative forces inherent in the culture of the organisation. The implications of this metaphor are therefore important. Greater project authority and time are necessary to complete projects that encounter a strong, negative cultural current. Conversely, less formal authority and fewer dedicated resources are needed to complete projects in which the cultural currents generate behaviours and cooperation that foster project success.

The key issue is the degree of interdependency between the parent organisation and the project team. In cases where the prevalent organisational culture supports the behaviours essential to project completion, a weaker, more flexible project management structure can be effective.

When the dominant organisational culture inhibits collaboration and innovation, it is advisable to insulate the project team from the dominant culture. Here, it becomes necessary to create a self-sufficient project team. If a dedicated project team is impossible because of resource constraints, then at least a project matrix should be used where the project leader has dominant control over the project. In both cases, the managerial strategy is to create a distinct team subculture in which a new set of norms, customs and values evolve that will be conducive to project completion.

SNAPSHOT *from* PRACTICE : Articulating an organisation's culture

The Organizational Culture Inventory (OCI) is a frequently used organisational assessment tool that can explore corporate culture, company culture and workplace culture. It is applicable to all types of organisations.

A large service-based company in Australia was about to take an organisational restructuring project forward to adjust its internal management structure, leadership style and culture, to better match the needs of:

- requirements from government

- changing strategy (after all, structure follows strategy—refer to *How Strategy Shapes Structure* (Kim & Mauborgne 2009))

- replacement of the company's ERP system.

To ascertain how the corporate, company and workplace culture was operating, the company undertook an OCI survey. Based on sample data, sourced from the OCI website, the *before* state (as developed by Drs RA Cooke and JC Lafferty of Human Synergistics International) could have looked similar to Figure 5.18.

By analysing data produced by the survey (also as developed by Drs Cooke and Lafferty of Human Synergistics International), the project was able to determine where adjustments would have to be carried out. These adjustments represented gaps between what was currently occurring (the as-is state) in the organisation compared with what was required to occur (the to-be state).

Figure 5.19 is an example of what a to-be state might look like (as developed by Drs Cooke and Lafferty of Human Synergistics International). The identified gaps represented packages of work that had to be attended to in the project. These were appropriately identified and included in the project schedule and were resourced (by employing organisational change consultants) and costed into the project's budget.

By taking the guesswork out of complex issues and effectively capturing the feelings of employees, this more fact-based approach can be useful for establishing new routines, leadership styles, values and rituals in the reorganised organisation.

The authors acknowledge the existence of many other tools that can assist an assessment of organisational cultural dimensions.

Figure 5.18 The *before* or *as-is* state of the company

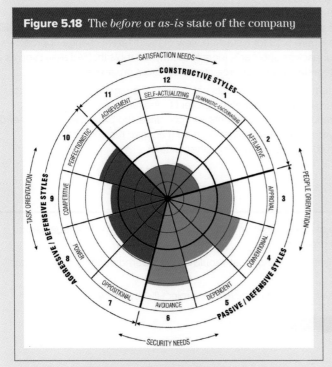

Source: Organizational Culture Inventory® (OCI®): Research & Development by Robert A. Cooke, Ph.D. and J. Clayton Lafferty, Ph.D. Copyright © 1987–2018 by Human Synergistics International. All Rights Reserved. Used by permission.

Figure 5.19 The *required* or *to-be* state of the company

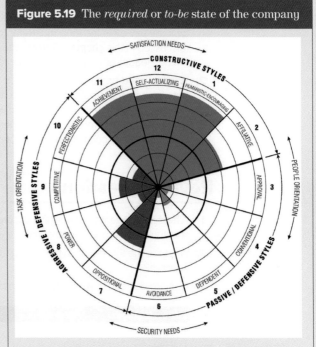

Source: Organizational Culture Inventory® (OCI®): Research & Development by Robert A. Cooke, Ph.D. and J. Clayton Lafferty, Ph.D. Copyright © 1987–2018 by Human Synergistics International. All Rights Reserved. Used by permission.

5.8 | Working across international cultures

In today's globalised marketplace, projects often traverse international boundaries. This means that a project leader not only has to establish positive professional working relationships with stakeholders who may not be in the same continent or country, but who may come from a very different culture to the one the project leader is accustomed to working in. If this is the case, the project leader could:

- Learn from a trusted in-country stakeholder (if one is available), for example, by sharing experiences about the project and describing how each would typically approach differing situations in their home-country. This would assist in establishing a positive rapport.

- Identify and learn about cultural differences and cultural norms ahead of time, so relationships begin on the best possible grounds. A tool that is gaining commercial popularity (based on research) to help facilitate this process is Hofstede's Six Dimensions of International Culture (Geert Hofstede n.d.). Readers are encouraged to review Hofstede's model and country comparison tool (Hofstede Insights 2018a, 2018b) at www.hofstede-insights.com/product/compare-countries/.

Summary

This chapter has examined two major supplemental factors to the management of projects, neither of which can be ignored in today's contemporary project management environments.

1. Project leaders should recognise the importance of OCM and the importance of the project leader's ability to successfully embrace and promote OCM practices within the project environment—for example, leveraging commercially available techniques and regularly applying these techniques (e.g. ADKAR, Kotter and the change leader's roadmap, among many others that are available). Students are advised to independently learn more about these techniques.

    The project leader should not underestimate the importance of engaging with stakeholders and creating an environment of stakeholder co-creation. Time invested in quality stakeholder engagements will typically pay off in the long run. Refer to Figure 5.19 for a stacked view of the different change approaches (discussed in this chapter). Select one, unpack its approach, identify the myriad tools that will assist you as a change leader or project leader and integrate it with your project management processes.

2. We discussed organisational culture in terms of how this affects not only the management of the project, but also how the project considers culture in the delivery of the project to the functions and employees affected by its implementation. When working across continents and countries, the project leader will need to consider how different cultures operate so that stakeholders can be managed more effectively and communications can be tailored to local cultural norms (among other factors).

Review questions

1. Why is it important to assess the culture of an organisation before deciding what project management structure should be used to complete a project?

2. What are the three main types of organisational change that should be considered during the pre-project activities?

3. As a project leader, what OCM activities would you include in your project (list by life cycle stage)?

Life cycle stage	Activity
Pre-project	
Initiation	
Planning	
Execution	
Closure	
Operations	

Figure 5.20 Stacked change models around the predictive lifecycle

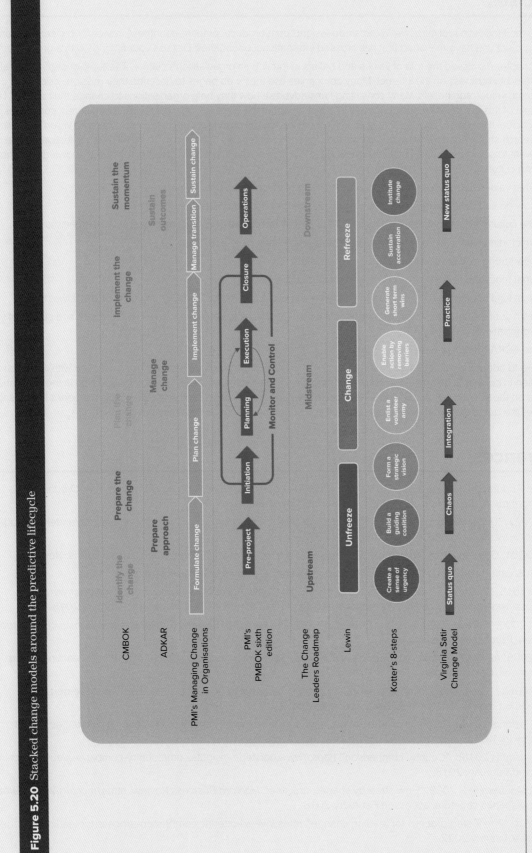

Exercises

1. Using the Hofstede tool (https://www.hofstede-insights.com/product/compare-countries/), review two differing countries for a project you have managed that has crossed international boundaries. Discuss your findings with a group member.

2. This chapter discussed the role of values and beliefs in forming an organisation's culture. The topic of organisational culture is big business on the internet. Many companies use their web pages to describe their mission, vision, and corporate values and beliefs. Many consulting firms advertise how they help organisations to change their culture. The purpose of this exercise is for you to obtain information about the organisational culture for two different companies of your choice. If you wish, you can simply search for the key words *organisational culture* or *corporate vision and values*. The search should identify numerous companies for you to potentially use to answer the following questions. (*Note:* You may want to select companies that you would like to work for in the future so you can extend your knowledge of their working culture.)

   a. What values and beliefs are championed by each of these companies?

   b. How do you think the organisations would each deliver projects within their culture?

3. Use the cultural dimensions listed in Figure 5.21 to assess the culture of your current (or previous) organisation.

   a. Which dimensions were easy to evaluate, and which ones were not?

   b. How strong is/was the culture of your organisation?

   c. What functions does/did the culture serve for your organisation?

   d. What kind of projects are/were easy to implement in your organisation, and why do you think this is/was so?

   e. From your experience, what kind of projects would be difficult to implement, given the structure and culture of your organisation?

4. For the ADKAR template (see Figure 5.21):

   You are to adopt the role of an end user (or customer) for a project you have recently been involved with. For each question in column 3, complete the corresponding blank in column 4 and then score each question in the circle shown, based on the scoring criteria provided. Next, review the results you have captured with a project leader's hat on and answer the question: "What do these results tell you about the change acceptance of your project?"

References

Ackerman Anderson L & Anderson D 2010, *The Change Leader's Roadmap: How to Navigate Your Organization's Transformation*, 2nd edition, John Wiley & Sons Inc, United States.

Belyh A 2022, "Understanding the Kubler-Ross change curve", Cleverism, https://www.cleverism.com/understanding-kubler-ross-change-curve/, accessed January 2022.

Collins J 2001, *Good to Great: Why Some Companies Make the Leap and Others Don't*, HarperCollins, New York.

Cooke RA & Lafferty JC 1987, *Organizational Culture Inventory*. Human Synergistics, Plymouth, USA.

D'Onfro J 2015, "The truth about Google's famous '20% time' policy", Business Insider Australia, https://www.businessinsider.com.au/google-20-percent-time-policy-2015-4?rw=UK&IR=T, accessed February 2018.

Fisher JM 2000, "Creating the future?", in Scheer JW (ed), *The Person in Society: Challenges to a Constructivist Theory*, Geissen, Psychosozial-Verlag.

Hiatt JM 2006, *ADKAR®: A Model for Change in Business, Government and Our Community*, Prosci Learning Centre Publications, Colorado, USA.

Hofstede G n.d., "The 6-D model of national culture", https://geerthofstede.com/culture-geert-hofstede-gert-jan-hofstede/6d-model-of-national-culture/, accessed April 2022.

Hofstede Insights 2018a, "National culture", https://www.hofstede-insights.com/models/national-culture/, accessed February 2018.

Hofstede Insights 2018b, "Country comparison", https://www.hofstede-insights.com/country-comparison/australia,china/, accessed February 2018.

Kim WC & Mauborgne R 2009, "How strategy shapes structure", *Harvard Business Review*, https://hbr.org/2009/09/how-strategy-shapes-structure, accessed February 2018.

Kotter JP n.d., "The 8-step process for leading change", https://www.kotterinc.com/8-step-process-for-leading-change/, accessed January 2022.

Figure 5.21 ADKAR template

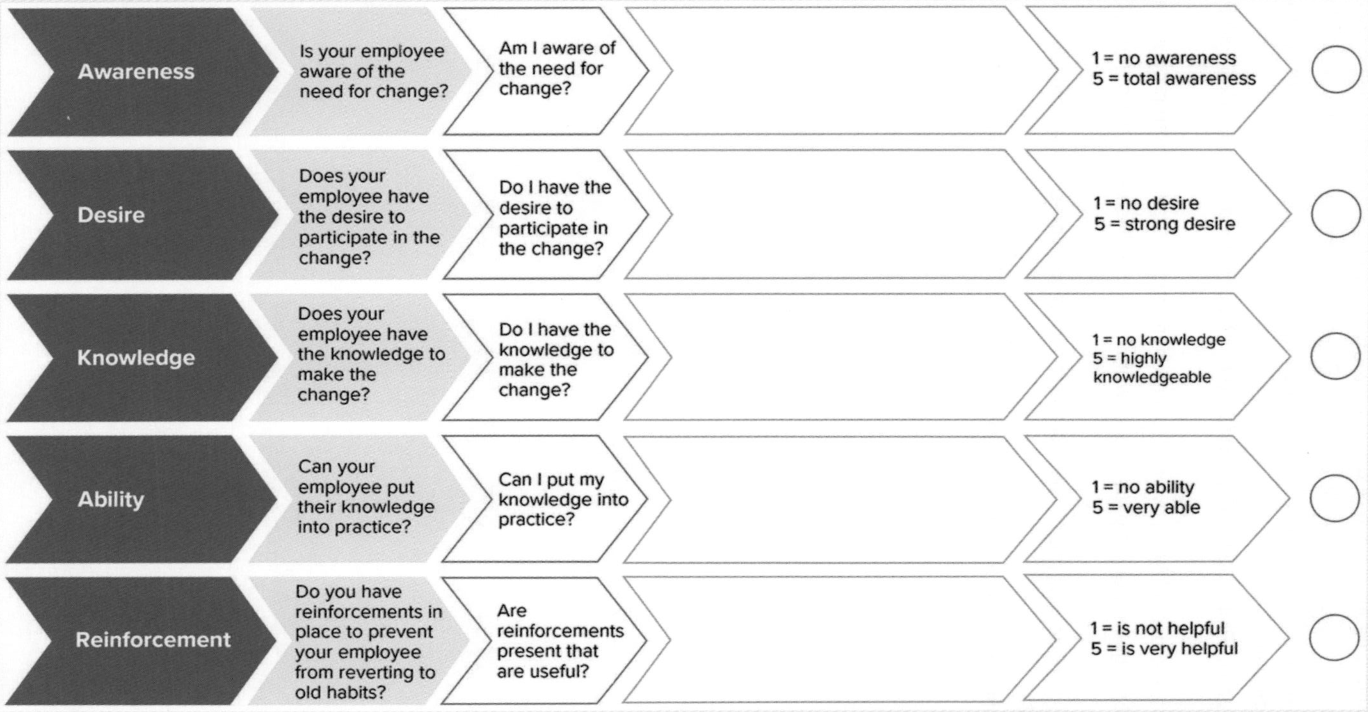

Awareness	Is your employee aware of the need for change?	Am I aware of the need for change?		1 = no awareness 5 = total awareness	◯
Desire	Does your employee have the desire to participate in the change?	Do I have the desire to participate in the change?		1 = no desire 5 = strong desire	◯
Knowledge	Does your employee have the knowledge to make the change?	Do I have the knowledge to make the change?		1 = no knowledge 5 = highly knowledgeable	◯
Ability	Can your employee put their knowledge into practice?	Can I put my knowledge into practice?		1 = no ability 5 = very able	◯
Reinforcement	Do you have reinforcements in place to prevent your employee from reverting to old habits?	Are reinforcements present that are useful?		1 = is not helpful 5 = is very helpful	◯

Kotter JP 2012, Leading Change, Harvard Business Review Press.

Lewin K 1943, "Defining the 'field at a given time'", *Psychological Review*, vol. 50, no. 3, pp. 292–310.

MindTools, "Lewin's change management model", https://www.mindtools.com/pages/article/newPPM_94.htm, accessed January 2022.

NAB 2011, *Annual Review 2011*, National Australia Bank.

Project Management Institute (PMI), 2013, *Managing Change in Organisations: A Practice Guide*, PMI.

Project Management Institute (PMI) 2017, *A Guide to the Project Management Body of Knowledge*, 7th edition, PMI.

Project Management Institute (PMI) 2021a, *A Guide to the Project Management Body of Knowledge (PMBOK® Guide)*, 7th edition, Newton Square, PA.

Project Management Institute (PMI) 2021b, *The Standard for Project Management (ANSI/PMI 99-001-2021)*, 7th edition, Newton Square, PA.

Prosci n.d., "Prosci 3-phase process", https://www.prosci.com/methodology/3-phase-process, accessed January 2022.

Satir Workshops, "Satir change model", http://www.satirworkshops.com/files/satirchangemodel.pdf, accessed January 2022.

Strategies for Managing Change n.d., https://www.strategies-for-managing-change.com/force-field-analysis.html, accessed May 2022.

William Bridges Associates, "Bridges transition model", https://wmbridges.com/about/what-is-transition/accessed January 2022.

PART 3

Performing project initiation

CHAPTER 6
Project integration management

Learning elements

6A Understand the integrative nature of project management and the subtle complexities of managing projects in real-world environments.

6B Understand the importance of project design and how this informs development of the Project Charter and later the project scope.

6C Develop the ability to apply integrative thinking (systems thinking) to make connections between activities across and within knowledge areas.

6D Delve deeper into specific integrative activities that may be considered within each knowledge area (scope, schedule, cost, quality, resources, risk, stakeholders, communication and information, and procurement)

6E Understand the criticality of managing variations (changes to the project).

6F Have an awareness of project closure.

6G Apply concepts to retain and capture project knowledge.

In this chapter

6.1 Introduction

6.2 Project chartering and the project leader

6.3 Project design and the integrated Project Management Plan

6.4 Executing the work and delivering

6.5 Managing project control

6.6 Managing variations (change requests)

6.7 Managing project finalisation

6.8 Managing project knowledge

6.9 Integrative thinking

Summary

6.1 : **Introduction**

Project integration management spans several activities to ensure the project content and the management of the project are successfully integrated across the project life cycle. It is important, from a practical perspective, to realise that project integration requires thinking in a deeper, integrative manner—across the accumulation of information gained by implementing aspects of each of the other **knowledge areas**.

Integration may be referred to as the glue that holds together components from the knowledge areas (scope, cost, resources, quality, schedule, communication and information, stakeholders, risk and procurement). It seeks to ensure that activities are consolidated and unified; that interrelationships between the knowledge areas are coherent; and that conflicts, contradictions and discrepancies do not exist between knowledge areas (PMI 2017).

The activities that drive integration across the life cycle discussed in this chapter encompass:

- establishing the project, including developing the **Project Charter**, and determining and assigning the authority of key stakeholders including the project leader and project sponsor

- project planning and design, including developing the **integrated Project Management Plan (integrated PMP)**. The integrated PMP integrates all the planning aspects of the other nine knowledge areas (scope, cost, resources, quality, schedule, communication and information, stakeholders, risk and procurement). *Note:* Integration—the topic of this chapter—is the tenth of a total of 10 knowledge areas. This includes integrating an activity planned in one area (e.g. scheduling) and reviewing impacts to any of the other knowledge areas (e.g. resources, risk and procurement).

- managing variations (integrated change control) across the project, including implementing approved variations the updates to **deliverables**, project processes, project documents, including the integrated PMP

- managing project finalisation, including the closure of a stage or phase, contracts for portions of outsourced work or other project closure activities

- managing project knowledge, including requisite protocols and systems to ensure this is taking place in an effective manner.

Some of these integrative activities are summarised across the life cycle in Figure 6.1. Although governance is considered an integrative item, in today's projects it can be quite impactful, therefore a discussion on governance is provided in Chapter 7 "Governance and projects".

The final part of this chapter outlines some of integrative activities that need to be considered across the knowledge areas of scope, schedule, cost, quality, resources, stakeholders, communication and information, risk and procurement.

Remember: *Integration* is a more holistic technique that may not be intuitive to new project leaders until they have experienced several projects under differing conditions. It pertains to being able to think widely and deeply across the entire project and business context; examples of applying this integrative approach as a project leader could include:

- continued checking that the final product, service or the result benefits are designed (planned) into the project; remember the saying "design with the benefits in mind"

Figure 6.1 Project integration activities

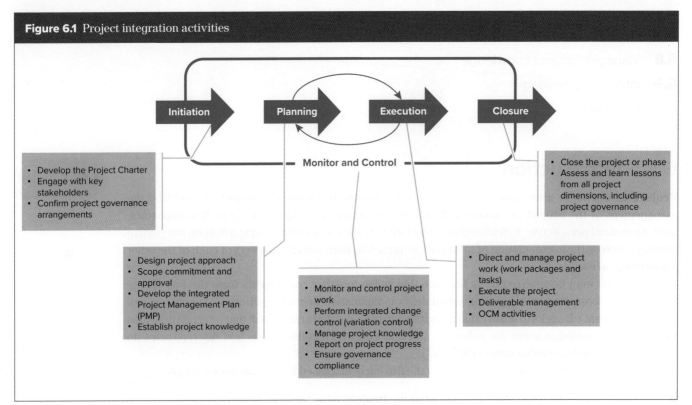

© 2022 Dr Neil Pearson

- ensuring a comprehensive integrated PMP that encompasses all integrated activities is produced and later maintained

- producing timely project data so analysis and reporting of this information can inform improved decision-making in the project and beyond (e.g. the program within which the project sits). When a decision is made in the project, does this take into consideration the greater whole and granular work activities? Has the decision been thought through in terms of what its potential implications may be?

- asking whether the project team is enabled to share information across the project, and wider afield with the business. What about sharing information outside of the organisation, for example, with partners to whom work has been outsourced?

- asking whether all considerations of closure, benefits and the delivered product(s) have been fully understood as the project transitions through the project life cycle stages towards, and including, the final handover to the business before final project closure

- managing changes to the **triple constraints**—scope, time, cost—and ensuring they are fully understood in relation to impacts across the knowledge areas and beyond

- noting if aspects of the life cycle approach been tailored to fit the emphasis, size and risk profile of the project

- asking if any additional plans (to the integrated PMP) been developed (e.g. to meet industry-specific requirements such as a workplace health and safety management plan, or an environmental management plan)

- asking whether integrative project management information systems (technology and tools) have been established to capture and share knowledge and information across the project (whether virtual or physical in nature).

As can be seen from this short list of examples, integration is a truly multifaceted concern.

PMBOK Seventh edition updates (PMI 2021)

The knowledge area content of the PMBOK sixth edition (PMI 2017) has in the seventh edition (PMI 2021) been largely dispersed into assumed content within the **performance domains.** Integration is now seen as a higher-order component discussed within the context of *product management*, *systems thinking principle* and *tailoring principle*; a brief summary follows.

Product management

Product management (introduced in Chapter 1 "Contemporary project management") pertains to the **product life cycle** and how this may traverse programs and projects. The implication is that the product life cycle (as illustrated in Chapter 1, Figure 1.7) will, over the life of the product, be delivered, maintained and disposed of by potentially multiple programs and projects. This is illustrated in Figure 6.2.

Figure 6.2 Integration of product management

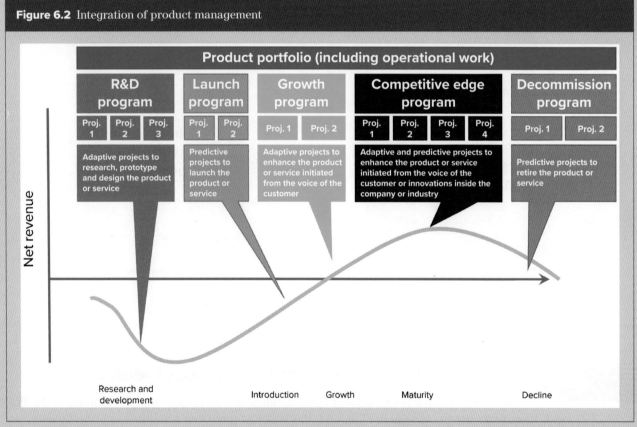

© 2022 Dr Neil Pearson

Principle: Systems thinking

The concept of thinking in systems or systems thinking was introduced in Chapter 1, section 1.4.4. Integration in relation to systems covers the two dynamics of any project: thinking in terms of systems from the management of the project—what has been termed *integrative thinking* in this chapter; and also thinking in terms of systems in relation to the business system being changed as a result of this project. Both are important in terms of ensuring integration takes place within the project environment and also of the product, service or result produced from the project into the business.

Principle: Tailoring

Integrative thinking performance domains is reinforced in this principle, which is discussed further in this chapter. Think about what elements of managing a project are required to what depth in order to create a tailored approach to the management of the project that does not impose overly arduous requirements on the project leader.

Regardless of PMBOK seventh edition updates, if as suggested by PMBOK seventh edition we have selected to use a predictive project management life cycle, then, as a project leader, subject to tailoring, we still have to ensure the relevant items discussed in this chapter are attended to.

Figure 6.3 indicates the PMBOK sixth edition *knowledge areas* approach versus the PMBOK seventh edition *performance domains* approach. Regardless, at the centre of each is the consideration that work done in one area has likely consequences in other areas, whether we call this *integration*, *interactions* or some other more complex term such as *systems thinking*. Experienced project leaders realise the value of taking this holistic approach and do not consider each knowledge area or performance domain in isolation.

Figure 6.3 Integration or interactions; we have to integrate our thinking

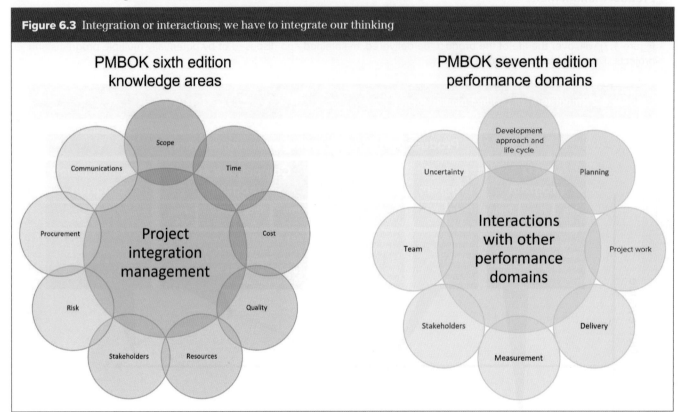

6.2 | **Project chartering and the project leader**

The first topic in a predictive context is the Initiation of the project, and the drafting of the Project Charter document. As seen in Figure 6.4, this is one of three key activities the project leader carries out in the Initiation stage.

Note: The figure also indicates that in chartering we are mindful of interactions with other systems introduced in this text thus far: organisational change management, benefits (value), and the strategic portfolio/program environment.

The Project Charter is a summary document that provides a formal agreement of the project's existence between the project's sponsor (the business) and the project leader. In most organisations, the Project Charter provides the go-ahead for the project to start—that is, to progress from the Initiation stage to the Planning stage within the predictive life cycle (PMI 2017). *It is the project sponsor that influences the choice of project leader to take the Business Case and develop the Project Charter as the Charter is effectively an agreement between the project sponsor and the project leader to start the project.*

Figure 6.4 Chartering and the predictive life cycle

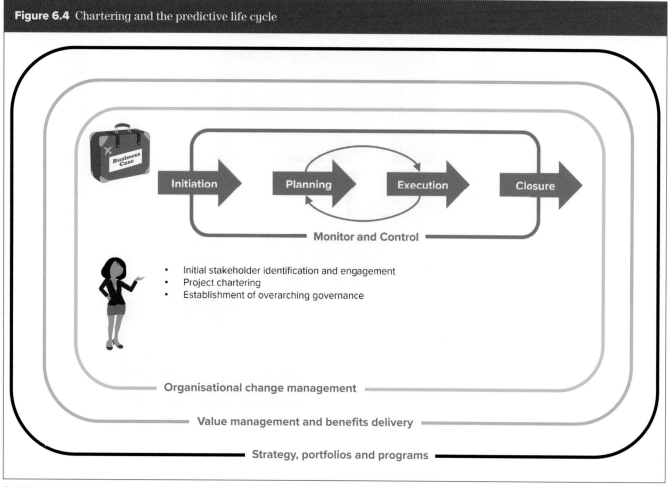

Initiation → Planning → Execution → Closure

Monitor and Control

- Initial stakeholder identification and engagement
- Project chartering
- Establishment of overarching governance

Organisational change management

Value management and benefits delivery

Strategy, portfolios and programs

Projects must, at their outset, have a sound understanding of the problem to be tackled and the goal to be achieved (within a **Business Case**). Before the project is scoped, the charter ensures a consistent understanding of the problem, the value to be derived from the project and its alignment to strategy (PMI 2017). Subsequent scoping and planning detail how this is to be done.

Figure 6.5 illustrates (from a project perspective) how the charter enables the linkage of work between the higher-level program, portfolio and strategy (green arrow), and how the benefits (yellow arrow) are progressively unpacked, understood and expressed in a measurable way. The Business Case provides solid foundations between the business world and the start of the project environment.

The charter should articulate (among other key factors for the organisation) items such as:

- *Project background:* Why the project has come into existence.
- *Project objectives:* Described using the SMARTA acronym (see Chapter 4 "Strategy, project selection and the Business Case", Table 4.1).
- *Project benefits and disbenefits:* Disbenefits are expected undesirable outcomes—they can, for example, take the form of a loss of value to a department or person (termed the *disbeneficiary*) because of the project.
- *Strategic alignment:* Which elements of strategy it assists in delivery and the expected effect on any objectives and key performance indicators (KPIs).

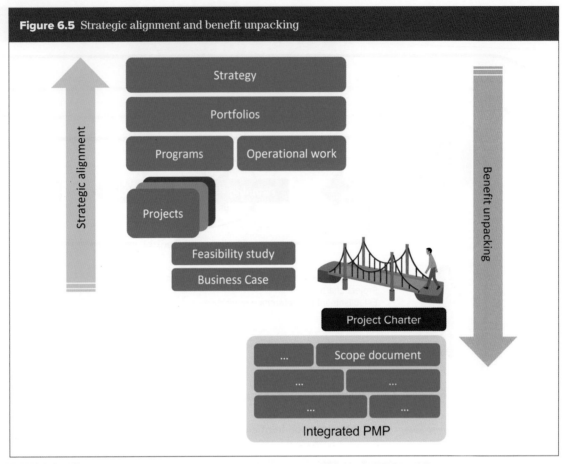

Figure 6.5 Strategic alignment and benefit unpacking

© 2022 Dr Neil Pearson

- *Project vision statement:* What the customer's world or internal company environment will look like (vision) at the end of the project. Useful to convey a consistent message to all stakeholders engaged on the project. Refer to Figure 6.6 for writing styles of project vision statements.
- *Key stakeholders:* Only the key stakeholders at this point and their role in the project.
- *Indicative budget:* With tolerances clearly outlined (+/– 40% accuracy?). (Refer to Chapter 9 "Estimating".)
- *Indicative timeline (with milestones):* With expectations set to reflect that this is subject to change during the further scoping and subsequent detailed planning.
- *Key risks:* The key risks associated with the project.
- *Assumptions:* Statements of truth about project conditions (e.g. access to stakeholders).
- *Constraints:* What will constrain the project (e.g. availability of resources or materials).
- *Signatures of approval:* To gain acceptance of the project's boundaries and green light to proceed into full scope development in the Planning stage.

The Project Charter effectively integrates the project into the organisation's wider reasons for the project and clearly identifies the project leader, who is accountable both for delivering the benefits and achieving the project's objectives.

Figure 6.6 Project vision styles

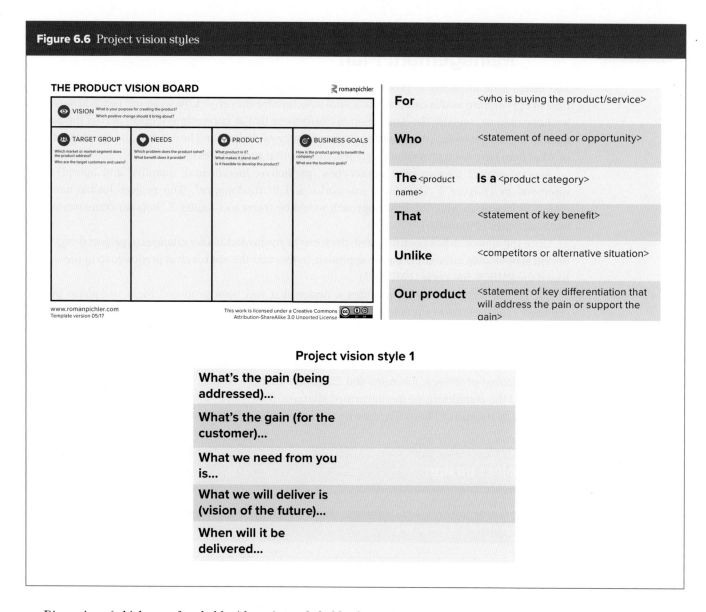

Project vision style 1

Discussions (which are often held with senior stakeholders) can present the project leader with an opportunity to start building a positive working rapport and establishing constructive professional working relationships. It is important to ensure that meetings are planned and well organised to support the smooth flow of discussions and to ensure the proposed content is covered and decisions recorded.

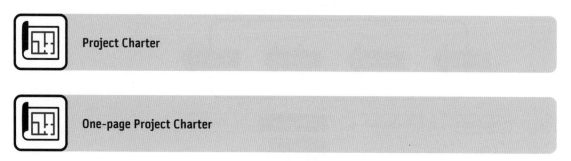

The charter establishes initial expectations and paves the way for further planning to take place, including defining the scope of the project and the next integrative activity—building the integrated PMP. The PMI states that without a Project Charter there is no project.

6.3 Project design and the integrated Project Management Plan

Too often, little attention is given to a project's approach and design. This potentially presents a missed opportunity as this can provide a vital structure for the project. To wrap our heads around this, we have only to consider the Agile (Scrum) movement that is currently sweeping across the project management community (emphasising the importance of design) and how this may impact the design of what may have been previously a staged, incremental **project design**.

Several project management approaches (predictive, incremental, adaptive and hybrid) were discussed in Chapter 2 "Popular frameworks and methodologies". The project leader now has many choices as to what the best approach would be (refer to Chapter 2 "Popular frameworks and methodologies", Figure 2.5).

Once the approach has been selected, the focus of the project leader changes to project design. The design is obviously influenced by the approach; in this text the approach is predominately predictive, based the PMBOK life cycle (PMI 2017).

"In Theory: Project design" indicates a design that has been proposed for a two-phase project (Figure 6.7). Phase 1 takes a predictive approach and could, for instance, consider wider project planning for the whole project (its multiple phase approach). The output of Phase 1 could be detailed current state process models pertaining to the current *as-is* process for hospital admissions. Phase 2 (after some further detailed planning) then involves moving into the future state design, development and delivery of the improved processes, job roles and IT system changes, which, due to constrained stakeholder access and the complexity of the integrated changes, then moves into an Agile approach for project Execution. At the end of Phase 2, a more traditional (predictive) whole-of-project closure takes place.

IN THEORY Project design

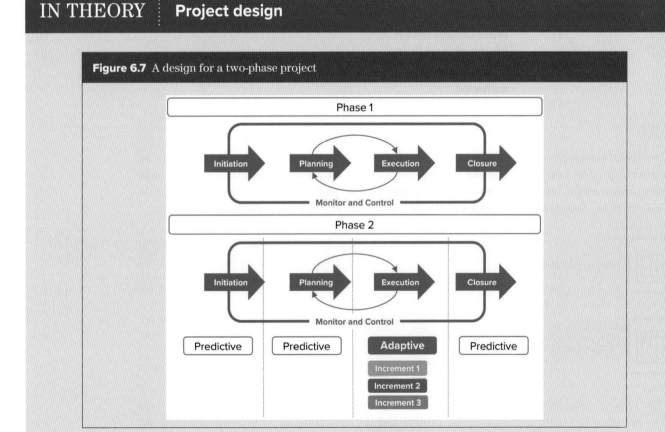

Figure 6.7 A design for a two-phase project

Leveraging the predictive approach brings some stability to the whole project around the planning of resources, costs and timescales (a request from senior management), but later the adaptive approach provides flexibility in the development and implementation of the *to-be* processes, job designs and Information and Communication Technology (ICT) changes. In the adaptive component of the design the business receives three increments of product, which are shipped to the business and implemented at the end of each increment (remember an increment is typically made up of multiple sprints—refer to Chapter 3 "Agile (Scrum) project management"). The two phases are then closed in a traditional, predictive manner.

The complete project design would have been documented as a component of the integrated PMP (normally within the scope document, one of the first key documents produced). It is, in fact, about tailoring the project life cycle approach and building a design that will enable the most efficient use of project resources, while fitting in with the operational business environment to implement the changes being sought by the project.

There are many factors to consider when designing the project approach (again, an example of integrative thinking!) such as:

- the physical design of the blocks of work
- the effect of predictive, adaptive (iterative) or hybrid approaches on the design
- events taking place in the business and in the external environment
- constraints in relation to the use of resources (human and other)
- other programs and projects taking place at the same time
- the operational activities or business-as-usual activities
- the complexity and uncertainty of the requirements
- the risk profile of the project
- the need for the business (or customer) to receive smaller, more frequent releases of product
- the major deliverables to be produced from the project.

The effort placed into a project's design early on will pay dividends throughout the entire project. Often, project leaders do not attend to and consider the intricacies and complexities of design before detailed planning starts and have inadvertently set stakeholder expectations on an incorrect course. If the design is captured in the project scope document, it becomes one of many project artefacts that make up the integrated PMP.

6.3.2 **The integrated Project Management Plan**

The integrated PMP is a concatenation of all the plans and artefacts from each of the knowledge areas, plus any other supporting documents (refer to Figure 6.8). The artefacts on the right of the figure represent the more static documents that establish *how* we are going to manage that particular area. We attend to these at the start of each area so there are common governance and business rules as to how that knowledge area is to be applied in this project's environment. The artefacts on the left are the living documents of the project's content; these express in varying levels of detail all the work to be done, its costs, resources, the risk profiles, stakeholders, and relevant communications. These sit among a myriad of other information that, once planned and approved, form the basis of the baseline Project Management Plan that will be subsequently executed.

- *For smaller projects:* The key components of the integrated PMP could be contained within a single contiguous document, with headings to cover content from both sides—the governance/process management side and the project's living side.
- *From medium to large:* The integrated PMP is more likely to be a compendium of documents held together under document control and release control, on a secured shared network drive, with multiple folders possibly containing many dozens of project artefacts.

Figure 6.8 The integrated Project Management Plan

← **More process-/governance-based**   **More project content-based** →

Scope Management Plan	Scope document, project approach (design), work breakdown structure (WBS), product breakdown structure (PBS), requirements traceability matrix
Schedule Management Plan	Timelines, milestone charts, project schedule, time estimating information
Cost Management Plan	Project budget, cost estimating information, quotes (RFQ)
Quality Management Plan	Quality plans, continuous improvement trackers, quality control activities (identified and built into WBS), quality reports
Resource Management Plan	Resource assignment matrix (RAM), skills matrix, team charter, role descriptions, agreements and contracts, RASCIs
Communications Management Plan	Communications register, template communications (including project status reports), meeting agendas and actions, knowledge repositories
Risk Management Plan	Risk and issues register, risk reporting (heat map)
Procurement Management Plan	Tenders, contracts, supplier selection grids, performance/payment schedules
Stakeholder Management Plan	Stakeholder register, agreements, role descriptions, RASCIs

- Governance Management Plan
- Organisational Change Management Plan (OCMP)
- Configuration Management Plan
- Requirements Management Plan

© 2022 Dr Neil Pearson

The PMBOK seventh edition (PMI 2021) retains management plans but the 10 knowledge areas outputs move into the *commonly used artefacts* section (sub-section 4.6.3 Plans). The partial list of artefacts is shown in Table 6.1.

Table 6.1 Main artefacts in PMBOK seventh edition

Plan artefacts	Strategy artefacts	Log and register artefacts	Hierarchy artefacts	Baseline artefacts	Report artefacts
Change (Variation) Control Plan	Business Case	Assumption log	Organisational breakdown structure	Budget	Quality report
Communications Management Plan	Project brief	Change log	Product breakdown structure	Milestone schedule	Risk report
Cost Management Plan	Project Charter	Issue log	Resource breakdown structure	Performance measurement	Status report
Scope Management Plan	Project vision statement	Lessons Learned Register	Risk breakdown structure	Project schedule	
Procurement Management Plan	Roadmap	Risk Register	Work breakdown structure	Scope	
Project Management Plan		Stakeholder Register			
Quality Management Plan					
Requirements Management Plan					
Resource Management Plan					
Risk Management Plan					
Schedule Management Plan					
Stakeholder Engagement Plan					
Test Plan					

Source: Adapted from Project Management Institute (PMI) 2021, *A Guide to the Project Management Body of Knowledge 7th edition, AND The Standard for Project Management,* https://www.pmi.org/pmbok-guide-standards/foundational/pmbok, accessed December 2021

The purpose and details of each of the subsidiary management plans (in the Table 6.1 "Plan artefacts" column) and associated artefacts are discussed within the respective knowledge area chapter.

Although it may at first appear that a project leader is taking a knowledge area approach to planning a project, hopefully they are taking a more holistic (integrative) approach to consider all the other knowledge areas in any and all decisions. In Figure 6.9, for example, given the simple task of an item being procured, with an integrative hat on, the project leader must consider many facets beyond the item simply being procured. Consider why good project leaders are often rewarded well. They typically have the ability to direct, and to think, in an integrative manner for the many hundreds of tasks and components that can make up a typical project.

Figure 6.9 Example of integrative thinking

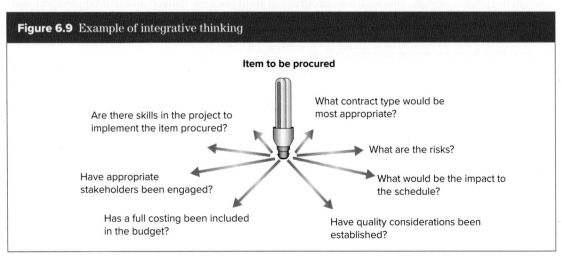

Monty is an early-career project leader. It is his first full life cycle project, where he is leading a small project team to design and deliver an information technology infrastructure library service desk process, and all the associated team and structural changes that must take place. On approval of the project's charter, Monty diligently runs through each of the other nine knowledge areas, crafting the individual subsidiary plans and associated project management artefacts.

It takes some weeks of discussions with the key subject matter experts to workshop, design and gain agreement on the work to be undertaken. Before Monty submits his plans to the relevant committee for approval (to progress into the Execution stage of the project), he asks a seasoned fellow project leader, Olivia, to review the key outputs to ensure potential questions are discussed before meeting with the approval committee.

Olivia comes back to Monty with some interesting questions, including:

- Why haven't the communication costs been accounted for in the project budget?

- Why have resources been costed but are not allocated in the Resource Allocation Matrix (RAM)?

- Why are work packages present in the **work breakdown structure** (WBS) but not visible in the project's Gantt chart?

- Why do the scope document's deliverables appear while other deliverables do not appear in the WBS?

- Why has only line management been involved in the position changes indicated in the reworked service desk organisational structures, and not the human resource manager too?

Monty is at first a little annoyed that he had overlooked such questions. Olivia quietly reassures him that many early career project leaders frequently overlook the integration of all aspects of project management, including making integrative connections across the knowledge areas. Monty thanks her for her words of wisdom and reviews all the plans, including subsidiary plans and other project management artefacts, for integrative thinking.

What would have happened if the approval committee had approved the plans, trusting Monty as a professional project leader? Most likely delays, variation requests and scope creep, and a poor track record for Monty.

6.4 | **Executing the work and delivering**

In executing the project, the baseline integrated PMP becomes the playbook for the rest of the project. The focus is on the allocation of **work packages** and tasks to resources for work to now start, be monitored and ultimately completed, with the goal of achieving the project's deliverables. Deliverables should be considered in the design of a project. If a purely predictive life cycle approach was taken towards the management of the project, a project leader might introduce deliverables all the way through the project design. This indicates progress to stakeholders, gains continued buy-in and hands over progressive deliverables to the business. Deliverables assist the project leader by chunking the work into manageable components, which can be delivered to the business (customer) for sign-off. Figure 6.10 indicates a design along such lines.

The signing-off of the deliverable is usually a formal process, the result of which is an approved deliverable acceptance form. Chapter 18 "Project execution" reviews this process in more detail.

Another key activity of the project leader undertaken during Execution is the allocation and doing of that work.

Behind each deliverable there could be several work packages, which enable the completion and delivery of the deliverable to the business. Figure 6.11 illustrates this relationship between the work packages enabling the delivery of a deliverable and the project team member(s) being allocated to a work package (resource allocation).

The continual cycle of verifying resource availability and the allocation of work to resources is critical during the execution of the project. It is the most hands-on management part of the project work, where the project leader interacts closely with those responsible for delivering the work packages.

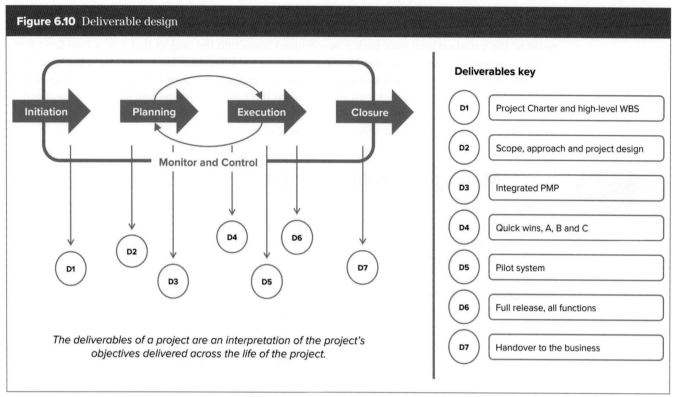

Figure 6.10 Deliverable design

The deliverables of a project are an interpretation of the project's objectives delivered across the life of the project.

Deliverables key

D1	Project Charter and high-level WBS
D2	Scope, approach and project design
D3	Integrated PMP
D4	Quick wins, A, B and C
D5	Pilot system
D6	Full release, all functions
D7	Handover to the business

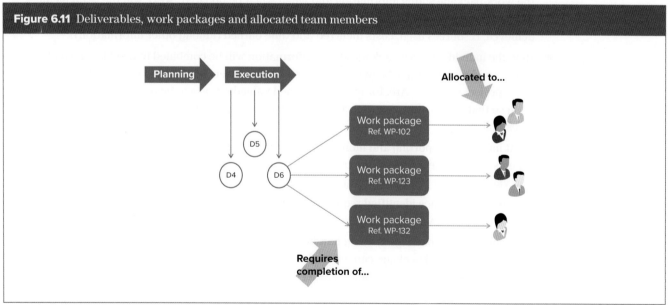

Figure 6.11 Deliverables, work packages and allocated team members

Requests to change the project (for whatever reason) are captured as variation requests. These variation requests can affect planned work. Chapter 8 "Defining the scope of a project" covers the process of variation request management in detail. From an integrative perspective, when a variation request is requested, and as part of the analysis of that variation request, the assigned project team member must ask: Is there any impact to any of the other knowledge areas as a result of this variation? If so, what is the impact? The resulting findings would be documented and returned to the project leader for review in a variation impact analysis document.

An approved variation request would have resulting approved actions (across any of the other knowledge areas), which would then be reflected into the relevant parts of the integrated PMP. The result of the variation may have such a pronounced impact on the project that a new baseline (scope baseline, schedule baseline or cost baseline) must be established. This is then the new or revised baseline from which the project starts to execute. Additionally, a record of baselines is also kept so we know exactly what occurred with references to the baseline version and documents updated as a result. The reader will be able to see this tracking of baselines within the Scope Management Plan (refer to Chapter 8 "Defining the scope of a project").

6.5 | Managing project control

The reporting, reviewing and decison-making based on project information will ensure that the work is in accordance with the planned work to be carried out, as documented in the baselined Project Management Plan. As we know, the integrated PMP is a compendium of all the individual knowledge area management plans and other associated artefacts that were developed during the Planning stage of the project. If performance differences are encountered (between what was planned and what is occurring during Execution), these would be highlighted through the reporting and reviewing of project information (adapted from PMI 2017).

The project approach (predictive, incremental, adaptive, hybrid) will influence how project tracking will take place. The key integrative concern is to ensure that tracking is integrated into the relevant components of the Project Management Plan and into the practices of the project team. The following points therefore need to be considered.

- The project data required and how project tracking information is to be tracked. Who will update the work package status information and when will it be updated? Also, will the team member who is allocated to the work package update information at the end of every day on the value achieved, resources used, costs incurred and time burned (among other information)?

- How the individual work package status information will be combined to produce the daily, weekly and monthly reports that are required by the project leader (and other stakeholders) to track project progress. Are, for example, earned valued reports to be produced and analysed daily so that trends, discrepancies and respective root-cause analyses and corrective actions can be established?

- What impact the reporting and monitoring of this information will potentially have on other aspects of the project. Does, for example, a risk need to be raised, or an issue escalated because of a variance from planned activity—remember, integrative thinking!

- Whether the variance identified requires the project leader to raise a variation request that is submitted into the variation management process for consideration.

- Whether the work package is being handled by an outsourced party. If so, how much insight into that outsourced package can we see? Does the resulting variance breach any contractual agreements that need to be escalated as a risk or issue through the respective escalation processes?

- Wider in scope, but also relevant, is the need to periodically check back with the sponsor and the documented Business Case, to ensure the project remains strategically aligned, that the business environment has not changed, and that the Business Case continues to remain valid and on-track to deliver the benefits and objectives.

If the project, or part of the project, is more adaptive (Agile) in nature, then information on sprints, sprint backlog items and their tracking through the development team (by updating *done story points* against each story) would still be reported daily via the burndown and burnup charts. Refer to Chapter 3 "Agile (Scrum) project management".

6.6 : **Managing variations (change requests)**

Variation (change) control is included within project integration management as it is a process that spans the entire life cycle of the project, but in practice is only strictly applied after the baseline integrated Project Management Plan has been approved. The variation management process includes the raising and approval of a variation request, the analysis of the variation and its approval (or rejection). Chapter 8 "Defining the scope of a project" covers the process of variation management in more detail, providing an example variation management process.

In modern project management, the project leader needs to consider the impact of variations beyond what is referred to as the *triple constraints* of scope, time and cost to also include quality, risk, resources and the organisation's strategy, known collectively as the *seven constraints*. Refer to Figure 6.12.

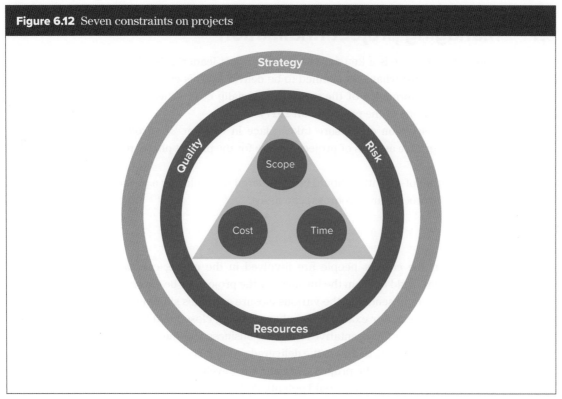

Figure 6.12 Seven constraints on projects

© 2022 Dr Neil Pearson

Project integration has many facets that must be reflected within a variation management process. For example:

- Has the project leader communicated the process to be followed for any variation requests to all members of the project team?
- Is the project team aware of any templates or ticket logging process for capturing the variation request?
- Has the project team member communicated the stages and timings of the process the variation request must go through to the requestor of the variation (typically a person in the business)?
- Has an integrative analysis of the variation request taken place to consider, at minimum, the impact to the knowledge areas and beyond (i.e. are there specific knowledge areas that need to be appended to the PMBOK knowledge areas that must be considered in the project environment—for construction this would include workplace health and safety and environmental considerations)?
- What is the outcome of the process? Does it require a re-baselining of the scope, budget (costs) or schedule?

- How is the approved variation request to be implemented? (If not approved, has this been communicated back to the requestor?)

- What lessons can be learned? Have these been recorded in the **Lessons Learned Register** and actioned, so the issue is not encountered again? For example, if the estimating process and calculation for a work package were incorrect and components were missed in the estimation of costs, the lesson learned would be to update how estimating is carried out so future estimates are not underestimated for these types of work packages.

Integration and ensuring project integrity remains true and honest can be a complex activity for the project leader to oversee and ensure it is carried out in a transparent and ethical manner. Hence, project integration management considers this to be an integrative process that continually operates across all stages of the project life cycle.

6.7 : **Managing project finalisation**

Closing the project or a phase is a key activity of the project leader. It is where what was delivered is directly compared against what was planned to be delivered. This could include aspects of benefit (value) delivered, the performance of the project (especially cost, schedule, resources and quality elements) and the resourcing of the project (PMI 2017).

A comprehensive discussion on closure takes place in Chapter 21 "Project closure". Here, we consider the more integrative aspects of project closure for the project phase, project contracts or the project itself.

The integrative nature of activities should be considered when closing a phase, contract or project. A 3P approach (people, process and progress) can assist.

6.7.1 **People**

Consider first whether the correct people are involved in the phase, contract or project closure activity. Representatives could be from the business or the project, or be external to the organisation. Integratively, the people represented at the various closure activities should cover the key aspects of the phase, contract or project. For example, if a phase is being closed that has implemented working software to the business, then representatives from the business and the project should be present at the project phase closure meeting, to assess the delivered product according to the original scope (plus any approved variations). If only the project team and the development team were present at such a meeting, the perspective of acceptance would potentially be skewed. Ensuring the correct people are present at the closure activity is vital to ensuring a holistic (integrative) approach is achieved. If people have left the project (and/or the organisation) and are no longer available, key learnings may be lost. Therefore, taking steps to capture this information before it is lost forms part of an integrative approach.

The second consideration is where people will move to following closure of the phase, contract or project. With a contract, this may be clean-cut, with little resource management required. At project closure, however, there can be many aspects to consider when it comes to project team members moving back into their substantive positions in the business (requiring human resource involvement). This encompasses being able to capture subject matter expertise that has been gained over time while working on the project.

Decisions will need to be made about how the organisation can best leverage this knowledge at project closure. For example, perhaps it is appropriate that the project team member takes on a new, more senior role in the organisation so their skills, knowledge and expertise can continue to be leveraged in the business—they will effectively follow the project back into the business and become the subject matter expert. These topics and more are discussed in Chapter 19 "Project leaders and project teams" and Chapter 21 "Project closure".

6.7.2 **Process**

This topic is more applicable for the **lessons learned** review, which would be an agenda item on the project closure meeting. Lessons learned will also form part of the post-implementation review meeting, from a project approach, processes and guidelines review. The project leader will, integratively, consider each of the knowledge areas at the project closure meeting to ensure all activities left in progress are successfully closed out. A project checklist is typically used to assist the project leader to do this. At the post-implementation review (i.e. after the closure of the project), the business will look to learn greater lessons, going beyond how the project operated across the knowledge areas. Wider organisational processes will be brought into question, such as processes outside the project, the organisation's human resource processes, the procurement process, the portfolio alignment process, business case gateway reviews, and benefit definition and tracking. Any learnings that can be passed back to the owners of these organisational processes will hopefully assist in the delivery of future projects. The process and protocols of learning lessons would form part of the project's Scope Management Plan, for example. The lessons learned process is discussed in Chapter 21 "Project closure".

6.7.3 **Progress**

The project leader will consider the following issues:

- Aspects of how project tracking and reporting functioned, for example, whether the project was able to accurately provide status updates to inform quality decision-making.
- The variation control process, from turnaround times to the volume of requests. If there were many variation requests for a particular area of the project, does this indicate an improvement opportunity that needs to be addressed before future projects start up?
- The deliverable acceptance process and the design of deliverables in the project: Did the project obtain the correct balance and granularity of deliverables?
- How products, services and results transitioned between phases (within the project or at contract closure from a third party into the business, or at project closure from the project to the business/ customer).
- How the Business Case remained current throughout the project. Were benefits validated at key points to ensure delivery of the project's benefits remained on track?

Note: A similar process is achieved in Agile, at the end of each sprint (and increment) via the sprint review meeting and the sprint retrospective meeting (refer to Chapter 3 "Agile (Scrum) project management").

6.8 : **Managing project knowledge**

In today's information-rich environments, the project leader and the project team will need to consider several dynamics around information. For example:

- What information is required to be maintained by the project, as opposed to in the business?
- Who can have access to what information and at what level (i.e. create, read, update, delete)?
- In what medium is the information best presented (e.g. wiki, discussion forum, intranet site)?
- Who within the project is responsible for maintaining the information?
- How and when is the information announced or communicated?

Addressing these and other questions will require engaging with stakeholders so protocols and tools can be put in place to enable successful data, information and knowledge-sharing in the

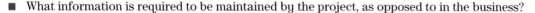

project environment. Ensuring formal documents or repositories of information are established ensures that a single, known source of truth exists for that subset of project information.

For example, members of the project team should be able to access the common project Lessons Learned Register, so they can seek information that helps to inform work packages they may have been assigned. Building and maintaining a formal lessons learned document requires a certain amount of work and effort, but without it a project team will have no single source of information to turn to regarding potentially project-saving lessons that have been learned through prior projects. For example, valuable lessons may have been learned from project end-stage reviews (or from each sprint retrospective in adaptive project management), which may otherwise be lost. What this approach promotes (whether predictive or adaptive) is the capturing of tacit knowledge (i.e. knowledge that is in people's heads) into a more explicit format—in this case, the Lessons Learned Register (which is considered explicit—written down).

 Lessons Learned Register

In the socially aware world of contemporary project management, project stakeholder management skills and the ability to manage and (appropriately) share knowledge and information have become must-have skills for the project leader and project team members. The environment (culture) of the organisation may influence the style (or mediums) used in knowledge sharing. At times, it may be appropriate for the project leader (with suitable backing) to politely challenge the use of traditional mediums of communication/knowledge sharing that may continue to exist in old-school organisations. Conversely, it may be that the project leader needs to adapt to more contemporary social media practices and must be prepared to change their approaches according to the organisation's and project's needs.

Consider the following suggestions for tools for sharing knowledge (and information), adapted and extended from PMBOK (PMI 2017, p. 103).

- Networking events can bring together internal, external (or a combination of) stakeholders in a social atmosphere.
- Communities of practice and special interest groups can bring together stakeholders who are focused around a particular area of interest.
- Discussion forums and discussion groups can leverage social media technologies (e.g. Yammer, Confluence).
- Knowledge fairs and cafés can promote innovation and idea generation, as well as knowledge sharing.
- Coaching, mentoring and training are good ways to share knowledge and information.
- Stories tend to resonate well with people. The project may have an elevator pitch or a 60-second story that is used to illustrate the pain being experienced by the customer, the desired future state after the project, and how this will be achieved. Stories have been used for millennia to pass on knowledge and still remain a powerful medium.
- Workshops that are designed for a specific objective are a common format used for sharing and eliciting information in a project environment.
- Meetings can, if structured by a well-thought-out agenda, produce outcomes for more formal, in-depth discussions.
- Observation (or shadowing) is a useful technique for probing tacit knowledge around a particular job function.

"In Theory: Information sharing" provides an example of where the project leader has actively identified information and communication requirements and has put in place the technology that is needed for supporting the integrative nature of information and knowledge sharing across all aspects of the project.

IN THEORY : Information sharing

Leading a global project across multiple geographically dispersed locations can present numerous challenges. On this occasion, the challenges were in being able to share and communicate (sometimes business-sensitive) information across a diverse set of stakeholders. The company had recently adopted Oracle Beehive and the project leader adopted the software package as the repository, conferencing and information-sharing hub for the project.

Features of Oracle's enterprise solution include:

- enterprise messaging—calendar, email, tasks and contacts
- team collaboration—discussion groups, wikis, document sharing and search capability
- synchronous collaboration—conferencing, chat, presence and voice chat.

1. The project leader established the protocol that everyone in the project team had to be logged onto instant messaging with a status flag showing their availability (e.g. whether available, in a meeting, on a critical path activity or away).

2. All virtual meetings were recorded and made available to team members who could not attend the live meetings due to significant differences between respective time zones. The recordings included voice and video and any shared desktop screens.

3. A project wiki was maintained for all project terminology and the documents were secured and shared from within the collaborative environment.

4. An intranet site, built on top of the corporate document management system, was constructed to share information with the rest of the business (set up as part of the communication strategy for the project).

5. Various discussion groups were established to cover such topics as data migration, technical configuration and business rule changes.

6. Calendars were shared across the team to see into tasks allocated and other business-as-usual commitments.

Although these facilities are available in many social media platforms, the benefits of using a tool such as Oracle Beehive were in its enterprise presence (i.e. all organisation employees and contractors used a single platform).

The project leader (Pearson) should review and implement tools that will assist in managing knowledge and information. The project leader in this case was complimented at the end of the project for having facilitated high-quality communication and information-sharing beyond expectations.

6.9 : Integrative thinking

To help the project leader understand how important it is to think integratively (in systems), it often helps to think in multiple dimensions and the connections and intricacies between them. This type of thinking can be done at any level from the more holistic *where does the project sits within the external and internal business environment* (as illustrated in Figure 6.13), to systems specific, to the project's content requiring subject matter expertise to unpack and understand.

As numbered on Figure 6.13, within the boundaries of the project:

1 Think backwards! Are factors that have already been established or work approved now being changed and therefore require re-confirmation or approval to move forward? What lessons have been learned from previous projects?

Figure 6.13 Dimensions of integrative thinking

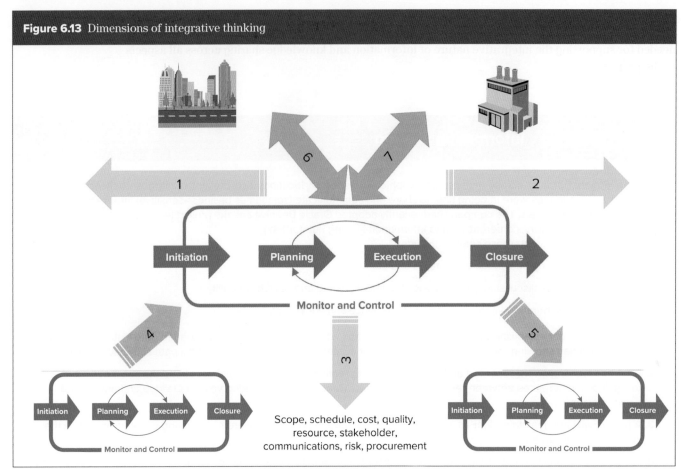

© 2022 Dr Neil Pearson

2 Think forwards! What is the impact on events that have yet to occur in the project, for example, from a variation that is occurring now? What has already been confirmed? What else needs to be done? What needs to be changed? And what should now *not* be done?

3 Think more deeply into, and across, the other knowledge areas. For example, if a new stakeholder is introduced, what communications are required? Does this change the structures for reporting? What effect will this have when implementation takes place? Don't forget to include your organisation's/industry's additional plus-plus knowledge areas, for example, workplace health and safety and the environment.

Upstream and downstream to the project:

4 Check for integrative effects on downstream projects (check this also if there is a degree of parallelism taking place between projects). If you change a deliverable, does this have an impact on considerations other project leaders may have to consider in their projects? Know your upstream and downstream dependencies and manage them closely.

5 Check for integrative effects when a project upstream of the project changes and affects work in the project. What impact is there to schedules? Have the risk profiles changed? What other changes are required?

Externally and internally to the business:

6 Consider what impact project decisions may have on the current and future environment: this may be from a compliance perspective, or may be driven from a company ethics perspective (e.g. outwardly displaying that your organisation is an environmentally considerate organisation). Alternatively, consider what impacts the external environment could have on your project.

7 Finally, consider the impacts of the project on the business. For example, if a new process is introduced, how does this impact on operational employees? Will this raise any organisational change management activities or communication requirements that now need to be planned into the project? What is occurring in the business environment and does this impact the project? If so, what must be done about it?

What you have in effect is a system, and your system thinking skills as a project leader will ensure all the interactions and feedback loops are being considered.

The remaining sections of this chapter review each of the other knowledge areas (scope, schedule, cost, quality, resources, risk, stakeholders, communication and information, and procurement) and present, by predictive life cycle stage, key activities couched in an integrative manner.

Note: There are many terms included in these integration summary tables which are explored further in other chapters.

6.9.1 **Project scope integration**

Project scope integration includes aspects of project and processes, through to the validation of the scope document and deliverables at project closure. Typical activities carried out in relation to scope integration can be seen in Table 6.2.

Table 6.2 Project scope integration

Life cycle stage	Integrative activity
Initiation	■ Develop the scope, captured in the scope document and accompanying WBS. ■ Review lessons learned from past projects and how these apply to the current project. ■ Develop the initial WBS. Reflect the thinking and work from all the other knowledge areas back into the WBS. ■ Estimate the project's overall (projected) cost and duration, and then gain agreement with executive management at the Initiation stage of the project. ■ Set expectations around the accuracy of estimating around the initiating, scoping and detailed planning activities that follow. ■ Develop and communicate the Scope Management Plan, including the variation management (or change request) process. ■ Gain approval of the project scope document and the Scope Management Plan, before proceeding into detailed planning. The scope document becomes the scope baseline for the project. ■ Review lessons learned regarding scope management from previous projects and what is being done in this project to mitigate negative lessons or leverage positive lessons from previous projects.
Planning	■ Continue development of the integrated PMP, based on the pre-approved scope. ■ Apply the variation process to any scope changes once scope is agreed. ■ Continue to validate the project's objectives (and Business Case), typically at the project Steering Committee meetings or gateway review points. ■ Continue to improve the project scope control processes as documented in the Scope Management Plan. ■ Continue to validate the project objectives, scope and benefits and make sure work being planned will deliver the benefits; recall the saying *design with the benefits in mind!*
Execution	■ Ensure the scope document is aligned to approved scope variations and, if necessary, re-baseline the scope. ■ Continue to improve the project scope control processes. ■ Deliver the deliverables, as defined in the project scope document and project schedule, ensuring deliverables are signed off appropriately.
Monitor and Control	■ Apply the variation process for any change to the project. Review the impact of the variation across the other knowledge areas and update project documentation as required on approved variation requests.
Closure	■ Validate results produced by the project against what was defined within the scope document (including the project's objectives, outcomes, outputs and benefits)—did the project deliver what it promised to deliver? ■ Review all variations to ensure the delivery of approved variations to scope took place and that there are no outstanding requests. ■ Capture scope lessons learned. ■ Hand over final project deliverables to the relevant business owners/customer.

6.9.2 **Project schedule integration**

Table 6.3 outlines some of the integrative activities a project leader would consider from a project schedule integration aspect.

Table 6.3 Project schedule integration

Life cycle stage	Integrative activity
Initiation	■ Develop the Schedule Management Plan, and, for example, capture how you want completion of work packages to be reported. ■ Develop the high-level timeline or project schedule to include in such documents as the Project Charter. ■ Review lessons learned regarding schedule management from previous projects and what is being done in this project to mitigate negative lessons or leverage positive lessons from previous projects.
Planning	■ Continue to develop the WBS and work packages. ■ Leverage the WBS to determine high-level estimates for the duration of work packages and tasks. This would also include an estimation of resource requirements to determine how long each resource is required for and the costs associated with that resource. ■ Continue to develop the Schedule Management Plan. ■ Develop the detailed project schedule, including obtaining more detailed/accurate estimates than were required at the Initiation stage. ■ Allocate resources and costs to the project schedule (using a software package to ease the maintenance of schedule data). ■ Review the project schedule to look for efficiency-maximising opportunities (including opportunities to fast-track and crash the project schedule). Crashing, for example, might have integrative aspects to resolve with resourcing. ■ Update the scope document with the list of scheduled milestones and deliverables. ■ Obtain baseline approval of the project schedule prior to the Execution stage; this then becomes the schedule baseline. ■ Communicate the Schedule Management Plan and the project schedule to the project team and other stakeholders as required.
Execution	■ Allocate activities and work packages to internal personnel and external contractors, as defined in the project schedule or resource allocation matrix (RAM). ■ Obtain approvals when deliverables are delivered to the customer. ■ Update the project team on the project's schedule, typically at project team meetings where the previous, current and following week's allocations and statuses are discussed.
Monitor and Control	■ Monitor the performance of work packages and update the project schedule with tracking information. ■ Maintain project schedule and reflect variations back into the WBS. ■ Monitor the schedule baseline for discrepancies between, for example, planned and actual activity durations. Invoke the variation process for any changes to the project schedule, to ensure the variation request has been appropriately analysed and the full impact of a request on the schedule is captured for later approval/no approval. On approval, the project schedule could potentially be re-baselined. Maintain a history of the schedule baselines. ■ Ensure milestones and deliverables are achieved, and report on milestone and deliverable progress. ■ Closely monitor activities on the project schedule's critical path. ■ Report on project progress in a defined and agreed format. ■ Project status reporting may include the preparation of earned value management (EVM) information.
Closure	■ Final project reporting for time, schedule baseline versus actual schedule (including any approved variations). ■ Check to ensure that all tasks/work packages have been completed according to the project schedule. ■ Capture scheduling lessons learned. ■ File relevant scheduling information in the project library.

© 2022 Dr Neil Pearson

Integration of the schedule aspects of the project forms one of the most critical activities for a project leader. Communication is key to ensuring that all involved in the project know what work packages (and associated tasks) they are accountable for delivering, monitoring progress to ensure the project remains on track, and identifying any issue early on in relation to the non-completion of work packages or delays to work packages.

6.9.3 **Project cost integration**

Project cost management is often a complex activity. It involves bringing together many sources of information (the WBS, estimating information, information systems, and accounting policies and procedures) and skills (project accountants, finance representatives, sponsor and project leader) to arrive at a realistic project budget. Some of these activities, captured against each stage of the project life cycle, are shown in Table 6.4.

Table 6.4 Project cost integration

Life cycle stage	Integrative activity
Initiation	■ Estimate costs across the WBS for each resource identified. This has integrative links with the identification and the estimation of resources duration. Remember, resources for which costs are being estimated, such as raw materials, plant, human resources and equipment can be quite wide in nature. ■ Review the WBS from a *make or buy* analysis perspective as this may influence the type of cost estimating that is carried out. ■ Develop the Cost Management Plan, including any finance or project accounting related governance. ■ Identify and possibly gain approval of any identified large capital items and long lead-time items (integrative links to procurement). ■ Identify funding sources and signatories to obtain release of funds into the project. ■ Insert funding sources into the project budget and review the project's cashflow. ■ Request access to corporate systems, such as financial and Enterprise Resource Planning (ERP) systems. ■ Review lessons learned regarding cost management from previous projects and what is being done in this project to mitigate negative lessons or leverage positive lessons from previous projects.
Planning	■ Continue to develop the WBS and work packages from a cost perspective. Have all resources and miscellaneous costs been identified? ■ Use estimating techniques to ensure improved accuracy, to bring the project budget within the industry-accepted +/− 5–10% estimating accuracy, or as specified by the organisation's governance. ■ Continue to develop the Cost Management Plan. ■ Baseline setting of the project budget and approval of the project budget, prior to the Execution stage; this forms the cost baseline. ■ Communicate both the Cost Management Plan and the project budget to the project team and others, as required. ■ Arrange for the setting up of project financial structures in financial and ERP systems, according to company policy.
Execution	■ Continue to maintain the WBS, project schedule (network) and the project budget to ensure all elements of the project are kept aligned. ■ Update corporate systems with financial information and approvals, ranging from contractor and project staff timesheets to invoices and purchase orders. ■ Ensure those with allocated work packages know the budget for the work package and where the money has been allocated within the work package. ■ Ensure those executing work packages know in which system or meeting, for example, cost information is reported and how.
Monitor and Control	■ Monitor the baseline project budget for the impact of variations. ■ Invoke the variation process for any changes to the budget, to ensure the variation(s) have been appropriately analysed and their full impact is approved or not approved before any documents are updated and the project budget is re-baselined and reissued. ■ Report on the project's progress as part of project status reporting. *Note:* The project status report may include the preparation of EVM information. This would include cost figures such as planned value (PV), actual costs (AC) and earned value (EV). Refer to your organisation's EVM guidelines (or resources such as https://www.standards.org.au/standards-catalogue/sa-snz/other/ob-014) in relation to what is included in such calculations. ■ Monitor the cost performance of work packages, to ensure completion within agreed cost parameters (in addition to scope, time and quality parameters).
Closure	■ Final project reporting, cost baseline versus actual, including any approved variations. ■ Update the organisation's corporate systems with final project costs. ■ Close access to systems, to prevent any future projects from booking costs to the account codes set up for this project. ■ Capture cost-related lessons learned.

© 2022 Dr Neil Pearson

6.9.4 **Project quality integration**

The integration of quality across the project life cycle requires a complex interaction of project management actors, including the customer or recipient of the deliverables to agreed quality criteria. Table 6.5 provides an overview of the functions of quality across the life cycle of a project in the context of project quality integration management.

Table 6.5 Project quality integration

Life cycle stage	Integrative activity
Initiation	■ Establish the quality assurance and quality control process requirements for the product, service or result being produced by the project. This will involve understanding the exact quality requirements of the customer. ■ Establish quality assurance and quality control processes from a project management perspective: audits, reviews and gates and the quality of project artefacts. ■ Brainstorm the initial Quality Assurance (QA) and Quality Control (QC) planning grid (covered in Chapter 13 "Project quality management"). ■ Establish the *cost of quality* to the project. ■ Establish the *cost of poor quality* to the project (i.e. costs associated with poor-quality products, services or results that have to be rectified (reworked) within the project). ■ Document quality in the scope document and gain agreement on the broad specifications for quality with sponsor, client or customer. ■ Review lessons learned regarding quality from previous projects and what is being done in this project to mitigate negative lessons or leverage positive lessons from previous projects.
Planning	■ Build the Quality Management Plan: detail all aspects of quality assurance and quality control (from both project management and product or service perspectives). This is likely to result in multiple quality plans to cover each of the major areas of quality in your project. ■ Gain approval for the Quality Management Plan.w ■ Review any risks associated with decisions made around quality assurance and quality control. ■ Establish any additional work packages, tasks or deliverables arising because of quality assurance and quality control planning. You are in Planning so enriching the WBS is a part of the journey to make sure all activities are included in the project design. ■ Ensure the planned durations of existing work packages and tasks allow for quality activities (that are a direct result of building quality into the project). ■ Ascertain the cost of building quality aspects into the project and articulate this cost, ensuring the project's budget includes necessary coverage of these costs. We call this the *cost of quality*, and it is discussed further in Chapter 12 "Project cost management". ■ Ensure work packages include all relevant quality assurance criteria and quality control mechanisms.
Execution	■ Ensure the recipient of the work package understands the implications of the quality criteria they and the work package will be performance managed against. ■ Consider holder-specific quality meetings with the customer and suppliers (as required) to raise/ensure awareness about, and control of, quality. ■ Sign off deliverables to include acceptance to the stated quality criteria. ■ Continually seek efficiencies in the project's delivery through continuous improvement processes.
Monitor and Control	■ Tightly manage the control of quality. ■ Raise variations for quality variances (quality issues). ■ Put in place action plans for rectification, post-root-cause analysis.
Closure	■ Ensure all project and product or service quality outputs/outcomes have been achieved. ■ Obtain final quality sign-offs, as required. ■ Interact with suppliers about final defect lists and any procurement-related activities (such as withholding payments) (i.e. integration with project procurement activities). ■ Record lessons learned in relation to quality for future projects.

© 2022 Dr Neil Pearson

As indicated in Table 6.5, there are many considerations and complexities involved in applying quality as an integrative process across the life cycle of a project. Quality aspects should not be underestimated. The impact on the project's final success or failure could range from *life critical* to *irreversible reputational damage* (both to the project and the organisation as a whole).

6.9.5 **Project resource integration**

It is important to consider resourcing related activities across the entire life cycle. This becomes ever more complex in today's business environments as resources regularly come and go from projects. Table 6.6 indicates some of the main activities the project leader is likely to become involved with.

Table 6.6 Project resource integration

Life cycle stage	Integrative activity
Initiation	■ Identify resource requirements in developing the WBS and in subsequent estimating. ■ Capture the human resource requirements within the project Resource and Skills Matrix. ■ Capture other resource commitments in a resourcing matrix and/or the project schedule. These could include tools, equipment, raw materials and so on. ■ Develop the Resource Management Plan, including identifying any organisation processes and procedures that must be adopted into the project (typically recruitment, performance management and termination) in relation to human resources. Establish project governance in relation to human resource aspects. Identify how the team/individuals are to be rewarded (consider cost implications and capture these in the project budget). ■ Define the project's organisational structure, roles and supporting role fact sheets and/or role-position descriptions. ■ Establish the project's culture. ■ Identify early on, and make arrangements for, resources (e.g. human, tools, equipment) that are in high demand, or for which there is a general skills shortage. ■ Review lessons learned regarding resource management from previous projects and what is being done in this project to mitigate negative lessons or leverage positive lessons from previous projects.
Planning	■ Continue to develop the Resource Management Plan (ensure all types of resources are considered, human and other). ■ Capture and analyse all resource details in the Resource and Skills Matrix, including the training needs analysis, details of certifications and performance dynamics (KPIs and targets). ■ Analyse the resource types and identify the most efficient method of using these resources across the life cycle of the project. Allocate resources to the project schedule and carry out resource levelling, as required. ■ Start recruiting the project team. ■ Establish a project team agreement (if required) and project identity. ■ Develop a RASCI (who is Responsible for the task, who is Accountable for the task and what has been done, who will provide Support for the implementation of the activity/process/service, who can be Consulted about the task and who should be Informed about task progress or decisions in the task).
Execution	■ Ensure a project kick-off meeting is carried out. Establish project ground rules and principles. ■ Build (acquire and recruit) the project team. ■ Acquire other resources (tools, equipment and raw materials) required by the project. ■ Engage with contract and procurement activities for the acquisition of resources as required. ■ Organise and induct project team members. ■ Allocate tasks to the project team. ■ Carry out team meetings and team-building activities. ■ Build relationships. ■ Manage and resolve conflict. ■ Manage resource commitments and availability. ■ Update resources used in the project schedule, so EVM information generated is accurate.
Monitor and Control	■ Monitor the performance of the project team. ■ Monitor resource usage and adjust work allocation. ■ Performance monitor external resources and address issues as they arise.
Closure	■ Have a closure workshop (party). Remember that, in general, people need closure and thanks—recognition of some kind, whether this is a group celebration or individual thanks. ■ Release staff from the project—contract, secondment or other. ■ Conduct final team and individual performance reviews. ■ Pay retention and other bonuses, as agreed. ■ Capture resource lessons learned. ■ Link to contracts and procurement for the closing of any other resource-related contract terms and conditions.

© 2022 Dr Neil Pearson

As can be seen, the integrative elements of resource management can be extensive, as the type and quantity of resources usually peaks during the execution of the project.

6.9.6 **Project stakeholder integration**

Stakeholder management can be complex. This is unsurprising if we consider the variety of experience and industries of individual or groups of stakeholders. The impact they can potentially have across the project management life cycle, and on the knowledge areas, can be significant. Therefore, stakeholder management can be an intensive activity for the project leader. Table 6.7 provides a snapshot of some of the activities the project leader may need to consider with regards to stakeholder management.

Table 6.7 Project stakeholder integration

Life cycle stage	Integrative activity
Initiation	■ Identify stakeholders—within the project, subject matter experts, in the business and external to the business (including potential paying customers). Ensure a comprehensive stakeholder identification activity takes place. Create the first cut of the Stakeholder Matrix. ■ Engage with the sponsor to identify stakeholders they consider should be included in the project. ■ Establish which stages and knowledge areas each stakeholder will contribute to. ■ Analyse the stakeholders: work out, for instance, where power/interest sits. ■ Analyse the stakeholders from an organisational change management perspective. ■ Hold a stakeholder *meet and greet session* to set initial project expectations (expectation management). Build rapport and co-ownership of the project (stakeholder co-creation). ■ Define role expectations of the stakeholder to the project and of the project to the stakeholder, with role descriptions and RASCI matrices. ■ Ensure key stakeholder involvement in the project design. ■ Identify any organisational governance (or policy/policies) where stakeholders are to be considered, and the mechanisms for contacting them. It is possible that contact with some stakeholders (most commonly external groups) may only be possible via existing internal stakeholders in the organisation who might not be directly a part of the project. ■ Review lessons learned regarding resource management from previous projects and what is being done in this project to mitigate negative lessons or leverage positive lessons from previous projects.
Planning	■ Gain further stakeholder involvement and buy-in into the detailed design of the project. ■ Generate interest in stakeholder co-ownership. ■ Identify new stakeholders as planning progresses, and as further subject matter experts are involved. ■ Review the project information and communication aspects of existing and new stakeholders. ■ Identify costs associated with stakeholder engagement activities and ensure these are included in the project budget. ■ Plan for the engagement of stakeholders: Who in the project team is primarily responsible for managing the working relationship and business activities with stakeholders? ■ Manage organisational politics and associated company dynamics as the impact of the project design becomes apparent.
Execution	■ Ongoing stakeholder management and identification of new stakeholders—for example, stakeholders who are to receive the finished deliverables and/or final product. ■ Manage the handover of deliverables to stakeholders. ■ Address concerns. If concerns become issues, the project leader will have to become involved in clarifying and resolving the issues. ■ Integrate your organisational change management activities into the integrated PMP and Organisational Change Management Plan.
Monitor and Control	■ Carry out stakeholder surveys to ascertain how engagement with stakeholders is perceived and follow up with appropriate actions. ■ Monitor for changes to stakeholder contribution—are they losing interest and why? ■ Review and update stakeholder management strategies.
Closure	■ Communicate the project's success to all project stakeholders. This may require generating several different messages to the different types of stakeholders on the project. ■ Personally thank all stakeholders involved in the project (you never know when you may require input from a stakeholder in future projects!). ■ Capture and action stakeholder lessons learned for future projects.

© 2022 Dr Neil Pearson

6.9.7 **Project communication and information integration**

Project communication is integral to all aspects of the project life cycle. Table 6.8 illustrates some of the activities that a project leader will have to make arrangements for within the project environment.

Table 6.8 Project communication and information integration

Life cycle stage	Integrative activity
Initiation	■ Develop the Communications Management Plan. ■ Initiate the Communications Matrix. ■ Develop the project's big picture and early communication of this vision to the various stakeholder groups. ■ Develop the Project Charter. ■ Establish the project library. ■ Identify and gain access to project management information systems and/or corporate ERP/financial systems. ■ Review lessons learned regarding communications management from previous projects and what is being done in this project to mitigate negative lessons or leverage positive lessons from previous projects.

Life cycle stage	Integrative activity
Planning	■ Continue to develop the Communications Management Plan and communicate the plan to the project team. ■ Develop the Communications Matrix in more detail. ■ Closely manage sending of communications identified in the Communications Matrix. ■ Monitor feedback from the communications sent and include/consider in project reviews/meetings. ■ Develop, review and distribute project status reports. ■ Initiate the Communications Sent Register to record formal communications sent from the project. You never know when you may have to quickly access a communication sent from the project. ■ Maintain the project library and any project management information system. ■ Establish (and subscribe to) any electronic communication tools required to communicate with virtual team members. ■ Put in place systems to capture and share knowledge and information across the project team.
Execution	■ Address concerns to avoid any issues. If concerns become issues, the project leader will have to become involved in clarifying and resolving them. ■ Continue to send communications as identified in the Communications Matrix. ■ Develop, review and distribute project status reports. ■ Conduct project team meetings. ■ Maintain the project library and any project management information system. ■ Integrate your organisational change management activities into the integrated PMP and Organisational Change Management Plan.
Monitor and Control	■ Monitor feedback from sent communications. Ensure you have clear and active feedback mechanisms in your project. ■ Monitor changes to stakeholders and the impact it may have on the current messages and modes of communication—do they need adjusting? ■ Conduct project team meetings and take feedback. Adjust your project management processes and governance if necessary.
Closure	■ Prepare final project status report(s). ■ Ensure all project documentation is updated within any project management information systems/project library before archiving project information. ■ Capture communications lessons learned. ■ Conduct post-implementation reviews.

© 2022 Dr Neil Pearson

6.9.8 **Project risk integration**

A lot of benefit is achieved by applying each knowledge area across the life cycle of the project. Risk is especially important when applied in an integrative manner. Some of the key elements of project risk integration are shown in Table 6.9.

Table 6.9 Project risk integration

Life cycle stage	Integrative activity
Initiation	■ Establish the risk context within the external environment, the organisation and within the project. ■ Seek advice on the risk management framework and the process to be applied to the project from the project management office. ■ Develop the Risk Management Plan and define how the risk management process is to be applied. ■ Identify high-level risks for inclusion in the scope document. This may also necessitate opening up the project Risk Register to analyse the risk rating of any identified risks. Remember: Risks can be sourced from an activity that has been defined in any of the knowledge areas. ■ Plan an approach to risk management in the project (i.e. identifying specific risk roles and responsibilities. These are typically captured in the Risk Management Plan. ■ Develop the initial Risk Register. ■ Review lessons learned regarding risk management from previous projects and what is being done in this project to mitigate negative lessons or leverage positive lessons from previous projects.

(Continues)

Table 6.9 Project risk integration *(Continued)*

Life cycle stage	Integrative activity
Planning	■ Undertake detailed risk-identification, analysis, evaluation, treatment and contingency planning. Risk identification could involve workshops and brainstorming session(s), using risk identification techniques such as RBS, WBS, Delphi and PERT. ■ Continue to review all other project activities taking place (including, but not exclusively, the other knowledge areas) to identify any relevant risks and capture the risks. ■ Further develop the Risk Register. ■ Continue to develop the Risk Management Plan and its approval. ■ Communicate the Risk Management Plan and its approach to the project team.
Execution	■ Invoke the variation process when a risk becomes an issue. ■ When a risk becomes an issue, be suitably prepared by having contingency plans developed for high-probability/high-impact risks. ■ Communicate risks. This could be at regular team meetings or in project status reports. ■ Make improvements to the risk management process as opportunities arise through the lessons learned process.
Monitor and Control	■ Monitor risks (as you would for any dimension of the project). Watch for changes to individual risk profiles and new risks that may occur as the project progresses. ■ Report on risk as part of the project status report.
Closure	■ Close out any risks (and make sure the business is aware of any open risks in handover documentation). ■ Report the final project Risk Register as part of the final project closure report. ■ Capture risk lessons learned.

© 2022 Dr Neil Pearson

6.9.9 Project procurement integration

Procurement is integral to all aspects of the project life cycle: from initial *make or buy* decisions on long lead-time items through to project closure (ensuring all suppliers have delivered to mandated specifications and contractual agreements). Key activities of procurement (as distributed across the project life cycle) are captured in Table 6.10.

Table 6.10 Project procurement integration

Life cycle stage	Integrative activity
Initiation	■ Establish the procurement approach across the project. ■ Define roles and responsibilities in relation to procurement activities within the project. ■ Document all procurement management processes and governance in the Procurement Management Plan. ■ Engage with the organisation's procurement, contracts and legal departments to bring standard policy and procedure into the project environment, thereby establishing the governance policy and procedures for the project. ■ Identify the initial requirements for items to be procured, especially in relation to long lead-time items and large capital purchases. ■ Gain approval (according to the governance procedure) of any long lead-time item and large capital purchases. These typically fall outside the accountability of the project leader and may reside instead with governance committees (such as the project steering committee and/or sponsor). ■ Review lessons learned regarding procurement management from previous projects and what is being done in this project to mitigate negative lessons or leverage positive lessons from previous projects. This may extend to projects outside the organisation, where information is available (e.g. in trade magazines, journals and press releases).
Planning	■ Continue development of the Procurement Management Plan. ■ Review the WBS and decide on make or buy decisions in relation to work packages. ■ Review the WBS and ensure coverage of any procurement activities that are having to be undertaken (i.e. require time and resources). ■ Establish any tender processes, roles and responsibilities. ■ Identify and plan the approach to be taken for all other (non-long-lead time and large capital) purchases that have been identified during the detailed planning of the project. ■ Develop any required tender documents. *Note:* The development of tender documents can consume considerable time and resources. Ensure allowances for this in the project schedule, budget and RAM. ■ Allow time for the procurement, contracts and legal departments to review and adjust contracts, according to organisational policies and procedures. ■ Review all procurement activities (and their potential impacts on the project schedule). ■ Review risks from a procurement perspective and include any risks on the project Risk Register.

Life cycle stage	Integrative activity
	■ Publicise open tenders and/or invite suppliers to closed tenders. Again, ensure any lead times are incorporated into the project schedule and incorporate potential knock-on effects in the turnaround times of tenders. ■ Once the successful suppliers have been selected from the tender process, engage each in contract negotiations. Establish all the contract performance criteria (linkages to quality) and related schedule of payments (linkages to budget) as a part of contract negotiations.
Execution	■ Make payments against the agreed schedule of payments (progress payments) according to the performance criteria that were contractually agreed. ■ Maintain records of deliverables and any outstanding defects for later reconciliation during the project and at project closure. ■ Apply the project variation management process to any deviations in scope and changes to the project that are a result of changes to procurement activities or non-conformance (quality aspects). ■ Continue to manage stakeholders and build relationships with suppliers to ensure alignment with project objectives. Trust in the supplier relationship is not (unfortunately) automatic and must be built and maintained across all stages of the project life cycle, from Initiation through to Closure.
Monitor and Control	■ Monitor contract performance criteria and take corrective actions where necessary (this may be included as a part of the quality continuous improvement process). ■ Monitor changes in procurement-related risks and raise any new risks as and when these occur.
Closure	■ Conduct final assessments of contract deliverables, based on the defined acceptance criteria. ■ Agree on defect or fix lists and the payments to be withheld until such problems have been resolved. On a cautionary note, be aware that although standard percentages are usually agreed within a contract for such situations, if the monetary value of the defect(s) exceeds the monetary percentage withheld, it may be possible for the supplier to walk away from the contract by declaring bankruptcy. ■ Hand over warranties and guarantees to the business. ■ Review the performance of all suppliers and contractors and notify the procurement and contracts department of the outcomes of this assessment. Especially highlight where performance has been sub-par and where consideration should be given to potentially not using those suppliers/contractors for future projects. ■ Capture procurement lessons learned for the benefit of future projects. ■ Conduct final, formal, contract close-out activities, as defined in the organisation's procurement and contracts policies and procedures.

© 2022 Dr Neil Pearson

Table 6.10 shows the complexity and variation of procurement activities to be considered in the Initiation, Planning, Execution and Closure stages of the project.

Summary

The complex nature of integrative thinking has been explored throughout this chapter, including:

■ developing the Project Charter and the overall project approach and project design
■ the importance of integrating artefacts generated through planning the individual knowledge areas into an integrated PMP
■ the integrative nature of assessing variations to the project and the impact of the variation to all areas of the project, including scope, schedule, resources, costs, quality, risk, stakeholders, communication and information, and procurement
■ ensuring the ability to collect information in an accurate manner is built into the project so project reporting can later take place
■ allocating and managing project work
■ ensuring systems exist for the collection and sharing of project information across and outside the project
■ closing of a project stage or the whole project and making sure any lessons learned are captured and leveraged
■ recognising the importance of ensuring good governance foundations are laid and built upon for the project (refer to Chapter 7 "Governance and projects")
■ discussing integrative thinking across the knowledge areas with some typical day-in-the-life-of dot points to inspire your integrative thinking!

This chapter has also linked to material covered in future chapters of this text where further detail and discussion of the various topics and techniques is found.

Remember: Think in an integrative manner, in systems and connections.

The British Computer Society's POPIT™ model (as adapted in Figure 6.14) can be applied to how the project leader needs to continually think integratively and holistically about how the project impacts on the organisation, the people, the processes, the information flows and the technology that enables the flow of information.

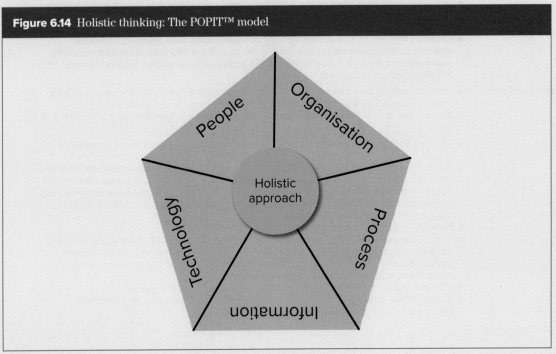

Figure 6.14 Holistic thinking: The POPIT™ model

© 2022 Dr Neil Pearson

Source: Adapted from Yeates D, Cadle J & Paul D 2014, *Business Analysis,* 3rd edition, BCS Learning & Development, The Chartered Institute for IT ©Assist Knowledge Development

Review questions

1. What are the triple constraints?
2. What are the extended seven constraints, and why are they important to project integration management?
3. What are the components of an integrated PMP?
4. Why is deliverable design important?
5. What is the importance of having a Project Charter?
6. Why is integrated change control essential in the management of change requests?
7. Provide six techniques (with examples) of sharing project knowledge (and information).
8. What is integrative thinking and systems thinking?

Exercises

1. Using the information in Figure 6.5, draft a similar diagram for the Golden Years Admissions Business System Replacement (ABS-R). Ensure you include deliverables across the entire life cycle of the project, so you can show progress to the management team and the customer. Be prepared to share design with the wider class.

2. For a project you have worked on recently, create a Lessons Learned Register; assume you are in Initiation stage. Ensure you consider both positive and negative lessons and remember to include how you addressed these lessons in your project.

References

Project Management Institute (PMI) 2017, *A Guide to the Project Management Body of Knowledge,* 6th edition, PMI.

Project Management Institute (PMI) 2021a, *A Guide to the Project Management Body of Knowledge (PMBOK® Guide),* 7th edition, Newton Square, PA.

Project Management Institute (PMI) 2021b, *The Standard for Project Management (ANSI/PMI 99-001-2021),* 7th edition, Newton Square, PA.

Yeates D, Cadle J & Paul D 2014, *Business Analysis,* third edition, BCS Learning & Development, The Chartered Institute for IT.

CHAPTER 7
Governance and projects

Learning elements

7A Understand what governance is and why it is critical for a project leader to define governance arrangements.

7B Be able to identify governance for the project environment within which the project sits.

7C Be able to design, document and communicate a projects governance using various tools and techniques.

7D Have the ability to monitor and review the application of governance throughout the project.

7E Be able to enhance the tactical operation of the project by adjusting and/or continually improving the governance mechanisms that are in place.

7F Understand the role of a project management office and the links with project governance.

In this chapter

7.1 Introduction to governance in the project context

7.2 Identify governance

7.3 Develop a governance plan

7.4 Monitor governance

7.5 Review governance

7.6 The project (program) management office

Summary

7.1 Introduction to governance in the project context

Project governance is often a too-little, too-late activity that a project leader attends to because a situation (or issue) has occurred. Even though project governance has become a fashionable phrase in some circles, it is still relatively poorly attended to in many project environments.

Project governance should be:

- well-planned and thought through as early as possible in the management of the project. At the project level, key governance must be established, ideally prior to the Initiation stage. It could even be considered an activity to carry out in the pre-Initiation stage, and in organisations that have a project management office (PMO), it could be heavily influenced or even mandated by the PMO as the project is established.

- tailored to meet the organisation environment, customer and project.

- captured in easily accessible documents. Company policy and procedures, and protect artefacts, such as the project's various management plans, the project-wide **RASCI** (see section 7.3.1), and reflected into role descriptions and even employment **job descriptions.**

- communicated and agreed with all the relevant parties (roles) involved, within the project environment and beyond the project team.

Project management is the act of applying processes, skills, knowledge and tools to achieve specific project objectives. This differs from **project governance,** which is frequently described as the ability for executives and senior management teams to effect or exercise oversight, ensuring strategies are implemented and business benefits realised.

Clearly, project governance exists in organisations above the management of projects. Without effective governance, projects exist only to deliver the outcomes and outputs of a single project; how these projects deliver business benefits and collectively organisation strategies is encoded in the governance of the organisation.

Let's step back from these definitions and present a picture of the potential layers of governance that could exist in an organisation in relation to portfolio, program and project management. Refer to Figure 7.1.

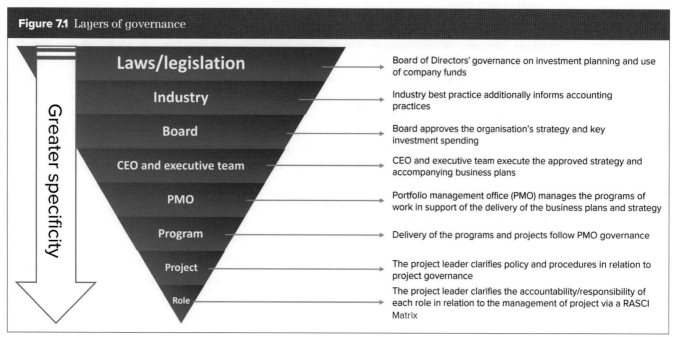

Figure 7.1 Layers of governance

Laws/legislation — Board of Directors' governance on investment planning and use of company funds

Industry — Industry best practice additionally informs accounting practices

Board — Board approves the organisation's strategy and key investment spending

CEO and executive team — CEO and executive team execute the approved strategy and accompanying business plans

PMO — Portfolio management office (PMO) manages the programs of work in support of the delivery of the business plans and strategy

Program — Delivery of the programs and projects follow PMO governance

Project — The project leader clarifies policy and procedures in relation to project governance

Role — The project leader clarifies the accountability/responsibility of each role in relation to the management of project via a RASCI Matrix

Greater specificity

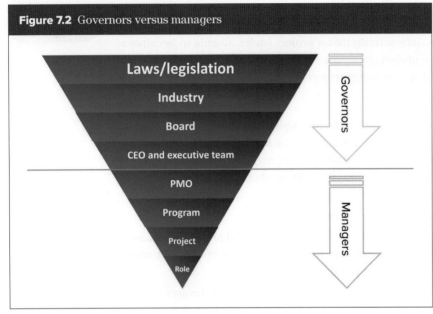

Figure 7.2 Governors versus managers

The left side of Figure 7.1 (the inverted triangle) illustrates the layers of governance, while the right side are examples of how a project is managed and how each level sees their role.

We can apply the phrase "governance is what governors do; and management is what managers do" to our world of project management (Rowlings 2022). Refer to Figure 7.2. Note that the line between the two perspectives simply indicates that the governance and its interpretation increases in specificity, from high-level organisational governance (e.g. on good financial practices) through to specific business rules being enacted by different roles in the project environment.

It has been established that successful organisations have clear, active governance in place, and that the relevant governance is cascaded down throughout the organisation. As project leaders we have to be aware of two specific classes of governance in order to successfully deliver our projects:

1. *Project governance that affects how our project is run:* For example, a gated project management methodology, such as the traditional life cycle approach (Initiation, Planning, Execution, Monitor and Control, and Closure) could be issued by the organisation's PMO, project management policies and guidelines.

2. *Governance that applies to the design and delivery of the product, service or result that the project produces:* For example, if we were on a construction project and had to comply with noise legislation, governance would be internalised with the roles/business rules with the design (Planning) and delivery (Execution) of the project. This has to be identified by the project leader and project team.

The different approaches outlined in Chapter 2 "Popular frameworks and methodologies" encapsulate various amounts of governance within their respective approaches. In some approaches, the governance is presented more as guidelines (such as the *Project Management Body of Knowledge* (PMBOK)); in other approaches the governance is quite directive and forms the backbone of the approach (such as PRINCE2). Our role as project leaders is to make it clear—to any role involved in the project or interfaces with the project—the relevant governance that will guide that role in the activities they undertake. We are in effect **tailoring** the governance arrangements to the project where relevant, or adopting wholeheartedly the governance provided to us.

So, what can happen if appropriate governance does not exist or is inadequate? Effects can include:

■ indecision leading to project issues

■ finger pointing and project failure

■ no committee agreement on, for example, variation requests

■ less effective decisions leading to softer project outcomes

■ inadequate risk management leading to issues and triple constraints impacts

■ outcomes not meeting required quality standards

■ schedule slippage due to weak project decision-making.

This list is only indicative, but does show the need for firm, structured, documented and communicated project governance.

7.1.1 The three pillars and four principles of project governance

Before progressing into specific governance activities, let us first review a common vocabulary around an approach to conceptualising governance and a number of principles that should in general be adopted by practising project leaders.

The **three pillars of project governance** are widely adopted as: structure, people and information.

1. *Structure:* From the initial project selection boards, to the PMO's project performance committees, to the project steering committee and Change Control Board (CCB), these all represent elements of structure around the project.

2. *People:* The roles within the above structure. For example, the chair of the CCB, its role description and accompanying RASCI, and the incumbent in that role being a suitable candidate with, for example, no conflicts of interest.

3. *Information:* The information (based on project data) that informs the people in the structure of various levels of project-related management information. This could vary from risk heat maps (discussed in Chapter 16 "Project risk management") to project status reports and variation requests.

Many governance systems are accompanied by principles, which are usually behavioural traits we wish to see in and guide those who are implementing governance. Principles are especially important at the higher levels of governance, as governance statements can be quite broad, lacking specific details of application we are interested in as a project leader. Good governance is transparent, written down (not in the heads of people), fair and inclusive, and promotes accountability.

We will become more familiar with the role of principles as we progress further into the chapters of this text. For example, the Project Management Institute (PMI) has defined a set of principles as a part of the PMBOK seventh edition (PMI 2021); these are intended to drive behaviours in how the project leader delivers the project.

The **four principles of project governance** are as follows:

■ *Principle 1: Ensure a single point of accountability for the success of the project.* One of the key roles on any project is the *project sponsor* (Refer to the sixth edn. p. 469). They are the accountable business representative for successful delivery of the project. They can make or break the success of a project. *Note:* The project sponsor is also referred to as the *project owner* or *senior responsible owner.*

■ *Principle 2: Ensure project ownership is independent of asset ownership, service ownership or other stakeholder group.* The allocated project sponsor should not have other conflicting or complementary roles in the organisation that could compromise the success of the project. For example, a project that is going to adversely affect the asset management systems and processes in an organisation should not be sponsored by the asset manager. However, the asset manager would be a stakeholder in the project.

■ *Principle 3: Ensure separation of stakeholder management and project decision-making activities.* For example, a project may have a user group who influence project decisions. This user group is not a deciding factor in, for example, a Change Control Board, who are focused on making the correct decisions to keep the project on track to achieve its outputs and outcomes (deliverables). The user group are stakeholders in the project, and the Change Control Board are there to make governance decisions in relation to variations to the project in order to protect the triple constraints: scope, time and cost.

■ *Principle 4: Ensure separation of project governance and organisational governance structures.* For example, the project leader wouldn't make a change request to a senior functional manager who may have known disagreements to the project. The project management framework would stipulate an independent Change Control Board made up of various voting members to review all project variations regardless of source or impact.

By following these principles, the project ensures sound committed leadership, and that any decisions are made by appropriate governance bodies with suitable skills and knowledge, working on behalf of the organisation's interest and not any individual's interest. Some of the tools discussed in the next section, such as the RASCI and various management plans, assist the project leader in documenting the relevant governance, and further to this communicate the governance to the required parties (the project team and stakeholders) as required.

7.1.2 Application of governance to project management

It is the project leader's responsibility to ensure that all the appropriate governance is established during the Initiation (and into the Planning) stage of the project. During project Execution and as a part of Monitor and Control of the project, the project leader ensures that governance is being adhered to, raising any governance issues so they can be rectified as appropriate. During Monitor and Control, project information is also reported to the appropriate stakeholders as defined in the project's Information and Communications Management Plan (e.g. within the project status report). At project Closure, the project leader has a number of governance-related activities to enact, including the closure of the project, final reporting, lessons learned, **Business Case** delivery and benefit (value) realisation.

Governance is captured within a number of mediums. These typically include rules, policies, procedures, norms, relationships, systems and processes, but could extend to laws, legislation and best practice (e.g. the PMBOK itself).

Figure 7.3 summarises some of the governance activities discussed in this chapter as they relate to the management of a project.

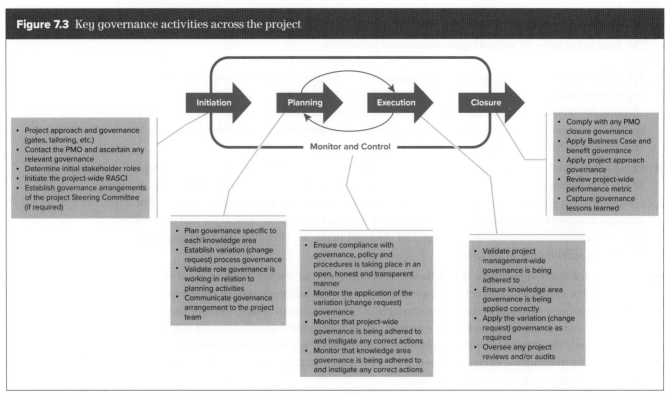

Figure 7.3 Key governance activities across the project

So, how does all this relate to the management of a project at the project leader level? To answer this question, we can review of some of the key activities a project leader engages in during the typical stages of a traditional project life cycle (Table 7.1).

Table 7.1 Indicative governance activities by predictive stage

Stage	Project leader activities
Initiation	■ Establish the project approach, agree how this would be tailored to the project being managed. ■ Contact the organisation's project management office (PMO) (if present in the organisation) and discuss all relevant governance that is required to be brought into the project environment. This includes higher-level governance around benefit (value) management and program and portfolio reporting arrangements. ■ Establish the gates the project has to progress through, the information required at these gate reviews, and the governance surrounding the decisions made at these gates. Refer to Chapter 2 "Popular frameworks and methodologies". ■ Ensure all checks have been made in relation to acceptance of the project's Business Case, as this will form the basis of chartering discussions. ■ Appoint a suitable **project sponsor**—are they on board and a positive influence on the project in the business? ■ Establish governance arrangements for the project **Steering Committee** (if required) (sometimes referred to as a project control board). ■ Identify further project stakeholders and a formal project role allocated where necessary. ■ Create the initial project-wide RASCI to capture governance - created and/or tailored within the project environment. ■ Create the initial Governance Planning Canvas (refer to the next section in this chapter and Figure 7.5). What laws, legislation and legal considerations need to be adhered to from a governance perspective? These should be identified from both an industry/organisational perspective and the also from a project content perspective. The former is more obvious as the project leader is typically a subject matter expert in an industry (e.g. mining, construction, information technology) and would be across any relevant laws, legislation and legal considerations; the latter is related to the content of the project and what it is delivering as a product, service or result and will be more specific to the project. ■ Establish the process for governance escalation and capture in the project-wide Governance Management Plan.

Planning	■ Plan governance specific to each knowledge area: discussed at the knowledge area level in detail within each knowledge area respective chapter.
	■ Establish variation (change) process governance. How does the organisation's variation process work with the profile of the project? Does the project have a greater degree of uncertainty and require a more frequent review of variations in the project?
	■ Ensure the agreed (in the Initiation of the project) governance, policy and procedures are being enacted correctly.
	  • If "Yes"—good outcome, can it be improved?
	  • If "No"—investigate why and correct—if required escalate the breach (transparency).
	■ Continue development of the project-wide RASCI for governance.
	■ Prepare for the upcoming governance stage (or phase) gate review.
	■ Communicate governance arrangement to the project team.
	■ Establish performance criteria that will inform, for example, governance committees (e.g. the Steering Committee cannot make a decision on whether to approve a variation without accurate information on the project's schedule, budget and contingency funds).

Execution	■ During project Execution ensure that all governance is being applied in a consistent manner. This could be at a macro level (e.g. the correct application of the agreed tailored project management approach) or a micro level (e.g. the agreed Schedule Management Plan and the manner in which work package status progress is calculated and reported). ■ Prepare for the upcoming governance stage (or phase) gate review. ■ Validate project-wide governance is being adhered to. ■ Apply the variation (change request) governance as required. ■ Oversee any project reviews and/or audits. The PMO may have in place governance around quarterly project reviews and random knowledge area auditing (e.g. in the area of procurement or risk).
Monitor and Control	■ Ensure compliance with governance, policy and procedures is taking place in an open, honest and transparent manner (ethical and principles-bases project management). ■ Monitor the application of the variation (change request) governance. ■ Monitor the project-wide governance is being adhered to and instigate any corrective actions. ■ Monitor knowledge area governance is being adhered to and instigate any corrective actions.
Closure	■ Ensure the benefits have been delivered and accounted for in accordance with the benefits (value) management governance. ■ Ensure the wider Business Case has been delivered as stated. ■ Ensure the scope of the project has been delivered as agreed. ■ Extract lessons learned from the project for the management of future projects. This could be in relation to the project management framework and governance, or more specific to each knowledge area (e.g. lessons learned in relation to the procurement governance, policy and procedures). ■ Prepare final project reporting to satisfy the project management framework governance requirements. This would include the final project closure report and the post-implementation review (discussed in Chapter 21 "Project closure"). ■ Complete any PMO governance for project closure. ■ Ensure the project has completed its project closure checklist (discussed in Chapter 21 "Project closure"). ■ Prepare for the final governance stage (or phase) gate review.

A simple governance framework is illustrated in Figure 7.4. The next four sections of this chapter take each activity in the process and provide techniques, tools and discussion from a project leader's perspective.

Figure 7.4 A generic project governance framework

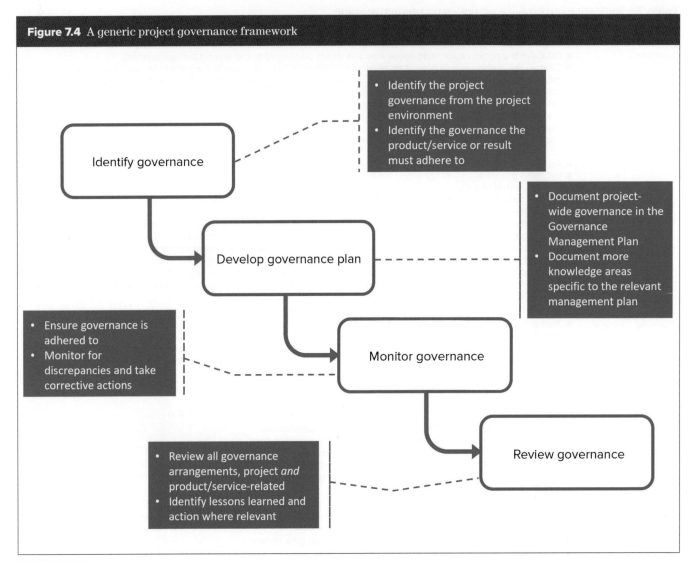

 ## 7.2 | Identify governance

The starting point for identifying governance should be to recognise the two primary groupings of governance a project leader considers.

1. *Governance that directly relates to the management of the project,* whether this is sourced from governments, industry, the organisation or sub-functions within the organisation in relation to the management of portfolios, programs and projects.

2. The more difficult one is *governance that relates to the product, service or result* being produced by the project. For example, if the project is to design, prototype and establish manufacturing for a new kind of airbag system, the product will have to comply with the governance, laws and legislation of each country the product will be deployed to. We therefore need to consider these in our research and development of the design to ensure the product is built to comply.

To this aim, the author (Pearson) has designed the Governance Planning Canvas to assist the project leader workshopping all the relevant tiers of governance in the project environment and in support of delivery of the product, service or result produced from the project (Figure 7.5).

Figure 7.5 The Governance Planning Canvas

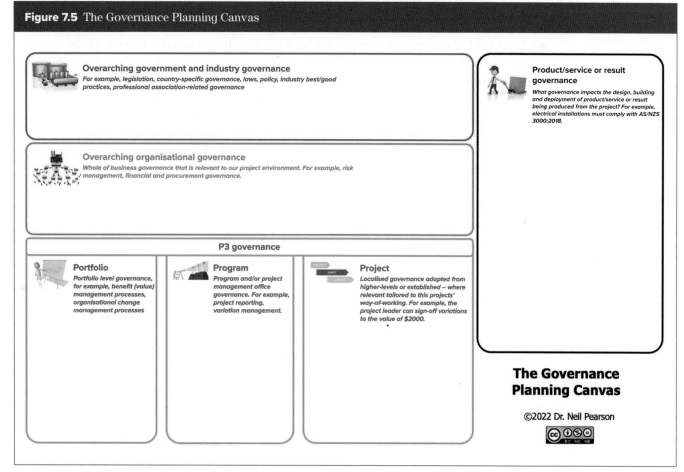

© 2022 Dr Neil Pearson

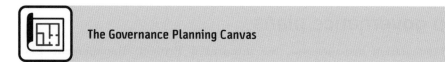

The Governance Planning Canvas

7.2.1.1 Governance that directly relates to the management of the project

The blue, orange and green on Figure 7.5 is the focus of this chapter; however, don't forget to cover off the second part of the canvas (black), which relates to any governance that the end-product, service or result must comply with as this too will result in tasks to be built into the project design! The segments to be considered here are:

- *Blue:* Overarching government and industry governance—this considers the highest level of governance from a value system perspective. Is the investment strategically aligned? Does it represent good use of company funds? Aa a director of the airbag company and a member of the Australian Institute of Company Directors I would have to be basing such decisions on researched facts, presented and approved at various committees—this is governance.

- *Orange:* Overarching organisational governance—This could be based in many of the company's disciplines, such as risk management, human resources, contract and procurement. As a project leader, an assessment of the project and all the organisational level governance would be made; for example, if the airbag project were to rely heavily on procurement of contracted-out components, it would be pertinent to ensure that the governance around contracting and procurement was agreed and, if necessary, tailored to the project context.

- *Green:* Portfolio, program and project (P3) governance first identifies any applicable governance and then questions whether that governance needs to be tailored.

  - *Portfolio:* For example, as a project leader, what benefit management process exists, how does this affect on-boarding benefit owners (stakeholders) to the project, how are benefits reported and when?

  - *Program:* For example, as project leader, am I obligated under the program reporting governance to collect and subsequently report on project performance metrics (e.g. cost, time, quality, customer happiness) in a particular format? What is this governance? How does it impact my project in terms of project data I now need to collect? How does it get reported (red, amber, green), to which committee, at what time in the month?

  - *Project:* For example, the project leader can sign off variations to the value of $2,000, or as a project leader, do I need to tailor to this project's environment the frequency of the Change Control Board, which approves/disapproves project variations to a more frequent tempo?

7.2.1.2 Governance around the product, service or result being produced

The right section (black) of Figure 7.5 provides the opportunity to identify specific governance that the product/service or result being produced from the project must comply with. An *idea shower workshop* with key subject matter experts (SMEs) is a way to identify governance that may affect how the product or service is made and deployed. In the airbag example, is there governance about manufacturers' accountabilities and responsibilities globally. (For example, in relation to a global product recall, who does what? In the case of a global product update, who is responsible for fixing and who pays?). Capture this governance and review the impact on the design of the product or service (within the product breakdown structure) and in the work to be done by the project (the work breakdown structure) as well as how this is to be allocated to individuals in the organisation (accountabilities and responsibilities).

7.3 | Develop governance plans

In Chapter 6 "Project integration management", the **integrated Project Management Plan** (integrated PMP) was introduced (refer to Figure 7.6). The documents on the left of the figure capture the various levels of governance from a project perspective. Any governance that pertains to overarching project governance—including government and industry governance, organisational governance or P3 governance—would generally be documented in the project's overarching Governance Management Plan and supporting artefacts (such as the project-wide RASCI). However, governance that pertains to a specific knowledge area (that is generally more detailed and topic specific) tends to be captured in the individual Knowledge Area Management Plan.

The artefacts on the right side capture governance as it pertains to the design and development of the product/service or result being produced by the project. This could include work packages to ensure compliance with laws and legislation, specifications or standards that are being built into the project's deliverables. Deliverables themselves could have sign-off criteria that reflect compliance to various governance that the project's deliverables have to operate within when handed over to the operational business.

Figure 7.6 The integrated Project Management Plan

More process-/governance-based	More project content-based
Scope Management Plan	Scope document, project approach (design), work breakdown structure (WBS), product breakdown structure (PBS), requirements traceability matrix
Schedule Management Plan	Timelines, milestone charts, project schedule, time estimating information
Cost Management Plan	Project budget, cost estimating information, quotes (RFQ)
Quality Management Plan	Quality plans, continuous improvement trackers, quality control activities (identified and built into WBS), quality reports
Resource Management Plan	Resource assignment matrix (RAM), skills matrix, team charter, role descriptions, agreements and contracts, RASCIs
Communications Management Plan	Communications register, template communications (including project status reports), meeting agendas and actions, knowledge repositories
Risk Management Plan	Risk and issues register, risk reporting (heat map)
Procurement Management Plan	Tenders, contracts, supplier selection grids, performance/payment schedules
Stakeholder Management Plan	Stakeholder register, agreements, role descriptions, RASCIs

Governance Management Plan

Organisational Change Management Plan (OCMP)

Configuration Management Plan

Requirements Management Plan

© 2022 Dr Neil Pearson

7.3.1.1 Example

The airbag project you are working on has been party funded by a government grant. With the grant comes a number of accountabilities and responsibilities for various business rules and decisions. As project leader, you decide the best place to capture this governance would be in the project's Governance Management Plan.

- *Governance Management Plan:*
  - A Steering Committee is to be established for the airbag project. The Governance Management Plan includes a note about the committee and its purpose and refers the reader to the Steering Committee Charter. The Steering Committee Charter outlines all the governance related to that committee, including its membership, the quorum and the decision-making scope.
  - Inclusions for how the business and project interact in the definition, management and realisation of benefits (value), as captured in the Business Case, charter and project scope documents from a project perspective.
  - This includes the selection of the project management approach—predictive, incremental, adaptive or hybrid—and the framework being applied in this project. Typically this would come from the PMO; if not present in your organisation, the advice would be to document this in your project-wide Governance Management Plan
- *Risk Management Plan:* The project is adopting the PMO's risk management guidelines; however, the guidelines do not accommodate the escalation of risk from the project to the parent program. You put in place the PMBOK *escalate* mitigation strategy for risk treatment and capture this within the Risk Management Plan, as this is knowledge area governance.
- *Schedule Management Plan:* The project has adopted the PMO's governance on the choice of scheduling tool (in this case Microsoft Project). This is captured in the Schedule Management Plan. Additionally, as the project leader, you define how time is to be reported at project status meetings for the work packages using the *interval rule:* rounding down to the nearest 25 per cent band (i.e. 25%, 50%, 75% or 100% complete). Again, this is knowledge area specific—agreed, documented and communicated to the project team.
- *Communications Management Plan:* This covers industry legislation for the storing and security of information, and how freedom of information requests would be met within the target set by the legislation covering the jurisdiction in which the project takes place. As the project is partly funded by a government grant, what are the implications for the project in terms of access to internal information, including how funds are allocated and spent?

Templates to support the detail behind this example are included in the additional resources.

 Governance Management Plan

 Steering Committee Charter

Some links and further examples of the types of governance a project may be subject to have been included in Table 7.2.

Table 7.2 Further examples of governance

Category	Title	Link
Government and Industry	Corporate Governance Principles and Recommendations (ASX)	www.asx.com.au/documents/asx-compliance/cgc-principles-and-recommendations-3rd-edn.pdf
	AS/NZS ISO 14001:2016 Environmental Management Systems - Requirements with Guidance for Use	https://infostore.saiglobal.com/en-au/standards/as-nzs-iso-14001-2016-100725_saig_as_as_211642/
	Freedom of Information Act 1982	https://www.oaic.gov.au/freedom-of-information/foi-act
	AS/NZS 4801 Occupational Health and Safety Management Systems	https://www.saiglobal.com/Assurance/ohs/ASNZS_4801_OHS_Standard.htm
	AS/NZS ISO 9001:2016 Quality Management Systems - Requirements	https://infostore.saiglobal.com/en-au/Standards/AS-NZS-ISO-9001-2016-1845270/
	The Company Directors Corporate Governance Framework	www.companydirectors.com.au/Director-Resource-Centre/Corporate-Governance-Framework
	AS ISO 21504:2016 Project, Programme and Portfolio Management - Guidance on Portfolio Management	https://infostore.saiglobal.com/en-au/Standards/AS-ISO-21504-2016-1865515/ https://infostore.saiglobal.com/en-au/standards/iso-21500-2021-600570_saig_iso_iso_2934707/
	ANSI/PMI 99-001-2017 The Standard for Project Management	https://www.pmi.org/pmbok-guide-standards/foundational/pmbok/sixth-edition https://www.pmi.org/pmbok-guide-standards/foundational/pmbok
P3	AS/NZS ISO 31000:2009 Risk Management - Principles and Guidelines	https://infostore.saiglobal.com/en-au/standards/as-iso-31000-2018-1134720_saig_as_as_2680492/
	High-level governance	https://www.qut.edu.au/about/governance-and-policy
	Policies supporting governance	www.mopp.qut.edu.au
Organisational governance	Procedures	Details processes and work instructions that support the delivery of process in an organisation

© 2022 Dr Neil Pearson

7.3.1 The RASCI Matrix

The tool of choice for many project leaders to capture governance and business rules and decisions is a project-wide RASCI Matrix. The RASCI Matrix allows the mapping of rules and decisions (governance) to roles.

A snippet of a RASCI Matrix has been included in Table 7.3. The RASCI Matrix gives the project leader an opportunity to bring all the governance rules relating to project roles together. The RASCI Matrix captures the business rules and/or the decisions, mapped against the roles in an easily accessible matrix format.

Table 7.3 The RASCI Matrix

Business rule/decision	Category	Role			
		Project leader	Project team	Project sponsor	Steering Committee
Approval of purchase orders >$50K	Procurement	A	R	I	
Approval to move from one stage (gate review) to the next	Governance	R	S	R	A
Approval of variation requests ≤ .5 day and ≤$500 non-contiguous	Variation process	AR	R	I	I
Approval of variation requests > .5 day and >$500	Variation process	R	R	I	A

© 2022 Dr Neil Pearson

The letters in the intersection of a RASCI Matrix indicate:

- ***Responsible:*** Who is primarily responsible for making sure the rule or decision is enacted? There can be multiple people involved in taking responsibility. The *R* represents the role that is actually doing the work!

- *Accountable:* The person who has sole accountability for ensuring the decision/rule is enacted. There should only be one person or group in this role. The *A* represents with whom the buck stops—a single point of accountability!

- *Supports:* The people who are to support the accountable/responsible person. They could, for example, be carrying out part of the work, providing information or administrative services.

- *Consulted:* Here you are seeking to identify the people who must be consulted (e.g. the business user or customer).

- *Informed:* This refers to the people who must be informed of the decision (or rule) outcome. Again, these could be persons who are external to the project, the project team, or other formal roles identified by the project.

These steps will assist in building a RASCI Matrix:

- *Step 1:* Define all roles within the project (e.g. project leader, project team, project sponsor, Change (variation) Control Board, procurement manager, communications manager, change leader, SMEs) and enter these roles across the horizontal.

- *Step 2:* Capture the business rule/decisions down the vertical. There could be dozens to hundreds of these on a typical medium-sized project!

- *Step 3:* Categorise the rule (this makes for easier filtering of the rules later on).

- *Step 4:* Allocate the RASCI letters across the roles as appropriate.

- *Step 5:* Validate the allocated RASCI letter against the role, with the roles involved.

Remember, there can only ever be one *A* or accountable person/group per rule/decision. Roles can have multiple allocations, for example, a role can be both accountable and responsible (*AR*).

The RASCI can provide a useful tool to help ameliorate team conflict where there is dispute over who does what, or who makes which decisions in the project. The project leader could use a spreadsheet to build the RASCI Matrix, as illustrated in Table 7.4.

RASCI Matrix

The roles associated with the RASCI Matrix are usually defined to varying levels of detail, starting with a general description of the role, through to more detailed role descriptions documenting the outlines for each role (reporting relationships, decisions responsible for, and key duties).

Project Roles

All business rules should be categorised (and even sub-categorised) in the RASCI so that sets of rules can be reviewed together—for example, the project leader and project team can review all rules related to the category of *procurement* together and question: Are they complete? Are there business rules missing? Are they overlapping or duplicated? Categorising business rules (or decisions) enables the project leader and project team to see gaps that might cause issues in the project once the project moves into the Planning and Execution stages, and to address them early.

Note: The RASCI Matrix can be used for many purposes in a project environment, governance, business rules to support processes such as the variation process, or in the allocation of work packages and tasks to roles.

Table 7.4 Snippet of a project-wide governance RASCI

Project-wide Governance RASCI

Reference	Governance Category	Sub-category	Business Rule	Project Management Office	Project Steering Committee	Project Sponsor	Project Manager	Project Team Member	Change Manager	Project Scheduler	Contracts Administrator
BR-003	Project	Schedule Management	Create project schedule in Microsoft Project				AR			R	
BR-005	Program	Schedule Management	Manage & maintain links to dependencies between all Milestones, (including program tracking, program outcomes & strategic) investments)	A			C				
BR-006	Project	Schedule Management	Linking project milestones to program outcomes and strategic milestones	AR			R				
BR-008	Project	Governance	Acceptance of approved scope, change requests, project closure documentation		A	R	R		I	C	I
BR-010	Business	Business Case	Creates the Business Case for proposed investments	C		AR					
BR-013	Project	Information Management	Update investment details in Microsoft Project Server (including budgets, resourcing, parameters etc.)	AR		C					
BR-017	Project	Financial Management	Create the project financial structure in the organisations financial accounting system	AR			R				
BR-018	Project	Schedule Management	Create and update project work packages in the organisations project management information system	R			AR			R	R
BR-019	Program	Risk & Issue Management	Review escalated project risks and issues status, and manage unacceptable expectations	AR	C	R	R				
BR-023	Project	Information Management	Provide project progress against baseline project management plan		A		AR			R	
BR-024	Project	Stakeholder Management	Champion of the project. Support the project manager in the active marketing of the project to all relevant stakeholders		R	AR	R	R			
BR-025	Program	Business Case	Ensure the vision and business case for the project is clearly articulated to all stakeholders and aligns with the strategic direction of the organisation	AR		R	R				
BR-026	Project	Stakeholder Management	Ensure the project's deliverables appropriately reflect the interests of key stakeholders		R	AR	R				
BR-027	Project	Stakeholder Management	Negotiate membership of the project steering committee ensuring that its composition adequately reflects the interests of all stakeholders	AR		R	R				
BR-028	Project	Stakeholder Management	Endorse the selection of a project manager with skills and experience commensurate with the project's profile, cost, complexity and risk	R		AR					
BR-029	Business	Business Case	Provide strategic advice and direction to the project manager and team in planning, implementing and finalising the project		I	AR	I				
BR-031	Project	Integration Management	Ensure that the detailed project management plan (PMP) are complete before commencement of the project		I	AR	R	R	R	R	R
BR-034	Project	Business Case	Ensure that barriers to the successful completion of the project and realisation of business benefits that are outside the control of the project manager are addressed or escalated as appropriate		A	R	R				
BR-037	Project	Stakeholder Management	Provide recognition to the project manager and project team for project progress and achievement		A	R	I	I			
BR-039	Project	Information Management	Review of the project status report	I	A	R	R	C	C	C	C
BR-040	Project	Organisational Change Management	Development of the organisational change management transition plan		I	I	R		AR		
BR-045	Business	Governance	Make and interpret policy decisions and business decision for the project within the organisations governance framework		I	AR	R				
BR-047	Project	Risk & Issue Management	Ensure escalated issues are resolved promptly		A	R	R				
BR-049	Project	Scope Management	Review and endorse (NOT approve) project change requests and assess associated project or roll-on business impacts		AR	R	R				
BR-050	Business	Organisational Change Management	Support the hand-over process to ensure that the outcomes of the project are sustainable			AR	R		R		
BR-051	Project	Stakeholder Management	Provide leadership to the project				AR				
BR-053	Project	Governance	Enforces project management standards down into the project	AR			R				
BR-054	Project	Governance	Assists project manager in negotiating governance gates and policy	A		R	R				
BR-060	Project	Information Management	Provide timely information to enable informed decision making by the project sponsor			C	AR				

SNAPSHOT *from* PRACTICE : A populated RASCI template improves PMO governance outcomes

A project management office (PMO) wanted to improve the consistency in the application of governance across all projects under its control. Due to this organisation being a government-owned corporation, governance arrangements were often complex and involved input from multiple roles. To compound this complexity often projects were managed by contract project leaders who had limited knowledge of the mechanisms and processes of their employing organisation.

(Continues)

Snapshot from Practice: A populated RASCI template improves PMO governance outcomes (*Continued*)

The PMO was exposed to multiple (albeit non-intentional) governance breaches. When investigated, the PMO ascertained that for new project leaders and contract project leaders there was no single go-to document that outlined all the roles and the project management-related business rules and decisions. Each project leader was making a brave attempt to navigate the many policies and procedures across all the required departments—procurement, finance, HR, asset management, information technology, to name but a few. The outcomes of each individual project leader in doing this included mixed outcomes in interpreting the policy and procedures that existed in the organisation, missed governance, and issues being raised from the project leader because the desired outcomes were not being achieved.

After consulting the project leaders, the PMO committed to creating a master pre-populated RASCI template. The RASCI included in excess of 30 different roles from all areas of the business, over 1500 business rules categorised into 20 different categories. The RASCI became a part of the project management framework; further to this, it was a mandatory requirement that project leaders either follow the governance captured in the RASCI, or propose to the PMO adjustments for consideration in the context of their project environment (an example of tailoring). The success of the populated RASCI template resulted in fewer project governance issues, and streamlined who carried out what business rule or decision.

Further developments to the pre-populated RASCI included role descriptions for each of the 30-plus different roles. Where roles were recruited positions in the project organisational structure, pre-written HR-assessed job descriptions were provided. This created an environment of synergy across all projects in relation to job descriptions, role descriptions and the responsibilities and accountabilities (RASCI) of each role.

A by-product of this integrated RASCI was the identification of governance, overlaps, conflicts, gaps and omissions. The RASCI tool was used to facilitate discussions and clarify the overlaps, conflicts, gaps and omissions in governance so individual projects would not have to waste time in doing so.

7.3.2 Further techniques for capturing governance

Some governance may be diagrammatically illustrated as well as being supported by a RASCI. For example, refer to Figure 7.7, which illustrates the governance bodies and how they relate to each other and the project. This would be supported by a detailed RASCI outlining all the business rules and decisions, and which role is *responsible, accountable, supports, consulted* and *informed*. Remember, a role in a RASCI Matrix can also take on a committee (e.g. project Steering Committee), board (e.g. project **Change Control Board**) or group (e.g. end-user group).

Just as an individual role in a RASCI Matrix would have a role description and potentially job description, a committee, board or end-user group would have a charter that includes information such as:

■ purpose and objectives

■ meeting frequency

■ meeting structure and membership

■ relationships to other entities

■ objectives/activities

■ key decisions the entity is accountable for

■ the quorum (members) required to make these decisions.

 Change Control Board Charter

It is to committees such as the Steering Committee that governance would be reported—at the outset of the project with the initial (or baseline) integrated PMP and subsequently in project progress reports. Other techniques for capturing and documenting governance include:

■ *Flow charts:* Using simple flow chart symbols to indicate activities and decisions. An example is provided in Chapter 15 "Project information and communications management", for a communications preparation and approval process

Figure 7.7 The project with its relationship to other committees

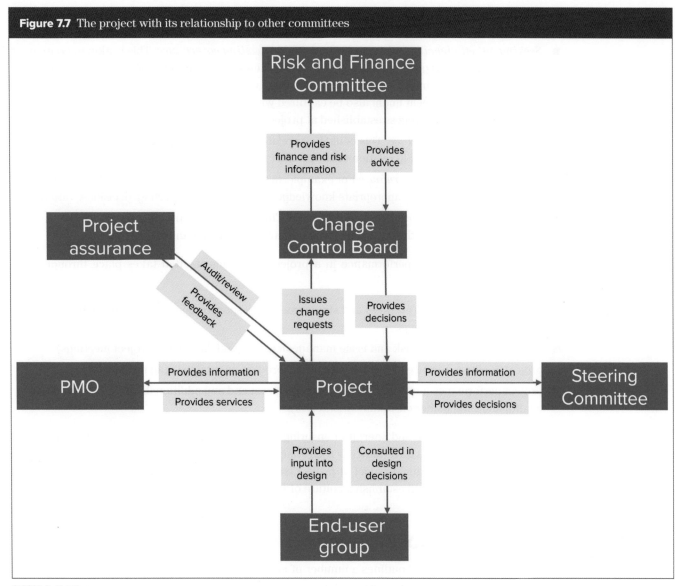

© 2022 Dr Neil Pearson

- *Swimlane diagrams:* Using a business process modelling notation. An example is provided in Chapter 8 "Defining the scope of a project", for the variation (change request) management process
- *Embedding governance into information technology systems:* Examples are financial delegations in a finance package, HR approvals in the HR system, or workflows in the project management information system
- *Written governance documents, policies or procedures* (as discussed throughout this chapter): Examples are the *project management framework document,* a popular PMO governance document to capture the approach, roles, governance and processes related to the management of projects.

7.4 Monitor governance

Once governance has been established, documented and approved into the project environment the project leader is then responsible for ensuring the following.

- *Any existing governance is applied in a consistent, ethical and transparent manner:* This could mean pushing the outcomes of applying governance upwards to the project sponsor, Steering

Committee and/or PMO. It could also mean, in some instances, enforcing governance to members of the project team and external contractors.

■ *Seeking out efficiencies and improvements to the existing governance:* This is akin to continuous improvement across governance processes and systems. Techniques like PDCA and DMAIC for managing continues improvements are discussed in Chapter 13 "Project quality management". Continuous improvement might also be captured within the project's lessons learned process (another governance process established at project outset).

■ *Identifying new governance:* This could be in relation to the management of the project or might result as a piece of work in relation to the product or service being produced by the project.

■ *The result of applying governance:* For example, in tracking project progress/schedule, budget or quality is fed back into the appropriate knowledge area for action (reporting, decisions, variations).

■ *Capturing lessons learned around governance:* This also involves practising continuous improvement to ensure the governance systems are kept current and effective.

Monitoring of governance performance in a project environment often takes place through these activities:

■ project meetings, team (progress and status) meetings, sponsor update meetings, external contractor status meetings

■ Steering Committee for risk and issue management (beyond day-to-day project meetings)

■ project quality assurance of the project and the product or service being produced

■ project performance metrics, around scope, time, cost and any additionally defined metrics (e.g. quality and stakeholder/customer satisfaction).

Project leaders invest time and energy in ensuring governance of the project kicks off in a defined direction; making sure this governance is then enacted becomes the subsequent focus, so monitoring project governance is a critical aspect of project leadership. Being consistent, open, transparent and ethical in your approach will establish a culture of firmness and trust within the project environment.

7.5 : **Review governance**

Chapter 21 "Project closure" outlines a number of activities that the project leader undertakes at the Closure stage of the project or project phase.

Learnings in relation to governance will be incorporated into lessons learned throughout the project approach, in the project closure activities and in the post-implementation review. As with any lesson learned, the key is to ensure accountable owners are allocated to any improvement actions and that a check-back is carried out to ensure those actions have been acted on.

■ Is there any project governance (e.g. the project management framework, the variation management process, the committees and boards established, the templates, the process and information technology systems) that are advised to be improved for future projects?

■ Is there governance in the wider organisation (e.g. procurement, financial delegations, strategic, HR, legal and contract management) that is advised as requiring improvement for future projects?

Governance is an integral element of a project leader's role in establishing a project, planning a project, ensuring the project is executed under the governance and business rules and in closing out a project. Governance lines of communication and information flow should be clear to all those in the project team, and beyond in any board, committee or user group. It is the project leader's accountability to ensure that they use suitable tools and techniques to communicate governance; these would include combinations of a Governance Management Plan, RASCI Matrix, role descriptions and job descriptions, committee charters, and of course each individual Knowledge Area Management Plan.

7.6 : The project (program) management office

PMOs were originally developed as a response to the poor track record many companies had in completing projects on time, within budget and according to plan. Today, PMOs come in many different shapes and forms. One interesting way of classifying PMOs was set forth by Casey and Peck (2001), who describe certain PMOs in terms of being: (1) a weather station, (2) a control tower or (3) a resource pool. Each of these models performs a very different function for its organisation.

- *A weather station:* The primary function of the weather station PMO is to track and monitor project performance. It is typically created to satisfy top management's need to stay on top of the portfolio of programs and projects underway in the organisation. Staff provide an independent forecast of project performance. The questions answered for specific projects include: How are our projects progressing? Which ones are on track? Which ones are not? How are we doing in terms of cost? Which projects are over or under budget? What are the major problems confronting projects? Are contingency plans in place? What can the organisation do to help the project?

- *A control tower:* The primary function of the control tower PMO is to improve project execution. It considers project management as a profession to be protected and advanced. The PMO identifies best practices and standards for project management excellence. They work as consultants and trainers to support project leaders and their teams.

- *A resource pool:* The goal of the resource pool PMO is to provide the organisation with a cadre of trained project leaders and professionals. It operates like an academy for continually upgrading the skills of the organisation's project professionals. In addition to training, this kind of PMO also serves to elevate the stature of project management within the organisation.

The project leader should be aware of the PMO arrangement within which they are operating, as it will undoubtably impact the roles and governance that will need to be embedded at the project level as opposed to the governance that exists at higher levels.

So far, we have touched on how PMOs are considered to be part of a project's organisational structure. This section defines the different types of PMOs and also takes a look at some of their respective functions. To help unpack some of the types of PMOs that could occur at different levels of a project organisation's structure, refer to Figure 7.8.

At the most strategic point in the organisation there could be (what we have termed here) the *Office of Strategy Management:* this is where strategy is designed (architected), developed, planned, aligned, reviewed, communicated, cascaded and adapted. The PMO reports into the Office of Strategy Management and provides status updates on how the portfolios are delivering on the organisation's strategy.

1. Level 1, portfolio management office (Portfolio-MO); besides reporting progress towards the strategic objectives (as outlined previously), the Portfolio-MO (among its many functions) designs, develops, plans and reviews the portfolios of strategic and operational work and ensures aggregated information is available to the senior management teams.

2. Level 2, the program management office (Program-MO) may be established to manage a single program of work (such as an accident and emergency ward refit) or may be established to support multiple programs of work. Either way, its primary concerns are providing direct support and program(s) reporting.

3. Level 3, the project management office (Project-MO) is usually established on the same principle as the Program-MO, but is focused specifically on the project delivery level of an organisation. It is usually found supporting larger, more complex projects.

Some common themes can be found across all the levels (1, 2, or 3) and a management office may focus on one or more of the levels. The PMI terms these *supportive, controlling and directing.* A particular management office (e.g. a Program-MO or Project-MO) might provide the features of all

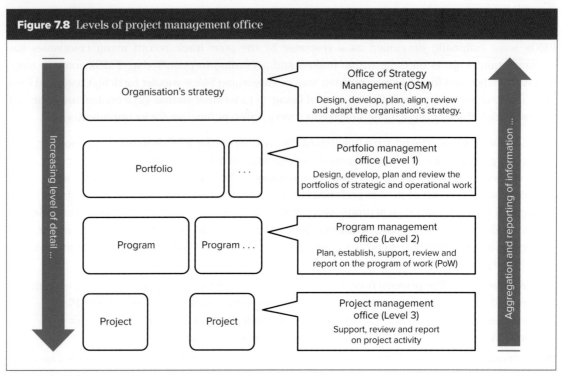

Figure 7.8 Levels of project management office

© 2022 Dr Neil Pearson

three or might focus on the controlling theme. From initial discussions, the project leader should be able to quickly identify whether the PMO is supportive, controlling or directive.

■ Supportive PMOs guide the projects within their remit, often providing project management guidelines, templates and training to support a consistent delivery of projects. They will often offer registers of lessons learned for project leaders to review and inform current projects so that negative lessons are not repeated and positive lessons are leveraged. Their role is guiding and they often do not have high levels of control.

■ Controlling PMOs introduce gate reviews with must-do activities that projects must satisfy in order to progress through the life cycle (e.g. project leaders must ensure that the Business Case remains valid and is updated with current findings to ensure the project will deliver the intended benefits (financial or other) that were originally stated). Controlling PMOs may also introduce a standard variation management process and Change Control Board to approve (or reject) variations to the project before the project leader can commit them into the project.

■ Directive PMOs take controlling a step further by taking a vested interest in the progress of the project throughout its entire life cycle. Project leaders are assigned to the project by the PMO and report directly to the PMO.

The upshot of this is that when you (as a project leader) ask whether a PMO exists, you can be more specific, as this will influence how you leverage the PMO in the project's organisational structure and ascertain what level of governance and control will be applied—it will therefore help you to manage expectations.

A PMO can, and does, mean different things to different organisations, depending on the purpose of the PMO. Table 7.5 shows supportive, controlling and directive features against portfolio, program and project.

Table 7.5 Portfolio, program and project: Supportive, controlling and directive features

Management office theme	Portfolio	Program	Project
Supportive	Forecasting supply and demand (e.g. of resources) at the portfolio level. Maintaining and promoting the shared use of a portfolio-level Lessons Learned Register.	Program management information systems and repositories. Program management information and knowledge management, and the transfer of information between programs. Program management education and training in the governance and procedures to be adopted. Maintaining and promoting the shared use of a program-level Lessons Learned Register. Providing pooled organisational change management resources to the program. Coaching, mentoring, training and oversight.	Leading information and knowledge transfer between projects in the program for tacit and explicit knowledge and information. Coaching, mentoring, training and oversight. Coordinating communication across projects as required. Maintaining and promoting the shared use of a cross-project Lessons Learned Register. Providing pooled organisational change management resources to projects being administered by the PMO. Establishing project leader communities of practice or other sharing mediums across projects
Controlling	Forecasting supply and demand for a portfolio that can be further broken down into supply and demand for projects and programs. Aggregating and providing performance results of the portfolio, most likely reporting to the Office of Strategy Management or executive management team. Identifying and analysing risks, and planning risk responses at a portfolio level.	Providing aggregated reporting across the program to the program managers and the portfolio management office. Identifying and analysing risks, and planning risk responses at a program level. Program management audits (including advisory health checks). Terminating projects and, ultimately, the program. Managing shared resource pools across the program. Maintaining a records library of all program and project artefacts (project archive). Maintaining a master program schedule, tracking dependencies between projects in/across the program down to an individual task level.	Terminating projects. Providing aggregated reporting across all projects administered by the PMO to the project leaders and also to the PMO. Identifying and analysing risks, and planning risk responses across all projects administered by the PMO. Managing shared resource pools across all projects administered by the PMO. Monitoring compliance with project management standards, policies, procedures and templates by means of project audits (often referred to as *project health checks*). Maintaining a records library of all project artefacts to ensure reinvention of the proverbial wheel does not waste resources on future projects.
Directive	Establishing the portfolio management methodology, best practices and standards for use as guidelines, while formulating the methodology and standards for project and program management. Defining a portfolio management strategy. Providing portfolio oversight and managing the overall portfolio value to ensure the delivery of the organisation's strategy and/or business plans.	Identifying and developing program management methodology, best practices and standards. Developing and managing program policies, procedures, templates and other shared artefacts. Establishing required committees, including the Steering Committee and Change Control Board.	Identifying and developing the project management methodology, best practices and standards. Developing and managing project policies, procedures, templates and other shared documentation. Defining roles and responsibilities, defining a project-level RASCI. Establishing required committees, including the Steering Committee and Change Control Board.

Source: Adapted and extended from the Project Management Institute (PMI) 2013, *The Standard for Portfolio Management,* third edition, p. 18; PMI 2013, *The Standard for Program Management,* third edition, p. 64; PMI 2017, *A Guide to the Project Management Body of Knowledge,* p. 49

Referring to Table 7.5, the project leader should be able to identify:

- which of the level(s) of management office exists (portfolio, program and/or project)
- the predominant, or mix, of themes the management office uses in its approach. If, for example, the PMO is geared towards the supportive theme, does the project leader have more flexibility

in the project management approach they can select and its tailoring towards the project environment?

■   the key features offered by the management office, and the degree of optionality or compliance the project leader has.

Note on terminology: The reader may also see the terms *PM3* (portfolio management, program management, project management), *P3M* (portfolio, program and project management) or *P3O* (portfolio, program, project offices) used.

Summary

Figure 7.9 summarises the different contexts of governance outlined in this chapter. Typically, a project's governance will be a subset of all these areas of governance. Identifying what governance is relevant to the project is the purpose of the Governance Planning Canvas introduced in this chapter. Once governance has been identified, it is formalised within the project environment and captured in key project artefacts, for example, the Governance Management Plan, the project-wide RASCI Matrix or knowledge area management plans. Governance is then communicated to all those who have a role in the governance proceedings. During project Execution, governance is applied and monitored to ensure compliance; we learn from our actions and course-correct as necessary. At the end of the project all governance is reviewed and lessons are sought for future projects and to improve the PMO and wider business activities (such as procurement, human resources or procurement departments).

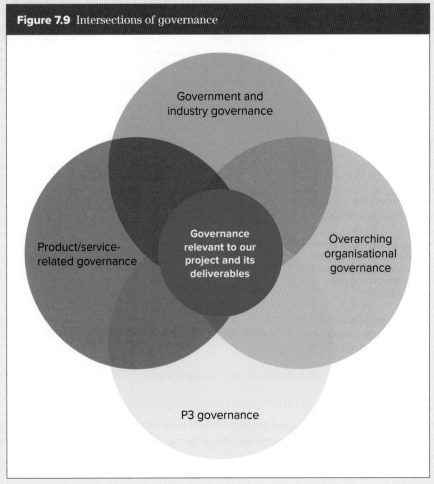

Figure 7.9 Intersections of governance

Government and industry governance

Product/service-related governance

Governance relevant to our project and its deliverables

Overarching organisational governance

P3 governance

Review questions

1. Would the CEO and executive team be classified as governors or managers?
2. Describe the three pillars of project governance.
3. Describe the four principles of project governance.
4. If taking a holistic approach to project governance, what two key documents (tools) would the governance be captured within?
5. If taking a knowledge area approach, which documents would be key in capturing governance?
6. What are the typical layers of governance a project leader should be aware of?
7. Which of the four principles would support the following statement: *A project leader reviews the membership of the existing Change Control Board and notices that two of the projects key stakeholders who hold high power and high influence are a part of this Change Control Board. The project leader makes a recommendation to the project sponsor that membership of this board should be revised.*
8. The Change Control Board has the final decision on whether a change is accepted into the project or rejected. This would be covered by which pillar described in this chapter?
9. The project leader is accountable and responsible for ensuring change requests are submitted to the Change Control Board within five working days (where possible). How would this business rule be represented in the project-wide RASCI?

Exercises

1. As a project leader for a project in your workplace, and encompassing knowledge gained from this chapter, review Table 7.6 and identify any new or changed governance items you will now be considering in your project.

Table 7.6 Governance identification

Area	An example to direct your thinking	Your items*
Project management approach	The organisation's project management framework will be adopted with the following modifications: • An interactive presentation of gate reports will be made to enable a quicker Q&A cycle at the go/no-go gate, with decisions taken in real-time where possible. • The change request process cycle time will be modified from 10 business days to within five business days.	
PMO	Project status reporting must be provided in accordance with the PMO project reporting guidelines.	
Scope management	In the event of a new baseline scope document being approved, it is the accountability of the project leader to ensure the entire project team is briefed on the changes. The project administrator is responsible for ensuring the new scope baseline is appropriately updated in the project management information system.	
Schedule management	Work packages will be reported on by the allocated individual at the end of each day by providing to the project scheduler the following information: planned value (PV), actual costs (AC) and earned value (EV).	
Cost management	Contractors are not approved to pay expenses via company credit cards.	
Quality management	Work packages when completed must be returned to the project scheduler with an appropriate quality certificate or sign-off document.	
Resource management	The project scheduler is responsible for issuing any new project schedule baselines.	
Procurement management	Procurement tenders must be approved in accordance with the corporate procurement policy.	
Stakeholder management	The project leader is accountable for ensuring all stakeholders are managed by a single contact in the project team.	
Communications information management	The project leader approves all final communications to the external customer before final delivery of the communication.	

(Continues)

Table 7.6 Governance identification (*Continued*)

Area	An example to direct your thinking	Your items*
Risk management	The risk process adopted by this project must comply with the ISO 31000:2018 standard	
Requirements management	Each individual requirement must be owned by a single business analyst in the project.	
Organisational change management	The project leader is accountable for and contributes towards the contents of the project's Organisational Change Management Plan.	
Benefits (value) management	The business owners nominated for each benefit to be delivered by the project will be informed of any status as to the realisation of the potential benefit.	

© 2022 Dr Neil Pearson

* You could idea-storm all these items/activities using sticky notes, and then use the affinity technique (looking for items/activities of likeness) to bring like items together in groups. Your trainer will demonstrate this technique in the classroom.

2. Take the third column, 'Your items' of Table 7.6, and transfer them into the start of the project-wide RASCI Matrix. You will have to adjust your *governance item* into business rule/decision language and work out the appropriate distribution of the responsible, accountable, support, consulted and informed (RASCI). Each of your items may generate multiple business rules and/or business decisions.

References

Casey W & Peck W 2001, "Choosing the right PMO setup", *PM Network,* vol. 15, no. 2, pp. 40–47.

Project Management Institute (PMI) 2013, *The Standard for Portfolio Management,* 3rd edition, PMI.

Project Management Institute (PMI) 2013, *The Standard for Program Management,* 3rd edition, PMI.

Project Management Institute (PMI) 2017, *A Guide to the Project Management Body of Knowledge,* sixth edn, PMI.

Project Management Institute (PMI) 2021a, *A Guide to the Project Management Body of Knowledge (PMBOK® Guide),* 7th edition, Newton Square, PA.

Project Management Institute (PMI) 2021b, *The Standard for Project Management (ANSI/PMI 99-001-2021),* 7th edition, Newton Square, PA.

Rowlings T 2022, "Don't confuse project governance with project management", Frame Group, https://www.framegroup.com.au/dont-confuse-project-governance-with-project-management/, accessed December 2021.

PART 4

Performing project planning

CHAPTER 8

Defining the scope of a project

Learning elements

8A Understand the importance of scoping a project and how this defines what the project is to achieve.

8B Understand how the Scope Management Plan differs from the scope document.

8C Develop a comprehensive scope document and understand some of the practical techniques that can be applied in developing its content.

8D Have a basic understanding of requirements gathering and capturing in a project environment.

8E Further understand the importance of the work breakdown structure and how this differs from a product breakdown structure and an organisation breakdown structure.

8F Define and establish a process for variation management in the project environment.

In this chapter

8.1 Introduction

8.2 Planning scope management

8.3 Defining the project scope

8.4 Capturing requirements

8.5 Creating the work breakdown structure (WBS)

8.6 Integrating the WBS with the organisation

8.7 Estimating the WBS

8.8 Variation request management

Summary

8.1 : Introduction

One of the most critical (and often one of the most difficult) activities within a project life cycle involves being able to successfully define the many and varied aspects of a project at its outset. This is because the project leader and the project team often start out with only minimal information (typically a partial Business Case and Project Charter based on this), have only a limited stakeholder network and have only a broad idea of the problem to be solved.

The early stages of developing an outline serve to ensure that all subsequent project tasks are identified and that participants of the project understand *what is to be done*. Once the outline and its details are defined, an integrated Project Management Plan (PMP) can be developed to schedule work and allocate budgets (which is discussed in later chapters). The process of scoping a project from inception through to approval prior to the Execution stage is discussed in detail within this chapter. Once the scope baseline is established, this information can be later used for control as the project moves from the Planning stage to the Execution stage. The chapter concludes with a discussion on how the project scope is verified in the Closure stage of the project, to ensure that what was planned and agreed in the scope document (plus any approved **variation requests**) was delivered to the customer's expectations.

Before venturing into a detailed discussion about the development of the project scope document, let's first look at some commonly used techniques that can help to explore and define a project's parameters. Frequently used terminology (which is in alignment with the Project Management Institute's (PMI's) *Project Management Body of Knowledge* (PMBOK)) is also introduced.

- ■ *Project Charter:* This is a summary document, which in most cases provides a formal agreement of the project between the project sponsor (the business) and the project leader. In some organisations, the Project Charter provides the go-ahead for the project, whereas in others the go-ahead will come as a result of the project leader having sought and obtained agreement on the wider scope of the project. Either way, the Project Charter is a formal, approved document that provides a high-level perspective of the key attributes of the project's scope. The Project Charter is discussed in Chapter 6 "Project integration management".

- ■ *Scope Management Plan:* This plan captures the more static processes and governance aspects of how project scope is to be approved and managed. The **variation management process (VMP)** is also formalised within the Scope Management Plan (if not available from the Project Management Office). The variation process will be followed throughout the project for all variation requested to the scope of the project, no matter how seemingly insignificant.

- ■ *Scope document:* This document defines the full and complete picture of the scope of work to be undertaken. The scope document is taken further into the Planning stage of the project as it is this scope from which detailed planning takes place. The scope document always needs to be approved by relevant stakeholders and/or the project steering committee before proceeding into the detailed planning of the project and the development of the integrated Project Management Plan (integrated PMP).

- ■ *Work breakdown structure (WBS):* The WBS provides a whole-of-project perspective on the **deliverables**, packages of work and tasks that must be carried out in order to deliver the defined deliverables of the project and, therefore, the product, service or result produced from the project.

- ■ *Estimating artefacts:* In order to arrive at time, cost and resource estimates for the project, an estimation of the required **work packages** and tasks within the WBS will need to be undertaken. *Note:* There is a general industry understanding that projects (during their Initiation stage) should be estimated within an accuracy of +/− 30–40%. In comparison, note that at the end of the project Planning stage, this will typically be within an accuracy of +/− 5–10%. So, from the Project Charter to the scope document through to the detailed integrated Project Management Plan, the level of accuracy will improve significantly.

■ *Technical/product requirements:* As well as documents that support the management of the project, numerous content-specific artefacts will be generated. These could include a detailed **product breakdown structure (PBS)** and technical specifications—more typically these are referred to as *requirements* in a business sense or could be a bill of materials (BOM) in a physical sense. This chapter will take a more in-depth look at the types of requirements and the process of requirements gathering, analysing and capturing (documenting).

Figure 8.1 illustrates the flow of information as it will occur within and beyond this chapter. As can be seen, establishing a clear scope, understanding *what* the product, service or result is to be delivered (PBS) and *how* this is to be delivered (WBS) informs and focuses the project leader's efforts in relation to detailed planning.

Before detailing the process of scoping out a project, it is important to understand the differences between *product scope* and *project scope.*

■ The product or service scope is all the features and functions expected from the product, service or result. For example, a house build might have requirements around the layout of rooms and the colour and quality of finishes; these are all specific to the product.

■ The project scope includes all the activities (work) that must be performed to develop and deliver the product, service or result. For example, there may be a requirement that the customer attends a design centre to select all the internal and external finishes of the house.

This chapter's discussion of scope adopts the assumption that project scope includes the necessary features and functions of the product in all aspects of project documents produced, from the scope statement and the WBS, through to all other parts of the integrated PMP and associated artefacts.

Before moving onto the work of drafting the scope management plan, scope document and WBS, let us first review where in the predictive life cycle we are operating (Figure 8.2).

Referring to Figure 8.2, this chapter will cover all those activities outlined in *A*. The scoping artefacts developed are usually subject to preliminary approval at *B* before detailed planning takes place at *C*. This is to ensure the project leader, project sponsor and key stakeholders have a solid understanding of the scope before large amounts of planning energy (resources, time and cost) are put into developing the detailed integrated PMP—the plan from which the project is executed.

Before the actual scoping work is carried out, the first thing to consider is the governance and processes in relation to scoping activities. These form some of the ground rules for everyone in the project. This governance is captured in the Scope Management Plan and relevant entries into the project-wide RASCI (refer to Chapter 6 "Project integration management").

8.2 | Planning scope management

The Scope Management Plan details governance, process and guidelines on how scope will be planned, approved and managed in the project environment. The Scope Management Plan should be established and agreed alongside the project's scope document early in the scoping activities. The contents of a Scope Management Plan could include the following.

1. *The process to be applied for all project variation requests:* This is the key process that outlines the steps to be taken on any variation request being raised.

2. *The process for scope verification:* This outlines the process around due diligence and verification of the scope document prior to its final approval. Does your organisation have, for example, a list of due diligence signatories from each department head affected by or interested in the project who must review and sign the scope document before formal approval by the project sponsor? If so, the process and people would be captured here.

Figure 8.1 The flow of key activities into and out of scoping

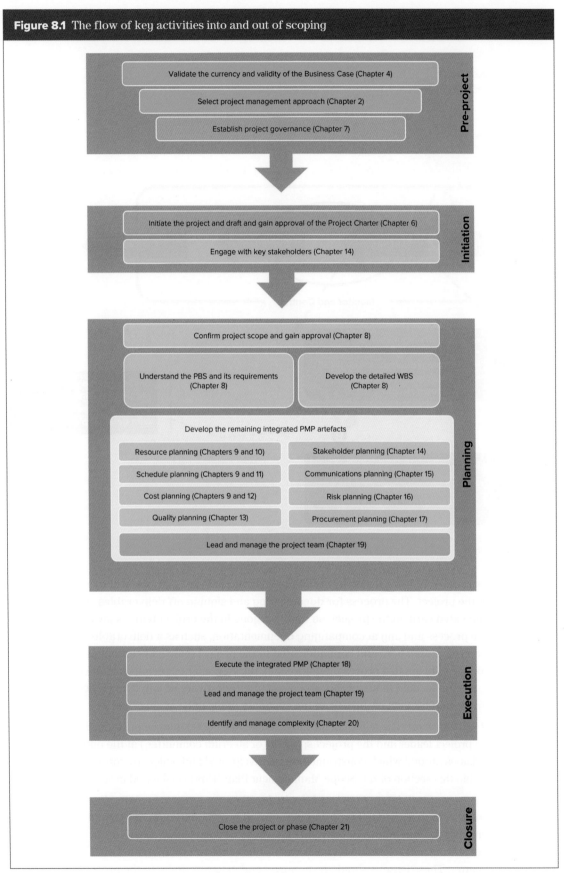

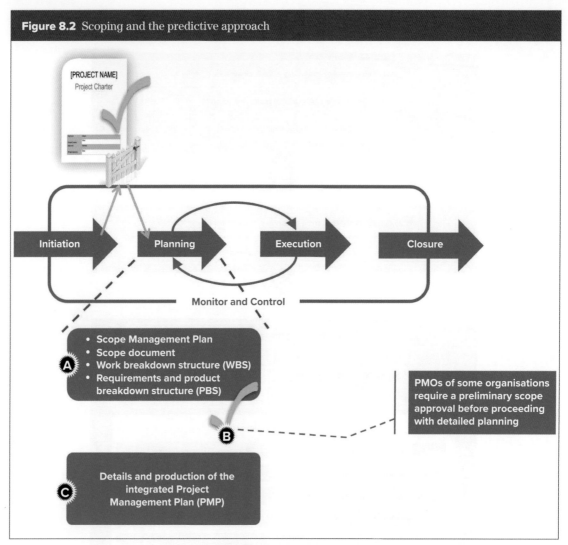

Figure 8.2 Scoping and the predictive approach

© 2022 Dr Neil Pearson

3. *The process for deliverable acceptance:* Deliverables (outcomes or outputs) will be delivered throughout the project. The process for documenting and signing off deliverables is defined and communicated early in the project, so that everyone in the project team is aware of the process. The process and any accompanying documentation, such as a deliverable acceptance form, would be captured here and communicated to the project team so everyone is following a planned, consistently applied process. Additionally, the customer or recipient of the deliverables will also be communicated to about this process so they are aware of any documents, time and approach to signing off deliverables from the customer perspective.

4. *Constraint management:* The triple constraints (scope, time, cost) may be prioritised in discussions between the project leader and the project sponsor (or steering committee) at the outset of the project. Decisions around which constraints are relatively rigid and which are more fluid should be captured within this section of the Scope Management Plan. This is discussed in section 8.3.2.

5. *How lessons learned will be captured and applied within the project:* Applying lessons learned from previous projects should not be a one-off event at project Initiation but should be considered as an opportunity for continuous improvement purposes. Project team meetings provide an ideal setting for capturing and reflecting on what went right, what went wrong and what could have been done better. These lessons should be actioned and incorporated into the project as well as being recorded for post-project improvement.

6. *Baseline history:* This is a history of every re-baseline from the original baseline created at the Planning stage gate review (i.e. when the scope is first baselined)

Note: Elements of 1, 2, 3 and 5 could be captured in the project-wide RASCI discussed in Chapter 7 "Governance and projects".

 Scope Management Plan

8.3 : Defining the project scope

Defining the project scope sets the stage for developing a more detailed Project Management Plan later in the Planning stage. Project scope is a definition of the result, or vision, of your project. The primary purpose of project scope is to define (as clearly as possible) the deliverable(s) of the project and what is and what is not going to be included in the work of the project. Despite how fundamental and essential defining scope is, this process is frequently overlooked, even in well-managed large government organisations and corporates as well as small-to-medium sized enterprises.

Research clearly shows that a poorly defined scope is one of the most frequently mentioned reasons in challenged projects. In a study involving more than 1400 project leaders in the United States and Canada, Gobeli & Larson (1990) found that approximately 50 per cent of planning problems related to an unclear definition of scope and goals. Even studies today suggest a strong correlation between project success and clear scope definition. The scope document directs customer and project participants' focus to the project's purpose throughout the life of the project and should be continually verified as the project progresses. The scope must be controlled for variations to the scope of the project throughout the project, but strictly after baseline scope approval.

The scope should be developed under the direction of the project leader (with the inclusion of the project sponsor and customer). The project leader is responsible for seeing that there is agreement with the sponsor and customer on project objectives, deliverables (at each stage of the project), technical requirements and so forth. For example, a deliverable in the early stages might be developing specifications; for the second stage, prototypes for testing; for the third, initial production run to introduce to market; and finally, marketing promotion.

Your project scope document will be referred to by the project sponsor, customer and project team for planning and measuring project progress. *Scope* describes what is expected to be delivered to the customer(s) during and when the project is complete. The project scope should define the results that are to be achieved in specific, tangible and measurable terms. The project leader should leave no stone unturned and must be very specific and accurate in their use of language. In today's project environment, assumptions are no excuse for non-delivery of the product, service or result!

8.3.1 Typical project scope contents

Project scope is the keystone that interlocks all the elements of a project's dimensions. To ensure that the scope definition is complete, you may wish to use the typical contents of a project scope document as a checklist that is shown in Table 8.1.

Table 8.1 Typical project scope document contents

Number	Scope document element
1.	Project background
2.	Project approach
3.	Project benefits/disbenefits
4.	Strategic alignment
5.	Impact if not approved
6.	Dependencies
7.	Project vision statement
8.	Project acceptance criteria
9.	Project organisational structure
10.	Key stakeholders
11.	Project objectives
12.	Deliverables (output and outcomes)
13.	Inclusions/exclusions (in scope/out of scope)
14.	Constraints
15.	Assumptions
16.	Technical requirements (including quality considerations)
17.	Risk analysis
18.	Overall project timeline and milestones
19.	Overall project cost and funding sources
20.	Organisational change impact
21.	Lessons learned review
22.	Approvals and version control
23.	Product breakdown structure (PBS)
24.	Product acceptance criteria
25.	Work breakdown structure (WBS) and dictionary

Although this list appears extensive, it is relevant to projects of all sizes, risk and complexity. If due diligence is not paid to define, document and agree on these aspects, a project would be considered to be poorly scoped (with associated potential repercussions). The author's (Pearson's) top 25 items to include in a generic scope document are further outlined in the following pages (each item has been supported by a short definition, for clarity).

1. *Project background:* This provides a general background to the project as to why it is taking place and the situation that led up to the project being required. This is the *story* behind the project coming into being. This provides a useful narrative to readers outside the project, by setting the scene of the project.

2. *Project approach:* This provides detail on how the project will be undertaken—for example, whether there will be a staged or phased approach, whether the project will follow industry or best-practice methodologies (such as a software development life cycle (SDLC) approach), how the project will be approached within the organisational culture, and how the project will leverage techniques such as rolling wave planning, phases or increments in its design and approach.

3. *Project benefits:* These should have been captured in the Business Case that kicked off the request to initiate the project. The project leader needs to ascertain the accuracy of these benefits and define which benefits will be delivered by the project, and which will be enabled by the realisation of the project (some benefits of the project defined within the Business Case may only be realised after the project has completed, during business-as-usual operations). Benefits should be measurable (quantifiable) where possible but will undoubtedly be a mix of both tangible and intangible benefits. Benefits should also have a benefit owner. The project leader should also consider the project's disbenefits. Disbenefits are expected undesirable outcomes. An example of a disbenefit is the loss of value of a person or department arising from the project; the person or department would be termed the *disbeneficiary.*

4. *Strategic alignment:* The project leader provides details of the alignment of the project to the department's Business Plan, and/or the organisation's strategy; it captures which (if any) key performance indicators will be improved by implementing the project. If the project is being carried out for an external customer, the project leader will have to consider whose alignment is stated here: the organisation's perspective or the customer's raison d'être? The project leader in today's contemporary project environment should nearly always be in receipt of a Business Case or similar document where these parameters will be outlined. Verify and check these when provided to ensure what has been promised at higher echelons in the organisation can actually be delivered by the project leader!

5. *Impact if not approved:* By scoping the project, the project leader will gain a good understanding of the impact on the business if the project is not approved. The reasons behind the decision not to approve the project should always be documented so the sponsor, customer and business have a clear understanding of the consequences to the business if the project does not go ahead.

6. *Dependencies:* The project leader is responsible for determining whether the project is dependent on the completion of any other projects or activities in the company; for example, an upstream project must be completed before activities in this project can be executed. Also, a review of which projects or activities in the company are dependent on this project completing should be undertaken (often referred to as *downstream* projects).

7. *Project vision statement:* Tell the story and paint that picture of what the end-state looks like. A useful technique is to create a 60-second pitch. A form of this was considered in Chapter 3 "Agile (Scrum) project management", in the project vision statement.

8. *Project acceptance criteria:* Project acceptance criteria bring together multiple elements of the scope document. They could include criteria related to:
   - acceptance of the project deliverables
   - acceptance of the final output of the project (quality perspective)

- acceptance of the project benefits
- the performance baselines of scope/schedule/time.

Additional criteria could be more subject specific, such as:

- acceptance criteria around a technical or soft (user interface) design
- acceptance criteria around usability of a product (meets user requirements)
- all the validated (signed-off) requirements have been delivered
- the project has not breeched any laws, legislation or policies.

Acceptance criteria can be difficult to pull together but when done successfully provide another focus point for the project leader and project team.

9. *Project organisational structure:* This illustrates the structure and reporting lines of all personnel identified to be involved in the project and whether these reporting lines are matrix (dotted line) or direct (solid line). Providing those who are reviewing the scope with a *visual* of the project's organisational structure helps them to see (at a high-level indication) the size of the human resource commitment that is being made to the project.

10. *Key stakeholders:* Although the Stakeholder Matrix may be initiated during the scoping of the project, at minimum the scope document should contain a list of the key stakeholders involved in the project. It should set out their individual role, what you (as project leader) want from them, and, conversely, what they want from the project. Their relative power and interest in the project should also be indicated. *Note:* A *stakeholder* is anyone who has an interest in the project or is impacted by the project.

11. *Project objectives:* What are the objectives of the project? (Reflect back to the SMARTA acronym introduced in Table 4.1 in Chapter 4 "Strategy, project selection and the Business Case".) By applying the SMARTA technique to the project's objectives, the project leader ensures that each individual written objective is specific, measurable, assignable, realistic, time-bound and agreed. The project's objective answers the questions of *what, when and how much?* In today's project management environment, it is also important to define the critical success factors (CSFs) of the project. This means thinking holistically about what factors provide a picture of the project's success and what must be achieved for this to occur. An example of an objective versus a CSF is given below:

- Objective: Achieve fresh supplies from farm to customer in 24 hours for 75 per cent of organic fresh produce we handle.
- CSF: Sustainment of successful relationships with local suppliers.

12. *Deliverables:* Deliverables are often categorised into two types—*outputs*—usually associated with the tangible (physical) aspects that the project is to deliver (e.g. training manuals, a new financial system, a building, a bridge); and *outcomes*—associated with changes in behaviours (e.g. the new finance system is adopted by all company users and people are confident in using it—providing benefits to the organisation in the faster recovery of monies owed).

13. *Inclusions (in scope) and exclusions (out of scope):* Most project leaders are very adept at documenting what is included within the project. However, what about what is specifically *not* included within the scope of the project? If out-of-scope items are not documented, this can lead to situations where undocumented assumptions arise later on in the project: for example, where one party assumes these were included in the scope of the project (typically the customer) while the other party makes the assumption that they were not included in the scope of the project (typically the project sponsor).

A commonly used tool for understanding scope is the **context diagram**. A context diagram indicates scope by indicating the actors (users, ICT system or group) and their high-level interaction with the product, service or result. For example, an actor *employee* in an HR kiosk development project could want to *lodge a leave request* or *query remaining leave*. These are activities that are in the scope of the project.

Figure 8.3 is a partial context diagram for a taxi and driver registration system.

Figure 8.3 Context diagram: New taxi registration system

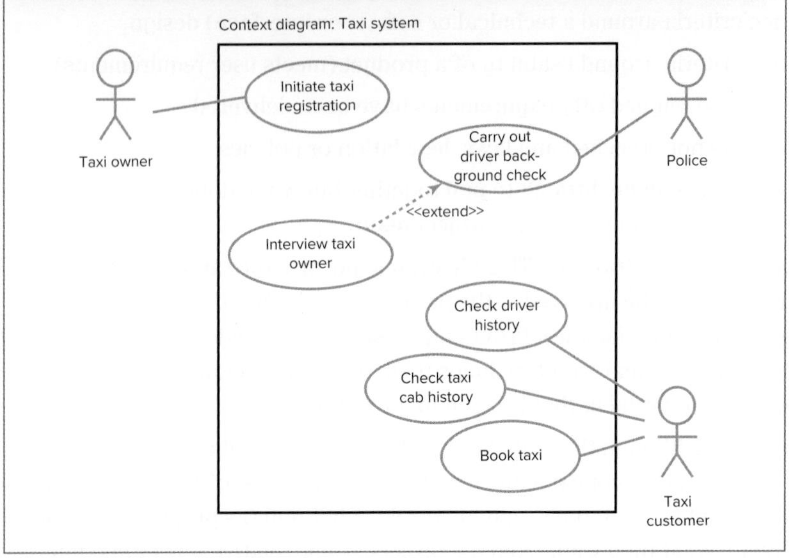

Context diagram: Taxi system

- Initiate taxi registration
- Carry out driver back-ground check
- Interview taxi owner
- <<extend>>
- Check driver history
- Check taxi cab history
- Book taxi

Taxi owner

Police

Taxi customer

© 2022 Dr Neil Pearson

A popular variant to the context diagram is the *rich picture*. This is more informal in nature. The rich picture captures essential considerations for inclusion in the scope of the system being considered. Figure 8.4 illustrates a rich picture for how a patient is currently admitted into a care home. The thought bubbles on the diagram indicate the importance of building rich pictures—these indicate the feelings/emotions of the people (actors) involved in the process. Rich pictures can provide insights into the current system of events or future system of events that are to be considered. They provide an ideal way of engaging hands-on with your key subject matter experts (SMEs).

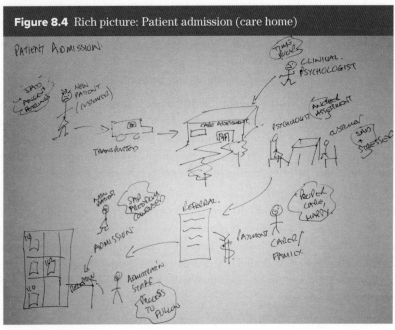

Figure 8.4 Rich picture: Patient admission (care home)

© 2022 Dr Neil Pearson

14. *Constraints:* This refers to documented conditions that are known to have a constraining effect on the project. They may be financial or related to the conditions in which the project is taking place (e.g. there is resource scarcity). Any constraints raised should be assessed for hidden risks.

15. *Assumptions:* What are the known (confirmed) assumptions for the project? Assumption statements are accepted as *true without proof.* Assumptions are circumstances and/or activities that need to occur for the project to be successful, but are outside the control of the project team. For example, an assumption for a large construction project could be *no shortage or cost increases in the supply of cement to the project.* Any assumptions raised should also be assessed for hidden risks.

16. *Technical requirements (including quality considerations):* Here, the scope would (at a high level) seek to document the technical aspects of the product and/or service being produced (e.g. the known technical requirements for a large-bore water pump). These requirements would also form the basis of planning for the quality assurance aspects of the product or service being produced. Remember from Chapter 1 that these are all too often poorly articulated, even in today's projects!

17. *Risk analysis:* The project sponsor is often a good source of information about high-level risks to the project from a business perspective. The customer may additionally have some concerns they want to articulate at project outset. However, ultimately, the responsibility of identifying high-level risks during project scoping falls to the project leader. They must ensure not only that high-level risks are identified, but that the probability/likelihood (the chance) of such risks occurring and their impact/consequence (the effects if the risk occurs) are also analysed.

18. *Overall project timeline and milestones:* The WBS will be started as part of the development of the scope document. This will inform (through the estimating activities) the overall project timeline, milestones, assumptions and end-date. A milestone is a significant event in a project and occurs at a point in time—milestones are zero-duration activities (it is the work done prior to the milestone that delivers it!). Milestones should be natural, important control points in the project. They should be easy for all project participants to recognise. The timeline presented within the scope document assists in clarifying understanding of the major milestones with those responsible for scope approvals. The timeline in scoping may also be supported with a high-level project schedule, usually in the form of a Gantt chart, which provides a level of detail to those interested in reading beyond the timeline.

19. *Overall project cost and funding sources:* The same techniques can be applied as per above, but with the goal of arriving at an overall project estimate for costs. It is also useful to consider the identification and approval (with the project scope document) of any long lead-time items and/or large capital items. These items may require special approvals, earlier than planned in the project life cycle. *Note:* In estimating costs, the project leader will also be considering the resource commitment (as this will have to be estimated from both a cost and time perspective).

20. *Organisational change impact:* Most projects deal with change from one state (the *as-is* state) to another planned state (the *to-be* state, or planned outcome of the project). The project scope document should contain a review of the organisational change impact of the project on the business. Some of the questions the project leader needs to address during this early stage of the project include whether the business is ready for the change proposed by the project, what other changes are occurring at the same time that might need coordinating with this project, and whether the project needs to employ the services of a specialist change consultant. Chapter 5 "Organisational change management and cultures" discussed the topic of organisational change management in detail.

21. *Lessons learned review:* The scope document should capture the sources and lessons learned from previous projects that are relevant to this project, both for projects within and outside the organisation. This helps to ensure that mistakes and successes of the past are considered when designing the current project.

22. *Approvals and version control:* All project documents should have version and distribution control information on their front page. This ensures that when the scope document is reviewed, all stakeholders involved in the review are using the same version of the document.

Note: Often valuable meeting time is lost in trying to ascertain which versions of the documents are around a meeting table. As part of the governance process (gated life cycle) the project scope document should be reviewed extensively by all key stakeholders and by the project sponsor and customer, with appropriate sign-offs obtained before the project moves into the Planning stage.

23. *Product scope description:* otherwise known as the *product breakdown structure* (PBS) in other approaches such as PRINCE2 and the APM Body of Knowledge. A PBS, as indicated in Figure 8.5, provides solely a breakdown of the product (blue square) into its sub-assemblies (grey parallelogram), and the sub-assemblies into components internally built (green trapezium) or components externally sourced (orange oval). PBSs are different from WBSs in that they only show the make-up of the parts of the product or service, and do not include the work required to be done to construct the final product.

Figure 8.5 Example product breakdown structure

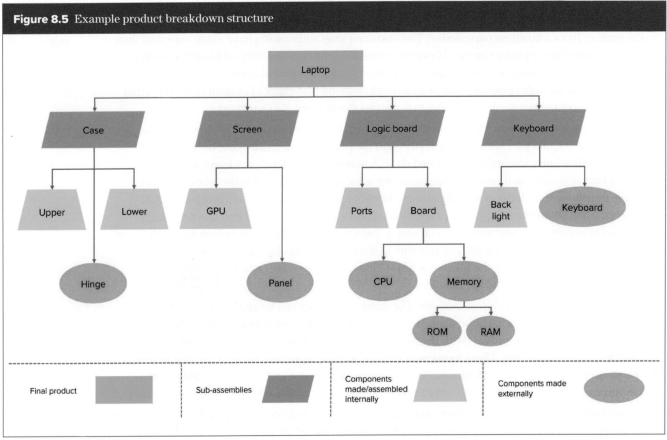

© 2022 Dr Neil Pearson

In Chapter 17 "Project procurement management", the concept of a **bill of materials (BOM)** is also discussed. A BOM is similar in nature to a PBS, typically presented as an indented list of sub-assemblies and components with additional columns for information such as supplier, quantity, and make or buy decision.

24. *Product acceptance criteria:* Based on the PBS, the acceptance criteria against each component, sub-assembly and the final product would be defined. This is akin to identifying the quality assurance criteria in the BOM.

In relation to the product, service or result to be produced by the project, the two key aspects a project leader must be clear about is a detailed breakdown of:

■ *what* the product, service or result is, whether this is captured as a PBS, BOM, Requirements Matrix or other

■ *how* the product, service or result is to be made by the project, including any required project management activities (i.e. the WBS)

25. *WBS:* How the deliverables of the project are to be designed, developed and implemented in the project (i.e. this is the work the project has to do in order to deliver the end product, service or result). Refer to section 8.5 for a detailed explanation of a WBS and the associated WBS dictionary items.

Scoping a project should not be considered a *tick-and-flick* activity. It is a serious endeavour to ensure that all parties agree on what is to be achieved by the project, how long it will take, at what cost and what exactly will be delivered at the end of the project. Refer to "Snapshot from Practice: Whether a project is large or small, scope is important—Relationships Australia Queensland", where it can be seen that, even for small projects, scope is just as important as for large projects.

The scope document is a living document that travels with the project—subject to variations. After all, the project leader needs a scope baseline document that has been agreed on and approved, against which variations to scope can be managed (e.g. to prevent **scope creep**). Figure 8.6 aptly depicts the type of mismatch in understanding that can occur if a project is not correctly scoped.

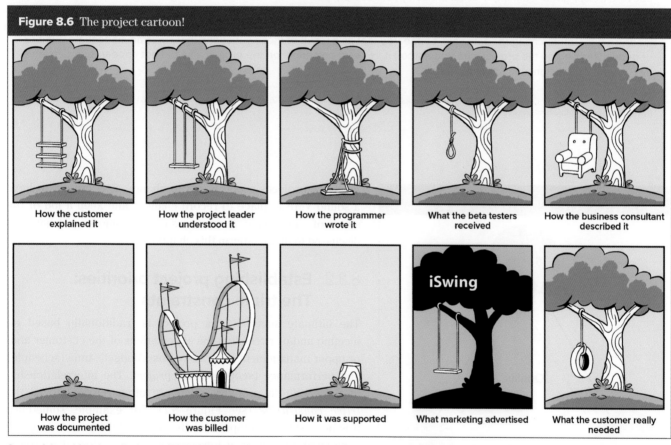

Figure 8.6 The project cartoon!

How the customer explained it

How the project leader understood it

How the programmer wrote it

What the beta testers received

How the business consultant described it

How the project was documented

How the customer was billed

How it was supported

iSwing — What marketing advertised

What the customer really needed

Source: Adapted from https://archive.ph/20130719182750/; http://www.businessballs.com/treeswing.htm and www.projectcartoon.com.

The list of top 25 items for inclusion in a scope document offers typical potential scope inclusions. It is typical, since different industries and companies will have specific items relevant to their industry and organisational practices. Many companies engaged in contract work refer to the scope document as a *scope statement* or *project initiation document (PID)*.

Many projects suffer from scope creep, which is the tendency for the project's scope to usually expand (change) over time (usually because of the customer's changing requirements, specifications and priorities). Scope creep (jokingly referred to as *hope creep*), can be reduced by not only having a well-written scope document, but also by having a process to manage project variations, as and when they occur. A scope statement that is too broad is an invitation for scope creep. Scope creep can have a positive or negative effect on the project, but in most cases it means added costs and possible delays. Changes in requirements, specifications and priorities frequently result in cost overruns and delays. Review the two examples provided in "Snapshot from Practice: Scope creep".

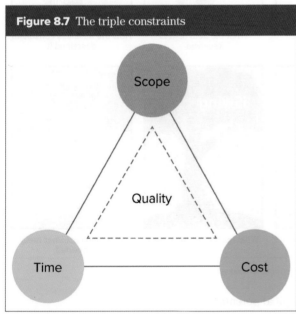

Figure 8.7 The triple constraints

© 2022 Dr Neil Pearson

Note: Refer to Chapter 6 "Project integration management", section 6.6 for a discussion on the seven project constraints that are now more frequently considered, and also Chapter 3 "Agile (Scrum) project management", Figure 3.18, for an illustration of constraints in the adaptive (Agile) life cycle context.

If the project's scope needs to change, it is critical to have a sound VMP in place to record changes and keep a log of the status of all changes. The process of managing scope change is discussed in detail later in this chapter.

8.3.2 Establishing project priorities: The triple constraints

The ultimate success of a project is traditionally based on meeting and/or exceeding the expectations of the customer and/ or upper management in terms of cost (budget), time (schedule) and performance (scope) of the project. The interrelationship of these criteria produces what are often referred to as the *triple constraints* (see Figure 8.7). For example, sometimes it is necessary to compromise the scope of the project to get it completed quicker or at lower cost. Often, the longer a project takes, the more expensive it becomes. However, a positive correlation between cost and schedule may not always be true. Other times, project costs can be reduced by using cheaper, less efficient labour or equipment that extends the duration of the project. Likewise, project leaders are often forced to expedite or crash certain key activities by adding additional labour, thereby raising the original cost of the project. *Note:* The triple constraints are often referred to in a more casual manner as the *iron triangle*.

It is important to recognise the significance of quality being at the centre of the triple constraints. If other dimensions (scope, cost and time) change, the project leader is tasked with ensuring that quality does not suffer in light of other variations (if quality suffers there is a likelihood the customer will not accept deliverables). This is indeed a difficult balancing act at the best of times. One of the primary jobs of a project leader is to manage the trade-offs between time, cost and scope. To do so, a project leader must define and understand the nature of the priorities of the project. They need to have a candid discussion with the project sponsor to establish the relative importance of each criterion. For example, what happens when the customer keeps adding requirements? Or, if midway through the project, a trade-off must be made between cost and speed—which criterion has priority? How will this impact the governance around the variation management process?

One technique found in practice that is useful for this purpose involves completing a constraint preference matrix for the project, to identify which of the constraints are more rigid or more flexible.

- *Rigid:* The constraint is more fixed. The sponsor is less open to discussions and changes in relation to this constraint.
- *Flexible:* There is some ability to move based on this constraint being affected by a variation later on in the project.
- *Fluid:* The constraint has greater ability to withstand movement because of change in this project environment.

Figure 8.8 indicates such a constraints preference matrix based on the **seven constraints** previously introduced.

Figure 8.8 Constraints preference matrix

	Rigid	Flexible	Fluid	Comments
Scope		◎		
Time	◎			
Cost			◎	
Quality	◎			
Resources		◎		
Risk	◎			
Alignment	◎			

© 2022 Dr Neil Pearson

Priorities vary from project to project. For example, for many software projects, time to market is critical, and companies like Microsoft may defer original scope requirements to later versions, in order to win the race to the market first. Alternatively, for special event projects (e.g. conferences, sports events, tournaments), time is constrained once the date has been announced, and if the budget is tight, the project leader may have to compromise the scope of the project in order to complete it on time.

Some would argue that all three criteria are always constrained and that good project leaders should seek to optimise each criterion. If everything goes well on a project and no major problems or setbacks are encountered, their argument may be valid. However, this situation is rare, and project leaders are often forced to make tough decisions that benefit one criterion while compromising the others. The purpose of this exercise is to define and agree on what the priorities and constraints of the project are upfront during scoping, so that when push comes to shove, the right decisions can be made—or at least favourable options presented to the project sponsor, based on their constraint preferences.

Whether a project is large or small, scope is important— Relationships Australia Queensland

Scope is key for gaining an agreement between all parties involved in the project. On a recent ISO: 9001 project that one of the authors (Pearson) was involved in, a short-term contract to deliver specific components of a larger ISO project had to be scoped before a contract value could be placed on the project. The sponsor, the operations manager and the quality manager were adopting a light-PRINCE2 approach towards the project, and they therefore set about establishing the scope of the project (or, as referred to in PRINCE2, the project initiation document (PID)). The scoping activities included the author in some pre-contract work, to establish exactly what was required from the project. Buy-in from all parties significantly assisted the process of clarifying and focusing the project from the outset. Although the project was to run for only six weeks, it was important that very close attention was paid to establishing its scope. The non-negotiable constraints for the project were time (the project had a fixed duration of six weeks) and cost; the scope was subject to several constraints and assumptions, as illustrated in Figure 8.9.

Figure 8.9 Managing the triple constraints

	Rigid	Flexible	Fluid	Comments
Scope			◎	Extended items such as the levels into which the process is broken down can be adjusted given time is fixed.
Time	◎			Completion date cannot be extended due to contractor availability and the requirement to start the new year with a new direction.
Cost	◎			Funding not negotiable.
Quality	◎			Quality not negotiable.
Resources			◎	Additional resources coached to take on work could be located if required.
Risk		◎		Review on an as-required basis.
Alignment	◎			The objectives of the project are aligned to a strategic ISO 9001 initiative and cannot be altered.

© 2022 Dr Neil Pearson

Assumptions placed around scope (performance) constraints included statements about:

- accessibility to resources, the executive team (including the CEO) and other senior management
- accessibility to key SMEs in the business
- identification and on-boarding of two key supporting business analysts to shadow the author, so that active knowledge transfer could take place.

Based on the scope, some specific deliverables (both output and outcome) were defined, as indicated in Table 8.2. What this table demonstrates is that all parties knew exactly the scope of the project agreements, and everybody was on the same page from the outset, before contracts were signed.

As the sponsor had a solid knowledge of a project management approach, constructive and robust discussions around the scope of the project took place. Whether a project is small or large, the importance of scoping cannot be overstated. As a side note, the six-week project did produce the defined deliverables, on time, to budget and within the resource constraint— the company worked extremely hard to make the resources available at the correct time.

Table 8.2 Scope outputs and outcomes

Deliverables: outputs	Deliverables: outcomes
■ Level 0 process zone—defined for all processes, and nominated process owners were agreed to and assigned to each process.	■ Holistic process understanding by the executive team and directs: Process Policy is agreed and understood.
■ Process workshop for executive team ×2.	■ Process owner role description is agreed and signed up to.
■ Process workshop for each executive team member and nominated representatives.	■ Process owners are owning the nominated processes and starting to engage in mapping (at a high level) the Level 1 process maps.
■ Process Policy developed and communicated.	■ The process owners are gathering continuous improvement requests and are prioritising these in a register for review as a process owner team.
■ Continuous Improvement (CI) Policy and CI register development, communication and application.	
■ Business analysis process mapping guidelines, Requirements Gathering Template and Measure Definition Template developed and applied.	■ BA role established and coached through development of the first processes.
■ As-is process for service area translated into business process model and notation with business analyst (BA) resources.	■ Process owners generally understand the business process notation, and nominated representatives have the ability to develop basic processes.
■ BA position description agreed with human resources and BA role(s) recruited (from internal resource pool). Internal resources trained in business analysis skills and process modelling skills.	■ Communication of the role of processes in the organisation, the links to quality and the general process notation to the whole of the business are understood.
■ Selection and implementation of organisation process management technology, to support ongoing mapping of all organisational processes (for ISO accreditation).	

There are likely to be natural limits to the extent managers can constrain, optimise or accept any one criterion. It may be acceptable for the project to slip one month behind schedule but no further, or to exceed the planned budget. Likewise, it may be desirable to finish a project a month early, but after that, cost conservation should be the primary goal. Some project leaders document these limits as part of creating the Priority Matrix.

In summary, developing a constraint preference matrix for a project before the project begins is a useful exercise. It provides a forum for clearly establishing priorities with the project sponsor, so as to create shared expectations and avoid misunderstandings. The priority information is essential to the planning process, where adjustments can be made in the scope, schedule and budget allocation. Finally, the matrix can be useful throughout the project to check priorities considering pending variations.

Something to be conscious of is the fact that priorities may change during a project. For example, the customer may suddenly need the project completed one month sooner, or new directives from top management may emphasise cost-saving initiatives. The project leader therefore needs to be vigilant so they can anticipate and confirm changes in priorities and make appropriate adjustments.

 Scope Document

8.4 │ **Capturing requirements**

The whole process and approach of capturing requirements within a project environment (whether a software, construction or service project) have become more structured, and techniques that have predominantly evolved from the world of software engineering are increasingly being used across all industries and projects. Requirements originate from the Initiation, and Planning stages (and even from the Execution stage, through variations). The challenge lies in accurately collecting and analysing requirements to ensure the product, service or end result can be later validated to ensure it meets what was expected (and defined in the original requirements).

Many projects fail because of inadequate requirements gathering and poorly defined requirements. A requirement is a criterion or condition (business rule), or capability of a product, service or result that is required to be captured (elicited), documented and validated in order that the project can ultimately deliver it. If a complete set of requirements is not captured, documented, and validated, the chances are that the project will not deliver what the customer requires. It is the role of the project leader to guide the collection of requirements from a product scope perspective (most probably supervising a team of engineers of business analysts to do so). From a project scope perspective, it is the project leader's responsibility to ensure this is carried out in a complete and comprehensive manner. Remember, the product owner carried out a similar task in the formation and maintenance of the product backlog (refer to Chapter 3 "Agile (Scrum) project management").

Figure 8.10 illustrates the requirements management process that is adopted in this text. This process was based on industry experience—the process illustrated does, however, adopt elements from both the PMI's *Requirements Management: A Practice Guide* (PMI 2016) and the British Computer Society's *Business Analysis* fourth edition (BCS 2020).

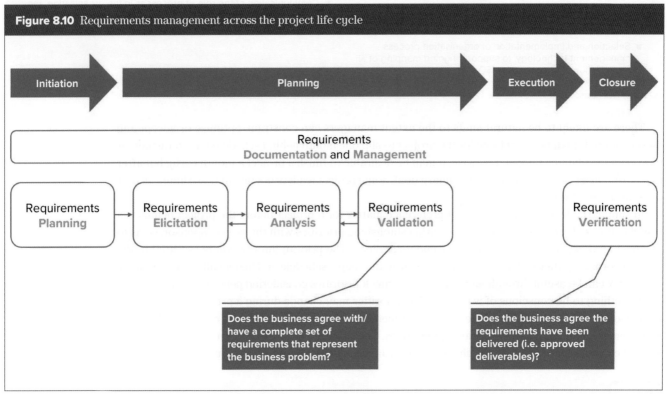

Figure 8.10 Requirements management across the project life cycle

© 2022 Dr Neil Pearson

Let's examine the stages of this requirements management process and how these relate to activities not only in scoping the project but as ongoing activities throughout the project life cycle.

1. *Requirements planning:* As the project kicks off and the project team is formed, the project leader must consider how requirements are to be managed, including:

   ■ establishing the process for requirements management, as illustrated in Figure 8.10

   ■ ensuring the correct tools and training to support the process are actioned

   ■ developing the Requirements Management Plan, and setting out the process, tools and techniques used to support the management of requirements in the project environment (if not available from other areas of the business)

   ■ agreeing with the project team on how requirements will be socialised with other stakeholders, via a business requirements specification document or other means

■ agreeing with the business a protocol for the prioritisation of requirements (refer to MoSCoW, in Chapter 3 "Agile (Scrum) project management").

 Requirements Management Plan

2. *Requirements elicitation:* During the Planning stage of the project life cycle, the project team (including the project leader) will generate potentially hundreds of requirements. These will be captured in various working documents, which will typically cause problems in maintaining requirements. Therefore, a suitable tool should be made available to assist with capturing the requirements in a consistent manner.

A basic tool could be as simple as setting up a Microsoft Excel spreadsheet, which will then allow for the capture and subsequent analysis of requirements (i.e. de-duplicating, creating atomic (singular) requirements, and reusing requirements (e.g. within different business rules)). A snapshot of a simple spreadsheet is illustrated in Table 8.3. This type of document is often referred to as a *Requirements Register*.

Table 8.3 Requirements Register

Requirement ID	Requestor/originator	Requirement category	Requirement	Project team member assigned	Link to WBS ref(s)	Module delivered in	Priority
R3.5	User group	Solution, functional	\<As a/an> Employee \<I want to > lodge a request for leave \<so that> I can take a well-earned break from work.	Development Team 1	WBS 5.7	TBA	Must
R3.6	User group	Solution, functional	\<As a/an> Employee \<I want to > be able to see what leave requests I have lodged and their status \<so that> I can manage my leave allowance.	Development Team 1	WBS 5.7	TBA	Should
R3.9	HR Director	Business, general	Interfaces must comply with internal Ux guidelines and branding.	Project level guidance	WBS 1.1	TBA	Must

© 2022 Dr Neil Pearson

Note: This is a cut-down matrix; however, it does indicate requirement traceability backwards to the originator of the requirement and requirement traceability forwards to the team member assigned the WBS item, and forwards again to the module the requirement would be released in.

Requirements elicitation is an important step that necessitates active engagement with the project's stakeholders to extract and capture requirements. Common techniques used in this process include the following.

■ Observation: A project team member observes a stakeholder when they are carrying out tasks and uses questions to clarify information about the tasks. The observer might have to visit different employees carrying out the task at different times, to gain a true understanding of the task and future requirements to be considered by the project.

■ Interviews: A project team member interviews one or multiple stakeholders to ascertain requirements. These might have to be cross-referenced to ensure a unique set of requirements is generated.

■ Focus groups: A group of (usually external or customers of the system) stakeholders is brought together to focus on a particular topic for discussion and negotiation, and ultimately an agreed set of requirements. Several focus group sessions may need to be carried out to fully explore and define the requirements to the required level from the customer's perspective.

- Workshops: Workshops can be run in many ways (from brainstorming sessions to fish-bowl sessions). They can be (especially in the early days) quite creative and exploratory in nature. The idea is to bring a group of people together to gain agreement on a set of requirements to be taken forward by the project.
- Scenarios: Getting stakeholders to talk/act through various scenarios to explain/demonstrate how they would use a particular product or service. The arising scenarios would be captured, and requirements would subsequently be extracted for later verification.
- Surveys/questionnaires: Typically used for large, geographically dispersed groups. Development of surveys is a specialist task that, when executed well, can yield successful and useful results.

3. *Requirements analysis:* In this chapter, it has been pointed out that missing or incorrect requirements are cited as one of most frequent reasons why projects fail. This emphasises that not only is the whole requirements management process important, but so too is making sure that the collected requirements are appropriately analysed. Analysis will include working out if requirements:

- are atomic—consider only one feature or item at a time (i.e. not concatenated covering multiple items)
- don't overlap—this is where part of one requirement appears in another requirement
- are not duplicated—total duplication of a requirement elsewhere in the project, often collected by different project team members
- don't appear multiple times—if they do, split them out and make them atomic (i.e. each requirement statement must only cover a single requirement)
- are irrelevant—are they are required and do they directly relate to the problem? Otherwise, why are we looking at them in this project?
- are feasible—technically, financially (they can be funded) and business feasible (they can be implemented in the business)
- don't conflict—contradicting or conflicting requirements must be resolved
- are free of solutions—the business reason for why the solution is being suggested must be ascertained
- are comprehensible—use clear, plain English and avoid jargon and acronyms; and use concise, verb–noun, or the Agile approach: *As a _____, I want to _____, so that I can _____.*
- are consistent—across the whole group of requirements (i.e. requirements are defined to a similar level of detail)
- are unambiguous—no assumptions are made in the interpretation of a requirement
- are correct—they describe something that is required to meet the objectives
- are testable—the solution can be tested to confirm the requirement has been met
- are traceable—from the requirement's source to where it was deployed (software or product in use by consumers)
- are prioritised—requirements with business input take on the same MoSCoW approach (refer to Chapter 3 "Agile (Scrum) project management").

Business analysts often refer to this list as *requirements filters* (BCS 2020) as each requirement is filtered through these criteria to ensure they are well formed.

4. *Requirements validation:* This is considered to be more of an internal process, to validate the requirements collected with the stakeholder (internal or external to the organisation) are complete (are what they want), accurate, signed-off and testable (often referred to as *CAST*). This should mean that when the project or service is built during the Execution stage of the project, it meets the CAST requirements (i.e. it demonstrates the features and functions that the

customer wants—and no more!). This is similar to the INVEST acronym introduced in Chapter 3 "Agile (Scrum) project management".

5. *Requirements verification:* Usually occurs at certain points in a predictive project, for example, when a deliverable is handed over to the business, when the project reaches a particular phase or stage gate, or at the end of the project. When any of these events occur, the product (service or result) will be verified against the previously agreed CAST requirements. If the deliverable does not meet requirements, decisions must be made about which direction this issue/shortfall needs to be taken in. Would, for example, rework correct the issue/shortfall that has been identified? How much effort is this rework? Who is going to pay for it? Does a variation need to be lodged?

Remember: Quality requirements generate good results for the project only when the work around building and developing the requirements is successfully engineered (designed) into the WBS (or equivalent).

Requirements are generally classified into differing categories. Table 8.4 depicts a commonly encountered categorisation system (based on BCS 2020). The table also provides information about where in the project life cycle the category of requirement is likely to be identified and captured. Examples from different types of projects are given to help explain this *fit*.

Table 8.4 Requirement types

Type	Description	Life cycle stage	Example
Business: General	High-level business requirements related to: ■ business policies ■ legal ■ branding ■ cultural ■ language.	Initiation Planning (scoping) or sprints	■ All external (customer) interfaces must meet the organisation's branding standards. ■ The final product must meet product safety standards, as laid down by the country of sale (e.g. vehicle jacks must comply with AS/NZS 2693 Vehicle Jacks); https://www.productsafety.gov.au/standards/vehicle-jacks). ■ The system must comply with financial regulations and services legislation.
Business: Technical	Overarching technical requirements related to: ■ hardware ■ software ■ interoperability.	Initiation, Planning (scoping) or sprints	■ The system must produce outputs that are compatible with Microsoft Office 365. ■ The application must operate on the company's Standard Operating Environment, based on Apple OSX. ■ The product must operate on all European electrical sources.
Solution: Functional	Any feature required by the business in the final solution related to: ■ creation of data ■ reading/retrieval of data ■ update/maintenance of data ■ procedural requirements ■ disposal/deletion of data ■ usage of a product or service.	Planning or sprints	■ The payroll system must ensure a full audit trail of all payments is maintained. ■ As an events manager, I want to be able to query all events by artist so I can answer customer enquiries. ■ As a user of a mobile phone, I want to be able to record any voice call so I can comply with legal requirements. ■ As a user of a building, I want to be able to release the front door lock from the inside of my apartment so I do not have to open the front door lock in person.
Solution: Non-functional	Technical specifications related to: ■ performance ■ access ■ security ■ usability ■ capacity ■ backup and recovery ■ achieving and retention ■ maintainability ■ business continuity.	Planning or sprints	■ The payroll system must compile the pay data file (sent to the payroll bureau) in a compatible file type. ■ The door release must occur within three seconds of being activated. ■ The mobile phone network must connect calls within six seconds of the call being initiated. ■ Only the payroll manager can access the pay details of executive managers.

8.5 Creating the work breakdown structure (WBS)

Once the scope of the project has been defined (including the identification of deliverables), the work of the project can be successively subdivided into smaller work elements. The outcome of this hierarchical decomposition process is called the *work breakdown structure* (WBS).

The PMI considers the construction of a WBS so critical to the proceedings that a separate practice standard was written to support the subject area. For information beyond this text, the reader is encouraged to refer to the *Practice Standard for Work Breakdown Structures* (PMI 2019).

Using a WBS helps to provide a project leader with a degree of confidence that all product components (the PBS or BOM) and work elements are integrated together and form a basis for further planning. Basically, the WBS is a visual description of the project, with different levels of detail. It provides a well-developed description of the project and helps the project leader to ensure that just the right scope and nothing more and nothing less is achieved. In practice, the scope document and WBS are developed in parallel—as one often informs the other.

Figure 8.11 shows three styles commonly used in practice. The WBS begins with the *project* as the final deliverable! *Major deliverables* are identified first, and then the *sub-deliverables* needed to accomplish the larger deliverables are defined (if required). The process is repeated until the detail below a deliverable can be accurately estimated, is manageable, and a team/individual can be made responsible for carrying out the work. This level is often referred to as the *work package*. The rule of thumb is that a work package should not exceed 80 hours total effort as they become unmanageable and troublesome to report on and therefore control. If the project leader has to break the work packages down further (for understanding and estimating purposes), then *tasks* below the work package could be defined.

On some occasions, a cost/control account is introduced between the deliverable and work package, to provide an accounting control point.

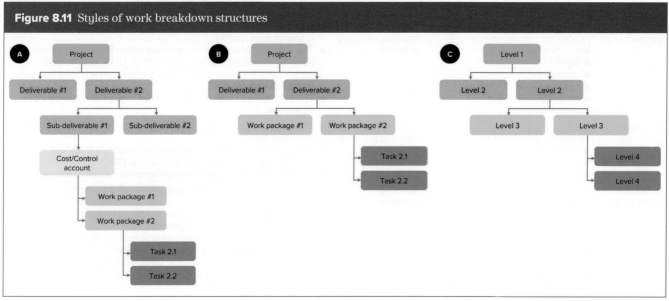

Figure 8.11 Styles of work breakdown structures

The phraseology is less important than the concept of decomposing the work into work packages and tasks in order that the project is planned 100 per cent. The PMI touts that if the work is not in the WBS then it is not in the project! In this text we will be using the WBS as a reference point from which to identify and estimate resources, and their durations and costs, and then subsequently create three key project artefacts: the project schedule, the project budget and the Resource Allocation Matrix (RAM). The WBS is therefore a pivotal artefact.

8.5.1 How WBS helps the project leader

The WBS defines all the elements of the project in a hierarchical framework and establishes their association with the project. Think of the project as a large work package that is successively broken down into smaller work packages: the total project is the summation of all the smaller work packages. This hierarchical structure facilitates the evaluation of cost, time, resources and technical performance at all levels in the organisation over the life of the project. The WBS also provides management with information appropriate to each level.

Each item in the WBS requires resources and time and introduces costs. With this information it is possible to identify the resource requirements and to develop the project budget and the project schedule (Gantt chart). The WBS also serves as a reference point for tracking cost and work performance during the Execution stage.

As the WBS is developed, organisational units and individuals are assigned responsibility for executing work packages; this integrates the work and the organisation. This **organisation breakdown structure (OBS)**, as it is referred to, is discussed later in this chapter.

The WBS provides the opportunity to *roll up* (sum) the budget (the planned costs) of the smaller work packages into larger work elements, so performance can be later measured.

The WBS can also be used to define communication channels and assist in understanding and coordinating many parts of the project. The structure shows which work and organisational units are responsible for what. Problems can be quickly addressed and coordinated because the structure integrates work and responsibility. The WBS assists the project leader to answer the questions: What must be done? How long will it take? How much will it cost? And Who (or what) will do that work?

On reviewing the "Snapshot from Practice: Lesson from history—Sydney Opera House", one can reflect on how this project may have been planned if contemporary scoping and variation management principles had been applied.

Figure 8.12 shows a simplified WBS for the design of a Smartwatch project.

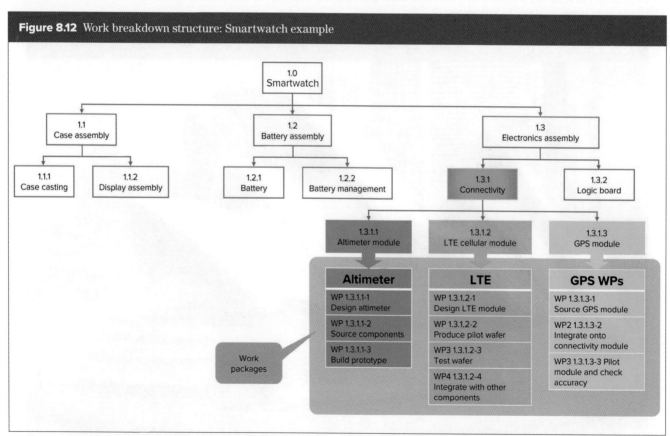

Figure 8.12 Work breakdown structure: Smartwatch example

© 2022 Dr Neil Pearson

8.5.2 **WBS development**

Refer back to Figure 8.12. At the top of the chart (referred to as *Level 1* in PMBOK) is the project end item (i.e. a deliverable product or service). Level 2 shows a partial list of deliverables necessary for developing a Smartwatch. One deliverable is the connectivity (shaded orange), which is made up of three sub-deliverables: altimeter module, LTE cellular module and GPS module. Finally, each of these sub-deliverables requires work packages that will be completed by an assigned team or individual.

Each deliverable will be successively divided in this manner. Note that it is not necessary to divide all elements of the WBS to the same level. Work packages are short-duration pieces of work that have a definite start and end-point, consume resources and represent a cost to the project. A work package lead is responsible for seeing that the package is completed on time, within budget and according to technical specifications (quality). Practice suggests a work package should not exceed 80 hours (or one reporting period). If a work package has a duration exceeding 80 hours, checkpoints or monitoring points should be established within the duration, say, every two to five days. This allows progress and problems to be identified before too much time has passed (and costs have been incurred). Alternatively, the work package should ideally be broken down into smaller work packages. Each work package of the WBS should be as independent of other packages of the project as possible.

SNAPSHOT *from* PRACTICE : **Lesson from history: Sydney Opera House**

The Sydney Opera House is a worldwide iconic piece of architecture known for its unique design (Figure 8.13). It was the result of a New South Wales competition to design the nation's national opera house in 1957. Jørn Utzon was selected as the winner in 1958, and the rest is history. The project cost was initially estimated at AUD7 million, but it came in vastly overbudget at AUD102 million, with a schedule blow-out from four years to 14 years. So, what went wrong and how can we continue to learn from this historic project?

Figure 8.13 Sydney Opera House

Alan L Meakin/Shutterstock.com

Many a post mortem into the root causes has been carried out, with common themes emerging.

There was most certainly evidence reported in the press at the time that the Labour Premier, Joe Cahill, jumped the gun by authorising the go-ahead of the project based on Jørn Utzon's designs and drawings. Little attention was given to agreeing the scope of the project and thoroughly investigating all the client's needs (the client being the New South Wales Government). Even though the design was structured into the key stages (Stage 1, the podium; Stage 2, the outer shells; and Stage 3, the interiors), the NSW government gave the go-ahead before Jørn Utzon had finished the designs—never mind converting the design into engineering drawings from which construction should have started.

In addition to the scope being little more than architectural drawings, major amendments were made by the government during its failed start, such as changes to the number of auditoriums from the two that initially appeared in Jørn Utzon's designs to four.

There were clear stakeholder issues between the NSW Government and Jørn Utzon, when in 1967 he walked off the project, leaving no further design sketches, and thinking he would be asked back. This was compounded when the person who was later to become lead engineer, Ove Arup, and a hastily assembled team were left to fill in the blanks with only a casual arrangement between Utzon and Arup. Utzon was never asked back to the project; although in 2003 he was awarded the Pritzker Prize for architecture, he never returned to Australia and never saw the final product.

With continued challenges and lack of ownership combined with poor estimates, the costs and subsequent schedule blew out massively.

The building was finally opened by Queen Elizabeth II in 1973. The unforeseen final cost blowout was never offset by any future benefits. The Sydney Opera House continues to be one of the world's top draws for tourists and is estimated to bring in tourist revenue in excess of AUD700 million annually—if only that benefit had been defined in the Business Case.

Looking back on historic project failures in our industry and beyond can often bring home the seriousness of why lessons learned are an important aspect to be considered before starting any project. The lessons here are all too clear:

- no Business Case

- lack of sponsorship

- confused decision-making

- few plans in advance, more planning on the go

- poor estimating

- lack of understanding of client requirements

- poor stakeholder management

- the project was run from ongoing changes (variations) rather than a plan!

Sources: Adapted from Martin CGO 2012, "The Sidney [sic] Opera House construction: A case of project management failure", https://www.eoi.es/blogs/cristinagarcia-ochoa/2012/01/14/the-sidney-opera-house-construction-a-case-of-project-management-failure/; Irvine J 2013, "Why Sydney's Opera House was the world's biggest planning disaster", https://amp.couriermail.com.au/news/why-sydneys-opera-house-was-the-worlds-biggest-planning-disaster/news-story/9a596cab579a3b96bba516f425b3f1a6, accessed April 2022.

Note: There is an important difference between a deliverable/sub-deliverable and a work package. Typically, a deliverable/sub-deliverable includes the outcomes of more than one work package (providing a way of grouping work); therefore, the deliverable/sub-deliverable does not have a duration of its own and does not consume resources or cost money directly. The duration of a deliverable/sub-deliverable can be derived from identifying which work package must start first (earliest) and which package will be the last to finish; the difference from start to finish becomes the duration for the sub-deliverable.

Each work package (or tasks) usually has associated information collected, documented and potentially in a form to be communicated to the work package lead and team members responsible for carrying out the work. This is often referred to as the **WBS dictionary** item. The WBS dictionary is a detailed catalogue of each work package and tasks, and contains many items (typically one for each WP!).

Typical items captured against each WBS dictionary item are indicated in Table 8.5.

Table 8.5 WBS dictionary item

WBS dictionary item	Description
Unique identifier	Each work package is uniquely identified
Description	Defines the work to be done (what)
Timings	Identifies the time to complete a work package (how long) and any related milestones
Budget	Identifies a (time-phased) budget to complete a work package (cost)
Resources	Identifies resources needed to complete a work package (how much people, plant and equipment and raw materials)
Work package lead	Identifies a single person responsible for delivering and monitoring the work package (who)
Performance	Identifies monitoring points for measuring progress (control)
Acceptance/quality	Includes specifications so quality can be checked (how well)
Documentation	Includes all required artefacts to execute the package (required information)

© 2022 Dr Neil Pearson

A house build is used as an example for the WBS in Figure 8.14, and Table 8.6 illustrates an example of the contents of the work package or pack or the WBS dictionary item.

Figure 8.14 Work breakdown structure: House build example

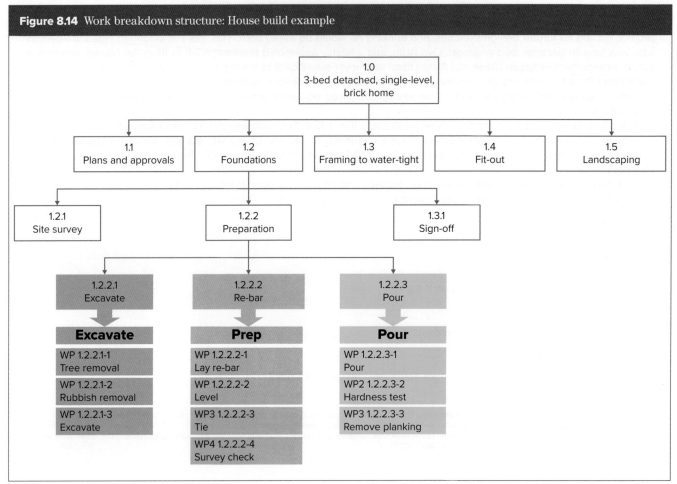

© 2022 Dr Neil Pearson

Table 8.6 WBS dictionary item or pack contents

Work package	WP 1.2.2.1-1
Task description	Felling and removal of all trees, as identified on the site plan by the chartered surveyor. All tree material, including the removal of stumps, is be carried out by the required date
	Trees for removal have been marked with a fluorescent-orange band tied around the base of the tree
Associated	Mark site, Chartered Surveyor
Milestone	Foundations complete
Assigned to	CutAbove Tree Services
	Contact: Ash 0999 912 000
Start/End	Start 10 April
	End 14 April
Resources	CutAbove Tree Services to supply all required equipment
	Project to provide safety supervisor onsite
Budget	As quoted $10,800 (incl. GST)
Contract	Contract to CutAbove Tree Services attached
Quality	Adherence to AS/NZS 4801
Documentation	Refer attached site plan
	Copy of contract
Other	Safety induction to be carried out prior to entry on site

© 2022 Dr Neil Pearson

The level of detail in a work package varies. However, in some industries the pack of information that makes up the work package can be extensive. Inclusions typically found in the pack include technical specifications, plans/drawings/diagrams, quality assurance information, quality control information costs, and contracts. The use of packs and work packages is prevalent in some industries, especially in construction (private and public). Although there is a cost to producing the packs (time in the project), the benefits to the project and those allocated the task is seen to far outweigh this.

By retaining a WBS dictionary of items in an organisation, subsequent projects can re-use WBS items to construct a new WBS based on defined packages of work, thereby saving effort by reusing work done in previous projects. This is especially important where an organisation tends to be a contractor to similar types of projects. The WBS dictionary can also provide a good source of estimating information and, when mined historically, inform current estimating activities. Large government and military projects often leverage WBS dictionaries.

 WBS and Work Package Dictionary

Creating a WBS from scratch can be a daunting task. Project leaders can take advantage of relevant examples from previous projects to begin the process and leverage WBS dictionaries if they exist. However, WBSs are the product of group effort. If the project is small, the entire project team may be involved in breaking the project down into its components (e.g. in an idea-shower workshop). For large, complex projects, the people responsible for the major deliverables are likely to meet to establish the first two or three levels of the WBS. In turn, further detail would be delegated to people responsible for specific work. Collectively, this information would be gathered and integrated into a complete WBS. The final version would be reviewed by the core project team for accuracy, completeness and detail. Relevant stakeholders (most notably customers and sponsors) would be consulted to confirm agreement and to carry out revisions when appropriate, as well as subject matter experts (SMEs) from a detailed subject perspective.

Project teams developing their first WBS frequently forget that the structure should be end-item, output-oriented. First attempts often result in a WBS that follows the organisational structure—design, marketing, production finance. If a WBS follows the organisational structure, the focus will be on the organisation's function and processes rather than on the project's output or deliverables. In addition, a WBS with a process focus will become an accounting tool that records costs by function rather than a tool for output management. Every effort should be made to develop a WBS that is output-oriented in order to concentrate on agreed deliverables.

8.5.3 Practice techniques used to develop the WBS

Development of the WBS can be undertaken as a team activity and a method commonly used for this involves sticky notes. First, empty a room, leaving only a table that has sticky notes on it. Next, invite various groups or individuals to come into the room to idea-shower development of the WBS. Differently coloured sticky notes can be used to represent different levels of the WBS, the different groups responsible for doing the work, or to indicate which groups/individuals added the items to the WBS. Once the WBS has been captured to the required level of detail, it should be moved into a software package (e.g. Microsoft Visio, OmniGraffle (on Mac)), or into specialist tools such as Matchware (www.matchware.com/en/products/mindview/default.htm) so it can be circulated to a wider group for input and review.

Another technique that can be used is *mind-mapping*. Mind-maps almost duplicate the structure of a WBS, but in a more free-flowing creative format. To create a mind-map, first start with the project's name as the centre node and then build out curved lines (deliverables) one at a time; each new line added is akin to a new level being added on the more formal WBS structure. Whiteboards or mind-mapping tools (orchestrated by a facilitator—normally the project leader) provide ideal platforms for constructing mind-maps. The author (Pearson) has used a number of tools to mind-map projects (e.g. www.ayoa.com and www.thebrain.com).

A structured English list format is also commonly used, which involves an indented list of numbered points being developed. Engineers and logical thinkers tend to prefer this style as it provides them with a format that is familiar to them in their daily roles. There is no single correct way for constructing a solid, comprehensive and well-devised WBS. The key is to understand the preferred working style of the people who are to be involved in development and the end goal to be achieved. Ideally, the project leader should not be the facilitator of the idea-shower session if they are also to be involved in the development of the WBS. In this scenario, consider using an independent facilitator instead. By using sticky notes, whiteboards or software tools, there is always an opportunity to make changes on the fly as individual or groups of sticky notes can be moved around.

8.6 | Integrating the WBS with the organisation

The WBS can be used to link the organisational units responsible for performing the work with the work. In practice, the outcome of this process is the OBS set adjacent to the WBS. Frequently, the traditional organisational structure can be used, or the project organisational structure if the project is completely performed by the project team.

The OBS assigns the lowest organisational unit the responsibility for doing the work packages. Herein lies a major strength of using the WBS and OBS together as they can be integrated. The intersection of deliverables with the organisational unit creates a project control point that integrates work and responsibility. At the intersection point, for example in Figure 8.15(a), the cost account against which to post costs in the project has been indicated in the work package. There are other variations on this intersection point, for example if the OBS is sufficiently detailed, down to job/role level, then the intersection can be used to map work package to the job/role (i.e. this is akin to creating a RAM). Refer to Figure 8.15(b).

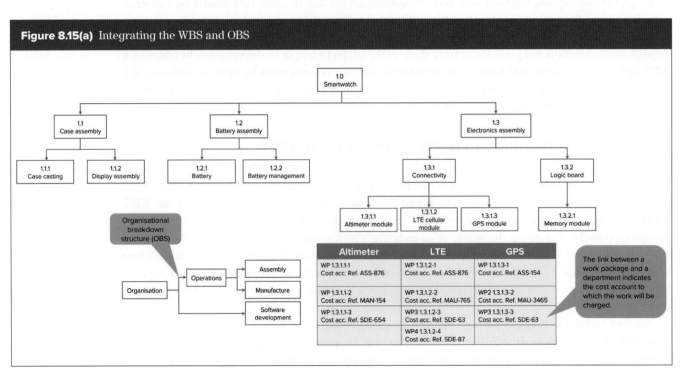

Figure 8.15(a) Integrating the WBS and OBS

Figure 8.15(b) WBS, OBS and resource assignment

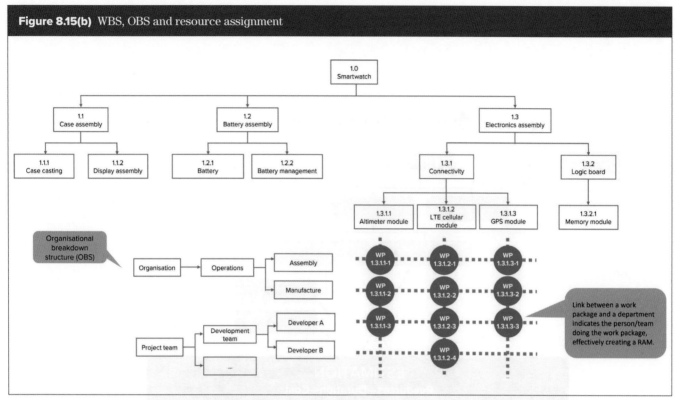

© 2022 Dr Neil Pearson

Note: The OBS is not the same as the project's organisation chart, which outlines the project's report structure and roles. Later, we will use the intersection as a cost account for budgetary control of projects. For example, in Figure 8.15(a) the LTE cellular module element requires completion of work packages whose primary responsibility will include the assembly and manufacture. Control can be checked from two directions—outcomes and responsibility. In the Execution stage of the project, progress can be tracked vertically on deliverables (client's interest) and tracked horizontally by organisational responsibility (management's interest).

8.7 | Estimating the WBS

Once the WBS has been captured, refined and (for the most part) socialised within the project team, the WBS will need to be translated into a format that facilitates general access and ease of maintenance. The WBS provides an ideal structure for estimating (which is the focus of the next chapter, Chapter 9 "Estimating").

Estimating at the Planning stage of the project life cycle is geared towards defining the overall timeframe and budget for the project, to a tolerance that is typically +/− 5–10%. The typical journey at this point in the proceedings is captured in Figure 8.16. An estimate of the resources, durations and costs should be made against each work package, or at the individual task level below the work package. From this estimating information, it is then possible to take the:

■ work package (or task) information as the resources allocated and create the RAM, which assigns resources to work (refer to Chapter 10 "Project resource management")

■ work package (or task) and the duration information and derive a timeline for the project, or the project schedule when relationships between work package (or tasks) is added into the activity (refer to Chapter 11 "Project schedule management")

■ resource, duration and cost information to create the project's budget, adding in cross-project costs not accounted for at the work package (or task) level (refer to Chapter 12 "Project cost management").

The WBS is typically maintained throughout the life of the project. However, the content of the WBS will move into other tools the project leader can leverage to further plan, monitor and control against.

Figure 8.16 WBS forming the basis of detailed planning

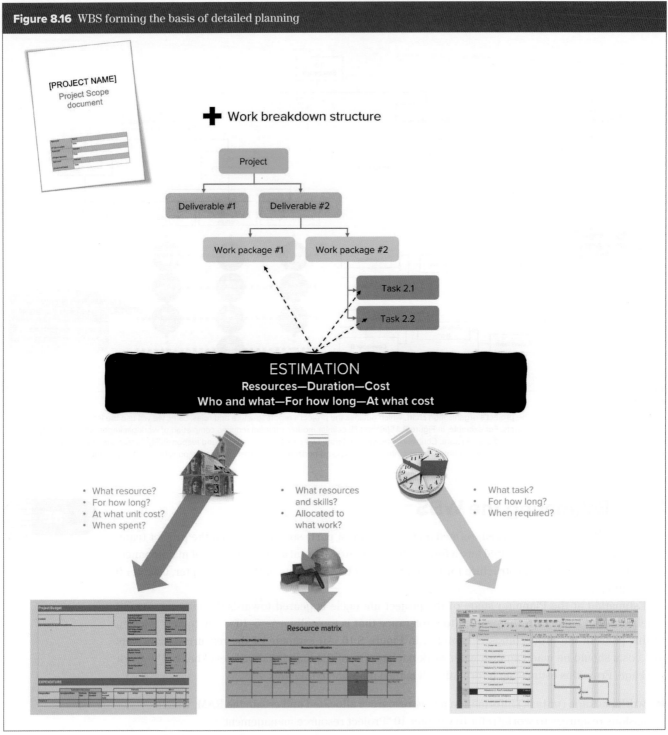

© 2022 Dr Neil Pearson

As illustrated in Figure 8.16, the task and duration information for each work package (or task) is typically captured in a project scheduling software package—Microsoft Project is a popular choice. However, financial information may be maintained within a spreadsheet or within the organisation's Enterprise Resource Planning system, or project account system.

In its visual form, the WBS makes a useful addition to the scope document since it provides readers of the scope document with a whole-of-project perspective and a breakdown of the elements of the project.

Note: The PMI introduced the *100 per cent rule*, implying that if a work package (and associated tasks) is not captured within the WBS, then it is not part of the project. With changes in thinking (such as a more adaptive approach to project management), this is now open to some debate. This, however, does not stop the project leader including planning packages in the WBS that indicate that further detailed planning is required when the project approaches that deliverable/work package (i.e. the concept of rolling wave planning). A modified Smartwatch WBS indicating planning packages is illustrated in Figure 8.17.

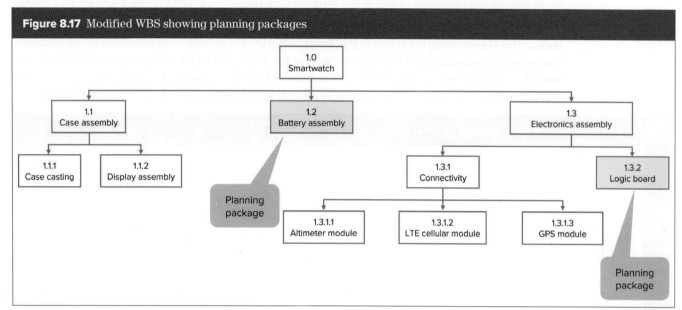

Figure 8.17 Modified WBS showing planning packages

© 2022 Dr Neil Pearson

8.8 : Variation request management

A major aspect of any project is **variation management** (also referred to as *change request management*). Going forward in this text, it will be referred to as *variation management*, as this clearly differentiates it from organisational change management, introduced in Chapter 5 "Organisational change management and cultures".

As outlined in section 8.2, this process is typically documented within the Scope Management Plan.

Even in the best planned projects, not every detail of a project plan will materialise as expected, resulting in variations to the project's scope. Coping with and controlling project variations can be a formidable challenge for some project leaders. Variations come from many sources such as the project's customer, project owner, SMEs, project leader, team members, and from risks that eventuate into issues, among many other sources. Most variations fall into the following three categories:

1. *Scope changes for project design changes or additions:* These can represent significant variations if, for example, the customer requests a new feature or a redesign that will improve the product.

2. *Implementation of contingency plans:* When risk events do occur (and become issues), these can result in changes to baseline costs and schedules.

3. *Improvement changes suggested by project team members.*

Because change is inevitable, the establishment of a well-defined process that captures variations and reviews (analyses) and implements the resulting changes is essential. A project variation management process (VMP) involves recording, analysing and controlling variations from the project baselines of scope baseline, costs baseline and schedule baseline (as a result of gaining approval of the integrated PMP at the end of the Planning stage before proceeding into the Execution stage). In practice, most VMPs are designed to accomplish the following:

1. identify the proposed variation

2. record the proposed variation

3. analyse the impacts of the variation across the knowledge areas

4. review, evaluate and approve or disapprove the variation

5. update project documentation as necessary based on the decision (Step 4), re-baseline scope, time, cost artefacts if required

6. communicate variations to all parties affected (e.g. requestor, project sponsor and project team).

Figure 8.18 illustrates a swimlane process diagram that captures these steps. **Swimlane diagrams** such as this are becoming the common way to articulate project management processes in organisations. The horizontal swimlanes can represent a role (e.g. the project leader), a group (e.g. the Change Control Board), or an ICT system (not used in this swimlane diagram). Common notations used are based on unified modelling language (UML) or business process model and notation (BPMN), as used in this figure.

Figure 8.18 Variation control swimlane process

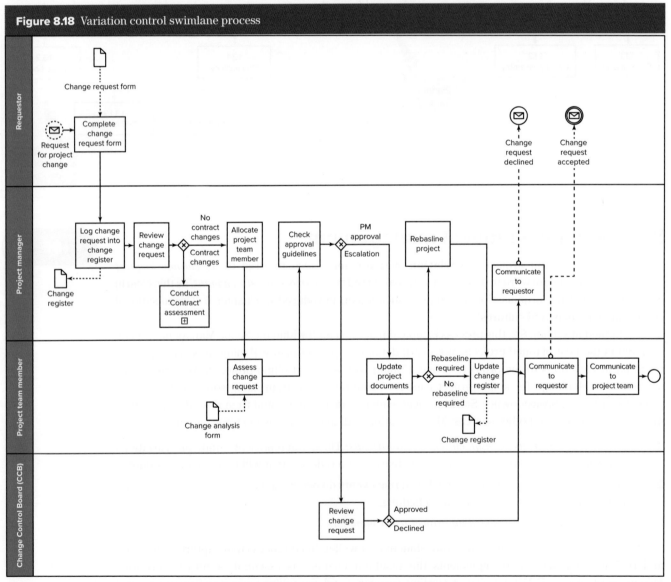

© 2022 Dr Neil Pearson

On small projects, the VMP may simply entail approval being sought from the project sponsor. On larger projects, more elaborate decision-making processes will be established, with different governance levels (approvals) having to be gained for different impact levels of the variation. For example, changes in performance requirements may require multiple sign-offs (including sign-offs by the project sponsor and client), whereas the project leader can usually independently authorise something such as switching suppliers, or a cost overrun of a fixed amount (e.g. $5,000), subject to contingency arrangements. Regardless of the nature of the project, the goal is to establish the process for introducing necessary variations to the project in a timely and effective manner.

Assessing the impact of the variation on the project is particularly important. Often, solutions to immediate problems have adverse consequences on other aspects of a project. For example, if, in overcoming a problem with the exhaust system for a hybrid car, the design engineers add a new element that contributes to the overall prototype's weight, this may cause allowable weight parameters to be exceeded. It is important that people with appropriate expertise assess the implications of the variation. On construction projects, this is often the responsibility of the architecture firm, while software architects perform a similar function with software development endeavours.

Project leaders often use variation request forms and registers to track proposed variations. An example of a simplified variation request is depicted in Figure 8.19. Typically, variation request forms include a description of the change, the impact of it not being approved and (dated) requestor signatures. Keep in mind that variation requests acknowledge and receipt the request, but do not

Figure 8.19 Sample variation request form

Variation request

Project name	
Originator	**Name:**
	Signature:
Date raised	
Change ID	*[To be issued by the project to enable traceability.]*

Background to the variation

Document the background to the events leading up to the variation.

Statement of the variation

The ORIGINATOR provides a clear statement of the variation being requested.

Why is the variation necessary?

Provide a clear description of why the variation is necessary.

What are the consequences if the variation is not approved?

Describe what the consequences are estimated to be if the variation is not approved or included within the current project scope.

indicate that the request has been accepted at this stage. A lesson learned from years of practice in recording variations is to always ensure that the requestor of the variation fully completes the initial variation request form. As a project leader or project team member, it is too easy to incorrectly interpret a variation, say after a busy meeting, or after a discussion at a coffee machine, or when information is passed to you second hand.

1a Variation Request

1b One-page Variation Request

The analysis of the variation is critical as it needs to consider all dimensions of the project (remember the integrated thinking concept introduced in Chapter 6 "Project integration management"); to this end, most projects will have a form where the impact of the variation, and its overall time/cost recommendations, can be captured. Often, these forms, complete with the project's recommendation, are the input into the Change Control Board or project Steering Committee, for final decision.

1c Variation Request Analysis

An abridged version of a variation request register for the Smartwatch project is presented in Figure 8.20. These types of registers are used to monitor where the variation request is within the VMP. It is not uncommon in most projects to have multiple (dozens) of variations on the go at any one time. The register provides a summary and status of all variations, including useful information such as the source, date of the request, project team member assigned, cost estimates and the current status.

Figure 8.20 Variation Request Register

Variation Request Register

Change ID	Description (as documented by the ORIGINATOR in the Change Request)	Originator	Assigned To (person responsible for the Change Analysis)	Status (refer to 'look-up' tables for definitions)	Recommendation	Date Decision Made	Documents Updated incl. Version #	Originator Notified	Follow-up Actions
1	Need to include Haptic feedback module in logic board WBS ID 1.3.2	Research and Project Director	Project Manager	Logged					
2	Power consumption of LTE module over allowed specification.	Intel	Design Engineer - Sarah Smith	In progress					
3	Case casting, to be produced in 3 different colours (gold, grey, black), not the original two (grey, black).	Marketing Director	Design Engineer - Sarah Smith	Approved	Change to manufacturing process to allow tint to be applied.	05/02/2018	Manufacture tint specifications.	Meeting, 05/02/2018 Gold tint specification added to manufacturer's specs.	None.
4	Changeable watch strap movement to be added to case casting design.	Marketing Director	Legal Department	Not Approved	Patent infringement of competitor product.	23/01/2018		eMail, Ref. Change ID4 Strap Movement, filed in project Change Request library.	None.

Logged—Request has been logged and assigned to the appropriate group/individual.
In progress—The assigned group/individual is currently reviewing the request and its impact on the project.
Approved—The request has been approved by the appropriate governing bodies.
Park list—The request has not been approved, but has been placed on the 'park' list for the next release/stage/project.
Not approved—The request has been rejected and will not be implemented for the reasons stated.

1d Variation Request Register

If the VMP is not integrated within the project environment and made the responsibility of all to undertake with any variation, then the project runs the risk of scope creep and eventual erosion of any plans, potentially leading to termination of the project in some cases. Thus, the key to a successful VMP is to carefully document all variations and educate the project team to follow this process at all costs, for all variations, regardless of how insignificant they may first appear!

The benefits derived from a VMP include:

- inconsequential variations are discouraged by the formality of a process
- costs of variations are maintained in the variations request register
- integrity of the scope, WBS and performance measures is maintained
- allocation and use of budget and management reserve funds are tracked
- responsibility for implementation is clarified
- effect of variation is visible to all parties involved
- implementation of variations is monitored
- scope variations will be quickly reflected (if approved) in baseline and performance measures, from which project execution then takes place.

Clearly, variation management is important and requires that an individual or a particular group be responsible for approving variations, keeping the process updated and communicating variations to the project team and to relevant stakeholders. Project control depends heavily on keeping the VMP current. As a bonus, a historical record of variations can be used to satisfy customer enquiries, identify problems in post-project audits, and to feed information into the lessons learned register, for the benefit of future projects.

Summary

Clearly defining your project is the first and most important step in project management. Some organisations even have a sub-gate in planning to approve project scope before the subsequent detailed planning and production of all the project's other artefacts.

This chapter has highlighted the following.

- The absence of a clearly defined project scope document consistently shows up as a major reason for project failures. Closely coupled with this is the absence of a VMP, meaning that after the scope has been documented and agreed, there is little control over scope creep. Projects, therefore, often go beyond the original scope of the project, incur extra costs and overrun scheduled completion dates (sound familiar?).
- Project scope definition and the WBS are the pivotal artefacts affecting every subsequent aspect of planning and therefore execution of the project.
- The scope provides a focus and emphasis on the result of the project. Establishing project priorities allows managers to make appropriate trade-off decisions (recall the discussion on the Constraints Preference Matrix, Figure 8.8).
- The project's scope document is the single source of scope for the project and must be defined with a high degree of accuracy, completeness, buy-in, agreement and with a holistic (overarching) consideration of the project and business environment.
- Articulation of governance and processes for the management of scope (including the VMP) is captured in the Scope Management Plan. This must be communicated and reinforced to the project team.

■ We have underscored the importance of having an established requirements management process and associated tools (documented in the Requirements Management Plan) and the criticality of ensuring that requirements are well formed, applying all the requirements filters.

Review questions

1. What are the main elements of a typical scope document?
2. What questions does a project objective answer? What would be an example of a good project objective?
3. What technique is useful for having a robust discussion with the project sponsor on the rigidity of the project's constraints?
4. What kind of information can be captured against a work package (or task)?
5. What is the 100 per cent rule, and how does the adaptive or rolling wave planning approach to projects affect it?
6. What are the key steps in a variation management process (VMP)?
7. How can a Scope Management Plan assist in communicating process and governance?
8. What is the OBS in the context of ascertaining the impact of work on departments/roles?
9. What are the key categories of requirement types?

Exercises

1. Develop a WBS for a project you are working on. Use the sticky note style of approach.
2. Develop a WBS for an organisation with 12 employees about to undergo an office move to a greenfield site. Be sure to identify the deliverables and the organisational units (people) responsible for the work packages. Develop a corresponding OBS that identifies who is responsible for what, based on Figure 8.15(a) or 8.15(b).
3. Your roommate is about to submit a scope statement for a spring concert sponsored by the entertainment council at the University of Queensland (UQ). UQ has over 32 000 undergraduate students and 11 000 postgraduate students. This will be the first time in several years that UQ has sponsored a spring concert. The entertainment council has budgeted $40,000 for the project. The event is to occur on 5 September. Since your roommate knows you are taking a class on project management, they have asked you to review their scope statement and make suggestions for potential improvements. They consider the concert to be a résumé-building opportunity for them and therefore want to be as professional as possible. Below is the draft of the scope statement they have prepared to date. What suggestions would you make about the draft's contents, and why?

UQ SPRING MUSIC CONCERT

Project objective
To organise and deliver a six-hour music concert

Deliverables
1. Concert security
2. Contact local newspapers and radio stations
3. Separate beer garden
4. Six hours of musical entertainment
5. Design a commemorative concert T-shirt
6. Local sponsors
7. Food venues
8. Event insurance
9. Safe environment

Milestones
1. Secure all permissions and approvals
2. Sign a big-name artist

3. Contact secondary artists

4. Secure vendor contracts

5. Advertising campaign

6. Plan set-up

7. Concert

8. Clean-up

Technical requirements

1. Professional sound stage and system

2. At least five performing acts

3. Restroom facilities

4. Parking

5. Compliance with UQ and Brisbane City/local council requirements/ordinances

Constraints

1. Seating capacity for 8000 students

2. Concert must be over at 12:15 am

Assumptions

1. Performers are responsible for travel arrangements to and from UQ.

2. Performers must provide own liability insurance.

3. Performers and security personnel will be provided with lunch and dinner on the day of the concert.

4. Vendors contribute 25 per cent of sales to concert fund.

5. Below are four mini-case studies from practice. Break into small groups and (a) analyse the case and (b) provide five recommendations to the project sponsor as to: What do you do? What impact do your decisions have on the project's cost, schedule and performance?

Project A

You've just taken over a project from another project leader and have come back from a very uncomfortable meeting with your business sponsor. In the meeting, the sponsor told you how dissatisfied he is with the project's performance to date and that he's getting ready to pull the plug on the project entirely. Deadlines keep slipping, the application isn't complete, and the sponsor feels like he can't get in touch with anyone to give him an update on the project's status and progress.

From conversations with your project team, you learn that requirements still haven't been finalised and the team is waiting for input before being able to proceed on several key parts of the application. Despite that, they've been able to push forward in other areas, and are quite proud of the work they've done. However, they haven't had a chance to show it to the sponsor.

To complicate matters further, your boss has made it clear that this project must be completed on schedule because he needs the resources for another project.

What do you do? What impact do your decisions have on the project's cost, schedule and performance?

Project B

Your project team has finished gathering the requirements and developing the solution design. Your team is broken into two main groups. The first group consists of the project leader, business analysts and management, and is located in Australia. The second group consists of the development and quality assurance teams, and is located in India.

The work WBS was developed based on estimates from the teams in India. The development team has agreed to provide daily updates to you about progress against the WBS to make sure the project's milestones are going to be met. However, by the time the development team gets close to the first milestone, it becomes obvious that it is falling behind, even though its daily updates indicate that it was on track. In addition, the team has adopted a different design approach from the one agreed upon at the beginning of the project.

The lack of meaningful updates from the development team, along with a different design track, has jeopardised the entire project by rendering the whole plan obsolete. Your team is now at risk of not delivering the project.

What do you do? What is the impact to cost, schedule and performance?

Project C

You have just taken over as the program manager of a large program with multiple tracks and a go-live scheduled in three months. At the first meeting with the project sponsors and key stakeholders, you find out that the business requirements are not complete and, in some cases, not started. Furthermore, the project scope is not realistic to be able to meet the upcoming go-live and, overall, the project teams are confused due to a lack of communication and understanding of priorities.

What do you do? What impact do your decisions have on the project's cost, schedule, and performance?

Project D

You've just been assigned to take over a new project from an outgoing project leader. It is a high-visibility project that is using a development methodology that is new to you and to your company. In your transition meetings with the outgoing project leader, she assures you that development is complete and that all you must do is shepherd the project through acceptance testing and release. As a result, you released several project team members, as scheduled.

The acceptance testing does not go as smoothly as planned. The application has more defects than anticipated, and some core functionality cannot be tested. The project team doesn't feel like it is getting the direction it needs to continue moving forward, and furthermore, the business sponsor has asked you when she can expect to test application functionality that you didn't know was in the scope. Your project's deadline is rapidly approaching, and inter-project dependencies make it unlikely that you will be able to push your launch date.

What do you do? What impact do your decisions have on cost, schedule, and performance?

References

British Computer Society 2020, *Business Analysis*, 4th edition, British Computer Society.

Gobeli DH & Larson EW 1990, 'Project management problems', *Engineering Management Journal*, vol. 2, pp. 31–6.

McDonald S 2012, "QLD Health payroll: IT 'train wrecks' preventable", *CIO*, 7 June, https://www.cio.com.au/article/426920/qld_health_payroll_it_train_wrecks_preventable, accessed February 2018.

Project Management Institute (PMI) 2016, *Requirements Management: A Practice Guide*, PMI.

Project Management Institute (PMI) 2017, *A Guide to the Project Management Body of Knowledge*, 6th edition, PMI.

Project Management Institute (PMI) 2019, *Practice Standard for Work Breakdown Structures*, 3rd edition, PMI.

Project Management Institute (PMI) 2021a, *A Guide to the Project Management Body of Knowledge (PMBOK® Guide)*, 7th edition, Newton Square, PA.

Project Management Institute (PMI) 2021b, *The Standard for Project Management (ANSI/PMI 99-001-2021)*, 7th edition, Newton Square, PA.

CHAPTER 9
Estimating

Learning elements

9A Understand the different levels of estimating accuracy.

9B Understand factors that influence estimating in practice.

9C Comprehend and apply different approaches to estimating, including top-down and bottom-up.

9D Be able to apply the numerous estimating techniques as appropriate to resources, durations and costs.

In this chapter

9.1 Introduction

9.2 Factors influencing the quality of estimates

9.3 What is being estimated?

9.4 Estimating guidelines for resources, duration (time) and costs

9.5 Top-down versus bottom-up estimating

9.6 Methods for estimating project resources, durations (time) and costs

9.7 Additional estimating considerations

Summary

9.1 | Introduction

Estimating is the science of placing a quantity of resources, for a required duration, with known costs against a work package or the tasks of a work package, depending on the detail of the work breakdown structure (WBS). The level of effort the project leader will put into estimating is often influenced by the stage of the predictive life cycle and the governance of the organisation. Figure 9.1 indicates the key estimating activities and suggested governance accuracy for the predictive life cycle.

Figure 9.1 Key estimating activities across the predictive life cycle

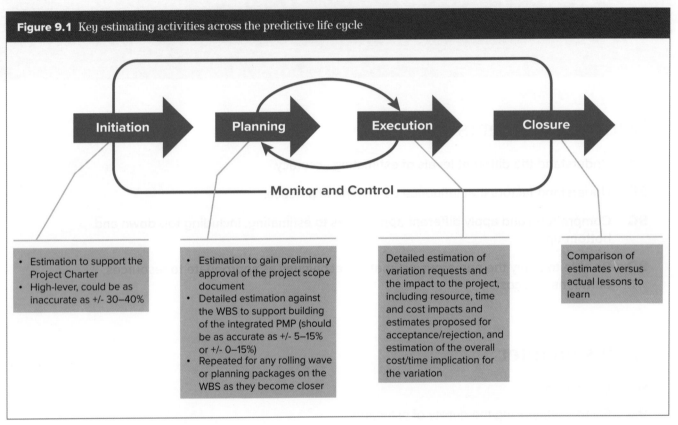

© 2022 Dr Neil Pearson

As can be seen in Table 9.1, the techniques and tools of estimating have commonalities across the estimation of durations (time), costs and resources (human and other). So, rather than discussing the topic of estimating three times in each respective chapter, we have instead pooled the estimating techniques and discussion into this chapter to make an easily accessible combined estimating resource.

Where there is an urgent need to start work on a project, a project leader may be tempted to minimise or avoid the effort needed to follow through on estimating resources, durations (time) and costs. This is a huge (and often costly) mistake to make. There are important reasons why it is necessary to invest the effort and time needed to complete estimating in the project (appropriate to the stage of the life cycle it is in) and manage the expectations of your organisation and the project stakeholders.

Estimates of resources, durations and costs are needed to:

- support fact-based decisions with key project stakeholders
- determine whether the project is worth doing
- determine how long the project should take
- schedule the work (work packages and/or tasks) of the project
- determine resources required (human and other)
- develop time-phased budgets based on all-inclusive estimated costs

- assist in establishing the scope baseline, the cost baseline and the schedule baseline
- enable a determination of how well the project is progressing (from the baselines) in subsequent project stages
- provide accurate estimates in relation to any variation request so its impact to the project (typically during the Execution stage) can be determined.

Table 9.1 Estimating resources, duration, cost: references to PMI and text chapters

Knowledge area	Description	PMBOK 6th edition	Tools and techniques	Relates to chapter in this text
Project resource management	This includes the processes to estimate all the actual resources required by the project, including details of quantities, how they are to be sourced and any associated resources required to enable these key resources.	p. 307	Expert judgement Bottom-up estimating Analogous estimating Parametric estimating Data analysis Project management information system Meetings	Chapter 10 "Project resource management"
Project schedule management	This includes the processes to estimate time units for any identified resources required by the project.	p. 173	Expert judgement Analogous estimating Parametric estimating Three-point estimating Bottom-up estimating Data analysis Decision-making Meetings	Chapter 11 "Project schedule management"
Project cost management	This includes the processes to estimate costs for, and associated with, any identified resources required by the project.	p. 231	Expert judgement Analogous estimating Parametric estimating Bottom-up estimating Three-point estimating Data analysis Alternatives analysis Reserve analysis Cost of quality Project management information system Decision-making (voting)	Chapter 12 "Project cost management"

Estimating is the process of approximating the resources required and the time and cost of completing the project's deliverables. Estimating processes are frequently classified as **top-down** and **bottom-up** (further explained in Figure 9.4). The time available and project stage will often influence whether top-down (high-level) or bottom-up (detailed) estimates are sought. Top-down estimates are usually applied by project leaders when time is short, or when in the Initiating stage of the project. Project leaders will often derive estimates from analogy, group consensus or mathematical relationships. The project team members, however, typically perform bottom-up estimates (when time has been allowed for the extra detail to be appropriately researched). Their estimates are based on estimates of each element found in the WBS, usually at the lowest level (work package or task). Bottom-up estimating is normally carried out in the Planning stage of the project to ensure that estimates of the project are as accurate as possible and within defined tolerances.

All project stakeholders desire accurate time, cost and resource estimates, but they generally also understand the inherent uncertainty in all projects and the effort that estimating often consumes. Inaccurate estimates, however, lead to false expectations and customer dissatisfaction. Accuracy may be improved with greater effort, but of course estimating costs time and therefore money! It is usually worth the time and effort involved, because of the obvious benefits that can be gained (realistic expectations and customer satisfaction being but two). In essence, project estimating becomes a trade-off for the following reasons.

- Estimates serve as a baseline for comparing actual costs, times (durations) and resources (used) throughout the life cycle of the project.

- Project status reports depend on reliable estimates as their major input for measuring variances so that corrective action(s) can be taken as needed.
- Estimates become the planned baseline at the start of the project's Execution stage.
- Ideally, the project leader, and in most cases the customer, would prefer to have a database of detailed time (duration), cost and resource estimates for every work package in the project—regrettably, such detailed estimating is not always possible or practical.
- Project estimating is a complex process; estimates of time, costs and resources together allow the project leader to develop a time-phased budget and a resource-loaded project schedule, which are imperative for project control.

Before we delve fully into estimating, let's explore some of the more holistic factors that influence it.

9.2 : **Factors influencing the quality of estimates**

A typical statement in the field of project management revolves around the desire to have a 95 per cent probability of meeting time and cost estimates. Past experience is a good starting point from which to develop time, cost and resource estimates. However, estimates based on past experience almost always need to be refined by other considerations to reach the 95 per cent probability level. Factors related to the uniqueness of the project will have a strong influence on the accuracy of estimates. Project, people and external factors will all need to be carefully considered to improve the quality of estimates.

9.2.1 **Planning horizon**

The quality of the estimate will depend on the planning horizon—estimates of current events will be closer to 100 per cent accurate, but this accuracy will be reduced the more distant (further into the future) the events are. The accuracy of time, cost and resource estimates should improve as we move from the Initiating stage to the point where individual work packages and tasks are defined within the Planning stage.

The **estimating trumpet** produced by R. Max Wideman (Figure 9.2) provides an industry standard for expectations that prevail across the project industry and can therefore be used when setting expectations with executive management, sponsors, steering committees and customers. This, after all, is the principle of **rolling-wave planning**.

Rolling-wave planning is the technique of only planning in detail the work that is to be undertaken in the near term. As the project leader moves forward in the project, work that was possibly indicated as a planning package on the WBS will be expanded and planned in detail when the time has arrived to do so. There may be many reasons why a work package has not been developed into a detailed plan but left for expansion in the future; for example, the currently unknown outcomes of preceding work packages may need to be known to carry out the planning, or it is not a good use of resources to plan a future work package in detail now, when nearer-term work packages require attention. This is also a common occurrence in adaptive approaches.

9.2.2 **Project duration**

Long projects typically experience the most problems when estimates have been prepared months (and sometimes years) in advance. If estimates do not include a stated factor for potential increases in costs, durations or resources, this can accordingly affect accuracy. For example:

- Some projects have failed to consider that changes to workplace health and safety legislation may occur—this has consequently extended the durations of some activities and has led to new activities being introduced into the overall project.

Figure 9.2 The estimating trumpet

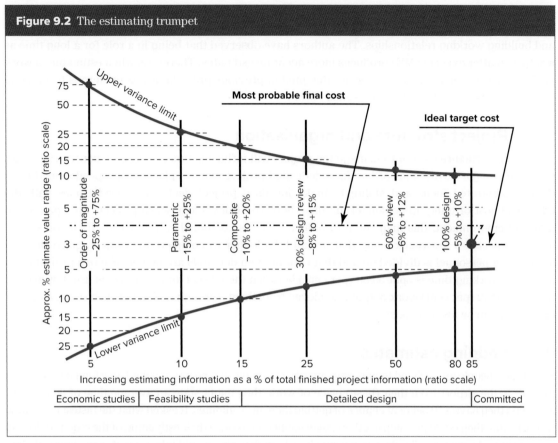

- The time required to implement a new technology project often has a propensity to expand in an increasing, non-linear fashion, as unrealistic estimates of work were committed to.

- Sometimes, poorly written scope specifications for new technology required in a project also result in errors in estimating durations as the technology is essentially cutting-edge or green field and patterns for estimating are often not available or reported on in industry.

Note: There are occasions when estimated costs reduce, for example (as one of the authors has experienced) where technology has replaced humans and therefore the cost has been lower than original estimates.

Given that (generally) the level of uncertainty around estimating increases in long-duration projects, careful consideration needs to be paid to how these types of projects should be approached. Generally, the simple three-month rule is applied to estimates—any estimate older than three months needs to be re-estimated or re-confirmed with the supplier. Indeed, most reputable suppliers state how long their estimate is valid for.

9.2.3 **People**

A people factor can also be responsible for errors being introduced into duration (time), cost and resource estimates. For example, the accuracy of estimates will depend on the skills of the people making them. A close match of people skills to the work package being estimated will undoubtedly beneficially influence both productivity and learning time taken. Similarly, whether members of the project team have worked together before on similar projects is likely to influence the time it takes to coalesce members into an effective team. Sometimes, factors such as staff turnover can impact the process of estimates. It should be noted that adding more people to a project increases time spent communicating. Typically, people have only five to six productive hours available for each working day; the other hours are taken up with indirect work such as meetings, paperwork, answering email and building working relationships. The authors have observed that being in a role for a long time as a subject matter expert (SME) produces more accurate estimates. Therefore, when estimating a work package that is complex, has not been attempted in previous projects or has numerous technology considerations, pick or pay for a seasoned SME.

9.2.4 **Project structure and organisation**

The project structure chosen to manage the project will influence time, cost and resource estimates. One of the major advantages of having a dedicated project team in place is the speed gained from their concentrated focus and ability to make localised project decisions. Speed comes with the additional cost of tying up personnel full time, however. Conversely, when projects are operated in a matrix environment, this may serve to reduce costs as personnel can be more efficiently shared across projects—a drawback being that it may take longer to complete the project, given that the attention of personnel is divided up and that coordination demands are higher. Where a project team member's working time is split 50/50 (per cent) between the project and business as usual, it may be that only 40/40 (per cent) work output is achieved from them (through no fault of their own), as 20 per cent will likely be lost in task switching.

9.2.5 **Padding estimates**

Sometimes, people are inclined to **pad** estimates. For example, if a person is asked how long it takes them to drive to the airport from their (base) place of work, they might state an average time of 30 minutes, assuming they have a 50 per cent chance of getting there in 30 minutes. If asked what the fastest timeframe would be that they could possibly get there, they might then reduce their estimation of the required driving time down to 20 minutes. Finally, when asked how long the drive would take them if they absolutely had to be there to meet with your customer, it is likely that they would increase their estimate to say, around 50 minutes, to ensure they would not be late. This similarly occurs in work situations when the project leader is asked for time, cost and resource estimates—project leaders may be inclined to add a little padding to increase the probability of accuracy and to reduce the probability (risk) of inaccuracy (i.e. being late). If everyone at all levels of the project were to add a little padding to reduce such risk, the project's duration (time), cost and resource (commitment) would be seriously overstated. This phenomenon often causes some managers or customers to call for a 10–15 per cent cut in time and/or cost estimates for the project, but of course, the next time this game is played, the person estimating cost and/or time is highly likely to hike (pad) their estimate to 20 per cent or more. Clearly, such games defeat the chance of being able to achieve realistic estimates and yet realistic estimates are what are needed to be competitive.

As a professional in the discipline, it is the project leader's responsibility to ensure that clear governance is established around the use of padding. Some project leaders establish a clear policy of *no padding*, stating that an appropriate contingency will be added to the project. Contingency is typically held by the sponsor or the project management office (PMO) and to gain access to funds sitting in the contingency account, the project leader has to make use of the variation management process (outlined in Chapter 8 "Defining the scope of a project").

9.2.6 **Organisational culture**

Organisational culture can significantly influence project estimates. In some organisations, estimate padding is tolerated (and even privately encouraged in some cases). Other organisations place a premium on accuracy, and strongly discourage estimating gamesmanship.

Organisations vary in terms of the importance they attach to estimates. The prevailing belief in some organisations is that detailed estimating takes too much time and is not worth the effort, or that it's impossible to predict the future and therefore why bother estimating? Other organisations subscribe to the belief that accurate estimates are the bedrock of effective project management. As

can be understood therefore, organisational culture shapes every dimension of project management and estimating is not immune to this influence.

9.3 : **What is being estimated?**

Before looking at some of the tools and techniques used in estimating, we must first consider what is being estimated against each of the work packages (and tasks). When a project leader estimates a work package, they need to consider what resources are required, how long these resources are required for (the time/duration) and the cost of these resources, plus any additional items required to successfully complete the work package. This order is important as the information builds from *resources to durations to costs*.

Note: There are obvious exceptions to this rule; for example, the project leader may decide to buy the work package into the project, in which case the focus will on be duration and cost—the resources required in the main are the concern of the supplier doing the work package.

9.3.1 **Resources**

Resource is the generic term used in project management for any item that is consumed by the project. The range of potential resources needed for a project can vary considerably and are of course impossible to accurately document in full. Having said this, Table 9.2 provides a snapshot of some of the more commonplace resource types frequently encountered.

Table 9.2 Typical types of resources used by projects

Resource category	Examples
Human resources	Internal employees (full or part time), contractors, temps, consultants, secondments, volunteers, freelancers
Tools	Testing equipment, compressors, drills, desktop computers, telephones, tablet devices, access to information (libraries), internet, software licences, laptops, test equipment, pens, paper
Plant	Office facilities, warehouse (storage) space, production lines, operational shop-floor environments
Equipment	Utes, cars, hoists, scissor lifts, trucks, desks, filing cabinets, printers, network equipment, servers, telephone systems (PABX)
Raw materials	Concrete, fill, steel, roofing tiles, fencing panels, circuit boards, plastic pellets (nurdles), lithium, copper, wood, cables
Capital	Funding sources, cash flow into the project, loans, equity, venture capital
Services	Consultancy, maintenance, facilities, data centre services, cleaning, catering, security
Other	Paper, printers, books, insurance, training, consumables, subscriptions, energy consumption

© 2022 Dr Neil Pearson

The range of resource types will be refined as the project leader builds out the work packages and starts to estimate the resources required to complete each work package. The project resource/skills matrix is often used to capture details of the human resources required, allowing for further analysis of this dimension (refer to Chapter 10 "Project resource management"). The cost information will have implications for the project budget (refer to Chapter 12 "Project cost management") and time information for the project schedule (refer to Chapter 11 "Project schedule management"). This illustrates the integrative nature of project management and the complexity involved in juggling the many dimensions of a project.

9.3.2 **Time**

Once resources have been identified against items within each work package, the duration that each of these will be required for needs to be captured (estimated). For some kinds of resources this is a relatively straightforward task; for example, if a specialist contractor is required for 10 workdays of effort or a cement pump is required for two weeks on site. Other resource costs (such as those relating to human resource costs or costs associated with equipment that is needed in an ad hoc way over an extended period) will need somewhat more of a holistic consideration.

A project leader must ask themselves whether it is most cost efficient to deploy the resource to only the required tasks it has been identified against or whether it is more efficient to keep the resource for a longer duration, or even for an entire phase of the whole project. Take, for example, plant and equipment costs: there will be costs associated with bringing the item on site, set-up time, tear-down time and transport costs. Does having to carry out this sequence multiple times on a project exceed the cost of renting for the whole stage? The same applies to human resources: if an electrical tester is required for several activities towards the end of the project, does the project leader pay a higher day rate and take the risk of whether this resource will be available after it has been released, or would it be more efficient for the project to place the resource on a short-term contract? The project leader will only be able to make such efficiency decisions once identification of the requirement of that resources has taken place across all the work packages that require the use of it. Where possible, for like groups of resources normalise the units of time used, whether this be in hours, part days, days, weeks, etc. as this will make scheduling of these resources an easier task.

9.3.3 Costs

Detailed cost estimates are made against the resources identified for each work package and/or task on the WBS, along with any other overarching project costs and miscellaneous costs identified. These costs could fall broadly into the categories of fixed direct costs, fixed indirect costs, variable direct costs and variable indirect costs. The total project cost estimate can be broken down in this fashion to focus control and improve decision-making (i.e. it is clearer to see where costs are being allocated to at a high level).

Often organisations will have their own structure around how the project should account for costs incurred (e.g. a chart of accounts or set of project accounting codes). The project leader should seek advice from the organisation's finance department (and/or PMO) about how to allocate and record costs within their project environment.

Typically, what is being estimated from a cost perspective is based on whether the deliverable or work package is to be made in the project (all its component pieces, e.g. materials, have to be bought in and resources have to assemble and make the item), or whether the deliverable or work package is be outsourced in some form—in which case the cost could be a single large cost that includes all the materials and work, perhaps provided as a quote or response to a tender to the project leader.

Table 9.3 shows how costs are estimated against a work package.

Table 9.3 Example: Estimating a work package

Work package	WP3.2 Develop Guardian application eForm
Resources/effort	2 × developers, 10 days 1 × tester, 2 days 1 × Business Analyst, 3 days
Costs	Developer $850/day Tester $1,100/day Business analyst (BA) $1,000/day
Calculations	2 × developers × 10 days = 20 days' effort 20 days × $850 = $17,000 1 × tester × 2 days = 2 days' effort 2 days × $1,100 = $2,200 1 × BA × 3 days = 3 days' effort 3 days × $1,000 = $3,000 Hire of conference room to host focus group = $400 Lunch and drinks for invited focus group participants = $150
Total costs	$17,000 + $2,200 + $3,000 + $400 + $150 = **$22,750**

© 2022 Dr Neil Pearson

Let's next review the techniques for estimating the resources (and quantities), for how long (duration/effort) and at what cost.

9.4 Estimating guidelines for resources, duration (time) and costs

The process of estimating must be clearly understood to ensure all aspects have been considered and that crucial elements are not overlooked. A commonly asked question about estimating is simply: I'm in the Planning stage, where do I start? The simple answer is: With resources at the work package level or if developed into tasks at the task level.

Figure 9.3 illustrates one of the author's (Pearson's) workflow when estimating the work package and task levels.

Managers recognise time, cost and resource estimates must be accurate to gain an understanding of (in the Initiation stage), be able to refine (in the Planning stage) and track (in the Execution stage) the performance of the project. There is substantial evidence to suggest that poor estimates are a major factor in many projects that have failed. Therefore, every effort should be made to see that initial estimates are as accurate as possible. Making a choice to not produce estimates leaves a great deal to luck, and this scenario would not be acceptable to most professional project leaders and most modern organisations.

Even though a specific project will not have been carried out before due to its uniqueness in some way, a project leader can follow eight guidelines to develop useful work package (or task) estimates:

1. *Responsibility:* At the work package level, estimates should be made by the person(s) most familiar with the task. Draw on their subject matter expertise (the reason these stakeholders are termed *subject matter experts* or SMEs). Except for super-technical tasks, those who are responsible for getting the job done on schedule and within budget are usually first-line supervisors or technicians who are experienced and familiar with the type of work involved. These people generally will not have a preconceived duration for a deliverable in mind. They will instead give an estimate based on their experience and best judgement. A secondary benefit of using those who are responsible for getting the job done is the potential buy-in from them that is gained when they see that the estimate materialises when they implement the work package (or task). If those involved are not consulted, it will be difficult to hold them responsible for a failure to achieve the estimated duration—if they are subsequently allocated the work package or task to deliver. Finally, drawing on the expertise of team members who will be responsible helps to build communication channels early.

2. *Use several people to estimate:* It is well known that a resource, duration or cost estimate usually has a better chance of being realistic when several people with relevant experience and/or knowledge of the task are consulted. It is, of course, true that people will each bring different biases to the table, based on their unique work and life experiences, but a discussion of individual differences in their estimates can lead to a consensus (and tends to eliminate extreme estimate errors)—recall the Planning Poker game introduced in Chapter 3 "Agile (Scrum) project management".

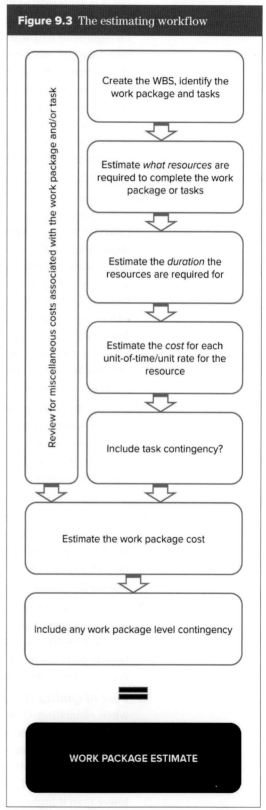

Figure 9.3 The estimating workflow

Review for miscellaneous costs associated with the work package and/or task

Create the WBS, identify the work package and tasks

Estimate *what resources* are required to complete the work package or tasks

Estimate the *duration* the resources are required for

Estimate the *cost* for each unit-of-time/unit rate for the resource

Include task contingency?

Estimate the work package cost

Include any work package level contingency

WORK PACKAGE ESTIMATE

© 2022 Dr Neil Pearson

3. *Normal conditions:* When task time, cost and resource estimates are determined, they will have been based on certain assumptions. Estimates should be based on normal conditions, efficient methods and a normal level of resources. Normal conditions are sometimes difficult to discern, but it is necessary to have a consensus in the organisation as to what *normal conditions* means in the project. If the normal workday is eight hours, then the time estimate should be based on an eight-hour day; if the normal workday is two shifts, then the time estimate should be based on a two-shift workday. A time estimate should reflect efficient normal methods of use for the resources that are to be available. The time estimate should represent the normal level of resources, people or equipment. For example, if three programmers are available for coding, or two road graders are available for road construction, the time and cost estimates should be based on these normal levels of resources (unless it is anticipated the project will change what is currently viewed as normal). Possible conflicts in the demand for resources on parallel or concurrent activities should not be considered at this stage. The need for adding resources will be examined when scheduling is discussed in Chapter 11 "Project schedule management".

4. *Time units:* The specific time units to be used should be selected early in the Initiating stage of the project. All task time estimates need to use consistent time units. Estimates of time must consider whether normal time is represented by calendar days, workdays, work weeks, person days, single shift, hours, and so on. In practice, *workdays* is the dominant choice for expressing task duration. However, in projects such as a heart transplant operation, minute increments would probably be more appropriate to use as a time unit. An example of a project that is known to have used minutes as the time unit involved the movement of patients from an old hospital to a new purpose-built hospital across town. Since the project encompassed moving patients for whom a move could be life-endangering, minutes were used to ensure patient safety and emergency life-support systems were on standby in case these were needed. The point is network analysis requires a standard unit of time. When software programs allow more than one option, some notation should be made of any variance from this standard unit.

5. *Independence:* Estimators should treat each work package as being independent of other work packages in the WBS. First-line managers usually consider tasks independently; this is good. Top managers are prone to aggregating many tasks into a one-time estimate and then they deductively make the individual task time estimates add to the total. Each task time estimate should be considered independently of other activities, and later in the planning process (at scheduling) efficiencies should be sought.

6. *Contingencies:* The concept of contingency is further discussed in Chapter 12 "Project cost management". All those involved in estimating should be aware of the ground rules around when and how contingency is to be considered. Some estimators pad in their heads, some include no padding and others add a declared pad amount—this can become confusing and lead to inaccurate (confused) estimates.

7. *Carrying out a risk assessment of the estimate helps to avoid surprises:* It is obvious that some work packages/tasks will carry more time and cost risks than others. For example, introduction of a new technology usually carries more time and cost risks than a proven technology that has been implemented hundreds of times. Simply identifying the degree of risk lets stakeholders consider alternative methods and alter process decisions.

8. **Cost of quality (CoQ):** Quality affects many areas of a project and needs to be considered when estimating. Quality will affect the choice of equipment used, the people used and the quality of raw materials, and ultimately will affect what and who is used in the project. Higher-quality materials and resources (in general) will affect who and what services are considered in estimating. Usually there is a higher cost to the project when higher-quality (more expensive resources) are used. For example, an estimate provided by lower-cost providers will be lower than if higher-end (higher-quality) providers are used—but there again, the quality

expectations from the lower-cost provider would also be lower! Chapter 13 "Project quality management" provides a more extensive discussion on quality and how it affects many aspects of a project.

9.5 | Top-down versus bottom-up estimating

Since the process of estimating costs money, deciding how much time and detail to devote to the process can be difficult. When considering estimating, you (as a project leader) may be faced with statements such as:

- "Rough order of magnitude is good enough. Spending time on detailed estimating wastes money!"
- "Time is everything; our survival depends on getting there first! Time and cost accuracy is not an issue."
- "The project is internal; we don't need to worry about cost."
- "The project is so small; we don't need to bother with estimates. Just do it!"
- "We were burned once; I want a detailed estimate of every task by the people responsible."

However, there are sound reasons for using top-down or bottom-up estimates, and Table 9.4 depicts conditions that suggest when one approach might be preferred over another.

Table 9.4 Conditions that may influence the choice of top-down or bottom-up estimating

Condition	Top-down estimates	Bottom-up estimates
Strategic decision-making	X	
Cost and time important		X
High uncertainty (risk)	X	
Internal, small project	X	
Fixed-price contract		X
Customer wants details		X
Unstable scope	X	
Public money being spent		X
Public–private projects		X

© 2022 Dr Neil Pearson

Refer to Figure 9.4. Top-down estimates are usually derived from someone who uses their subject matter experience and/or personal sources of information to determine the project's duration, typical resources needed and, therefore, total cost. These estimates are sometimes carried out at a whole-of-project level, or more typically at the first few levels of the WBS. These estimates are often made by managers who have very little knowledge of the processes of project management. For example, in a speech, the mayor of a major city exclaimed that a new law building would be constructed at a cost of AUD23 million and would be ready for occupancy in two years. Although the mayor probably asked for an estimate from someone, it is not clear who this came from—there is every chance (but you hope not) that it came from a lunch-time meeting with a local contractor who wrote an estimate (or guesstimate) on a paper napkin! This is, of course, an out-there example, but in a relative sense, this type of scenario is often played out in reality, raising questions such as: Do these estimates represent low-cost, efficient methods? Do the top-down estimates of project time, cost and resources become a self-fulfilling prophecy, in terms of setting time, cost and resource parameters?

If possible and practical, the project leader will want to push the estimating process down to the work package (or task) level for bottom-up estimates, yet establish efficient methods for doing this. Good sense suggests that project estimates should come from the people who are most knowledgeable

Figure 9.4 Top-down versus bottom-up estimating

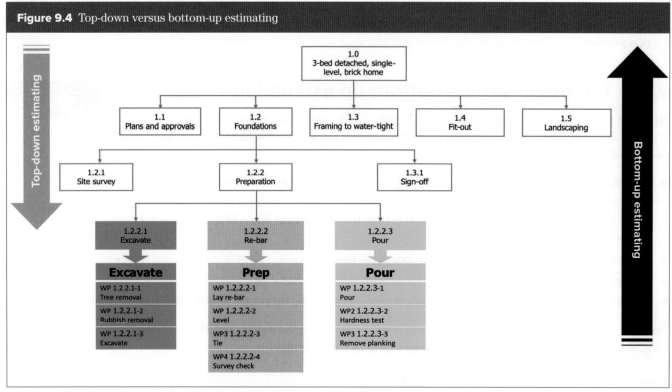

© 2022 Dr Neil Pearson

about the estimate needed. Using several people who have relevant experience with the task can also help to improve time, cost and resources estimates.

A bottom-up approach at the work package level can serve as a check on cost elements in the WBS by rolling up the tasks associated with a work package and work packages into deliverables. Similarly, resource requirements can be checked. Later, the time, resource and cost estimates from the work packages can be consolidated into the project schedule, resource matrix and the project budget—all of which are used to control the project during the Execution stage.

SNAPSHOT *from* PRACTICE   Macmahon—Hope Downs rail project

Macmahon Holdings, a Perth-based mining services and construction company, announced that its CEO of 12 years was stepping down and slashed its profit forecast for the year (2012–13). But why?

The company had serious problems with its Hope Downs 4 rail earthworks project for Rio Tinto, including delays and increased costs in order to meet deadlines.

A management review identified further issues. Different parts of the project were then rescheduled.

Where the failure in estimating occurred was not made clear, but the example clearly exemplifies the costs of not attending to estimating correctly. Where do you think the process fell down?

Source: Adapted from Wilson-Chapman A 2012, "Macmahon CEO gone, shares halved", News Limited, https://www.news.com.au/finance/business/macmahon-shares-plummet-on-downgrade/news-story/193125a7a42f07011e6ce60b892ba388, accessed October 2012.

The assumption is that any movement away from the low-cost, efficient method will increase costs (e.g. overtime). The preferred approach in defining the project is to make rough top-down estimates, develop the WBS/organisation breakdown schedule, make bottom-up estimates, develop schedules and budgets, and reconcile differences between top-down and bottom-up estimates. Hopefully, these steps will be done before final negotiation with either an internal or external customer.

In conclusion, the ideal approach is for the project leader to allow enough time for both the top-down and bottom-up estimates to be worked out, so an integrated Project Management Plan (based on reliable estimates) can be offered to the customer. In this way, false expectations are minimised for all stakeholders and negotiation is reduced. (Review "Snapshot from Practice: Macmahon—Hope Downs rail project".)

9.5.1 Phase estimating and rolling-wave planning

Some projects, by their very nature, cannot be rigorously defined because of the uncertainty of the design of the final product. These projects are often found in aerospace research and development projects, Information and Communications Technology (ICT) projects, new technology projects, construction projects and research projects, where design is incomplete, and the previous phase informs the next phase of the project. In these projects, **phase estimating** is frequently used.

Phase estimating is used when an unusual amount of uncertainty surrounds a project, and it is impractical to estimate times and costs for the entire project. Phase estimating uses a two-estimate system over the life of the project. A detailed estimate is developed for the immediate phase and a macro (high-level) estimate is made for the remaining phases of the project. Figure 9.5 depicts the phases of a project and the progression of estimates over its life (the arrows represent the change in levels of detail in estimating made). As an example, when the project need (Business Case) is determined, a macro estimate of the project cost, duration and resources is made, so analysis and decisions can be made. Simultaneously, a detailed estimate is made for deriving specifications (Initiating) and a macro estimate for the remainder of the project. As the project progresses and specifications are solidified, a detailed estimate for design (Planning) is made and a macro (high-level) estimate for the remainder of the project is calculated. Clearly, as the project progresses through its life cycle and more information is available, the reliability of the estimates should be improving.

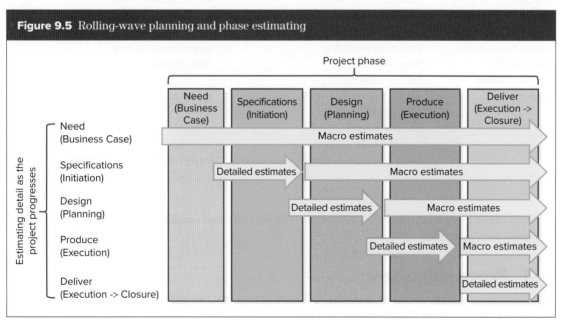

Figure 9.5 Rolling-wave planning and phase estimating

© 2022 Dr Neil Pearson

Phase estimating is preferred by those working on projects where the final product is not known and the level of uncertainty is significant—for example, the integration of internet technology into home appliances (the *internet of things*). The commitment to cost and schedule is only necessary over the next phase of the project, and commitment to unrealistic future schedules and costs based on poor information is avoided. This progressive macro/detailed method provides a stronger basis for using schedule and cost estimates to manage progress during the next phase.

Unfortunately, your customer (internal or external) will likely be pressing for an accurate estimate of time, cost and resource commitment the moment the decision is made to implement the project. Additionally, the customer who is paying for the project often perceives phase estimating as a blank cheque, because costs and schedules are not firm over most of the project life cycle beyond the current phase. Even though the reasons for phase estimating are sound and legitimate, most customers have to be persuaded of its legitimacy. A major advantage for the customer is the opportunity to change features and re-evaluate or even cancel the project in each new phase. In conclusion, phase estimating is very useful in projects that possess huge uncertainties concerning the final nature (shape, size, features) of the project.

9.6 Methods for estimating project resources, durations (time) and costs

This section reviews a number of commonplace estimating tools and techniques that are used in estimating resources, durations (time) and costs. These tools and techniques are commonly found in a wide range of disciplines (e.g. from project management to engineering). Table 9.5 illustrates the commonality between tools and techniques across the three knowledge areas of time, costs and resources in the Project Management Institute's *A Guide to the Project Management Body of Knowledge* (*PMBOK® Guide*) (PMI 2017).

Table 9.5 Estimating techniques

Time	Cost	Resources
Expert judgement	Expert judgement	Expert judgement
Analogous estimating	Analogous estimating	Analogous estimating
Parametric estimating	Parametric estimating	Parametric estimating
Three-point estimating	Three-point estimating	–
Bottom-up estimating	Bottom-up estimating	Bottom-up estimating
Data analysis	Data analysis	Data analysis
Decision-making	Decision-making	–
Meetings	–	Meetings
–	Alternatives analysis	–
–	Reserve analysis	–
–	Cost of quality	–
–	Project management information system	Project management information system

© 2022 Dr Neil Pearson

Each of the tools and techniques in Table 9.5 (along with some additional techniques) will now be described with examples.

9.6.1 Expert judgement

Like the consensus approach, this is where SMEs are drawn into the estimating process. As an SME for a particular subject area, they bring a vast knowledge base of experience to the project. Using SMEs to estimate components of the project can potentially provide years of insights and experience on the item being estimated. Expert judgement can therefore prove to be a very useful estimating resource—providing information that the project leader or others in the project team would otherwise not have access to. For example, as project leader you are often (although you should not need to be) an SME. On a large office relocation project, one of the authors brought in a specialist cabling company to figure out the best way to provide flexible cabling layouts for phone and multiple data points per seat. The specialist cabling company made the recommendation to use raised floors, with moveable data/phone housing tiles that were placed on longer-than-normal cable runs: this allowed the floor space and density of phones/cables to be altered to infinite combinations by simply lifting floor tiles. Without the expert judgement of the specialist cabling company, the best solution and therefore cost may not have been arrived at so efficiently.

9.6.2 **Analogous method**

Analogous means *similar or alike in such a way as to permit the drawing of an analogy* (a similarity between the alike features of two things). When applied to project management, we are usually comparing the estimates of the project (or components of a project) with past similar projects, to inform and formulate our estimate. The **analogous estimating** method requires that good historical data is available to make comparisons against.

This method is suitable for use where the current project closely follows past projects in features and costs. Analogous estimates can be made quickly with little effort and with reasonable accuracy. This method is very common in projects that are relatively standard but have some small variation or customisation. When comparing, it is advisable to check how current the comparison project is— out-of-date project comparison will lead to inaccurate estimates. For example, a current project has to build a two-car shed with workshop for a house build project. Instead of spending time obtaining quotes for the work, the project leader could look at previous similar projects. If the two-car shed with workshop cost $23,500 a year ago on a similar project, a figure close to this would be used on the current project (perhaps consider the increased prices of steel and labour shortages due to pandemic supply chain issues). By using analogy, we have removed guesswork and applied facts based on a previous known project.

9.6.3 **Parametric estimating**

Parametric estimating is a technique where data on various parameters of a previous project are used to make a current estimate of the work to be carried out. The relationship between the historic parameters (such as weight, size, cost, complexity, manpower) are used to estimate the current requirements.

For example, contractors frequently use the number of square metres to estimate the cost and time involved in building a house: for example, if a carpet layer knows, say, that the square metres required is length × width, and the cost of the floor material is $120/sq. metre, the labour $200/sq. metre, and the floor area is 15 metres × 23 metres, a total cost can be calculated based on current rates. Parametric techniques such as cost per square metre can form the source of top-down estimates and are typically more accurate than the analogous method, with the level of detail in the data being the accuracy factor. For example, as part of a Microsoft Office conversion project, 36 different computer workstations needed to be converted. Based on past conversion projects, the project leader determined that on average, one person could convert three workstations per day. Therefore, the task of converting the 36 workstations would take three technicians four days. Similarly, to estimate the wallpapering allowance on a house renovation, the contractor figured a cost of $5 per square metre of wallpaper and $2 per metre to install it, for a total cost of $7. By measuring the length and height of all the walls, they were able to calculate the total area in square metres and multiply it by $7.

9.6.4 **Three-point estimate**

The **three-point estimate** (**PERT**) has become a popular way of arriving at a (weighted) average. The PERT formula considers three estimates: a low (optimistic) estimate, an average (most likely) estimate and a high (pessimistic) estimate. The formula for the three-point estimate is:

$$\frac{\text{optimistic} + (4 \times \text{most likely}) + \text{pessimistic}}{6}$$

An example is illustrated in Figure 9.6 (based on Chapter 8 "Defining the scope of a project", Figure 8.14). The PERT formula typically results in a slightly higher estimate than would be achieved if the most likely option were selected. However, if all of these (typically) small increases were taken across the whole project, the result could be a noticeably higher overall project cost and / or time estimate for the project. The challenge here is in obtaining the number of estimates required and the time involved in obtaining them. Overall, this approach is seen to provide a more realistic estimate.

Figure 9.6 PERT estimating

WBS ID	Description	Duration estimate in units of .5 days			
		Optimistic best-case scenario	Most likely	Pessimistic worst-case scenario	PERT
1.2.2.1	Excavate				
WP 1.2.2.1-1	Tree removal	4	5	7	5.2
WP 1.2.2.1-2	Rubbish removal	1	1.5	2	1.5
WP 1.2.2.1-3	Excavate	2	5	8	5.0
1.2.2.2	Re-bar				
WP 1.2.2.2-1	Lay re-bar	3	4	7	4.3
WP 1.2.2.2-2	Level	0.5	1	2	1.1
WP 1.2.2.2-3	Tie	2	2.5	3	2.5
WP 1.2.2.2-4	Survey check	0.5	1	2.5	1.2
1.2.2.3	Pour				
WP 1.2.2.3-1	Pour	1	1	3	1.3
WP 1.2.2.3-2	Hardness test	0.5	0.5	1	0.6
WP 1.2.2.3-3	Remove planking	1	3	6	3.2

© 2022 Dr Neil Pearson

9.6.5 **Consensus methods**

This could perhaps occur in the Initiation stage of a project where managers in a top-down fashion use their pooled experience to make estimates. It could similarly be applied during the Planning stage, at a work package or task level, where SMEs come together and make a consensus decision on the estimating approach to a piece of work and the resulting values it produces. The Delphi method and NGT approach can both assist in the process of arriving at a consensus. The author (Pearson) has applied the NGT technique amongst a group of SMEs at the work package level to arrive at a consensus agreement on the estimate value to be taken forward.

9.6.6 **Alternative analysis (a type of data analysis)**

Alternative analysis considers the different alternatives to delivering the deliverable, work package or task. Alternative analysis can be applied at a higher level in the project to determine which of a set of options could be the best choice, for example, whether an organisation buys in a software package to manage payroll, employs a service company to provide the payroll processing, or the project develops a customised software solution inhouse. Similarly, an alternative analysis might be considered in a bottom-up approach when estimating a discrete piece of work by simply considering: What alternatives to achieving the same end-state exist?

Take, for example, the refurbishment of an ore processing plant: the project has work packages defined that cover the refurbishment of several silos. What potential alternatives does the project leader have?

1. Erect scaffold towers, clean and prepare surfaces, paint, tear down scaffold towers, at a cost of AUD3.5 million.

2. Build a switch-out silo and switch out each silo in turn, enabling the other silos to remain in service, at a cost of AUD2.5 million.

3. Use a custom-designed Z-lift to refurbish each silo in situ, at a cost of AUD1.5 million.

This is often why project leaders go to tender (request for proposal) when looking at unusual pieces of work.

9.6.7 Reserve analysis

Reserve analysis is used to determine the amount of contingency and management reserve needed for the project. Refer to Chapter 12 "Project cost management" for a detailed explanation of this technique.

9.6.8 Cost of quality

Chapter 13 "Project quality management" discusses the impacts of both the cost of quality (COQ) and the cost of poor quality (COPQ), and how these impact the discussion of general project quality with the customer. Generally, the higher the level of quality specified by the customer, the more increase in costs there will be due to additional quality activities, more expensive raw materials/components and additional quality control checks required to ensure compliance with specifications. The customer should be in a position where they can assess the COQ against the COPQ. For example, a customer might specify a lower quality for a component of a smartwatch, knowing that this will increase the number of product returns later in the product life cycle. Quality costs and this is a conscious decision led by the customer. The project leader might, however, have to provide the COQ—this is what the specified level of quality the customer wants will cost to achieve in the project.

9.6.9 Vendor bid analysis

Again, as with some of the other methods, the vendor bid method can be applied in both a top-down and bottom-up approach. Although mostly used to obtain quotes for work packages in a bottom-up approach, it can also be applied to a complete branch of the WBS at a higher level (this may be relevant when a whole part of the project is to be contracted out or outsourced in some form). In this method, vendors are provided with the work package details and asked to provide details of costs and timing. Depending on which stage the project is at, this may influence the type of information requested. For example, during the project Initiating stage, a *request for information* or a *request for quote* might be appropriate methods for approaching vendors; however, as the project moves into the detailed Planning stage, a *request for tender* would be a more appropriate format to employ. Chapter 17 "Project procurement management" details the differing types of tenders that are available to the project leader.

9.6.10 Estimating tools and IT systems

The best way to improve estimates is to collect and archive data on past project estimates: planned values versus actuals. Archiving this historical data (for both planned and actuals) provides a valuable knowledge base of information that can be drawn upon to help improve project cost, time and resource estimations in current and future projects. Creating an estimating database is a best practice approach, supported by leading project management organisations (such as the PMI, the Association for Project Management and PRINCE2). Companies that are disciplined about their estimating approach will often capture large amounts of data over a long time and use this data to produce estimates of future work. Internal estimating tools typically reside within spreadsheets and databases: an example of this might be an energy utility company that has vast amounts of historical data on completed projects, down to a work package and task level—each work package successfully captures details of the resources that were used, the durations they were needed for, and their associated costs. This data can therefore be mined to inform estimate data for standard jobs in current and future projects.

Externally, many companies provide simple online estimating tools for their customers to use to generate estimates (thus saving the company time and money in having to perform estimating tasks for the customer). These types of tools are often seen on equipment hire websites, where the customer selects the required equipment, nominates the duration of the hire period, the insurance level required and other selections as appropriate, and the estimating tool then provides them with an online quote.

Two key rules to remember when setting up estimating tools are: (1) ensure the data is maintained (remember the saying "rubbish-in, rubbish-out"!) and (2) allow for variables. For example, what if (in the case of the utility company example) the geological make-up of the ground for which a quote was prepared was not considered in the estimation tool? If normal ground conditions were assumed in the estimating tool, how much would the estimate be out by if rock was encountered?

If the tool is not available internally to the organisation based on actuals, ask the question: Is there a tool available externally? For example, when estimating the house build as illustrated in the WBS (Figure 9.3), the project leader would tap into established industry resources (e.g. the Rawlinson's Guide at https://www.rawlinsonswa.com.au/post/rawlinsons-wrote-the-book-on-construction-cost-estimating).

9.6.11 **Lessons learned**

Mining lessons learned from previous projects can be helpful in influencing not only how estimating is to be approached in your current project, but also what is to be estimated. Some lessons learned will be related to the how, or the process, of estimating. These lessons could be about developing and updating sub-processes such as the one indicated in Figure 9.2. If we can be more efficient about *how* we estimate, then valuable time and resources may be freed up to allow a more concentrated focus on the *what* of estimating. For example, a lesson learned from a previous project indicated that GST (tax) and shipping and handling costs (among other miscellaneous costs) were frequently being omitted from estimates. The project team therefore collectively idea-showered a mandatory checklist that had to be signed by the project team member to verify completeness as part of quality control of the estimating process.

Other lessons will relate to the *what* component of *what we are estimating*. A lesson learned from a previous project used in this text indicates that in a three-bedroom plus garage house-build, the use of environmentally friendly products in its construction increased build costs by 35 per cent across the entire project. Learning from past projects (whether the lesson is positive or negative) is an essential exercise project leaders must leverage.

9.6.12 **Function point methods for software and system projects**

In the software industry, software development projects are frequently estimated using weighted macro variables called **function points**, or major parameters such as number of inputs, number of outputs, number of enquiries, number of data files and number of interfaces. These weighted variables are adjusted by adding in a complexity factor. The total adjusted count provides the basis for estimating the labour effort and cost for a project (usually using a regression formula derived from data of past projects). Refer to https://www.estimancy.com/en/2018/09/25/story-points-vs-function-points/ for a brief overview of function points and a close relative, **story points** (discussed in Chapter 3 "Agile (Scrum) project management").

9.6.13 **Template methods**

If the project is similar to past projects, then the costs from past projects can be used as a starting point for the new project. Differences in the new project can be noted and previous times and costs adjusted to reflect these differences. For example, a ship repair dry-dock organisation has a set of standard repair projects (e.g. templates for overhaul, electrical, mechanical) that are used as starting points for estimating the cost and duration of any new project. Differences from the appropriate standardised project are noted (for durations, costs and resources) and changes are made. This approach enables the organisation to develop a potential schedule, estimate costs and develop a budget in a very short time-span. Development of such templates in a database can quickly reduce estimate errors.

9.6.14 Range estimating

Let's start by first considering when **range estimating** should be used: range estimating works best when work packages have significant uncertainty associated with the time, cost or resource dimensions involved for completing the work package.

If the work package is routine and carries little uncertainty, then using the person who is most familiar with the work package to estimate is usually the best approach. They will either know durations (time), costs and resources from past experience, or know where to find this information and so should be able to estimate work package durations (time), costs and resources relatively easily. However, when work packages have significant uncertainty associated with time (duration), cost and resources, it is prudent to have a policy that requires three estimates to be given—*low*, *average* and *high*. The low to high estimates give a range within which the average estimate will fall. Determining the low and high estimates for the activity will be influenced by factors such as complexity, technology, newness and familiarity.

How are estimates obtained? Since range estimating works best for work packages that have significant uncertainty, having a group determine the low, average and high cost or duration gives the best results. Group estimating tends to refine extremes by bringing more evaluative judgments to the estimate about potential risks. The judgement of others in a group helps to moderate perceived extreme risks associated with a time, cost or resource estimate. Involving others in making estimates gains buy-in and credibility for the estimate. Figure 9.7 presents an abridged estimating. The group estimates show the low, average and high values for each work package. The confidence (risk) level column is the group's independent assessment of the degree of confidence that the actual time required will be very close to the estimate. In a sense, this number represents the group's evaluation of many factors (e.g. complexity, technology, experience) that might impact the average time estimate.

Figure 9.7 Range estimating

| WBS ID | Description | Duration estimate in units of .5 days | | | | |
		Low estimate	Average estimate	High estimate	Range	Confidence level
1.2.2.1	Excavate					
WP 1.2.2.1-1	Tree removal	4	5	7	3.0	low
WP 1.2.2.1-2	Rubbish removal	1	1.5	2	1.0	high
WP 1.2.2.1-3	Excavate	2	5	8	6.0	medium
1.2.2.2	Re-bar					
WP 1.2.2.2-1	Lay re-bar	3	4	7	4.0	medium
WP 1.2.2.2-2	Level	0.5	1	2	1.5	high
WP 1.2.2.2-3	Tie	2	2.5	3	1.0	low
WP 1.2.2.2-4	Survey check	0.5	1	2.5	2.0	low
1.2.2.3	Pour					
WP 1.2.2.3-1	Pour	1	1	3	2.0	high
WP 1.2.2.3-2	Hardness test	0.5	0.5	1	0.5	high
WP 1.2.2.3-3	Remove planking	1	3	6	5.0	low

© 2022 Dr Neil Pearson

Group range estimating allows the project leader and owner to assess the confidence associated with project times (and/or costs). This approach helps to reduce surprises as the project progresses. The method also provides a basis for assessing risk, managing resources and determining the project contingency fund. Range estimating is popular in software and new product projects, where up-front requirements are fuzzy and not well known.

9.6.14.1 Affinity grouping

Here items (e.g. work packages, tasks for requirements) are reviewed and dropped into predefined sizing groups. For example, the T-shirt sizes previously introduced could be the buckets into which work could be dropped. Figure 9.8 provides an example of this for the house build project, where project team members have transferred the work packages to sticky notes and then undertaken an idea-shower to position the work into the right-size T-shirt. These activities can engage with project team members; however, as a technique, this is more top-down based.

Figure 9.8 Affinity grouping and T-shirt sizing

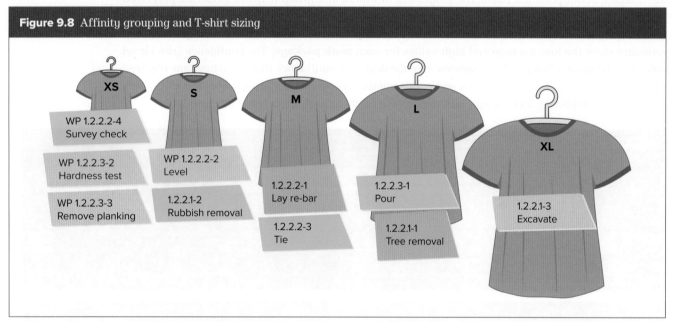

© 2022 Dr Neil Pearson

This is a technique you are more likely to experience in the adaptive Agile (Scrum) approach to initially estimate the first cut of the product backlog.

9.6.14.2 Wideband Delphi

Wideband Delphi is an estimating technique where SMEs produce individual estimates and then meet as a project group to discuss until consensus has been reached.

Obtaining accurate estimates is a challenge. Committed organisations accept the challenge of coming up with meaningful estimates and invest heavily in developing their capacity to do so. Accurate estimates reduce uncertainty and support a discipline for effectively managing projects. See Table 9.6 for a summary of the differences between top-down and bottom-up estimates.

Table 9.6 Estimating techniques in relation top-down and bottom-up estimating

Tool/technique	Approach	
	Top-down	Bottom-up
Expert judgement	Applied to the top levels of the WBS.	Applied to items within each work package, to compare/validate against other methods.
Analogous estimating	Applied to the top levels of the WBS.	Applied to items within each work package, or at a work package level.
Parametric estimating	Applied to the top levels of the WBS.	Applied to items within each work package, or at a work package level.
Three-point estimate	Can be applied to a section of the WBS when used in conjunction with other techniques such as vendor bid analysis.	Applied to items within each work package.
Consensus methods and Delphi	Applied to the top levels of the WBS.	Applied to items within each work package.
Alternative analysis	Applied to the approach taken to accomplish the project at higher levels of the WBS.	Applied to items within each work package, or at a work package level.
Reserve analysis	Contingency applied to the whole project level of the WBS or the control level.	Contingency applied at the task and work package level.
Cost of quality	Applied to the whole project.	Applied at the task and work package level.
Vendor bid analysis	On a section of the WBS which may be outsourced in its entirety.	Applied to items within each work package, or at a work package level.
Estimating tools and systems	–	Applied to items within each work package, or at a work package level.
Function point methods for software and system projects	–	Applied to items within each work package, or at a work package level.
Template methods	–	Well-defined jobs within a work package.
Range estimating	–	Applied to items within each work package.
Lessons learned	Applied at the project level from previous projects' lessons.	Applied at the task and work package level from previous projects' lessons.
Affinity grouping	Applied at the deliverable to work package level, provides a broad classification of the work.	
Wideband Delphi	Consensus voting, typically occurring at the deliverable / sub-deliverable level, due to the nature of the activity.	

© 2022 Dr Neil Pearson

9.7 | Additional estimating considerations

9.7.1 Level of detail in estimating

Top management interests usually centre on the total project and major milestone events that mark major accomplishments, for example *Build oil platform in the North Sea* or *Design a prototype*. Middle management might centre on one segment of the project or on one milestone. Front-line managers' interests may be limited to one work package. One of the benefits of the WBS is the ability to aggregate task level information, so each level of management can have the kind of information that is necessary to make decisions. Getting the level of detail in the WBS to match management needs for effective implementation is crucial; yet achieving this delicate balance is difficult.

The level of detail in the WBS varies with the complexity of the project, the need for control, the project size, its cost, duration, resource commitments and other factors. If the structure reflects excessive detail, there is a tendency to break the work effort into departmental assignments. This tendency can become a barrier to success, since the emphasis will be on departmental outcomes, rather than on deliverable outcomes. Excessive detail also means more work, which may not be required given the factors noted previously. On the other hand, if the level of detail is not adequate, an organisational unit may find the structure falls short of meeting its needs. Fortunately, the WBS has built-in flexibility. Participating departments may expand their portion of the structure to meet their specific needs. For example, the engineering department may wish to further break down work on a deliverable into smaller packages such as electrical, civil and mechanical. Similarly, the marketing department may wish to break a new product promotion into TV, radio, periodicals and social media.

9.7.2 **Refining estimates**

As described earlier, detailed work package estimates are aggregated and rolled up by deliverable to control packages, and subsequently to the project level to provide the total planned cost of the project. Similarly, estimated durations are entered into the project schedule to establish and determine the overall duration of the project. Experience tells us that for many projects, total estimates do not materialise, and the actual costs and schedule of some projects significantly exceed original work package estimates. In order to compensate for the difficulty of obtaining cost and schedule estimates, some project leaders adjust total costs by some multiplier (e.g. total estimated costs × 1.20). The practice of adjusting (padding) original estimates by 20, or even 100 per cent, begs the question: Why? After investing so much time and energy on detailed estimates, why could the numbers be so far off? There are several reasons for this, most of which can be traced to the estimating process itself and the inherent uncertainty of predicting the future. Some of these potential reasons are outlined here.

- *Interaction costs are hidden in estimates:* According to best practice, each task estimate is supposed to be done independently. However, tasks are rarely completed in a vacuum. Work on one task is dependent upon prior tasks, and the hand-offs between tasks require time and attention. For example, people working on prototype development need to interact with design engineers after the design is completed, whether to simply ask clarifying questions or to make adjustments in the original design. Similarly, the time necessary to coordinate activities is typically not reflected in independent estimates. Coordination is reflected in meetings and briefings as well as time necessary to resolve disconnects between tasks. Time, and therefore cost, devoted to managing interactions rises exponentially as the number of people and different disciplines involved increases on a project.

- *Normal conditions do not apply:* Estimates are supposed to be based on normal conditions. While this is a good starting point, it rarely holds true in real life. This is especially true when it comes to the availability of resources. Resource shortages, whether in the form of people, equipment or materials, can extend original estimates. For example, under normal conditions, four bulldozers are typically used to clear a certain site size in five days, but the availability of only three bulldozers would extend the task duration to eight days. Similarly, the decision to outsource certain tasks can increase costs as well as extend task durations, since time is added to acclimatising outsiders to the particulars of the project and the culture of the organisation.

- *Things go wrong on projects:* Design flaws are revealed after the fact, extreme weather conditions occur, accidents happen, and so forth. Although you shouldn't plan for these risks to happen when estimating a particular task, the probability and impact of such events needs to be considered as part of the risk analysis. Refer to Chapter 16 "Project risk management".

- *Changes to project scope and the integrated Project Management Plan:* As the project leader progresses further and further into the project, they obtain a better understanding of what needs to be done to accomplish it. This may lead to major changes in project documents. Likewise, if the project is a commercial project, changes often must be made midstream to respond to new demands by the customer and/or competition. Unstable project scopes are a major source of cost overruns. While every effort should be made up-front to nail down the project scope, it is becoming increasingly difficult to do so in our rapidly changing world.

The reality is that for many projects, not all the information needed to make accurate estimates is available, and it is impossible to predict the future. The dilemma is that without solid estimates, the credibility of the project plan is eroded. Deadlines become meaningless, budgets become rubbery and accountability becomes problematic.

Challenges like those described above will influence the final time, cost and resource estimates. Even with the best estimating efforts, it may be necessary to revise estimates based on relevant information before establishing a baseline schedule and baseline budget. Effective organisations adjust estimates of specific tasks once the risks, resources and particulars of the situation have been more clearly defined. They recognise that the rolled-up estimates generated from a detailed estimate based on the WBS are just a starting point. As they delve further into the project planning process, they make appropriate revisions in the time, cost and resource commitments of specific activities. They factor the final assignment of resources into the project budget and project schedule. For example, when they realise that only three instead of four bulldozers are available to clear a site, they adjust both the time and cost of that activity. They adjust estimates to account for specific actions to mitigate potential risks on the project. For example, to reduce the chances of design code errors, they would add the cost of independent testers to the schedule and budget. Finally, organisations adjust estimates to take into account abnormal conditions. For example, if soil samples reveal excessive ground water, they accordingly adjust foundation costs and times.

There will always be some mistakes, omissions and adjustments that will require additional changes to estimates. Every project should have in place a variation management process to accommodate these situations and the impact on the project baselines.

Summary

Estimating is all too often taken as a comparatively less important activity in projects. However, it forms the bedrock for all subsequent planning activities, based on the fact that a 100 per cent complete WBS has first been prepared. Figure 9.9 repeats the planning workflow we are now firmly within. It shows that, based on a 100 per cent complete WBS, the stage we have just completed is that of estimating—the estimation of what resources, for how long at what cost. As indicated, this estimating information then feeds into the activities of planning resources, planning the project schedule and planning the project budget—all derived from the WBS and the estimated work packages/tasks.

Ensure the following when estimating.

- Manage expectations around the level of accuracy that needs to be achieved and that is acceptable to the business. A reference point exists in the *estimating trumpet* but the reader should additionally research their own industry's expectations and apply the industry rules as necessary.
- Consider the many and varied factors that additionally affect estimating, such as the planning horizon, project duration, people, structure, padding and culture.
- Understand what is being estimated: resources (human or other), plant, equipment, raw material(s), capital, and others.
- Understand the general estimating process, as illustrated in Figure 9.2 in this chapter, not forgetting that while the resources are a major source of items to estimate, there are also many other ancillary items that will need to be identified and estimated.
- Understand the general approaches to estimating, including top-down (broad-range) estimates, bottom-up (detailed) estimates and the hybrid approach of phase or rolling-wave estimating, where detailed (bottom-up) estimates are achieved for immediate work, and work in the future is estimated at a higher level (top-down).
- Understand the large number of estimating tools and techniques available to the project leader. These include expert judgement, analogous estimating, parametric estimating, three-point estimating, bottom-up estimating, data analysis, decision-making, meetings, alternatives analysis, reserve analysis, cost of quality (COQ), estimating tools, affinity grouping and Wideband Delphi.

The level of effort that is gone into should follow the old saying of *no more than is necessary and sufficient*. It is well known that up-front efforts to clearly define project objectives, scope and specification vastly improve the accuracy of time, cost and resource estimates. *Remember:* For internal project leaders, you are only as good as your last project, so define a complete WBS and estimate accurately; for external project leaders, you are often the face of profits for your organisation—get it wrong and there could be more than your personal career on the line; the organisation's existence could well be affected.

Figure 9.9 Estimation in the workflow of planning

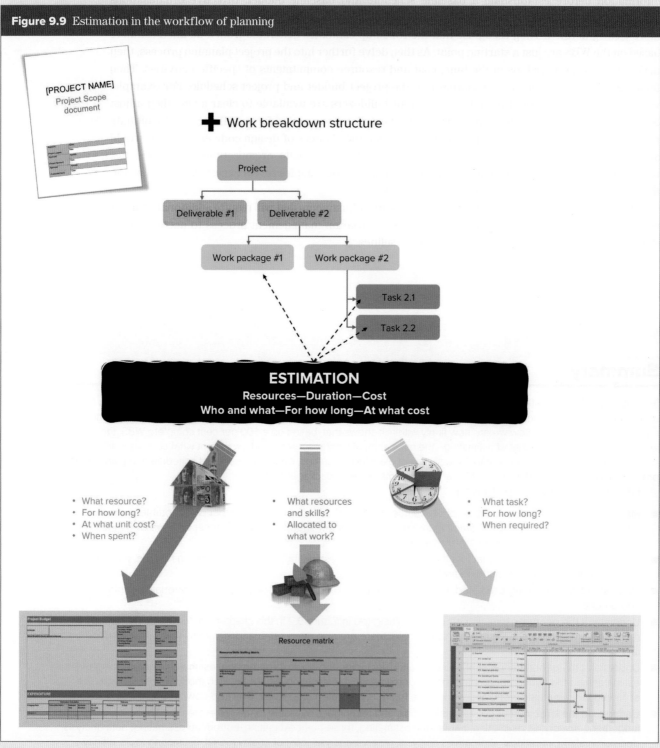

Review questions

1. What is your understanding of the wider definition of *resources*?
2. Explain the difference between analogous and parametric estimating.
3. What is the general sequence of events that typically occurs when estimating at the work package level / task level?
4. What are the key typical estimating activities carried out by a project leader across the predictive life cycle?

5. In what situations would a project leader use phase estimating or rolling-wave planning in relation to estimating?

6. What is the three-point formula and how does it affect estimates?

7. How, mathematically, does the range estimate differ from the three-point estimate?

Exercises

1. The estimating trumpet illustrates the tolerances and expectations around levels of estimating accuracy across the life cycle. How do the tolerances resonate with your organisation's expectations around estimating?

2. You are about to embark on a project to introduce a project management information system that integrates the functions of scheduling, risk management and social media (blogs, forums and wikis), which must also allow contractors to log into the system to update work package performance status. How would the vendor bid analysis and expert judgement approaches be applied in this situation? What is the value in applying both techniques? What would be the downside of applying both techniques?

3. Refer to one of your own recent projects and review the different estimating tools and techniques that have been outlined in this chapter. For the estimating techniques you originally used in the project, reflect on what led you to use the technique and whether you would use a different technique or multiple techniques in the future. What lessons are there to be learned?

4. Using the information provided in Table 9.7, estimate a number of work packages and/or tasks. Include at least two estimates below the Foundations deliverable. Capture your responses in a format similar to Table 9.8.

Table 9.7 Estimating information

| | Duration | Effort | Cost | | | Material costs | Resources | Assumptions |
			Quote 1	Quote 2	Quote 3			
Land preparation	8 days							
Survey and stake-out		1 day				N/A	Project leader (costs covered elsewhere) Contractor #4	The site is a standard 800 sq/m block; previous projects were quoted an average of $200 per 200 sq/m
Foundations	7 days							
Excavate		1 day (all quotes)	$800	$1,500	$2,500		Contractor #1 Site supervisor .5 day @ $300	Including materials
Lay re-bar		1 day (all quotes)	$500	$600	$650		Contractor #2 Site supervisor .5 day @ $300	
Pour concrete		.5 day (all quotes)	$100 sq/m	$120 sq/m§	$150 sq/m		Contractor #3 Site supervisor .5 day @ $300	The area to be poured is 30 sq/m

© 2022 Dr Neil Pearson

Table 9.8 Estimating format

Parameter	Calculations	Comments
Duration		
Resources/effort		
Cost	Total cost = $	
Assumptions		

© 2022 Dr Neil Pearson

References

Project Management Institute (PMI) 2017, *A Guide to the Project Management Body of Knowledge*, 6th edition, PMI.

Project Management Institute (PMI) 2021a, *A Guide to the Project Management Body of Knowledge (PMBOK® Guide)*, 7th edition, Newton Square, PA.

Project Management Institute (PMI) 2021b, *The Standard for Project Management (ANSI/PMI 99-001-2021)*, 7th edition, Newton Square, PA.

Wideman RM 2002, "The estimating accuracy trumpet", http://www.maxwideman.com/issacons3/iac1331/sld003.htm, accessed 16 July 2019.

Wilson-Chapman A 2012, "Macmahon CEO gone, shares halved", News Limited www.news.com.au/business/companies/macmahon-shares-plummet-on-downgrade/story-fnda1bsz-1226477144064, accessed October 2012.

CHAPTER 10

Project resource management

Learning elements

10A Understand the planning aspects of project resource management, including the development of the Resource Management Plan.

10B Be able to successfully identify the resources required to accomplish a project.

10C Be aware of project considerations in the acquisition of resources.

10D Understand the links between resources, schedules and estimating.

10E Gain an understanding of how to monitor and control project resources and avoid some common pitfalls.

10F Understand key resource activities that take place within Closure.

In this chapter

10.1 Introduction

10.2 Planning resource management

10.3 Resource identification and assignment

10.4 Acquiring resources

10.5 Monitoring and controlling resources

10.6 Resource closure

Summary

10.1 | Introduction

In this chapter, we will review some of the more practical aspects in the identification of resources, in planning resources and in managing the practicalities of resource commitments. This chapter focuses on the wider discussion of the varied resource commitments projects require. Figure 10.1 represents typical resource management activities discussed further in this chapter; these could mainly be described as the *hard aspects* related to resource management. Chapter 19 "Project leaders and project teams" contains a discussion on the *softer aspects* of human resource management, including principles-based project management, **team building**, codes of ethics, leadership, conflict and general project team management.

Figure 10.1 Resource management activities

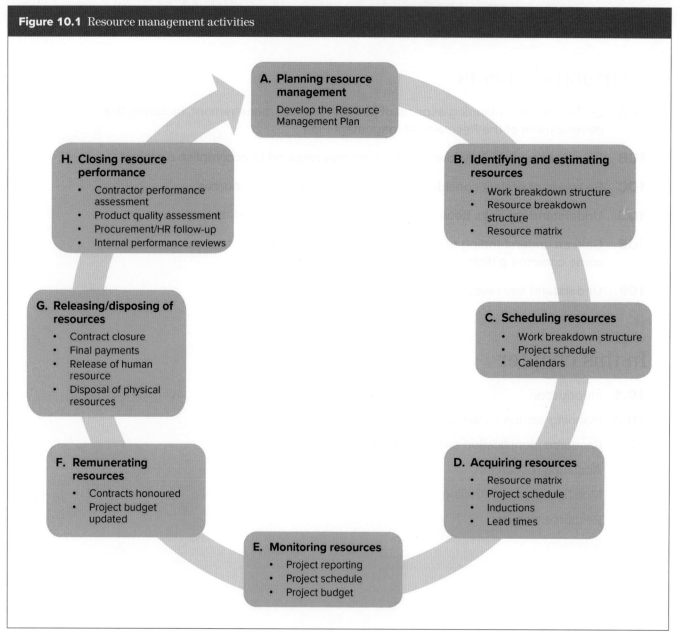

© 2022 Dr Neil Pearson

Note: The boxes in Figure 10.1 have been labelled for reference purposes only and do not necessarily represent a strict sequence of activities.

The project leader experiences the iterative nature of this cycle, especially during the Execution stage of the project, where resources are continually loaded into the project. It is for this reason that some projects assign dedicated project schedulers to the project: to maintain the project schedule, carry out resource allocations, manage resource allocations (e.g. resource conflicts), monitor the status of **work packages** and prepare reports for consideration by the project leader.

This chapter also has strong links with Chapter 9 "Estimating", which discusses the process of taking the **work breakdown structure (WBS)** and using this as reference point for **resource identification** at the work package and/or **task** level. This chapter takes a holistic approach to the identification of all resources required by the project, and, as illustrated in Figure 10.2, the chapter additionally takes the work and resource data a step further, culminating in the development of the **Resource Matrix** or **Resource Allocation Matrix (RAM)**.

Figure 10.2 Scope—estimate—plan

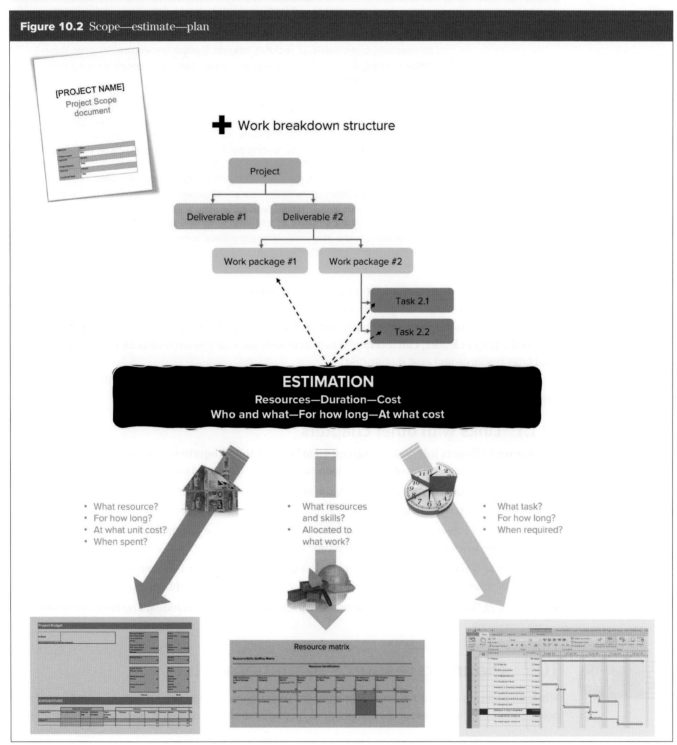

The Project Management Institute, in the sixth edition of *A Guide to the Project Management Body of Knowledge* (PMI 2017), widened its definition of *resource* to formally encompass not just human resources but all resources required by a project. Of course, project leaders have been considering the wider implications of all resources required by the project (human and other) for some time now. This chapter extends this thinking and therefore necessarily encompasses human and all other **resource types** throughout its narrative.

Table 10.1 Extended list of resource types (categories) with examples

Resource type	Example
Human resources	Internal employees (full or part time), contractors, temps, consultants, secondments, volunteers, freelancers
Tools	Testing equipment, compressors, drills, desktop computers, telephones, tablet devices, libraries (corporate, online, or societal), internet, laptops, test equipment, pens, paper
Plant	Office facilities, warehouse (storage) space, production lines, operational shop-floor environments, service centres
Equipment	Vehicles (utes, cars, trucks), hoists, scissor lifts, trucks, excavators, test equipment, compactors, cranes, personal protective equipment, environmental protection
Office equipment	Desks, filing cabinets, partitions, air-conditioning unit, chairs, photocopiers (print stations), fax, shredders, printers, lighting, whiteboards, TVs, projectors, videoconferencing
Raw materials	Concrete, fill, steel, roofing tiles, fencing panels, circuit boards, plastic and plastic pellets (*nurdles*), lithium, copper, wood, cables, cloth, gravel, chemicals, glass, metals
Financial capital	Funding sources, cash flow into the project, loans, equity, venture capital
Services	Consultancy, maintenance, facilities, data centre services, cleaning, catering, security
Information technology	PCs, laptops, smartphones, tablets, servers, monitors, printers, network equipment, software—purchased, software as a service, telephone systems (PABX), software licences
Other	Paper, printers, books, insurance, training providers, consumables, subscriptions, energy consumption, safety equipment

© 2022 Dr Neil Pearson

Note: The resource types in Table 10.1 may possibly relate to the way your organisation accounts for resources within its financial, procurement and other policies. It would therefore be worth checking with the organisation's relevant departments whether a list of pre-defined resource types exists, so you, as the project leader, can leverage this in activities such as resource identification and allocation (and later resource and cost monitoring).

The first activity is to plan resource management, so information on such elements as resource categories are discovered early in this process and leveraged.

10.1.1   Links with other chapters

■ Chapter 6 "Project integration management" covers the integrative aspects of project resource management across each of the knowledge areas (refer to Table 6.6).

■ Chapter 9 "Estimating" covers the linkage between resource identification and estimating the quantity of resources required.

■ Chapter 11 "Project schedule management" takes the resource information and assigns this against the work package or task on a time basis.

■ Chapter 12 "Project cost management" takes the resource requirement, when it is due to fall in terms of time in the project's budget, and the costs; it then creates the time-phased project budget.

■ Chapter 21 "Project closure" wraps up all aspects of the project including any final discussions on resources.

10.2 | Planning resource management

When considering project resource management (refer back to Figure 10.1, box A), a project leader needs to consider how resources are going to be planned and managed. A **Resource Management**

Plan—one of the subsidiary plans to the integrated Project Management Plan (integrated PMP)—is therefore used to accomplish this.

The Resource Management Plan encapsulates the legislation, policy and procedure, best practice and **governance** (among other items) that impact the management of resources in this project environment. The plan is supported by a number of other living project artefacts, such as the **Skills Matrix**, the **Resource Assignment Matrix (RAM)**, and/or the **RASCI Matrix**, the bill of materials and the WBS.

Typical contents of the Resource Management Plan (based on people resources but could equally be applied to other major resource types) are outlined here.

1. *Human (and other) resources strategy and approach:* This initial section of the Resource Management Plan describes the general strategy and approach to resource management for this project environment. For example, it might set out whether the use of contractors is preferred or whether the project is to *second* resources from the business. This general approach section sets the tone of the project and indicates the preferred management approach towards the recruitment (**acquiring resources**), management of resources and release of resources from the project. Seconding resources to the project has the benefit of building skills and knowledge in those people, who can then take this back to the business when the project is closed or the resources released from the project.

2. *Policy and procedure:* This identifies any relevant organisational resource-related policy and procedures applicable to the project environment. Typical organisational process assets the project may need to adopt could include the following.

   People resource related:

   - recruitment policy and procedures
   - performance management guidelines
   - learning and development guidelines
   - staff release policy and procedures
   - contracting-out policy and procedures
   - staff remuneration policy and procedures.

   Other resources related:

   - asset management **policy and procedures**
   - maintenance policy and procedures
   - facilities policy and procedures.

3. *Project organisational structure:* Although the project organisational structure is typically illustrated in the project scope document, it is not uncommon to also see the structure documented within the Resource Management Plan, supported by a more in-depth discussion on team dynamics, organisational culture and **role** descriptions.

4. *Key resources:* Although the resource matrix captures all the required information to be collected on each, the project leader may also wish to have a snapshot view available of the key resources on the project. See Tables 10.2(a) and 10.2(b).

Table 10.2(a) Examples of key human resources

Role	Description	Comments
Project officer	Provides administration support to the project, including document management, financial status reporting and other reporting, as specified in role description.	Role Fact Sheet—Project Officer
Contract manager	Develops, reviews, and manages all contractual arrangements (human or other).	Role Fact Sheet—Contracts Manager

Table 10.2(b) Examples of other key resources

Resource	Description	Comments
Corporate file server	The corporate file server is evaluated to ensure that it can store the large volumes of project information that will be generated, and to ensure data can be accessed, updated, searched, and extracted expediently.	Service Request SR-76534 (logged with internal IT support)
Backhoe machinery	Required in the *foundations* work package.	Contact the site preparation department to undertake a resource availability check

© 2022 Dr Neil Pearson

5. *Governance (roles and responsibilities):* As with management plans introduced in previous chapters, use the RASCI Matrix early in the project to ensure that resource-related business rules and/or decisions are clearly articulated and implemented. The human resources component of the RASCI typically enables miscellaneous resource governance (business rules and decisions) to be defined and captured, for example regarding what is to occur if a conflict situation arises, or what happens if role clarity needs to be achieved. An example of a simple RASCI Matrix is included as Table 10.3.

Table 10.3 RASCI Matrix

ID	Business rule / decision	Category	Project sponsor	Project leader	Project support	Project Steering Committee	Project team	Organisational HR manager	Finance and Payroll Department
BR11	Approval of any people-related resource to the project	Resource		R	A	I	I	C	I
BR14	Ensure project induction has taken place	Resource		AR	R		R		
BR16	Ensure contractor background check has been done before contract release	Resource		AR	R			C	C

© 2022 Dr Neil Pearson

6. *Recognition and reward:* Outline the arrangements (if required) for a clear and transparent recognition and reward system for the project team (as a group), plus details of any individual reward arrangements—remember to ensure arrangements are in line with the organisation's policy and procedure.

7. *Project team agreement:* If necessary, establish a project team agreement. This may contain the project's values and behaviours in relation to working together and supporting each other as a team. It should be signed by all project team members and displayed in a prominent place within the project environment and reinforced by the project leader and all contributing team members (refer to Chapter 19 "Project leaders and project teams"). Remember, we did a similar activity for the Scrum team.

8. *Project induction arrangements:* Capture the project's induction process. This may be an addition to any company induction arrangements. The project induction process could cover items such as:
   - role clarification
   - meeting the project team members
   - signing on to any team agreements
   - a walkaround of the project environment
   - introduction to the project management framework and methodology
   - walkaround and introduction to key stakeholders.

9. *Unions and agreements:* Include details of union-negotiated **enterprise bargaining agreements (EBAs)** or other union agreements that impact the way resources can be deployed on this project.

10. ***Workplace health and safety (WHS):*** Document how WHS applies to the project environment and state whether this is office-centric, or more specific to onsite arrangements that must be established and maintained during the life of the project.

11. ***Team Development Plan****:* Outline the approach to be taken towards team development. This could range from planned team-building activities to aspects of how the project team is going to function across a global virtual team environment. Note that there may be both schedule and budgetary implications, which may not have been identified through the development of the work packages within the WBS.

12. *Risk review:* Ensure a risk review of resource activities is carried out and that any risks identified are captured in the project's Risk Register under the category of, for example, *Resource*.

13. *Lessons learned:* Ensure that a review of any **lessons learned** from prior similar projects is undertaken, and that any relevant lessons learned are entered into the project's Lessons Learned Register under the category of *Resource*. Action any activities in relation to lessons and how they are to be managed in this project.

14. *Assumptions and constraints:* Consider what assumptions are being made in relation to resources for the project (remember an assumption is an *assumed statement of truth*). Also, capture any resource factors that may constrain the project (e.g. a particular skills shortage or access to a particular piece of equipment). The project leader should also be cognisant of how marketplace conditions may inform assumptions and constraints. Assumptions and constraints should also be reviewed for risk.

As with all management plans, although it is important to document resource dynamics, the actual *value* aspects of these typically emanate from discussions, consultations and decisions that have collectively produced an agreed set of statements that can be communicated to all members of the project team. Such analysis undoubtedly opens other questions, which may, for example, result in a risk being raised, a new task being added into the WBS, a variation being made to a work package, a variation to a lead/lag time on a task in the schedule, or an additional cost to be included in the project budget.

If the Resource Management Plan has been created as an integrated Resource Management Plan, it is likely the information on human and other resources will be integrated together in a single plan. More commonly, two distinct plans are developed, one covering human resources and the second covering other (physical) resources, as illustrated in Figure 10.3.

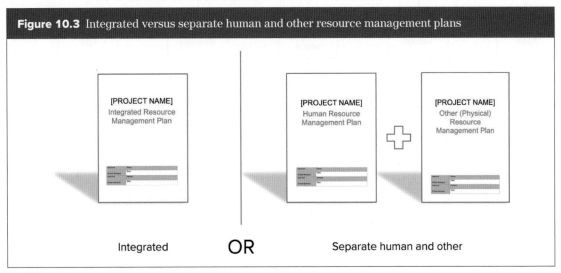

Figure 10.3 Integrated versus separate human and other resource management plans

© 2022 Dr Neil Pearson

 Resource Management Plan

10.3 | Resource identification and assignment

A comprehensive identification of the resources needed by a project is an essential element of any project, and a project leader (assisted by the project team) can use a variety of techniques to help them identify required resources. Refer to Figure 10.1, box B and Figure 10.2 Scope—estimate—plan; in the workflow of capturing information against the WBS, at this point the project leader would be carrying out, for example, identification of resources against the WBS, but could be applying any of the following techniques to assist them in ensuring a comprehensive identification of resources takes place:

- developing a **resource breakdown structure (RBS)**
- leveraging the WBS
- reviewing lessons learned from previous projects
- leveraging pre-defined resource categories, the **chart of accounts** or project accounting codes.

These approaches are discussed below.

10.3.1 Resource breakdown structure

An RBS, much like a WBS, is a hierarchical decomposition, but the RBS is a decomposition of resource categories. When an RBS is being developed, it is important to involve project team members (and other subject matter experts) in the process, to ensure differing perspectives are tabled for consideration. Development of the initial RBS usually involves an idea-shower workshop (using sticky notes), to draw out all the potential resources that will be required to achieve the project. Figure 10.4 illustrates an RBS for part of the House Build example. Captured here in a hierarchical format are the results of the idea-shower workshop with SMEs and project team members.

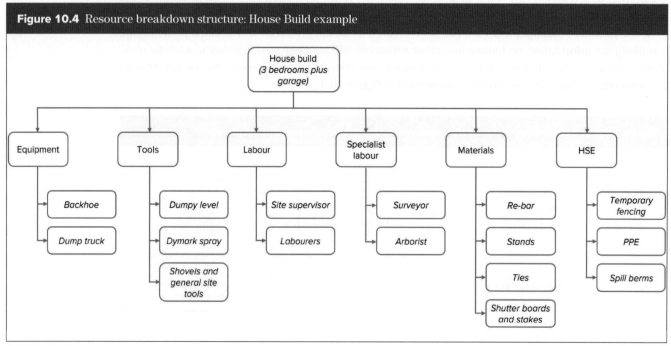

Figure 10.4 Resource breakdown structure: House Build example

© 2022 Dr Neil Pearson

There are some advantages to an idea shower, as this approach allows a less structured methodology and inspires more creative avenues to be explored—as opposed to more structured thinking based on the WBS. This hopefully increases opportunities for identifying resource items that have not previously been considered beyond the WBS, for example resources used across the entire project and not just potentially allocated to a work package. Also, by inviting appropriate SMEs to participate, the project leader should be able to leverage the opportunity, using it as part of the stakeholder engagement strategy by engaging with stakeholders face to face.

If we compare the RBS generated in Figure 10.4 with our original WBS-focused estimating carried out in Chapter 9 "Estimating", you will see differences—for example, additional HSE resources were identified here but missed in the WBS-focused identification of resources for estimating. This brings home the importance of using multiple techniques to ensure items are not missed at the identification stage.

10.3.2 Leverage the WBS

Leveraging the WBS can be carried out in a bottom-up or top-down approach.

- *Bottom-up approach:* The WBS (at the work package or task level) provides an ideal opportunity to collect detailed resource requirements. This approach is ideal when in the Planning stage of the project. Figure 10.5 illustrates this, based on the House Build project, where resource identification has taken place at the work package level.

Figure 10.5 Example work breakdown structure (WBS) and resource identification: House Build example

WBS ID	Description	Resource type	Source	Arrangement	Estimating calulations
1.2.2.1	Excavate				
WP 1.2.2.1-1	Tree removal				
	Temporary fencing and signage	HSE	Coats Hire	Contract	
	ACME tree removal	Contract		Contract	
WP 1.2.2.1-2	Rubbish removal				
	Backhoe	Equipment (internal)		xCharged	
	Dump truck	Contract		Contract	
	Backhoe operator	Resource (internal)			
WP 1.2.2.1-3	Excavate				
	Backhoe	Equipment (internal)		xCharged	
	Dump truck	Contract		Contract	
	Backhoe operator	Resource (internal)			
	Surveyor	Contract		Contract	
	Site supervisor	Resource (internal)		Prorated	
1.2.2.2	Re-bar				
WP 1.2.2.2-1	Lay re-bar				
WP 1.2.2.2-2	Level				
WP 1.2.2.2-3	Tie				
WP 1.2.2.2-4	Survey check				
1.2.2.3	Pour				
WP 1.2.2.3-1	Pour				
WP 1.2.2.3-2	Hardness test				
WP 1.2.2.3-3	Remove planking				

Refer to Chapter 9 "Estimating"

© 2022 Dr Neil Pearson

- *Top-down approach:* The project leader can identify resources from a top-down (higher-level) perspective. This approach is ideal for identifying the key resources (human and other) required by the project when in the Initiation stage—for example, resource commitments at the higher level; deliverable, sub-deliverable or even planning packages.

The WBS or bill of materials might also capture information about how resources will be acquired into the project. (See also "Snapshot from Practice: Defining a WBS and identification of resources".)

If, for example, a WBS deliverable-level item was tagged as being an outsourced component (from a make or buy analysis), then the project leader would not be required to make an estimate of this resource requirement for this deliverable-level item; instead an initial *request for information* or even *request for quotation* can be obtained from potential suppliers (refer to Chapter 17 "Project procurement management"). The project leader can then review these proposal responses and carry out a *map and gap* between what the supplier is stating would be provided in terms of resources, and what additional resources may be required to be supplied by the project. Simple techniques such as the map and gap provide clarity and reduce the need for assumptions (potentially leading to variations being raised later in the project).

SNAPSHOT *from* PRACTICE | **Defining a WBS and identification of resources**

On a recent project, one of the authors (Pearson) worked with an outside consulting company to define a repeatable WBS structure against which resource types could be allocated. This project started off by clearly identifying the top-level deliverables of the project, resulting in 11 modules of a software redevelopment project.

For each of these 11 modules, a repeatable approach was taken to the high-level work packages that had to be achieved. These high-level work packages included:

1. development capture of *as-is* process for the application area

2. assessment and prioritisation of future requirements of the application area

3. gap analysis of the *as-is* process to the high-priority requirements identified

4. assessment of impact to the technology, people and structure of the organisation

5. definition (design) of the *to-be* in terms of process, people, organisations, information and technology requirements

6. design of the epics, increments and sprints from this resulting design (per point 5)

7. development of the schedule to build the required artefacts

8. implementation considerations for the *to-be* design.

These repeatable work packages were applied to each of the 11 modules. Subsequently, the project leader and consultants were able to carry out a high-level identification of the resources required to complete each work package.

Although this activity took some weeks to complete, at the end of the exercise a total high-level resourcing profile of the 11 modules, and therefore the project cost, could be obtained. This informed the Business Case and scoping of the project during the scoping and enabled better management decisions to be made on the affordability of, and therefore the approach to be taken to, the subsequent design of the project, before proceeding further into the detailed Planning stage of the project.

10.3.3 Lessons learned and previous projects

Although leveraging lessons learned can be very helpful to project leaders, this opportunity is (quite surprisingly) sometimes overlooked. Taking a lessons learned approach towards resource management simply means looking at previous, similar projects to learn valuable lessons; in this case the focus is about lessons in relation to resources. For example, a lesson might be around the skill level of consultants used on a business process re-engineering project. The project was promised *experienced* business analysts and the work was estimated based on this resource being experienced; however, when the work was executed, it became apparent that the business analysts were junior, took longer and required more coaching. In this project, the project leader would now ask for detailed résumés of all consultants before engagement to ensure they had sound industry knowledge, had practised over several years and had excellent references (checked).

10.3.4 Leverage pre-defined resource categories, the chart of accounts or project accounting codes

This is almost a checklist style of approach and may manifest in different forms. For example, in one project the author (Pearson) was provided with a list of **project account codes**, resource types, and rates planned and actual from the organisation's project accounting system for a similar past project.

This gave the project an instant insight into all the resources used by that project with the benefit of providing planned and actual rates. Another example might be the provision of how all resources are to be accounted for with the organisation's chart of accounts.

Review the chart of accounts at https://business.vic.gov.au/tools-and-templates/chart-of-accounts-example. This again offers inspiration for types of resources that be or may not be relevant to consider for a project. Towards the end of the list there are categories such as rent, wages, advertising, freight, utilities—as a project leader you can therefore raise the questions: Are any of these resource types required in our project? Have we missed any that need to be considered? Do we now have a formal type or category name that we should use in the project to align with the company's accounting practices?

By applying multiple resource identification techniques, the project leader (in conjunction with the project team and other SMEs) should be able to carry out a comprehensive resource identification for the project.

10.3.5 Resource assignment

A technique often used to validate work (the WBS) and who/what resources will do this work is the Resource Allocation Matrix (RAM). It is most often presented as a hybrid WBS and RASCI Matrix. Figure 10.6 illustrates a partial RAM for the House Build example.

Figure 10.6 Example RAM by RASCI

WBS ID	Description	Human resources				Contractor resources			Physical resources	
		Project leader	Site supervisor	Surveyor	Backhoe operator	Contractor: trees	Contractor: concrete	Hire company: Coats (fence)	Backhoe	Dump truck
1.2.2.1	Excavate									
WP 1.2.2.1-1	Tree removal		A			AR				
WP 1.2.2.1-2	Rubbish removal		A		R				S	S
WP 1.2.2.1-3	Excavate		A	R	R				S	S
1.2.2.2	Re-bar									
WP 1.2.2.2-1	Lay re-bar									
WP 1.2.2.2-2	Level									
WP 1.2.2.2-3	Tie									
WP 1.2.2.2-4	Survey check									
1.2.2.3	Pour									
WP 1.2.2.3-1	Pour									
WP 1.2.2.3-2	Hardness test									
WP 1.2.2.3-3	Remove planking									

© 2022 Dr Neil Pearson

The RAM indicates who (which role in the project) is accountable, responsible, consulted, informed or supports each of the work packages in the WBS. In building the RAM, the project leader and project team must think hard about what resources would be accountable (only one role can take this role), who would be responsible, who would support (the responsible), and who would be consulted and informed.

Other versions of the RAM might not be driven by the RASCI but by *effort required*, as illustrated in Figure 10.7, where the quantity of resources are indicated in the intersection of role to work package. This approach allows for extracting various other information, as in this example totals of each type of resource—these can be informational, providing input into discussions with maybe the resource owner in the organisation about resource availability.

Figure 10.7 Example RAM by effort

WBS ID	Description	Duration/days (from estimation) using PERT	Human resources				Contractor resources			Physical resources	
			Project leader	Site supervisor	Surveyor	Backhoe operator	Contractor: trees	Contractor: concrete	Hire company: Coats (fence)	Backhoe	Dump truck
1.2.2.1	Excavate										
WP 1.2.2.1-1	Tree removal	5.2		1			2.0				
WP 1.2.2.1-2	Rubbish removal	1.5		1		1.0				1.0	1.0
WP 1.2.2.1-3	Excavate	5		1	0.5	1.0				1.0	1.0
	Work package (effort .5/day increments) by resource*		0	3	0.5	2	2	0	0	2	2

*Not duration of work package

1.2.2.2	Re-bar
WP 1.2.2.2-1	Lay re-bar
WP 1.2.2.2-2	Level
WP 1.2.2.2-3	Tie
WP 1.2.2.2-4	Survey check

1.2.2.3	Pour
WP 1.2.2.3-1	Pour
WP 1.2.2.3-2	Hardness test
WP 1.2.2.3-3	Remove planking

© 2022 Dr Neil Pearson

RAM

10.3.6 Capturing further resource information

The capturing and analysis of project team roles at this stage is vital. Most project leaders will maintain an all-encompassing Skills Matrix or similar—collating detailed information on particularly human resources (although a similar matrix could be developed for physical resources for your industry). Additional information for human resources captured in this matrix could include the following.

1. *Resource/skills identification:* Required skills are identified against each WBS item/work package (as are the resource loading, cost and duration for the required resource). This component of the matrix is typically populated during the development of the WBS and the estimating activities of the project (during the Initiation or Planning stage of the project life cycle). Refer to Table 10.4.

Table 10.4 Resource identification information

Information captured	Description
Work package	A link to the WBS, where the resource was identified.
Resource category	A category for the resource—such as tester, developer, electrician. This is useful for when the project leader wishes to look at the total requirements of a resource category, across the whole project. Decisions can then be made on how to source this resource to the project (e.g. full time versus contracted when needed).
Resource skills	The skills the resource needs to have. These could, for example, range from specific skills, such as .NET programming skills, to softer skills such as **change management** skills.
Resource name(s)	Actual resource name if known at this time.
Project stage	State in which stage of the project the resource is primarily going to be deployed.
Resource loading	Is the resource *front-loaded* (used heavily at the start of the project/stage), *back-loaded* (used heavily at the end of the project/stage) or *normally loaded* (an even usage of the resource throughout the whole stage/project)?
Estimated resource usage percentage	Estimated usage of the resource—obtained via the estimating activities carried out in the Initiation and Planning stages of the project.
Estimated duration required	In real terms, how long is the resource required for (i.e. number of hours/days/weeks/months)?
Resource calendar	Is the resource available for a standard working week, or is it only available on certain days of the week? Is the resource based on a shift calendar situation such as those used in the mining industry?

2. *Staffing management information:* This section of the matrix should indicate the sources of the resources and whether these are to be obtained from within the organisation or externally. How a resource is to be released upon project completion should also be addressed. For contracted resources this is an easy task. However, for internal resources that have been seconded to the project from the business, there may be several stages that have to occur to move the resource back to its substantive position in the business, especially if a backfill has been put in place. Refer to Table 10.5.

Table 10.5 Staffing management information

Information captured	Description
Internal resource source	Is the resource to be sourced internally and, if so, from where within the organisation?
External resource source	If the resource is to be sourced externally, which agency or company may be able to provide the resource?
Resource acquisition strategy	How will the project leader bring this resource into the project? Will the resource be subject to special approvals? Does the project leader have to go through (sometimes a lengthy) internal recruitment process (as documented in the organisation's internal recruitment policies and procedures)? How does it impact the project schedule?
Resource funding	How is the resource to be funded—directly to the project budget, to be internally cross-charged, or will the resource be covered in company overheads?
Estimated cost	What are the estimated costs of the resource? Is there a day rate arrangement, or a standard rate arrangement of cross-charging for internal resources?
Extension considerations	If use of the resource needs to be extended, what associated considerations will the project need to include? If use of the resource is extended, does the rate change, for example? Is a retainer fee appropriate to keep the resource on the project's books?
Release strategy	What considerations have to be put in place when the resource is released from the project? For example, if the resource (a person) was seconded from within the organisation and their position in the business has been back-filled by another person, will this mean the project leader will have two resources to make arrangements for? As release considerations can be complex, the project leader should consider the release strategy at the point when the resource is identified, thereby setting the expectations and hopefully a smooth transition of resources from the project when they are no longer required.

© 2022 Dr Neil Pearson

3. *Training needs analysis:* This section aims to identify qualifications, certifications (trade or professional) and insurances that may be required. An analysis should be undertaken to identify any gaps in training, as these might have implications for the project in terms of training that needs to be provided, and the associated cost(s) and schedule implications of this. For example, if we require *trades* on the project to carry out electrical testing, then not only would they need relevant qualifications, but also current industry/government body certification(s). If their certification(s) were to expire during project execution, this could place the project in an awkward situation. Refer to Table 10.6.

Table 10.6 Training needs analysis

Information captured	Description
Required certifications	What certifications must the resource have, from a legal and compliance perspective? For example, an electrical tester must hold certifications from state/territory or regulatory bodies in order to practice. Identify what these are and check that these are valid for the duration of the activities they have been assigned to.
Expiration date	A record of when these certifications are due to expire.
Required qualifications	What qualifications must the resource hold? For example, is a degree in electrical engineering required?
Training gaps	Given that resources with the necessary skills, certifications and qualifications may not be readily available, how will these be obtained from the project environment? There may be integrative implications to the project schedule (e.g. downtime of the resource while the resource is trained) and/or a cost implication (e.g. the cost of training or certification), which must be included within the project budget.
Insurances/company registrations/visa requirements	The project leader must ensure that the company, contractor or consultant holds current and relevant insurances (some of these may have been reviewed as part of procurement activities). If a resource is being brought in from overseas, have appropriate checks been made to ensure they hold a relevant work visa?
Employment status	The location of the resource within the recruitment process needs to be tracked to check whether they are progressing through the process on schedule, so they can join the project at the right time. Recruitment processes are notorious for not going according to plan! For example, if no suitable personnel are identified in initial recruitment interviews, delays will ensue. Role(s) will have to be readvertised, new applications sifted through and interviews organised and held for a second group of candidates.
Company induction	What company inductions does the resource have to progress through? Are the induction programs in line with the project schedule or does the project need to make special arrangements with the HR department?
Project induction	Has the resource been suitably inducted into the project environment? It is not unusual to have a project induction in medium-to-large projects.

© 2022 Dr Neil Pearson

4. *Performance management:* This section shows how an individual will be performance managed within the project environment. Questions should be asked around: What key performance indicators (KPIs) are to be set? What targets are to be achieved? Refer to Table 10.7.

Table 10.7 Performance management information

Information captured	Description
Performance management arrangements	How is the resource to be performance managed? If the resource was recruited directly to the project, it would be the project leader's responsibility to put in place the necessary performance management schedules. If, however, the resource already reports to a line manager in the business as their functional manager, what arrangements will be put in place (with the line manager) to performance manage them?
Performance indicators and targets	A project leader should define a set of performance indicators and targets that must be achieved by the resource. These may, or may not, be linked to performance payments or bonuses.
Achievement (tracked during the project and at project closure)	Performance should be tracked for each resource on an ongoing basis, as this makes being able to make any recommendations at the end of the project easier (e.g. when deciding whether to recommend bonus payments, if any are available).

© 2022 Dr Neil Pearson

 Skills Matrix

The same thinking can be developed and applied to identified equipment (Table 10.8) and identified materials (Table 10.9).

Table 10.8 Capturing of equipment resource information

Identify	Example
What is it?	Z-lift
What features should it have?	Stabilisers and safety cut-out for instability
How is it maintained? By whom?	Hire company
Who is to supply it?	Coates Hire
Is a backup supplier required; if so, who is it?	Kennards Hire
What quantity is required?	2
What is the cost by (unit)?	$550/day
Are there set-up and tear-down costs?	Delivery and removal included in hire rate
Who's responsible for breakdowns?	Hire company
How fast is a repair guaranteed?	1 business day

© 2022 Dr Neil Pearson

Table 10.9 Capturing of material resource information

Identify	Example
What is it?	Concrete
What grade/quality is required?	Suitable for site class re. AS 2870
How is quality tested?	Core sample(s)
How is it supplied (unit)?	Cubic metre
Who is to supply it?	ABC contractor
Is a backup supplier required, if so, who is it?	XYZ contractor
What quantity is required?	30 cubic metres
What is the cost by (unit)?	$300 cubic metre
Are there delivery costs?	Included
Are there delivery requests?	Site supervisor and site team must be onsite and ready to accept delivery for pouring

© 2022 Dr Neil Pearson

Although the task of building and maintaining this level of information may, at first, seem excessive, the reality is that, given the vast potential for delays in activities to occur and for money to be burned unnecessarily in a project, taking the time to prepare and maintain this type of information can pay great dividends in the long term.

Ultimately this allocation of resources to work is usually captured on the project schedule (refer to Chapter 11 "Project schedule management"). Figure 10.8 shows the results of investing time in professional scheduling software, which can assist in this task greatly. This figure shows a partly developed project Gantt chart being created by the project officer (or in larger projects a dedicated project scheduler).

Figure 10.8 Microsoft Project resource assignment

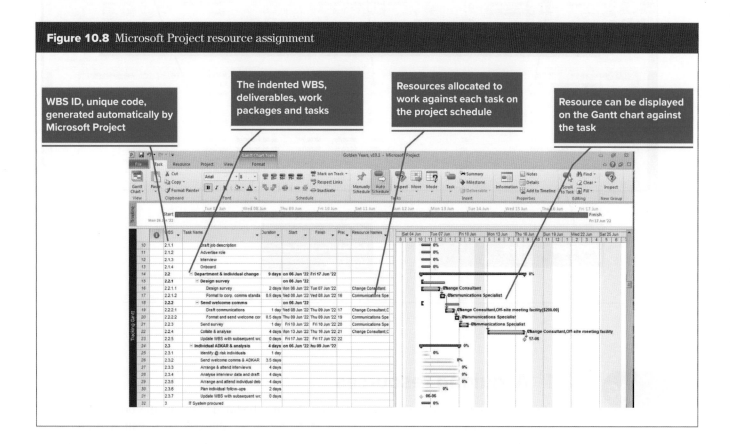

The resources are entered into a different form in **Microsoft Project** before being assigned to the task. An example of a work-in-progress entry of resources into the Microsoft Project resource sheet can be seen in Figure 10.9.

Figure 10.9 Microsoft Project resource set-up

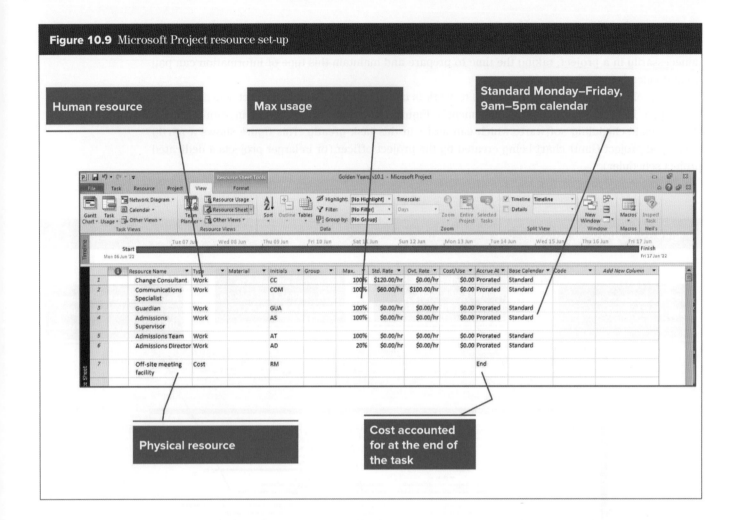

10.4 | Acquiring resources

Once the resources have been identified, estimated and scheduled—that is, the project leader not only knows *what* resources are required, but also *how much* the resources will cost and *when* those resources will be required—the project can next take steps towards acquiring these required resources. The project leader should be able to negotiate resources from those able to provide resources to the project. If the project leader cannot successfully negotiate resources, it can fall to the project sponsor to do this on the project leader's behalf (PMI 2017). On paper this sounds simple, but the act of acquiring resources can be fraught with challenges that can affect the planning of the project. For example:

1. *Organisational politics kick in:* Executives and managers play a political game to retain resources on lower-priority projects because giving up resources might indicate to others that work in their department is slow, or they strategise to retain their staff headcount, which they perceive as influencing their power in the organisation. Unfortunately, these types of activities are still commonplace in many organisations (whether commercial, government or other).

2. *A resource is withdrawn:* A department or function might suddenly withdraw resources at short notice (Murphy's Law states this will occur just before the resource is scheduled to start a work package!) This could be in response to any number of situations, but typically is due to firefighting a crisis in the operational side of the business.

3. *The business restructures due to changes in market conditions:* This should not be a surprise but if it does occur during the project, it could cause substantial resource issues.

4. *There are restrictions to resources from the outset.*

   ■ The project leader typically does not have direct control over the resources required.

   ■ The resources could be subject to union, enterprise or collective bargaining arrangements, and therefore cannot be released from business-as-usual activities, without the individual required having to leave a job and join the project as a contractor (not unheard of).

   ■ The resources could be in a supply-and-demand relationship where others (project and companies) with deeper pockets are able to secure supplies.

Tips that may help the project leader to stave off potential problems around resource acquisition include:

■ *For internally identified resources:* Identify who the controlling stakeholder is so they can be brought into the primary stakeholder circle of the project. Identify what strategies must be actioned to ensure their continued buy-in and commitment to the project to secure needed resources to the project. A commitment in email gained from them will not form an internal department-to-department contract. Ascertain the WIFFM factor for the releasing manager; they could be receiving a benefit from the project?

■ *For externally sourced resources:* The project leader needs to professionally engage with the supplier and, again, develop the required stakeholder engagement strategy. It may be that the project leader must commit to pre-contract conditions or retainers to secure the resource to the project. This technique is prevalent where internal resources are not available, and externally the resource is in scarce supply.

A checklist to support the acquisition of human and other resources could include items such as:

● Is the resource available at the timeslot required by the project?

● If the timeslot changes, how does this affect the resource availability?

● Does the cost of the resource include any hidden costs (e.g. does the project pay superannuation payments in addition to the cross-charge for the resource)?

● Are the resource costs within the expectations of the project?

● Does the resource (if human) have the correct skills and competencies to be employed in the required role?

● Is the project willing to address skills and competency gaps and fund training/scheduling?

● Does the resource (if human) have the relevant industry experience?

● Will there be difficulties in communicating with the resource (if human) in terms of language, cultures or, more commonly, time differences?

When considering the acquisition of resources, a project leader must contemplate:

■ any *pre-work* required during the Planning stage of the project to ensure that resources will be available when they are required, and in the correct amounts they are needed (i.e. there are no unwanted surprises). For example, a work package that requires contractor ABC would require an additional work package to recruit the resource, this work package being started some eight weeks prior to when the contractor is actually required to start a work package.

■ resource-readiness (in the Execution stage of the project), such as ensuring required resources are scheduled to the project at the right time (i.e. on time). It is no good, for example, having expensive heavy-lift equipment on site at the right time if its operator has not been inducted into site WHS practices, has not completed necessary administrative paperwork, and so on. This alone could result in schedule slippage as the equipment is ready but the operator is not. Resources need to be aligned with the activity they are required for.

Acquiring physical resources means engaging with suppliers (most probably external to the organisation) to obtain the physical resources (e.g. equipment and materials). Acquiring these physical resources is likely to take on one of the procurement options outlined in Chapter 17 "Project procurement management".

10.5 Monitoring and controlling resources

The project schedule will drive when resources are planned to be onboarded to the project, in readiness for the resource to be used. The project leader must consider **resource scheduling** carefully (whether human or other resources), as during the monitoring and controlling stage of these resources, the project leader will be using the project's schedule as a baseline from which to monitor any variances in resource usage, once the project enters the Execution stage. The project leader needs to carefully consider what they are monitoring in terms of resources. For instance:

1. Was the resource made available at the scheduled time it was planned for in the project schedule?

2. Does the project schedule represent (and has it been updated with) all variation requests? Also, has the subsequent impact of the variation request on resources to be used in the future also been checked as a part of the variation analysis (refer to Chapter 8 "Defining the scope of a project", section 8.8).

3. If a project is using pooled resources, organised by a project management office (PMO) (discussed in Chapter 11 "Project schedule management"), the project leader will need to check whether other projects pulling on the same pooled resources have changed their needs for the resource. It may be that the resource will now not be available when it is needed, due to slippage of time in a dependent project.

4. For human resources, have personnel arrived with the requisite (mandatory) skills? Were they inducted into the project in time to start work on allocated work packages, at the scheduled start time?

5. Also, for human resources, has anything changed in the political landscape/marketplace that may affect resourcing of the project? For example, has a new mine site been announced that pays above market rates—if so, what is/could be the impact to resources on the project?

6. If (physical) resources (such as tools and equipment) are committed to the project over a longer duration, what backup arrangements have been put in place to mitigate the risk of the original resource identified not being available?

7. Do (physical) resources (such as tools and equipment) committed to the project over a longer duration have an appropriate maintenance schedule and has this been accounted for in the project's schedule and budget?

8. Is the expected output rate (performance) being obtained from the resource? Were expectations of what the resource could produce overly optimistic? This could apply to human resources (e.g. number of story points attended to by a developer) and to physical resources (e.g. number of tonnes of dirt shifted per hour by a backhoe). Procedures must be established in the project at the relevant WBS level to track such metrics and allow for identification of where variances are occurring so corrective actions can be taken (usually via the project's variation management process).

9. What happens when an internal resource that has been committed to the project is suddenly not available at the exact point the project requires it? Hopefully, the project leader has read this book and has carried out a risk review of all WBS resource allocations during the Planning stage of the project. In this case, they will have a risk contingency plan to fall back on.

10. Have *quality of work* and *schedule of payments* been appropriately linked to the resource's allocated work, so the project leader knows when a resource has produced the correct quantity and quality of work, which then triggers payment for the work achieved? Miscommunication

about the work achieved in a project and lack of payment for that work has been known to lead to the withdrawal of resources from a project until payment has been received for work done! This could be a potential delay to the project.

11. Being allocated lesser-quality resources in lieu of planned higher-quality resources—for example, an experienced developer is initially promised to the project, but a graduate with no experience is provided instead; or a planned concrete pump, capable of 140 cubic metres/hour was promised, but a 65 cubic metres/hour pump turns up on site.

The project leader must therefore ensure there are the correct checks and balances in place to ensure that resources turn up at the scheduled time, produce the promised outputs and are remunerated accordingly.

10.6 Resource closure

Referring to Figure 10.1, box G, it can be seen that the resource discussion is now moving towards the resource closure activities. The project may have resources that:

■ are not consumed during the project that will have to be released or disposed of at the end of the project; this could be quantities of raw materials that have to be sold and funds recovered into the project, or waste materials that must be paid for by the project for their disposal

■ were used in the project, but which the project leader has to release, for example for:

● human resources, this could mean releasing contractors, returning internally sourced employees back to business-as-usual operations, or promoting project team members to project roles on other projects (discussed in Chapter 21 "Project closure")

● physical resources, this could be the return of equipment to a hire/lease company, the environmentally considerate disposal of unused raw materials, or sale of equipment no longer required.

When resources of any type are onboarded into the project (at the resource acquisition stage), it is important to also consider how that resource will exit the project at project closure (if it is not fully consumed during the project). The project leader should ensure that suitable arrangements have been considered, any risks identified, associated costs included in the project budget and work package, and tasks included in the project schedule. Refer back to Table 10.4.

Lessons learned in relation to resources would also be captured in the project-wide Lessons Learned Register. Some lessons could relate to the various human resource, recruitment, approval, onboard and release policies and procedures—if so, the project leader should debrief the HR manager before departing the project; the same applies to any other department where organisational practices in relation to project environments do not provide the best outcome.

Summary

This chapter has focused on several topics around the identification, information capture relating to, and scheduling of resources that are required to complete a project. The identification and estimating of resources was also discussed in Chapter 9 "Estimating", where the focus was on estimating against the WBS. This chapter has taken a more holistic approach to resource management in a project environment, including:

■ the identification of all resource types required by a project, including human resources, tools, plant, equipment, raw materials, capital, services and any other relevant category of resource

■ the use of the RBS, the WBS, the RAM and other techniques to ensure a comprehensive approach is taken towards the identification of resources and the allocation of these resources against the project's work packages and tasks

■ considerations to be aware of when allocating resources and onboarding these to the project at the required time in the project

■ the monitoring and controlling of resources, which is particularly critical during the Execution stage of the project, and how to avoid some common issues that may arise.

The next chapter tackles the subject of project schedule management, which includes the scheduling of the resources identified as discussed in this chapter within a professional scheduling package.

Review questions

1. What does a Resource Management Plan highlight the need for, when undertaking resource management?
2. Provide eight examples of resource types (or categories).
3. Why is a RASCI useful in planning project resource management?
4. Why is a RAM useful?
5. What additional project-led information can be useful to a project leader when they are planning human resource needs?
6. Name three resource identification techniques.
7. Identify a minimum of four factors that can affect the acquisition of resources.
8. Why do we monitor and control resources?
9. What are the key activities a project leader must attend to in project resource management?
10. What is likely to happen once the first allocation of the human resource to work packages and tasks occurs, and when is this communicated to the project team?

Exercises

1. For a project you are currently working on (individually at your organisation), capture notes (on flip-chart paper) of how you categorise the types of resources and how this links to any accounting mechanisms.
2. Discuss in your study groups (or make notes as an individual) some of the issues you have personally experienced when monitoring and controlling resources in a project you have worked on.
3. Capture three lessons learned in relation to resources (human or other) from projects you have worked on in the past or are working on currently.

References

Project Management Institute (PMI) 2017, *A Guide to the Project Management Body of Knowledge*, 6th edition, PMI.

CHAPTER 11

Project schedule management

Learning elements

11A Understand the basis of project schedule management and a typical workflow of events.

11B Establish sound scheduling governance and other factors, and capture the information in the Schedule Management Plan.

11C Understand the significance of building a realistic project schedule.

11D Understand the relationship between activities and resources in a scheduling context.

11E Be able to identify and diagnose some of the more common issues in project scheduling.

11F Be aware of key monitoring and controlling activities.

In this chapter

11.1 Introduction

11.2 Planning schedule development

11.3 Developing the project schedule

11.4 From work package/task to network

11.5 From network to project schedule

11.6 Advanced scheduling techniques

11.7 Advanced schedule efficiency techniques

11.8 The resource scheduling challenge

11.9 Assigning and monitoring project work

11.10 Multi-project resource optimisation

Summary

11.1 | Introduction

Project schedule management is probably one of the more complex areas of project management. Devising an elegant project schedule that represents all the work of the project in a considered manner can provide many challenges. To support the development of project schedules, we will continue in further developing the following artefacts as inputs into the scheduling workflow:

1. the **work breakdown structure (WBS)**, work packages and tasks

2. estimating to a more accurate level the duration/effort and resources required to accomplish the work packages and tasks

3. developing and understanding **project network** diagrams as a way of understanding the concepts behind the **Gantt chart**, and in improving our sequencing ability.

As a result of the above, this chapter will also take the reader through the basic steps of developing a project schedule, often referred to as the *Gantt chart*, loading the resources against the schedule, and the subsequent optimisation of the schedule.

These general scheduling activities are indicated in Figure 11.1.

Figure 11.1 General scheduling activities

A. Planning schedule management
- Develop the Schedule Management Plan
- Variation management process (VMP)
- Project-wide RASCI

B. Reviewing WBS
- Work breakdown structure
- Further estimating

C. Scheduling activities
- Work breakdown structure
- AON diagram
- Gantt chart
- Resource information
- Calendars
- Milestone chart

D. Seeking efficiencies
- Crashing
- Fast-tracking
- Resource utilisation
- Schedule baseline approval

E. Monitoring and controlling schedule
- Project reporting
- Project schedule
- Milestone tracking
- Variation management

F. Closing schedule
- Planned and variations versus actual
- Final schedule status reporting

This chapter will take the WBS, work packages and tasks (Chapter 8 "Defining the scope of a project"), and the resources and durations/effort assigned (Chapter 9 "Estimating" and Chapter 10 "Project resource management") to provide the typical workflow most project leaders (or project schedulers, if this a full-time role in the project) will work through. The workflow we are working through from a practice perspective is captured in Figure 11.2, where in this chapter we review the activities that are taking place in relation to the core project data of work (work package and tasks), duration/effort and resources. We bring this data together to create the all-important project schedule, often represented as a Gantt chart, and today less frequently the **activity-on-node (AON)** network diagram.

Figure 11.2 Scope—estimate—plan

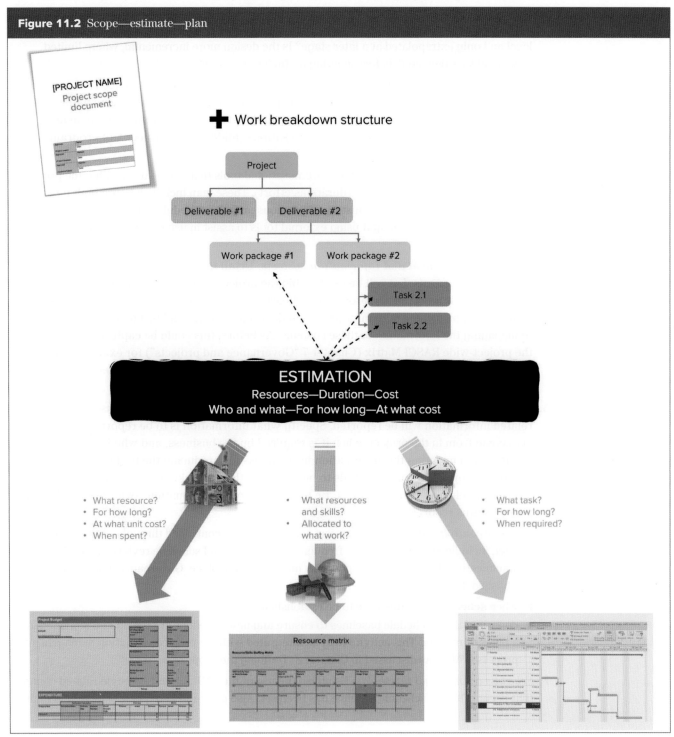

11.2 | Planning schedule development

As with all the areas of knowledge, we must first plan and establish the governance and guidelines around the schedule management work. The output of these planning activities is the integrated Project Management Plan (integrated PMP) subsidiary plan artefact, referred to as the **Schedule Management Plan**. Before we examine the detail in how to craft and optimise project network diagrams and project schedules, let us first review the typical contents of the Schedule Management Plan:

1. *The schedule management approach:* Describe the overarching strategy and approach towards the scheduling of the project. What is the design of the project from a time perspective? Is the project being broken into multiple stages, and the rolling-wave planning technique being applied—therefore there are WBS *planning packages* that will be planned at a top-down level and only extrapolated at a later stage? Is the design more incremental, where limited functionality is delivered, before layering on further features?

2. *Policy and procedures:* Identify any company or project management office (PMO) policy and procedures that must be adopted by the project in relation to schedule management (e.g. adoption of Microsoft Project as the scheduling tool for milestone management and reporting, as documented in the organisation's guidelines to project and program schedule management).

3. *Time estimation tools:* Document any organisational tools that will be used within the project for the further estimation of time (durations/effort). These may include inhouse built tools that provide estimates based on the history of previous projects' schedule, budget, resourcing and other data. Do the same thing if using external tools to assist in using industry guidelines and online resources.

4. *Schedule management and information systems:* Detail the project's information management systems that will be used within the project for the management of the project schedule and, if reported, the production of earned value management (EVM) data. This would be supplemented with information on the project's roles and responsibilities in relation to managing the information in these systems. As before, this could be captured within the project-wide RASCI Matrix (Chapter 7 "Governance and projects") for example, and categorised as "Schedule", so these business rules and decisions can be filtered and cut-and-pasted here for communication to the project team.

5. *Schedule/time reporting arrangements:* Identify within which project reports schedule-related information will be reported. Specify what information is to be reported on, where it is to come from in the project, when it is required by the business, and who is responsible for collating and updating this information in readiness for producing the project status report. If a lot of project information needs to be reported, this will take time, effort, resources and, ultimately, costs to the project. Be lean with project information—who reads a 30-page project status report?

6. *Schedule control:* Define how the project schedule will be controlled throughout the life of the project, including details about the frequency of updates and schedule reviews, as well as how communicating the schedule and progress made will take place. Governance also needs to be established, for example about:

   ■ when **schedule baselines** are to be established
   ■ control of these schedule baselines to ensure any new baselines are issued and managed in a planned manner. This activity may be integrated with the project's variation management process (VMP) (as discussed in Chapter 8 "Defining the scope of a project").

7. *Schedule changes and thresholds:* Establish the use of the VMP for any schedule-related changes that occur after the schedule baseline has been set. Also captured here are any threshold limits

the project leader holds (as agreed by the Steering Committee), for example: "The project leader can approve variations with a schedule impact only of <.5/day slippage to the critical path, but must also report these slippages to the Steering Committee". Again, this could be captured in the VMP governance and/or within the project-wide RASCI.

8. *% complete rules:* The project leader should agree and document how *% complete* for a work package/task is to be determined. Document, then communicate these rules to the project team. For example, consider which of the below (or other) rules is to be applied by anyone leading or working on a work package:

   ■ 0/100 rule: This rule assumes credit is earned for having performed the work once it is completed. Hence, 100 per cent of the time/budget is earned when the work package / task is completed. This rule could be used for work packages / tasks that have very short durations.

   ■ 50/50 rule: This approach allows 50 per cent of the value of the work package budget to be earned when it is started, and 50 per cent to be earned when the package is completed. This rule is also popular for work packages / tasks of a short duration and small total costs.

   ■ Interval rule: Some organisations use a fixed interval per cent complete rule (rounding down to 25%/50%/75%/100% intervals). The intervals can, however, take on any set of interval values, as defined by the organisation. Note that intervals of thirds are also popular.

   ■ Actual per cent complete: Based on the work package leads *% complete* calculation; can be subjective if rules around how to calculate are not documented.

   ■ EVM: provision of earned value management data, using project data and EVM calculations.

9. *Schedule management roles and responsibilities:* Describe the roles and responsibilities in relation to the management of the schedule, how data is updated (entered) and by whom, and verified and reported on (for example).

10. *Assumptions and constraints:* Consider what assumptions are being made in relation to the schedule factors for the project. (Remember: An *assumption* is an assumed statement of truth.) Also, capture information about what schedule factors may constrain the project. For example, if access to a particular resource type is restricted, this will impact the schedule with the effect of extending the duration of any assigned work packages/tasks.

11. *Risk review:* Ensure that a risk review of any scheduling activities is carried out and that identified risks are entered into the Risk Register under the category of "Schedule". Either reflect those risks in this part of the Schedule Management Plan or make reference to the Risk Register filtered to the category of "Schedule".

12. *Lessons learned:* Document lessons learned from relevant previous projects (either internal or external to the organisation) regarding schedule management, and state how this project will be designed to avoid or exploit these lessons.

 Schedule Management Plan

11.3 | Developing the project schedule

Once the governance around project scheduling has been determined, the task of developing the project schedule can start. The project schedule is developed from the information generated in building the WBS and from the estimation of resources, the effort required and the overall duration of each work package.

In today's busy project environments, it is here the project leader would transfer all the information in a project scheduling software (Gantt chart); however, it is very useful to aid the understanding of what is happening automatically when a Gantt chart is created by first looking at the activity on node (AON) network diagram.

Both the AON and Gantt chart are graphic visualisations of the work to be carried out. They both depict project activities (work packages/tasks), the logical sequences involved and the interdependencies of the activities to be completed. The AON also depicts the timepoint for activities to start and finish, along with details of the *longest path(s) through the network, but the shortest time that the project can be completed in*—referred to as the **critical path**.

The project network is the framework that is used for the project information system that will be used by the project leader to track the project and to make decisions concerning project time, cost and performance. Developing the project network takes time, and therefore it costs money. Are networks worth the struggle, then? The answer is a resounding *Yes!* The network is easily understood by others because it presents a graphic representation of the flow and sequence of work through the project. Once the network is developed, it can very easily be modified or changed when unexpected events occur as the project progresses (e.g. to model changes to the project). For example, if materials for a task are delayed, the impact can be quickly assessed and the whole project revised in only a few minutes with an appropriate software package (such as Microsoft Project). These revisions can subsequently be communicated to all project participants quickly and efficiently, once baselined only after any changes have been through the VMP.

The project network also provides other invaluable information and insights: it provides the basis for scheduling resources and tracking costs, and it enhances communication that melds all managers, teams and individuals together in meeting the time, cost and performance objectives of the project. It provides a calculated estimate of the project's duration, rather than picking a project completion date from a hat or merely applying someone's preferred date. The network provides times when activities can start and finish, and when they can be delayed. It provides the basis for budgeting the cash flow of the project. It identifies which activities are *critical* and therefore which should not be delayed if the project is to be completed as planned. It highlights which activities to consider if the project needs to be compressed to meet a deadline.

There are other reasons why project networks are worth their weight in gold. Basically, they minimise surprises by getting the schedule out early, thereby allowing corrective feedback to take place. It's no wonder that practitioners commonly claim that the project network represents three-quarters of the planning process. Perhaps this is an exaggeration, but nonetheless it signals the perceived importance of the project network as a guidance tool that can support project leaders working in the field. Although this is one of the more complex knowledge areas of project management, time invested in becoming familiar with these tools and techniques not only provides benefits for planning the current project, but also can facilitate diagnosis and replanning when things do not go as planned.

11.4 | **From work package/task to network**

As mentioned previously, the most common route in contemporary project management is to go from a well-defined and estimated WBS directly into the project schedule (or Gantt chart) within a scheduling software application. However, from a learning perspective, taking a step back and understanding the AON network diagram as a means to calculate the critical path will pay back in scheduling later multiple times as you will be able to comprehend float (**slack**) and the true impact of the critical in greater depth. This sequence is depicted in Figure 11.3.

Project networks are developed from the WBS. In practice, you will have to make some decisions before embarking on this process of moving the WBS (with estimating information for duration and effort) to the AON, in order to take the bones of the AON into a project scheduling package and create the project schedule.

Figure 11.3 From WBS to AON to project schedule (Gantt chart)

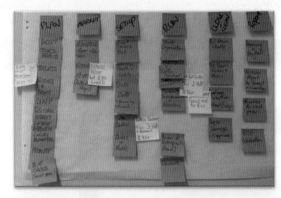

Work breakdown structure (WBS) plus estimating information

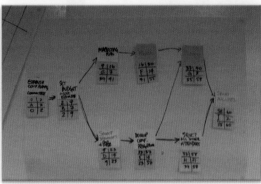

Activity on node (AON) network diagram

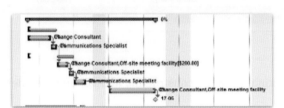

Project schedule, Gantt chart

IN THEORY | Duration and effort

When we were talking about estimating, a discussion on duration versus effort was deferred to this chapter on scheduling—so let's look at the differences.

In drafting the WBS, refer to Figure 11.4, part A, the deliverable and its associated work packages were idea-showered. In *estimating*, the effort (in days) required for each work package was estimated. However, to obtain the *duration* for the deliverable, we cannot simply sum the effort of each work package; we must think about the sequence of the work packages, which will then provide us with a truer duration for the deliverable. If we had summed up the effort for each work package, a figure of 39 days would have resulted.

Referring to Figure 11.4, part B, the process of sequencing the work packages has been started and we can now see if we take the effort of each of the longest tasks in the sequence (i.e. the critical path for this segment of the WBS) that the duration of the work package is actually 26 days.

Therefore (without scheduling the WBS) it is often difficult to provide a *time estimate* based solely on the WBS. The same activity could have been carried out if it were a work package broken down into tasks—the same principle applies.

(Continues)

In Theory: Duration and effort (*Continued*)

If we were then to additionally layer on the resource availability (the resource calendars), then Figure 11.4, part B would likely change again. This is why later in this chapter we layer resources onto the schedule!

Figure 11.4 Effort versus duration

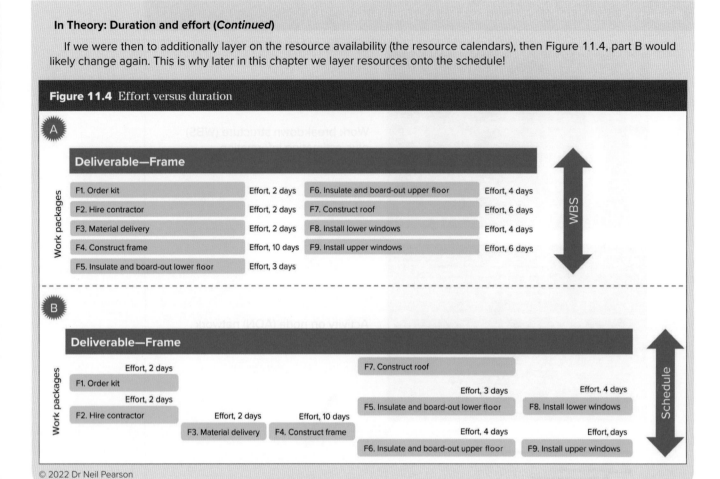

© 2022 Dr Neil Pearson

Let's now step through this process of taking the WBS, constructing an AON and then developing the resulting project schedule (Gantt chart).

The process starts with the WBS; there are three scenarios that need to be considered before sequencing the work to be done into an AON diagram.

1. If the WBS has been developed down to work package only level, then the work packages become the activities on the AON diagram. Later the deliverables or sub-deliverables that the work packages roll-up into become the summary tasks in, for example, Microsoft Project.

2. If the WBS has been developed down to the task level, then the tasks become the activities on the AON diagram. Later the work packages that the tasks roll-up into become the summary tasks in, for example, Microsoft Project.

3. If the WBS has some work packages and other work packages broken down into tasks, then use the lowest level across the entire AON, whether this is a hybrid of work packages for some elements of the WBS and tasks below a work package for other elements of the WBS. *Note:* Where a work package has been broken into tasks, we ignore the work package itself—only the tasks below the work package become activities on the AON.

There is an overhead in the project (and the business!) to being overly zealous in the breaking down of work packages into many, many tasks. It goes without saying that the more detail that is captured, the more work (and potential complexity) there is in managing it—it is indeed a fine line to decompose work packages to a level of comfort for managing the project and being overly detailed and incurring project overheads in micro-managing the detailed tasks later in the monitoring and controlling of the project.

Referring to Figure 11.5, the architect has provided some more detail on the House Build—Frame deliverable, providing the work packages and effort for each. The architect has also provided some

Figure 11.5 WBS House Build

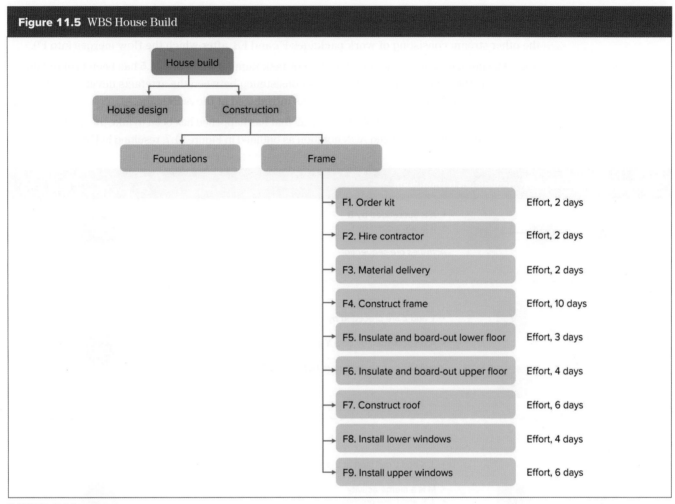

© 2022 Dr Neil Pearson

advice on working in this part of the world at this time of year: "Labour is cheap, the weather is inclement, the roof should be priority before any internal work starts".

Step 1: Sequence (in this case) the work packages

The first step is to take the work packages and develop the sequence and **relationships** between the work packages in the AON diagram. Bear in mind when you do this, dummy nodes may have to be introduced to sequence successfully.

With the advice of the architect, we have simply taken the work packages and sequenced, applying AON notation as outlined in Figure 11.7. This has resulted in the AON as represented in Figure 11.6.

Figure 11.6 Step 1: WBS to AON

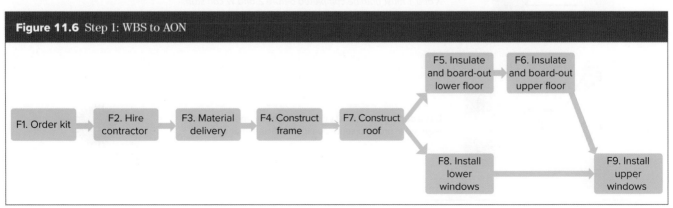

© 2022 Dr Neil Pearson

Here it can be seen that work packages F1 through F4 are sequential, and F7 becomes a *split node* into two **parallel** streams of activity, one stream consisting of work packages F5 and F6, the other stream consisting of work packages F7 and F8, after which the flow merges into F9.

Note: The unique (work package reference) or task number in Figure 11.5 has been brought down into AON as the same identifier. This keeps consistency between the artefacts developed and saves confusion if a new number scheme was introduced at the AON stage.

So, at this point in building the AON diagram, all that has happened has been to take the work packages (or tasks) and sequence applying AON notation as outlined in Figure 11.7, resulting in Figure 11.6.

Figure 11.7 Common AON sequencing terminology

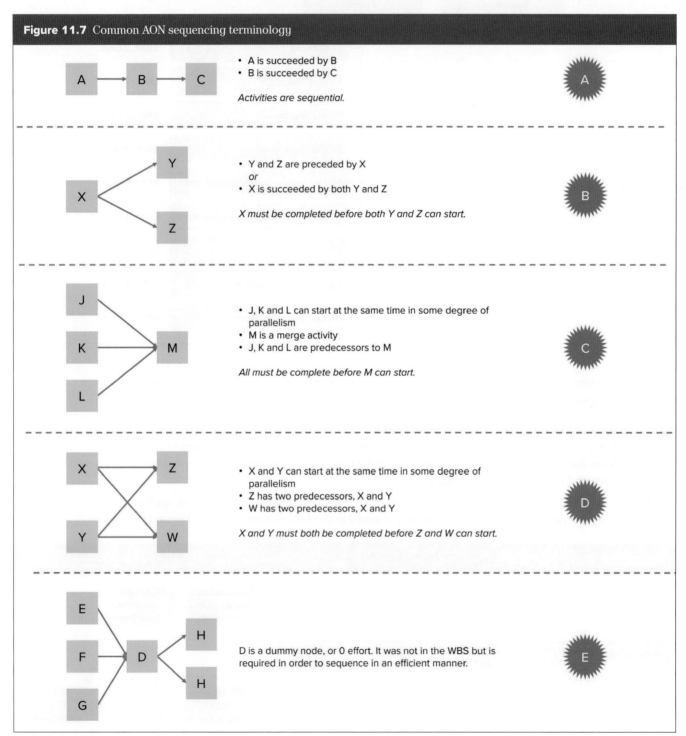

• A is succeeded by B
• B is succeeded by C

Activities are sequential.

• Y and Z are preceded by X
   or
• X is succeeded by both Y and Z

X must be completed before both Y and Z can start.

• J, K and L can start at the same time in some degree of parallelism
• M is a merge activity
• J, K and L are predecessors to M

All must be complete before M can start.

• X and Y can start at the same time in some degree of parallelism
• Z has two predecessors, X and Y
• W has two predecessors, X and Y

X and Y must both be completed before Z and W can start.

D is a dummy node, or 0 effort. It was not in the WBS but is required in order to sequence in an efficient manner.

Step 2: Add in the effort/durations from as estimated

(For more on estimating, refer to Chapter 9 "Estimating".)

We do this on what has been termed the *AON data node*, which adds information that will be calculated over the coming steps. For this step, all we need to add to our AON is the work package name (but remember, we could be doing this at the task level; therefore, it would be the task name), and the duration for each work package (or at the task level, the duration of the task).

Let's look at an example AON data node and the information it contains before applying it to our House Build—Frame example. Figure 11.8 indicates an annotated AON data node.

Figure 11.8 AON data node

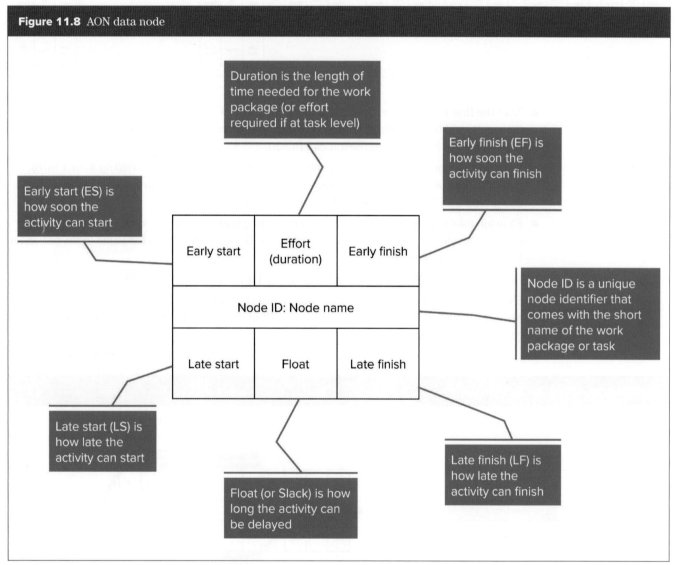

© 2022 Dr Neil Pearson

Step 2 is therefore to take the Step 1 output (the sequenced AON, Figure 11.6) and format using the AON data node, adding in the duration (effort) information of the work package. Figure 11.9 indicates the result of doing this.

Step 3: The forward pass

The forward pass uses the duration (effort) information (for each individual work package or tasks) and calculates *how soon the project can be completed*. It reveals the earliest possible completion date or what will be become our expected project completion time. Refer to Figure 11.10 while reading this method.

Figure 11.9 Step 2: Applying the AON data node and estimating information

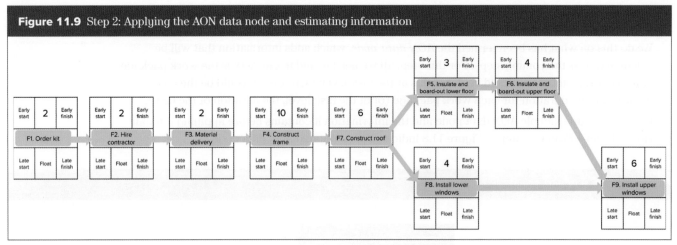

© 2022 Dr Neil Pearson

- Take the first node. The earliest F1 can start is at 0 days (1 day will reveal the same result by the way!). Add to the **early start (ES)** of 0 the duration, so $0 + 2 = 2$. This will be the **early finish (EF)** of F1 (i.e. the earliest it can finish).

- We repeat this process for F2, where the ES is *the maximum of any preceding node's early finish*. F2 has only one preceding node so the ES of F2 becomes 2; adding the duration of 2 to this gives F2 an EF of 4. The same logic applies to F3, F4 and F7.

- F5 again takes on the maximum EF of its preceding nodes, so the 22 comes forward to the ES of node F5; add the duration of 3, which gives an EF of 25. F8 follows the same logic, so has an ES of 22 and an EF of 26.

- F6 takes the EF of F5 as the ES (i.e. 25); adding 4 gives the EF of F6 as 29.

- F9 takes the maximum EF of its preceding nodes (F6 and F8) as the ES (i.e. the 29 of F6); this becomes the ES of F9. Adding the 6 gives the EF of 35 days. Therefore, the earliest this project can finish is in 35 days.

Remember: The ES of the succeeding node is the maximum EF of all its preceding nodes!

Figure 11.10 Step 3: The forward pass

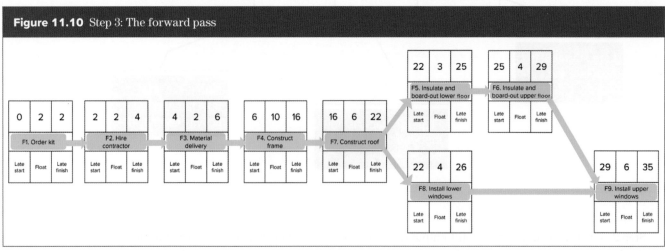

© 2022 Dr Neil Pearson

Step 4: The backward pass

The goal of the backward pass is to calculate the *latest* each node can be started (the **late start** or **LS**) and the latest each node can be finished (the **late finish** or **LF**). Refer to Figure 11.11 while reading the method that follows.

- Taking F9 (the last node) and the early finish of EF 2 and bring it down into the latest finish of node F9, then take away the duration to arrive at the node's latest start of 29.

- The 29 flows back into both the LF of nodes F6 and F8. For F6, take the duration 4 off the 29, resulting in an LS of 25. For node F8, apply the same logic, giving an LF of 29 and an LS of 25.

- For F5, take the LS of node F6 as the EF, then take away the duration 3, resulting in an LS of 22.

- For node F7, we take the *minimum of the succeeding late starts*. F5 is 22 and F8 is 25 so we bring back the 25 and place this in the LF of F7, take away the duration and the LS becomes 16.

- Node F4 LF takes on the 16 of F7; taking the duration of 6 away from 16 leaves an LS of 6. Apply the same logic to nodes F3 through to F1.

The network should balance out on the backward pass ending at zero.

Remember: The LF of the preceding node is the minimum LS of all its succeeding nodes!

Figure 11.11 Step 4: The backward pass

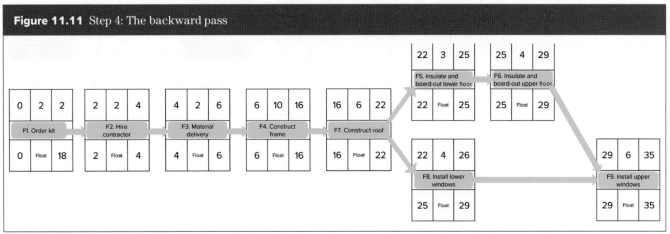

© 2022 Dr Neil Pearson

Step 5: Calculating the float and identifying the resulting critical path

The critical path is defined as the *longest path through the project network, but the shortest time in which the project can be completed.*

It is the path (or paths) where nodes do not have any float (i.e. LF − EF = 0 or LS − ES = 0). Refer to Figure 11.12 and calculate the float.

Figure 11.12 Step 5: Calculating the float

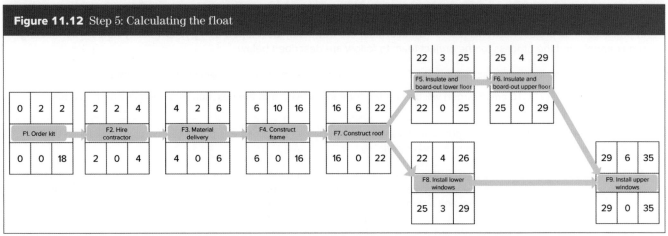

© 2022 Dr Neil Pearson

Starting with "F1. Order kit", take away the ES from the LS (or the EF from the LF) and place the result value in the "Float" position on the AON data node. So, for F1 this would be an LF of 2 − EF of 2 = 0; the zero has been placed in the "Float" box on the node. This same process is repeated for each node in the network diagram.

Once this has been done, sit back and look at the network diagram. For all those activities that have a zero float (i.e. they cannot be moved without impacting the end date of the project), mark a red line through the network—this is the critical path of the project.

Remember: The critical path(s) is/are the path(s) with the longest duration through the network, but which represents the shortest time to complete the project. Refer to Figure 11.13.

Figure 11.13 Identifying the critical path

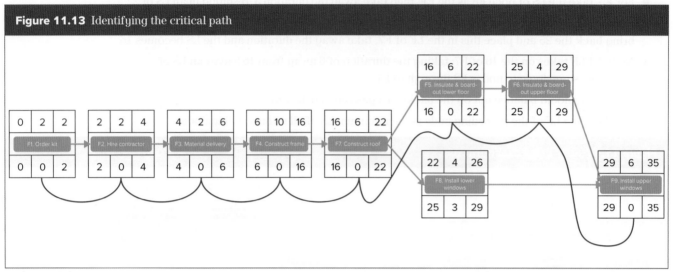

© 2022 Dr Neil Pearson

In this example only node F8 has any float, so F8 could float (be delayed by) up to three days without materially impacting the critical path of the project. If F8 went over to four days, then it would impact the critical path and we would have to recalculate all the values again from Step 3 to identify the new critical path.

Note: It is possible to have multiple critical paths through a network. In this case the project leader has more risk in the project and needs to ensure frequent monitoring and reporting of all those nodes on the multiple critical paths takes place.

In practice, small project networks (25 to 100 activities) are frequently developed using yellow sticky notes. The meeting requirements and the process for the project team to follow are described below.

1. There should be a meeting facilitator and (of course) the project team members present at the meeting.

2. One sticky note (7 × 10 cm or larger) will be needed for each activity, and the description of the activity should be printed on the note.

3. An erasable whiteboard (a long, approximately one-metre-wide piece of butcher's paper can be used in place of the whiteboard if none is available) and a marker pen.

All the yellow sticky notes are placed within easy view of all the team members. The team begins by identifying activities (activity stickers) that have no predecessors. Each of these activity stickers is then attached to the whiteboard (or butcher's paper, if used). A start node is drawn, and a dependency arrow is connected to each activity.

Given the initial network start activities, each activity is next examined for any immediate successor activities. These activities are attached to the whiteboard and dependency arrows drawn. This process is continued until all the yellow sticky notes are attached to the whiteboard with dependency arrows. (Note: The process can be reversed, beginning with those activities that have no successor activities and connecting them to a project end node. The predecessor activities are selected for each activity and attached to the whiteboard with dependency arrows marked.)

When the process is complete, the dependencies are recorded using the project software that develops a computer-designed network, along with the critical path(s) and early, late and slack times. This methodology sensitises team members early on to the interdependencies between activities of the project. This methodology also empowers team members by allowing them input into the important decisions they must implement later.

The critical path

The **critical path method** has long been considered an absolutely necessary activity in the generation of a project schedule to baseline and subsequently monitor from. The following comments were made by highly experienced project leaders when asked about the significance of the critical path in managing projects.

- "I try to make it a point whenever possible to put my best people on critical activities or on those activities that stand the greatest chance of becoming critical."

- "I pay extra attention when doing risk assessment to identifying those risks that can impact the critical path (either directly or indirectly) by making a non-critical activity so late that it becomes critical. When I've got money to spend to reduce risks, it usually gets spent on critical tasks."

- "I don't have time to monitor all the activities on a big project, but I make it a point to keep in touch with the people who are working on critical activities. When I have the time, they are the ones I visit to find out first-hand how things are going. It's amazing how much more I can find out from talking to the *rank and file* who are doing the work and by reading the facial expressions of people—much more than I can gain from a number-driven status report."

- "When I get calls from other managers asking to borrow people or equipment, I'm much more generous when it involves resources working on non-critical activities. For example, if another project leader needs an electrical engineer who is assigned to a task with five days of slack, I'm willing to share that engineer with another project leader for two to three days."

- "The most obvious reason the critical path is important is because these are the activities that impact completion time. If I suddenly get a call from above saying they need my project done two weeks earlier than planned, the critical path is where I schedule the overtime and add extra resources to get the project done more quickly. In the same way, if the project schedule begins to slip, it's the critical activities I focus on to get back on schedule."

11.5 | From network to project schedule

There are many software scheduling packages in the marketplace; one of the most popular is Microsoft Project.

Note: The professional advice would be to build a Business Case for the standardisation of the selection and embedding of a program and project scheduling tool across the whole organisation.

Due to the continuing release of the many various software packages in the marketplace, this text will not be stepping through how to create a project schedule in a software tool. However, the House Build AON will be taken forward to the construction of a schedule (in this case, Gantt chart), using Microsoft Project as the scheduling tool. The steps that will now be progressed through in the remaining sections of the text largely follow the workflow indicated in Figure 11.14.

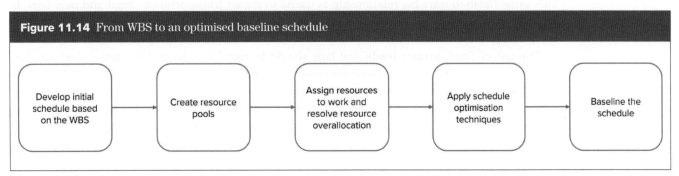

Figure 11.14 From WBS to an optimised baseline schedule

© 2022 Dr Neil Pearson

The basic terminology used to schedule will first be introduced.

11.5.1 **Finish-to-start (FS) relationship**

The finish-to-start relationship represents the typical, generic network style used in the early part of the chapter. The generic finish-to-start relationship is illustrated in Figure 11.15.

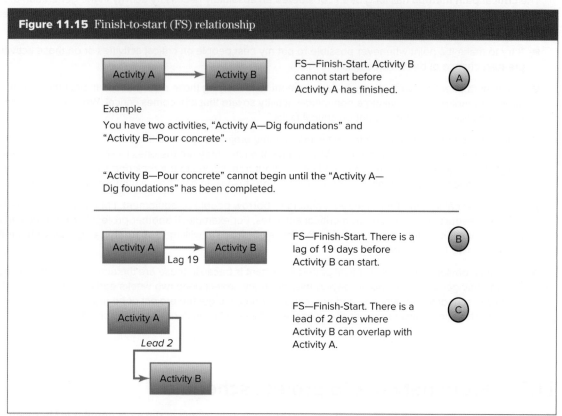

Figure 11.15 Finish-to-start (FS) relationship

FS—Finish-Start. Activity B cannot start before Activity A has finished. (A)

Example

You have two activities, "Activity A—Dig foundations" and "Activity B—Pour concrete".

"Activity B—Pour concrete" cannot begin until the "Activity A—Dig foundations" has been completed.

FS—Finish-Start. There is a lag of 19 days before Activity B can start. (B)

FS—Finish-Start. There is a lead of 2 days where Activity B can overlap with Activity A. (C)

© 2022 Dr Neil Pearson

There are situations where the next activity in a sequence must be delayed even when the preceding activity is complete. For example, removing concrete forms (Activity B) cannot begin until the poured cement has cured for two time units (Activity A). Figure 11.15B shows this **lag relationship**. Finish-to-start lags are frequently used when ordering materials. For example, it may take one day to place orders but 19 days to receive the goods. The use of finish-to-start allows the activity duration to be only one day and the lag 19 days. This approach ensures the activity cost is tied to placing the order only, rather than charging the activity for 20 days of work. This same finish-to-start lag relationship is useful to depict transportation, legal and mail lags. In Figure 11.15C, Activity B (the successor task) will start two days before the predecessor activity being completed.

The use of finish-to-start **leads** and lags should be carefully checked to ensure their validity. Conservative project leaders, or those responsible for the completion of activities, have been known to use lags as a means of building in a *pad* factor to reduce the risk of being late. A simple rule to follow is that the use of finish-to-start lags must be justified and approved by someone responsible for a large section of the project. The legitimacy of lags is not usually difficult to discern. The legitimate use of the additional relationship shown can greatly enhance the network by more closely representing the realities of the project.

11.5.2 **Start-to-start (SS) relationship**

The generic start-to-start relationship is illustrated in Figure 11.16A.

Figure 11.16 Start-to-start (SS) relationship

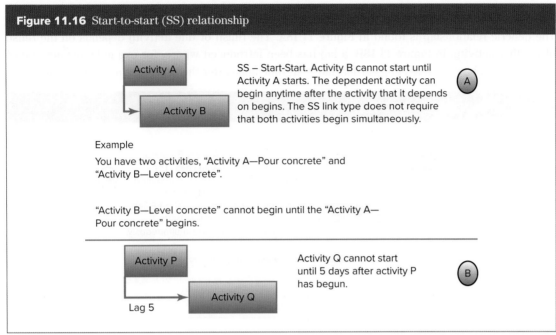

Activity A

Activity B

SS – Start-Start. Activity B cannot start until Activity A starts. The dependent activity can begin anytime after the activity that it depends on begins. The SS link type does not require that both activities begin simultaneously.

(A)

Example

You have two activities, "Activity A—Pour concrete" and "Activity B—Level concrete".

"Activity B—Level concrete" cannot begin until the "Activity A—Pour concrete" begins.

Activity P

Activity Q

Lag 5

Activity Q cannot start until 5 days after activity P has begun.

(B)

Typical start-to-start relationships are shown in Figure 11.16. Figure 11.16A shows the start-to-start relationship with zero lag, while Figure 11.16B shows the same relationship with a lag of five time units. It is important to note that the relationship may be used with or without a lag. If time is assigned, it is usually shown on the dependency arrow of an AON network (or the arrow joining the activities on a Gantt chart).

In Figure 11.16B, Activity Q cannot begin until five time units after Activity P begins. This type of relationship typically depicts a situation in which you can perform a portion of one activity and begin a following activity before completing the first. This relationship could be used on the pipe-laying project, for example (Figure 11.17). The start-to-start relationship can reduce project delays by using lag relationships.

It is possible to find compression opportunities by changing finish-to-start relationships to start-to-start relationships. A review of finish-to-start critical activities may point out opportunities that can be revised to be parallel, by using start-to-start relationships. For example, in place of a finish-to-start activity "Design house, then build foundation", a start-to-start relationship could be used in which the foundation can be started, say, five days (lag) after design has started—assuming the design of the foundation is the first part of the total design activity. This start-to-start relationship with a small lag allows a sequential activity to be worked on in parallel and compression of the duration of the critical path. This technique is referred to as **fast-tracking** and is further described later in this chapter. This same concept is frequently found in projects in which **concurrent engineering** is used to speed completion of a project. Start-to-start relationships can depict the concurrent engineering conditions and reduce network detail. Of course, the same result can be accomplished by breaking an activity into small packages that can be implemented in parallel, but this latter approach increases the network and tracking detail significantly.

Figure 11.17 Use of lags

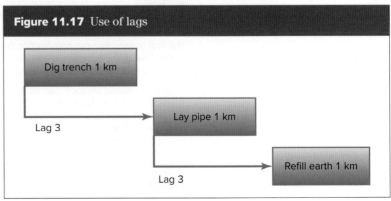

Dig trench 1 km

Lag 3

Lay pipe 1 km

Refill earth 1 km

Lag 3

11.5.3 **Finish-to-finish (FF) relationship**

The generic relationship is found in Figure 11.18A. The finish of one activity depends on the finish of another activity. In Figure 11.18B, a lag has been introduced where, for example, the activity of testing cannot be completed any earlier than four time units after the prototype activity is complete.

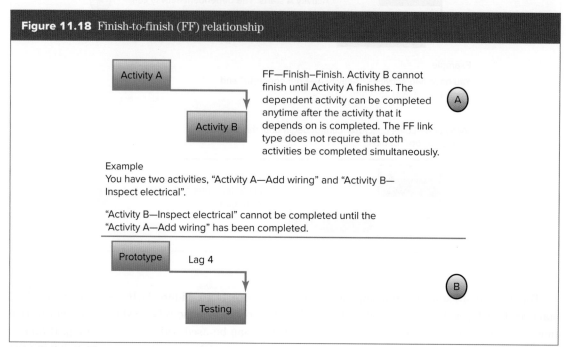

Figure 11.18 Finish-to-finish (FF) relationship

Activity A

FF—Finish–Finish. Activity B cannot finish until Activity A finishes. The dependent activity can be completed anytime after the activity that it depends on is completed. The FF link type does not require that both activities be completed simultaneously.

Activity B

A

Example
You have two activities, "Activity A—Add wiring" and "Activity B—Inspect electrical".

"Activity B—Inspect electrical" cannot be completed until the "Activity A—Add wiring" has been completed.

Prototype   Lag 4

Testing

B

© 2022 Dr Neil Pearson

11.5.4 **Start-to-finish (SF) relationship**

This relationship represents situations in which the finish of an activity depends on the start of another activity (refer to Figure 11.19A). For example, system documentation cannot end until three time units after testing has started (see Figure 11.19B). Here, all the relevant information to complete the system documentation is produced after the first three days of testing.

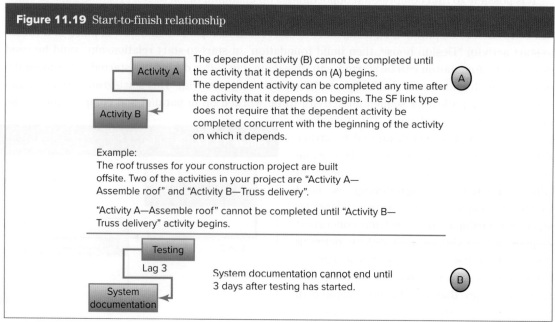

Figure 11.19 Start-to-finish relationship

Activity A

The dependent activity (B) cannot be completed until the activity that it depends on (A) begins. The dependent activity can be completed any time after the activity that it depends on begins. The SF link type does not require that the dependent activity be completed concurrent with the beginning of the activity on which it depends.

Activity B

A

Example:
The roof trusses for your construction project are built offsite. Two of the activities in your project are "Activity A—Assemble roof" and "Activity B—Truss delivery".

"Activity A—Assemble roof" cannot be completed until "Activity B—Truss delivery" activity begins.

Testing

Lag 3

System documentation

System documentation cannot end until 3 days after testing has started.

B

© 2022 Dr Neil Pearson

11.5.5 Combinations of lag relationships

More than one type of lag relationship can be attached to an activity. These relationships are usually start-to-start and finish-to-finish combinations tied to two activities. For example, the "Bug-fix" activity cannot begin until two time units after the "Code" activity has started. Code must be finished four time units before bug-fix can be finished (refer to Figure 11.20).

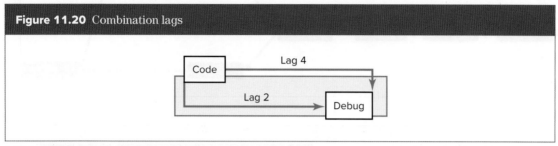

Figure 11.20 Combination lags

© 2022 Dr Neil Pearson

Figure 11.21 shows a recreation of the AON network (Figure 11.21A) in Microsoft Project as a Gantt chart (Figure 11.21B). Figure 11.21C is a Microsoft Project network view of the same Gantt chart. You will note on the network view that the critical path has been calculated and highlighted in red. The same can be achieved on the Gantt chart, by baselining the schedule and viewing the *tracking Gantt*. This uses the concept of creating the schedule (time) baseline. This can be seen in Figure 11.21D, where the project leader (or maintainer) has the ability to now enter actual percentage complete (the top red bar of the two bars for each task) to compare against a baseline planned value (the bottom grey bar). It will also be noted that the top bar indicates the critical path in red, with non-critical path tasks in blue.

As noted previously, creating the *network diagram—AON* is not often carried out by project leaders, but it can be an intermediary method for unpacking and exploring alternatives to sequencing complexity before committing into a scheduling software package.

Figure 11.21 Using Microsoft Project: (A) AON network diagram, (B) Gantt chart (schedule), (C) network (represented from the Gantt chart) and (D) baselined Gantt chart (schedule)

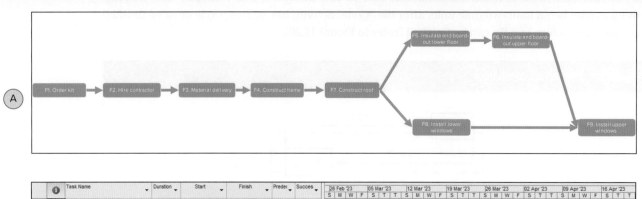

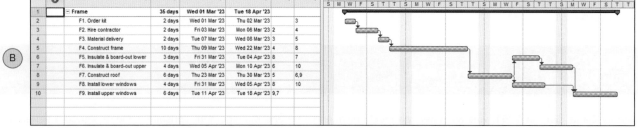

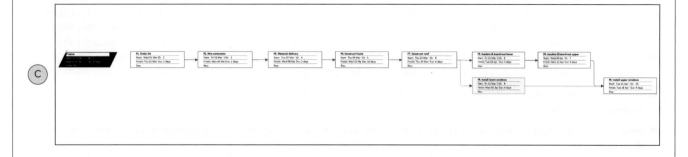

However, it is a very common, and indeed good, practice to construct a robust WBS and then with the estimating information build the project Gantt chart in the organisation's preferred scheduling software package.

1. The transfer of the WBS into the Gantt chart is a very simple process. To get from Figure 11.5 (the WBS) to Figure 11.21B (the Gantt chart), essentially the deliverables and sub-deliverables become *summary tasks*. A work package, if it has tasks below, will also become a summary task. If a work package does not have tasks below then the work package is considered a task in Microsoft Project.

2. Once the structure has been created in Microsoft Project, then the duration is entered into the "Duration" field.

3. Next the relationship between the tasks is created. This can be done in different ways: it is preferable to use the "Successor" and "Predecessor" fields to enter the relationship rather than drag the cursor between tasks.

4. Last, consider if any of the advanced scheduling techniques (in the next section) need to be attended to.

This process is nicely captured in the YouTube video clip: https://www.youtube.com/watch?v= zLuQLkGzHOM.

11.6 : **Advanced scheduling techniques**

The previous two sections have demonstrated a level of proficiency in taking a WBS and creating an AON and/or Gantt chart. This would provide the project leader and project team with a basic schedule for the project. However, there are numerous further techniques and terminology associated with project schedule management (introduced below); they can typically be applied to either AON or Gantt charts.

- **Total slack**: This tells us the amount of time a task can be delayed without delaying the project. Stated differently, total slack is the amount of time a task can exceed its early finish date without affecting the project end date or an imposed completion date. Total slack or *float* for a task is simply the difference between the LS and ES (LS − ES = total slack) or between LF and EF (LF − EF = total slack).

- **Free float** (*or free slack*): This is how long a task can be delayed, without delaying the ES of the successor task. Free float is calculated by subtracting the EF date of the current task node from the ES date of the succeeding task node (i.e. Free float = ES of succeeding activity node − EF of current activity node). *Note:* If two tasks are converging into a single task, only one of these two tasks may have a free float.

  Example: As indicated in Figure 11.13, there is only one activity node that has any free float—this is node F8, "Install lower windows". This node can be delayed by three days without impacting the overall project end date. If it was delayed by exactly three days, though, it would become a second critical path. If task F8 went over to four days, the project's network would have to be recalculated, and no doubt task F8 would now become part of the new critical path calculated.

- *Uncertainty and the project schedule:* A more advanced technique known as the *Monte Carlo* technique can assist if there is uncertainty (or risk) in relation to tasks on the schedule, in particular those on the critical path. This involves estimating the impact of possible risks on project schedule and budget.

  Good introductions to this topic are located at the following links:

  - www.youtube.com/watch?v=xtKWN2sHec4
  - www.youtube.com/channel/UCh3WQGV3vQAR0kdTJPlNwvQ

  (*Note:* The authors do not endorse this product, the video clips form a good definition and simple example of the application of the Monte Carlo technique.)

- *Risk:* Once a project schedule has been optimised after resource allocation, then the residual (or baseline) schedule should have a risk assessment carried out. Any work packages and/or tasks that carry significant risk in being achieved should have an appropriate risk raised on the project risks register. These could be categorised under the heading of "Schedule risk", to aid identification and review.

- **Sensitivity:** Sensitivity is used against a number of different techniques in advanced scheduling. However, some project leaders apply the word *sensitivity* to the critical path. For example, for a network with only one critical path with non-critical tasks, having significant total float would be described as *insensitive*. A network which has perhaps multiple critical paths, which are similar in criticality, and any noncritical tasks have limited total float, would be described as *sensitive*. For example, if the network illustrated in Figure 11.13 must be described in terms of sensitivity, it would be described as *insensitive*. The network has only one critical path, with only one non-critical task which has three days' float. Three days' float is quite lenient when you consider most of the other tasks are less than this in duration!

- *Multiple starts and multiple ends:* It is perfectly feasible that a project network may have multiple starts and multiple ends. Caution is advised, though, in reviewing the network and questioning if this is the case or is it more the reality that the project does have a defined *dummy* start task (with a zero duration) or a start task that has been omitted (project kick-off, one day duration), which acts as a *burst* task to the succeeding tasks to take place (refer to Figure 11.7B). The same discussion applies for the end tasks.

- **Dangler paths:** When developing a project schedule as a project leader (or scheduler), we need to be mindful of not having what we refer to as *dangler paths*—paths that go nowhere (i.e. a path that comes to a dead end and has not been linked to a succeeding task or the projected end task). Dangler paths should be picked up and a relationship with a succeeding task in the network should be established. Why? A change on the dangler path could have potential impacts to subsequent activities and even the end date of the project; if not linked, this would not show up on the schedule's subsequent tasks.

- **Laddering:** Laddering is where a long task may have other associated tasks that can take place before the long task completes 100 per cent. In such cases we need to take the long task and break it into smaller repetitive tasks, each with its associated sub-tasks. Referring to Figures 11.22 and Figure 11.23, it can be seen how to approach such a situation.

In Figure 11.22, all code is developed before being tested, before being piloted, prior to release.

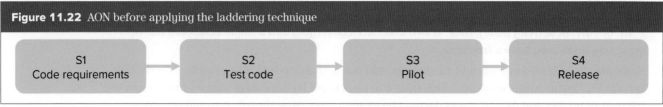

Figure 11.22 AON before applying the laddering technique

© 2022 Dr Neil Pearson

In Figure 11.23, the code has been split into three modules, each of the modules being tested, piloted and released in a laddered effect.

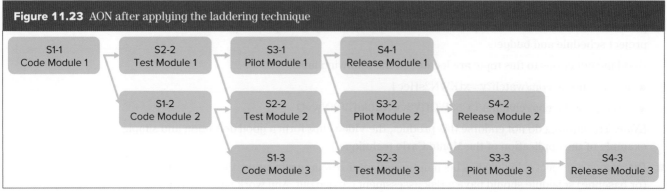

Figure 11.23 AON after applying the laddering technique

© 2022 Dr Neil Pearson

So, what we are saying is that a more efficient design can be achieved by applying the laddering technique. A project leader may do this for several reasons, such as more efficient use of resources, more frequent delivery to the business, and better control over the project. *Note:* Techniques such as laddering could also form the basis for discussion in the approach section of the Schedule Management Plan (refer to section 11.2).

■ *Leads and lags:* The use of leads and lags has been developed to offer greater flexibility in schedule (also network) development. There are two types—delay (lag) and overlap (lead). Delay is indicated by a positive value and is called *lag time*. It specifies that the successor task will start only after X number of days (time units), when the predecessor task is completed (e.g. based on a finish-to-start relationship). A lag directs a successor activity to be delayed. Lag time is a delay between tasks that have a dependency. For example, if you need a two-day delay between the finish of one activity and the start of another, you can establish a finish-to-start dependency and specify two days of lag time. Note: In Microsoft Project, enter the lag time as a *positive* value.

Overlap is indicated by a negative value and is called *lead time*. It specifies that the successor activity will start X number of days before the predecessor task is completed (e.g. based on finish-to-start relationship). A lead allows acceleration of a successor task. Lead time is the overlap between tasks that have a dependency. For example, if a task can start when its predecessor is half finished, you can specify a finish-to-start dependency with a lead time of 50 per cent for the successor task. Note: In Microsoft Project, enter the lead time as a negative value.

The use of *leads* and *lags* in project networks occurs for two primary reasons. First, when activities of long duration delay the start or finish of successor activities, the network designer normally breaks the activity into smaller activities to avoid the long delay of the successor activity; and second, leads and lags can be used to constrain the start and finish of an activity.

Refer to Figure 11.24 for a simple example of including a lag and lead in the House Build example introduced earlier. *Note:* We have assumed that "F2. Hire Contractor" will only take place after 20 days of wait time; however, we wish to have the contractor on site one day before material delivery—therefore there is a lead time of one day between "F3. Material Delivery" and its predecessor "F2. Hire Contractor". Once the lags and leads were introduced into the network, all Steps 1 through 5 were then reapplied to the new information introduced (i.e. the lag and lead times). As can be seen in Figure 11.24, the critical path has not changed but the earliest project finish date now extends to 54 days.

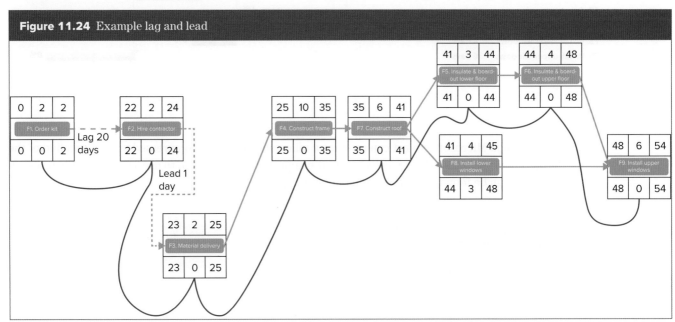

Figure 11.24 Example lag and lead

■ ***Milestones:*** Milestones are important to consider in the construction of a project schedule. We identified milestones as a part of the scoping activities in Chapter 8 "Defining the scope of a project". A milestone is a *zero-duration* task in the project schedule. It is the activities that precede the milestone where all the work is done. The milestone represents a point in time. A milestone should increase visibility for the project team and stakeholders and act as a point in time to determine whether the desired state has been achieved or not. In defining milestones in such a manner and elevating their purpose, they act as visible control points, indicating to all concerned achievement. For the House Build project, let us now introduce several milestones that perhaps would have been defined in the scope document of the project.

- Milestone 1, design completed
- Milestone 2, foundations completed
- Milestone 3, framing completed
- Milestone 4, roof completed.

Milestones 3 and 4 are relevant to the part of the project currently being scheduled. If these two milestones are now inserted into the schedule, they become visually apparent and draw attention to delivery and sign-off. A milestone is typically represented by the diamond shape and is entered as a zero duration (Figure 11.25). *Remember:* It is the work done before the milestone that achieves the milestone—there is no work done at the milestone!

Figure 11.25 Example Gantt chart with milestones

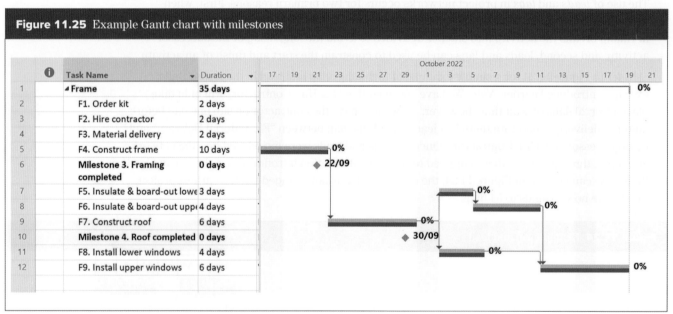

© 2022 Dr Neil Pearson

Although Microsoft Project can produce a milestone summary/compressed project timeline of the project, it is useful as a *design technique* to the approach to scheduling to use a more flexible tool—an example can be found in the following template.

 Visual Timeline

- ***Hammock activities:*** Figure 11.26 adds in a hammock activity to the House Build example (refer to activity "F10. Hammock Activity Site Supervisor"). This simply indicates in this instance that a fixed resource is required to supervise the work across activities F4 and F7. Maybe the project leader in this instance wanted to highlight the difference between work that is contracted against work that is internal (the site supervision).

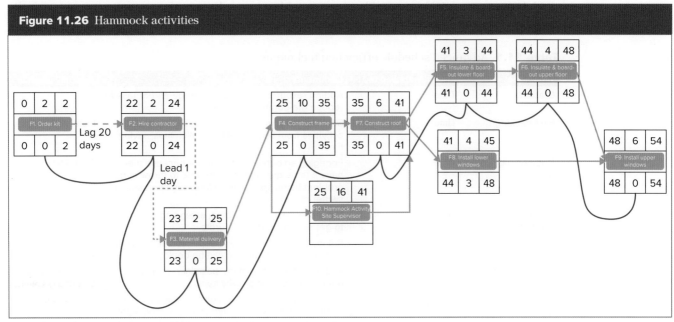

Figure 11.26 Hammock activities

The duration for the introduced hammock activity node is derived from the ES of Activity F4 and the EF of Activity F7; that is, the difference between 41 and 25, or 16 time units. The hammock duration will change if any ES or EF in the network changes. Hammock activities are very useful in:

- assigning and controlling indirect project costs
- aggregating sections of the project—similar to developing a sub-network, but the precedence is still preserved
- presenting a macro (collapsed/high-level) network to senior management
- grouping activity nodes, which can facilitate getting the right level of detail for specific sections of a project.

As seen in the examples in this section, the techniques are synonymous with both network diagrams and project schedules, as in effect they are merely different graphical representations of the same information.

11.7 Advanced schedule efficiency techniques

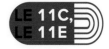

Sitting alongside the advanced scheduling techniques are *advanced schedule efficiency techniques*. These techniques could, for example, be applied:

- in the initial design of the project schedule, during project planning
- during the analysis of a variation request
- when an issue occurs.

Table 11.1 provides a summary of these techniques and shows where the technique is primarily applied (but can be used for other purposes). Referring to Chapter 8 "Defining and managing the scope of a project", section 8.3.2 "Establishing project priorities: The triple constraints", the notion of managing the triple constraints was introduced where a discussion around constraints preferences was made by the project sponsor. When looking across the techniques in this section, remember this discussion as it will influence which technique you might apply! For example, if *cost* was deemed as rigid, but *time* was fluid, we would not use **crashing** to resolve a variation request, as we typically know crashing involves adding extra resources and therefore cost.

Table 11.1 Advanced schedule efficiency techniques

Technique	Primarily applied to . . .	Comments	Typically impacts
Crashing	Time	Adding resources to a work package and/or task to reduce the duration (not effort).	Cost
Fast-tracking	Time	Seeking schedule efficiencies by resequencing activities from sequential to parallel; thus, saving time.	Risk
Outsourcing project work	Time	Engaging an outsourced provider because they have a large quantity of a resource to throw at the problem being solved; therefore, can complete in a swifter manner.	Cost, Risk
Scheduling overtime	Time	Using the existing workforce, extending their hours to get over a short-term hurdle.	Cost, Risk
Doing it twice—fast, and then correctly	Cost	Put in place a temporary cheaper solution until the more permanent solution can be deployed.	Cost, Risk, Time
Reducing project scope	Scope	Reducing the scope of the baselined project, removing the least-priority items.	Risk, Cost, Time, potentially Quality
Compromising quality	Quality	Reducing the quality of the end product, service or result. Must be customer led as they will be signing off deliverables against the revised quality criteria.	Risk, Quality

© 2022 Dr Neil Pearson

11.7.1 **Crashing**

The most common method for shortening project time is to assign additional human resources and/or equipment (resources) to activities—thereby *crashing* or shortening the project schedule. However, there are limits as to how much speed can be gained by adding human resources. Doubling human resources from (for example) two people to four people will not necessarily reduce completion time by half. In reality, the project leader would probably only gain one-and-a-half times the productivity, not twice the productivity, as factors such as interactions, communication, confusion and access to other resources (e.g. stakeholders) would significantly impact the utilisation rate of the additional resource.

This effect is often referred to as *Brooks law*—adding human resources to a late software project makes it later. Frederick Brooks formulated this principle from his experience as a project leader for IBM's System/360 software project during the early 1960s. While subsequent research confirmed the general veracity of Brooks' prediction, it also discovered that adding more people to a late project does not always cause the project to be further delayed. The linchpin is whether new staff are added early on, so there is sufficient time to make up for lost ground once the new members have been fully assimilated. *Remember:* Crashing tends to lead to increased cost and increased risk, among other factors.

11.7.2 **Fast-tracking**

Sometimes it is possible to rearrange the logic of the project network so that critical activities are carried out in parallel (concurrently) rather than sequentially (one after another). When this alternative is given serious attention, it is amazing to observe how creative project team members can be in finding ways to restructure sequential activities to now be in parallel. As noted earlier in this chapter, one of the most common methods for restructuring activities is to change a finish-to-start relationship to a start-to-start relationship. For example, instead of waiting for the final design to be approved, manufacturing engineers can begin building the production line as soon as key specifications have been established. Changing activities from sequential to parallel usually requires closer coordination among those responsible for the activities affected but can produce tremendous time savings. Remember: Fast-tracking tends to lead to a decrease in time but an increase in risk.

11.7.3 **Outsourcing project work**

A common method for shortening the project time (and sometime costs) is to subcontract out a deliverable, work package or even task. The subcontractor may have access to superior technology or human expertise that will accelerate the completion time of the activity. For example, contracting for a backhoe could accomplish in two hours what it can take a team of labourers two days to do. Likewise, by hiring a consulting firm that specialises in .NET development, a firm may be able to halve the time it would take for less-experienced internal programmers to do the work. Subcontracting also frees up resources that can be assigned to a critical activity and will ideally result in shorter project duration.

11.7.4 **Scheduling overtime**

The easiest way to add more labour to a project is not to add more people, but to schedule overtime. If a team works 50 hours a week instead of 40, it might accomplish 20 per cent more. By scheduling overtime, it may be possible to avoid the additional costs of coordination and communication encountered when new people are added. If the personnel involved are salaried workers, there may be no real additional cost for the extra work. Another advantage is that there are usually fewer distractions when people work outside normal hours.

Overtime has its disadvantages. First, hourly workers may be paid time-and-a-half for overtime and double time for weekends and holidays. Sustained overtime work by salaried employees may incur personal costs (e.g. divorce, burnout, turnover). The latter is a key organisational concern when there is a shortage of workers, or the worker is assigned to a critical path activity. Furthermore, it is an oversimplification to assume that, over an extended period, a person will be as productive during their eleventh hour at work as they are during their first hour of work. There are natural limits to what is humanly possible, and extended overtime may lead to an overall decline in productivity when fatigue sets in.

Overtime and working longer hours are the preferred choice for accelerating project completion, especially when the project team is salaried. The key is to use overtime judiciously. Remember that a project is a marathon and not a sprint! You do not want to run out of energy before the finish line.

11.7.5 **Doing it twice—fast, and then correctly**

If you are in a hurry, try building a *quick and dirty* short-term solution (or prototype), and then go back and do it the right way. For example, the Sydney Olympics used this strategy when finalising the volleyball tournament. This was originally slated to be held in an inside venue; however, a temporary stadium was constructed on the world-famous Bondi Beach with over 10 000 seats.

11.7.6 **Reducing project scope**

Probably the most common response for meeting unattainable deadlines is to reduce or scale back the scope of the project. This invariably leads to a reduction in the functionality of the project. For example, a new car will average only 7.8 L/100 km instead of 11.4, or the software product will have fewer features than originally planned. While scaling back the scope of the project can lead to big savings in both time and money, it may come at a cost of reducing the value of the project to the customer. If the car gets lower mileage, will it stand up to competitive models? Will customers still want the software minus the features?

The key to reducing a project scope without reducing value is to reassess the true specifications of the project. Often requirements are added under *best-case, blue-sky* scenarios and represent desirables, but not essentials. Here it is important to talk to the customer and/or project sponsors and explain the situation—"You can get it your way but not until February". This may force the customer to accept an extension or to add money to expedite the project. If not, then a healthy discussion needs to take place regarding what the essential requirements are and what items can be compromised to meet the deadline. A more intense re-examination of requirements may improve the value of the project by getting it done more quickly and for a lower cost.

Calculating the savings of the reduced project scope begins with the WBS. Reducing functionality means certain deliverables (or requirements) can be reduced or even eliminated.

11.7.7 Compromising quality

Reducing quality is always an option, but it is rarely acceptable (or used). If quality is sacrificed, it may be possible to reduce the time of an activity on the critical path. Some car manufacturers will compromise on quality in production (for a known problem), and then carry out a recall at the dealership before the car is delivered to the customer. This can be more economical than stopping the production line. There are also considerations beyond the project life cycle back into the product life cycle to consider; for example, an organisation might reduce quality specifications in building a bridge to minimum safety requirements, but in doing so substantially increase the bridge's operational and maintenance costs post-project.

Refer to "Snapshot from Practice: The fastest house in the world", which discusses how these techniques can be applied.

SNAPSHOT *from* PRACTICE : The fastest house in the world

17 December 2002—after revving up their power tools and lining up willing volunteers, Shelby County's Habitat for Humanity broke the world record for the fastest house ever built, clocking in at 3 hours, 26 minutes and 34 seconds. The former record holder (New Zealand's Habitat Affiliate Mannakau) had held the record for three years at 3 hours, 44 minutes and 59 seconds. The Alabama project beat the New Zealand record by 18 minutes.

"This was different than any construction project that I've ever been a part of," said project leader Chad Calhoun. "The minute-by-minute schedule, the planning of each precise movement, the organisation of all the teams and materials could not have gone more smoothly on build day. All the long hours of planning definitely paid off."

In preparation for the build, Habitat volunteers put the foundation in place and constructed prefabricated wall panels. Once the whistle blew at 11 am on 17 December, the exterior wall panels were raised into place, followed by the interior panel, which took only 16 minutes. Special colour-coded teams of workers connected the wiring and plumbing, put in insulation, installed appliances, laid carpeting and tiles, installed light fixtures, painted the house inside, applied vinyl siding outside and attached assembled front and back porches.

At the same time, the roof was constructed on the ground next to the house. Once the roof was completed—approximately one-and-a-half hours later—a Steel City crane lifted the 6350-kg roof assembly into place. Crews attached the roof while others completed the interior work. There was even time to lay sod, plant shrubbery and decorate a Christmas tree in the front yard—all within the official build time of 3 hours, 26 minutes and 34 seconds.

The recipient of this gift was Bonnie Lilly, a single mother and nursing technician who had applied to Habitat for Humanity three times before she was selected to receive the three-bedroom, two-bath home. "It's amazing," Lilly said. "Who am I to have this happen for me? A world record, hundreds of people coming together to build my house—I still can't believe it."

Habitat for Humanity is an international charitable organisation that builds simple, affordable houses and sells them on a no-interest, no-profit basis to needy families.

Source: Drummond E 2002, 'Shelby county habitat for humanity breaks world record', CSR Wire, www.csrwire.com/press_releases/24660-The-House-That-Love-Built-Really-FAST-And-Just-in-Time-for-Christmas-Kicker-Habitat-For-Humanity-Breaks-World-Record-Set-By-New-Zealand, accessed February 2018.

In practice, the methods most used to adjust the project schedule are scheduling overtime, outsourcing and adding resources (crashing) as each of these maintains the essence of the original plan. Options that depart from the original project plan include doing it twice, changing scope and compromising quality.

11.8 : The resource scheduling challenge

Project leaders operate in a world of constraints, whether these are based on cost, time, resources or other factors. Therefore, when carrying common activities in a project environment, the project leader must be able to guide the project team on theory, best practice and good practice. When it comes to scheduling resources on the project schedule, this is no different. A project leader, when estimating the project's WBS, needs to also consider asking a number of questions and stating the resulting constraints and assumptions around using that resource on the project.

- *People:*
  - Can sufficient quantity be obtained when needed?
  - Are the available resources junior, or moderately or expertly skilled?
  - Do the resources need to be obtained outside the organisation?
  - Is there a shortage of the skill in the industry?
- *Equipment:*
  - Is the equipment available when required?
  - Is it used repeatedly throughout the project or as a one-off?
  - Does the equipment have to be obtained from external sources?
  - How quickly can the equipment be obtained?
  - Are there set-up and tear-down considerations?
- *Materials:*
  - How far in advance does ordering take?
  - Can we store them?
  - Are they perishable?
  - Are they available in the marketplace?
  - Are there supply chain problems?

Answers to these and many other questions will not only influence the project schedule development but also how the resources are allocated to the work packages and tasks. For example, if the project leader knows in advance that a resource is constrained it will immediately affect the manner in which the schedule will be constructed. The more common way to allocate resources is to build the project schedule and then allocate the resources. If, subsequent to this, if there are resources that have been over-allocated, for example, it is then necessary to carry out *resource optimisation*. That is the subject of the next section.

11.8.1 Resource optimisation

Resource optimisation is the application of the following two techniques as appropriate to problem:

1. *Resource levelling:* Adjusting the start and finish dates of a scheduled work package and/ or task to balance the demand from the work on a resource with its supply. With the available resources, when will the work be finished?

2. ***Resource smoothing:*** Adjusting the activities (work packages and/or tasks) on the project schedule such that they do not exceed the supply (quantity) of the resource. This means delaying work in the schedule to smooth out the peaks and troughs of the resource. Although removing flexibility in the schedule, the schedule should be doable by the desired "end" date required.

In reality the project scheduler will use a combination of these individually or combined to achieve the desired effect. Refer to Table 11.2 for a comparison of the two techniques.

Table 11.2 Resource optimisation

Resource levelling	Resource smoothing
Adjust the start and finish dates of a scheduled work package and/or task to balance the demand from the work on a resource with its supply.	Adjust the activities (work packages and/or tasks) on the project schedule such that they do not exceed the supply (quantity) of the resource.
Remove all conflicting resources issues.	Protect the critical path and end-date of the project; not all resource conflict may be removed.
May not require additional resources as the start/end dates are adjusted to account for the resource supply.	May require additional resources to address any remaining conflicting resource issues.
The project end-date will probably be pushed out as a result of applying this technique.	The goal is to protect the project end-date and critical path.
Available float is used for resource levelling, therefore may change the critical path.	Activities only delayed within their free and total float. No change in the critical path (ideally).
Project duration will be extended.	Project duration stays the same (ideally).

© 2022 Dr Neil Pearson

It is important to remember that, if resources are truly limited and activity time estimates are accurate, the resource-constrained schedule will materialise as the project is implemented—not the time-constrained schedule! Therefore, failure to schedule limited resources can lead to serious problems for a project leader. Creating a resource-loaded schedule before the project begins leaves time for considering reasonable alternatives, and ironing out any known resource constraint issues before the schedule is approved to the baseline project schedule from which the project will be later executed.

If the scheduled delay is unacceptable or the risk of being delayed too high, the assumption of being resource constrained can be reassessed. Cost–time trade-offs can be considered. In some cases, priorities may be changed.

Resource schedules provide the information needed to prepare time-phased work package budgets with dates (i.e. we will know exactly when a resource is used and be able to account for this in the time-phased project budget as the *planned value*). Once established, resource-loaded schedules provide a quick means for a project leader to gauge the impact of unforeseen events such as turnover, equipment breakdowns or transfer of project personnel. Resource schedules also allow project leaders to assess how much flexibility they have over certain resources.

The following set of figures aims to take the reader through the workflow of creating a resource pool, allocating resources and optimising resources given certain events—such as resource over-allocation. The below lettered points describe each step.

- *Step A:* Figure 11.27A shows the previous Gantt chart for the House Build project. No resources have yet been added.

- *Step B:* Figure 11.27B shows a resource of Site Supervisor being added to the pool of resources that will be available to allocated to tasks (work packages or tasks in the WBS!) in a later step. A standard calendar has been used for the resource, which means when the resource is allocated to a task it will use an 8 am − 5 pm day and not work weekends.

- *Step C:* Figure 11.27C shows the allocation of resources to tasks. The upper screen is the baseline tracking Gantt chart; the lower screen is the task detail where, among other things, the resource can be allocated to the task—as seen in the highlighted dropdown. In this case the Site Supervisor was allocated to both tasks F5 and F8.

- *Step D:* Figure 11.27D shows the result of allocating the same resource at 100 per cent usage to two tasks that are (at present) being carried out in parallel. As the highlight indicates, Microsoft Project will display a red person next to tasks that have resource overallocations. Given the Site Supervisor has been allocated to two parallel tasks, Project has now highlighted this.

- *Step E:* Figure 11.27E indicates the resource graph, which in this case, when the Gantt chart activities on the upper screen are brought into focus, highlights the resource allocation graphically. It can be seen that the Site Supervisor was allocated to two tasks simultaneously, so a 200 per cent loading of the resource has taken place.

- *Step F:* Figure 11.27F—to resolve the problem of this overallocation, the project leader (or scheduler) could:

  - Option 1. Review the activities and optimise the resource allocation—because both activities are ground-floor activities, we could potentially halve the resource allocation, so the Site Supervisor spends 50 per cent on F5 and 50 per cent on F8.

  - Option 2. Activity F5 could be rescheduled to a new time, thereby avoiding the clash with the resource Site Supervisor. This would in real life mean negotiating with the board/insulation installer. Note: Because F5 is on the critical path, this would not be our first choice.

  - Option 3. Activity F8 could be rescheduled to a new time, therefore avoiding the clash with the resource Site Supervisor. This would in real-life mean negotiating with the window installer. Note: F8 is not on the critical path.

  Let's assume Option 3 is taken. When the F8 task is right clicked, several options are presented in relation to how this resource overallocation can be resolved. In this case "Reschedule to Available Date" is selected.

- *Step G:* Figure 11.27G shows the result of selecting this option (highlighted). F8 has been slipped to start on the Friday; no work is done over the weekend, but the following Monday to Wednesday have been scheduled. Thus, our four-day F8 activity has used all available total float (three days) for the activity as it has been slipped by the three-day duration of F5.

- *Step H:* Figure 11.27H shows the result of this is an updated schedule, whereby the schedule now has two critical paths. The project leader must make sure that tasks F5 and F8 are completed on time for task F9 to start. Any slippage in either F5 or F8 will in this case cause the project schedule to slip and the end date of the project to move out. *Note:* The red person has been removed from the two tasks as the resource overallocation has now been resolved.

Note: Microsoft Project offers many ways to review and resolve resource overallocations.

The scenario described in the steps is just one example of what a project leader and/or scheduler face daily, not only when planning the project, but also when executing the project and monitoring and controlling it. The situation will be different each time, and using the skills as a human to analyse the content of the tasks and what is desired, combined with the calculated information provided by the scheduling tool, will help to make the best decision possible. Letting the scheduling package alone automatically recalculate the schedule should not be relied upon as it may not (and probably will not) have the desired effect you as a project leader and project team had in mind!

Figure 11.27 Example: Resource levelling

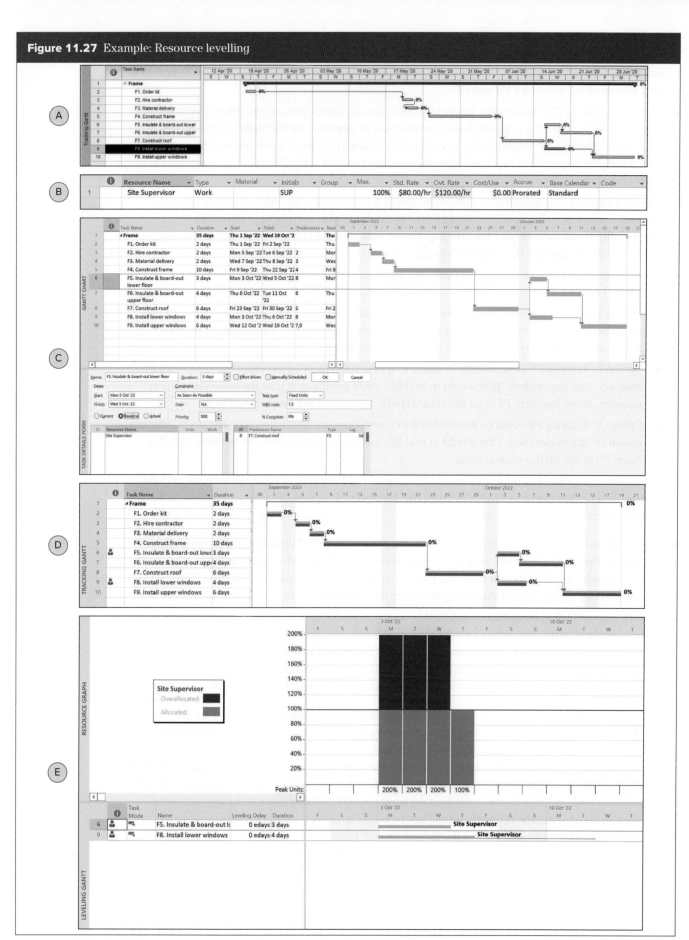

Figure 11.27 Example: Resource levelling *(Continued)*

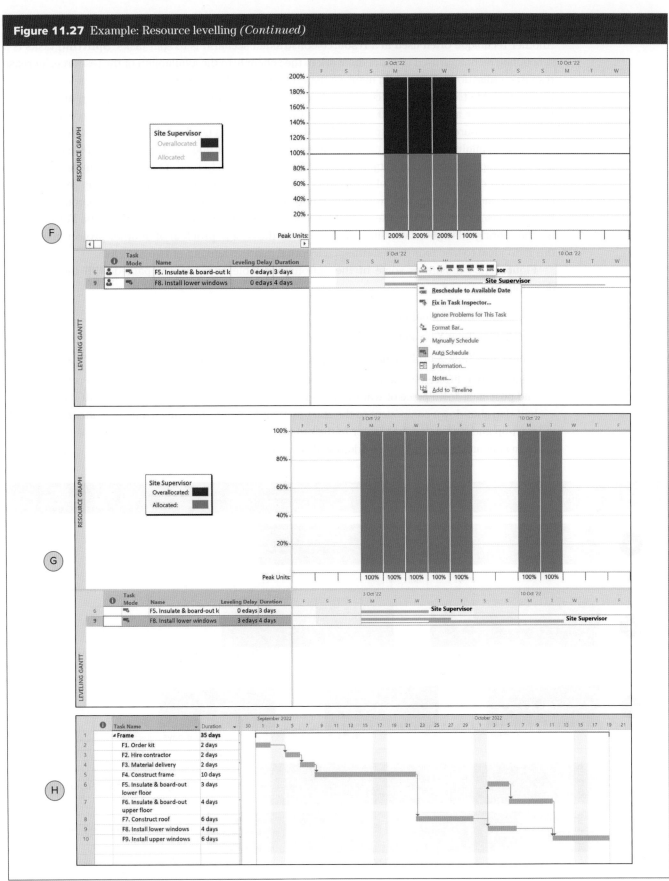

11.8.2 Splitting tasks

Another technique often used in a resource-constrained scenario is to split tasks. **Splitting** tasks is a scheduling technique used to adapt the work in the schedule to the availability of the resource, increase resource utilisation, or generally improve the efficiency of the schedule. For example, a key resource is not available to carry out 10 contiguous days of work on the project; however, they are available for 10 days over a 15-day period. By splitting the work, we get to keep the key resource. Finding an alternative resource might be expensive, could be external and need a contract, could take time to get up to speed, might not have the exact required skills, etc.; splitting—although on the face of it taking five days longer—would in reality be a lot quicker than having to recruit maybe an outside resource!

Splitting can be a useful tool if the work involved does not include large start-up or shut-down costs (e.g. moving equipment from one activity location to another). The most common error is to interrupt *people work*, where there are high conceptual start-up and shut-down costs. For example, having a bridge designer take time off to work on the design problem of another project may cause this individual to lose four days shifting conceptual gears in and out of two activities.

Figure 11.28 illustrates some of the options available and is accompanied with the following description:

- A indicates the original task unsplit.
- B indicates Task X broken into two equal duration tasks—Task X and Task Y.
- C indicates Task X broken into three equal duration tasks—Task X and Task Y and Task Z.
- D indicates a different scenario that can occur when splitting; in this case there is a pre-start-up and post shut-down piece of work to the split tasks. Say we introduce a start-up half-day and a half-day shut-down component to the start of Task X. When split, this would now incur additional start-up and shut-down time (refer to the red areas). This is illustrated in D where the task has been split and is now taking an additional two half-days = one day.

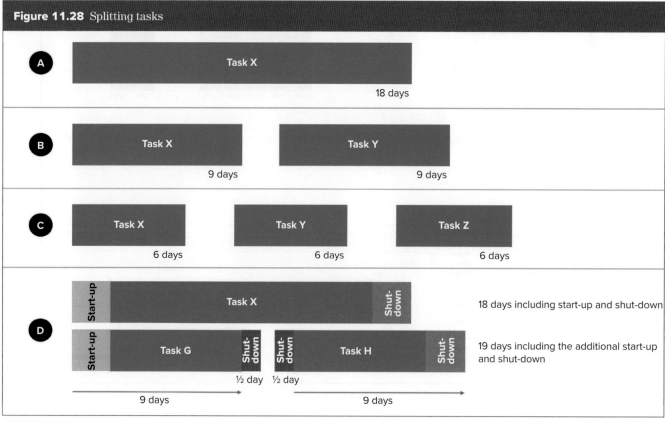

Figure 11.28 Splitting tasks

One of the strengths of today's project management software is the ability to identify and provide options for resolving resource allocation problems. A project leader who uses Microsoft Project to plan projects shared with us the following checklist for dealing with resource conflicts after preliminary assignment of resources has been made.

1. Assess whether you have overallocation problems (see red in the resource sheet view).

2. Identify where and when conflicts occur by examining the resource usage view.

   Resolve the problem by replacing overallocated resources with appropriate resources that are available. Then ask if this solves the problem. *If not*, use the levelling tool and choose the level within slack option. Does this solve the problem? (Are resources still over-allocated?) Check the sensitivity of the network and ask if this is acceptable. *If not*, consider splitting tasks. Make sure to readjust task durations to consider additional start-up and shut-down time.

3. If (2) does not work, then use level tool default option and ask if you can live with the new completion date. *If not*, negotiate for additional resources to complete the project. *If not possible*, consider reducing project scope to meet deadline.

   While this checklist makes specific references to Microsoft Project, the same steps can be used with most project management software.

11.8.3 Critical chain scheduling

The **critical chain method** of scheduling extends the critical path method by considering the constrained resources allocated, particularly on the critical path (discussed previously in this chapter), then extending this concept and introducing different buffers along the path (chain). Critical chain scheduling is the result of the work of Elliyahu M. Goldratt in *Critical Chain* (1997), which took inspiration from his earlier work on the theory of constraints. His focus in *Critical Chain* was to take our thinking beyond what is critical in term of tasks and propose that it is the resources that are critical (work is driven by resource availability). Inherent to all of us is the tendency to overestimate a task, start late on a task (and hopefully finish on time) and allow time for gold-plating or enhancing the work we have done to the requirements. This in the critical chain method is stripped out of the task estimate of duration/effort and introduced back into the schedule as a buffer. How much of the task duration/effort is moved into the buffer depends on the project leader; often 50 per cent of the time is taken away and brought back in as buffer. Assuming half the tasks on the project use all the buffer and half the tasks on the project use none of the buffer, the project *should* deliver on schedule. The critical path plus the total of all the task buffers is therefore communicated to management as the project finish date. Figure 11.29 illustrates the critical path method versus the critical chain method.

Figure 11.29 Critical path method versus critical chain method

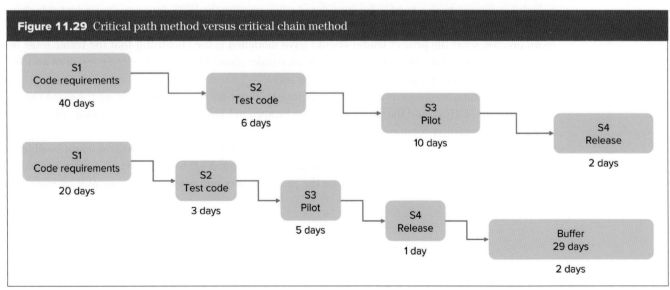

So, how is time managed at a task level? A task will deliver within its buffer; at a project level, the sum of the actual tasks delivered should hopefully never exceed the percentage of buffer available for that portion of the project. Refer to Figure 11.30 where "S1. Code Requirements" went over the 20 days to an actual of 30 days, then 10 days of buffer have been used, leaving 19 days of buffer for the remaining tasks. Looking at the schedule, it is unlikely that the remaining tasks would use those 19 days (as 10 days of that buffer are from "S1. Code requirements", which delivered late but still within the buffer time allowed).

Figure 11.30 Example: Critical chain method

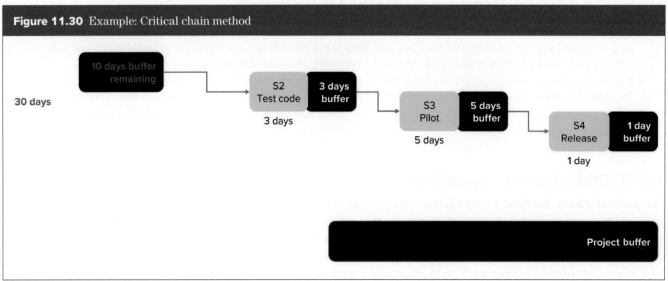

11.8.4 Slowing the work

There are occasions when slowing down preceding tasks to a delayed successor task can also work to the advantage of the project leader. It could be that resources on these preceding activities can be moved or shared with other tasks that are now on the critical path, therefore shortening the overall project duration.

11.8.5 Schedule constraints

Schedule constraints also need to be considered when moving the WBS data into the project schedule. For example, in the House Build task, "P. Frame delivery" (Figure 11.21) is expressed as 15 days; to be more precise, what the project leader should have modelled is the constraint that the frame must be delivered on a fixed date for any subsequent work to take place. This fixed date is a constraint and, for example, in Microsoft Project can be entered as such.

This scheduling technique is indicated in Figure 11.31, where the action of setting the event can be seen in Figure 11.31(a), and the result of this can be seen in Figure 11.31(b), with the constraint noted in the 'i' or information column.

Note: The duration was changed to one day to improve the schedule. You will no doubt be able to see many improvements to the way this schedule was designed—this is all part of coming up with a professional, realistic project schedule that the project leader and project team can later execute and deliver against.

Figure 11.31(a) Adding a time constraint

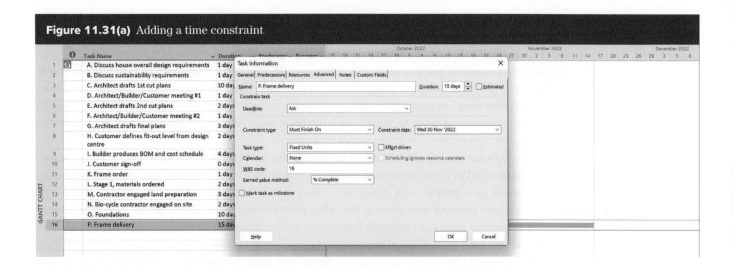

Figure 11.31(b) Results of adding a time constraint

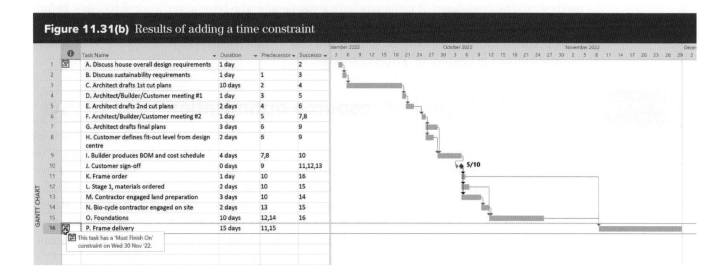

11.9 Assigning and monitoring project work

Chapter 18 "Project execution" discusses in more detail some of the project leader's activities in relation to the execution of the project schedule, and the monitoring and controlling of the project schedule, including:

- work package/task assignment
- work completion
- work performance
- reporting on work (including schedule forecasting).

When making individual assignments, project leaders should match, as best they can, the demands and requirements of specific work with the qualifications and experience of available participants. In doing so, there is a natural tendency to assign the best people to the most difficult tasks. Project leaders need to be careful not to overdo this. Over time, these people may grow to resent the fact that they are always given the toughest assignments. At the same time, less-experienced participants may resent the fact that they are never given the opportunity to expand their skill/knowledge base. Project leaders need to balance task performance with the need to develop the talents of people assigned to the project.

Project leaders not only need to decide who does what, but who works with whom. Several factors need to be considered in deciding who should work together. First, to minimise unnecessary tension, managers should pick people with compatible work habits and personalities but who complement each other (i.e. one person's weakness is the other person's strength). For example, one person may be brilliant at solving complex problems but sloppy at documenting their progress. It would be wise to pair this person with an individual who is good at paying attention to detail. Experience is another factor. Veterans should be teamed up with new hires—not only so they can share their experience but also to help socialise the newcomers to the customs and norms of the organisation. Finally, future needs should be considered. If managers have some people who have never worked together before but who have to later in the project, they may be wise to take advantage of opportunities to have these people work together early on so that they can become familiar with each other. This topic is discussed further in Chapter 18 "Project execution".

11.10 | Multi-project resource optimisation

For clarity, we have discussed resource allocation issues within the context of a single project. Resource allocation often occurs in a multi-project environment, where the demands of one project must be reconciled with the demands of another project. Organisations must develop and manage systems for efficiently allocating and scheduling resources across several projects with different priorities, resource requirements, sets of activities and risks. The system must be dynamic and capable of accommodating new projects as well as re-allocating resources once project work is completed. While the same resource issues and principles that apply to a single project also apply to this multi-project environment, application and solutions are more complex, given the interdependency among projects.

The following lists three of the more common problems encountered in managing multi-project resource schedules. Note that these are macro manifestations of single-project problems that are now magnified in a multi-project environment.

1. *Overall schedule slippage:* Because projects often share resources, delays in one project can have a ripple effect and delay other projects. For example, work on one software development project can grind to a halt because the coders scheduled for the next critical task are late in completing their work on another development project.

2. *Inefficient resource utilisation:* Because projects have different schedules and requirements, there are peaks and valleys in overall resource demands. For example, a firm may have a staff of 10 electricians to meet peak demands when, under normal conditions, only five electricians are required. In the construction industry you can improve efficiency and resource allocation by understanding the difference in the effective operation of each machine—for example, moving dirt up to 100 meters is much more efficient with a bulldozer than a scraper (100–500 metres) or a dump truck (500+ metres).

3. *Resource bottlenecks:* Delays and schedules are extended because of shortages of critical resources that are required by multiple projects. For example, at one Lattice Semiconductor

facility, project schedules were delayed because of competition over access to test equipment necessary to debug programs. Likewise, several projects at a forest commission area were extended because there was only one silviculturist on the staff.

To deal with these problems, more and more companies create project offices or departments to oversee the scheduling of resources across multiple projects. One approach to multiple project resource scheduling is to use a first come, first served rule. A project queue system is created in which projects currently underway take precedence over new projects. New project schedules are based on the projected availability of resources. This queuing tends to lead to more reliable completion estimates and is preferred on contracted projects that have stiff penalties for being late. The disadvantages of this deceptively simple approach are that it does not optimally use resources or consider the priority of the project.

Summary

Many project leaders feel the project network (schedule) is their most valuable project document. It is, in fact, just one of many project artefacts that can be used to capture the dynamics of a project. This chapter has introduced the following.

- The importance of establishing governance, policy and processes around the planning of schedule management across the life cycle of the project. This more static information is typically captured in the Schedule Management Plan—one of the subsidiary plans to the integrated PMP.
- The concept of AON networks as a way of fundamentally understanding how activities in a project are scheduled, and how the all-important critical path is calculated—and what this means to the project.
- The development of the project schedule or Gantt chart, from information already researched and captured in the WBS (refer to Chapter 8 "Defining the scope of a project"), combined with the estimating information (refer to Chapter 9 "Estimating") captured against the WBS.
- Several techniques for optimising the overall project schedule. These include the two key techniques of crashing: adding additional resources (usually to activities on the critical path) to shorten the duration of activities, and fast-tracking—reviewing activities to ascertain opportunities for carrying out previously sequential activities to more in parallel (the degree of overlap might be just part of the activity's duration).

The project leader must be on top of the project schedule as this makes up one of the project baselines (i.e. the schedule baseline) against which changes to the project are assessed to ensure scope creep does not occur from a schedule perspective. As illustrated in this chapter, project schedule management involves more than just successfully pulling together a Gantt chart (using a tool such as Microsoft Project). Instead, project schedule management requires a deeper understanding of how to leverage the theory of relationship types, crashing, fast-tracking and other advanced techniques to successfully deliver the project within a realistic time frame.

Review questions

1. How does the WBS differ from the project network?
2. How are WBS and project networks linked?
3. Why bother creating a WBS? Why not go straight to a project network and forget the WBS?
4. Why is *slack* important to the project leader?
5. What is the difference between *free slack* and *total slack*?
6. Why are *lags* used in developing project networks?
7. What is a *hammock activity* and when is it used?

8. What are five common reasons for *crashing* a project?

9. What are the advantages and disadvantages of reducing project scope to accelerate a project? What can be done to reduce the disadvantages?

10. Why is scheduling overtime a popular choice for getting projects back on schedule? What are the potential problems for relying on this option?

11. "Reducing the project duration increases the risk of being late." Explain.

12. How does resource scheduling reduce flexibility in managing projects?

13. How can outsourcing project work alleviate the three most common problems associated with multi-project resource scheduling?

14. Explain the risks associated with levelling resources, compressing or crashing projects, and imposed durations or catch-up as the project is being implemented.

Exercises

1. Draw an AON network diagram for the following list of tasks obtained as a result of a workshop between the builder and customer for how they are to approach the House Build project. (Note: The earlier design was dismissed by the customer due to lack of involvement.) What is the project duration in days?

ID	Task description	Predecessor	Duration
A	Discuss house overall design requirements	–	1
B	Discuss sustainability requirements	A	1
C	Architect drafts first cut plans	B	10
D	Architect/Builder/Customer meeting #1	C	1
E	Architect drafts second cut plans	D	2
F	Architect/Builder/Customer meeting #2	E	1
G	Architect drafts final plans	F	3
H	Customer defines fit-out level from design centre	F	2
I	Builder produces BOM and cost schedule	G, H	4
J	Customer sign-off (milestone)	I	0
K	Frame order	J	1
L	Stage 1, materials ordered	J	2
M	Contractor engaged, land preparation	J	3
N	Bio-cycle contractor engaged on site	M	2
O	Foundations	L, N	10
P	Frame delivery	K, O	15

2. The architect has advised there is a wait time for the final plans of 25 days, and the frame kit manufacturer has informed the project leader of a 15-day delivery delay. Introduce these into your AON network diagram and see what effect it has on the critical path and project length.

3. Move the AON network diagram from Exercise 1 into a scheduling package of your choice. Use a standard calendar where 8 am – 5 pm is the standard day, with 12 – 1 pm as the lunch break, and weekends are not considered working days. What happens to the project duration now? Why does this differ from the AON constructed in Exercise 1?

References

APM 2022, "Difference between 'resource smoothing' and 'resource levelling'", https://www.apm.org.uk/resources/find-a-resource/difference-between-resource-smoothing-and-resource-levelling/, accessed May 2022.

Drummond E 2002, "Shelby county habitat for humanity breaks world record", CSR Wire, www.csrwire.com/press_releases/24660-The-House-That-Love-Built-Really-FAST-And-Just-in-Time-for-Christmas-Kicker-Habitat-For-Humanity-Breaks-World-Record-Set-By-New-Zealand, accessed February 2018.

Goldratt EM 1997, *Critical Chain*, The North River Press.

Project Management Institute (PMI) 2017, *A Guide to the Project Management Body of Knowledge*, 6th edition, PMI.

Project Management Institute (PMI) 2021a, *A Guide to the Project Management Body of Knowledge (PMBOK® GUIDE)*, 7th edition, PMI.

Project Management Institute (PMI) 2021b, *The Standard for Project Management (ANSI/PMI 99-001-2021)*, 7th edition, PMI.

CHAPTER 12

Project cost management

Learning elements

12A Be able to successfully plan project cost management.

12B Understand how project costs are arrived at.

12C Be able to construct a time-phased project budget.

12D Have an awareness of how to monitor and control project costs.

12E Understand and set project contingency.

12F Be aware of considerations for completing and closing cost management activities.

In this chapter

12.1 Introduction and important considerations for project cost management

12.2 Cost management planning

12.3 Identification, estimation and categorisation of costs

12.4 Time-phased project budgets

12.5 Project cost control and monitoring

12.6 Contingency planning

12.7 Cost closure

Summary

12.1 : Introduction and important considerations for cost management

Project cost management includes many facets of budgeting, including the planning of costs; the estimating of costs against the **work breakdown structure (WBS)**; the building of the project budget; the controlling of costs; and the presentation of the costs in a format that is of value to the project management office (PMO), management and the project sponsor. The goal is to have a structured presentation of cost data and information, at a suitable level of detail, which will enable the project leader—later in the project life cycle—to track spend, and analyse and report on any **variances** (adapted PMI 2017).

This chapter covers the subject of project cost management; the reader should note that several topics relevant to this chapter have been covered in preceding chapters (refer to Figure 12.1).

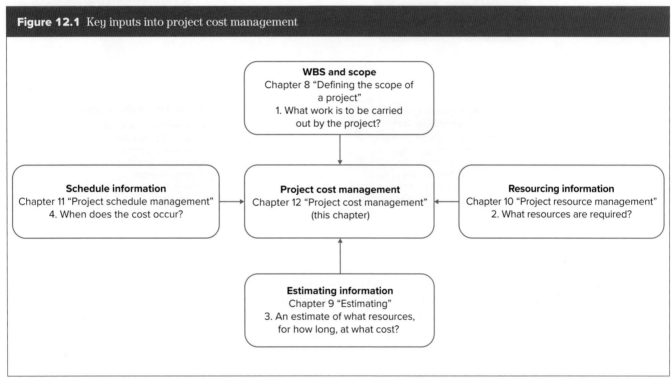

Figure 12.1 Key inputs into project cost management

WBS and scope
Chapter 8 "Defining the scope of a project"
1. What work is to be carried out by the project?

Schedule information
Chapter 11 "Project schedule management"
4. When does the cost occur?

Project cost management
Chapter 12 "Project cost management" (this chapter)

Resourcing information
Chapter 10 "Project resource management"
2. What resources are required?

Estimating information
Chapter 9 "Estimating"
3. An estimate of what resources, for how long, at what cost?

© 2022 Dr Neil Pearson

12.1.1 General cost activities

Figure 12.2 highlights some of the general cost management activities that would be undertaken by a project leader, most probably supported by project support staff along with subject matter experts (SMEs) in the business such as project accountants or commercial managers. Unlike scheduling, project costs management is not a complex activity; however, it does require attention to a lot of details, especially on larger projects where there could be hundreds—if not thousands—of line items in the project budget.

Let's look at some of the scenarios and questions that must be answered through project cost management activities (these are by no means exhaustive):

■ *Scope:* What is the relationship between the scope of the project and the environment within which the project is to operate—is there, for example, the requirement to have a large amount of **contingency** and have this contingency managed in a controlled manner?

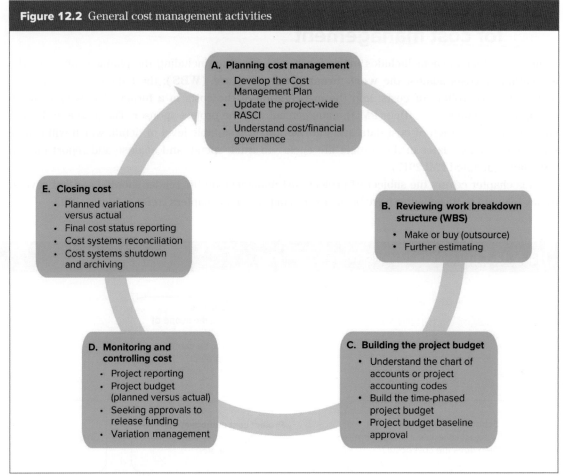

Figure 12.2 General cost management activities

© 2022 Dr Neil Pearson

- ■ *Risk:* Are there any costs associated with mitigating risks (e.g. insurance costs) or in avoiding risk completely by introducing new work packages into the design of the project—if so, what are the associated costs? How is the contingency for the project influenced by the project's overall risk? Does risk management determine the amount of contingency held against the project? This will be discussed in more detail in Chapter 16 "Project risk management".

- ■ *Quality:* What is the **cost of quality (CoQ)** to the project? There are obvious implications to costs when considering higher quality: higher-quality parts and additional quality-related tasks within the work packages equate to higher costs. Alternatively, what is the cost of not carrying out quality work now (rework in the project) and in the future when the project is handed over to the business?

- ■ *Communications and stakeholder management:* Depending on the project, there could potentially be considerable costs associated with some project communications. For example, on projects requiring frequent community stakeholder engagement, the costs for venue hire, publicity and travel must be factored in, and so too the costs associated with using print media (newspapers and journals), social media and other internet platforms to reach the targeted audience.

- ■ *Resources:* Human resource and other resource requirements obviously add costs to the project (e.g. the hiring of contractors for a project are typically higher than using internal resources). Costs associated with the training and development of the business users of a system when rolling out a platform to all employees of an organisation can be significant; project team-building activities, and bonus and retention payments all need to be accounted for in the project budget. Costs such as these are often overlooked.

- *Procurement:* These are costs associated with schedules of payments, contractor payments and other costs associated with procuring products and/or services to the project (at the correct time-point in the project's schedule). Have sufficient funds been released into the project budget to meet these commitments?

As set out above, costs can arise from many sources across the life cycle of a project, and from any of the knowledge areas covered in this text.

During the Initiation stage of the project, the project leader needs to particularly consider the costs of **large capital items** and **long-lead-time items**.

12.1.2 **Large capital items**

The project leader should specifically identify any large capital items that will have to be procured for the project. Large capital items may require several special considerations for the following reasons.

- *The scale of the cost of the items:* Large capital items are often investments that require substantial up-front outlay, and their cost could exceed the total of all other project costs.

- *Approvals required for their purchase:* Due to the scale of their investment, large capital items may need approvals outside of the organisation's standard procurement processes. The CEO, executive team and company board may have to be approached to canvass such approvals.

- *The processes of procurement and negotiating contracts can be lengthy:* Due to the scale of the investments and the types of purchase made, tendering, selecting suppliers and contract negotiations can take extended periods of time, which need to be factored into the project schedule and accounted for in the project budget.

- *Financial cash-flow considerations:* How will large capital purchases be funded? Do contracts necessitate substantial up-front deposits to be made, before the project is approved at the Initiation stage and before project funding is released? How and when will the remaining balances be paid (i.e. via a series of staged payments or via a single large payment on delivery)? The project leader will need to ensure the project has the required cash flow (funding) at the right times to be able to meet the cost commitments and will therefore need to consider this as part of the project cost management and project procurement management planning (refer to Chapter 17 "Project procurement management").

Examples of large capital items could include large bore tunnelling equipment, electrical transformers, heavy-duty equipment, buildings and office space and equipment for data centres. Sometimes, large capital items fall into the long-lead-time category, meaning they are not only expensive to acquire, but also take a considerable amount of time to acquire and to therefore become available for use in the project.

12.1.3 **Long-lead-time items**

Items that have a long lead time must be identified early in the project life cycle. These items are typically required for activities on the **critical path**, which adds complexity. Long-lead-time items need to be:

- identified early, as essentially the project may not be able to start producing its deliverables without the presence of these items—sometimes these items are identified and commitments made pre-project as part of developing the Business Case (a good idea)

- approved outside the project management life cycle (i.e. approvals are obtained prior to project kick-off)—when this occurs, there must exist a high degree of certainty that the project is going to proceed into the Initiation stage and onto the Planning and Execution stages; otherwise, expensive commitments and contractual obligations could be entered into, and the project does not proceed or takes a revised approach.

Long-lead-time and large capital purchases: The Clem Jones Tunnel (CLEM7) project

RiverCity Motorway contracted the design and construction of this tunnel to the Leighton Contractors and Baulderstone Bilfinger Berger Joint Venture (LBB JV). Construction of the AUD3 billion tollway commenced in September 2006 and was completed in March 2010: seven months ahead of schedule. Tunnelling on the CLEM7 was undertaken by two tunnel-boring machines named Matilda and Florence, plus several smaller roadheader machines. Digging the south-bound tunnel, Florence completed her journey from Bowen Hills to Woolloongabba on 16 April 2009. She was followed approximately six weeks later on 26 May 2009 by Matilda, whose breakthrough into the access shaft at Gibbon Street, Woolloongabba, signalled the end of tunnelling for the project.

Matilda and Florence are the largest of their type in the world and excavated 75 per cent of the tunnel. The tunnel-boring machines operated like a moving factory, excavating the rock, erecting the concrete tunnel lining and placing the road base as they went. Some of the dimensions of the tunnelling machines are outlined here:

- cost—AUD50 million per machine

- diameter—12.4 metres

- length—261 metres

- weight—4000 tonnes

- cutters—78 tungsten carbide tipped 48 centimetre disc cutters

- manufacturer—Herrenknecht (Germany)

- tunnelling rate—up to 20 metres per day

- operating crew—22 people per shift.

These machines represented a significant capital purchase by the project. However, they were only two of many large capital items that had long lead-times. The ventilation equipment also represented significant purchases. In 2008 a Rivercity Motorway investor update indicated that "To date, 70 percent of the final mechanical and electrical design has been completed and procurement is well advanced with all major long lead time items ordered. The mechanical and electrical contractor, United Group, has taken delivery of the first three batches of jet fans (119 in total). The first three shipments of smoke dampers (28 in total) have also arrived in Brisbane. Factory acceptance tests have been continuing in Australia and overseas for items such as ventilation outlet axial fans and transformers".

Figure 12.3 A tunnel-boring machine

Shutterstock/Oleg Totskyi

Source: The text is adapted from Queensland Government, www.brisban. qld.gov.au/traffic-transport/roads-infrastructure-bikeways/tunnels-bridges-major-roads/CLEM7/Construction-facts-figures/index.htm and Rivercity Motorway 2008, "Tunnel boring machine breaks through at Kangaroo Point", www.asx.com.au/asxpdf/20081223/pdf/31fbhvzlkd2dtr.pdf, accessed December 2012

For an example of the procurement of long-lead-time and large capital items in a project environment, refer to "Snapshot from Practice: Long-lead-time and large capital purchases: The Clem Jones Tunnel (CLEM7) project". Other costs are typically identified from the WBS, the work packages and the tasks, as discussed later in this chapter.

Also often contemplated early in the cost process is the **make or buy analysis**. Simply put, the project leader will have to make decisions about whether to buy in components (at the deliverable or work package level) to the project, or make these within the project. As an example, a project might be considering the implementation of a payroll system and the project leader would therefore need to decide whether to purchase a commercial off the shelf package (COTS), or whether to develop a payroll package as part of the project. These decisions are often driven by cost, yet other factors such as skills, time and risk may also be important, in which case, these factors will also need to be considered as a part of the make or buy decision. Chapter 17 "Project procurement management" considers the make or buy decision in further detail.

These early considerations for project cost management and the resulting decisions made are often captured in the project's **Cost Management Plan**, along with other information related to how cost management will take place in this project.

This text has taken the workflow as indicated in Figure 12.4; this chapter will soon take the WBS, complete with resources, schedule and estimates (including of costs), in order to produce the project budget, which will be **baselined** (at the end of the Planning stage) for later monitoring and controlling against during the Execution stage of the project.

Figure 12.4 The general workflow from WBS to project budget

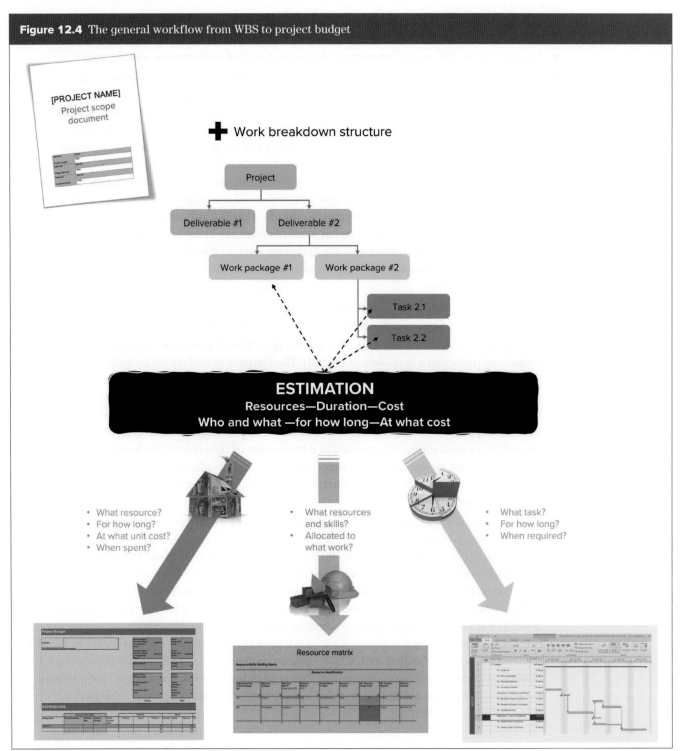

12.2 | Cost management planning

The Cost Management Plan captures various information that assists in understanding how cost estimating was applied, and the basis of the project's cash flow, governance, policy and procedure around the management and approval of the project budget, among other information. It is a document that supports the understanding of the resulting project budget and informs how the budget will be managed during the running of the project. The typical contents of a Cost Management Plan could include the following.

- *Glossary:* Definitions of all financial terms used, basis for calculations and explanations.

- *Cost approach:* The general strategy and approach to cost management on the project.

- *Governance, policy and procedure:* As a project leader it is important to know what organisational policy and procedures must be adopted into the project environment. On medium to large projects, it is useful to include both finance and procurement department representatives as stakeholders to the project. Some organisations have commercial managers (or similar role), through which the project leader and project team direct all questions on financial governance, policy and procedure. Details of the organisation's governance, policy and procedure (from a financial perspective) should be clearly articulated in the Cost Management Plan and communicated to all members of the project team who have financial responsibilities. It is important not only to capture what the interactions are at the corporate levels of the organisation, but also what arrangements are being put in place at a local project level in relation to discretionary spending, such as the use of company credit cards, spending limits and expense codes, the approval of expense claims within the project and timesheet approvals.

- *Contingency:* This is an amount of funds allocated for events that are outside the approved project budget and includes the governance around how these funds are accessed.

- *Estimating policy and tools:* Any activity that is estimated should be recorded in an estimating repository (typically a spreadsheet or tool). The estimating tool would include information on the WBS reference; what was estimated; the estimating technique applied; what stage of the project life cycle it was conducted within; who carried out the estimating and who provided the estimate information; and how long the estimate is valid for, especially if provided by an external supplier. It is also important to document any estimating assumptions, so that when the source of each estimate is queried at a later stage of the project, the basis upon which the estimate and assumptions were made will be clear. This allows for transparency in the estimating process and for lessons learned to be captured, to improve the current project and future projects.

- *Systems:* Finance, **enterprise resource planning (ERP)** systems and/or **project accounting systems**. These can be complex and daunting for the project leader and those in the project team responsible for maintaining the financial information within them. Clear guidelines should be established (and communicated) to all those who are required to access these systems, on how to use these systems in the project environment. The range of access type will also vary extensively, for example, access to a time-sheeting module for consultants, a reporting application for the project administrator, or access to the wider ERP system for the project accountant to maintain details of work packages, tasks and work orders. The project leader must become familiar with which systems are optional and which are mandatory for the maintenance of project cost information. The project leader must also ensure that a request for access to systems is initiated and that appropriate training for all those who have access to these systems is carried out.

- *Roles and responsibilities:* Any business rules in relation to the management of costs could be captured in the project-wide RASCI and categorised with the tag *Cost* for easy identification. An example of such a business rule could be *Expense claims greater than $100 must be approved*—the project leader would be both Accountable (A) and Responsible (R) and the Project Administrator could also be a Support (S) role to the project leader.

- *Make or buy analysis:* Review the WBS and decide whether to make in the project, or buy into the project. Capture what is to be bought, the deliverable or work package, the approach (e.g. COTS or outsource) and the procurement route intended to be taken (e.g. purchase order, contract or tender).

- *Long-lead-time and large capital items:* Once identified, the requirements, value and timelines for acquiring long-lead-time and large capital items (along with funding and approvals) should be documented.

- *Funding sources:* Most project budgets represent an outflow of money based on approved funding for the project. The approved budget for the project is typically not released in one chunk of funds; more frequently, funds will be released upon certain milestones being achieved, or by approval within the gated life cycle (refer to Chapter 2, section 2.9.3). In developing the project budget, the project leader must consider the timing and sources of the funds and incorporate them within the project budget as cash in-flows. Although the accounting for these cash in-flows would appear in the project budget, the details of the timing and amounts, funding sources and approvals would typically be documented within the Cost Management Plan.

- *Assumptions and constraints:* Consider what assumptions are being made in relation to cost factors for the project. (*Remember:* An *assumption* is an assumed statement of truth.) Also, capture what cost factors may constrain the project (e.g. ensuring funds are released in a timely manner to meet contractual arrangements and to ensure a good working relationship with suppliers is maintained).

- *Lessons learned:* Ensure that a review of any lessons learned from prior similar projects is undertaken, and that any relevant lessons learned are entered into the project's Lessons Learned Register under the category of *Cost*. Action any activities in relation to lessons and how they are to be managed in this project.

 Cost Management Plan

Now that the basis of costing has been established, the discussion will move into the processes of building the time-phased budget, controlling costs and the closure of costs-related activities.

12.3 Identification, estimation and categorisation of costs

Costs can occur and be associated to almost any activity in the planning of a project. Table 12.1 illustrates some of the sources of costs (and cost-related information) by knowledge area. *Note:* Although the WBS when estimated for resources, effort and costs provides an excellent source of information for the work packages and tasks, there are other costs that need to be considered that might fall outside the WBS.

Table 12.1 Examples of costs by knowledge area

Knowledge area	Sources of costs
Scope	The actual costs involved in the Initiation and Planning stages of the project must be accounted for—these are not free! Project leader costs, cross-charges for any stakeholders involved, potential SMEs and even a developing project team, accommodation and office/site resources. It might be that the project leader plans Planning and puts a cost/time on these activities. Producing the integrated Project Management Plan (integrated PMP) (which is a result of the Planning stage) could have a considerable cost associated with its development. Both these costs (the Initiation and Planning costs) must be captured within the project budget to provide a realistic whole-of-life-cycle project cost to the organisation.
Time	In Chapter 11 "Project schedule management", the discussion on duration versus effort was considered. Budgeting looks at both. We may, for example, have a machine operator required for 10 days' effort allocated to a task within a work package; however, because the machine is expensive to bring on site and we will need it in a work package 20 days later, the machine is kept on site for 30 days; thereby saving the set-up and delivery costs, which would be greater than keeping the machinery on site. These differences on how resources are deployed in the project schedule from a time perspective to how they are better utilised from a cost perspective need to be reconciled.
Quality	There is a cost to good quality. There are additional cost implications to the quality of the goods and/or services bought into the project, and additional costs in ensuring quality is produced within the work packages / tasks. Higher-quality goods and/or services generally have a higher cost.
	From a Business Case perspective, the above costs of building quality into the project can be set against the costs of poor quality (COPQ) occurring in the business when the project is handed over, or even within the project if rework has to be carried out.
Resources	Identify all the resources required to achieve each deliverable, its work package and tasks. Do not forget the project leader, project administrator (project officer), project accountants (to manage information in the company's ERP system) or other costs associated with whole-of-life project costs, such as rental of office space for the project team, electricity, ICT support, and so on. These could, for example, be allocated against the top-level Project box on the WBS.
	The project leader is a good example of a resource that is across the whole project. We don't typically assign the project leader as a resource against each work package where they are used and cost them into the work package; rather we assume the project leader as a fixed cost across the entire duration of the project. If resources are seconded to the project, there could be a cost in recruiting the back-filling positions in the operational business; these costs are likely to be payable by the project. So, in building the project budget, consider resources consumed beyond those identified at the work package and tasks levels.
Procurement	This includes early identification of long-lead-time items and large capital items. The bill of materials (BOM) and/or product breakdown structure (PBS) provide an important list of all the products (and their parts) and/or services required by the project to produce the product, service (or result) from the project. The BOM is discussed in Chapter 17 "Project procurement management". The project leader's review of the WBS with a *make or buy* decision will determine how the work package resources required will be brought into the project. Internal resources tend to be more cost-effective; however, if the approach of the project is to outsource large sections of the WBS and there are many suppliers, then the cost of tendering, putting in place contracts and subsequently performance monitoring those contracts could form a large component of the project schedule and project budget. Ultimately the contract terms and conditions for performance and payment will be a consideration for the project leader to include in the project budget, as it will represent money out, at specific points in time (i.e. time-phased).
Information and communications	Information sharing often requires ICT systems to support the collection and dissemination of project information. These systems could potentially need purchasing for the project. For example, as project leader you may decide to use the Atlassian Confluence software package to share knowledge in your project team. This would represent a direct cost to the project if these were not a part of the standard desktop environment.
	Any communication activity has a cost associated with it, whether this is the resources assigned to write, review and distribute electronic communications or prepare print communications. Print communications could also have additional costs such as announcements in mainstream newspapers—costing many thousands of dollars.
	Some projects may have dedicated human resources employed in respect to communications, such as a full-time communications manager.
Risk	Risks are typically assessed for costs across multiple dimensions.
	If risk workshops are carried out, invited SMEs and external consultants represent costs that need to be planned and accounted for. Mitigation plans (controls) that have been put in place to reduce risks will take time and effort in the project and therefore have an associated cost.
	For higher risks that cannot be reduced, there could be a potential cost to the business if they do occur and become active issues. The project leader may have to consider these costs in the contingency costs calculated for the project. **Expected monetary value (EMV)** is often used in risk analysis to provide an indication of the financial impact of a risk if it were to become an issue. This in turn may influence the size of the contingency retained for the project.
Stakeholders	Some stakeholder engagements incur considerable costs. For example, say you have a town-hall meeting, open to members of the public, for the announcement of a new hospital wing. You'd have to hire the venue, staff the venue, produce quality information booklets and have a feedback mechanism in place to publish responses to questions—all this costs money. Multiplying this with many other community and stakeholder engagements could result in a substantial communications budget.

Knowledge area	Sources of costs
Integration	Integration activities are not free to the project. For example, if we say on average a project will receive around 20 to 30 variation requests, consider how much time and effort goes into assessing the impact of variation (a project team member is assigned), approving/disapproving the variation, if approved—the effort required to update the project documents and potentially re-baselining the project. Again, some inclusions should be made to cover within the project budget. If the project leader has to carry out extensive project reporting as required by the organisation's PMO then again the cost of collecting this information at the task level and upwards needs to be considered, as does the administrative overhead to the project. Is a full-time project officer required to maintain, analyse and report on project information? Project Closure also has a cost associated with it. The project leader and key project administrative staff may have to be retained for a number of weeks to attend to all the closure activities as specified in the organisation's project governance.
Cost	Besides the project budget the cost knowledge area also considers the project contingency. How is contingency calculated? Is this based on a flat percentage or based on the risk profile of the project? The project leader is going to have to provide an open, transparent and calculated figure, and establish the governance around how contingency is accessed and tracked.
Organisational change management (OCM)	Although not a knowledge area, it is a source of potential costs, especially in soft projects where additional OCM activities have been planned into the work packages and tasks. There could even be a full-time OCM manager in the project. Again, all these costs need to be accounted for in the project budget.

© 2022 Dr Neil Pearson

This table provides an indication of how broadly as a project leader you must consider the costs to the project. The table is by no means exhaustive. The project leader and project team should review their project's WBS and check whether such costs have or not been considered, think integratively, think in terms of the entire business system that is potentially being impacted, and think beyond the deliverables and work packages for holistic, all-of-project-level costs.

Some organisations may have industry-specific cost checklists as an aide-mémoire for the project leader to check whether the listed cost is relevant and has been considered in their project.

 Cost Checklist

12.3.1 Recap of estimation of costs

Estimating was discussed extensively in Chapter 9 "Estimating". As a recap, estimating includes the following.

1. *Estimating resources:* This is the task of estimating the resources required by the project activities. Resources could be human or other (e.g. raw materials, facilities, plant and equipment) (PMI 2017). As well as the resource, the project leader and team should identify the quantity of the resource required.

2. *Estimating durations/effort:* This is the task of estimating how long a resource is needed, in terms of a time period. For some resources, this could be measured in hours or days; for others, it could be weeks or months. The objective is to accurately identify how long each resource is required for, inclusive of factors such as lead times, set-up times and tear-down times.

3. *Estimating activity costs:* This task aims to accurately identify the costs associated with the resource for the required time period. The costs could be estimated using an overall figure or more likely indicate the cost for the resource by (for example) per hour, per day, per use or per weight (PMI 2017).

The process of estimating should answer:

- what is required (e.g. skills, tools, equipment, raw material) and how many
- for how long (i.e. the duration of the *what*)
- when in the project timeline of events
- at what cost to the project.

At this point we should have identified and estimated all the costs relevant to the project or, if taking a rolling-wave planning approach for the stage, in detail. The next key activity for the project leader is preparing the actual project budget.

12.3.2 Cost categorisation

Accountants may require that the project leader accounts for project costs using standard accounting practices, whether this is to account for identified costs in broad categories (such as those indicated in Table 12.2) or on a more granular level (such as those indicated in an example **chart of accounts**, Table 12.3).

Table 12.2 Broad categories of costs

Fixed direct costs	Fixed indirect costs	Variable direct costs	Variable indirect costs
Direct costs are costs that are directly attributable to the project. They are chargeable to a specific work package.	Indirect costs cannot be directly attributed to the project but usually occur because of a direct cost. Sometimes referred to as general and administrative costs (G&A costs).	Variable costs change with the amount of some quantity being costed.	Variable indirect costs arise because of an indirect cost being attributed to the project. Sometimes referred to as G&A costs.
Examples: concrete, purchase of personal computers, hiring of staff, project leader's salary, lease of office space, bonus payments.	Examples: superannuation payments for hired staff, office maintenance costs because of leasing/ purchasing premises.	Examples: costs of ICT support: every time the project calls the service desk they are charged for the call, but the final cost depends on how many calls are made; mobile phone charges for a project team of 180 people.	Examples: a leave-loading for hired staff (which is obviously affected by the amount of holiday taken); the amount of time cleaning crews spend on cleaning.

© 2022 Dr Neil Pearson

Table 12.3 Extract from a chart of accounts

Code	Category	Capitalised (Y/N)
COMMUNICATIONS		
1001	Communications (internal)	N
1002	Communications (external)	N
1003	Venue hire	N
1004	Print shop printing	N
1005	Print media (newspapers, etc.)	N
PERSONNEL		
5001	Contractors	N
5002	Labor hire	N
5003	Recruitment	N
5004	Wages and salaries	N
5005	Travel and subsistence	N'
EQUIPMENT		
8001	Equipment repairs (not maintenance)	N
8002	Equipment maintenance	Y
8003	Equipment purchase	Y
8004	Equipment consumables	N
8005	Equipment rental	N
MATERIALS		
10001	Steel work	Y
10002	Concrete	Y

© 2022 Dr Neil Pearson

The project leader will have to ensure that all costs identified when being transferred into the project accounting system are allocated to their appropriate account code for later tracking and reporting. This could be as simple as maintaining a "Look-up" column in your project budget spreadsheet, to capture the account code.

12.4 Time-phased project budgets

Time-phased project budgeting is one of the simplest ways to arrange the costs in carrying out the project stage, or phase. In constructing the time-phased project budget, the costs captured are **planned costs**—that is, they are the estimated costs that we plan to spend at a point in time on the project schedule.

Inputs into developing the project budget, as discussed in the previous sections, include:

- all the clearly identified costs from estimating the WBS work packages and tasks
- other holistic project costs that fall across the overall project that may not have been included within the work packages and tasks

- the BOM for the product, service or result (if not fully covered in the WBS)
- the project's cash in-flows (income) and the timing of these within the project budget.

Without an accurate time-phased project budget, it would not be possible for the project leader to monitor and control **actual costs** spent against the **planned costs**, and report on the **variance** between the two (planned costs − actual costs).

12.4.1 Time-phased project budget, by category

The project budget is typically maintained within either a spreadsheet (for most small to medium-sized projects) or in the organisation's finance/ERP/project accounting system (for larger projects). When maintained in spreadsheets, project budgets are usually organised as simple expenditure and income, split along a time frame. Taking the WBS (introduced in Chapter 8, reproduced here as Figure 12.5) and estimating information, the process of moving the relevant information into the time-phased budget will next be explained.

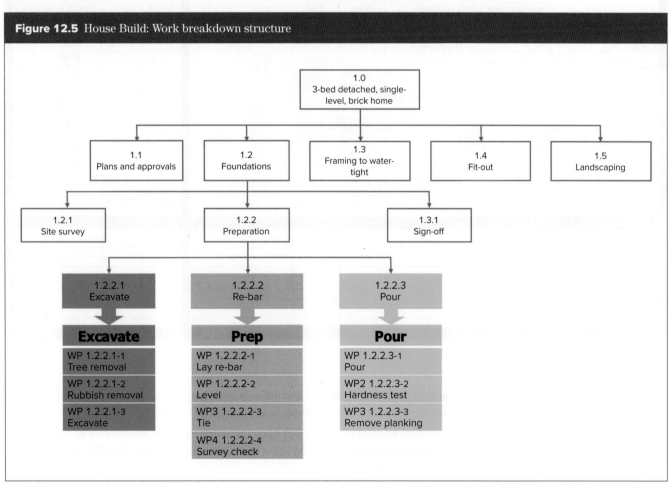

Figure 12.5 House Build: Work breakdown structure

© 2022 Dr Neil Pearson

Let's now start to develop a time-phased project budget spreadsheet for the *foundations* deliverable. It is important to note that the time-phasing (i.e. at what time-point the costs fall) is known, as the project leader would have created the project schedule and would therefore know when a work package (or task) is scheduled to take place. This work package / task information as to when it is scheduled is when the costs would normally fall within the time-phased budget.

Referring to Figure 12.6, the reader will also be able to see that the **planned, actual, variance (PAV)** approach has been taken to planning so subsequent tracking (controlling) of costs in the project can occur. As this is the project budget by category example, the reader will be able to see that down the left side of the spreadsheet costs have been allocated to cost categories (the chart of accounts or **project accounting codes**).

The time-phase has been simplified to months (along the horizontal); the project leader would of course use a time-phase appropriate to how they want to track and control project costs. This could be daily for a two-week mine shutdown, weekly for a two-month office move project or monthly for a two-year bridge construction. The time-phase should be suitable for how the project leader wants to track and control costs, for example a project leader might want to control costs on a weekly basis but can cumulate the weekly costs to provide the PMO with a monthly status report.

Figure 12.6 Time-phased project budget, by category

	Project Account Code	Estimate Calculations	March Planned	March Actual	March Varience	March Comments	April Planned	April Actual	April Varience	April Comments
Expenditure										
Equipment										
Backhoe	8005	Quote $1000/day rental	$10,000.00	$11,000.00	-$1,000.00	GST missing off invoice			$0.00	
					$0.00				$0.00	
Materials					$0.00				$0.00	
Steel rebar	10001		$4,500.00	$4,500.00	$0.00				$0.00	
Bar posts & ties	10001		$500.00	$500.00	$0.00				$0.00	
Concrete 60 cubic meters	10002	Quote MPA25 $306 cubic meter			$0.00		$18,360.00	$18,360.00	$0.00	
					$0.00				$0.00	
Labour					$0.00				$0.00	
Surveyor	5001	$1000/day	$1,000.00	$1,000.00	$0.00		$1,000.00	$1,000.00	$0.00	
Backhoe operator	5002	$500/day	$5,000.00	$5,000.00	$0.00				$0.00	
General Labourer 1	5002	$200/day	$2,000.00	$1,800.00	$200.00	Off-sick 1 day	$400.00	$400.00	$0.00	
General Labourer 2	5002	$150/day	$1,500.00	$1,500.00	$0.00		$300.00	$300.00	$0.00	
					$0.00				$0.00	
Overheads					$0.00				$0.00	
Project leader	5004	Fixed internal xCharge	$2,000.00	$2,000.00	$0.00		$2,000.00	$2,000.00	$0.00	
					$0.00				$0.00	
		Totals	$26,500.00	$27,300.00	-$800.00		$22,060.00	$22,060.00	$0.00	
Income										
Funding release: Foundations			$48,560.00							
Funding release: Framing										
Funding release: Fit-out										
Funding release: Landscaping										
Net Position										
Total planned		$48,560								
Total actual		$49,360								
Net		$800								

- *Planned:* The **baseline** (estimated planned and subsequently approved) value for the stage of the project. In this case the foundations deliverable was planned to be $48,560.

- *Actual:* The actual value charged to the project once the work has been completed. In this case the foundations deliverable actually incurred costs of $27,300 (in January) plus $22,060 (in February), giving a total of $49,360.

  Variance: *Variance = Planned − Actual* (i.e. $48,560 − $49,360 = −800). Thus resulting in an overspend of $800.

  A negative number indicates the actual spend is greater than was planned, and a positive number indicates the spend is under budget, that is, the actual is below what was planned. In the example, the variance is the planned value of $48,560 minus the actual value of $49,360, which equals minus $800. So, at this point in time the project is $800 overspent. In the spreadsheet (see Figure 12.6) a

"Comments" column can be used to capture the reason(s) why. These financial positions can then be reported on in the project status report and the reasons for the difference articulated.

Note: These time-phased project budgets are also known as the *project cash flow statements*; much like a business's cash flow, they show expenditure against income over a set period of time.

The project leader's choice of categories in the "Expenditure" column determines how the categories of costs are going to be tracked within the spreadsheet. In this example, the column "Project account code" for expenditure used the account codes introduced in Table 12.3. Remember that the other options for categorisation of costs included:

- chart of accounts
- project accounting codes
- fixed direct/fixed indirect categories
- variable direct/variable indirect categories.

Note: These categorisations of costs would be captured in the Cost Management Plan, and communicated to all those involved in managing project costs, thereby a consistent approach is taken to recording cost items against the correct category; we also keep an important stakeholder happy— the commercial manager (or finance department)!

Within the "Income" row (Figures 12.6 and 12.7), the funding releases have been captured. Calculating down the columns enables the project leader to control variances along the time dimension. For example, in January the planned expenditure minus the actual expenditure equals minus $800, so we can immediately see the project has overspent.

Calculating along the rows would enable the project leader to calculate the total for each category and subcategory; for example, the total planned cost of the "general labourer 1" comes in at $2,000 (January) + $400 (February) = $2,400 (total not shown in this excerpt of the spreadsheet).

This enables the project leader to ask questions such as:

- Have we overspent on a resource type?
- By how much? For what reason?
- Was the estimate carried out using incorrect information?
- Do the estimating tools need to be updated?
- Can we access such a quantity of that resource?
- Have we moved outside of any constraints?
- What lessons learned can be drawn?

12.4.2 Time-phased project budget, by WBS

Another variation of the time-phased project budget is to track costs by the control account, work package and/or task. Figure 12.7 provides an illustration. The project budget shown in Figure 12.7 is again based on the partial House Build WBS in Figure 12.5. This method for developing the project budget provides a very detailed methodical approach to the preparation of the budget and allows for the tracking of planned, actual and variance details against each work package and/or task and across time. Note that the time dimension for both these examples has been defined as months; however, on shorter, fast-paced projects, the project leader may select a more frequent time dimension such as weeks or, in some cases, days! The disadvantage of tracking by WBS is that the project budget can become very large; the advantage is that it tracks to the timeline of the project schedule—and indeed some project leaders take the cost information and track from within a software scheduling package such as Microsoft Project. Microsoft Project allows for the costs against each work package to be entered directly into the tool.

Figure 12.7 Time-phased project budget, by WBS

		Project Account Code	Estimate Calculations	March Planned	March Actual	March Varience	March Comments	April Planned	April Actual	April Varience	April Comments
Expenditure											
1.2.2.1	Excavate										
WP 1.2.2.1-1	Tree removal					$0.00				$0.00	
WP 1.2.2.1-2	Rubbish removal					$0.00				$0.00	
WP 1.2.2.1-3	Excavate					$0.00				$0.00	
	Surveyor	5001	$1000/day	$1,000.00	$1,000.00	$0.00				$0.00	
	Backhoe	8005	Quote $1000/day rental	$10,000.00	$11,000.00	-$1,000.00	GST missing off invoice			$0.00	
	Backhoe operator	5002	$500/day	$5,000.00	$5,000.00	$0.00				$0.00	
						$0.00				$0.00	
1.2.2.2	Rebar					$0.00				$0.00	
WP 1.2.2.2-1	Lay rebar					$0.00				$0.00	
	General Labourer 1	5002	$200/day	$2,000.00	$1,800.00	$200.00				$0.00	
	General Labourer 2	5002	$150/day	$1,500.00	$1,500.00	$0.00				$0.00	
	Steel rebar	10001		$4,500.00	$4,500.00	$0.00				$0.00	
	Bar posts & ties	10001		$500.00	$500.00	$0.00				$0.00	
WP 1.2.2.2-2	Level					$0.00				$0.00	
WP 1.2.2.2-3	Tie					$0.00				$0.00	
WP 1.2.2.2-4	Survey check					$0.00				$0.00	
	Surveyor	5001	$1000/day			$0.00		$1,000.00	$1,000.00	$0.00	
						$0.00				$0.00	
1.2.2.3	Pour					$0.00				$0.00	
WP 1.2.2.3-1	Pour					$0.00				$0.00	
	General Labourer 1	5002	$200/day			$0.00		$400.00	$400.00	$0.00	
	General Labourer 2	5002	$150/day			$0.00		$300.00	$300.00	$0.00	
	Concrete 60 cubic meters	10002	Quote MPA25 $306 cubic meter			$0.00		$18,360.00	$18,360.00	$0.00	
						$0.00				$0.00	
WP 1.2.2.3-2	Hardness test					$0.00				$0.00	
WP 1.2.2.3-3	Remove planking					$0.00				$0.00	
						$0.00				$0.00	
						$0.00				$0.00	
Overheads						$0.00				$0.00	
Project leader		5004	Fixed internal xCharge	$2,000.00	$2,000.00	$0.00		$2,000.00	$2,000.00	$0.00	
						$0.00				$0.00	
			Totals	$26,500.00	$27,300.00	-$800.00		$22,060.00	$22,060.00	$0.00	
Income											
Funding release: Foundations				$48,560.00							
Funding release: Framing											
Funding release: Fit-out											
Funding release: Landscaping											
Net Position											
Total planned		$48,560.00									
Total actual		$49,360.00									
Net		$800.00									

© 2022 Dr Neil Pearson

In both examples, the transfer of costs to the month in which they occurred has been sourced from the project schedule (i.e. when the cost occurred in terms of when that work package or task was scheduled to take place), hence the workflow that has been followed in Chapter 9 "Estimating", and replicated in this chapter as Figure 12.7.

Whichever style of project budget is developed, it can be expanded to record and track a host of other financial-related information. There is value in doing so to allow more complete analysis for both performance reporting and lessons learned analysis. For example, in Figures 12.6 and 12.7, additional columns could be inserted to track:

- estimating information, including:
  - estimate value(s)
  - source of the estimate
  - estimate method (e.g. three-point, parametric, alternative analysis)
  - estimate expiration (most quotes are only valid for a limited time)

- invoice information, including:
  - invoice number(s)
  - dates issued/paid
  - supplier name
  - schedules of payments
  - notes on supplier performance
  - references to contract terms and conditions
- quality criteria, including quality assurance criteria that must be met before payment
- tracking information, including:
  - tracking totals—planned, actual and variance
  - work package totals
  - project account code totals
  - earned value information.

Note: The sum of the planned values, totalled by month, and then all the months totalled together would equate to the planned value for the project. This planned value for the entire project is typically set on approval of the integrated PMP at the end of the Planning stage before the project moves into the Execution stage (i.e. it is the **cost baseline**). Any variations to the project definitely require a variation request to be raised and would be assessed from this cost baseline (in conjunction with the other two baselines—the *scope baseline* and the *schedule baseline*).

12.4.3 Time-phased project budget, by WBS and OBS

The third type of perspective of the time-phased project budget is to take the time-phased project budget by WBS and layer onto the budget the organisational breakdown structure (OBS); this enables the project leader to see where the costs fall by department in the organisation. Not all projects will require this view of the budget, but it has been included to illustrate how different presentations of the project budget can assist the project leader in communicating different perspectives of the cost component of the project to the different stakeholders (Figure 12.8).

In Figure 12.8, it is possible to see the impact from a cost perspective against each of the construction company's departments. This has additionally been split into three total lines to capture planned labour costs, planned equipment costs and planned material costs. The project leader could use this information, for instance, to discuss with department managers the upcoming resource commitments required from each of them.

So, at this point we have a time-phased project budget, either structured by cost category or WBS. The Cost Management Plan and project budget are components of the integrated PMP and with all the planning artefacts at the end of the Planning stage would be taken for approval. At this point, the project budget becomes the baseline budget from which the project starts Execution.

 Budget Spreadsheet

Figure 12.8 Budget with organisational breakdown structure (OBS)

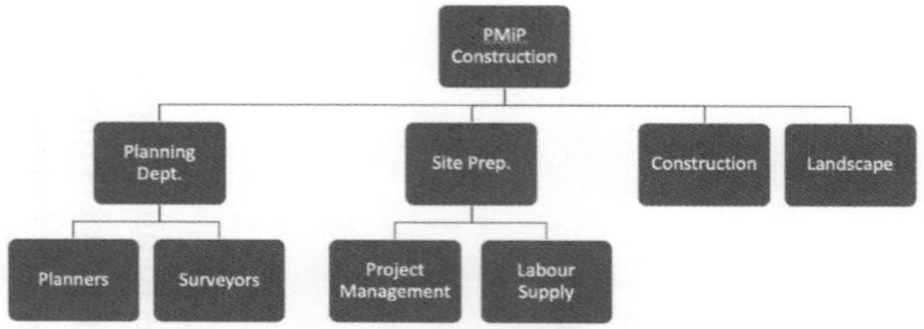

12.5 Project cost control and monitoring

Many things can potentially go adrift during the Execution stage; these are wide-ranging and varied.

- Costs increase from the time of the estimate to the time the project enters the Execution stage—for example, if there is an increase in labour charges that cannot be accommodated by the organisation that quoted the original costs. This is especially prevalent in the construction/mining industry with the ebb and flow of large (multi-billion dollar) projects and the supply/demand for key resources.

- The time it actually took to complete an activity (work package) blows out, thereby increasing costs.

- Unplanned findings occur during a work package, which were not planned for in the original estimate—this is especially true in construction projects once the first hole is dug and a water pipe or communications cable is suddenly discovered that was not on the plans of any council or utility company!

- Natural forces change the market conditions—for example, when Cyclone Yasi hit northern Queensland in 2011, many utility and infrastructure companies had to redeploy resources to emergency projects, taking away from planned project activity.

What can the project leader do in such cases? Refer to Chapter 8 "Defining the scope of a project", where the variation management process (VMP) was introduced. Whatever the reason, where a cost overrun has occurred, the project leader (or preferably the requestor of the variation) should raise a variation request and seek appropriate approvals per the VMP. The outcome of the variation analysis might be to accept the variation and approve an increase to the budget or more likely pull funds from the contingency set aside for the project (hopefully a risk had been raised and an EMV amount allocated into the contingency for such events).

The key to cost control is to monitor closely the spend that is taking place and, using simple tools such as a project budget spreadsheet (or reports from the company's financial/ERP/project accounting system), monitor the planned costs (estimated) versus the actual costs incurred and be able to justify the reasons for over- or even under-spend.

Various charts can be plotted using such time-phased information, such as a simple graph of planned spend and actual spend. See Figure 12.9, which relates to the progress of the House Build project and plots the data on cumulative planned costs and cumulative actual costs.

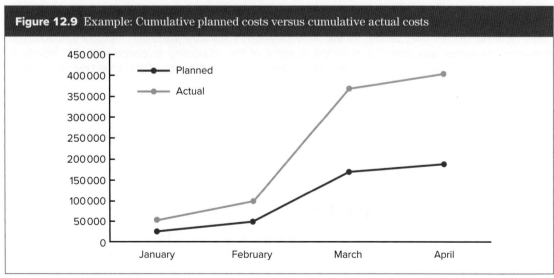

Figure 12.9 Example: Cumulative planned costs versus cumulative actual costs

© 2022 Dr Neil Pearson

Simple charts such as this assist the project leader to control the quality and performance of the project itself. In all stages of the project life cycle, but especially in the Execution stage, the project leader is accountable for tracking this information and taking pre-emptive actions based on the data.

In addition to tracking the planned costs against the actual costs, the project leader can use more advanced techniques such as earned value management (EVM) to forecast the actual values for the project at completion in addition to schedule related metrics.

In monitoring and controlling the project budget, one of the project leader's biggest headaches can be in reconciling the costs actually incurred, when they occurred and matching to this to the company's accounting practices of issuing and paying invoices. A tip here is to diligently stick with the project schedule and the project budget—for example, when a work package is completed and the monies allocated spent, this is what gets recorded in the project budget; do not, for instance, delay accounting for the money until the invoice has been paid by the finance department. This is because there could be substantial time differences between the two events occurring and trying to reconcile can otherwise become an endless administrative task. The KISS (*keep it simple, stupid*) principle definitely applies here: when the work package is complete (at its allocated time-point), the money has effectively been spent and should be recorded as such in the project budget.

The "Snapshot from Practice: Project accounting guidelines" illustrates how project environments must support the business in all senses of the word. It also illustrates the value as a project leader in consulting with your PMO, and/or the finance department to capture any such financial governance (early in the project) within the project's Cost Management Plan.

SNAPSHOT *from* PRACTICE : Project accounting guidelines

While jointly managing a PMO for a large energy distribution company in Australia, one of the authors (Pearson) was involved in establishing governance, processes, policies and templates for the business change, project management framework (PMF). Among the various policies developed was a policy related to capitalisation of assets.

When the value of money leaves a company, the company reports it as an expense. Expenses reduce profit. Every $1 in wages that you pay a teenager who staffs your ice cream stand is $1 that leaves your company, so it reduces your profit by $1. But the value of money spent on assets doesn't leave the company, so it's not recorded as an expense and therefore doesn't reduce profit. The value remains on the balance sheet. This is asset capitalisation (Merritt n.d.)

So, by capitalising assets correctly, such as a $20,000 ice cream maker for the business mentioned above, an organisation can gain by a depreciation of the assets over the life of the asset, as the ice cream maker will not be worth $20,000 in, say, five years' time.

The principle can be applied in most countries, according to the local tax laws. As the energy distributor was an Australian Government-owned corporation, codes of accounting practices related to government were applicable. Sourcing information on asset capitalisation and depreciation of software assets, the author discovered a different set of guidelines, as documented in Accounting Guidance Note No. 2007/1—Accounting for Internally Developed Software (Australian Government 2007). Armed with this information, the author was able to capture the essence of the accounting guidance note and include instructions for project leaders on what could/could not be capitalised within the relevant section of the project management framework (PMF).

Sources: Merritt C n.d., "What does capitalizing assets mean?", Chron, http://smallbusiness.chron.com/capitalizing-assets-mean-65016.html); Australian Government 2007, Accounting Guidance Note No. 2007/1—Accounting for Internally Developed Software, Department of Finance and Deregulation, https://www.finance.gov.au/publications/accounting-guidance-notes/docs/AGN_2007-1-Internally-Developed-Software.pdf), accessed February 2018.

12.6 : Contingency planning

It was stated earlier in the chapter that **contingency** is an amount of funds allocated for events that are outside the approved project budget. There are several questions to be answered when allocating contingency funds:

■ How much should be allocated for contingency?

■ How does the project leader/the project gain access to the contingency funds?

■ What approvals need to take place?

In practice, contingency funds are usually retained by the PMO, project sponsor or project Steering Committee. Access to these contingency funds is via the VMP. There are various approaches to calculating contingency.

■ Industry thinking on contingency amounts often makes reference to the *general risk profile* of the project. Low-risk projects typically hold back around 10 per cent of the total planned project budget in a contingency fund, with amounts of 30 per cent held back for high-risk projects.

■ More specifically the project will hold a contingency amount based on the actual risk profile of the project using the expected monetary value (EMV) approach. This is an amount of contingency held back as a result of the risk analysis and the probability and costs associated with each risk. Chapter 16 "Project risk management" discusses this approach further.

■ The Project Management Institute (PMI) illustrates the contingency amounts as indicated in Figure 12.10. This figure has been annotated to assist the reader in interpreting how the contingency amount is arrived at.

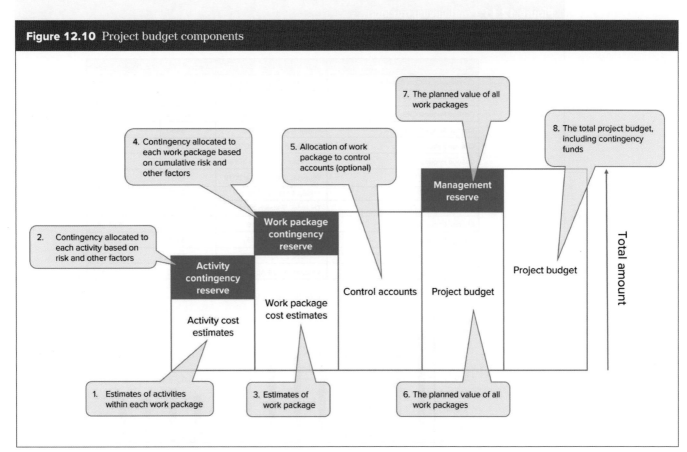

Figure 12.10 Project budget components

Source: Adapted from the Project Management Institute (PMI) 2017, *A Guide to the Project Management Body of Knowledge*, 6th edition, PMI, p. 255

In essence (relating to Figure 12.10), there are therefore two types of reserves:

1. Project reserves, accounted for within the activity and work packages, which are:

■ under the control of the project leader and are subject to the integrated variation management process

■ used to deal with known unknowns

■ openly declared and included in the **cost baseline**.

2. Management reserves, accounted for as a specified amount on the summation of the control accounts, which are:

   ■ subject to the integrated variation management process (and therefore) management approval

   ■ used to manage unknown unknowns

   ■ included in the project budget.

After approval of a variation request to gain access to reserves, including documenting why the funds are needed, the project budget would be increased by the agreed amount, which would also result in an increase to the project's cost baseline—in fact, it could mean re-baselining the project budget (and schedule) and issuing a new baseline from which the project continues executing.

Some project leaders track the amounts of contingency calculated at each of the levels indicated in Figure 12.10 to ensure that contingency reserves are not being depleted too quickly, too early in the project—a sure sign that the project may be heading for disaster. An example of a simple contingency tracking chart is in Figure 12.11.

Figure 12.11 Contingency tracking

Reason	Date	Amount	Contingency "pool"
Contingency @ Cost Baseline	Thursday, 29 November 2018	$35,000	$35,000
Change Request CR2	Thursday, 6 December 2018	$4,350	$30,650
Change Request CR3	Friday, 7 December 2018	$2,000	$28,650
Change Request CR4	Friday, 4 January 2019	$450	$28,200
Change Request CR9	Tuesday, 8 January 2019	$579	$27,621
Change Request CR12	Thursday, 7 February 2019	$652	$26,969
Change Request CR16	Thursday, 21 February 2019	$987	$25,982
Change Request CR19	Friday, 1 March 2019	$456	$25,526
Change Request CR23	Thursday, 7 March 2019	$10,897	$14,539
Change Request CR24	Monday, 1 April 2019	$156	$14,383
Change Request CR25	Tuesday, 2 April 2019	$765	$13,618
Change Request CR31	Tuesday, 23 April 2019	$300	$13,318
Change Request CR32	Wednesday, 24 April 2019	$100	$13,218

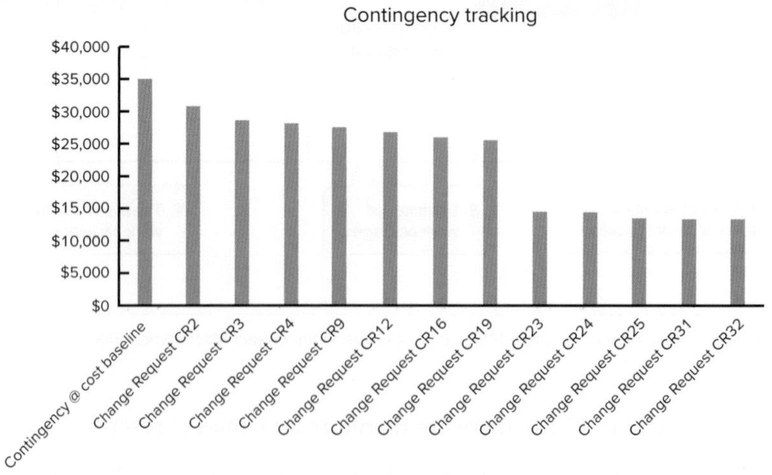

© 2022 Dr Neil Pearson

A simple contingency tracker is also included in the budget spreadsheet template.

Budget Spreadsheet

12.7 : Cost closure

Although there is no formal cost closure in the project cost management knowledge area, the PMI does cover costs to a limited extent in the "Project closure" section of the *Project Management Body of Knowledge (PMBOK® Guide)* (PMI 2017). This text takes a similar approach, and in Chapter 21 "Project closure", project cost closure is considered. For completeness of the present chapter, some project cost closure activities are captured here.

1. Final project reporting (baseline plus approved variations versus actual), and updating the organisation's corporate systems with final project costs. It is important to ensure that the final situation is represented in corporate systems; this could include the final reconciliation of invoices, paying invoices and capturing of outstanding invoices. Outstanding invoices (and approval to pay) would be handed over to the organisation's finance department, as you as project leader will have probably moved on to your next project and will not be waiting around for final payment of invoices in the context of the wider organisation finance procedures.

2. Running any final financial reports from financial systems and including as annexes to the project's final status report.

3. Closing down access to systems and project account codes. This is to prevent any future projects from booking costs to the account codes setup for this project. Unscrupulous project leaders have been observed to book costs to *balanced and closed* project account codes to hide overruns in costs on their projects!

4. Capturing cost-related lessons learned. Whether these are related to the processes that drive cost management in the project or from the actual estimating activities and cost variations encountered during the delivery of this project.

5. Providing a final statement of the project budget. With increases/decreases logged as a result of variation requests, and a final balance of the project and narrative as to whether the project was within budget or not.

6. Ensuring capitalisation and depreciation of assets and any other relevant financial guidelines have been applied according to the policies of the organisation.

12.7.1 Premature project closure

If a project is prematurely closed (for whatever reason) the project leader would carry out a full project closure including all the cost-related activities. *Remember:* A **sunk cost** is a loss that should be recorded. The project leader, Steering Committee and management team must declare the sunk costs of the project and move forward.

12.7.2 Project heath checks and audits

Project budgets and adherence to the governance captured in the Cost Management Plan, and associated financial policies and procedures, are often targets (along with project procurement management) for internal **health checks** or more stringent external audits. The project leader must have confidence in the transparent manner in which the project budget was initially created and in the subsequent monitoring and controlling of the project budget, variation management adherence, and appropriate access to contingency funds. Keep honest books and you'll soar through these audits with flying colours!

Summary

Project cost management requires attention to detail. Project cost management takes various inputs from the project schedule management (such as the WBS and their associated work package dictionary items—refer Chapter 8 "Defining the scope of a project"), project resource identification and scheduling, and estimation. Leveraging these artefacts enables the project leader to form an accurate project budget, subsequently baselined in order to monitor and control costs against. This chapter has considered the following.

- The Cost Management Plan governs and captures business rules around how costs are managed and reported in the project, along with other items such as policy and procedure, contingency, estimating, use of corporate systems, long-lead-time and large capital items, funding sources and lessons learned.
- Project cost management has its origins in the development of the project scope document, and the WBS (work packages and tasks).
- The estimation of all resources attached to the WBS plus wider (holistic) project costs all provide information that forms the basis for budgeting the project.
- From this information, the subsequent development of the time-phased project budget can take place.
- The cost baseline (the planned value of the project) represents the sum of the cost accounts (if used, or deliverables) and therefore the sum of the work packages and tasks. *Remember:* If your budgeted costs are not time-phased, you really have no reliable way to measure performance—when monies were planned to be spent and what was actually spent.
- The project leader is accountable for monitoring and controlling costs throughout the life cycle of the project. This includes the financial viability of the project, ensuring that there is sufficient funding to cover the outgoings of the project. The project leader must also report on costs as a part of the project's status report, and is involved in making hard choices; however, with a well-planned, detailed project budget that is time-phased, the project leader will be armed with the best information upon which to make these decisions.

Review questions

1. What types of project cost accounting structures can be applied to the categorising of costs?
2. Why is it important to establish links with the finance department of the organisation when drafting the Cost Management Plan?
3. What is the purpose of *contingency* and how can access be gained to contingency funds?
4. What types of systems are typically used to track project budgets, and whose responsibility is it to ensure that appropriate access is maintained to these systems?
5. What is the significance of identifying long-lead-time items and large capital items early in the project life cycle?
6. What is the project *cost baseline* and how is it arrived at?
7. When should the change/variation process be invoked from a cost control perspective?
8. What additional information can be gained from simple spreadsheet budgets to monitor and control project costs (remember PAV, and tallies across the rows)?

Exercises

1. Review the Template—Project Budget. Which budget would be best suited to a project you have worked on recently? Did you have such cost information? Or do you need to create a version of the spreadsheet that would work for your project environment?
2. Develop a Cost Management Plan for a recent project you have worked on using the template provided: don't forget to review the template first and identify any additional headings that would be required in your project environment.
3. Either:
   - A—Review recent project management press articles, or
   - B—Use projects within your organisation

   and identify six lessons learned from a cost perspective. Reflecting on these lessons learned, suggest ways in which these could be leveraged (for positive lessons) or avoided (for negative lessons) in a project you have worked on.

References

Australian Government 2007, Accounting Guidance Note No. 2007/1 – Accounting for Internally Developed Software, Department of Finance and Deregulation, https://www.finance.gov.au/publications/accounting-guidance-notes/docs/AGN_2007-1-Internally-Developed-Software.pdf), accessed February 2018.

Merritt C n.d., "What does capitalizing assets mean?", Chron, http://smallbusiness.chron.com/capitalizing-assets-mean-65016.html), accessed February 2018.

Project Management Institute (PMI) 2017, *A Guide to the Project Management Body of Knowledge*, 6th edition, PMI.

Project Management Institute (PMI) 2021a, *A Guide to the Project Management Body of Knowledge (PMBOK® Guide)*, 7th edition, PMI.

Project Management Institute (PMI) 2021b, *The Standard for Project Management (ANSI/PMI 99-001-2021)*, 7th edition, PMI.

Queensland Government, www.brisbane.qld.gov.au/traffic-transport/roads-infrastructure-bikeways/tunnels-bridges-major-roads/CLEM7/Construction-facts-figures/index.htm, accessed December 2012.

Rivercity Motorway 2008, "Tunnel boring machine breaks through at Kangaroo Point", www.asx.com.au/asxpdf/20081223/pdf/31fbhvzlkd2dtr.pdf, accessed December 2012.

CHAPTER 13
Project quality management

Learning elements

13A Establish what *quality* means in the project environment.

13B Be able to establish a culture and process around continuous improvement in the project environment.

13C Understand and apply quality assurance (QA) and quality control (QC) techniques.

13D Understand the different tools and techniques used to control and monitor quality.

13E Be able to investigate defects by applying root-cause analysis techniques.

In this chapter

13.1 Introduction

13.2 Quality and project management

13.3 Continuous improvement

13.4 Planning for quality

13.5 Quality of the project management

13.6 Carrying out quality control

13.7 Reporting quality performance

13.8 Root-cause analysis

Summary

13.1 | Introduction

Quality is a critical aspect of project management. Its definition forms the basis of:

- understanding and articulating the required level of quality, from the **voice of the customer (VOC)** perspective

- management of the triple constraints. The triple constraints were introduced in Chapter 8 "Defining the scope of a project" (Figure 8.7) and as noted, *quality* sits at the centre of the triangle. The project leader essentially manages the aspects of scope, time and cost while trying to protect (or not impede) the quality criteria of the project. There may be a point where quality must be sacrificed (by agreement) to complete the project on time and on cost

- setting the criteria to which deliverables will be later assessed in order to be signed off by the customer.

Many aspects of quality are woven throughout the project life cycle; however, discussions around quality should start from the very outset of a project, within the Initiation stage of the project life cycle.

The two key aspects of quality the project leader must consider are:

1. *Quality of the project management:* The focus here is on setting the project management quality expectations, deciding how these will be measured and how improvements will be made during the life cycle of the project—for example, specifying how and when project health checks will take place to ensure conformance to project governance criteria and guidelines.

2. *Quality of the product, service or result produced by the project:* Here, the focus is on the product, service or result being produced from the project, for the customer of the project. These criteria are often referred to as the *voice of the customer* or VOC. For example, a touch screen display forming part of an aircraft cockpit console would require identifying the required specifications; defining the tolerances for these specifications; and defining how quality will be checked, at what point in the proceedings, and by whom.

Both aspects need to be present in order for the management of the project and the production of the product, service or result to produce the expected quality results. There are some common activities associated with project quality, as captured in Figure 13.1.

| PMBOK | Seventh edition updates (PMI 2021) |

In the recent update to the *Project Management Body of Knowledge* (PMBOK) seventh edition, *Quality* now appears as a principle: "Build Quality into Processes and Deliverables" (PMI 2021b, p. 47). The name of this principle alone reinforces what has been promoted in this text for the last three editions: that as project leaders we need to be mindful of both (1) quality of the project management, and (2) quality of the product, service or result produced by the project.

Figure 13.1 General project management quality activities

A. Planning quality management
- **Understand the voice of the customer (VOC)**
- **Establish the project's continuous improvement process**
- **Create the first cut of the project's Quality Management Plan**
- **Update the project-wide RASCI with any quality governance, business rules and decisions**

B. Planning for quality
- **Identify and specify the quality criteria (start with an idea shower using the QA/QC grid)**
- **Develop detailed quality plans as required**
- **Review the work breakdown structure (WBS) and other project artefacts for quality-related specifications and control activities that need to be included in the WBS and others artefacts**

C. Seeking continuous improvements
- **Seek and action continuous project management-related improvement opportunities**
- **Seek and action continuous product/service-related improvement opportunities**
- **Maintain the Continuous Improvement Register**

D. Monitoring and controlling quality
- **Quality reporting of any defects/issues/non-conformances**
- **Deliverables signed off by customer based on quality**
- **Performance payments to suppliers based on quality not time/quantity**

E. Quality at Closure
- **Lessons learned**
- **Final deliverables to quality specifications**
- **Final handover**
- **Review the Continuous Improvement Register handover to outstanding requests to the business (where appropriate)**

© 2022 Dr Neil Pearson

 **LE 13A**

13.2 | Quality and project management

Before delving further into a discussion of quality and project management, it's important to first clarify understanding of some of the common terminology that will be used in this section.

When scoping a project, discussions must move from talking about requirements for quality at a high, overarching level and move towards a tight definition of the criteria of quality. Perceptions of what will constitute quality will have been discussed with the customer and will have been translated into broad-brush quality requirements during the Initiation stage of the project or, in fact, even before project development, within the Business Case. The customer's quality requirements are often referred to as the *VOC*. The VOC is critical—after all, if the project does not understand what the customer wants and how success is measured, how can accurate requirements be defined for what needs to be delivered from the project? It is therefore the project leader's responsibility to ensure that the customer's perceptions and their requirements are researched, clarified, documented and agreed upon. This forms part of the project Initiation activities and flows into the Planning stage of the project, where the development of the **Quality Management Plans** and other associated artefacts is carried out.

The overall objective therefore is to define and manage quality because, as illustrated in Figure 13.2, the cost to rectify poor quality logarithmically increases across the life cycle of the project. When poor quality is passed into *business as usual*, the cost to rectify problems increases significantly. If poor quality reaches the customer, the cost is even greater as the company brand and reputation are often affected. A case in point is the Samsung Galaxy Note 7 mobile phone and its exploding batteries—this **defect** issue is reported to have cost Samsung more than USD5 billion (Swider 2017).

Figure 13.2 Cost to rectify quality defects across and beyond the project life cycle

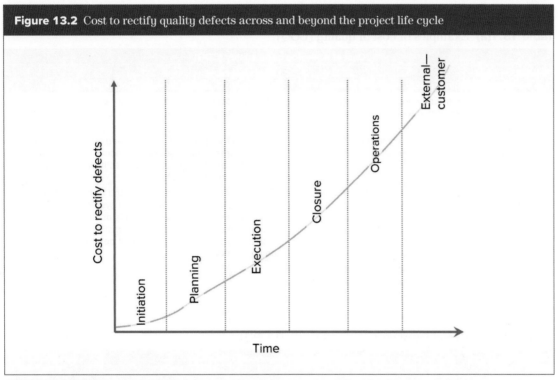

© 2022 Dr Neil Pearson

13.2.1 **Cost of quality (COQ) and cost of poor quality (COPQ)**

During discussions about quality, the project leader is likely to be asked what the **cost of quality (COQ)** is for the product or service being designed. COQ includes both: (1) the cost of preventing a defect or rework (i.e. the costs incurred as a resulting of achieving quality), and (2) the **cost of poor quality (COPQ)**—costs generated when poor quality occurs (e.g. rework in the project, and potentially recalls and reputation damage post-project).

For example, if Samsung had invested more into the prevention side of quality (COQ), by ensuring the Galaxy Note 7 batteries manufactured by one of their own subsidiaries fitted the Note 7 case, it would have reduced or probably not had to count the COPQ (i.e. the USD5 billion in costs of recalls, replacements and reputation damage).

When the COQ is incorporated into the design of the final project and resulting product or service, it could have many implications, including the following.

- *Estimation of the project costs:* Higher quality usually means higher costs, whether in the components purchased, or in the use of higher-quality service providers.

■ *The need to consider the impact on the time taken to complete activities:* It may now take longer and require additional steps, for example, to carry out additional quality control tasks within work packages.

■ *The design of comprehensive quality control processes and general continuous improvement activities:* To ensure that quality is being applied and improved throughout the life of the project (e.g. we are improving our own project management processes and other processes in the business such procurement, contracts, finance and human resources).

If insufficient attention is paid to quality in general, many potential costs to the project can arise when deliverables are handed over (or post-project). These can include, for example, not achieving the required product or service project quality, product or service defects, unnecessary rework, non-conformance and dissatisfied customers (Table 13.1a).

Table 13.1(a) Examples of cost of quality (COQ)

Cost of achieving good quality (COQ)	
Prevention costs (i.e. the costs of building quality into the process)	**Appraisal costs** (i.e. the costs associated with checking for quality)
Additional processes are developed and compliance to these processes are ensured, to achieve the quality outcomes.	Costs associated with the time and resources expended in conducting audits and project health checks.
Training costs associated with training project staff and contractors to ensure quality requirements are understood and met.	Checking the quality of products and services produced by the project. These additional checks to ensure the process is producing outputs correctly are costs that should be identified in the project.
Increase in the cost of components to ensure these are at the required level of quality.	Testing components individually and further testing the integrated set of components as a system in the final product or service. If the product is destroyed during testing, this is referred to as *destructive testing* (and has a greater cost, which is the cost of destroying the part being tested).
Costs associated with purchasing the correct tools and equipment to carry out quality control activities.	

© 2022 Dr Neil Pearson

Table 13.1(b) Examples of cost of poor quality (COPQ)

Cost arising from poor quality (COPQ)	
Internal failure costs (i.e. the costs associated with reworking the defective product or service before it reaches the customer)	**External failure costs (i.e. the costs associated with a defective product (or service) reaching the customer)**
Failing to *do it right the first time* necessitates additional time and cost to complete.	Customer dissatisfaction and longer-term reputational damage (loss of future business).
The costs of reworking defective parts or service elements (e.g. a service desk ticket that is not resolved correctly and must be re-opened and reworked by the service desk agents).	Increased risk of legal action being taken against the project and/or the organisation.
A process fails to deliver the required outputs and must be shut down until the root causes have been identified and corrected—before the process can be re-started.	Excessive warranty/defect claims, resulting in a cost to the project and/or organisation, in terms of rectification during and/or post-project.

© 2022 Dr Neil Pearson

In most situations, the project leader will work with the customer to define and negotiate acceptable levels of quality that meet both the customer's expectations and the project leader's ability to deliver these within agreed budget, time and scope parameters (the triple constraints!)

The project leader could already be aware of the COPQ such as those shown in Table 13.1(b). This is because documents such as the Business Case or the Project Charter may have already outlined them. For example, the Project Charter's problem statement might include aspects of poor quality. See "Snapshot from Practice: Simple paving quandary" for an example of lessons in project quality.

Simple paving quandary

A local council in Queensland established a project for a major shopping centre redevelopment. The redevelopment required a substantial amount of external paving to be relaid. In designing the project, the designers and engineers omitted to factor in the Australian Standards for quality specifications for pavers. The design utilised a natural paving material where the tolerances of the paver used were not consistent across its surface. When the client was involved in the sign-off of a deliverable for a section of the laid pavers, the surface was measured to ensure that a +/− 2 mm variance across the surface of the paver had been adhered to. As the pavers were a natural material, they did not meet these requirements and quality came into question. It was apparent that the client, project leader and designer did not have a clear understanding of the quality requirements of the pavers, even though in this case there were well-documented Australian Standards available for reference and inclusion as the quality criteria (e.g. AS/NZS 4455.2:2010 "Masonry Units, Pavers, Flags and Segmental Retaining Wall Units"). The standards had not been identified by any party in the project: not by the designer, the paving company representative or the project leader.

Figure 13.3 Simple paving quandary

This snapshot shows the effect of the COPQ in the project management processes, in not identifying the relevant quality criteria, resulting in a cost to the project and probably the customer—after all, someone must pay for the rectification of the poor quality!

13.3 Continuous improvement

Before proceeding with the project aspects of **quality assurance (QA)** and **quality control (QC)**, let's first delve into some of the background behind the process of continuous improvement and how this impacts the management of quality in a project environment.

Continuous improvement is an [overarching] ongoing effort to improve products, services, or processes. These efforts can seek 'incremental' improvement over time or 'breakthrough' improvement all at once (ASQ 2018a).

PMBOK **Seventh edition updates (PMI 2021)**

Continuous improvement is also recognised in the *Project Management Body of Knowledge* (PMBOK) seventh edition (PMI 2021a, p. 144), where as a part of *Tailoring* the topic of implementing ongoing improvement is discussed. There are many advantages to involving team members in continuous improvement processes as it fosters a sense of ownership, empowerment and pride. It also affirms the project leader's trust in individual team members, which, in turn, fosters improvement and innovation.

There are several commonly applied approaches to continuous improvement, including the **Plan, Do, Check, Act** cycle; the **Plan, Do, Study, Act** cycle; **Lean Six Sigma**; and, to a lesser extent today, **total quality management (TQM)**.

13.3.1 **Plan, Do, Check, Act (PDCA)**

Many **ISO 9001** accredited organisations follow the PDCA approach towards continuous improvement (ISO 9001 promotes PDCA as the preferred continuous improvement approach). PDCA (Figure 13.4) was popularised by W Edwards Deming. Deming later changed the word *Check* to *Study*, arguing that we don't just check to see if something worked, or did not work—but rather we study this with interest, to understand more deeply what exactly happened. Refer to Table 13.2 for a definition and application of how the PDCA cycle might form the basis of continuous improvement in a project environment.

Figure 13.4 The Plan, Do, Check, Act (PDCA) cycle

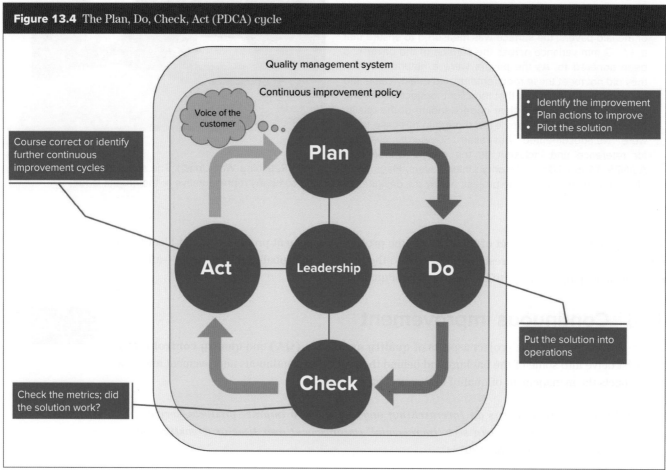

© 2022 Dr Neil Pearson

Table 13.2 Plan, Do, Check, Act (PDCA) defined and applied

	PDCA defined	PDCA ISO 9001* definition	PDCA example (applied to the management of a project)
Plan	Define the problem to be addressed, collect relevant data, and analyse this data to ascertain the problem's root cause. Decide upon a measurement to baseline the process and understand what it is currently delivering.	Establish the objectives of the system and its processes, and the resources needed to deliver results in accordance with customers' requirements and the organisation's policies and identify and address risks and opportunities.	An issue has been identified with the variation management process (VMP). Approvals for variation requests must wait until the next weekly meeting of the Change Management Board (CMB). This is delaying project progress and frustrating the client.

	PDCA defined	**PDCA ISO 9001* definition**	**PDCA example (applied to the management of a project)**
Do	Develop and implement a solution; typically, a *to-be* process with associated documents and system changes.	Implement what was planned.	The project leader asked the project coordinator to investigate the situation. The project coordinator provided the following recommendations: ■ Revise the VMP. ■ Devolve accountability for approval of variation request to the project leader for variations <\$3,000 in value and/or less than 0.5-day schedule slippage. ■ CMB to meet twice weekly for 30 minutes. These variations are subsequently implemented in the project's VMP and communicated to the project team.
Check	Confirm the results of *before* (baseline) and *after* (implemented solution) data. Did we achieve what we expected?	Monitor and (where applicable) measure processes and the resulting products and services against policies, objectives, requirements and planned activities and report the results.	Check variation requests are being attended to in a timelier manner. Check the client's satisfaction with the revised process.
Act	Embed the change, inform others about process changes, and make recommendations to improve the process in the next PDCA cycle.	Take actions to improve performance, as necessary.	Further improve the VMP by introducing an automated workflow to improve audit-tracking and integration with the project management information system.

Source: Adapted from International Organization for Standardization (ISO) 2015, ISO 9001 "Quality Management Systems–Requirements", 5th edition

Some project leaders like to capture continuous improvements; a simple form could resemble the online template.

PDCA Tracker

13.3.2 Lean Six Sigma

Lean Six Sigma was introduced in Chapter 2 "Popular frameworks and methodologies". **Six Sigma** is a metric, a methodology and a management system. As a methodology it focuses on understanding customer requirements, alignment of key business processes, basing control on data and embedding sustainable outcomes in the business. As a management system, the focus is on ensuring strategic alignment, using high-performing teams to attack specific continuous improvement projects to ensure results are sustained in the business. Six Sigma's continuous improvement approach involves applying the Define, Measure, Analyse, Improve and Control (DMAIC) process (as introduced in Chapter 2 "Popular frameworks and methodologies"). The core principle of Lean Six Sigma is to create customer value while minimising waste. This means creating increased value for customers, with fewer resources and a focus on the key processes that do not produce waste.

Lean Six Sigma brings both approaches together but drives the process of improvement through the DMAIC process, rather than through the ISO-preferred approach of PDCA. Table 13.3 provides an example of the same variation request issue (Table 13.2) through the DMAIC process.

As demonstrated in Tables 13.2 and 13.3, implementing a continuous improvement approach into a project environment ensures quality, measurable improvements are being made to the project's processes (in this case).

The same approaches could also be taken to the technical content of the product, service or result being produced by the project. For example, a technical engineer undertaking some development work discovers a more efficient method of doing this within the project. This should be treated as a continuous improvement opportunity, perhaps applying the PDCA principle.

Table 13.3 Define, Measure, Analyse, Improve and Control (DMAIC) continuous improvement example

	DMAIC defined	DMAIC example (applied to the management of a project)
Define	Define and understand the problem being investigated in this cycle of continuous improvement.	An issue has been identified with the variation management process (VMP). Problem statement: Approvals for variations must wait until the weekly meeting of the Change Management Board (CMB). This is delaying project progress (by an average of three days per variation request) and frustrating the client (lowering the project's customer engagement survey score by two points). Goal statement: Ensure minor variations are attended to immediately (within one working day) and improve the customer engagement survey by 1.5 points, within two weeks of making improvements to the VMP. The customer was interviewed to find out what was critical to them—the cycle time of the process was confirmed as their key critical to quality (CTQ) measure.
Measure	Understand the *as-is* process, measure and establish a baseline from which to improve.	The project leader asked the project coordinator to investigate the situation. The project coordinator mapped the current as-is process as a swimlane diagram and measured the average: ■ cycle time (minutes) to complete a variation request ■ delay time (minutes) introduced by waiting for the CMB. The as-is process was baselined.
Analyse	Analyse the data and process to understand the root causes to the problem.	The project coordinator analysed the as-is process for value, waste and flow (these are key lean techniques) and also took a further exploratory data analysis of the work in progress variations and cycle time of the process. From the value and flow analysis, it was observed there was a lot of waste in waiting for the CMB. They also detected some defects in variation requests—these were being sent back to the customer as all the information on the variation had not been completed. These two root causes: (1) delays waiting for the CMB, and (2) incorrect information provided by customer were taken forward to the Improve stage of DMAIC.
Improve	Make suggestions for improving the root causes and seek approval for the best solution(s) to implement in the business.	In relation to delays waiting for the CMB, the recommendation was to (1) revise the VMP and devolve accountability for approval of the variation request to the project leader for variations <$3,000 in value and/or less than 0.5-day schedule slippage, and (2) change the frequency and duration of the CMB to a twice-weekly meeting of 30 minutes. In relation to incorrect information provided by customer, the variation request was made into an online form, with mandatory fields complete with explanations of how to complete the form. These variations are subsequently approved by the project sponsor and implemented in the project environment. The VMP was remeasured to see if the variations had had a positive effect on the VMP: ■ the average cycle time (minutes) to complete a variation request ■ the average delay time (minutes) introduced by waiting for the CMB ■ customer engagement survey.
Control	Hand over the solution to the business—in this case project.	The VMP was communicated to the customer and all project staff. The process was then measured weekly to ensure the improvements were being adhered to and the variation was being sustained. Additionally, a suggestion was made to further improve the VMP by introducing an automated workflow of variation requests to improve audit-tracking and integration with the project management information system.

© 2022 Dr Neil Pearson

13.3.3 Total quality management (TQM)

Total quality management (TQM) focuses on achieving 100 per cent customer satisfaction and zero defects, in business processes and quality supply chains. The main principles of TQM include prevention, zero defects, getting things right the first time, "quality involves everyone", continuous improvement and employee involvement. TQM is arguably rapidly falling out of use in favour of Lean Six Sigma.

To monitor and control the volume of continuous improvement opportunities taking place in the project at any one time, the project leader may also wish to maintain a simple register of continuous improvement requests and their status. Continuous improvements made may also be a part of the project leader's performance metrics for a project, so tracking in this way provides tangible metrics.

Register—Continuous Improvement Requests

13.4 Planning for quality

PMBOK sixth edition (PMI 2017) recommends capturing quality in several key documents. The outputs of planning QA and QC are often outlined in the project's Quality Management Plan, whereas the control of quality during project execution often manifests itself in the QC activities to be carried out with the work packages and tasks in the work breakdown structure (WBS), supported by the various QC documents such as **run charts**, reports and **checklists**, reported on during the Execution of the project.

Some QA criteria could already have been captured in the various project management documents (described in earlier chapters of this text). For example:

- The Requirements Register (refer to Chapter 8 "Defining the scope of a project") has acceptance criteria against each individual requirement for checking the quality of the requirement meets the agreed specification of the requirement provided to us by the business/customer.

- Business general and business technical requirements could have been outlined in the scope document and/or the Business Case. Business general requirements are high-level business requirements related to business policies, legal, branding, cultural requirements and language. These are effectively QA standards, against which quality must be monitored to ensure compliance takes place.

- Business technical requirements are overarching technical requirements related to hardware, software and interoperability. Again, these are QA standards, against which quality must be monitored to ensure compliance takes place.

- Story cards in a Scrum (Agile) approach capture on the rear of the card the acceptance criteria— this is the quality assurance standard against which the story must be tested (within the sprint) and later verified on delivery to the customer (at the sprint review meeting) (refer to Chapter 3 "Agile (Scrum) project management").

Tables 13.4(a) and 13.4(b) illustrate how planning for quality assurance and quality control (in the Planning stage) differs from carrying out quality control (in the Execution stage).

Table 13.4(a) Planning quality assurance (QA) and planning quality control (QC)

Project Management in Practice (Pearson et al.)	PMBOK sixth edition (PMI 2017)	Example: Service industry	Example: Construction industry
Planning the QA criteria—the standards to which we must ensure actual quality is compared. Planning for QC—the activities (processes, tools and techniques) that will later be applied in the project. Execution stage to control quality, thereby ensuring we are meeting the QA criteria.	Refer to PMBOK p. 271 "Plan quality management" definition. Refer to PMBOK p. 271 "Manage quality" definition.	A. For the project management— developing a comprehensive variation management process (VMP) (refer Chapter 8 "Defining the scope of a project"). B. For the deliverables produced by the project—developing a customer engagement process for a new ICT implementation of a CRM system (e.g. Figure 13.7).	C. For the project management— developing an escalation process for checking and validating deliveries from suppliers to the project (onsite). D. For the deliverables produced by the project—developing a process for testing electrical fittings, including how measures will take place according to the electrical standard that has to be legally adhered to.

© 2022 Dr Neil Pearson

Table 13.4(b) Doing quality control (based on the planned criteria and control task defined in Table 13.4(a) A, B, C, D)

Project Management in Practice (Pearson et al.)	PMBOK sixth edition (PMI 2017)	Example: Service industry	Example: Construction industry
The activities of executing the planned processes (above), using the defined tools and techniques to measure the actual outputs/ outcomes from the project and the product, service (or results) being built by the project. Checking for variances between the planned QA criteria and what the project actually produced and taking appropriate action.	Refer to PMBOK p. 271 "Control quality" definition.	A. For the project management— checking (measuring) that 100% of variations requested to the project were put through the project's formal variation management process. B. For the deliverables produced by the project—verifying the process of customer engagements results in an improved customer satisfaction score.	C. For the project management—checking (measuring) that deliveries received are valid and correct. Escalating issues to the site supervisor for action with supplier when deliveries are not correct. D. For the deliverables produced by the project—measuring the number of electrical fittings that did not meet the electrical standards. Logging these variances and taking appropriate action to rectify faults and identify the root causes to put in place a further continuous improvement.

© 2022 Dr Neil Pearson

QA is about defining the standards, specifications, measures and QC processes to be used, as well as stating when the QC checks will take place and by whom. *Note:* We are only planning the QC at this stage, not actually carrying out the processes to actively check the quality—this activity is discussed in a later section of this chapter (when we start to do work and deliver deliverables!).

The author (Pearson) proposes that the preparation of QA includes the processes of what the PMI terms *plan quality management—the process of identifying quality requirements and/or standards for the project and product and documenting how the project will demonstrate compliance*—the last part of this statement implies the planning of QC.

QA and plan quality management activities include the planning of QC mechanisms, as follows.

1. Understanding the VOC by analysing and gaining agreement about the relevant quality criteria to be applied to the product or service being produced by the project. This is probably the most important quality activity—to understand the VOC quality requirements and make these explicit (written down and measurable).

2. Ensuring the formal documentation (to a detailed level) of requisite QA criteria, including standards, technical specifications, policies, procedures and processes are further developed based on 1. above.

3. Reaching agreement and documenting how quality is to be measured, when it is to be reported and what approvals must take place, by whom and when.

4. Establishing any baseline project performance measurements before project commencement; therefore, allowing for measurement against this baseline during the QC of the project later.

5. Including training and education of internal or external staff responsible for ensuring that quality deliverables are achieved by the project. *Remember:* Quality is everyone's responsibility, but it is ultimately the project leader's accountability to ensure that everyone involved in the project adopts a quality ethos.

6. Defining quality governance aspects by asking who is responsible and accountable for all the defined aspects of quality? For example, state who is responsible for checking the quality of a particular component during a specified work package within the project, and who the issue will be escalated to, should this measurement be out of tolerance.

7. Complying with any overarching quality systems that may exist within an organisation (e.g. ISO 9001:2015 "Quality management systems—Requirements" or ISO 14000:2015 "Environmental management systems—Requirements with guidance for use"). This would also include adoption by the project of any overarching continuous improvement processes, as discussed earlier in this chapter.

Understanding QA in respect to overall project quality management planning is the important first step. The project leader must then make sure this is taken forward and captured at the various levels of detail, as the project moves from the Initiation stage through to the Planning stage. The Quality Management Plan clearly defines the QA requirements and how QC will be carried out to ensure these requirements are met. Remember that quality almost always impacts on other project activities, such as the project schedule, the project budget, quality-related risks and the inclusion of quality specifications in procurement-related activities (e.g. contract conditions). More detailed considerations to be factored into the project are outlined as follows.

1. Considerations to factor into the project schedule may include the following.
   - Ensuring work packages include the necessary time for quality activities to be carried out. We know that building QC into a task or work package is more efficient than checking for quality after the task has completed.

■ Defining governance and embedding this governance in all project activities to successfully manage quality in the project environment. We know that planning for prevention of defects is better than spending time on rectifying defects.

■ Adding extra work packages to carry out QC measures and checks if required. We normally build quality into the work package producing the work and, only if necessary, checks after the work is completed.

■ Scheduling training and education programs within the project about quality. This will impact the availability of resources (people) that would otherwise be committed to doing tasks on the project—but we know this is a worthwhile investment.

2. Considerations to factor into the project budget may include the following.

■ Higher costs of components: Components built to higher standards cost more money and will impact the final project budget—we know the level of specification is set with the customer and expectations that "What you pay for is what you get" run true not just in projects but all aspects of business.

■ Higher costs of skilled staff, or higher-end service providers: Employing a major consulting company will cost more than a local business, but we know we are paying for top-notch consultants; therefore, the result should be of higher quality.

■ Complying with company-wide accreditations such as ISO 9001 will incur additional costs: The impact to the project must be made transparent by including additional work packages to cover compliance work.

■ Including a contingency to allow for continuous improvement processes to be applied within the project environment: Continuous improvement takes time and effort—we generally pursue continuous improvement requests that deliver the best value for the project.

■ Including contingency for rework: Most projects encounter some rework in high-risk areas.

3. Considerations to factor into the project risk may include risks associated with:

■ non-conformance internally: Is there a risk to the project budget, schedule and scope if poor quality work is produced and has to be rectified?

■ possible damage to reputation: Will a defect reach the customer, and what will be the risk to the organisation's image and reputation if this occurs?

■ product malfunction and harm to persons: What is the potential risk to the business if this occurs?

■ rework for activities where there are substantial costs to the project (e.g. for reworking a defective output).

So how can we as project leaders ensure that we are taking a considerate and inclusive approach to the identification of the relevant QA criteria and how we plan to manage these in the project?

A simple idea-shower technique used in the Initiation stage and further detailed in the early Planning stage can assist in identifying the important aspects of quality that will be further defined in the required Quality Management Plans, as illustrated in Figure 13.5.

It provides a useful way to idea shower the initial quality criteria of both the project itself and the product or service being produced by the project. This tool can be used in a workshop session to collate various perspectives of quality that need to be investigated through the project Initiation and Planning stages.

Note: For each QA activity listed in the left side of the table, there needs to be corresponding QC actions *planned* in the right side of the table—these could lead to additional tasks being required within the relevant work package!

How does this look in terms of physical artefacts in the project? Figure 13.6 indicates some of the documentary artefacts you as a project leader may be generating, or, if a project officer, contributing to the generation of.

Figure 13.5 Quality assurance/quality control planning grid

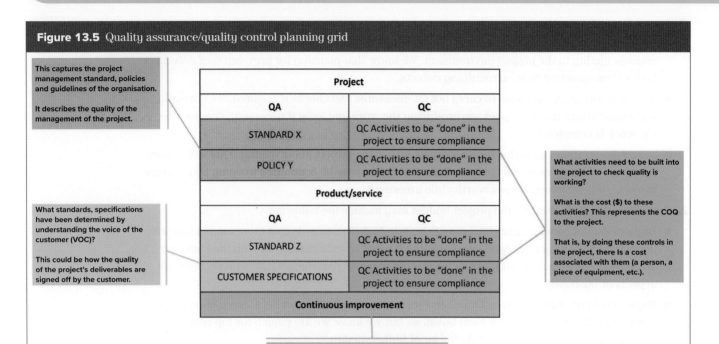

This captures the project management standard, policies and guidelines of the organisation.

It describes the quality of the management of the project.

What standards, specifications have been determined by understanding the voice of the customer (VOC)?

This could be how the quality of the project's deliverables are signed off by the customer.

Project	
QA	QC
STANDARD X	QC Activities to be "done" in the project to ensure compliance
POLICY Y	QC Activities to be "done" in the project to ensure compliance
Product/service	
QA	QC
STANDARD Z	QC Activities to be "done" in the project to ensure compliance
CUSTOMER SPECIFICATIONS	QC Activities to be "done" in the project to ensure compliance
Continuous improvement	

What activities need to be built into the project to check quality is working?

What is the cost ($) to these activities? This represents the COQ to the project.

That is, by doing these controls in the project, there Is a cost associated with them (a person, a piece of equipment, etc.).

The project would adopt the organisation's policy and procedures on continuous improvement. For ISO accredited organisations, this is most likely to be the PDCA approach.

© 2022 Dr Neil Pearson

Figure 13.6 Documents generated from the QA/QC planning grid

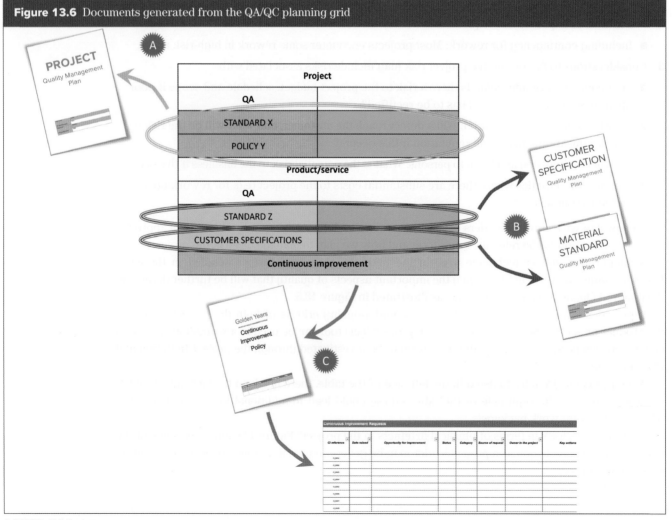

© 2022 Dr Neil Pearson

Note: In Figure 13.6 each major QA and QC area has generated a separate Quality Management Plan; for example, there is a Quality Management Plan for the management of the project (A), and other separate Quality Management Plans for more specific areas of the product being produced by the project (B); this is a common situation to be in as a project leader. (C) represents the organisation's continuous improvement policy and the project's register of continuous improvements.

Within each of the Quality Management Plans on larger projects it may be necessary for the project lead and, if employed, a dedicated project quality manager, to break down the QC activities to a very granular level. An example of such a breakdown is included as Table 13.5.

Table 13.5 Detailed mapping of quality assurance criteria and quality control mechanisms

Source or standard	Quality criteria	Category	Acceptable tolerance	Occurrence	Control approach	Responsibility
Product specification sheet for new low-energy/ low-heat light enclosure	Enclosure meets the product specifications, electrical contacts earthed to housing	Electrical	100% of sample selected meeting design installation drawings, with no earthing issues	Random	Correct installation of enclosure and earth connection according to design drawings and specifications	Site manager

© 2022 Dr Neil Pearson

For an example of the QA and QC *planning* grid, refer to Table 13.6 and the "Snapshot from Practice: Apartment build".

Table 13.6 Quality assurance/quality control planning grid, with examples

Project management	
Quality assurance planning: What standards, technical specifications and policies are to be applied to the management of the project?	Quality control planning: How are the defined quality assurance attributes to be controlled? What are the processes, measures, tolerances and responsibilities?
Project management office (PMO), project governance requirements and project management framework	Carry out project health checks at scheduled intervals within each stage of the project life cycle.
PMO gateway reviews process	Project documents presented at each gateway in the project management life cycle for approval, before proceeding to the next stage of the project.
Harmonised with relevant workplace health and safety legislation	Health and safety audits carried out at random intervals by the internal audit department. Results and recommendations presented to the project Steering Committee for actioning.
ISO/NZS/AS 31000:2009 "Risk management—Principles and guidance" (risk management framework)	The corporate risk department spot checks the project to ensure good risk management practices are being applied. Results and recommendations are presented to the project Steering Committee for actioning.
Product, service or result produced by the project	
Quality assurance planning: What standards, technical specifications and policies are to be applied to the end-product or service being created?	Quality control planning: How are the defined quality assurance attributes to be controlled? What are the processes, measures, tolerances and responsibilities?
Construction example: Compliance with AS 2870:2011 "Residential slabs and footings"	External independent surveyor to check at the recommended stages in the laying of waffle foundations. Issues to be escalated to the project leader for immediate attention. Risk identified due to recent press reports of issues in the use of such slabs (e.g. https://www.cornellengineers.com.au/beware-waffle-slabs/)
Service example: Compliance with the *Freedom of Information Act 1982* (FOI Act) (https://www.oaic.gov.au/freedom-of-information/rights-and-responsibilities)	Random check student records post data migration to ensure compliance with the FOI Act. Discrepancies to be brought to the attention of the project leader immediately for root-cause investigation.
Continuous improvement approach	
The project operates under a continuous improvement approach as outlined in the ISO 9001 guidelines for the organisation. All project team members are reminded to apply the PDCA cycle to the project's internal process to seek and make improvements in processes. The project leader will need to approve all suggestions before a project team member makes any changes to the project's processes.	

© 2022 Dr Neil Pearson

SNAPSHOT
from PRACTICE　　**Apartment build**

During a workshop on quality (hosted by the project leader), held during the Initiation stage of a project to build a low-rise five-storey block of apartments, discussions turned to two aspects of quality in the project: project management quality and electrical system quality. Table 13.7 is an extract of the QA/QC idea-shower grid in which the project leader had started to capture discussions from the workshop.

Table 13.7　Example: Planning quality assurance and quality control idea-shower grid

Project management	
Quality assurance planning: What standards, technical specifications and policies are to be applied to the management of the project?	Quality control planning: How are the defined quality assurance attributes to be controlled? What are the processes, measures, tolerances and responsibilities?
Project management office (PMO), project management framework (PMF)	To ensure the PMF is being adhered to by the project, the PMO is to carry out random project health check assessments periodically throughout the life cycle of the project. Any deviations from the PMF will be reported back to the project leader within three days of the health check being carried out; non-compliances will be prioritised so that continuous improvements can be scheduled and made to the project processes in a timely manner.
Compliance with relevant state/territory workplace health and safety legislation (https://www.safeworkaustralia.gov.au/)	As detailed in the additional Workplace Health and Safety (WHS) Plan, the project office (and site environments) will be subject to all the requirements of the relevant WHS legislation as deemed necessary and overseen by the site safety officer. The necessary control processes are to be documented in the WHS Plan, including the WHS reporting status, defined measures, targets and tolerances, and the roles and responsibilities of the people involved.
Product, service or result produced by the project	
Quality assurance planning: What standards, technical specifications and policies are to be applied to the end-product or service being created?	Quality control planning: How are the defined quality assurance attributes to be controlled? What are the processes, measures, tolerances and responsibilities?
Compliance with AS/NZS 3000:2007 "Electrical installations" (https://www.saiglobal.com/PDFTemp/Previews/OSH/as/as3000/3000/3000-2007.pdf)	Testing each fused circuit against the standard. Certificate of test(s) by the insured registered electrical contractor (who is independent of the company). Checklist of all circuits maintained and details of the number of failed tests provided to the project leader daily, for a subsequent root-cause analysis and improvement of the installation processes as required.
Product specification sheet for new low energy/low heat light enclosure	Random check of light enclosure during project construction to ensure compliance with the product specification sheet. Each sample of light enclosures tested is to be reported (in written format) to the site manager for a root-cause analysis and rectification actions. A histogram of faulty lighting enclosures is to be sent to the project leader daily.
Continuous improvement approach	
All employees of Acme Building are expected to contribute to the continuous improvement of all aspects of the project management process (including all tools and templates used) and must actively seek and report to the project leader quality improvements to the building being constructed.	

© 2022 Dr Neil Pearson

It is important to recognise that the QA criteria against which the project QC checking will take place may not yet exist in the form of standards or technical specifications and that these may have to be developed within the project. If this is the case, the process of integrating them will need to be considered carefully, given that this may result in a task (or work package) having to be scheduled and budgeted in the Planning stage of the project.

Remember to draw on both internal and external resources while developing ideas captured in the QA/QC grid. For example, internal QA sources could include:

■ PMO policies and procedures

■ organisational project management framework and/or the standards upon which these are based (e.g. PMBOK, PRINCE2 and Agile)

■ gateway review processes (e.g. the Office of Government Commerce Gateway Review Process, https://www.gov.uk/government/publications/ogc-gateway-review-0-strategic-assessment-guidance-and-templates)

- internal business processes, such as procurement, finance, recruitment, contracting and human resource management.

External sources on the other hand could include:

- International Organization for Standardization (www.iso.org)
- American National Standards Institute (www.ansi.org)
- sites that offer compendiums of standards, such as SAI Global (www.saiglobal.com and www. standards.org.au)
- manufacturers' product specifications
- codes of practice
- industry standards
- government legislation and policies (often mandatory)
- most importantly, the VOC.

This section has outlined the importance of identifying, capturing and agreeing from the outset aspects of quality planning for the project and the product or service being produced from the project.

13.5 | **Quality of the project management**

As noted in Figure 13.6, the project could have multiple Quality Management Plans to support its delivery. Let's look at a generic Quality Management Plan, with a more overarching project management quality perspective.

1. *Quality strategy:* Describe the importance of quality to the project and state how this relates to rigour around the management of the project and of the product or service being produced by the project. The quality strategy may also indicate a quality motto, signalling the importance of quality to the project, and the fact that it is the responsibility of *everyone* working on the project (whether in a permanent, contract or temporary role) to adopt a proactive attitude and response to providing quality outcomes.

2. *Policy and procedure:* Identify any relevant organisational quality policies and procedures that have to be applied within the project environment. This could include the following:
   - AS/NZS ISO 9001:2015 "Quality management systems"
   - AS/NZS ISO 14001:2016/16/19 "Environmental management systems"
   - PMBOK sixth edition is a standard (ANSI/PMI 99-001-2017)
   - PMBOK seventh edition is a standard (ANSI/PMI 99-001-2021)
   - ISO 21500:2016 "Guidance on project management"
   - AS/NZS ISO 31000:2018 "Risk management principles and guidelines"
   - organisational continuous improvement process
   - organisational innovation process
   - Lean Six Sigma.

   Describe how the identified policies will be tailored to this project's particular environment.

3. *Quality escalation process:* A quality defect or non-compliance in this project will be treated as a quality issue. Document what will occur when a quality defect/non-compliance occurs. This may be either:
   - the project's standard issue escalation process as documented in the project's Scope Management Plan, or
   - a more specific process for the escalation of quality issues can be documented in this section of the Quality Management Plan. Typically, this could be a simple flowchart (with the

business rules additionally captured in the project-wide RASCI). The process should clearly define the steps to be taken, all pertinent documentation, and the people/committees involved in the process of managing quality issues in the project.

Consider how the following aspects are to be documented and communicated in your project environment.

Relating to issues for the management of the project:

- non-conformance policy/process (project)
- corrective action policy/process (project)
- continuous improvement policy/process (project).

Relating to issues in the product or service being produced by the project:

- non-conformance policy/process (customer product or service)
- corrective action policy/process (customer product or service)
- continuous improvement policy/process (customer product or service).

Note: In most cases the latter set related to the product or service should be treated as imperative as these could affect non-delivery to the customer, or the customer not signing off a deliverable due to quality defects.

4. *Continuous improvement process:* The approach to continuous improvement—this explains whether a PDCA or DMAIC process will underpin the activities that all the project team may be involved in, in relation to either (1) improving the processes around the project management of the project and/or (2) improving the product, service or result produced by the project. Refer to section 13.3.

5. *Quality roles and responsibilities:* This section should describe the roles and responsibilities of the quality function within the project. For example, the project leader is accountable for ensuring time/cost project performance information is presented as annotated earned value management (EVM) charts. Some larger projects could employ a full-time project quality manager, in which case they could be responsible for a lot of the quality activities taking place on the project; in other circumstances the responsibilities are shared between the project team members.

6. *The quality (QA/QC) planning grid (Figures 13.5 and 13.6), which outlines the high-level quality requirements:* This provides an ideal way to idea shower and capture the standards, policies, technical specifications and legislation that have to be adhered to by the project, and the control mechanisms to be put in place to monitor the quality of these when produced in the project, in addition to the big-ticket items in relation to the quality of the product or service being produced by the project (detailed in further individual Quality Management Plans, Figure 13.6).

7. *Quantification and articulation of knock-on effects to the cost and time requirements of the project, arising from undertaking planned QA and QC activities:* For example, if a stringent approach to quality is to be taken in the building of a high-tech component of a satellite, what are the additional costs and schedule implications to doing this—what is the COQ for including these extra activities? Is the customer aware of these and accepting of them in the project's overall budget? Are they aware of the cost of poor quality (i.e. they lose control of a multi-billion dollar satellite in space with no way to rectify!)

8. *The assumptions and constraints related to planning and controlling quality in the project.*

9. *Risk:* This involves assessing activities for potential quality risks, by carrying out a risk assessment and updating the project's Risk Register, as appropriate.

10. *Links to other project documents that contain a detailed breakdown of each item (e.g. standard, specification, requirement, legislation) as captured in the quality criteria grid, from both a QA (what) and QC (how) perspective:* This may generate numerous additional quality plans for certain components of the project.

Quality Management Plan

In summary, the Quality Management Plan assists in:

■ removing discrepancies between the perceptions and perspectives of the sponsor, the customer and the project, by articulating and agreeing the key QA requirements of the project and how the QC aspects are planned to take place during the delivery of deliverables and/or the Execution stage of the project

■ ensuring appropriate measures and control mechanisms (processes and checks) are put in place for each criterion prior to project execution

■ documenting and agreeing on the approach to continuous improvement in the project environment (PDCA or DMAIC)

■ clarifying the key project processes, roles and responsibilities in relation to quality.

Decisions made in the early planning of quality can have long-lasting effects on the deliverables of the project. Figure 13.2 amply illustrates this.

"Snapshot from Practice: VET Quality Framework" describes a situation where a project leader begins to identify the QA and QC aspects required of an organisation when registering to become a registered training organisation in Australia.

SNAPSHOT *from* PRACTICE : **VET Quality Framework**

A non-accredited training organisation has recently made the strategic decision to become a registered training organisation (RTO). In order to do so, the organisation must comply with the guidelines of the Australian Skills Quality Authority (ASQA). A project was established by the director of the organisation and the project is currently in the Planning stage. The project leader has started to review the quality aspects of the project, to prepare for developing the project's Quality Management Plan, and in doing so has located the following information.

■ The VET Quality Framework is aimed at achieving greater national consistency in the way providers are registered and monitored and in how standards in the vocational education and training (VET) sector are enforced.

■ The VET Quality Framework comprises the:

  ● standards for National VET Regulator (NVR) RTOs

  ● fit and proper person requirements

  ● financial viability risk assessment requirements

  ● data provision requirements and the Australian Qualifications Framework.

Due to the nature of the registration process, RTOs must adopt these standards (quality assurance criteria) and further develop quality control processes for the RTO as a part of the project. The project leader documents these requirements in the project's Quality Management Plan.

Further to this, the project leader has been in contact with stakeholders in their stakeholder network from other RTOs and has been given ideas about two key processes for the control of quality in the RTO, which they consider the project must produce. The project leader documents these in the Quality Management Plan and adds two additional work packages to the project's work breakdown structure (WBS). The work packages are titled: "Development of the course student feedback sheet and continuous improvement process" and "Development of the facilitator course feedback sheet and continuous improvement process".

(Continues)

The project leader now tasks a business analyst (BA) to review the VET Quality Framework guidelines and take on the further development of the project's Quality Management Plan. The BA is asked to bring any further work packages resulting from the review to the attention of the project leader as these will subsequently need to be included in the project's WBS, project budget and other project documents.

Source: VET information sourced from Australian Skills Quality Authority (ASQA) n.d., "VET Quality Framework", ASQA, https://www.asqa.gov.au/about/australias-vet-sector/vet-quality-framework, accessed May 2022

13.5.1 Processes: Helpful techniques

The world of quality brings together a number of process modelling techniques, whether these processes are related to the:

1. project management-related processes such as the variation management process introduced in Chapter 8 "Defining the scope of a project", or

2. deliverables of the project, for example, a customer engagement process for the introduction of a new customer relationship management (CRM) system.

One of the more popular techniques for mapping out a process involves developing a *SIPOC*. The SIPOC is a relatively simple tool that is used to map out a process at a high level—we could use this technique during the scoping of the project, for example. Figure 13.7 illustrates a partial SIPOC,

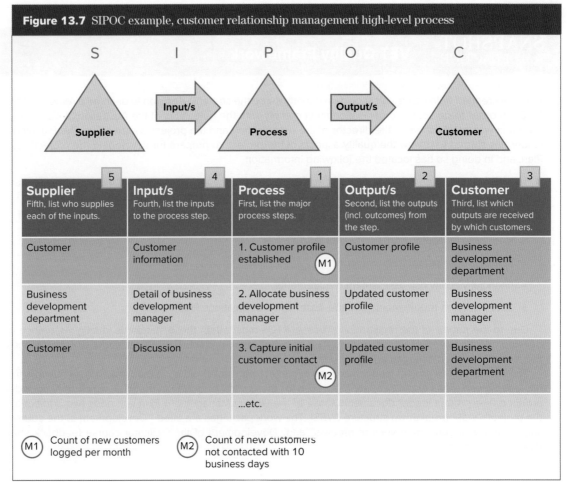

Figure 13.7 SIPOC example, customer relationship management high-level process

Supplier [5]	Input/s [4]	Process [1]	Output/s [2]	Customer [3]
Fifth, list who supplies each of the inputs.	Fourth, list the inputs to the process step.	First, list the major process steps.	Second, list the outputs (incl. outcomes) from the step.	Third, list which outputs are received by which customers.
Customer	Customer information	1. Customer profile established (M1)	Customer profile	Business development department
Business development department	Detail of business development manager	2. Allocate business development manager	Updated customer profile	Business development manager
Customer	Discussion	3. Capture initial customer contact (M2)	Updated customer profile	Business development department
		...etc.		

(M1) Count of new customers logged per month

(M2) Count of new customers not contacted with 10 business days with a simple example of introducing a new CRM system (it focuses the project leader on the underlying business process; the CRM system is just the enabler to the process). Understanding the scope of the process is important as it will influence the scope of the project.

The order in which to construct the SIPOC is indicated in the (SIPOC) table headings. When developing a SIPOC, start with the process (1), define the outputs (2) and map which customer (3) these are delivered to. Then come back and detail the inputs (4) and who supplies (5) these inputs. Finally, add a key to the table as shown in Figure 13.7. Don't just number the tiles—add an object (square) with the number inside it. Additionally, M1, M2, etc. indicate where the process is to be measured (these could be turned into **operational level agreements** with/between internal departments or even **service level agreements** with/between external parties). These measures could even be the quality criteria used to measure the success of the project later, from either an internal or an external customer perspective.

Beyond the SIPOC (taking the understanding of the process to the next level of detail) are the process models themselves. Here, the project leader could use a variety of process modelling techniques, with the simplest being a **flowchart**. In practice, the most commonly used modelling technique however is a process **swimlane diagram**.

Processes and flowcharts are instrumental in being able to achieve quality in a repeatable, measurable way. Processes and flowcharts model the activities to be completed for a particular activity. In modelling the activities, existing or new measures can be overlaid onto the process. When a process or flowchart of activities can be measured, then the quality of that process can be measured and therefore subsequently monitored and controlled. A simple flowchart (with measures shown) is illustrated in Figure 13.8.

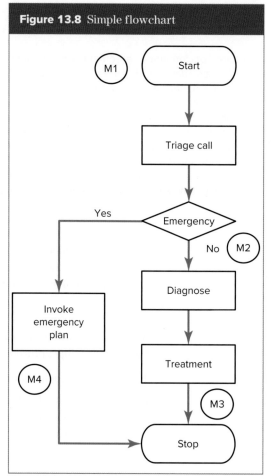

Figure 13.8 Simple flowchart

© 2022 Dr Neil Pearson

In Figure 13.8, four measures take place: M1—the number and time of calls going into the system; M2—the number and time of calls/requests that are not emergency-related; M3—the number and times of calls/requests post-emergency response; and M4—the number and time of non-emergency calls, post-diagnosis and treatment. From this simple flowchart, it would be possible (for example) to calculate the time taken for a request at M1 to be triaged and responded to as an emergency (M4). This information could then be tracked on a **control chart** for analysis as part of a project deploying an emergency response service desk. Refer to "Snapshot from Practice: Service desk project, measuring the process", for an example of the importance of process measurement.

SNAPSHOT *from* PRACTICE Service desk project, measuring the process

A large software company had initiated a project to establish a 24/7, multilingual, internal ICT service desk. The project had multiple streams of work running concurrently, including streams to develop the telephony infrastructure, survey and agree on languages, decide on the best business locations to geographically locate the three service centres, and a stream to define the staffing requirements and develop all the internal service processes.

The project leader was actively involved in the design of the *staffing requirements and development of all the internal service processes* stream and negotiating the service desk measures about what the quality of service would look like when implemented in the business.

Based on IT Infrastructure Library (ITIL) best practice, the service desk processes were developed. However, discussions continued on how process quality was to be measured. Ultimately the process measures would form part of the service desk

(Continues)

Snapshot from Practice: Service desk project, measuring the process (*Continued*)

agents' performance agreements when handed over to the business at the end of the project. The project leader recounts Eli Goldratt's adage of, "Tell me how I will be measured, and I will tell you how I will perform". After numerous workshops, a suite of process measures was agreed. When the processes were piloted with the measures, it was pleasing to see that the extra time spent on unpacking these measures—to ensure they provided control over the process and provided a good measure of performance of the service desk agents—had paid dividends.

Quality is not just for project leaders who are at the coal face of project management, wishing to have efficient project management processes. The success of project leaders is also driven by the quality of the artefacts that are designed, developed and delivered into the business at the end of the project. The output for this project team was a carefully crafted set of processes and measures that enabled the quality of the processes, outputs and outcomes to be measured, while at the same time allowing for measured performance of the service desk agents, which also promoted good team behaviours.

Another popular approach to capturing processes is to use a swimlane diagram. Two industry best-practice approaches to capturing processes in the swimlane format include: business process model and notation (BPMN) and **unified modelling language** (UML will be left for the reader to explore in other texts).

In BPMN, actors (a role, department/group or IT system) are represented as swimlanes combined with a special set of notation (symbols) and a set of business rules, which ensures all elements of a process are fully captured. In a project environment this has the benefit of capturing the:

1. project management processes, to achieve quality in the management of the project

2. processes related to the deliverables of the project, so the end product or service, once handed over to the business/customer, has repeatable processes to support ongoing operations (in business as usual).

For a detailed resource on BPMN, refer to the Object Management Group's website at www.omg.org/spec/BPMN/2.0/ and for an accessible snapshot to the BPMN notation, refer to www.bpmb.de/images/BPMN2_0_Poster_EN.pdf.

Note: An example of a project variation management process using the BPMN notation was introduced in Chapter 8 "Defining the scope of a project" (Figure 8.18). These BPMN-style swimlane diagrams are fast becoming the de facto standard in businesses to capture organisational processes. The project leader will frequently find that they are either modifying (improving) existing swimlane diagrams as a part of the project's deliverables or designing new processes (in the swimlane format) to be handed over to the business at the end of the project as a declared output of the project.

Opportunities for continuous improvement can come from both formal project QC mechanisms and from informal channels (such as suggestion boxes or innovation registers). Together, they can create a learning project environment where ideas for continuous improvement are captured, reviewed and brought on board to improve the project management processes and the product or service being produced by the project. In addition to the formal documentation of continuous improvement processes, there will be opportunities to discuss continuous improvement opportunities across various forums, such as at project team meetings, project Steering Committee meetings, supplier meetings, performance and peer reviews, open suggestion boxes and innovation-recognition programs. A good project leader is always interested in eliciting feedback—seeking to find out:

1. What went well (and why)?

2. What didn't go well (and why)?

3. What would we do differently next time?

Now that the basis for quality assurance has been established, captured, and communicated via the Quality Management Plan and other artefacts (e.g. swimlane diagrams), the focus turns towards controlling quality.

13.6 Carrying out quality control

Moving from the identification of QA criteria to the measurement of quality once the project is active (typically in the Execution stage) is referred to as *doing QC*. (In the previous section we explored how the project leader must plan both the QA aspects of what to measure and the QC process of how this will be carried out in the project, as the latter will represent work packages or tasks in the WBS.) We are now doing all the control activities captured in earlier Quality Management Plans, placed into the WBS and subsequent project schedule, and included as items in the project budget if necessary.

QC necessitates two key activities:

1. Checking that the project itself is meeting quality requirements for the management of the project. For example, check whether all the project approvals being obtained are in accordance with the project governance criteria established in the project management framework.

2. Checking the quality of the product, service or result being produced by the project. For example, the redesign of a braking system of a hybrid fuel cell / battery car requires the manufacturers to consider the additional adjusted weight of the vehicle. One of the components (the brake hose) therefore has to be checked at various stages in the design, prototype and production stages to ensure the part meets the requirements (i.e. is within the tolerances specified in the technical specifications by the customer). The arising QC data is plotted on a run chart and checked at the quality review meetings.

QC is often visible in the project environment due to the presence of various visual representations of data (e.g. charts, graphs, statistical reports). QC provides the project leader, the project team and the suppliers of products and services to the project with a method by which quality can be continually monitored. This enables the identification of variances so corrective action can be taken. Taking corrective action (via the continuous improvement process) is key to controlling quality. Corrective action that is taken quickly to remedy the root cause(s) of a problem may potentially stave off future repetitions of the threat to quality. Controlling quality starts from the definition and agreement of the quality specifications (QA) and the QC mechanisms for the project captured in the relevant Quality Management Plan. The task of monitoring these defined quality requirements typically commences from Execution onwards. The quality requirements for the product or service being produced are usually controlled during the Execution stage of the project, when activities start to produce project deliverables.

A project leader should make sure they have numerous tools available to assist with the collection and analysis of data and subsequent presentation of QC information. In this section we will review some commonly used techniques that can help support a project leader to control the quality of the project along its many dimensions. The sample tools are drawn from many of the quality methodologies that were discussed earlier in this chapter, for example, Lean Six Sigma. Each technique can be used either in isolation or can be combined with other techniques to provide opportunities for further analysis.

SNAPSHOT *from* PRACTICE   Quality control in mining

Ensuring ore quality is maintained is a key concern for mining operations. BHP Billiton embarked on a USD554 million project (completed in 2012) to shift its crushing and conveying facilities at its Escondida copper mine (Atacama Desert, 170 km southeast of Antofagasta in northern Chile) as the quality of ore begins to deteriorate.

Although the mine remains one of the most productive for the company to date, the quality of ore has fallen by 30 per cent in the past 10 years—and a decline of this magnitude means lower production rates and lower profits. BHP Billiton, of course, realises this and has announced that it is "studying a number of additional opportunities to improve access to higher grade ore and increase processing capacity over the years to come" (BHP Billiton 2011). High-grade ore is also of importance to shareholders, making good quality control systems and sampling techniques two of the top priorities for mining projects.

(Continues)

Snapshot from Practice: Quality control in mining (*Continued*)

Sampling is an important step, not just in quality control, but also in planning future operations. Following months of soil sampling and surface reconnaissance, BHP Billiton identified high-priority targets within its lucrative Lluvia-Jojoba project. Work took place around the Creston Pit and a broad zone of combined gold–copper soil geochemical anomalies was discovered. "Elevated gold and copper values in soil are generally considered to be a good proxy for identifying areas where ore-grade gold and copper deposits may be located sub-surface," contractor NWM said in a statement.

Another contractor, RSV Gem, was undertaking a drilling phase at a goldmine 120 kilometres north of Harare in Zimbabwe, although it received a setback when previous samples were vandalised, highlighting the upmost importance

Figure 13.9 Quality control in mining

Shutterstock/Jason Benz Bennee

of having clear quality control measures in place. Drilling also helps to confirm the results of earlier sampling. "Given the better-than-expected grades at depth, the company also plans to drill holes more than 800 metres to test this 'plunge extension', which is open-ended," chief executive officer Vimal Bansi told Mining Weekly. He highlighted that the second drilling program was needed to comply with the South African Mineral Resources and Reserves Code for quality assurance and quality control assay protocol.

Of course, quality control does not end when ore is sampled and confirmed, or indeed once the mineral leaves the mine site, as recent advancements in the area show. Neels Els, project leader at Dump and Dune Drillers, spoke to Mining Weekly about the benefits of in-line sampling of minerals in trucks as they are transported to power stations and export terminals, saying this process can enhance quality control processes. "For power stations, up-to-date information on the quality is important and can affect the operation of the stations, which is why we are offering this system to take samples as trucks or trains pass on the way to their end destination," he explained.

The company's auger drill is mounted on an arm which takes a sample for testing from every truck that passes, and the company says it has also seen success when it has been used on coal stockpiles and discards and plans on extending its use in the future. As with many other aspects of mining operations, automation is also being seen as a way of simplifying and ensuring the accuracy of quality control systems.

Source: Adapted from Mining IQ Editorial, "Quality control in mining", Mining iQ, www.miningiq.com/technical-services-and-production/articles/Quality-control-in-mining/, accessed January 2013

Some of the more popular techniques for controlling the actual quality of the project itself or the components of the project, service or result being produced are described below.

13.6.1 **Run chart**

A **run chart** represents some variable (data) collected over time. Taking the concept of light enclosures introduced in Table 13.8 (see "Snapshot from Practice: Apartment build"), the project leader has received the information from the site supervisor as plotted in Figure 13.10. As a project leader we should be able to read charts such as this one and be able to identify various patterns. If patterns can be identified, we can ask why (at the identified point in time) did a defect occur, and initiate a **root-cause analysis** to find out what is happening.

The run chart can help the project leader to analyse data and facilitates being able to look for any patterns. Some typical patterns that are often seen in run charts are illustrated in Figure 13.11.

Figure 13.10 Run chart example (Execution stage)

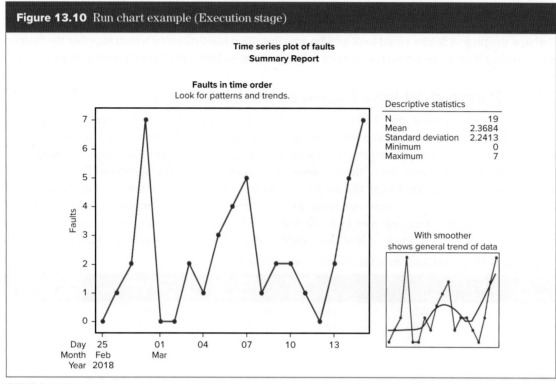

Time series plot of faults
Summary Report

Faults in time order
Look for patterns and trends.

Descriptive statistics	
N	19
Mean	2.3684
Standard deviation	2.2413
Minimum	0
Maximum	7

With smoother
shows general trend of data

© 2022 Dr Neil Pearson

Figure 13.11 Run chart patterns

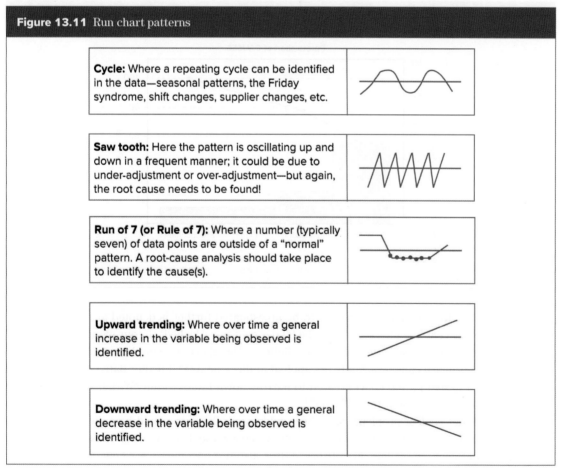

Cycle: Where a repeating cycle can be identified in the data—seasonal patterns, the Friday syndrome, shift changes, supplier changes, etc.

Saw tooth: Here the pattern is oscillating up and down in a frequent manner; it could be due to under-adjustment or over-adjustment—but again, the root cause needs to be found!

Run of 7 (or Rule of 7): Where a number (typically seven) of data points are outside of a "normal" pattern. A root-cause analysis should take place to identify the cause(s).

Upward trending: Where over time a general increase in the variable being observed is identified.

Downward trending: Where over time a general decrease in the variable being observed is identified.

© 2022 Dr Neil Pearson

In the case of Figure 13.10, perhaps the project leader should investigate what was happening on 28 February, 7 March, and 14 and 15 March (as there is an underlying sawtooth pattern in the data). Perhaps the project leader could look at who was installing the fittings or which supplier the fittings were coming from, to ascertain root causes to the problem so they can put corrective actions in place.

13.6.2 Pareto chart (also known as the 80/20 rule)

The **Pareto chart**, named after Vilfredo Pareto (an 18th century Italian statistician), is a chart that contains bars and a line graph. The bars represent the categories under review (always presented in descending order) and the line represents the cumulative percentage total. The purpose of the chart is to identify where the majority of the problems lie, to enable these to be addressed first. Hence, the Pareto chart is also referred to as the *80/20 rule*, as we are seeking to identify where, potentially, 80 per cent of problems may have occurred due to 20 per cent of their causes, in order to address them. We will use the data captured in Table 13.8 (in relation to the quality criteria of the lighting enclosure) to create an example of how this would be plotted using a Pareto chart (Figure 13.12).

Table 13.8 Collected fault data for the lighting enclosure

Causes	Defects	% of total	% of total calculation	Cumulative %	Cumulative % calculation
Wiring	25	55.6	(25/45) × 100	55.6	55.6
Installation	10	22.2	(10/45) × 100	77.8	55.6 + 22.2
Product fault	5	11.1	(5/45) × 100	88.9	77.8 + 11.1
Other	5	11.1	(5/45) × 100	100.0	88.9 + 11.1
Total	45				

© 2022 Dr Neil Pearson

Figure 13.12 Pareto chart example

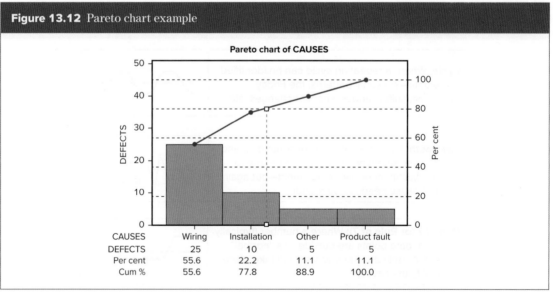

© 2022 Dr Neil Pearson

The cut-off for the categories that need to be investigated further is denoted at the point where the cumulative per cent line intersects with the 80 per cent line (dashed). In our example, this would include the cause "Wiring" and the cause "Installation". The chart is a simple but effective tool for articulating the primary causes of faults (as applied in this example). Further data could be sourced on Wiring and a nested Pareto chart created to narrow down faults within "Wiring"—perhaps there was one overriding fault type within "Wiring"?

Once the 80 per cent of problems have been addressed, the data would be collected again and plotted on a new Pareto chart. If the corrective actions have worked, a new set of causes, again falling within the 80 per cent cut-off line, are observed. It is also not uncommon for new causes to appear when resampling the data.

13.6.3 **Control charts**

Control charts are special types of run charts. They are graphs used to study how a process changes over time. Data are plotted in time order. A control chart always has a central line for the average, an upper line for the upper control limit and a lower line for the lower control limit. These lines are determined from data. By comparing current data to these lines, you can draw conclusions about whether the process variation is consistent (in control) or is unpredictable (out of control, affected by special causes of variation) (ASQ 2018b).

In Figure 13.13, the upper of the two charts is the first part of the control chart. In this case, it is indicating that the process is not in control and producing stable results. The red data-point on the 6th of the month should be investigated, as it is showing what is called a *special cause*. The project leader would carry out a root-cause analysis, identifying the cause of the problem, and subsequently put in place corrective actions. *Note:* The upper control limit (UCL) and lower control limits (LCLs) are calculated from the data-points, and the UCL represents + 3 standard deviations above the mean, and the lower control limit (LCL) represents −3 standard deviations below the mean. (For detail on control charts, see https://www.isixsigma.com/tools-templates/control-charts/a-guide-to-control-charts/.)

Figure 13.13 Control chart example

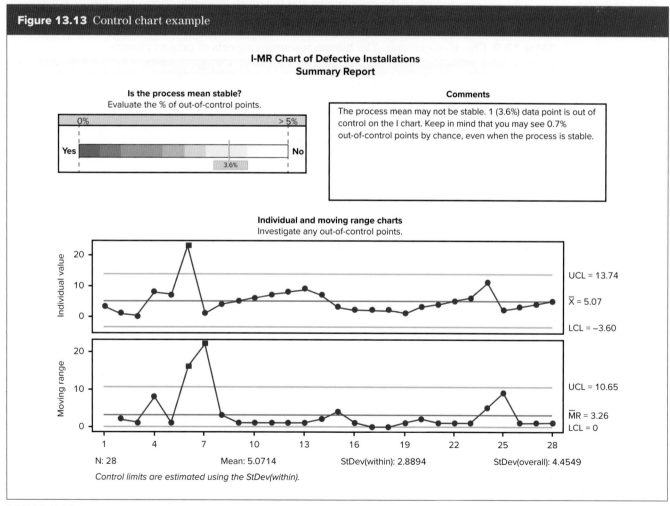

Note: The charts in this section of the text were created using a popular Lean Six Sigma statistical package known as Minitab (www.minitab.com/en-us/). The reader is encouraged to explore such tools to research how the data can potentially be visualised for projects they are involved with.

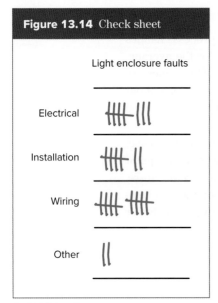

Figure 13.14 Check sheet

Light enclosure faults

Electrical

Installation

Wiring

Other

© 2022 Dr Neil Pearson

13.6.4 **Check sheets**

Check sheets are often used to collect ad hoc data that occur in a non-planned manner. The check sheet (Figure 13.14) facilitates the collection information in an ad hoc manner, enabling this to subsequently be put into other types of QC charts (such as a Pareto chart or a run chart). The check sheet is a simple tool that uses a *five-bar gate* to record counts.

13.6.5 **Checklists**

Although not a quantitative tool, checklists are useful for ensuring that tasks have been carried out and are used in a variety of instances within project management. For example, Table 13.9 shows a project closure checklist for various human resource components for project closure.

Checklists can also take on a more product or service focus, for example a checklist for the installation of a light enclosure (used in previous examples). Here, a checklist could be used both as a QC document by the installation engineer and as a quality audit document by the site supervisor, who could take a random sample of the installations and run down this same checklist to ensure compliance had been met against each outlined step.

Table 13.9 Checklist example: The human resources aspects of project closure

Closure—human resources	Date checked	Checked by whom?	Comments/actions
Have the team members been thanked for their individual contributions?			
Have the project successes been communicated to the various stakeholder groups?			
Have arrangements been made to release or return staff?			
Have relevant project team members been performance-appraised and have their line managers been briefed on their performance?			
Have contractors been released, contracts closed-out and procurement *blacklists* populated with the details of any under-performing contractors/organisations?			
Have the project successes been celebrated (project closure celebrations)?			

© 2022 Dr Neil Pearson

13.6.6 **Benchmarking**

Benchmarking provides a reference point against which to measure. Different types of benchmarking exist depending on what is to be compared, including:

■ *Internal benchmarks:* Here, the area that is to be improved is measured before the project takes place. Therefore, when the project is progressing and at project completion, a benchmark of what was measured before the project's commencement can be applied.

■ *External benchmarks:* With this approach, the internal data is compared against benchmark data from external sources. These external sources could be industry bodies or sources of information available in the public domain (such as annual reports and financial statements).

■ *External best practice benchmarks:* This is a variation of external benchmarking. However, rather than being a straight comparison to external sources, *best practice* implies structure and research. See for example, the PMI's *maturity assessment tool* called OPM3 (Organisational Project Management Maturity Model). Organisations can survey the maturity of project management within their organisations, and this can be compared with previous surveys within their organisation. It can also be compared with best practice within the industry or sector and overall, against all organisations (who have published) their data in the OPM3 database.

13.6.7 **Histograms**

Histograms are simple charts that allow the continuous data along the horizontal axis to be placed into *bins* and then counted (the frequency on the vertical axis). What this indicates is how close the data are to the normal distribution (as the red overlaid line shows). Also, reading the pattern of the data allows a project leader to move into root-cause analysis mode so they can start to ask themselves: Why do I see that pattern in the data?

Figure 13.15 shows data collected from a project involving piloting a call centre. The chart shows the "buckets" or "bins" along the horizontal (x) axis for call length, with the vertical (y) axis showing the frequency of calls of that length. As we expect, the curve follows the normal or Gaussian distribution with the overlaid red curve (indicative).

With some charts such as the histogram (run chart and box plot), it is possible to layer on the customer's agreement; the operational level agreement (OLA)—typically used between departments in an organisation, or the service level agreement (SLA)—typically used between the organisation and its external paying customers. When this is done, it becomes quite easy to see where such agreements are not being met.

By looking at Figure 13.16, the project leader knows there is a problem; ultimately, the customer will not sign off on the call centre until the process and system only generate values below the upper specification limit (USL). The chart also indicates a lower specification limit (LSL), which has artificially been placed to the far left, because there was no lower limit set by the customer. In this case, the nearer to zero the number, the happier the customer is likely to be (as call will be shorter). *Note:* The USL and LSL are specification values set by the customer, not control lines (UCL and LCL) which are calculated from the data, as we observed in the control chart.

13.6.8 **Bar charts**

Bar charts facilitate the comparison of frequencies (counts of) discrete categories (bins) of data. The categories that are being compared are placed along one axis and a measured value is shown on the other axis. In Figure 13.17, the project leader is monitoring the number (frequency) of variation

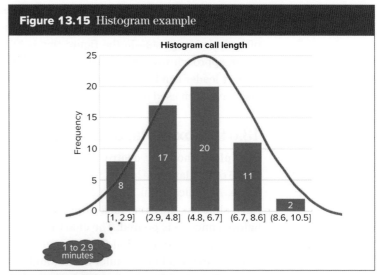

Figure 13.15 Histogram example

© 2022 Dr Neil Pearson

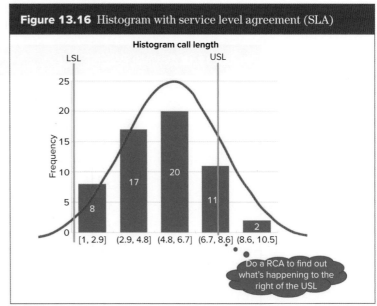

Figure 13.16 Histogram with service level agreement (SLA)

© 2022 Dr Neil Pearson

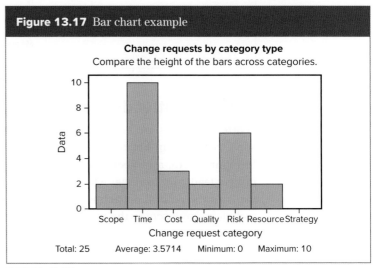

Figure 13.17 Bar chart example

© 2022 Dr Neil Pearson

requests for each of the seven types (categories) of constraints. Using this type of visual depiction of the data, the project leader can monitor (and therefore see) the categories which contain the majority of variation requests—in the figure this is "Time". The project leader can then (again) take a root-cause approach towards questioning why this is. Once the root cause(s) have been identified, the project leader can instigate necessary actions to make needed changes. (*Note:* A Pareto chart could also have been used to visually depict this data.)

13.6.9 Box plots, or box and whisker diagrams

Box plots show the centre (median), 25th and 75th percentiles and the whiskers represent the range of the data (the lowest to the highest value). Box plots are useful when comparisons are being made. As indicated in Figure 13.18, two shifts on a 24-hour construction site are being compared. Each shift has the same task of placing ties on the reinforced steel bar (re-bar) to hold it in place before concrete is poured. The chart represents the data collected by the site supervisor at the end of a typical 24-hour period. The data clearly reveals that Shift A (the night shift) has a far greater range in the number of faults in ties, and the middle 50% of the data (the box) also has a greater range. But why? The project leader would go and see what is happening on the site with the site supervisor, as neither would want the project delayed. They would work together to investigate root causes, making recommendations and setting follow-up actions for what needs to be changed.

Figure 13.18 Box plot example

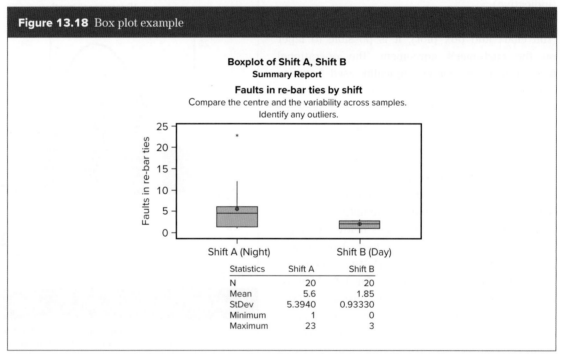

© 2022 Dr Neil Pearson

13.6.10 Scatter diagrams

Scatter diagrams are used to visualise the correlation between two variables—that is, there is some relationship between two variables, but we cannot say there is causation (x causes y). In Figure 13.19, a project was piloting a payroll system and looking at different variables. The project leader noticed that when defects (errors) in the pay run increased, the number of enquiries made to the payroll department also increased. The project leader used a variety of root-cause techniques to discover the root cause(s) and implemented a change in the pilot system before the system went live.

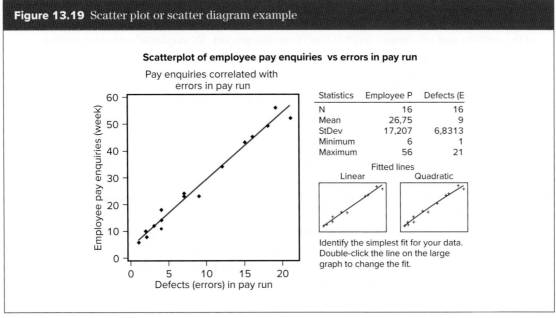

Figure 13.19 Scatter plot or scatter diagram example

© 2022 Dr Neil Pearson

Note: Some of the charts in this section of the text were created using a popular Lean Six Sigma statistical package known as Minitab (www.minitab.com/en-us/) The reader is encouraged to explore such tools to research how the data can potentially be visualised for projects you are involved with.

Such diagrams with supporting narrative could make up some content of the project's quality report along with quality defects, rework and other issues, with their corresponding recommendations for corrective actions.

13.7 Reporting quality performance

There are several tools available for monitoring quality, in order that corrective actions can be establish to improvement the practices and work in the project environment (and beyond). In summary, the project leader is monitoring and controlling quality across the two dimensions introduced earlier:

1. Across the quality of the management of the project. Quality performance metrics could be built around the criteria:

   ■ measures of cost performance, EVM, or a simple planned value versus actual costs, and whether this has required the use of any contingency funds set aside

   ■ measures of schedule performance, EVM or milestone slippage

   ■ measures of scope variance (variation requests), number of requests raised and approved, use of contingency

   ■ measures of customer satisfaction, complaints raised, positive feedback

   ■ audits and reviews, number of nonconformances

   ■ value and benefits, partial delivery or full delivery of a benefit or value statement

   ■ suppliers, non-conformances (i.e. raw material not delivered to required project quality specifications).

   With other defined metrics together, these provide a good indication as to the quality of the management of the project.

2. Across the deliverables being produced from the project. Are these to customer specifications and standards? (for example). These performance metrics give a good indication as to the quality of the outputs and outcomes (deliverables) from the project. Examples of customer quality performance criteria are.

- number of defects or non-conformances in the project's outputs
- conformance or non-conformance to a standard (ISO or other)
- deliverables signed off by customer without issues raised (i.e. no rework to be carried out in the project)
- conformance or nonconformance to specific customer specifications.

With other defined metrics, together, these provide a good indication as to the quality of the deliverables being produced by the project, and whether these meet the customer (requirements) specifications—or not!

Although a short section in this chapter, defining and reporting on the quality performance metrics really does focus the project leader and project team. These metrics would be documented in various places throughout the project documentation, such as the scope document, Business Case and Quality Management Plans; however, it is good practice to bring all these various metrics together and create a performance dashboard of the project.

13.8 | **Root-cause analysis**

In the previous QC section, numerous mentions of root-cause analysis were made. This section investigates the process of root-cause analysis and suggests two common techniques often applied by a project leader in their endeavour to find the root cause or, more often, multiple causes to problems.

Root-cause analysis is often used within project environments to seek out the cause of a problem(s) so that this can be dealt with. Figure 13.20 indicates a simple root-cause process.

A root-cause analysis involves:

1. *Identify the problem:* What specifically is occurring? (There are usually discernable symptoms.)

2. *Define and understand the problem:* Ask initial questions to seek proof (e.g. when is the problem occurring, how often, what is affected?). Understanding the context and the environment in which the problem exists is part of this step.

3. *Identify the root causes:* There are numerous tools and techniques available. Two techniques, reviewed later in this section, are the **5 whys** and **fishbone** diagrams. This step is concerned with identifying the root cause(s) to the defined problem. It is often the case that there will be a combination of (multiple) causes with one overriding cause. If the project leader identifies multiple root causes they should prioritise the causes as there might not be time within the project to attend to all causes identified and only the ones that deliver the best value to the project and/or customer would be implemented.

4. *Implement corrective actions:* Once the root cause(s) has been identified, corrective action(s) can be brainstormed and agreed upon. This may mean, for example, updating processes and work instructions, carrying out training, or

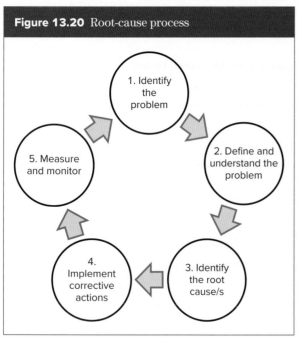

Figure 13.20 Root-cause process

putting additional QC steps into a work package or task. The corrective action will depend on the problem itself and its identified root cause(s).

5. *Monitor and measure:* Once corrective action(s) have been implemented, the project (or business) must continue to actively measure and monitor the situation, to ensure the problem does not reappear. It is highly likely, given that project leaders work within a culture of continuous improvement, that a different problem will appear, and when this occurs the cycle will be started once more.

In Step 3, it was pointed out that several RCA tools and techniques are available and the 5 whys and fishbone diagrams were mentioned. As promised, an explanation of these now follows.

13.8.1 Five whys

Akin to a toddler's seemingly never-ending questions of "but why...?", the **5 whys** technique involves asking the question "why" in the context of the last response (answer) provided to a question. Essentially, the preceding question's answer forms the basis for the next question. Figure 13.21 provides an example of the 5 whys.

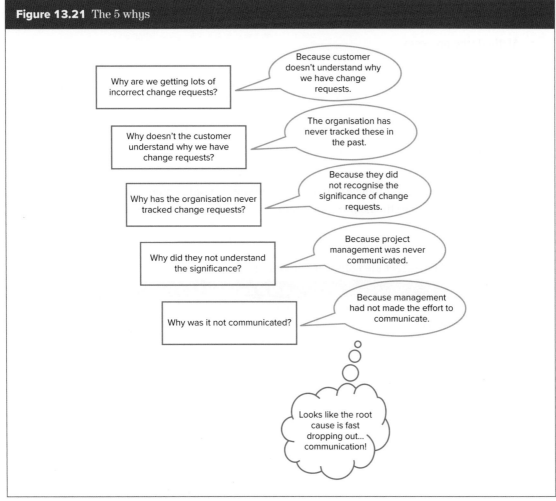

Figure 13.21 The 5 whys

© 2022 Dr Neil Pearson

Note: The 5 whys is just a tag line; you may find that fewer "whys" or more commonly, more "whys" are needed to get to the root cause of a problem. How do you know when the root cause has been reached? Typical signs are that no further value is added by asking another "why" or the response to a "why" starts to repeat (and point to) the same cause (as in this example). Another signifier of the root cause is when a work instruction level is reached or an environment factor around work instructions is reached, as these are usually at a base level in the organisation or the project.

13.8.2 The cause–effect diagram (fishbone or Ishikawa diagram)

A fishbone or **cause–effect diagram** can be used to analyse a problem to identify its root causes. Steps taken in a root-cause workshop leveraging the fishbone technique could resemble the following:

1. A problem has been identified and the project leader has defined (and now understands) the problem. The project leader recognises that containment actions may need to be put in place as a temporary stop-gap.

2. The project leader puts together an idea-shower team that includes members of the project team, subject matter experts and an external consultant. The project leader sets out the fishbone method at the idea-shower workshop and encourages participants to use this to brainstorm the root causes of the problem.

3. The project leader draws up the large bones on the fish and labels them:
    a. Manpower (human resources of any gender)
    b. Machine (tools and technology)
    c. Method (the process)
    d. Materials
    e. Measurement
    f. Mother nature
    g. Management
    h. Maintenance
    i. ?

    Leaving a question mark (?) indicates that other categories might emerge during the idea shower, and these can be added to the fishbone diagram as new categories to idea shower under. Refer to Table 13.10.

Table 13.10 Cause and effect idea-shower categories

8 Ms of manufacturing	8 Ps of marketing	3 CPOs of service
Manpower (human resources of any gender)	Product or service	Culture
Machine (tools and technology)	Price	Communication
Method (the process)	Promotion	Customer
Materials	Place	People
Measurement	Process	Process
Mother nature	People	Politics
Management	Physical evidence	Organisation
Maintenance	Performance	Objectives
		Operations

© 2022 Dr Neil Pearson

4. The project leader hands a pack of sticky notes to each idea-shower session attendee and asks them to write down every potential cause of the problem they can think of (from every conceivable different angle). After two hours the team is exhausted but is pleased by the large number of potential causes they have brainstormed (Figure 13.22).

Figure 13.22 Simple cause–effect diagram

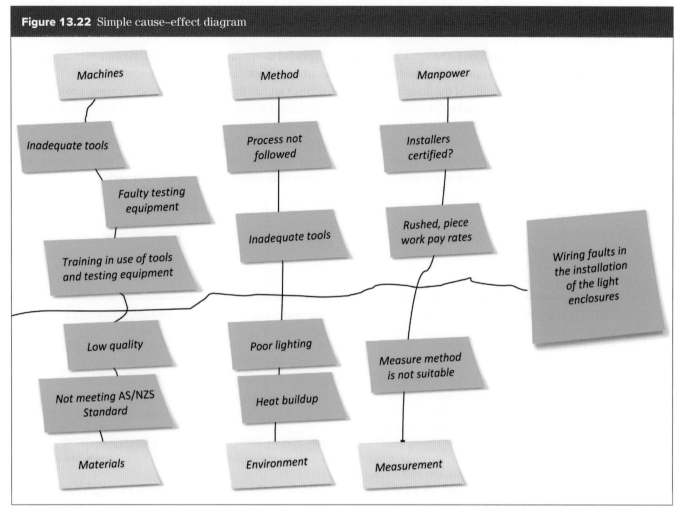

5. Next, the project leader summarises and clarifies the suggested causes with the team. After this, the project leader allocates usually the large bones on the fish (the suggested potential causes) to each member of the project team, asking them to investigate and report back the next morning with facts, evidence or data that prove the problem identified *is not* a cause of the problem, or *is* a cause of the problem. This continues until all potential causes have either been decided as *causes* or *not related causes* and ruled out of the discussion.

6. By midweek, the project team members are leaning towards three potential causes as being the root cause(s) of the problem. These suggestions are investigated by going and seeing, and indeed, prove to be the root causes!

7. Improvement actions are agreed upon, the process is improved, the work instructions are updated and further training is carried out.

8. The project leader comes back a week later to measure and check that improvements have indeed cured the problem.

The cause–effect diagram forms a powerful tool for team involvement around why a problem is occurring. Depending on the severity of the problem being investigated, the project leader may consider halting related tasks, until the root cause of the problem has been identified and mechanisms have been put in place to rectify the process. Once the problem has been identified and dealt with, tasks can resume.

The 5 whys and fishbone techniques can be applied beyond the realms of investigations into exploring issues about quality. These techniques are useful at any point where a root cause needs to be identified.

In relation to the quality of the management of the project and its defined performance criteria, project audits are a popular approach: where, for example, the PMO schedules a formal audit or less formal review of how the project management is taking place. Is it following the project management framework and gate reviews; are the financial rules being adhered to; and is contract and procurement being carried out in a fair, open and honest manner (according to guidelines)? These reviews are an essential feedback tool for the project leader, with discrepancies being attended to through (for example) the continuous improvement approach.

Summary

Quality is everyone's responsibility and therefore ensuring that clear quality criteria are established, both from a project management perspective and a product or service perspective, is critical. The project leader is ultimately responsible for ensuring that definitions of quality are articulated, agreed, documented, actioned and achieved by applying the processes, tools and techniques outlined in this chapter. This chapter has introduced the following concepts.

- Ensuring an environment and culture of continuous improvement is promoted in the project environment—to continually learn from and adjust (improve) processes and systems that govern the project.
- Articulating assurance standards (specifications) against which the product, service or results will be measured, to gain sign-off of the project and its deliverables.
- Managing (or controlling) quality throughout the project life cycle, particularly during the Execution stage. By using visual representations of data, the project leader can identify where problems exist and work to identify their root cause(s) and put corrective actions into place.
- Carrying out root-cause analysis as a matter of routine work to ensure time is spent on the right things. The project leader can use the 5 whys and the fishbone (cause–effect) techniques to gain group involvement and participation when seeking out the true root causes to a problem.

The project leader is responsible for ensuring perceptions of quality, as viewed by the key stakeholders in the project (the sponsors, customers and suppliers), are captured as tangible, agreed and measurable quality criteria ("we listen to the VOC"). This can be a challenging endeavour. However, if perceptions are left unarticulated and undefined, this will undoubtedly lead the project down a disorderly path of troublesome issues. The adage "fit for purpose" does not define quality, but merely indicates a perspective as seen from an individual viewpoint. It is the project leader and project team's responsibility therefore to ensure that relevant, measurable quality criteria are established at the outset of the project. Quality needs to be taken on board as being every project member's responsibility and needs to be controlled effectively, especially throughout the Execution stage of the project, when the customer's deliverables will be being produced.

Remember the old archery analogy, as illustrated in Figure 13.23—we need both precision and accuracy taking place within our project environments.

Figure 13.23 Precision and accuracy

Do know know if you have precision and accuracy in your project?

Arrows clustered tightly in one area of the target, even if they are not clustered in the bullseye, are considered to have high precision.

Targets where the arrows are more spread out but equidistant from the bullseye are considered to have the same degree of accuracy.

Targets where the arrows are both tightly grouped and within the bullseye are considered both accurate and precise.

Precise measurements are not necessarily accurate measurements, and accurate measurements are not necessarily precise measurements.

© 2022 Dr Neil Pearson

Review questions

1. Provide some examples of quality performance criteria critical to the success and acceptance of a project.
2. What is the difference between quality assurance and quality control?
3. What continuous improvement policies and guidelines exist in your organisation?
4. What is the purpose of the Quality Management Plan?
5. Which types of tools would be useful for investigating the root cause of a problem?
6. How can checklists be used within a project environment?

Exercises

1. What would the QA/QC planning grid (see Figure 13.5) look like for a project you have been involved in?
2. Apply the fishbone technique to a problem you have recently encountered and then comment on what this technique reveals.
3. For a project you have worked on, reflect on section 13.6 "Carrying out quality control", and think about what should have been measured and controlled using data visualisations. Make a list of the visualisation techniques and what you could have used them for.
4. For one of the data visualisations identified in Exercise 3, with real or hypothetical data mock up the visualisation.

References

American Society for Quality (ASQ) 2018a, "Continuous improvement", ASQ, http://asq.org/learn-about-quality/continuous-improvement/overview/overview.html, accessed February 2018.

American Society for Quality (ASQ) 2018b, "Control chart", ASQ, http://asq.org/learn-about-quality/data-collection-analysis-tools/overview/control-chart.html, accessed February 2018.

Australian Skills Quality Authority (ASQA) n.d., "VET Quality Framework", ASQA, https://www.asqa.gov.au/about/australias-vet-sector/vet-quality-framework, accessed February 2018.

BHP Billiton 2011, "BHP Billiton approves USD554 million investment at Escondida", 24hGold, www.24hgold.com/english/news-company-gold-silver-bhp-billiton-approves-usd554-million-investment-at-escondida.aspx?articleid=697199.

International Organization for Standardization (ISO) 2015, ISO 9001 "Quality Management Systems – Requirements", 5th edition.

Mining IQ Editorial, "Quality control in mining", Mining iQ, www.miningiq.com/technical-services-and-production/articles/Quality-control-in-mining/, accessed January 2013.

Project Management Institute (PMI) 2017, *A Guide to the Project Management Body of Knowledge*, 6th edition, PMI.

Project Management Institute (PMI) 2021a, *A Guide to the Project Management Body of Knowledge (PMBOK® Guide)*, 7th edition, PMI.

Project Management Institute (PMI) 2021b, *The Standard for Project Management (ANSI/PMI 99-001-2021)*, 7th edition, PMI.

Swider M 2017, "Here's why the Samsung Galaxy Note 7 batteries caught fire and exploded", Techradar, www.techradar.com/news/samsung-galaxy-note-7-battery-fires-heres-why-they-exploded, accessed February 2018.

CHAPTER 14

Project stakeholder management

Learning elements

14A Understand the overall process of stakeholder management, including stakeholder identification, stakeholder analysis and stakeholder engagement.

14B Be able to apply the basic concepts of stakeholder co-creation to engagements with stakeholders.

14C Be able to holistically plan stakeholder management.

14D Be able to apply various stakeholder management tools to the identification of stakeholders.

14E Be able to apply various stakeholder management tools to the analysis of stakeholders.

14F Understand some of the complexities in the process of stakeholder management.

14G Be able to successfully and cleanly close down stakeholder relationships at the end of the project.

In this chapter

14.1 Introduction

14.2 Stakeholder co-creation

14.3 Planning stakeholder management

14.4 Identifying stakeholders

14.5 Analysing stakeholders

14.6 Engage and monitor stakeholders

14.7 Closing down stakeholder relationships

Summary

14.1 : Introduction

Over-eager project leaders sometimes try to push their own agenda onto others, thinking this will spur on successful completion of a project. However, what they soon find out is that a project's success depends on the cooperation of a wide range of individuals, the majority of whom do not directly report to them as project leader. For example, during the course of a systems integration project, a project leader is surprised by how much time they are spending negotiating and working with vendors, consultants, technical specialists and other functional managers. Instead of working with the project team and other stakeholders to complete the project, they find themselves being constantly pulled by the demands of different groups of people who are not directly involved in the project but who nonetheless have a vested interest in its outcome. As a result, the project leader starts to work longer hours to try to disentangle the situation, but this only leads them further towards the shadowy path of burnout and project disbandment by stakeholders.

This chapter reviews the processes of **stakeholder identification**, **stakeholder analysis** and the building of lasting **stakeholder strategies** (collectively referred to as *stakeholder management*).

PMBOK : **Seventh edition updates (PMI 2021)**

The *Project Management Body of Knowledge* (PMBOK) seventh edition (PMI 2021) has promoted the topic of stakeholders in several ways.

First, stakeholders are a "project management principle" within the *Standard for Project Management*. Second, stakeholders are also a "performance domain" within the *Guide to the Project Management Body of Knowledge*. Third, "Tailoring" considers the wider context of stakeholders in the project environment. Fourth, there are implications to stakeholders through the majority of the "Principles", in "Stewardship" for example, as it implies both internal and external consideration of aspects of integrity, care, trustworthiness and compliance. This demonstrates the integrative nature of the project (PMI 2021a, p. 24), without expressly having a separate "Integration" knowledge area—it is a skill that good project leaders seem to excel at.

Fifth, the number of tools highlighted in the seventh edition has been expanded to include power/impact, attitude, beliefs, expectations, degree of influence, proximity to the project and interest in the project. Although PMBOK does not provide any further information on these tools, this text aims to unpack these and others so that readers have a deeper understanding of how they can be applied in practice.

These observations on stakeholder management practice old and new have been distilled into a few general stakeholder management activities carried out in most projects regardless of approach (predictive through adaptive) (Figure 14.1).

As we progress through this chapter, take note of the definition of a stakeholder: Individuals/ organisations that are directly/indirectly involved in a project, who are affected negatively/positively by the outcomes of project decisions/performance.

Project leaders should carefully assess whether an individual or a group is a stakeholder; the more stakeholders, the more lines of communication, the more to manage, the more chance of conflict and confusion—choose wisely and manage empathetically.

With this said, we will first consider the concept of **stakeholder co-creation**, as this influences all activities—seeking to build and deliver value for the business, the stakeholders and the project team. We are now in partnership with our stakeholders, not subservient to them; both parties wish to see success, and to achieve success both parties must work together with a shared goal and shared values.

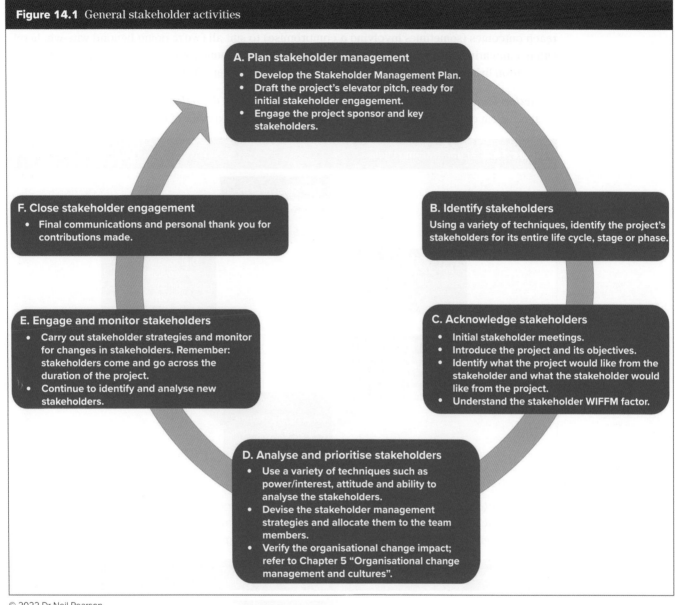

Figure 14.1 General stakeholder activities

A. Plan stakeholder management
- Develop the Stakeholder Management Plan.
- Draft the project's elevator pitch, ready for initial stakeholder engagement.
- Engage the project sponsor and key stakeholders.

B. Identify stakeholders
Using a variety of techniques, identify the project's stakeholders for its entire life cycle, stage or phase.

C. Acknowledge stakeholders
- Initial stakeholder meetings.
- Introduce the project and its objectives.
- Identify what the project would like from the stakeholder and what the stakeholder would like from the project.
- Understand the stakeholder WIFFM factor.

D. Analyse and prioritise stakeholders
- Use a variety of techniques such as power/interest, attitude and ability to analyse the stakeholders.
- Devise the stakeholder management strategies and allocate them to the team members.
- Verify the organisational change impact; refer to Chapter 5 "Organisational change management and cultures".

E. Engage and monitor stakeholders
- Carry out stakeholder strategies and monitor for changes in stakeholders. Remember: stakeholders come and go across the duration of the project.
- Continue to identify and analyse new stakeholders.

F. Close stakeholder engagement
- Final communications and personal thank you for contributions made.

© 2022 Dr Neil Pearson

14.2 | Stakeholder co-creation

Co-creation (sometimes referred to as *sustainable project management*, *connected enterprise* or *value creation*) is an emerging trend in stakeholder engagement. In summary, stakeholder co-creation is a form of cooperation in which all participants (**stakeholders**) influence the process and the result. This topic is introduced here, before the process of stakeholder management is discussed, so that readers can familiarise themselves with this concept and thus can layer it onto discussions as the chapter progresses.

In practical terms, stakeholder co-creation is the close, trusted, positive, open-minded, supportive (with synergy), collaborative engagement of stakeholders to create project value (outputs, outcomes and benefits) that really does add value to recipients (customers and society). For example, if a project leader were working on plans for the development of a new low-rise block of 20 apartments on the fringe of a suburban neighbourhood, they would need to engage in open dialogue with a range of stakeholders (i.e. neighbourhood citizens, the local council, local environment groups, potential customers for the apartments) to create value for all within a cooperative environment. On paper, this may sound easy, but in practice, the project leader will need to create the environment for this to take place in a trusted manner. Complexities and dynamics must be understood at a deeper level, common ground must be found at all stages of engagement, and conflict and negotiation must be managed to reach outcomes (sometimes involving a compromise) to suit all (we're going beyond win–win here!). Often, innovative (future-oriented) solutions will need to be found for complex problems. Stakeholder co-creation brings other techniques into the project environment. These include:

■ *Action learning:* The project leader and project team take a *do, reflect and learn* approach, to inform the current cycle of engagement and be able to adjust the next cycle of engagement (see Figure 14.2).

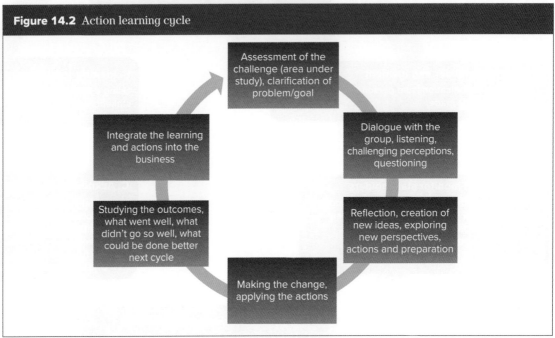

Figure 14.2 Action learning cycle

© 2022 Dr Neil Pearson

■ *Organisational development for internally focused projects:* This is where a planned and systematic approach towards enabling sustained organisational performance, through the involvement of the organisation's people, is taken (see Figure 14.3).

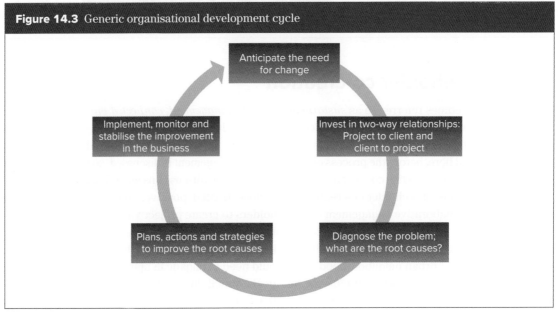

Figure 14.3 Generic organisational development cycle

© 2022 Dr Neil Pearson

■ *Sustainable development:* Where the aims are to deliver products and services that are sustainable in the real world (see Figure 14.4)—considering not just the green aspects of sustainability, but taking a more holistic approach to sustaining outcomes over the long term.

Figure 14.4 Generic sustainable development cycle

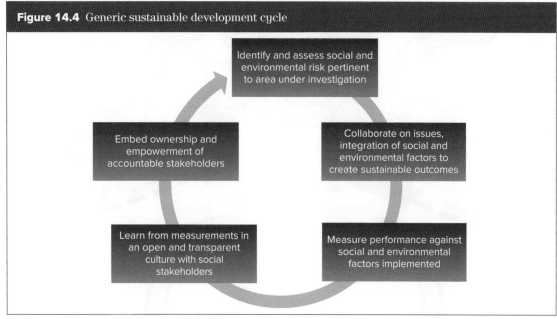

© 2022 Dr Neil Pearson

At the crux of stakeholder co-creation is the concept of understanding, creating and then delivering value to the project stakeholders. Value involves ultimately understanding what each stakeholder does value—which, of course, will be different for each, according to their own unique perspective. For example, in an apartment build, the customer of the apartment might seek a **value proposition** of *high-end, accessible with full amenities;* but the neighbourhood citizen might seek *low environmental impact, fits with the landscape of the community and is suitably landscaped to minimise visual impact.* Understanding the differing stakeholders' value propositions and their complexities and interplays helps the project leader to unpack any conflicts. This insight is key to working towards creating value in stakeholder co-creation (Figure 14.5). In the past, project leaders may have casually sought to understand the **"What's in it for me?" (WIIFM)** factor. Co-creation takes this further by understanding the true value proposition for each impacted stakeholder, and sub-groups of stakeholders, working towards maximising value to all.

When developing the concept of stakeholder co-creation and identifying what this means to the respective stakeholders, the project leader could use diagrams that combine elements of the **stakeholder network diagram** and **rich pictures** (introduced in Chapter 8 "Defining the scope of a project"), business systems and systems thinking to create a pictorial representation of the co-creation ecosystem.

■ The stakeholder network diagram indicates stakeholders, relationships, networks and interactions.

■ The rich picture diagram indicates activities, artefacts and, most important, emotions—what is being *felt.*

■ Systems thinking and business systems incorporate the wider landscape and its interconnectedness.

When these are combined and applied to groups, such as crowds of people, movements of people, communities of people, clubs of experts and coalitions of parties, the project leader can start to understand the true value of what stakeholders are seeking and how the resulting ecosystem feeds and reacts to those within it. Refer back to Figure 14.5 for an example of the result of carrying out a co-creation workshop.

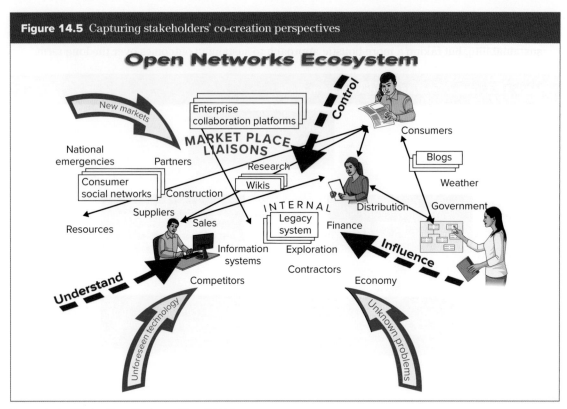

Figure 14.5 Capturing stakeholders' co-creation perspectives

Source: Axelrod Becker Consulting Inc. and SageNet LLC

The reader is encouraged to review further resources on stakeholder co-creation, for example:

- https://organisatieleren.be/co-creation
- https://fronteer.com/what-is-co-creation/
- www.pmi.org/learning/library/value-cocreation-stakeholders-research-project-9529 (PMI membership required)
- www.youtube.com/watch?v=VxXt-JMX0Fg

14.3 │ Planning stakeholder management

In parallel with the dynamic information relating to the stakeholders of the project (i.e. stakeholder identification and analysis), the project leader would also be establishing the governance, policy and roles around stakeholder management for the project. This is again articulated in a management plan, in this case the **Stakeholder Management Plan**. Below is a summary of the key contents of such a plan.

- *Strategy and approach:* This section of the plan describes the general strategy and approach to stakeholder management within the project environment. Is it co-creation principles, for example?

- *Policy and procedure:* Identify any relevant organisational stakeholder engagement policy and procedures that must be applied within the project environment. For example, the organisation could have rules for the contact of certain external stakeholders, which must be channelled only through the nominated members of the Senior Management Team within the organisation.

- *Information systems:* Document any systems (central repositories of information) where stakeholder information must be maintained. For example, some organisations use **Customer Relationship Management (CRM)** systems to maintain information on stakeholders.

- *Stakeholder management roles and responsibilities:* This section should describe the various roles and responsibilities project team members have in relation to the management of stakeholders and stakeholder decision-making capabilities. This information could have been captured in the project-wide RASCI and referenced back to this section of the Communications Management Plan.

- *Stakeholder survey:* A **stakeholder survey** is to be sent out periodically to all stakeholders during the project Planning and Execution stages to gauge stakeholder feedback from current stakeholder engagement strategies. This will supplement any feedback discussed at team meetings and unsolicited feedback received directly from stakeholders to members of the project team.

- *Risk review:* Ensure a risk review of any stakeholder activities is carried out, and that identified risks are entered into the Risk Register under the category of "Stakeholder".

- *Assumptions and constraints:* Consider what assumptions are being made in relation to stakeholders for the project. (*Remember:* An assumption is an *assumed statement of truth.*) Also capture what stakeholder factors may *constrain* the project. For example, this could be access to certain stakeholders at rigid times.

- *Lessons learned:* Ensure that a review of any lessons learned from prior similar projects is undertaken, and that any relevant lessons learned are entered into the project's Lessons Learned Register under the category of "Stakeholders". Action any activities in relation to lessons and how they are to be managed in this project.

 Stakeholder Management Plan

Included with the text is an online template providing more details as to the contents of the Stakeholder Management Plan. *Note:* The purpose of these management plans is to capture project-wide governance, policy, tools, business rules (RASCI), processes and other more static information, in this case stakeholder-based information.

14.4 Identifying stakeholders

Ultimate success is not determined by whether a project is completed on time, within budget or according to specifications, but rather by whether the customer is satisfied with what has been accomplished. Customer satisfaction is the bottom line. Bad news travels faster and further than good news. A happy customerer is likely to share their satisfaction about a particular product or service with another person. An unhappy customer, however, is statistically likely to share their discontent with up to eight other people! Project leaders need to cultivate positive working relations with clients to preserve their reputations.

When new project leaders do find time to work directly on the project, they often adopt a hands-on approach towards managing it. They choose this style, not because they are power-hungry egomaniacs, but because they are eager to achieve results! They often quickly become frustrated by how slowly things operate, by the number of people who may have to be brought on board, and the difficulty of gaining some people's cooperation. Unfortunately, as this frustration builds, the natural temptation is to exert more and more pressure and to get more heavily involved in the project. When this happens, the project leader tends to quickly earn the reputation of being a *micro manager* and subsequently may lose sight of the real role they play in guiding a project.

Some new managers never break out of this paradigm. Others soon realise that authority does not equal influence and that being an effective project leader involves managing a much more complex and expansive set of interfaces than they had previously anticipated. They encounter a web of relationships that require a much broader spectrum of influence than they had initially felt was either necessary or even possible.

Consider for example, a significantly sized project (such as creating a new product or installing a new information system), which will, most likely, encompass working with several different groups of stakeholders. There will be a core group of specialists assigned to complete the project, and this group is likely to be supplemented at different times by professionals who will work on specific segments of the project. There will also be groups of people (within the performing organisation) who will, either directly or indirectly, become involved throughout the entire project life cycle. This will typically include top management and the customer, to whom the project leader will be accountable. There will also be other managers who will provide resources and/or may be responsible for specific segments of the project, as well as for administrative support services (such as human resources (HR) and finance).

Depending on the nature of the project, there may also be several different groups outside the organisation that will influence the success of the project; the most important of these of course will be the customer for whom the project is being designed. Identifying and mapping these stakeholders and their various relationships is extremely useful. Brainstorming the identification of stakeholders and understanding the relationships between them is critical not only at the Initiation stage of a project (for the initial key stakeholders to be engaged with), but also at the start of each of the other stages of the project life cycle—and even sometimes multiple times within each stage. Figures 14.6(a), (b), (c) and (d) represent a few different approaches for stakeholder identification. Each of these approaches could be accomplished by carrying out a sticky note team idea-shower session. *Remember:* The more inclusive the project leader can make such activities, the better the chance of identifying all stakeholders, and the greater the buy-in from the project team and the stakeholders.

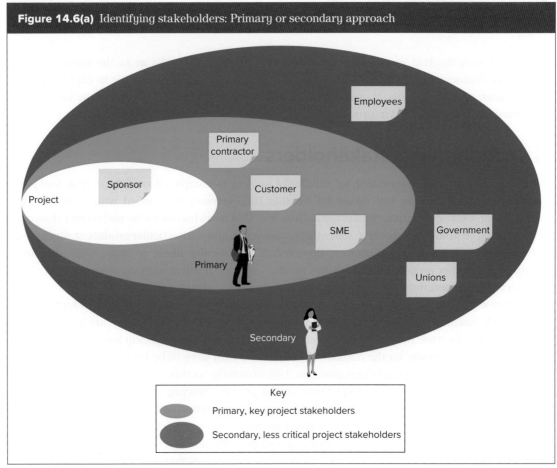

Figure 14.6(a) Identifying stakeholders: Primary or secondary approach

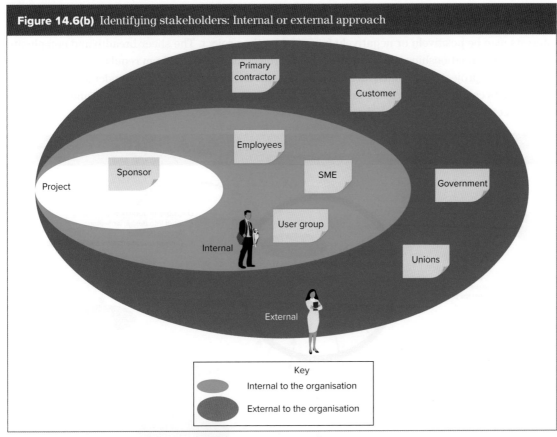

Figure 14.6(b) Identifying stakeholders: Internal or external approach

© 2022 Dr Neil Pearson

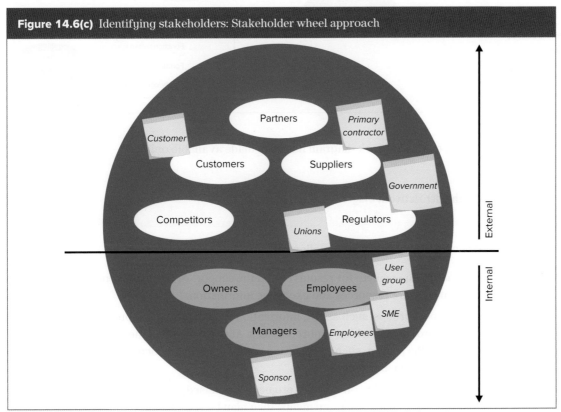

Figure 14.6(c) Identifying stakeholders: Stakeholder wheel approach

© 2022 Dr Neil Pearson

Source: Adapted from Yeates D, Cadle J & Paul D 2020, *Business Analysis*, 4th edition, BCS Learning & Development, The Chartered Institute for IT

Each stakeholder will bring different expertise, perspectives, priorities and agendas to the project. Stakeholders are people and organisations who are actively involved in the project, or whose interests may be positively or negatively impacted by the project. The sheer breadth and complexity of stakeholder relationships is what distinguishes project management from regular management. To be effective, a project leader must identify the right stakeholders in the project, understand how these stakeholders can affect the project, develop trusted relationships in a short timespan, and define how the project team can engage with them.

Figure 14.6(d) Identifying stakeholders: The stakeholder network diagram

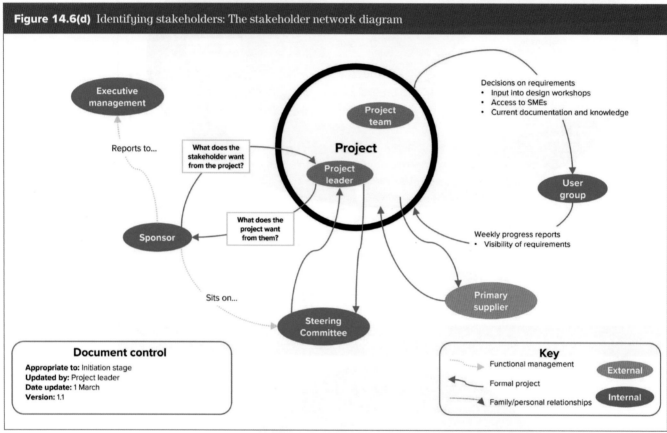

© 2022 Dr Neil Pearson

A template based on this network diagram has been made available online.

 Stakeholder Network Diagram

Typical stakeholder groups include the following.

- Project leaders naturally compete for resources and the support of top management. At the same time, they often must share resources and exchange information.

- Administrative support groups, such as HR, information system operators, purchasing agents and maintenance staff, provide valuable support services. At the same time, they impose constraints and requirements on the project, such as requiring expenditure to be documented and the delivery of information to be timely and accurate.

- Functional managers (depending on how the project is organised) can play a minor or major role in the project's success. In matrix arrangements, they may be responsible for assigning project personnel, resolving technical dilemmas and overseeing the completion of significant segments of project work. Even in dedicated project teams, the technical input from functional managers may be useful, and their acceptance of completed project work may be critical. Functional managers usually want to cooperate up to a point—but only up to a certain point as they will also be concerned with preserving their status within the organisation and minimising the disruptions the project may cause to their own day-to-day operations.

- Top management approves funding of the project and establishes priorities within the organisation. Top management also defines *success* and makes decisions about rewards for accomplishments. Significant adjustments in budget, scope and schedule typically need top management's approval. Top management will have a natural, vested interest in the success of the project, but at the same time must be responsive to what is best for the entire organisation.

- Project sponsors champion the project and use their influence to gain approval for it. Their reputation is tied to the success of the project, and they need to be kept informed of any major developments. They defend the project when it comes under attack and are key project allies.

- Contractors (in some cases) may conduct all the actual work, with the project team coordinating their contributions. In other cases, they are responsible for ancillary segments of the project scope. Poor work outcomes and schedule slips can affect the work of the core project team. While contractors' reputations depend on them doing good work, they must also balance their contributions with their own profit margins and their commitments to other clients.

- Government agencies typically place constraints on project work. Permits need to be secured. Construction work must be built to code. New drugs must pass a rigorous battery of tests. Other products must meet safety standards (e.g. workplace health and safety standards).

- Other organisations (depending on the nature of the project) may directly or indirectly affect the project. For example, suppliers provide necessary resources for completion of the project work, and delays, shortages and poor quality can bring a project to a standstill. Public interest groups may apply pressure on government agencies. Customers often hire consultants and auditors to protect their interests on a project.

Stakeholders are often grouped into **primary stakeholders**, who are the individuals and groups most affected by the outcomes of the project; and **secondary stakeholders**, who are the individuals or groups not directly affected by the outcome of the project, but who still have an interest in it. Secondary stakeholders often help by aiding the primary stakeholders. These relationships are interdependent, in that a project leader's ability to work effectively with one group will affect their ability to manage other groups. For example, functional managers are likely to be less cooperative if they perceive that top management's commitment to the project is waning. Conversely, the project leader's ability to buffer the team from excessive interference from a client is likely to increase their standing with the project team.

Other good sources of stakeholders can be identified from:

- discussing with the project sponsor about who they identify as being a stakeholder in the project
- reviewing the **organisational chart** and assessing (given the nature of the project) who, from a functional organisational perspective, is likely to be interested in or impacted by the project.

14.4.1 **The Stakeholder Register**

Identifying stakeholders, according to the approach used in Figures 14.6(a), (b), (c) and (d), forms the start of the process of actively identifying a project's stakeholders. As part of this process, the project leader will develop what is often referred to as the **Stakeholder Register**. This document is used by the project leader to maintain (and regularly review) details of stakeholders.

Information collected at the stakeholder identification stage could include (among a whole host of other information) the following.

- The stakeholder's name.
- The stakeholder's functional role (e.g. the position the stakeholder has in the organisation's structure).
- The stakeholder's contact details and (optionally) the contact details of a secondary stakeholder who can be contacted when the primary stakeholder is unavailable. It may also be the project's preference that the secondary stakeholder should have the same decision-making accountability as the primary stakeholder.
- Information about whether the stakeholder is **internal** or **external** to the organisation; this could affect the available channels of communication and the messages being sent.
- Details of *what the stakeholder wants from the project* (i.e. capturing the agreed expectations of what they will receive from the project). This could range from, for example, receiving project updates through to outcome-related activities.
- Details of *what the project wants from the stakeholder* including agreement on their decision-making ability, and any information and/or resources they are to provide to the project.
- Current perceptions and knowledge; this forms the start of change management activities for the project—by capturing perceptions and knowledge, the project leader knows what perception the stakeholder has of the *as-is* current state.
- Desired perceptions and knowledge; this is the project's assessment of where the project must move the stakeholder—from the as-is state to the project's vision or *to-be* future state.
- Details of any stakeholder personal preferences, pet hates (e.g. about when/when not to contact them), any points of passion (positive or negative), how they wish to be addressed; having this kind of information to hand can help navigate around particularly prickly stakeholders. But be careful how this information is captured and shared among project team members!
- Stakeholder management strategies and actions on individual members of the project management team to ensure within the project team there is a responsible person who is going to build and maintain the relationship with the stakeholder.

An extensive Stakeholder Register has been included in the online resources, which also include numerous tools for analysing stakeholders (which is discussed later in this chapter).

 Stakeholder Register

SNAPSHOT *from* PRACTICE : The project leader as conductor

The role of a project leader is comparable to that of a conductor. The conductor of an orchestra integrates the divergent sounds of different instruments to perform a given composition and make music. Similarly, the project leader integrates the talents and contributions of different specialists to complete the project. Both must be good at understanding how the different players contribute to the performance of the whole. Both are almost entirely dependent upon the expertise and know-how of the players. The conductor does not have command of all the musical instruments. Likewise, the project leader usually possesses only a small proportion of the technical knowledge needed to make decisions. As such, the conductor and project leader both facilitate the performance of others rather than actually perform.

Conductors use their arms, baton and other non-verbal gestures to influence the pace, intensity and involvement of different musicians. Likewise, project leaders orchestrate the completion of the project by managing the involvement and attention of project members. Project leaders balance time and process and induce participants to make the right decisions at the right time, just as the conductor induces the wind instruments to perform at the right moment in a movement. Each controls the rhythm and intensity of work by managing the tempo and involvement of the players. Finally, each has a vision that transcends the music score or project plan, and, to be successful, each must earn the confidence, respect and trust of their players.

The project management organisational structure being used will influence the number and degree of external dependencies that will need to be managed. One advantage of creating a dedicated project team is that it reduces dependencies (especially within the organisation) because most of the resources are assigned to the project. Conversely, a functional matrix structure increases dependencies, with the result that the project leader is much more reliant upon functional colleagues for work and staff.

The old-fashioned approach to managing projects emphasised directing and controlling subordinates. The contemporary perspective emphasises engaging with project stakeholders and anticipating change. Project leaders need to be able to assuage (relieve) customer concerns, sustain support for the project at higher levels of the organisation, and quickly identify problems that threaten project work, while at the same time defending the integrity of the project and the interests of the project participants. Within this web of relationships, the project leader must find out what needs to be done to achieve the goals of the project and build a cooperative network for accomplishing this (stakeholder co-creation). Project leaders undertake and achieve this without expecting or demanding cooperation. This necessitates using sound communication skills, leveraging political capital and tapping into a broad influence base. (See "Snapshot from Practice: The project leader as conductor", for more about what characterises a project leader.)

14.5 : Analysing stakeholders

Analysing identified stakeholders is an ongoing activity for the project leader. The management of stakeholders is truly a cross-life-cycle effort: different stakeholders will require different levels of attention during the different stages of the project life cycle, as stakeholders come and go from the project. For example, the project leader may have a frequent contact with the project sponsor or senior business users during the Initiation stage of a project, but during the Planning stage of the project, the management of stakeholders may shift to the business users (who are going to be the recipients of the outputs and outcomes of the project). During the Execution stage, the project sponsor may require exception reports on progress from the project leader. Being able to analyse stakeholders and design strategies to manage them is critical to project success—but, as with just about everything in project management, stakeholders change.

14.5.1 Power/Interest grid

The **Power/Interest Grid** (Figure 14.7) is often used for assessing and managing a stakeholder's power and interest throughout the project life cycle.

By mapping power and interest (on a relative scale of high to low), the project team can review the position of each stakeholder and apply appropriate strategies for managing them. The intersections on the Power/Interest Grid are frequently annotated as follows.

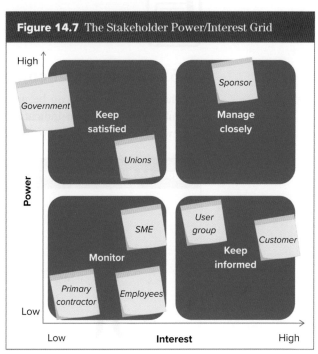

Figure 14.7 The Stakeholder Power/Interest Grid

© 2022 Dr Neil Pearson

- *Manage closely (high power/high interest):* These stakeholders are actively managed. They not only have a high interest in the project, but also have the power to influence (in either a positive or negative manner). Examples of these types of stakeholders include the project sponsor, key users and funding providers.

- *Keep satisfied (high power/low interest):* These stakeholders need to be kept satisfied. This type of stakeholder could, for example, be an external government department that doesn't have a direct interest in the project but could influence its outcome. For example, when managing a (non-government) project that is subject to government legislation, the government would likely have little to no direct interest in the project itself. However, should a change in government policy occur, this could potentially have major implications for the project.

- *Keep informed (low power/high interest):* Here, stakeholders could hold important influence, despite not being high on the power dimension. In this situation, they must be kept informed about relevant information and decisions. Examples might be technical experts, executive assistants and the general user base affected by the project.

- *Monitor (low power/low interest):* These are the minimum-maintenance stakeholders. Keep them informed and monitor for any changes in their power and/or interest. Send them a weekly newsletter or provide an intranet page for them to review.

Knowing where your stakeholders are positioned on the Power/Interest Grid and understanding the dependencies (relationships) that exist between these stakeholders can involve a bit of detective work. The project leader will be on a journey of discovery to work out how this network is interlinked and intertwined!

Note: Within the Stakeholder Register template online, you will find different versions of the Power/Interest Grid, covering combinations of:

- power/interest (four segments)
- modified power/interest (six segments)
- power/influence
- influence/impact.

 **Stakeholder Register**

14.5.2 Stakeholder continuum analysis

Another technique that can be used is to place stakeholders on a continuum. This continuum will resemble the continuum indicated in Figure 14.8, where a stakeholder is positioned on a scale, somewhere from project "Opposer" through to project "Promoter".

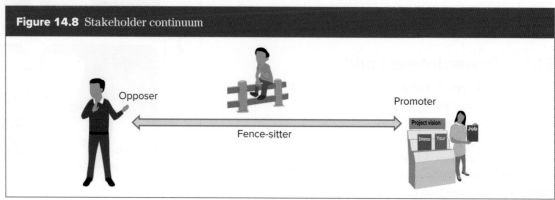

Figure 14.8 Stakeholder continuum

Opposer

Fence-sitter

Promoter

Another tool is the Stakeholder Engagement Grid (explained in Table 14.1). This maps the current (C) and desired (D) level of engagement by the stakeholder.

Table 14.1 Stakeholder Engagement Grid

Stakeholder	Role	Unaware	Resistant	Neutral	Supportive	Leading
Jane Smith	Project Sponsor				C	D

Key
- Unaware: Unaware of the project and any potential impacts.
- Resistant: Aware of the project and its potential impacts and is resistant to change.
- Neutral: Aware of the project yet neither supportive nor resistant.
- Supportive: Aware of the project and potential impacts and supportive of the change.
- Leading: Aware of the project and potential impacts and actively engaged in the success of the project.

C: Current position
D: Desired position

© 2022 Dr Neil Pearson

Our stakeholder strategies formulated from analysing the grid will be to either:

1. promote the stakeholder, as they are not using their position/influence/role, etc. to maximise results for the project. A typical strategy to promote a stakeholder might be for the project team to formulate communications for them, which they then send out in their name.

2. cool down the stakeholder, as, although they are supportive, maybe they are not respected in the operational area, their loyalties are misguided, they are supportive for the wrong reasons, or they are just simply meddling in project activities. Here, strategies might include one-to-one engagements carried out by the project leader and coaching; failing that, using the one-up rules and discussions with their manager to cool down the engagement. Cool-down strategies have to be carefully thought out as they could result in a *blocker*.

14.5.3 Stakeholder attitude

The **stakeholder attitude** tool assesses the attitudes of stakeholders. The tool can provide insights into how a stakeholder's attitude could positively or negatively affect the project. It is similar in nature to the stakeholder continuum.

The project leader and project team could again, in a workshop style, rate the attitude of each stakeholder previously identified and use this information to design/update the resulting stakeholder management strategies and communications. Table 14.2 provides an attitude scale to assess stakeholders against, with some notes on common situations that may affect the project.

Table 14.2 Stakeholder attitudes

Attitude	Notes
Champions will actively work for the success of the project.	The project sponsor should be of this mindset and attitude; if not, consider what needs to be carried out as a strategy to promote the stakeholder's attitude, or, in worse cases, request a more suitable project sponsor.
Supporters are in favour of the project but will probably not be very active in promoting it.	Managers of the areas being affected by the project should be active supporters. Can they see the project vision, do they understand how it will assist them to work better, faster, smarter, and so on?
Neutral stakeholders express no opinion either in favour or against the project.	Otherwise known as *fence-sitters*, who can fall either way at any time. Try and elicit deeper thoughts as to what their position could be in order to define appropriate stakeholder management strategies.
Critics are not in favour of the project but are probably not actively opposed to it either.	Critics need to be managed in a positive way to better understand the project vision and what its strategically aligned goals are. Find out why they are being critical.
Opponents will actively work to disrupt, impede or derail the project.	Opponents need to managed away and out of the project (as with blockers) if they are not willing to state factually their grievances. Projects often do not have the luxury of overinvesting time in turning opponents around into supporters. If the first attempt to do so fails, escalate the risk to the project sponsor.
Blockers are stakeholders who will just obstruct progress (possibly for reasons outside the project itself).	Find out why they are blocking. If this cannot be quickly turned around, consider alternative strategies. Escalate to the project sponsor for a more senior discussion. Failing that, remove from the project's stakeholders.

Source: Adapted from Yeates D, Cadle J & Paul D 2020, *Business Analysis*, 4th edition, BCS Learning & Development, The Chartered Institute for IT

With attitudes, the project leader needs to get to the root cause of why critics, opponents and blockers are the state they are in—again, one-to-one meetings and working the stakeholder network will hopefully shed light on the issue so we can work to address it (ask a direct *why* question). With supporters and champions, we want to sustain and leverage, but monitor to ensure this support does not change or wane (ask what we can do to help you promote the project's vision).

14.5.4 Contribution/Commitment Grid

The **Contribution/Commitment Grid** (Figure 14.9) provides a more detailed insight into the stakeholder's involvement in the project.

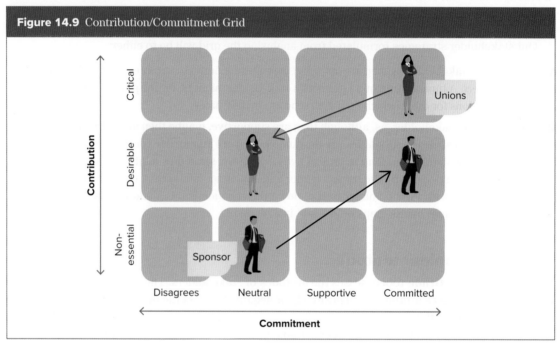

Figure 14.9 Contribution/Commitment Grid

© 2022 Dr Neil Pearson

The degree to which a stakeholder is required to contribute to a project to ensure its success depends on several factors, including the:

■ stakeholder's position and authority within the organisation

■ degree to which the project is reliant upon the stakeholder to provide a product or service to the project

■ level of social influence the individual has and the degree to which the individual is familiar with specific aspects of the business.

Each of these factors can be analysed in more detail during the stakeholder analysis. The outcome is summarised in a contribution index, with the following values.

■ *Critical:* The stakeholder has the power to make the project succeed or to prevent it from succeeding altogether.

■ *Desirable:* The project can be completed even without an active contribution from the stakeholder, but this would have a serious impact on the quality, elapsed time and cost of execution. The stakeholder can act as an advocate for the project to peers.

■ *Non-essential:* Although the stakeholder can contribute to the project, their contribution is either not essential or can be more easily obtained from other stakeholders. *Note:* An individual with a contribution index below *non-essential* may not be a stakeholder of the project.

Each stakeholder will display a different level of commitment to the project throughout the life of the project.

- *Committed (wants to make the project happen):* The stakeholder has made a commitment to contribute to the project (preferably in writing) and is available to do so. Their commitment may be documented in the form of an agreed plan, describing what will be provided and by when, or in other forms of written communication (e.g. email, memo, letter, contract, statement of intent).
- *Supportive (wants to be involved in making the project happen):* The stakeholder is well informed and sees value in what is being produced from the project. The stakeholder understands their contribution and is willing to provide it, although no formal commitment has been entered into.
- *Neutral (will let the project happen, shows indifference):* The stakeholder may or may not be informed about the project and, while they do not disagree, they are not actively involved in any capacity, or may be indifferent about the project's objectives and outcomes.
- *Disagrees (will try to stop the project from happening):* The stakeholder may or may not be informed but does not see value in the project and the work being performed. They would rather not be involved in the project, and in fact would prefer the work not to be carried out at all.

As a result of this analysis, the project leader could add the following items to the Stakeholder Register.

- Current commitment level: The project leader may update the Stakeholder Register following a meeting, by placing supervisor Helena's details in the critical/neutral segment of the grid.
- Desired commitment level: After discussions with the project team, the project leader wishes to move supervisor Helena into the critical/committed segment of the grid.
- Action steps: These are the steps that the project team needs to take with the stakeholder in order to move the stakeholder's position from the current commitment level to the desired commitment level.

Note: Figure 14.9 shows the positions of two stakeholders. The red line indicates a stakeholder who considers themselves to have more importance than the project deems them necessary to have, so actions are about downwardly managing this stakeholder. The blue line indicates the opposite: a stakeholder is assessed as being of lesser importance than the project requires so actions are about upwardly managing this stakeholder. In both cases, the stakeholder actions (or strategies) will be determined to move the stakeholder into the best position for the project's success and these actions will be allocated to project team members for follow-up.

14.5.5 Stakeholder frequency analysis

A simple technique to categorise the amount of frequency of contact a stakeholder requires is to use a diagram similar to Figure 14.10. The figure indicates ellipses with frequency timings (adjust the timings to suit your project environment). Simply dropping a stakeholder into the band promotes thinking with your project team. As project leader you can also stand back and look at the overall loading of frequencies across all stakeholders; if a large proportion of stakeholders require frequent contact, it could affect various dimensions of your project—for example, how much of your time as project leader and the time of the project team will be required to maintain the relationships and communications with the stakeholder? Can these individual stakeholders be consolidated into groups of stakeholders to make management more efficient? Does the project require a dedicated organisational change manager or communications specialist to assist you and the project team?

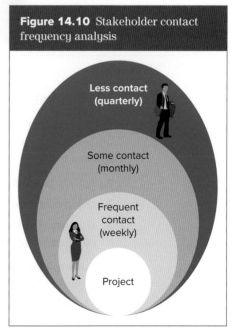

Figure 14.10 Stakeholder contact frequency analysis

Less contact (quarterly)

Some contact (monthly)

Frequent contact (weekly)

Project

© 2022 Dr Neil Pearson

14.5.6 **Stakeholder proximity/priority**

A similar technique can be applied to **stakeholder proximity/priority**. However, with proximity it's important to define what the stakeholder is in proximity to (e.g. a specific deliverable, a stage in the project life cycle or phase). For example, in Figure 14.11 the proximity has been mapped in relation to the "HR kiosk design". Those closest to the proximity context should have a higher priority in that piece of work being undertaken in the project. Red (hot) indicates high proximity (priority), in this case to the HR kiosk design, through to cold (blue), which indicates lower proximity (priority). The stakeholders have also been separated into internal and external, as this may influence our engagement strategies and subsequent communications (refer to Chapter 15 "Project information and communications management").

Figure 14.11 Stakeholder proximity (priority) analysis model

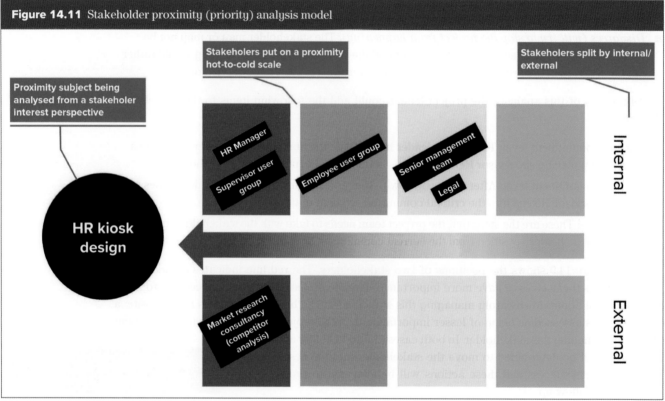

14.5.7 **Salience model**

The stakeholder **salience model** (proposed by Mitchell, Agle & Wood 1997) allows a project leader to further assess the salience or importance of stakeholders relative to the project. The model has three dimensions:

1. *Power:* The authority/influence of a stakeholder on the project (objectives).
2. *Legitimacy:* How genuinely involved a stakeholder is in the project.
3. *Urgency:* The degree to which a stakeholder's requirements call for immediate attention. Consider two factors here—time-sensitivity and criticality.

Refer to Figure 14.12. As a project leader (and team), attention should be given to those stakeholders with power; legitimate claims; and critical, time-sensitive requests (i.e. those stakeholders at the intersection of all three ellipses (dimensions)).

Figure 14.12 Salience model

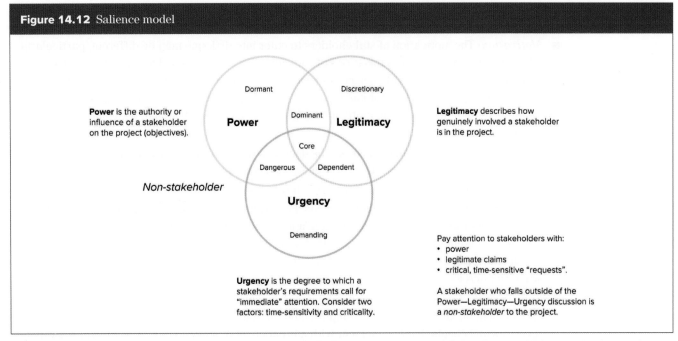

Source: Adapted from https://www.brighthubpm.com/resource-management/81274-what-is-the-salience-model/#the-salience-model-diagram, original concept in Mitchell, Agle, and Wood, Toward a Theory of Stakeholder Identification and Salience: Defining the Principle of Who and What Really Counts (1997, The Academy of Management Review 22, 853–886)

A stakeholder who falls outside the power/legitimacy/urgency discussion is of course a *non-stakeholder* to the project.

It is possible to combine a number of these stakeholder analysis techniques on a single visual; this can assist in thinking integratively within the stakeholder knowledge area and beyond. A good example of this can be found at Stormbal 2016 at https://www.stormbal.com/100/stakeholder-analysis-tool-interest-power-proximity-attitude.

Stakeholder Register

14.6 Engage and monitor stakeholders

No matter what tools are used to identify, and then subsequently analyse, the project's stakeholders, the project leader must be cognisant of the fact that perceptions about stakeholders can change. Some of this change will occur within the project while other changes may occur that are beyond the understanding of the project leader. There are many complexities involved with managing stakeholders, and the tools mentioned in this chapter so far have all been around stakeholder identification and analysis. In the Cranfield University School of Management report *Stakeholder Engagement: A Road Map to Meaningful Engagement*, Neil Jeffery (2009) provides a useful summary of some of the complexities involved in managing stakeholders. Included in his summary are:

■ *Trust:* Trust must be established (often quickly) to gain a healthy stakeholder relationship. It is often the factor that underpins the relationship before other aspects can be truly developed. The building of trust is a fundamental prerequisite to meaningful engagement, as is a focused effort to deepen the level of trust during engagement. One of the greatest steps in building trust is to understand the motivation of your stakeholders.

- *Motivation:* The motivation of stakeholders to enter into dialogue may be different, particularly when the two parties are organisations of radically differing ethos, values and culture (e.g. a commercial company providing services to a project being run by a not-for-profit organisation). In such cases, it is important for each party in the engagement process to recognise, analyse and understand the underlying motivation of the other as a critical step in emphasising and strengthening the relationship.

- *Embeddedness of stakeholder thinking:* The degree to which an organisation can achieve meaningful stakeholder engagement depends on how embedded concepts are across the organisation.

- *The importance of accurate representation:* It is important to achieve accurate representation of all your stakeholders and stakeholder types. For example, if you are engaging with a population mixed across race, religion, gender, region, age, class, sexual orientation and education (or even time-poor stakeholders), it is important that you elicit views that represent this diversity as well as consider effective ways to engage with a cross-section of the stakeholder population, which will differ across groups.

- *Tone from the top:* Appropriate leadership is fundamental in the building of meaningful engagement by an organisation, exemplified by the role of the CEO in convincing employees, investors and clients that engagement with a broader set of stakeholders is worthwhile. Even if an organisation has the appropriate capabilities and organisational culture to allow meaningful engagement to develop, without the approval and active leadership (through both words and deeds) of its CEO, it is unlikely to be successful.

- *Organisational behaviour:* Understanding an organisation and being able to successfully analyse the nature of its organisational behaviour and culture is key to forecasting how engagement with stakeholders will develop, what critical issues and challenges may arise and how meaningful relations may be achieved. Depending on its culture, the organisation may respond in a different way to stakeholders.

- *Non-productive engagement behaviour:* Sometimes non-productive engagement can exist; this is when previous engagement has not produced a positive outcome and therefore has been abandoned by either or both parties. Several challenges can arise from this situation as a result of the engagement issue not being resolved: either it can re-emerge later as a more difficult subject to address, or the abandonment of the issue can further inflame already difficult stakeholder relations.

SNAPSHOT *from* PRACTICE : Complex stakeholder management—a simple solution

A large business change project had to establish a way of tracking stakeholder discussions across a multi-country project team. The project team, because of the stakeholder analysis, had decided to split the management of stakeholders.

Fred managed three executives; Sarah managed another three; and the project leader, Louise, managed a further two. While managing these eight stakeholders, the project team adhered to their project rule that they would only ever liaise with their nominated stakeholders and would never cross-discuss project matters with other team members' stakeholders. This made perfect sense from a stakeholder management perspective in that trust, understanding and engagement were quickly established with the various executives. However, the project team had to work out the technicalities for sharing stakeholder information with the rest of the team members and for allowing a platform for questions to be posted to a nominated project team member, ready for any upcoming meetings that project team member had.

The solution for managing this level of complexity of stakeholder information came in the form of leveraging the functionality of a customer relationship management (CRM) software package. The project adopted vtiger (www.vtiger.com/crm/), a CRM cloud-based software solution, so all stakeholder information could be shared among the project team instantly, with notifications set to gain updates on stakeholders when entries were made in a stakeholder's record.

Some of the complexities that can quickly develop when managing multiple, often senior-level stakeholders are illustrated in "Snapshot from Practice: Complex stakeholder management—a simple solution".

In Chapter 8 "Defining the scope of a project", it was emphasised that ultimate success is not determined by whether the project is completed on time, within budget or according to performance specifications, but whether the customer is satisfied with what has been accomplished. Customer satisfaction is the bottom line.

Customer satisfaction is a complex phenomenon, but one simple (and useful) way of viewing it is in terms of met expectations. According to the *met expectations model*, customer satisfaction is a function of the extent to which the perceived performance (or outcome) exceeds expectations. Mathematically, this relationship can be represented as the ratio between perceived performance and expected performance (see the equation that follows). When performance falls short of expectations (ratio <1), the customer is dissatisfied. If the performance matches expectations (ratio =1), the customer is satisfied. If the performance exceeds expectations (ratio >1), the customer is very satisfied, or even delighted.

$$0.90 \text{ Dissatisfied} = \frac{\text{Perceived performance}}{\text{Expected performance}} = 1.10 \text{ Very satisfied}$$

High customer satisfaction is the goal of most projects. However, profitability is another major concern. For example, completing a construction project two weeks ahead of schedule may involve significant overtime expenses. Similarly, exceeding reliability requirements for a new electronic component may involve considerably more design and debugging effort. Under most circumstances, the most profitable arrangement occurs when the customer's expectations are only slightly exceeded. Returning to the mathematical model: with all other things being equal, one should strive for a satisfaction ratio of 1.05, not 1.5!

The met expectations model of customer satisfaction highlights the point that whether a client is dissatisfied or delighted with a project is not based on hard facts and objective data, but on perceptions and expectations. For example, a customer may be dissatisfied with a project that was completed ahead of schedule and under budget if they thought the work was of poor quality and that their fears and concerns were not adequately addressed. Conversely, a customer may be very satisfied with a project that was over budget and behind schedule if they felt the project team protected their interests and did the best job possible under adverse circumstances.

Project leaders must be skilled at managing customer expectations and perceptions. Too often they deal with these expectations after the fact when they try to alleviate a client's dissatisfaction by carefully explaining why the project cost more or took longer than planned. A more proactive approach is to begin to shape expectations up-front and to accept that this is an ongoing process throughout the life of a project. Project leaders need to direct their attention both to the customer's base expectations (the standard by which perceived performance will be evaluated) and to the customer's perceptions of actual performance. The goal is to educate clients so they can make a valid judgement as to project performance.

Managing customer expectations begins during the preliminary project approval stage of negotiations. It is important to avoid the temptation to oversell the virtues of a project to win approval, because this may create unrealistic expectations that may be too difficult, if not impossible, to achieve. At the same time, project proponents have been known to lower customer expectations by underselling projects. If the estimated completion time is 10 to 12 weeks, they will promise to have the project completed within 12 to 14 weeks, therefore increasing the chances of exceeding customer expectations by getting the project completed early.

From the initiation of the project, through its planning and onto execution, while the project is being monitored and controlled, until its final close-out, stakeholders are integral to almost everything undertaken in the project—in fact the raison d'être of the project is that there is a customer that requires something of value!

In engaging with the stakeholders, the strategies that are being applied are those that the project leader and project team captured in the Stakeholder Register as a result of the identification and subsequent analysis of each stakeholder (individual or group). It is these strategies that are effectively enacted during the stage or phase of the project we happen to be in.

The project leader must remember that stakeholders change due to many circumstances.

- The incumbent of a role might leave the company, and the role (a stakeholder in our project) might not be filled, or not filled within the duration of our project, and we must locate a suitable alternative stakeholder.

- A stakeholder could be promoted in their role. Does this mean they now have more power/interest in the project and start to exert this for their own agenda? Or does this mean they become disinterested in the project and start to block its progress as they now have more pressing matters to attend to?

- A stakeholder could for reasons not determined be a supporter one day and an opponent the next. As a project leader we must in this case quickly find out why their attitude has changed—no doubt a one-to-one meeting at their preferred coffee shop is required!

- A stakeholder's network has changed and has now become a board member at a major contractor to our project. What should we do as a principle-based project leader?

These paragraphs represent but a few of a plethora of reasons why stakeholders change in a project. As a project leader we would be reviewing our initial stakeholder identification, analysis and stakeholder management strategies on an ongoing basis throughout the entire project life cycle and adjusting as stakeholders and stakeholder dynamics change.

Another way of engaging with your stakeholders and gaining raw feedback at selected points in the project is to carry out a survey. A well-constructed stakeholder survey can provide an important feedback loop to the project leader, project team and reassure the project sponsor. A survey template is available online to provide ideas around content for a stakeholder survey, but as with all the templates made available with this text, it should be checked for relevance to your project. Survey responses could be returned anonymously to a drop-box at the Project Management Office or solicited by email.

Stakeholder Survey

These surveys could also be run from an online survey platform such as www.surveymonkey.com or https://crowdsignal.com, for example.

14.7 : Closing stakeholder relationships

Towards the end of the project, or when a certain time event completes, a stakeholder may no longer be required by the project. The project leader should be mindful of these timings and ensure an intentional debrief and thank you is provided. Even if there have been a few bumps in the road, it is, where possible, always best to ensure the relationship is left on good terms. It is surprising how stakeholders come around again in future projects within the organisation, within the industry or even within a geographic region.

Reflect on lessons learned with the stakeholder: What went right? What went wrong? What would we do differently next time? Record these in the project's Lessons Learned Register for future projects.

Summary

Stakeholder management, with all its social and political complexities, can be the crux of many projects.

- Stakeholder management is closely associated with the knowledge area of project communication and information management—and the two are often considered together. Figure 14.1 indicates the cycle of activities that usually take place with each stakeholder—from stakeholder identification through to stakeholder analysis, and the actioning of strategies resulting from this analysis.
- This chapter reviewed several tools that can be leveraged to identify, analyse and manage stakeholders, such as the Power/Interest Grid, the Contribution/Commitment Grid and the concept of stakeholder co-creation.
- Stakeholder management starts from the word *go* on a project and does not end until the project deliverables have been successfully handed over to the business and the project team has been disbanded. As with project communications, stakeholder management can consume a large proportion of the project leader's face-to-face time and energy, but if stakeholders have been selected wisely, this is not wasted time.
- Stakeholder management has close ties with the work being carried out in the area of organisational change management (OCM) (refer to Chapter 5 "Organisational change management and cultures"). As a project leader or a member of a project team, we should be aware of the core OCM reactions we might be observing when meeting with stakeholders and the inferences this has for OCM strategies, stakeholder strategies and stakeholder communications.

Review questions

1. Why would you use multiple ways to identify stakeholders?
2. What is stakeholder co-creation?
3. What information would be included in a typical Stakeholder Register?
4. Why is it important to build trust with stakeholders?
5. What does mapping stakeholders in the Contribution/Commitment Grid enable the project leader to do?
6. What does the salience model enable the project leader to deduct?
7. What is the definition of a stakeholder?
8. What could be included in the Stakeholder Management Plan?

Exercises

1. Idea storm a stakeholder identification technique discussed in this chapter (refer to Figures 14.6(a), (b), (c) and (d)) for a current project you are involved in.
2. On the internet, research additional information on stakeholder co-creation. Look for examples in your industry. Comment on how well your company embraces this kind of thinking.
3. For the stakeholders identified in Exercise 1, apply the stakeholder analysis tool stakeholder proximity (priority): would this have helped you to prioritise stakeholder engagements more effectively?

References

Jeffery N 2009, *Stakeholder Engagement: A Road Map to Meaningful Engagement*, Doughty Centre for Corporate Responsibility, Cranfield School of Management.

Mitchell RK, Agle BR & Wood DJ 1997, "Toward a theory of stakeholder identification and salience: Defining the principle of who and what really counts", *Academy of Management Review*, vol. 22, no. 4, pp. 853–86.

Also, on his own home page https://www.ronaldmitchell.org/publications/Prepub%20version%20SPW.pdf https://www.ronaldmitchell.org (You choose whichever way is easier/cheaper!)

Project Management Institute (PMI) 2017, *A Guide to the Project Management Body of Knowledge*, 6th edition, PMI.

Project Management Institute (PMI) 2021a, *A Guide to the Project Management Body of Knowledge (PMBOK® Guide)*, 7th edition.

Project Management Institute (PMI) 2021b, *The Standard for Project Management (ANSI/PMI 99-001-2021)*, 7th edition.

Yeates D, Cadle J & Paul D 2020, *Business Analysis*, 4th edition, BCS Learning & Development, The Chartered Institute for IT.

CHAPTER 15

Project information and communications management

Learning elements

15A Understand the context for project communications.

15B Be able to apply various communication models to your project communications.

15C Undertake the identification and planning of communications, given the range of stakeholders that exist on a typical project.

15D Understand the different styles and purposes of project reporting.

15E Understand the concept of data, information, knowledge and wisdom (DIKW) and how this manifests in the various project management information flows.

In this chapter

15.1 Introduction

15.2 Background to communications in projects

15.3 Communication models

15.4 Further communication considerations

15.5 The Communications Management Plan

15.6 Planning, developing and tracking communications

15.7 Project reporting

15.8 Project Management Information Systems (PMIS)

Summary

15.1 Introduction

Stakeholders, communications to stakeholders and the sharing of project information are all interconnected. This chapter focuses on the information and communication aspects, as a detailed discussion on project stakeholder management took place in Chapter 14 "Project stakeholder management". To some extent, the assumption leading into this chapter is that most stakeholders we are communicating to would have been identified as a result of stakeholder identification. Subsequent to this, communications planning tends to take place on two fronts:

1. the formal communications planning for communications related to the content of the product, service or result being developed by the project to both internal and external stakeholders (e.g. a newsletter sent to all employees updating them on the upcoming new features of the employee kiosk)

2. in relation to the formal project communications, which relate to the day-to-day running of the project (e.g. an exception project status report prepared and then delivered verbally to the project Steering Committee).

Some of the questions we are trying to answer in relation to stakeholders and project communications include:

- Who needs what information?
- What level of information is required?
- When is the information required?
- Where is the information to be made available?
- Why is the information being provided (what's the purpose)?
- How is the information to be provided (what channels)?

The general activities involved in the workflow of communications have been captured in Figure 15.1.

These activities are explored throughout this chapter. However, let's first look at how the knowledge area of "Project Communications Management" (PMI 2017) now appears in the restructured *A Guide to the Project Management Body of Knowledge (PMBOK® Guide)* and *The Standard for Project Management* (PMI 2021).

PMBOK	Seventh edition updates (PMI 2021)

The PMBOK seventh edition does not include a principle or performance domain specifically on the subject of communications. Communications, however, appears predominately within the Planning Performance and Project Work Performance domains.

The Project Management Institute (PMI), within the "Models, Methods, and Artifacts", also mentions a few models to aid in understanding the theory behind communication (discussed later in this chapter).

A technical project leader becomes very astute at the identification of stakeholders, planning *on paper* the communications required; however, without understanding the theory of communications, all this detailed planning creates, at best, a confused set of stakeholders. The next two sections take a brief tour of the background of communications and subsequently introduce several models to assist us as project leaders in being better communicators. Aside from communications in project management, communication is a huge discipline in its own right; taking the time to brush up on communication skills, learn about new models and trial new social media technologies is an ongoing challenge for project leaders.

Figure 15.1 General project communication activities

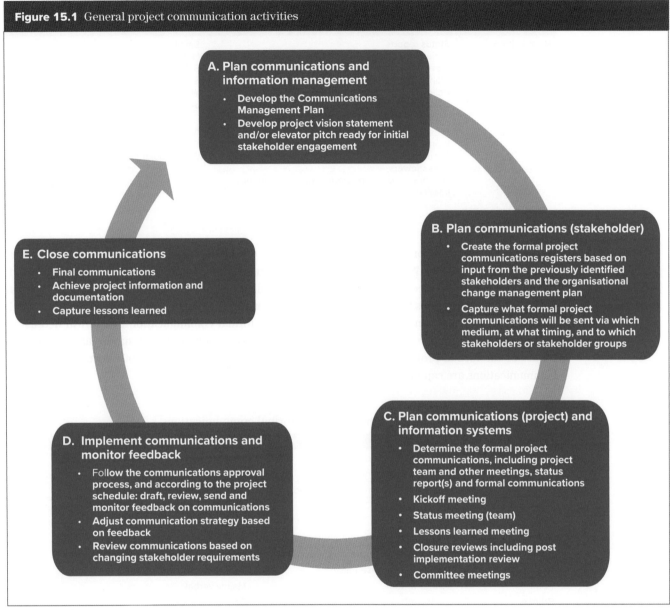

© 2022 Dr Neil Pearson

15.2 | Background to communications in projects

15.2.1 Formal or informal communications

Project leaders should be able to distinguish what messages will require **formal communications** versus **informal communications**. As a project leader we focus on the more formal, point-in-time communications, but at the same time recognise that many and varied informal communications will be taking place between project team members and various stakeholders. Remember: The more (in quantity) formal communications there are on a project, the more tasks will be required to ensure project team members are made responsible for carrying out the authoring, reviewing and approving of communications. Table 15.1 outlines some of more common project formal versus informal communications.

Table 15.1 Project formal and informal communications

	More formal	More informal
More written	Status reports Variation requests Meeting minutes Plans and artefacts Policy, procedures, and guidelines Decision Registers (Meeting) Action Registers	Email Notes SMS/texts Social media (not moderated) Whiteboard notes Sticky notes
More verbal	Presentations Workshops Focus groups Idea showers Demonstrations (e.g. product demonstration) Interviews	Ad hoc discussions Coffice (or coffee shop) meetings Water cooler chats Voicemails or voice messages

© 2022 Dr Neil Pearson

Most of the formal communications are the result of planning communications—for example, it could be a review of the WBS to identify formal communications required at the work package and/or task level in the project design. Informal communications are more ad hoc and spontaneous in nature. On most occasions there would be no requirement to make an informal communication formal; however, an informal communication might require a formal communication to confirm details of, for example, a discussion with promises made, but these are more ad hoc in nature and not usually a part of the formal project communications planning. The characteristics of informal and formal communications are captured in Table 15.2.

Table 15.2 Characteristics of formal versus informal communications

Basis	Formal	Informal
Origin	Deliberately structured	Spontaneous and unstructured
Nature	Planned, systematic and authorised	Unplanned, unsystematic and unauthorised
Flow	Prescribed through chain of command	Unofficial/casual channels
Flexibility	Rigid	Flexible
Authority	Official channels	Unofficial
Purpose	To achieve business requirements	To satisfy personal need
Speed	Takes time to arrange, do and follow up	Fast, often on the spur of the moment
Accuracy	Accurate, legal, representative	Distorted, rumours, gossip
Form	Verbal and written	Mainly verbal
Source	Can be traced	Cannot be traced

© 2022 Dr Neil Pearson

15.2.2 **Communication direction**

Figure 15.2 shows the dimensions of *upwards, downwards, horizontal* and *outward* communications that a project leader must consider when targeting communications to the various levels of an organisation, both internal and external to it. When a message is sent, it can be communicated in different ways—the wording of the communication will often need to be adjusted for each level, as appropriate. The intent of the message will be the same; it will be the direction it is targeted in that differs. For example, senior management in the first instance require compact factual summaries (upwards), peer managers need to know why they must carry out activities (horizontal), employees want to know what's in it for them (downwards), and a customer may need to know critical safety information (outwards).

Figure 15.2 Directions of communication

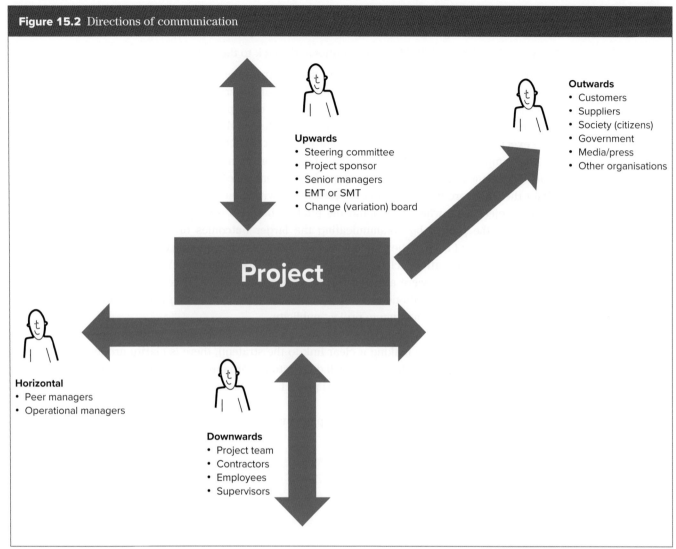

© 2022 Dr Neil Pearson

15.2.3 Pitching the project

Ensuring that everyone in the project team is *singing from the same song sheet* is critical to the project. The authors have been in a position where incongruent, inconsistent and inaccurate stories of the project were received by senior stakeholders from project team members.

At the outset (beginning) of a project, the big picture may unintentionally be forgotten as the project is *chunked* down into its relative components/processes. The simplest and most powerful way to ensure the project team knows and sends a consistent message about the project from the outset is to create a compelling project **elevator pitch (EP).**

An EP is a condensed story of the project that can be delivered (pitched) within 90 seconds. The concept of an EP was initially developed to enable a pitch to be quickly delivered to stakeholders (a captive audience) while travelling up eight floors (of a typical office building) in an elevator. An EP typically answers the following questions (which are embedded within the story of the pitch):

1. What is the *pain point* being experienced?—by the stakeholders

2. Who's sponsoring it and why?—alignment to the organisation's strategy

3. What are the business outcomes?—a vision of the future

4. How are we going to get to these outcomes?—the steps to be taken

5. What's in it for me (WIIFM)?—the emotional tie back to the stakeholder.

Ensuring all project team members are singing from the same song sheet ensures a consistent message is sent by the project. This is a fundamental imperative and yet, quite surprisingly, many projects fail to afford sufficient time to developing a clear project statement that can be repeatedly delivered and understood by any stakeholder (regardless of their role or interest in the project, that is, from executive to on-the-ground subject matter expert (SME)).

An example of good practice was exhibited in a program the author (Pearson) was working on, which was made up from nine other sub-projects. Great success was achieved by not only having an EP for the whole program, but also for each project within the program. This not only ensured clarity for the project team when developing the pitches, but also provided clarity for every stakeholder involved in the project by communicating the larger outcomes of the whole program, and the component focus of each of the projects. The pitches were subsequently captured in a flyer leaflet and left with stakeholders after each meeting. The flyer was also casually left in meeting rooms frequented by peer managers who were affected by the project's outcomes. This example shows the creative side of project communications as the project leader must continually review all methods used for communication to ensure maximum project publicity.

A useful inclusion to have in an EP is the articulation of the link between the project and the organisation's strategy. By making a clear link to the strategy, there is clarity around the origins of the project and the benefits the project will deliver to the organisation. Another technique like the EP was introduced in Chapter 3 "Agile (Scrum) project management", that of the project vision (refer to section 3.5.1 "The product vision").

The online resources include two vision/pitch builders.

Tool—Project Vision Statement

Tool—60" Pitch Builder

15.2.4 Organisational considerations

The project leader, through carrying out such activities as the cultural survey (outlined in Chapter 5 "Organisational change management and cultures") will (hopefully) be able to pick up on the culture and style of communication that predominates in the organisation. These ingrained patterns of communications that have evolved over time could be significant to the project leader in establishing a project norm for communicating with the organisation. It is often more productive to go with the flow of the existing communication approaches than establish new and perhaps challenging approaches to communication. If, for example, the organisation has been operating successfully on the *cascade* style of communication, why would a project leader move to a *pull* model of communications and risk the reputation and success of the project?

15.2.5 Communication challenges

Project communications factors frequently appear on project failure lists. However, to understand more deeply the point of failure is key to ensuring that lessons are learned and not repeated. Unpacking communication issues further could result in identifying some of the more commonly experienced challenges involved with communication, which include the following.

■ *Lack of communication:* Symptoms of lack of communication include *flapping* and statements of uncertainty being made by stakeholders.

■ *Miscommunication:* This can manifest in many forms, for example, by not spending enough time developing and reviewing communications before sending them, or selecting an inappropriate **communication medium**.

■ *Timing of communication:* As with all aspects of communication, the timing of events is critical. If the communication is sent too soon, the message may be forgotten or may lose impact. Send it too late, though, and the receiver(s) may not have sufficient time to make any necessary arrangements. A useful technique from practice is to include communication tasks on the project schedule and highlight these in a differently coloured overlay to indicate the importance of planning, reviewing and sending project communications.

As project leaders, we should acknowledge and leverage aspects of non-verbal communications. **Non-verbal communications** make up around 55 per cent of all communication, so selecting the correct medium is critical to project success. This is especially true during the Initiating and Planning stages of the project, where people first engage with each other within the project environment. Gestures, tone and facial expressions alone can portray a vast range of meanings (which we often miss in the world of social media-driven communication strategies).

Too much communication: Just as there can be a lack of communication or there may be miscommunication, there can also be too much communication; this too can be detrimental to the project. Many employees talk of *information overload syndrome*, where recipients of communications can no longer associate with a specific event, they feel overwhelmed by the volume of communications or the communications are not targeted. It's important therefore that the project leader is selective in what communications are sent, to whom and when—to ensure any communications sent are attended to in an appropriate manner by the receiver of the communication (and not just junked or filtered).

Project communications need to be well planned. Like most elements of project management, quality time spent planning communications is seldom wasted. So, what are some of the benefits of paying careful attention to communication within the project? In their book *Communication: Your Key to Success*, Taylor & Lester (2009) point out some of the potential benefits of having good communication within a project environment (per a project management context), including:

■ reduced conflicts, rumour-mongering, misunderstandings, stress, errors and mistakes

■ increased productivity, motivation, cooperation and success

■ better (smoother) problem-solving, decision-making, image and reputation, and workflow.

The challenge is therefore to ensure a planned and considered approach is taken by the project leader to ensure a successful outcome is achieved with the stakeholders. To assist us in this task, several communication models will be introduced.

15.3 : **Communication models**

As a project leader, having some knowledge about communication theory and practices can greatly assist us in positioning communications, authoring communications and understanding how communications are perhaps perceived by the recipient. This section tackles a few of the more theoretical models and concepts, but they all have practical applications in the project environment.

15.3.1 **Styles of communication**

Stakeholders have differing priorities in how they want to interact with the project. The project will have different priorities on the urgency of the information that comes from it. These priorities must be balanced, this being another consideration in the planning of communications. The PMI promotes three predominant styles of communications:

1. *Interactive communication:* This is often the most common type of communication, where two parties are in direct face-to-face contact (physical or virtual), including most frequently meetings, information-gathering sessions, workshops, focus groups, interviews and idea showers, among many other popular formats. Interactive communication is often referred to as *rich* due to the many dimensions it can take, ranging from the verbals to the non-verbals in communication. The non-verbals are said to make up the larger part of the interaction; consequently, a section is devoted to this topic later in this chapter.

2. *Push communication:* Here communications are pushed from the project. The communication is more directive than consultative in nature and frequently there is little to no loop for feedback. Announcements would be a good example, where the decision has been made (with or without involvement of key stakeholders), with the act of announcing effectively pushing the information onto the recipients. Push communications have a place in projects; however, the project leader should be wary of overusing them. In the event of an urgent communication, if the recipients have been overwhelmed by numerous push communications, our urgent matter could be directed elsewhere.

3. *Pull communication:* Here, stakeholders pull the information they require from published sources. For example, an intranet page could be established where stakeholders are free to pull information as and when required. We of course need to establish what information they require so that it is available to be pulled.

Regardless of the type of communication style employed, a project leader must be cognisant of the complexities that are involved with project communication as an endeavour.

15.3.2 Lines of communication

A frequently encountered communication model to be aware of as a project leader is the **lines of communication**. The larger the project becomes and/or the more stakeholders that become involved in the project, the greater the number of potential lines of communication there will be. Consider the two project teams shown in Figure 15.3 and the potential lines of communication within each.

Calculating the lines of communication is as simple as applying the formula:

$$\frac{n(n-1)}{2}$$

where *n* is the number of people being communicated with.

We can see that Team A has three lines of communication whereas Team B has 10. By adding only two stakeholders into the mix, the lines of communication have increased significantly. Just consider this scenario on a project with dozens of active stakeholders, all of whom must be communicated with, or a project team with tens of people! The principle applies either way.

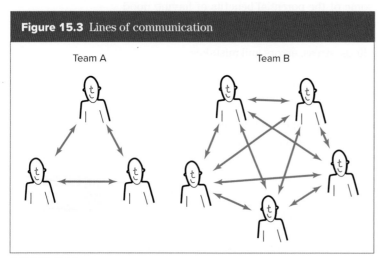

Figure 15.3 Lines of communication

© 2022 Dr Neil Pearson

15.3.3 Sender–receiver model

The discipline of project management often refers to the **sender–receiver model**. This model, sometimes known as the *Shannon and Weaver model* (Verdú & McLaughlin 2000) articulates a simple model of communication. As we know, communication can only take place between two (or more) individuals (or groups). When the sender sends the message, regardless of the medium, the message is open to distortion, deletion, deflection or, more frequently, incorrect translation. Some organisations refer to this as *noise*, meaning that an intended message may not achieve its desired intent (Figure 15.4). Once a message has been received and digested, the receiver will often seek clarification via a feedback loop. In a face-to-face situation the feedback loop can be as simple as the receiver saying, "Can I recap on what we have just agreed?" But if the chosen communication medium is email, how does the receiver confirm or provide constructive feedback? Remember, communication is a two-way process.

Figure 15.4 The sender–receiver model

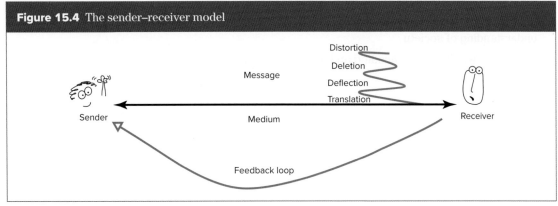

© 2022 Dr Neil Pearson

Although some critics have raised concerns about the Shannon and Weaver model, the author (Pearson) believes that it is situation-dependent in application; therefore, the project leader should also consider:

- the impact if the communication is sent to multiple parties (e.g. a mass email) as the model assumes a one-to-one situation
- potential variations in how the message will be interpreted. *Remember:* A person is an individual and their perspective may differ from the perspective of others. This may also be compounded by cultural and other factors.
- the power-interest relationships of those at the receiving end of the message.

15.3.4 SMCR model (Berlo's model)

The **SMCR model** stands for *source, message, channel, receiver* (see Figure 15.5). The SMCR model accounts for a variety of human variables that are present in person-to-person communications. It is often applied to the communication of emotionally complex messages. There is an assumption in

Figure 15.5 The SMCR model

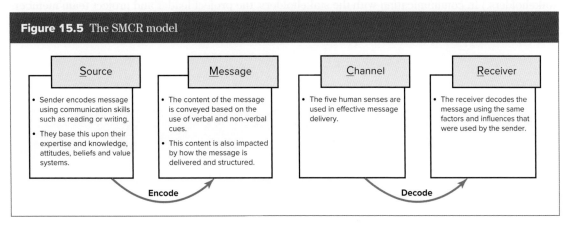

using this model that the receiver should be on the same platform as the sender (to ensure a smooth flow of information). The receiver should have good communication skills to understand what the sender is trying to convey, and have the right attitude and a sufficient level of knowledge to be on par with the receiver.

The sender (or source) encodes the message to be sent. This involves:

- their communication skills—their ability (skills) to communicate (e.g. their reading, writing, speaking and listening skills)
- their attitude towards their audience, towards the subject matter and even towards oneself
- their knowledge about the subject
- their social system—includes their values, beliefs (cultural), their religion and general understanding of society
- the culture within which encoding and decoding take place.

The message consists of:

- content—the content of the message to be delivered
- elements—aspects such as language, gestures and body language
- treatment—the way in which the message is conveyed/delivered
- structure—the structure of the message (i.e. how it is arranged)
- code—how it is sent, and in what form.

The channel provides an understanding of the senses used in the delivery of the message: hearing and sight (and touch, smell, taste) are also a part of the model.

The receiver of the message then decodes the message. All the elements of the sender or source (see above) apply once more, given the assumption of the model, that is, the receiver should be on the same platform as the sender.

Shannon and Weaver's model of communication and the SMCR model provide useful visualisations to assist with understanding the basics of communications theory. They also provide a worthwhile insight into how some forms of communication may be constructed. Although it would be practically impossible to apply the models to every type of formal project communication, the principles of the models nonetheless give a good understanding of the dynamics of the communication process.

So far, this chapter has provided a general background to communication, having looked at some examples of communication models that are often referenced by project leaders. We must bear in mind, however, that before identifying a suitable plan for project communications, the project leader needs to first identify and analyse the project's stakeholders. (Chapter 14 "Project stakeholder management" discussed activities involved in identifying and managing often complex networks of stakeholders.) In communicating with the stakeholders, the project leader and project team members should be aware of the non-verbal side of communications and the importance of picking up on these non-verbals as a part of the holistic approach to communications.

PMBOK ┊ **Seventh edition updates (PMI 2021)**

The sender–receiver and SMCR model are very similar in intent to the **Browaeys and Price model of communication**, which was introduced in the seventh edition of the *PMBOK® Guide* (PMI 2021).

15.3.5 Axes of effectiveness and richness

Alistair Cockburn developed a model that describes the communication channels along the **axes of effectiveness and richness**.

> *To make communications as effective as possible, it is essential to improve the likelihood that the receiver can jump the communication gaps that are always present. The sender needs to touch into the highest level of shared experience with the receiver. The two people should provide constant feedback to each other in this process so that they can detect the extent to which they miss their intention* (Cockburn 2006).

If we refer back to the Agile Manifesto and the principles introduced in Chapter 3 "Agile (Scrum) project management", which Alistair Cockburn later contributed to, we note the manifesto item "Individuals and interactions over processes and tools", and its supporting principles, "Business people and developers must work together daily throughout the project" and "The most efficient and effective method of conveying information to and within a development team is face-to-face conversation" (Agile Manifesto 2001). As the author (Pearson) has said many times to his project team members, "Don't hide behind email, go and see…"

15.3.6 The gulf of execution

In computing, the gulf of execution is a term for the gap between a user's end-goal and the steps they need to take to achieve that goal. To reduce this gap, designers need to limit the number of steps in the process, thereby making the experience more user-friendly. In addition, there is a **gulf of evaluation** (gap) between an external stimulus and the time it takes a person to understand what it means.

In project communications this could be applied to the received communication and the ability of the recipient to execute its contents. The sender–receiver, SMCR and Browaeyss and Price models are more focused on environmental factors surrounding the sending, receiving and comprehension of the message, rather than the execution of its contents.

So, what could we build into a project as a project leader while planning communications to cover off concerns with the gulf of execution? This is where having target users in the business, prototype labs or customer representatives comes in. The author (Pearson), while project leader to a global consolidation project, had nominated in-country representatives, and, as a part of the communications process (documented in the **Communications Management Plan**) the author of any global communication had to ensure a representative (in the country receiving the communication) had thoroughly read and executed the actions in any communications. Although this process took longer to execute, the benefits paid back from the first communication sent—fewer queries and less rework in the project. The gulf of execution had been reduced.

15.4 Further communication considerations

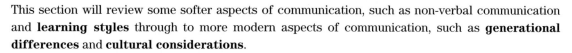

This section will review some softer aspects of communication, such as non-verbal communication and **learning styles** through to more modern aspects of communication, such as **generational differences** and **cultural considerations**.

15.4.1 Non-verbal communications

Albert Mehrabian (who is Professor Emeritus of Psychology at UCLA in the United States) writes about non-verbal communication in the following way:

> *Our speech-orientated culture is just beginning to take note of the profound and overlooked contribution of nonverbal behavior to the processes of communication. This contribution of our actions rather than our speech is especially important, since it is inseparable from the*

feelings that we knowingly or inadvertently project in our everyday social interaction and determines the effectiveness and well-being of our intimate, social, and working relationships.

Mehrabian goes on to suggest that:

People who have a greater awareness of the communicative significance of actions not only can ensure accurate communications of their own feelings but can also be more successful in their intimate relationships, in . . . work that involves the persuasion, leadership, and organization of others (Mehrabian 1972, p. 2).

Mehrabian's 7-38-55 Rule of Personal Communication is illustrated in Figure 15.6. The percentages of 7, 38 and 55 are supported by lists of potential behaviours that might be experienced by a project leader or by a stakeholder during an engagement. In the Barlow sender–receiver model, communications were being sent and received; here, in the 7-38-55 model, what is being sent and received are the non-verbal cues.

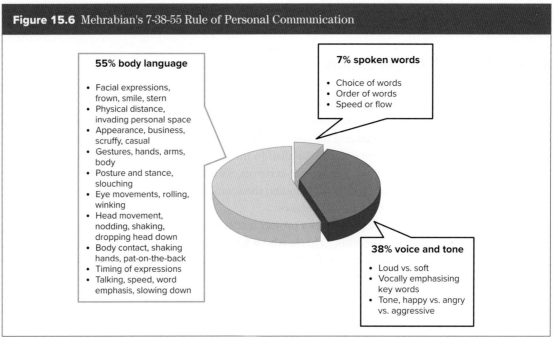

Figure 15.6 Mehrabian's 7-38-55 Rule of Personal Communication

55% body language
- Facial expressions, frown, smile, stern
- Physical distance, invading personal space
- Appearance, business, scruffy, casual
- Gestures, hands, arms, body
- Posture and stance, slouching
- Eye movements, rolling, winking
- Head movement, nodding, shaking, dropping head down
- Body contact, shaking hands, pat-on-the-back
- Timing of expressions
- Talking, speed, word emphasis, slowing down

7% spoken words
- Choice of words
- Order of words
- Speed or flow

38% voice and tone
- Loud vs. soft
- Vocally emphasising key words
- Tone, happy vs. angry vs. aggressive

© 2022 Dr Neil Pearson

Source: © Mehrabian 1972. List of traits compiled by Dr Neil Pearson 2018

Non-verbal cues are classified as: touch (haptics), body language (kinesics), distance (proxemics) and voice (paralanguage). Bearing this in mind, reflect on how you, as project leader, might interpret what is being communicated in the following scenario:

A stakeholder is sitting across the table from you with their arms folded, and they are predominately looking at people who are walking past the glass-walled meeting room. The stakeholder glances at you briefly from time to time. Their notepad is closed and their pen rests on top of it. In response to your question, "How are you feeling about working with me on this project?", they say, "I really want to work with you in this project". What do you as the project leader read into this situation? What's the non-verbal takeaway message(s) potentially being communicated? Why did we not pick up on the signals and address them in the moment?

There is a dichotomy of behaviours going on here, both verbal and non-verbal and so you, as project leader, would need to probe further to establish whether your hunch is correct.

The PMI recognises the importance of non-verbal communication. It makes various references to non-verbal communication, including:

- as a must-have skill of the project leader
- in dealing with stakeholders
- in communications.

There are many examples of non-verbal communications, including body language, eye movement, physical gestures, voice tone and facial expressions. The art of picking up cues used in non-verbal communication is captured in the **neuro-linguistic programming (NLP)** approach. NLP is "used for personal development and for success in business. NLP is the practice of understanding how people organise their thinking, feeling, language and behaviour to produce the results they do" (NLP Academy 2018).

When you next meet with stakeholders, project team members or the project sponsor, in your role as project leader, try to be cognisant of not only what they are verbally saying to you, but also what their non-verbal cues may be telling you about what they are really thinking! Even when trained in the art of NLP, being able to practise NLP skills in the moment can take time to master. However, it is a communication skill that can help to provide a well-rounded understanding of what a person is saying and what they are indirectly saying (therefore communicating), which can help to foster a more in-depth understanding of their true message and move towards a more trusting relationship with your stakeholders.

15.4.2 Learning styles: visual, auditory, kinesthetic (VAK) model

There are many different learning styles. Getting the best out of people necessitates being able to assess and understand how project team members, the project sponsor and other stakeholders learn. This knowledge can benefit a project leader as it means they can tailor communications to be more engaging for their audience.

Fernald, Keller, Orton, Gillingham, Stillman and Montessori were some of the first psychologists and teaching specialists to develop what is popularly known as the *visual, auditory, kinesthetic (VAK)* model in the 1920s. The model depicts how individual learning styles influence the way a person learns and postulates the distribution of learning styles found in the general population. Figure 15.7 illustrates the observed reported styles of learning.

If a project leader is struggling to communicate effectively with a group of individuals (or a single individual), they should consider whether this is because the person(s) doesn't fall into the 65 per cent population group of visual learners, but instead naturally uses either an auditory or a kinesthetic style of learning. This fascinating area of work became a research focus for Neil Fleming (of New Zealand). In 1987 Fleming became the first person to systematically present a series of questions that could be used by teachers, students and employees to work out individual learning styles. Fleming added a fourth mode—*reading/writing*—and the model became known as VARK (Vark Learn 2018).

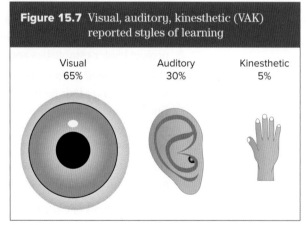

Figure 15.7 Visual, auditory, kinesthetic (VAK) reported styles of learning

Visual 65%   Auditory 30%   Kinesthetic 5%

© 2022 Dr Neil Pearson

Fleming's VARK questionnaire can be accessed at: http://vark-learn.com/the-vark-questionnaire/. It is helpful for investigating situations such as the one outlined previously. Why not try the survey for yourself and investigate your own learning style?

Bearing in mind earlier discussions about non-verbal cues, let's now consider how an individual's learning style could potentially be revealed by their use of non-verbal cues. Look at Table 15.3 for some suggestions—remember the NLP approach introduced earlier in this section, which would teach you how to pick up on such cues.

Table 15.3 What VAK can help to tell us about stakeholders

Learning style	Watch their eyes	Listen to what they say
Visual (see it)	Looking upwards	I get the picture. I can visualise that. I see how it works! I see the landscape you're working in ...
Auditory (hear it)	Looking straight ahead	That rings a bell! Sounds good to me. I hear what you're saying.
Kinesthetic (do it)	Looking downwards	That feels about right. How does that grab you? Let me try ...

© 2022 Dr Neil Pearson

15.4.3 **Generational communications**

In a typical organisation there could be up to five different generations working side by side in the workplace. Project leaders will have to create environments where multiple ways to communicate will exist to ensure engagement occurs successfully across the generations. This will necessitate being cognisant of different communication styles and preferences, given that each person is highly likely to be more comfortable using the communication style that their generation grew up with.

Table 15.4 represents commentary that has been collected from various resources. It is presented as a heads-up for project leaders regarding what to be cognisant of when they are involved in working out information and communication requirements in a project environment.

Note: It is important that the project leader always consults with the project team directly to ascertain and agree on the overall preferred information and communication style.

15.4.4 **Cultural differences**

The topic of culture has been discussed in Chapter 5 "Organisational change management and cultures". Three perspectives of culture often experienced by project leaders are as follows.

1. *Project culture:* This is established by the project leader to build an open, honest, transparent and trusted environment that project team members and engaged stakeholders can work within. The project leader establishes and enforces the project culture.

2. *Organisational culture:* This comprises the values, structures, politics, agendas and leadership styles (among other factors) that influence the project culture (and the culture into which the final product, service or result will be deployed). The project leader has limited control over the organisation's culture but may be able to influence it in a positive manner through the good behaviours of the project team.

3. *International cultures:* This impacts how stakeholders behave and how information is interpreted across international boundaries.

These *perspectives of culture* will influence all types of communication:

■ *Written report or document:* This includes the words used and how these are translated (interpreted) by the receiver, whose native language might not be the same as the sender's.

■ *Face-to-face meeting (where a nod might mean no!):* Differences in cultural non-verbal cues should be thoroughly researched and understood before face-to-face engagement to prevent any potentially embarrassing faux pas and misunderstandings occurring.

■ *Virtual meeting:* If one of the communication *feedback channels* is missing (e.g. non-verbal cues cannot be seen), how can we be sure that discussions are being interpreted correctly by either party?

Contemporary project leaders must consider at least all the above aspects when developing the strategy to be used for information sharing and for communication (as documented in the Communications Management Plan). This also applies to the development of the communications

Table 15.4 Information and communication preferences across generations

Generation	Silent generation (traditionalists) 1925–45	Baby boomers 1945–60	Generation X 1961–80	Generation Y (millennials) 1981–95	Generation Z ("I" generation) 1995–2010	Generation Alpha 2010–present day
Date range (approx.)	Silent generation (traditionalists) 1925–45	Baby boomers 1945–60	Generation X 1961–80	Generation Y (millennials) 1981–95	Generation Z ("I" generation) 1995–2010	Generation Alpha 2010–present day
Defining events and technology associated with the generation	■ Automobile ■ Wartime rationing ■ Defined gender roles	■ Television ■ Landing on the moon ■ Cold War ■ Freedom of speech ■ The nuclear family ■ Nuclear arms race and superpower play-offs	■ Personal computer ■ Compact disc ■ Early mobile technology ■ Dual incomes and greater independence from the nuclear family ■ Dial-up internet	■ Tablets and smart phones ■ 9/11 ■ Reality TV ■ Google ■ Online social movement groups ■ Born into the internet (*digital natives*) ■ High-speed internet	■ Artificial intelligence ■ 3D printing ■ Global warming ■ Crowdsourcing ■ Social media ■ Always-on internet (over mobile data) and social media platforms	■ Streaming technology ■ Virtual world through to metaverse
Communication trends	■ Formal letters written communications	■ Telephone	■ eMail and text messages (SMS)	■ Text messages and social media	■ Hand-held communication devices	■ Virtual over face to face
Career expectations	■ Job for life, security, loyalty to the organisation	■ Organisational careers, loyal to the company, climbing the corporate ladder, ability to work from home	■ Loyal to the profession, not the employer ■ More flexibility in working arrangements	■ Entrepreneurs ■ Digital working ■ Dependence on instant feedback and gratification ■ Over-compensated	■ Pop-up businesses ■ Move around organisations freely and frequently ■ Confident but without experience	
Meeting medium	■ Face-to-face, let's have a conversation	■ Call me on my phone, and let's have a conversation	■ Online—send me an email and we can meet if required	■ Online face-to-face conferencing ■ Information length and depth starts to reduce—a move to Google approach; don't waste time on details	■ Online, social media ■ Smaller, and small chunks of information without depth ■ Social consequence of online communication decreasing the ability to successfully meet face-to-face in a business environment	■ Have only known the 21st century ■ Brought up with technology in their hand ■ Heavily influenced by digital communications of many mediums ■ Snapchat and TikTok

SNAPSHOT *from* PRACTICE   Culture shock!

One of the authors of this book (Pearson) was involved in a strategic planning project for a Pacific Island community which involved working with government staff and community stakeholders. After the project had concluded, he reflected on lessons he had learned about information and communication management by contemplating the following questions.

What went well?

1. *Meetings:* Trying to arrange face-to-face meetings with some of the stakeholders was difficult. What was found to work well was physically getting out of the office to meet stakeholders on their own turf. Despite it being a very hot and humid climate, making the effort to go out to the environments in which stakeholders lived and worked exhibited commitment and a willingness to experience and take part in their culture. This garnered their respect and buy-in to the project.

2. *Communication with language:* Recognising and adjusting to the fact that English was a second language on the Island when seeking ideas about how to communicate the final outcomes of the project. As a result, it was agreed that it would be culturally accepted if the final presentation was made to the whole department at various morning teas using a narrated PowerPoint. The stakeholders felt respect was demonstrated for their input to the project by being invited to the morning teas and narration was carried out by various members of the community to demonstrate buy-in. Photographs were used in the presentation to illustrate the relevance and benefits of the project to the community.

3. *Communication beyond the written word:* It was necessary to think outside the box about how to communicate with some stakeholders as some did not read English. This had the potential to render communication about some ideas challenging for the project leader, but he adapted his communication style to the situation by using descriptive narrations, visuals (photographs, drawings), non-verbal cues, stories and making sure that verbal communication took precedence over any written report or annotated chart.

What didn't go so well?

■ It was difficult to foster a deep understanding of existing island politics and the hierarchical clan-based culture that existed. It made the project feel like it had only a cursory understanding of the environment. Given the short period of time that the author was in contact with stakeholders, a lot of cultural information had to be absorbed and acted upon correctly.

What could be done better next time?

■ To deeper understand the actual ability of the managers to achieve corporate targets in what was at times a tough environment (politically, culturally, physically and environmentally)—where targets had never realistically been applied to any role in the past.

Successful communication was possible because trust was developed between the project leader and the community (stakeholders). To build this trust, the assistance of respected community members (including several elders) was gained, and they came together to deliver the key project messages to their departments and the wider community. In addition, a script was created for the final presentation, which local people took turns to narrate (each representing an allocated government department/area of interest). Although a simple idea, the cross-engagement between community and government (departments) created a positive rapport and a commitment to the project's goal. This, in turn, helped to break down some barriers between the community and government officials.

Figure 15.8 shows a sample slide (one of many) from the final presentation, which was narrated by a government department member who was also a part of the island community.

Taking the time to find out about a stakeholder's preferred way of receiving and sharing information, for example, by asking them some simple questions when you meet them, can facilitate successful ongoing project communication. For example, it's easy to ask them whether they would like to have information on the project shared in the form of a status report or a short weekly meeting.

Figure 15.8 Example of a narrated slide, as used during the final communication stage

THEMES TO DELIVER OUR OBJECTIVES

Community Engagement

This theme encompasses greater transparency and engagement of the community by establishing repeatable communication channels. Providing Sections with a platform to engage and share information with the community on available services.

© 2022 Dr Neil Pearson

themselves (as documented in the **Communications Register**). Project leaders must take care to ensure that messages are not lost in translation and should work towards all communications being as culturally and linguistically unambiguous and neutral as possible, so as not to unintentionally put stakeholders off-side. This can be tricky to achieve, and miscommunication and misinterpretation are regularly cited as reasons for projects failing because of poor communications.

Planning and addressing how project communications will take place with the various stakeholder groups is sometimes either overlooked or has insufficient attention paid to it. Care and attention need to be devoted to development of the **Communications Management Plan** (discussed later in this chapter) and the associated project communication documents (such as the Communications Register) to ensure the mediums, tools, methods, timing and hierarchies of communication are fully understood and documented for later development and distribution during the Executing stage of the project.

15.5 The Communications Management Plan

As with the previous knowledge areas that have been discussed, a management plan should be developed before planning and developing communications. The Communications Management Plan is typically developed during the Planning stage of the project. Artefacts such as the Stakeholder Register and a communications risk analysis would typically be considered within the Initiating stage of the project.

A typical Communications Management Plan includes the following sections.

1. *Communications strategy and approach:* This section of the plan describes the general strategy and approach to communications management within the project. For example, in a community-based project, you would describe what the general approach to communicating with the community will be. *Note:* This is not the place for detailed communications identification and planning, as this takes place in the Communications Register (discussed later in this chapter). The intention here is to conceptualise the overall approach to be taken with individuals and groups both internal or external to the organisation.

2. *Policy and procedure:* Identify any relevant organisational communication and marketing policies and procedures that must be applied within the project environment. The organisation may have style guides that have to be followed for all corporate internal, and most certainly external, communications. There may also be guidelines on the use of logos or trademarks and processes to follow in relation to the development of any external communication collateral.

3. *Project reporting arrangements:* Detail the project reporting requirements, including all status reports that are to be generated by the project, who these are for, and their frequency (see Table 15.5 for an example). *Note:* It is common practice to include blank template reports as appendices to the Communications Management Plan, the format of these reports having been agreed by the project leader and the recipient of the report.

Table 15.5 Project reporting requirements

Report	Who	Frequency	Format
Executive tracking report	Executive management	Monthly	Refer CMP Appendix X
Project status report	Project Management Office	Fortnightly	Refer CMP Appendix Y
Team progress report	Project team	Weekly	Refer CMP Appendix Z

© 2022 Dr Neil Pearson

Note: CMP = Communications Management Plan

4. *Project team directory:* In addition to the stakeholder contact information contained in the Stakeholder Register, it is useful to capture all the project team's contact details. This may include phone numbers and email addresses not available outside the project team. Another useful aspect to consider is the contact's availability. For example, does the project require a 24/7 contact person or (alternatively) on-call arrangements? A simple table (as illustrated in Table 15.6) would

suffice for this. The authors have experienced times on projects where the availability of key project staff during go-live weekends (e.g. of large ICT systems) is required. It is therefore useful to capture formal details of these arrangements within the Communications Management Plan.

Table 15.6 Project team contact information

Role	Name	Email(s)	Phone number(s)	Availability
Project leader	Sarah Jones	s.jones@company.com.au	+ 61 XXXX XXX XXX	8 am – 8 pm incl. weekends
Project officer	John Smith	j.smith@company.com.au	+ 61 XXXX XXX XXX	8 am – 4 pm weekdays only
Database administrator	Ellen Jones	e.jones@company.com.au	+ 61 XXXX XXX XXX	On-call 24/7

© 2022 Dr Neil Pearson

5. *Committee/project meeting arrangements:* Identify and document the project's formal meetings (e.g. who is to attend and the frequency and format of the meetings). Refer to Table 15.7 for an example. Also include a **committee charter** for each committee as an appendix to the Communications Management Plan (once developed and agreed by the committee). In addition to the committee's objectives, the charter should include the quorum of people required and motions to be passed/decisions to be made at the meeting. Another good practice is to schedule the meetings for the life of the project at the outset, using the organisation's calendar system. This gives maximum notice to required meeting attendees, with the aim of hopefully avoiding conflicts with their availability as the project progresses.

Table 15.7 Project meeting(s) schedule

Meeting	Who	Frequency	Format	Charter, agenda, or other documents
Team meeting	Project team Project leader	Weekly	Fridays Calendar invites established Apologies to the project leader	Refer to Team Meeting Agenda, Appendix X*
Technical review meeting	Project leader SME Project technical lead	Fortnightly	As required project technical lead to build relationships with SME	Refer to CMP Appendix X

© 2022 Dr Neil Pearson

Note: CMP = Communications Management Plan; SME = subject matter expert

* A team meeting agenda and meeting effectiveness scoring system is included in the online resources.

 Project Team Meeting Standing Agenda

6. *Communication roles and responsibilities:* This section should describe all the roles and responsibilities of the communications function within the project. This could be presented as a narrative; or a supporting category could be created in the project-wide RASCI (discussed in Chapter 7 "Governance and projects") and either cut and pasted into this document or referenced from this document. Refer to Table 15.8 for an example of a RASCI covering two simple business rules.

Table 15.8 Communication RASCI

					Role					
Ref.	Rule/Decision	Category	Comments	Sponsor	Project leader	Project support	Project Steering Committee	Supplier	Corporate communications	Project communications manager
23.	Approval of communications to external suppliers	Communications			A	R		I	C	R
24.	Approval of external community engagement communications	Communications		C	C	R	I		A	R

© 2022 Dr Neil Pearson

7. *Communication review process:* As illustrated in the simple flowchart in Figure 15.9, documenting the review process up front ensures that the message has the best chance of being received in the manner it was intended. This is especially important for formal communications.

Figure 15.9 Communication review process

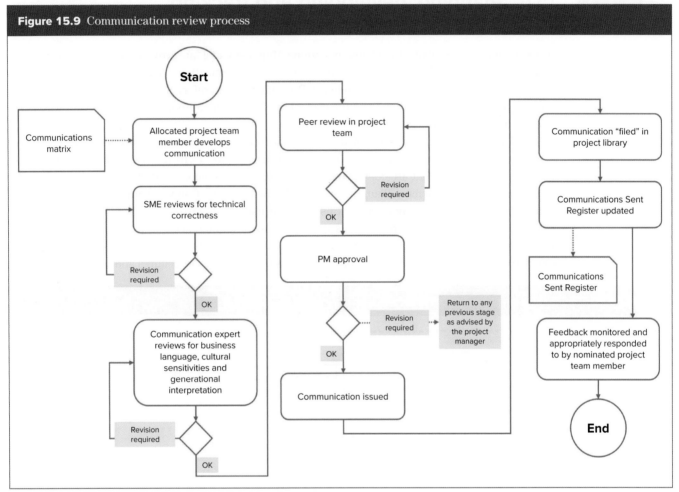

© 2022 Dr Neil Pearson

8. ***Project Management Information System (PMIS):*** The PMIS details the project's information management systems to be used within the project. This could range from corporate ICT systems to more specific project-related information systems. The project leader should also consider the security of access to these systems, as much of this information will be confidential to the project team, or even to specific roles within the project team.

9. *Risk review:* Review any communication activities to be carried out and identify risks. Ensure these are captured within the project's Risk Register. Either reflect those risks in this part of the Communications Management Plan or make reference to the Risk Register.

10. *Lessons learned:* Ensure that a review of any lessons learned from prior similar projects is carried out and that any relevant lessons learned are entered into the Lessons Learned Register under the category of "Communications". Alternatively, document the communications lessons learned directly within the Communications Management Plan.

Numerous project details will have to be raised, discussed and resolved when defining the Communications Management Plan. Documenting these within the Communications Management Plan will provide a point of reference for everyone in the project team.

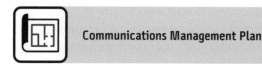

Communications Management Plan

15.6 Planning, developing and tracking communications

Previous discussions about the Communications Management Plan provided guidance around the governance, processes, roles and responsibilities of communications. These earlier discussions in developing the Communications Management Plan will have therefore paved the way to the planning of each (formal) communication from the project, including who authors the message and who is the receiver of the message.

The Stakeholder Register (a detailed list of what formal communications are planned to be sent) is a good place to start a review of communications. Figure 15.10 illustrates the typical project management artefacts that are considered at this stage in the communication planning process—the Communications Management Plan, the Stakeholder Register, the Communications Register (planned communications) and the **Communications Sent Register** (a library of sent communications). *Note:* Many other project management artefacts also input into the communications planning process, such as the scope document, Organisational Change Management Plan, cultural assessment, **work breakdown structure (WBS)** and organisational process assets (e.g. policies, procedures and guidelines).

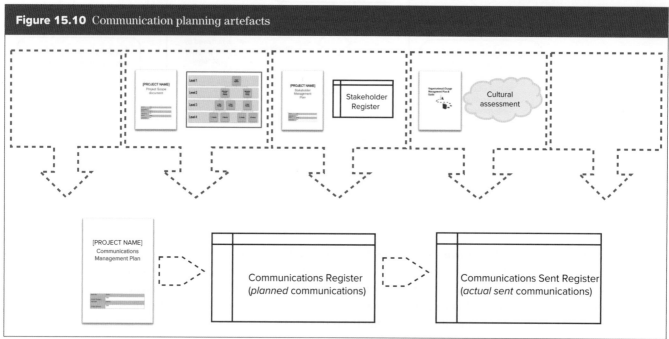

Figure 15.10 Communication planning artefacts

It is important to note that for simple projects, there is normally a strong correlation between planned communications and identified stakeholders. However, in more complex projects, there may be other project communications that cut across different groups of stakeholders to present a unified message. The starting point for this next planning activity is assumed to be the Stakeholder Register (i.e. a list of all stakeholders who have a stake in the project). Building the Stakeholder Register was discussed in detail in Chapter 14 "Project stakeholder management".

The Communications Register helps the project leader to identify and capture formal communications that are planned to take place against each stakeholder. Refer to Table 15.9 for a simplified example of a Communications Register.

Table 15.9 Example of a Communications Register

Stakeholder	Message	Medium	Frequency	Feedback channel	Author	Approver	Direction
Sponsor	Project status report	Status report template via email	Weekly (Thursday)	Email to project leader	Project officer	Project leader	Project → stakeholder
Supplier (software development agency)	Burndown chart	Approved template via email	Daily	Project leader collator for supplier feedback	Supplier	Supplier	Supplier → project
User group	Project newsletter	Intranet site	Weekly	Email to project officer	Project officer	Project leader	Project → stakeholder
Project Management Office	Project status report	Status report template via email	Weekly (Friday)	Email to project leader	Project officer	Project leader	Project → stakeholder

© 2022 Dr Neil Pearson

Some of the main information that might be captured within the Communications Register is explored in the following list.

1. *Message sending:* This is probably the most important field as it should describe WHY and WHAT message is being sent. For example, "status update" does not provide the WHY, and a more suitable response could be "Weekly progress reports on an informal basis to enable a swifter decision process".

2. *Stage:* Captures the project life cycle stage within which the communication is planned to be sent (or all stages). By reviewing the planned communications by stage, the project leader can assess the total communication commitment required by the project. This in turn may influence decisions around what communication assistance might be required.

3. *Responsible for authoring:* Who in the project team is responsible for writing the communication? If the project leader decides to add tasks to the schedule (and/or WBS), requiring a communication be prepared, the responsible resource can then be allocated to the task.

4. *Reviewer:* Who in the project team or in the general business community is to review the message? Referring to the communication models introduced earlier, if the project leader can bring stakeholders in the business on board to review (from the business perspective) the communications being sent from the project, this should (in theory) narrow the gap between the sender and the receiver.

5. *Approver:* Who in the project team is responsible for signing off the communication? (In most circumstances, this would be the project leader.)

6. *Method of feedback:* The simple sender–receiver model of communication highlighted the notion of a feedback loop (Figure 15.4). The planned method of feedback should be captured against each communication and appropriate arrangements made for reviewing and actioning this feedback.

   Some common channels for receiving feedback from the stakeholder include:

   ■ phone—calling a project team member directly

   ■ email—to an individual project team member's email account or, which is often more frequently preferred, to a generic email account that can be monitored by any nominated project team member

   ■ call centre—in some large projects, the organisation's internal or external service desk might be briefed to answer calls

   ■ social media—if social media channels have been established by the project (e.g. in a large community-based project targeting generations Y and Z and Alpha), these will need constant monitoring.

7. *Responsible for monitoring feedback:* The person(s) nominated (with regard to number 6 in this list) would be responsible for monitoring feedback and for taking appropriate actions.

8. *Medium(s):* The selected medium(s) for the communication. Potential mediums could include email, fax, phone, web conference, videoconference, voice conference, social media, TV, radio, newspapers, flyers, posters, internet sites, intranet sites, signs, SMS, leaflet drops and face-to-face communication (individual or groups).

9. *Frequency:* The frequency of communication (e.g. daily, weekly, monthly, ad hoc).

10. *Costs:* Capturing the costs associated with the communication: In some projects, these could be substantial and would therefore have implications to the project budget (remember your integrative thinking!)

Refer to the online template to review this and further information which can be captured while planning communications.

 Communications Register

So where are communications sourced from? Many techniques can be used for identifying communication requirements, including the following.

■ *Sourcing from the Stakeholder Register:* This (as indicated in Figure 15.11) is the most popular method. Most stakeholder engagements require some formal project communications.

■ *Sourcing from the WBS:* In reviewing the WBS (the deliverable, work packages and tasks), the project team are often able to identify various communications requirements associated with the deliverable or work package or task.

■ *Scope document:* The project leader should always consider the original project scope and any commitments made in the scope document that require a communication consideration.

■ *Communications manager:* A different perspective might be achieved about project communications if a communication specialist is brought into the project. For example, perhaps a more holistic big-picture view of the project may be gained that had not been successfully captured in any of the detailed individual stakeholder communications. Some projects employ full-time communications managers while others bring in the organisation's corporate communications manager to review the Communications Management Plan and Communications Register, to receive impartial feedback.

■ *Organisational change manager:* Integration of organisational change management (OCM) activities and communications with the core activities must take place. Otherwise, there could be duplicate messages being sent, conflicting messages being sent, or confusion created by not taking a consolidated approach to communications holistically across all project activities.

■ *From the project team:* Leverage the team and their growing relationships with stakeholders to input into the planning of communications.

In developing the Communication Register, you will notice that there are various **multiplicities of communication**. Typically, a communication multiplicity takes on one of three types, as indicated in Figure 15.11.

During the Initiation and Planning stages of the project, identifying communications (while potentially carrying out communications) is a critical aspect of managing the project. Communications is a discipline in its own right, so any professional assistance that can be brought into the project environment will aid the overall writing, validating and distribution of its communications.

One of the authors (Pearson) has experienced projects where key formal communications have been outlined, drafted, reviewed and agreed while building the Communications Register—we know what is expected to occur at certain points in the project, so using idle time early on can make for timely communications later on in the project. This takes the planning of communications to a new level and is a definite move away from reactive communications.

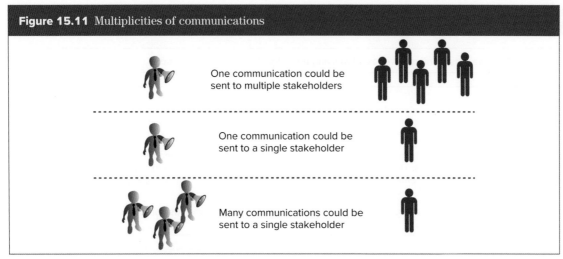

Figure 15.11 Multiplicities of communications

One communication could be sent to multiple stakeholders

One communication could be sent to a single stakeholder

Many communications could be sent to a single stakeholder

© 2022 Dr Neil Pearson

15.6.1 Developing communications

Communications are typically developed (written) in the Executing stage of the project as they become due in line with the project schedule. Many models exist that provide structure around the development of the communication content. These models include **CPORT** and the **4Cs**.

15.6.1.1 CPORT

CPORT is a simple set of guidelines developed out of practice to assist in the development of communications. CPORT stands for:

- **C**ontext of the communication
- **P**urpose of the communication
- **O**bjectives of the communication
- **R**esources affected by the communication
- **T**iming—when do the effects of the communication take place?

CPORT acts as a checklist in the development of the communication. It is very much medium-independent so can be applied to any communication (Figure 15.12).

15.6.1.2 The 4Cs

In a similar vein to CPORT are the 4Cs of truth about communication.

The 4Cs of truth about communication are more substantial in nature than CPORT, and are the subject matter of *The 4Cs of Truth about Communication* (Albanese 2007). Albanese describes the 4Cs in the following way.

1. *Comprehension is the first C:* Your message or ad needs to be quickly comprehended by your intended target. If you have to explain what your advertising or marketing message means, it has probably missed the mark with limited impact.

2. *Credibility is the second C:* Your brand's message must make sense to the consumers relative to the way they perceive it. Consumers are smart and if you serve up a context for thinking about your brand that is completely implausible, you will lose them immediately.

3. *Connection is the third C:* Consumers need to feel your message; they need to make a personal connection with what you are saying. They need to viscerally respond, "That's me!"

4. *Contagiousness is the fourth C:* Consumers need to feel energised and motivated to do something based on your message—whether it's to pass on to their friends and colleagues, to think about your brand in a different way, to find out more information—whatever—they need to act (Albanese 2007).

Figure 15.12 CPORT style of communication

Subject: XXX: Project Name: 20 characters of informative text identifying the subject of the communication.

- Where XXX is one of:
- A: = Action Required
- FYI: = For Your Information
- U: = Urgent Action Required

The format of the email included the following headings. *Note:* These took on a CPORT style but were modelled on the sender–receiver model (i.e. a feedback loop was provided). The headings in the email were left so the reader could easily locate the information in the email. Further to this, the whole email had to fit within an 800 × 600 screen size with the complete message having to be visible without the receiver having to scroll.

This template and the guidelines for its use were captured in the Communications Management Plan as part of the communications strategy for the project.

What is being announced?
A short paragraph clearly describing the announcement.

Who is affected?
The people affected by the communication. As the organisation did not have a comprehensive distribution list, it was decided to send communications to the whole stakeholder group (i.e. the 15 000 employees), and to include this section of the email to indicate the various roles that would be affected by the communication.

When will it take place?
In this section a long date format and Coordinated Universal Time (UTC) were used. Additionally, a link was provided to a time-converter website, giving the receiver the ability to calculate the date and time of the communication in their local country's time zone.

Where do I go for further information?
As the email message was constrained in length, the detailed instructions were developed in Microsoft® Word, exported to a PDF that was uploaded to the project's intranet site and a link (tested first!) inserted into the communication.

Who do I contact for further information?
In the majority of cases, this was always a real person and contact phone number. This was supported by a reply-to generic email address that was set up specifically for project communications.

© 2022 Dr Neil Pearson

SNAPSHOT *from* PRACTICE   **Mass email communications**

The consolidation of information and communication technology systems is always on the books of many large corporations. One of the authors (Pearson) had the experience of working on a large consolidation project, involving the consolidation of a customer ticketing system that was used by tens of thousands of customers, and supported internally by a user base of 15 000 employees (at all levels across the organisation).

Communicating internally with 15 000 employees provided an interesting challenge from the outset. Employees were located around the globe and were from a multitude of multinational and multicultural backgrounds—but the business language was English. It was soon discovered, through delivering project communications, that English is not interpreted in the same way across the globe! To ensure a clearly identifiable project image, the author put together a standard format for all email communications, which included:

- an identifiable project logo and project name, to enable the user base to identify formal project communications above any noise in the business

- an intranet site containing project information, copies of communications, frequently asked questions (FAQs) and detailed technical and business process documents

- a pre-communicated format for emails. This was the most successful element of communications in the project. The format of emails was predetermined by the project (refer to the mock-up in Figure 15.13), and this was communicated to all 15 000 employees on the distribution list

- a communications manager and a review process that included business representatives from key countries across the globe.

CPORT and the 4Cs provide a good basis for constructing the communications message. (Recall that a communications review and approval process was included in the Communications Management Plan.) From experience we know that no matter how well the project thinks it has prepared a communication, the acid test will come from those who receive the communication; hence, the importance of establishing a review process that includes input from representative stakeholders in the business. You can read about the application of CPORT and the 4Cs to a large back-office consolidation project in "Snapshot from Practice: Mass email communications".

As can be imagined, the number of formal communications sent from a project across all mediums can be quite extensive.

Communications Message

15.6.2 Tracking sent communications

Keeping a record of sent communications is just as critical as planning the communications in the first place. How many times have you, as project leader, been asked to go back to a communication sent three months ago on a project? How did you locate it? How much time did it take to find out who it was sent to?

A handy resource a project leader may want to create is a simple Communications Sent Register that can be used to record all formal communications sent from the project. Table 15.10 illustrates this kind of register.

Table 15.10 Simple Communications Sent Register

Date	Message	Reference/link to a copy of the communication sent	Medium	Who sent to (distribution list or other)	Feedback received	Feedback allocated to
Monday 14 Jan 2018	Notify users of the project status, indicating what changes they will see to the organisation structure	Comms_Users_ Organisation.doc	Email	All company employees	Sarah Jones suggested clarity by using diagrams to represent changes to the structure	Project leader

© 2022 Dr Neil Pearson

This section has reviewed the process of identifying, developing and tracking communications. These activities could be distributed to various project team members, as indicated below.

- The project leader could be responsible for instigating the communications strategy and for planning communications on the project.
- The task of developing (writing) communications might reside with the allocated project team member and/or SMEs from the business working on the project.
- The task of tracking and monitoring communications could be the responsibility of the project officer.
- If the project has a full- or part-time communications manager allocated to it, then it may be the case that the project leader devolves responsibility to them for all project communications.

These roles/rules could be added to the project-wide RASCI, to clearly indicate where accountabilities and responsibilities lie in relation to project communications. The Communications Sent Register is a tab within the online Communications Register.

Communications Register

15.7 **Project reporting**

Performance reporting of the project is crucial to communicating the status of the project to the project management office (PMO), the project sponsor, the Steering Committee and other stakeholders, as documented in the Communications Management Plan (and/or Communications Register). Most of the information on which the project status report is based will be distributed among the many other project artefacts that the project leader (and project team) will be maintaining as part of day-to-day activities on the project. However, bringing this information together (compiling the report), validating the report (reviewing), distributing the report and fielding subsequent questions can be quite an involved process, which should not be underestimated by the project leader. In some cases, it may be advisable to include a repeating communications task on the project schedule, as this will focus the project leader's attention on achieving any reporting deadlines (along with those involved in extracting data from ICT systems and presenting them as information in a report format). *Remember:* The project status report should be treated as a two-way opportunity to communicate with its recipients, and the project leader should actively seek feedback on elements of the report, such as changed risks and escalated issues, or decisions to be made.

Some outputs of project performance reporting include:

■ work achieved in the current reporting period
■ work achieved against planned work (baselines for schedule, cost and scope)
■ forecast of future work to be achieved (including time and cost)
■ value of work achieved (using metrics such as **earned value management** (EVM))
■ analysis of risks and issues
■ summary of outstanding and approved variation requests and the impact on baselines
■ information on team health
■ other information as required or mandated in the project reporting system. (PMI 2013)

Most project leaders will become familiar with two key types of project reports: **full reporting** and **exception reporting**. As the name suggests, full reporting provides a comprehensive report on all dynamics of the project, usually in considerable detail, covering the areas of scope, schedule, cost, quality, resources, communications, risk, stakeholders (including organisational change) and procurement. A typical full report may include information such as:

■ an executive summary
■ validation of scope and/or Business Case to ensure validity of the project
■ cost analysis
■ schedule (time) analysis, including milestones/deliverables summaries
■ previous week, current week, next week tasks and supporting narrative
■ risk profiles for high and extreme risks, plus details risks of changed and new risks
■ issues raised (as a result of risks turning into issues) or other project issues
■ outstanding project variation requests, their status and impact analysis summary
■ resource utilisation in the previous week, current week, next week format
■ quality nonconformances
■ contract status and performance tracking.

The other key type of report that is becoming more popular with project leaders and executives alike is the exception report. Here, only exceptions from the agreed baselines (scope, time, cost) are highlighted with plans for rectifications presented, with additional summary information on issues, variations and nonconformances. Table 15.11 indicates some of the advantages and disadvantages of each type of report.

Table 15.11 Key reporting types: advantages and disadvantages

Full reporting	Exception reporting
Advantages	**Advantages**
Covers all the major project dimensions in comprehensive detail.	Focuses executive management's attention on changes to the agreed/approved baseline plan (not the entire status of all aspects of the project).
	More efficient for project leaders and the project team to prepare (less time-consuming).
Disadvantages	**Disadvantages**
Can consume a lot of project management time to generate.	Presents only exceptions (so achievements may be underplayed).
Can result in executive management information overload.	Executive management has to request details on/may be unaware of original/re-baselined project data and information.
Does not focus executive management's attention on the exceptions or issues that need attending to.	

© 2022 Dr Neil Pearson

How the project report is delivered may also vary from organisation to organisation. Most project leaders will be familiar with documenting the project in a written report format and sending this (usually via email) to executive management, the project Steering Committee and/or the PMO. After delivery of the report, there should be timely feedback and/or a questions loop (where the project leader responds to questions, or the questions on decisions and guidance are provided by the recipient of the report).

Some organisations provide a forum, such as a project review meeting (or Steering Committee meeting) with key stakeholders, where the project leader will be asked to deliver the report and verbally make a summary and field questions. The project leader must be prepared to answer on-the-fly, on-the-spot questions with this face-to-face approach as the discussion progresses.

15.7.1 Performance dashboards

Steering committees, executives and even some PMOs prefer RAG dashboards to provide a snapshot of the project's status at any one time. These dashboards could be automated in large projects or where investments in ICT systems have been made. Quite often they are a distillation of multiple data sources that the project leader has brought together in a manual format using a **red—amber—green (RAG)**-style one-page format. Figure 15.13 illustrates such a dashboard created as a Microsoft PowerPoint presentation as part of a presentation to support the delivery of either a full or an exception report.

Available online are two templates that can be edited to form the basis of a project exception report, and an accompanying presentation with a copy of Figure 15.14.

 Project Status Report (Exception Format)

 Project Status Report (Presentation Format)

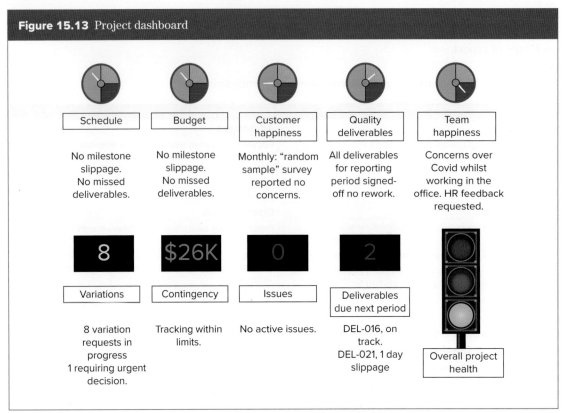

Figure 15.13 Project dashboard

© 2022 Dr Neil Pearson

Remember: The organisation's PMO or project Steering Committee will influence the format and delivery style of the project status report; their engagement early in the project will ensure these groups of stakeholders are kept informed as the project progresses, in the format they require and specify.

From a communications planning perspective, the project leader must plan what formal project status reports are to be produced as this could have implications for:

- time—the inclusion of a repeating task in the project schedule if assistance from other project resources is going to be required

- data upon which the report (information) and its accompanying narrative will be built—the project leader must ensure the data can be sourced, collated and validated in order to report on. Have, for example, time sheets been completed and entered into the project accounting system so actual hours and therefore costs can be calculated?

- systems, format and presentation—systems for project reporting are becoming more ICT enabled, with live performance dashboards updated from corporate systems becoming the norm for medium-to-large projects.

 ## 15.8 : **Project management information systems (PMIS)**

PMIS vary in their complexity according to their purpose. For example, complex tools might include the type of systems offered by Artemis and Primavera, whereas simple systems may involve the use of inhouse file-server-based project libraries. In today's project environment, a PMIS is critical for being able to efficiently store, manage, search, distribute and maintain a whole host of project-related information. Projects typically not only include a myriad of project management-related documents, but also many thousands of artefacts that are related to the development of project-specific content.

Establishing a PMIS is an activity the project leader must consider at the outset of the project, to ensure a structured, easily accessible and central (authoritative) source of information exists. Some types of PMIS are discussed in the list below. *Note:* In practice, a combination of systems is usually used so that a comprehensive environment for storing and maintaining various types of project and project-related information is possible.

- *Corporate systems:* These may range from the organisation's enterprise resource planning (ERP) systems to its financial systems. ERPs typically track information on work orders, packages of work and costs allocated. Finance systems may support the project in terms of managing its budget and the reconciliation of purchase orders and invoices. They will also provide financial statements for the project. In some cases (when combined with scheduling information), EVM reports can be produced.

- *Scheduling and resource-management systems:* Most high-end scheduling systems such as Microsoft Project Server offer features far beyond the scheduling and tracking of tasks on a typical project. Most offer the ability to allocate resources and resource usage, and track progress and costs assigned to each task (work package) in the project. Resource pools can be established for shared resources.

- *File sharing:* Most projects have a project library of some description, usually shared from a central file-sharing system provided by the organisation's ICT department. The project team then can create a file structure that is relevant to the project. Access to such systems can be tailored so that permissions to the sub-directories of information can be secured to specific groups of people within, and beyond, the project team.

- *Intranets:* Systems such as Microsoft SharePoint offer repositories for files while also offering features such as integrated calendars and the ability to create wikis, forums and blogs. Typically, these need to be set up and maintained by an administrator within the project. This is potentially a responsibility of the project officer; however, the project leader must ensure the person allocated to this role has the necessary training to manage the system and to make maximum use of the features it offers.

- *Document management systems (DMS) and content management systems (CMS):* Both offer a high degree of formality in terms of managing artefacts (e.g. documents). Configuration management (CM) (see next section), workflow and document versioning are key features of these systems. Some of the more commonly encountered DMS include TRIM (a records management system from HP), Xerox Docushare and OpenText ECM suite.

- *Integrated PMIS:* These are specific tools aimed at solving multiple aspects of information management in the project environment. These would provide facilities for scheduling and budget management (often integrated into corporate ICT systems), in addition to general CM, reporting and information-sharing features. These systems also have the ability to manage information across the nine knowledge areas of the PMBOK. As indicated previously, due to the complex nature of such a system, the authors recommend the integration of multiple systems that provide best-in-class features required by the project.

15.8.1 Configuration management (CM) and document management systems (DMS)

As indicated above, the project could potentially generate thousands of artefacts, ranging from project management documents through to test plans and codes. The collection/development, analysis and dissemination of all these artefacts on the project requires some formality. Historically referred to as *version control*, CM has become the norm for managing the many and varied project artefacts in anything but simple projects. The project leader must decide which key artefacts will be subject to what levels of CM. In its simplest form, CM could be a version and distribution control added to the front of documents.

■ Version control aims to track the changes made to a document through the life of the project. The benefits to the project are a known state of a document, ensuring that when it is reviewed or approved, the readers/recipients are aware of which version is being reviewed and approved. This may take the form of a simple version tracking table that is inserted on the front page of the document (Table 15.12). The naming standard and versioning numbering system must also be established within the Communications Management Plan.

Table 15.12 Document version control

Version	Description of change	Changed by	Date
1.0	Initial document	Project leader	1 March
1.01	Updated WBS	Project leader	5 March

© 2022 Dr Neil Pearson

■ Distribution control differs from version control and involves tracking to whom (stakeholders) the document was issued, and on what date. From a project perspective, this ensures that readership of controlled documents is clearly articulated and tracked. If a document must be re-released or recalled, the author of the document knows exactly who to contact. Again, this may be in the form of a simple distribution-tracking table that is inserted on the front page of the document (Table 15.13).

Table 15.13 Document distribution control

Version	Released to	Released by	Date
1.01	Project sponsor	Project leader	5 March

© 2022 Dr Neil Pearson

Note: Documents must not be forwarded to other parties without the prior consent of their author(s).

When artefacts are placed inside a DMS, more complex workflows can be achieved. For example:

■ Documents may only be checked out by approved people and must be checked in once editing has been completed.

■ The document might be part of a workflow process, where the document is moved along a predefined workflow of people for editing and approval.

■ The author will be responsible for maintaining the meta data (data about data) for the document, such as its author, purpose and any key word search terms, and security privileges (among a whole host of other information). This facilitates being able to search and retrieve the documents at a later stage.

■ Version control will be applied by the system, creating the ability to refer to previous controlled copies of a document if needed.

■ Administrators will have to establish role and security permissions to protect the documents within the system.

PMISs vary widely. From a project management perspective, the concepts of version and distribution control should always be considered when establishing a PMIS at the project Initiation stage. For simple projects, a manual version and distribution control is a minimum requirement, and this is usually established and monitored by the project officer. For complex projects, a PMIS can deliver many benefits, although the cost of the systems administration must be borne in mind.

As a final note to this section on document management and configuration management, the reader's attention is brought back to the discussion on quality. If your organisation is an accredited quality organisation that holds accreditations such as ISO 9001, your project will have to inherit the organisation's Quality Management Systems in relation to document management and CM. The project leader may also wish to consider adopting best practice and standards for document management within the project. Examples are ISO 10007-2017 "Quality management systems—Guidelines for configuration management", and AS/NZS ISO 30301:2012 "Information and documentation—Management systems for recordkeeping—Requirements". These are in addition to any legal requirements to which your organisation or industry is subject.

15.8.2 Project knowledge management

Before examining what knowledge is within a project environment, let's first look at some definitions of data, information, knowledge and wisdom (DIKW). The project leader must be able to differentiate between the different tiers (see Figure 15.14) in order to manage the source and to capture data that are relevant, accurate, timely, complete and reliable (the infamous five qualities of data!). Figure 15.14 indicates the tiers of DIKW, with a couple of examples from a project perspective.

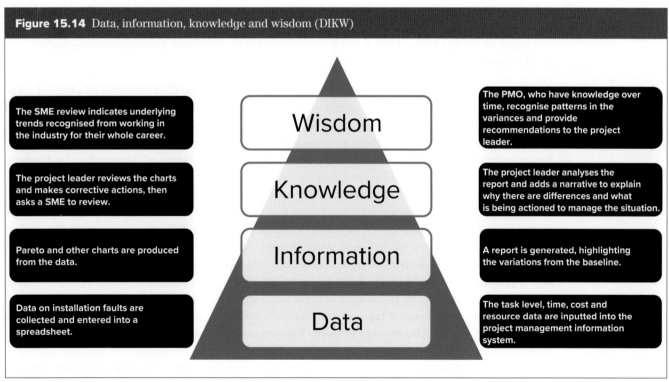

Figure 15.14 Data, information, knowledge and wisdom (DIKW)

The SME review indicates underlying trends recognised from working in the industry for their whole career.

The project leader reviews the charts and makes corrective actions, then asks a SME to review.

Pareto and other charts are produced from the data.

Data on installation faults are collected and entered into a spreadsheet.

Wisdom

Knowledge

Information

Data

The PMO, who have knowledge over time, recognise patterns in the variances and provide recommendations to the project leader.

The project leader analyses the report and adds a narrative to explain why there are differences and what is being actioned to manage the situation.

A report is generated, highlighting the variations from the baseline.

The task level, time, cost and resource data are inputted into the project management information system.

© 2022 Dr Neil Pearson

Below is an excerpt from AS 5037-2005 "Knowledge management—A guide":

Data: *Any manifestation in the environment, which may include symbolic representations that, in combination, may form the basis of information.*

Information: *Data in a context to which meaning has been attributed.*

Knowledge: *A body of understanding and skills that is constructed by people and increased through interaction with other people and with information. The literature is replete with* *many contested definitions of knowledge. There is no single agreed definition of knowledge or one unifying theory of knowledge management. Knowledge has many facets:*

1. *It can be highly personal and subconsciously understood. Knowledge resides in a person's mind and may include aspects of culture or 'ways of doing things' (often referred to as tacit knowledge).*
2. *It can be recorded as information in a document, image, film clip, or some other medium.*
3. *It can be considered as a component of an organisation's asset base* (Standards Australia 2005).

Source: Standards Australia 2005, AS 5037-2005 Knowledge Management—A Guide. Reproduced by McGraw Hill LLC with the permission of Standards Australia Limited under licence CLE0822MGH. Copyright in AS/NZS vests in Standards Australia and Standards New Zealand. Users must not copy or reuse this work without the permission of Standards Australia or the copyright owner.

Wisdom is often described as being "knowledge over time". A fundamental challenge that project leaders face (a challenge that is typical for operational managers across the business) is to be able to capture knowledge. Project leaders need to consider two types of knowledge—explicit and tacit knowledge.

■ **Explicit knowledge** can be more easily expressed and transferred between people without loss of meaning; it is usually recorded in a medium such as a document, image, process model, ICT system, in policy and procedure manuals, and process and operating procedures.

■ In contrast to explicit knowledge, **tacit knowledge** is difficult to articulate. It cannot easily be transferred without close personal contact, demonstration and involvement. Tacit knowledge refers to highly personal knowledge that resides in a person's head (mind) and includes physical skills, as well as aspects of culture or ways of doing things. Importantly, tacit knowledge cannot be easily captured, but it can be transferred in discussion or via observation—much like apprenticeships.

Most project leaders are aware of project data, for example, the data elements of planned value and earned value. They will also be aware of the potential for information to be gained from an EVM analysis (a graph of the results that have been plotted). We know that to read the EVM graph, the reader uses known information about positive and negative variances (i.e. they use their knowledge). However, a project leader will actively apply their (potentially, vast array of) knowledge (i.e. wisdom) amassed over their entire career when making decisions on how best to, for example, get a project back on track. Wisdom is tacit knowledge and is often hard to express and capture.

But herein lays the challenge: How to identify knowledge that can easily be made explicit, and how to pass on tacit knowledge between the members of the project team? This is no easy task! The project leader can create an open environment where knowledge transfer is supported (and in some cases rewarded). The project leader can initiate coaching and mentoring across the project, peer reviews, and/or promote the use of various software tools, but at the end of the day it requires people to be in an environment where there is a culture of knowledge sharing (not knowledge hoarding). Remember: When we impart knowledge, it takes on the form of information to others. When they internalise this information, it becomes knowledge to them. Wisdom is a refined state of knowledge that is gained over time, and through vast experience.

Some organisations deploy social media tools to promote information sharing across geographically diverse project teams, two examples being Yammer (www.yammer.com) and Confluence (www. atlassian.com). These tools provide secure environments that project teams can use to communicate and share information. Remember: When using such systems, declare them in the Communications Management Plan, along with information about who has what access levels.

Note: As with all the other software tools that are referred to in this book, the authors do not advise, recommend or support any one tool over another. You must carry out a full needs analysis according to your project's requirements before adopting any software tools. The examples and hyperlinks provided to resources are indicative only of what is widely available in the marketplace, and you must form your own opinion as to their suitability and relevance to your project.

Summary

It is often said in project management circles that project communications management can make or break a project. Crafting the vision of the project from the get-go is important to laying successful foundations for the project.

- Moving on from stakeholder identification and analysis (discussed in Chapter 14 "Project stakeholder management") is the activity of identifying formal project communications to be sent to these stakeholders.
- To arrive at a set of clearly defined communication protocols, the project leader must consider which model is the most fitting for communicating with a particular stakeholder. The project leader, supported by the project team and/or communications manager, defines the details of each communication. Some of the items considered at this point include the identification of the message that is being sent, the medium to be used and how frequently the communication will be sent. All this communication information will be captured in the Communications Register.
- The governance aspects of communication—such as project roles and responsibilities, review processes, and organisational policy and procedure—are among the items that need to be captured within the Communications Management Plan. This is then communicated to the entire project team so a consistent approach to communications is taking place.
- When it comes to sending a communication, the author, a reviewer and an approver will all become involved. The initial development (writing) of a formal communication could be carried out within the project by a project team member (or in some cases SME) before it is progressed through multiple reviews (technical, cultural, generational) and final approval is given. Once approved and sent, the communication can be recorded in the Communications Sent Register.
- During the formal communication process, the project leader will be involved in many informal communications with the project team: capturing knowledge within organisational process and systems, developing project status reports, and the ongoing and critical role of building and maintaining relationships with the stakeholders and the project team.
- A project leader needs to carefully consider their manner and the verbal and non-verbal messages they are sending, and how these messages are received and perceived by other stakeholders and project team members. Knowing the 7-38-55 model and being able to understand non-verbal cues are important project leader skills. A project leader needs to be able to pick up on these non-verbal cues so they can diplomatically question statements and claims made by a stakeholder, for example, whether the stakeholder's non-verbal cues contradict what is verbally being said. NLP, knowledge of which can be acquired through taking a professional development training course, can help to foster an awareness of the non-verbal cues that may be used during face-to-face communication.
- Communication across project teams is likely to encompass a range of generations, as well as learning and communication needs and styles. It is therefore important to consider the likely generational impact of project communications. For example, if a Yammer social media group is set up to facilitate a discussion of project ideas, would this exclude certain generations from being able to confidently participate or contribute (e.g. through lack of social media know-how, or having no interest in online discussions)?
- It is important to be aware of how information is shared and communicated across the different generations that are employed in the organisation's workforce.
- Project communications can be one of the most rewarding activities of project management. When executed well, the benefits of good communication can be significant; it can break down cultural and age barriers, facilitate information-sharing, canvass new ideas, promote change and foster positive team rapport (among other benefits). However, if communication is not planned and executed well, a project may be at risk of failure or non-acceptance by the project's customers.

Review questions

1. What is the significance of carrying out a detailed stakeholder analysis before developing the Communications Register?
2. Outline your understanding of project communications.
3. What are the models of communication that are introduced in this chapter?
4. Why is it important to understand the complexities in lines of communication?
5. What topics could be addressed within the project Communications Management Plan?

6. What methods can be used to identify communications?

7. What is the purpose of the 4Cs of truth about communication and CPORT when writing communications?

8. What are the four directions of communication the project leader may have to consider when planning communications?

9. What is a project management information system (PMIS)?

10. What are non-verbal cues, and why are they important to a project leader?

11. What is VARK? Why is it important?

Exercises

1. Ask a colleague in the room about the status of a current project they are involved with. Ask them some easy and some more difficult questions: take note of any non-verbal cues that may reveal their inner thoughts about what is really going on in the project and how they feel about this.

2. Use the table below to indicate/suggest what type of communication might be the most appropriate in each stated situation. A response to the first situation is provided by way of an example to help get you started.

Situation	Your response
A request for a change to the scope of a work package	*The person who requested the variation is asked verbally to complete a variation request form*
Status (steering committee) presentation	
Scheduling a project meeting	
Workshop to carry out a root-cause analysis of a problem	
Conducting a bidder workshop	
Notifying a project team member of poor performance (first occasion)	
Notifying a project team member of poor performance (second occasion)	
Making a change to the terms and conditions of a contract	
Confirming a discussion regarding project reporting improvements with the PMO	

3. Think about how having multiple generations in your workplace may affect the way in which communications take place. What (if any) challenges have you experienced when communicating across differing generations? How did you resolve these challenges?

   Share your observations with a person in the training room who is from a different generation to yourself (if possible) to hear their perspective.

References

Agile Manifesto 2001, "Principles behind the Agile Manifesto", http://agilemanifesto.org/principles.html, accessed February 2018.

Albanese I 2007, *The 4Cs of Truth in Communication*, 1st edition, Paramount Marketing Publishing.

Berlo D 1960, *The Process of Communication: An Introduction to Theory and Practice*, Holt, Rinehart and Winston, New York, pp. 23–24.

Cockburn A 2006, *Agile Software Development: The Cooperative Game*, 2nd edition, Addison-Wesley Professional.

Mehrabian A 1972, *Silent Messages: Implicit Communication of Emotions and Attitudes*, Albert Mehrabian, Wadsworth Publishing Company, p. 2.

NLP Academy 2018, "What is NLP?", NLP Academy, www.nlpacademy.co.uk/what_is_nlp/, accessed February 2018.

Project Management Institute (PMI) 2013, *A Guide to the Project Management Body of Knowledge*, 5th edition, PMI.

Project Management Institute (PMI) 2017, *A Guide to the Project Management Body of Knowledge*, 6th edition, PMI.

Project Management Institute (PMI) 2021a, *A Guide to the Project Management Body of Knowledge (PMBOK® Guide)*, 7th edition, PMI.

Project Management Institute (PMI) 2021b, *The Standard for Project Management (ANSI/PMI 99-001-2021)*, 7th edition, PMI.

Standards Australia 2005, AS 5037-2005 "Knowledge management—A guide".

St Louis M 2017, "How to spot visual, auditory, and kinesthetic learning executives", Inc.com, https://www.inc.com/molly-reynolds/how-to-spot-visual-auditory-and-kinesthetic-learni.html, accessed February 2018.

Taylor S & Lester A 2009, *Communication: Your Key to Success*, Marshall Cavendish Corporation, Singapore.

Vark Learn 2018, "Introduction to VARK", http://vark-learn.com/introduction-to-vark/, accessed February 2018.

Verdü S & McLaughlin SW 2000, *Information Theory: 50 Years of Discovery*, IEEE Press.

CHAPTER 16

Project risk management

Learning elements

16A Be able to apply the ISO Standard for risk management (ISO 31000:2018) to the project environment, for both threat and opportunity risks.

16B Be able to plan and establish a project-wide risk management system.

16C Understand the significance of establishing the context of risk in a project environment.

16D Understand and apply some of the fundamental risk management tools that are found in a project environment, for identification, analysis and evaluation of risks in both their inherent and residual states.

16E Respond to the challenges of monitoring and controlling risk during the execution of a project.

16F Be able to consider the impact of risk to the project's budget and to contingency reserves.

In this chapter

16.1 Introduction

16.2 Risk management overview

16.3 The Risk Management Plan

16.4 Step 1: Establishing the risk context

16.5 Step 2: Risk identification

16.6 Step 3: Risk analysis

16.7 Further complexity in risk analysis

16.8   Step 4: Risk evaluation

16.9   Step 5: Risk treatment

16.10 Step 6: Contingency planning

16.11 Opportunity risk explored

16.12 Common approaches to handling risk

16.13 Budgets, contingency and risk

16.14 Risk monitoring and review

16.15 Communication and consultation

16.16 Close risk management

16.17 Risk management tools

      Summary

16.1 | Introduction

To put risk into perspective, a project leader needs to recognise that the essence of project management is risk management. Every technique in this book is really a risk management technique; each technique tries to prevent something adverse from happening. Project selection systems try to increase the likelihood that projects will contribute to the strategic objectives of the organisation. Project scope documents are designed to avoid costly misunderstandings and to reduce scope creep from the project's outset. As will be discovered in this chapter, managing risk depends on having a communicated risk management process in place. However, in any project team, there must be an understanding of the fact that *things can happen*, that risks are never static, and **issues** both immediate and eventuated are required to be managed. It is the responsibility of the project leader to ensure there is a clear understanding that it is okay to talk about risk, to point risks out, to review and update risk status, and to bring issues to the attention of the project leader. The project leader needs to establish an open, trusted environment where risk can be challenged and discussed as a part of daily conversations and where the risky subject is not avoided (and is therefore already on the way to becoming an issue).

Risk is an integral part of project management. However, due to the varied nature of risk, it can be difficult to identify, despite the project leader's best efforts. According to **ISO 31000:2018 "Risk management—Guidelines"**, *risk* is defined as the "effect of uncertainty on objectives". Therefore, it could be stated that a project risk offers the potential for an event to cause a deviation from *the expected*, in either a positive or a negative manner.

So, if a risk is defined as a *potential* deviation in the project, what then constitutes an *issue*? In general, an issue is a negative event that has *already* occurred (this topic is discussed later in this chapter). Establishing clear terminology within the project's **Risk Management Plan** should be the first step towards ensuring there is shared understanding of processes, roles, and terms used. The consequences of some potential risk events, such as schedule slippages, cost overruns, equipment malfunction or changes in technical requirements, can be anticipated. However, other forms of risk can extend beyond most people's imagination; take, for example, the 2008 global financial meltdown and the 2020 global pandemic.

While some forms of risk can have positive consequences (such as an unexpected price reduction in materials), the focus of this chapter is what can potentially go wrong, and the risk mitigating processes we can employ to divert/avoid as much risk as possible away from the project. The processes applied in this chapter are based heavily on the risk management standard AS ISO 31000:2018, which is an identical adoption of ISO 31000:2018 (the global standard). This standard has been widely adopted by organisations within Australia (and wider afield) as the basis for the risk management policy and procedure in their organisations, from corporate risk to workplace health and safety risk, to project risk. Risk management strategies attempt to recognise and mitigate the potential for unforeseen trouble spots to occur when the project is implemented. Risk management identifies as many risk events as possible (what can go wrong?), aims to minimise their impact (what can be done about the event before the project begins?), manages responses to the events that do materialise (**Contingency Plans**) and provides contingency funds to cover risk events that do materialise. For an example of how a project leader must always actively *scan* for risks beyond what is immediately in front of them, refer to "Snapshot from Practice: Land titles".

The general project risk management activities appear in Figure 16.1; these and more will be explored over the course of this chapter.

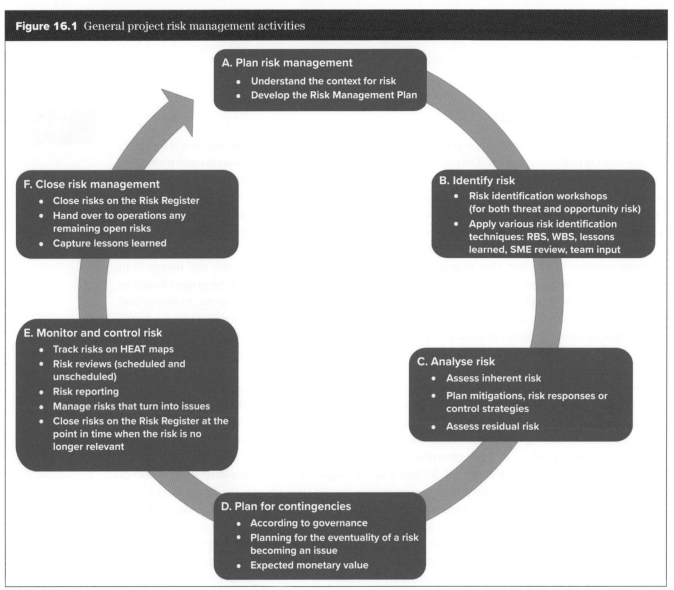

Figure 16.1 General project risk management activities

PMBOK | **Seventh edition updates (PMI 2021)**

Risk is discussed within the *Project Management Body of Knowledge* (*PMBOK® Guide*) seventh edition, where it appears as a principle in the *Standard for Project Management* (PMI 2021b, p. 53). "Optimize Risk Response" can be summarised as continuously evaluating all risk to increase positive risks (opportunities) and reduce negative risks (threats). The responses should always be cost effective and realistic.

The Project Management Institute publishes an additional guide on risk, *The Standard for Risk Management in Portfolios, Programs, and Projects* (PMI 2019).

16.2 Risk management overview

Figure 16.2 graphically shows the risk management challenge. The chances of a risk event occurring (e.g. an error in time estimates, cost estimates or in a technology design) are greatest during the Initiation, Planning and tailoring off during Execution stages of a project. The cost impact of a risk event in the project is less if the event occurs earlier rather than later. This is because the early stages of the project represent the period when the opportunity for minimising the impact, or for working around a potential risk, exists. Conversely, as the project passes the halfway implementation mark, the cost of a risk event occurring increases rapidly. For example, the risk event of a design flaw occurring after a prototype has been made will have a greater cost/time impact than if the event occurred early in the Planning stage of the project. Clearly, identifying project risk events and deciding on suitable responses before the project delivers is a more prudent approach to take than not attempting to manage risk.

Risk management requires a *proactive* rather than a *reactive* approach. It is a preventive process designed to ensure that surprises are reduced and that any negative consequences associated with undesirable events (often referred to as a **threat risk**) are minimised. It also prepares the project leader to act when a time, cost and/or technical advantage is possible (an **opportunity risk**). The successful management of project risk affords the project leader better control and can significantly improve the chances of project objectives being reached on time, within budget, and for meeting required technical (functional) performance.

The potential sources of project risks are unlimited. Threat risks can originate from many sources that may be external or internal to the organisation. External threat risks could include raw material price increases, supply chain issues, fluctuating exchange rates and government regulations. Internal threat risks may include having limited office space, having restricted resources and having rigidly set funding. Whatever the source of the risk, the project leader must make every attempt to identify all risks, carry out actions in the project to mitigate (control) each risk and put in place plans (contingency) to manage the risk if it eventuates into an issue.

To assist in the processing of risk, project leaders will typically adopt the risk management process of the parent organisation. In many cases this risk management process will be based on ISO 31000:2018. If such a process does not exist in the parent organisation, then it will be the project leader's responsibility to define, and subsequently communicate, such a process for risk management in their project. This risk management process would then be documented in the project's Risk Management Plan (discussed later in this chapter).

Refer to the the risk management process image per ISO 31000:2018. The process is surrounded

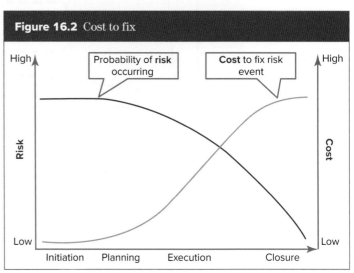

Figure 16.2 Cost to fix

© 2022 Dr Neil Pearson

Figure 16.3 Risk management process

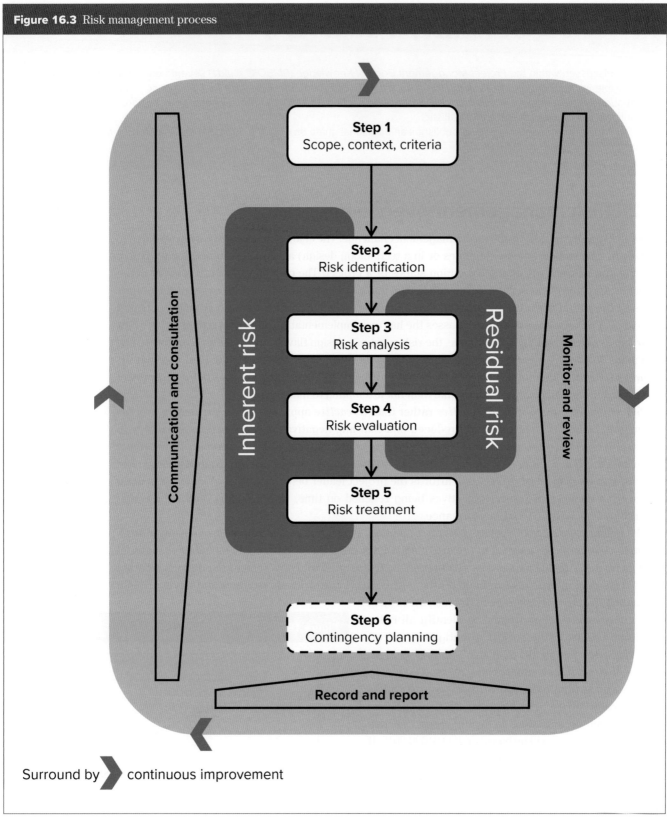

Source: Adapted from ISO 31000:2018 "Risk Management—Guidelines".

by the framework; the framework in the ISO standard defines how basically the risk management process down the centre is subject to continuous improvement. The process down the centre defines the key activities (this is a not a process), assessing the **risk context**, **risk identification**, **risk analysis**, **risk evaluation** and **risk treatment**. The process is supported by communication and consultation, monitoring and review, and recording and reporting. All these steps will be worked through; however, turning the standard into a workable risk management process requires consideration of a more practical workflow, therefore the sequence of Figure 16.3 is used in this chapter. The key difference is clarity around the identification, analysis, evaluation and treatment of the initial risk (opportunity or threat) identified and then the steps of analysis and treatment being applied to this inherent risk (before the controls have been enacted) to form what is termed the *residual* risk priority. That is, once the treatment has been determined for the initial *inherent* risk, its actions must be carried out in the project before the risk is reduced to its *residual* level.

Therefore, the workflow that will be progressed in this text will be: initial risk identification, inherent risk analysis and evaluation, risk treatment and, where relevant, residual risk analysis and evaluation; and further to this, where residual risks are running high—the planning of contingency.

SNAPSHOT *from* PRACTICE | **Land titles**

Australian resources (mines), energy (gas) and large-scale agricultural users of native title land in Western Australia were thrown into jeopardy after a Federal Court decision invalidated a large number (estimated at over 200) of native title land use agreements. This includes the debated, and still contentious, AUD16 billion Carmichael coal mine project in Queensland, Australia.

Some communities risk losing substantial development funding through Indigenous land-use agreements.

This example demonstrates the importance of continually scanning the external environment for all potential risks to the project. Although a heated topic in Australia, this same debate is impacting other projects across the globe, from Alaska to South America.

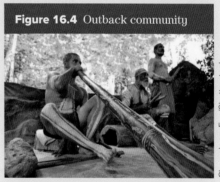

Figure 16.4 Outback community

ChameleonsEye/Shutterstock

Source: Adapted from McKenna M 2017 "Native title call a risk to projects", *The Australian*, 8 February, https://www.theaustralian.com.au/national-affairs/indigenous/native-title-call-a-Risk-to-projects/news-story/70e29506ce805d373497f75cb3518608, accessed February 2018

Establishing the basis for risk management is one of the first activities the project leader must attend to, as the risk management process (and the terminology used in the process) will serve to inform the project team and project stakeholders on all aspects of risk management, throughout the project life cycle. Remember: The risk management process is there to put structure around the processing of risk; being *risk aware* and making the project team risk aware is a matter of changing the culture so that people identify risk and are empowered to raise risks in a transparent and trusted culture.

16.3 | **The Risk Management Plan**

Throughout this chapter, reference is made to the **Risk Management Plan**. This section outlines the typical contents of a Risk Management Plan.

1. *Risk context:* The context of risk needs to be captured at both the organisational level and at the project level. The project leader needs to consider the overarching **risk context** within which the project will operate—that is, is the context *risk-averse* or *risk-taking* and how does this transfer into the project environment? There could be cases where the general context of risk is to be risk-averse but the project being worked on is out of context and represents a major innovation being brought to market and is inherently risky. Knowing the context and being able to articulate it can set expectations for the project team and greater stakeholder community (Step 1 in Figure 16.3).

2. *Risk methodology:* Refer to any corporate risk management frameworks or methodologies that exist (e.g. the process as illustrated in Figure 16.3) and are to be applied to the management of risk within the project environment. Provide commentary on how risk terminology has been tailored to the project environment, including the following.

   ■ The categorisation methodology used to categorise risks. Some projects use the 10 knowledge areas (PMBOK); other projects use more bespoke categories. Either way, the categorisation will assist the project leader and project team in reviewing categories of risks later in the project.

   ■ Definitions of terminology and details of scales as appropriate, for example:

      ● the probability (likelihood) of the risk occurring (e.g. 5 = certain, 4 = probable, 3 = expected, 2 = uncertain, 1 = improbable)

      ● the impact (consequence) if the risk occurred (e.g. 5 = very high, 4 = high, 3 = medium, 2 = low, 1 = unlikely)

      ● the proximity of the risk to the present time (one week, one month, two months, etc. or by project stage). This can be useful in prioritising risks that must be fully defined and monitored which are closer to a piece of work taking place in the project.

   Note: ISO 31000:2018 does not define probability, impact, proximity or any other scaled element. It is for the owning organisation to define, agree and establish in governance detailed definitions of the scale of probability, impact and proximity.

3. *Risk roles and responsibilities:* Leverage the project-wide RASCI (refer to Chapter 7 "Governance and projects"), to capture the roles and responsibilities associated with risk management in the project (such as issue escalation, changes to individual **risk profiles**, and continuous improvements to the risk process). *Note:* This differs from the ownership of individual risks, which is captured in the **Risk Register** (discussed later in this chapter).

4. *Risk escalation process:* Capture the general risk escalation process. Some of this may be documented in the project-wide RASCI; however, a simple flowchart may make this more accessible to the project team in times of need. This needs to be linked to the risk control strategy *escalate*, which is introduced into the sixth edition of PMBOK (PMI 2017) and discussed later in this chapter.

5. *Risk reporting:* Detail where and how reported risk should be documented. This ensures that project management information is maintained to appropriate levels for reporting of risk to take place in an efficient and effective manner. Will, for example, **risk heat maps** (see later in this chapter) be presented for discussion at the weekly status meeting?

6. *Scheduled risk audits and health checks:* Document details on when and by whom any risk audits are scheduled to be carried out. Additionally, note any planned **risk workshops** to revisit all risks at key time-points in the project schedule to ensure a proactive approach to the monitoring of risk.

7. *Lessons learned:* Review any lessons learned from prior, similar projects regarding the management of risk. For negative lessons, document how they relate to the project and what is being done in the project to ensure they are not repeated. For positive lessons, document how the project can apply or improve on the lesson.

The Risk Management Plan is a relatively static document established early during the Planning stage. It is there to provide the governance for risk, and the processes and definitions of how risk is to be managed in the project. The online Risk Management Plan contains further details on all entries typically found in such a management plan.

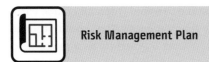

Risk Management Plan

The next sections of this chapter review the steps outlined in Figure 16.3.

16.4 Step 1: Establishing the risk context

Organisations invariably operate within environments of risk. Understanding the external environment in which the organisation operates (and in which your project is operating) is key to knowing not only what potential risks may already exist, but also informs the project about potential external risks that may arise—this is the *context of risk*. The internal risk context defines the internal environment within which the organisation seeks to achieve its objectives. Both external and internal contexts will influence the **risk appetite** of the project. For example, if the organisation is particularly risk-averse, the project leader may need to use strategies to treat risk to reduce the probability and impact of the risk. In this scenario, effectively the project is changed to include activities to reduce the risk to as low a level as possible, or to remove the risk altogether. Mining companies and government entities typically take this approach when dealing with any potential workplace health and safety risks, or when there is a threat to the organisation's reputation. In some companies, the approach to risk is completely the opposite; they are risk-takers and have a higher tolerance towards risk-taking. For example, an innovation project to bring a new product to the market might have a higher financial risk tolerance—it may be willing to fund (venture and equity funding) and manage financial risk to the project and to the organisation that other organisations would simply consider unacceptable.

The project sponsor can be a useful source of information when establishing the context of risk for the project. The person in charge of enterprise risk management in the organisation may influence the risk appetite of the project. It can therefore be useful to draw both stakeholders into initial discussions about the context of risk, usually during the Initiating stage of the project when initial high-level project risks are identified.

Some organisations use the **ALARP** acronym to establish the context of risk management in their organisation. ALARP stands for "as low as reasonably practicable", implying that the project will have done all that is reasonable to prevent problems and dangers. The ALARP approach requires each risk to be analysed separately and followed by the implementation of appropriate mitigation strategies right down to its lowest level. There is a move in some industries to move away from ALARP and use "so far as is reasonably practicable" (**SFAIRP**). There is a subtle difference between the two; with ALARP, you're aiming for *low*, which can in some cases mean taking steps beyond what is actually practicable; therefore the preference is moving to use the more considered application of SFAIRP, namely that *what can be done should be done, unless it is reasonable to do something less.*

16.5 Step 2: Risk identification

Risk identification is the most critical step: if we fail to identify risk, then we cannot manage it. The project leader must lead the identification of risk by trying to generate a list of all possible risks that have the potential to affect the project. To achieve this, the project leader (typically) pulls together (during the Initiating stage) a risk workshop, comprising core team members and relevant stakeholders. The team uses idea showering and other problem-identifying techniques to identify potential risks. Participants are encouraged to keep an open mind and to generate as many ideas about probable sources of risk as possible. Many projects have been derailed by an event that members had initially thought was completely improbable and not captured. Fortunately, there are many techniques that can be used to identify risks. A common mistake to avoid (typically made early in the risk identification process) is focusing on *objectives* rather than on *events* that could produce consequences. For example, team members may identify *failing to meet a schedule* as a major risk, when what they need to focus on are the actual events that could cause this to happen (e.g. poor estimating, adverse weather conditions, shipping delays). Focusing on **root causes** of events will lead to better strategies to mitigate the risk later.

16.5.1 Risk identification: Risk breakdown structure

Many organisations use a **risk breakdown structure (RBS)**, in conjunction with work breakdown structures (WBS), to help project teams identify and eventually analyse risks. Figure 16.5 provides a generic example of an RBS, where the project leader has identified categories and subcategories of risk (leaving question marks for the team to identify further categories); the team has subsequently started to identify (using yellow sticky notes) the actual risks under each subcategory. The focus at the outset should be on risks that can affect the whole project, as opposed to a specific section of the project or network. The categories and subcategories for the RBS can be predetermined by the project leader or, if an idea-showering approach is used, can be determined by the group during the idea-showering session itself. Typical categories of risk include communications, compliance, enterprise, brand, environmental, finance, health and safety, human resources, legal, physical, political, quality, social, reputational and technological—to name but a few. A similar approach to that taken in the development of the WBS can be applied to the idea showering of the RBS (i.e. using sticky notes in a formal risk identification workshop). Some organisations supply a list of mandatory risk categories that must be considered by the project leader in workshopping the RBS (e.g. see Table 16.1). *Note:* The project leader should always idea shower beyond any mandated categories and always keep an open mind. *Remember: If a risk is not identified, it cannot be assessed and controlled.* Idea shower wide and deep to ensure all risks are identified, even if later assessed to be of low priority.

Figure 16.5 A risk breakdown structure (RBS) idea shower

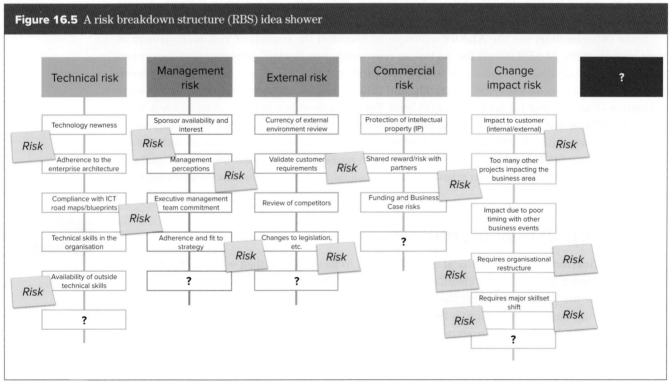

16.5.2 Risk identification: Work breakdown structure

After risks have been identified at a high level, across the whole project using a defined set of categories, a risk identification across more specific areas can be carried out. The WBS is an effective tool for identifying specific risks. A review of each work package (and task, if relevant) should be undertaken, and the following asked:

- What risks are present in carrying out the activities within the work package and/ or tasks?
- What risks are present when multiple activities in a work package and/or tasks are carried out at the same time?

Although this can take some effort, it provides another potential perspective on risks that may exist at a detailed level within the project.

Using the RBS and WBS reduces the chance of a risk event being missed. The WBS and RBS are complementary; it is not a case of either/or but applying both techniques.

Table 16.1 An example of mandatory risk categories

Risk category	Subcategory
Technical risk	Technology newness Adherence to the enterprise architecture Compliance with ICT roadmaps/blueprints Technical skills in the organisation Availability of outside technical skills
Management risk	Sponsor availability and interest Management perceptions Executive management team commitment Adherence and fit to strategy
External risk	Currency of external environment review Customer requirements validated? Review of competitors Changes to legislation, etc.
Commercial risk	Protection of intellectual property (IP) Shared reward/risk with partners Funding and Business Case risks
Change impact risk	Impact to customer (internal/external) Too many other projects impacting the business area Impact due to poor timing with other business events Requires organisational restructure Requires major skillset shift

© 2022 Dr Neil Pearson

16.5.3 Risk identification: Risk profiles

A **risk profile** is another useful tool. A risk profile is a list of questions that is used to address common areas of uncertainty that are often found on a project. These questions are predominantly developed (and refined) from previous, similar projects; Table 16.2 provides a partial example of such

Table 16.2 Partial risk profile for a product development project

Area of uncertainty	Example question
Technical requirements	■ Are the requirements stable? ■ Do the requirements have defined and agreed tolerances?
Design	■ Does the design depend on unrealistic or optimistic assumptions? ■ Does the design require uncharted territory to be navigated?
Testing	■ Will testing equipment be available when needed? ■ Will testing resources be available?
Development	■ Is the development process supported by a compatible set of procedures, methods and tools? ■ Does the development process include peer reviews?
Schedule	■ Is the schedule dependent upon the completion of other projects? ■ What other projects are dependent upon our project?
Budget	■ How reliable are the cost estimates? ■ What is the contingency included, given the risk context and profile?
Quality	■ Are quality considerations built into the design? ■ Are we in compliance with the customer's quality management system?
Management	■ Do people know who has authority for what? ■ What is the Steering Committee accountable for?
Work environment	■ Do people work cooperatively across functional boundaries? ■ Can company politics derail the project?
Staffing	■ Are staff members inexperienced, or is the company understaffed? ■ Are staff members appropriately trained?
Customer	■ Does the customer understand what it will take to complete the project? ■ Is the customer seen as a partner?
Contractors	■ Are there any ambiguities in contractor task definitions? ■ Which contract types are to be avoided to reduce risks?

© 2022 Dr Neil Pearson

a risk profile. Good risk profiles are tailored for the type of project being undertaken. For example, developing an information system is different from building a new car and therefore risk profiles are specific to the project's subject matter. Risk profiles recognise the unique strengths and weaknesses of the organisation, and they address both technical and managerial risks. For example, the profile shown in Table 16.2 asks questions about the design (whether the design depends upon unrealistic assumptions) and work environment (do people cooperate across functional boundaries?)

Risk profiles are usually generated and maintained by staff from the project management office (PMO). They are updated and refined during the post-implementation review (PIR) (refer to Chapter 21 "Project closure"). When kept up to date, these profiles can be a powerful resource for the project leader to have on tap in the risk management process. The collective experience of the organisation's past projects resides in these questions. However, remember that risk profiles should be used in conjunction with RBS, WBS and other far-reaching techniques, and not used as the only tool to identify risks.

16.5.4 Risk identification: Lessons learned

Lessons learned registers and historical records can either complement risk profiles or be used when formal risk profiles are not available. Project teams can investigate what happened on past, similar projects to identify potential risks. For example, a project leader can check the on-time performance of selected vendors to gauge the potential threat of any shipping delays. ICT project leaders can access best practice papers detailing other companies' experiences of converting software systems. Enquiries should not be limited to recorded data. Savvy project leaders also tap into the tried and tested wisdom of highly experienced project leaders (and their peer networks).

16.5.5 Risk identification: Delphi method

The **Delphi method** is another useful tool for helping to identify risk. It is a structured (initially anonymous) method that solicits information from a panel of stakeholders. Typical steps in using this method might resemble the following.

- *Step 1:* Identify the group of stakeholders to be included in the task of identifying risks.
- *Step 2:* Send a request (e.g. an email) to each group member anonymously (as each group member should not know who the other members are), requesting they identify risks around the brief of the project you give to them.
- *Step 3:* Collate the responses (usually a deadline for their response is placed on the request) and start to pull together a structured list of the responses received.
- *Step 4:* Send the list back out to the group (anonymously) and, again, gather responses. (The list should start to expand as each member of the group extrapolates on the anonymous responses provided by others.)

Repeat Steps 3 and 4 until no more content is added to the list.

- *Step 5:* Send the final list of identified risks to the group.
- *Step 6 (optional and not part of the formal Delphi method):* Bring the group together in a workshop-type format to debate any differing perspectives. This is the first time each group member will discover who else was invited to respond, so be prepared to facilitate the group during discussions.

A benefit of the Delphi method is that personalities are kept out of the risk identification process. Since the group is working anonymously, the focus is kept on risk identification, and not on personality clashes, personal plans or political agendas!

In identifying risk, it is often the case that only the symptoms of a risk are captured and not the real root cause of the risk, which, after all, should be the focus of the risk analysis. Two techniques (not the only techniques available) that can assist the project leader to get to the root cause of a risk (or problem) are the **5 whys** and the cause and effect (fishbone) technique (refer to Chapter 13 "Project quality management"). As a brief recap: the 5 whys technique involves repeatedly asking the question "Why?", with the goal being to peel away the layers of symptoms to reveal the core problem. Using this process, it may be the case that even more risks are identified. Ultimately, this process aims to get to the real risk that needs to be managed, rather than its symptoms. Although the process is referred to as the *5 whys*, in practice it may be necessary to ask either fewer or more "Why" questions to get to the actual cause of the risk.

16.5.6 Risk identification: SWOT

A **SWOT analysis** is a useful tool for helping to understand the project's risk context and for facilitating the identification of high-level risks. Usually carried out in the Initiating stage of the project life cycle, the SWOT analysis can provide a holistic perspective on risk for the overall project. The SWOT technique examines the project from four perspectives: strengths and weaknesses (from an internal perspective) and opportunities and threats (from an external perspective). The SWOT analysis also examines the degree to which strengths and opportunities offset the more harmful threats and weaknesses. Another way to view a risk SWOT identification is that strengths and opportunities represent positive (or opportunity) risks, and threats and weaknesses represent negative (or threat) risks.

16.5.7 Risk identification: Review of all project assumptions and constraints

There are inherent risks in stating **assumptions** (whether as part of the scope document or within any of the other knowledge area management plans). The project leader must therefore review all assumptions made across the project, assess whether these are true and scrutinise what risks lie in making such assumptions. The same approach can be applied to **constraints**. Constraints represent a potential source of risk since, if we are immediately constraining the project in some dimension (e.g. funding or resource shortage), we are potentially introducing risk into the project. Constraints (as with assumptions) should always be reviewed from a risk perspective.

The risk identification process should not be limited to only the project's core team. Input should be solicited from customers, sponsors, subcontractors, vendors and other stakeholders. Relevant stakeholders can be formally interviewed or included on the project's risk management team. Not only can these key players potentially offer up a valuable perspective, but by involving them in the risk management process, they may become more oriented towards the project's success. One of the keys to success around risk identification is *attitude*. While a can-do attitude is essential during implementation, project leaders should encourage critical thinking when it comes to risk identification as the goal is to identify potential problems before they happen.

16.5.8 Risk identification: Subject matter expert review

As with any topic in life, getting an external subject matter expert (SME)—in this case to review the project from a risk perspective—can bring fresh eyes to the subject and identify risks that are often sitting right under our noses. You may find that SMEs can be sourced internally in your organisation, in which case ensure there are ground rules established to allow for critical but friendly feedback.

The RBS, WBS and risk profiles are useful tools for making sure no stone is left unturned. However, when these tools are applied well, the number of identified risks can seem overwhelming and a little discouraging. Initial optimism might be replaced with griping and cries of "What have we got ourselves into?!" It is important that project leaders set the right tone at this juncture and push forward with completing the risk management process, so members regain confidence in themselves and in the project. It is also at this point that the project leader should start to develop another key artefact: the **Risk Register**.

Risk Register

During risk identification, the project leader will typically collect information on the following.

1. *Risk ID (RID):* This will be a unique reference number allocated to a particular risk (bear in mind that a typical project may identify hundreds of potential risks).

2. *Risk name:* A simple name for the risk.

3. *Risk description:* A clear and detailed description of the risk.

4. *Risk category/subcategory:* Typically, each risk category will be the same as the categories of risk identified in developing the RBS. This is a useful way to later filter the Risk Register for analysis and reporting purposes.

5. *Opportunity/threat risk:* A classification of whether the risk presents a *threat* or an *opportunity* to the project.

6. *Risk source (date/person/source):* Records *when*, *where*, and *by whom* the risk was identified. This is a useful reference tool, because if further information/questions are raised around the risk, either the person who raised the risk can be contacted or the source (a document or otherwise) can be referred to.

Once a thorough and inclusive risk identification has been carried out, and the information collated in a Risk Register, the task of risk analysis takes place next. A partial example Risk Register is included as Table 16.3.

Table 16.3 Risk identification: House Build example

Risk identification							
Risk ID	Risk name	Risk category	Risk or issue	Opportunity or threat	Date raised	Raised by	Risk owner
RID-0001	Abnormal ground conditions discovered when taking core samples of site.	Foundations	Risk	Threat	3 March	Site supervisor	Project leader
RID-0002	Unstable ground requires additional groundwork prior to foundations.	Foundations	Risk	Threat	5 March	Site supervisor	Project leader
RID-0003	Inclement weather days exceed "wet days" built into schedule.	Foundations	Risk	Threat	3 March	Site supervisor	Project leader

© 2022 Dr Neil Pearson

16.6 Step 3: Risk analysis

Risk analysis involves developing a clear understanding about an identified potential risk. In carrying out the analysis, the **probability** (likelihood) and **impact** (consequence) of the risk occurring will be determined. Step 2 required a list of potential risks to be produced. Not all these risks will deserve attention as some will be trivial and can be ignored; however, others will pose serious threats to the welfare of the project and therefore must not be ignored. Project leaders must develop methods for sifting through the list of risks, eliminating inconsequential or redundant ones, and stratifying noteworthy ones, in terms of their importance and urgency. Again, the project leader will need to ensure that there are clear definitions and scales in place to transparently support the terms *probability* (likelihood) and *impact* (consequence). *Note:*

- *Probability* refers to the probability of the event occurring. (This is otherwise known as the *likelihood* of the risk occurring.)

- *Impact* refers to the impact of the event. (This is otherwise known as the *consequence* of the risk if the event occurs.)

Simply stated, risks need to be evaluated in terms of the probability of the event occurring and the impact if it does occur. The risk of a project leader being struck by lightning at a work site would have major negative impact on the project, but the probability of this happening, in reality, is so low that it is not worthy of further consideration. Conversely, people do change jobs, so an event such as the loss of key project personnel within an organisation would have not only an adverse impact but would also have a high probability of occurring. If it is likely to occur within a particular organisation, it may be wise for the organisation to be proactive and to mitigate the risk by developing incentive schemes for retaining specialists and/or engaging in cross-training to reduce the impacts of turnover. It is here that another term will be introduced: *inherent*. Before any mitigation (control) strategies are applied to manage risk in the project, the project leader will review the probability of the risk eventuating and its potential impact/repercussions. In Step 5, the project leader recalculates what level the risk still might pose after mitigation (control) strategies have been applied; this is known as the *residual* risk. This simple workflow is illustrated in Figure 16.6.

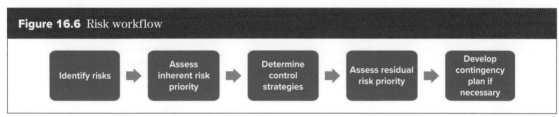

Figure 16.6 Risk workflow

© 2022 Dr Neil Pearson

The quality and credibility of the risk analysis process requires that different levels of risk probabilities and impacts are defined. These definitions vary and should be tailored to the specific nature and needs of the project. For example, a relatively simple scale ranging from *very unlikely* to *almost certainly* may suffice for one project, whereas another project may use more precise numerical probabilities (e.g. 0.1, 0.3, 0.5). Impact scales can be a bit problematic since adverse risks will affect project (or business) objectives differently. For example, a component failure may cause only a slight delay in the project schedule but lead to a major increase in project cost. If controlling cost is a high priority, then the impact would be severe. If, on the other hand, time is more critical than cost, the impact would only be minor.

Because impact ultimately needs to be assessed in terms of project priorities, different kinds of impact scales are used. Some scales simply use rank-order descriptors, such as *low, moderate, high* and *very high*, whereas others use numeric weights (e.g. 1–10). Also, some will focus on the project in general, while others will focus on specific project objectives. The project leader therefore needs to define up-front what will distinguish a weighting of 1 from a weighting of 3, or a *moderate* impact from a *severe* impact. The documentation of risk analysis can be evidenced in various risk assessment forms used by different companies. A simple inherent risk analysis, using a spreadsheet, is included as Table 16.4 by way of an example.

Table 16.4 Simple risk analysis: House Build example

Risk identification		Inherent risk (unmitigated risk)		
Risk ID	**Risk name**	**Probability***	**Impact†**	**Inherent RPN (Probability × Impact)**
RID-0001	Abnormal ground conditions discovered when taking core samples of site.	3	4	12
RID-0002	Unstable ground requires additional groundwork prior to foundations.	2	4	8
RID-0003	Inclement weather days exceed "wet days" built into schedule.	3	3	9

© 2022 Dr Neil Pearson

* Probability scale
1 Rare
2 Unlikely
3 Possible
4 Likely
5 Almost certain

† Impact scale
1 Insignificant
2 Minor
3 Moderate
4 Major
5 Catastrophic

This risk analysis is the current state of the risk before any mitigation (control) strategies have been applied; it is often referred to as the *inherent risk*. In addition to evaluating the probability and impact of risk events occurring, the project team can assess when the event might occur. This is often referred to as *proximity*. Again, a proximity scale would be defined up-front. If this is applied to the same identified risks, it could result in Table 16.5.

Table 16.5 Risk analysis (including proximity): House Build example

Risk identification		Inherent risk (unmitigated risk)			
Risk ID	Risk name	Probability*	Impact†	Proximity‡	Inherent RPN (Probability × Impact × Proximity)
RID-0001	Abnormal ground conditions discovered when taking core samples of site.	3	4	5	60
RID-0002	Unstable ground requires additional groundwork prior to foundations.	2	4	2	16
RID-0003	Inclement weather days exceed "wet days" built into schedule.	3	3	2	18

© 2022 Dr Neil Pearson

* Probability scale	† Impact scale	‡ Proximity scale
1 Rare	1 Insignificant	1 Before project handover
2 Unlikely	2 Minor	2 Within 20 days
3 Possible	3 Moderate	3 Within 10 days
4 Likely	4 Major	4 Within 5 days
5 Almost certain	5 Catastrophic	5 Immediate

Inclusion of the proximity of the risk (i.e. how near it could occur to the current date) assists the project leader in prioritising which risk needs to be attended to first. In this example, RID-0001, when multiplied by the proximity weight of 5, changes the priority of the risk and highlights that the risk should be attended to immediately.

16.7 Further complexity in risk analysis

Refer back to Figure 16.3. The project leader can take the risk analysis further still, by extending the impact rating. In some organisations, impact ratings may be assessed along a greater range of criteria. Table 16.6 provides an example of how impact scales could be defined, given the project objectives of cost, time, scope and quality.

Table 16.6 An example of how impact scales could be defined

Relative or numerical scale				
Impact rating	Cost	Time	Scope	Quality
1 Very low	Insignificant cost increase	Insignificant time increase	Scope decrease barely noticeable	Quality degradation barely noticeable
2 Low	<10% cost increase	<5% time increase	Minor areas of scope affected	Only very demanding applications are affected
3 Moderate	10–20% cost increase	5–10% time increase	Major areas of scope affected	Quality reduction requires sponsor approval
4 High	20–40% cost increase	10–20% time increase	Scope reduction unacceptable to sponsor	Quality reduction unacceptable to sponsor
5 Very high	>40% cost increase	>20% time increase	Project result is rendered useless	Project result is rendered useless

© 2022 Dr Neil Pearson

Table 16.6 demonstrates certain conditions that might be stated in impact scales regarding how a risk could potentially impact major project objectives (examples are provided for negative risks only). But how would this be integrated into the overall risk impact score? In Table 16.7 the reader can see that the single "Impact" column of the risk analysis has been replaced by the four project objective criteria of Table 16.6: cost, time, scope and quality. The overall risk ranking score is now calculated by adding the four impact criteria together and then multiplying the result by the probability:

(Cost + Time + Scope + Quality) × Probability. This needs to be carried out for both the inherent and residual risk analysis (residual risk will be covered later in this section).

Table 16.7 Impact considered over multiple impact criteria

| Risk name | Probability | Impact | | | | Overall inherent risk |
		Cost	Time	Scope	Quality	
Abnormal ground conditions discovered when taking core samples of site.	3	4	4	1	2	33
Unstable ground requires additional groundwork prior to foundations.	2	2	5	1	4	24
Inclement weather days exceed "wet days" built into schedule.	3	2	5	2	5	42

© 2022 Dr Neil Pearson

There are obvious benefits in looking at the impact in this way, including the fact that the project is informed exactly about which area would be impacted the most if the risk were to occur. The project leader must be mindful of these splits in monitoring and controlling the risk. The PMI discusses the "reviewing categories" of urgency, proximity, dormancy, manageability, controllability, detectability, connectivity, strategic impact and proximity (PMI 2017, p. 424).

Some risk management software packages will allow different approaches to be taken and therefore offer the benefit of being able to visualise risks on various charts. Figure 16.7 presents an inherent risk visualisation of risks, with probability plotted on the vertical axis, impact on the horizontal axis, and the size of the bubble (in this case) representing proximity. Charts can be modified for other criteria. For example, the size of the bubble could represent the cost to the project if the risk occurs.

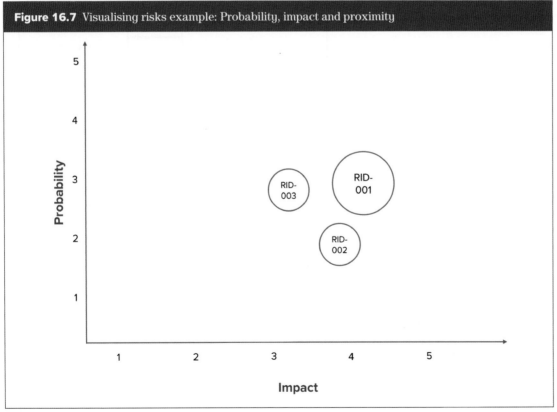

Figure 16.7 Visualising risks example: Probability, impact and proximity

© 2022 Dr Neil Pearson

In addition to the qualitative risk analysis techniques, the project leader could take a more quantitative approach to the analysis of risk using techniques such as PERT, decision trees and simulations (Monte Carlo).

16.7.1 **PERT**

The **program evaluation and review technique (PERT)** and **PERT simulation** can be used to review activity and project risk. PERT (and similar techniques) take a more macro perspective by looking at overall cost and schedule risks. The focus is not on individual events, but rather on the probability of the project being completed on time and within budget. These methods are useful in assessing the overall risk of the project and the need for items such as contingency funds, additional resources and longer task durations. A PERT simulation assumes a statistical distribution (range between optimistic and pessimistic) for each activity duration; it simulates the network (perhaps over 1000 simulations) using a random number generator. The outcome is the relative probability (called a *criticality index*) of an activity becoming *critical* under the many different, possible activity durations for each activity. A PERT simulation also provides a list of potential critical paths, and the probabilities of each occurring. Having this information available can greatly facilitate the identification and assessment of schedule risk.

16.7.2 **Decision trees**

Decision trees are used to assess alternative courses of action, using **expected monetary value (EMV)**. They use a quantitative assessment of risk to understand all the possible outcomes for a given set of related project risks. An example of a **decision tree analysis** for a software project is provided in Figure 16.8. The project has three possible decisions: stay with the existing software, buy a new software

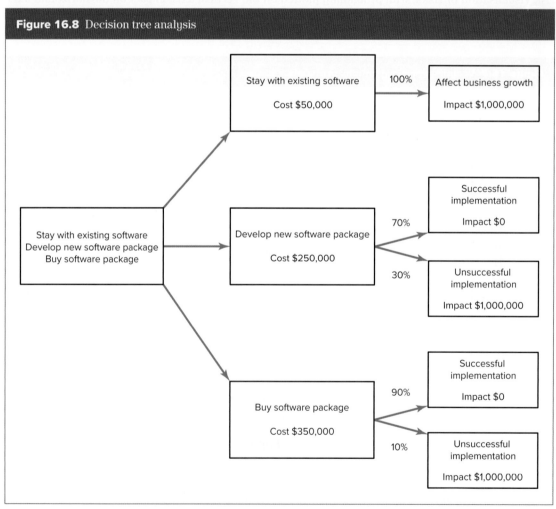

Figure 16.8 Decision tree analysis

package, or develop a new software package. Each decision in turn has a tree of probable outcomes (with an attached probability of that outcome occurring) and the cost (impact) should that outcome occur. The idea of decision tree analysis is to quantitatively analyse which decision would be best.

- *Step A:* Define the decisions/problem.
- *Step B:* Define the decision tree of possible outcomes.
- *Step C:* Attach the probability of each outcome occurring.
- *Step D:* Attach the impact of each outcome in dollars ($).
- *Step E:* Calculate the expected monetary value of each decision (in this example, this would be the impact if that decision is not successful).

  For example:

  - Stay with the existing software: $1 \times \$1,000,000 = \$1,000,000$
  - Buy software package: $0.1 \times \$1,000,000 = \$100,000$
  - Develop new software package: $0.3 \times \$1,000,000 = \$300,000$

- *Step F:* Add in the costs of taking each decision.

  For example:

  - Stay with the existing software: $\$1,000,000 + \$50,000 = \$1,050,000$
  - Buy software package: $\$100,000 + \$350,000 = \$450,000$
  - Develop new software package: $\$300,000 + \$250,000 = \$550,000$

- *Step G:* The DECISION! From the calculations above, it can be seen that "Buy software package" is the most cost-balanced option, based on the probability of the risk occurring, the impact to the business if it occurs and the cost of taking that decision path.

16.7.3 Monte Carlo technique

The **Monte Carlo technique** is another quantitative technique. Monte Carlo simulation is a technique used to understand the impact of risk and uncertainty in financial, time, cost and other forecasting models. A Monte Carlo simulator helps one visualise most or all the potential outcomes, thus enabling one to have a better idea regarding the risk of a decision.

Although not frequently used in small and medium projects, for large, risky projects the technique offers a more statistical approach to assessing risk outcomes. The model works by taking a range of values for each risk (optimistic outcome, most realistic outcome and pessimistic outcome) and running hundreds (or even thousands) of simulations between these values, to obtain estimates of likely outcomes (PMI 2017). *Note:* This is an advanced topic and the reader is advised to pursue specific information before using this technique—a useful internet resource is provided at: https://www .youtube.com/watch?v=4Hz58TV70k4

So, let's pause to consider where the project leader will be within the risk process at this point; by the end of Step 3: Risk analysis, they will have a solid idea of the risk profile of the project (potential risk), having taken the appropriate steps to analyse and ascertain the inherent risk score for each risk that was identified in Step 2: Risk identification. The project leader therefore should have a good idea by now of the overall inherent risk profile of the project.

16.8 Step 4: Risk evaluation

This step in the process could be referred to in various ways, depending on the industry preference. Common terms include *risk treatment, risk mitigation, risk response, controls,* and *intervention actions.*

Although ISO 31000:2018 separates **risk evaluation** from **risk analysis**, in practical terms, both are carried out simultaneously: that is, in identifying the probability and impact of a risk and evaluating the overall risk rating of each risk, the project leader will make decisions about which risks pose a higher threat to the project (or greater opportunity if the risk is an opportunity risk).

In Step 5: Risk treatment (examined below), the options available to the project leader for reducing the risk profile (probability and/or impact) of each identified risk are explored.

By this stage in the risk management process, the inherent risk rating for each identified risk will have been captured in the project's Risk Register, including details of:

- the probability (likelihood) rating of the risk occurring
- the impact (consequence) of the risk if it occurs
- the overall risk rating, usually in a simple calculation (Probability × Impact), which gives an overall risk rating to the risk, often referred to as the **inherent risk priority number (RPN)**. *Note:* The definitions of probability and impact, and the scales and any weighting systems to be applied to all project risks, are documented in the Risk Management Plan but applied to the risks in the Risk Register
- the proximity of the risk, how close in time could the risk occur, which assists the project leader in prioritising which risks to attend to first
- optional **detection difficulty**—"How do we known radioactive water is leaking below the nuclear melted core?"; and **early warning indicators**—"Sensor reading in subtrain water aquifer detects abnormal levels of radiation".

16.9 | STEP 5: Risk treatment

When a risk event has been identified and assessed, a decision must be made concerning which risk response is the most appropriate for it. Responses to threat risks can be classified as **escalate** (introduced in the sixth edition of PMBOK (PMI 2017)), *mitigate, avoid, transfer* or *accept*. Responses to opportunity risks include *escalate, exploit, share, enhance* and *accept. Note:* This stage has many different phrases, such as risk treatment, risk mitigation, risk response and risk controls.

16.9.1 Inherent threat risk response options

Different methodologies have different terminology for categories of risk responses towards differing threat risks. Table 16.8 illustrates the threat risk terminology used by PMBOK, PRINCE2, Praxis and APM.

Table 16.8 Threat risks: Response terminology

PMBOK	PRINCE2	Praxis	APM
Escalate			
Avoid	Avoid	Avoid	Avoid
Transfer	Transfer	Transfer	Transfer
Mitigate	Reduce	Reduce	Reduce/mitigate
Accept	Accept	Accept	Accept
	Fallback*		Contingency plan
	Share		

© 2022 Dr Neil Pearson

Note: PMBOK = Project Management Body of Knowledge; APM = Association for Project Management
* Only happens when the risk occurs and the Contingency Plan is actioned

Some organisations will have specific controls that must be applied to the risk depending on the inherent risk score (RPN). Figure 16.9 illustrates an approach that is often used to assist a project leader in applying in a consistent manner the correct control strategy.

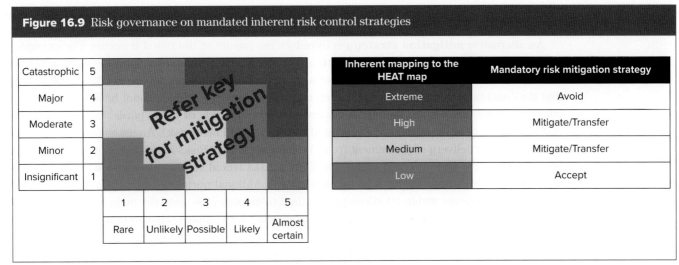

Figure 16.9 Risk governance on mandated inherent risk control strategies

Catastrophic	5					
Major	4					
Moderate	3					
Minor	2					
Insignificant	1					
		1	2	3	4	5
		Rare	Unlikely	Possible	Likely	Almost certain

Inherent mapping to the HEAT map	Mandatory risk mitigation strategy
Extreme	Avoid
High	Mitigate/Transfer
Medium	Mitigate/Transfer
Low	Accept

© 2022 Dr Neil Pearson

The threat risk response categories are now examined using the PMBOK approach.

16.9.2 Escalate risk

In the sixth edition of PMBOK (PMI 2017), an additional risk response is introduced—*escalate*—which needs to occur when the project leader, team and/or sponsor agree that the threat is outside the scope/authority of the project. The escalation must be to a named party who will take over accountability for the risk. Parties typically involved in escalations include the program management office (PMO), the portfolio management office or the business (e.g. if the risk turns out to be a general business risk) (PMI 2017).

The project leader should be aware of this new risk strategy and update any tools used (such as a Risk Register) to encompass this strategy and communicate to the project team what this strategy is, and how it would be applied in the project.

16.9.3 Mitigating risk

There are basically two strategies for mitigating risk: (1) reduce the probability that the event will occur and/or (2) reduce the impact that the adverse event could potentially have on the project. Most risk teams focus first on reducing the probability of risk events occurring since there will be no need to consider the (potentially costly) second strategy if this approach is successful.

Testing and prototyping are frequently used to prevent problems from surfacing later in a project. An example of testing could, for instance, relate to an information systems project where the project team is responsible for installing a new operating system in the team's parent company. Before implementing the project, the team tests the new system on a smaller isolated network. By doing so, it discovers a variety of problems and is able to come up with solutions, before full implementation. The team may still encounter problems with the installation, but the number and severity of problems is likely to be greatly reduced.

Most often, it is beneficial to identify the root causes of an event. For example, the fear a vendor will be unable to supply customised components on time may be attributable to (1) poor vendor relationships, (2) design miscommunication or (3) lack of motivation. As a result of this analysis, the project leader may decide to *do lunch* with the vendor to engage with them and build trust, or invite the vendor to attend design meetings and restructure the contract to include incentives for on-time delivery. Other examples of how the probability of the occurrence of risks could be reduced include

(1) scheduling outdoor work to be conducted during the summer months, (2) investing in up-front safety training and (3) choosing high-quality materials and equipment.

An alternative **mitigation strategy** is to reduce the impact of the risk if it occurs. For example, a new bridge project for a coastal port is to use an innovative, continuous cement-pouring process, developed by an Australian organisation, to save large sums of money and time. The major risk is that the continuous pouring process for each major section of the bridge cannot be interrupted. Any interruption will necessitate the whole cement section (hundreds of cubic yards) being torn down and started over (or the structural integrity of the section will be at risk). An assessment of *possible risks* centres on delivery of the cement from the cement factory. Risks identified are that trucks may be delayed, or the factory could break down. Such risks would result in tremendous rework costs and delays. Risk is therefore reduced by having two additional portable cement plants built nearby on different highways within 30 kilometres of the bridge project in case the main factory supply is interrupted. These two portable plants carry raw materials for a whole bridge section, and extra trucks are on immediate standby each time continuous pouring is required. Similar risk reduction scenarios are apparent in system and software development projects where parallel innovation processes are used in case one fails.

16.9.4 Avoiding risk

Risk avoidance involves changing the project plan to eliminate the risk or condition. Although it is impossible to eliminate all risk events, some specific risks may need to be avoided before you launch the project. For example, adopting proven technology instead of experimental technology can eliminate technical failure. Choosing an Australian supplier as opposed to a supplier in a country prone to political unrest would virtually eliminate the chance that political unrest might disrupt the supply of critical materials (unless, of course, it was dependent on a supply chain of raw materials). *Note:* Avoiding a risk event by redesigning the project could potentially introduce new risks, which would have to be assessed.

16.9.5 Transferring risk

Passing risk to another party is common practice; however, such a transfer does not change the risk. Passing risk to another party almost always results in having to pay a premium for this exemption. Fixed-price contracts are a classic example of risk being transferred from an owner to a contractor. The contractor understands that their organisation will have to cover the cost of any risk event that materialises; therefore, a monetary risk factor is added to the contract bid price. Before electing to transfer the risk, the owner should decide which party is in the strongest position to be able to best control activities that might lead to the risk occurring. Also, serious consideration needs to be given to whether the contractor is capable of absorbing this risk. It will be imperative to clearly identify and legally document details of their responsibility for absorbing the risk.

Another, more obvious, way of transferring risk is through insurance. In many instances this is impractical because being able to clearly define the project risk event and its conditions to an insurance broker who is unfamiliar with the project can be difficult and usually expensive. Of course, low-probability and high-impact risk events such as *acts of God* (e.g. lightning) are more easily definable and insurable. Other financial instruments may be used to transfer risk, for example, performance bonds, warranties and guarantees.

On large international construction projects, like petrochemical plants and oil refineries, host countries often insist on contracts that enforce build–own–operate–transfer (BOOT) conditions. Here, the project is expected to not only build the facility, but also to take over ownership until its operation capacity has been proven and all debugging has occurred before final transfer of ownership to the client occurs. In these cases, the host country has effectively transferred the financial risk of ownership until the project has been fully completed and capabilities have been proven. As with avoiding risk, transferring risk may introduce new risks to the project, requiring analysis.

16.9.6 **Accepting (retaining) risk**

In some cases, a conscious decision is made to accept the risk of an event occurring. Some risks are so large that it is not feasible to consider transferring or reducing the event (e.g. an earthquake or flood). The project owner assumes the risk because the chance of such an event occurring is slim. In other cases, risks that are identified in the budget reserve can simply be absorbed if they materialise. The risk is retained by developing a Contingency Plan to be implemented if the risk materialises. In a few cases, a risk event can be ignored, and a cost overrun accepted, should the risk event occur. In other cases, the probability and impact of the risk are low, and the risk is accepted—no further actions are carried out in the project.

16.9.7 **Continuing the risk discussion**

The more effort that is given towards risk response before the project begins, the better the chances will be for minimising project surprises. Knowing ahead of time whether the response to a risk event means that it will be retained, transferred or mitigated will greatly reduce stress and uncertainty. Again, control is possible with this structured approach. Once a mitigation strategy has been agreed, it may be necessary to plan actions for reducing the overall risk rating to a residual level. This information should be captured in the Risk Register. The Risk Register should now track the following information about each identified risk.

- *Mitigation strategy:* For threat risks, this would be one of mitigating, avoiding, transferring or accepting (retaining).
- *Mitigation Plan:* Details the actions to be carried out in the project. This could be as simple as noting that additional insurance is required or may introduce additional tasks into the WBS that have to be resourced within the project.
- *Cost (to mitigate):* What are the associated costs of carrying out the mitigation strategy?
- *Mitigation owner:* Who in the project is responsible for ensuring that the activities outlined in the mitigation plan are carried out and, once completed, are reported back to the project leader?
- *Probability:* Once the mitigation strategy and plan have been applied, where does this leave the risk in relation to the probability of it occurring?
- *Impact:* Once the mitigation strategy and plan have been applied, where does this leave the risk in relation to the impact, if it does occur?
- *Overall residual risk:* The revised "Probability × Impact" calculation, which gives an overall RPN rating to the residual risk.
  - If accepting the risk, there is no change to the probability and impact values.
  - If mitigating against the risk, there should be a change to the probability and/or impact, depending on what the mitigation actions contained.
  - If transferring the risk, there could potentially be a change to the probability and/or impact, depending on what the mitigation actions contained. *Note:* New risks could be identified as a result of the transfer strategy.
  - If avoiding the risk, the project would be replanned to ensure the risk is not present; therefore, there would be no residual risk rating as the risk would effectively have been removed. *Note:* New risks could be identified because of the replanning.

So, what would our risk analysis now look like, given the previous example? Let's extend the risk table by adding in the mitigation strategy (sometimes referred to as *controls*), plan and owner, and then review and update the values of probability and impact and the overall risk rating for what we now refer to as the *residual RPN* (Table 16.9).

Table 16.9 Mitigation and residual risk assessment

Risk identification		Inherent risk (unmitigated risk)			Mitigation planning			Residual risk (mitigated risk)		
Risk ID	Risk name	Probability*	Impact†	Inherent RPN	Strategy	Mitigation actions	Mitigation owner	Probability*	Impact†	Residual RPN
RID-0001	Abnormal ground conditions discovered when taking core samples of site.	3	4	12	Mitigate	1. Take core samples earlier in the project. 2. Include costs in first stage payment by customer.	1. Project leader 2. Finance director	1	4	4
RID-0002	Unstable ground requires additional groundwork before foundations.	2	4	8	Avoid	1. Replan the project schedule to include additional steps in the land procurement strategy, so land is not purchased that has a high cost of pre-work.	1. Procurement manager	1	4	4
RID-0003	Inclement weather days exceed "wet days" built into schedule.	3	3	9	Accept			3	3	9

© 2022 Dr Neil Pearson

Note: **RPN** = risk priority number

* *Probability scale*
1 Rare
2 Unlikely
3 Possible
4 Likely
5 Almost certain

† *Impact scale*
1 Insignificant
2 Minor
3 Moderate
4 Major
5 Catastrophic

Once all the actions/controls have been applied in the project, this will generate the *residual RPN* that the project leader will want to monitor when monitoring and controlling the project during the Executing stage. If the controls have not been fully actioned in the project, the project leader should monitor the *inherent RPN* instead, as the risk has not yet been reduced to its residual value.

16.10 Step 6: Contingency planning

A **Contingency Plan** is an alternative plan that will be used if a possible foreseen risk event becomes a reality (i.e. an issue). The Contingency Plan represents actions that will be carried out when the risk eventuates and becomes an issue. A key distinction between a risk response (mitigation strategy) and a Contingency Plan is that a response is part of the actual Risk Register, while a Contingency Plan is referred to within the Risk Register, but is normally a whole plan of actions that only goes into effect after the risk occurs and becomes an *issue*.

Like all plans, the Contingency Plan answers the questions of *what, where, when, who* and *how much*. The absence of a Contingency Plan when a risk event occurs can cause a manager to delay or postpone the decision to implement a remedy. This postponement can lead to panic and a situation in which the first remedy suggested is latched onto. Such *after-the-event* decision-making, made under pressure, can be potentially dangerous and costly. Contingency planning evaluates alternative remedies for possible foreseeable events before the risk event occurs and so the best plan can be selected from alternatives. Such early contingency planning facilitates a smooth transition to the remedy, or work-around plan. The availability of a Contingency Plan can significantly increase the chances for project success. Conditions for activating the implementation (sometimes referred to as **triggers**) of the Contingency Plan should be decided and clearly documented in the Risk Register, against each risk, as required. For high-priority risks, where there is a residual risk high probability and/or impact of the risk becoming an issue and having to be managed, the plan should include a cost estimate. All parties that will be affected should agree to the Contingency Plan and have the authority to make commitments if the plan is enacted. Because the implementation of a Contingency Plan will embody some disruption in the sequence of work, all Contingency Plans need to be communicated to team members so that surprise and resistance are minimised. Table 16.10 illustrates risk contingency planning.

Taking the Risk Register to its final stage in this process requires the following information to be noted against each risk for which it was necessary to have a Contingency Plan in place. (*Note:* Typically, this will be risks that have a high-probability and high-impact rating.)

■ *Contingency (event) Action Plan:* If the risk becomes an issue, what is the planned sequence of events to be taken to manage the situation? (At times, these plans can be extensive and may have to be documented elsewhere, with a reference to the plan captured in the Risk Register.)

■ *Trigger:* Details of what triggering event causes the plan to be invoked.

■ *Contingency (event) Plan owner:* Who is going to take charge of managing the Contingency Plan once the trigger event has occurred?

■ ***Cost of contingency:*** What are the potential costs to the project in invoking the Contingency Plan?

Within the inclusion of contingency planning (not formally a step within ISO 31000:2018), the process of identifying, analysing, evaluating and treating risks is now complete. The majority of risk planning is carried out during the Planning stage of the project. However, when new risks are identified during the progression of the project, or when the status of risks changes, the same process must be repeated. Risks will also be closed with the passing of time.

Table 16.10 Risk contingency planning

Risk identification		Inherent risk (unmitigated risk)			Mitigation planning			Residual risk (mitigated risk)			Contingency planning			
Risk ID	Risk name	Probability	Impact	Inherent RPN	Strategy	Mitigation plan	Mitigation owner	Probability	Impact	Residual RPN	Contingency action plan	Trigger	Contingency plan owner	Cost of carrying out the contingency plan
RID-0003	Inclement weather days exceed "wet days" built into schedule.	3	3	9	Accept			3	3	9	Employ contract-rate labourers. Crash and fast track project schedule to allow parallel activities with additional resources.	Wet weather days exceed industry standard buffer included in project schedule.	Project leader	AUD500/day/ contractor
RID-0017	Concrete pump machine breakdown.	3	5	15	Accept			3	5	15	Standby arrangements with local hire company put in place.	Pump breakdown, not serviceable within 15 minutes.	Site Supervisor	AUD3000/ half-day

© 2022 Dr Neil Pearson

Note: RPN = risk priority number

16.11 : Opportunity risk explored

So far, this chapter has focused on threat (or negative) risks to the project (i.e. what can go wrong on a project). There is a flip side: there can be positive risks on a project that, when well managed, have the potential to enhance project outcomes. This is commonly referred to as **opportunity (or positive) risk**. An opportunity is an event that can have a positive impact on project objectives. For example, unusually favourable weather can accelerate construction work, or a more favourable contract to supply fuel at cheaper prices may create savings that could be used to add value to a project. Essentially, the same process that is used to manage threat risks is applied to opportunity risks. Opportunities are identified, assessed in terms of likelihood and impact, responses are determined, and Contingency Plans can even be established to take advantage of the opportunity if it occurs. The major difference between managing negative risks and opportunity risks is in the response approach taken, as treatment strategies are different for opportunity risks. Table 16.11 illustrates opportunity risk terminology used by PMBOK, PRINCE2, Praxis and the Association for Project Management (APM).

Table 16.11 Opportunity risks, response terminology

PMBOK	PRINCE2	Praxis	APM
Escalate			
Exploit	Exploit	Exploit	Exploit
Share	Share	Share	Share
Enhance	Enhance	Enhance	Enhance
Accept			
	Reject	Reject	Accept

© 2022 Dr Neil Pearson

As outlined in Table 16.11, when dealing with an opportunity risk, the project leader must consider how potential benefits from the opportunity risk are to be managed and enhanced within the project. To help unpack this, let's look at an example of an opportunity risk presented in a Risk Register (Table 16.12).

Table 16.12 Opportunity assessment

Risk identification		Inherent risk (unmitigated risk)			Mitigation planning			Residual risk (mitigated risk)		
Risk ID	Risk name	Probability*	Impact†	Inherent RPN	Strategy	Mitigation actions	Mitigation owner	Probability*	Impact†	Residual RPN
RID-0004	Attaining a high Nationwide House Energy Rating Scheme (NatHERS) and National Australian Built Environment Rating System (NABERS) enables a premium selling price to "green" customers.	1	4	4	Enhance	Undertake a construction review and build to NatHERS and NABERS standards highest rating.	Project leader	4	5	20

© 2022 Dr Neil Pearson

Note: RPN = risk priority number
* *Probability scale*   † *Impact scale*
1 Remote   *1 Minor*
2 Low   *2 Moderate*
3 Medium   *3 Major*
4 Probable   *4 Substantial*
5 Certain   *5 Transformative*

The inverse (to that of a threat risk) is happening to the overall risk ranking of the opportunity risk. This is because we want to enhance the opportunity and reap rewards greater than were planned when it does occur. Therefore, the residual RPN for an opportunity risk should always be higher that the inherent RPN! Threat risk we want to reduce; opportunity risk we want to enhance.

- *Exploit:* This tactic seeks to eliminate the uncertainty associated with an opportunity to ensure the risk definitely occurs. Examples include assigning your best personnel to a critical burst activity to reduce time to completion, or revising a design to enable a component to be purchased rather than developed internally.

- *Share:* This strategy involves allocating some or all the ownership of an opportunity to another party who is best able to capture it for the benefit of the project. Examples include establishing continuous improvement incentives for external contractors, or joint ventures.

- *Enhance:* This is the opposite of mitigation, in that action is taken to increase the probability and/or the positive impact of an opportunity. Examples include choosing site location based on favourable weather patterns or choosing raw materials that are likely to decline in price (so savings are made).

- *Accept:* Accepting an opportunity means being willing to take advantage of it if it occurs, but not taking action to pursue it.

While it is only natural to focus on threat risks, it is sound practice to engage in active opportunity risk management as well. The process around how to analyse an opportunity risk is like that of a threat risk, with some adjustments in how the terminology is applied. Consider the following.

- *Opportunity probability:* How likely is the opportunity to happen? (We want it to happen, given that it is an opportunity.)

- *Opportunity impact:* How helpful would it be if it did happen? (We want to exaggerate its impact so we can reap greater rewards.)

With risk response or enhancement (not mitigation) strategies, we are trying to (1) make the opportunity happen and (2) make it better: that is, we want to exploit and maximise opportunities, so the resulting (residual) probability and impact is higher (i.e. we want to increase the probability of it occurring, and enhance the impact). We would therefore put in place an Enhancement (not mitigation) Action Plan and implement the actions. Refer to Table 16.12.

Remember: We wish to minimise threats and leverage opportunities.

16.12 : **Common approaches to handling risk**

Some of the most-encountered methods used for handling risk are discussed in the following sections. Although the choice of approach may vary from project to project, there are some prevailing common themes that a project leader should be aware of.

16.12.1 **Technical risks**

Technical risks are specific to each subject matter domain. For example, technical risks in an information technology project could be around the commissioning of server hardware; although the hardware might be delivered without damage, it starts to fail when it has been run up and soak-tested. Obviously, a root-cause analysis would take place; but the fact remains that the risk of hardware failing during soak-testing has now eventuated and the Contingency Plan needs to be invoked.

16.12.2 **Schedule risks**

Some organisations will defer dealing with the threat of a project coming in late until this situation surfaces. Contingency funds are set aside to expedite or *crash* the project to get it back on track. Crashing, or reducing, the project's duration is accomplished by shortening (compressing) one or more activities on the critical path. However, this approach brings additional costs and risks. Some

Contingency Plans can avoid costly procedures. For example, schedules can be altered by working activities in parallel, or by using start-to-start lag relationships. Also, using the best people on high-risk tasks may relieve, or lessen, the chance of some risk events occurring. This approach could potentially be combined with fast-tracking the schedule (refer to Chapter 11 "Project schedule management").

16.12.3 Schedule risks and time buffers

Just as contingency funds are established to absorb unplanned costs, managers can use time buffers to cushion potential delays in the project. Like contingency funds, the amount of time buffered will depend upon the inherent uncertainty of the project (i.e. the more uncertain the project, the more time should be reserved for the schedule). The strategy is to assign extra time at critical moments in the project. For example, buffers are added to:

- activities with severe risks
- merge activities that are prone to delays due to one or more of the preceding activities being late
- non-critical activities, to reduce the likelihood that they will create another critical path
- activities that require scarce resources, to ensure the resources are available when needed.

In the face of overall schedule uncertainty, time buffers are sometimes added to the end of the project. For example, a 90-day project may have a 10-day project buffer. While the extra 10 days would not appear on the schedule, they would be available if needed. Similar to management reserves, time buffers typically require the authorisation of top-level management.

16.12.4 Cost risks

For projects that have a long duration, some contingency will need to be built in to accommodate price changes (which are usually upwards). An important point to remember when reviewing pricing is to avoid the potential trap of only using one lump sum to cover price risks. For example, if inflation has been running at about 3 per cent, some managers will add 3 per cent for all resources used in the project. This lump-sum approach does not address exactly where price protection is needed and fails to provide opportunities for tracking and control. On cost-sensitive projects, price risks should be evaluated item by item. Some purchases and contracts will not change over the life of the project. Those that may change should be identified, and estimates made of the potential magnitude of those anticipated changes. This approach ensures control of contingency funds as the project is implemented.

16.12.5 Funding risks

What if the funding for the project is cut by 25 per cent, or completion projections indicate that costs will greatly exceed available funds? What are the chances of the project being cancelled before completion? Seasoned project leaders recognise that a complete risk assessment must include an evaluation of funding supply. This is especially true for publicly funded projects. Just as government projects are subject to changes in strategy (and political appetites), business firms also frequently undergo changes in their priorities. They may also face staff changes in top management personnel, and the pet projects of a new CEO may replace those of the business's former CEO. Resources may become tight, and one sure way to fund new projects is to cancel existing projects. Severe budget cuts or lack of adequate funding can have a devastating effect on a project. Typically, when such a fate occurs, it becomes necessary to scale back the scope of an existing project to *what is possible*. (*All-or-nothing projects* are ripe targets for budget-cutters.) This was the case for the United States Army's Comanche helicopter after the decision was made to move away from manned reconnaissance aircraft. The *chunkability* of an existing project can act as an advantage. For example, a motorway resurfacing project may not get fully completed but the project will still have added value for each kilometre that has been fully completed and left safer.

On a much smaller scale, some funding risks may exist for more pedestrian projects. For example, a building contractor may find that due to a sudden downturn in the stock market, a private individual can no longer afford to build their dream house on land the contractor owns, or an ICT consulting organisation may be left empty-handed when a major client files for bankruptcy. In the former case, the contractor may have, as a contingency, the option of building and selling the house on the open market; unfortunately, the ICT consulting organisation would likely have to join a (potentially) long line of creditors.

16.13 : Budgets, contingency and risk

Work carried out in identifying and assessing risk can be used to make financial decisions about the mitigation of risks and can inform the level of contingency that must be retained in the project reserves. This information can ultimately also indicate how much the management reserve is likely to be affected by the overall risk in the project (these reserve types were discussed in Chapter 12 "Project cost management"). The PMI describes risks as *known unknowns* because although the risk has been identified (it is known), it is not known (in reality) if the risk will occur (unknowns).

16.13.1   Decision: Inherent risk versus the cost to mitigate the risk

The project leader needs to consider what the cost to the project would be if the risk did occur (in its unmitigated state) compared with what the cost would be of putting mitigation strategies (controls) in place. If the cost of the controls is greater than the cost of the risk occurring, then the project leader might decide not to implement the controls. For example, there is a risk that the project leader will leave the project. This inherent risk is analysed and the cost, if the project leader leaves, is estimated to be $5,000. The mitigation strategy is to employ a trainee project leader to shadow the experienced project leader, at a cost of $15,000 to the project. Based on these numbers alone (not considering any other associated risks), the project leader makes a financial decision (in conjunction with the project sponsor), not to employ a shadow project leader and to instead run the risk that they (the project leader) may not be present for the entire project. This is an example of where costs inform decision-making (i.e. the cost of the risk occurring in its unmitigated (controlled) state is less than the cost to mitigate, therefore the decision is made not to mitigate).

16.13.2   Higher RPN residual risks and expected monetary value (EMV)

If a risk (regardless of what controls have been applied) remains at a high level, there is a likelihood that contingency planning could be enacted. The project leader therefore needs to consider the costs of these contingency plans occurring. Two options should be considered: the total cost of the contingency plans or a weighted cost. In Table 16.13, the project leader could (for all risks where there's high probability and high impact) take the raw sum of the "contingency plan costs" forward to the sponsor for inclusion in the management reserve or, more commonly, take the sum of the "weighted costs" (i.e. the expected monetary value) forward to the sponsor for inclusion as the project's contingency. Using EMV as a method to calculate contingency relies on a few factors:

- the project is risk driven (i.e. a thorough job of identifying risks is done across all aspects of the project)
- each risk's probability and impact (inherent and residual) are based on a more quantitative assessment
- a fairly accurate monetary value can be placed on the cost to the project if the risk does occur (contingency dollars).

Refer to Table 16.13 for an example of how to calculate the EMV.

Table 16.13 Expected monetary value (EMV)

Risk	Residual probability	Contingency plan	Contingency plan cost	Weighted cost
Concrete pump machine breakdown.	60% (0.6*) probability of occurring	Standby arrangements with local hire company put in place.	$3,000	0.6* × $3,000 = $1,800
Rain days exceed avg. of past five years due to climatic events.	70% (0.7*) probability of occurring	Build time extended by 20 days, retentions paid to labour and equipment companies.	$36,000	0.7* × $36,000 = $25,200

© 2022 Dr Neil Pearson

Probability scale
1 Remote ≤ 20%
2 Low > 20% ≤ 40%
3 Medium > 40% ≤ 60%
4 Probable > 60% ≤ 80%
5 Certain > 80 ≤ 100%

In this table, EMV has been calculated on the residual probability and also the cost of implementing the Contingency Plan.

16.14 | Risk monitoring and review

Referring to Figure 16.3, the reader will have noticed a "Monitoring and review" component to the process. Typically, the results of the six steps of risk management are summarised in the Risk Register. As indicated within each step, the Risk Register details all identified risks, including descriptions, categories, the probability of their occurrence, impacts, responses, Contingency Plans, owners and status. The Risk Register is the backbone of **risk monitoring and review**. Risk monitoring and control involves:

- ensuring the risk mitigation strategies (controls) are being actioned by the assigned project team member
- monitoring contingency triggering events, early warning indicators, and initiating Contingency Plans as required
- escalating risks that move out of project control, per the newly introduced *escalate* risk response category
- watching for new risks and logging these into the Risk Register for subsequent analysis
- monitoring existing risks for changes in conditions that will affect the profile of the risk.

A risk heat map, as shown in Figure 16.10, is a very popular medium for helping to visualise and facilitate the reporting of risk status. In this case, the diagram has two heat maps.

- The heat map on the left side maps out key risks for threat risks (and is usually presented on a green, amber and red colour scale). The colour red would indicate (in monitoring and controlling risks) that the risk has a high potential to breach, and therefore turn into an issue, at which point its Contingency Plan would be instigated. It may be that the project leader is, at this time, already carrying out actions to further reduce the probability/impact of this risk, if it is in such a position on the Risk Register. Generally, risks should be moving from top right (red) to the bottom left (green) as the project leader seeks to reduce the threat of the risk, and eventually close the risk when time/conditions have passed, and the risk is no longer valid.
- The heat map on the right side represents opportunity risks. The project leader would want to increase the probability of the risk occurring and would be looking to extend its impact if it does occur. Risks would therefore be moving from the bottom right to the top left of the grid.

The visual heat map (and its associated risk summary) would form a component of a typical project status report, as risks are *always* reported on. If a risk does become an issue, then the governance and processes that have been put in place in the risk escalation process subsection of the Risk Management Plan would be invoked.

Figure 16.10 Key risk monitoring and control activities

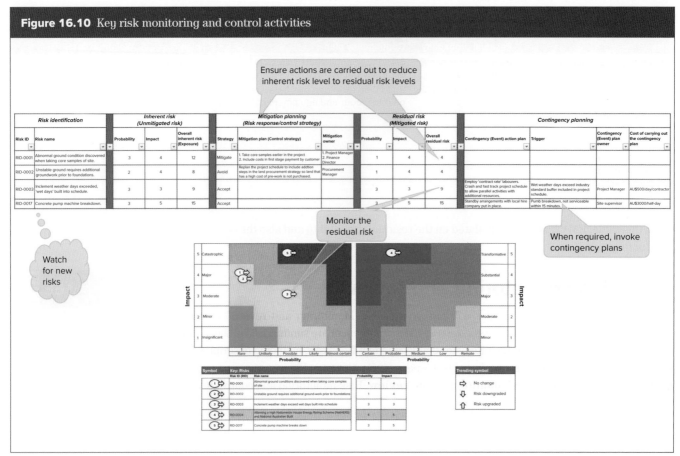

Project leaders need to monitor risks just as they track project progress. Risk assessment and updating must be part of every status meeting and project progress report. The project team must be on constant alert for new, unforeseen risks (unknown unknowns). Management needs to be sensitive to the fact that others may not be forthright in acknowledging new risks and problems. Admitting that there might be a bug in a design code, or that different components are not compatible, may be seen to reflect poorly on an individual's performance. If the prevailing organisational culture is one where mistakes are punished severely, then it is only human that people will want to protect themselves from admonishment. Similarly, if bad news is greeted harshly and there is a propensity to *kill the messenger*, participants will naturally be reluctant to speak freely. The tendency to suppress bad news is compounded when individual responsibility is vague, and the project team is under extreme pressure from top-level management to get the project done quickly.

Project leaders need to establish an environment in which participants feel comfortable that they can raise concerns and admit mistakes. The norm should be that revealing mistakes is acceptable, whereas hiding mistakes is intolerable. Problems should be embraced, not suppressed. Participants should be encouraged to identify problems and new risks. The key to this is the project leader's own attitude and actions, as they must actively demonstrate a positive, supportive attitude. On large and/or complex projects, it may be prudent to repeat the risk identification/assessment exercise to identify fresh information. Risk profiles should be reviewed to test if the original responses still hold true. Relevant stakeholders should be brought into the discussion and the Risk Register will need to be updated. While this may not be practical on an ongoing basis, project leaders should touch base with stakeholders regularly or hold special stakeholder meetings to review the status of risks on the project.

A second tactic for controlling the cost of risks is to document responsibility. This can be problematic in projects involving multiple organisations and contractors. Responsibility for risk is frequently passed on to others with a dismissive comment along the lines of: "That's not my concern". This mentality is dangerous. Each identified risk should be assigned (or shared) by mutual agreement of the owner, the project leader and the contractor, or the person with line responsibility for the work package or iteration of the project. Risk costs, when identified as part of risk planning, should be included in the project budget. However, when a risk eventuates and becomes an issue, the project leader may have to apply to the Steering Committee and/or sponsor to draw on project contingency funds. Having line personnel participate in the process focuses attention on the budget reserve, control of its rate of usage, and early warning about potential risk events. If risk management is not formalised, responsibility and responses to risk will be ignored—"It's not my area…"

The project leader needs to be prepared for independent risk audits. These may be carried out as routine health checks by the PMO or by the organisation's corporate risk department (the timing of these scheduled risk reviews could be documented in the Risk Management Plan). However, in some instances, these may be externally initiated by boards or by governing bodies, and therefore the project leader might not necessarily know about them in advance (unscheduled risk review). *Note:* If your organisation has a gateway review process (such as the OGC Gateway Review process), risk will be examined in detail at these reviews.

16.14.1 Risk closure

Remember, once the risk event has passed, the risk should be closed and the Risk Register updated appropriately. It is important to remove unnecessary **noise**, so that focus is retained on current risks. The bottom line is that project leaders (and team members) need to be vigilant and constantly on the lookout for potential risks so any new land mines that could potentially derail a project can be expediently defused. Risk assessment must be part of the recurring agenda of status meetings, and when new risks emerge, these need to be analysed and incorporated into the risk management process.

16.15 Communication and consultation

Referring to Figure 16.3, you will notice a "Communication and consultation" component to the process. This component is to remind the project leader that risk planning is not, and should not be, carried out in isolation. Internal and external stakeholders bring with them many differing backgrounds, perspectives and experiences. In considering risk, it is especially important that these are included in activities, so that risk can be identified and mitigated. By creating a consultative approach to risk management, the project leader can:

■ establish the risk context, both in regard to the external environment and the internal (organisational) environment

■ draw in stakeholders to ensure their interests (from a risk perspective) are understood and captured

■ bring together people with different or complementary backgrounds, to assist in a more complete risk analysis of the project

■ seek input about how to deal with the risk from the people involved in the analysis.

Consultation is key to understanding not only the risks, but also the process being applied to the management of risks in the project. From a communication perspective, the details of risks should appear in all formal project management status reports produced from the project. Risks will be an agenda item at team meetings and Steering Committee meetings.

16.16 | Close risk management

Towards project closure, the Risk Register should essentially (if all went to plan!) be full of closed risks that did not eventuate into issues. Some of the activities at project closure in relation to risk management would therefore include:

- close, as appropriate, remaining risks in the Risk Register
- hand over to operations remaining open risks that are not related to the project but to the operational running of the system
- capture lessons learned in relation to risks, and the management of risk
- close risk-related issues, where a risk eventuated and resulted in an *issue*, ensure that the issue has been resolved and there are no remaining actions.

16.17 | Risk management tools

This chapter has leveraged Microsoft Excel for capturing, tracking and monitoring risk examples. For projects where a lot of risk must be managed, project leaders may like to look to the wide range of tools that are available in the marketplace. Some examples are provided in Table 16.14.

Table 16.14 Risk management tools

Tool	Weblink
Oracle Crystal Ball	https://www.oracle.com/applications/crystalball/
Cura	https://www.curasoftware.com
Active Risk	https://sword-grc.com
@Risk	https://www.palisade.com/Risk/
RiskyProject	https://intaver.com
SiteSafe	https://safesitehq.com
SAS	https://www.sas.com/en_us/software/model-risk-management.html

© 2022 Dr Neil Pearson

Note: While this list is provided as an example, the authors do not endorse any of the tools listed and this list cannot be relied upon to be current, complete or accurate. You must form your own opinion when selecting any product.

Summary

To put project risk into perspective, the project leader needs to recognise that the essence of project management is risk management. Every technique discussed in this text is really a risk management technique: each in its own way tries to prevent something adverse from happening. Project selection systems try to increase the likelihood that projects will contribute to the strategic objectives of the organisation. Project scope documents, among other things, are designed to avoid costly misunderstandings from the project outset. This chapter has covered the following.

- Project leaders need to understand the context for risk in the industry, the environment, the organisation and the project, so expectations around risks and how these are managed can be established with the project sponsor and other stakeholders.
- RBSs reduce the probability that some vital part of the project will be omitted or that budget contingency estimates are unrealistic. Along with other risk identification techniques, it ensures that risks are identified, because if we fail to identify risk it cannot be managed and is likely to come back and bite us!
- From this perspective, project leaders engage in risk management activities to compensate for the uncertainty inherent in project management and the fact that things never go according to plan. Risk management is proactive,

not reactive. It reduces the number of surprises and leads to a better understanding of the most likely outcomes of threat (negative) events.

■ Although many managers believe that in the final analysis, risk assessment and contingency will depend upon subjective judgement, some standard method for identifying, assessing and responding to risks should be included in all projects. The very process of identifying project risks forces a level of discipline at all levels of project management and stands to improve project performance.

■ Contingency plans increase the chance that the project can be completed on time and within budget. Contingency plans can be simple workarounds or elaborately detailed plans. Responsibility for risks should be clearly identified and documented. It is desirable and prudent to keep a reserve to hedge against project risks. Control of reserves should remain with the project sponsor or Steering Committee. Use of contingency reserves should be closely monitored, controlled and reviewed throughout the project life cycle.

Experience clearly indicates that using a formal, structured process to handle possible foreseen and unforeseen project risk events minimises surprises, costs, delays, stress and misunderstandings. Risk management is an iterative process that occurs throughout the life cycle of the project. When risk events occur, or changes are necessary, using an effective change control process to quickly approve and record changes/variations will facilitate performance being measured against the schedule and budget. Ultimately, successful risk management requires a culture in which project threats are embraced, not denied, and problems are identified, not hidden.

Ten golden rules of project risk management

■ Rule 1: Make risk management part of your project. This is essential to the success of project risk management. If you don't truly embed risk management into your project, you cannot reap the full benefits of this approach.

■ Rule 2: Identify risks early in your project. The first step in project risk management is to identify the risks that are present in your project. This requires an open mindset that focuses on future scenarios that may occur.

■ Rule 3: Communicate about risks. Failed projects show that project leaders were frequently unaware of the big hammer that was about to hit them. The frightening finding was that frequently someone in the project organisation did see the hammer but didn't inform the project leader of its existence.

■ Rule 4: Consider both threats and opportunities. Project risks have a negative connotation: they are the bad guys that can harm your project. However, modern risk approaches also focus on positive risks: the project opportunities.

■ Rule 5: Clarify ownership issues. Some project leaders think they have finished once they have created a list of risks. However, this is only a starting point. The next step is to clarify who is responsible for what risk.

■ Rule 6: Prioritise risks. A project leader once told me, "I treat all risks equally". This makes project life simple. However, it doesn't deliver the best results possible. Some risks have a bigger impact than others.

■ Rule 7: Analyse risks. Understanding the nature of a risk is a precondition for a good response, therefore take some time to have a closer look at individual risks and don't jump to conclusions without knowing what a risk is about.

■ Rule 8: Plan and implement risk responses. Implementing a risk response is the activity that adds value to your project. You prevent a threat occurring or minimise negative effects. Execution is key here. The other rules have helped you to map, prioritise and understand risks. This will help you to make a sound risk response plan that focuses on the big wins.

■ Rule 9: Register project risks. This rule is about bookkeeping: Maintaining a risk log enables you to view progress and make sure you won't forget a risk or two. It is also a perfect communication tool that informs your team members and stakeholders about what is going on (Rule 3).

■ Rule 10: Track risks and associated tasks. The Risk Register you have created as a result of Rule 9 will help you to do this. Tracking tasks is a day-to-day job for the project leader. Integrating risk tasks into that daily routine is the easiest solution.

Source: Adapted from Jutte B n.d., "10 golden rules of project risk management", https://www.projectsmart.co.uk/risk-management/10-golden-rules-of-project-risk-management.php, accessed May 2022.

Review questions

1. "Project risks can/cannot be eliminated even if the project is carefully planned." Explain.
2. The chances of risk events occurring and their respective costs increasing change over the project life cycle. What is the significance of this phenomenon to a project leader?
3. What is the difference between *avoiding* a risk and *accepting* a risk?
4. What is the difference between *mitigating a risk* and *contingency planning?*
5. Explain the difference between *opportunity* risk and *threat* risk.

6. Why are the WBS and RBS complementary in identifying risk?
7. What are the parallels between a standard such as ISO 31000:2018 and the Risk Management Plan?
8. What does the control strategy *escalate* mean to the project leader?

Exercises

1. Review the process in Figure 16.3 and the process for risk management you have been involved in on a recent project. Identify the similarities and differences. What would you now consider to improve your project's risk management process?

2. Although we introduced a set of project management principles in Chapter 2 "Popular frameworks and methodologies", consider purely the context of risk and define a set of principles which could be used to promote better risk management practices in your project.

3. Review the arrows surrounding Figure 16.3. What does this mean in a project context?

References

International Organization for Standardization 2018, ISO 31000:2018 "Risk management—Guidelines".

Jutte B n.d., "10 golden rules of project risk management", https://www.projectsmart.co.uk/risk-management/10-golden-rules-of-project-risk-management.php, accessed May 2022.

McKenna M 2017, "Native title call a risk to projects", *The Australian*, 8 February, https://www.theaustralian.com.au/national-affairs/indigenous/native-title-call-a-Risk-to-projects/news-story/70e29506ce805d373497f75cb3518608, accessed February 2018.

Project Management Institute (PMI) 2017, *A Guide to the Project Management Body of Knowledge*, 6th edition, PMI.

Project Management Institute (PMI) 2019, *The Standard for Risk Management in Portfolios, Programs, and Projects*, PMI.

Project Management Institute (PMI) 2021a, *A Guide to the Project Management Body of Knowledge (PMBOK® Guide)*, 7th edition, PMI.

Project Management Institute (PMI) 2021b, *The Standard for Project Management (ANSI/PMI 99-001-2021)*, 7th edition, PMI.

CHAPTER 17

Project procurement management

Learning elements

17A Understand the role of procurement within a project environment.

17B Understand the procurement decisions and options available to a project leader.

17C Be able to plan, identify procurement items and understand the make or buy decision.

17D Be aware of the steps involved in tendering and the common tender types.

17E Be aware of the steps involved in contracting and the common contract types.

17F Apply the essential elements of contract negotiation to ensure contracts are based on solid foundations.

17G Negotiate successfully and deal with difficult situations.

17H Understand the activities involved in procurement closure.

In this chapter

17.1 Introduction

17.2 Procurement and projects

17.3 Identifying procurement requirements

17.4 Procurement Management Plan

17.5 Decision: Purchase order

17.6 Decision: Tender, including supplier selection

17.7 Decision: Contracts and contract types

17.8 Outsourcing project work

17.9   Partnering practices

17.10   Procurement closure activities

Summary

17.1 | **Introduction**

Project **procurement** management is greater than contracting. Procurement considers many activities to identify, source, procure and manage suppliers, resources, tools, equipment etc. to the project. A key factor to bear in mind during procurement activities is the obligation being made by the project leader (as a representative of the organisation) to enter into mutually binding (legal) agreements, where there is a monetary exchange for goods and services.

Procurement requires the skills and knowledge of others beyond the immediate project team, such as from the procurement, contract and legal departments of an organisation. Procurement can therefore be one of the more challenging areas, especially for junior and learning project leaders, as the repercussions of making an ill-informed decision can ripple beyond the project, often with serious litigation consequences—*praemonitus, praemunitus*: forewarned is forearmed!

As with all material covered in this text, project leaders operate under a code of practice and are expected to be ethical in all their dealings (covered further in Chapter 19 "Project leaders and project teams"). To this aim it is expected that all dealings in relation to procurement are carried out with **probity**.

> *Probity is evidence of ethical behaviour in a particular process. For Queensland Government procurement, demonstrating probity means more than just avoiding corrupt or dishonest conduct. It involves proactively demonstrating that any procurement process is robust and the outcome beyond reproach. Probity requires acting such a way that there can be no perception of bias, influence, or lack of integrity. This requires ethical conduct that exceeds the legal requirements. To this end probity within procurement should not be a last minute add on but must be integrated into all stages of the procurement process* (Queensland Government 2019).

Source: https://www.hpw.qld.gov.au/__data/assets/pdf_file/0016/3337/probityintegrityprocurement.pdf, accessed February 2022, CC BY 4.0 https://creativecommons.org/licenses/by/4.0/

Note: Procurement is one area of project management whose ethical requirements vary by country, state and industry; project leaders are advised to always consult the relevant procurement specialists in the location in which they are working.

Ethical procurement in a project context gives a project leader the opportunity to get involved in various activities. In some small-to-medium enterprises, and most certainly in large corporates, the project leader may be constrained by law, policies and procedures in relation to what they can do themselves and what they must rely on others to do on their behalf. Ensuring healthy relationships with procurement, contract and legal departments is essential. The general procurement activities that a project leader could become involved in are shown in Figure 17.1.

PMBOK	**Seventh edition updates (PMI 2021)**

Procurement appeared as a knowledge area in the sixth edition of PMBOK (PMI 2017). In the seventh edition, it appears as one of many sub-components of the Planning Performance Domain (PMI 2021a, p. 65).

Procurement also appears within the Project Work Performance Domain as the sub-component "Working with Procurements" (PMI 2021a, p. 74), where working with other stakeholders in the business is stressed. This area of project management is highly regulated, not only from within the organisation but also by external factors such as legislation and industry practices.

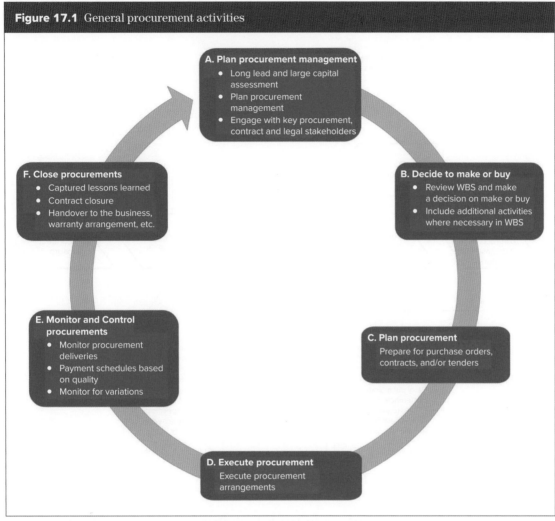

Figure 17.1 General procurement activities

A. Plan procurement management
- Long lead and large capital assessment
- Plan procurement management
- Engage with key procurement, contract and legal stakeholders

B. Decide to make or buy
- Review WBS and make a decision on make or buy
- Include additional activities where necessary in WBS

C. Plan procurement
Prepare for purchase orders, contracts, and/or tenders

D. Execute procurement
Execute procurement arrangements

E. Monitor and Control procurements
- Monitor procurement deliveries
- Payment schedules based on quality
- Monitor for variations

F. Close procurements
- Captured lessons learned
- Contract closure
- Handover to the business, warranty arrangement, etc.

© 2022 Dr Neil Pearson

17.2 Procurement and projects

The procurement process can be a challenging area of project management for most project leaders, as it requires the possession of many skills (such as communication, analysis, negotiation and business acumen). Although a one-size-fits-all approach is not applicable for procurement, there are, nonetheless, certain key decisions (or routes through the process) that will determine in each procurement instance the type of activities that project leaders will become engaged in (refer to Figure 17.2).

One of the project leader's principal activities (during the early stages of establishing the procurement function within the project) will be to review all the organisation's procurement, contracting and legal policies and procedures. Most project leaders will therefore establish contact with the relevant stakeholders in each of these areas early on in the project, in order to establish that the governance between the project and the relevant department is agreed and that appropriate routes through this (potential) minefield are established and agreed.

Involving the procurement department as a stakeholder on a project that will require procurement support not only assists in building relationships, but it also ensures the project leader is briefed correctly on all relevant organisational policy and procedures. The information acquired from this should be documented within the Procurement Management Plan for later dissemination and communication to the project team.

Establishing early positive interfaces (and governance) between the project and the organisation's procurement department helps to build trust and encourages appropriate governance is followed in the

Figure 17.2 Procurement decision: Purchase order, contract or tender?

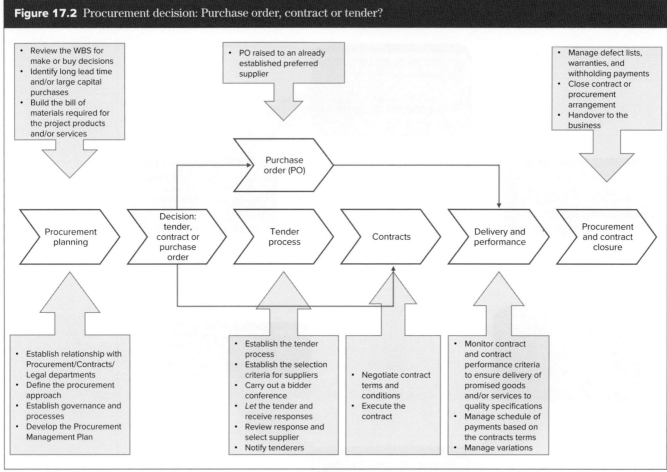

project. On large projects, it not uncommon to have individuals dedicated to running the procurement and contracting function and reporting to the project leader. Such people may be contracted in for the duration of the project or seconded to it from the relevant department. The latter situation has the obvious benefit of bringing knowledge and experience of company procurement policy and procedures into the project. But contracting procurement managers from outside the organisation requires them to get up to speed on organisational policy and procedures before they can become fully functional on the project.

17.3 Identifying procurement requirements

Some procurement requirements should be considered early in the project life cycle, and in some instances even pre-project, within the Business Case proposal. Although broad-brush statements might have been made about the investments approach to procurement, the Business Case should specifically address the following.

■ *Long-lead-time items:* When a product (or service) being procured into the project has a **long lead time**, this timeframe needs to be carefully recognised and factored in, as it has the potential to delay the project's start, and/or delay the start of critical project tasks. **Long-lead-time items** can artificially extend the project duration by weeks (and some cases months) so taking these items out of the project life cycle and building the relevant steps into the investment Business Case can make sense. For example, say a large energy distribution network requires 20 transformers, and the only global supplier of such items has stated an 18-month lead time on this quantity. The procurement and timing of these items as a strategic business case that will ultimately deliver the upgraded network through a project needs to be carefully considered—hence the use of programs and portfolios.

■ *Large capital items:* These items do not routinely fall into a standard project management financial governance process. The tendering and contracts process can be complex and require high levels of input from senior stakeholders on the project. As with long-lead-time items, **large capital items** should be given early and special attention to ensure minimal impact on schedules, budgets and the overall project design. In the above example, the transformers do not only take 18 months to deliver, but the supplier has requested for a substantial deposit (non-refundable) to be made. Not only is this outside any project approval limits, it is contractually committing the organisation to the process with possible high break fees and loss of large deposits—regardless of whether the project goes ahead or not. Again, this is why organisations run portfolios and programs of work.

The project leader (supported by the project team) will need to make decisions about whether to **make or buy** during early procurement planning activities. When identifying the items to be procured, the project leader will be making decisions about whether the product or service is effectively being made within the project (as a deliverable of the project), or whether it is to be procured into the project. Refer to "Snapshot from Practice: Investing in investigations" as an example of investing in the decision as to whether to make or buy.

The range of items identified during the development of the work breakdown structure (WBS) and associated project planning documents is often quite extensive and can include:

■ simple procurement of off-the-shelf products (e.g. a piece of equipment or a software package)

■ bespoke products that are specially designed and manufactured for the project (e.g. a steel structured building for use in regional Australia where extreme environmental factors exist)

■ procurement of services (e.g. the provision of waste removal from a construction site)

■ the employment of contractors and full-time hires to the project (e.g. the recruitment of a procurement manager on a fixed-term contract to the project)

■ the procurement of a large item of capital equipment (e.g. an electrical transformer to supply a small township).

These are a just few examples of the types of procurements that are typically encountered on projects of all sizes and complexities. The reasons why items might be procured into a project and the type of procurement (contract) that is therefore entered into will be influenced by many factors. For example:

■ It may be that the time constraints of the project do not allow certain items to be made within the project.

■ Value-for-money decisions indicate that the cost of making an item within the project is far greater than that of procuring the item into the project.

■ The risk in making the item is not within the risk profile of the project and the risk cannot be transferred, via procurement of the item, to another party.

■ Resource availability might be a concern to the project, especially if the project leader is unsure of being able to obtain the required skills to make the item within the project; the decision is therefore made to procure.

■ Specialist skills/products might not be available within the organisation; therefore, the project must procure these items into the project environment.

Once identified, items to be procured are usually captured in some form of **bill of materials (BOM)**. A BOM is a hierarchical decomposition of all the items required by the project; although its origins are in manufacturing, it is equally applicable to the service industry. The BOM could be represented as a hierarchical structure, much like the WBS, or it could take the form of a spreadsheet with nested rows, indicating the breakdown of each component into its subsequent components. Figure 17.3(a) represents a visual approach, and Figure 17.3(b) a spreadsheet approach, for a fit-out of a new hot-desking office.

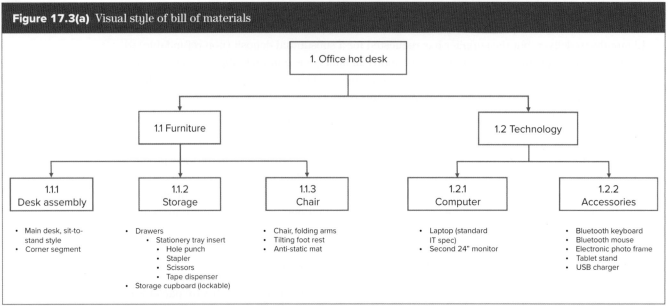

Figure 17.3(a) Visual style of bill of materials

© 2022 Dr Neil Pearson

Figure 17.3(b) Spreadsheet-style bill of materials

© 2022 Dr Neil Pearson

Typical information captured in a BOM includes:

- *BOM unique reference:* Indented for each sub-component of the BOM so it can be referred to in work package or tasks, for example.
- *Item name:* If possible, research and use industry standard names.
- *A description of the item:* Capture all requirements and specifics that may get overlooked in the bigger picture. These could later be included as additions to specifications of the product and become contractual.

- *Make or buy decision:* How is the item to be primarily acquired? If mixed (make and buy), break it down into sub-components so it is clear which item is coming from where.
- *Related BOM items:* Cross-reference any other related items in the BOM, so if a sub-component is changed, the impact on any other items can be assessed.
- *Quantity assurance criteria (e.g. standards, specifications):* Define any overarching quality requirements (such as those of the relevant AS/NZS standard) or requirements specific to the BOM item (different tolerances for our project).
- *Quality control activities (e.g. who, how, cost, tools):* Who is going to check the quality of the product on delivery? Remember: In project procurement, suppliers do not get paid because they have made a delivery; they get paid because the delivery is the right quantity, on time, and to the defined quality specifications.
- *Cost known:* Accurate cost if known.
- *Cost estimate:* If estimated and has yet to be confirmed.
- *Phase, stage or date required:* The list can be prioritised by those items required sooner, so arrangements can start to be made. Otherwise, the project might not have the item in time for when it is needed!
- *Procurement type:* Contract, tender or **purchase order (PO)**—again, can help prioritise work. Items that are needed sooner that will require a tender will need immediate attention as tendering can be a long process that has, for example, the potential to delay the project.
- *Source/supplier:* If known, check existing preferred suppliers as it is nearly always easier to use an existing supplier that is on the organisation's approved list than it is to go through a supplier selection process.
- *The people responsible for procuring in the project team/organisation's contracts department:* These could even be linked to work packages and tasks.
- *Transport considerations:* Who pays? Is it included in the cost? Are there any tactical difficulties in gaining access (e.g. at certain times of the day)?
- Storage/security considerations: Are the items of high value (such as technology) and do they need secure storage at site before they can be deployed?
- *Packaging/disposal considerations:* Who is responsible? If we are a sustainable project, how much will it cost to have all the packing, for example for 2000 new desktop computers, removed in a green/sustainable manner?
- *Penalties (e.g. for late delivery):* Are these critical path items? If so, do we wish to put penalty payments against them to encourage prompt attention by the supplier?
- *Risk assessment:* What are the risks associated with the procurement activity? These would be entered into the project's Risk Register.

A simple BOM template has been included in the online resources; however, check your organisation's guidelines as these may be required to be constructed within an enterprise resource planning (ERP) system (or similar), using standard component codes, etc.

 Bill of Materials (BOM)

The BOM usually accompanies the project's Procurement Management Plan, and together they guide the project in what to procure (the BOM) and how to procure (the Procurement Management Plan). Let's now review a typical Procurement Management Plan.

17.4 Procurement Management Plan

As with the other knowledge areas, procurement has a management plan. This could take the format of a standalone document, or a section of a one-document integrated Project Management Plan. A Procurement Management Plan is typically used to capture the following information.

- *Governance:* This includes the relevant roles and responsibilities of those involved in procurement-related activities. Using the RASCI Matrix (introduced in Chapter 7 "Governance and projects"), it defines appropriate governance arrangements (e.g. PO sign-off limits and tender reviewer arrangements).

- *Organisational policy and procedures in relation to procurement, contracting and legal processes:* On procurement-heavy projects, it is standard working practice to have a dedicated procurement manager (or representative) on the project. The person who holds this role should have and be able to leverage a vast amount of information and knowledge about the organisation's policy and procedures. Capturing the essence of this information within the Procurement Management Plan assists other project team members to understand the procurement process and policies of the organisation and their roles.

- *Procurement governance (roles and responsibilities):* This section should describe all the roles and responsibilities of the procurement function within the project environment. For example, in a project that is likely to have many approvals for medium-value items, and where the project leader has a low approval limit, then the project leader may wish to challenge this as the approver (typically the project sponsor) could quickly become a bottleneck to the project functioning. Would it make more sense for the project leader to have devolved responsibility to sign off the bulk of these medium-value items?

- *Adjustments to standard contract terms and conditions (T&Cs):* Outline if there are tailored project-related T&Cs that will need to be included in specific or all contracts related to the project. For example: Whose variation process is being used? What performance reporting information will the project get access to? Is a pandemic being considered as *force majeure*?

- *Requirements of long-lead-time items and large capital purchase items:* Ensure that any items that fall outside the standard procurement cycles of the project are clearly highlighted. This would include documenting when they are needed by the project and when the latest order and approval for order of these items can take place. There may be supporting tenders and sign-off documents if these items need to be purchased before a succeeding stage of the project.

- *Audit requirements:* Is procurement activity subject to scheduled audits? What information must be maintained by the project? What is the process for an unscheduled audit—do all involved in procurement have to put a hold on work and be directed to other duties until the audit feedback has been provided?

- *Purchasing assumptions:* Define any assumptions around the procurement of items to the project. For example, copper wire will fluctuate in price in line with the metals market indices; therefore, are allowances in funding these items made in the estimating process or the contingency process based on risk?

- *Market conditions:* Capture the background to the prevailing market conditions that will influence decisions, such as make or buy or the PO/tender/contract decision.

- *Risk analysis of procurement activities:* This is usually captured within the project-wide Risk Register, identifying potential risks in, for example, using a particular supplier, the choice of materials selected or delivery times.

- *Review of procurement lessons learned:* This includes lessons from previous projects, and how these have been accommodated within the current project.

Refer to the online Procurement Management Plan for further inclusions to consider. As with any template, ensure you as a project leader review the contents and ensure it includes all aspects you are required to cover in your project environment.

Procurement Management Plan

Once the activities of procurement planning have been attended to, the focus will move towards a detailed review of the WBS, the make or buy decision, and the steps to be subsequently taken. Refer to Figure 17.4, which provides an example of the decision and workflow that may take place in practice.

The type of procurement decides the workflow through the procurement process; that is, how the item is to be procured—whether by PO (direct to a supplier), by contract (to an already established supplier) or by a full **tender process**. Decisions such as this and the business rules behind the decision would be captured in the Procurement Management Plan (usually as references to existing organisational policy and procedures).

Figure 17.4 The procurement decision

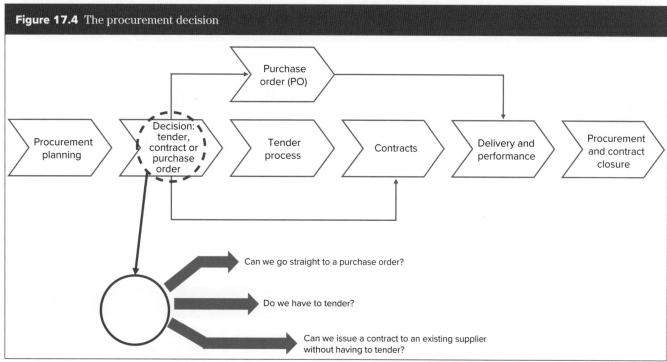

© 2022 Dr Neil Pearson

The next sections of this chapter discuss elements that are relevant to this workflow and to the decisions that a project leader may have to make.

17.5 Decision: Purchase order

LE 17B

Raising POs is often the simplest route for obtaining a product and/or service into the project. An organisation will typically already have established who its preferred suppliers are, so there will be no need for the project leader to perform this arduous task of supplier selection/tendering. Once the BOM has been developed (see Figure 17.3), the project leader/project team will (for PO route items) agree which of the company's preferred suppliers is to be used and then start to issue POs at the required time(s). As part of this approach, it is essential that the project schedule is consulted, to ensure the selected supplier's lead times allow delivery within sufficient time for the WBS work package to start on time. Normally, organisations have multiple preferred suppliers that cover the same products, so if one preferred supplier cannot deliver the quantity on time then alternative, or even multiple, supplier arrangements can be made.

If large numbers of POs are likely to be issued by the project, arrangements should be made with the procurement and/or finance departments to ensure these will be turned around and processed in a timely manner. This is important as we may want to mitigate risk around delays to the WBS work packages and/or tasks. Alternatively, it might be prudent to consider whether a procurement and/or finance department employee could be seconded into the project to carry out all PO activities for the project, thereby providing knowledge, consistency and attention to the continual flow of POs.

Remember that POs have a workflow associated with them that goes beyond raising the initial PO and flows into the Execution, Monitor and Control and Closure stages of the project, as illustrated in Figure 17.5.

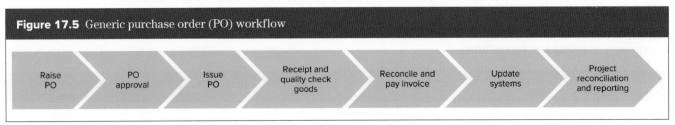

Figure 17.5 Generic purchase order (PO) workflow

© 2022 Dr Neil Pearson

17.6 Decision: Tender, including supplier selection

Most organisations have a centralised procurement and purchasing section with an established preferred supplier list and/or preferred panels. The project leader therefore may have to adopt and use these preferred supplier agreements when sourcing required products and/or services, in accordance with the organisation's procurement policies and procedures. *Note:* Preferred supplier agreements are usually reviewed periodically, and suppliers will be advertised for, interviewed and selected according to predetermined criteria. When no supplier exists for the products and services that the project requires, or the value of the work is such that it cannot be just given to an existing supplier, then the project leader will have to undertake the complete tendering process as indicated in Figure 17.6.

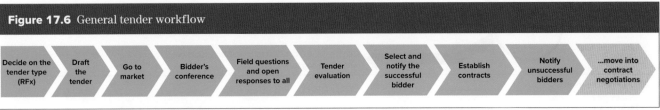

Figure 17.6 General tender workflow

© 2022 Dr Neil Pearson

Standing offer arrangements (SOAs) are another type of agreement for preferred suppliers. They involve establishing an arrangement to obtain frequently used products and/or services over a set period—meaning the project does not need to undertake formal procurement processes in this regard. As with preferred supplier agreements, SOAs can save the project leader both time and energy. Both arrangements have obvious benefits for the organisation, including the following.

- contract terms and conditions have already been established
- prices have already been agreed
- delivery schedules have already been negotiated
- insurance has been arranged

■ company background checks have been satisfied (*Note:* Dun & Bradstreet (global marketplace) and Company360 (Australian marketplace) are popular sites for researching company backgrounds and financial information.)

■ trusted business relationships enable value-adding between supplier and buyer.

Issues can arise for a project when products and/or services fall outside preferred supplier agreements or SOAs. In this situation, the project leader might consider one of two commonly used practices.

1. *Ad hoc purchasing:* This is usually associated with low-value, low-risk and small-volume purchases. Three quotations are obtained and the supplier representing the best value is selected.

2. *Direct sourcing:* This is usually used where specialist products and/or services are required, but only a limited number of suppliers (or even a sole supplier) are available in the marketplace. Direct sourcing usually occurs with assistance from the organisation's procurement department to set up the required arrangements.

17.6.1 **Tenders and the tender process**

Before contract negotiations are entered, the project leader (supported by the project team) may first have to undertake a formal **tender process**. If so, one of the first decisions to make is to decide whether the tender should take the format of an **open tender** (where the tender is open to any tenderer in the marketplace to tender to supply the required goods and/or services) or a **closed tender** (where only selected tenderers are invited to respond to the tender proposal). Closed tenders are sometimes referred to as *limited tenders* or *selective tenders*.

Whether an open or closed tender process is used, the process usually proceeds through several steps, typically including:

■ *Step 1:* The tender process is planned, and decisions are made regarding who should participate in it, from both within the project team and the wider organisation. This is sometimes referred to as *RFx, x* being the type of tender being sought (see Table 17.1 for tender types).

■ *Step 2:* The tender documents are prepared. This requires the involvement of legal, procurement and contracts personnel from a due-diligence perspective. In preparing the tender documents for release to the marketplace, the organisation needs to prepare the evaluation criteria. Some government polices mandate that the evaluation criteria, weighting and analysis methodologies are prepared before opening a tender for responses (refer to Step 3 and Step 4). And, further to this, that the criteria are published with the tender document, in an open and transparent manner.

■ *Step 3:* Optionally a **bidder conference** is run. Also known as a *contractor/vendor conference*, this meeting takes place at the release of the tender to the suppliers or general. Its aim is to ensure that all tenderers have a clear understanding of the procurement requirements.

■ *Step 4:* The tender is opened for responses (in the case of an open tender), or suppliers are invited to tender (in the case of a closed tender). From a project-scheduling perspective, it must be borne in mind that since open tenders are typically left in the marketplace for around four to eight weeks, there is potential for some subsequent project tasks to be delayed, and this must therefore be factored into the work packages and tasks on the final project WBS and project schedule. Also, it is during this stage of the tender process that decisions will need to be made regarding how tender questions and responses are to be handled to ensure minimal delays. *Remember:* In either an open or closed tender environment, if one tenderer asks a question, the response must be propagated to all registered tenderers, so the process remains open and transparent and no preferential information is provided to any one tenderer.

■ *Step 5:* The tender is closed. Responses are collated and distributed to the relevant parties for analysis.

- *Step 6:* The tenders are analysed by applying the evaluation criteria and weighting (this is defined in Step 2).
- *Step 7:* The successful supplier is notified.
- *Step 8:* The contract is established.
- *Step 9:* Once the successful supplier is contractually bound, the unsuccessful tenderers are duly notified.

Table 17.1 Types of tenders

Request for information	A **request for information (RFI)** is used to gather information to assist in the decision-making process before any formal commitments are made. RFIs can be used to obtain estimates during any stage of the project management life cycle, but are particularly useful during the scoping stage as they can obtain information that may assist the project in its early design. An RFI is similar to an expression of interest (EOI), or a registration of interest (ROI).
Request for quotation	A **request for quotation (RFQ)** provides a detailed specification of the product and/or services being sought to be procured. RFQs are written in a formal, structured manner, with a high degree of specificity. This ensures a consistent approach can be taken in the analysis of the tenders. Contents of an RFQ could include: - purpose and background - process for questions and clarifications - technical specifications - tolerances and quality specifications - drawings and blueprints - terms and conditions - a draft contract. An RFQ is synonymous with an invitation to bid (ITB).
Request for proposal	A **request for proposals (RFP)** is, in essence, the reverse of a RFQ. Rather than specifications being defined within the tender and the tenderer responding to them line by line, an RFP requires the tenderer to set out a design to solve the problem posed in the tender. This approach makes it difficult to set up a standard set of criteria as the designs received back by the project could be vastly different in their approach and therefore an *apples-with-apples* comparison cannot be simply made. Each must be taken on its own merits and an informed consensus decision must be made by the review group as to which one provides the best overall response to the problem.
Request for tender	A **request for tender (RFT)** is a more formal (and official) expression of the intent to secure a supplier for a product and/or service. In addition to the information sought in an RFQ, an RFT will ask for information about the company's financial stability, insurance cover and reputation (references should be sought). In some circumstances (e.g. government tenders), it will be indicated how the RFTs will be evaluated (the criteria of evaluation). The weighting of each of the criteria to be evaluated is typically kept confidential. The RFT might also be presented as an invitation to tender (ITT)!

The timing of Steps 7, 8 and 9 is critical; it is not wise to notify the successful and unsuccessful tenderers of the outcome of the tender process at the same time in case the successful tenderer subsequently withdraws its interest and no longer wishes to be considered. This would place the project in a weaker position by having to return to an (already notified and initially unsuccessful) second-choice tenderer.

When selecting a supplier (see Step 6), a simple spreadsheet can be used as a tool for setting out scores allocated to each criterion (for an example, see Table 17.2). Note that the actual number of criteria could be quite extensive, covering the criterion contained within the tender document, plus any further criteria required from a due-diligence perspective (such as financial performance of the tenderer).

There are different ways to approach the scoring of each criterion. It is not uncommon for all financial and contractual aspects to be assessed by the procurements and contracts department while the project leader focuses on the project-specific requirements. Another method that may be used includes taking a workshop approach towards scoring each criterion. This involves key stakeholders within the organisation discussing and scoring the potential suppliers' responses (tender responses) as a group and arriving at a transparent consensus agreement on the final selection of the supplier.

Table 17.2 Tenderer Selection Matrix

Criteria	Weight %	Tenderer #1 Overall score = 0.00		Tenderer #2 Overall score = 0.00	
		Score (out of 100)	Weighted score	Score (out of 100)	Weighted score
Coverage of requirements	2.5		= weight × score		= weight × score
Financial performance	10.0				
Company reputation	5.0				
Past experience in this area	5.0				
Safety record in executing	5.0				
Risks management of contract	10.0				
Performance reporting of contract	7.0				
Meets technical design requirements	4.0				
Favourable payment terms	7.0				
Ability to deliver on results	8.0				
After-delivery service	3.5				
Supplier history	12.0				
Dun & Bradstreet rating	11.0				
Demonstrates value for money	10.0				
	Total score		= sum of the above		= sum of the above

© 2022 Dr Neil Pearson

A basic supplier selection template has been included in the online resources.

 Supplier Selection

A more radical (but seldom used) method involves sending out copies of the submitted tenders to key internal stakeholders, requesting that they individually place a score against each criterion. The resultant scores are subsequently brought together in the form of a master spreadsheet and the overall averages are calculated. If there is a consensus in overall opinion, that supplier will be selected. However, if there is a large variation in opinions, a workshop would need to be organised to facilitate a resolution of the decision.

It is critical that the project leader selects the correct type of tender to use at each stage of the project life cycle and therefore they should appropriately seek input from the contracts and procurement departments.

New trend: Once the successful tenderer has been chosen and notified, and prior to the **main contract** coming into force, the project may wish to enter a **trial engagement** to assess the practicalities of the contract from both sides.

17.7 Decision: Contracts and contract types

 LE 17E

Having established the requirements for procurement and undertaken necessary tendering and/or supplier selection activities, the next stage in project management procurement is to consider the different types of contracts that may be entered into. Contracts can be highly complex and are designed to be legally binding. Since there can be detrimental legal and financial repercussions if a contract's terms are broken, it is highly advisable for project leaders to engage with their organisation's procurement and contract department to determine which **contract types** are favoured by the organisation, and to canvass assistance in constructing a well-defined, legally appropriate contract that protects the organisation's interests.

Some of the contract types that may be considered include:

- **versions of build, own, operate, transfer (BOOT)**
- **partnerships**

- **fixed-price contracts**
- **cost-reimbursable contracts**
- **time and materials contracts**.

These three types of contracts contain similar elements; however, the sequence of the elements differentiates the type of overall contract.

17.7.1 Build, own, operate, transfer (BOOT)

The contract sets out that the initial asset is to be built by a specifically named contractor and that once the asset has been built, it is to be operated by this named contractor (or sometimes a new organisation that has been set up specifically to operate the asset will be named). The ownership of the asset, at this point, stays with the contracting organisation. However, at a future time, the asset is handed back to the original organisation that let the contract. For example, say a government wishes to build a toll bridge between two major highways. The government would contract all elements of build, own and operate to the contracting organisation. The contracting organisation in this example could be a conglomerate of large construction companies. Once the construction has been completed (the build would be classified as a large, complex project), the asset could be transferred to an organisation specifically set up to operate the asset. If operation of the asset has been set to 25 years, after this point it would be returned to the government for ongoing ownership and operation.

17.7.2 Build, own, operate (BOO)

Here, the contract would be established but there would be no intention of transferring the asset (e.g. a toll bridge between the two major highways) back (to the government) at a future point in time. The asset would remain under the ownership of the organisation that built and subsequently operated it (until the organisation decided to sell the asset).

17.7.3 Build, operate, transfer (BOT)

The difference here is that the asset remains in the ownership of the organisation that let the contract originally (e.g. the government would be the owner in the above example). The building and the subsequent operation of the asset remain the domain of the contracted organisation.

The reasoning behind why a particular contract type is selected over another will vary. However, using the example of the toll bridge provided earlier:

- The BOOT method would enable some elements of risk to be borne by the contracting organisation. Assuming that research has indicated the revenue from the toll bridge will exceed the cost of the build-and-operate activities over the life of the ownership of the asset (i.e. the revenue from the toll bridge over the 25 years of ownership would outweigh the cost of building it and its subsequent operation), this would make the contractor a profit.
- With a BOO contract, the government would have a limited interest in any ownership of the asset, and both the risk and the reward would be borne by the contracting organisation.
- With a BOT contract, the asset would remain the property of the government; however, so would any associated responsibilities. The risk and reward of building and operating the toll bridge would rest with the contracting organisation. There are many complexities involved in such contracts.

Refer to "Snapshot from Practice: CLEM7 tunnel, Brisbane, Australia", for an example of a BOOT arrangement.

17.7.4 Partnerships

A partnership is where two or more parties conduct business together, sharing the profits but also the risk. Partnerships are usually entered into on a 50/50 basis (this ratio can vary) and may exist under the guise of joint ventures, strategic alliances, consortia and teaming. Partnerships can be complex but are often used where equal control of a project is deemed necessary. Costs fall equally between both parties, and any profits made are distributed equally between both parties (unless specified otherwise).

17.7.5 Fixed-price contracts

Fixed-price contracts come in many variations.

- *Firm fixed price (FFP):* FFP contracts are the most commonly occurring type of contract, where the price (and the seller's margin) is fixed. The price of items is fixed at the time of contract and is only subject to change if the scope of the work changes. The risk is borne by the seller, so if, for example, more effort is required to produce the goods (because the seller did not include a necessary stage of production), the seller still must deliver the goods to the buyer at the agreed cost.
- *Fixed-price incentive fee (FPIF):* As with an FFP contract, the price component of the contract is fixed; however, there is an agreement on how the margin component is constructed. For example, if the seller delivers ahead of time (without compromising on quality), they may be eligible for a performance-based incentive payment.
- *Fixed price with economic price adjustment (FP-EPA):* This type of contract is found less frequently and is more usually applied when a contract extends over a long period of time, or where items in the contract are subject to fluctuations that are not controllable by the seller. For example, if a seller is supplying copper cable over a long-term contract, parties to the contract need to recognise that there will potentially be a daily fluctuation in the price of this raw material on the metals exchange; therefore, there should be provisions in the contract for price adjustments to be made (within agreed tolerances).

Note that while *incentive* in the fixed price arrangement reduces the risk to the seller, cost reimbursable contracts reduce the risk to the buyer as an incentive.

17.7.6 Cost-reimbursable contracts

In a **cost-reimbursable contract**, the legitimate costs of completed work are billed back to the organisation on whose behalf the work has been completed. Within this arrangement there will be a profit belonging to the contracting organisation, as agreed within the terms of the existing contract. There is a level of uncertainty with these types of contracts.

- *Cost plus fixed fee (CPFF):* A fixed fee is agreed upon for an estimated amount of work (determined during project estimating). This fee and the agreed allowable costs are subsequently billed back to the supplier.
- *Cost plus incentive fee (CPIF):* As with CPFF, the seller is reimbursed for all allowable costs. The remaining fee is determined on an incentive basis. The schedule of incentive fees is agreed as part of the contract negotiations and is based on various performance criteria. For example, if laying cable underground, the seller will be paid for agreed costs and, based on the performance schedule, receives an incentive payment that depends on the rate of cable laid over a particular period.
- *Cost plus award fee (CPAF):* The buyer meets all agreed costs, but the award component is paid only on completion of a larger, more comprehensive, overall performance goal.

Taking the cable-laying scenario outlined in CPIF, this might mean that receipt of payment would depend upon the successful completion of all cable being laid into the ground and successful testing (as working to required specifications) of the entire cable run.

17.7.7 Time and material (T&M) contracts

T&M contracts are a hybrid of both cost-reimbursable and fixed-price contracts. These are often used when a predetermined volume of work cannot be forecast, so the risk must be more balanced between the buyer and the seller. Using the cable-laying scenario once more, if there are variations in the ground to be excavated to lay the cable that cannot be determined, the supplier might not be able to enter into a fixed price contract and may simply opt for a T&M contract, where material costs would be covered with an amount fixed per-hour of labour used.

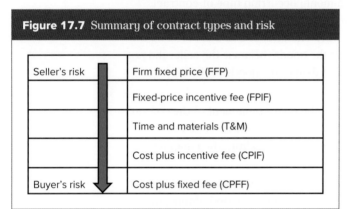

Figure 17.7 Summary of contract types and risk

© 2022 Dr Neil Pearson

As demonstrated, there are numerous types of contracts available. Project leaders may consider using a particular type of contract during the Initiating and Planning stages of the project but might use more of a risk-transferral type of contract during project Executing stage, where the *unknown* elements become *known* elements. This is illustrated in Figure 17.7.

Project leaders should *always* liaise with their organisation's legal (contracts and procurement) team before entering any kind of contract; there are many potential pitfalls, therefore it is best to always seek professional, specialist advice. This is the case whether working with local, national or globally positioned organisations.

17.7.8 Contracts: Six essential elements of a contract

When the successful tenderer is notified, the purchasing organisation and supplier will enter formal contract negotiations. Elements that must exist for a contract to be legally binding are illustrated in Figure 17.8.

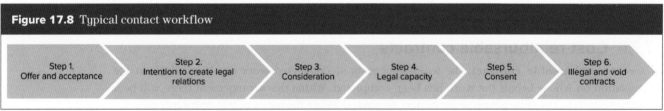

Figure 17.8 Typical contact workflow

© 2022 Dr Neil Pearson

- *Step 1:* A contract is formed when an offer by one party is accepted by the other party.
- *Step 2:* A contract does not exist just because there is an agreement between two or more people. The parties to the agreement must intend to enter into a legally binding agreement. The law is not so concerned with what the parties subjectively intended, but with what a reasonable person would consider the parties intended in the circumstances in which the agreement was reached. Such an intention will rarely be stated explicitly in a written document but will be inferred from matters such as the nature of the relationship between the parties and the nature of the agreement.
- *Step 3: Consideration* is the price paid for a promise made by one party to the other party. The price must be something of value, although it need not be money. Consideration may be a right, interest or benefit going to one party, or some forbearance, detriment or loss given, undertaken, tolerated, or suffered by the other party.

- *Step 4:* Not all people are free to enter a valid contract. Contracts involving the following may have issues related to consent and legal capacity.
  - people who have a mental impairment
  - young people (minors)
  - bankrupts
  - corporations (people acting on behalf of a company); and
  - prisoners.
- *Step 5:* Entering into a contract must involve the elements of free will and proper understanding of what each of the parties is doing. In other words, the consent of each of the parties to a contract must be genuine. Only where the essential element of proper consent has been given is there a contract that is binding upon the parties.
- *Step 6:* The law will not enforce all contracts. A contract (or a term of a contract) that involves illegal conduct may be void and unenforceable. Whether contracts that are illegal by statute will be deemed void and unenforceable depends on the particular statute and the ordinary principles of statutory interpretation. Contracts absolutely prohibited by statute will be deemed to be void, whether the parties know of the illegality or not.

Source: Adapted from https://fls.org.au/law-handbook/consumers-contracts-the-internet-and-copyright/how-contract-law-works/elements-of-a-contract/, accessed February 2022.

When entering contract negotiations involving internal or external legal parties, the project leader should consider allowing additional time for these activities to take place. When dealing with **contract law** and contracts, as already pointed out, it will be necessary to consult internal specialist expertise, but it is also prudent to obtain the professional expertise of external legal practitioners. The author (Pearson) has experienced long lead times for contract reviews by legal departments, sometimes weeks—these need to be factored into the project schedule so as to not impede a subsequent work package and/or task taking place.

More information on the elements of a contract can be found at: https://fls.org.au/law-handbook/consumers-contracts-the-internet-and-copyright/how-contract-law-works/elements-of-a-contract/ (Fitzroy Legal Service 2022).

Note: These elements of a contract can vary between states as well as from country to country; always check with a subject matter expert in your organisation before committing to any agreements, written or verbal.

17.7.9 Extended contract considerations

The project leader should clearly specify any inclusions to be set out within the standard terms and conditions of the contract. For example:

- *Dispute arrangements:* The procedure to be followed in the event of a contractual dispute (which cannot be resolved between the two parties) should be clearly set out and defined. The following are points to consider.
  - The conditions required for an element of the contract to be in dispute.
  - A designated independent third party should be specified and agreed upon, to host and facilitate dispute resolution meetings.
  - The location for any dispute resolution meetings needs to be agreed upon in advance in the contract. This can be particularly important if suppliers are offshore.
  - The contract needs to set out how the costs of this independent third party are to be met by the two main contracting parties.
- *Subcontracting:* The contract should clearly indicate whether any subcontracting is to be allowed. Some contracts specifically state that no subcontracting is to be allowed. Buyers often

do this to ensure that the quality, safety record, financial status and reputation of the primary contractor are not diluted by subcontracting to a third party (who may be unknown to the buyer).

- *Non-disclosure agreements/confidentiality:* Relates to how information, and whether customer information or new product design information, is to be protected from the marketplace and from competitors. For example, the classification *commercial in confidence* (and other classifications of information) may be used between the two parties. The contract should clearly define the information classifications to be used and set out how, and the extent to which, information needs to be protected.

- *Intellectual property (IP):* In today's ever-litigious and information-based society, having a clear understanding of IP, copyright, patents and trademarks is critical to legally protecting non-tangible project and organisational assets, as well as tangible products.

- *Performance and payment schedules:* Clearly documented performance targets (based on quality criteria) need to be linked to payment schedules. Detaching the payment schedule from performance targets is a common error. The project must receive quality-based products and/or services (within defined tolerances), which then attract a payment.

- *Non-agreement/contract dissolution:* Clauses setting out how the contract is to end should both parties mutually agree to dissolve the contract (and where dispute arrangements are not invoked).

- *Defects and withholding arrangements:* Contract clauses setting out the process and timeframes for defect correction and the amounts to be withheld/retained in the event of outstanding defects at project closure.

SNAPSHOT *from* PRACTICE | CLEM7 tunnel, Brisbane, Australia

RiverCity Motorway Group contracted the design and construction of the CLEM7 tunnel (a 6.8 km tolled motorway connecting five of Brisbane's major highways) to Leighton Contractors and Baulderstone Bilfinger Berger as a joint venture (LBB JV). Upon successful construction of the CLEM7, the operation of the tunnel and tollways was handed over to Queensland Tollway Company (RiverCity Motorway Group). RiverCity Motorway Group was established to build, own and operate the venture, with the planned eventual transfer back to the City of Brisbane after a 45-year concession period.

Figure 17.9 Cars in a tunnel

Ingram Publishing/SuperStock

The CLEM7 project provides not only a good example of a joint venture between two major construction partners (Leighton Contractors and Baulderstone Bilfinger Berger), but also a good example of a BOOT project. The CLEM7 project also provides significant insight into lessons learned for the way these large public infrastructure projects are planned: the RiverCity Motorway Group collapsed (in 2011) with debts of AUD1.3 billion. The cause was stated to be largely due to the general public's (wide-ranging) refusal to use the tunnel due to perceived exorbitant toll charges (similar situations to this occurred around the Lane Cove and Cross City tunnels in Sydney, Australia).

What lessons can we take away from such a failed project?

Even though the build component was completed to schedule (actually, ahead of schedule in this case) and to cost, it was not apparent whether the customer (i.e. the very basis of the initial Business Case) had been considered and involved adequately enough.

A project leader is often faced with many potentially litigious decisions during the contract negotiation process. The involvement of representation from internal organisational resources (at minimum) is therefore critical to ensure that the contract negotiation is watertight, fair, transparent and will deliver what the project leader has defined. External professional legal advice should always be sought where there is uncertainty or where further clarity is needed.

In Australia, there are also standards available for general conditions of contract, such as AS 2124 B-1992, now superseded by AS 4000 B-1997.

17.7.10 The art of negotiation

Effective negotiation is critical for successful collaboration. All it takes is one key problem to explode to convert a sense of *we* into an *us versus them* situation. Negotiation is pervasive throughout all aspects of project management work. For example, project leaders must negotiate the levels of support and funding they will receive from top management. They must negotiate staff and technical input from functional managers. They must coordinate with other project leaders and negotiate project priorities and resource commitments. They must negotiate within their project team to determine assignments, deadlines, standards and priorities. Project leaders must also negotiate prices and standards with vendors and suppliers. It is clear therefore that a project leader must have a firm understanding of how the negotiating process works in practice, possess the requisite negotiation skills and be able to leverage tactics often used during robust negotiations. When combined, these elements can help to foster project success.

Many people approach the negotiating table as if they are in a contest. They believe that each negotiator is out to win as much as they can for their side. Their measure of success is how much they gain, compared with the other party/parties. While this approach may be applicable when negotiating the sale of a house, it is not true for project management: project management is not a contest!

The people working on the project (whether they represent different companies or differing departments within the same organisation) are not enemies nor competitors, but rather allies or partners. They have formed a temporary alliance to complete a project and for this alliance to work, a certain degree of trust, cooperation and honesty is required. Although the parties within this alliance may have different priorities and standards, they are bound by the success of the project. If conflicts escalate to the point where negotiations break down and the project comes to a halt, then everyone loses.

Unlike the bartering process with a street vendor when a person (the potential buyer) can simply walk away if they can't reach agreement, the people involved in project work must continue to work together. Therefore, it is fitting for them to work together to resolve disagreements in a way that contributes to the long-term effectiveness of their working relationship.

Conflict in a project can actually be good! When dealt with effectively, conflict can lead to surges of innovation, better decision-making and more creative problem-solving. Project leaders must accept this aspect of negotiation and realise that negotiation is, essentially, a two-part process: the first part of the process deals with reaching an agreement, and the second part deals with the implementation of that agreement. It is the implementing stage, not the agreement itself, that determines the success of negotiations. All too often, managers reach an agreement with someone, only to find out later that they failed to do what they agreed to do, or that their actual response fell far short of expectations. Experienced project leaders recognise that implementation is based on satisfaction—not only with the outcome, but also with the process by which the agreement was reached. If someone feels bullied or tricked into doing something, this will invariably be reflected in a half-hearted performance.

Experienced project leaders do the best they can to merge individual interests with what is best for the project, to come up with effective solutions to problems. Fisher & Ury (1991) champion an approach to negotiating that embodies these goals. It emphasises developing *win–win* solutions while protecting yourself against those who would take advantage of your forthrightness. Their approach is called **principled negotiation** and is based on the four following key points (which are discussed in the following sections):

1. Separate the people from the problem.
2. Focus on interests, not positions.

3. Invent options for mutual gain (the win–win position).

4. When possible, use objective criteria.

17.7.10.1 Separate the people from the problem

Strong adversarial-type personalities can sometimes derail substantive issues that are under consideration. Instead of attacking the problem(s), people begin to attack each other. Once people feel attacked or threatened, their energy naturally goes into defending themselves, and not into solving the problem at hand. What needs to happen, therefore, is for them to focus on the problem—not on the other person—during the negotiation. This means avoiding personalising the negotiation and not framing the negotiation as a contest. Instead, focus needs to be kept on the problem to be resolved. In Fisher and Ury's (1991) words: "Be hard on the problem, soft on the people".

By keeping their focus on the issues and not on personalities, negotiators are better able to let the other person blow off steam without getting emotionally involved. When dealing with important problems, it is not uncommon for people to become upset, frustrated and angry. However, an angry attack is highly likely to produce an angry counterattack, and the discussion quickly escalates into a heated argument: an emotional chain reaction.

In some cases, people use anger as a means of intimidating and forcing concessions because the other person wishes to preserve the relationship. When people become emotional, negotiators should keep a cool head and remember the old German proverb "Let anger fly out the window". In other words, in the face of an emotional outburst, imagine opening a window and letting the heat of the anger fly out of the window. Avoid taking things personally and redirect personal attacks back to the question at hand. Don't react to the emotional outburst but try to find the issues that triggered it. Skilled negotiators keep their cool under stress and, at the same time, build a bond with others by empathising and acknowledging common sources of frustration and anger.

While it is important to separate the people from the problem during actual negotiations, it is beneficial to have a friendly rapport with the other person before beginning negotiations. Such rapport is consistent with the social network tenet of building a relationship before you need it. Reduce the likelihood of misunderstandings and getting off on the wrong foot by having a history of interacting in a friendly, responsive manner with the other person. If, in the past, the relationship has been marked by healthy give-and-take, in which both parties have demonstrated a willingness to accommodate the interests of the other, then neither individual is likely to adopt an immediate win–lose perspective. Furthermore, a positive relationship adds a common interest beyond the specific points of contention. Not only do both parties want to reach an agreement that suits their individual interests, but they also want to do so in a manner that preserves their relationship. Each is therefore more likely to seek solutions that are mutually beneficial.

17.7.10.2 Focus on interests, not positions

Negotiations often stall when people focus on positions:

■ "I'm willing to pay $10,000." "No, it will cost $15,000."

■ "I need it done by Monday." "That's impossible, we can't have it ready until Wednesday."

While such interchanges are common during preliminary discussions, managers must prevent this initial posturing from becoming polarised. When such positions are stated, attacked and then defended, each party figuratively begins to draw a line they will not cross. This line creates a win–lose scenario in which someone has to lose by crossing the line to reach an agreement. As such, the negotiations can become a war of wills, with concessions being seen as a loss of face.

The key is to focus on the interests behind your positions (what you are trying to achieve) and separate these goals from your ego as best you can. Not only should you be driven by your interests, but you should try to identify the interests of the other party. Ask why it will cost so much or why it can't be done by Monday. At the same time, make your own interests come alive. Don't just say that it is critical that it be done by Monday; explain what will happen if it isn't done by Monday.

Sometimes, when the true interests of both parties are revealed, there is no basis for conflict. Take, for example, the Monday versus Wednesday argument. This argument could apply to a scenario involving a project leader and the production manager of a small, local firm that is contracted to produce prototypes of a new generation of computer mouse. The project leader needs the prototypes on Monday to demonstrate to a users' focus group. The production manager says this is impossible. The project leader says this would be embarrassing because marketing has spent a lot of time and effort setting up this demonstration. The production manager again denies the request and adds that he has already had to schedule overtime to meet the Wednesday delivery date. However, when the project leader reveals that the purpose of the focus group is to gauge consumers' reactions to the colour and shape of the new devices, not the finished product, the conflict disappears. The production manager tells the project leader that she can pick up the samples today if she wants because production has an excess supply of shells.

When focusing on interests, it is important to practice the communication habit: "Seek first to understand, then to be understood". This involves what Stephen Covey (1990) calls *empathetic listening*—allowing a person to fully understand another person's frame of reference. This approach reveals not only what that person is saying but also how they feel. Covey (1990) asserts that people have an inherent need to be understood. He goes on to observe that satisfied needs do not motivate human behaviour; only unsatisfied needs do—"People try to go to sleep when they are tired, not when they are rested" (Covey 1990). The key point is that until people believe they are being understood, they will repeat their points and reformulate their arguments. If, on the other hand, you satisfy their need by seeking first to understand, then the other party is free to understand your interests and focus directly on the issues at hand. "Seeking to understand", however, requires discipline and compassion. Instead of responding to the other person by asserting your agenda, respond by summarising both the facts and feelings behind what the other person has said to check the accuracy of comprehension.

17.7.10.3 Invent options for mutual gain (the win–win position)

Once the individuals involved have identified their interests, they can explore options for mutual gain. This is not easy. Stressful negotiations inhibit creativity and free exchange. What is required is collaborative brainstorming in which people work together to solve the problem in a way that will lead to a win–win scenario. The key to brainstorming is separating the *inventing* from the *deciding*. Begin by taking 15 minutes to generate as many options as possible. No matter how outlandish any option is, it should not be subjected to criticism or immediate rejection. People should feed off the ideas of others to generate new ideas. When all possible options have been exhausted, sort through the ideas that have been generated and focus on those that have the greatest possibilities.

Clarifying interests and exploring mutual options creates the opportunity to dovetail interests. Dovetailing means one person identifies options that are of low cost to them but of high interest to the other party. This is only possible if each party knows what the other's needs are. For example, in negotiating a price with a parts supplier, a project leader learned from their discussion that the supplier was in a cash flow squeeze after purchasing a very expensive fabrication machine. Needing cash was the primary reason the supplier had taken such a rigid position on price. During the brainstorming session, one of the options presented was to prepay for the order, instead of following the usual payment on delivery arrangement. Both parties seized on this option and reached an amicable agreement in which the project leader would pay the supplier for the entire job in advance, in exchange for a faster turnaround time and a significant price reduction. Such opportunities for win–win agreements are often overlooked because the negotiators become fixated on solving their own problems and fail to look for opportunities to solve the other person's problems.

17.7.10.4 **When possible, use objective criteria**

Most established industries and professions have developed standards and rules to help deal with common areas of dispute. For example, both buyers and sellers rely on the *blue book* to establish price parameters for a used car. The construction industry has building codes and fair practice policies to resolve proof of quality and safe work practices. The legal profession uses precedents to adjudicate claims of wrongdoing.

Whenever possible, you should insist on using external, objective criteria to settle disagreements. For example, a disagreement arose between a regional airline and the independent accounting team entrusted with preparing its annual financial statement. The regional airline had made a significant investment by leasing several used airplanes from a larger airline. The dispute involved whether this lease should be classified as an operating or capital lease. This was important to the airline because if the purchase was classified as an operating lease, the associated debt would not have to be recorded in the financial statement. However, if the purchase was classified as a capital lease, then the debt would be factored into the financial statement and the debt/equity ratio would be much less attractive to stockholders and would-be investors. The two parties resolved this dispute by deferring to formulas established by the Financial Accounting Standards Board. As it turns out, the accounting team was correct but, by deferring to objective standards, it was able to deflect the disappointment of the airline managers away from the accounting team and preserve a professional relationship with that airline.

17.7.10.5 **Dealing with unreasonable people**

Most people working on projects realise that, in the long run, it is beneficial to work towards mutually satisfying solutions. Still, occasionally you encounter someone who has a dominant win–lose attitude about life and they are difficult to deal with. Fisher & Ury (1991) recommend using *negotiation jujitsu* when dealing with such a person. That is, when the other person begins to push, don't push back. As in the martial arts, avoid pitting your strengths against another's directly; instead, use your skill to step aside and turn that person's strength to your ends. When someone adamantly sets forth a position, neither reject it nor accept it. Treat it as a possible option and then look for the interests behind it. Instead of defending your ideas, invite criticism and advice. Ask why it's a bad idea and discover the other's underlying interest.

Those who use negotiation jujitsu rely on two primary weapons. They ask questions instead of making statements. Questions allow for interests to surface and do not provide the opponent with something to attack. The second weapon is silence. If the other person makes an unreasonable proposal or attacks you personally, just sit there and don't say a word. Wait for the other party to break the stalemate by answering your question or coming up with a new suggestion.

The best defence against unreasonable win–lose negotiators is having what Fisher & Ury refer to as a "strong **BATNA**" (Best Alternative To a Negotiated Agreement). They point out that people try to reach an agreement to produce something better than the result of not negotiating with that person. What results would be the true benchmark for determining whether you should accept an agreement? A strong BATNA gives you the power to walk away and say, "No deal unless we work towards a win–win scenario".

Your BATNA reflects how dependent you are on the other party. If you are negotiating price and delivery dates and can choose from several reputable suppliers, then you have a strong BATNA. If, on the other hand, there is only one vendor who can supply you with specific, critical material on time, you have a weak BATNA. Under these circumstances you may be forced to concede to the vendor's demands. At the same time, you should begin to explore ways of increasing your BATNA for future negotiations. This can be done by reducing your dependency on that supplier. Begin to find alternative substitutable materials or negotiate better lead times with other vendors.

Negotiating is an art (as well as a science), and there are many intangibles involved in the process. In this section, we have reviewed some useful and time-tested principles (based on the celebrated work of Fisher & Ury 1991) that can help to foster effective negotiations. Given the significance of negotiation in project management, Fisher & Ury's work is a helpful time-tested resource, and there are many other resources available that can be of use. Negotiation training workshops can provide opportunities to practise these skills face to face and you should also take advantage of day-to-day interactions to sharpen your negotiating acumen.

17.8 Outsourcing project work

If the decision is made to buy into the project, then the process of **outsourcing** may come into play. The term *outsourcing* has traditionally been applied to transferring business functions or processes (e.g. customer support, ICT, accounting) to other (often offshore) companies. For example, when you call your internet provider to solve a technical problem, you may end up speaking with a technician who is in another country. Outsourcing now means that significant chunks of project work are contracted out. For example, HP and Dell work closely with other hard drive manufacturers to develop next-generation laptops. Toyota and Daimler AG collaborate with suppliers to develop new car platforms. Apple works with Samsung and LG on screen technology.

The shift towards outsourcing is readily apparent in the film industry. During the golden era of Hollywood, huge, vertically integrated corporations made movies. Studios such as MGM, Warner Brothers and 20th Century Fox owned large movie lots and employed thousands of full-time specialists, including set designers, camera operators, film editors and directors. Star actors like Humphrey Bogart and Marilyn Monroe were signed to exclusive studio contracts for a set number of films (e.g. six films over three years). Today, most movies are made by a collection of individuals and small companies who come together to make films project by project. This structure allows each project to be staffed with the talent most suited to its demands, rather than choosing from only those people the studio employs directly. This approach is also being applied to the creation of new products and services in contemporary marketplaces.

Figure 17.10 depicts a situation in which a zero-gravity reclining chair is being developed. The genesis for the chair comes from a mechanical engineer who developed the idea in their garage.

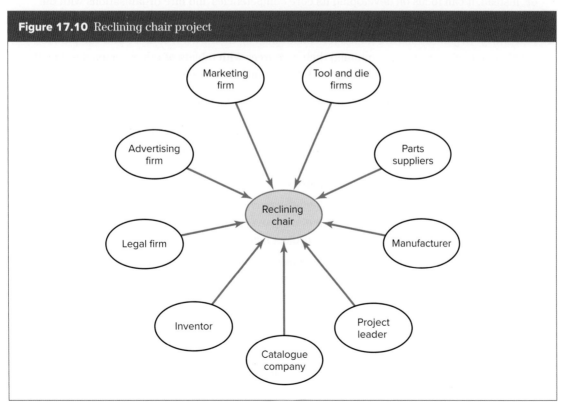

Figure 17.10 Reclining chair project

The inventor negotiates a contract with a catalogue organisation to develop and manufacture the chair. The catalogue organisation in turn creates a project team of manufacturers, suppliers and marketing organisations to create the new chair. Each participant adds their expertise to the project. The catalogue organisation brings its brand name and distribution channels to the project. Marketing organisations refine the design, develop packaging and test potential market names. Engineering organisations provide customised parts, which are delivered to a manufacturing organisation that will produce the chair. A project leader is assigned by the catalogue organisation to work with the inventor and the other parties to complete the project.

Many outsourced projects operate in a virtual environment in which people are linked by internet-enabled communications. They may rarely, if ever, see one another face to face. On other projects, participants from different organisations may work next to each other, for example, on a construction site or in shared office space. In either case, people come and go as services are needed, much as in a matrix structure. But they are not formal members of one organisation, they are technical experts who form a temporary alliance with an organisation, fulfil their contractual obligations and then move on to the next project.

The advantages of outsourcing project work are many:

- *Cost reduction:* Companies can secure competitive prices for contracted-out services, especially if the work can be outsourced offshore. Furthermore, overhead costs are dramatically cut since the company must no longer internally maintain the contracted services.

- *Faster project completion:* Not only can work be done more cheaply, but it might also be done faster. Competitive pricing means that more resources will potentially be available for the same dollar-cost. Furthermore, outsourcing can provide access to equipment and tools that can accelerate the completion of project tasks. For example, by contracting a backhoe operator, you can accomplish in four hours what it might take a landscaping crew four days to complete.

- *High level of expertise:* A high level of expertise and technology can be brought to bear on the project. The company no longer has to keep up with technological advances as this is taken care of. Instead, it can focus on developing its core competencies and hire organisations with the know-how to work on relevant segments of the project.

- *Flexibility:* Organisations are no longer constrained by their own resources and can pursue a wide range of projects by combining their resources with talents of other companies. Small companies can instantly go global by working with offshore partners.

The disadvantages of outsourcing project work are less documented, but here are a few:

- *Coordination breakdowns:* Coordination of professionals from different organisations can be challenging, especially if the project work requires close collaboration and mutual adjustment. Breakdowns are exacerbated by physical separation, with people working in different buildings and different cities, or even different countries.

- *Loss of control:* There is potential loss of control over the project. The core team depends on other organisations they have no direct authority over. While long-term survival of participating organisations depends on performance, a project may falter when one partner fails to deliver.

- *Conflict:* Projects are more prone to interpersonal conflict since the different participants do not share the same values and priorities, and potentially, culture. Trust, which is essential to project success, can be difficult to forge when interactions are limited, and people come from different organisations.

- *Security issues:* Depending on the nature of the project, trade and business secrets may be revealed. This can be problematic if the contractor also works for your competitor.

- *Confidentiality:* This is another concern and companies must be very careful when outsourcing processes like payroll and insurance information.

Few people disagree that reducing costs is the primary motive behind outsourcing project work. However, recent industry polls indicate a shift away from simply opting for the best low-cost deal and a shift towards securing services from companies that provide the best value in terms of both cost and performance. Performance is not simply limited to the quality of specific work, but also an ability to collaborate and work together. Companies are doing their homework to determine, "Can we work with these people?"

SNAPSHOT *from* PRACTICE | **Investing in investigations**

A university clearing house whose primary value-adding function was to match students to university courses (while carrying out numerous back-office checks) was involved in an ongoing program to replace its legacy ICT systems. Due to the size and complexity of the systems, the CEO committed to "investing in investigating" the best option for the future development of the systems, prior to embarking upon a strategy for their actual replacement.

The project gained commitment and funds to employ the services of a highly regarded software development company that had a sound local reputation for investigating various options for the redevelopment of such critical "core value-adding" systems of organisations.

The options the company considered for the replacement of systems included:

1. *Option A:* The internal redevelopment of systems—employing internal Agile teams to carry out requisite redevelopment activities over an extended time frame.

2. *Option B:* An external modular/phased redevelopment of components on a cleverly sequenced time line of modules.

3. *Option C:* An external "big-bang" development approach to core modules—replacing large tracts of functionality in one go.

   From a procurement perspective, each option would have resulted in different approaches to the procurement of resources to the project:

   ■ Option A would have resulted in many short-term contracts for the recruitment of external contract developers.

   ■ Option B would have been a phased contract, where being able to proceed onto the next phase would be determined by whether delivery of the preceding module had been successful.

   ■ Option C would have required a much longer contractual engagement to be entered, most probably involving a long tendering process to select the supplier to the project.

"Investing in investigations" to help determine and select the best deployment method enabled the business to more comprehensively consider the long-haul costs of each option. Other considerations included the fit with the revenue stream of the organisation. Synergies with the business must never be ignored as contracts are generally legally binding once formally entered, and if they need to be broken (exited) quickly because the funding model changes, this could potentially break a company in high exit fees and legal costs.

The organisation made a wise choice after reviewing the consultant's report findings about each of the potential options: Option A was selected above any of the other approaches as the funding and control factors, combined with a modular approach (which enabled better quality access to internal stakeholders), were seen as critical to the project's long-term success.

17.8.1 Best practices in outsourcing project work

This section describes some of the best practices we have observed being used by organisations that excel in project management (see Table 17.3). Although the list is by no means comprehensive, it reflects strategies used by organisations with extensive outsourcing experience. These practices reveal an underlying theme in how organisations approach contracted work on projects. Instead of the traditional master–slave relationship between project and provider or buyer and seller, all parties work together as partners, sharing the ultimate goal of a successful project.

Table 17.3 Best practices in outsourcing project work

Project area	Best practice
Requirements and procedures	Well-defined requirements and procedures
Training	Extensive training and team-building activities
Conflict management	Well-established conflict management processes
Review	Frequent review and status updates
Location	Co-location when needed
Contracts	Fair and incentive-laden contracts
Outsourcing	Long-term outsourcing relationships

© 2022 Dr Neil Pearson

Differences between the traditional approach and the **partnering** approach towards managing contracted relationships are summarised in Table 17.4. Partnering requires more than a simple handshake! It typically entails a significant commitment of time and energy to forge and sustain collaborative relations among all parties. This commitment is reflected in the seven best practices outlined in Table 17.3.

Table 17.4 Key differences between partnering and traditional approaches towards managing contracted relationships

Partnering approach	Traditional approach
Mutual trust forms the basis for strong working relationships.	There is suspicion and distrust; each party is wary of the motives for the other's actions
Shared goals and objectives ensure common direction.	Each party's goals and objectives, while similar, are geared to what is best for them.
Joint project team exists with high level of interaction.	There are independent project teams; teams are spatially separated with managed interactions.
Open communications avoid misdirection and bolster effective working relationships.	Communications are structured and guarded.
Long-term commitment provides the opportunity to attain continuous improvement.	Single project contracting is normal.
Objective critique is geared towards candid assessment of performance.	Objectivity is limited, due to fear of reprisal and lack of continuous improvement opportunities.
Access to each other's organisational resources is available.	Access is limited, with structured procedures and self-preservation taking priority over total optimisation.
Total company involvement requires commitment from CEO to team members.	Involvement is normally limited to project-level personnel.
Integration of administrative systems equipment takes place.	Duplication and/or translation takes place with attendant costs and delays.
Risk is shared jointly among the partners, which encourages innovation and continuous improvement.	Risk is transferred to the other party.

© 2022 Dr Neil Pearson

17.9 : **Partnering practices**

17.9.1 **Well-defined requirements and procedures**

Convincing people from different professions, organisations and cultures to work together is difficult. If expectations and requirements are unclear or open to debate, it is even harder. Successful organisations are very careful when selecting the work to be outsourced. They often choose to contract only work with clearly defined deliverables and measurable outcomes. For example, contractors hire electrical firms to install heating and air-conditioning systems, electronic firms use design firms to fabricate enclosures for their products, and software development teams outsource the testing of versions of their programs. In all these cases, the technical requirements are spelled out in detail. Even so, communicating requirements can be troublesome, especially with offshore providers, and extra care must be taken to ensure that expectations are clearly understood.

Not only do requirements have to be made clear, but the different organisations' project management systems need to be integrated. Common procedures and terminology need to be established so different parties can work together. This can be problematic when you have organisations with more advanced project management systems working with less developed organisations.

Proficient companies address this issue up-front instead of waiting for problems to emerge by carrying out an initial assessment of the fit between the provider's project management methods and their own project management system. This fit then becomes a prime consideration when they choose vendors. Work requirements and deliverables are spelled out in detail in the procurement process. Significant time and energy are invested into establishing project communication systems to support effective collaboration.

When working with other organisations on projects, it is important to consider (and protect) your organisation's security (and that of its customers). Security extends beyond competitive secrets and technologies to include access to information systems. Organisations must establish robust safeguards to prevent access to sensitive information and the introduction of viruses into its systems from less secure provider systems. Information technology security therefore necessitates additional cost and risk, and this will need to be addressed up-front, before project work is outsourced.

17.9.2 **Extensive training and team-building activities**

Often, managers become so preoccupied with the plans and technical challenges involved in a project that they assume that people issues will simply work themselves out over time. Smart organisations recognise, however, that people issues are just as important, if not more important, than many technical issues and they therefore train their personnel to work effectively with people from a wide variety of other organisations and countries. This training is pervasive. It is not limited to management but involves all people, at all levels, who interact with and are dependent upon outsourcers. Trainees may attend a class about how to generally negotiate effectively or may learn specific requisite skills (e.g. how to work effectively with programmers whose first language is not the same as yours). Team members are provided with a theoretical understanding of any barriers to collaboration and are taught skills to overcome these.

Training is augmented by inter-organisational team-building sessions that are designed to forge healthy relationships before the project begins. Team-building workshops involve key players (engineers, architects, lawyers, specialists and other staff). In many cases, organisations find it useful to hire an outside consultant to design and facilitate the sessions. The consultant is typically well versed in inter-organisational team building and can provide an impartial perspective to the workshop. The length and design of team-building sessions will depend on the experience, commitment and skill level of the participants. For example, in one project, where the business owner and contractors were relatively inexperienced in working together, a two-day workshop was convened. The first day was devoted to ice-breaking activities and establishing the rationale behind partnering. The conceptual foundation was supported by exercises and mini-lectures on teamwork, synergy, win–win and constructive feedback. The second day began by examining the problems and barriers that had prevented full collaboration in the past. Representatives from the different organisations were each (separately) asked to answer the following questions:

- What actions do the other group(s) engage in that create problems for us?
- What actions do we engage in that we think create problems for them?
- What recommendations would we make to improve the situation?

The groups shared their responses and asked questions to seek clarification about anything that was not clear to them. Agreements and disparities in the lists were noted and specific problems were identified. Once problem areas were noted, each group was assigned the task of identifying its specific interests and goals for the project. Goals were shared across groups, and special attention was devoted to establishing what goals they had in common. Recognition of shared goals was critical for transforming the different groups' stances into a cohesive team position. Team-building sessions often culminate with the creation of a **Partnering Charter** that is signed by all participants. This charter states the common goals for the project, as well as the procedures that will be used to achieve these goals (see Figure 17.11 for an example of the first page of such a charter).

Figure 17.11 Generic Partnering Charter

LOGO

PARTNERING CHARTER BETWEEN X AND Y

Our mission is to ensure an open, honest and transparent stance is taken to all our partnering operations to ensure outcomes for all parties are maximised.

THROUGH OUR JOINT OBJECTIVES

To understand and question what the customer wants and strive to deliver maximum value to them

Cultivating an environment of trust in all our dealings

Taking responsibility for our environment in the present and ensuring no known implications for future generations are created

To be equitable in all our dealings, with no bias on age, gender or cultural background, for example

To ensure our physical and mental well-being is being considered in all transactions, everyone who comes to work returns home in a healthier state

Quality is everyone's responsibility, quality is never compromised

Risk is shared and always raised, all activities are carried out in an environment where open communications are valued

Issues are resolved in a collaborative, constructive environment, root causes are identified and shared ownership is taken

Conflicts are depersonalised and based on facts, information and data. Outcomes are focused on value to the customer

Decisions are not determined in isolation but in collaboration with parties from all sides of the agreement

Project management is done under a one shared approach, we all seek opportunities to improve this approach on a daily basis

17.9.3 **Well-established conflict management processes**

Conflict is inevitable on most projects. When handled effectively and constructively, disagreements can actually elevate performance. However, if it is not quickly extinguished, smouldering dysfunctional conflict can ignite and severely undermine project success. Outsourced activities are susceptible to conflicts since people are unaccustomed to working together and will have different values and perspectives (they are, after all, employed by different organisations and are loyal to their employer). Smart organisations invest significant time and energy up-front to establish the rules of engagement, so disagreements are handled constructively.

Escalation is the primary control mechanism for dealing with and resolving problems. The basic principle of escalation is that problems should be resolved at the lowest level of the management hierarchy, within a set time limit (e.g. one business day) or they are escalated to the next tier/level of project management. If escalation occurs, then that level/tier has the same time limit applied to resolve the problem or it gets passed on to the next higher level. *No action* is not an option, nor can one participant force concessions from the other by simply delaying a decision. While there is certainly no shame in pushing significant problems up the hierarchy, at the same time managers should be quick to point out to subordinates any problems or questions that they should have been able to resolve on their own without escalating the matter.

If possible, key personnel from their respective organisations should be brought together to discuss any potential problems and to formulate problem-solving responses. This usually occurs as part of the coordinated series of team-building activities as discussed earlier. Particular attention is devoted to establishing the *change control process* as problems often erupt around this. People who are or will be dependent upon each other in the project need to try to identify potential problems that may occur, so they can agree in advance how these should be resolved.

Principled negotiation emphasises collaborative problem-solving and is the norm for resolving problems to reach agreement in project management situations. This approach is discussed in detail later in this chapter but is mentioned here to foster a link between conflict management and resolution and partnership working.

17.9.4 **Frequent review and status updates**

Project leaders and other key personnel from all organisations involved will meet on regularly to review and assess project performance. Collaborating as partners is considered to be a legitimate project priority (which is assessed along with time, cost and performance). Teamwork, communication and timely problem resolution are all evaluated. This provides a platform for identifying any problems to do with not only the project, but also with working relationships, so that these can be resolved quickly and appropriately.

An increasing number of companies are using online surveys to collect data from project participants about the quality of working relations they experience (see Figure 17.12 for a partial example). With this data to hand, one can then gauge the pulse of the project and identify any issues that need to be addressed. Comparing survey responses, period by period, means that areas that need to be improved or problems that need to be solved can be tracked over time. In some cases, follow-up team-building sessions are arranged—to focus on specific problems and to recharge collaboration.

Finally, when the time comes for celebrating a significant milestone, no matter who is responsible, all parties (if possible) should be invited to join in the celebration. This not only reinforces a common purpose and project identity, but also helps to establish positive momentum for the next stage of the project.

Figure 17.12 Sample online survey

Evaluation of partnering process: attitudes, teamwork, process.
(Collected separately from owner and contractor participants, and then compared and aggregated.)

1. Communications between the owner/contractor personnel are

1	2	3	4	5
Difficult, guarded				Easy, open, up-front

2. Top management support of partnering process is

1	2	3	4	5
Not evident or inconsistent				Obvious and consistent

3. Problems, issues, or concerns are

1	2	3	4	5
Ignored				Attacked promptly

4. Cooperation between owner and contractor personnel is

1	2	3	4	5
Cool, detached, unresponsive, removed				Genuine, unreserved, complete

5. Responses to problems, issues, or concerns frequently become

1	2	3	4	5
Personal issues				Treated as project problems

© 2022 Dr Neil Pearson

17.9.5 Co-location when needed

One of the best ways to overcome inter-organisational and intercultural friction is to have people from each organisation working side by side on the project. Smart companies rent or make available necessary accommodation(s) so all key project personnel can work collectively together. This allows a high degree of face-to-face interaction that is helpful when coordinating activities, solving difficult problems and forming a common bond. This is especially relevant in complex project situations where close collaboration from different parties is required for success. For example, the Australian Government often provides common (shared) office space for key contractors responsible for developing disaster response plans.

Our experience tells us that co-location is often very important and therefore well worth the added expense and inconvenience (within limits, of course). When this is not practically possible, the travel budget for the project should contain ample funds to support timely travel to the different organisations.

Co-location is less relevant for independent work that does not require ongoing coordination between professionals from different organisations. This would be the case if discrete, independent deliverables like beta testing or a marketing campaign are being outsourced as the normal channels of communication should be able to handle any coordination issues.

17.9.6 Fair and incentive-laden contracts

The goal when negotiating contracts is to reach a fair deal for all involved. Managers need to recognise that cohesion and cooperation will be undermined if one party feels they are being unfairly treated by others. They should also realise that negotiating the best deal in terms of price alone could come back to haunt them (e.g. shoddy work; or change order gouging, where a seller sets prices at a much higher level than is considered fair or reasonable).

Performance-based contracts, in which significant incentives are established based on the priorities of the project, are becoming increasingly popular. For example, if time is critical, then contractors accrue payoffs for beating deadlines; if scope is critical, bonuses are issued for exceeding performance expectations. At the same time, contractors will be held accountable; penalty clauses will be executed if they (or their business, depending on their legal status or business registration type) fail to perform up to standard, and/or meet deadlines, and/or fail to control costs.

17.9.7 Long-term outsourcing relationships

Many companies recognise that major benefits can be enjoyed when outsourcing arrangements extend across multiple projects and are long term. For example, Corning (specialists in materials science) and Toyota are among the many organisations that have forged a network of long-term strategic partnerships with their suppliers. Among the many advantages of establishing long-term partnerships are the following.

- *Reduced administrative costs:* The costs associated with bidding and selecting a contractor are eliminated. Contract administration costs are reduced as partners become knowledgeable about their counterpart's legal concerns.

- *More efficient utilisation of resources:* Contractors have a known forecast of work, while owners can concentrate their workforce on core businesses and avoid the demanding swings of project support.

- *Improved communication:* As partners gain experience with each other, they develop a common language and perspective, which reduces misunderstanding and enhances collaboration.

- *Improved innovation:* The partners are able to discuss innovation and associated risks in a more open manner and share risks and rewards fairly.

- *Improved performance:* Over time, partners become more familiar with each other's standards and expectations and can apply lessons learned from previous projects to current projects.

Working as partners in project environments demonstrates a conscious effort on the part of management to form collaborative relationships with personnel from different organisations to work towards the successful completion of the project. For outsourcing to work, there needs to be effective negotiation to merge (while protecting) interests and to discover solutions to problems in the project.

17.10 Procurement closure activities

Figure 17.13 (in three parts) illustrates some additional end-of-project procurement activities and indicates how they may be taken forward by the organisation post-project.

Further project closure procurement considerations are covered in Chapter 21 "Project closure", but mentioned here are:

- capturing procurement lessons learned
- final performance payments
- final contract dispute resolution
- supplier evaluation.

In addition to the handover of remaining procurement activities to the relevant business department and/or the operation department, the project leader should carry out an open and honest evaluation of the supplier; this will inform lessons learned and additionally be fed back to the contract, procurement and legal departments to inform the future projects (and the business in general) about using the supplier, or not.

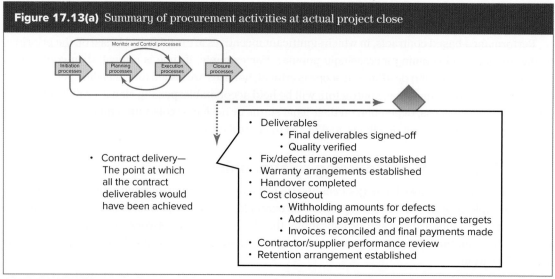

Figure 17.13(a) Summary of procurement activities at actual project close

- Contract delivery—
The point at which
all the contract
deliverables would
have been achieved

- Deliverables
  - Final deliverables signed-off
  - Quality verified
- Fix/defect arrangements established
- Warranty arrangements established
- Handover completed
- Cost closeout
  - Withholding amounts for defects
  - Additional payments for performance targets
  - Invoices reconciled and final payments made
- Contractor/supplier performance review
- Retention arrangement established

© 2022 Dr Neil Pearson

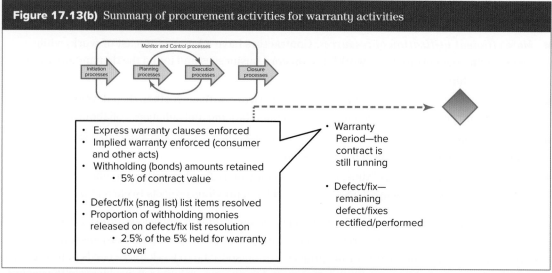

Figure 17.13(b) Summary of procurement activities for warranty activities

- Express warranty clauses enforced
- Implied warranty enforced (consumer and other acts)
- Withholding (bonds) amounts retained
  - 5% of contract value

- Defect/fix (snag list) list items resolved
- Proportion of withholding monies released on defect/fix list resolution
  - 2.5% of the 5% held for warranty cover

- Warranty Period—the contract is still running

- Defect/fix— remaining defect/fixes rectified/performed

© 2022 Dr Neil Pearson

Figure 17.13(c) Summary of activities at formal contract discharge, after any warranty/defect arrangements have expired

- Discharge of a contract occurs when the contract is legally completed.
- Hopefully it occurs for you when all involved parties complete the contract as agreed!
- The alternative is accord*
- Final supplier performance review

- Contract discharge

© 2022 Dr Neil Pearson

*An agreement (accord) between two contracting parties to accept alternate performance to discharge a pre-existing duty between them and the subsequent performance (satisfaction) of that agreement.

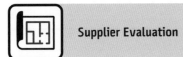

Supplier Evaluation

Summary

Procurement can be quite an arduous activity from a project leader's perspective, and the complexities of the procurement function in a project environment should not be underestimated. Potential impacts on the project schedule and project resources must be considered in some detail to ensure adequate time and resources are made available, not only to prepare tenders and negotiate contracts, but also to *performance manage* them throughout the life of the project.

- Procurement activities often involve other parts of the organisation, such as the procurement and contracts department(s) or, in some situations, the legal department.
- Engaging representative stakeholders (with their respective knowledge from areas of the business) can reap great dividends as the project progresses.
- Paying particular attention to the finer details of the terms and conditions of contracts is important as this can help to remove as much uncertainty (from both a buyer's and seller's perspective) as possible. We have looked at the importance of tightly defining the requirements of items to be procured, discussing how this becomes especially important when the contract is executed as these criteria can provide the basis for performance management of the contract, and resulting payments to the supplier.
- Building positive professional relationships with suppliers is an important function within procurement. Creating professional two-way trust and building understanding of the project requires a project leader to invest time, energy and robust communication skills.
- During closure of the project, the project leader must ensure that all activities are directed towards contract closure and that all products and/or services have been delivered to specification and relevant payments have been made. Any defect arrangements and lists of defects need to be agreed and appropriate (or pre-agreed) amounts of monies held back.
- Once all warranties and outstanding defects have been handed over to the business as part of project closure, the project leader will be responsible for notifying the procurement and contracts department of any lessons learned. This is especially important for lessons learned regarding non-performance or sub-performance by any supplier or contractor.

Review questions

1. Define your understanding of project procurement.
2. What is the make or buy decision?
3. What are the differences between the tender types RFI, RFQ, RFP and RFT?
4. What are the elements of a legally binding contract?
5. When would a time and materials (T&M) contract be used?
6. What is the key difference between a fixed price contract and a cost-reimbursable contract?
7. What are the key steps involved in a tender process?
8. What steps can be taken during negotiation to assist in a constructive outcome for all parties involved?
9. What are some benefits of outsourcing? When is outsourcing likely to be used in a project context?

Exercises

1. In the case of the CLEM7 tunnel example provided (see "Snapshot from Practice: CLEM7 tunnel, Brisbane, Australia"), what do you think could have been done in the project to better assess potential customer demand for using the tunnel and the toll pricing to be levied?

2. What additional organisation-specific activities would you include in the integration of procurement that may not be covered in Table 6.10 "Project procurement integration", in Chapter 6 "Project integration management"?

3. Reflect on a recent project you have been involved in that necessitated contractual negotiations. What lessons learned came out of that project from a contract or wider procurement perspective?

References

Covey SR 1990, *The Seven Habits of Highly Effective People*, Simon & Schuster, New York.

Field C 2012, "Elements of a contract", *Law Handbook*, Fitzroy Legal Service, www.lawhandbook.org.au/handbook/ch12s01s02.php#Ch125Se60983, accessed September 2012.

Fisher R & Ury W 1991, *Getting to Yes: Negotiating Agreement Without Giving In*, 2nd edition, Penguin Books, New York.

Fitzroy Legal Service 2018, *The Law Handbook 2018*, www.lawhandbook.org.au/, accessed February 2018.

Project Management Institute (PMI) 2017, *A Guide to the Project Management Body of Knowledge*, 6th edition, PMI.

Project Management Institute (PMI) 2021a, *A Guide to the Project Management Body of Knowledge (PMBOK® Guide)*, 7th edition, PMI.

Project Management Institute (PMI) 2021b, *The Standard for Project Management (ANSI/PMI 99-001-2021)*, 7th edition, PMI.

Queensland Government 2019, *Probity and Integrity in Procurement*, https://www.hpw.qld.gov.au/__data/assets/pdf_file/0016/3337/probityintegrityprocurement.pdf, accessed February 2022.

PART 5

Performing project execution

CHAPTER 18
Project execution

Learning elements

18A Understand the change in cadence from planning to executing the approved baselined Project Management Plan.

18B Be able to associate with several day-in-the-life situations leveraging all the hard planning work done.

In this chapter

18.1 Introduction

18.2 Moving from planning to execution

18.3 A day in the life

Summary

18.1 | Introduction

As we move from the Planning stage to the Execution stage, the project leader will have to prepare themselves for the marathon: the activities for most projects to this point have been the warm-up phase. Execution takes a different cadence and pace—a pace that must be sustainable without burning out the project team, or on occasions the **stakeholders** who surround the project team. As any marathon runner will tell you, pace is key—they want to pass that finish line and gain the recognition.

This chapter recaps on some of the key processes that are important to the project leader and introduces further processes to support delivery; however, the bulk of the chapter covers day-in-the-life scenarios covering the execution of a project, built around the knowledge introduced in this text thus far. *Day in the life* is an important technique used in organisations to paint a picture of how the project management approach is used on a day-to-day basis in certain scenarios during the execution of a project. We hope you find these day-in-the-life scenarios useful.

The project Execution stage is typically an absolute hive of activity; it is the stage where typically resource loading is at its greatest and cumulative costs are rising steeply as money is spent. This ramp-up of resources and costs is often visualised as represented in Figure 18.1.

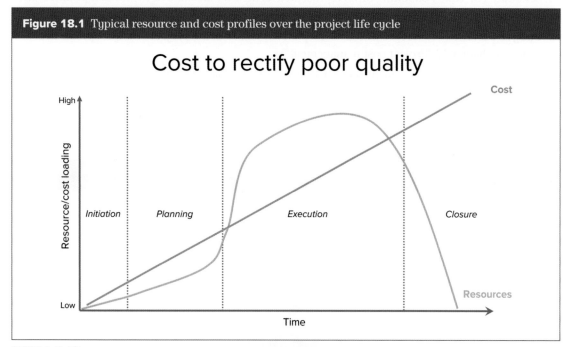

Figure 18.1 Typical resource and cost profiles over the project life cycle

© 2022 Dr Neil Pearson

PMBOK | Seventh edition updates (PMI 2021)

The seventh edition of the *Project Management Body of Knowledge* (PMBOK) (PMI 2021) has taken a similar approach to execution (delivery) of a project, covering the nuances of how the knowledge complements the work to be done. The work to be done and all its dynamics are of course contained in the integrated Project Management Plan (integrated PMP). The integrated PMP will have been **baseline** approved before its execution.

This chapter covers material introduced in PMBOK seventh edition that appears within three PMBOK project performance domains.

1. Project Work Performance Domain

2. Delivery Performance Domain

3. Measurement.

18.2 | Moving from Planning to Execution

Moving from Planning to Execution could be carried out from several different perspectives, given the existence of life cycle approaches such as predictive (sequential, overlapping or phased), incremental, adaptive and hybrid (refer to Chapter 2 "Popular frameworks and methodologies"); therefore, the information presented in this chapter will need to be contextualised for your project's approach and environment. What has most certainly happened is that selected work packages and tasks designed for the Execution stage will have probably already started towards the end of the Planning stage; rarely is there a clean break in activities considered as Planning. There is a short period of delay until the **integrated PMP** is approved, before Execution can start. The flow of work is typically more seamless and will ramp up slowly as Planning nears completion.

18.2.1 Baselines and baseline management

The baseline plan provides the project leader, **project sponsor** and Steering Committee with elements for measuring performance. The integrated PMP contains the information for four baselines:

1. **schedule (or time) baseline**, often represented as the first baseline of the tracking Gantt chart (refer to Chapter 11 "Project schedule management")

2. **budget baseline**, often represented as the planned values in the project's budget spreadsheet (refer to Chapter 12 "Project cost management")

3. **scope baseline**, as captured in the scope document (refer to Chapter 8 "Defining the scope of a project")

4. **performance baseline**, which contains all the other key performance metrics upon which the project and project leader will be performance managed.

This process is represented in Figure 18.2.

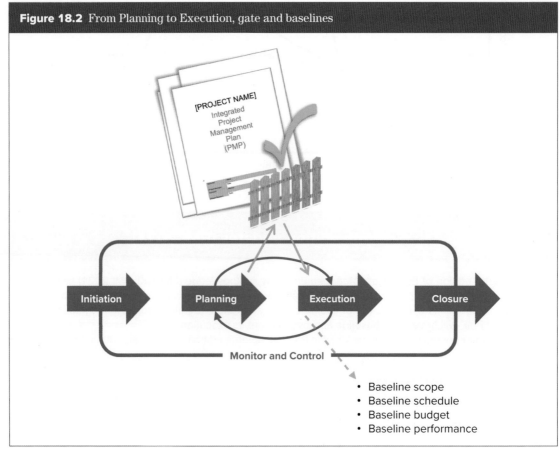

Figure 18.2 From Planning to Execution, gate and baselines

© 2022 Dr Neil Pearson

This approved integrated PMP is often referred to as the *baseline plan*, and it is from this plan that subsequent monitoring and controlling of the various parameters of the project takes place as the project is executed. Remember, the baselines that are always baselined at this time in the integrated PMP are the **scope baseline**, **cost baseline** and **schedule baseline**. The fourth baseline, the **performance baseline**, will be discussed further as it is becoming more frequently requested by project management offices (PMOs) and management alike. The scope, schedule and cost baselines help us manage the **triple constraints** and look more critically at project variations; however, the general performance of the delivery of the project also needs to be considered across other dimensions.

In relation to key metrics generated by the project, the majority are **lag** or **lagging** indicators—they compare data after the event and tell us something has happened. Good sets of metrics also include indicators that are **lead** or **leading** indicators, which are more forecast based and perhaps indicate that something could happen in the future.

Some example performance metrics for the triple constraints of scope, time and cost can be found in Table 18.1.

So, what other metrics are PMOs, management, the project sponsor and the project leader interested in monitoring? These will vary from project to project, depending on your project environment and the content of the project. These other metrics are collectively referred to as the **performance baseline**; some examples are indicated in Table 18.2.

Table 18.1 Scope, time and cost indicators: Lagging and leading

Lagging	Leading
Scope	
Number of variation (change) requests raised, related to scope	Stakeholder workshop indicates a disconnect between project team and business users
Number of new features added to the product increases	
Objectives met	
Time	
Milestone slippage	Upcoming shortage of a key skill reported in the industry media
Deliverable delivery late	
Work package and task slippage in project schedule	
EVM data such as SPI and SV	EVM forecast data such as EAC, ETC, TCPI
Cost	
Actual costs greater than planned costs	Increasing market/indexes (such as currency or metals)
	Inflation
EVM data such as SPI and SV	EVM forecast data such as BAC

© 2022 Dr Neil Pearson

Note: BAC = budget at completion; EAC = estimate at completion; ETC = estimate to complete; EVM = earned value management; SPI = schedule performance index; SV = schedule variance; TCPI = to complete performance index

Table 18.2 Performance baseline indicators, lagging and leading

Lagging	Leading
Quality	
Number of defects (or non-conformances)	Improvement ideas suggested and incorporated into product design
Time to rework	
Cost to rework	
Cost of scrap (the ones that failed rework)	
Safety	
Lagging lost time injury frequency rate (LTIFR)	Average compliance of internal workplace health and safety (WHS) verification audits
Medically treated injury frequency rate (MTIFR)	WHS training delivery
Average time lost rate (ATLR)	
Lost time injury incidence rate (LTIIR)	
Customer	
Number of complaints per period	Net promoter score (NPS)
Number of product returns	Forward sales of a non-released product
	Leads or referrals
Sustainability and environment	
Number of environmental breaches	Rising levels before an event is triggered
Number of environmental complaints	
Stakeholder	
Stakeholder satisfaction survey	Suggestion box responses put into action
Stakeholder complaints	

(Continues)

Table 18.2 Performance baseline indicators, lagging and leading (*Continued*)

Lagging	Leading
Miscellaneous	
Number of deliverables signed off with no rework	360-degree evaluations of team members
Number and variance in milestones not delivered to planned schedule	Training delivered prior to rollout on a new system
Benefit delivered or not delivered	Tracking towards a benefit delivery
Risks eventuated into an issue	Threat risk profile moving upwards
Burn rate of cashflow	Earned value management forecast indicators
Lines of code developed	Code conforms to internal quality criteria
Six-month employee performance review	Employees making weekly progress towards meeting performance criteria

© 2022 Dr Neil Pearson

Once a suitable mix of performance measures has been identified and agreed, the project leader then needs to define the measure in further depth. This is to ensure:

■ there is an agreed definition of the measure

■ there is an agreed calculation based on authoritative sources of data

■ the data can be collected in the project so the measure can be produced

■ how the measure is to be reported is agreed.

Read "Snapshot from Practice: Environmental performance" for a further review of the wide and varied measures that should be considered by a project.

On occasions the author (Pearson) has used the online Measure Definition Template to capture detailed descriptions of a project's key performance metrics. These descriptions, including baseline measurement, have proven invaluable. A lesson learned from many junior project leaders is forgetting to baseline the performance measure; this is built into the baseline approval of scope, time and cost—but what about all those other performance metrics you defined? Did you remember to baseline them so a later comparison against the tracking values or end or project values can be made?

 Measure Definition Template (MDT)

A project leader charged with ensuring all project safety concerns are addressed should be certain to involve relevant subject matter experts at an early stage since, as with quality, all aspects of implementing safety measures will undoubtedly add activities to the project and therefore costs and time; however, safety should never be compromised at the expense of other project criteria.

Environmental performance reporting can be as important as safety as the financial costs of environmental incidents, including plant, animal, and human, can be exorbitant. An example of this is the 2010 BP Deepwater Horizon oil platform disaster—aside from the unfortunate initial loss of life, the subsequent clean-up operations cost BP USD38 billion, and the costs are still rising. Adverse environmental impacts can take the form of:

■ pollution incidents, including run-off, tailings and chemical spills

■ damage to environmentally sensitive land areas, involving damage to flora, fauna and wildlife by chemical or mechanical means

■ cultural heritage impacts, including the encroachment into, and destruction of, traditional and historical Aboriginal land.

Defining and ensuring relevant environmental performance criteria are adhered to and reported on is another aspect of project performance that a project leader must sometimes consider. One of the most common standards that shapes how environmental performance is managed in an organisation (or within a project that takes on environmental aspects) is the standard ISO 14001:2015 "Environmental management systems—Requirements with guidance for use".

18.2.2 Variations and the variation management process

The **variation management process (VMP)** was discussed in Chapter 8 "Defining the scope of a project". We are now in the Execution stage of the project, so the golden rule of variation management must be applied: "no changes to the project's constraints unless an approved variation request exists". As illustrated in Figure 18.2, the baselines are set at the end of the Planning stage. It is these baselines, scope, time and cost that are being compared with the actual scope, actual cost and actual schedule. Therefore, any variations to these baselines must follow the VMP so that they can be captured, analysed, reviewed and approved into the project. This may result in approved variations:

- with only minor changes to selected project documents; in this case a document may be *versioned* and then released (communicated) to the project team

- that are more major and fundamentally affect the project's schedule, budget and/or scope. In this case the project leader should consider re-baselining the project, issuing new documents and then restarting Execution from these **re-baselined** documents. Therefore, in the project's Scope Management Plan, a baseline history table is introduced so the project leader can track the issuing of the re-baselined project and the reason it was re-baselined. Refer to the online template, where the VMP process has been documented, along with a baseline table for tracking the re-baselining of the project.

Scope Management Plan

18.2.3 Deliverables and the deliverable acceptance process

Obtaining deliverable acceptance by the customer is a major and critical activity throughout project Execution and into the project Closure stage. Delivery of some **deliverables** to the customer will be straightforward. Others will be more complex and difficult. Ideally, there should be no surprises. This necessitates having a well-defined scope, plus an effective **variation request** system with active customer involvement (customer involvement is critical to acceptance). *Note:* Experienced project leaders will rarely have a single sign-off of the project's deliverables at the end of a project. This is because best practice indicates that deliverables should be planned into the project schedule and signed off as they are delivered throughout the entire project life cycle. This process is illustrated in Figure 18.3, where a number of deliverable IDs (DIDs) are indicated along the life cycle of the project. Each deliverable would be formally signed off using a **deliverable acceptance form**, thereby reducing the uncertainty (**risk**) of final acceptance at project closure.

Deliverable Acceptance

It is possible that some deliverables will not immediately be accepted. A deliverable could be accepted with conditions, which could mean some rework in the project. The deliverable form with the corrected deliverable could at a later stage be presented for confirmation. If not accepted, the reasons for non-acceptance must be clearly documented, and a root-cause investigation initiated as to why.

In projects where there is a lot of deliverable activity, the project leader may wish to keep a Tracking Register of the status of all deliverables: planned, in delivery or delivered (refer to the online template).

Deliverable Tracking Register

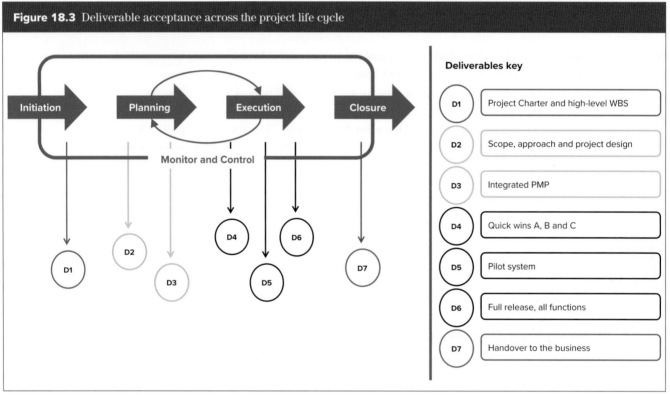

Figure 18.3 Deliverable acceptance across the project life cycle

© 2022 Dr Neil Pearson

As captured in the Tracking Register, the reader will notice that some deliverables could be highlighted as *quick wins* or *low-hanging fruit*, where a short burst of effort achieves a deliverable that is usually made highly visible to the project recipients, as if to say "We are delivering, and early".

The swimlane process diagram (or equivalent) for the deliverable acceptance process would be another artefact established within the Scope Management Plan by the project leader early in the project life cycle.

18.2.4 What's the difference between a milestone and a deliverable?

This is a frequently asked question in project management, and it not infrequently results in confusion. Table 18.3 captures the key differences.

Table 18.3 Deliverable or milestone?

Deliverable	Milestone
Tangible—delivering something of value to the customer, typically a project output, but could also be outcome based or a mix of both	Tangible or a marker to achievement, most likely a point-in-time marker for the project leader to track progress towards project goals rather than something that is delivered to the customer
Important to the customer	Important to the project/project team
Point-in-time marker for an expected delivery to the customer	Point-in-time marker for achievement in the project/project team
Could be tied to project performance and a resulting payment from the customer	Could be tied to performance but typically not payment
Could be a reason for project celebration	Could be a reason for a project "pat on the back"

© 2022 Dr Neil Pearson

18.3 A day in the life

Performance, variations and deliverables are just a few of the activities a project leader would become involved in during project Execution. Below are several short day-in-the-life scenarios a project leader could become involved in, with links to existing topics covered in this text to help assist in further understanding some typical project leader actions.

18.3.1 Kick-off

You, the project leader, have hired a venue for the project **kick-off meeting**, and have invited the project team, key stakeholders, project sponsor and Steering Committee members. You have prepared a short presentation that steps through the key dimensions of the project scope. The presentation ends with an open Q&A session. At the Q&A session the questions are captured and are subsequently turned into what forms the internal project frequently asked questions (FAQs), which is maintained on the project's intranet page. The kicker for the project team comes after the presentation and Q&A session—a surprise open morning tea for all stakeholders who have been initially identified by the team. This informal and impromptu networking session starts to form relationships within and beyond the project team. After the kick-off meeting, you send to the team an email following up with any remaining questions (communications feedback loop), with a link to the latest project documentation and an invitation for the first formal project **team meeting**.

Key areas of this scenario are covered in:

- Chapter 15 "Project information and communications management"
- Chapter 19 "Project leaders and project teams".

18.3.2 Let's get moving . . .

While people are in attendance for the kick-off meeting, it makes sense to keep the team around for the first formal project team meeting. This first meeting is all about work allocation (schedule, resources) and how project performance data is reported back to the project leader and project coordinator. You have stressed to the project team that this is to be 100 per cent face to face with no virtual dial-in, and have budgeted for this as a part of the project's budget (cost—travel).

The meeting starts and you bring printed summary work package packs with some key artefacts for the work package leaders.

These work package packs contain:

- work package work breakdown structure (WBS)-dictionary item summary sheet (refer to Figure 18.4)
- copies of the blueprints and designs
- a schedule segment that covers all work packages issued at the meeting, so work package leaders can see the relationships between work and fellow work leaders
- a copy of any risks relevant to this part of the project.

Figure 18.4 Example: WBS-dictionary item

WP Tree Removal	
Work Package Reference	WP 1.3.1.1-1
Description	Felling and removal of all trees, as identified on the site plan by the chartered surveyor. All tree material, including the removal of stumps, is to be carried out by the required date. Trees for removal have been marked with a fluorescent-orange band tied around the base of the tree.
Tasks	1.1.1 Activity—Mark Site, Chartered Surveyor 1.1.2 Activity—Peg Site, Site Supervisor 1.1.3 Activity—Etc.
Milestone	Foundations complete.
Assigned to	CutAbove Tree Services. Contact: Ash: 0999 912 000
Start/End	Start: 10 April End: 14 April
Resources	***Provided by Project:*** Project is to provide safety supervisor on-site. ***Provided by Contractor/Supplier:*** CutAbove Tree Services to supply all required equipment.
Budget	As quoted: $10,800 (incl. GST)
Contract	Contract to CutAbove Tree Services attached.
Quality Standards/ Acceptance Criteria	Adherence to AS/NZS 4801.
Quality Control Activities	o Have a "watcher" when wood chipper is in operation, with 1 m of the "kill switch" o Have a "watcher" in place when any aerial work is being undertaken. o Photos (before and after) of any tree completely felled must be kept to prove no kisted or endangered trees have been incorrectly felled.
Technical	Refer attached site plan.
Attachments	Copy of contract. Site plan.
Reporting Arrangements	Outline how the work package will be reported back to the Project Manager.
Dependencies	Project XYZ, 5.5 Work Package.
WHS	Safety induction to be carried out prior to entry on site.
Environmental	N/A

You allow for a 30-minute review of the work packages by the work package leaders and any contributors, after which an open Q&A session (communications) takes place to mitigate any potential risks.

In the second part of the meeting you take everyone through the formal project management information system, with a demonstration of the project-specific status update screen (SUS). The SUS was specifically created by the project because of a request by the work package leaders during the Planning stage.

The meeting ends at 3.30 pm with a motivational speech from a local personality and all attendees are released for the day.

Key areas of this scenario are covered in:

■ Chapter 11 "Project schedule management"
■ Chapter 12 "Project cost management".

18.3.3 Time for a status team meeting

The status meeting (scheduled communication) starts promptly at 9.30 am; as with all meetings going forward, it is a hybrid physical and virtual meeting. You provide a two-minute management update, with a short five-minute Q&A. To keep the meeting to time, you have decided to opt for the Agile 4L's (loved, loathed, longed for, learned). Each attendee is given two minutes to provide this style of update (refer to Chapter 3 "Agile (Scrum) project management"). You really want to focus on the team side; after all, it is a team meeting. At the "Let's get moving" meeting, you put in place a formal method for project performance data, which appears to be working well. The meeting is over by 10 am, allowing the team to get back to their work.

You return to your work area and reflect on the team meeting, picking out areas that need fine-tuning (**continuous improvement**) and putting actions in place which mainly fall on you and the project coordinator to attend to (servant leadership). After the team meeting, you routinely send out the project schedule segment, which covers the work packages in progress, to provide an open, visible status to all.

Key areas of this scenario are covered in:

■ Chapter 15 "Project information and communications management"
■ Chapter 19 "Project leaders and project teams".

18.3.4 Status report time

It is the end of the first month and it is time to produce the project status reports. You refer to the project schedule and see the **exception report** must reach the PMO on or before the last working day of the month. The reporting arrangements were already established and piloted in the Planning stage of the project. Picking up the template reports, there is a dashboard report for the Steering Committee and an exception report for the project sponsor. You start to pull the information from the various project information systems.

■ Schedule data are the responsibility of the project coordinator.
■ The master project budget is yours to maintain as project leader.
■ The team update the weekly status update system (SUS) with their end-of-week summaries.
■ The project leader maintains the Risk Register.
■ All variations are the responsibility of the project leader.

All this governance was established at the Planning stage. In a perfect world, the project leader would have a rehearsed process of pulling the data from each system and massaging them into the pre-arranged report format, adding in the resulting narrative (information, knowledge, wisdom).

On this occasion you pull all the information together into the **dashboard (red, amber, green or RAG-style) report**, and the exception report. It is the day before the report is due and you are writing the report narratives but sense that the report information is *too perfect*: is the project really exactly on track with the schedule, with no **issues**, no variations, no elevated risks, no budget variances and no decisions for the Steering Committee? You ask another peer project leader to review the report and she pulls some financial information from the project account system (ignoring your master project spreadsheet) for the same period. She flags to you some financial concerns that don't reconcile.

Later that day, after talking with the company's commercial manager, you realise your project is being run on an accrual basis, while the accounting system is based on a cash system. You agree on the accrual method, as when a work package is complete the money has been spent from the project at that time. You update your project-wide governance RASCI and include a narrative with the report stating that, according to the project's master budget, the project is showing no variances; however, due to misunderstanding concerning the company's financial accounting standard, a full reconciliation won't be provided until the next reporting period.

You send out both status reports in an open and transparent manner. You also decide to include a cut-down version of the project schedule as the detail in the master schedule is likely to distract the Steering Committee and project sponsor from the big-picture progress and decisions. This chart is to take the form of a **milestone slippage** chart (Figure 18.5).

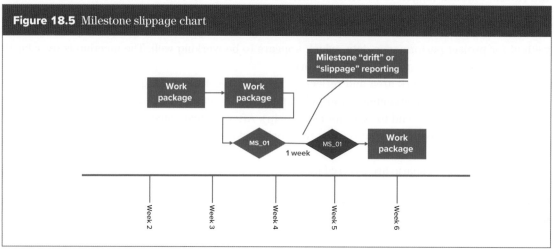

Figure 18.5 Milestone slippage chart

© 2022 Dr Neil Pearson

Key areas of this scenario are covered in:

- Chapter 11 "Project schedule management"
- Chapter 12 "Project cost management"
- Chapter 15 "Project information and communications management".

18.3.5 Caring for the team

Deliverable DID_0003 has been delivered to the customer. It has been a hard slog for the team, but sticking to the principle of *no team burn-out* that the team placed on the team charter, you have ensured no overtime (free or billed) has occurred. The hard slog is rewarded by an extended team meeting where you bring in a local mobile barista van for the day (where project team members can access free coffee and snacks). It's a small reward but the project team really appreciates the effort.

You have also asked the team for ideas for the next unscheduled team reward—they can make their suggestions by posting an anonymous card into the suggestion box at reception. You have a team encouragement fund that is approved by the project sponsor.

As the end of the first month approaches, you have scheduled one-on-ones with each team member. These are confidential meetings where the team member can bring any project-related or personal matter up for discussion, although you and the project sponsor have a general open-door policy.

At a one-on-one, a team member mentions they are having problems with an issue at home and would like to work from home for the next two weeks. You are supportive and say you will notify the team, and ask the team member if they have all the suitable equipment at home to work in a WHS-suitable environment. You check with Human Resources as a matter of course to ensure company policies are being adhered to.

The discussion with the team member focuses on their work package being on the critical path—you want to gain confirmation that the individual can complete it and does/does not require assistance from team members working on tasks that have some slack.

The team is not aware of any conflicts but, by looking across all the one-on-ones, you are able to pick up on some potential conflict that might occur as the next two work packages become due for allocation. There are some subject matter expert (SME) decisions to be made! Pre-empting the situation, you call a consensus workshop between the work package leaders and SMEs. You lay out the ground rules for the meeting and, after some robust conversations, the SMEs agree on a way forward (consensus). After the meeting, the two work package leaders thank you for the discussion.

Key areas of this scenario are covered in:

- Chapter 14 "Project stakeholder management"
- Chapter 19 "Project leaders and project teams".

18.3.6 Those pesky stakeholders

When identifying and analysing the stakeholders in Planning, you and the project team agreed that one "some interest, high power" stakeholder is requiring more than *keep satisfied* strategies. You confirm that considerable time and energy is being devoted across the team to managing this one stakeholder. You pull the team together and ask for all communications to be directed through you. After a couple of days, you collect all the communications that would be flowing to that stakeholder and make your observations. However, before jumping to any conclusions you drop by the stakeholder's office and invite them for a quick coffee at a coffee shop away from the work location. Before long, the stakeholder reveals they are being cross-questioned by team members for duplicate information that has often been provided to other members in the team.

Back at your desk, you decide to immediately update the stakeholder management strategy to one that channels all questions and responses through a single team member, and supplement this with a project stakeholder decision log. This log must be updated by all project team members with any stakeholder questions and decisions. All team members are required to review the log for entries made by other team members. You realise this is additional work in the project, but you also realise that stakeholders are critical to the outcomes of this project. The lesson learned entered in the project's Lessons Learned Register is to review the cross-team communications with stakeholders and build that into the stakeholder management strategy. You introduce a stakeholder complexity tool to assist with future project idea showers when one stakeholder has multiple lines of contact (see Figure 18.6).

Key areas of this scenario are covered in Chapter 14 "Project stakeholder management".

Figure 18.6 Unpacking stakeholder complexity

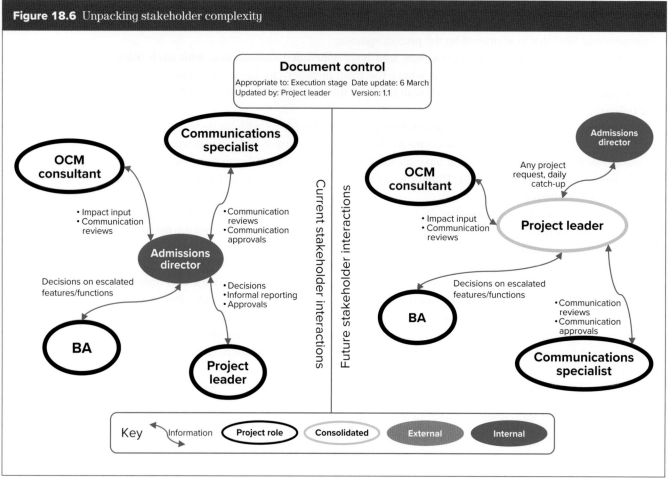

© 2022 Dr Neil Pearson

18.3.7 Don't panic, we have a Contingency Plan

At last week's team meeting, one of the team raised a concern with a risk that was looking like it was going to increase, as a supplier had indicated general supply chain issues. The project team member has dropped into your office one morning after receiving an overnight communication from China. Due to the recent pandemic, the supplier has now confirmed they have no idea when the technology will be delivered to the project for configuration. You immediately review the impact on the project, subsequently change the *risk* to an *issue*, and immediately send a notification through to the project sponsor (per the risk escalation process that was documented in the Planning stage within the Risk Management Plan). The sponsor responds immediately with the advice that the **Contingency Plan** should now be invoked before it becomes too late.

An emergency impromptu team meeting is called. You summarise the issue and bring the team's attention to the Contingency Plan. There are certain tasks that will now be allocated to team members who were working on work packages related to or impacted by the supply issue. The individuals with allocated tasks are asked to dial into a war-room conference in the morning to provide updates.

The next morning there is positive news: between two of the tasks allocated, a supply can be sourced; however, as costed in the Contingency Plan, this is going to impact the cost of supply by 30 per cent. This is within the contingency set aside for this event occurring and also within the project's cumulative contingency limits, so you give the immediate go-ahead to continue through the contingency steps, notifying the previous supplier only after contracts with the two new suppliers have been signed.

Risk averted, you had to do minimal planning, panicking and delaying, and instead gracefully enacted the Contingency Plan, in this case with team members who would be directly impacted.

Key aspects of this scenario are covered in Chapter 16 "Project risk management".

18.3.8 The project sponsor has some questions

The sponsor has been going through the next year's business planning process and has not been paying sufficient attention to your project. You raised this with them at the last monthly report. It is now two weeks later, and the sponsor has asked you to attend a brown-bag lunch with them and a peer manager. No further information was given at the time, but you suspect, from the lack of responses to the issue raised at the previous monthly meeting, the commitment of the sponsor.

The peer manager starts to ask a lot of questions about the status of the project, and you are able to respond with appropriate information to every question and return with a series of questions around the sponsor role in a high-profile project. This immediately brings a response from the current sponsor, who has recognised that they cannot be committed to the project (remember the chicken and pig story in Chapter 3 "Agile (Scrum) project management"?) They confirm that the peer manger is to take over the role of project sponsor.

On leaving the room you immediately seize the opportunity and suggest they go out for a coffee the next morning to establish how you are to communicate and work together. They fail to show for the coffee meeting. This does not bode well, and you walk to their office, only to find your path blocked by a determined personal assistant. The alarm bells are ringing. Your attempts at gaining access to the previous sponsor are equally blocked.

On returning to your desk, you raise an immediate issue (not identified as a risk) to the Steering Committee and ask, as defined in the Steering Committee Charter, for a special convening of the committee to discuss the sponsorship of the project.

Key aspects of this scenario are covered in Chapter 14 "Project stakeholder management".

18.3.9 What! An audit today?

It is 9am as you walk into the project area. All is suspiciously quiet. Turning the corner, you see two grim-looking official people sitting in your office. They announce that they are immediately to be given full access to all procurement records for the purpose of a compliance audit on behalf of the government audit office. After confirming their official ID, you ask them to step through the process that will be progressed through—your concern is not that any procurement-related document, process or artefact is out of place, but that these unannounced officials don't impact the work being done by people who are likely to be taken offline to act as *runners* to the officials in providing information, or subjected to lengthy audit interviews.

Within the hour you have agreed on the names of the individuals who will be brought into the process at what time and immediately call an all-hands meeting with the two officials in the room. You have given them access to your office. You stir up some office banter and provide a round of coffees to the project team to reassure them that this is a routine audit, albeit an unscheduled one.

By the end of the third day, the auditors provide an interim report with a few advisories—nothing major to note. You call a project team meeting while the auditors are still present and ask for (continuous) improvement ideas as to how the advisories can be improved. The auditors are impressed and leave the project area with confidence that they have a professional project leader working on this contract.

Key areas of this scenario are covered in:

- Chapter 14 "Project stakeholder management"
- Chapter 13 "Project quality management"
- Chapter 17 "Project procurement management".

18.3.10   **A variation has been requested**

As you walk to your next stakeholder meeting, a senior stakeholder stops you and suggests a variation to the scope of the project to include some additional modules that they think will add considerable value to the project. Using your next meeting as an excuse, you thank the stakeholder for their request and inform them that you will be in contact later in the day.

Your meeting ends and on returning to your desk you immediately send to the senior stakeholder and their personal assistant a copy of the Variation Request Form, with the variation process fact sheet that outlines the key steps in the process that will be followed.

Some days later (doesn't this show the urgency of the request?) you receive the completed variation request; on logging this into the Variation Request Register, you notice that the scope of the variation has already been reduced by the requestor.

Reviewing the project schedule, you see that one of the non-critical work packages has two days' slack, and so allocate the variation request to the work package leader, asking them to carry out an analysis but spend no longer than 50 per cent of the float for their work package. They review the variation request and confirm back to you that this is doable, and they will get back to you with the results of the analysis in two days' time.

You receive an email with the analysis at the end of the second day. First, the overall impact to the project is some $20,000—this is way beyond your approval limit and will have to be sent to the Steering Committee for approval; second, the recommendation is to outsource the requested functions to a third-party supplier, which, as indicated in the analysis report, will introduce additional risk. The variation request is sent to the Steering Committee, who sit weekly for a brief amount of time (you established this routine in Planning as you knew the project would require weekly guidance and not fortnightly or monthly sittings). Their response comes back as declined, with the recommendation that the variation to scope is logged as a Phase 2 enhancement.

You set up a 30-minute face-to-face meeting with the requestor for the next morning and provide the feedback to them in a positive manner: "This was a really good enhancement idea, but due to company funds and knock-on effect to other project activities, it was the recommendation of the Steering Committee to take the variation forward but in Phase 2 of the project."

Back at your desk, you update the Variation Request Register and feed back to the team member who did the analysis the outcome of the request. The loop is closed, and the predetermined VMP (designed in the Planning stage) has worked like clockwork.

Key areas of this scenario are covered in:

- Chapter 8 "Defining the scope of a project"
- Chapter 14 "Project stakeholder management".

18.3.11   **Value is delivered!**

As you sit back after the project team celebration and the reward they selected (a desk head and shoulder massage!), you consider the deliverable just delivered to the customer. It was a major deliverable and actually contributed a large percentage to one of the project's Business Case **benefit** statements. It is also the end of the month and you are in the midst of preparing the monthly exception report. In addition, you include a copy of the benefits table from the Business Case with an update on how benefit delivery is progressing, providing a measured statement with evidence of the partial achievement of a declared benefit.

The Steering Committee is impressed that not only has the benefit been delivered but that the remaining benefits declared are at this point on track to be delivered by the scheduled completion date of the project. They also make a continuous improvement request to you to include this benefit tracking information as a part of the monthly status report. You log the improvement in the Continuous Improvement Register and allocate the actions of updating the exception report template to the project officer.

Key areas of this scenario are covered in:

- Chapter 4 "Strategy, project selection and the Business Case"
- Chapter 13 "Project quality management"
- Chapter 15 "Project information and communications management".

18.3.12 We have a supplier performance issue

You find yourself at the team meeting making notes about defects in components delivered from an existing preferred supplier of the company and now the project. This is not the first week that reports of defects from this company have been made. You ask the project officer to build some Pareto charts of suppliers of this component. It takes the project officer a couple of days to compile the information, but once the job has been done, they meet with you to present two very nicely formed Pareto charts. The first Pareto chart clearly indicates that over 90 per cent of the defects on this component are coming from one supplier. The second Pareto chart indicates that components from this supplier are routinely defective in two areas, these two areas representing over 80 per cent of the defects.

Armed with this data, you call a meeting with the supplier in question, and you present the facts in the Pareto chart in a questioning manner. You don't want to apportion blame as the supply of these parts is linked to critical path activities. You ask the supplier if they could kindly review the data and carry out a root-cause analysis to see if the data are true—you jokingly offer to pay a day's rate if they do not find any root causes that they need to address!

A couple of days later you receive a call from the supplier, thanking you for bringing to their attention the component defects. They will recall all current components, and as a thank you make your project the first recipient of a fresh batch of modified components. They also ask that you keep tracking the components for the next few shipments to ensure that no secondary defects bubble to the top of the Pareto that exceed the tolerances set out in the contract. This was a good outcome for project and supplier, as you reflect on those upcoming work packages that could have been in jeopardy if relations had turned sour over this small issue.

Key areas of this scenario are covered in:

- Chapter 13 "Project quality management"
- Chapter 17 "Project procurement management".

18.3.13 That weekly newsletter

The communications specialist who is seconded to the project on a part-time basis has asked you to provide a positive news story from the project to include in the latest weekly newsletter that is sent (push communication) to all 10,000 employees in the organisation about the upcoming *employee kiosk launch*. You poll the project team, and a team member comes up with the idea of putting a supermarket check-out kiosk in reception, but the computer will have the employee kiosk (potentially shippable product) loaded up instead—available for any employee to walk up and try. You agree and ask the team member and communications specialist to set up the demo kiosk in time for the article to be included in the next newsletter. Harnessing the ideas of others and giving them the credit certainly works in this case. The kiosk is still there in reception as you walk past four weeks after project handover.

Key areas of this scenario are covered in:

- Chapter 15 "Project information and communications management"
- Chapter 19 "Project leaders and project teams".

This section has hopefully provided the new, or even experienced, project leader and project officer some ideas around the day-to-day activities they are likely to be involved in, from projects small to large, these are common situations! In Execution there is a definite playbook for each of the key areas of project management; these playbooks are essentially the processes that have been planned and tailored to the project environment, which the project leader enacts given any situation. Atlassian has captured this concept in the Team Playbook (https://www.atlassian.com/team-playbook). Although it is more geared towards Agile, the principle works well in a more predictive project environment. The examples provided above are essentially playbooks or, as the American sport of gridiron calls them, *plays*.

These scenarios have covered the key areas of project Execution, which typically include:

- project scope management, variations and the impact on the triple constrains (scope, time, cost)
- stakeholder management
- tracking time, budget and resources against the baseline approved Project Management Plan
- deliverable presentation, management and sign-off
- management of the project team, including conflict and performance
- ensuring communications are providing the right balance of information, at the right time and to the relevant stakeholders
- **quality** across all aspects of the project, the deliverables from the project and the quality of outsourced work to the project.

Summary

This chapter reviewed some day-in-the-life scenarios that relate to activities carried out in the project Execution stage. As a summary of this chapter, a checklist of activities typically experienced during project Execution has been included as Table 18.4. *Note:* This table is not exhaustive and should be combined with the Monitor and Control activities.

Table 18.4 Common Execution stage activities

Knowledge area	Activities
Scope	■ Continually watch for variations and ensure the VMP is always applied to avoid any scope creep through management of the triple constraints. ■ Manage project baseline information and, if required, re-baseline and issue project documentation. ■ Report milestone achievement in charts such as a milestone slippage chart. ■ Seek continuous improvements to the scope management process as opportunities arise. ■ Capture scope-related lessons learned.
Schedule (Time)	■ Allocate work packages and tasks to project team members and external contractors, as planned in the project schedule or Resource Allocation Matrix (RAM). ■ Apply the deliverable management process, ensuring all deliverables are signed off accordingly. ■ Ensure updated work package and task information is provided back to the project so status on progress can be maintained. ■ Provide various reports from a schedule perspective. These could be tracking Gantt charts, earned value management (EVM) reports or simple milestone slippage reports. ■ Maintain the schedule to ensure the flow of work is maintained in light of other activities project team members may be involved with (refer to section 18.3.10 "A variation has been requested"). ■ Maintain baseline history of the project schedule. ■ Seek continuous improvements to the schedule management process as opportunities arise. ■ Capture time-related lessons learned.
Cost	■ Manage the project reserves, tracking access to the reserves as a result of approved variations or risk Contingency Plans being triggered. ■ Track invoices and their payment. ■ Track timesheets and approvals. ■ Ensure when money leaves the project (i.e. when a work package is completed), it is it accounted for as spent. ■ Continue to maintain the WBS, project schedule and the project budget to ensure all elements of the project are kept aligned. ■ Update corporate systems with financial information and approvals, ranging from contractor and project staff timesheets to invoices and purchase orders. ■ Ensure those with allocated work packages know the budget for the work package and where the money has been allocated to within the work package. ■ Ensure those executing work packages know how they are to report cost information. ■ Seek continuous improvements to the cost management process as opportunities arise. ■ Capture cost-related lessons learned.

Table 18.4 Common Execution stage activities (*Continued*)

Quality	<ul><li>Ensure the recipient of the work package understands the implications of the quality criteria they and the work package will be performance-managed against.</li><li>Consider holding specific quality meetings with the customer and suppliers (as required) to raise/ensure awareness about, and control of, quality.</li><li>Sign off deliverables, to include acceptance of the deliverable to the agreed quality criteria.</li><li>Seek continuous improvements to the quality management processes as opportunities arise.</li><li>Capture quality-related lessons learned.</li></ul>
Resource	<ul><li>Ensure a project kick-off meeting is carried out. Reinforce the project ground rules and principles.</li><li>Acquire, recruit and build the project team according to the upcoming work packages.</li><li>Acquire other resources—tools, equipment and raw materials—required by the project.</li><li>Ensure procurement and contract activities are carried out in sufficient time to enable the scheduled work packages to take place when planned.</li><li>Organise the induction of project team members.</li><li>Carry out team meetings and team-building activities to ensure a harmonious team is maintained.</li><li>Manage and resolve conflict within the team in a fair, open and honest manner.</li><li>Manage resource commitments and availability and adjust, for example, the project schedule and project budget.</li><li>Seek continuous improvements to the resource management process as opportunities arise.</li><li>Capture resource-related lessons learned.</li></ul>
Stakeholder	<ul><li>Manage stakeholder relationships and identify new stakeholders.</li><li>Manage the handover of deliverables to stakeholders.</li><li>Address stakeholder concerns and update the stakeholder engagement strategies as appropriate.</li><li>Ensure an integrated approach between the **organisational change management (OCM)** activities and the project activities in relation to stakeholder management strategies are coordinated so as to avoid any conflicting situations.</li><li>Seek continuous improvements to the stakeholder management process as opportunities arise.</li><li>Capture stakeholder-related lessons learned.</li></ul>
Communication	<ul><li>Execute the communications as planned in the project schedule and the Communications Register.</li><li>Monitor the feedback loops of communications and adjust the project's communication approach and communications as necessary.</li><li>Develop, review and distribute project status information to the relevant stakeholders, project sponsor, Steering Committee and project team.</li><li>Conduct project team meetings.</li><li>Maintain the project library and, if being used, the project management information system (PMIS).</li><li>Ensure an integrated approach between the OCM activities and the project activities in relation to stakeholder communications coordinated so as to avoid any conflicting situations.</li><li>Seek continuous improvements to the communications management process as opportunities arise.</li><li>Capture communications-related lessons learned.</li></ul>
Risk	<ul><li>Monitor risks, be prepared to raise issues and invoke any Contingency Plans for high-probability/high-impact risks.</li><li>Carry out risk reporting for both threat and opportunity risks in the format of heat maps.</li><li>Carry out ad hoc risk review workshops to ensure no risk is left unaddressed.</li><li>Solicit feedback on changes to risk profiles at team and other meetings.</li><li>Seek continuous improvements to the risk management process as opportunities arise.</li><li>Capture risk-related lessons learned.</li></ul>
Procurement	<ul><li>Make payments against the agreed schedule of payments (progress payments), according to the performance criteria contractually agreed.</li><li>Maintain records of deliverables and any outstanding defects for later reconciliation during the project, and at project closure.</li><li>Continue to manage stakeholders and build relationships with suppliers to ensure alignment with project objectives. Trust in the supplier relationship is not (unfortunately) automatic and has to be built and maintained across all stages of the project life cycle, from Initiation through to Closure.</li></ul>

© 2022 Dr Neil Pearson

Review questions

1. How does a tracking Gantt chart help communicate project progress?

2. Why is it important for project leaders to resist variations to the project baselines?

3. Beside a scope, cost, and schedule performance, what other aspects of project performance may have to be reported on and why?

4. What types of reports could the project leader be asked to prepare and present during the execution of a project?

5. What is the difference between a milestone and a deliverable?

6. Why are deliverables included throughout the project life cycle?

7. What are the typical resource and cost profiles for a project?

8. What is the difference between a leading and lagging indicator?

Exercises

1. This chapter has made reference to the EVM technique, but this topic is too lengthy to explain in a general project management text; therefore, the reader is encouraged to review the following three short video clips on EVM.
   - Part 1 www.youtube.com/watch?v=UggTFk2EiUg
   - Part 2 www.youtube.com/watch?v=jJi1FxC2e64
   - Part 3 www.youtube.com/watch?v=-MJEYc48Cjs

   Then seek other resources that would assist you in your understanding of EVM.

2. Reflecting on a recent project in your organisation, capture at least six lessons learned: these should be a mixture of negative and positive lessons.

Lesson (Describe what the lesson was)	Positive or negative lesson?

3. For a recent project, identify or record the additional performance metrics beyond those associated with scope, time or cost that were used to track other areas of project performance.

Measure	Lead or lag	Purpose

References

Project Management Institute (PMI) 2017, *A Guide to the Project Management Body of Knowledge*, 6th edition, PMI.

Project Management Institute (PMI) 2021a, *A Guide to the Project Management Body of Knowledge (PMBOK® Guide)*, 7th edition, PMI.

Project Management Institute (PMI) 2021b, *The Standard for Project Management (ANSI/PMI 99-001-2021)*, 7th edition, PMI.

CHAPTER 19

Project leaders and project teams

Learning elements

19A Understand the role of the modern project leader, as well as the attributes of the multifaceted project leader and codes of ethics.

19B Understand leadership as it pertains to the project leader and project teams.

19C Understand and tackle the challenges involved with sourcing project teams.

19D Understand and tackle the challenges of building project teams (including training, coaching and mentoring team members).

19E Understand and tackle the challenges of managing project teams (including managing performance and team conflict).

19F Understand and tackle the challenges of disbanding project teams.

19G Understand managing virtual project teams.

19H Be able to define servant leadership and understand how the approach is leveraged in the Scrum environment and its applicability to the project leader.

In this chapter

19.1 Introduction

19.2 Understanding the role of a contemporary project leader

19.3 Managing versus leading a project

19.4 Building and leveraging your networks

19.5 Ethics and the project leader

19.6 Building trust: The key to exercising influence

19.7   The project leader as a leader

19.8   Project teams

19.9   Building project teams

19.10   Managing project teams

19.11   Disbanding project teams

19.12   Servant leadership

Summary

19.1 | **Introduction**

This chapter discusses the various skills and abilities a project leader needs to successfully initiate, plan, execute, monitor and control, and close a project. Many of the skills and abilities are soft skills-related, and as the adage goes: "The hard stuff is the easy stuff, the soft stuff is the hard stuff". Soft skills are seen as the Achilles' tendon of project leaders, especially those in the early stages of their career or project leaders coming from individual contributor roles, maybe as previous **subject matter experts (SMEs)** in the business. Project leadership is what the author (Pearson) refers to as a *social* role—a considerable amount of the project leader's time will be consumed by project team leadership activities, stakeholder and supplier management and related communications. This chapter brings together the soft aspects of project leadership into one resource—for example, Chapter 10 "Project resource management" focused on the *hard* side of resource management (identification and allocation of resources) and did not particularly discuss its soft side.

This chapter has three main themes:

1. the skills and abilities of a project leader

2. project teams, from sourcing them, building and managing them, through to disbanding them

3. the topic of **servant leadership** as not only a preferred leadership style of the Scrum master (refer to Chapter 3 "Agile (Scrum) Project Management") but also as a leadership style that can be adopted in other project management approaches such as the predictive approach.

As introduced in Chapter 1 "Contemporary project management", in the industry there is a shift in focus on recruiting project managers who *get the job done* to project leaders who *get the job done, keeping the team happy and customer satisfied*, or as the author (Pearson) says: "There are very good technical project managers, but are they a good project leader?". Those who have been interviewed recently for a project management role might have noticed the number of questions asked about teams, leadership, communication and stakeholder engagement. This represents the shift in the industry to emotionally intelligent project leaders, as opposed to sound project managers—the difference between management versus leadership is also discussed in this chapter.

PMBOK | **Seventh edition updates (PMI 2021)**

The seventh edition of the *Project Management Body of Knowledge* (PMBOK) (PMI 2021) has further promoted the soft side of project management. Two of the 12 principles directly relate to the contents of this chapter, those being the project management principles of:

■ creating a collaborative team environment.
   Within this principle several topics are outlined, including team agreements, organisational structures, processes to assist the team in achieving the work, the RASCI in relation to team roles, and ethical codes of behaviour.

- demonstrating leadership behaviours.

  This principle focuses on differentiating between a good project *leader* and a project *manager,* listing a number of project leadership traits: agreed goals, motivational vision, reaching consensus, overcoming obstacles, negotiating and resolving conflict, communication styles, mentoring team members, skill development, collaborative decision-making, active listening, empowering teams, team cohesiveness and responsibility, showing empathy, being self-aware, harnessing change, acknowledging mistakes and learning, and leading by example.

The *Team* is also a performance domain relating to the people who are tasked with, and contribute to, achieving the project goals.

Where a solid discussion on teams and leadership takes place, including: centralised leadership, the traditional project manager role versus the distributed style, where team members are empowered individuals responsible for managing themselves as a team. This is the Agile (Scrum) style of servant leadership, which we capture in this chapter in section 19.12. The Project Management Institute (PMI) includes details on this style of project leadership in the seventh edition (PMI 2021a, pp. 17–19). Further topics included in Team Performance Domain are:

- *Team development:* Vision, roles and responsibilities, day-to-day running of the team and guidance—guiding the team in good behaviours and the right direction.

- *Team culture:* Transparency, integrity, respect, positive discourse (where conflict arises, resolve though dialogue), support, courage and celebrating success.

- *High-performing project teams:* Open communication, shared understanding, shared ownership, trust, collaboration, adaptability, resilience, empowerment and recognition.

- *Leadership skills:* Establishing and maintaining vision, critical thinking, motivation, interpersonal skills (including emotional intelligence) and conflict management.

  Supporting the Principles (Teams and Leadership) and the Performance Domain (Team) are several models:

- *Motivation models:* Herzberg's hygiene and motivational factors; Pink's intrinsic versus extrinsic motivation; McClellan's theory of needs; and McGregor's Theory X, Theory Y and Theory Z (McGregor)

- *Team development models:* **Tuckman and Jensen's team development model** and **Drexler and Sibbet's team performance model**.

The starting point for this chapter is therefore the principles and ethics. Ethics are considered a profession's interpretation of morals; the PMI code of ethics (responsibility, respect, fairness and honesty), discussed later in this chapter, would be a representation of this. The principles introduced in PMBOK seventh edition are complementary to the code of ethics and provide more specific guidance relating to how we as project leaders go about our activities. The 12 principles that the PMI introduced are:

1. Be a diligent, respectful and caring steward

2. Create a collaborative project team environment

3. Effectively engage with stakeholders

4. Focus on value

5. Recognise, evaluate and respond to system interactions

6. Demonstrate leadership behaviours

7. Tailor based on context

8. Build quality into processes and deliverables

9. Navigate complexity

10. Optimise risk responses

11. Embrace adaptability and resiliency

12. Enable change to achieve envisioned future state (PMI 2021a, p. 146).

Or alternatively, if an open-source approach is preferred, then leverage the resources such as the nearly universal principles of projects (NUPP), described in Chapter 2 "Popular frameworks and methodologies" and dot-pointed below:

- *NUP1:* prefer results and the truth to affiliations

- *NUP2:* preserve and optimise energy and resources

(Continues)

PMBOK: Seventh edition updates (PMI 2021) (*Continued*)

■ *NUP3:* always be proactive

■ *NUP4:* remember that a chain is only as strong as its weakest link

■ *NUP5:* don't do anything without a clear purpose

■ *NUP6:* use repeatable elements (NUPP 2019).

19.2 Understanding the role of a contemporary project leader

In today's complex, fast-paced business environment, there is no room for *accidental* project leaders. Project leaders need to be trained professionals who have the relevant knowledge and experience in project management. They should have acquired formal qualifications in project management (e.g. the Certificate IV, Diploma or Advanced Diploma in Project Management), or industry certifications and memberships (e.g. PMP, CSM, AgilePM, IPMA—refer to Chapter 1, Table 1.6 "Project management qualifications and certifications (Australia and international)"). This will enhance their chances of successfully leading projects of all complexities and sizes.

Figure 19.1 illustrates the key skill groups the author (Pearson) sees successful project leaders possessing. The following points expand on these skill groups.

■ *Subject matter expertise:* Although there is much debate on this point, most organisations (through their **recruitment** processes) ensure that, in addition to sound project management abilities and qualifications, the candidate will have relevant industry experience. One school of thought is that if the project leader has an already-proven track record in project management then, in theory, they should be able to manage a project of almost any content. Another school of thought is to employ only project leaders who have a background in the industry/sector/subject area. If you find yourself currently in the jobseekers' market looking for your next project management position or contract, you will probably find that the latter school of thought is the more prevalent. As a profession, however, the former applies, as project management is taught as a generic skill, which is portable across many sectors and industries.

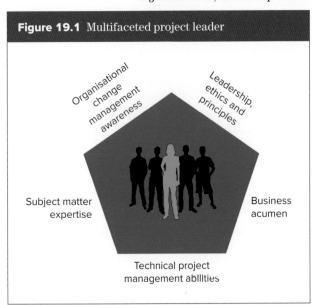

Figure 19.1 Multifaceted project leader

© 2022 Dr Neil Pearson

■ *Organisational change management awareness:*
Organisational change management (OCM) is a specialist skill (not to be confused with routine project variation management, which is carried out as a part of monitoring and controlling a project). Most projects involve changing the status quo; the project sets out to move from a current (*as-is*) state to a new (*to-be*) state. Managing the organisation and the people within the organisation through this change is the role of an organisational change manager. On large, complex projects, the organisational change manager role may be specifically recruited to an organisation. At other times, the organisation may employ an organisational change specialist who sits within the human resources (HR) department, who can be seconded to the project for short durations to provide expertise. However, unfortunately the author's (Pearson's) experience has been a total lack of OCM resources in organisations; therefore, from a project

leader's perspective, this creates the requirement to upskill as a project leader as you will be dealing with organisational change almost on a daily basis from the very announcement of the project (refer to Chapter 5 "Organisational change management and cultures").

- *Leadership, ethics and principles:* Leadership skills are often acquired through general leadership and work experience. They may include communication, negotiation, performance management, team/people management, time management, customer service, mentoring, presentation and decision-making skills. While nearly all these skills can be taught from a theoretical perspective, they can be greatly enhanced by real-life experience, and through coaching and mentoring received in the workplace. **Ethics** and **principles** are more normalised in the project management industry as covered in the introduction to this chapter, with resources being available to establish norms in a project environment.

- *Technical project management abilities:* These are the skills, tools and techniques that enable the project leader to successfully carry out the management of a project. Scoping the work, estimating, scheduling, managing budgets, managing project variations and risk management are but a few of the project management activities a project leader will be involved with. As a project leader, we seek qualifications such as the Australian Certificate IV and Diploma in Project Management Practice, or the globally accepted PMP certification to demonstrate such skills.

- ***Business acumen:*** Project managers need to understand the business the project is operating in, the strategic alignment of the work, the benefits expected and the customer for whom the work is delivering value to. Chapter 4 "Strategy, project selection and the Business Case" covered these aspects, although they tend to appear throughout all chapters of the text as they guide the project. A maintained Business Case becomes the North Star for the project.

As can be seen from Figure 19.1, the project leader will be *a jack of all trades and a master of one* (project leadership, of course!). Project management is, at first glance, an apparently misleading discipline. While there is an inherent logic in the progression from formulating a project scope statement, creating a work breakdown structure (WBS), developing a project schedule, adding resources, agreeing baselines, and reaching milestones, when it comes to implementing and completing projects, this logic quickly disappears, and project leaders encounter a much messier world, filled with inconsistencies and paradoxes. Effective project leaders must be able to deal with the contradictory nature of the work; some of these contradictions will now be considered.

- *Innovate and maintain stability:* Project leaders have to put out fires, restore order and get the project back on track. At the same time, they need to be innovative and develop new, more efficient ways of doing things. Innovations can unravel stable routines, however, and spark new disturbances that must be dealt with.

- *See the big picture while getting your hands dirty:* Project leaders must see the big picture and how their project fits within the larger strategy of their organisation. They must also often get deeply involved in project work and technology. After all, if they don't worry about the details, who will? Being able to operate at both ends of the spectrum is vital, but never lose sight of the fact that you are a project leader, leading a team to a vision or end state.

- *Encourage individuals but emphasise team:* Project leaders must motivate and cajole and entice individual performers while at the same time maintaining teamwork. They have to be careful to be fair and consistent in their treatment of team members, while at the same time treating each member as a unique individual.

- *Hands-off/hands-on:* Project leaders must intervene, resolve stalemates, solve technical problems and insist on specific approaches. At the same time, they must recognise when it is appropriate to sit on the sidelines and let other people figure out what to do. Empowerment is key. But those being empowered must know what boundaries to operate within and when to ask for help as it is okay to ask for help.

- *Flexible but firm:* Project leaders must be adaptable and responsive to events and outcomes that occur on the project. At the same time, they must hold the line at times and persevere when everyone else wants to give up.

- *Individual versus team versus organisational loyalties:* Project leaders need to forge a unified project team whose members stimulate one another to extraordinary performance. But at the same time, they have to counter the excesses of cohesion and the team's resistance to outside ideas. They have to cultivate loyalties to both the team and the parent organisation. Individuals also have loyalties that confuse the mix.

Managing these contradictions (and others) requires finesse and balance. Finesse involves being able to skilfully move back and forth between opposing behavioural patterns. For example, most of the time project leaders actively involve others in discussions and decision-making, move by increment and seek **consensus**. There are other times when project leaders must act as autocrats and take decisive, unilateral action. Seeking a balance involves recognising the danger of extremes. Too much of a good thing invariably becomes harmful. For example, many managers tend to always delegate the most stressful, difficult assignments to their best team members. This habit often breeds resentment among those chosen ("Why am I always the one who gets the tough work?") and never allows the weaker members to develop their talents further.

There is no one management style or formula for being an effective project leader. The world of project leadership is too complicated for formulas! Successful project leaders have a knack for being able to adapt their approach styles to meet the demands of specific circumstances within a situation.

So, what qualities and abilities should one look for in an effective project leader? Many authors have addressed this question and have generated list after list of skills and attributes they associate with being an effective manager. When reviewing these lists, one sometimes gets the impression that to be a successful project leader requires someone with superhuman powers! While we agree that not everyone is suited to being an effective project leader, there are a number of core traits and skills that can (potentially) be learned by an individual to support their successful performance in the role of project leader. A number of these will now be outlined.

- *Systems thinker:* Project leaders must be able to take a holistic rather than a reductionist approach to projects. As well as breaking up a project into individual pieces (planning, budget) and managing it by understanding each part, a systems perspective focuses on trying to understand how relevant project factors collectively interact to produce project outcomes. The key to success then becomes managing the interaction between different parts, and not the parts themselves. For example, if you are the project leader tasked with developing and embedding a new purchasing function within an organisation, you would not simply take the purchasing process and break it down into its constituent parts. Looking at the purchasing function from a systems perspective, you would look at where it fits within the organisation. It would, for instance, have interactions with the finance department, finance systems, warehousing, contracting, order fulfilment, customers and suppliers.

- *Personal **integrity:*** Before you can lead and manage others, you must be able to lead and manage yourself! Begin by establishing a firm sense of who you are, what you stand for and how you should behave. This inner strength provides the buoyancy to endure the ups and downs of the project life cycle and the credibility essential to sustaining the trust of others.

- *Proactive:* Good project leaders take action before it is needed to prevent small concerns from escalating into major problems. They spend much of their time working within their sphere of influence to solve problems and not dwelling on things they have little control over. Project leaders can't be whiners!

- *High **emotional intelligence (EQ):*** Project management is not for the meek. Project leaders must have command of their emotions (and often emotions do run high in a project environment) to respond constructively to others when project matters intensify. Refer to "In Theory: Emotional intelligence" to read more about this quality.

■ *General business acumen:* Because the primary role of a project leader is to integrate the contributions of different business and technical disciplines, it is important that they have a general grasp of business fundamentals and how the different functional disciplines interact to contribute to a successful business. A contract project leader who is new to an organisation may have to be careful not to inadvertently get on the wrong side of required people and/or departments that are going to be involved in the project. Project leaders often look to the project sponsor or executive for useful guidance about potential pitfalls to be avoided.

■ *Effective time management:* Time is a manager's scarcest resource (it is finite!). Project leaders must be able to allocate their time wisely and quickly adjust their priorities. They need to balance their interactions, so no one feels ignored.

■ *Skilful Eurocrat (a politician of a union of many countries):* Project leaders must be able to deal effectively with a wide range of people and win support for and endorsement of their project. They need to be able to sell the virtues of their project without compromising the truth. It is often said that a good project leader will not be found sitting at their desk maintaining the project schedule but will instead be found away from their desk, communicating and managing relationships with those involved.

■ *Optimist:* Project leaders have to display a can-do attitude. They must be able to find rays of sunlight in a dismal day and keep people's attention positive. A good sense of humour and a playful attitude are often a project leader's greatest strength.

■ *Storyteller:* Project leaders need to be able to construct a sound, compelling story of the future that will encourage anyone, at any level, to join the project journey. However, the story should include the *point of pain* (why we are doing this project), where we are moving from, how we are going to get to the end point, and what this end point will look like. Good leadership and optimistic storytelling skills can help to foster a re-energised, newly optimistic dimension to a project.

In recent years, the PMI has formally recognised the mix of skills that are needed by a project leader; the PMI refers to this mix as the *talent triangle* (PMI 2017). It includes a mix of skills, including technical project management, leadership, and strategic and business management. A brief explanation of these three skills follows.

■ *Technical project management:* This category includes all the technical project management skills within the project environment. These will vary from project environment to project environment—for example, the Scrum master has a specific set of skills that are different to those of a project leader undertaking a more predictive approach to managing a project. Each would be employed based on their respective technical project management skills. Note that the PMI's 10 knowledge areas cover aspects of technical project management.

■ *Leadership:* On large projects, the project leader could have dozens to hundreds of people reporting to them directly and indirectly, so they must lead—be able to establish the **shared vision** and bring everyone who is involved in the project (including stakeholders outside the project) on board to take the journey towards success. To do this, they need to foster an optimistic, positive and collaborative approach. The ability to **build trust**, negotiate and resolve conflict(s), act ethically and be considerate are some of the skills that fall into this category. They need to know their own leadership style and understand concepts such as EQ (refer to "In Theory: Emotional intelligence").

■ *Strategic and business management:* In Chapter 4 "Strategy, project selection and the Business Case", we covered many aspects of this skillset, for example, understanding the process of *strategy formation* (taking into consideration the internal and external environments); defining the vision, mission, values and strategic goals; selecting investments, leading to the development of the portfolio, programs and projects, through to the Business Case, which creates the focus for why the business needs to carry out the program/project.

Along with the ability to make the strategic linkage, the modern project leader must have a good degree of business acumen and be able to understand financial accounting and what business the organisation is in! They must be astute about finances, risk, value (benefits), costs (and funding) and the extended set of constraints (of scope, time, cost, quality, risk, resources) and the organisational strategy (refer to Chapter 4 "Strategy, project selection and the Business Case"). *Note:* See also the discussion in Chapter 6 "Project integration management", Figure 6.12 "Seven constraints on projects". Some potential pathways towards understanding and (further) developing EQ are:

- EQ workshop training, self-study and tailored courses that help to upgrade one's general business perspective and capacity for systems thinking
- supplementary professional development that can help individuals to improve their EQ, build their leadership skills, and grow their negotiation and conflict skills (plus numerous other skills, potentially, depending on the training course)
- coaching and mentoring that involve having practical work-based learning experiences. Trainees learn from their peers' expertise and experience and may even be coached by senior staff (such as senior project leaders and technical experts).

IN THEORY   Emotional intelligence

Emotional intelligence (EQ) is the ability or skill of perceiving, assessing and managing your own emotions and/or those of others. Although the notion of EQ emerged in the 1920s, it was not until Daniel Goleman published his book *Emotional Intelligence* (in 1995) that the concept captured the attention of business people and the public alike. Goleman divided EQ into the following five emotional competences:

1. Self-awareness—knowing your emotions, recognising feelings as they occur and understanding the link between your emotions and your behaviour. Self-awareness is reflected in confidence, realistic assessment of personal strengths/weaknesses and ability to make fun of oneself.

2. Self-regulation—being able to control disruptive impulses and moods and respond appropriately to situations. Self-regulation is reflected in trustworthiness and openness to change.

3. Self-motivation—being able to gather up your feelings and pursue goals with energy, passion and persistence. The hallmarks of self-motivation include a strong desire to achieve and internal optimism.

4. Empathy—being able to recognise the feelings of others and tuning into their verbal and non-verbal cues. Empathy is reflected in the ability to sustain relationships and in cross-cultural sensitivity.

5. Social skills—being able to build social networks and rapport with different kinds of people. Social skills include being able to lead change, resolve conflicts and build effective teams.

It is clear how EQ can positively contribute to being an effective project leader. In Goleman's view, the competences build on each other hierarchically. At the bottom of the hierarchy is *self-awareness*. Some level of self-awareness is needed to move to *self-regulation*. Ultimately, social skills require all four of the other competences in order to begin to be proficient at leading others. Experts believe that most people can learn to significantly increase their EQ, and numerous training programs and materials have emerged to help individuals realise their EQ potential.

Sources: Adapted from Bradberry T & Graves J 2005, *The Emotional Intelligence Quick Book: How to Put Your EQ to Work*, Simon & Schuster, New York; Cabanis-Brewin J 1999, 'The human task of a project leader: Daniel Goleman on the value of high EQ', PM Network, November 1999, pp. 38–42.

However, no workshop, training program or mentoring experience can transform a pessimist into an optimist or provide a sense of purpose when there isn't one. Optimism, integrity and even being proactive are not easily developed traits; a person needs to have this natural drive and interest.

19.3 Managing versus leading a project

In a perfect world, the project leader would simply implement the integrated Project Management Plan (PMP) and the project would be completed. The project leader would work with others to formulate a schedule, organise a project team, keep track of progress, and announce what needs to be done next (and then everyone would charge along). Of course, no one lives in a perfect world, and rarely does everything go according to plan. Project participants get tetchy; they fail to complement each other; other departments are unable to fulfil their commitments; technical glitches arise; work takes longer than expected. The project leader's job is to get the project back on track. As a good manager, they expedite certain activities; figure out ways to solve technical problems; serve as a peacemaker when tensions rise; and make appropriate trade-offs among time, cost and scope of the project.

However, project leaders do more than put out fires and keep the project on track. They also innovate and adapt to ever-changing circumstances. They often have to deviate from what was planned and introduce significant changes to, for example, the project schedule to respond to unforeseen threats or opportunities. For example, customers' needs may change, requiring significant design changes midway through the project. Competitors may release new products that dictate crashing project deadlines. Working relationships among project participants may break down, requiring a reformulation of the project team. Ultimately, what was planned or expected in the beginning may be very different from what was accomplished by the end of the project.

Project leaders are responsible for integrating assigned resources to complete the project according to plan. At the same time, they need to initiate changes in plans and schedules as persistent problems make plans unworkable. In other words, managers want to keep the project going while making necessary adjustments along the way. According to Kotter (2007), these two different activities represent the distinction between *management* and *leadership*. Management is about coping with complexity, while leadership is about coping with change.

Good *management* brings about order and stability by formulating plans and objectives, designing structures and procedures, monitoring results against plans, and taking corrective action when necessary. *Leadership* involves recognising and articulating the need to significantly alter the direction and operation of the project, aligning people to this new direction, and motivating them to work together to overcome hurdles produced by the change and to realise new objectives.

Strong leadership, while usually desirable, is not always necessary to be able to successfully complete a project. Well-defined projects that encounter no significant surprises require little leadership, as might be the case in constructing a conventional apartment building, where the project leader simply administers the project plan. Conversely, the higher the degree of uncertainty encountered on a project—whether in terms of changes in project scope, technological stalemates, breakdowns in coordination between people and so forth—the more leadership is required. For example, strong leadership would be needed for a software development project in which the parameters are always changing to meet developments in the industry.

It takes a talented person to perform both roles well. Some individuals are great visionaries who are good at exciting people about change. Too often, though, these same people lack the discipline or patience to deal with the day-to-day drudgeries of managing. Likewise, there are other individuals who are very well organised and methodical and yet they lack an ability to inspire others.

Strong leaders can compensate for their managerial weaknesses by having trusted assistants who oversee and manage the details of the project. Conversely, a weak leader can complement their strengths by having assistants who are good at sensing the need to rally project participants. Still, one of the things that renders good project leaders so valuable to an organisation is their ability to both manage and lead a project. In doing so, they recognise the need to manage project interfaces and build a **social network** that allows them to find out what needs to be done and can obtain the cooperation that is necessary to achieve this.

19.4 : Building and leveraging your networks

19.4.1 Mapping networks and dependencies

The first step towards building a network is to identify those on whom the project depends for its success. The project leader (and their key assistants) therefore need to ask the following questions:

- Whose cooperation will we need?
- Whose agreement or approval will we need?
- Whose opposition would keep us from accomplishing the project?

Many project leaders find it helpful to draw a map of these dependencies. Two such maps have been discussed in previous chapters of this text but are reproduced here to reinforce the importance of this concept (Figure 19.2 (a) and (b)).

Figure 19.2(a) Networks with dependencies (macro project level)

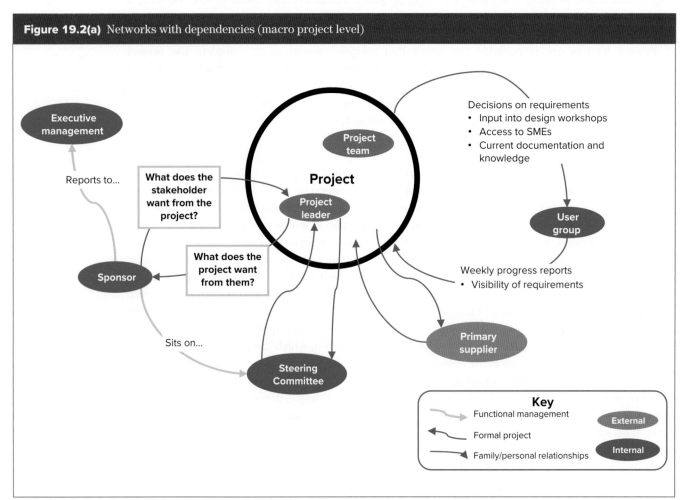

Figure 19.2(b) Networks with dependencies (micro level)

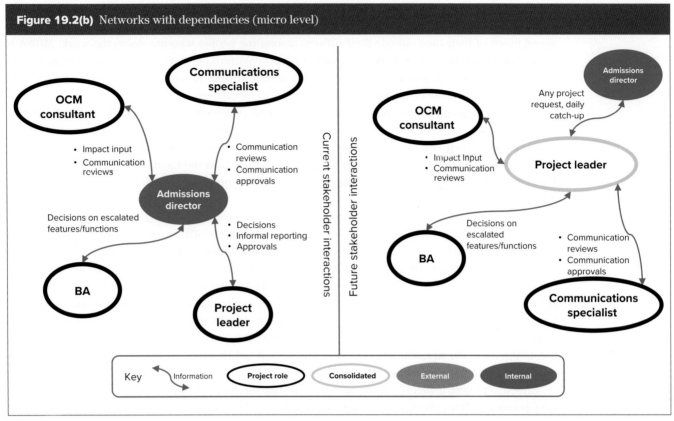

It is always better to overestimate rather than underestimate networks. All too often, talented and successful project leaders are derailed because they are blindsided by someone whose position or power they had not anticipated. After identifying who the project will depend on, the project leader can, effectively, step into their shoes to see the project from that person's perspective. For example:

- What differences exist between me and the people on whom I depend (goals, values, pressures, working styles, risks)?
- How do these different people view the project (supporters, indifferents, antagonists)?
- What is the current status of the relationship I have with the people on whom I depend?
- What sources of influence do I have relative to those on whom I depend?

Once the project leader starts this analysis, they can begin to appreciate what others value and what currencies (if any) they might be able to offer as a basis on which to build a working relationship. The project leader will also begin to realise where potential problems may lie—professional working relationships in which they have a current *debit* or no convertible *currency* to trade. Diagnosing the project from another person's point of view can help the project leader to anticipate the other person's reactions and feelings about project decisions and actions. This information is vital for selecting the appropriate influence strategy and tactics and for conducting successful negotiations. Chapter 14 "Project stakeholder management" investigated several tools for analysing these different stakeholder perspectives.

19.4.2 Management by wandering around (MBWA)

The preceding example illustrates the next step in building a supportive social network. Once the project leader has established which key players will determine success, they next need to initiate contact and begin building a relationship with those players. A management style that can help foster positive professional working relationships is what employees at Hewlett-Packard refer to as **management by wandering around (MBWA)**. MBWA reflects the fact that good managers tend to spend much of their time outside their offices, among the people who are doing the work. MBWA is somewhat of a misnomer as there is actually a purpose/pattern behind the wandering. Through face-to-face interactions, project leaders can stay in touch with what is really going on in the project and can seek to enhance the cooperation that is essential to its success.

Effective project leaders initiate contact with key players to keep abreast of developments, anticipate potential problems, provide encouragement, and reinforce the objectives and vision of the project. They can intervene to resolve conflicts and prevent stalemates from occurring. By staying in touch with various aspects of the project, they become the focal point for information on it. Participants turn to them to obtain the most current and comprehensive information about the project, which reinforces their central role as the project leader.

We have observed less effective project leaders who have deliberately avoided taking a MBWA approach. They typically attempt to manage projects from their offices and computer systems. They proudly announce their *open-door policy* and encourage others to come to see them when a problem or an issue arises, but to them, no news is good news! This allows their contacts to be determined by the relative aggressiveness of others. People who take the initiative to seek out the project leader get too high a proportion of the project leader's attention compared with people who are offsite and therefore cannot easily pop in to speak with them and people who are more passive and therefore may be reluctant to bother the project leader by approaching them directly. This behaviour supports the adage "only the squeaky wheel gets greased", and yet this type of arrangement can breed real resentment within the project team.

Effective project leaders find the time to regularly interact with more distant stakeholders. They keep in touch with suppliers, vendors, top management and other functional managers. In doing so, they maintain familiarity with the different parties, sustain friendships, discover opportunities to work more effectively, and better understand the motives and needs of others. They remind people of commitments and champion the cause of their project. They also shape people's expectations. Through frequent communication, they alleviate people's concerns about the project, dispel rumours, warn people of potential problems, and lay the groundwork for dealing with setbacks in a more effective manner.

Unless project leaders take the initiative to build a network of supportive relationships, they are likely to see a manager (or other stakeholder) only when there is bad news or when they need a favour (e.g. they don't have the data they promised, or the project has slipped behind schedule). Without prior, frequent, easy, give-and-take interactions about non-decisive issues, an encounter prompted by a problem is likely to provoke excess tension. The parties are more likely to act defensively, interrupt each other and lose sight of the common problem.

Experienced project leaders recognise the importance of building relationships before they need them. They initiate contact with key stakeholders at times when there are no outstanding issues or problems, and therefore no anxieties and suspicions. On these social occasions, they engage in small-talk and responsive banter. They respond to others' requests for aid, provide supportive counsel and exchange information. In doing so, they establish credit in that relationship—which will allow them to deal with more serious problems down the road. When one person views another as being pleasant, credible and helpful (based on previous contact), they are much more likely to be responsive to requests for help and be less confrontational when problems arise. A word of warning when applying the MBWA technique: Be careful the team do not see it as *tokenist leadership*; if you are sincere, take time, listen, sit down and show empathy. Finally, WBWA is often associated with walk the talk (WTT) (i.e. *do as you speak*). The two, when combined in a sincere manner, can send powerful messages.

19.4.3 Managing upward relations

Research consistently points out that project success is strongly affected by the degree to which a project has the support of top management. Such support is reflected in an appropriate budget, responsiveness to unexpected needs, and a clear signal to others in the organisation of the importance of cooperation.

Visible top management support is not only critical for securing the support of other managers within an organisation, but is also a key factor in the project leader's ability to motivate the project team. Nothing establishes a manager's right to lead more than their ability to defend. To win the loyalty of team members, project leaders must be effective advocates for their projects. They must be able to get top management to rescind unreasonable demands, provide additional resources and recognise the accomplishments of team members. This is more easily said than done, of course. Working relationships with upper management is often a common source of consternation. Project leaders are typically heard saying things along the lines of:

- "They don't know how much it sets us back, losing [name] to another project!"
- "I would like to see them get this project done with the budget they gave us!"
- "I just wish they would make up their minds as to what is really important!"

While it may seem counterintuitive for a subordinate to manage a superior, smart project leaders devote considerable time and attention to influencing and garnering the support of top management. Project leaders have to accept profound differences in perspective and become skilled at the art of persuading superiors. Many of the tensions that arise between upper management and project leaders do so because of differences in perspective. Project leaders become naturally absorbed with what is best for their project. To them, the most important thing in the world (well, at least in their working day) is their project! Top management should have a different set of priorities. They will be concerned with what is best for the entire organisation. It is only natural for these two interests to conflict at times. For example, a project leader may lobby intensively for additional personnel (sourced from other departments), only to be turned down because top management believes the other departments cannot afford a reduction in their staff. Although frequent communication can minimise differences, the project leader has to accept the fact that top management is inevitably going to see the world differently.

Once project leaders accept that disagreements with superiors are more a question of perspective than substance, they can focus more of their energy on the art of persuading upper management. But before they can persuade superiors, they must first prove loyalty. Loyalty, in this context, simply means that most of the time project leaders must show that they consistently follow through on requests and adhere to the parameters established by top management (without a great deal of grumbling or fuss). Once project leaders have proven their loyalty to upper management, senior management is likely to be much more receptive to challenges and requests. Project leaders must cultivate strong ties with upper managers who are sponsoring the project. As noted earlier, these are usually high-ranking executives who have championed the approval and funding for the project and thus their reputations will be aligned with the project.

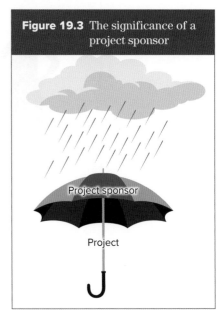

Figure 19.3 The significance of a project sponsor

Project sponsor

Project

© 2022 Dr Neil Pearson

Sponsors will defend the project when it is under attack in upper circles of management. They shelter the project from excessive interference (see Figure 19.3). Project leaders should always keep such people informed of any problems that may cause embarrassment or disappointment. For example, if costs are beginning to outrun the budget, or a technical glitch is threatening to delay the completion of the project, then the project leader must make sure the sponsors are the first to know.

Timing is everything: for example, a request for additional funding made the day after disappointing third-quarter earnings are reported is less likely to be accommodated than if the request were submitted four weeks earlier. Good project leaders pick the optimum time to make an appeal to top management. They enlist their project sponsors to lobby their cause. They also realise there are limits to top management's accommodations. Here, the Lone Ranger analogy is appropriate—"You have only so many silver bullets, so use them wisely".

Project leaders need to adapt their communication pattern to that of the senior group. For example, one project leader recognised that top management tended to use sports metaphors to describe business situations, so she framed a recent slip in schedule by admitting that "we took two steps backwards, but one step one forwards". Smart project leaders learn the language of top management and use it to their advantage.

Finally, a few project leaders admit ignoring chains of command. If they are confident that top management will reject an important request and that what they want to do will benefit the project, they do it without asking permission. While acknowledging that this is very risky, they claim that bosses typically won't argue with success.

19.4.4 Leading by example

A highly visible, interactive management style is not only essential for building and sustaining cooperative relationships, but it also allows project leaders to utilise their most powerful leadership tool—their own behaviour. Often, when faced with uncertainty, people look to others for cues as to how to respond and they demonstrate a propensity to mimic the behaviour of their superiors. A project leader's behaviour symbolises how other people should work on the project. Through their behaviour, they can influence how others act and respond to a variety of issues related to the project. To be effective, project leaders must lead by example (see Figure 19.4).

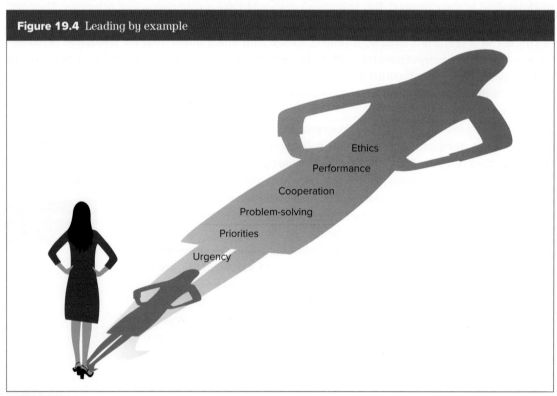

Figure 19.4 Leading by example

Ethics
Performance
Cooperation
Problem-solving
Priorities
Urgency

© 2022 Dr Neil Pearson

Next, we look at six aspects of how to lead by example.

19.4.4.1 Urgency

Through their actions, project leaders can convey a sense of urgency that can permeate project activities. This urgency, in part, can be conveyed through stringent deadlines, frequent status report meetings, and aggressive solutions for expediting the project. The project leader uses these tools like a metronome to pick up the beat of the project. At the same time, such devices will be ineffective if there is not also a corresponding change in the project leader's behaviour. If they want others to work faster and solve problems quicker, then they need to work faster themselves: they need to hasten the pace of their own behaviour. They should accelerate the frequency of their interactions, talk and walk more quickly, get to work sooner, and leave work later. By simply increasing the pace of their daily interaction patterns, project leaders can reinforce a sense of urgency in others. However, on the flip side, don't be in a constant state of urgency, or (like a vaccine), over time the effect will wear off.

19.4.4.2 Priorities

Actions speak louder than words. Subordinates and others discern project leaders' priorities by how they spend their time. If a project leader claims that a particular project is critical but is then perceived as devoting more time to other projects, then all their verbal reassurances are likely to be unheard. Conversely, a project leader who takes the time to observe a critical test, instead of simply waiting for a report about the test, affirms the importance of the testers and their work. Likewise, the types of questions project leaders pose can communicate priorities. For example, by repeatedly asking how specific issues relate to satisfying the customer, a project leader can reinforce the importance of customer satisfaction.

19.4.4.3 Problem-solving

How project leaders respond to problems sets the tone for how others tackle problems. If bad news is greeted by verbal attacks, then others will be reluctant about being forthcoming. If the project leader is more concerned with finding out who is to blame instead of how to prevent problems from happening again, then others will tend to cover their tracks and cast the blame elsewhere. If, on the other hand, project leaders focus more on how they can turn a problem into an opportunity, or how to learn from a mistake, then others are more likely to adopt a more proactive approach towards problem-solving. As a project leader, we should be seeking to locate the facts behind the **root cause** of the problem and not jump to attributing blame or playing the *blame game*.

19.4.4.4 Cooperation

How project leaders act towards *outsiders* influences how team members interact with outsiders. If a project leader makes disparaging remarks about the "idiots in the marketing department", for example, then this (often) becomes the shared view of the entire team. If project leaders set the norm of treating outsiders with respect and being responsive to their needs, then others will more likely follow suit.

19.4.4.5 Performance

Veteran project leaders recognise that if they want participants to exceed project expectations, they must themselves exceed others' expectations in their role of project leader. They establish a high standard for project performance through the quality of their daily interactions. They respond quickly to the needs of others, carefully prepare and run crisp meetings, stay on top of all the critical issues, facilitate effective problem-solving and stand firm on important matters. However, the contemporary project leader will know that performance is not about peaks and troughs, but about sustainment.

19.4.4.6 Ethics

How others respond to ethical dilemmas that arise during a project will be influenced by how the project leader has responded to similar dilemmas. In many cases, team members base their actions on how they think the project leader would respond. If project leaders deliberately distort or withhold vital information from customers or top management, then they are signalling to others that this kind of behaviour is acceptable. Project management invariably creates a variety of ethical dilemmas—we will now look at this topic in more detail.

19.5 : **Ethics and the project leader**

Questions of ethics have already arisen in previous chapters, which discussed, for example, potential padding of cost and time estimations and the exaggeration of project pay-offs in project proposals. Ethical dilemmas involve situations where it is difficult to determine whether conduct is right or wrong. For example, is it acceptable to falsely assure customers that everything is on track when, in reality, you are only telling them this to prevent them from panicking and making matters worse?

Project leaders often report that they have encountered ethical issues in their work. Examples include being pressured to alter status reports, the backdating of signatures, the shading of documentation to mask the reality of project progress, falsification of cost accounts, safety standards being compromised to accelerate progress, and approving shoddy work.

Project management is complicated work and, as such, ethics invariably involve grey areas of judgement and interpretation. For example, it may be difficult to distinguish the deliberate falsification of estimates from genuine mistakes, or the wilful exaggeration of project pay-offs from genuine optimism. It becomes problematic when trying to determine whether unfulfilled promises were deliberate deceptions or, alternatively, an appropriate response to changing circumstances. To provide greater clarity about business ethics, many companies and professional groups publish a code of conduct. Cynics see these documents as simply *window-dressing*, while advocates argue that they are important (albeit limited) first steps. In practice, personal ethics do not lie in formal statutes but at the intersection of one's work, family, education, profession, religious beliefs and daily interactions. Most project leaders report that they rely on their own private sense of right and wrong—what one project leader called their *internal compass*. A common rule of thumb for testing whether a response/a choice is ethical involves imagining that whatever you choose to do is going to be reported on the front page of your local newspaper and, potentially, in social media (e.g. see "Snapshot from Practice: The ethical project leader"). Would you be comfortable with your choice/decision? Could you live with it? What would be the impact to the business? Would the choice/decision endanger lives of customers or the community?

Unfortunately, scandals at Enron, Worldcom, Arthur Andersen and, more recently, Carillion PLC (which went into compulsory liquidation in 2018) and Evergrande have demonstrated a propensity for some highly trained professionals to abdicate personal responsibility around their actions and to obey the arguably somewhat unethical directives of superiors. Top management and the culture of an organisation can play decisive roles in shaping members' beliefs of what is right and wrong. Some organisations indirectly encourage ethical transgressions by fostering a *win at all costs* mentality. Pressures to succeed can obscure consideration of whether the ends justify the means. Conversely, there are organisations that place a premium on fair play and, as a result, command an enhanced market position by virtue of being perceived as trustworthy.

SNAPSHOT *from* PRACTICE : **The ethical project leader**

Being a member of a professional organisation brings with it a commitment. In Australia, whether you are a senior executive and a member of the Australian Institute of Company Directors (AICD), a medical doctor and a fellow of a professional college, an electrician and a member of Master Electricians Australia, or a project leader and a member of the Australian Institute of Project Management (AIPM), your membership of such organisations will entail signing up to a code of ethics.

Several elements are discussed in the AIPM code of ethics, including *professional conduct*:

"**1.** Act with Integrity

- 1.1 Be honest and trustworthy
- 1.2 Demonstrate respect for others
- 1.3 Act with a clear conscience

   2. Practice Competently

      ■ 2.1 Maintain and develop knowledge and skills

      ■ 2.2 Act on the basis of adequate competency

   3. Demonstrate Leadership

      ■ 3.1 Uphold the reputation of the profession

   4. Act with Responsibility

      ■ 4.1 Engage responsibly with the community

      ■ 4.2 Foster health, safety and wellbeing

      ■ 4.2 Balance the needs of the present with the needs of the future" (AIPM 2014).

To position your ethical behaviour, ask yourself what you would do in the following situation. You have a close friend working in your project. They are found to be taking a bribe from a supplier to the project. Only you (as the project leader) know about this and you have only just discovered it is happening. Reporting the behaviour would mean losing a much-needed project resource at a critical point in the project's execution.

What would you do in this situation?

a. Keep quiet.

b. Contact your organisational HR department and professional body.

c. Confront your friend yourself.

d. Call the police immediately and present your facts.

The best way to approach such a situation would be (b), as you would not be ignoring the situation, and you would not need to confront your friend directly, but appropriate disciplinary action could be taken by the HR department and/or the professional body so the unethical behaviour is (hopefully) discontinued.

Many project leaders claim that ethical behaviour is its own reward. By following your own *internal compass*, your behaviour expresses your personal values. Others suggest that ethical behaviour is doubly rewarding—not only will you be able to sleep soundly at night, but you will also develop a positive reputation as a person who has sound integrity. As will be explored in the next section, such a reputation is essential to establishing the trust necessary to exercise influence effectively. When joining the PMI, we subscribe to the ethics of PMI, which include responsibility, respect, fairness and honesty.

■ Responsibility is our duty to take ownership for the decisions we make or fail to make, the actions we take or fail to take, and the consequences that result.

■ Respect is our duty to show a high regard for ourselves, others, and the resources entrusted to us. Resources entrusted to us may include people, money, reputation, the safety of others, and natural or environmental resources. An environment of respect engenders trust, confidence, and performance excellence by fostering cooperation—an environment where diverse perspectives and views are encouraged and valued.

■ Fairness is our duty to make decisions and act impartially and objectively. Our conduct must be free from competing self-interest, prejudice, and favouritism.

■ Honesty is our duty to understand the truth and act in a truthful manner both in our communications and in our conduct (PMI n.d.).

Review the full ethics guidance at the following internet resource: www.pmi.org/-/media/pmi/documents/public/pdf/ethics/pmi-code-of-ethics.pdf?sc_lang_temp=en

19.6 | Building trust: The key to exercising influence

Trust can be defined as believing that "someone is good and honest and will not harm you, or that something is safe and reliable" (Cambridge Dictionary n.d.).

There are many dimensions of trust (either implied or stated) across the project environment. For example:

■ The project team trusts the project leader to create a safe working environment.

■ The project leader trusts the project sponsor to be open and honest with them in all their dealings.

■ The project management office (PMO) trusts the project leader to provide an accurate and honest project status.

■ Stakeholders trust the project has the business's interests ahead of any individual or organisational agendas.

■ Project team members trust stakeholders are being honest about the requirements necessary from a new computer system.

The significance of trust can be discerned by its absence. Imagine how different a working relationship is when you distrust the other party, as opposed to when you trust them. When people distrust each other, they often spend inordinate amounts of time and energy attempting to discern hidden agendas and the true meaning of communications, and then securing guarantees to promises. They are much more cautious with each other and can be hesitant about cooperating. Here is what one line manager had to say about how he reacted to a project leader he did not trust:

> *Whenever Jim approached me about something, I found myself trying to read between the lines to figure what was really going on. When he made a request, my initial reaction was 'no' until he proved it.*

Conversely, trust maintains smooth and efficient interactions. When you are trustworthy, people are more likely to take your actions and intentions at face value when circumstances are ambiguous. For example, here is what a functional manager had to say about how he dealt with a project leader he trusted:

> *If Sally said she needed something, no questions were asked. I knew it was important or she wouldn't have asked.*

Trust is an elusive concept. It is hard to nail down in precise terms WHY some project leaders are trusted and others are not. One popular way to understand trust is to see it as a function of character and competence. *Character* focuses on personal motives (i.e. do they want to do the right thing?), while *competence* focuses on the skills necessary to realise motives (i.e. do they know the right things to do?).

A list of tips for trust-building behaviours can be found in the web resource "Build trust and be transparent" (Murray 2010). Some of the tips found in this web resource have been adapted and contextualised as follows.

■ *Be accountable for your actions:* "Accountability involves claiming your own power and marshalling your internal resources to achieve better results. Accountability asks *What can I do to make a difference?* Accountable behaviour enables you to take charge of your thoughts, feelings and actions."

■ *Act consistently with your words:* "People will pick up immediately when you espouse one value with your words but demonstrate the opposite of that value through your actions."

■ *Live your values and communicate them regularly:* "Review the primary values that allow you to inspire trust in others: honesty, responsibility, respect, fairness and compassion. First, ask yourself how often and how clearly you communicate and share these values with others. When facing a difficult situation, openly refer to these values and draw on them to make the best decision. Next, assess how well you live out these values in your daily routine and in your interactions with others."

■ *Admit mistakes and take blame:* "We all make mistakes at work, and the negative consequences usually spill over and impact others. To maintain the respect and trust of co-workers, your boss, customers, vendors, and suppliers, don't hesitate to own your mistakes." And be professional in accepting the mistakes of others. Mistakes can be seen as learning opportunities—employees rarely deliberately make mistakes; there is usually a cumulation of events.

■ *Listen for understanding:* "The very act of listening can build trust. By taking the time to listen and really seek to understand the opinion of others, you are demonstrating respect and acknowledging their unique perspective." Practise **active listening**—it is harder than you think!

■ *Act with integrity and ethics:* "The most important action you can take to build trust in the workplace is to be honest and ethical. When speaking and communicating with others, tell the truth."

■ *Be an advocate for a fear-free culture:* "Warren Bennis of the University of Southern California discovered in his research that effective leaders build trust by being consistent and predictable in their behaviour and attempting to truly listen and understand the perspective of others."

■ *Face reality:* "In our conversations with others, we would all like to tell the truth as part of doing business, tackling new challenges, or resolving hard issues. However, the task can be difficult, as we often fear that a difficult conversation will turn into an angry confrontation, stirring up emotions and causing a distraction."

■ *Provide honest feedback:* "One of the primary responsibilities of a leader is to provide feedback to others, especially the people who report directly to you. The act of providing feedback can help establish trust, but only if you have the courage to be honest."

■ *Build trust with openness:* "The common, initial reaction to a mistake is to blame someone else. However, even apparently random errors occur due to the convergence of multiple contributing factors; sometimes the cause is people, sometimes the cause is the work process itself. You will never be able to discover true causes for problems unless you have a fear-free culture. Blaming individuals causes people to shut down their communication and limits their willingness to communicate the facts honestly."

Stephen Covey resurrected the significance of *character* in leadership literature in his best-selling publication *Seven Habits of Highly Effective People* (1989). Covey criticised popular management literature as focusing too much on shallow human relations skills and manipulative techniques, which he labelled *the personality ethic*. He argued that at the core of highly effective people is a character ethic that is deeply rooted in personal values and principles such as dignity, service, fairness, and the pursuit of truth and respect.

One of the distinguishing traits of good character is consistency. When people are guided by a core set of principles, they are naturally more predictable because their actions are consistent with these principles. Another feature of good character is openness. When people have a clear sense of who they are, and what they value, they are more receptive to others. This trait provides them with the capacity to empathise and the talent to build consensus among divergent people. A further quality of good character is a sense of purpose. Managers who have good character are driven not only by personal ambitions but also by motivations for the common good. Their primary concern is what is best for their organisation and for the project, not what is best for them personally. The willingness to subordinate personal interests to a *higher purpose* generally garners the respect, loyalty and trust of others.

A concept that keeps our trust factor in check as well as providing a useful tool to position where loyalties lie with others as project leader is the **trust equation**. Brought to fame in the book, *The Trusted Advisor* (Maister, Green & Galford 2000), it provides an equation where a quotient (score) is given to the following factors.

■ CREDIBILITY has to do with the words we speak. In a sentence we might say, "I can trust what she says about intellectual property; she's very credible on the subject."

■ RELIABILITY has to do with actions. We might say, "If he says he'll deliver the product tomorrow, I trust him, because he's dependable."

■ INTIMACY refers to the safety or security that we feel when entrusting someone with something. We might say, "I can trust her with that information; she's never violated my confidentiality before, and she would never embarrass me."

■ SELF-ORIENTATION refers to the person's focus. Whether the person's focus is primarily on him or herself, or on the other person. We might say, "I can't trust him on this deal—I don't think he cares enough about me, he's focused on what he gets out of it." Or more commonly, "I don't trust him—I think he's too concerned about how he's appearing, so he's not really paying attention" (Trusted Advisor n.d.).

Source: Adapted from The Trusted Advisor, by Maister, Green and Galford, 2000, https://trustedadvisor.com/why-trust-matters/understanding-trust/understanding-the-trust-equation, accessed February 2022.

Referring to Figure 19.5, you can calculate a score by using a simple numeric 1 (low) to 5 (high) and work out your or others' trust quotient. As indicated in the equation, as "self-orientation" is a single variable below the division line, it will significantly impact the outcome of the equation.

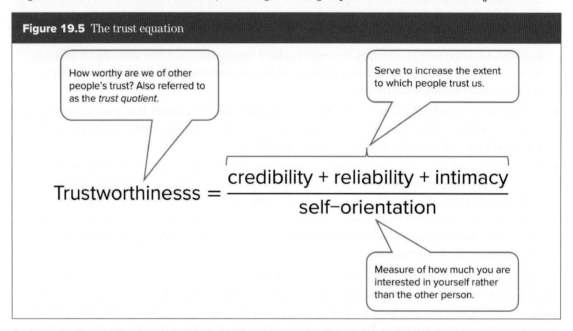

Figure 19.5 The trust equation

> How worthy are we of other people's trust? Also referred to as the *trust quotient*.

> Serve to increase the extent to which people trust us.

$$\text{Trustworthinesss} = \frac{\text{credibility} + \text{reliability} + \text{intimacy}}{\text{self-orientation}}$$

> Measure of how much you are interested in yourself rather than the other person.

Refer to the two scenarios in Figure 19.6.

Figure 19.6 Trust scenarios

$$\text{Trustworthinesss} = \frac{\text{credibility} + \text{reliability} + \text{intimacy}}{\text{self-orientation}}$$

Scenario A: You are negotiating a contract for a large software system purchase with a pushy account manager. The numbers stack up as:

$$\frac{3 + 4 + 4}{5} = 2$$

Scenario B: You are negotiating a contract for a large software system purchase with an attentive account manager who is listening to the problem and your concerns. The numbers stack up as:

$$\frac{3 + 4 + 3}{1} = 10$$

It is clear which account manager we would like to be dealing with.

19.7 | **The project leader as a leader**

Knowing your personal leadership and management style is key to understanding reactions from those around you. Figure 19.7 illustrates a leadership continuum. As can be seen, the manager's approach is placed on a continuum, from an autocratic style of management through to a democratic style of management.

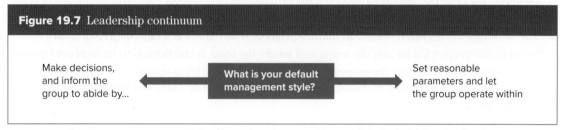

Figure 19.7 Leadership continuum

Make decisions, and inform the group to abide by...

What is your default management style?

Set reasonable parameters and let the group operate within

© 2022 Dr Neil Pearson

The continuum indicates the relationship between the level of freedom that a manager chooses to give to a team and the level of authority applied by the manager. As the team's freedom is increased, the manager's authority decreases. Most managers have a preferred style. However, there are times when a manager may move between styles. For example, when a difficult decision has to be made within the project that has been the result of executive discussions, the project leader may move to a more *autocratic* decision style. The different blends of authority and *freedoms of subordinates* are outlined as follows.

- *The manager makes and announces the decision:* In this style, the project leader reviews all appropriate options in light of goals, issues, priorities, schedules and so on, and decides which action to take and subsequently informs the project team of the decision. Although the project leader does need to consider how their team will react, and must be prepared for questions, the team plays no active part in making the decision.

- *The manager sells the decision to the group:* The project leader chooses which action to take (as in the previous approach style) but explains (*sells*) the decision to the project team. In doing so, the project leader is more likely to be viewed as recognising the project team's importance (and concern).

- *The manager presents ideas and invites questions:* The project leader presents their decision, along with additional ideas (options) they have come up with. The project team is then invited to ask questions and to discuss the rationale for these ideas with the project leader. This style starts to gain buy-in from the project team, as there is a higher level of team involvement and discussion (leading to a more empowered project team).

- *The manager presents a tentative decision that is subject to change following discussion:* The project leader discusses and reviews the provisional decision they have arrived at with the project team on the basis that the project leader will take on board the views of the project team before a decision is finalised. Here, the project team is more empowered to influence the project leader's final decision.

- *The manager presents the problem, canvasses suggestions and makes appropriate decisions:* The project leader presents a situation to the project team. The project team is encouraged and expected to contribute ideas, suggest suitable options and offer enabling perspectives. The project team and the project leader then discuss all suitable options before a final decision is arrived at. The project team's input is seen as being highly valued, with its members contributing to the project and the decisions being made.

- *The manager defines limits and asks the group for the decision:* In this style, the project leader effectively delegates responsibility for making a decision to the project team (albeit within the project leader's stated limits). This style of approach really empowers the project team; however, the project leader still has to mitigate any risks that may result from the proposed decision.

- *The manager permits subordinates to function within superior defined limits:* Here, the project leader provides greater freedom for decision-making, but only within a set of parameters. For example, the project leader may increase the project team's spending authority for the team to be able to make quicker, context-based decisions.

- *The manager allows full freedom:* In mature projects where there is a high degree of trust between the project leader and the team, and where the team is considered to be high performing, the project leader may give the project team full freedom. The team operates as the project leader would in the mode of *makes decisions and announces decisions*. (Adapted from Tannenbaum & Schmidt 1973.)

As a project leader, know your default style, as this is the style you will revert to in times of stress—and it is exactly at these times that you need to make a conscious decision about what style is most appropriate (which might be the opposite of your default style!).

19.8 | Project teams

19.8.1 Sourcing project teams

Sourcing project teams includes decisions around the selection of the project sponsor and project leader, through to sourcing all the other required members of the project team. It is the project team that typically takes the most planning to acquire. This section on sourcing project teams will review some of the situations a project and project leader may be in at the outset of the project.

19.8.2 Project sponsor

At the stage where the project's Business Case is issued (by the relevant management office), a sponsor for this Business Case would have been agreed (and a project leader may also have been identified). The portfolio/program/project management office needs to carefully consider the choice of project sponsor—after all, it is well known that having the right fit and attitude of project sponsor greatly increases the project's success. It is not uncommon for mature management offices to use a checklist approach towards checking sponsor and project alignment. The author (Pearson) observes some of the following traits of good sponsors:

- Promote understanding of the root cause of the problem and do not dive in and address the symptoms

- Understand the 80/20 rule and when *good enough* is sufficient to provide a workable solution to the business

- Corral the best team possible, using the power of influence at management level to obtain the best resources for the most critical projects

- Be the umbrella that shields the project, project leader and project team from unnecessary *noise* in terms of politics, company culture and other distracting factors

- Offer the most positive, proactive support to the project

- Ensure the project leader and project team have clearly defined accountabilities and ensure they make good on them

- Listen, take advice wisely and make sound decisions in a timely manner

- In times of changing business environments, know when to prematurely terminate a project based on the presenting facts

- Be clear, concise and factual in their communications
- Be ethical in all their dealings.

In selecting the project sponsor, the issuer of the Business Case must also consider the following.

- *The organisation's hierarchy:* Is it flat or hierarchical? Does position in the hierarchy affect the level of authority the sponsor may have, and if so, to what extent? For example, would the implementation of customer relationship management (CRM) software be best sponsored by the director of marketing, or the director of business development?

- *The organisation's culture:* Are the necessary levels of empowerment and accountability being passed to the nominated sponsor in the organisation, to enable the project to be appropriately driven and directed?

- *The politics of the organisation:* Would weak political players not have the ability to resolve escalated issues and gain the right backing from around the boardroom table? For example, if the business development department is seen as being aloof, would the project have greater success if it was sponsored by the director of marketing?

The project sponsor can make or break a project and so their selection requires careful consideration. If the above considerations have not been taken into account when the project leader is appointed, then what leverage will the project leader have to question the choice of appointed project sponsor? Would they be able to gain a more suitable sponsor for the project if this needs to be challenged? Mature project organisations should be able to entertain such a challenge without repercussions.

19.8.3 Project leader

Once the project sponsor has been established, the next role to be recruited is that of the project leader (and the project leader subsequently establishes the remainder of the project team). There are many potential considerations to take into account when sourcing a project leader. Some factors that come into play include the following.

- *The degree to which the organisation is projectised:* For example, are there career project leaders *benched* in the PMO, ready to take on the next project, or is the organisation more functional in design and a functional manager is to take on the role of managing the project?

- *The organisation's HR and recruitment policy:* For example, some organisations do not have permanent project leaders—their resourcing strategy is to go to the market to recruit project leaders with previous experience in the required subject domain.

- *Secondment:* If project leader skills exist in the organisation as part of the functional hierarchy but are not used full time, then a person who possesses the requisite skills will be seconded from their substantive role to manage the project on a full-time basis. Once the seconded person's project management responsibilities are complete, they return to take up their functional role within the organisation once more.

- *Contracting:* Contracting in a project leader to work on a particular project is common. If carefully selected, contract project leaders can bring with them technical project management skills and strong leadership, strategic and business-management skills (as noted in the PMI's talent triangle and Pearson's **multifaceted project leader**—refer back to Figure 19.1).

Regardless of the avenue from which a project leader is sourced, it is essential that they possess the behavioural traits that were discussed earlier in this chapter to increase the likelihood of project success. A higher weighting may therefore be given at **interview** to the individual's leadership skills (and their cultural fit to the organisation), in combination with their business leadership skills. This is because it is far easier to subsequently train an individual to fill any technical gaps than it is to adjust ingrained behaviours and traits.

19.8.4 **Recruiting project members**

The process of selecting and recruiting project members will vary across organisations. Two important factors affecting recruitment will be the importance of the project and the management structure being used to complete it. For high-priority projects, considered as critical for the future of the organisation, the project leader may be given almost carte blanche to select whomever they deem to be necessary (from across the business and outside). For less significant projects, a project leader may need to persuade personnel from other areas within the organisation to join the team.

In many matrix structures, the functional manager will control who is assigned to the project and the project leader will therefore have to work with the functional manager to obtain necessary personnel. Even in a project team where members are selected and assigned on a full-time basis to the project, the project leader must be sensitive to the needs of others. There is no better way to create enemies within an organisation than to be perceived as unnecessarily robbing other departments of essential personnel. Experienced project leaders stress the importance of asking for volunteers. This desirable step often is outside the manager's control. Still, the value of having team members volunteer for the project as opposed to being assigned cannot be overlooked. Agreeing to work on the project is the first step towards building personal commitment to it. Such commitment will be essential to maintain motivation when the project hits hard times and extra effort is required.

When selecting and recruiting team members, project leaders naturally look for individuals who have the necessary experience and knowledge or technical skills critical for being able to complete the project. At the same time, there are some less obvious considerations that also need to be factored into the recruitment process.

■ *Ability to problem-solve:* If the project is complex and *fuzzy*, the manager will want people who are good at working under uncertainty and who have strong problem-identification and problem-solving skills. These same (often highly creative) people are very likely to be bored and less productive when working on straightforward projects that are highly predictable.

■ *Availability:* Sometimes, the people who are most often available are not actually the ones wanted for the team. Conversely, it may be that a recruited person is already overcommitted when recruited, and if so, they are unlikely to offer much value to the team.

■ *Technological expertise:* Managers should be wary of people who know too much about a specific technology. That may sound counterintuitive, but technology buffs who like to *study and tinker* may sometimes find it hard to settle down and perform the work.

■ *Credibility:* The credibility of the project is enhanced by the reputation of the people involved in it. Recruiting enough winners lends confidence to the project.

■ *Political connections:* Astute managers frequently recruit individuals who already have a good working relationship with key stakeholders. This is particularly true for projects operating in a matrix environment in which a significant portion of the work will be under the domain of a specific functional department, and not the core project team.

■ *Ambition, initiative and energy:* These qualities can make up for a lot of shortcomings in other areas and should not be underestimated.

■ *Attitude, ability and willingness to perform as part of a team:* These traits are often harder to pick up in an interview situation by an inexperienced manager. Personality profiling can assist in identifying a person who has a healthy attitude and who is a team player.

Where recruitment of project resources is taking place the project leader is often called upon to draft **job descriptions**, which are typically assessed by the HR department for fit to role title and to determine pay-grade information. So, ensuring the suitable use of keywords is key. A project leader is leading and managing a team to deliver something of value to a customer, whereas a project coordinator is assisting the project manager in the maintenance of project information. Words must be used carefully; to this end it is best to review the industry **best practice**. For example, the International

Centre for Complex Project Management presents a competency standard aimed as complex project managers (at https://iccpm.com/wp-content/uploads/2018/09/CPM-Competency-Standard-V4.1.pdf). Capturing the job description with key competencies is best achieved by using a company standard proforma, an example of which is included in the online templates.

 Position Description

The PMI also offers a competency development framework that may assist in defining competencies and can also be of use when drafting **performance agreements** for the core project roles (e.g. project leader and project coordinator) (at www.pmi.org/pmbok-guide-standards/framework/pm-competency-development-3rd-edition).

A template to assist in pulling together performance development plans is included in the online templates. As a project leader, when onboarding the candidate, one of the first tasks is to agree the levels of performance and the contribution expected. These could include contribution to the baseline performance measures introduced in Chapter 18 "Project execution", Tables 18.1 and 18.2.

 Performance Agreement

In relation to interviewing candidates for roles in the project environment, preparation is key whether you are a project sponsor seeking an ethical, emotionally intelligent leader who can mange projects, or a project leader seeking a motivated, highly skilled communicator who can work with various stakeholders and collect and collate information as a project coordinator. Recruitment is also a transparent process internally, which includes the interview script, the interview scoring and the interview notes. For this reason, most organisations will have a proforma for defining the key interview questions up-front, the scoring of these questions and the recording of any other behavioural (non-verbal) observations that the interviewers noted at the interview. It also assists the interview team after the interview to go back to notes and make an informed, consensus-based decision on which of the (usually many) candidates is to be selected. Hiring into the organisation is an expensive endeavour—hiring the wrong candidate to the project can be disastrous. A skeleton interview preparation script is included in the online templates.

 Interview Question Script

And a more detailed project leader interview script is also provided.

 Project Manager Questions

19.9 Building project teams

One of the challenges project leaders often face in building a team is the lack of full-time involvement of team members. Specialists work on different stages of the project and spend much of their time and energy elsewhere. They are often members of multiple teams, with each team competing for their time and allegiance. Project expert David Frame (1995) points out that for many specialists, a specific project is an abstraction and consequently, their level of motivation suffers. Refer to "In Theory: Motivation models". Project leaders need to try to make the project team as real as possible to the participants by developing a unique team identity to which participants can become emotionally attached. Team meetings, the co-location of team members, team names and **team rituals** are common vehicles for achieving a sense of team identity. These approaches are unpacked further as follows.

■ *Effective use of meetings:* Periodic project team meetings provide an important forum for communicating project information. A less obvious function of project meetings is to help establish a concrete team identity. During project meetings, members see that they are not working alone. They are part of a larger project team, and project success depends on the collective efforts of all the team members. Timely gatherings of all the project participants help define team membership and reinforce a collective identity.

■ *Co-location of team members:* The most obvious way to make the project team real is to have members work together in a common space. This is not always possible in matrix environments where involvement is part time and members are working on other projects and activities. A worthwhile substitute for co-location is the creation of a project office (sometimes referred to as the *project room*). Such rooms act as the common meeting place and contain the most significant project documentation. Frequently, their walls are covered with Gantt charts, cost graphs and other outputs associated with project planning and control. These rooms serve as a tangible sign of project effort.

■ *Creation of project team identity:* By giving a team a name, the project team gains an identity and becomes much more tangible. Frequently, an associated team (or project) logo is also created. Again, the project leader should rely on the collective ingenuity of the team to come up with the appropriate name and logo. These symbols can then be printed on stationery, T-shirts, coffee mugs, etc. to help signify team membership and can also be used to embellish project communications.

■ *Get the team to build or do something together as a team early on:* Nothing reinforces a sense of a team more than working on something together. Holding a team BBQ, to which everyone brings a plate of food, can help to foster positive relations between team members in a relaxed manner.

■ *Team rituals:* Just as corporate rituals help establish the unique identity of a firm, symbolic actions at the project level can also contribute to a unique team subculture. For example, on one project, team members were given ties with stripes that corresponded to the number of milestones on the project. After reaching each milestone, members would gather and cut the next stripe off their ties to signify progress. Ralph Katz (2004) reports it was common practice for Digital Equipment's alpha chip design team to recognise people who found a bug in the design by giving them a phosphorescent toy cockroach. The bigger the bug that was discovered, the bigger the toy cockroach received. Such rituals help to set project work apart from mainstream operations and reinforce a special status.

IN THEORY | Motivation models

Hygiene and motivational factors (Frederick Herzberg)

According to Herzberg, the absence of hygiene factors causes dissatisfaction among employees in the workplace. To remove dissatisfaction in a work environment, these hygiene factors must be present; however, their presence does not ensure satisfaction entirely. Eliminating dissatisfaction is only one-half of the task (refer to Table 19.1). Herzberg often referred to hygiene factors as *KITA* factors, which is an acronym for *kick in the ass*—the process of providing incentives or threat of punishment to make someone do something. The other half would be to increase satisfaction (motivators) in the workplace.

Table 19.1 Hertzberg motivators (satisfaction) and hygiene factors

Motivators (satisfaction)	Hygiene factors	
Challenging work	1. Company policies	
Recognition for achievement	2. Supervision	
Responsibility	3. Relationship with boss	Order of importance
Opportunity (to do something meaningful)	4. Work conditions	
Involvement in decision-making	5. Salary	
Sense of importance (in the organisation)	6. Relationship with peers	

Based on this, there are four possible combinations:

1. *High Hygiene + High Motivation:* The ideal situation where employees are highly motivated and have few complaints.

2. *High Hygiene + Low Motivation:* Employees have few complaints but are not highly motivated. The job is viewed as a paycheck.

3. *Low Hygiene + High Motivation:* Employees are motivated but have a lot of complaints. A situation where the job is exciting and challenging but salaries and work conditions are not up to par.

4. *Low Hygiene + Low Motivation:* This is the worst situation, where employees are not motivated and have many complaints.

Intrinsic versus extrinsic motivation (Dan Pink)

Dan Pink defines autonomy as "the desire to lead your own life". He argues that giving employees autonomy is effective in the workplace. However, this runs contrary to traditional management practices. Pink presents two types of motivation, intrinsic and extrinsic.

1. Intrinsic motivation: Involves engaging in an activity because we find the activity itself rewarding. The rewards that they receive are secondary to the satisfaction of completing the activity. The intrinsic motivators Pink defines are:

   ■ Autonomy—the desire to lead your own life

   ■ Mastery—wanting to improve

   ■ Purpose—a cause bigger than yourself.

2. Extrinsic motivation focuses on the reward that you receive for completing an activity. The *carrot and stick* effect has numerous shortcomings, including that the:

   ■ carrot is the reward—when rewarded, a person will be motivated to behave that way in the future

   ■ stick is the punishment—when behaviour is punished, people are less likely to behave in that way in the future.

   Pink argues that intrinsic motivation is the key to great results, as extrinsic rewards will only take you so far. However, extrinsic rewards must be present—we want to be paid for our work! (Pink 2009). Take time to review Dan Pink's TED talk at: www.ted.com/talks/dan_pink_the_puzzle_of_motivation

Theory of needs (David McClelland)

McClelland argues that we all have three types of motivation:

■ The need for achievement, working on medium-complexity tasks with results based on effort

■ The need for affiliation, creating and maintaining social relationships

■ The need for power, where a high value is placed on discipline.

(Continues)

In Theory: Motivation models (*Continued*)

His research showed that 86 per cent of the population were dominant in all, two, or one of the motivational factors, and further to this that those holding top management positions had a high need for power and a low need for affiliation. He also observed that people with a high need for achievement are best given projects in which they can succeed through their own efforts—a project leader?

Theory X, Theory Y and Theory Z (Douglas McGregor)

Theory X managers tend to take a pessimistic view of their people and assume that they are naturally unmotivated and dislike work. As a result, an authoritarian management style is often applied. Managers think the team members need to be prompted, rewarded or punished to ensure they complete tasks.
This style of management assumes that workers:

- dislike their work

- avoid responsibility and need constant direction

- have to be controlled, forced and threatened to deliver work

- need to be supervised at every step

- have no incentive to work or no ambition, and therefore need to be enticed by rewards to achieve goals.

Theory Y managers have an optimistic, positive opinion of their people, and they use a decentralised, participative management style. This encourages a more collaborative, trust-based relationship between managers and their team members.
This style of management assumes that workers are:

- happy to work on their own initiative

- happy to be more involved in decision-making

- are self-motivated to complete their tasks

- enjoy taking ownership of their work

- seek and accept responsibility, and need little direction

- view work as fulfilling and challenging

- solve problems creatively and imaginatively.

Although our assumptions about what motivates our people will impact which of these two approaches we take, our choice can also be influenced by other factors such as:

- the organisational structure (many layers of management or flat)

- the type of work that employees do (repetitive or challenging)

- the skill level (novice to experienced).

It goes without saying which approach has the greater benefits for the organisation and the employees. The question we have to ask is: As a project leader, which approach should we be promoting?

Theory Z was added later by William Ouchi. Theory Z is about creating an environment that motivates employees through long-term employment, respect for the employee, individual responsibility and more informal managerial control.
Theory Z managers:

- work to be proactive, but do not overly micromanage

- try to build long-term relationships

- work to cultivate individual responsibility rather than assume its existence or lack of existence

- have more informal control over subordinates

- work to create more group collaboration (MindTools n.d.; Render 2009).

Source: Adapted from Mind Tools n.d., "Theory X and Theory Y", www.mindtools.com/pages/article/newLDR_74.htm, accessed February 2022; Pink D 2009, "The puzzle of motivation", TED Global, www.ted.com/talks/dan_pink_the_puzzle_of_motivation accessed February 2022; Render J 2019, "MacGregor's XY Theory and Ouchi's Theory Z", https://agile-mercurial.com/2019/06/28/macgregors-xy-theory-and-ouchis-theory-z/, accessed February 2022.

19.9.1 Creating a shared vision

Unlike project scope statements, which include specific costs, completion dates and performance requirements, the project **vision** involves fewer tangible aspects of project performance. It refers to an image that the project team (and project customer) share of how the project will look at completion, how they will work together and/or how customers will accept the project. At its simplest level, a shared vision is the answer to the question, "What do we want to create?" Visions come in a variety of shapes and forms; they can be captured in a slogan or in a symbol or can be written as a formal project vision statement.

What a vision *is* is not as important as what it *does*. A vision inspires members to give their best effort. Moreover, a shared vision unites professionals with different backgrounds and agendas behind a common aspiration. It helps motivate members to subordinate their individual agendas and do what is best for the project. As has been wisely observed, "In the presence of greatness, pettiness disappears". Visions also provide focus and help communicate fewer tangible priorities, helping members make appropriate judgement calls. Finally, a shared vision for a project fosters commitment to the long term and discourages expedient responses that collectively dilute the quality of the project.

Visions can be surprisingly simple. For example, the vision for a new car could be expressed as a *pocket rocket*. Compare this vision with the more traditional product description—*a sports car in the mid-price range*. The pocket rocket vision provides a much clearer picture of what the final product should be. Design engineers would immediately understand that the car will be both small and fast and that the car should be quick when pulling away, nimble in turns and very fast on straight sections. Obviously, many details would have to be worked out, but the vision would help establish a common framework for making decisions.

There appear to be four essential qualities of an effective vision (see Figure 19.8): First, its essential qualities must be able to be communicated—a vision is worthless if it only resides in someone's head! Second, visions must be challenging, but also realistic. For example, a task force directed at overhauling the curriculum for a university program in business at a university is likely to roll its eyes if the dean announces that their vision is to compete against the world-renowned Harvard Business School in the United States. Conversely, developing the best undergraduate business program in the state may be a realistic vision for that task force. Third, the project leader must believe in the vision— passion for the vision is an essential element of an effective vision. Finally, the vision should be a source of inspiration to others.

Once a project leader accepts the importance of building a shared vision, the next question is how to get a vision for a particular project. Project leaders don't *get visions!* They act as catalysts for the formation of a shared vision. In many cases, visions are inherent in the scope and objectives of the project. People get naturally excited about being the first ones to bring a new technology to the market or solve a problem that is threatening their organisation. Even with mundane projects, there are often ample opportunities for establishing a compelling vision. One way is to talk to various people involved in the project and find out early on what gets them excited about the project. For some, it may be doing a better job than on the last project, or the satisfaction seen in the eyes of customers when the project is over. Many visions evolve reactively in response to competition. For example, we expect that Apple has the vision to make a watch that delivers beyond a fitness tracking device to a device that predicts and monitors health, being able to detect strokes and heart attacks— this vision is prevalent in the media but is yet (as of 2022) to be made accurately functional in the device, having no blood sugar, body temperature or blood pressure monitoring capabilities.

Some experts advocate engaging in formal vision-building meetings. These meetings generally involve several steps, beginning with members identifying different aspects of the project and

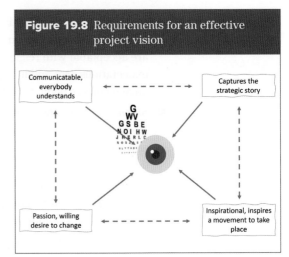

Figure 19.8 Requirements for an effective project vision

Communicatable, everybody understands

Captures the strategic story

Passion, willing desire to change

Inspirational, inspires a movement to take place

© 2022 Dr Neil Pearson

generating ideal scenarios for each aspect. For example, on a construction project the scenarios may include *no accidents, no lawsuits,* or *how we are going to spend our bonus for completing the project ahead of schedule.* The group reviews and chooses the scenarios that are most appealing and translates these into vision statements for the project. The next step is to identify strategies for achieving the vision statements. For example, if one of the vision statements is that there will be no lawsuits, members will identify how they will have to work with the owner and subcontractors to avoid litigation. Next, members volunteer to uphold each statement. The vision, strategies and the name of the responsible team member are published and distributed to relevant stakeholders.

In more cases than not, shared visions emerge informally. Project leaders collect information about what excites participants about the project. They test bits of their working vision in their conversations with team members, to gauge the level of excitement the early ideas elicit in others. To some extent they engage in basic market research. They seize opportunities to galvanise the team, such as by rejecting a disparaging remark by an executive that the project will never get done on time. Consensus in the beginning is not essential. What is essential is a core group of at least one-third of the project team that is genuinely committed to the vision. They will provide the critical mass to draw others on board. Once the language has been formulated for communicating the vision, then this statement needs to be a staple part of every working agenda and the project leader should be prepared to deliver a persuasive presentation-type speech at a moment's notice. When problems or disagreements emerge, all responses should be consistent with the vision.

Much has been written about visions and leadership. Critics argue that vision is a glorified substitute for shared goals. Others argue that it is one of the things that separates leaders from managers. The key is discovering what excites people about a project, being able to articulate this source of excitement in an appealing manner and protecting and nurturing this source of excitement throughout the duration of the project.

This text has previously introduced a few tools to assist in building the project vision statement; refer to Chapter 3 "Agile (Scrum) project management", section 3.5.1.

19.9.2 Tuckman and Jensen's five-stage team development model

Just as most infants develop in predictable ways during their first months of life, many experts argue that groups also tend to develop in a predictable manner. One of the most popular models used to explain this process was developed by Bruce Tuckman (1965). Although developed a while ago now, this model is still often used to explain team formation and development. It comprises five stages (see Figure 19.9) through which groups develop into effective teams. *Note:* The model originally contained only four stages, but the fifth—"Adjourning"—was added in 1977 jointly by Bruce Tuckman and Mary Ann Jensen.

- *Forming:* During this initial stage, members get acquainted with each other and understand the scope of the project. They begin to establish ground rules by trying to find out what behaviours are acceptable with respect to both the project (what role they will play, what performance expectations are) and interpersonal relations (who's really in charge). This stage is completed once members begin to think of themselves as being part of a group.

- *Storming:* As the name suggests, this stage is marked by a high degree of internal conflict. Members accept that they are part of a project group but resist the constraints that the project and group put on their individuality. There is conflict over who will control the group, how decisions will be made and to whom work is allocated. As these conflicts are resolved, the project leader's leadership becomes accepted, and the group moves to the next stage.

- *Norming:* The third stage is one in which close relationships develop and the group demonstrates cohesiveness. Feelings of camaraderie and shared responsibility for the project are heightened. The norming stage is complete when the group structure solidifies, and the group establishes a common set of expectations about how members should work together.

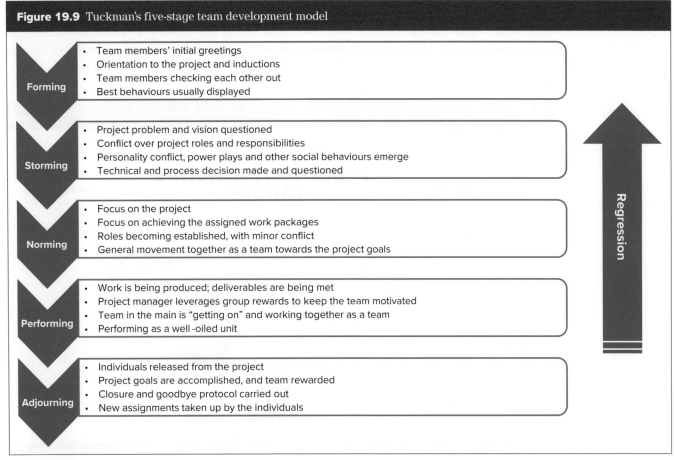

Figure 19.9 Tuckman's five-stage team development model

Forming
- Team members' initial greetings
- Orientation to the project and inductions
- Team members checking each other out
- Best behaviours usually displayed

Storming
- Project problem and vision questioned
- Conflict over project roles and responsibilities
- Personality conflict, power plays and other social behaviours emerge
- Technical and process decision made and questioned

Norming
- Focus on the project
- Focus on achieving the assigned work packages
- Roles becoming established, with minor conflict
- General movement together as a team towards the project goals

Performing
- Work is being produced; deliverables are being met
- Project manager leverages group rewards to keep the team motivated
- Team in the main is "getting on" and working together as a team
- Performing as a well-oiled unit

Adjourning
- Individuals released from the project
- Project goals are accomplished, and team rewarded
- Closure and goodbye protocol carried out
- New assignments taken up by the individuals

Regression

© 2022 Dr Neil Pearson

- *Performing:* The team's operating structure at this point is fully functional and accepted. The focus of group energy has moved from getting to know each other and how the group will work together to accomplishing the project goals. This for the project leader is the hardest state at which to maintain the team, having to apply their EQ at its peak.

- *Adjourning:* For conventional work groups, performing is the last stage of their development. However, for project teams, there is a completion stage: during this stage, the team prepares for its own disbandment. High performance is no longer a top priority. Instead, attention is devoted to wrapping up the project. Member responses will vary during this stage. Some members will be upbeat and will bask in the project team's accomplishments. Others may feel down over the loss of camaraderie and (potentially) loss of friendships they have gained with people during the project's life.

Tuckman's model has several implications for those working on project teams. The first is that the model provides a framework for the group to understand its own development. Project leaders often find it useful to share this model with their teams. It can help members accept the tensions of the "Storming" stage and direct their focus to moving towards the more productive stages. Another implication is that it stresses the importance of the "Norming" stage, which contributes significantly to the level of productivity experienced during the "Performing" stage.

It should be noted that teams can (and often do) regress to prior stages of the model. For example, when a new team lead is brought into the project team, the team may regress, albeit temporarily, into the "Forming" or "Storming" stages of the model. Project leaders must take an active role in shaping group norms that will contribute to ultimate project success. The project leader must be able to quickly identify unacceptable behaviours and intervene with corrective actions.

19.9.3 Drexler and Sibbet's team performance model

When teams come together, they have a predictable set of questions. If you can understand this progression as a project leader you can almost preempt the questions and assist the team move through the process. This progression is often represented as a *bouncing ball*, as illustrated in Figure 19.10.

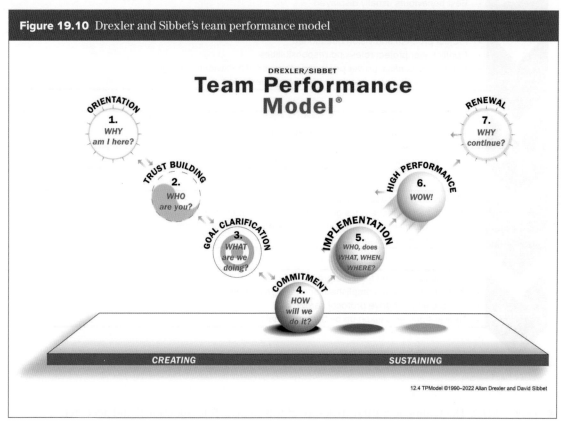

Figure 19.10 Drexler and Sibbet's team performance model

Source: https://www.thegrove.com/methodology/team-performance-model, accessed February 2022.

Working between the sky (freedom) and the ground (constraints that keep us grounded) gives the diagram on the left side (creating), comprising the following four stages.

1. *Orientation stage:* Why are they part of a group? If people don't get an answer to the Why, they leave the process.
2. *Trust-building stage:* Who are they going to work with? If people don't get an answer to the Who, they go back to the Why.
3. *Goal-clarification stage:* What the group is doing?
4. *Commitment stage:* How are they going to work together (in terms of, for example, staff, money, time, materials)?

The right-hand side of the model takes us back to freedom (a place we gravitate towards), which gives rise to the following considerations.

■ *Implementation stage:* the Who, What, When and Where of the implementation.

■ *High-performance stage:* the Wow.

■ *Renewal stage:* Why should we continue?

The model also has certain exit and/or regression points (much like Tuckman & Jensen). For example, if an individual cannot find answers to the orientation stage (and *Why am I here?*) they are likely to exit. Similarly in the trust-building stage, if the Who cannot be answered then it is likely the individual will go back to the Why. More details can be found at www.thegrove.com/methodology/team-performance-model

Tuckman and Jensen and Drexler and Sibbet offer insights into what we as project leaders must understand and provide information about to help the team build. The concern in a project environment is that teams need to build quickly and change focus from personal dynamics to work, as the project will almost immediately have to start accomplishing (work packages) and delivering (deliverables). This compression of time is where the emotionally intelligent project leader really displays their leadership skills.

19.9.4 Situational factors affecting team development

Experience and research indicate that high-performance project teams are much more likely to develop under the following conditions:

- A team size of 5 plus or minus 2 team members
- Members volunteer to serve on the project team
- Members serve on the project from beginning to end
- Members are assigned to the project full time
- Members are part of an organisational culture that fosters cooperation and trust
- Members report solely to the project leader
- All relevant functional areas are represented on the team
- The project involves a compelling objective
- Members are located within conversational distance of each other.

It is rare that a project leader is assigned a project that meets all these conditions. For example, many projects' requirements dictate the active involvement of more than 10 members and may consist of a complex set of interlocking teams comprising more than 100 professionals. In many organisations, functional managers or PMOs assign project members, with little input from the project leader. To optimise resource use, team member involvement may be part time and/or participants may move in and out of the project team on an *as-needed* basis. In many corporations a **not invented here (NIH)** culture exists that discourages collaboration across functional boundaries.

Team members often report to different managers and, in some cases, the project leader will have no direct input over team members' performance appraisals and advancement opportunities. Key functional areas may not be represented during the entire duration of the project but may only be involved in a sequential manner. Not all projects have a compelling objective. It can be hard to get members excited about mundane projects such as a simple product extension or a conventional apartment complex. Finally, team members are often scattered across different corporate offices and buildings or, in the case of a virtual project, across the entire globe. It is important for project leaders and team members therefore to recognise the situational constraints they are operating under, and to do the best they can within these constraints. It would be naïve to believe that every project team has the same potential to evolve into a high-performance team. Under less-than-ideal conditions, it may be a struggle just to meet project objectives. Ingenuity, discipline and sensitivity to team dynamics are therefore essential in maximising the performance of a project team.

19.9.5 Building high-performance project teams

Project leaders play a key role in developing high-performance project teams. They recruit members, conduct meetings, establish a team identity, create a common sense of purpose or a shared vision, manage a reward system that encourages teamwork, orchestrate decision-making, resolve conflicts that emerge within the team and rejuvenate the team when energy wanes (see Figure 19.11). Project leaders take advantage of situational factors that naturally contribute to team development, while improvising around those factors that inhibit team development. In doing so, they exhibit a highly interactive management style that exemplifies teamwork and, as discussed in the previous chapter, manage the interface between the team and the rest of the organisation.

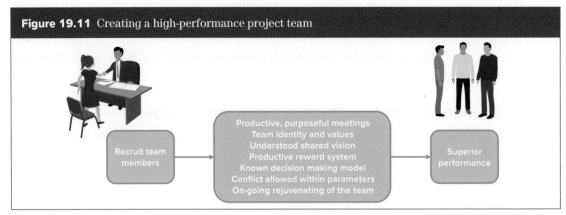

Figure 19.11 Creating a high-performance project team

Recruit team members

Productive, purposeful meetings
Team identity and values
Understood shared vision
Productive reward system
Known decision making model
Conflict allowed within parameters
On-going rejuvenating of the team

Superior performance

© 2022 Dr Neil Pearson

When building high-performance project teams, as with all factors in project management, we need to consider the integrative aspects of human resource management. The following are examples of questions a project leader ought to consider when building the team:

- Do I need to budget for **team-building** activities?
- What is the impact to the project schedule?
- What is the best way to reward the project team (both financial and non-financial)?
- What are the **early warning indicators (EWIs)** that the team is drifting?
- Are we communicating in an accepted manner?

19.9.6 Generational theory and project teams

Whether they represent *generational theory*, *multi-generational teams* or *age diversity*, workplaces today are often a rich melting pot of different cultures, ages and genders. The project leader needs to understand the dynamics of the project team from a personality perspective, and be able to consider many other varied dimensions. For example, when a younger, relatively inexperienced person is recruited into a highly experienced project team, how does this change team dynamics? Keeping an open mind and sense of positivity, coaching and mentoring can alleviate tensions—almost everyone we encounter at work can teach us something new or provide a different perspective.

Fresh ideas can invigorate a stale environment, and new tools and ways of communicating should be embraced. Try asking rhetorical questions to explore the potential of tools and skills that may, at first, seem alien to some project environments. For example, "How might social media technologies assist us in achieving or promoting the outcomes of the project?"

If the younger person will be supervising older team members, prepare the team to accept the person as the boss. Give the person the support they need; after all, it was your decision to employ that person in the role so you must have confidence in their ability. Your role as project leader is to achieve the project's success (and ultimately your own success). Consider putting into place suitable coaching and mentoring arrangements for anyone in the team who needs it, or establishing a whole-of-team mentoring arrangement, where everyone in the team has access to a mentor.

Younger supervisors or managers should also openly show respect for the wealth of knowledge and experience that older team members may have. Remember that older generations can be very adaptable and open to new ideas. Bringing in a new technology or theory may greatly assist the project, but a naively enthusiastic approach often fails. In this instance, it is better to make a case for change and provide examples showing where the technology has worked with other projects.

Understanding that some generations prefer face-to-face time as opposed to screen-time modes of communicating means that provision should be made for in-person communication, as well as email, tweets and instant messaging. Of course, whether face-to-face or electronic communication takes place, it is important to be considerate of what is being communicated, as well as when and to whom. Accept that meetings have a purpose and that meeting people and building relationships in business is usually a face-to-face activity (or a telephone call when communicating with more remotely located employees or stakeholders).

Intergenerational differences are frequently brought to the fore in workplaces. The current economic climate means there has been an increase in the number of mature-aged workers seeking to stay in or return to work. In specialist areas, personnel may be called back from retirement due to resource shortages. A good project leader must be aware of any generational differences, but also of cultural differences. For example, in the Middle East, the working week typically starts on a Sunday and ends on a Thursday (Friday being the Muslim holy day). In China, the way of business is *Guanxi*, meaning *relationships* or *connections*. Guanxi can best be described as a network of elaborate relationships that promote trust and cooperation. Establishing Guanxi in a sincere, supportive manner, based on mutual respect, is a fundamental aspect of Chinese culture and of doing business in China. In Japan, *Wa* (harmony), *Kao* (the notion of *face* and personal pride) and *Omoiyari* (empathy and loyalty) are encouraged in society, and are also carried through into the Japanese business culture. When using resources from other countries, make sure there is a general awareness throughout the project of any cultural needs and expectations that must be met. After all, it is a truly global environment that projects operate within today.

19.9.7 Orchestrating the decision-making process

Most project decisions do not require a formal meeting to be held to discuss alternatives and determine solutions. Instead, decisions are made in real time as part of the daily interaction patterns between project leaders, stakeholders and team members. For example, through a routine "How's it going?" question, a project leader discovers that a mechanical engineer is stuck trying to meet the performance criteria for a prototype he is responsible for building. The project leader and engineer go down the hallway to talk to the designers, explain the problem and ask what, if anything, can be done. The designers distinguish which criteria are essential and which ones they think can be compromised. The project leader then checks with the marketing group to make sure these modifications are acceptable. They agree with all but two of the modifications. The project leader goes back to the mechanical engineer and asks whether the proposed changes would help solve the problem. The engineer agrees. Before authorising the changes, the project leader calls the project sponsor, reviews the events and gets the sponsor to sign off on the changes. This is an example of how, by practising MWBA, project leaders can consult team members, solicit their ideas, determine optimum solutions, and create a sense of involvement that builds trust and commitment to decisions.

Projects can encounter problems that require the collective decision-making and wisdom of team members, as well as relevant stakeholders. Group decision-making should be used when it will improve the quality of important decisions. This is often the case with complex problems that require the input of a variety of different specialists. Group decision-making should also be used when strong commitment to the decision is needed, and there is a low probability of acceptance if only one person makes the decision. Participation is used to reduce resistance and secure support for the decision. Group decision-making would be used, for example, to deal with controversial problems that could have a major impact on project activities, or when trust is low within the project team. Some guidelines for managing group decision-making are provided below.

19.9.7.1 **Facilitating group decision-making**

Project leaders play a pivotal role in guiding the group decision-making process. They must remind themselves that their job is not to decide, but to facilitate discussion within the group so that the team reaches a consensus on the best possible solution. **Consensus** within this context does not mean that everyone supports the decision 100 per cent, but that they all agree on what the best solution is, under the circumstances. Facilitating group decision-making essentially involves four major steps. Each step is briefly described below, and suggestions are provided for how to manage the process.

1. *Problem identification:* The project leader needs to be careful not to state the problem in terms of choices (e.g. should we do X or Y?). Rather, the project leader should identify the underlying problem to which these alternatives, and probably others, are potential solutions. This allows group members to generate alternatives, not just choose among them. One useful way of defining problems is to consider the gap between where a project is (i.e. the present state) and where it should be (the desired state). For example, the project may be four days behind schedule, or it could be that the prototype weighs two kilograms more than the specifications. Whether the gap is small or large, the purpose is to eliminate it. The group must find one or more courses of action that will change the existing state into the desired one. If defensive posturing arises during the problem identification discussion, then it may become appropriate to postpone the problem-solving step, if possible. This allows for emotions to subside and members to gain a fresh perspective on the issues involved.

2. *Generating alternatives:* Once there is general agreement as to the nature of the problem(s), the next step is to generate alternative solutions. If the problem requires creativity, then an **idea shower** is commonly recommended: the team generates a list of possible solutions, writing these up on a flipchart or whiteboard, and runs through each suggestion one by one, as a collective. Before this takes place, the project leader would first ban criticism and would remind participants to be respectful of each other's ideas. Members would be encouraged to piggyback on others' ideas by extending them, or by combining ideas to form a new idea. The object is to create as many alternatives as possible, no matter how outlandish they may appear to be. Some project leaders report that for tough problems, they have found it beneficial to conduct such sessions away from the normal work environment; a change of scenery (to neutral ground) often appears to stimulate fresh creativity. Design thinking (incorporating **convergent** and **divergent thinking**) is also becoming a popular approach to generating alternatives. Refer to "In Theory: Design thinking".

IN THEORY : Design thinking

- There are various approaches that may be used to generate options and define solutions.

- One such approach is known as ***design thinking***. This approach:

  - encourages the use of product design concepts and techniques such as prototyping, learning from trying out ideas, divergent and convergent thinking and, most importantly, keeping a customer focus in mind

  - helps to uncover innovative options that may not have been identified when using more traditional approaches

  - is highly iterative as practitioners work through various stages, revisiting each stage as necessary to develop and deliver an outcome or product that will address the defined problem and meet the needs of customers.

  Refer to Figure 19.12.

Figure 19.12 Design thinking cycle

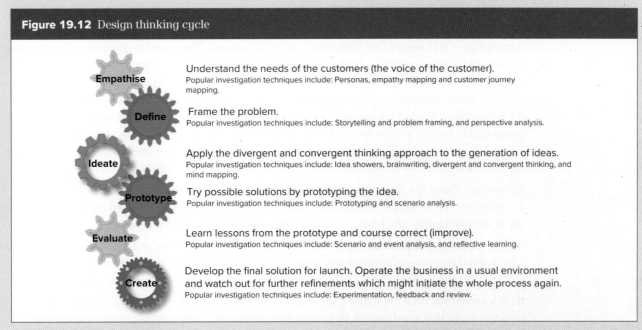

Empathise — Understand the needs of the customers (the voice of the customer).
Popular investigation techniques include: Personas, empathy mapping and customer journey mapping.

Define — Frame the problem.
Popular investigation techniques include: Storytelling and problem framing, and perspective analysis.

Ideate — Apply the divergent and convergent thinking approach to the generation of ideas.
Popular investigation techniques include: Idea showers, brainwriting, divergent and convergent thinking, and mind mapping.

Prototype — Try possible solutions by prototyping the idea.
Popular investigation techniques include: Prototyping and scenario analysis.

Evaluate — Learn lessons from the prototype and course correct (improve).
Popular investigation techniques include: Scenario and event analysis, and reflective learning.

Create — Develop the final solution for launch. Operate the business in a usual environment and watch out for further refinements which might initiate the whole process again.
Popular investigation techniques include: Experimentation, feedback and review.

© 2022 Dr Neil Pearson

A short explanation can also be found at: https://youtu.be/-ySx-S5FcCl

Within the "Ideate" stage, the cycle of divergent and convergent thinking is mentioned—this technique takes practice but, when mastered, can generate rich ideas (refer to Figure 19.13).

- The constant focus is on addressing the problem or opportunity to achieve a desired outcome.

- The needs and goals of customers are always kept in mind as this is a customer-centric approach.

- Participants work collaboratively and engage in both divergent and convergent thinking.

- Where possible, customers are involved in the design thinking process in order to support co-creation of products and value.

Figure 19.13 Divergent and convergent thinking

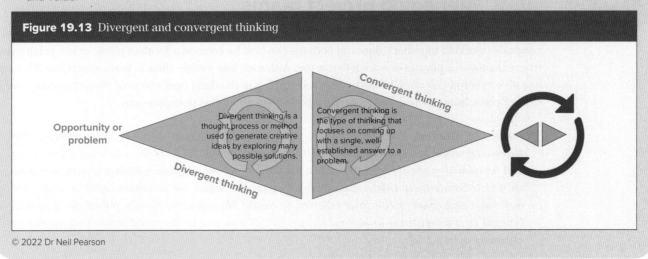

Opportunity or problem

Divergent thinking is a thought process or method used to generate creative ideas by exploring many possible solutions.

Divergent thinking

Convergent thinking is the type of thinking that focuses on coming up with a single, well-established answer to a problem.

Convergent thinking

© 2022 Dr Neil Pearson

3. *Reaching a decision:* The next step is to evaluate and assess the merits of alternative solutions. During this stage it is useful to have a set of criteria for evaluating the merits of different solutions. In many cases, the project leader can draw upon the priorities for the project and have the group assess each alternative in terms of its impact on cost, schedule and performance, as well as on the reduction of the problem gap. For example, if time is critical, then the solution that solves the problem as quickly as possible would be chosen.

During the course of the discussion, the project leader attempts to build consensus among the group. This can be a complicated process. Project leaders need to provide periodic summaries to help the group keep track of its progress. They must protect those members who represent the minority view and ensure that such views get a fair hearing. They need to guarantee that everyone has an opportunity to share opinions and no one individual or group dominates the conversation. (It may be useful to bring a two-minute timer along and use this to regulate speaking time.) When conflicts occur, managers need to apply some of the ideas and techniques that are discussed in the next section. Project leaders need to engage in consensus-testing to determine what points the group agrees on and what sources of contention remain. They need to be careful not to interpret silence as agreement and need to confirm agreement by asking direct questions. Ultimately, through thoughtful interaction, the team agrees on the solution that is best for the project.

Remember: There is a difference between **majority** and consensus in a team decision-making environment. For example, if a team of eight people decide to move forward on a matter but only six of the eight agree, the team could leave the room in one of two states:

a. If a majority decision-making ground rule was practised, then six people would leave the room singing the praises of the decision while the other two could be in a more negative state and may not openly support the decision (e.g. when asked about it outside the room).

b. If a consensus decision-making ground rule was practised, then the project leader would press home that even though there may have been some initial disagreements in the room, everybody has now agreed to support this decision to move forward in a positive manner. When asked outside the room on the decision made, everyone would equally and positively support the decision made.

4. *Follow-up:* Once the decision has been made and has been implemented, it is important for the team to find the time to evaluate its effectiveness. If the decision failed to provide the anticipated solution, then the reasons why this occurred should be explored and the lessons learned added to the collective memory bank of the project team for future reference.

19.10 : **Managing project teams**

The energy and drive of teams is captured in the term *synergy*, which is derived from the Greek word *sunergos* (working together). Synergy perhaps can best be seen on a football pitch, or in a relay team, where teammates play as one to defeat a foe. Although less visible than in team sports, positive and negative synergy can often be both observed and felt in the daily operations of project teams. Here is a description from one team member we interviewed about this phenomenon:

> *Instead of operating as one big team, we fractionalised into a series of subgroups. The marketing people stuck together, as well as the systems guys. A lot of time was wasted gossiping and complaining about each other. When the project started slipping behind schedule, everyone started covering their tracks and trying to pass the blame on to others. After a while, we avoided direct conversation and resorted to email. Management finally pulled the plug and brought in another team to salvage the project. It was one of the worst project management experiences in my life.*

This same individual (fortunately) was also able to recount a more positive project team experience they had had:

> *There was a contagious excitement within the team. Sure, we had our share of problems and setbacks, but we dealt with them straight on and, at times, were able to do the impossible. We all cared about the project and looked out for each other. At the same time, we challenged each other to do better. It was one of the most exciting times in my life.*

It is interesting to note that the following set of characteristics is commonly associated with **high-performing teams** that exhibit **positive synergy**.

- The team shares a sense of common purpose, and each member is willing to work towards achieving project objectives.
- The team identifies individual talents and expertise and uses them, depending on the project's needs at any given time. At these times, the team willingly accepts the influence and leadership of the members whose skills are relevant to the immediate task.
- Roles are balanced and shared to facilitate both the accomplishment of tasks and feelings of group cohesion and morale.
- The team exerts energy towards problem-solving rather than allowing itself to be drained by interpersonal issues or competitive struggles.
- Differences of opinion are encouraged and freely expressed.
- To encourage risk-taking and creativity, mistakes are treated as opportunities for learning rather than reasons for punishment.
- Members set high personal standards for performance and encourage each other to realise the objectives of the project.
- Members identify with the team and consider it an important source of both professional and personal growth.

High-performing teams become champions, create breakthrough products, exceed customer expectations, and get projects done ahead of schedule and under budget. They are bonded together by interdependency and a common goal or vision. They trust each other and exhibit a high level of collaboration.

Some project leaders carry out ad hoc surveys, seeking anonymous information from the team meetings on how they are feeling: this tool can be good when there are competing personality types operating in the team, where extroverts can monopolise the airspace, leaving the introverts thinking but having a feedback loop. The **team survey** can be useful to provide this feedback loop from your team. It could of course just be used to capture ideas for general team improvement. A skeleton survey template is included in the online resources.

 Team Survey

19.10.1 **Managing project reward systems**

Project leaders are responsible for managing the reward system that encourages team performance and *above and beyond* effort. One advantage they have is that often project work is inherently satisfying, whether it is manifested in an inspiring vision or a simple sense of accomplishment. Projects provide participants with a change of scenery, a chance to learn new skills and an opportunity to break out of their departmental cocoon.

Most project leaders we talk to advocate the use of group rewards. Because most project work is a collaborative effort, it only makes sense that the reward system would encourage teamwork. Recognising individual members, regardless of their accomplishments, can distract from team unity. Project work requires a high degree of interdependence, so it can become problematic to distinguish who truly deserves additional credit. Cash bonuses and incentives need to be linked to project priorities. It makes no sense to reward a team for completing its work early, if controlling cost was the number one priority. One of the limitations of lump-sum cash bonuses is that all too often they are consumed by the household budget to pay the dentist or mechanic. To have more value, rewards need to have lasting significance. Many companies convert cash into holiday rewards (sometimes with corresponding time off work). For example, one firm rewarded a project team for getting the job done ahead of schedule with a four-day, all-expenses-paid trip to Walt Disney World for the members' entire families. That holiday will not only be remembered for years, but it also acknowledged spouses and the team members' children who, in a sense, also contributed to the project's success. Similarly, other firms have been known to give members home computers and entertainment centres. Wise project leaders negotiate a **discretionary budget** so they can reward teams who surpass milestones with gift certificates (e.g. to popular restaurants) or tickets to sporting events. Impromptu pizza parties and barbecues are also positive ways to celebrate key accomplishments (poll your teams for ideas of what they would appreciate as rewards).

Sometimes, project leaders have to use negative reinforcement to motivate project performance. For example, Ritti (1982) recounts the story of one project leader who oversaw the construction of a new, state-of-the-art manufacturing plant. His project team was working with several different contracting firms. The project was slipping behind schedule, mostly because of a lack of cooperation among the different players. The project leader did not have direct authority over many of the key people, especially the contractors from other companies. He did, however, have the freedom to convene meetings at his convenience. So, the project leader instituted daily coordination meetings, which all principals involved in the project were required to attend at 6.30 am. The meetings continued for about two weeks until the project got back on schedule. At that time the project leader announced that the next 6.30 am meeting was cancelled (and no further meetings were needed as the project did not slip behind schedule again).

While project leaders tend to focus on group **rewards**, there are times when they need to reward individual performance. This is done not only to compensate extraordinary effort, but also to signal to the others what exemplary behaviour looks like. Some examples of rewards that can be used to motivate and recognise individual contributions include the following.

■ *Letters of commendation:* While project leaders may not have responsibility for their team members' performance appraisals, they can write letters commending their performance. These letters can be given directly to the individual and/or to the worker's supervisor(s) (and can be placed in their personnel files to document their positive contribution towards the project/the organisation).

■ *Public recognition for outstanding work:* Outstanding workers should be publicly recognised for their efforts. Some project leaders begin each status review meeting with a brief mention of those project workers who have exceeded their project goals.

■ *Job assignments:* Good project leaders recognise that, while they may not have much budgetary authority, they do have substantial control over *who does what, with whom, when* and *where*. Good work should be rewarded with desirable job assignments. Managers should be aware of team member preferences and, when appropriate and possible, seek to accommodate them.

■ *Flexibility:* If done judiciously, a degree of flexibility (being willing to make exceptions to rules) can be a powerful reward—for example, allowing members to work at home when a child is sick, or excusing a minor imprudence as a learning opportunity, can engender long-lasting loyalty.

We reiterate, however, that individual rewards should be used judiciously, and the primary emphasis should be on group incentives. Nothing can undermine the cohesiveness of a team more than members beginning to feel that others are getting special treatment (favouritism) or that they are being treated unfairly. Camaraderie and collaboration can quickly vanish, only to be replaced by bickering and obsessive preoccupation with group politics. Such distractions can absorb a tremendous amount of energy that otherwise would be directed towards completing the project. Individual rewards typically should be used only when everyone in the team recognises that a member is deserving of special recognition.

19.10.2 Managing conflict within the project

Disagreements and conflicts naturally emerge within a project team during the life of a project. Participants will disagree over priorities, allocation of resources, the quality of specific work, solutions to discovered problems and so forth. Some conflicts support the goals of the group and improve project performance. For example, two members may be locked in a debate over a design trade-off decision involving different features of a product. They argue that their preferred feature is what the primary customer truly wants. This disagreement may force them to talk to or get more information from the customer, with the result that they realise neither feature is highly valued and the customer wants something else. On the other hand, conflicts can also hinder group performance. Initial disagreements can escalate into heated arguments, with both parties storming out of the room and refusing to work together.

19.10.3 Encouraging functional (healthy) conflict

The demarcation between **functional** and **dysfunctional conflict** is neither clear nor precise. In one team, members may exchange a diatribe of four-letter expletives and eventually resolve their differences. Yet in another project team, such behaviour would create irreconcilable divisions, and would prohibit the parties from ever working together productively again. The distinguishing criterion is how the conflict affects project performance, not how individuals feel. Members can be upset and dissatisfied with the exchange, but as long as the disagreement furthers the objectives of the project, then the conflict is functional. Project leaders should recognise that conflict is an inevitable (and even a desirable) part of project work; the key is to encourage functional conflict and manage dysfunctional conflict.

A shared vision can transcend the incongruities of a project and establish a common purpose to channel debate in a constructive manner. Without shared goals, there is no common ground for working out differences. In the previous example involving the design trade-off decision, when both parties agreed that the primary goal was to satisfy the customer, there was a basis for more objectively resolving the dispute. Therefore, agreeing in advance which priority is most important—cost, schedule or scope—can help a project team decide which response is most appropriate.

Sometimes it's not the presence of conflict but the absence of conflict that is the problem. Sometimes, because of compressed time pressures, self-doubt and the desire to preserve team harmony, members are reluctant to voice objections. This hesitation robs the team of useful information that might lead to better solutions and the avoidance of critical mistakes. Project leaders need to encourage healthy dissent to improve problem-solving and innovation. They can demonstrate this process by asking tough questions and challenging the rationale behind recommendations. They can also orchestrate healthy conflict by bringing in people with different points of view to critical meetings. Project leaders can legitimise dissent within the team by designating someone to play the role of *devil's advocate* or by asking the group to take 15 minutes to come up with all the reasons the team should not pursue a course of action. Functional conflict plays a critical role in obtaining a deeper understanding of the issues and coming up with the best decisions possible.

One of the most important things project leaders can do is model an appropriate response when someone disagrees or challenges their ideas. They need to avoid acting defensively and instead encourage critical debate. They should exhibit effective listening skills and summarise the key issues before responding. They should check to see if others agree with the opposing point of view. Finally, project leaders should value and protect dissenters. Organisations tend to create too many *yes men* but the emperor needs to be told when he doesn't have any clothes on!

19.10.4 Managing dysfunctional conflict

Managing dysfunctional conflict is a much more challenging task than encouraging functional conflict. First, dysfunctional conflict is hard to identify. A manager might have two highly talented professionals who dislike each other, but in the heat of competition they produce excellent results.

Is this a pleasant situation? No. Is it functional? Yes, as long as it contributes to project performance. Conversely, sometimes functional conflict degenerates into dysfunctional conflict. This change occurs when technical disagreements evolve into irrational personality clashes or when failure to resolve an issue causes unnecessary delays in critical project work.

The second major difficulty project leaders face is that there is often no easy solution to dysfunctional conflict. Project leaders must decide among several different strategies to manage it. Following are five possibilities.

1. *Mediate the conflict:* The manager intervenes and tries to negotiate a resolution by using reasoning and persuasion, suggesting alternatives and the like. One of the keys is trying to find common ground. In some cases, the project leader can make the argument that the win–lose interchange has escalated to the point that it has become lose–lose for everyone and now is the time to make concessions.

2. *Arbitrate the conflict:* The manager imposes a solution to the conflict after listening to each party. The goal is not to decide who wins but to have the project win. In doing so, it is important to seek a solution that allows each party to save face; otherwise, the decision may provide only momentary relief.

3. *Control the conflict:* Reducing the intensity of the conflict by smoothing over differences or by interjecting humour is an effective strategy. If feelings are escalating, the manager can adjourn the interaction and hope cooler heads prevail the next day. If the conflict continues to escalate, project assignments may need to be rearranged (if possible) so the two parties don't have to work together.

4. *Accept it:* In some cases, the conflict will outlive the life of the project and, though a distraction, it is something the project leader must live with.

5. *Eliminate the conflict:* Sometimes the conflict has escalated to the point that it is no longer tolerable. In this case the manager removes the members involved from the project. If there is a clear *villain* then only that person should be removed. If, as is often the case, both parties are at fault, then it would be wise if possible, to remove both individuals from the project. Their removal would give a clear signal to the others on the team that this kind of behaviour is unacceptable.

Project leaders establish the foundation for functional conflict by establishing clear roles and responsibilities, developing common goals or a shared vision, and using group incentives that reward collaboration. Project leaders must be adroit at reading body language to identify unspoken disagreement. They also have to keep in touch with what is going on in a project to identify small problems that might escalate into big conflicts. Well-timed humour and redirecting the focus to what is best for the project can alleviate some of the interpersonal tensions that are likely to flare up on a project team.

The **nominal group technique (NGT)** process can be a useful tool when trying to gain team agreement on several issues. By applying the NGT process, the team can generate a prioritised list of issues that need to be addressed.

Many other instruments can be deployed to assist in diagnosing team conflict. Some commonly encountered ones include:

- *Team management systems (TMS):* A system of assessments and feedback instruments that support individuals, teams and organisations to effect positive and lasting change and achieve higher performance in the workplace (www.tmsoz.com).

- *Myers-Briggs type indicator:* A tool for helping to gain a basic understanding of personality type (www.myersbriggs.org).

- *Belbin team roles:* Reports that can help to select/develop high-performing teams, raise self-awareness and increase personal effectiveness (www.belbin.com).

- *Other tools:* Disc360 (www.everythingdisc.com)

- *The Colour Wheel* (https://inside-inspiration.com.au/factsheets/insights-discovery-personal-effectiveness-program-factsheet.pdf).

Using team performance and personality tools such as those listed above can help a project leader not only to identify personality types within their project team, but they can also help them to ascertain strategies that can be employed to foster positive team and individual interactions, even facilitating a quicker "storming" (Tuckman) stage by ensuring people know their traits, and know how to interact with people on the opposite side of the assessment. For example, TMS has a particular focus on team dynamics and provides suggestions for how people in conflict could work better with each other. TMS is debriefed on two levels: an individual level report, and a facilitated team debrief to all members of the team.

19.10.5 Rejuvenating the project team

Over the course of a long project, a team sometimes drifts off course and loses momentum. If this happens, the project leader needs to realign the team with the project's objectives and accelerate. There are both formal and informal ways of doing this. Informally, the project leader can institute new rituals like the toy cockroaches discussed earlier to reenergise a team. On one project that was experiencing rough going, the project leader stopped work and took the team bowling to relieve frustrations. Another option is to have the project sponsor give a *pep talk to the troops*. In other cases, a friendly challenge can reinvigorate a team. For example, one project sponsor offered to cook a five-course meal if the project got back on track and hit the next milestone.

Sometimes, more formal action needs to be taken: the project leader may recognise the need for a team-building session devoted to improving the work processes of the team. This meeting is particularly appropriate if they sense that the team is approaching a transition point in its development. The goal of such a session is to improve the project team's effectiveness through better management of project demands and group processes. It is an inward look by the team at its own performance, behaviour and culture for the purpose of eliminating dysfunctional behaviours and strengthening functional ones. The project team critiques its performance, analyses its way of doing things and attempts to develop strategies to improve its operation.

As important problems are discussed, alternatives for action are developed. The team-building session concludes by deciding on specific action steps for remedying problems and setting target dates for *who will do what, when*. These assignments can be reviewed at project status meetings or at a special follow-up session.

It has become fashionable to link team-building activities with outdoor experiences. The outdoor experience—whether it is hiking or canoeing, for example—places group members in a variety of physically challenging situations that must be mastered through teamwork, not individual effort. By having to work together to overcome difficult obstacles, team members are supposed to experience increased self-confidence, more respect for another's capabilities and a greater commitment to teamwork. No empirical data is available to support such exotic endeavours, other than the enthusiastic support of the participants. Such activities are likely to provide an intense common experience that may accelerate the social development of the team. Such an investment of time and money communicates the importance of teamwork and is considered by some as a perk of being on the project. At the same time, unless the lessons from these experiences can be immediately transferred to actual project work, their significance is likely to vanish.

19.10.6 Conducting project meetings

The first project **kick-off meeting** is critical to the early functioning of the project team. According to one veteran project leader:

> *The first team meeting sets the tone for how the team will work together. If it is disorganised, or becomes bogged down with little sense of closure, then this can often become a self-fulfilling prophecy for subsequent group work. On the other hand, if it is crisply run, focusing on real issues and concerns in an honest and straightforward manner, members come away excited about being part of the project team.*

There are typically three objectives that project leaders try to achieve during the first meeting of the project team. The first is to provide an overview of the project, including the scope and objectives, the general schedule, as well as the method and procedures. The second is to begin to address some of the interpersonal concerns captured in the team development model: Who are the other team members? How will I fit in? Will I be able to work with these people? The third and most important objective is to begin to model how the team is going to work together to complete the project. The project leader must recognise that first impressions are important; their behaviour will be carefully monitored and interpreted by team members. This meeting should serve as an exemplary role model for subsequent meetings and reflect the leader's style.

The meeting itself comes in a variety of shapes and forms. It is not uncommon in major projects for the kick-off meeting to involve one or two days, often at a remote site, away from interruptions. This retreat provides sufficient time for preliminary introductions, beginning to establish ground rules and establishing relationships. One advantage of offsite kick-off meetings is that they provide ample opportunity for informal interaction among members during breaks, meals and evening activities; such informal interactions are critical to forming positive working relationships. However, many organisations either do not have the luxury of holding elaborate retreats or the scope of the project and the level of involvement required by different participants does not warrant such an investment of time. In these cases, the key operating principle should be KISS (*Keep it simple, stupid!*—a design principle coined within the US Navy in 1960). Too often, when constrained by time, project leaders try to accomplish too much during the first meeting, and in doing so, issues do not get fully resolved and members come away with an information headache. The primary goal is to run a productive meeting, and objectives should be realistic given the time available. If the meeting is only one hour, then the project leader should simply review the scope of the project, discuss how the team was formed and provide an opportunity for members to introduce themselves to the team.

19.10.6.1 Establishing ground rules

Whether as part of an elaborate first meeting or during follow-up meetings, the project leader must quickly begin to establish operational ground rules for how the team will work together. These ground rules involve not only organisational and procedural issues, but also normative issues on how the team will interact with each other. Although specific procedures will vary across organisations and projects, some of the major issues that will need to be addressed include the following.

19.10.6.2 Planning decisions

1. How will the Project Plan be developed?
2. What tools will be used to support the project?
3. Will a specific project management software package be used? If so, which one?
4. Who will enter the planning information?
5. What are the specific roles and responsibilities of all the participants?
6. Who needs to be informed of decisions? How will they be kept informed?
7. What is the relative importance of cost, time and performance?
8. What are the deliverables of the project-planning process?
9. What format is appropriate for each deliverable?
10. Who will approve and sign off at the completion of each deliverable?
11. Who receives each deliverable?

19.10.6.3 Tracking decisions

1. How will progress be assessed?
2. At what level of detail will the project be tracked?

3. How will team members get data from each other?

4. How often will they get these data?

5. Who will generate and distribute reports?

6. Who needs to be kept informed about project progress, and how will they be informed?

7. What content/format is appropriate for each audience?

8. Meetings:
   - Where will meetings be located?
   - What kind of meetings will be held?
   - Who will run the meetings?
   - How will agendas be produced?
   - How will information be recorded?

19.10.6.4 Managing variations decisions

1. How will variations be instituted?

2. Who will have approval authority?

3. How will variations be evaluated?

19.10.6.5 Relationship decisions

1. What department or organisations will the team need to interact with during the project?

2. What are the roles and responsibilities of each organisation (reviewer, approver, creator, user)?

3. How will all involved parties be kept informed of deliverables, schedule dates, expectations, etc.?

4. How will the team members communicate among themselves?

5. What information will and won't be exchanged?

Checklists like these are only a guide; items should be added or deleted as needed. Many of these procedures will have already been established by precedent and will only have to be briefly reviewed. For example, Microsoft Project or Oracle Primavera may be the standard software tool for planning and tracking. Likewise, a specific firm is likely to have an established format for reporting status information. How to deal with other issues will have to be determined by the project team. When appropriate, the project leader should actively solicit input from the project team members and draw upon their experience and preferred work habits. This process also contributes to their buying into the operational decisions. Decisions should be recorded and circulated to all members.

During the course of establishing these operational procedures, the project leader, through word and deed, should begin working with members to establish the norms for team interaction. Below are examples of some norms that researchers have found to be associated with high-performance teams.

- Confidentiality is maintained; no information is shared outside the team unless all agree to it.
- It is acceptable to be in trouble, but it is not acceptable to surprise others. Tell others immediately when deadlines or milestones will not be reached.
- There is zero tolerance for bullying a way through a problem or an issue.
- Agree to disagree, but when a decision has been made, regardless of personal feelings, move forward in consensus.
- Respect outsiders, and do not flaunt one's position on the project team.
- Hard work does not get in the way of having fun.

One way of making these norms more tangible is by creating a **team charter** that goes beyond the scope statement of the project and states in explicit terms the norms and values of the team. This charter should be a collaborative effort on the part of the core team. Project leaders can lead by proposing certain tenets, but they need to be open to suggestions from the team. Once there is general agreement to the rules of conduct, each member signs the final document to symbolise commitment to the principles it contains. Unfortunately, in some cases, charters become meaningless because the charter is signed and filed away, never to be discussed again. To have a lasting effect, the charter must be a legitimate part of the project-monitoring system. Just as the team reviews progress towards project objectives, the team assesses the extent to which members are adhering to the principles in the charter.

Project leaders play a major role in establishing team norms through personal example. If they freely admit mistakes and share what they have learned from the mistakes, other team members will begin to do the same. At the same time, project leaders need to intervene when they believe such norms are being violated. They should talk to offenders privately and clearly state their expectations. The amazing thing about groups is that once a group is cohesive, with well-established norms, the members will often police themselves. For example, one project leader confided that his team had a practice of having a small beanbag present at every meeting. If any one member felt that a colleague was exaggerating or being dishonest, they were obliged to toss the beanbag towards the feet of the speaker!

A common activity at the kick-off meeting is to agree and sign up to the team charter; this is a popular activity in Agile (Scrum) projects as Chapter 3 "Agile (Scrum) project management" indicated (Figure 19.14).

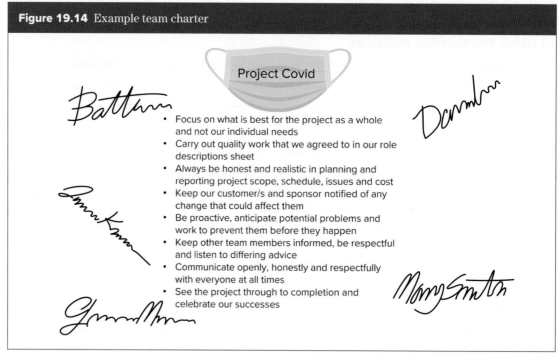

Figure 19.14 Example team charter

Project Covid

- Focus on what is best for the project as a whole and not our individual needs
- Carry out quality work that we agreed to in our role descriptions sheet
- Always be honest and realistic in planning and reporting project scope, schedule, issues and cost
- Keep our customer/s and sponsor notified of any change that could affect them
- Be proactive, anticipate potential problems and work to prevent them before they happen
- Keep other team members informed, be respectful and listen to differing advice
- Communicate openly, honestly and respectfully with everyone at all times
- See the project through to completion and celebrate our successes

© 2022 Dr Neil Pearson

19.10.7 Managing subsequent project meetings

The project kick-off meeting is one of several kinds of meetings required to complete a project. Other meetings include status report meetings, problem-solving meetings and audit meetings. Issues unique to these meetings will be discussed in subsequent chapters. For now, here are some general guidelines for people chairing meetings.

1. Start meetings on time—regardless of whether everyone is present.
2. Prepare and distribute an agenda before the meeting.
3. Identify an adjournment time.
4. Periodically take time to review how effective previous meetings have been.

5. Solicit recommendations and implement changes.

6. Assign good record keeping.

7. Review the agenda before beginning, and tentatively allocate time for each item.

8. Prioritise issues so that adjustments can be made given time constraints.

9. Encourage active participation of all members by asking questions instead of making statements.

10. Summarise decisions and review assignments for the next meeting.

11. Prepare and distribute a summary of the meeting to appropriate people.

12. Recognise accomplishments and positive behaviour.

Tracking the multitude of meetings that are typical for a project action can be facilitated using a tracking spreadsheet (e.g. Table 19.2). In practice, the action-tracking log would be displayed in the room (via a projector) and so it can also be shared via a videoconferencing system with project team members who are remotely located. This would enable all meeting participants to see the actions, who they were assigned to, and their current status in a live format, as the meeting progressed. Once the meeting had concluded, the spreadsheet could be filtered (by meeting date and status) and the resulting contents cut and pasted into an email and sent out to all attendees. This active form of meeting action tracking ensures there is complete visibility and accountability for achieving actions, and that actions are immediate (there are no formal minutes to write and approve).

Table 19.2 Action tracking

Meeting action tracker							
Meeting date	Meeting name	Action ref. #	Raised BY	Action ON	Due date	Actions to be taken	Status (Open/Closed)

© 2022 Dr Neil Pearson

 Action Tracker

A useful technique, available via the Scrum framework, is the *sprint retrospective* (refer to Chapter 3 "Agile (Scrum) project management"). This is where the previous reporting period is reviewed, and a focused discussion takes place based on the following questions:

1. What worked well?

2. What didn't work well?

3. What could have been done better?

4. What lessons learned were identified?

The purpose of this review is to ensure that useful information is shared and that channels of communication remain open between the project team and the project leader in a process of continual learning or continuous improvement. Meetings are often considered as anathema to productivity, but this does not have to be the case. The most common complaint is that meetings last too long. Establishing an agenda and adjournment time therefore helps participants to budget their discussion time and provides a basis for expediting proceedings. Record keeping can be an unwelcome, tedious task. Using software tools to record decisions and information in real time can facilitate the communication process. Careful preparation and consistent application of these guidelines can make meetings a vital part of projects.

19.10.8 Managing virtual project teams

Building a high-performance project team from a mixture of part-time and full-time members can be a challenging task. This is exacerbated when team members work offsite and cannot engage in face-to-face interactions. Such would be the case for a **virtual project team** in which the team members are geographically situated so that they may seldom, if ever, meet face to face as a team. For example, when one of the authors (Pearson) was project managing a large back-office consolidation of ICT systems at Oracle Corporation in the United States, he was in regular meetings with virtual team members in the United Kingdom, parts of Europe and in Australia. Can you imagine the logistics of organising an all-hands meeting with multiple time-zone differences, cultures and availabilities?

When team members are spread across different time zones and continents, opportunities for direct communication become constrained. Electronic communication, such as videoconferencing, email and teleconferencing, takes on more importance in virtual projects because this is the primary means of communication. Two of the biggest challenges involved in managing a virtual project team are developing trust and developing effective patterns of communication. Unlike when working as a traditional team, where members can see whether someone has done what they say they have done, virtual team members often have to depend on the word of distant members. At the same time, it can be difficult to trust someone whom you may have met only once or twice, or maybe not at all. Now, of course, through Skype, Zoom and other electronic communication mediums, people can see each other and read the non-verbals—for example, physical actions and voice tones. Geographic separation prohibits informal social interactions, which are often important in building camaraderie among team members. As one virtual team member complained, "You can't have a beer together over the internet!".

So how can a project leader facilitate the development of trust within a virtual team? If it is impossible to hold a face-to-face meeting at the beginning stage of team formation, a manager will need to orchestrate an exchange of social information (i.e. who everyone is and background information about each person) during the initial virtual interchange. They also need to set clear roles for each team member. Ideally, specific tasks should be assigned to each member so everyone can make an immediate contribution to the project. Trust within projects that necessitate a lot of virtual interaction grows by fostering team member reliability, consistency and responsiveness. The project leader must consistently display enthusiasm and an action orientation in all messages; this spirit will then hopefully spread to other team members.

The second major challenge for managing a virtual project team is to establish effective patterns of communication. Emails and physical documents are great for communicating hard facts—but not the feelings that may lie behind these facts; nor do they allow for real-time communication. Conference calls and project chat rooms can help, but they also have their limitations. Videoconferencing is a significant improvement over non-visual electronic forms of communication. With the explosion of social media tools such as Skype, Zoom, GoToMeeting, Microsoft Teams and others, this has become far more accessible to organisations of all sizes. The maxim is match the technology to the communication need. Following are some guidelines developed by 3M for use on its distributed projects.

- *When to email:* To distribute important information and news in a one-to-one or one-to-many frame of reference.

- *When to use electronic team boards (such as Yammer and Trello):* To encourage discussion and flesh out diversity of opinion on issues.

- *When to videoconference:* When you need to see each other's faces and expressions. This is important during the early stage of a project, when you are building relationships and developing a common understanding of what needs to be done. Also use when working on critical decisions and/or contentious issues. Remember: 80 per cent of the conversation is via non-verbal cues (refer to Chapter 15 "Project information and communications management").

- *When to use conference calls:* When people in different locations are working with common documents, presentations, sketches and models. Use for status report meetings and to sustain social camaraderie.

- *When to fly:* To build or repair trust. Use the travel budget to get all key players together early on to instil commitment to the goals of the project and engage in team-building activities.

Even with the best communication system available, managers have to overcome the problem of time zone differences, cultural nuances and finding a convenient time for people to conference. The tips below can help to alleviate some communication problems and enhance the performance of virtual teams.

- *Keep team members informed about how the overall project is going:* Develop a central access point to provide members with updated project schedules. Team members need to know where they fit into the big picture.

- *Don't let team members vanish:* Virtual teams often experience problems when trying to get in touch with each other. Use internet-based scheduling software to share project and project team members' calendars. Call team members regularly and make some of these calls social, not work related.

- *Establish a code of conduct to avoid delays:* Team members need to agree not only on what, when and how information will be shared, but also on how and when they will respond to it. Develop a priority system to distinguish messages that require immediate response from those with longer time frames.

- *Establish clear norms and protocols for surfacing assumptions and conflicts:* Because most communication is non-visual, project leaders cannot watch body language and facial expressions to develop a sense of what is going on. They need to probe deeper when communicating, to encourage members to explain their viewpoints, actions and concerns more clearly. They must double-check comprehension.

- *Share the pain:* Do not require everyone to conform to your time zone and preferences. Rotate meeting times so that all team members have a turn working according to their clock.

To some extent, managing a virtual project team is no different from managing a regular project team. The key is working within the constraints of the situation to develop effective ways for team members to interact and combine their talents to complete the project. There are many tools available to assist the project leader in a virtual environment; some of these are captured in Table 19.3.

Table 19.3 Virtual team management tools*

Category	Purpose	Tool
Conferencing	To facilitate voice, video and screen-sharing (of a computer screen) across multiple parties.	www.webex.com www.gotomeeting.com www.gotowebinar.com www.gototraining.com www.skype.com www.eztalks.com www.zoom.com
Stakeholder management	To manage and share stakeholder information. These tools come from a customer relationship management (CRM) background but in recent times have been applied to manage stakeholders in a project environment.	www.salesforce.com/ www.zoho.com www.vtiger.com/crm/
Team information-sharing	These tools can be used to share information and provide social media-style tools for team communications. Some of these tools offer a private environment, which general social media tools do not.	www.atlassian.com/software/confluence/ www.yammer.com www.confluence.com www.trello.com Google apps for business Microsoft teams www.dropbox.com www.box.net
Cloud-based project management environments	Useful tools that go beyond traditional project scheduling, to supplement the scheduling of activities to project team members.	www.zoho.com/projects/ www.liquidplanner.com http://gantter.com www.aconex.com www.basecamp.com
Social media tools	Everyday social media tools that can be leveraged within the project environment.	www.twitter.com www.facebook.com Google Hangouts https://slack.com
Virtual whiteboard and workspaces	Great for workshops, idea showers or just group engagement.	https://miro.com/index/ www.mural.co/features https://lucidspark.com/product

The authors do not recommend any of these tools per se; always do your research based on your project's requirements.

19.11 : Disbanding project teams

Saying goodbye at the end of a project for some team members can be a life-changing event. Over the life cycle of a project, team members often acquire new skills and abilities that make them more employable and more suited to other roles in, or beyond, the organisation. As the project moves towards making its final deliverables, progressively more and more team members will be leaving the project. This progressive loss of team members will be noticed by those remaining in the team and will act as a stark reminder that they too will have to leave the project soon. This may affect the morale of the remaining team, and the project leader must be able to identify this and step in to raise team spirits and keep the spirit of the project alive through to final closure. Working relationships will have been made, trust gained and a community will have been built, so the project leader must work diligently with individuals to manage their release from the project in a controlled manner. When recruiting team members, a good, integrative project leader will do the following.

1. Establish an approximate time frame for when the person is to be released from the project.

2. Establish the conditions of the release; for example, if the person was contracted then the contract will be terminated according to the terms and conditions of the contract. If the person was internally sourced, they may be going back to their substantive position back in the business (this could potentially mean a drop in pay, which the HR department may need to coach them to prepare for).

3. Carry out the required performance reviews, as required by the organisation's HR department and according to company policy. This may include end-of-project/contract bonuses or other arrangements.

4. Carry out the required exit interviews, according to the HR department and company policies.

5. Thank the team member for their contributions to the team.

6. Celebrate the successes of the team by holding a closure party to show the project leader, sponsor and organisation's gratitude for individual and team commitments in having completed the project successfully.

Other considerations will include ensuring the core project team is present to be able to participate in the formal project closure meeting and in the post-implementation review. Both the project and the business will want to capture lessons learned, for example.

Remember: Just as Tuckman and Jensen observed (refer to section 19.9.2), "Adjournment" is recognised as a stage in the team development model. For a successful team, "Adjournment" will be a positive experience; however, for individual team members, there can be a sense of loss (almost a time of mourning) as farewells are said, and a whole new engagement has to be found.

19.12 : Servant leadership

The final section of this chapter takes the reader back to Chapter 3 "Agile (Scrum) project management", where the role of Scrum master was discussed in detail. Scrum (and its Agile variants) promote the use of servant leadership as the preferred style for managing the Scrum team. Robert K Greenleaf formalised servant leadership into an approach that can be applied in any team environment:

> *The servant-leader is servant first... It begins with the natural feeling that one wants to serve, to serve first. Then conscious choice brings one to aspire to lead. That person is sharply different from the person who is a leader first, perhaps because of the need to assuage an unusual power drive or to acquire material possessions* (Greenleaf 1970).

The underlying principle therefore is that a servant leader leads by serving. In the case of Scrum, the Scrum master is the servant leader, among their other roles. The servant leader promotes social competency skills to elicit the best attributes from the development team, product owner and others around them. Some of the key traits of a servant leader would include the following.

■ *Listening and understanding:* If a Scrum master (or traditional project leader) takes the time to listen attentively to a person who is explaining a problem or issue they have encountered in a project, they are more likely to be able to help develop solutions. When in "listening mode", a Scrum master (or traditional project leader) is more easily able to gain insights into what the problem/situation is and is likely to provide advice based on what works. They are less likely to go into a "directing" mode and therefore hopefully pursue a coaching mode instead, from which the individual team member can learn.

■ *Language and imagination:* "Nothing is meaningful until it is related to the hearer's own experience". Communicating needs to be just enough to help the person make the leap from hearing to learning from experience.

■ *Withdrawal:* This means finding one's optimum by learning when to "retreat" (even if only for a moment), in order to reorient oneself. Withdrawal considers how to best make use of scarce resources and conserve energy, to deal with emergencies that will occur from time to time: "The servant-as-leader must constantly ask: *How can I use myself to serve best?*"

■ *Acceptance and empathy:* "The servant as leader always empathizes, always accepts the person but sometimes refuses to accept some of the person's effort or performance as good enough".

■ *Know the unknowable:* Beyond conscious rationality, beyond academic intelligence, the servant leader needs to "have a sense for the unknowable and be able to foresee the unforeseeable".

■ *Foresight:* This is the central ethic of leadership—"Prescience, or foresight, is a better than average guess about what is going to happen when in the future". It is the information gap between what we know (reports of information) and what may happen in the future.

■ *Awareness and perception:* This means picking up on the wider "sensory experience" of the environment—the modern concept of being in the moment and being fully aware of one's surroundings.

■ *Persuasion:* Whether attempting to persuade a group or an individual, persuasion must be "gentle but clear and persistent persuasion" which does not exert compliance through position power.

■ *One action at a time:* This is often the way that great things are achieved.

■ *Conceptualising:* Whether to a group or an individual, the servant leader needs to conceptualise and communicate thoughts and feelings in manner that makes them accessible to others (Greenleaf 1970).

The elements above have been adapted from Greenleaf's original text, to try to communicate the subtleties of how a servant leader behaves. For a traditional project leader, these can be hard to grasp and even harder to apply—how can one really *serve and lead* a project team? The PMI's *Agile Practice Guide* (PMI 2017b, p. 35) talks about a shift from "managing coordination" to "facilitating coordination". Facilitators encourage participation, shared understanding, shared responsibility (as it's the team that brings the project over the line, not a single person), collaboration and communication (and the removal of bottlenecks or impediments).

The Project Times promotes Greenleaf's thinking and has managed to illustrate the essence of servant leadership (see www.projecttimes.com/articles/the-art-and-science-of-servant-leader-in-agile-scrum-world/). The author (Pearson) has tried to recreate this state of "zen" between the key roles in Figure 19.15.

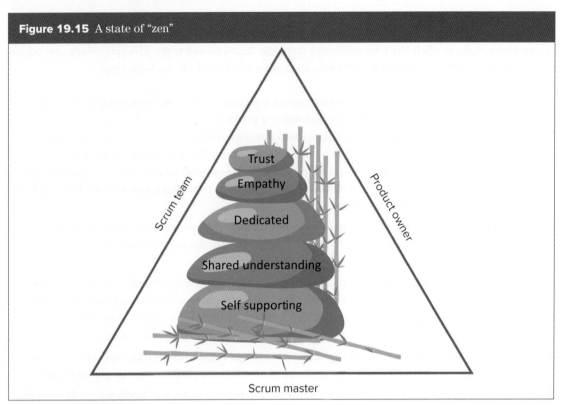

Figure 19.15 A state of "zen"

© 2022 Dr Neil Pearson

The trick for the Scrum master is to keep themselves, the product owner and Scrum team equally balanced and in tune, creating almost a state of "zen" between the key roles. So, what can the Scrum master do in practice?

- Promote Scrum practices across the product owner, development team and those who interact with the Scrum master.
- Assist the Scrum team by removing impediments and serving the team so that it can focus on delivering the sprint goal.
- Protect the team from outside interruptions (business) and distractions from inside the team.
- Coach the product owner in their vital role of supplying the prioritised list of stories from the business.
- Ensure team members don't overcommit. Overtime is not part of the Scrum brief, and the sprint velocity informs the capability of the development team.
- Assist the team to achieve the sprint goal—serving the team by ensuring it has the necessary environment, tools and systems.
- Use insight and experience to ensure potential future issues are avoided, or at least minimised.
- Promote a positive culture during tough times, which is commensurate with the culture in the good times.
- Listen, observe and seek *inner direction* when coaching the team to work in an optimal way.

Although the servant leader qualities have been applied to the Scrum master's role, the principles are equally as relevant for other styles of leadership—for example, for a traditional project leader:

- Listen as well as direct, remembering that communication is a two-way interaction.
- Take an interest in the people who make up the project team; avoid treating them as disposable resources.

■ Employ the power of persuasion to keep the team productive and the sponsor (and other stakeholders) committed.

■ Apply the trust equation (e.g. https://trustedadvisor.com/why-trust-matters/understanding-trust/understanding-the-trust-equation) and actively reduce any self-interested approach.

■ Recognise the contributions of the project team: say "thank you" and continue the positive motivation of the team.

Interest is currently building in applying the subtleties of servant leadership not only within Scrum projects but also in traditional project leader-led multi-generational, multi-cultural, multi-country teams. There is no better time to be reading about the servant-leadership approach than now and to consider implementing it—one step at a time, of course.

Summary

The chapter has considered several *softer* topics in relation to the project leader, including the following.

■ A cross-section of skills: These are the skills that a modern project leader must have to be considered well-rounded and capable of working in a business environment. Numerous skills have been considered under Pearson's concept of the multifaceted project leader (refer to Figure 19.1).

■ The ethical project leader: In today's fast-paced, high-pressure environments, a project leader must remain ethical and moral in all their dealings, no matter how pressured they may be. Professional project management organisations require member project leaders to demonstrate ethical behaviour and strong personal integrity.

■ Trust and the project leader: "Trust withers through neglect." This is particularly true under conditions of rapid change and uncertainty that naturally engender doubt, suspicion and even momentary bouts of paranoia. Project leaders must maintain frequent contact with key stakeholders to keep abreast of developments, assuage concerns, engage in reality testing and focus attention on the project. Frequent face-to-face interactions reaffirm mutual respect and trust in each other.

This chapter also unpacked the stages of sourcing, developing, managing and disbanding project teams. Discussions encompassed the following.

■ Selecting the best project sponsor for the project (and not basing selection on the politics of the business) and where the project leader has the trust and openness of the business to question any pre-allocated project sponsors.

■ Recruiting the project leader and the project team: What to look for, including current industry demands of an organisational cultural fit; strong communication skills; flexibility; and multi-skilled, experienced employees.

■ Developing the project team, including the consideration of roles and responsibilities and the use of the RASCI Matrix to resolve conflict around role and responsibility assignment.

■ The Tuckman and Jensen team development model: How the project leader should be able to identify which stage the team is at within this model and how they can resolve and move forward from issues with the team. Additionally, the Drexler and Sibbet team performance model, where individuals and team seek answers to critical questions, without answer they may exit or reverse back a stage and question again (refer to Figure 19.10).

■ How maintaining a team performance and reward system is important to a project that delivers consistently: The project leader must build considerations into all aspects of the project, from budgets to schedules, to ensure time is allowed for positive team building.

■ Disbanding a team: When a team disbands, individual and team considerations need to be managed by the project leader. These should not be overlooked. Tuckman and Jensen's "Adjourning" stage within their team development model reflects this stage of the project.

The final section of the chapter reviewed the servant leadership approach to the management of a team. Although primarily applied to Scrum (Agile and their variants) approaches to project management, there is a lot that a modern project leader can learn from servant leadership and can apply in a traditional project environment.

Project leaders often work under less-than-ideal conditions to develop a cohesive team that is committed to working together and completing the project to the best of their abilities. They must recruit personnel from other departments and manage this temporary involvement of team members. They must bring strangers together and quickly establish a set of operational procedures that unite their efforts and contributions. They must be skilled at managing meetings, so meetings do not become a burden but rather a vehicle for progress. Project leaders need to forge a team identity and a shared vision that commands the attention and allegiance of participants. They need to use group incentives to encourage teamwork and identify when it is appropriate to recognise individuals for special acknowledgment. Project leaders must encourage functional conflict that contributes to superior solutions, while being on guard against dysfunctional conflict that can break a team apart.

Review questions

1. What are the elements of an effective project vision? Why are they important?
2. Why should a project leader emphasise group rewards over individual rewards?
3. What is the difference between *functional* and *dysfunctional* conflict on a project?
4. When would it be appropriate to hold a formal team-building session on a project?
5. What are the unique challenges to managing a virtual project team?
6. Where do you normally sit on the leadership style continuum?
7. What is the difference between *leading* and *managing* a project?
8. Why is it important to build a relationship before you need it?
9. Why is it critical to keep the project sponsor informed?
10. Why is trust a function of both character and competence?
11. Which of the traits/skills associated with being an effective project leader is the most important? Which is the least important? Why?
12. What is *servant leadership*?
13. What should you consider when disbanding a project team or releasing an individual project member?
14. What is the difference between *consensus* and *majority* decision-making? How might each type of decision-making potentially affect project image?

Exercises

1. Create 12 questions that you could use at an interview for a project leader that would test their (your!) soft skills and leadership ability. Please do not refer to the two online interview templates!
2. Review the trust equation video (http://trustedadvisor.com/why-trust-matters/understanding-trust/understanding-the-trust-equation) and (using a scale of 1 = high, 10 = low) assess where you would place yourself and at least three other (de-identified) stakeholders you may have interacted with recently. What did you find?

    The following two exercises are to be based on a recent project you have been involved in. This project may be a student project, a work project, or an extracurricular project.

3. Analyse how effectively the group managed meetings. What did the group do well? What did the group not do well? If the group were formed again, what specific recommendations would you make about how the group should manage meetings?
4. Answer the following questions:
   - How strong is the team identity on this project and why?
   - What could participants do to strengthen team identity?
   - What kind of informal activities could be used to rejuvenate the team?
   - Why would these activities work?
5. Access the Project Management Institute website and review the standards contained in the ethics section: www.pmi.org/-/media/pmi/documents/public/pdf/ethics/pmi-code-of-ethics.pdf?v=6af21906-e593-4b63-8cee-abeb4137f41d&sc_lang_temp=en

    How useful is the information for helping someone decide what behaviour is appropriate and inappropriate?

References

3M, "Leading a distributed team", www.3m.com/meetingnetwork/readingroom/meetingguide_distribteam.html, accessed February 2018.

Australian Institute of Project leaders (AIPM) 2014, *Code of Ethics and Professional Conduct*, AIPM, https://www.aipm.com.au/documents/aipm-key-documents/aipm_code_of_ethics_2015.aspx, accessed February 2018.

Bradberry T & Graves J 2005, *The Emotional Intelligence Quick Book: How to Put Your EQ to Work*, Simon & Schuster, New York.

Cabanis-Brewin J 1999, "The human task of a project leader: Daniel Goleman on the value of high EQ", *PM Network*, November, pp. 38–42.

Cambridge Dictionary n.d., "Meaning of 'trust' in the English dictionary", https://dictionary.cambridge.org/dictionary/english, accessed February 2018.

Covey SR 1989, *The Seven Habits of Highly Effective People*, Simon & Schuster, New York.

Frame JD 1995, *Managing Projects in Organizations*, Jossey-Bass, San Francisco.

Greenleaf RK 1970, *The Servant as Leader*, https://www.greenleaf.org/what-is-servant-leadership/, accessed July 2018.

The Grove n.d., "The Drexler/Sibbet team performance model", https://www.thegrove.com/methodology/team-performance-model, accessed February 2022.

Katz R 2004, "How a team at Digital Equipment designed the 'alpha' chip", *The Human Side of Managing Technological Innovation*, 2nd edition. Ed. Ralph Katz, Oxford University Press, New York, pp. 121–33.

Kotter JP 2007, "Leading change: Why transformation efforts fail", *Harvard Business Review*, January, pp. 1–7.

Maister DH, Green CH & Galford M 2000, *The Trusted Advisor*, The Free Press, New York.

Mind Tools n.d., "Theory X and Theory Y", https://www.mindtools.com/pages/article/newLDR_74.htm, accessed February 2022.

Murray S 2010, "Build trust and be transparent", RealTime Performance, http://www.realtimeperformance.com/blog/build-trust-and-be-transparent/, accessed February 2018.

NUPP 2019, "NUPP – Nearly universal principles of projects", https://nupp.guide, accessed February 2022.

Pacelli L 2005, 'Top ten attributes of a great project sponsor', Paper presented at PMI Global Congress 2005—North America, Project Management Institute.

Pink D 2009, "The puzzle of motivation", TED Global, https://www.ted.com/talks/dan_pink_the_puzzle_of_motivation accessed February 2022.

Project Management Institute (PMI) n.d., *Code of Ethics and Professional Conduct*, https://www.pmi.org/-/media/pmi/documents/public/pdf/ethics/code-values-card.pdf?v=44578e34-7742-4156-8ce0-034489794fe4&sc_lang_temp=en, accessed February 2022

Project Management Institute (PMI) 2017a, *A Guide to the Project Management Body of Knowledge*, 6th edition, PMI.

Project Management Institute (PMI) 2017b, *Agile Practice Guide*, PMI.

Project Management Institute (PMI) 2021a, *A Guide to the Project Management Body of Knowledge (PMBOK® Guide)*, 7th edition, PMI.

Project Management Institute (PMI) 2021b, *The Standard for Project Management (ANSI/PMI 99-001-2021)*, 7th edition, PMI.

Render J 2019, "MacGregor's XY Theory and Ouchi's Theory Z", https://agile-mercurial.com/2019/06/28/macgregors-xy-theory-and-ouchis-theory-z/, accessed February 2022.

Ritti RR 1982, *The Ropes to Skip and the Ropes to Know: Studies in Organizational Behaviour*, Wiley, New York.

Scrum Alliance, "The art and science of the servant leader", https://www.scrumalliance.org/community/articles/2014/august/the-art-and-science-of-servant-leader, accessed February 2018.

Tannenbaum R & Schmidt WH 1973, "How to choose a leadership pattern", *Harvard Business Review*, May–June, p. 12.

The Trusted Advisor n.d., "Understanding the trust equation", https://trustedadvisor.com/why-trust-matters/understanding-trust/understanding-the-trust-equation, accessed February 2022.

Tuckman B 1965, "Developmental sequence in small groups", *Psychological Bulletin*, vol. 63, no. 6, pp. 384–99.

Tuckman BW & Jensen MC 1997, "Stages of small group development revisited", *Group and Organizational Studies*, vol. 2, pp. 419–27.

CHAPTER 20

Complex project management

Learning elements

20A Understand the nature of complex project management.

20B Be able to evaluate a project's complexity, taking into consideration key dimensions of complexity.

20C Understand the nature of forming actions and strategies to address complexity in projects.

20D Be aware of the necessity to monitor complexity.

20E Understand complexity at closure and handover to the operational business.

In this chapter

20.1 Introduction

20.2 Thinking practices to assist the project leader

20.3 Evaluating project complexity

20.4 A generic complexity framework

20.5 Framework Part A: Pre-project complexity assessment

20.6 Framework Part B: Detailed complexity assessment

20.7 Framework Part C: Monitor project complexity

20.8 Framework Part D: Review and capture knowledge

20.9 Framework Part E: Assess handover and operational complexity

Summary

20.1 : **Introduction**

Complexity has no boundaries; it is an intricate web of interrelations that informs us that maybe this project is going to have challenges. As the adage goes, *forewarned is forearmed* (i.e. prior knowledge of possible problems gives us a tactical advantage).

The **International Centre for Complex Project Management (ICCPM)** defines **complexity** as follows.

> *Whilst there is no universally accepted definition for Complex Project Management, at the point of ICCPM's establishment it was agreed between its founding organisations that complex projects are those that:*
> - *Are characterised by uncertainty, ambiguity, dynamic interfaces, and significant political or external influences; and/or*
> - *Usually run over a period which exceeds the technology cycle time of the technologies involved; and/or*
> - *Can be defined by effect, but not by solution (ICCPM n.d.).*

Complexity theory underpins our ability to understand complex systems, and indeed we know that some projects are described as being in a *constant state of flux*. If we can identify these projects and the **dimensions of complexity** (flux), then we are in a better place to manage these dimensions. So, what is **complexity theory**?

Figure 20.1 On the edge of chaos

Complexity thinking is based on interactions, relationships, patterns and non-static elements coming together. Complexity is often found in natural systems, such as weather systems, in global political systems, and in some project environments!

The non-static components of a complex system, like the formation of a snowflake, is often a unique event, like a cloud forming a coming-together of energy, dynamics and forces in constantly-changing formations.

These systems exist on a continuum, calm weather to story weather, where it is reported the most productive place on this continuum is on that of chaos–after the lazy calm weather, but before the storm!

PMBOK : Seventh edition updates (PMI 2021)

In the *Project Management Body of Knowledge* (PMBOK), the Project Management Institute (PMI) includes the "Navigate Complexity" principle, which states that complexity arises from the many elements (humans or systems) interacting during the project life cycle.

PMBOK stresses the importance of continually monitoring the complexity of a project and adjusting activities as and when required.

In the seventh edition of PMBOK there is a performance domain (the "Uncertainty Performance Domain") within which complexity elements are discussed (PMI 2021a, p. 252). It covers topics such as general uncertainty, ambiguity, volatility, risk and complexity.

Within complexity, considerations are discussed around the following.

■ *Systems-based complexity:* Where a system of interrelated elements is captured with the aim of decoupling—breaking the system apart to understand its components; and also with the aim of simulation—of components of the system to understand patterns and their effects on the overall system.

■ *Reframing:* (a) Diversity—where complex systems are viewed from different perspectives using different modes of thinking, from idea showers, to the Delphi technique to design thinking and the divergent and convergent thinking techniques; and (b) Balance—using different sets of data (e.g. forecast, random and known) to explore system responses.

■ *Process-based complexity:* Here techniques such as iteration—where the system is built iteratively (or incrementally), one component at a time, and after each iteration questions are asked and lessons sought on what occurred; or engagement—where the stakeholder is actively engaged to *assumption bust* any work carried out; and fail safe—where consideration is given to redundant components that replace or support a *graceful degradation* of a system where critical components exist.

If asked to idea shower phrases related to project complexity, those indicated below would come to the front of mind:

■ ambiguity

■ uncertainty

■ unpredictability

■ dynamic and dynamics

■ social structures, natural structures

■ interrelationships, connectedness

■ funding and budgets not aligned

■ team size and non-standard structures

■ strategic viewpoint (rapidly changing environment)

■ stakeholder engagement networks, dispersed and varied

■ long extended projects.

Distilling these down into factors considered by a few approaches would produce a table of factors that are still not globally agreed, with only some alignment of the factors. Table 20.1 indicates factors of complexity as introduced by various emerging contributors.

Table 20.1 Factors of complexity

ICCPM	PMBOK seventh edition (PMI 2021b)	Navigating Complexity (PMI 2014)	Managing Complex Projects: A New Model (Hass 2009)
Structural complexity	Human behaviour	Human behaviour	Details: number of variables and interfaces
Technical complexity	System behaviour	System behaviour	Ambiguity: lack of awareness of events and causality
Directional complexity	Uncertainty and ambiguity	Ambiguity	Uncertainty: inability to pre-evaluate options
Temporal complexity	Technological innovation		Unpredictability: inability to know what will happen
Socio-cultural complexity			Dynamics: rapid rate of change
			Social structure: numbers and types of interactions

Sources: International Centre for Complex Project Management (ICCPM) n.d. "What is complex project management?", https://iccpm.com/about-complex-project-management/, accessed February 2022; Project Management Institute (PMI) 2021b, *The Standard for Project Management (ANSI/PMI 99-001-2021),* 7th edition, PMI; Project Management Institute (PMI) 2014, *Navigating Complexity: A Practice Guide,* PMI; Hass K 2009, *Managing Complex Projects: A New Model,* Management Concepts Press, Kindle Edition.

So, what does a complex project look like? The author (Pearson) proposes the following profiles, as illustrated in Figure 20.2.

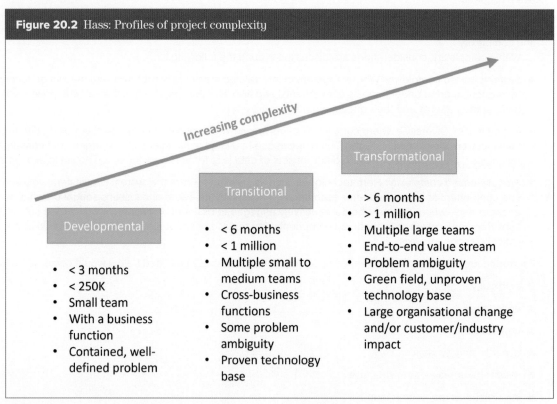

Figure 20.2 Hass: Profiles of project complexity

Increasing complexity

Developmental
- < 3 months
- < 250K
- Small team
- With a business function
- Contained, well-defined problem

Transitional
- < 6 months
- < 1 million
- Multiple small to medium teams
- Cross-business functions
- Some problem ambiguity
- Proven technology base

Transformational
- > 6 months
- > 1 million
- Multiple large teams
- End-to-end value stream
- Problem ambiguity
- Green field, unproven technology base
- Large organisational change and/or customer/industry impact

Source: Adapted from Hass, Kathleen. *Managing Complex Projects: A New Model* (p. 49, Fig 3-3). Management Concepts Press. Kindle Edition.

Complexity is an additional factor in managing projects large or small that runs across the life cycle of the project. Some of the key activities fitted to the **predictive** project life cycle are indicated in Figure 20.3. However, there seems to be consensus that **adaptive** approaches such as Scrum and Agile are generally more suited to addressing some of the main concerns of complex projects. Refer to Chapter 3 "Agile (Scrum) project management".

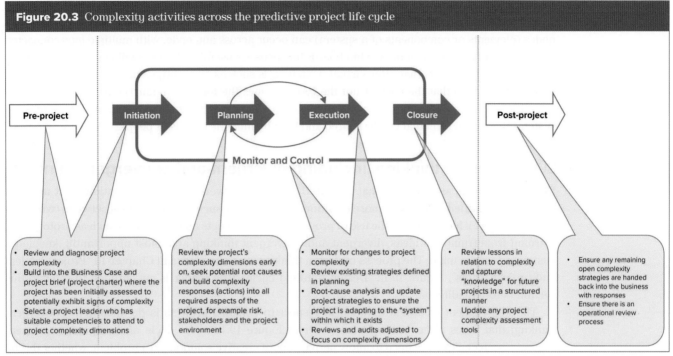

Figure 20.3 Complexity activities across the predictive project life cycle

© 2022 Dr Neil Pearson

20.2 Thinking practices to assist the project leader

The project leader who deals with complex projects must use thinking techniques beyond simple linear thinking, such as **systems thinking** (interconnectedness beyond the business system), **divergent** and **convergent thinking,** and creative thinking techniques such as **design thinking.** These techniques will assist the project leader in making connections between dimensions that result in strategies that reduce, mitigate and avoid complexity in the project.

20.2.1 Systems thinking

Systems thinking was briefly introduced in Chapter 1 "Contemporary project management". Here we are interested in interconnected systems. Often parallels are drawn with natural biological systems. Humans need food, water and air to breathe: water produces the food, whether animal or plant based; plants exchange gases, which in turn enrich the air we breathe—this simplified example shows the interconnectedness of the natural world that has evolved over millions of years. Disturbing just one element of the system has untold impacts across the system—take, for example, humans creating excessive CO^2 levels.

As a project leader, being able to conceptualise, analyse and visualise in terms of systems will greatly assist in the management of complex projects. Complex projects have a net of interconnected dimensions; the project leader must identify and understand the connections to make informed actions—these actions are ultimately incorporated into the various dimensions of the project's artefacts.

The idea of systems thinking was conceptualised by von Bertalanffy (1969):

[A] system is a complex of interacting elements and that they are open to and interact with their environments. In addition, they can acquire qualitatively new properties through emergence, thus they are in a continual evolution.

Given the majority of the population is visual (as opposed to auditory or kinetic) in terms of learning style, how could we represent a system in a visual medium? This is not easy, as connections between nodes (elements or components of a system) can occur across any node, with multiple interconnected connections often being common. Whiteboards and pens are useful tools, especially in small workgroup formats. Free-form tools that offer virtual whiteboards such as Miro (https://miro.com) are of use but require training so that the content not the tool becomes the focus (e.g. miro.com); accessible (non-scientific) tools such as TheBrain (www.thebrain.com) offer some possibilities to explore interconnected systems in a visual form that can be shared and built by multiple groups of people.

20.2.2 Design thinking, including divergent and convergent thinking

Design thinking is an approach that is geared towards uncovering innovative options that may not have been identified when using more traditional approaches, such as gap analysis between two states (*as-is* and *to-be*). It encourages the use of product design concepts and techniques such as prototyping, learning from trying out ideas, divergent and convergent thinking and, most importantly, keeping a customer focus in mind. The process of design thinking was introduced in Chapter 19 "Project leaders and project teams", Figure 19.12 "Design thinking cycle". The reader is encouraged to refer to this section before reading on.

The key element of design thinking in respect to complex projects is the divergent–convergent thinking that takes place within Ideate (refer to Figure 19.12). This cycle of divergent–convergent thinking is a technique designed to allow perhaps more creative solutions to a problem, whether this be a strategy (actions) to address complexity, or strategies to better address complex project risks (outside the accept/avoid/mitigate/transfer options). The divergent–convergent cycle is indicated in Figure 20.4. The constant focus is on addressing the problem or opportunity to achieve a desired outcome.

The needs and goals of customers are always kept in mind as this is a customer-centric approach. Participants work collaboratively and engage in cycles of divergent then convergent thinking. Where

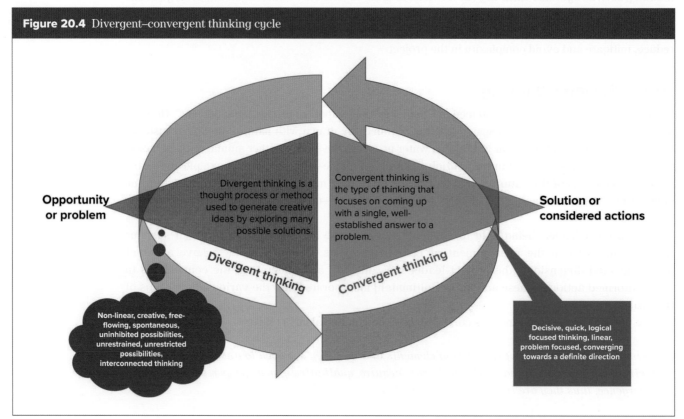

Figure 20.4 Divergent–convergent thinking cycle

possible, customers are involved in the design thinking process to support co-creation of products and value (Paul & Cadle 2020).

Divergent thinking is characterised by: non-linear creative, free-flowing, spontaneous, uninhibited possibilities; unrestrained, unrestricted possibilities; and interconnected thinking. Convergent thinking is characterised by decisive, quick, logical, focused thinking. When the two modes are combined in cycles, the problem and the options (solutions) to the problem are deeply explored, then focused, then explored and focused until no new insights are brought to the possible solution. As those who have worked on complex projects will know, standard diagnostic approaches often don't provide the answer; often, there is no simple answer but a set of connected actions that together may reduce the risk of certain conditions coming to fruition at the same time (a *perfect storm* event).

20.2.3 **Creative versus logical thinking**

The divergent–convergent thinking cycle is influenced by the Nobel Prize-winning research that Roger Wolcott Sperry and others conducted on left- and right-brain functions in the 1960s. He identified that the left brain is associated with more logical, factual, fact-driven patterns, whereas the right brain is associated with more holistic, imaginative and feeling patterns. Sperry's research has in recent years been casually (and non-scientifically) associated with so-called *left brain – right brain thinking*, which in a business context has been used to illustrate the distinctly different types of thinking we may adopt at different times to make sense of our world. We are not, however, only one type of thinker: both halves of the brain work together to produce results!

This can alternatively be construed as thinking in more creative ways as opposed to more logical ways. Some common traits of creative thinking versus logical thinking are captured in Table 20.2.

Table 20.2 Creative versus logical thinking traits

Creative thinking traits	Logical thinking traits
Curious	Filtering
Sensitive (receptive)	Logical
Feeling (emotions)	Factual
Risk taking	Rational
Open	Linear
Uninhibited	Simplifying
Unrestrained	Categorising
Story-making	Attentive (to detail)
Complex	Investigative
Build on lessons learned	Critical
Conceptual thinking	Systems thinking (interconnectedness)

© 2022 Dr Neil Pearson

These two thinking patterns are evident in divergent–convergent thinking, while systems thinking pulls from both, seeking to explore connections rather than making connections. As to the techniques that support creative versus logical thinking, we could scour the internet and research archives and locate many dozens of techniques that favour either mode of thinking. A sample of the more common techniques is included in Table 20.3.

In essence we must identify the situation we are about to enter and ensure appropriate approaches are used. On occasions, project leaders must be logical thinkers (e.g. when scheduling work packages and tasks); at other times they must use more exploratory techniques, such as understanding empathetically the customer's experience, or when exploring strategies to address complex divergent–convergent cycles!

The remaining sections of this chapter detail the generic project **complexity framework**, and associated techniques that may assist a project leader within each stage of the framework. When exploring and developing actions and strategies, leverage the techniques of systems thinking, design thinking and creative versus logical techniques.

Table 20.3 Creative versus logical thinking techniques

Creative thinking techniques	Logical thinking techniques
De Bono's six thinking hats	Decision trees/decision tables
Rich pictures	Processes
Mind maps	Questioning
Idea showers	Deductive reasoning
Storyboards	Root-cause analysis
Brain shifter	Critical friends
Metaphorical thinking	Based in research
Customer journey maps	Use case diagrams
Crawford slip/Delphi method	Critical thinking
Design thinking	Structured English, pseudo code
Personas	State charts
Soft systems methodology (conceptual world versus real world)	Systems (thinking) descriptions and diagrams

© 2022 Dr Neil Pearson

 LE 20B

20.3 | **Evaluating project complexity**

The quest to understand and enumerate project complexity starts when developing the Business Case that will support the project, where an initial evaluation of project complexity is undertaken. Hass (2009) promotes the use of *spider diagrams* or **radar charts** to visualise the scale of complexity across the dimensions where complexity is *possibly* present.

SNAPSHOT *from* PRACTICE | **Grand Egyptian Museum (GEM)**

In 2002 the Egyptian Government announced the start of a project to build the world's largest museum to house in excess of 100 000 treasures from the country's rich historic past. A competition to design what was to be called the Grand Egyptian Museum (GEM) was opened to architectural companies across the world. In 2003 the winner was announced, an entry from a company in Dublin, Ireland.

On reviewing some of the information available, it is apparent that the project from the outset was to face some significant challenges. Extracting relevant information from various sources, the author (Pearson) has attempted to map dimensions on a radar chart (or *spider diagram* as Hass calls them). The criteria used for assessing complexity were inspired by the criteria from Hass (2009) (Figure 20.5).

Mirko Kuzmanovic/Shutterstock.com

To summarise such a highly complex project is not an easy task. With brevity in mind, some of the notable factors behind this complex project are indicated in Table 20.4.

From the outset, some of these dimensions could have been predicted from the very start, including the design and physical location challenges, the multiple funding sources of such a huge project, and the risks around resources (physical and human), cost and schedule dimensions. Construction began in 2005. From 2011 political instability and subsequent unrest besieged the project for several years. This impacted tourism directly linked to some of the funding sources for the project—the factors compounded. The GEM unofficial website indicates a revised opening in 2018 after the delays, but as of February 2022 the earliest proposed opening date is November of 2022, some 20 years after the initial design competition was won! This begs the question: Could more have been done earlier to assess complexity?

Source: Adapted from Grand Egyptian Museum 2022, "Grand Egyptian Museum", https://grandegyptianmuseum.org, accessed February 2022

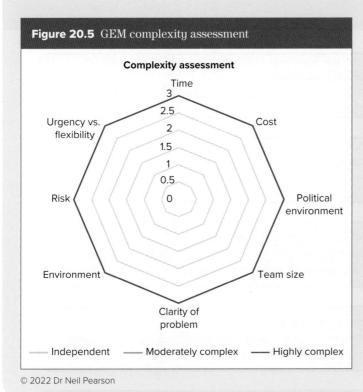

Figure 20.5 GEM complexity assessment

Complexity assessment

(Radar chart axes: Time, Cost, Political environment, Team size, Clarity of problem, Environment, Risk, Urgency vs. flexibility; scale 0–3)

— Independent — Moderately complex — Highly complex

© 2022 Dr Neil Pearson

Table 20.4 GEM brief complexity analysis

Complexity factor	GEM example
Time	>20 years
Cost	AUD1.2 billion and counting (reported GBP£600 million in 2019)
Political environment	Unstable during the early project with a less than one year hiatus due to political unrest
Team size	Many hundreds of contractors
Clarity of problem	There was a design in principle (by the winner of the competition), but it had to be turned into detailed architectural plans that took into account the harsh, ever-changing physical environment
Environment	World heritage area, site of soft shifting sands
Risk	High levels in terms of funding, environment, political conditions
Urgency versus flexibility	Replace insecure ageing central museum

© 2022 Dr Neil Pearson

20.4 A generic complexity framework

Projects do not necessarily start out as complex projects—they might do, but they can also become complex during the life of the project. Therefore, an organisation that exhibits contemporary project management awareness in items such as those discussed in Chapter 1 "Contemporary project management" may fare better. It may have practices in place to identify complex projects initially and also the learning mechanisms to identify changes to a project's **complexity profile** throughout its life cycle. Intelligent project management organisations value:

■ understanding customer value and the customer experience

■ compression of the product or service life cycle

■ business systems and systems thinking

■ organisational change management

■ organisational learning (introduced as action learning in Chapter 14 "Project stakeholder management").

Such organisations are more likely to identify and be able to manage complexity when it does arise, as practices are already embedded in organisational behaviours.

There is commonality between the aforementioned bodies (see Table 20.1 "Factors of complexity") in this chapter around a framework for complexity in project management, as captured in Figure 20.6.

Supplementing this with formal tools in the project environment such as decision tools and **complexity assessment** tools can assist the organisation to be forearmed.

Figure 20.6 Generic complexity framework

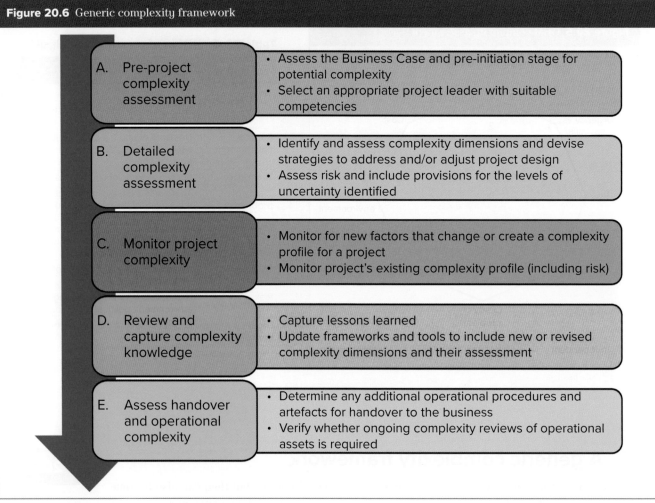

A.	Pre-project complexity assessment	• Assess the Business Case and pre-initiation stage for potential complexity • Select an appropriate project leader with suitable competencies
B.	Detailed complexity assessment	• Identify and assess complexity dimensions and devise strategies to address and/or adjust project design • Assess risk and include provisions for the levels of uncertainty identified
C.	Monitor project complexity	• Monitor for new factors that change or create a complexity profile for a project • Monitor project's existing complexity profile (including risk)
D.	Review and capture complexity knowledge	• Capture lessons learned • Update frameworks and tools to include new or revised complexity dimensions and their assessment
E.	Assess handover and operational complexity	• Determine any additional operational procedures and artefacts for handover to the business • Verify whether ongoing complexity reviews of operational assets is required

20.5   Framework Part A: Pre-project complexity assessment

Turning intuition and wisdom into a more tangible assessment is required. This can be done via several prudent questions being asked, or by the application of tools to assist in our decision-making. At this pre-project stage an assessment is being made of the problem and its approach.

20.5.1   Problem root cause verified?

The first check to make is that the root cause has been identified and decisions are not being made on veiled symptoms. For this, tools mentioned in Chapter 13 "Project quality management", such as the 5 whys and fishbone (cause–effect, Ishikawa) diagrams can be used. However, as we are dealing with complexity, more complex process-based tools are available (which, as a side benefit, would assist in capturing knowledge), such as the Apollo **root-cause analysis** methodology: www.apollorootcause .com/page/about/apollo-root-cause-analysis-method

20.5.2   Complex or complicated?

The next step is to assess the problem (the one driving the project) and its complexity. Here, another established framework is drawn into the picture. As the Praxis framework reported:

> *The Cynefin Framework was created by Dave Snowden of Cognitive Edge as a tool to help decision-making in complex social environments. . . . The Cynefin framework has relevance*

to projects, programmes, and portfolios because the P3M approach has to be tailored to the context of the work. Factors such as complexity and uncertainty need to be understood before deciding whether to manage the work as a project or programme, or perhaps deciding whether iterative approaches (such as Agile) are relevant or not (Praxis 2019).

The **Cynefin framework** (as illustrated in Figure 20.7) provides a decision-making framework around the problem situation being faced, with further research by others indicating early identification of the project management approach.

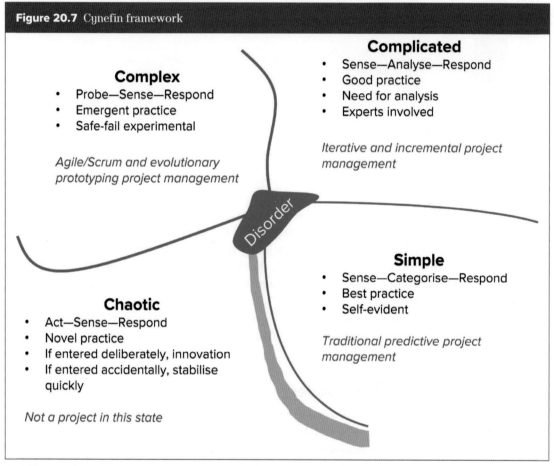

Figure 20.7 Cynefin framework

Complex
- Probe—Sense—Respond
- Emergent practice
- Safe-fail experimental

Agile/Scrum and evolutionary prototyping project management

Complicated
- Sense—Analyse—Respond
- Good practice
- Need for analysis
- Experts involved

Iterative and incremental project management

Disorder

Simple
- Sense—Categorise—Respond
- Best practice
- Self-evident

Traditional predictive project management

Chaotic
- Act—Sense—Respond
- Novel practice
- If entered deliberately, innovation
- If entered accidentally, stabilise quickly

Not a project in this state

Source: Adapted from The Cynefin Co 2022, "The Cynefin framework", https://thecynefin.co/about-us/about-cynefin-framework/, accessed June 2022

The creators of the Cynefin framework have produced an excellent explanation of its purpose and use in the following video clip, which readers are strongly encouraged to watch before continuing to read this chapter: www.youtube.com/watch?v=N7oz366X0-8

As this is a sense-making framework, the data precedes the framework and therefore the patterns (framework) emerge from the data in interconnected complex social processes.

The implications for us as project leaders are that when starting to consider a complex, complicated or simple problem, the trajectory of management might not remain the same as when we make sense of our current situation; throughout the project we may have to adopt more adaptive approaches or drop back into more predictive approaches. Hass confirms this thinking as illustrated in Figure 20.8 (adapted). Where a scale of "Independent", "Moderately complex" and "Highly complex" is presented, within later chapters of her text Hass discusses the most suitable approaches given the complexity of the project. Again we see more waterfall (predictive) approaches being applied to "Independent" projects, and more adaptive approaches used in "Highly complex" projects. For example, if we are

Figure 20.8 Project management approach selection

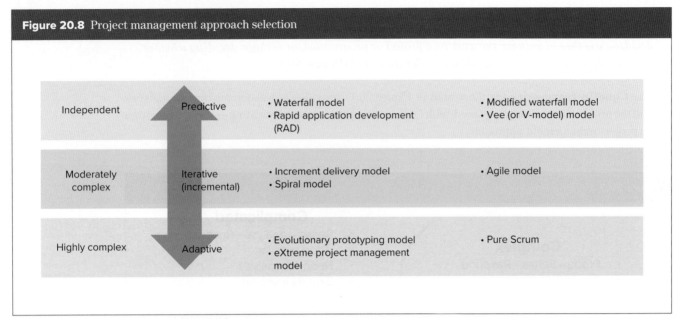

Source: Adapted from Hass K 2009, *Managing Complex Projects: A New Model,* Management Concepts Press, Kindle Edition, p. 78

building a new warehouse from a blueprint on known ground conditions, our project is likely going to be "Independent" and use a predictive approach (e.g. we could use the PMI life cycle approach); however, if we are researching a new vaccine for a global pandemic we are in the Cynefin "Complex" or initially chaotic area, or, as Hass categorises it, the "Highly Complex" area, where we are likely to use adaptive (e.g. Scrum or Agile) techniques, with the aim of quickly and efficiently ruling out candidates that safe-fail in trial.

Other research on the assessment of complexity related to the initial project approach taken is available from: https://pmworldlibrary.net/wp-content/uploads/2021/05/pmwj105-May2021-Ika-Couillard-Garon-coping-with-project-complexity.pdf

20.5.3 **Competent project leader?**

Another dimension to be considered as the project is initiated is the appointment of a suitably competent project leader. Here we would look to **competency** assessments geared towards the assessment of a project leader's **complex project management** competencies, which go beyond those frameworks for standard project leader competencies. There are two notable contributions in this area—the ICCPM and Hass—but others, such as the **International Project Management Association (IPMA)** levels, are also recognised.

The ICCMP expands the concept of a competency framework for project leaders nurturing complex projects, offering nine *views*, with several sub-items within each view. Sub-items are rated across three levels of competency: practitioner, competent and leader (leader being the highest level). The nine views are:

- View 1—Systems Thinking and Integration
- View 2—Strategy and Project Management
- View 3—Business Planning, Lifecycle Management, Reporting & Performance Measurement

- View 4—Change and Journey
- View 5—Innovation, Creativity and Working Smarter
- View 6—Organisational Architecture
- View 7—Leadership and Communication
- View 8—Culture and Being Human
- View 9—Probity and Governance (ICCPM 2012).

Although some of these competency views seem relatively benign on the surface, when drilled into they do probe more advanced traits of a project leader who is capable of managing complex projects. The full competency standard is available at https://iccpm.com/wp-content/uploads/2018/09/CPM-Competency-Standard-V4.1.pdf

20.5.4 **Initial risk assessment**

At the pre-project stage, a project complexity risk assessment would also be considered. The approach and process to such risk management activities is documented in Chapter 16 "Project risk management". Running such a risk identification at this stage in relation to complexity would be the focus for the workshop. Rather than looking at a wide scope of risk, the focus for the workshop is risk related to potential project complexity. Generally, the consensus of research tells us that **risk** and **complexity** are correlated (Figure 20.9).

The question is therefore what factors of risk would represent a good starting point from which to assess the risk of complexity. As project leader, the normal risk identification techniques apply—the **risk breakdown structure (RBS),** risk categories, idea showers and sticky notes, review of the work breakdown structure (WBS) activities; and of course we could use the dimensions or factors of risk as categories to generate (identify) risks from. Some of these factors or dimensions are included in Table 20.5.

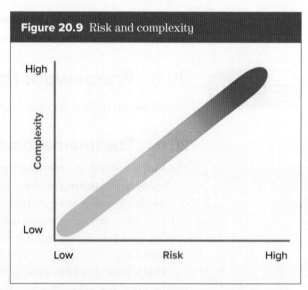

Figure 20.9 Risk and complexity

© 2022 Dr Neil Pearson

Table 20.5 Factors and dimensions of complexity from which to generate risks

IPMA perspectives	Hass dimensions of complexity
Capability perspectives:	■ Time/cost
	■ Team size
■ Input-related complexity	■ Team composition and performance
■ Process-related complexity	■ Urgency and flexibility of cost, time and scope
■ Output-related complexity	
■ Risk-related complexity	■ Clarity of problem, opportunity and solution
	■ Requirement's volatility and risk
Context perspectives:	■ Strategic importance
	■ Political implications
■ Strategy-related complexity	■ Multiple stakeholders
■ Organisation-related complexity	■ Level of organisational change
■ Sociocultural-related complexity	■ Risks, dependencies and external constraints
	■ Level of ICT complexity
Management/leadership perspectives:	
■ Team-related complexity	
■ Innovation-related complexity	
■ Autonomy-related complexity	

Sources: International Project Management Association (IPMA) n.d.(a), "How we define complexity in projects, programmes and portfolios", https://www.ipma.world/individuals/certification/complexity/, accessed June 2022; Hass K 2009, *Managing Complex Projects: A New Model,* Management Concepts Press, Kindle Edition, pp. 44–5

Using these dimensions and factors provides the categories from which to idea shower risks. Leveraging the Risk Register to record and track these risks as a set of interrelated risks by categorising them as *project complexity* will mean that they can be later located and reviewed.

20.5.5 Lessons learned

Lessons learned can be a significant input, initially into the conception and design of the project but also during the project to improve ongoing outcomes. They also leave a history to inform future projects of **lessons learned** (positive or negative). The activity is placed here in pre-project complexity assessment as we would be seeking lessons from other internal or industry projects to inform the start-up of the project. The topic of lessons is discussed further in the next section.

At this stage in the author's (Pearson's) **generic complexity framework**, we have:

- a pre-initiation (pre-project) assessment of the project complexity
- advice on the best approach (life cycle) to apply (predictive through adaptive) at the project's inception
- required project leader competencies
- project complexity risk assessment.

20.6 Framework Part B: Detailed complexity assessment

We will return to Hass and a few additional resources in this area of more detailed assessment.

20.6.1 The International Project Management Association (IPMA) tool

The tool is located at: www.ipma-usa.org/project-management-complexity-evaluation-tool

It progresses through several perception-based responses to questions around possible dimensions of complexity. The same parameters from the "Snapshot from practice: Grand Egyptian Museum (GEM)", when fed into the questionnaire, produced the result captured in Figure 20.10.

The survey recommends the skill competency level or the project manager. The IPMA Level A is described as:

"IPMA level A certification is the highest internationally recognised level as project, programme and/or portfolio professional... You are a professional amongst professionals, recognised by your peers and your customers. You truly deserve your position: project director, programme director or portfolio director" (IPMA n.d.(b)).

20.6.2 Hass complexity actions

Hass considered dimensions of complexity (as introduced in "Snapshot from Practice: Grand Egyptian Museum (GEM)", where again a perceptions-based score is attributed to the dimension identified. These scores are then visualised on a spider (or radar) chart for further analysis.

Hass dedicates individual chapters of her book to the following combinations of project complexity:

- large, long-duration projects
- large, dispersed, culturally diverse project teams
- highly innovative, urgent projects with aggressive scopes and schedules
- ambiguous business problems, opportunities and solutions
- poorly understood, volatile requirements
- highly visible strategic projects, often politically sensitive
- complex, large-scale change initiatives
- projects with significant dependencies and external constraints
- high level of ICT complexity.

Figure 20.10 IPMA complexity questionnaire for the GEM project

international
project
management
association

Home » Project Management Complexity Evaluation Tool

What Level of Certification Am I Qualified For?
Management Complexity Evaluation Tool

Use this page to evaluate the complexity of your projects, programs, and portfolios. After rating all ten indicators, review the overall score to see which level this project, program, or portfolio qualifies for.

Instructions:

1. For each of the ten Complexity Indicators below, select the option button that best describes your project, program, or portfolio.

2. After evaluating all Complexity Indicators, review your result at the bottom of the page. It identifies the certification level where this project, program, or portfolio can be used as valid experience. Note that the result does not show until you have rated all ten indicators.

Complexity Indicators	Very low	Low	High	Very high
1. Objectives and assessment of results (output-related complexity): this indicator covers the complexity originating from vague, exacting, and mutually conflicting goals, objectives, requirements, and expectations.	○ Very low	○ Low	○ High	◉ Very high
2. Processes, methods, tools, and techniques (process-related complexity): this indicator covers the complexity related to the number of tasks, assumptions and constraints, and their interdependence; the processes and process quality requirements; the team and communication structure; and the availability of supporting methods, tools, and techniques.	○ Very low	○ Low	◉ High	○ Very high
3. Resources including finance (input-related complexity): this indicator covers complexities relating to acquiring and funding the necessary budgets (possibly from several sources); the diversity or lack of availability of resources (both human and other); and the processes and activities needed to manage the financial and resource aspects, including procurement.	○ Very low	○ Low	○ High	◉ Very high
4. Risk and opportunities (risk-related complexity): this indicator covers complexity related to the risk profile(s) and uncertainty levels of the project, program, or portfolio and dependent initiatives.	○ Very low	○ Low	○ High	◉ Very high
5. Stakeholders and integration (strategy-related complexity): this indicator covers the influence of formal strategy from the sponsoring organization(s) and the standards, regulations, informal strategies, and politics which may influence the project, program, or portfolio. Other factors may include the importance of outcomes for the organization; the measure of agreement among stakeholders; the informal power, interests, and resistance surrounding the project, program, or portfolio; and any legal or regulatory requirements.	○ Very low	○ Low	○ High	◉ Very high

	Very low	Low	High	Very high
6. Relations with permanent organizations (organization-related complexity): this indicator covers the amount and interrelatedness of the interfaces of the project, program, or portfolio with the organization's systems, structures, reporting, and decision-making processes.	○ Very low	○ Low	○ High	◉ Very high
7. Cultural and social context (socio-cultural complexity): this indicator covers complexity resulting from socio-cultural dynamics. These may include interfaces with participants, stakeholders, or organizations from different socio-cultural backgrounds or having to deal with distributed teams.	○ Very low	○ Low	○ High	◉ Very high
8. Leadership, teamwork, and decisions (team-related complexity): this indicator covers the management and leadership requirements from within the project, program, or portfolio. This indicator focuses on the complexity originating from the relationship with the team(s) and their maturity and hence the vision, guidance, and steering the team requires to deliver.	○ Very low	○ Low	◉ High	○ Very high
9. Degree of innovation and general conditions (innovation-related complexity): this indicator covers the complexity originating from the degree of technical innovation of the project, program, or portfolio. This indicator may focus on the learning and associated resourcefulness required to innovate and/or work with unfamiliar outcomes, approaches, processes, tools, or methods.	○ Very low	○ Low	◉ High	○ Very high
10. Demand for coordination (autonomy-related complexity): this indicator covers the amount of autonomy and responsibility that the project, program, or portfolio manager/leader has been given or has taken/shown. This indicator focuses on coordinating, communicating, promoting, and defending the project, program, or portfolio interests with others.	○ Very low	○ Low	○ High	◉ Very high

Based on your average score (3.7), your suggested certification level is "IPMA Level A, Certified Project, Program or Portfolio Director."

Press the Print this Page button to print this worksheet. These results are **not** saved. [Print This Page]

This tool is for your use in evaluating the management complexity of the projects, programs, and portfolios you are planning to use to support your experience claims. Note that most other PM certifications available in the USA do not consider the management complexity of the work you manage.

Note for Managers:
You can use this tool on a prospective basis to match your Project, Program, or Portfolio Managers to future assignments. You can also use it to identify areas of exposure to risk.

More Information

- Certification Program Overview
- What IPMA Certification Level is Right for Me?
- Make a Certification Payment
- Certification FAQs
- Evaluate the Management Complexity of your Program or Project
- Certification Site Map

Downloads

- ICB4, the IPMA Individual Competence Baseline
- IPMA-USA Fee Schedule
- Exam and Interview Dates
- Certification Application
- Sample Exams
- Recertification Application

IPMA
international
project
management
association

PM-SAT
Self-Assessment
Tool for PM
Learning

SEARCH

Change
Agents
Blog

© 2017 IPMA-USA

Source: IPMA-USA, https://www.ipma-usa.org/project-management-complexity-evaluation-tool

By way of an example, in the discussion on how to manage poorly understood, volatile requirements, Hass proposes several techniques for consideration, from completing a rigorous analysis prior to project funding through to insisting on adequate customer, end-user and technical involvement.

Again, by using such advice, the project leader is better informed as to what actions might need addressing within the design of the project.

20.6.3 Detailed risk response

Uncertainty was introduced as a key phrase associated with complex projects. Wherever there is **uncertainty** in a project, the amount of time dedicated to risk management activities should increase. Taking information presented in Chapter 16 "Project risk management", we modify certain elements of the process described.

- In risk identification we are really trying to identify the unknown-unknowns, so getting close to the edge of risk identification is paramount. This may mean spending additional time with a varied group of internal and external stakeholders, viewing risk from varying perspectives with individuals who may not see the world in the same manner as we do.

- In mitigating the risk, the standard five strategies—accept, avoid, mitigate, transfer, escalate (or combinations of)—might not fit the response we have to consider, so don't be constrained by categories; after all, we are on the edge of **chaos** and our strategies may be unique responses to a complex system of interactions.

- In monitoring risk, our practices are constant and ongoing and adaptive, supplemented by planned events such as team meetings and risk review workshops.

20.6.4 Review of prior complexity lessons learned

Lessons learned make yet another appearance in this chapter on complexity. At this stage in the proceedings, it is a matter of checking previous lessons captured from complex projects and assessing which are relevant to this current project. From the lesson, actions and strategies will once again be formed for inclusion in the project's design and later implementation.

Whichever techniques are applied, the result will be strategies and actions to assist in the management of complexity and in the design of the project.

At this stage in the author's generic complexity framework, we have:

- a detailed understanding of the project's complexity dimensions
- strategies designed to address complexity and reduce risk built into the design of the project.

There are no templates to support the project leader in this space; however, the author (Pearson) has used a software tool called "TheBrain" (www.thebrain.com) to map the interconnectedness of complicated and complex projects to assist in later analysing this captured information.

20.7 : Framework Part C: Monitor project complexity

Using existing tools identified earlier in the chapter (such as the PMI navigating complexity assessment questionnaire) the project leader and project management office (PMO) should be vigilant when it comes to:

- attending to existing identified complexity dimensions; if necessary, change our original strategies designed into the project pre-initiation, initiation and later the more detailed project planning artefacts
- being receptive to new complexity dimensions appearing—we should not be complacent about what we did identify and manage to avoid because of past and current strategies; rather we should have our complexity radar on high alert for changes to the system within which our project is operating and be prepared to radically (if necessary) change our approach and work.

Consider this a part of your project's radar! Refer to Figure 20.11. When should these reviews be carried out?

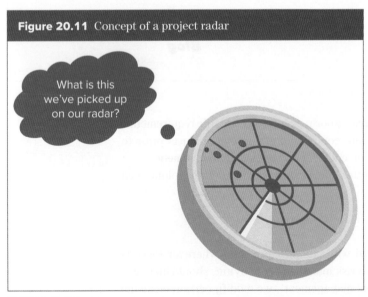

Figure 20.11 Concept of a project radar

What is this we've picked up on our radar?

- As the project is being executed, these **complexity reviews** are background checks in continual checks and balances taking place by the Level A project leader. Any cues, triggers or instincts should be investigated and, if appropriate, considered in future project delivery decisions and work.

- As a formal scheduled review by entities such as the PMO—where active checking of the complexity status is intentionally carried out at a scheduled point in time (e.g. at a gateway review).

- As a formal unscheduled review—where, due to factors identified by the review body, these could be external triggers (e.g. political change) or internal triggers (e.g. project status) of the unscheduled review.

- As a function of a project audit—not purely targeting complexity but the overall management of the project in its entirety.

Other techniques such as risk monitoring are operating at a heightened level of alert due to the imminent threat of entry of an unknown target appearing on our project's radar.

As we are going about our work, reflect on the Cynefin framework, as at times in the project we may have to completely change the entire project's course, or temporarily move into a different space on the Cynefin framework to regain our direction. Monitoring project complexity is no easy task: learn lessons, adapt rapidly and continue delivery.

In addition to the content of the project, the artefacts (e.g. policy, processes, guidelines, templates) related to the management of the project should also be reviewed for their suitability to the complexity of the project, and analysed and redesigned so as not to constrain the project.

At this stage in the author's (Pearson's) generic complexity framework, we have updates to:

- existing complexity strategies (actions) for continued execution of the project and/or identification of new dimensions of complexity for inclusion in the project's execution

- the way we perceive the management of the project.

20.8 Framework Part D: Review and capture knowledge

The capturing of lessons learned is an ongoing process in complex projects as these inform learnings and direction of current and future projects. This is an adaptive network of connections, where lessons learned will not be just simple statements of learning but will be connected in *sets* that together provide the greater lesson. Remember: The key purpose of the lessons learned activity is move knowledge *from our heads* to a more explicit medium (the Lessons Learned Register) so that it can be reviewed, used and matured, as illustrated in Figure 20.12.

Continuous improvement opportunities might result from lessons learned. These improvement opportunities could impact the complexity framework and techniques, the general project management framework and PMO activities, and could also have an impact wider afield in the organisation, such as improvements to recruitment, risk, procurement, contracting and other organisational processes. Refer to Chapter 13 "Project quality management" for descriptions of continuous improvement approaches, such as Plan, Do, Check, Act (PDCA) and Define, Measure, Analyse, Improve, Control (DMAIC).

At this stage in the author's (Pearson's) generic complexity framework, we have:

- a growing list of lessons learned, which will inform future projects or future work on this project

- specific continuous improvement actions to improve the framework and techniques made available in the organisation.

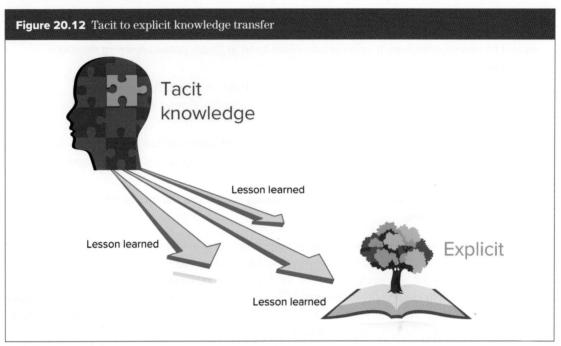

Figure 20.12 Tacit to explicit knowledge transfer

© 2022 Dr Neil Pearson

20.9 Framework Part E: Assess handover and operational complexity

So, let's take an extreme example to demonstrate what we see as complexity in operations as a result of project delivery. The Northrop Grumman B-21 Raider is touted as the world's most advanced, very long-range, large, heavy-payload stealth intercontinental strategic bomber. Developed for the United States Air Force, it will be able to deliver conventional and thermonuclear weapons. It is not due for release until 2027. Whether in the air or on the ground, the operational running and maintenance of such a high-tech asset is not simple, nor complicated, but a more complex endeavour where operational systems will require extensive redesign and adaptability in their day-to-day operations. If we compare this with taking our domestic car to a mechanic for its routine service, the comparison in complexity once the asset is in operations can be made!

The complex project's operational asset (product, service or result delivered from the project), is operating in a much more complex environment, one which must be prepared in a similar manner to the complexities of developing the asset initially. These handovers can take months or years to reach full operational potential and could be further projects of a program that take this renewed focus forward into the operational side of the business.

At this stage in the author's (Pearson's) generic complexity framework, we have complexity mappings of ongoing system interactions that must be managed in the operational business to ensure continued operation of the project's final deliverables.

Summary

This short introduction to the topic of project complexity has used a generic framework of key activities to be considered in the identification, planning and ongoing management of complexity in a project environment. The framework is supported by several techniques drawn from prevailing best practice at each stage to assist the project leader in establishing a protocol for dealing with the complexity in projects. These have been summarised in Figure 20.13.

Figure 20.13 Summary: A generic complexity framework and supporting techniques

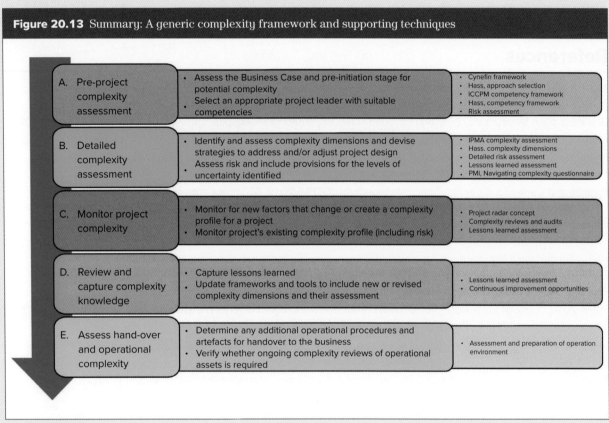

© 2022 Dr Neil Pearson

Because of the nature of complexity, the project leader and supporting roles will have to be practised in techniques such as systems thinking (interconnectedness), design thinking (including divergent and convergent thinking), and creative and logical thinking techniques, as more structured linear modes of approach and thinking will probably not make the connections between dimensions and craft strategies that reduce, mitigate and avoid complexity in the project.

Review questions

1. What phrases could be associated with complexity?
2. What are the author's generic complexity model key stages and what is their purpose?
3. Using the Cynefin framework as a reference point, what are the three key decisions where a project approach could be used and what options in terms of approaches are available?
4. What is the significance of lessons learned in complex projects?
5. How does risk relate to project complexity, and what does this mean in terms of risk management in the project?
6. What three thinking practices could assist us in exploring and defining, for example, strategies and actions for inclusion in the project?

Exercises

1. Using the Hass dimensions of complexity (refer to Figure 20.6), select a megaproject of interest from the Wikipedia list (https://en.wikipedia.org/wiki/List_of_megaprojects) and generate a Hass spider diagram or radar chart. Capture your justification for scoring each dimension.

2. For the project in Exercise 1, carry out the IPMA Management Complexity Evaluation Tool (www.ipma-usa.org/project-management-complexity-evaluation-tool). Capture your reasons for the score. Compare with the results from Exercise 1. Did the two profiles assess differently?

References

The Cynefin Co 2022, "The cynefin framework", https://thecynefin.co/about-us/about-cynefin-framework/, accessed June 2022.

Grand Egyptian Museum 2022, "Grand Egyptian Museum", https://grandegyptianmuseum.org, accessed February 2022.

Hass K 2009, *Managing Complex Projects: A New Model,* Management Concepts Press, Kindle Edition.

International Centre for Complex Project Management (ICCPM) n.d. "What is complex project management?", https://iccpm.com/about-complex-project-management/, accessed February 2022.

International Centre for Complex Project Management (ICCPM) 2012, "Complex project manager competency standards", https://iccpm.com/resource-centre/cpm-standards/, accessed June 2022.

International Project Management Association (IPMA) n.d.(a), "How we define complexity in projects, programmes and portfolios", https://www.ipma.world/individuals/certification/complexity/, accessed June 2022.

International Project Management Association (IPMA) n.d.(b), "Become recognised as a professional – Certification", https://www.ipma.world/individuals/certification/certified-projects-director-level-a/, accessed February 2022.

Paul D & Cadle J 2020, *Business Analysis,* 4th edition, BCS, United Kingdom.

Praxis 2019, "Cynefin framework", https://www.praxisframework.org/en/library/cynefin-framework, accessed June 2022.

Project Management Institute (PMI) 2014, *Navigating Complexity: A Practice Guide,* PMI.

Project Management Institute (PMI) 2021a, *A Guide to the Project Management Body of Knowledge* (*PMBOK® Guide*), 7th edition, PMI.

Project Management Institute (PMI) 2021b, *The Standard for Project Management* (*ANSI/PMI 99-001-2021*), 7th edition, PMI.

Von Bertalanffy L 1969, *General System Theory: Essays on Its Foundations and Development,* Braziller Inc.

PART 6

Performing project closure

CHAPTER 21
Project closure

Learning elements

21A Understand the background to successfully closing out a project, considering project reporting, human resources, financials, procurement, contracts and lessons learned.

21B Understand the different conditions under which a project might enter the Closure stage.

21C Further understand the key activities undertaken at the project Closure stage.

21D Understand performance across the multiple dynamics of a project, including project performance, team performance, individual performance and contractor/supplier performance.

21E Be able to take a rigorous approach to the capture of, analysis of and subsequent learning from lessons learned.

21F Be able to describe how benefits are delivered within the project and/or handed over into the business for post-project delivery.

In this chapter

21.1 Introduction

21.2 Types of project closure

21.3 Closure activities

21.4 Performance evaluation

21.5 Lessons learned

21.6 The Business Case, benefits and scope realisation

21.7 Project celebration

Summary

21.1 Introduction

Every project comes to an end; a project is by definition time-bound. But how many project participants get excited about closing out a project? The deliverables are complete, ownership is already in the process of being transferred to the operational business (customer), and everyone's focus is on *what next for me?*—hopefully a new, exciting project. The careful and skillful management of the Closing stage is just as important as the management of any other stage of the project.

Observation tells us that organisations that manage the review and closure of projects prosper. Organisations that don't manage either of these endeavours will tend to have projects that drag on forever and are never truly handed over to the operational business. Lessons won't be learned and the project will have a lacklustre impact on the organisation. **Project closure** is a definite stage, a finite end to the project, the finish banner of what has felt like a marathon at times.

Closing out a project can necessitate a seemingly daunting number of tasks. Traditionally the project leader alone was responsible for seeing that all tasks and loose ends were completed, tied up and signed off. This is no longer true, as in today's project-driven organisations, which often have many projects occurring simultaneously, responsibility for completing closure tasks often gets split between the project leader, the **project management office (PMO)**, the finance department, procurement and contracts departments and others. As when the deliverables have finally been handed over to the customer, the project tends to go into a swift administrative shutdown, as the people employed in it are released and costs closed. Many activities overlap, occur simultaneously, and require coordination and cooperation between stakeholders.

There are several activities that need to be undertaken during the Closure a stage of a project, including performance evaluation and the evaluation of **lessons learned** (Figure 21.1).

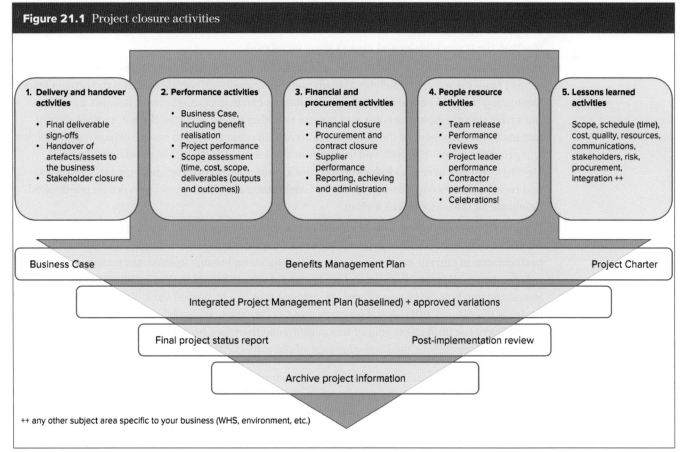

Figure 21.1 Project closure activities

© 2022 Dr Neil Pearson

- *Delivery and handover activities:* Final handover of deliverables to the operational business and/or customer is a key part of closure. It ensures formal acceptance and sign-off of these deliverables as well as a formal sign-off of the entire project (acknowledging all the previous deliverables made throughout the Execution stage). Handover of all the artefacts occurs as promised and consistent with documents such as the project scope document and wider **integrated Project Management Plan** (integrated PMP). These could include physical items (outputs) as well as confirmation of outcomes (e.g. an employee satisfaction survey tells us employees are happier because of the ICT-enabled business change project).

- *Performance activities:* The project was established on the basis of a **Business Case** (including defined benefits), a **Benefits Management Plan** (if the benefits are documented separately to the Business Case), a Project Charter and a project scope document (which includes **specific, measurable, achievable, realistic** and **timely (SMART)** objectives and deliverables). As discussed in Chapter 18 "Project execution", this also includes the **performance baseline**, **scope baseline**, **cost baseline** and **schedule (time) baseline**. Across these documents and baselines, some measures must be assessed, and data collected, analysed, reviewed and reported on. This is not an insignificant task and may require more resources than just the project leader (i.e. a **business analyst** or project coordinator may be involved as an assistant).

- *Financial and procurement activities:* The focus at project closure is on ensuring the project is approved and accepted by the customer. Other **closure activities** include closing accounts, paying invoices, reassigning equipment, releasing and reassigning personnel, finding new opportunities for project staff, closing facilities and the final report. Checklists are used extensively to ensure tasks are not overlooked. In many organisations, closure tasks are largely carried out by the PMO, in coordination with the project leader. The final project closure report is the responsibility of the project leader. However, responsibility for carrying out the **post-implementation review (PIR)** is usually assigned to a PMO staff member (to take an independent perspective), who assembles input from selected stakeholders (e.g. the customer, the sponsor, the project leader and project team members).

- *People resource activities:* The process of evaluation involves assessing the performance of the project team (as a group), individual team members, suppliers, contractors and the project leader. Evaluating the performance of these major players can generate important insights into who (and who not) to employ or enter into contracts within future projects. Such activities usually include the involvement of the human resources (HR) department to ensure organisation policies and procedures are being adhered to. Other activities include the physical release of people, closing down any access to **Information and Communications Technology (ICT)** systems and recall of assets (e.g. phones, laptops). Celebratory activities should also not be overlooked. Celebrate all the successes as a team.

- *Lessons learned activities:* This is known as the *retrospective* in the Scrum approach. Lessons that have been learned through previous project experience(s) can be applied to inform improved performance in current and future projects. Today, many lessons learned workshops are run by independent facilitators. Post-project reviews held with the team help to catch any remaining issues and any holistic (whole-of-project) lessons that can be passed back into the greater business operations. PIRs should be carried out before the team is disbanded and/or before key people leave the project—timing of this activity can therefore be critical and should be built into the project's schedule at the Planning stage of the project.

The results of stage, phase or project closure are typically made explicit (i.e. they are documented) within several project-related documents, including the Business Case, the **Benefits Management Plan** and the **Lessons Learned Register**, among other documents. These, together with the final project closure report and the post-implementation review report, should be presented to various groups of stakeholders in the business and eventually **archived** in the project library for reference by future project leaders. Table 21.1 summarises who the audience might be for such documents.

Table 21.1 Key project closure documents

Document	Role			
	Project sponsor	Project management office	Business as usual	Future project leaders
Business Case	√	√		
Benefits Management Plan	√		√	
Lessons Learned Register		√	√	√
Project closure report	√	√		
Post-implementation review (PIR)		√		√
Project library (archive)		√		√

© 2022 Dr Neil Pearson

This chapter begins by pointing out that projects can be closed for many reasons: not all projects end with a clean finish. Regardless of the conditions for ending a project, the general closure process will be similar, although the endings may differ significantly. *Wrap-up* or *closure* tasks are tasks that represent all the activities that must be resolved before the project is closed. After this has occurred, an evaluation of project performance takes place and lessons learned are examined and recorded in detail. Actions are set to ensure these lessons are applied to the business and future projects.

21.2 Types of project closure

LE 21B

On some projects, the end of the project may not be as clear as hoped for. Although the scope document may define a clear ending for a project, its actual ending may or may not correspond to that. Fortunately, the vast majority of projects do eventually meet their well-defined end. The different types of closure can be described as **normal**, **premature**, **phase** (or stage), **perpetual**, **failed project** or **changed priority**, as outlined below.

21.2.1 Normal

The most common circumstance for project closure is simply a completed project. For many development-type projects this will mean handing over a final design to production, and the subsequent creation of a new product or service line. For internal ICT projects (e.g. major system upgrades or the creation of a new inventory control system), the end of the project will occur when its deliverables are incorporated into ongoing operations. Typically, some modifications to the scope, cost and/or schedule will have occurred during the project's life cycle (variations), although these would have been reviewed, approved and included into the scope of the project and therefore its final deliverables.

21.2.2 Premature

The premature ending of a project could arise for any number of reasons—for example, due to a change of management, a change of businesses strategy, a faltering/slowing down of the economy, the sponsor moving onto other priorities, or the project failing to progress through a gateway review because the Business Case is no longer valid. Gateway reviews are often nicknamed *kill-points* for that very reason.

Completion also arrives prematurely for a few projects due to some parts of the project being eliminated. For example, in a new product development project, the marketing manager may insist on being supplied with production models before they have been tested: "Give the new product to me now, the way it is. Early entry into the market will mean big profits! I know we can sell a bazillion of these. If we don't do it now, the opportunity will be lost!"

In this scenario, the pressure will be on the project leader to finish the project and send it to production as quickly as possible. However, the implications and the risks associated with making the decision should be carefully reviewed and assessed by senior management and all stakeholders. All too frequently, perceived benefits turn out to be illusory, dangerous and hugely risky.

21.2.3 Phase (or stage)

Although this chapter discusses steps towards closing a project at its ultimate end, it should be noted that most elements of project closure can also be applied at the end of each stage of the project life cycle, or at particular phases in the project design. To help clarify this, refer to Chapter 2 "Popular frameworks and methodologies", Figures 2.20, 2.21 and 2.22, and consider where closure activities could be applied in each of these approaches.

21.2.4 Perpetual

Some projects never seem to end! A major characteristic of this kind of project is constant add-ons, suggesting the presence of a poorly conceived project scope and a poorly applied project management approach. Organisations should regularly review all project activity and ensure no perpetual projects exist, and if any are identified, bring them to a swift close via the formal project closure steps. Yes, there may be a phase 2 project, with further work, but this is another subsequent project, not a perpetual extension of the current one.

21.2.5 Failed project

Failed projects are usually easy to identify and are easy for a review group to close. However, every effort should be made to communicate the reasons for termination of the project. In any event, project participants should not be left with any kind of stigma for having worked on a project that failed. Many projects will fail because of circumstances beyond the control of the project team.

21.2.6 Changed priority

Organisation priorities often change, and their strategies will therefore shift in direction. For example, during the 2008–13 global financial crisis (GFC), many organisations shifted their focus away from money-making projects towards cost-saving projects. The COVID pandemic affected many organisations' operational activities, with priorities (and projects) realigned to continue business in the new order of the world. Each organisation's oversight group will continually revise project selection priorities to reflect changes in organisational direction based on many factors, in particular changes to the organisation's external environment and competition. Projects that are already in progress may need to be substantially altered or cancelled. Thus, a project may start as a high priority but see its ranking erode or crash during its project life cycle, as conditions change.

Remember: In any of these situations that represent a non-normal close, the project leader and the organisation should be aware of the **sunk costs** that have been made; these would be recorded in the final project status report.

The next sections of this chapter review some of the key closure activities in more detail.

21.3 ⋮ Closure activities

By this stage, the major challenges for the project leader and for the team members will be over. However, getting the project leader and the project participants to wrap up remaining items in order to fully complete a project can be difficult. It's like asking, "The party is over—now who wants to help clean up?" Much of this work is mundane and tedious. Motivation and staff retention can be chief challenges. For example, accounting for equipment and completing final reports are often perceived as dull administrative tasks by project professionals, who are action-oriented individuals. The project leader's task therefore is to keep the project team focused on the remaining project activities and on final delivery to the customer, until the project is fully complete. Communicating a closure and review plan and schedule early on allows the project team to (1) psychologically accept the fact that the project will end and (2) prepare themselves to move on. The ideal scenario would be to have each team member's next assignment ready at the stage that the current project's completion is announced.

Project leaders need to be careful to maintain their enthusiasm for completing the current project and must continue to hold people accountable for deadlines, which are prone to slip during the waning stages of the project.

Implementing the closure process can include many activities. Some organisations develop lengthy lists for closing projects as they gain experience over time. These can be very helpful for ensuring that nothing is overlooked. Implementing Closure includes the following key activities:

1. Gaining final deliverable (outcomes and outputs) acceptance from the customer (final deliverable sign-off)

2. Shutting down physical resources (e.g. releasing to new uses, finalising leases)

3. Releasing project team members, including handling the movement of permanent borrowed team members back to their substantive positions in the business

4. Closing accounts and seeing that all invoices are settled (refer to Chapter 12 "Project cost management")

5. Closing procurements and supplier contracts (refer to Chapter 17 "Project procurement management")

6. Creating a **final project status report** and archiving the project library

7. Congratulating the project team and celebrating

8. Communicating (hopefully successful) outcomes and thanks to the wider project stakeholder community

9. Reviewing the Business Case, benefits, **critical success factors (CSFs)** and key performance indicators (KPIs).

Administering the details of closing out a project can be intimidating. Some organisations have checklists of dozens of closure checks and tasks! These checklists deal with closure details relating to items such as facilities, teams, staff, customers, vendors and the project itself. A partial example administrative closure checklist is shown in Table 21.2.

Note: Most good PMOs will have such checklists available to the project leader.

Table 21.2 Project closure checklist

	Date checked	Comments/actions	Responsible
Scope and performance			
Have all deliverables (outputs and outcomes) been accounted for and delivered from the project?			
Have the project objectives and CSFs been achieved?			
Have all variations been recorded in the Variations Register, and appropriate lessons learned extracted for the management of future project scope?			
Have all variation requests been fully completed and closed as appropriate?			
Were there any major omissions from the scoping of the project that offer lessons learned for the organisation?			
Have all business owners been notified, and have they agreed to the handover of the relevant deliverables? Have these final deliverables been formally signed off?			
Have the Business Case benefits been measured and reported on to the appropriate management and other stakeholders?			
Have the project's baselines (scope, time, cost and performance) been reported against? Are there any lessons learned to be extracted?			
Has handover of any phase 2 project ideas captured during this project taken place back to the project sponsor and/or PMO for possible follow-up projects?			

(Continues)

Table 21.2 Project closure checklist (*Continued*)

	Date checked	Comments/actions	Responsible
Time (schedule)			
Have all work packages and tasks been completed according to the project schedule?			
Has an updated project schedule been prepared, finalised and included in the final project closure report?			
Have lessons from any missed/delayed work packages and tasks been identified?			
Have estimates, formulas and methods for duration estimation been filed in the project library for use in future projects?			
Has a review of the scope baseline plus any approved variations against the planned baseline schedule been carried out and reported on?			
Cost/financial/procurement			
Have all outstanding invoices been recorded?			
Have all contracts been closed out (formal written notice)?			
Have all purchase orders been checked and delivered and payment issued?			
Has access to financial systems been revoked?			
If the project team is disbanded before financial closure of the project takes place, has a responsible commercial manager (or other) been assigned to do final closedown of the project accounts?			
Have rental or lease equipment agreements been closed, equipment returned and deposit(s) recovered?			
Has a fix (defect) list been agreed with suppliers and appropriate withholding amounts retained by the business?			
Has a final certificate (of practical completion/other) been issued to the client?			
Have estimates, formulas and methods for cost estimation been filed in the project library for use in future projects?			
Have contractors been released, contracts closed-out and procurement *blacklists* revised with underperforming organisations?			
Have any left-over raw materials or waste been disposed of in an environmentally considerate manner?			
Have all warranties/guarantees been handed over to relevant persons within the organisation?			
Have final formal contract close-out activities (as defined in the organisation's policies and procedures) been undertaken for all contracts?			
Quality			
Has evidence of deliverables (to quality standards/specifications) been retained as part of the deliverable acceptance process, and filed in the project library?			
Have quality lessons learned been extracted from the project and documented in the Lessons Learned Register, final project closure report and PIR?			
Have all quality records been retained and filed in the project library for future projects' reference?			
Has the quality of the management of the actual project been assessed and any continuous improvements been captured for the PMO to improve project management processes for future projects?			
Team (human resources)			
Has the team been thanked for their individual contribution?			
Have arrangements been made to release or return staff?			
Have relevant project team members been performance-appraised and (as required) have their line managers been briefed on their performance?			
Has access to ICT systems been revoked?			
Have the project successes been celebrated (project closure party)?			
Does the HR department need to be included in a career counselling capacity?			
Have all personal project assets been reclaimed from the project team members (e.g. phones, laptops and other tools and equipment)?			
Have all final exit interviews been scheduled, carried out, and HR copied in on relevant documentation?			
Has payment of retention and other bonuses, as agreed based on actual performance, been agreed and set up for payment?			

	Date checked	Comments/actions	Responsible
Risk			
Have all risks been closed-out cleanly?			
Are there any open risks that require handing over to business as usual with the final deliverables?			
Has the Risk Register been updated and filed in the project library?			
Have lessons in relation to the management of the project been captured in the Lessons Learned Register?			
Did any opportunity risks materialise, and were these successes delivered and communicated to appropriate stakeholders?			
Sponsor/customer			
Have all project deliverables been completed and approved (accepted), including approved variation requests?			
Is all acceptance testing complete and have any outstanding issues been resolved or placed on an agreed defect list?			
Have all business owners of the project's outcomes, outputs and benefits been notified?			
Have relevant *benefit owners* been notified, and have they accepted responsibility for the tracking of ongoing project benefits handed into the business post-project?			
Has an in-depth project review and evaluation interview with the customer been conducted?			
Have the users of deliverables been interviewed to assess their satisfaction with the deliverables? With the project team? With vendors? With training? With support? With maintenance?			
Communications and other stakeholders			
Has the project closure and success been communicated to the wider internal project stakeholders?			
Have all external stakeholders to the project been notified of the project outcomes and what it means to them?			
Have records of all project communications been filed in the project library?			
Has an in-depth project review and evaluation interview been conducted with the customer?			
Have users been interviewed to assess their satisfaction with the project deliverables, with the project team, with vendors, with training, with support, with maintenance etc?			
Project administration			
Has the project library been updated (to include details of final and accurate project financials)?			
Has an end-of-project lessons learned (retrospectives) workshop been carried out and lessons captured?			
Have lessons beyond the project environment been passed to accountable departmental managers to attend to (e.g. improvements to HR processes or procurement processes)?			
Has the final project closure report been signed and accepted by relevant bodies, including the project sponsor and Steering Committee?			
Has the PMO been notified and provided with all documents and project information?			
Has the PMO or appropriate body (either external or internal to the organisation) carried out a PIR?			
Have all major project decisions been recorded and lessons learned extracted for future projects?			
Have the organisation's enterprise resource planning (ERP) system, finance system, project management information system and other systems been updated as required with the final project details?			

 Checklist—Project Closure

21.3.1 Final deliverable acceptance

Experienced project leaders will rarely have a single sign-off of the project's deliverables at the end of a project. This is because best practice indicates that successful projects have deliverables designed and planned into the project schedule and signed off as they are delivered throughout the entire project life cycle. This process is illustrated in Chapter 18 "Project execution", Figure 18.3 "Deliverable acceptance, across the project life cycle", where several deliverable IDs (DID) are indicated along the life cycle of the project. Each deliverable would be formally signed off using a **deliverable acceptance** form, thereby reducing the uncertainty (risk) of final acceptance at project closure.

The conditions for completing and transferring the final project deliverables should be established at the Planning stage. A completed software program offers a good example of how specific details will need to be worked out in advance: for instance, if the user has problems using the software, will the customer withhold final payments? Who will be responsible for supporting and training the user base? What if handover documentation is not ready in time for operational use? If these conditions are not clearly defined within the integrated PMP, getting acceptance/approval of delivery can be troublesome. Some projects define CSFs within the project scope document. These, along with the deliverables and objectives, are then used to confirm delivery and to secure final payments and/or final sign-off of the project from the customer.

21.3.2 Readiness assessment

In Chapter 5 "Organisational change management and cultures", the concept of a business readiness assessment was introduced. If your project has a concept of a go-live to the customers (whether these are internal or external to the organisation) it is good practice to administer some form of readiness survey (discussed in Chapter 5 "Organisational change management and cultures"). Whether this is carried out in the Closure stage as a part of final handover or in the Execution stage will depend on the design of your project. The readiness survey will contain information about the readiness of all levels of users of the system. There could be some *wash-up tasks* to be carried out in the project as a result of carrying out such assessments, but undoubtedly these will make for a smoother final go-live and handover—and a happy customer.

21.3.3 Project team disbandment

A gradual release of the project team typically occurs during the latter half the Execution stage into the Closing stage. For some team members, termination of the activities they have been responsible for ends before the project is delivered to the customer, in which case reassignment of these participants needs to take place well before the final finish date. For the remaining (full-time, part-time and contract) team members, their release schedule should have been determined when they were brought into the project—this discussion was captured in the resource Skills Matrix (refer to Chapter 10 "Project resource management")—so there should be no surprises. The different situations the project leader could find themselves in include the following.

- Team members being returned to their former functional (substantive) roles in the business. Project leader may have to negotiate with the operational line manager as to when this occurs, as their substantive position could have been filled with a temporary replacement, in which case the temporary incumbent would have to be released.

- Team members being assigned to new operational positions as part of the handover, subsequently playing an active role in the operation of the new product or service once it has been handed over to the business. This provides a solid base for knowledge transfer between the project and the handover to the business.

- For contracted workers, the end of their assignment to this project. Contract end dates are known when the contractor is brought onto the project.

21.3.4 **Procurement and contracts**

Since many work invoices will not be submitted until after the project is officially over, closing out contracts can be messy and fiddly as there may be multiple loose ends that need to be tied up: it is realistically improbable that all submitted invoices will have been finalised, billed and then paid (settled). Also, when contractors are used, there is a need to verify that all the contracted work has been performed to the terms of their contract (performance and quality-based payments are now the norm). Keeping contract records—such as progress reports, invoices, change records and payment records—is imperative and will be vital as evidence should a contract dispute or lawsuit arise. All too often, dealing with paperwork (and record-keeping in general) is left on the back burner in the haste to meet looming deadlines, but this only creates major headaches later when final documentation is drawn up.

21.3.5 **Splitting closure**

Some organisations split the project Closure stage into two sub-stages:

1. *Closure:* This represents all the aspects of formal administrative project closure, minus any ongoing financial aspects of the project. This is where the *soft aspects* of HR are managed, the project library is archived, the project closure reports are drafted and final sign-off is achieved.

2. *Finalisation:* Here, only the final accounting and invoicing aspects remain, and these can be carried out without the expense of retaining the project team (and often the project leader). The final financial, procurement and contracting aspects of the project could be handed over to the relevant department in the business to handle rather than keeping expensive project staff around to carry out these administrative duties. Items to be reconciled and then handed over would include outstanding invoices, schedules of payments, performance acceptance criteria, withholding arrangements, warranties and fix-lists.

21.3.6 **Creating the final project report**

The final project report summarises project performance and provides useful information for continuous improvement. Although the final report will be customised to your organisation, its content typically includes the following: an executive summary, a review and analysis of each dimension (knowledge area), any recommendations, and of course key lessons learned.

■ *Executive summary:* This summary simply highlights key findings and facts relating to the project's implementation—whether the project objectives (and CSFs) were met for the customer. For example, are stakeholders satisfied that their strategic intents have been met? What has been user reaction to the quality of the deliverables? Are the project deliverables being used as intended, and are they providing the expected benefits? Final time, cost and scope performances are listed. Any major problems encountered and addressed are noted here, as are summaries of key lessons learned.

■ *Review and analysis:* Data are collected to record the project history, management performance, and lessons learned, to improve future projects. Analysis examines in detail the underlying causes of problems, issues and successes. The analysis section includes a succinct, factual review of all dimensions of the project, for example, project CSFs, objectives, deliverables, the procedures, and systems used, quality outcomes and organisational resources. It is common to collect data from both an organisational and project team viewpoint. The PMO or closure facilitators often use questionnaires and surveys to pick up on issues and events that need to be examined further. For example, 'Was the organisational culture supportive and correct for this type of project? Why? Why not?'; or 'Did the team have adequate access to organisational resources—people, budget, support groups, equipment?'. The project will also provide project schedules, cost comparisons, scope data and other data needed to tell the story of performance. The review and analysis should aim to cover all the knowledge areas of scope, time, quality, cost, resources, communications and information, risk, procurement, stakeholders, and integration. Without a full analysis of each knowledge area and other specific areas to your industry such as environment and workplace health and safety, there is potential to miss elements that may provide useful information for lessons learned for future projects. When undertaking this analysis, the project leader must consider three questions (for each of the dimensions):

1. What was planned?
2. What was changed?
3. What was delivered?

- *Recommendations:* Usually, review recommendations represent major improvement actions that should take place. They can be technical in nature and focus on solutions to problems that surfaced. For example, to avoid rework, the report for a construction project may recommend shifting to a more resilient type of building material. In another situation, there may be a recommendation that a vendor or contractor relationship be either terminated or sustained.

- *Lessons learned:* Lessons learned arguably offer the most valuable ongoing contribution from the closure process. These should be collected from a number of workshops, for example workshops with:

  - the project team and key subject matter experts (SME)
  - the customer of the project, who may be internal or external to the organisation
  - various subgroups of other stakeholders to assess what went well, not so well, or would be done differently next time.

The positive attributes of being able to empower and inform others in future projects needs to be highlighted. In practice, new project teams looking for insights for a new project on find that studying past project reports (for projects that are similar to the project they are about to start) can reap valuable rewards. Team members frequently remark: "The recommendations were good, but the 'lessons learned' section really helped us to avoid many pitfalls and made our project implementation smoother". It is for precisely this reason that lessons learned have taken on greater prominence in the project management field and warrant an extended discussion at the end of this chapter. Three key questions to ask when capturing lessons learned are:

1. What went well?
2. What didn't go so well?
3. What would we do differently next time?

Lessons learned are not just a one-off activity that is carried out at the end of the project. Although a formal lessons learned workshop is a planned activity that should be held at the end of the project (or stage), in modern project environments it is also common to seek and exploit lessons learned at project team meetings, at reviews and during heath checks and audits throughout the life cycle of a project. See "Snapshot from Practice: Gateway review lessons learned".

 Project Closure Report

 21.4 : **Performance evaluation**

Many project closure activities support the process of reviewing what actually went on in the project. Performance reviews—of the project team, of the contribution made by each individual and the **performance of suppliers** and of **contractors**—all form components of the **performance review** and Closure stage of the project. Note that some of these aspects will have already been considered (planned for) during HR activity planning (set out in Chapter 10 "Project resource management"). Other aspects, such as contractor performance, were introduced in Chapter 17 "Project procurement management"; a concluding discussion on their performance is provided in this section.

SNAPSHOT *from* PRACTICE — Gateway review lessons learned

Lessons learned are frequently hidden within the accumulation of project management documentation, or in the heads of individuals; but more often, they are simply not captured and are lost. Governments, as well as corporates and small-to-medium enterprises, are becoming increasingly aware of the potential significance of losing such rich knowledge and information. They realise that not capturing, publishing and passing this type of knowledge and information back into the organisation for the benefit of future programs and projects represents a significant missed opportunity.

The New Zealand Treasury actively seeks to capture lessons learned from projects via gateway reviews in a series of formal reports. In its gateway reviews—lessons learned reporting, the reasons stated for investing effort into publishing a formal lessons learned report are given as, "These lessons learned are observations gained from Gateway reviews which highlight opportunities for project and programme management improvements in New Zealand Government agencies." Many of the projects reviewed during this period involved cross-government and multi-jurisdictional initiatives, which can be inherently more complex than single agency projects. This gateway report summarises the key themes in order of frequency as indicated in Table 21.3.

Table 21.3 Lessons learned themes

	Report 4, 2017 (Reviews 151–200)	Report 3, 2015 (Reviews 101–150)	Report 2, 2013 (Reviews 051–100)
1	Governance	Governance	Business Case
2	RAID (Risks, Assumptions, Issues, Dependencies)	Sourcing strategy/ management	Risk & issue management
3	Business case	Business case	Governance
4	Transition into service	Risk & issue management	Sourcing strategy/management
5	Sourcing strategy/management	Programme/Project management	Transition into service
6	Programme & Project Management	Stakeholder management	Programme & Project management
7	Stakeholder management	Resourcing	Resourcing
8	Resourcing	Benefits realisation	Stakeholder management
9	Benefits realisation & management	Transition into service	Benefits realisation
10	Management of change	Programme/Project planning	Management of change
11	Financial planning & management	Management of change	Programme/Project planning
12	Programme/project planning	Capturing lessons learned	Financial management
13	Capturing lessons learned	Methodology	Methodology
14	Methodology	Financial management	Dependency management

Source: https://www.treasury.govt.nz/information-and-services/state-sector-leadership/investment-management/review-investment-reviews/gateway-reviews/gateway-reviews-lessons-learned, accessed February 2022 CC BY 4.0 https://creativecommons.org/licenses/by/4.0/

Project leaders are increasingly looking to events from the past to inform events of the future. Formal lessons learned may be found in publications, in lessons learned databases and in centralised processes. The lessons that have been learned should be leveraged in future project environments, to ensure (often expensive) mistakes and missed opportunities are not ignored. The list in Table 21.3 indicates areas that maybe we should be wary of! (*Note:* This edition of *Project Management in Practice* brings more focus to governance by the introduction of a new chapter, Chapter 7 "Governance and projects".)

Sources: The Treasury 2017a, "Gateway reviews—lessons learned", https://www.treasury.govt.nz/information-and-services/state-sector-leadership/investment-management/review-investment-reviews/gateway-reviews/gateway-reviews-lessons-learned, accessed February 2022; The Treasury 2017b, *New Zealand Gateway Reviews Lessons Learned Report 2017*, https://www.treasury.govt.nz/sites/default/files/2018-03/gateway-lessons-learned-report-jul17.pdf, accessed February 2022

21.4.1 Post-implementation review (PIR)

The purpose of a project closure report is to capture the facts of the project, whereas the purpose of a PIR is to assess how well the project, the project team and the project leader performed. PIRs are often carried out by a person who is external to the actual project (e.g. they may work for the PMO or may be sourced externally to carry out this specific task). The timing of a PIR is critical as the aim is to capture knowledge from people on the project, but of course if these people have already left the project, the value in carrying out a PIR will be somewhat diluted. When conducting the review, use the following guidelines.

- *Ask for openness:* Some aspects of the project might not have gone as expected, but these are often where greater learnings take place.
- *Be objective:* Avoid emotions and politics; stick to the facts.
- *Be future focused:* Remember that although we can look back with hindsight, we are capturing lessons for future projects.
- *Address both positive and negative perspectives:* Both perspectives are equally important at this stage in the review. A simple technique for gaining quick responses is the $3 + 3$ questionnaire, where stakeholders are asked to list three positive and three negative aspects of the project. The technique gives equal weight to both positive and negative aspects (it is too easy otherwise to focus on negative aspects rather than positive ones).

A PIR interview and subsequent data/information analysis (leading to the final PIR report) will typically cover the following areas.

- *Gap analysis:* What was originally defined? What was actually delivered? What got changed on the way?
- *Determination of the achievement of the project goals:* Did the product or service delivered meet the requirements that were originally defined? Were these to the quality defined? And ultimately, was it what the customer wanted?
- *Stakeholder satisfaction:* Were the stakeholders satisfied with the behavioural aspects of the project leader's and team's performance as well as with what was delivered?
- *Benefit review:* If benefits were to be delivered as part of the project, have these been checked? What benefits are still to be realised by the business and who in the business is going to take accountability for bringing them to fruition?
- *Future work:* Capture any future work not included within the scope of the project that should be reported back to the project sponsor, Steering Committee and PMO, which could be packaged as continuous improvement work or new projects. These could also include rejected variations (changes) to this project.
- *Lessons learned:* Are there wider lessons for the organisation that go beyond the project perspective? There could be lessons for the PMO, to improve the project management framework, templates and other intellectual properties; there could be lessons for HR in terms of how people are recruited into projects, for procurement, contracts, or legal departments, among others.

 Post-implementation Review

21.4.2 **Team evaluation**

The evaluation of team performance is essential for encouraging positive changes in behaviour and to support individual career development and continuous improvement (e.g. through inhouse organisational learning processes or via individual sponsorship to undertake external training).

Evaluation implies measurement against specific criteria. Experience proves that the stage for evaluation must be set before the project commences: the expectations and standards to be met need to be known (as do any constraints) and a supportive organisational culture needs to be in place. If this isn't the case, the effectiveness of the evaluation process will suffer.

In a macro sense, evidence suggests that performance evaluation is often not performed well; there are two major reasons for this that are cited by practitioners:

1. Evaluations of individuals are left to be carried out by the team member's own home department supervisor(s)

2. Most organisations do not go beyond typical measures of team performance centred on time, cost and specifications—although these measures are important and critical, organisations should consider evaluating the team-building process, the effectiveness of group decision-making and problem-solving processes, group cohesion, evaluating the level of trust among team members, and the quality of information that was exchanged. Measurement of customer and user satisfaction with project deliverables (i.e. the project results) is often missed completely. Yet, project success depends significantly on satisfying these important factors. The quality of the deliverables is the responsibility of the team.

To carry out an evaluation of the project's team performance, first define the criteria against which they will be evaluated. This process was outlined in Chapter 19 "Project leaders and project teams", and is further discussed below.

■ Do standards for measuring performance exist? Peter Drucker was once quoted as saying, "If you can't measure it, you can't manage it" (Drucker Institute 2013). It is important therefore to be able to assess whether the goals (and the expected targets for these goals) were made clear for both the team and the individuals within the team. Were they challenging? Were they attainable and attained? Did they lead to positive consequences?

■ Are individual and team responsibilities and performance standards known by all team members?

■ Are team rewards adequate? Do they send a clear signal that senior management believes that the synergy of teams is important?

■ Is a clear career path for successful project leaders in place?

■ Was the team empowered to manage short-term difficulties?

■ Is there a relatively high level of trust emanating from the organisational culture?

■ Team evaluation should go beyond time, cost and specifications. The characteristics of highly effective teams discussed in Chapter 19 "Project leaders and project teams" can easily be adapted as measurements of team performance.

■ What organisational learning can be taken away from the process of team and individual performance management? Was this fed back into the relevant areas of the business, e.g. to the HR department and/or the line manager?

In practice, the team evaluation process takes many forms—especially when evaluation goes beyond time, budget and specifications. A typical mechanism for evaluating teams is a survey administered by the HR department. The survey is normally restricted to team members, but in some cases, other project stakeholders interacting with the team may also be included. A sample of a survey can be seen in Table 21.4. After the survey results have been tabulated, the team will meet with the facilitator and/or senior management to review the results.

Table 21.4 Sample team evaluation and feedback survey

Question	Comments and observations
1. Did the team share a sense of common purpose?	
2. Was each member willing to work towards achieving the project's objectives?	
3. Was respect shown for other points of view and ideas?	
4. Were differences of opinion encouraged and freely expressed?	
5. Was it possible to achieve consensus on project decisions, in the main?	
6. Did the majority of interactions among team members occur in a comfortable, open, honest and supportive atmosphere?	
7. Were all project meetings properly managed and run effectively?	
8. Did the team's communication methods and the frequency and content of communications meet your personal needs?	
9. Were project tasks shared equally within the project team and were the skills of individuals leveraged in an effective manner?	
10. Was working on the team project a valuable experience for you?	
11. Did you learn new skills and/or gain beneficial experience by being involved in this project?	
12. Did your supervisor display empathy and were they able to listen to your concerns and ideas?	
13. Were you able to speak freely with your supervisor, even if you disagreed with the decisions being made?	
14. Was the feedback on your performance accurate, timely and constructive?	
15. Did you feel you were a member of a well-functioning, co-operative team?	
16. Did the project management environment employ a continuous improvement process that improved the process and procedures of the project?	
17. Did you clearly understand the needs of the customer and did the project reflect these needs?	
18. Were you able to inform other people that you were proud to be working on this project?	
19. Were you able to achieve an overall balance between the project's requirements and your personal life?	

© 2022 Dr Neil Pearson

 Team Survey

This session is comparable to the team-building sessions that were described in Chapter 19 "Project leaders and project teams", except that the focus here is on using the survey results to assess the development of the team, its strengths and weaknesses, and the lessons that can be applied to future project work. The results of team evaluation surveys are helpful in changing behaviour to better support team communication, the team approach and a continuous improvement of team performance.

21.4.3 **Performance reviews**

Organisations vary in the extent to which their project leaders will be actively involved in the appraisal process of team members. In organisations where projects are managed within a functional organisation, the team member's area manager, not the project leader, will be responsible for assessing performance. The area manager may solicit the project leader's opinion about the individual's performance on a specific project; this will be factored into the individual's overall performance. In a **balanced matrix**, the project leader and the functional manager will jointly evaluate an individual's performance. In a **project matrix**, and for project organisations in which the lion's share of the individual's work is project related, the project leader will be responsible for appraising their individual performance. One process that appears to be gaining wider acceptance is the multi-rater appraisal or **360-degree feedback**, which involves soliciting feedback concerning a team member's performance from everyone their work affects. This would include therefore not only project and functional managers, but also peers, subordinates and even customers. Refer to Chapter 19 "Project leaders and project teams" for further details on performance and feedback.

Performance appraisals generally fulfil two important functions. The first is developmental in nature; the focus is on identifying individual strengths and weaknesses and developing action plans for improving performance. The second is evaluative and involves assessing how well the person has performed in order to determine salary or merit adjustments. These two functions are not compatible. Employees, in their eagerness to find out how much pay they will receive, tend to tune out constructive feedback on how they can improve their performance. Likewise, managers tend to be more concerned with justifying their decision than engaging in a meaningful discussion about how the employee can improve their performance. It is difficult to be both a coach and a judge. As a result, several experts on performance appraisal systems recommend that organisations separate performance reviews (which focus on individual improvement) and pay reviews (which allocate the distribution of rewards).

In some matrix organisations, project leaders conduct the performance reviews, while the area managers are responsible for carrying out pay reviews. In other cases, performance reviews will be part of the project closure process, with pay reviews being the primary objective of the annual performance appraisal. Other organisations avoid this dilemma by allocating only group rewards for project work and provide annual incentive awards for individual performance (such as shares and bonus payment).

We will now discuss reviews that are designed to improve performance, as pay reviews are often outside the project leader's jurisdiction.

21.4.3.1 Individual reviews

Organisations employ a wide range of methods to review the performance of individuals working on a project. In general, the review methods used to assess individual performance tend to centre on the technical and social skills an individual has brought to the project and to the team. Some organisations rely simply on an informal discussion between the project leader and the project member. Other organisations may require project leaders to submit written evaluations that describe and assess the individual's performance on a project. Many organisations use rating scales that are similar to a team evaluation survey; the project leader rates the individual according to a certain scale (e.g. from 1 to 5) on a number of relevant performance dimensions (e.g. teamwork, customer relations, communication). Some organisations augment these rating schemes with behaviourally anchored descriptions of what constitutes a "1 rating", a "2 rating" and so forth. Each method has its strengths and weaknesses; unfortunately, in many organisations, the appraisal systems are designed to support mainstream operations and not unique project work. The bottom line is that project leaders must use the performance review system that is mandated by their organisation as best they can.

Regardless of the method used, the project leader needs to sit down with each team member and discuss their individual performance, both at the outset of the project and periodically throughout the project, as well as at project closure. The following list offers some general tips for conducting performance reviews (but of course project leaders must use their own discretion, according to their organisation's requirements).

1. Always begin the process by asking the individual to evaluate their contribution to the project; (1) this approach may yield valuable information that you were not aware of before; (2) this approach may also provide an early warning for situations in which disparity exists between assessments; and (3), this method helps to reduce the judgmental nature of discussions as it fosters a balanced and open dialogue.

2. Avoid (where possible) drawing comparisons with other team members. Instead, assess the individual in terms of established standards and expectations. Comparisons tend to undermine cohesion and divert attention away from what the individual needs to do to improve their performance.

3. When you have to be critical, focus the criticism on specific examples of behaviour, rather than on the individual personally (make sure you have gathered the facts before the meeting). Describe in specific terms how the behaviour affected the project.

4. Be consistent and fair in your treatment of all team members. Nothing breeds resentment more than if individuals feel (or hear through the grapevine) that they are being held to a different standard than other project members.

5. Treat the review as only one point in an ongoing process. Use it to reach an agreement as to how the individual can improve their performance.

Managers and subordinates alike may dread a formal performance review. Neither may feel comfortable with the evaluative nature of the discussion that is to take place and the potential for misunderstandings and hurt feelings to arise. Much of this anxiety can be alleviated if the project leader is doing their own job well: project leaders should constantly be giving team members feedback throughout the project so individuals already have a pretty good idea of how well they are performing/have performed and how the manager therefore feels before the formal meeting. Post-project angst can be avoided if pre-project expectations are discussed and are regularly reinforced during project performance.

In many cases, the same process used for reviewing the performance of team members will also be applied to an evaluation of the project leader's performance. Many organisations augment this process (given the importance of the project leader's position to their organisation). This is where the 360-degree review is becoming increasingly popular. In project-driven organisations, the PMO will typically be responsible for collecting information from customers, vendors, team members, peers and other managers about a specific project leader's performance and approach. This methodology offers tremendous potential for helping to foster the development of more effective project leaders if carried out well.

As well as being generated for (and by) performance reviews, data can also be collated to inform lessons learned.

21.4.4 Contractor and supplier performance

As well as assessing team and individual performance, it is important to review the performance of contractors and suppliers. Contractors may be subject to similar types of review processes, but the way in which the gathered information is used will vary according to the maturity of the organisation. It is important to capture information about good and poor performances by contractors and suppliers; it is very easy for this knowledge to be lost when the project closes. Who this information ought to be shared with within the organisation needs careful consideration: reflect on what some of the implications of not sharing this information might be (e.g. re-employing under-performing contractors, using suppliers that didn't perform to requirements).

Contractors often work as individuals, making it relatively easy to capture information about their performance. However, there must be a clear understanding of whose responsibility it is to inform the HR department about contractor performance, both good and poor. The project leader might be asked to make recommendations about who to use for future projects (and who it might be advisable to avoid in the future).

Good contractors should be documented as being suitable to work on future projects. This type of information can be both practical and useful, since contractors may not have specific HR records within the organisation and therefore, from a procurement perspective, might be viewed as (just) another contract that has been established and closed. Many organisations that regularly use contracted resources are increasingly realising the benefits of holding registers of approved (tried and tested) contractors and consultants (often populated with details of their past performance also). A project leader therefore potentially will have a rich repository readily available to them, to assist them with decision-making. *Note:* Government organisations in Australia are subject to the *Freedom of Information Act 1982* (Cth), so contractors may have a legal right to check the information held about them and to ask for any incorrect information to be rectified or removed from such registers.

Supplier performance should also be reviewed. Supplier performance can make or break a project, especially when their commitment to the project is against critical path project activities. All suppliers should therefore be reviewed. Sample review criteria are demonstrated in Table 21.5. *Note:* In some organisations, the contract and procurement departments will already have a predefined supplier survey for the project leader to complete. As project leader, you will therefore need to check this.

Table 21.5 Supplier performance review

Criteria	Weight	Score	Total score*
Timeliness of deliveries/service provided			
Completeness of deliveries/service provided			
Non-agreed changes to product or service specifications			
Met all contract terms and conditions			
Friendliness of service and support			
Ability and willingness to correct defects in a timely manner			
Recommended to give repeat business			
Provided status and tracking information required by the project			
Quality of product or service was consistent with agreed quality requirements			
Ability to accommodate changes to requirements, in line with project change requests			

*Total score = Weight × Score

© 2022 Dr Neil Pearson

Refer to the online template.

Supplier Evaluation

Each criterion shown in Table 21.5 (and any others your organisation deems necessary) should be reviewed against a set of predefined scores (this ensures an *apples-with-apples* comparison of suppliers can be made later, rather than risking an *apples-with-oranges* comparison). For example:

1. Unsatisfactory—fails to react or respond/deliver in timely manner

2. Fair—occasionally fails to react or respond/deliver in timely manner

3. Satisfactory—acts and responds to agreed parameters

4. Good—acts or responds/delivers in timely manner above agreed parameters

5. Outstanding—continually acts or responds/delivers in timely manner, exceeding all expectations.

Once supplier reviews have been completed, the project leader must ensure the performance feedback is disseminated to all appropriate departments within the organisation. Be sure to notify the contracts and procurement department and the finance department as this will enable a permanent track record to be created, so when future projects come along the benefits of hindsight will be readily available.

21.5 | Lessons learned

Lessons learned represent analysis that is carried out during the project and at the project Closing stage. Lessons learned attempt to capture both positive and negative project learnings (i.e. what has been gleaned). This analysis considers what worked and what didn't. Lessons learned, sometimes referred to as *post-mortems*, *post-project reviews* or *retrospectives*, have long been part of the project management approach. Peter Senge's *The Fifth Discipline: The Art and Practice of the Learning Organisation* (1990) drew focus towards the institutionalisation of organisational learning. Figure 21.2 illustrates a typical lessons learned process.

Although analyses of past processes often prove to be useful for closure and lessons learned, it is true to say that often their real value is not fully leveraged. Large, multinational companies with projects spread across the globe can find it challenging to effectively mine captured lessons learned. Smaller organisations also sometimes struggle to reap the potential rewards to be gained by examining lessons learned. The same project mistakes therefore tend to continue year after year, project after project. In the words of one executive: "Lessons learned are worth their weight in gold!

Figure 21.2 Lessons learned across the project life cycle

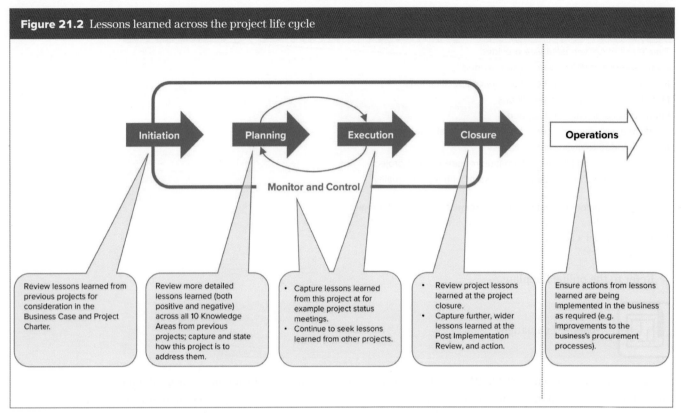

Initiation → Planning → Execution → Closure → Operations

Monitor and Control

Review lessons learned from previous projects for consideration in the Business Case and Project Charter.

Review more detailed lessons learned (both positive and negative) across all 10 Knowledge Areas from previous projects; capture and state how this project is to address them.

- Capture lessons learned from this project at for example project status meetings.
- Continue to seek lessons learned from other projects.

- Review project lessons learned at the project closure.
- Capture further, wider lessons learned at the Post Implementation Review, and action.

Ensure actions from lessons learned are being implemented in the business as required (e.g. improvements to the business's procurement processes).

© 2022 Dr Neil Pearson

I do not understand why we don't do a better job nurturing, dispersing, and implementing lessons learned though". Processes for capturing lessons learned continue to evolve, but countless practitioners acknowledge the existence of many types of barriers that can hinder or block the effective mining of lessons learned. A few of the most ubiquitous barriers are noted below.

- Lack of time to capture.
- Most lessons learned are captured when the project is complete; teams get little direction or support after the lessons are reported.
- Lessons learned often degenerate into blame sessions that became emotionally damaging.
- Lessons learned are not being used across different locations.
- Lessons learned while implementing the project are seldom used to improve the remaining work in the project.
- Too often, the lessons learned are not used in future projects because the organisational culture fails to recognise the value of learning.

What is needed to overcome these barriers is a strong methodology and management commitment to ensure lessons learned are identified, recorded, utilised and become ingrained in project and organisational culture. The key is to turn the lessons learned into actions and to have someone own the actions, so that something will get done about it in this project. The military has long used lessons learned to improve their operations (e.g. after each manoevre has taken place). Lessons learned have emerged as a strong process and management philosophy and are used by project-driven organisations around the world to mine the gold that the lesson has revealed. Lessons learned are championed by Norman Kerth in his text *Project Retrospectives* (2001) as follows:

> *A retrospective is a methodology that analyses a past project event to determine what worked and what didn't, develops lessons learned and creates an action plan that ensures lessons learned are used to improve management of future projects.*

The key point in conducting lessons learned analyses is to reuse solutions and to stop repetitive mistakes. A well-run lessons learned workshop should have several embedded, distinguishing characteristics to help ensure its effectiveness and value.

- It should be run by an independent facilitator.
- It should include a minimum of three *in-process* learning gates during the project life cycle.
- The workshop has an owner.
- A repository that is easy to access and use is developed.
- Discipline is mandated to ensure lessons are reviewed and used in future projects.
- Lessons found relevant should have an owner and the actions tracked to ensure the learning (from either a positive or negative lesson) is embedded in the project work.

21.5.1 Initiating the review

The review process style depends primarily on organisational and project size. Every effort should be made to make a project review a normal process rather than a surprise occurrence. In small organisations and projects where face-to-face contact at all levels is prevalent, project closure may be an informal process and simply take the format of a staff meeting. But even in such an environment, the content of a formal project review should still be examined and covered, and notes should be made of the lessons that have been learned. In some organisations, review initiation comes from a formal project review group, often a PMO service; for example, all projects are reviewed at specific stages in the project life cycle (i.e. perhaps when a project is 10–20% complete in terms of schedule (or cost), and again when it is 50% complete, and at project completion). In most multi-project organisations, reviews (called *gates*) will be planned for the completion of major milestones. These types of reviews are not linked to percentage complete as milestones; either the requirements for completion have been reached or they have not. It is important to emphasise that regardless of how reviews are set up, they need to be set up in the project Planning stage (i.e. before the project begins), with time and resources allocated to this process. This is a popular activity for project coordinators to become deeply involved in.

21.5.2 Use of an independent facilitator

Project leaders should consider using an independent facilitator to collect and implement lessons learned, especially in organisations where blame takes place frequently. A facilitator will guide the lessons workshop through an analysis of project activities—those that went well, those that did not go so well and those that required changing. The facilitator develops a follow-up action plan that clearly sets out defined goals and accountability (who is responsible for what and by when).

21.5.2.1 Characteristics of a facilitator

All project reviews will necessitate deciding who will facilitate and who will be accountable for conducting the review. Perhaps nothing influences the success of a project review more than the selection of the closure facilitator. This person should not be randomly chosen from personnel in the PMO. Independence is the key consideration when selecting the facilitator, therefore at minimum, they should:

- have no direct involvement or direct interest in the project
- be perceived as impartial and fair
- have the respect of senior management and other project stakeholders
- demonstrate willingness to listen
- exhibit independence and the authority to confidently report review results, without bowing to recriminations and complaints from vested interests
- have the best interests of the organisation as their priority when making decisions
- have proven robust experience of working in the organisation or industry.

21.5.2.2 **Roles of a facilitator**

There are good reasons for using an independent facilitator. Lessons learned exercises can sometimes degenerate into griping sessions where blame is tossed about and individuals may feel that they are being attacked about their performance on the project. This can result in poor, guarded participation. When this happens, the focus strays away from concentrating on root causes and how to improve performance in future projects. The facilitator therefore needs to be careful to avoid blame and to ensure others do not apportion it. In this way, stakeholders can feel safe to provide input in an open, honest and constructive manner.

A trained independent facilitator is often capable of eliciting information that would not be forthcoming to the project leader. Project participants report they are far more willing to attend and contribute to a lessons learned session run by an independent facilitator who can often eliminate many political aspects of discussions that would otherwise hinder the process. Another advantage of using an independent facilitator is that they can deliver any bad news to the project sponsor or to senior management without fear of recriminations.

21.5.3 **Managing a review**

Having a facilitator available at the start of a project is the preferred situation to be in. This is because the lessons learned approach stresses that lessons learned during project execution should be gathered and then applied to change remaining work. If lessons learned are not captured early on, they may be lost; after all, people forget things, people leave the project etc. Capturing lessons midway through the project life cycle allows the way the remaining work is performed to be changed (some practitioners call this process *correcting course while the project is in flight*). Most lessons learned methods use a minimum of three gates during the project life cycle. In this way, the lessons can be applied for the remainder of the project's execution (refer to Figure 21.2).

It is critical to have a separate repository or library, where reports and lessons learned can easily be accessed and retrieved. The PMO or oversight committee are usually responsible for maintaining this repository and encouraging its use. It is not unknown for a brilliant closure report to be created, only for it to be filed into someone's folder (instead of in a repository or library), never to be seen again! This is truly a big mistake! Lessons learned are often the single best source of information a project leader or team can use when planning a future project. Repeatedly, project leaders recount how lessons learned have saved their lives by allowing them to avoid a pitfall. Presentations at organisational meetings or conferences constantly encourage others to use and develop lessons that have been learned. (The sharing of lessons learned may even provide an opportunity for the project leader to shine in front of senior management.)

21.5.4 **Overseeing a post-project review**

In the past, lessons learned were primarily collected from a post-project survey. Someone reviewed the answers, summarised the results and filed the document. A lessons learned facilitator will often use several questionnaires as a starting point for conducting a post-project lessons learned analysis. These surveys often offer clues about previously unrecognised, deeper problems. A facilitator relates each clue to areas needing improvement, which are often found by checking the changes running through the project's change request process. The hard data may point directly to areas that can be improved. In some cases, the data direct the facilitator to the area where a problem was solved.

21.5.4.1 **Process and methods review**

A process review begins with a review of the strategic intent of the project, the selection criteria, the Project Charter, the project objectives, project scope and the acceptance criteria. This starting point reinforces and clarifies the Business Case for the project and the final project deliverables. Additional data-gathering for the process review is initiated through a questionnaire distributed to all major project stakeholders for their response. Examples of some typical questionnaire questions are provided in Table 21.6. Although this sample questionnaire has some areas of omission, it could be used as a starting point for your own project.

Table 21.6 Project process review questionnaire

Question	Yes/no/comment
Were the project objectives and strategic intent of the project clearly and explicitly communicated?	
Were the objectives and strategy in alignment?	
Were the stakeholders identified and included in the planning?	
Were project resources adequate?	
Were people with the right skill sets assigned to this project?	
Were time estimates reasonable and achievable?	
Were the risks for the project appropriately identified and assessed before the project started?	
Were the processes and practices appropriate for this type of project? Should projects of a similar size and type use these systems? Why/why not?	
Did outside contractors perform as expected? Explain.	
Were communication methods appropriate and adequate among all stakeholders? Explain.	
Is the customer satisfied with the project product?	
Are the customers using the project deliverables as intended? Are they satisfied?	
Were the project objectives met?	
Are the stakeholders satisfied their strategic intents have been met?	
Has the customer or sponsor accepted a formal statement that the terms of the Project Charter and scope have been met?	
Were schedule, budget and scope standards met?	
Is there any one important area that needs to be reviewed and improved upon? Can you identify the cause?	
Were the project's deliverables (outputs and outcomes), benefits and objectives achieved?	

© 2022 Dr Neil Pearson

21.5.4.2 **Organisational review**

One of the themes of this text is that project performance is strongly influenced by organisational culture. It is therefore important to be able to assess what fundamental organisational cultural properties exist that have the potential to affect your project's success or failure, and/or which may become a hindrance to the project team. Again, survey questionnaires are easy, quick and somewhat inexpensive to develop in order to collect data expeditiously. Table 21.7 shows a partial organisational survey as found in practice.

Table 21.7 Organisational review questionnaire

Question	Yes/no/comment
Was the organisational culture supportive for this type of project?	
Was senior management support adequate?	
Were people with the right skills assigned to this project?	
Did the project office help or hinder management of the project? Explain.	
Did the team have access to organisational resources (people, funds, equipment)?	
Was training for this project adequate? Explain.	
Were lessons learned from earlier projects useful? Why? Where?	
Did the project have a clear link to organisational objectives? Explain.	
Were project staff properly reassigned?	
Was the HR department helpful in finding new assignments?	

© 2022 Dr Neil Pearson

It is rare that important problems or successes will not show up in answers to a well-developed questionnaire. With the survey information in hand, the facilitator will carry out one-on-one visits to project team members, the project leader and other stakeholders to dive deeper into an analysis of cause-and-effect impacts. Fundamentally, the attempt is to isolate whether *a lack of x resulted in y*. It is important to stay with the big lessons. For example, the facilitator might ask team members, "What was the biggest pain-point in the project?", and from the responses given they can then synthesise the collective wisdom.

Armed with the information gleaned from one-on-one sessions and from other sources, the facilitator can next lead a team lessons learned session. This type of session usually starts with a review (synopsis) of the facilitator's report and an attempt to elicit further (key) information from team members about any issues, stumbling points or contentions. In fact, one of the roles of the facilitator is to lead the team in exploring new ways for solving a problem. Once the team reaches consensus about key lessons learned, it next works together to develop and document an action plan for improving future projects. Each lesson learned should have at least one lesson that will improve current or future projects. One person needs to be assigned as the owner of the lesson and they will also serve as the go-to person if more information is needed. If possible, the facilitator should elicit senior management's commitment for implementing the lesson.

A switched-on facilitator will also review archived lessons so they can investigate whether there have been any noticeable trends across similar projects (e.g. they may consider whether there are affinities between problems and successes among many projects). They will also want to know whether resources have been inadequate or whether there is evidence that senior management has supported the mining of lessons learned, and they may also look for any fundamental organisational culture dimensions that affected project successes and failures, or that became a hindrance to project teams.

During a conversation with one PMO manager, it emerged that a facilitator had discovered a (quite obvious) problem that had been occurring for over four years across most of the organisation's multi-country projects. It is difficult to believe that no one picked up on a problem that was detrimentally affecting so many of the organisation's projects. In this US organisation, managers were simply too focused on schedules, performance and the bottom line. They neglected to establish a personal professional working relationship with their foreign counterparts—for example, they didn't ask about their counterparts' key interests, their family and any cultural matters that were important to them. Relationships were often strained and performance suffered. The outcome of the facilitator's input was that project participants in each country are now required to attend a cultural awareness class to learn about their counterparts' country, customs and culture, and project results have already improved dramatically.

21.5.5 Using lessons learned

Each lesson learned is assigned an owner (who is typically a team member who is interested in, and familiar with, the lesson learned). This team member/owner serves as the contact point for anyone needing information (e.g. expertise, contacts, templates) relating to the lesson learned.

The facilitator is also tasked with the job of ensuring there is a clear process in place to ensure lessons are used to improve the management of future projects. Some organisations mandate that the team allocated to a new project must review the lessons learned on similar, past projects. This mandate tactically ensures that the most significant lessons are institutionalised: there will be no future excuse for not having used past best practices and for not having avoided past mistakes. If previous project leaders (before your project) had completed lessons learned more effectively, your project might have avoided many mistakes. Of course, a requirement is archiving the lessons in a repository/library. But beyond that, a simple, easy to use, consistent format is necessary to ensure that information is easily found, used and updated over time. A blog can be used to receive user comments on how helpful the lesson is in improving a process or product.

21.5.6 Lessons learned repository

As we have stated, if lessons learned are to be used effectively, it is critical to have some type of a repository (or library) in place where reports and lessons learned can be deposited, accessed and easily retrieved. This is especially relevant in today's global marketplace where the global businesses will use some form of web-based system to facilitate information-sharing and to capture shared learning. The responsibility of maintaining and promoting an organisation-wide repository of lessons learned is normally the responsibility of the PMO or oversight committee. Usage of such a repository often depends on how easy it is to search for relevant information. Personnel will be discouraged from accessing the repository if information is difficult to find. For example, one project leader commented: "There are so many lessons learned items in the library, I can't find information that applies to my project!" At a minimum, the repository should classify projects by type or characteristics. Each project review is categorised because there are differences in the way projects with different characteristics are managed and handled in an organisation. The classification of projects by characteristics allows prospective readers, teams and project leaders to be selective in their search and use of report content.

A snapshot of part of a repository classification scheme that allows prospective project stakeholders to start their search for information related to their prospective project might show:

- project type (e.g. development, marketing, systems, construction)
- size (e.g. monetary, duration)
- number of staff
- technology level (e.g. low, medium, high, new)
- strategic or operational support
- product, service or hybrid
- make (develop internally) or buy (outsource).

Many other classification fields relevant to the organisation could be included so users can drill further down into the repository to search for projects that match the features of their prospective project.

The impetus for the success of lessons learned has been increasing recognition of their real value in improving the management of future projects. For example, Intel, which has project teams dispersed over 290 locations in 45 countries, has found the use of trained facilitators to be highly effective in the process of mining and using lessons learned. Intel continues to train 15 new facilitators each year. The lessons learned approach is now standard operating procedure in many project-driven organisations. They are often the single best source of information a project leader or team can use in planning their next project. Lessons learned are a main change agent for developing best project management practices across an organisation. The lessons learned approach represents a positive step towards ensuring lessons are both developed and implemented so that the efficiency and efficacy of future projects are improved.

 Lessons Learned Register

21.6 The Business Case, benefits and scope realisation

An emphasis on the delivery of value from project investments is (thankfully) trending upwards in the project management industry. Value (or the benefits to be realised) are rapidly becoming a project leader's area of responsibility, with accountability still residing thankfully with the project sponsor or recipient operational manager. This is evident if the reader refers to Chapter 2 "Popular frameworks and methodologies", where several project management approaches were introduced, including APM, Praxis and ISO 2100:500.

Most of these project management approaches included activities to not only identify benefits (pre-project or at project start-up), but also to realise benefits at project closure and handover benefits beyond the project to the operational business. Figure 21.3 illustrates a benefits management process across the predictive project management life cycle.

Figure 21.3 Integrating benefits management with the project life cycle

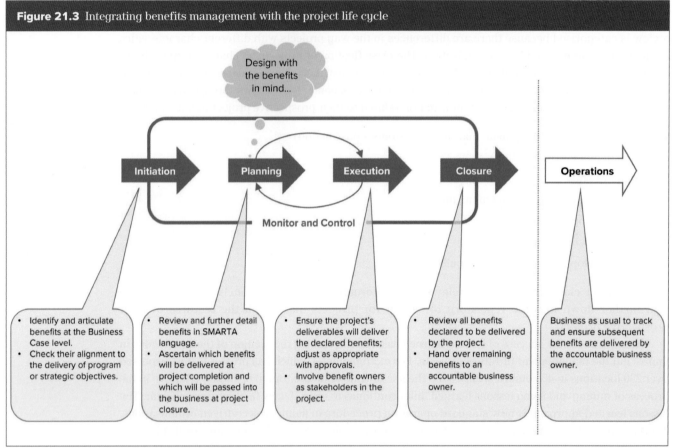

© 2022 Dr Neil Pearson

Figure 21.3 indicates two key activities that occur at project closure in relation to benefits.

1. Ensure that all planned benefits, as stated at the project's outset, are accounted for, and delivered at project closure. This would include any adjustments to the benefits that may have been agreed and approved at the various project gateway reviews. Measuring and reviewing benefits is no trivial activity and really draws on the project leader's ethics in terms of their being open, honest and transparent when declaring what benefits have been delivered against what was declared at the start of the project and adjusted at the gates throughout the project.

2. Ensure that benefits that go beyond the project are handed over to an accountable business owner for later realisation in the business. The project leader must ensure that the benefit is properly documented, communicated and handed over to the accountable business owner, in a professional manner.

As with all project tasks, these activities must be planned and should be included in the project's schedule, budget, and in relevant stakeholder and communication documents. The Business Case, for example, would be updated. More often, in today's modern project management organisations, a benefits realisation report would be prepared for presentation and handover to the business. Benefits management is a growing area of project management.

Some of the project performance documents and things to check for are summarised in Table 21.8.

Table 21.8 Project performance documents and checks

Document	Promises made	Checks to make	Roles involved
Benefits (Management) Plan	Benefits to the operational business unit or wider organisation	■ Did the project deliver the benefits? ■ Was part of a benefit delivered, leaving a gap to be captured in further projects?	■ Project leader ■ Project sponsor ■ Steering Committee ■ Operational business unit manager(s) ■ Project management office (PMO)
Business Case	As above, plus: Contribution to key performance indicators (KPIs). These could be internal KPIs related to contributing to the strategic objectives of the organisation or externally facing such as the improvement of a service level agreement with a customer	■ Measure and analyse the amount of movement a KPI made. ■ Did the KPI meet its target value or was there a shortfall? If there was a shortfall, carry out a root-cause analysis and state why.	■ Project leader ■ Project sponsor ■ Steering committee ■ PMO
Scope document or Project Initiation Document (PID)	Project objectives and project deliverables	■ Were the project objectives (outputs and outcomes) delivered as promised? ■ Were any quality issued raised? ■ Did the project meet its overall project objectives? If not, why not?	■ Project leader ■ Project sponsor ■ Steering Committee ■ PMO
Baselines, scope, time, cost and performance	The baselines cover the standard, and was the project delivered on time, on cost and to agreed scope (including approved variations). The performance baseline could include a multitude of metrics such as stakeholder engagement, customer happiness, number of defects etc.	■ Planned versus actual values for cost and time ■ Scope plus number and extent of variations ■ Performance per the metrics defined	■ Project leader ■ Project sponsor ■ Steering Committee ■ PMO

© 2022 Dr Neil Pearson

21.7 : **Project celebration**

The final closure activity for the project leader will be the project's closure celebration! Hopefully this will be an upbeat, jovial get-together that offers a chance to celebrate successes, brings closure and acts as an opportunity for goodbyes to be said. This celebration is an opportunity to recognise the efforts that project stakeholders have made. Even if the project did not reach its objectives and/or benefits 100 per cent, it is still appropriate to recognise the effort and goals that were achieved. If the project was a success, invite everyone who, in some way, contributed. Thank the team as a group and also thank each person individually. The spirit of the celebration should be one of gratitude towards the project team (and stakeholders) for a job well done, a job they are leaving with a positive feeling of accomplishment.

Summary

The project Closure stage is a full stage of the project life cycle. It is not a stage to skipped, nor one to take a token approach to. It is a stage that should be planned for and allowed time to complete in its entirety.

Several key aspects should be covered in closure, as follows.

■ Delivery and handover activities: Final handover of deliverables to the operational business and/or customer is a key part of closure. It ensures formal acceptance and sign-off of these deliverables and a formal sign-off of the entire project (acknowledging all the previous deliverables made throughout the Execution stage). It encompasses handover of all the artefacts as promised and as documented in the project scope document and wider integrated PMP. These could include physical items (outputs) as well as confirmation of outcomes (e.g. an employee satisfaction survey tells us our employees are happier because of the business change project).

■ Performance activities: The project was established on the basis of a Business Case (including benefits), a Benefits Management Plan (if the benefits are documented separately to the Business Case) and a project scope document (which includes SMART objectives). As discussed in Chapter 18 "Project execution", also included are the performance baseline, scope baseline, cost baseline and schedule (time) baseline. Across these documents and baselines there could be quite a few measures that must be assessed. and data collected, analysed, reviewed and reported on. This is not an insignificant task and may require more resources than just the project leader (i.e. a business analyst or project coordinator may be involved).

- Closure activities: The focus at project closure is to ensure the project is approved and accepted by the customer. Other closure activities include closing accounts, paying invoices, reassigning equipment, releasing and reassigning personnel, finding new opportunities for project staff, closing facilities and the final report. Checklists are used extensively to ensure tasks are not overlooked. In many organisations, closure tasks are largely carried out by the PMO, in coordination with the project leader. The final project closure report is the responsibility of the project leader. However, responsibility for carrying out the PIR is usually assigned to a PMO staff member, who assembles input from selected stakeholders (e.g. the customer, the sponsor, the project leader and project team members). In smaller organisations and projects, these closure activities are typically left to the project leader and the team.

- People resource activities: The process of evaluation involves assessing the performance of the project team (as a group), of individual team members, suppliers, contractors and the project leader. Evaluating the performance of these major players can generate important insights into who (and who not) to employ or enter into contracts with in future projects. Such activities usually include the involvement of the HR department to ensure organisation policies and procedures are being adhered to. Other activities include the physical release of people, closing down any access to ICT systems and recall of assets (e.g. phones, laptops). Celebratory activities should also not be overlooked. Celebrate all the successes as a team.

- Lessons learned activities: This is known as the *retrospective* in the Scrum approach. Lessons that have been learned through previous project experience(s) can be applied to inform improved performance in current and future projects. Today, many lessons learned workshops are run by independent facilitators. Post-project reviews held with the team help to catch any remaining issues and any holistic (whole-of-project) lessons that can be passed back into the greater business operations. PIRs should be carried out before the team is disbanded and/or before key people leave the project—timing of this activity can therefore be critical and should be built into the project's schedule at the Planning stage of the project.

Project closure is both a happy and sad time! It is where we celebrate the success of the project, but also where we say our goodbyes to people we have worked with, often for extended periods of time. The project leader must ensure that every person is thanked for their contribution before closing the doors on the project one last time.

And remember, make your projects more sustainable by recycling knowledge in the form of lessons learned.

Review questions

1. When and how might a project be closed?
2. What types of information would you expect to find in a post-implementation review (PIR)?
3. Why is it difficult to perform a truly independent, objective review?
4. Comment on the following statement: "We cannot afford to terminate the project now. We have already spent more than 50 per cent of the project budget".
5. Why should a project leader separate performance reviews from pay reviews? How do you do this?
6. Why is it important to review supplier and contractor performance?
7. Explain the activities in relation to benefits that occur across the project life cycle.
8. Why must a project leader revisit the Business Case, Benefits Plan and scope document at the project Closure stage?

Exercises

1. Taking the project closure checklist (refer to Table 21.2), review and add in any specific items that would need to be included from your organisation's perspective.
2. Interview a fellow project leader in your class and ask them to provide a minimum of two examples of when lessons learned have been used in a project they are familiar with.
3. In small groups, discuss how benefits are managed at project closure. Do your experiences differ from each other's? What recommendations would you make to improve the benefit management process in future projects and why?

4. Fred, a project manager, is currently closing out a project. The PMO is pressing him to release project staff and also for the final project deliverables to the business to be handed over. Fred, however, is resisting releasing some key members of the project team, given that the project has experienced some issues with its procurement and HR aspects.

The project has succeeded in providing quality outcomes to the business up to this point, and has been praised for its practices in engaging with the various business stakeholders and for the Agile approach taken towards communication with these stakeholders. The project sponsor has already congratulated the project team and project manager for having delivered some outstanding results to business operations. These results have really improved the effectiveness and efficiency of a key number of the business's processes and how these integrate with the existing ICT infrastructure.

Fred has prepared a project closure report and, pending final deliverables to the business, is getting ready for a mandatory presentation to the project sponsor and other key interested parties. The project closure report he has prepared is focused on reporting the triple constraints only and there appears to be no process in place with the PMO to facilitate a PIR. Fred has some concerns at this point and has therefore enlisted the skills of you, a more experienced project manager, to provide input into proceedings.

Your tasks as a more experienced project manager:

a. Prepare a briefing document about improvements that could be made to the:

- final project closure report
- process and timing of a PIR.

b. Produce a Lessons Learned Register of both positive and negative lessons as you (personally) perceive them, using the hooks provided in the case study. You will have to make assumptions, or maybe you have real-world experience you can bring into your responses.

c. Comment on some of the potential impacts that may be experienced due to the timing of releasing project team members in this case study (from both Fred's and the PMO's perspectives).

References

Drucker Institute 2012, "Measurement myopia", https://www.drucker.institute/thedx/measurement-myopia/, accessed June 2022.

Kerth N 2001, *Project Retrospectives: A Handbook for Team Reviews*, Dorset House Publishing Company.

Project Management Institute (PMI) 2017, *A Guide to the Project Management Body of Knowledge*, 6th edition, PMI.

Project Management Institute (PMI) 2021a, *A Guide to the Project Management Body of Knowledge* (*PMBOK® Guide*), 7th edition, PMI.

Project Management Institute (PMI) 2021b, *The Standard for Project Management (ANSI/PMI 99-001-2021)*, 7th edition, PMI.

Senge P 1990, *The Fifth Discipline: The Art and Practice of the Learning Organisation*, Doubleday/Currency.

The Treasury 2017a, "Gateway reviews—lessons learned", https://www.treasury.govt.nz/information-and-services/state-sector-leadership/investment-management/review-investment-reviews/gateway-reviews/gateway-reviews-lessons-learned, accessed February 2022.

The Treasury 2017b, *New Zealand Gateway Reviews Lessons Learned Report 2017*, https://www.treasury.govt.nz/sites/default/files/2018-03/gateway-lessons-learned-report-jul17.pdf, accessed February 2022.

Glossary

360-degree feedback A multi-rater appraisal system based on performance information that is gathered from multiple sources (superiors, peers, subordinates, customers).

5 Whys A method in which a series of five 'why' questions are asked to deepen understanding of the risk, or the root cause of a problem.

80/20 rule (Pareto rule) This rule states that 80% of effects come from 20% of causes.

A

activity Task(s) of the project that consumes time while people/equipment either work or wait.

Actual Cost of the Work Completed (AC) The sum of the cost incurred in accomplishing work. Previously this was called the actual cost of the work performed (ACWP).

acquiring resources The act of bringing resources onto the project just in time for the work packages and/or tasks they have been allocated to undertake.

action learning The practice of learning from actions (reflection) and putting the learnings back into the loop of making improvements.

active listening This means 80% listening and 20% talking.

adaptive Akin to the Agile/Scrum approach to managing a project.

ADKAR This is an OCM approach—the awareness, desire, knowledge, ability and reinforcement to change.

Agile Project Management (Agile PM) A family of incremental, iterative development methods for completing projects.

ALARP This stands for "as low as reasonably practicable". This technique is used to reduce risk to a practicable level.

alternative analysis This entails looking at different solutions to parts of the project's design, such as alternatives to carrying out a particular work package.

analogous estimating When looking at similar past projects to inform estimates on a current project.

Analytic Hierarchy Process (AHP) A method used to prioritise projects or investments, often implemented within Project Portfolio Management (PPM) software.

Activity-on-Node (AON) Method for drawing project networks. The activity is on the node (rectangle).

archived project information The act of filing the most up-to-date information and actuals associated with any element of a project into the project archive or library.

AS/NZS/ISO 31000:2009 The risk management standard describing the principles, framework and process for the management of risk. The standard is often applied to the management of risk in a project environment.

assumptions A statement of truth, assumed to be true within the project environment, e.g. availability of 'testers' during software testing. Assumptions should be reviewed from a risk perspective.

audits A formal quality check of the management of a project during which constructive advice on how to improve project outcomes is received.

B

balanced matrix A matrix structure in which the project manager and functional managers share roughly equal authority over the project. The project manager decides what needs to be done; functional managers are concerned with how it will be accomplished.

bar charts These are simple charts used to assist in visual presentation of data, for example quality date during the Execution of a project.

baseline A concrete document and commitment; it represents the first real plan with cost, schedule, and resource allocation. The planned cost and schedule performance are used to measure actual cost and schedule performance. Serves as an anchor point for measuring performance.

BATNA (Best Alternative To a Negotiated Agreement) A strong or weak BATNA indicates your power to negotiate with the other party.

benchmarking A technique of establishing a baseline measure from which to compare future performance. Can be carried out at a project level or on the project's product/service.

benefit (value) The defined business benefit (or the value) the customer is expecting from the project.

Benefit–Cost Ratio (BCR) A ratio of costs associated with carrying out the project, to benefits received from delivery of the project.

Benefits Management Plan A plan which contains detailed benefit profiles and guidelines on how benefits are to be tracked and delivered.

best practice An industry practice deemed as a 'standard' approach.

bidder conference A conference with registered bidders that announces and describes the tender and tender process to interested parties.

bill of materials (BOM)   A hierarchical decomposition for the product or service being produced by the project.

bottom-up approach   An approach to estimating, where estimates are made at the bottom-up (typically the task or work package) level.

bottom-up estimates   Detailed estimates of work packages usually made by those who are most familiar with the task (also called micro estimates).

box and whisker plot   A visualisation of a set of data, including the minimum number, maximum number and the middle 50% of data points around the median number.

brainstorming   Generating as many ideas/solutions as possible without critical judgment.

Bridges transition model   An OCM approach.

Browaeys and Price model of communication   A communication model which considers the effect of language, styles, stereotypes and relationships in sending messages to a receiver.

Budget baseline   The baseline (usually at the end of Planning) approved budget for the project.

Build–Operate–Transfer (BOT) contract   A variation of the BOOT contract (build, operate and transfer).

Build–Own–Operate (BOO) contract   A variation of the BOOT contract (build, own and operate).

Build–Own–Operate–Transfer (BOOT)   A risk management provision in which the prime contractor not only builds the facility, but also takes over ownership until its operation capacity has been proven before final transfer of ownership to the client.

build trust   The act of making stakeholders rely on you.

burndown/burnup   A chart to track the status of user stories completed withing a sprint (timebox).

business analyst   A formal role often used in projects to carry out various activities related to the analysis of the business in its current or to-be states.

Business Case   A document capturing the reason for the project's existence, the benefits to be delivered and the strategic alignment, amongst other important information.

Business Process Model and Notation (BPMN)   A process notation designed to model business processes within an organisation.

C

cause–effect diagram   A tool also known as the Ishikawa diagram, which assists in identifying the root causes of a problem.

change leaders roadmap   An OCM approach designed to support more transitional and transformative changes.

changed priority   Usually associated with the priority of the project—reflected in the Business Case—typically in relation to changes in the organisation's external environment.

chaos   A theory where decisions are made in response to a chaotic environment; refer to the Cynefin framework.

chart of accounts   A hierarchical numbering system used to identify tasks, deliverables, and organisational responsibility in the work breakdown structure.

checklists   A simple technique to assist in checking-off a list of items, for example a record of items to complete as project leader during the closure of a project.

checksheet   An often used tool used at various points in the project management life cycle to check that procedures, activities and tasks have been completed against a specified list of questions.

closed tender   Tendering to a closed (list) of suppliers. *See also* open tender.

closure activities   Activities administered by the project leader in the closure of a project. Typically, a checklist will be provided by the PMO to action.

commercial off the shelf package (COTS)   A term given to the purchase of commercial software packages, for example Microsoft Office.

committed   Often used to discuss a role's involvement in an Agile project: are you interested or committed? We only wish for the involvement of committed people in an Agile environment. Refer to the pig and chicken story in the text.

committee charter   A charter that describes the purpose, objectives and decision-making accountabilities of a committee, e.g. the project steering committee.

communication medium   The medium(s) through which the communication will be delivered, for example email, newsletter or social media channel.

Communications Management Plan   One of several management plans that define the governance, roles, procedures and other static predetermined procedures that are to be followed within the project environment.

Communications Register   A register of all formal, outgoing project communications. Useful to refer to in the event of questions being raised against past communications. Provides an audit trail of sent communications.

Communications Sent Register   A register of sent communications, which assists in locating information quickly, including who the communication was sent to (e.g. a distribution list if the medium were email).

competency   A skill of a role (e.g. project leaders should have formal competencies in organisation change management).

complex project management   The area of knowledge which captures best practice in the management of complex projects.

complexity The result of assessing a project and giving it a complexity classification, score or rating.

complexity assessment An assessment to evaluate the level of complexity a project may experience.

complexity assessment questionnaire A document used to gauge the level of complexity of a project.

complexity framework A framework which describes the stages for the identification, assessment and management of complex projects.

complexity profile A profile which describes the complexity of a project, usually articulated under a number of headings, for example *risk, change* and *stakeholders.*

complexity reviews Reviews of a project to assess its complexity, which are carried out in pre-project activities as well as periodically to ensure the project's profile is not becoming (more) complex.

complexity theory Formal academic theory around the general subject area of complexity.

concurrent engineering or **simultaneous engineering** Cross-functional teamwork in new-product development projects that provides product design, quality engineering, and manufacturing process engineering all at the same time.

consensus decision making Reaching a decision that all involved parties agree with and support.

constraints Statements which describe elements that will constrain the project (e.g. if a resource type is constrained, the project manager would review constraints in scoping and decide if any risks result).

context diagram A diagram used to capture the "big picture" of the business system within which the deliverables of the project will operate.

contingency A percentage of the total project budget held by the project steering committee/sponsor. Access to contingency funds is achieved through the project change/variation process.

contingency fund *See* contingency reserve.

contingency plan A plan that covers possible identified project risks that may materialise over the life of the project.

continuous improvement The act of seeking and actioning improvements in the management of the project and the project content (such as subject matter improvements).

contract A formal agreement between two parties wherein one party (the contractor) obligates itself to perform a service and the other party (the client) obligates itself to do something in return, usually in the form of a payment to the contractor.

contract law Formal law which informs how contacts are formed and administered. It can be industry, state and/or country specific.

contract types *See* contract

contribution/commitment grid A stakeholder analysis tool aimed at ascertaining where stakeholders sit in relation to

contribution/commitment and where the project manager/project team would like to see the stakeholder move.

control charts A method of reporting on usually the Quality of the projects outcomes and outputs. Usually generated as apart of Quality Control (QC) activities.

cost baseline The approved project budget as a result of the Planning phase of the project life cycle. This is the baseline from which Change (variation) Management would be applied to in order to control costs.

Cost Management Plan One of the knowledge area plans that identifies and tailors aspects of governance, policy, procedure and processes relating to cost management.

cost of contingency The value in $ of all the project's contingency, whether derived from EMV, summing padding, or other methods.

cost of poor quality (COPQ) The cost related to delivering poor quality in the project (e.g. this rework or re-testing. There is a cost associated with having to rework a work package or task as time and resources will add up to a $ value).

Cost of Quality (CoQ) The cost of not achieving quality in the project environment against the cost of implementing quality in the project environment. There are costs associated with carrying out quality (additional activities) as well as not carrying out quality (additional rework).

cost–benefit analysis *see* Benefit–Cost Ratio (BCR)

cost plus award fee (CPAF) A contract type that allows the contractor to be reimbursed for the costs of performing the work and earn an additional amount for good performance.

cost plus fixed fee (CPFF) A contract type where the contractor is paid for the normal expenses plus an additional fixed fee.

cost plus incentive fee (CPIF) A contract type that provides contractors with additional financial incentives for keeping the cost of the project as low as they can.

cost-reimbursable contract A contract type that reimburses the contractor for costs incurred on the project (usually within defined limits, that is, not open ended)

CPORT A technique to assist in the drafting of clear communications (context, purpose, objectives, resources and timing).

crashing Shortening an activity or project.

critical chain method A scheduling technique used as an alternative to PERT and the critical path method. Calculated buffers are used to manage schedule over/under runs in terms of time.

critical path The longest activity path(s) through the network. The critical path can be distinguished by identifying the collection of activities that all have the same minimum slack.

critical path method (CPM) A scheduling method based on the estimates of time required to complete activities on the critical path. The method computes early, late, and slack times for each activity in the network. It establishes a planned project duration if one is not imposed on the project.

critical success factors (CSFs) Factors (qualitative) in the business (or project) that define success; usually supported by a number of key performance indicators (quantitative).

cultural considerations The act of considering the impact of the project on cultures (company, people and/or countries) in the design and subsequent execution of any project activities.

current state The current as-is state the business operates in prior to any change being made.

Customer Relationship Management (CRM) A term used to describe software that maintains details on customers (stakeholders).

Cynefin framework A decision-making framework used to assist leaders in consciously making decisions based on the context at the time; simple, complicated and complex contents are considered.

D

daily Scrum meeting A short status meeting held daily by each team during which the team members synchronise their work and progress as well as report any impediments for removal by the Scrum master.

dangler An activity in a project schedule that has no relationship to any successor activities.

dashboard (red, amber, green or RAG-style) report A summary of important information (based on project data in this context) to highlight the key dynamics in a simple red, amber, green style.

data, information, knowledge, wisdom (DIKW) A knowledge management concept on how data becomes information, interpreted using knowledge or over time by experts who possess wisdom.

decision tree/decision tree analysis A method to assist in the selection of decisions or in the probability of risk alternatives.

defect An undesirable outcome from carrying out a piece of work, usually resulting in rework and therefore additional time/cost to the project.

deliverable A major product or result that must be finished to complete the project.

deliverable acceptance A formal documented process for the sign-off of deliverables.

deliverable acceptance form A formal documentation of a deliverable, usually signed off on acceptance by the relevant business representative (or customer).

deliverable tracking register A register of all deliverables and their status; for example: in progress, accepted or rejected.

delivery of value Delivering benefits (value) back to the organisation either during execution of the project, in the form of deliverables, and/or at the end of the project.

Delphi Technique or **Delphi Method** A group method to impartially collect perspectives and input into a problem or situation.

design thinking A theory used to assist in a more creative approach to problem-solving and solutioning.

detection difficulty A term used in an FMEA analysis to describe how difficult it could be to detect whether the risk could occur.

DevOps An approach that combines Agile development, Lean and operations management.

direct costs Costs that are clearly charged to a specific work package—usually labour, materials or equipment.

directions of project communications A technique used to "tailor" a communications message to different audiences (upwards, horizontal (peers), downwards or external).

discretionary budget An unspecified lump sum stating what the amount is for as well as what the maximum sum will be at the end of the project.

divergent and convergent thinking A technique used in the Ideation stage of design thinking to open up creative thinking (divergent) around solutions, to focus (convergent) and then to repeat the cycle. The idea is to seek solutions that at first might drop out of linear thinking.

DMAIC A continuous improvement technique (Define, Measure, Analyse, Improve, Control).

do it right the first time (DIRFT) A principle to get project team members (or others) to think about the cost of not doing it right the first time.

dysfunctional conflict Disagreement that does not improve project performance.

E

early finish (EF) The earliest an activity can finish if all its preceding activities are finished by their early finish times (EF = ES + DUR).

early start (ES) The earliest an activity can start. It is the largest early finish of all its immediate predecessors (ES = EF − DUR).

early warning indicators (EWIs) These are indicators which could be monitored to assess whether a risk is about to change from a risk (uneventuated) to an issue (eventuated/occurred).

Earned Value Management (EVM) or **Earned Value Analysis** A technique for measuring project performance and progress, based on a quantitative assessment of project progress and 'value' delivered.

Elevator Pitch (EP) A short snappy pitch which can be used in the communication of the project or elements of the project.

emotional intelligence (EQ) The ability or skill to perceive, assess, and manage the emotions of one's self and others.

enterprise bargaining agreements (EBAs)   A Union agreement which may contain information (constraints) on how the human resource can be used (e.g. travel is counted as working time, which could restrict the hours the resource is available for use).

Enterprise Resource Planning (ERP) system   Corporate IT systems that provide a repository of data on company information from project-related and financial, to resource information.

escalate   The act of taking a decision, issue or other matter to a higher authority.

estimating trumpet   A generic, industry-wide expectation setting of the level of detail required in estimation.

ethical behaviours   Behaviours which are promoted in order to ensure all dealings are carried out ethically.

ethics   Behaviours usually implemented through a set of principles or guidelines to ensure everyone is acting and behaving in an ethical manner.

event   A point in time when an activity(s) is started or completed. It does not consume time.

exception report   A report on the status of a project based on exceptions (deviations) from what was planned to take place (as documented in the baseline project management plan).

expected monetary value (EMV)   A technique to calculate project contingency based on the probability of a risk occurring and the costs incurred if the risk does occur. It is calculated by multiplying the probability (as a per cent) by the costs (e.g. 80 (80%)×($10,000) = EMV of $8,0000).

explicit knowledge   Knowledge which has been extracted from the minds of people and written down (i.e. made explicit).

F

Failure Mode and Effects Analysis (FMEA)   Each potential risk is assessed in terms of severity of impact, probability of the event occurring, and ease of detection.

fast-tracking   Accelerating project completion, typically by rearranging the network schedule and using start-to-start lags (i.e. planning tasks to occur in parallel as opposed to in sequence).

final project status report   The project leader's final formal report on all dimensions of the project as they actually stand at the end of the project.

finance/ERP system   *see* Enterprise Resource Planning (ERP) system.

firm fixed price (FFP)   A contract type where the contractor provides a fixed (firm) price for the work to be done that is not subject to adjustment and pushes risk towards the contractor in the event of something being missed by them in the price.

fishbone (cause–effect) diagram   A root-cause analysis technique that assists the project manager and project team in working out what the root cause(s) to a problem could be.

fixed-price or **"lump sum" contract**   A contract in which the contractor agrees to perform all the work specified in the contract at a predetermined, fixed price.

float   *see* slack.

formal communications   Formal, planned communications with stakeholders, as opposed to informal "water cooler" discussions and communications.

free slack   The maximum amount of time an activity can be delayed from its early start (ES) without affecting the early start (ES) of any activity immediately following it.

full reporting   A type of report that reports on all aspects of the projects progress. Usually includes aspects of scope, time, quality, cost, human resources, risk, procurement, communications and stakeholders.

function points   Points derived from past software development projects that assist in the estimating the amount of time to construct a new software project. Also referred to as a functional point analysis.

functional conflict   A behaviour that occurs when low to moderate levels of conflict improve the effectiveness of the team.

future state   The to-be state of the project as the business moves towards delivering the project.

G

Gantt chart   A graphic representation of project activities depicted as a time-scaled bar chart.

gap analysis   The difference between the current state (the way the business operates now) and the future state.

gates or **kill points**   A review point in the project life cycle where decisions are made on the viability of a project, or to seek approvals for a project to progress into the next phase or stage.

generational differences   Disparities in the way different generations behave, communicate and act. These should be considered in defining communications and the stakeholder management strategies.

going native   Adopting the customs, values, and prerogatives of a foreign culture.

governance   The framework that guides and directs aspect of the management of a project and potentially the product, service or result being produced. Project leaders should identify, and be prepared to integrate governance into all aspects of project delivery.

groupthink   A tendency of members in highly cohesive groups to lose their critical evaluative capabilities.

H

hammock activity   A special-purpose aggregate activity that identifies the use of fixed resources or costs over a segment of the project (e.g., a consultant). Derives its duration from the time span between other activities.

health checks   Informal audits of projects to provide guidance and corrective actions.

high-performing teams   Small teams that are empowered to make decisions and resolve conflict without the requirement or intervention of a team leader or manager.

histograms   A type of bar chart used to visualise data.

I

impact   A general term used to describe the significance of the organisational change that the project's deliverables (outcomes) has on the intended audience.

informal communications   Unplanned communications (e.g. "water cooler" discussions and coffee shop chats).

inherent risk priority number (RPN)   The probability multiplied by the impact rating for an individual risk before any mitigations (or controls) are implemented.

integrative thinking   The art of considering across all the different knowledge areas (e.g. a communications task could incur costs in media charges, effort to write, review and publish, and risks based on how it is received and acted upon).

integrity   An adherence to morality and ethics.

in-process project audit   Reviews that occur early in projects, allowing for corrective changes if needed on the project in question or others in progress.

investment business case   A business case based around a specific area of investment that an organisation may make.

ISO 9000   A set of standards governing the requirements for documentation of a quality program.

ISO 21500:2012   ISO's recent publication providing a standard around the management of projects.

Issue   Typically associated with the occurrence of a risk (i.e. a risk that has eventuated).

J

job description   An outline of a job within the project environment, usually supplemented with a more specific Role Description, to distinguish between multiple roles inside and beyond the organisation.

K

knowledge areas   The ten knowledge areas associated with the 6th edition of PMBOK: scope, time, cost, quality, stakeholders, risk, procurement, communications and integration

Kotter's 8-step process   An OCM approach where the eight steps provide guidance around the key activities a change sponsor should be cognizant of and able to delegate to employees working with change in an organisation.

L

laddering   A technique used in scheduling to make more efficient use of resources.

lagging   A technique used in scheduling where one activity is delayed by a certain time period before the next activity is able to start.

large capital items   Items requiring a significant capital investment to be made by the project, typically identified and approved early on in the project life cycle by authorities other than the project manager.

late finish (LF)   The latest an activity can finish and not delay a following activity (LF = LS + DUR).

late start (LS)   The latest an activity can start and not delay a following activity. It is the largest late finish (LF) of all activities immediately preceding it (LS = LF − DUR).

lead-time   Overlap between activities that have one or more dependencies.

leading by example   Exhibiting the behaviours you want to see in others.

lean   A quality philosophy based on reduction of waste in processes and supplier/value chains.

Lean Six Sigma   A continuous improvement approach that takes aspect of Lean (based on the Toyota Production System) and Six Sigma (devised out of statistical process constol at Motorola in the 1980s).

learning styles   The different ways or methods in which people learn (e.g. visual, auditory and kinetic).

LeSS or **Large-Scale Scrum**   A scalable Agile approach that allows for mutiple development teams.

lessons learned   The principle of informing the current dynamics of the project based on events (lessons learned) of previous projects; also applicable to current projects in order to continuously improve the current project and to inform any future projects of a similar nature. *See also* retrospectives.

Lessons Learned Register   A central repository used for capturing and actioning lessons learned across the project.

levelling   Techniques used to examine a project for an unbalanced use of resources, and for resolving resource over-allocations.

Lewin's force field analysis   An OCM tool that gives a perception-based score on the positive and negative forces of a particular change.

life cycle   The term applied to the phases a project will typically go through. Under PMBOK these phases include; Initiation, Planning, Execution and Closure. Monitor and Control cuts across the whole project.

lines of communication   The different ways in which information is passed on (communicated) to stakeholders within a project; the number of lines of communication are exponential in relation to the number of parties being involved in a communication exchange.

long lead-time items   Project items that take a long-time to procure, (e.g. a tunnel-boring machine with an 18-month lead time).

M

majority   A decsion-making mode where the decision of the largest portion of the group (majority) is taken. *See also* consensus decision making

management by wandering around (MBWA)   A management style in which managers spend the majority of their time outside their offices interacting with key people.

McKinsey 7-S   An analysis tool used to identify gaps between the current and future states.

Microsoft Project   A popular scheduling tool.

milestone   An event that represents significant, identifiable accomplishment toward the project's completion.

milestone slippage   The failure to meet the original planned dates for milestones.

mitigation strategy (risk response)   Types of strategies that can be applied to reduce, eliminate (or accept) identified risks prior to project start-up or during the Planning and Execution phases of the project.

Monte Carlo technique (simulation)   A method of simulating project activity durations using probabilities; identifies the percentage of times, activities, and paths that are critical over thousands of simulations.

multifaceted project leader   A person who demonstrates the skill groupings seen as important to sucessful project leaders (organisational change management awareness, leadership, ethics and principles, business acumen, technical project management abilities, subject matter expertise).

multiplicities of communication   *see* lines of communication

N

Net Present Value (NPV)   The present value of all future cash inflows and outflows calculated on a minimum desired rate of return discount.

neuro-linguistic programming (NLP)   The practice of understanding how people organise their thinking, feeling, language and behaviour to produce the results they do; includes the technique to assist the in reading non-verbal queues which stakeholders may exhibit.

noise   The distortion, deletion, deflection or incorrect translation of a message between the sender and the receiver so that the message does not achieve its desired intent.

nominal group technique (NGT)   A structured problem-solving process in which members privately rank-order preferred solutions.

non-verbal communication   The conveyance of meaning without using verbal cues (i.e. touch (haptics), body language (kinesics), distance (proxemics) and voice (paralanguage)).

normal, premature, phase (or stage), perpetual, failed project   The different states a project can be in at the beginning of the Closure stage.

nudge theory   An OCM technique to that deliberately deploys a factor that influences an individual's choice or behaviour (a nudge) in order to elicit the desired outcome in the individual's self-interest.

NUPP   Nearly Universal Principles of Projects; a set of general project management principles.

O

open tender   A tender which is open to the marketplace where any suitable supplier can respond to the tender. *See also* closed tender.

operational level agreements   A formal understanding (agreement) between two or more departments within an organisation.

opportunity (or positive) risk   An under-used but understood aspect of risk management where opportunity risks are identified and tracked in addition to the normal threat risks.

organisation breakdown structure (OBS)   A framework used to assign responsibility for work packages.

organisational change management (OCM)   The consideration of the impact a project (change) may have on the people, functions and management of an organisation.

Organisational Change Management Plan   A strategy that captures all the analysis and activities required to more sucessfully address specific organisational change management activities in support of delivering the project.

organisational chart   A representation of the formal structure of an organisation or project.

organisational culture   A system of shared norms, beliefs, values, and assumptions held by an organisation's members.

outcomes   Behaviour-based project deliverables (e.g. events, occurrences, changes etc.) that mark progress towards the project goal.

outputs   Tangible project deliverables (e.g. a training manual, training system, process for the assessment of training needs etc.).

outsourcing   Contracting the use of external sources (skills) to assist in implementing a project.

overlapping relationship   Tasks that can be started in parallel to a predecessor task to some degree through means of a leading time.

P

P3.express   A light predictive project management framework.

pad   The practice of including additional time, cost or resources in estimating.

padding estimates   Adding a safety factor to a time or cost estimate to ensure the estimate is met when the project is executed. Professional project management practice prefers the use of project contingencies instead of 'artificially' padding estimates of individual work packages.

parametric estimating   Estimating based on formulas or statistics.

Pareto chart   A chart which supports the identification of 80 per cent of the problems/faults, often used in quality control to identify the categories in which they occur.

partnering charter   A formal document that states common goals and cooperative procedures used to achieve these goals, signed by all parties working on a project.

partnerships   A contract agreement between two parties where risk and reward are equally shared.

path   A sequence of connected activities. *See also* critical path.

payback model   The time it takes to pay back the project investment (investment/net annual savings). This method does not consider the time value of money or the life of the investment.

performance agreement   An arrangement that lays out the performance of an individual in a project, their performance indicators and targets.

performance baseline   A standard against which to accredit the skill level of various project management roles (e.g. scope, time and cost).

performance review   In general, all review methods of individual performance centre on the technical and social skills brought to the project and team. These reviews stress personal improvement and are frequently used for salary and promotion decisions.

PERT method/PERT simulation (project evaluation review technique)   One of a number of tools used in the estimating of cost, time or resources that assumes a statistical distribution (range between optimistic and pessimistic) for each activity duration to provide a list of potential critical paths and their probability of occurrence.

phase estimating   This estimating method begins with a macro estimate for the project and then refines estimates for phases of the project as it is implemented.

Plan–Do–Check–Act (PDCA)   A light continuous improvement technique often applied and associated with the life cycle of a project.

Plan–Do–Study–Act (PDSA)   A light continuous improvement technique often applied and associated with the life cycle of a project.

planned costs   Projected expenditures (estimates) of a project.

planned, actual, variance (PAV)   The three values a project leader tracks against in the project budget for each time period.

policy and procedures   Documentation of guidelines, processes and other organisational assets for the project (e.g. project management guidelines, procurement, human resource related processes and contracts).

portfolio   A grouping of programs, projects and related operational work that delivers a greater set of benefits to the organisation when managed in a coordinated manner.

positive synergy   A characteristic of high-performance teams in which group performance is greater than the sum of individual contributions.

post-implementation review (PIR)   A formal assessment usually carried out by a function outside of the project to independantly assess success and identify wider lessons learned.

potentially shippable product   A deliverable produced at the end of a sprint which can potentially be put into production (shipped). Typically a number of sprints are carried out before being combined into an increment for shipping.

power/interest grid   A grid that allows the plotting of the power/interest of stakeholders on a project to ascertain their level of management.

predictive   A traditional project life cycle that follows the four stages of Initiation, Planning, Execution and Closure.

primary stakeholder   A stakeholder who has a direct interest in the outcomes and outputs of the project. *See also* secondary stakeholder.

PRINCE2®   An established project management methodology that provides a strongly process-driven and role-based approach to the management of projects.

principled negotiation   A process of negotiation that aims to achieve win/win results.

principles   General precepts that guide a project leader in the management of a project. *See also* NUPP.

probability (likelihood)   Assessment of a risk of something occurring given a set of conditions.

probity   The quality of having strong moral principles, honesty, decency and ethics.

process charts/flow charts   A method of capturing processes and procedures. *See also* BPMN.

procurement   *See* contractor and supplier evaluation.

product breakdown structure (PBS)   A hierarchical decomposition for the product or service being produced by the project. *See also* BOM.

product life cycle   The stages of change of a product during its lifespan (e.g. it is designed, developed, released, gains momentum, reaches a peak in sales and then declines, until the product is eventually retired and removed from circulation).

product management   The delivery, maintenance and disposal of a product through its lifespan.

product owner   The person responsible for managing the product backlog in Scrum so as to maximise the value of the project. The product owner represents all stakeholders.

program   A collection of related projects, grouped in order to be managed in a more efficient manner. Usually delivers greater benefits to the organisation than each project would individually.

project account codes   An index of project components provided by the finance department against which project spend must be coded to ensure compliance with organisational accounting practices.

project accounting system   A financial system which specifically targets the management of project budgets from a project perspective.

project change/variation management systems   A process that describes in detail exactly how project change/variations are to be logged, ranked, assessed, approved (or not) and funded. The change/variation process is typically documented in the scope management plan where not provided by the organisation's PMO.

project charter   A document that authorises the project manager to initiate and lead a project.

project closure   All of the activities of shutting down a project. The major activities are evaluation of project goals and performance, developing lessons learned, releasing resources and preparing a final report.

project design   The concept of having a sound approach and design of the project, established during the Initiation to early Planning stages of the predictive life cycle.

project governance   Formal documentation of how governance will take place in a project, who is accountable for each decision and how the project will be managed.

project integration management   Activities that ensure the project content and the management of the project are successfully integrated across the project life cycle.

project kick off meeting   Typically the first meeting of the project team.

project life cycle   The stages found in all PMBOK-based projects— Initiation, Planning, Executing, Closing and Monitoring and Controlling.

Project Management Body of Knowledge (PMBOK)   The body of knowledge produced by the Project Management Institute (PMI) that provides an industry standard, best practice approach to the management of projects.

project management office (PMO)   A centralised unit within an organisation that oversees and improves the management of projects. Often provides standards, process, templates and knowledge to assist project managers.

Project Management Plan (PMP)   The key document/s produced in the Planning phase of the project life cycle. The PMP usually covers the ten areas of knowledge within the Project Management Body of Knowledge (Scope, Time, Quality, Cost, HR, Communications, Risk, Procurement, Stakeholders and Integration).

Project Management Professional (PMP)   An individual who has met specific education and experience requirements set forth by the Project Management Institute, has agreed to adhere to a code of professional conduct, and passed and examination designed to objectively assess and measure project management knowledge. In addition, a PMP must satisfy continuing certification requirements or lose the certification.

project manager   The individual responsible for managing a project.

project network   An alternative technique or view of the project schedule that applies the activities on a node network diagram.

project organisation   An organisational structure in which core work is accomplished by project teams.

project partnering   A nonbinding method of transforming contractual relationships into a cohesive, cooperative project team with a single set of goals and established procedures for resolving disputes in a timely manner.

project performance metrics   Standards for measuring the performance of the project, such as on-time, on-cost to customer satisfaction etc.

Project Portfolio Management (PPM) systems   The concept of managing a coordinated set of projects as a program or portfolio to deliver a greater set of benefits to the organisation than individual projects.

project sponsor   Typically a high-ranking manager who champions and supports a project.

Prosci   An OCM approach that has ADKAR at its core.

Q

Quality Assurance (QA)   The criteria (standards) which define in a measurable manner that Quality that is to be achieved by the project and of the products and services produced by the project.

Quality Control (QC)   The task of ensuring (monitoring) the project QA criteria to ensure that quality is being delivered by the project.

Quality Management Plan   The document which captures the QA and QC planning aspects of quality on the project. This would include the standards being applied, how these are going to be controlled, and roles and governance around quality.

R

range estimating   Reviewing risk against a possible range of estimates, to make estimating decisions.

RASCI   An matrix which assists in determining which roles are accountable and/or responsible, and which ones support or are consulted/informed.

re-baseline   Typically occurs when significant variations have occurred during the execution of a project and the project's three key baselines (scope, time and cost) have to be updated and recommunicated to the project team before project execution continues using these new baselines.

recruitment and onboarding The act of bringing new team member onto the project.

Request for Information (RFI) A less formal information-gathering tender type that the project can use to solicit interest in a tender item.

Request for Proposal (RFP) A type of tender where the problem to solve is outlined and tenders respond with their (often unique) solutions. Often used instead of RTF.

Request for Quote (RFQ) Sits between a RFI and RFT to obtain a quote on a tender requirements.

Request for Tender (RFT) A type of tender where the project specifies exactly what the tenderer is expected to provide details of.

reserve analysis The evaluation of project planning artefacts to determine the amount of contingency (or reserve) remaining.

resource Any person, groups, skill, equipment or material used to accomplish a task, work package, or activity.

Resource Allocation Matrix (RAM) or **resource matrix** A matrix which records and then enables the subsequent analysis of resources to be used by the project.

Resource Assignment Matrix A matrix mapping roles to work in the project.

resource breakdown structure (RBS) A classification of the roles required in the project under categories.

resource identification Formal determination of resources required by the project using tools such as the RBS and WBS.

resource levelling Identifying overuse of a resource (human or other) and making adjustments to the project schedule in order to ensure the reource is not over committed.

Resource Management Plan One of the knowledge area plans that identifies and tailors aspects of governance, policy, procedure and processes relating to human resources or resources in general.

resource scheduling The allocation of resources to work packages or tasks on the project schedule.

resource smoothing A technique used to review how resources are used across a project and check for over (or under) allocation of a resource.

resource types Categories of resources, often used on an RBS to classify resources.

rich pictures A diagram abundant in information, often used to map out a business system and its interactions with the project as articulated by the business (including the feeling and emotions of the people involved in the business system).

risk The potential for an undesirable event to occur.

risk analysis (or risk evaluation) The step of analysing identified risks.

risk appetite The overall demand of the business within which the project operations in relation to risk (e.g. government departments tend to be risk-averse).

risk breakdown structure (RBS) A dissection of risks under pre-defined categories.

risk context The definition of risk at the business level and within the project. Does the organisation have a high or low tolerance to risk-taking and how does this apply to the project environment?

risk evaluation The appraisal of inherent risks and implementation of mitigation (control) strategies (e.g. Accept, Avoid, Transfer, Mitigate and Escalate).

risk heat maps A visual diagram indicating the status of risks plotted.

risk identification The process and tools used to exhaustively identify possible risks to the project.

Risk Management Plan (RMP) Part of the PMP defining the risk management approach and context, including any frameworks and methodologies which are to be applied to the project environment.

risk monitoring and review The process of tracking risks on an ongoing basis to assess changes to the residual risk status and checking for any new risks which emerge as the project progresses.

risk profile A list of questions that addresses traditional areas of uncertainty on a project.

Risk Register The register to capture identified risks and the subsequent analysis of the risks. Used as a tracking tool during the monitoring and controlling of the project.

risk treatment The treatment of unmitigated risks to reduce the probability and/or impact of that risk

rolling-wave planning or **iterative planning** The technique of planning for the near term in detail and medium to long term at a higher level.

root-cause analysis A tool used to brainstorm and analyse the fundamental reason behind a problem. Common technuqes used in root cause analsyis include the 5-Whys and the fishbone diagram.

run chart A visual presentation of quality control data to allow identification of trends and patterns for further analysis.

S

salience model A design based on the analysis of power, legitimacy, and urgency. Those which exhibit all three are seen as stakeholders requiring immediate attention.

schedule (time) baseline Approval of the project schedule at the end of planning, but before execution, that forms the baseline schedule. New baselines can also be established during execution of the project as a result of an approved variation request.

Schedule Management Plan   One of the knowledge area plans that identifies and tailors aspects of governance, policy, procedure and processes relating to schedule management.

scope baseline   The approved scope of the project as documented at the end of planning prior to its approval and execution. It is from the Execution stage that all variations must be logged as variation requests and assessed.

Scope creep   The tendency for the scope of a project to expand once it has started.

scope document   The key output of the Initiation phase of the project where all the dimensions of the project are defined and agreed.

Scope Management Plan   The management plan which documents the more static elements of scope management in a project environment. Included within the scope management plan would be: governance and approval of scope; the project change/variation process; issue escalation process; and deliverable acceptance process.

Scrum   An incremental, iterative development approach to managing projects with a well-defined set of roles and processes.

Scrum master   The person responsible for the Scrum process and its correct application.

Scrum team   The core team that undertakes the user stories and tasks to deliver a potentially shippable product at the end of the sprint.

Secondary stakeholder   Stakeholders which may be indirectly interested or affected by the project. *See also* primary stakeholder.

Sender–receiver model   A documented model of communication and the effects to consider in sending and receiving a communication.

sequential relationship   Where one task must be completed before the subsequent (successor) task can be started.

servant leadership   A leadership style based on the underlying principle of the leadership by serving, adopted by Scrum Masters in Agile project management and now also being taken up by project leaders with their direct project team.

service level agreement (SLA)   An agreement between the project (or organisation) and an external (paying) customer. *See also* operational level agreement

seven constraints   The impact of variations beyond the triple constraints (scope, time and cost), including quality, risk, resources and strategy (alignment).

SFAIRP   so far as reasonably practicable; a technique used to sensibly reduce risk down to a manageable level.

shared vision   A collective image that the project team (and customer) have of how the project will look at completion, how

they will work together and/or how customers will accept the project.

six elements of a contract   The general six steps of contract formation: Offer, Acceptance, Awareness, Consideration, Capacity and Legality.

Six Sigma   A metric, methodology and management system focusing on understanding customer requirements, alignment of key processes, basing control on data and embedding sustainable outcomes in the business.

Skills Matrix   A matrix of roles, skills, qualifications, certifications and other information deemed necessary to be maintained in the project environment.

Slack (SL)   Time an activity can be delayed before it becomes critical.

SMARTA   A term applied to the writing of project objectives: Specific, Measurable, Assignable, Realistic, Time-bound and Agreed.

SMCR model (Berlo's model)   A model that accounts for the variety of human variables present in person-to-person communications: Source, Message, Channel and Receiver.

Social network building   The process of identifying and building cooperative relationships with key people.

Splitting   A scheduling technique in which work is interrupted on one activity and the resource is assigned to another activity for a period of time, then reassigned to work on the original activity.

Sprint   A fixed period of time during which a Scrum teams works to turn the product backlog it has selected into an increment of product functionality.

Sprint backlog   A list of tasks that defines a Scrum team's work for a sprint. Each task identifies those responsible for doing the work and the estimated amount of work remaining on the task on any given day during the sprint.

sprint planning   An Agile ceremony where the product owner presents the priortised product backlog from which the higest priority (value) user stories are discussed for inclusion in the actual sprint.

Sprint planning meeting   A Scrum meeting at the beginning of each sprint where the team meets to determine what items in the prioritised backlog can be turned into functionality during the upcoming sprint and plan what work will be needed.

Sprint retrospective meeting   A Scrum meeting in which the team discusses the just concluded sprint and determines what could be changed that might make the next sprint more enjoyable and productive.

Sprint review meeting   A Scrum meeting in which the team demonstrates to the product owner and any other interested parties what it was able to accomplish during the sprint.

Stakeholder   Individuals and organisations that are actively involved in the project, or whose interests may be positively or negatively affected as a result of project execution or completion. They may also exert influence over the project and its results.

stakeholder analysis   The act of using assorted tools and techniques to evaluate the various dimensions of previously identified stakeholders.

stakeholder attitude   A technique to assess the attitude of a stakeholder, typically on a scale of blocker through to supporter.

stakeholder co-creation   A form of cooperation in which all participants (stakeholders, project team etc.) influence the process and the result to create project value, with both sides having an interest in being sucessful.

stakeholder identification   The initial and ongoing classification of stakeholders throughout the lifecycle of the project using various tools and techniques.

Stakeholder Management Plan   The management plan which defines the policy, process, guidelines and roles in relation to the management of stakeholders in the project environment.

stakeholder network diagram   A diagram used to indicate stakeholders, relationships, networks and interactions in a project.

stakeholder proximity/priority   A technique to analyse how close the stakeholder is to the project (in terms of time, specific deliverables, stages in the lifecycle etc.) and thus their priority.

Stakeholder Register   A list of all stakeholders and the associated information deemed useful to the project.

stakeholder strategies   Approaches to managing individual stakeholders resulting from stakeholder analysis.

stakeholder survey   A survey sent to stakeholders to gain feedback on how well the project team is interacting with them (e.g. the communications and feedback loops).

standing offer arrangement (SOA)   An established supplier agreement to under which goods and/or services are supplied to the project. The project leader could be mandated to leverage these agreements rather than sourcing new suppliers and establishing new agreements.

Steering Committee   A panel of people put in place to govern and approve items (e.g. variation requests), and who act as an escalation point for issues.

story points   An Agile estimation technique based on relative effort, used by the Scrum team during detailed estimating at the Spring Planning meeting.

subject matter expert (SME)   A stakeholder to the project who is an authority (expert) in their field.

sunk cost   A cost which has already occurred (sunk) and may have to be written off if the project is prematurely terminated.

sustainability   The consideration of the impact of the project deliverables on the people or environment to which the projects deliverables are to be handed so as to not overburden them.

Swimlane diagrams   A tool used to capture organisational and project processes; each swimlane represents the role within which work (activities) is carried out.

SWOT analysis   A technique to evaluate the internal strength and weakness, as well as external opportunities and threats, at the project or organisational level.

Systems thinking   A holistic approach to viewing processes that emphasises understanding the interactions among different processes as opposed to viewing processes as independent activities.

T

T&M contracts   A type of contract that sets out the rate for materials and time (of resources), often used when uncertainty exists.

tacit knowledge   Implicit knowledge or understanding residing within people's heads (i.e. not documented).

task   Actions or work to be undertaken. *See also* work package.

team building   A process designed to improve the performance of a team.

team charter   A charter between members of the project team that includes a motivational and value-based statement by which the team agrees to abide.

Team Development Plan   A section within the Resource Management Plan that outlines how the team will be managed, developed (e.g. team events and training) and rewarded.

team rituals   Ceremonial actions that reinforce team identity and values.

team survey   An impartial and often anonymous survey issued to the project team to understand their current feelings about working on the project; they are used to supplement performance reviews.

tender process   The process often defined within the organisation's process assets that outlines the steps/stages all tenders must progress through in order to comply with organisational governance requirements.

The 4C's of Truth about Communication   A tool that assists in the development of a communication message: Comprehension, Credibility, Connection and Contagiousness.

the triple constraints   Managing the interplay of scope, time and cost while trying to balance the performance (Quality) aspects of the project.

threat risk   A type of risk which has the potential to harm the project.

three pillars of project governance   Structure, People and Information

three-point estimate (PERT)   *See* T&M contracts

top-down estimates   Rough estimates that use surrogates to estimate project time and cost (also called "macro estimates").

total quality management (TQM)   A philosophy of Quality where everyone in the creation or consumption of a product or service has a responsibility to its continuous improvement.

total slack (TS)   The amount of time an activity can be delayed and not affect the project duration (TS = LS − ES or TS = LF − EF).

trial engagement   A preliminary (trial) arrangement with the contractor or supplier to assess the practicalities of the contract from both sides from which a longer term arrangement may result, subject to various performance criteria being met.

triple constraint   The competing demands of time, cost, and scope. These constraints frequently represent trade-off decisions to be dealt with by the project manager and/or sponsor.

trust   An important dynamic of confidence and expectation between the various project stakeholders that is built over time.

trust equation   A method of assessing the strength of a trust relationship; can be used by the project leader or team members.

U

unfreeze   The first stage in Lewin's change approach which involves dismantling what currently exists in order to facilitate change.

unified modelling language (UML)   A stack of models used by Business Analysts and technical grades to model aspects of a business system.

V

value   The benefits the business or customer gains from a project.

value proposition   The benefits the company is proposing to offer a customer.

variance   The difference between two values (e.g. the difference between what was planned to be spent and what was actually spent) that is often applied to cost variance.

variation management process (VMP)   Documentation of the process for handling any project variations, usually as a swimlane diagram. Also called a change control process.

variation management system   A structure or process for handling project variations.

variation request   A petition to change (vary) the project scope.

Virginia Satir change model   An OCM tool that prompts thinking about the impact of an organisational change on employees.

virtual project team   Spatially separated project team whose members are unable to communicate face to face. Communication is usually by electronic means.

Vision   *See* project vision

vocational education and training (VET)   The part of tertiary education and training system which provides accredited training in job-related and technical skills.

voice of the customer (VOC)   A technique focused on listening to and validating what the customer desires and then designing it into the project deliverables.

W

Warranty Period   The length of time in which a product is still under some form of guarantee with the seller (e.g. for a physical product this could be repairs for 12 months), delivered from project team to business as part of handover activities.

WBS dictionary   A database of WBS elements that is built as a resulting of creating a WBS across often multiple projects. Encourages the re-use of WBS items and the storing of estimate information so that lessons learned across similar projects can be captured.

weak matrix   A matrix structure in which functional managers have primary control over project activities and the project manager coordinates project work.

"What's in it for me?" (WIIFM)   A practice of looking for links to the work that/person who is impacted by the project to gain buy-in

work breakdown structure (WBS)   A hierarchical method that successively subdivides the work of the project into smaller detail.

work package   A task at the lowest level of the WBS, assigned to one person and limited to 40 hours of work where possible.

wrap-up activities   Events (activities) associated with the closing down of a phase or stage of a project.

For further information, also see:

1. https://www.pmi.org/pmbok-guide-standards/lexicon

2. https://www.smartsheet.com/complete-glossary-project-management-terminology

3. https://www.scrum.org/resources/scrum-glossary

Index

A

acceptance criteria 101
accepting (retaining) risk 525
acquiring resources 327
action learning cycle 448
activity-on-node (AON) 345
actual costs 395
adaptive approaches 32, 35, 652
ad hoc purchasing 549
adjourning stage 623
ADKAR *see* Awareness, Desire,
    Knowledge, Ability and
    Reinforcement-to-change
    (ADKAR)
administrative support groups 454
advanced schedule efficiency techniques
    367–371
advanced scheduling techniques 363–367
  dangler paths 364
  free float/free slack 363
  laddering 364
  Monte Carlo technique 363
  multiple starts and multiple ends 364
  risk assessment 363–364
  sensitivity 364
  total slack 363
affinity grouping 316
Agile 28, 218
Agile Alliance 72
Agile (Scrum) approach 29–30
  adaptation 47
  benefits 48–49
  disbenefits 49
  inspection 47
  Scrum study approach 47, 48
  timeline 46
  transparency 47
Agile Manifesto 72
AgilePM 72
Agile project environment 3
Agile project management 73
Agile triangle 75
AIPM *see* Australian Institute of Project
    Management (AIPM)
ALARP *see* as long as resonably possible
    (ALARP)
alternative analysis 312–313
analogous estimating method 310–311
APM *see* Association for Project
    Management (APM)
artefacts
  capture governance 244–245
  estimate 261
  integrated project management
    plan 213
  see also Scrum artefacts
as low as reasonably possible
    (ALARP) 511

Association for Project Management
    (APM) 31, 49–50
APM life cycle and approach 31
assumptions
  planning stakeholder management 451
  project scope 269
  risk identification 515
audits 405
Australian infrastructure projects
    144–146
Australian Institute of Project
    Management (AIPM) 5, 8
Awareness, Desire, Knowledge, Ability
    and Reinforcement-to-change
    (ADKAR) 177, 179–180
axes of effectiveness and richness 479

B

backward pass 354–355
balanced matrix 684
bar charts 435–436
baseline
  defined 575
  management 576–579, 396
  planning stage 389
BCR *see* benefit–cost ratio (BCR)
Belbin team roles 634
benchmarking 434
benefit–cost ratio (BCR) 129
Benefits Management Plan 672
Berlo's model 477–478
Best Alternative To a Negotiated
    Agreement (BATNA) 560–561
best practice 616
bidder conference 549
bill of materials (BOM) 270, 543
bottom-up approach 149
bottom-up estimate 299
  see also estimate(s)
Box plots 436
brainstorming 452
Bridges transition model 188, 189
Brooks law 368
Browaeys and Price model of
    communication 478
brown cow technique 98
budget baseline 576
build–operate–transfer (BOT) 552
  see also contracts
build–own–operate (BOO) 552
  see also contracts
build–own–operate–transfer (BOOT)
    524, 552
  see also contracts
build trust 599
burndown/burnup 78, 106
business acumen 597
business analyst 672

Business Case 209, 240, 672
business case benefit statements 588
business improvement 173
business process model and notation
    (BPMN) 428
business readiness assessment 177
business use case 267
buy analysis 388

C

capability 88
CAPM *see* Certified Associate in Project
    Management (CAPM)
capturing requirements
  analysis 278
  elicitation 277
  focus groups 278
  interviews 277
  management 276
  observation 277
  planning 276
  register 277
  scenarios 278
  types 279
  validation 278
  verification 279
  workshops 278
capturing techniques 250–251
cascading 128
cause–effect diagram 440–441
centralisation of processes 22
Certified Associate in Project
    Management (CAPM) 8
Certified Practicing Portfolio Executive
    (CPPE) 8
Certified Practicing Project
    Administrator (CPPA) 8
Certified Practicing Project Director
    (CPPD) 8
Certified Practicing Project Manager
    (CPPM) 8
Certified Practicing Senior Project
    Manager (CPSPM) 8
Change Control Board (CCB) 250
changed priority 673
change leader's roadmap methodology
    (CLMR) 183
Change Management Body of Knowledge
    (CMBOK) 180–81
change readiness assessment 177
change request management *see*
    variation management process
    (VMP)
chart of accounts 330
charts
  bar chart 435–36
  box plots/box and whisker
    diagrams 436

charts (*Continued*)
  burndown and burnup charts 106, 110
  control chart 433
  flowchart 427
  Gantt chart 344
  histograms 435
  Pareto chart 432
  scatter diagrams 436–437
checklists 434
check sheets 434
clearinghouse 563
closed tender 549
close risk management 536
closure activities
  defined 672
  final deliverable acceptance 678
  final project report 679–680
  procurement and contracts 679
  project team disbandment 678
  readiness assessment 678
  splitting closure 679
closure stage 13
CMBOK *see* Change Management Body
    of Knowledge (CMBOK)
co-creation, stakeholder 446–450
commitment stage 624
committed 94
committee charter 486
communication
  communication medium 475
  Communications Management Plan
    246, 479, 485
  Communications Register 485, 489–490
  Communications Sent Register 488
  communication timing 475
  4Cs 491–493
  see also project communications
competent project leader 660–661
complexity
  assess handover and operational
    complexity 666
  defined 650
  detailed complexity assessment 662–664
  dimensions of 650
  evaluating project 655
  generic complexity framework
    657–658
  monitor project complexity 664–665
  pre-project complexity assessment
    658–662
  profile 657
  review and capture knowledge 665–666
  risk 661
  theory 650
complex stakeholder management 464
compromising quality 370
concurrent engineering 359
conductor, project leaders as 456–457
configuration management (CM) 497–499
conflict management
  partnering 567
  project teams 633
connected enterprise 447
consensus 312, 598
constraint management 264

constraints
  preference matrix 273
  project scope 268
risk identification 515
contemporary agile status reporting 106
context diagram 267–268
Context, Purpose, Objectives, Resources,
    Timing (CPORT) 491
contingency 306, 385, 402
  contingency (event) action plan 527
  contingency plan 506, 527–528, 584
  cost of 527
continuous improvement 583
contract law 555
contractors 455
  contractor/vendor conference 549
  performance 680, 686–687
contracts
  art of negotiating 557–561
  build–operate–transfer (BOT) 552
  build–own–operate (BOO) 552
  build–own–operate–transfer
    (BOOT) 552
  cost-reimbursable contracts 553–554
  defined 551
  elements of 554–555
  extended contract considerations
    555–557
  fixed-price contracts 553
  partnerships 553
  procurement and 679
  time and material (T&M)
    contracts 554
contribution/commitment grid 460–461
control chart 427, 433
control tower 253
convergent thinking 628, 653–654
cooperation, project leader 607
corporate systems 497
cost
  cost baseline 399, 577, 672
  costs estimate 304
  cost management
    activities 385–387
    categorisation 394
    closure 405
    contingency planning 402–404
    control and monitoring 401–402
    general cost activities 385
    identification, estimation and
      categorisation 391–393
    large capital items 387
    long lead-time items 387–389
    planning 390–391
    recap of estimation 393–394
  Cost Management Plan 389
  cost of quality (CoQ) 306, 313, 386,
    411–412
  cost plus award fee (CPAF) 553–554
  cost plus fixed fee (CPFF) 553
  cost plus incentive fee (CPIF) 553
  cost-reimbursable contracts 553–554
  cost risks 531
  cost to rectify poor quality
    (COPQ) 411

CPORT *see* Context, Purpose, Objectives,
    Resources, Timing (CPORT)
CPPA *see* Certified Practicing Project
    Administrator (CPPA)
CPPD *see* Certified Practicing Project
    Director (CPPD)
CPPE *see* Certified Practicing Portfolio
    Executive (CPPE)
CPPM *see* Certified Practicing Project
    Manager (CPPM)
CPSPM *see* Certified Practicing Senior
    Project Manager (CPSPM)
crashing 368
creative thinking 654–655
critical chain method 377–378
criticality index 520
critical path 348, 355–357, 387
critical success factors (CSFs) 267, 675
cultural differences 479, 482
current state 124
Customer Relationship Management
    (CRM) 450
customer satisfaction 465
Cynefin framework 658

D

daily Scrum meeting 76, 78, 93–94
dangler paths 364
dashboard (red, amber, green or
    RAG-style) report 584
data, information, knowledge and
    wisdom (DIKW) 499
decision making 627–630
  contracts and contract types 551–561
  purchase order 547–548
  supplier selection 548–551
decision tree analysis 520–521
defect issue 411
Define, Measure, Analyse, Design, Verify
    (DMADV) approach 31, 50
  see also Design for Six Sigma (DFSS)
Define, Measure, Analyse, Improve,
    Control (DMAIC) 31, 50–53, 416
degree of flexibility 632
deliverable(s)
  acceptance 579–580, 678
  acceptance form 579
  defined 261, 579
  IDs (DIDs) 579
  milestone and 580–581
  project integration management 217
  project scope 267
  Scope Management Plan 264
Delphi method 312, 514–515
Design for Six Sigma (DFSS) 50
  see also Define, Measure, Analyse,
    Design, Verify (DMADV) approach
design thinking 628, 629, 653–654
detailed complexity assessment
  detailed risk response 663–664
  Hass complexity actions 662–663
  International Project Management
    Association (IPMA) tool 662
  review of prior complexity 664

detailed risk response 663–664
DevOps 118
DFSS *see* Design for Six Sigma (DFSS)
dimensions, of complexity 650
direct sourcing 549
disbandment, project teams 678
discretionary budget 632
divergent thinking 628, 653–654
DMADV approach *see* Define, Measure,
    Analyse, Design, Verify (DMADV)
    approach
DMAIC *see* Define, Measure, Analyse,
    Improve, Control (DMAIC)
document management systems (DMS)
    497–499
Drexler and Sibbet's team performance
    model 594, 624–625
dysfunctional conflict 633–635

E

early finish (EF) 354
early start (ES) 354
earned value management (EVM) 494
edge of chaos 664
80/20 rule 432
    see also Pareto chart
elevator pitch (EP) 473
emotional intelligence (EQ) 598–600
engagement and monitor stakeholders
    accurate representation 464
    embeddedness of stakeholder
        thinking 464
    leadership 464
    motivation 464
    non-productive engagement 464
    organisational behaviour 464
    trust 463–464
enterprise bargaining agreements
    (EBAs) 328
enterprise resource planning (ERP) 390
environmental performance 578
escalate risk 522, 523
escalation 567
estimate(s)
    activities 298
    costs 304
    guidelines 305–306
    level of detail in 317
    methods for 310–317
    phase estimating 309–310
    quality of, factors influencing 300
        organisational culture 302–303
        padding estimates 302
        people 301–302
        planning horizon 300
        project duration 300–301
        project structure and
            organisation 302
    refinement of 318–319
    resources 303
    techniques and tools 298–299
    time 303–304
    top-down *vs.* bottom-up 307–308
    trade-off reasons 299–300

estimating trumpet 300, 301
ethics, project leader 597, 607–609
exception report 494, 583
execution stage 13, 575
expected monetary value (EMV) 392,
    520, 532–533
expert judgement 310
explicit knowledge 500
external stakeholder 456
extrinsic motivation 619

F

failed projects 674
fast-tracking 359, 368–369
feedback survey 684
Fibonacci sequence 95
50/50 rule 347
file sharing 497
final project report 679–680
final project status report 675
financial criteria models 137–141
finish-to-finish (FF) relationship 360
finish-to-start (FS) relationship 358
firm fixed price (FFP) 553
fishbone diagrams 438
Fisher's personal transition curve 186
5 whys 438, 439, 515
    see also fishbone diagrams; root-cause
        analysis
fixed-price contracts 553
fixed-price incentive fee (FPIF) 553
fixed price with economic price
    adjustment (FP-EPA) 553
flavours of Scrum/Agile 47–48, 72
flowchart 423, 427, 510
    see also charts; modelling techniques;
        project management, quality of;
        risk escalation process
formal communications 471–472
forming stage 622
forward pass 354
4Cs of truth about communications
    491–493
    see also communication; project
        communications
framework 12, 28–32
free float/free slack 363
full reporting 494
functional conflict 633
functional managers 454–455
function point methods 314
funding risks 531–532
future state 124

G

Gantt chart 344
gap analysis 175
gates 65–66, 689
gateway review 681
generational communications 479, 482
generational theory 626–627
generic complexity framework
    657–658, 662

goal-clarification stage 624
governance
    activities 240
    application of 240–242
    defined 327
    generic project 242
    governors *vs.* managers 238
    identify 242–243
    indicative activities 241
    layers 237
    management plan 243–244, 246–247
        capturing techniques 250–251
        RASCI Matrix 247–250
    monitor 251–252
    principles 239–240
    product, service 244
    project (program) management office
        253–256
    review 252
    three pillars 239–240
Governance Planning Canvas 243
Guidance on project management 42
gulf of execution 479

H

hammock activities 367
handover assessment 666
hands-off/hands-on 597
Hass complexity actions 662–663
heath checks 405
high-performing teams 631
histograms 435
holistic approach 22–24
hope creep 271
HR kiosk design 462
human resources 327–328
100 per cent rule 289
hybrid life cycle 35–36
hygiene and motivational factors
    618–620
    see also motivation models

I

impact (consequence) 516
incremental approach 33, 35–36
independent facilitator
    characteristics of 689
    role of 690
independent, negotiable, valuable,
        estimable, small and testable
        (INVEST) 100, 102
individual reviews 685–686
informal communications 471–472
Information and Communications
        Technology (ICT) systems 672
information sharing 223
information technology projects 4
inherent risk 509, 517, 518
    threat response options 522–523
    vs. cost to risk mitigation 532
inherent risk priority number (RPN)
    522, 527
initial risk assessment 661

initiation stage 12
integrated information system 261
integrated PMISs 497
integrated project management plan
    (integrated PMP)
    artefacts 213–215
    defined 205
    governance plan 244–245
    integrative thinking 215
    planning to execution 576
    project closure 672
    project design 212–216
integration 205
integrative project management 64–66
integrative thinking 223–225
    communication and information
        230–231
    cost 226–227
    integrative project management 64
    procurement 232–233
    quality 227–228
    resource 228–229
    risk 231–232
    schedule 226
    scope 225
    stakeholder 229–230
    systems thinking 207
intellectual property (IP) 556
interactive communication 476
internal compass 608, 609
internal rate of return (IRR) 131
internal stakeholder 456
International Centre for Complex Project
    Management (ICCPM) 650
international cultures 198
International Organization for
    Standardization (ISO) 29, 42–45
International Project Management
    Association (IPMA) 8, 31, 660, 662
interval rule 347
intranets 497
intrinsic motivation 619
INVEST *see* independent, negotiable,
    valuable, estimable, small and
    testable (INVEST)
iron triangle 272
IRR *see* internal rate of return (IRR)
ISO *see* International Organization for
    Standardization (ISO)
ISO 21500:2021 Project, programme and
    portfolio management—context
    and concepts 11, 12, 29, 30, 33, 42,
    43–46
    closing (or terminating) project
        activities 45
    controlling project activities 45
    directing project activities 44
    high-level components 42–43
    initiating project activities 44
    managing delivery activities 45
    pre-project activities 44
    project context for delivering
        projects 43
    project management life cycle 43, 44

ISO 31000:2018 Risk management—
    Guidelines 505
issues 584

J

Jeffery, N. 463
Jensen, M.A. 622, 625, 642
job assignments 632
job descriptions 237, 616
Jobs, S. 127, 128

K

Kanban (board) 30, 53, 72, 89, 93, 102,
    105, 116
kick-off meeting 87, 88, 581, 635
knowledge areas 205, 208
Kotter's 8-step process 181–183
Kübler-Ross model 185

L

laddering 364
    hammock activities 367
    leads and lags 365
    milestones 366
lag or lagging indicators 577
lag relationship 358, 361
lag time 365
land titles 509
large capital items 387, 543
large infrastructure projects, Australia
    2022 4
Large-Scale Scrum (LeSS) 72, 116–118
leadership skills 597
lead or leading indicators 577
lead time 365
Lean Six Sigma 30, 50–53, 415
learning styles 479, 481–482
legitimacy, salience model 462
lessons learned
    independent facilitator 689–690
    initiating review 689
    post-project review 690–692
    and previous projects 332
    project resources 314
    project scope 269
    repository 692–693
    Resource Management Plan 329
    review managing 690
    using 692
Lessons Learned Register 220, 222–223, 672
LeSS *see* Large-Scale Scrum (LeSS)
letters of commendation 632
Lewin's force field analysis 175, 183–184
Lewin's unfreeze, change, refreeze
    model 185
limited tenders 549
lines of communication 476
    see also communication; project
        communications
logical thinking 654–655
long-lead-time 387–389, 542–543

M

main contract 551
major deliverables 280
majority, and consensus 630
make analysis 388
make or buy decision 543, 545
management by wandering around
    (MBWA) 603–604
mass email communications 492
McKinsey 7-S tool 186–188
met expectations model 465
micro manager 451
milestones 366
milestone slippage 584
mind-mapping 285
Minitab 437
miscommunication 475
mission and values 127
mitigation strategy 524
modelling techniques
    flowchart 427
    swimlane diagram 251, 427
monitor project complexity 664–665
Monte Carlo technique 363, 521
MoSCoW 78–79, 82, 86–87, 90, 96, 278
motivation models
    hygiene and motivational factors
        618–619
    intrinsic *vs.* extrinsic 619
    theory of needs 619–620
    Theory X 620
    Theory Y 620
    Theory Z 620
multifaceted project leader 3, 615
multiplicities of communication 490
multi-project resource optimisation
    380–381
multi-weighted scoring models 143–146
Myers-Briggs type indicator 634

N

negotiating contract
    BATNA 560–561
    focus on interests, not positions
        558–559
    objective 560
    separate people from problem 558
    win–win position 559
net present value (NPV) 131, 138, 139–140
neuro-linguistic programming (NLP)
    approach 481
NGT *see* nominal group technique (NGT)
noise 535
nominal group technique (NGT) 147–
    148, 634
non-agreement/contract dissolution 556
non-disclosure agreements/
    confidentiality 556
non-verbal communications 475, 479–481
normal stage, project closure 673
norming stage 622
not invented here (NIH) 625

NPV *see* net present value (NPV)
nudge theory 171, 188
NUPP 57–58

O

Object-Oriented Programming, Systems, Languages and Applications (OOPSLA) 72
OCM *see* organisational change management (OCM)
OOPSLA *see* Object-Oriented Programming, Systems, Languages and Applications (OOPSLA)
open tender 549
operational complexity 666
operational level agreements 427
opportunity risk 507, 516, 529–530
optional detection difficulty 522
organisational change management (OCM)
    ADKAR 177, 179–180
    approaches and tools 177, 178
    Bridges transition model 188, 189
    champions 174
    change leader's roadmap methodology 183
    CMBOK 180–181
    consultant 174
    defined 170
    development change 173
    Fisher's personal transition curve 186
    John Kotter's 8-step process 181–183
    Kübler-Ross model 185
    leaders 174
    Lewin's force field analysis 183–184
    Lewin's unfreeze, change, refreeze model 185
    management awareness 596–597
    manager 490
    McKinsey 7-S tool 186–188
    nudge theory 188
    planning 171–172
    predictive life cycle 175–177
    Prosci 177, 178
    roles 173–174
    sponsor 173–174
    transformational change 172
    transitional change 173
    types 172–173
    Virginia Satir change model 188, 189
Organisational Change Management Ian 171–172
organisational chart 455
organisational culture
    characteristics and functions 191–195
    countercultures 193
    day-to-day activities 190
    defined 190–192
    gaining efficiencies 191
    implications for project management 195–196
    quality of estimates 302–303

    stakeholder relationships 198
    support functions 191
organisational development 448
organisation breakdown structure (OBS) 281
orientation stage 624
outsourcing
    project procurement management 561–564
    project work 369
outstanding work 632
overlapping relationship 63

P

pad estimates 302
pair-wise criterion (analytic hierarchy process) 146–147
parallel streams 352
parametric estimating 311
Pareto chart 432
partnering
    co-location 568
    conflict management 567
    defined 564
    fair and incentive-laden contracts 568–569
    frequent review and status updates 567–568
    long-term outsourcing relationships 569
    requirements and procedures 564–565
    training and team-building activities 565–566
partnering charter 565
partnerships 553
passing risk 524
payback 131
performance agreements 617
performance appraisals 684
performance baseline 576, 577, 672
performance domains 207
performance evaluation
    contractor and supplier performance 686–687
    performance reviews 684–686
    post-implementation review (PIR) 681–682
    team evaluation 682–684
performance management information 336
performance reviews 680, 684–686
performing stage 623
perpetual stage, project closure 674
personal integrity 598
personas 99
P3.express system 56–58
phase estimating 309–310
phase (or stage), project closure 674
Plan–Do–Check–Act (PDCA) 52, 413–415
Plan–Do–Study–Act (PDSA) 52
planned, actual, variance (PAV) 396
planned costs 394, 395

planning horizon 300
Planning Poker 95
planning stage 12–13, 576
planning stakeholder management
    assumptions and constraints 451
    information systems 450
    lessons learned 451
    policy and procedure 450
    risk review 451
    roles and responsibilities 451
    stakeholder survey 451
    strategy and approach 450
PMBOK *see* Project Management Body of Knowledge (PMBOK)
PMBOKr Guide 31, 58–59, 65
PMBOKr Guide 2021 114
PMI Code of Professional Conduct 8
PMI's Agile Practice Guide 36
PMO *see* project management office (PMO)
POPIT™ model 234
portfolio management 23
    classification of investments 136–137
    multi-criteria selection models
        checklist models 142–143
        multi-weighted scoring models 143–146
        nominal group technique 147–148
        pair-wise criterion (analytic hierarchy process) 146–147
    priority team or portfolio management office responsibilities 154
    risks and dependencies 154–157
    selection criteria
        financial criteria models 137–141
        non-financial criteria 141–142
    senior management input 153–154
portfolio management office (Portfolio-MO) 253, 255
positive synergy 631
post-implementation review (PIR)
    defined 672
    performance evaluation 681–682
post-project review
    organisational review 691–692
    process and methods review 690–691
potentially shippable product 78, 105, 106
power/interest grid 457–458
power, salience model 462
Praxis framework 31, 53–56
predictive approaches 652
predictive life cycle 33, 34
    construction industry 28
    estimates 298
    organisational change management 175–177
    project chartering 208, 209
    PMBOK 61
premature project closure 405
premature stage, project closure 673
pre-project complexity assessment
    competent project leader 660–661
    complex or complicated 658–660
    initial risk assessment 661
    root cause 658

primary stakeholders 455
PRINCE2 *see* Projects IN Controlled
        Environments (PRINCE2)
    PRINCE2 Agile 115–116
principled negotiation 557
principles, ethics and 597
priorities, project leader 607
proactive approach 507
probability (likelihood) 516
probity 540
problem-solving, project leader 607
procurement 232–233, 679
product acceptance criteria 270
product backlog item (PBI) 95, 97–102
product backlog structure 88, 89
product breakdown structure (PBS)
        262, 270
product life cycle 207
product management 207
product or service roadmap *vs.* release
        schedule 80
product owner 75, 78–81
product scope 262
program(s)
    vs. portfolio 11
    vs. project 10–11
program evaluation and review
        technique (PERT) simulation 520
program management office (Program-MO)
        253–256
Program Management Professional
        (PgMP) certification 8
project
    account codes, 332, 396
    accounting systems 390
    celebration 695
    challenged factors 5
    characteristics of 9
    definition 8
Project Charter 205, 208–211, 261
project closure
    business case, benefits and scope
        realisation 693–695
    changed priority 674
    checklist 675–677
    closure activities 674–680
    defined 671
    failed projects 674
    lessons learned 687–693
    normal stage 673
    performance evaluation 680–687
    perpetual stage 674
    phase (or stage) 674
    premature stage 673
    project celebration 695
project communications
    axes of effectiveness and richness 479
    communication challenges 474–475
    communication direction 472–473
    communication medium 475
    communications management plan
        485–487
    CPORT 491
    cultural differences 482–485

formal or informal 471–472
    4Cs 491–493
    generational communications 482
    gulf of execution 479
    lack of communication 475
    lines of communication 476
    miscommunication 475
    non-verbal communications 475, 479–481
    organisational 474
    pitching 473–474
    sender-receiver model 476–477
    SMCR model 477–478
    styles of 475–476
    timing of 475
    tracking sent communications 493
    visual, auditory, kinesthetic (VAK)
        model 481–482
project complexity 661
project coordinator 672
project design 212
project duration 300–301
project execution
    audit 587
    baseline 575–579
    contingency plan 586–587
    deliverable acceptance process
        579–580
    kick-off meeting 581
    milestone and deliverable 580–581
    project sponsor 587
    stakeholders 575, 585
    status report time 583–584
    status team meeting 583
    supplier performance issue 589
    team caring 584–585
    value 588–589
    variation 579, 588
    weekly newsletter 589–590
project governance 237
    see also governance
project integration management 205
    activities 205–206
    executing work and delivering 216–218
    finalisation 220–221
    integrative thinking 223–225
        communication and information
            230–231
        cost 226–227
        procurement 232–233
        quality 227–228
        resource 228–229
        risk 231–232
        schedule 226
        scope 225
        stakeholder 229–230
    knowledge 220–223
    Project Charter 208–211
    project control 218
    project design 212–213
    variation control 219–220
project knowledge management 499–500
project leader 15–16, 123–124
    business acumen 597
    competent 660–661

as conductor 456–457
    creative *vs.* logical thinking 654–655
    design thinking 653–654
    divergent and convergent thinking
        653–654
    ethics 597, 607–609
    as leader 613–614
    leadership and principles 597
    management by wandering around
        (MBWA) 603–604
    managing upward relations 604–606
    managing *versus* leading 601–602
    mapping networks and dependencies
        602–603
    organisational change management
        (OCM) 596–597
    performance 607
    role of contemporary 596–601
    servant leadership 594, 642–645
    stakeholder management 454
    systems thinking 653
    teams 614–617
    technical project management
        abilities 597
    trust 610–612
project life cycle
    adaptive 35
    hybrid 35–36
    incremental 33, 35
    life-cycle model 12–15
    PMBOK 12–15
    predictive 33, 34
    project management approach
        selection 36–37
    uncertainty informs approach 33
project management 3, 10
    benefits management integration
        essence of 161–164
        traditional project management life
            cycle 161
    business systems and systems thinking
        18–20
    complexity 18
    corporate right-sizing 20
    definition 4
    demand for 4
    discipline of 4
    fundamentals 6
    holistic approach to 22–24
    impact of 3
    increased customer focus 20
    organisational change management 21
    portfolio management 23
    product or service life cycle 16, 18
    qualifications and certifications 6, 7
    quality of 423–428
    significance of 6
    small projects represent big problems
        21–22
    triple bottom line (planet, people and
        profit) 20
    value and the customer experience
        16, 17
Yin and Yang of 24

Project Management Body of Knowledge
(PMBOK)
integrative project management 62–64,
64–66
PMBOKr Guide 58–59
predictive approach 62–64
predictive life cycle stages 61
The Standard for Project Management
59, 60
and tailoring 61–62
project management information
systems (PMIS)
configuration management (CM) 497–499
defined 487
document management systems (DMS)
497–499
project knowledge management
499–500
Project Management Institute (PMI) 8
project management office (PMO) 36,
249–250, 253, 255, 514
project management principle 446
Project Management Professional (PMP) 8
project matrix 684
project meetings 638–639
project network 344, 348
project performance metrics 244
project portfolio management (PPM)
systems
features of 157–159
prominent PPM systems 159–160
project priority process 135
project procurement management
closure activities 569–571
contracts and contract types 551–561
defined 540
identifying requirements 542–545
management plan 546–547
outsourcing 561–564
partnering 564–569
procurement and projects 541–542
purchase order 547–548
supplier selection 548–551
project reporting 494–496
arrangements 485
project scope 262
acceptance criteria 266–267
approach 266
approvals and version control 269
assumptions 269
background 266
benefits 266
capturing requirements 275–276
analysis 278
elicitation 277
focus groups 278
interviews 277
management 276
observation 277
planning 276
register 277
scenarios 278
types 279
validation 278

verification 279
workshops 278
constraints 268
cost and funding sources 269
defined 265
deliverables 267
dependencies 266
exclusions 267–268
impact 266
inclusions 267–268
lessons learned review 269
objectives 267
organisational change impact 269
organisational structure 267
outputs and outcomes 275
product acceptance criteria 270
product breakdown structure 270
risk analysis 269
stakeholders 267
strategic alignment 266
technical requirements 269
tick-and-flick activity 271
timeline and milestones 269
triple constraints 272–273
typical document contents 265
variation request management 289–293
vision statement 266
work breakdown structure 271
defined 279
development 281–285
estimating 287–289
organisational units 286–287
phraseology 280
practice techniques 285–286
project leader 280–281
styles 280
project selection
Business Case 149–152
ranking proposals 152
responsibility for prioritising 152–153
Projects IN Controlled Environments
(PRINCE2) 28–29
around the world 40–41
principles 38
processes 39–40
tailoring 40
themes 38–39
project sponsor 614–615
baseline management 576
project stakeholder management
analysing stakeholders 457–463
closing stakeholder relationships 466
engage and monitor stakeholders
463–466
identifying stakeholders 451–457
planning stakeholder management
450–451
stakeholder co-creation 447–450
project structure 302
Project success factors, 1994-2020 6
project team directory 485–486
project teams
building 617–630
conducting project meetings 635–638

conflict management 633
disbanding 642
disbandment 678
dysfunctional conflict 633–635
functional conflict 633
generational theory and 626–627
project leader 615
project reward systems 631–632
project sponsor 614–615
recruiting project members 616–617
rejuvenating 635
sourcing 614
subsequent project meetings 638–639
virtual 639–641
project uncertainty 663
project vision 621
project-wide governance RASCI 249
prominent PPM systems 159–160
Prosci change triangle model 177, 178
proximity, risk 518
proxy product owner 79
pull communication 476
purchase order (PO) 545, 547–548
push communication 476

Q

quality assurance (QA) 413
quality control (QC) 413, 429–430
quality management
activities 410
carrying out quality control 429–437
continuous improvement 413–416
continuous improvement process 424
cost of poor quality 411–412
cost of quality 411–412
cost to rectify poor quality 411
escalation process 423–424
planning 417–423
planning grid 424
policy 423
quantification and articulation 424
reporting performance 437–438
requirements 410
risk 424
roles and responsibilities 424
root-cause analysis 438–441
strategy 423
Quality Management Plan 411, 417–418,
421, 423, 425–426, 428–429

R

radar charts 655
range estimating 315–316
RASCI *see* Responsible, Accountable,
Supports, Consulted, Informed
(RASCI)
reactive approach 507
readiness assessment 678
re-baselined documents 579
recruitment 596
red-amber-green (RAG), style 495
reducing project scope 369–370

refining estimates 318–319
request for information (RFI) 550
request for proposals (RFPs) 550
request for quotation (RFQ) 550
request for tender (RFT) 550
reserve analysis 313
residual risk 509, 517
residual RPN 525, 527
resource 303
  acquiring 338–340
  closure 341
  identification and assignment 330–338
  management 324
  monitoring and controlling 340–341
  optimisation 371–375
  types 326
Resource Allocation Matrix (RAM) 280,
    325, 333–334
Resource Assignment Matrix (RAM) 327
resource breakdown structure (RBS)
    330–331
resource conflicts and multitasking
    134–136
resource identification 325
resource levelling 371
Resource Management Plan 326–329
Resource Matrix 325
resource pool 253
resource scheduling 340
resource smoothing 372
Responsible, Accountable, Supports,
    Consulted, Informed (RASCI) 237
  RASCI Matrix 247–250, 327, 328
retrospective 672
rewards 632
rich picture 268
rich pictures 449
risk
  and complexity 661
  complexity in 518–521
  defined 505, 509, 516–518
  risk evaluation from 521
  roles and responsibilities 510
risk appetite 511
risk avoidance 524
risk breakdown structure (RBS) 512, 661
risk category/subcategory 516
risk closure 535
risk context 509–511
risk description 516
risk escalation process 510
risk evaluation 509, 521–522
risk handling
  cost risks 531
  funding risks 531–532
  schedule risks 530–531
  technical risks 530
  time buffers 531
risk heat maps 510
risk ID (RID) 516
risk identification
  assumptions and constraints 515
  defined 509, 511
  Delphi method 514–515

lessons learned 514
  risk breakdown structure (RBS) 512
  risk profiles 513–514
  subject matter expert review 515–516
  SWOT analysis 515
  work breakdown structure (WBS) 513
risk management
  budgets, contingency and 532–533
  close 536
  communication and consultation 535
  opportunity risk explored 529–530
  overview 507–509
  risk handling 530–532
  risk monitoring and review 533–535
  step 1 (risk context) 511
  step 2 (risk identification) 511–516
  step 3 (risk analysis) 516–521
  step 4 (risk evaluation) 521–522
  step 5 (risk treatment) 522–527
  step 6 (contingency planning) 527–528
  tools 536
Risk Management Plan 246, 505,
    509–510
risk methodology 510
risk mitigation 523–524
  residual risk assessment 526
risk monitoring and review 533–535
risk name 516
risk profiles 510, 513–514
Risk Register 510, 515–516
risk reporting 510
risk review, stakeholder 451
risk source 516
risk transfer 524
risk treatment
  accepting (retaining) risk 525
  continuing risk discussion 525–527
  defined 509
  escalate risk 523
  inherent threat risk response options
    522–523
  risk avoidance 524
  risk mitigating 523–524
  risk transfer 524
risk workshops 510
rolling wave planning 56, 64, 300,
    309–310
root-cause analysis 430, 658
rugby scrum 72
run charts 417, 430–432

S

sacred cow 133
salience model 462–463
SBOK see Scrum Body of Knowledge
    (SBOK)
Scaled Agile Framework (SAFe) 72
scatter diagrams 436–437
schedule baseline 346, 576, 577, 672
schedule constraints 378
scheduled risk audits 510
schedule management
  activities 344

advanced schedule efficiency
    techniques 367–371
advanced scheduling techniques
    363–367
assigning and monitoring project work
    379–380
development 346–348
  actual per cent complete 347
  EVM 347
  50/50 rule 347
  interval rule 347
  planning 346–347
  0/100 rule 347
multi-project resource optimisation
    380–381
from network to project schedule
    357–363
resource scheduling challenge
    371–379
from work package/task to network
    348–356
Schedule Management Plan 246, 346
schedule risks 530–531
scheduling and resource-management
    systems 497
scheduling overtime 369
scope baseline 576, 577, 672
scope creep 271, 272
scope document 261
Scope Management Plan 261
  activities 263
  captured and applied 264
  constraint management 264
  deliverable acceptance 264
  history 265
  predictive approach 264
  variation requests 262
  verification 262
Scrum (Agile) approach
  AgilePM 72
  Agile/Scrum software tools 116
  application of 74
  artefacts 96–102
  definition of 73
  DevOps 118
  events (see Scrum events
    (ceremonies))
  Kanban 72
  LeSS framework 116–118
  LeSS or Large-Scale Scrum 72
  overview of 76–78
  PMBOK and Agile 114–115
  PRINCE2 Agile 115–116
  and procurement 112–113
  product or service roadmap vs. release
    schedule 80–81
  product owner 78–81
  Release Schedule 81
  rugby scrum 72
  SAFe 72
  Scrum master 81–83
  SCRUMstudy 72
  team 83–87
  timeline 72

Scrum artefacts
  advanced topic cumulative flow
    diagram 106–109
  burndown and burnup charts 106, 110
  contemporary agile status reporting
    106, 110
  potentially shippable product 105, 106
  product backlog 97–102
  product vision 96–97
  sprint backlog 102–106
  sprint velocity 109, 111, 112
Scrum Body of Knowledge (SBOK) 73
Scrum events (ceremonies)
  creation of the initial product backlog
    88–91
  daily Scrum meeting 93–94
  kick-off meeting 87, 88
  sprint planning meeting 92–93
  sprint retrospective meeting 94–96
  sprint review meeting 94
The Scrum Guide 72
Scrum master 76, 81–83
SCRUMstudy's SBOK 78
Scrum team 76, 83–87
secondary stakeholders 455
selective tenders 549
sender-receiver model 476–477
sensitivity 364
sequential relationship 62
servant leadership
  Agile/Scrum style of 595
  defined 594, 642–645
  project leader 642–645
service level agreements 427
service scope *see* product scope
Shannon and Weaver model 476
shared vision
  creating 621–622
  defined 599
Six Sigma 415
Skills Matrix 327
slack 348
small, in multi-project environment 21
source, message, channel, receiver
  (SMCR) model *see* Berlo's model
social network 602
so far as is reasonably practicable
  (SFAIRP) 511
software tools 116, 641
  Microsoft Project
    resource assignment 337
    resource set-up 338
  Mountain Goat Software 88–89, 100
  Trello 85, 116
  virtual team management tools 641
specific, measurable, achievable,
  realistic and timely (SMART) 672
specific, measureable, achievable,
  realistic, time-bound and agreed
  (SMARTA) 129
spider diagram 655
splitting closure 679
splitting tasks 376
sprint 76, 92

sprint backlog 76, 102–106
sprint burndown chart 106–109
sprint planning meeting 76, 79, 92–93
sprint retrospective 76, 94–96
sprint review 76, 94
sprint velocity 109, 111, 112
stacked change models 199
stakeholder(s)
  analysis 446
  attitude 459–460
  defined 447
  engage and monitor 463–466
  engagement cycle 452
  identification 446
  internal or external 456
  project execution 575
  salience model 462–463
stakeholder co-creation
  action learning cycle 448
  organisational development 448
  sustainable development 449
stakeholder continuum 458–459
stakeholder frequency analysis 461
stakeholder management
  complex 464
  roles and responsibilities 451
  stakeholder management plan 450–451
Stakeholder Matrix 267
stakeholder network diagram 449
stakeholder proximity/priority 462
Stakeholder Register 455–457
stakeholder strategies 446
stakeholder survey 451
Standardised Enterprise Bargaining
  Agreements 112
standards
  ANSI/PMI 99-001-2021 29
  ISO 21500:2021 11, 12, 29, 30, 33, 42,
    43–46
  ISO 31000:2018 12
standing offer arrangements (SOAs) 548
start-to-finish (SF) relationship 360
start-to-start (SS) relationship 358–359
status report time 583–584
status team meeting 583
Steering Committee 246
  Steering Committee Charter 246
storming stage 622
story points 314
strategy
  definition 123
  management process
    dimensions 125
    implement strategies through
      portfolios, programs and projects
      131–132
    organisational level current/future
      state 124–126
    organisation's strategic objectives
      128–129
    organisation's vision, mission and
      values 126–128
    schematic of 125, 126
    from strategy to project 129–131

portfolio management 136–142
portfolio, program and project
  management system
    implementation gap 133
    organisational politics 133–134
    resource conflicts and multitasking
      134–136
  project leaders 123–124
strengths and weaknesses, external
  opportunities and threats
  (SWOT) 127
subcontracting 555–556
sub-deliverables 280
subject matter expert (SME) 112, 176,
  244, 515–516, 594
sunk cost 405, 674
supplier
  performance 680, 686–687
  performance issue 589
  selection 548–551
sustainability 20
sustainable development 449
sustainable project management 447
swimlane diagram 251, 427
SWOT analysis 515
synergy
  defined 630
  positive 631
systems thinker 598
systems thinking 3, 207, 208, 653

T

tacit knowledge 500
TAgile way *see* Traditional and Agile
  (TAGILE)
tailoring 207, 238
team building 324
  activities 626
  partnering 565–566
  positive 645
team charter 637
team development 625
Team Development Plan 329
team evaluation 682–684
team management systems (TMS) 634
team meeting 581
  time for status 583
team survey 631
technical risks 530
template methods 314
tender process 547–551
theory of needs 619–620
Theory X 620
Theory Y 620
Theory Z 620
threat risk 507, 516
360-degree feedback 684
three pillars of project governance 239–240
three-point estimate (PERT) 311–312
tick-and-flick activity 271
time 303–304
time and material contracts (T&M) 554
time buffers 531

time management 599
time-phased project budgeting 394–395
    by category 395–397
    by OBS 399–400
    by WBS 397–400
time units 306
top-down estimate 299
top management 455
total quality management (TQM) 416
total slack 363
Traditional and Agile (TAGILE) 37,
    113, 115
training needs analysis 335
trial engagement 551
triggers 527
triple constraints 9, 75, 206, 219,
    272–273, 409, 577
trust
    project leader 599, 610–612
    stakeholder management 463–464
trust-building stage 624
trust equation 611
Tuckman and Jensen's team development
    model 594, 622–623

U

uncertainty informs approach 33
uncertainty risk 579
unified modelling language (UML) 428
unions 328
urgency, project leader 606–607
urgency, salience model 462

V

value 3
value creation 447
value proposition 449
variance 385, 395
variation (change) control 219–220
variation management process (VMP)
    261, 289–293, 579
variation request management 289–293
variation requests 261, 579
vendor bid analysis 313
version control 497, 498
Virginia Satir change model 188, 189
virtual project teams 639–641
    management tools 641
vision, project 621
vision statement 127
visual, auditory, kinesthetic (VAK) model
    481–482
voice of the customer (VOC) 51,
    409, 410

W

WAgile *see* Waterfall and Agile
    (WAGILE)
Waterfall and Agile (WAGILE) 37, 113
    vs. Agile approaches 5
WBS *see* work breakdown structure
    (WBS)
weather station 253
weighted scoring models 149

"what's in it for me?" (WIIFM) factor 449
win–win position 559
work breakdown structure (WBS)
    Communications Management
      Plan 488
    cost management 385
    defined 279
    development 281–285
    dictionary 283
    estimating 287–289
    leverage 331–332
    organisational units 286–287
    phraseology 280
    practice techniques 285–286
    project leader 280–281
    Project Management Institute's
      (PMI's) 261
    project schedule 597
    resource management activities 325
    risk identification 513
    scheduling workflow 344
    styles 280
work package 216, 261, 280, 325
workplace health and safety
    (WHS) 328

Y

Yin and Yang of project management 24

Z

0/100 rule 347